Everything You Need to Know about MEDICAL TESTS

Everything You Need to Know about

MEDICAL TESTS

Reader's Digest

The Reader's Digest Association (Canada) Ltd., Montreal

READER'S DIGEST / CANADIAN STAFF

Project Editor: Andrew R. Byers
Designer: Cécile Germain
Copy Editor: Gilles Humbert
Production Manager: Holger Lorenzen
Production Coordinator: Susan Wong
Consultants: Mark Berner, MD, and
  Gamma-Dynacare Medical Laboratories, Ottawa

Books and Home Entertainment
Vice President: Deirdre Gilbert
Managing Editor: Philomena Rutherford
Art Director: John McGuffie

SPRINGHOUSE CORPORATION / STAFF

Senior Publisher: Matthew Cahill
Clinical Manager: Cindy Tryniszewski, RN, MSN
Art Director: John Hubbard
Senior Editor: Michael Shaw
Editors: Marcia Andrews, Peter H. Johnson, Pat Wittig
Copy Editors: Cynthia C. Breuninger (manager),
  Priscilla DeWitt, Mary Durkin, Lynette High,
  Kathryn A. Marino, Christina P. Ponczek,
  Doris Weinstock
Designers: Stephanie Peters (senior associate
  art director), Lesley Weissman-Cook (book designer),
  Elaine K. Ezrow, Donald G. Knauss, Amy Litz,
  Mary Ludwicki, Kaaren Mitchel, Mary Stangl
Typography: Diane Paluba (manager),
  Elizabeth Bergman, Joyce Rossi Biletz, Phyllis Marron,
  Valerie Rosenberger
Manufacturing: Deborah Meiris (director),
  Pat Dorshaw, T.A. Landis
Production Coordinator: Margaret A. Rastiello
Editorial Assistants: Mary Madden, Beverly Lane

This book shouldn't be used for self-treatment. It is a medical reference book and is not intended to be a substitute for diagnosis and treatment by your doctor. If you think you have any medical problem, you should consult your doctor.

Cover photo: M. Krasowitz/FPG/Masterfile

Printed in Canada

01 02 03 / 5 4 3 2 1

Address any comments about *Everything You Need to Know about Medical Tests* to
Editor, Books and Home Entertainment
c/o Customer Service, Reader's Digest
1125 Stanley Street, Montreal, Quebec H3B 5H5

For information about this and other Reader's Digest products or to request a catalogue, please call our 24-hour Customer Service hotline at 1-800-465-0780.

You can also visit us on the World Wide Web at
http://www.readersdigest.ca

Canadian Cataloguing in Publication Data

Main entry under title:
  Everything you need to know about medical tests

  Includes index.
  ISBN 0-88850-736-4

    1. Diagnosis—Popular works.   2. Medicine—Popular.
I. Title: Medical tests.
RC71.E94 2001   616.07'5   C00-901373-3

Contents

ADVISORY BOARD

CONTRIBUTORS & CONSULTANTS

Charol Abrams, MS, MT (ASCP) SH, CLS (NCA), CLSp (H), CLS Consultant, Philadelphia

Barbara A. Ankenbrand, RN, BS, MA, Professor of Nursing, Mt. Mercy College, Cedar Rapids, Iowa

Wendy L. Baker, RN, BSN, MS, Staff, Critical Care Medicine Unit, University of Michigan Hospitals, Ann Arbor

Debra C. Broadwell, RN, PhD, ET, Associate Professor of Nursing, Emory University, Atlanta

Lillian S. Brunner, MSN, ScD, LittD, FAAN, Nurse-Author, Brunner Associates, Inc., Berwyn, Pa.

Judith Byrne, BS, MT (ASCP), Affiliate Member, American Society of Clinical Pathologists

Ricardo L. Camponovo, MD, Consultant in Anatomic and Clinical Pathology, Scottsdale (Ariz.) Community Hospital

Luther Christman, RN, PhD, FAAN, Former Dean, College of Nursing, and Former Vice President, Nursing Affairs, Rush-Presbyterian-St. Luke's Medical Center, Chicago

James Robert Cronmiller, BS, MA, MS, Medical Technologist, Genesee Hospital, Rochester, N.Y.

Ellen Digan, MA, MT (ASCP), Professor of Biology and Coordinator, MLT Program, Manchester Community Technical College, Manchester, Conn.

Stanley J. Dudrick, MD, FACS, Program Director and Associate Chairman, Department of Surgery, St. Mary's Hospital, Waterbury, Conn.

Barbara Boyd Egoville, RN, MSN, Former Instructor, Critical Care Nursing, Lankenau Hospital School of Nursing, Philadelphia

John J. Fenton, PhD, DABcc, FNACB, Director of Chemistry, Crozer-Chester Medical Center, Chester, Pa., and Associate Professor of Clinical Chemistry, West Chester University of Pennsylvania

Sr. Rebecca Fidler, MT (ASCP), PhD, Former Chairperson, Health Sciences, Salem (W.Va.) College

Ruth Ann Fitzpatrick, MD, Director, Division of Endocrinology, Crozer-Chester Medical Center, Chester, Pa.; and Clinical Assistant Professor of Medicine, Hahnemann Medical College, Philadelphia

Nancy Flynn, RN, C, MSN, Clinical Educator, Bryn Mawr (Pa.) Hospital

Pamela W. Gitschier, MT, MS, Technical Chemistry Supervisor, St. Luke's Hospital, Bethlehem, Pa.

Sandra K. Goodnough Hanheman, RN, MSN, PhD, Clinical Professor, Graduate Program, Texas Woman's University College of Nursing, Houston

Mary Chapman Gyetvan, RN, BSEd, MSN, Independent Clinical Consultant, Springhouse Corporation, Springhouse, Pa.

John J. Hagarty, MD, Surgical Pathologist, Emeritus Director of Laboratories, and Attending Pathologist, Holy Redeemer Hospital, Meadowbrook, Pa.

Annette L. Harmon, RN, MSN, CEN, Assistant Director of Nursing, Newton-Wellesley Hospital, Newton-Lower Falls, Mass.

Connie S. Heflin, RN, MSN, Associate Professor of Nursing, Paducah Community College, Paducah, Ky.

Richard Edward Honigman, MD, FAAP, Pediatrician, Levittown, N.Y.

Joyce LeFever Kee, RN, MSN, Associate Professor, College of Nursing, University of Delaware, Newark

Mary Frances Keen, RN, DNSc, Associate Professor, University of Miami School of Nursing, Coral Gables, Fla.

Rose M. Kenny, MD, Associate Pathologist, Doylestown (Pa.) Hospital

Catherine E. Kirby, RN, MSN, Nurse Consultant, Nursing Technomics, National Technomics, West Chester, Pa.

Paul M. Kirschenfeld, MD, FACP, FCCP, Medical Director, Intensive Care Unit, and Program Director, Internal Medicine Residency Program, Atlantic City (N.J.) Medical Center

William E. Kline, MS, MT (ASCP), SBB, Director, Technical Services, St. Paul (Minn.) Red Cross

Marc S. Lapayowker, MD, Chairman, Department of Radiology, Abington (Pa.) Memorial Hospital

Gizell Maria Rossetti Larson, MD, Staff Neurologist, Nicolet Clinic, Neenah, Wis.

Peter G. Lavine, MD, Director, Coronary Care Unit, Crozer-Chester Medical Center, Chester, Pa.

Dennis E. Leavelle, MD, Associate Professor and Consultant, Mayo Medical Laboratories, Mayo Clinic, Rochester, Minn.

Michél E. Lloyd, MT (ASCP), SBB, Senior Technologist, St. Luke's Hospital, Bethlehem, Pa.

Thomas E. Mackell, MD, FAAOS, Orthopedic Surgeon, Doylestown (Pa.) Hospital

Lillian Madden, RN, MSN, CCRN, Clinical Educator, Misericordia Hospital, Philadelphia

Elizabeth Anne Mallon, MS, MT (ASCP), Transplant Coordinator, Thomas Jefferson University Hospital, Philadelphia

Marylou K. McHugh, RN, EdD, Director of Graduate Program, Department of Nursing, LaSalle University, Philadelphia

Joan C. McManus, RN, MA, Assistant Professor of Nursing, Bergen Community College, Paramus, N.J.

S. Breanndan Moore, MB, BCh, FRCPI, Chairman, Division of Transfusion Medicine, and Professor of Laboratory Medicine, Mayo Clinic and Mayo Medical School, Rochester, Minn.

Barbara A. Moyer, RN, MSN, Education Nurse Specialist, Lehigh Valley Hospital, Allentown, Pa.; and Assistant Professor, Allentown College of St. Francis de Sales, Center Valley, Pa.

John E. Nestler, MD, Fellow in Endocrinology, University of Pennsylvania, Philadelphia

Patricia J. Noone, RN, BSN, MEd, Senior Associate Professor of Nursing, Bucks County Community College, Newtown, Pa.

Gary M. Oderda, PharmD, MPH, Professor and Chairman, Department of Pharmacy Practice, College of Pharmacy, University of Utah, Salt Lake City

John J. O'Shea, MD, Chief, Lymphocyte Cell Biology Section, Arthritis and Rheumatism Branch, National Institute of Arthritis and Musculoskeletal and Skin Diseases, National Institutes of Health, Bethesda, Md.

Catherine Paradiso, RN, CCRN, MS, Clinical Nurse Specialist, St. Vincent's Medical Center of Richmond, Staten Island, N.Y.

Ara G. Paul, BS, MS, PhD, Dean and Professor, College of Pharmacy, University of Michigan, Ann Arbor

Mae E. Paulfrey, RN, MN, Assistant Professor, University of San Francisco School of Nursing

Barbara Madigan Preston, RN, MSN, Vascular Nurse Clinical Specialist and Consultant, Hospital of the University of Pennsylvania, Philadelphia

Frances W. Quinless, RN, PhD, CCRN, Assistant Professor, Rutgers University College of Nursing, Newark, N.J.

Linda T. Raichle, PhD, MT (ASCP), Laboratory Training Advisor, National Laboratory Training Network, Exton, Pa.

Teresa A. Richardson, MT, MLT (AMT), Medical Laboratory Technologist, Quakertown (Pa.) Community Hospital

Carolyn Robertson, RN, MSN, Diabetes Nurse Specialist, New York University School of Medicine

Thomas E. Rubbert, BSL, LLB, JD, Attorney, Pasadena, Calif.

Harrison J. Shull, Jr., MD, FACP, Assistant Professor of Medicine, Vanderbilt University, Nashville, Tenn.

Joan Simpson, MS, MT (ASCP), Consultant, Mansfield Center, Conn.

Marian J. Hoffman Sperk, RN, MSN, CNSN, Clinical Nurse Specialist-Nutrition, Lehigh Valley Hospital, Allentown, Pa.

Johanna K. Stiesmeyer, RN, MS, CCRN, Critical Care Clinical Educator, El Camino Hospital, Mountain View, Calif.

Basia Belza Tack, RN, MSN, ANP, Professor, School of Nursing, University of Washington, Seattle

Deborah Porter Thornton, MEd, MT (ASCP), SC, Assistant Professor, Medical Laboratory Science Program, Department of Molecular and Microbiology, University of Central Florida, Orlando

Richard W. Tureck, MD, Professor of Obstetrics and Gynecology; Director, In Vitro Fertilization and Embryo Transfer Program, University of Pennsylvania School of Medicine, Philadelphia

Cheryl A. Walker, RN, MN, CFNP, CANP, MBA, Assistant Professor, School of Nursing, University of Colorado Health Science Center, Denver

Ronald J. Wapner, MD, Director, Division of Maternal and Fetal Medicine, Thomas Jefferson University Hospital, Philadelphia

Martin Weisberg, MD, FACOG, Assistant Professor of Obstetrics-Gynecology, Psychiatry, and Human Behavior, Jefferson Medical College of Thomas Jefferson University, Philadelphia

Elaine Gilligan Whelan, RN, MSN, MA, Associate Professor of Nursing, Bergen Community College, Paramus, N.J.

Jay W. Wilborn, CLS, MEd, Program Director, MLT-AD, Corland County Community College, Hot Springs, Ark.

Beverly A. Zenk Wheat, RN, MA, Oncology Nurse Consultant, Stanford (Calif.) University Hospital

FOREWORD

High-tech tests, such as CAT scans and MRI scans, capture the headlines. But these are just some of the literally hundreds of tests performed every day to help doctors diagnose illnesses.

Some tests, such as those performed on blood samples, may seem commonplace and, except for the jab of a needle, uneventful to the person whose blood is being drawn. However, just as our blood replenishes all of our body's cells, this vital substance yields a bounty of clues to illnesses throughout the body. Testing the blood's enzymes, for instance, helps us diagnose heart attacks, diseases of the liver and pancreas, and certain inherited illnesses. Testing the blood's hormones helps us spot thyroid problems, infertility in men and women, and certain cancers. Testing the blood's sugars helps us detect diabetes and keep tabs on therapy for this potentially damaging disease.

Beyond blood tests, there are tests of urine, tests of tiny samples of tissue from the breast and internal organs, and tests of the fluids in the spine, around the lungs, and in the abdomen. There are also X-rays, vision and hearing tests, exercise tests, and scans of the heart, lungs, bones, and brain that use mildly radioactive substances to detect illness. In all, there are well over 400 tests. And this book tells you about each one in a clear, accurate, and readily understandable way.

Everything You Need to Know about Medical Tests helps you become informed and prepared for virtually any test that you or a loved one may undergo.

Prepared with the help of more than 70 doctors and medical authorities, this comprehensive reference offers information and advice that can't be found in any other reference for concerned consumers. To be understood appropriately, the tests in this book must be viewed as one part of the medical evaluation performed by your doctor, who will interpret the results in light of your medical history and physical exam. Of course, medical tests alone cannot provide the whole picture of an illness. But the more you know about them, the more you'll be able to participate in decisions about your health care.

For each test in the book, you'll find clear answers, usually in a page or two, to these essential questions:

- Why is this test done?
- What should you know before the test?
- What happens during the test?
- What happens after the test?
- Does the test have risks?
- What are the normal results?
- If the results are abnormal, what do they mean?

Besides this core information, you'll find many special features, each of them marked by a small picture. For instance, you'll find:

- *Self-Help:* what you can do to feel better or care for yourself
- *How Your Body Works:* easy-to-understand explanations and illustrations of how the eyes allow us to see, what the thyroid gland does, how sound travels through the ear to the brain, and many other fascinating body functions
- *Insight into Illness:* why an illness occurs and how it progresses — all clearly spelled out in words and illustrations.

With all of these features, *Everything You Need to Know about Medical Tests* will prove informative and indispensable time and time again.

Dr. S. Breanndan Moore
Chairman, Division of Transfusion Medicine
Professor of Laboratory Medicine
Mayo Clinic and Mayo Medical School
Rochester, Minn.

X-RAYS:
Screening for Illness or Injury

NERVOUS SYSTEM

SKULL X-RAYS

Although of limited value in evaluating head injuries, skull X-rays are extremely valuable for studying abnormalities of the base of the skull and the cranial vault. They also allow doctors to study skull problems present at birth as well as to evaluate bone defects of the skull caused by other diseases.

Skull X-rays evaluate the three groups of bones that make up the skull: the calvaria (called the vault of the skull), the mandible (known as the jaw bone), and the facial bones. The vault and the facial bones are connected by immovable joints that have irregular serrated edges called sutures.

Taken together, the bones of the skull are so complex that a complete exam requires several X-rays of each area.

Taken together, the bones of the skull are so complex that a complete exam requires several X-rays of each area.

Why is this test done?
Skull X-rays may be performed for the following reasons:
- To help detect fractures after a head injury
- To help diagnose tumors of the pituitary gland, a tiny oval-shaped organ attached to the brain
- To detect skull problems present at birth or caused by other diseases.

What should you know before the test?
- An X-ray technician will perform the test, usually in the radiology department. The test takes about 15 minutes and doesn't cause discomfort.
- You won't need to fast or avoid fluids before the test. But you'll need to take off your glasses or any jewelry that would be in the X-ray field. If you wear dentures, you'll have to remove them.

What happens during the test?
- You lie on an X-ray table or sit in a chair and are asked to stay perfectly still. Foam pads, sandbags, or a headband may be used to keep your head still and increase your comfort.

■ The technician usually takes five different X-rays of your head. The X-ray films are developed and checked for quality before you leave the area.

What are the normal results?

A radiologist interprets the X-rays. This special doctor evaluates the size, shape, thickness, and position of bones in your head, the blood vessels, and other structures. All should be normal for your age.

What do abnormal results mean?

Skull X-rays can often show fractures of the vault or base of the skull. However, they won't be able to show fractures of the base if the bone is dense there.

Skull X-rays can also show skull problems that are present at birth. In addition, they can show areas of the brain where too much calcium is present. Certain brain tumors, such as oligodendrogliomas or meningiomas, contain calcium.

Skull X-rays may reveal changes in skull structure caused by other illnesses, such as Paget's disease.

ANGIOGRAM OF THE BRAIN'S BLOOD VESSELS

Called *cerebral angiography* by doctors, this test involves X-rays of the brain's blood vessels after injection of a special dye into an artery in the neck, inner thigh, or other area. This dye shows up on X-rays once it reaches the brain and circulates through its blood vessels.

Usually, this test is performed when the doctor suspects an abnormality in the brain's blood vessels. The abnormality may have been suggested first by the results of a computerized axial tomography (CAT) scan of the brain or a spinal tap.

Why is this test done?

The angiogram may be performed for the following reasons:

■ To detect problems in the blood vessels within or leading to the brain (for example, aneurysms, malformation of blood vessels, thrombosis, narrowing, or blockage)

■ To study any blood vessel in the brain that is positioned unusually (because of a tumor, a blood clot, swelling, a spasm, increased pressure within the brain, or hydrocephalus)

■ To locate clips applied to blood vessels during surgery and to check the condition of these blood vessels.

What should you know before the test?

■ You'll learn about the test, including who will perform it, where it will take place, and how long it will last (usually 2 to 4 hours, depending on the tests ordered). You'll be positioned on an X-ray table, with your head immobilized, and you should remain still when asked.

■ Tell the doctor or nurse if you have allergies to iodine, iodine-containing substances (such as shrimp or scallops), or injected dyes used in other tests. You'll be told about possible side effects from the dye injected for the test.

■ You'll need to fast for 8 to 10 hours before the test.

■ You'll put on a hospital gown and remove all jewelry, dentures, and hairpins. Be sure to urinate before leaving the room.

■ You may receive a sedative and another drug 30 to 45 minutes before the test. You'll also receive a local anesthetic. (Some people — especially children — will receive a general anesthetic.)

■ You'll need to sign a form that gives your consent to perform the test. Be sure to read this form carefully and ask questions if you don't understand any portion of it.

What happens during the test?

■ You lie on an X-ray table while the site for the injection is shaved. You need to lie still with your arms at your sides.

■ A local anesthetic is injected. Then the artery is entered with a needle.

■ After X-rays verify the placement of the needle, the doctor injects the special dye. You may feel a brief burning sensation as the dye is injected. After the injection, you may feel warm and flushed, have a brief headache, or have a salty taste in your mouth. You may even feel nauseated and vomit.

■ After the injection, X-rays are taken, developed, and reviewed. Depending on the results, more dye may be injected and another series of X-rays taken.

■ When a satisfactory series of X-rays is obtained, the doctor removes the needle. A nurse checks for any bleeding and applies a bandage.

What happens after the test?

■ Typically, you'll rest in bed for 12 to 24 hours and receive pain medications. A nurse will check you hourly for the first 4 hours and then every 4 hours.

■ You'll have an ice bag over the injection area to ease discomfort and minimize swelling.

■ If the injection was made in the inner thigh area, keep your leg straight for 12 hours or longer. If it was made in the neck area, the nurse will check your swallowing and breathing.

■ After the test, you may resume your usual diet. Drink fluids to help pass the special dye.

Does the test have risks?

■ This test shouldn't be done if a person has liver, kidney, or thyroid disease.

■ It also shouldn't be done if a person is allergic to iodine or the test dye.

What are the normal results?

The test should show normal circulation through the brain's blood vessels.

What do abnormal results mean?

Changes inside the brain's blood vessels suggest a disorder, such as spasms, plaque, fistulas, arteriovenous malformation, or arteriosclerosis. Reduced blood flow to the brain's blood vessels may be related to increased pressure inside the brain.

If any blood vessels in the brain aren't in their usual position, this change may indicate a tumor, an area of swelling, or blocked flow of spinal fluid. If a tumor is present, the test can show blood vessels within a tumor, which can tell the doctor about the tumor's position and nature.

After the text, most people rest in bed for 12 to 24 hours and receive pain medications. An ice bag over the injection area helps ease discomfort and minimize swelling.

MYELOGRAPHY

This test evaluates an area of the spine called the *subarachnoid space*. It requires injection of a special dye. Because the dye weighs more than spinal fluid, it flows through the subarachnoid space to the dependent area when the person, lying face down on a special table, is tilted up or down. The test allows the doctor to see the flow of the dye and the outline of the subarachnoid space. X-rays are taken to provide a permanent record.

Why is this test done?

Myelography may be performed for the following reasons:

■ To find tumors and herniated disks that partially or totally block the flow of spinal fluid

■ To help detect arachnoiditis, spinal nerve root injury, or tumors.

What should you know before the test?

■ You'll need to fast and avoid fluids for 8 hours before the test. If the test is scheduled for the afternoon and hospital policy permits, you may have clear fluids before the test.

■ You'll be told about the test, including who will do it, where it will take place, and how long it will last (usually an hour or more). You'll need to stay overnight in the hospital.

■ Tell the doctor or nurse if you have allergies to iodine, iodine-containing substances (such as shrimp or scallops), or injected dyes used in other tests. You'll be told about the possible side effects from the dye injected for the test. You may feel some pain caused by your positioning during the test and the insertion of the needle.

■ Tell the doctor if you've ever had a seizure.

■ Just before the test, remove any jewelry or other metal objects that would obscure the X-rays.

■ You may receive some medication, such as an enema, a sedative to relax you, and a drug to reduce swallowing during the test.

■ You'll need to sign a form that gives your consent to perform the test. Be sure to read this form carefully and ask questions if you don't understand any portion of it.

The test can locate problems within or surrounding the spinal cord, such as herniated disks and tumors.

What happens during the test?

- You lie on your side at the edge of a table, with your chin on your chest and your knees drawn up to your abdomen.
- The doctor inserts a needle into your lower back, in an area between two disks. Some spinal fluid may be removed for routine tests.
- A nurse turns you onto your stomach and secures you with straps across your upper back, under your arms, and across your ankles. You'll need to extend your chin to prevent the dye from flowing beyond the test area.
- The doctor injects the dye and tilts the table so that the dye flows through the spinal area. You may feel a brief burning sensation as the dye is injected. After the injection, you may feel warm and flushed, have a brief headache, or have a salty taste in your mouth. You may even feel nauseated and vomit.
- Tell the nurse or doctor if you get a headache or have trouble swallowing or breathing deeply enough. You'll be able to rest periodically during the test.
- The doctor observes the flow of the dye and takes X-rays. After satisfactory X-rays are obtained, the doctor removes the needle. The nurse then cleans the needle site with an antiseptic solution and applies a small bandage.

The doctor injects the dye and tilts the table so that the dye flows through the spinal area.

What happens after the test?

- Typically, you'll rest in a hospital bed for 6 to 24 hours and receive pain medications. A nurse will check you every half-hour for the first 4 hours and then every 4 hours.
- Drink extra fluids. The nurse will want you to urinate at least once within 8 hours of the test.
- Tell the nurse if you have any back pain, headache, or stiff neck. If there are no complications, you may go home and resume your usual diet and activities the day after the test.

Does the test have risks?

Generally, myelography shouldn't be performed if a person has increased pressure inside the brain, allergies to iodine or the special dye, or infection at the puncture site.

What are the normal results?

Normally, the dye flows freely through the spinal area, showing no blockages or structural abnormalities.

What do abnormal results mean?

The test can locate problems within or surrounding the spinal cord, such as herniated disks and tumors. If the test confirms a spinal tumor, the person may be taken directly to the operating room.

Myelography may help locate or confirm a ruptured disk, spinal narrowing, or an abscess and may occasionally confirm the need for surgery. This test may also detect syringomyelia (an abnormality marked by fluid-filled cavities within the spinal cord and widening of the cord itself), arachnoiditis, and spinal nerve root injury.

EYE

X-RAYS OF THE EYE'S ORBIT

The orbit is the cavity that houses the eye and the lacrimal glands as well as blood vessels, nerves, muscles, and fat. (See *Structures revealed by X-rays of the eye's orbit.*) Because portions of the orbit have thin bones that break easily, X-rays of this area are commonly taken after a facial injury. They're also useful in diagnosing eye and orbit diseases.

Special X-ray techniques can reveal foreign bodies in the orbit or eye that are otherwise invisible. In some cases, X-rays are used with computerized axial tomography (CAT) scans and an ultrasound test to better define an abnormality.

Why is this test done?

X-rays of the eye's orbit may be performed for the following reasons:
- To help detect fractures and diseases of the orbit
- To help locate foreign objects in the eye.

What should you know before the test?

- You'll learn about the test, including who will perform it, where it will be performed, and the expected duration (about 15 minutes). The test is painless unless you've suffered a facial injury, in which case positioning may cause some discomfort. You'll be asked to turn your head from side to side and to flex or extend your neck.

Structures revealed by X-rays of the eye's orbit

X-rays of the eye's orbit reveal many small structures in the surrounding area. This illustration shows some of the common reference points.

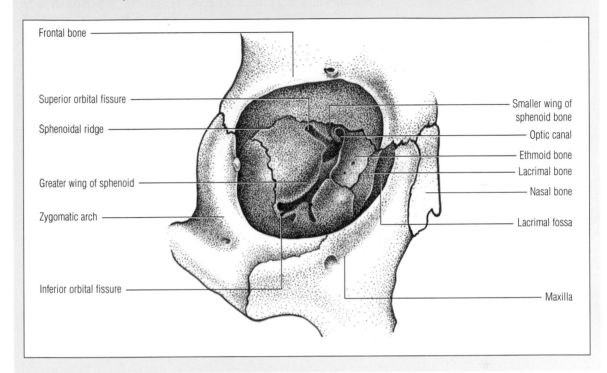

Frontal bone

Superior orbital fissure

Sphenoidal ridge

Greater wing of sphenoid

Zygomatic arch

Inferior orbital fissure

Smaller wing of sphenoid bone

Optic canal

Ethmoid bone

Lacrimal bone

Nasal bone

Lacrimal fossa

Maxilla

What happens during the test?

■ You lie on the X-ray table or sit in a chair. While the X-rays are taken, you have to remain still.

■ Usually, a series of X-rays is taken from different angles. These X-rays must be developed and inspected before you can leave.

What are the normal results?

The eye's orbit has a roof, a floor, and walls. The bones of the roof and floor are very thin. The floor bones, in fact, can be less than 1 millimeter thick. The walls are thicker. The X-rays should show no broken bones in the orbit or other problems.

What do abnormal results mean?

Broken bones from a facial injury are most common in the thin structures of the floor and ethmoid bone. Generally, enlargement of the orbit indicates a problem, such as a growing tumor. Destruction of the orbit's walls may indicate a malignant tumor or an infection. A benign tumor or cyst produces a clear-cut indentation of the orbital wall.

ANGIOGRAM OF THE EYE

In this test, called *fluorescein angiography* by doctors, a special camera takes rapid-sequence photographs of the eye. The photographs are taken after the injection of a special dye called *sodium fluorescein* into a vein in the arm. The dye lets the doctor see the appearance of blood vessels within the eye.

Why is this test done?

An angiogram of the eye may be performed to help find retinal problems, tumors, and circulatory or inflammatory disorders.

What should you know before the test?

■ You'll be told about the test, including who will do it, where it will take place, and that it usually about lasts about 30 minutes.

■ Tell the doctor or nurse if you have glaucoma or have ever had a bad reaction to dilating eyedrops. During the test, eyedrops will be instilled to dilate your pupils and a dye will be injected into your arm. Your eyes will be photographed with a special camera before and after the injection.

■ You'll need to sign a form that gives your consent to perform the test. Be sure to read this form carefully and ask questions if you don't understand any portion of it.

What happens during the test?

■ The nurse gives you eyedrops. Then you sit in the examining chair, facing the camera. You should loosen or remove any restrictive clothing around your neck.

■ You place your chin in the chin rest and your forehead against the bar. Then you open your eyes wide and stare straight ahead, while keeping your teeth together and maintaining normal breathing and blinking.

■ The nurse cleans your inner forearm with an antiseptic solution; then the dye is injected rapidly. You should maintain your position and continue to stare straight ahead.

■ You may experience nausea and a feeling of warmth. Tell the doctor or nurse how you feel, especially if the eyedrops or the dye makes you feel like vomiting, if you have a dry mouth or metallic taste, if you feel light-headed or faint, or if you start to itch.

■ As the dye is injected, 25 to 30 photographs are taken in rapid sequence. Each photograph is taken 1 second after the other.

■ The needle and syringe are removed carefully. Pressure and a dressing are applied to the injection site.

■ If late-phase photographs are needed, you'll sit and relax for 20 minutes. Then another 5 to 10 photographs may be taken.

What happens after the test?

■ Your skin and urine will be slightly discolored for a day or two afterward.

■ Your near vision will be blurred for up to 12 hours. During this period, you should avoid direct sunlight. You also shouldn't drive.

After the test, your near vision will be blurred for up to 12 hours. You should avoid direct sunlight and let someone else drive.

Does the test have risks?

■ The dye used in the test can cause nausea, vomiting, sneezing, numbness of the tongue, and dizziness. These sensations will go away shortly.

■ The dye rarely causes severe problems, such as breathing difficulty. The doctor will give an injection if this complication occurs.

What are the normal results?

After rapid injection, the dye reaches the retina in 15 seconds and fills its blood vessels. After filling the vessels, the dye recirculates through them about 30 to 60 minutes after the injection. Normally, there is no leakage of the dye from the retina's blood vessels.

What do abnormal results mean?

The test can detect tiny aneurysms, arteriovenous shunts, and formation of new blood vessels. It can also find eye diseases caused by high blood pressure. The test can reveal tumors and swelling or inflammation of the retina.

LUNGS & SINUSES

CHEST X-RAY

In this test, X-rays penetrate the chest and produce a black-and-white image on specially treated film. Normal areas of the lung let X-rays pass through them with little or no change. These normal areas look dark on X-ray film. In contrast, abnormal areas of the lung, such as foreign bodies, fluids, and tumors, change the X-rays. These abnormal areas look dense on X-ray film.

A chest X-ray is most useful when it's compared with previous X-rays. This comparison allows the doctor to detect changes.

Why is this test done?
A chest X-ray may be performed for the following reasons:
- To detect lung diseases, such as pneumonia, a collapsed lung, and lung cancer
- To detect problems in the chest area, such as cancer and heart disease
- To determine the location and size of a tumor
- To help evaluate lung condition and breathing.

What should you know before the test?
- You won't need to fast or limit fluids beforehand.
- You'll be given a gown without snaps to put on. And you'll need to remove any jewelry, such as a necklace, that may be in the X-ray field.
- You'll receive directions on how to breathe during the test.

What happens during the test?
- If a stationary X-ray machine is used, you stand or sit in front of it.
- If you're in a bed, a portable X-ray machine is used. The head of your bed will be raised.
- The nurse or technician tells you to take a deep breath and to hold it momentarily while each X-ray is being taken. Doing this provides the clearest view of your lungs.

Chest X-rays aren't usually done during the first 3 months of pregnancy because of the risk of birth defects.

Does the test have risks?

Chest X-rays aren't usually done during the first 3 months of pregnancy because of the risk of birth defects. However, when they're absolutely necessary, a lead apron will be placed over the mother's abdomen to shield the fetus from the X-rays.

What are the normal results?

To make an accurate diagnosis, the doctor reviews the results of the X-rays as part of a battery of tests. The doctor, for instance, might also look at the results of breathing tests and the physical exam.

What do abnormal results mean?

Chest X-rays can reveal dozens of different disorders. (See *Disorders revealed by chest X-ray.*)

Disorders revealed by chest X-ray

Chest X-rays can help detect disorders of the heart, lungs, ribs, and other structures. Some of the chief disorders they can help doctors find are:

- atherosclerosis
- bronchitis
- collapsed lung
- congestive heart failure
- cystic fibrosis
- emphysema
- fractures of the ribs or spine
- lung cancer
- pneumonia
- tuberculosis.

SINUS X-RAY

The sinuses — air-filled cavities lined with mucous membranes — lie within the maxillary, ethmoid, sphenoid, and frontal bones of the face. In this test, X-rays pass through the sinuses and react on specially sensitized film, forming an image that allows a doctor to study the sinuses.

Why is this test done?

A sinus X-ray may be performed for the following reasons:
- To detect injury or illness in the sinus area
- To confirm cancer or inflammation in the sinus area
- To determine the location and size of a malignant tumor.

What should you know before the test?

- You'll find out about the test, including who will perform it, where it will take place, and its expected duration (usually 10 to 15 minutes). You'll be asked to sit upright and to avoid moving while the X-rays are being taken to prevent blurring of the image.
- Your head may be immobilized in a foam vise during the test to help maintain the correct position. The vise doesn't hurt.

- You'll remove any dentures, all jewelry, and metal objects that could obscure the X-rays.

What happens during the test?

- You sit upright (with your head in a foam vise) between the X-ray tube and a film cassette.
- The X-ray tube is positioned at different angles and your head is placed in various standard positions while the sinuses are filmed.

Does the test have risks?

Sinus X-rays aren't usually done during pregnancy because of the risk of birth defects. However, when they're absolutely necessary, a lead-lined apron placed over the mother's stomach can shield the fetus.

What are the normal results?

Normal sinuses allow X-rays to pass through them. The sinuses are filled with air, which appears black on X-ray film.

What do abnormal results mean?

Sinus X-rays can detect sinus injury or fracture, sinus infections, and benign and malignant tumors.

CHEST FLUOROSCOPY

In this test, a continuous stream of X-rays passes through the chest and casts shadows of the heart, lungs, and diaphragm on a fluorescent screen. Because fluoroscopy reveals less detail than chest X-rays, it's used only when the doctor needs to look within the chest to detect or rule out a problem.

Why is this test done?

Fluoroscopy may be performed for the following reasons:

- To assess lung expansion and contraction during quiet breathing, deep breathing, and coughing
- To evaluate movement and paralysis of the diaphragm
- To detect blockages in the bronchi (the airways leading to the lungs) and lung disease.

What should you know before the test?

■ You'll learn about the test, including who will perform it, where it will take place, and its expected duration (usually 5 minutes).
■ During the test, you'll be asked to follow specific instructions — for example, to breathe deeply and to cough — while X-ray images are taken.
■ You'll remove all jewelry within the X-ray field.

What happens during the test?

During the test, the motion of your lungs and heart is observed on a screen. Special equipment may be used to intensify the images, or a videotape recording may be made for later study.

Does the test have risks?

Fluoroscopy should not be performed during pregnancy because of the risk of birth defects.

What are the normal results?

The normal diaphragmatic movement is synchronous and symmetrical.

What do abnormal results mean?

Diminished diaphragmatic movement may indicate lung disease. Diminished or paradoxical diaphragmatic movement may indicate paralysis of the diaphragm.

During fluoroscopy, the motion of your lungs and heart is observed on a screen. A videotape recording may be made for later study.

CHEST TOMOGRAPHY

This test provides clear X-rays of chest areas that are otherwise in the shadows of overlying or underlying structures. In this test, an X-ray tube and film swing around the person in opposite directions, creating a sharply defined X-ray picture of a specific area the doctor wishes to study. Because tomography exposes a person to high levels of radiation, it's used only to evaluate significant chest problems.

Why is this test done?

Chest tomography may be performed for the following reasons:

- To identify calcified or fatty deposits in dense lung tissue
- To locate tumors, especially those blocking a bronchus, one of the main breathing passages
- To find lesions, especially those located deep within the chest.

What should you know before the test?

- You won't need to fast or limit fluids beforehand. The test itself takes 30 to 60 minutes.
- You'll probably be warned that the test equipment is noisy because of rapidly moving metal-on-metal parts and that the X-ray tube swings overhead.
- You'll receive directions on breathing and movement during the test. You may be advised to close your eyes to prevent unintended movement.
- Just before the test, you'll need to remove all jewelry, such as a necklace, that's within the X-ray field.

Because tomography exposes a person to high levels of radiation, it's used only to evaluate significant chest problems.

What happens during the test?

- You lie on an X-ray table on your back and your side. The X-ray tube swings over you, taking many pictures from different angles.
- You need to breathe normally during the test but remain perfectly still. Foam wedges help you remain motionless.

Does the test have risks?

Because the test exposes a person to high levels of radiation, it's never performed during pregnancy.

What are the normal results?

A normal tomogram resembles a normal chest X-ray and shows no abnormalities.

What do abnormal results mean?

A radiologist interprets the X-ray films. A finding of calcium accumulation in the center of a lung nodule suggests a benign tumor. However, a nodule with an irregular border suggests a malignant tumor. A sharply defined nodule suggests a persistent inflammation called a *granuloma*.

The test can identify widening or narrowing of a bronchus and the extension of a tumor to the ribs or spine.

BRONCHOGRAPHY

This type of X-ray examines the breathing passages after a special dye is passed through a tube (called a *catheter*) into the trachea and bronchi. The dye coats the bronchial tree, permitting the doctor to see any anatomic deviations. Since the development of the computerized axial tomography (CAT) scan, bronchography is used less frequently.

Why is this test done?
Bronchography may be performed for the following reasons:
- To help detect bronchiectasis, bronchial blockages, lung cancer, cysts, and cavities
- To help pinpoint the cause of a bloody cough.

What should you know before the test?
- You'll find out about the test, including who will perform it, where it will take place, and its expected duration.
- You'll need to fast for 12 hours before the test.
- Tell the doctor or nurse if you have allergies to anesthetics, iodine, or the dyes used in any tests.
- If you have a cough, you may be given an expectorant before the test.
- If the test will be performed under local anesthesia, you'll receive a sedative to help you relax and to suppress the gag reflex. The anesthetic itself will have an unpleasant taste. During the test, you may experience some difficulty breathing. Be assured that your breathing passages won't be blocked and that you'll get enough oxygen. The catheter will pass more easily if you relax.
- If the test will be performed under general anesthesia, you'll receive a sedative before the test to help you relax.
- If you wear dentures, you'll need to remove them just before the test.
- You'll need to sign a form that gives your consent to perform the test. Be sure to read this form carefully and ask questions if you don't understand any portion of it.

If the test is to be performed under local anesthesia, you'll receive a sedative to help you relax and to suppress the gag reflex. The catheter will pass more easily if you relax.

What happens during the test?

- After a local anesthetic is sprayed into your mouth and throat, a bronchoscope or catheter is passed into the trachea, and the anesthetic and dye are given through it.
- You are placed in various positions during the test to move the dye into different areas of the bronchial tree.
- If you received a local anesthetic for the test, tell the doctor or nurse if you have trouble breathing, start to itch, or feel your heart pounding or fluttering. These are signs of an allergic reaction to the anesthetic or dye, which must be treated with medication.

What happens after the test?

- You won't be able to eat or drink until your gag reflex returns. It usually comes back in about 2 hours.
- You'll be asked to cough gently to help clear any remaining dye from your breathing passages. Another X-ray of your cleared breathing passages is usually done in 24 to 48 hours.
- If you have a sore throat, tell the nurse. You can have throat lozenges or a liquid gargle once your gag reflex returns.
- Don't resume your usual activities until the next day.

Does the test have risks?

- Bronchography shouldn't be done if you are pregnant, if you have allergies to iodine or the test dye, or if you have difficulty breathing.
- A person with asthma may have a spasm in the airway when the dye is given.
- A person with chronic bronchitis or emphysema may have a breathing passage blocked by the dye.
- Pneumonia can occur if the dye isn't cleared by coughing from your breathing passages.

What are the normal results?

The right bronchus is shorter, wider, and more vertical than the left bronchus. Successive branches of the bronchi become smaller in diameter and are free of any blockages or problems.

What do abnormal results mean?

Bronchography may show bronchiectasis or bronchial blockages due to tumors, cysts, cavities, or foreign objects. Findings must be correlated with the person's physical exam, medical history, and perhaps other tests.

ANGIOGRAM OF THE LUNGS

Also called *pulmonary arteriography* or *angiography* by doctors, this test evaluates the lungs' blood vessels to help identify the cause of a person's symptoms. In this test, X-rays are taken after the injection of a special dye into the pulmonary artery or one of its branches.

Why is this test done?

An angiogram of the lungs may be performed for the following reasons:

- To detect pulmonary embolism in a person who has symptoms but whose lung scan is inconclusive or normal
- To evaluate lung circulation before surgery in a person who was born with heart disease.

What should you know before the test?

- You'll learn who will perform the test and where and that it will take approximately 1 hour.
- You'll be told about the possible side effects from the dye injected for the test. Your heart rate will be monitored continuously during the procedure.
- Tell the doctor or nurse if you have allergies to anesthetics, iodine, shellfish (such as shrimp or scallops), or the dyes used in any tests.
- You'll need to fast for 8 hours.
- You'll receive a form that asks your consent to perform the test. Be sure to read this form carefully before signing it. Ask questions if you don't understand any portion of it.

The doctor injects a special dye that circulates through the blood vessels of your lungs as X-rays are taken.

What happens during the test?

- You lie on your back, the local anesthetic is injected, and a heart monitor is attached to you.
- The doctor makes a small incision in a vein in your forearm or groin area. Then the doctor inserts a small tube called a *catheter* into the vein and slowly moves it through the vein all the way to an artery in your lung.
- Next, the doctor injects the special dye, which circulates through your lungs' blood vessels while X-rays are taken. You may experience an urge to cough, a flushed feeling, nausea, or a salty taste for 5 minutes after the injection.
- After the X-rays are taken, the doctor slowly pulls the catheter back and removes it. The nurse applies a dressing over the catheter insertion site.

What happens after the test?

- You'll rest in bed for about 6 hours. A nurse will check your condition regularly during this time.
- The nurse will tell you about any restriction of activity. You may resume your usual diet after the test. Be sure to drink plenty of fluids.

Does the test have risks?

- The test can cause complications, such as a blockage of an artery, a tear in the heart, an irregular heartbeat from irritation of the heart, and kidney failure from a severe allergy to the test dye.
- The test shouldn't be done during pregnancy and in people who are allergic to iodine, shellfish, or the dyes used in medical tests.

What are the normal results?

Normally, the dye flows symmetrically and without interruption through the blood vessels of the lungs.

What do abnormal results mean?

Interruption of blood flow may be caused by an embolism (a clot that obstructs circulation), vascular filling defects, or stenosis.

HEART & BLOOD VESSELS

CARDIAC X-RAYS

These X-rays are among the most frequently used tests for evaluating heart disease and its effects on the blood vessels of the lungs. (See *The cardiac series,* page 24.) They show images of the thorax, mediastinum, heart, and lungs. In a routine evaluation, two different views are taken.

Why is this test done?
Cardiac X-rays may be performed for the following reasons:
■ To help detect heart disease and abnormalities that change the size, shape, or appearance of the heart and lungs
■ To check for the correct position of pulmonary artery and cardiac catheters and of pacemaker wires.

What should you know before the test?
■ You'll learn about the test, including who will perform it and where. The test exposes you to little radiation and is harmless.
■ You'll remove jewelry, other metal objects, and clothing above your waist and put on a hospital gown.

What happens during the test?
The procedure depends on how the X-rays are taken.

Front and back views
■ You stand up about 6 feet (2 meters) from the X-ray machine with your back to the machine and your chin resting on top of the film cassette holder.
■ The holder is adjusted to slightly extend your neck. You then place your hands on your hips, with your shoulders touching the holder, and center your chest against it.
■ You take a deep breath and hold it while the X-ray film is exposed.

The cardiac series

The cardiac series uses X-rays to provide a constant image of the heart in motion on a fluoro-scope screen. This allows the doctor to view the heart's chambers in motion from four directions, allowing a full study of the heart's action.

High radiation exposure

The cardiac series exposes a person to 15 to 20 times more radiation than conventional cardiac X-rays. It usually isn't performed on pregnant women and may be restricted in other people as well. In many cases, an echocardiogram is done instead. This test uses ultra-high-frequency sound waves to create an image of heart structures.

Left side view
- You extend your arms over your head and put your left side flush against the cassette.
- You then take a deep breath and hold it while the X-ray film is exposed.

Does the test have risks?

Cardiac X-rays usually aren't done during the first 3 months of pregnancy. However, when they're absolutely necessary, a lead shield or apron should cover the mother's stomach and pelvic area during the X-ray exposure.

What are the normal results?

The heart and lungs should have a normal size, shape, and condition on the X-rays.

What do abnormal results mean?

Cardiac X-rays must be evaluated in light of a person's medical history, physical exam, and the results of previous X-rays and electrocardiograms. An abnormal silhouette of the heart usually indicates enlargement of the left or right ventricle or the left atrium. The test can also show the first signs of congestion in the lungs' blood vessels.

X-RAYS OF THE LEG VEINS

Called *venography* or *ascending contrast phlebography* by doctors, this test checks the condition of the deep leg veins. It's the definitive test for detecting a condition called *deep vein thrombosis.*

Venography is expensive. A combination of three noninvasive tests — Doppler ultrasound, impedance plethysmography, and a nuclear scan with a radioisotope — provides an acceptable, but less accurate, alternative to X-rays of the leg veins.

Why is this test done?

X-rays of the leg veins may be performed for the following reasons:

- To confirm a diagnosis of deep venous thrombosis
- To distinguish blood clots from vein obstructions (such as a large tumor of the pelvis pressing on the leg veins)
- To evaluate vein problems present at birth
- To check how the valves within the deep leg veins work (especially helpful in identifying the cause of leg swelling)
- To locate a suitable vein for arterial bypass grafting.

What should you know before the test?

- You'll learn about the test, including who will perform it, where it will take place, and that it will last 30 to 45 minutes. You may feel a burning sensation in your leg during injection of the dye and some discomfort during the test. Complications from the dye are rare, but be sure to tell the doctor or nurse if you feel nauseated, have trouble breathing, or other problems.
- Tell the doctor or nurse if you have allergies to anesthetics, iodine, shellfish (such as shrimp or scallops), or the dyes used in any tests.
- You'll need to fast and to drink only clear liquids for 4 hours before the test.
- Just before the test, you should urinate, remove all clothing below the waist, and put on a hospital gown.
- You may receive a sedative if you're tense just before the test.
- You'll receive a form that asks your consent to perform the test. Be sure to read this form carefully before signing it. Ask questions if you don't understand any portion of it.

After the X-rays of your leg veins, you receive an injection of fluids to clear the dye from your veins.

What happens during the test?

- You lie on a tilting X-ray table so that the leg being tested doesn't bear any weight. You are told to relax this leg and keep it still. A tourniquet may be tied around your ankle.
- The doctor slowly injects the dye into a surface vein in your foot. Be sure to tell the doctor or nurse if you have nausea, severe burning or itching, tightness in the throat or chest, or trouble breathing.
- Using a fluoroscope, the doctor watches the movement of the dye through your leg veins and takes X-rays.
- After the X-rays, you receive an injection of fluids to clear the dye from your veins. Then the needle is removed and a bandage applied.

What happens after the test?

- The nurse will check your condition regularly. You'll receive pain medication to counteract the irritating effects of the dye.
- If the test indicates deep vein thrombosis, you'll receive medication and have to rest in bed with your leg supported or elevated.
- You'll be able to resume your usual diet.

Does the test have risks?

- The test isn't used routinely, because it exposes a person to relatively high doses of radiation and can cause complications, such as phlebitis, local tissue damage and, occasionally, deep vein thrombosis itself.
- Rarely, the dye used in the test causes a severe allergic reaction. Such reactions usually occur within a half-hour of the injection and require medication.

What are the normal results?

A normal test shows no problems in the leg veins.

What do abnormal results mean?

A test that shows consistent filling defects, an abrupt termination of a column of the test dye, unfilled major deep veins, or diversion of flow confirms a diagnosis of deep vein thrombosis.

DIGESTIVE SYSTEM

BARIUM SWALLOW

A barium swallow allows a doctor to examine the upper part of the digestive tract. When undergoing this test, a person drinks thick and thin mixtures of barium sulfate, a chalky drink with the consistency (but not the flavor) of a milk shake. The barium can be seen on an X-ray as it passes through the digestive tract.

This test is most commonly done as part of the upper GI series. It's usually performed when a person has a history of swallowing difficulty or vomiting.

Why is this test done?

A barium swallow may be performed for the following reasons:
- To diagnose hiatal hernia, a condition in which the stomach slides upward into the esophagus or along side it
- To diagnose pouches or sacs called *diverticula,* which may form in the upper digestive tract
- To diagnose esophageal varices, which are abnormal enlarged veins
- To detect narrowing of the upper digestive tract
- To identify ulcers, tumors, and polyps.

What should you know before the test?

- You'll need to fast after midnight the night before the test. (If an infant is being tested, feeding must be delayed to ensure full digestion of barium.)
- You'll learn about the test, including who will perform it, where it will take place, and its expected duration (about 30 minutes).
- You'll be asked to drink a barium preparation during the test. First, you'll receive a thick mixture, then a thin one. Altogether, you'll drink 12 to 14 ounces (about 350 to 400 milliliters) during the test.
- You'll be placed in various positions on a tilting X-ray table and X-ray films will be taken.
- Just before the test, you'll put on a hospital gown and remove any jewelry, dentures, hair clips, or other objects from the X-ray field.
- You'll receive a form that asks your consent to perform the test. Be sure to read this form carefully before signing it. Ask questions if you don't understand any portion of it.

What happens during the test?

- After you're secured on your back on the X-ray table, the table is tilted until you're upright. Then your heart, lungs, and abdomen are examined.
- Next, you take one swallow of the thick barium mixture, and X-rays are taken as the mixture moves through the pharynx, the uppermost part of your digestive tract.
- Then you're asked to take several swallows of the thin barium mixture. This part of the test examines your esophagus, which lies just downstream from your pharynx. During this portion of the test, you may be asked to swallow a "barium marshmallow" (a piece of soft white bread that has been soaked in barium).

A barium swallow may reveal problems in the pharynx, esophagus, or stomach.

■ As the test continues, you're secured to the X-ray table, which is tilted so that the movement of any barium through your esophagus can be seen.

■ Next, you take several more swallows of barium while your esophagus is examined and X-rayed. After the table is moved to a horizontal position, you take yet a few more swallows of barium and are X-rayed.

What happens after the test?

■ You'll be able to resume your normal diet. However, because you drank barium, your stools will be chalky and light-colored for 1 to 3 days.

■ If you don't have a bowel movement in 2 or 3 days, let your doctor know.

Does the test have risks?

A barium swallow shouldn't be done on any person who has a blocked intestine.

What are the normal results?

After the barium is swallowed, it pours over the base of the tongue into the pharynx. It's propelled by the normal digestive wave (which is called *peristalsis*) through the entire length of the esophagus in about 2 seconds. When it reaches the base of the esophagus, a sphincter opens and allows the barium to enter the stomach. After the barium passes, the sphincter closes. Normally, the barium evenly fills the pharynx and esophagus, and their linings look smooth and regular.

What do abnormal results mean?

A barium swallow may reveal problems in the pharynx, esophagus, or stomach. These problems include hiatal hernia, diverticula, and varices.

The test may detect narrowing, tumors, polyps, ulcers, and motility disorders, such as pharyngeal muscle disorders, spasms in the esophagus, and achalasia. However, a definite diagnosis commonly requires a biopsy or other tests.

UPPER G.I. AND SMALL-BOWEL SERIES

This test examines the upper and middle portions of the digestive tract (the esophagus, stomach, and small intestine). It requires ingestion of barium sulfate, a chalky drink with the consistency (but not the flavor) of a milk shake. Barium can be seen on X-rays as it passes through the digestive tract.

This test is performed when a person has:

- upper GI symptoms, such as difficulty in swallowing, vomiting, or burning or gnawing pain in the center of the stomach
- signs of small-bowel disease, such as diarrhea and unexplained weight loss
- signs of bleeding in the digestive tract, such as blood in vomit or dark, tarry stools.

Why is this test done?

The upper GI and small-bowel series may be performed for the following reasons:

- To diagnose hiatal hernia, a condition in which the stomach slides upward into the esophagus or alongside it
- To diagnose diverticula, which resemble pouches, in the upper digestive tract
- To diagnose esophageal varices, which are abnormal enlarged veins
- To help detect narrowing of the upper digestive tract
- To help diagnose ulcers, tumors, regional enteritis, and malabsorption syndrome
- To help detect motility disorders.

What should you know before the test?

- You'll need to follow a low-fiber diet for 2 or 3 days before the test. After midnight on the night before the test, you'll need to fast. If you smoke, you must stop after midnight.
- You'll learn about the test, including who will perform it, where it will take place, and its expected duration (up to 6 hours). Be sure to bring a good book along to pass the time.
- You'll be told about the barium preparation that you must drink during the test. First, you'll receive a thick mixture, then a thin one. Altogether, you'll drink 16 to 20 ounces (about 500 to 700 milliliters) during the test.

■ You'll be placed in different positions on a tilting X-ray table and X-ray films will be taken. During the test, your abdomen may be compressed to ensure proper coating of the stomach or intestinal walls with barium or to separate overlapping loops of your small intestine.

■ Just before the test, you'll put on a hospital gown and remove any jewelry, dentures, hair clips, or other objects from the X-ray field.

■ You'll receive a form that asks your consent to perform the test. Be sure to read this form carefully before signing it. Ask questions if you don't understand any portion of it.

What happens during the test?

■ After you're secured on your back on the X-ray table, the table is tilted until you're upright. Then your heart, lungs, and abdomen are examined.

■ You're asked to take several swallows of barium, and its passage through your esophagus is observed. Then X-rays are taken from many angles.

■ When barium enters your stomach, the doctor or an assistant may press your stomach inward to make sure that the barium coats it thoroughly.

■ You may be asked to sip barium through a perforated straw. As you do, a small amount of air also enters your stomach. This allows detailed examination and X-rays of the folds of your stomach. Next, you drink the remaining barium as the doctor observes the filling of the stomach and emptying into the duodenum, the first part of the small intestine.

■ Two series of X-rays of the stomach and duodenum are taken from different angles.

■ The passage of barium into the remainder of the small intestine is then observed, and X-rays are taken at 30- to 60-minute intervals.

What happens after the test?

■ You'll receive a cathartic or enema.

■ Your stools will be lightly colored for 1 to 3 days. However, if you don't have a bowel movement in 2 or 3 days, let your doctor know.

Does the test have risks?

The upper GI and small-bowel series shouldn't be done if a person has a blockage or tear of the digestive tract. Barium may worsen the blockage or seep into the abdominal cavity.

During the test, you're asked to take several swallows of barium, and its passage through your esophagus is observed. X-rays are taken from many angles.

What are the normal results?

After the barium is swallowed, it pours over the base of the tongue into the pharynx. It's propelled by contractions of the digestive tract (which is called *peristalsis*) through the entire length of the esophagus in about 2 seconds. When it reaches the base of the esophagus, a sphincter opens and allows the barium to enter the stomach. After the barium passes, the sphincter closes. Normally, the barium evenly fills the pharynx and esophagus, and their linings look smooth and regular.

As barium enters the stomach, it outlines the characteristic folds called *rugae*. When the stomach is completely filled with barium, its outer contour appears smooth and regular without evidence of flattened, rigid areas.

After barium enters the stomach, it quickly empties into the duodenum and reveals circular folds. These folds deepen and become more numerous in the next portion of the small intestine, the jejunum. The barium temporarily lodges between these folds, producing a speckled pattern on X-rays. As barium enters the ileum, the circular folds become less prominent and, except for their broadness, resemble those in the duodenum. The X-rays also show that the diameter of the small intestine tapers gradually from the duodenum to the ileum.

Normally, when the stomach is completely filled with barium, its outer contour appears smooth and regular without evidence of flattened, rigid areas.

What do abnormal results mean?

X-rays of the esophagus may reveal strictures, tumors, hiatal hernia, diverticula, varices, and ulcers. Benign strictures usually narrow the esophagus, whereas malignant ones cause erosive changes. Tumors produce filling defects in the column of barium, but only malignant ones change the mucosal contour. Nevertheless, biopsy is necessary for a definite diagnosis of both esophageal strictures and tumors.

Motility disorders, such as esophageal spasm, are usually difficult to detect because spasms are erratic and transient. Another test, called *manometry*, is generally performed to detect these disorders.

X-rays of the stomach may reveal tumors and ulcers. Malignant tumors appear as filling defects on the X-ray film and usually disrupt peristalsis. Benign tumors appear as outpouchings of the gastric mucosa and generally don't affect peristalsis. Ulcers occur most commonly in the stomach and duodenum, and these two areas are thus examined together. Benign ulcers usually show evidence of partial or complete healing and are characterized by radiating folds extending to the edge of the ulcer crater. Malignant ulcers, usually associated with a suspicious mass, generally have radiating folds that extend beyond the ulcer crater to the edge of the mass. However, biopsy is necessary for a definite diagnosis of both tumors and ulcers.

X-rays of the small intestine may reveal regional enteritis, malabsorption syndrome, and tumors.

BARIUM ENEMA

Also called a *lower GI exam,* this test involves X-ray examination of the large intestine. It's done for people with a history of altered bowel habits, lower abdominal pain, or the passage of blood, mucus, or pus in the stools.

In the single-contrast technique, barium sulfate is inserted into the rectum. In the double-contrast technique, barium sulfate and air are inserted into the rectum. The single-contrast technique shows a profile view of the large intestine. The double-contrast technique shows profile and frontal views. The latter technique best detects small tumors (especially polyps), early inflammatory disease, and the subtle bleeding caused by ulcers.

Why is this test done?

A barium enema may be performed for the following reasons:
- To help diagnose colon cancer, rectal cancer, and inflammatory disease
- To detect polyps, diverticula, and structural changes in the large intestine.

What should you know before the test?

- You'll learn about the test, including who will perform it, where it will take place, and its expected duration (30 to 45 minutes).
- You'll learn that the accuracy of the test depends on your cooperation with the prescribed diet and bowel preparation. A common bowel preparation technique includes restricted intake of dairy products and maintenance of a liquid diet for 24 hours before the test. You'll be encouraged to drink five 8-ounce (250-milliliter) glasses of water or clear liquids 12 to 24 hours before the test.
- You'll receive an enema or repeat enemas until no stools remain in your large intestine to obscure the X-rays.

■ You'll be placed on a tilting X-ray table and adequately draped. During the test, you'll be secured to the table and assisted to various positions.

■ You'll learn that you may experience cramping pains or the urge to defecate as the barium or air is introduced into the intestine. If so, breathe deeply and slowly through your mouth to ease this discomfort.

■ During the test, you must keep your anus tightly contracted against the rectal tube to hold the tube in position and help prevent leakage of barium. If the barium leaks out, the intestinal walls won't be adequately coated and the test results may be inaccurate.

■ You'll receive a form that asks your consent to perform the test. Be sure to read this form carefully before signing it. Ask questions if you don't understand any portion of it.

What happens during the test?

■ You lie on your back on a tilting radiographic table as X-rays of your abdomen are taken.

■ You are helped to a different position, and a well-lubricated rectal tube is inserted through the anus.

■ The doctor or assistant slowly delivers the barium enema through the tube, and the filling process is monitored. To aid filling, the table may be tilted or you may be assisted to a different position.

■ As the flow of barium is observed, X-rays are taken of significant findings. When the barium fills the intestine, overhead X-rays of the abdomen are taken. Then the rectal tube is removed. You're escorted to the toilet or provided with a bedpan and asked to expel as much barium as possible.

■ Afterward, an additional X-ray is taken.

■ A double-contrast barium enema may directly follow this examination or may be performed separately. If it's performed immediately, a thin film of barium remains in your intestine, coating the mucosa, and air is carefully injected to distend the bowel lumen.

What happens after the test?

■ You'll need to drink extra fluids because bowel preparation and the test itself can cause dehydration.

■ You should rest. This test and the bowel preparation exhaust most people.

■ You'll receive a cleansing enema to remove any remaining barium. Your stools will be lightly colored for 24 to 72 hours.

The accuracy of a barium enema test depends on your cooperation in following the prescribed diet and bowel preparation.

After the test, you'll need to drink extra fluids because bowel preparation and the test itself can cause dehydration.

Does the test have risks?

- A barium enema shouldn't be done if a person has a rapid heart rate, severe ulcerative colitis, toxic megacolon, or a suspected perforation in the intestine.
- This test should be performed cautiously if a person has a blocked intestine, ulcerative colitis, diverticulitis, or severe bloody diarrhea.
- The test can cause complications, such as a perforation of the colon, water intoxication, and barium granulomas.

What are the normal results?

In the single-contrast enema, the intestine uniformly fills with barium, and the colon's markings are apparent. The intestinal walls collapse as the barium is expelled, and the intestinal lining has a regular, feathery appearance on the X-ray.

In the double-contrast enema, the intestine uniformly expands with air and has a thin layer of barium providing excellent detail of the mucosal pattern. As the person is assisted to various positions, the barium collects on the dependent walls of the intestine by the force of gravity.

What do abnormal results mean?

Most colon cancers occur in the rectosigmoid region and are best detected by a different test called *proctosigmoidoscopy.* However, this test may reveal cancer located higher in the intestine.

X-rays also demonstrate and define the extent of inflammatory disease, such as diverticulitis and ulcerative colitis. Ulcerative colitis usually originates in the anal region and ascends through the intestine.

X-ray films may also reveal polyps, structural changes in the intestine (such as telescoping of the bowel), gastroenteritis, irritable colon, and some cases of acute appendicitis.

X-RAYS OF THE DUODENUM

X-ray examination of the duodenum, the first portion of the small intestine, is called *hypotonic duodenography.* It's performed after barium sulfate and air are delivered into the intestine by a catheter.

This test is done for people who have symptoms of duodenal or pancreatic disease, such as persistent upper abdominal pain. However, it requires other follow-up tests to confirm a diagnosis.

Why is this test done?

Hypotonic duodenography may be performed for these reasons:
- To detect small duodenal lesions and cancer of the pancreas
- To help diagnose chronic pancreatitis.

What should you know before the test?

- You'll learn about the test, including who will perform it, where it will take place, and its expected duration (approximately an hour). During the test, a tube will be passed through your nose into your duodenum to serve as a channel for the barium and air. As the air is introduced, you may experience a cramping pain. If you do, breathe deeply and slowly through your mouth to help relax the abdominal muscles.
- The drug glucagon or an anticholinergic drug may be given during the test. Glucagon can cause nausea, vomiting, hives, and flushing. The anticholinergic drug can cause dry mouth, thirst, a rapid heartbeat, difficulty urinating, and blurred vision. If you'll be receiving an anticholinergic drug, someone should accompany you home.
- You'll receive a form that asks your consent to perform the test. Be sure to read this form carefully before signing it. Ask questions if you don't understand any portion of it.
- Fast after midnight the night before the test.
- Just before the test, remove any dentures, glasses, necklaces, hairpins, combs, and constricting undergarments. Also, you should urinate.

After the test, you may burp the air the doctor introduced or pass gas. Because of the barium, your stools will look chalky white for 24 to 72 hours.

What happens during the test?

- While you're seated, a catheter is passed through your nose into the stomach. You then lie down on the X-ray table, and the catheter is advanced into the duodenum.
- The drug glucagon may be given through an arm vein. Or an anticholinergic drug may be injected into a muscle.
- The barium is instilled through the catheter, and X-rays are taken of the duodenum. Some of the barium is then withdrawn and air is instilled. Then additional X-rays are taken.
- When the required films have been obtained, the catheter is removed.

What happens after the test?

- If an anticholinergic drug was given, you'll need to urinate within a few hours after the test. If you're alone, you'll need to rest in a waiting area until your vision clears (in about 2 hours).

■ You may burp instilled air or pass gas. Because of the barium, your stools will look chalky white for 24 to 72 hours.

Does the test have risks?

■ Anticholinergic drugs shouldn't be given to anyone with severe heart disease or glaucoma.

■ Glucagon shouldn't be given to anyone who has severe diabetes.

■ A person with strictures in the upper digestive tract shouldn't undergo this procedure.

■ Elderly or very ill people may vomit from the test or may have heartburn.

What are the normal results?

When barium and air expand the duodenum, the mucosa normally appears smooth and even. The regular contour of the head of the pancreas also appears on the duodenal wall.

What do abnormal results mean?

Irregular nodules or masses on the duodenal wall could mean duodenal lesions, tumors of the pancreas, or chronic pancreatitis. Diagnosis requires further tests, such as endoscopic retrograde cholangiopancreatography, blood and urine tests, and ultrasound and computerized axial tomography (CAT) scans of the pancreas.

X-RAYS OF THE GALLBLADDER

Called *oral cholecystography* by doctors, this X-ray test examines the gallbladder after pills containing a special dye are swallowed. It's performed when a person has symptoms of gallbladder disease, such as pain on the upper right side of the abdomen, fat intolerance, and jaundice.

Why is this test done?

X-rays of the gallbladder may be performed for the following reasons:

■ To detect gallstones

■ To help diagnose inflammatory disease and tumors of the gallbladder.

What should you know before the test?

■ You'll find out about the test, including who will perform it, where it will take place, and its expected duration (usually 30 to 45 minutes, but a longer test may be necessary). You'll eat a meal containing fat at noon the day before the test and a fat-free meal in the evening. After the evening meal, you can only have water.

■ You'll receive several tablets that contain the special dye used in the test. Swallow the tablets one at a time at 5-minute intervals, with one or two mouthfuls of water. The tablets often cause diarrhea but rarely produce other problems, such as nausea, vomiting, stomach cramps, and painful urination. Tell the nurse immediately if you get any of these symptoms.

■ Tell the doctor or nurse if you have allergies to anesthetics, iodine, shellfish (such as shrimp or scallops), or the dyes used in any tests.

■ You may receive a cleansing enema the morning of the test. This clears the digestive tract for the test.

■ You'll receive a form that asks your consent to perform the test. Be sure to read this form carefully before signing it. Ask questions if you don't understand any portion of it.

The gallbladder normally appears pear-shaped, with smooth, thin walls. Its size varies.

What happens during the test?

■ You lie face down on the X-ray table, and the doctor takes and looks at X-rays of your abdomen.

■ You change positions and additional X-rays are taken.

■ You may then be given a fat stimulus, such as a high-fat meal or a synthetic fat-containing agent. The doctor will then observe the emptying of your gallbladder and take X-rays every 15 to 30 minutes. If the gallbladder empties slowly or not at all, these X-rays are also taken at 60 minutes.

What happens after the test?

■ If the results are normal, you can resume your usual diet. If they're abnormal, you may need to stay on a low-fat diet until a definite diagnosis can be made.

■ If gallstones are discovered, you'll need an appropriate diet — usually one that restricts fat — to help prevent attacks.

Does the test have risks?

The test shouldn't be done on a person with severe kidney or liver disease or with allergies to iodine, shellfish, or the dyes used for other diagnostic tests.

What are the normal results?

The gallbladder normally appears pear-shaped, with smooth, thin walls. Although its size varies, its basic structure — neck, infundibulum, body, and fundus — is clearly outlined on X-rays.

What do abnormal results mean?

The test can detect gallstones, the presence of cholesterol, polyps, and benign tumors. It also can show inflammatory disease such as cholecystitis — with or without gallstone formation.

When the gallbladder fails to contract following consumption of a fatty meal, it may indicate cholecystitis or common bile duct obstruction. If the X-rays are inconclusive, the test will have to be repeated the following day.

EXAMINATION OF THE BILE DUCTS

This test, which doctors call *percutaneous transhepatic cholangiography*, allows the doctor to examine the bile ducts (ducts that carry bile through the liver to the digestive system). It requires injection of a contrast dye directly into the ducts. The test is especially useful for evaluating a person with persistent upper abdominal pain after gallbladder removal and for evaluating a person with severe jaundice.

Why is this test done?

Percutaneous transhepatic cholangiography may be performed for the following reasons:
- To determine the cause of upper abdominal pain following gallbladder removal
- To distinguish between obstructive and nonobstructive jaundice
- To determine the location, the extent and, in many cases, the cause of gallbladder obstruction.

What should you know before the test?

- You'll learn about the test, including who will perform it, where it will take place, and its duration (about 30 minutes). During the test, you'll lie on a tilting X-ray table that rotates into vertical and horizontal positions. You'll be adequately secured to the table and assisted to different positions.

■ Tell the doctor or nurse if you have allergies to anesthetics, iodine, shellfish (such as shrimp or scallops), or the dyes used in any tests. Injection of the dye may produce a sensation of pressure and fullness and may cause brief upper back pain on the right side. The injection of the local anesthetic may sting the skin and produce transient pain when it punctures the liver capsule.

■ You may receive an antibiotic intravenously every 4 to 6 hours for 24 hours before the procedure.

■ You'll need to fast for 8 hours before the test. Just before the procedure, you may receive a sedative.

■ You'll receive a form that asks your consent to perform the test. Be sure to read this form carefully before signing it. Ask questions if you don't understand any portion of it.

The bile ducts should have a normal diameter and appear as regular channels, evenly filled with the dye.

What happens during the test?

■ You lie on your back on the X-ray table and are adequately secured. Then you'll receive an injection of the local anesthetic.

■ While you hold your breath at the end of expiration, the doctor guides a needle into the liver and slowly removes it while injecting the test dye. (See *How dye is injected directly into the liver*, page 40.)

■ Using a fluoroscope and monitor, the doctor checks the opacification of the bile ducts and takes X-rays as you're assisted into different positions. When the required X-rays have been taken, the needle is removed.

■ The nurse applies a dressing to the puncture site.

What happens after the test?

■ A nurse will check your condition regularly.

■ You should stay in bed for at least 6 hours after the test, preferably lying on your right side. This will help to prevent bleeding.

■ You can resume your usual diet.

Does the test have risks?

■ The test shouldn't be done in cases of cholangitis, massive ascites, an uncorrectable blood clotting disorder, or an allergy to iodine.

■ It carries the potential risk of bleeding, septicemia, bile peritonitis, and leakage of the dye into the peritoneal cavity.

What are the normal results?

The bile ducts should have a normal diameter and appear as regular channels evenly filled with the dye.

How dye is injected directly into the liver

To obtain a view of the bile ducts, the doctor performs a procedure called *percutaneous transhepatic cholangiography*. In this procedure, the doctor injects a special dye directly into the liver. This illustration shows the path of the needle through the liver into a structure called the *biliary radicle,* the primary root of the bile ducts.

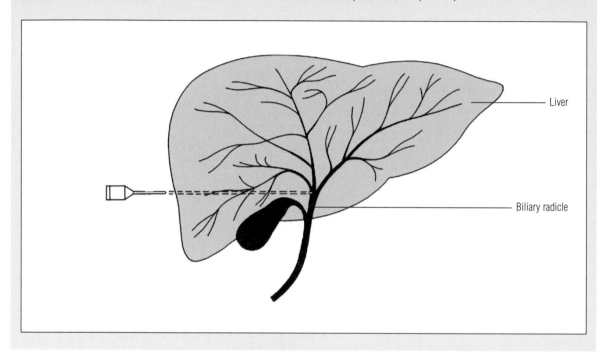

Liver

Biliary radicle

What do abnormal results mean?

Distinguishing between obstructive and nonobstructive jaundice hinges on whether bile ducts are dilated or of normal size. Obstructive jaundice is linked to dilated ducts. Nonobstructive jaundice is linked to normal-sized ducts. The obstruction may be caused by cholelithiasis, cancer of the bile ducts, or pancreatic cancer.

When ducts are of normal size and cholestasis is indicated, liver biopsy may be performed to distinguish among hepatitis, cirrhosis, and granulomatous disease.

EXAMINATION OF THE PANCREATIC DUCTS, LIVER, AND BILE DUCTS

A test called *endoscopic retrograde cholangiopancreatography* allows the doctor to examine the pancreatic ducts, liver, and bile ducts. This test uses X-rays and a special instrument called an *endoscope.* The X-rays are taken after the injection of a special dye through one of the endoscope's channels.

The test is performed when a person has confirmed or suspected pancreatic disease or obstructive jaundice of an unknown cause.

Why is this test done?

This test may be performed for the following reasons:
- To evaluate obstructive jaundice
- To diagnose cancer of the duodenum, the pancreas, and the bile ducts
- To locate stones and narrowing in the pancreatic ducts and hepatobiliary tree (the liver and bile ducts).

What should you know before the test?

- You'll learn about the test, including who will perform it, where it will take place, and its expected duration (30 to 60 minutes). At the start of the test, a local anesthetic will be sprayed into your mouth to calm the gag reflex. The spray has an unpleasant taste and makes the tongue and throat feel swollen, causing difficulty in swallowing. You'll also have an intravenous line inserted.
- You'll be told to let saliva drain from the side of your mouth during the test and that suction may be used to remove the saliva. A mouth guard will be inserted to protect your teeth and the endoscope. It won't interfere with your breathing.
- You'll be given a sedative before the insertion of the endoscope to help you relax, but you'll remain conscious during the test. You'll also receive an anticholinergic drug or the drug glucagon after insertion of the scope. The anticholinergic drug can cause dry mouth, thirst, a rapid heartbeat, difficult urination, and blurred vision. The glucagon can cause nausea, vomiting, hives, and flushing.
- When the doctor injects the dye for the test, be prepared to feel warm or flushed. Tell the doctor or nurse if you have allergies to anesthetics, iodine, shellfish (such as shrimp or scallops), or the dyes used in any tests.

- You'll need to fast after midnight before the test.
- Just before the test, remove any jewelry or constricting undergarments. You should urinate to minimize the discomfort of urine retention that may follow the test.
- You'll receive a form that asks your consent to perform the test. Be sure to read this form carefully before signing it. Ask questions if you don't understand any portion of it.

What happens during the test?

- After the nurse inserts an intravenous line, you get a local anesthetic that usually takes effect in about 10 minutes. If a spray is used, hold your breath while your mouth and throat are sprayed.
- You're given a basin to spit into. Because the anesthetic causes drooling, let the saliva drain from the side of your mouth.
- The nurse then inserts the mouth guard. While you're lying on your side, you receive a drug to help you relax.
- After you're relaxed, you bend your head forward and open your mouth. The doctor then guides the endoscope slowly into your stomach.
- You are then helped into a face-down position and are given an anticholinergic drug or glucagon. The doctor passes a small amount of air and the dye through one of the channels of the endoscope and examines the pancreas and the hepatobiliary tree. The doctor also takes X-rays, has them developed, and reviews them.
- When the required X-rays have been taken, the doctor may obtain a small biopsy specimen. Then the doctor removes the endoscope.

What happens after the test?

- The nurse will check your condition often: about every 15 minutes for 4 hours, then every hour for 4 hours, and then every 4 hours for 48 hours.
- You won't be able to eat or drink until your gag reflex returns. When it does, you can have fluids and a light meal.
- At the appropriate time, the nurse will remove the intravenous line.
- Tell the nurse if you have a sore throat. Soothing lozenges and warm saline gargles can ease discomfort.

Does the test have risks?

■ The test shouldn't be performed on a person with infectious disease, pancreatic pseudocysts, stricture or obstruction of the esophagus or duodenum, and acute pancreatitis, cholangitis, or heart or lung disease.

■ The test can cause cholangitis and pancreatitis.

■ The test can also cause breathing difficulty, low blood pressure, excessive sweating, a slow heartbeat, and laryngospasm.

What are the normal results?

The dye should uniformly fill the pancreatic duct, the hepatobiliary tree, and the gallbladder.

What do abnormal results mean?

The test may demonstrate obstructive jaundice. Examination of the hepatobiliary tree may reveal stones, strictures, or irregular deviations that suggest bile duct cirrhosis, primary sclerosing cholangitis, or cancer of the bile ducts.

Examination of the pancreatic ducts may also show stones, strictures, and irregular deviations that may indicate pancreatic cysts and pseudocysts, cancer, chronic pancreatitis, pancreatic fibrosis, and papillary stenosis.

Depending on test findings, a definite diagnosis may require further studies.

After you're relaxed, you bend your head forward and open your mouth. The doctor then guides the endoscope slowly into your stomach.

X-RAYS OF THE SPLEEN

This test, called *splenoportography,* consists of X-rays of the spleen's veins and portal system after the injection of a dye into the spleen itself. The test begins with measurement of splenic pressure and continues with X-rays that record the filling of the splenic and portal veins.

Why is this test done?

X-rays of the spleen may be taken for the following reasons:

■ To diagnose or evaluate portal hypertension (high blood pressure in the vein leading from the liver to the spleen).

■ To discover what stage of cirrhosis the person has.

What should you know before the test?

■ You'll learn about the test, including who will perform it and where and that it takes 30 to 45 minutes. You may feel a brief stinging sensation on injection of the local anesthetic and a brief warm or flushed feeling on injection of the test dye. You'll be alerted to report pain on your left upper side immediately.

■ Tell the doctor or nurse if you have allergies to anesthetics, iodine, shellfish (such as shrimp or scallops), or the dyes used in any tests. The dye used in this test can cause nausea, vomiting, excessive salivation, flushing, hives, sweating and, rarely, a severe life-threatening allergic reaction. These reactions usually occur 5 to 10 minutes after the injection.

■ Fast after the evening meal the day before the procedure.

■ About 30 minutes before the procedure, you'll receive a mild sedative and pain medication.

■ You'll receive a form that asks your consent to perform the test. Be sure to read this form carefully before signing it. Ask questions if you don't understand any portion of it.

What happens during the test?

■ You lie on your back on the X-ray table, with your left hand under your head. The left side of your chest and stomach are cleaned with antiseptics.

■ The doctor locates your spleen, takes an X-ray, and injects a local anesthetic.

■ You are directed to hold your breath as the doctor inserts the needle into the spleen. Breathe shallowly as the doctor connects a device to the needle to measure spleen pressure.

■ After measuring pressure, the doctor removes the device and injects the test dye. X-rays are then taken. When they're completed, the doctor removes the needle and applies a dressing.

What happens after the test?

■ The nurse will check you often: roughly every 15 minutes for 1 hour, then every 30 minutes for 2 hours, and then every hour for 4 hours.

■ Lie on your left side for 24 hours to minimize the risk of bleeding. Stay in bed for another 24 hours after that.

■ You can resume your usual diet. Drink fluids to promote excretion of the dye.

INSIGHT INTO ILLNESS

Understanding portal hypertension: Its causes and complications

Portal hypertension refers to high blood pressure in the vein leading from the liver to the spleen (the portal vein). It occurs because of increased resistance to blood flow, which may stem from a cause above, within, or below the liver. It may lead to a variety of complications, including an enlarged liver, an enlarged spleen, or esophageal varices, a condition marked by dilated, tortuous veins in the lower esophagus, which may start bleeding and lead to serious consequences.

Causes above the liver
- Incompetence of the heart's tricuspid valve
- Hepatic vein clot
- Constrictive pericarditis (inflammation of the sac surrounding the heart)

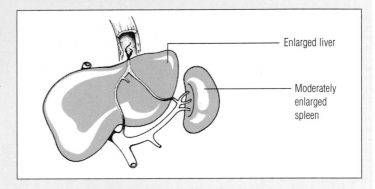

Enlarged liver

Moderately enlarged spleen

Causes within the liver
Cirrhosis

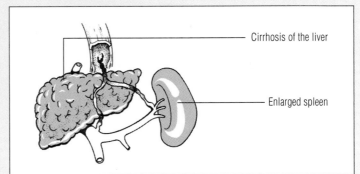

Cirrhosis of the liver

Enlarged spleen

Causes below the liver
Portal vein clot

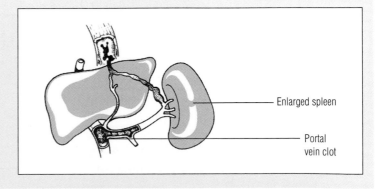

Enlarged spleen

Portal vein clot

Does the test have risks?

■ This test shouldn't be performed on a person with ascites, uncorrectable blood clotting problems, an enlarged spleen caused by infection, markedly impaired liver or kidney function, and an allergy to iodine.

■ This test may cause excessive bleeding that requires transfusion or, occasionally, splenectomy.

What are the normal results?

Spleen pressure normally measures 50 to 180 millimeters of water (3.5 to 13.5 millimeters of mercury). After the dye is injected into the spleen, it outlines splenic tributary veins and drains into the splenic and portal veins. Normal venous flow should be contained within these two vessels, without diversion into collateral veins.

What do abnormal results mean?

In portal hypertension, spleen pressure ranges from 200 to 450 millimeters of water (15 to 34 millimeters of mercury). The presence of collateral veins — often associated with esophageal varices, splenomegaly and, in some cases, an enlarged liver — can also indicate portal hypertension resulting from blocked portal venous flow. Results may also show thrombosis or occlusion in the splenic and portal veins provided venous flow isn't reversed. (See *Understanding portal hypertension: Its causes and complications,* page 45.)

The test may also show cirrhosis and, depending on the specific findings, may help determine its stage.

ANGIOGRAM OF THE ABDOMINAL BLOOD VESSELS

Called *celiac and mesenteric arteriography* by doctors, this X-ray test examines the abdominal blood vessels after the injection of a special dye. Injection of the dye into one or more arteries provides a map of the abdominal vessels. Injection into specific arterial branches, called *superselective angiography,* permits detailed study of a particular area.

This test is performed when endoscopy can't find the source of gastrointestinal bleeding or when barium studies, ultrasound scans, and nuclear medicine or computerized axial tomography (CAT) scans prove inconclusive in evaluating cancer. It's also used to evaluate cirrhosis and portal hypertension, to find blood vessel damage after abdominal injury, and to detect other blood vessel problems.

Why is this test done?

An angiogram of the abdominal blood vessels may be performed for the following reasons:

- To locate the source of gastrointestinal bleeding
- To help distinguish between benign and malignant tumors
- To evaluate cirrhosis and portal hypertension
- To evaluate blood vessel damage after abdominal injury
- To detect other blood vessels abnormalities.

What should you know before the test?

- You'll learn who will perform the test and where and that it takes 30 minutes to 3 hours, depending on the number of vessels studied. You'll receive a local anesthetic and feel a brief, stinging sensation as it's injected. You may also feel pressure when the doctor touches the area (over the femoral artery in the groin area) where the dye will be injected. But the local anesthetic will minimize the pain when the needle is introduced into the artery.
- You'll learn that the injection may cause a brief feeling of warmth or burning, a headache, a salty taste, and nausea and vomiting. Tell the doctor or nurse if you have allergies to anesthetics, iodine, shellfish (such as shrimp or scallops), or the dyes used in any tests.
- You'll need to lie still during the test to avoid blurring the films, and restraints may be used to keep you still. The X-ray equipment makes a loud, clacking sound as the films are taken.
- You'll need to fast for 8 hours before the test.
- Just before the test, put on a hospital gown and remove jewelry and other objects that might obscure anatomic detail on X-ray films. Then go to the bathroom to urinate.
- You'll receive a sedative just before the test, if the doctor prescribed one.
- You'll receive a form that asks your consent to perform the test. Be sure to read this form carefully before signing it. Ask questions if you don't understand any portion of it.

You'll need to lie still during the test to avoid blurring the films, and restraints may be used to keep you still. The X-ray equipment makes a loud, clacking sound as the films are taken.

What happens during the test?

- You lie on your back on an X-ray table, and a nurse inserts an intravenous line.
- X-rays are taken of your abdomen, and your pulse rate is checked.

- The nurse cleans the area around the injection site and shaves it.
- The doctor injects the local anesthetic and locates the femoral artery. Then the doctor inserts the needle and passes a catheter through it to the aorta, the major abdominal blood vessel.
- Next, the doctor injects the dye and takes a series of X-rays. After injecting into one or more major arteries, superselective catheterization may be performed.
- After the X-rays are completed, the doctor removes the catheter and applies a dressing.

What happens after the test?

- The nurse will check on you often to see if your pulses and the temperature and color of your leg are okay.
- You'll rest in bed for 4 to 6 hours. The leg with the puncture site must be kept straight.
- If you don't have an intravenous line, drink lots of fluids to speed the excretion of the dye.
- You may feel some temporary stiffness after the test from lying still on the hard X-ray table.

Does the test have risks?

- The test should be performed cautiously on a person with a blood clotting problem.
- The dye used in the test can cause an allergic reaction, which rarely is severe. Most reactions occur within a half-hour.
- Complications of the test include hemorrhage, thrombosis, an irregular heartbeat, and emboli caused by dislodging atherosclerotic plaques.

After the test, you'll rest in bed for 4 to 6 hours, and you must keep the leg with the puncture site straight.

What are the normal results?

The X-rays show no problems with the abdominal blood vessels.

What do abnormal results mean?

Gastrointestinal bleeding appears on the angiogram as the leakage of the dye from the damaged vessels. Severe upper gastrointestinal bleeding can be caused by conditions such as Mallory-Weiss syndrome, gastric or peptic ulcer, hemorrhagic gastritis, and an eroded hiatal hernia. Severe lower gastrointestinal bleeding can be caused by conditions such as bleeding diverticula and angiodysplasia.

The test can identify changes in blood vessels caused by abdominal cancer. It may also show the progression of cirrhosis.

Abdominal injury often damages the spleen and, less often, the liver. The test can reveal these injuries.

Various abnormalities affecting the diameter and course of an artery may appear on the angiogram. Atherosclerotic plaques or atheromas — fatty deposits inside the vessel — narrow the blood vessel and may block it.

KIDNEYS & URINARY TRACT

X-RAY OF THE KIDNEYS, URETERS, AND BLADDER

Called *KUB* for short, an X-ray of the kidneys, ureters, and bladder is usually the first step in testing the urinary system. This test determines the position of the kidneys, ureters, and bladder and helps detect major abnormalities.

This test has many limitations and nearly always must be followed by more elaborate tests, such as a computerized axial tomography (CAT) scan.

Why is this test done?

An X-ray of the kidneys, ureters, and bladder may be performed for the following reasons:
- To evaluate the size, structure, and position of the kidneys
- To screen for abnormalities in the region of the kidneys, ureters, and bladder.

What should you know before the test?

- You'll learn who will perform the test and where and that it takes only a few minutes.
- You won't need to fast or limit fluids.

What happens during the test?

- You lie on your back on an X-ray table, with your arms extended overhead.
- A single X-ray is taken.

Does the test have risks?

The test does involve exposure to a small amount of radiation. Men will have their groin area shielded by a lead apron to avoid irradiation of the testicles. Women, unfortunately, can't have their ovaries shielded because they're too close to the kidneys, ureters, and bladder.

What are the normal results?

Both kidneys should be about the same size. The ureters are only visible when an abnormality is present. The bladder may or may not be visible.

What do abnormal results mean?

Enlargement of both kidneys seen on the X-ray may be caused by polycystic disease, multiple myeloma, lymphoma, amyloidosis, or hydronephrosis. Enlargement of one kidney may be caused by a tumor, cyst, or hydronephrosis. Decreased size of one kidney suggests possible congenital hypoplasia, pyelonephritis, or ischemia.

This test may detect problems present at birth, such as abnormal location or absence of a kidney. It may also reveal polycystic disease, pyelonephritis, or kidney stones. In most cases, positive identification of kidney stones requires further testing.

An X-ray of the kidneys, ureters, and bladder is usually the first step in testing the urinary system.

NEPHROTOMOGRAPHY

This test provides images of sections or layers of the kidney and its blood vessels. In the test, special X-rays and other films are taken before and after the kidney is coated with a dye. Injected into the arm, this dye has special properties that cause it to show up on X-rays.

Nephrotomography can be performed as a separate test or as an adjunct to a test called *intravenous pyelography*. It's particularly helpful in identifying problems suggested by such other tests.

Why is this test done?

Nephrotomography may be performed for the following reasons:

- To differentiate a simple kidney cyst from a tumor
- To evaluate lacerations of the kidneys
- To find adrenal gland tumors when other tests indicate their presence but not their location.

What should you know before the test?

- You'll learn who will perform the test and where and that it takes less than 1 hour. During the test, you'll be positioned on an X-ray table and may hear loud, clacking sounds as the films are exposed. When the dye is injected, you may feel a burning or stinging sensation at the injection site, flushing, and a metallic taste.
- Tell the doctor or nurse if you have any allergies to shellfish (such as shrimp or scallops), iodine, or the dyes used in other diagnostic tests.
- You'll fast for 8 hours before the test.
- You'll need to sign a form that gives your consent to perform the test. Be sure to read this form carefully and ask questions if you don't understand any portion of it.

What happens during the test?

- You lie on an X-ray table as preliminary X-rays and tomograms are taken.
- After reviewing the preliminary tomograms, the doctor selects five vertical views of the kidney for filming. Then the doctor administers the test dye and takes additional tomograms.

What happens after the test?

- The nurse will check your condition regularly for 24 hours after the test.
- Tell the nurse if you feel flushed, nauseated, or itch or sneeze a lot. If you have these symptoms, the nurse will give you medication for them.

Does the test have risks?

Nephrotomography is performed with extreme caution on a person who has allergies to iodine or shellfish. Caution is also used when the test is being performed on a person with severe cardiovascular disease or multiple myeloma.

By examining images of sections or layers of the kidney, the doctor can differentiate a simple kidney cyst from a tumor.

What are the normal results?

The size, shape, and position of the kidneys should appear normal. No tumors, stones, or other abnormalities should be present.

What do abnormal results mean?

Among the problems detected by the test are simple cysts and tumors, areas of poor circulation, and kidney lacerations that occur following injury.

EXAMINATION OF THE URETHRA

X-ray examination of the urethra is called *retrograde urethrography*. Performed almost exclusively on men, this X-ray study uses a special dye that's injected or instilled into the urethra, the canal that carries urine from the bladder. The test allows the doctor to examine the full length of this canal.

Why is this test done?

X-ray examination of the urethra may be performed for the following reasons:
- To diagnose narrowing of the urethra, blockages, diverticula, and urethral problems present at birth
- To evaluate tears of the urethra or other injury
- To check the condition of the urethra after surgery.

What should you know before the test?

- You'll learn about the test, including who will perform it, where it will take place, and its expected duration (about 30 minutes). During the test, you may experience some discomfort when the catheter is inserted into the urethral opening and when the dye is instilled through the catheter.
- Tell the doctor or nurse if you have any allergies to shellfish (such as shrimp or scallops), iodine, or the dyes used in other diagnostic tests.
- You'll be told about the loud, clacking sounds as X-ray films are made.
- Just before the test, you may receive a sedative. The nurse will tell you to urinate.

■ You'll need to sign a form that gives your consent to perform the test. Be sure to read this form carefully and ask questions if you don't understand any portion of it.

What happens during the test?

■ You lie on the examining table as X-rays of the bladder and urethra are made. The doctor studies these X-rays to detect any stones, foreign bodies, or other problems.

■ The nurse cleans your penis with an antiseptic solution. The doctor then inserts the catheter into the urethra. The catheter has a small balloon at its end. The doctor inflates the balloon with a little water to prevent the catheter from slipping during the test.

■ The doctor injects the dye through the catheter. After three-fourths of the dye has been injected, the first X-ray film is exposed. The doctor injects the remainder of the dye and takes additional X-rays.

After the test, you'll be checked on regularly for 12 to 24 hours. Tell the nurse if you feel hot or have chills.

What happens after the test?

You'll be checked on regularly for 12 to 24 hours. Tell the nurse if you feel hot or have chills.

Does the test have risks?

The test is performed cautiously on a person with a urinary tract infection.

What are the normal results?

The urethra should appear normal in size, shape, and course.

What do abnormal results mean?

This test may reveal different problems, such as urethral diverticula, fistulas, narrowing, false passages, stones, and tears. It can identify problems present from birth, such as urethral valves and perineal hypospadias. It can also detect tumors, which are rare in the urethra.

EXAMINATION OF THE BLADDER

X-ray examination of the bladder is called *retrograde cystography*. During this procedure, a doctor inserts a catheter into the urethra, the slender channel through which urine flows from the bladder. After inserting the catheter, the doctor instills a special dye through the catheter into the bladder. The dye possesses properties that cause it to appear on X-rays.

The test can diagnose bladder rupture. It's also done for recurrent urinary tract infections (especially in children) and suspected fistulas, diverticula, and tumors.

The test should show a bladder with normal contours, capacity, and integrity. The bladder wall should be smooth, not thick.

Why is this test done?

This test is performed to evaluate the structure and integrity of the bladder.

What should you know before the test?

■ You'll learn about the test, including who will perform it, where it will take place, and its expected duration (about 30 to 60 minutes). During the test, you may experience some discomfort when the catheter is inserted into the urethral opening and when the dye is instilled through the catheter.

■ Tell the doctor or nurse if you have any allergies to shellfish (such as shrimp or scallops), iodine, or the dyes used in other diagnostic tests.

■ You'll be told that the X-ray machine makes loud, clacking sounds.

■ You'll need to sign a form that gives your consent to perform the test. Be sure to read this form carefully and ask questions if you don't understand any portion of it.

What happens during the test?

■ You lie on your back on the examining table, and a preliminary X-ray is taken. The doctor checks this X-ray before proceeding with the test.

■ Next, the doctor inserts a catheter through the urethra into the bladder, puts a clamp on the catheter, and gently instills the test dye through it.

■ The doctor takes one X-ray while you remain on your back and two more while you lie on each side. Next, the nurse may help you assume a jackknife position while the doctor takes yet another X-ray.

■ The doctor unclamps the catheter, which allows urine and the test dye to drain, and takes another X-ray. After this, the doctor removes the catheter.

What happens after the test

■ A nurse will check on you several times an hour for the first 2 hours after the test, then roughly every 2 hours for up to 24 hours.
■ The nurse will check the color and volume of your urine, which will probably contain some blood for a short time.
■ Tell the nurse if you feel hot, have chills, or simply don't feel well.

Does the test have risks?

■ This test shouldn't be performed during a severe urinary tract infection.
■ It also shouldn't be performed on any person with a blockage in the urinary tract.

What are the normal results?

The test should show a bladder with normal contours, capacity, and integrity. The bladder wall should be smooth, not thick.

What do abnormal results mean?

The test can identify pouches in the bladder wall called *diverticula*. It can also find tumors, stones or gravel, and blood clots.

EXAMINATION OF THE URETERS

This X-ray test, called *retrograde ureteropyelography*, examines the ureters, the two slender tubes that carry urine from the kidneys to the bladder. It's performed during cystoscopy, a procedure in which the doctor examines the bladder using a viewing instrument called an *endoscope*. During cystoscopy, the doctor will insert a catheter through one of the endoscope's channels into the ureters and gently instill a special dye. The dye possesses properties that cause it to appear on X-rays. (See *Spotting stones and other obstructions,* page 56.)

INSIGHT INTO ILLNESS

Spotting stones and other obstructions

X-ray examination of the ureters may detect blockages of urine flow in the kidneys and ureters. These blockages can be caused by a stricture, a tumor, a blood clot, or stones. Small stones may travel and become lodged in the ureter. A large blockage called a *staghorn stone* may form in the kidney.

Examples of various blockages are shown below.

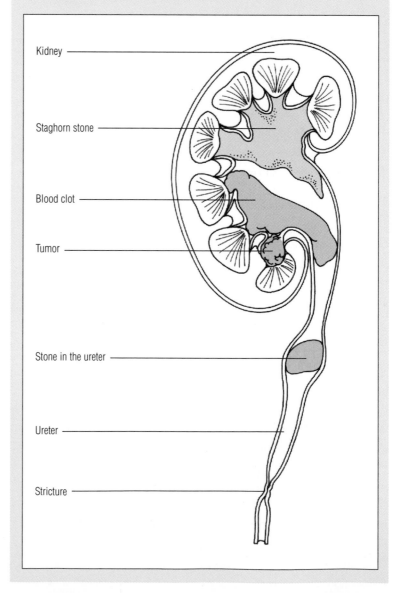

Kidney

Staghorn stone

Blood clot

Tumor

Stone in the ureter

Ureter

Stricture

Why is this test done?

This test is performed to check the structure and integrity of the kidneys and the ureters.

What should you know before the test?

■ You'll learn who will perform the test and where and that it takes about 1 hour. If a general anesthetic is to be used, you'll need to fast for 8 hours before the test. Generally, you should be well hydrated to ensure adequate urine flow.

■ During the test, you'll be positioned on an examining table, with your legs in stirrups. This position may be tiring.

■ If you don't receive a general anesthetic, you'll receive a sedative before the test. During the test, you may feel pressure when the endoscope is passed and when the dye is instilled. Also, you may feel an urgency to urinate.

■ You'll need to sign a form that gives your consent to perform the test. Be sure to read this form carefully and ask questions if you don't understand any portion of it.

What happens during the test?

■ You lie on your back on the examining table, with your legs in the stirrups.

■ After you receive an anesthetic, the doctor inserts the endoscope through the urethral opening and advances it into the bladder. Once there, the doctor can look at the bladder and insert a catheter into one or both ureters.

■ Next, the doctor instills a tiny amount of the test dye through the catheter and takes a series of X-rays.

■ Then the doctor removes the catheter, waits 10 to 15 minutes, and checks for retention of the dye. However, if the doctor finds a blockage in a ureter, the catheter may be kept in place to allow urine to flow.

What happens after the test?

■ The nurse will check on you often to see how you're feeling. You'll need to drink extra fluids.

■ The nurse will check the color and volume of your urine. You'll probably experience pain when you urinate, but the nurse will give you medication for as long as the pain lasts. Your urine will also contain some blood for a short time.

■ Tell the nurse if you have any pain or feel hot or have chills.

Does the test have risks?

Examination of the ureters will be done very carefully in a person with an ureteral blockage to prevent further injury.

What are the normal results?

The ureters should fill uniformly and appear normal in size and course.

What do abnormal results mean?

The test can reveal a blockage, most commonly at the junction of a ureter and the kidney. The blockage may be caused by a tumor, a blood clot, narrowing, or a stone.

EXAMINATION OF THE KIDNEYS

This X-ray test, called *antegrade pyelography*, examines the kidneys. It's performed when a blocked ureter makes it impossible to perform cystoscopy.

In this test, the doctor inserts a needle into the kidney, injects a special dye, and takes X-rays. The dye possesses properties that cause it to appear on X-rays.

Why is this test done?

X-ray examination of the kidneys may be performed for the following reasons:
■ To evaluate blockages in the kidneys or ureters caused by a stricture, stones, blood clots, or a tumor
■ To evaluate hydronephrosis
■ To check the condition of the kidneys or ureters before or after surgery.

What should you know before the test?

■ You'll learn about the test, including who will perform it and where and that it will take approximately 1 to 2 hours. During the test, the doctor will insert a needle into the kidney after giving you a sedative and a local anesthetic. Urine may be collected from the kidney for testing and, if necessary, a tube will be left in the kidney for drainage.

■ You may feel mild discomfort during injection of the local anesthetic and dye and also a brief sensation of burning and warmth from the dye.

■ Tell the doctor or the nurse if you have a blood clotting disorder. Also mention if you have any allergies to shellfish (such as shrimp or scallops), iodine, or the dyes used in other diagnostic tests.

■ You may need to fast for 6 to 8 hours before the test.

■ You may receive antibiotics before and after the test. Just before it, you may get a sedative to help you relax.

■ You'll need to sign a form that states your consent to perform the test. Be sure to read this form carefully and ask questions if you don't understand any portion of it.

What happens during the test?

■ You lie face down on the X-ray table. The skin over the kidney is cleaned with an antiseptic, and a local anesthetic is injected.

■ The doctor inserts a needle into the kidney, attaches tubing to it, and collects a little urine for testing.

■ Next, the doctor injects the test dye and takes X-rays.

■ If necessary, the doctor will insert a tube into the kidney to allow it to drain. If a tube isn't needed, the doctor removes the needle and tubing and applies a dressing.

As the test begins, you lie face down on the X-ray table. The skin over the kidney is cleaned with an antiseptic, and a local anesthetic is injected.

What happens after the test?

■ The nurse will check on you often to see how you're feeling.

■ The nurse will check the color and volume of your urine. You'll probably experience pain when you urinate, but the nurse will give you medication for as long as the pain lasts. Your urine will also contain some blood for a short time.

■ Tell the nurse if you have any pain or feel hot or have chills.

■ If the doctor leaves a kidney tube in place, the nurse will check that it's draining properly.

Does the test have risks?

This test shouldn't be performed on a person with a bleeding disorder.

What are the normal results?

After injection of dye, the kidneys and ureters should fill uniformly and appear normal in size and course. Normal structures should be outlined clearly.

What do abnormal results mean?

The test can show enlarged areas of the kidneys or ureters. This enlargement means a blockage, which can be caused by stricture, stones, blood clots, or a tumor.

The test can detect hydronephrosis. It also shows the results of a recent surgery.

EXAMINATION OF THE URINARY TRACT

The cornerstone of urologic testing, this test, called *intravenous pyelography*, evaluates the structure and function of nearly the entire urinary tract. It's commonly known by the abbreviation IVP. Another name for this test is excretory urography.

In this test, the doctor injects a dye into an arm vein. The dye, which has properties that cause it to appear on X-rays, flows to the kidneys. Once it's there, X-rays are taken. The dye continues to flow through the ureters, the slender tubes that connect the kidneys to the bladder. The doctor takes X-rays of the dye's passage through these structures.

Why is this test done?

Examination of the urinary tract may be performed for the following reasons:
- To evaluate the condition of the kidneys, ureters, and bladder
- To check for suspected kidney or urinary tract disease, such as kidney stones, tumors, urinary problems present at birth, or an injury to the urinary system
- To identify kidney problems as the cause of high blood pressure, a condition called *renovascular hypertension*.

What should you know before the test?

- You'll learn about the test, including who will perform it, where it will take place, and its expected duration.

- You may feel mild discomfort during the injection of the local anesthetic and a brief sensation of burning and warmth and a metallic taste in your mouth from the injection of the dye. During the test, the X-ray machine will make loud, clacking sounds.
- Tell the doctor or the nurse if you have a blood clotting disorder. Also mention if you have any allergies to shellfish (such as shrimp or scallops), iodine, or the dyes used in other diagnostic tests.
- Drink lots of fluids on the day before the test. For 8 hours before the test, you'll need to fast.
- You may receive a laxative on the night before the test to help give clearer X-rays.
- You'll need to sign a form that gives your consent to perform the test. Be sure to read this form carefully and ask questions if you don't understand any portion of it.

What happens during the test?

- You lie on your back on an X-ray table.
- The doctor takes a preliminary X-ray of your kidneys, ureters, and bladder. If this X-ray shows no obvious problems, the doctor goes ahead and injects the dye.
- About a minute later, the dye reaches the kidneys, and the doctor takes an X-ray. Additional X-rays are then taken at regular intervals, usually 5, 10, and 15 or 20 minutes after the injection.
- After the 5-minute X-ray is done, the doctor compresses the ureters. To do this, the doctor inflates two small rubber devices and places them on both sides of your stomach. The inflated devices block the ureters, without causing any discomfort, and keep the dye from flowing farther.
- After the 10-minute X-ray is done, the doctor removes the rubber devices. As the dye flows into the lower urinary tract, the doctor takes another X-ray of the lower halves of both ureters and then, finally, one of the bladder.
- At the end of the test, you'll urinate. The doctor then takes a last X-ray.

To prepare for the test, you'll drink lots of fluids the day before, fast for 8 hours and, possibly, take a laxative.

What happens after the test?

A nurse will check you for a delayed reaction to the dye.

INSIGHT INTO ILLNESS

Where stones form in the urinary tract

Stones may form in the kidneys or in the ureters, the two slender tubes that connect the kidneys and bladder. Stones can also form in the bladder.

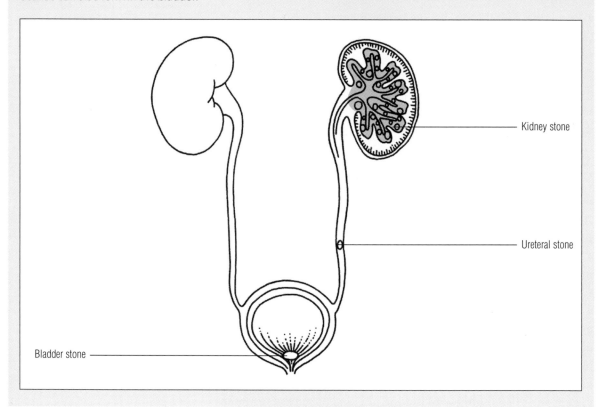

Kidney stone

Ureteral stone

Bladder stone

Does the test have risks?

The test shouldn't be performed on people with severe asthma or an allergy to the dye, unless they receive medication to avoid a serious reaction.

What are the normal results?

The kidneys, ureters, and bladder should show no evidence of tumors or other diseases.

What do abnormal results mean?

This test can demonstrate many abnormalities of the urinary system, including kidney or ureteral stones. (See *Where stones form in the uri-*

nary tract.) It can also show an abnormal size, shape, or structure of the kidneys, ureters, or bladder. It can detect an absent kidney or more than the normal two. Likewise, it can show polycystic kidney disease, tumors, renovascular hypertension, and urinary problems present at birth.

ANGIOGRAM OF THE KIDNEYS

This X-ray test allows examination of the kidneys and their blood vessels. In the test, the doctor injects a special dye into a blood vessel in the groin area. The dye possesses special properties that allow it to be seen on X-rays. When the dye reaches the kidneys, the doctor rapidly takes a series of X-rays.

Why is this test done?
An angiogram of the kidneys may be performed for the following reasons:
- To show the configuration of all the kidneys' blood vessels before surgery
- To determine the cause of renovascular hypertension
- To investigate kidney enlargement and nonfunctioning kidneys
- To evaluate chronic kidney disease or kidney failure
- To investigate kidney masses, blood vessel malformations, pseudotumors, and kidney trauma
- To detect complications following a kidney transplant, such as rejection of a new kidney.

What should you know before the test?
- You'll learn about the test, including who will perform it, where it will take place, and its expected duration (about 1 hour).
- You may feel mild discomfort during injection of the local anesthetic and a brief sensation of burning and warmth and a metallic taste in your mouth from the injection of the dye. During the test, the X-ray machine will make loud, clacking sounds.
- Tell the doctor or the nurse if you have a blood clotting disorder. Also mention if you have any allergies to shellfish (such as shrimp or scallops), iodine, or the dyes used in other diagnostic tests.
- For 8 hours before the test, you'll need to fast.

Angiogram of the kidneys may show narrowing of the renal artery by arteriosclerosis. This crucial finding confirms that high blood pressure is caused by a kidney problem.

- You'll put on a hospital gown and be asked to remove all jewelry or other metal objects that may obscure the X-rays.
- Just before the test, you'll receive a sedative and pain medication. The nurse will tell you to urinate.
- You'll need to sign a form that states your consent to undergo the test. Be sure to read this form carefully and ask questions if you don't understand any portion of it.

What happens during the test?

- You lie on the examining table, and a nurse inserts an intravenous line. The skin over the femoral artery, the blood vessel in the groin area where the doctor injects the dye, is cleaned with an antiseptic, and a local anesthetic is injected.
- The doctor then inserts a small tube called a *catheter* into the blood vessel and advances it, using a guide wire, to the aorta, the main blood vessel in the abdomen.
- The doctor injects the dye and takes X-rays.
- Next, to determine the position of the kidneys' arteries, the doctor injects additional dye and rapidly takes a series of X-rays.
- The doctor removes the catheter and applies pressure over the injection site for about 15 minutes to prevent bleeding. Then the doctor applies a dressing.

What happens after the test?

- You'll lie flat in bed for at least 6 hours. A nurse will check on you roughly every 15 minutes for 1 hour, then every 30 minutes for 2 hours.
- The nurse will check the dressing to make sure too much bleeding doesn't occur.

Does the test have risks?

This test shouldn't be done on a pregnant woman or on a person with bleeding tendencies, an allergy to the test dye, or kidney failure.

What are the normal results?

The test should show normal kidneys and blood vessels.

What do abnormal results mean?

An angiogram can show kidney tumors and cysts. The test can also show narrowing of the renal artery by arteriosclerosis. This crucial finding confirms that high blood pressure is caused by a kidney problem.

The test can detect kidney infarction, renal artery aneurysms, and renal arteriovenous fistula. It may show destruction and distortion of parts of the kidney in a person with severe or chronic pyelonephritis. The test may also indicate kidney abscesses or inflammation.

When angiography is used to evaluate kidney injury, it may detect blood clots, lacerations, shattered kidneys, and areas of infarction.

VENOGRAM OF THE KIDNEYS

This relatively simple X-ray test examines the main kidney veins and their tributaries. In this test, the doctor injects a special dye through a catheter placed in a blood vessel in the groin area. The dye possesses properties that cause it to appear on X-rays, which are taken when the dye reaches the kidney veins.

Why is this test done?
A venogram of the kidneys may be performed for the following reasons:
- To permit X-ray examination of the renal veins
- To detect renal vein thrombosis
- To evaluate kidney vein compression from tumors or retroperitoneal fibrosis
- To distinguish kidney disease and aneurysms from pressure exerted by an adjacent mass
- To evaluate kidney tumors and detect invasion of the kidney vein or inferior vena cava
- To detect kidney vein anomalies and defects
- To differentiate renal agenesis (absence of a kidney) from an undersized kidney
- To collect blood samples from the kidney to check for renovascular hypertension.

What should you know before the test?
- You'll learn about the test, including who will perform it, where it will take place, and its expected duration (about 1 hour). During

In preparation for these relatively simple X-rays, you'll need to fast for 4 hours and, possibly, follow a low-salt diet.

When studies of the right-side veins are completed, the doctor moves the catheter to the left kidney vein. More X-rays are taken.

the test, a catheter will be inserted into a vein in the groin area after you receive a sedative and a local anesthetic.

- You may feel mild discomfort during injection of the local anesthetic and a brief sensation of burning and warmth and a metallic taste in your mouth from the injection of the dye. During the test, the X-ray machine will make loud, clacking sounds.
- Tell the doctor or the nurse if you have a blood clotting disorder. Also mention if you have any allergies to shellfish (such as shrimp or scallops), iodine, or the dyes used in other diagnostic tests.
- For 4 hours before the test, you'll need to fast. However, if a blood sample will be taken as part of the test, you may need to follow a low-salt diet. You may also be instructed to temporarily stop taking any drugs for high blood pressure or, for women, oral contraceptives.
- You may receive a sedative before the test.
- You'll need to sign a form that gives your consent to perform the test. Be sure to read this form carefully and ask questions if you don't understand any portion of it.

What happens during the test?

- You lie on your back on the X-ray table. The skin over the right femoral vein near the groin is cleaned with antiseptic and draped.
- After injecting the local anesthetic, the doctor inserts a catheter into the femoral vein. Next, the doctor advances the catheter to the right kidney vein and injects the test dye. X-rays are taken.
- When studies of the right-side veins are completed, the doctor moves the catheter to the left kidney vein. More X-rays are taken.
- Next, the doctor may collect a blood sample from the kidney for testing. Then, the doctor removes the catheter, applies pressure to the site for 15 minutes, and applies a dressing.

What happens after the test?

- A nurse will check on you roughly every 15 minutes for 1 hour, then every 30 minutes for 2 hours. The nurse will also check the dressing to make sure too much bleeding doesn't occur. You'll be given pain medication and antibiotics.
- Tell the nurse if you don't feel well, especially if you have chills, feel hot, have trouble breathing, or feel pain.

Does the test have risks?

The test shouldn't be performed on a person with severe thrombosis of the kidney vein.

What are the normal results?

After injection of the dye, the kidney vein and tributaries should appear coated and have no abnormalities.

What do abnormal results mean?

The test can detect blockage of the kidney vein, tumors, and various venous anomalies, such as a missing kidney vein.

Lab tests of the kidney blood sample may indicate renovascular hypertension.

Voiding cystourethrography

This X-ray test examines the bladder and urethra after injection of a special dye through a catheter into the bladder. The dye contains special properties that allow it to be seen on X-rays, which are taken with the person in various positions. X-rays are also taken at the end of the test, during urination.

Why is this test done?

Voiding cystourethrography may be performed for the following reasons:
- To detect certain abnormalities of the bladder and urethra, such as vesicoureteral reflux, neurogenic bladder, an enlarged prostate, or diverticula
- To investigate recurrent urinary tract infection
- To investigate a suspected congenital anomaly of the lower urinary tract, abnormal bladder emptying, and loss of control over urination
- To evaluate an enlarged prostate, a narrowed urethra, and the degree of urinary impairment in men from a narrowed urethra.

What should you know before the test?

- You'll learn about the test, including who will perform it, where it will take place, and its expected duration (about 30 to 45 minutes).
- Tell the doctor or the nurse if you have a blood clotting disorder. Also mention if you have any allergies to shellfish (such as shrimp or scallops), iodine, or the dyes used in other diagnostic tests.
- You won't need to fast before the test.

- You'll need to sign a form that gives your consent to perform the test. Be sure to read this form carefully and ask questions if you don't understand any portion of it.

What happens during the test?

- You lie on your back on the examining table, and a catheter is inserted into the bladder.
- The doctor instills the dye through the catheter until the bladder is full. You may experience a feeling of fullness and an urge to urinate. Next, the doctor clamps the catheter and takes X-rays as you change positions.
- After the doctor removes the catheter, you change position again and urinate. During urination, the doctor takes four high-speed X-rays of the bladder and urethra.

What happens after the test?

- Drink lots of fluids to reduce burning on urination and to flush out any residual dye. The nurse will check the time, color, and volume of your urination.
- Tell the nurse if you feel hot or have chills.

Does the test have risks?

- Voiding cystourethrography shouldn't be performed if the person has a severe urethral or bladder infection, or a severe urethral injury.
- Men should wear a lead shield over their testicles to prevent radiation exposure during the test. Unfortunately, a woman's ovaries can't be shielded without blocking the bladder.

What are the normal results?

The structure and function of the bladder and urethra should be normal. There should be no regurgitation of dye into the ureters.

What do abnormal results mean?

The test may show urethral stricture, vesical or urethral diverticula, ureterocele, an enlarged prostate, vesicoureteral reflux, or neurogenic bladder. The severity and location of these conditions are then evaluated to determine whether surgery is necessary.

WHITAKER TEST OF KIDNEY FUNCTION

Also called a *pressure study* or *flow study*, this test evaluates kidney function. It combines X-rays with measurements of pressure and flow in the kidneys and ureters. (See *How the Whitaker test helps detect kidney blockage,* page 70.)

Why is this test done?
The Whitaker test may be performed for the following reasons:
- To detect a kidney blockage and to help determine if surgery is needed
- To further evaluate a blockage after other tests are done.

What should you know before the test?
- You'll learn about the test, including who will perform it, where it will take place, and its expected duration (about 1 hour).
- You may feel may feel some discomfort during insertion of the urethral catheter and injection of the local anesthetic and a brief sensation of warmth and burning after injection of the dye. During the test, the X-ray machine will make loud, clacking sounds.
- Tell the doctor or the nurse if you have a blood clotting disorder. Also mention if you have any allergies to shellfish (such as shrimp or scallops), iodine, or the dyes used in other diagnostic tests.
- For at least 4 hours before the test, you'll need to fast.
- You'll put on a hospital gown and be asked to remove all jewelry or other metal objects that may obscure the X-rays.
- Just before the test, you'll receive a sedative and antibiotics. The nurse will tell you to urinate.
- You'll be asked to sign a consent form.

What happens during the test?
- You lie on your back on an X-ray table.
- To prepare for measurement of bladder pressure, the doctor inserts a catheter through the urethra into the bladder.
- The doctor takes an X-ray of the urinary tract and then connects the catheter to a pressure-measuring device called a *manometer.*
- The doctor injects the dye into a vein. After a brief wait, the doctor injects a local anesthetic and makes a small incision to insert a cannula into the kidney.

How the Whitaker test helps detect kidney blockage

In the Whitaker test, many X-rays are taken of the upper urinary tract. X-ray results are compared with measurements of kidney and bladder pressures to detect evidence of blockages.

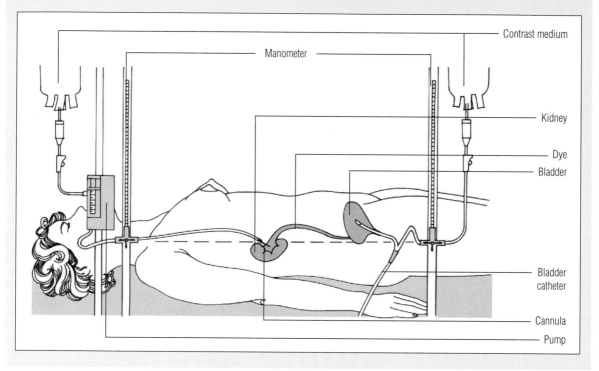

- You'll be asked to hold your breath as the doctor inserts the cannula into the kidney. Next, the doctor connects the tubing to the manometer.
- Now the doctor delivers the dye through the tubing as serial X-rays are taken and kidney pressure is measured. Bladder pressure is then measured.
- After the pressures are measured, the doctor removes the cannula and applies a dressing.

What happens after the test?
- You'll lie in bed on your back for 12 hours after the test.
- The nurse will check on you often, watching the color, frequency, and amount of urination. Some blood in the urine will appear for a brief time.
- Tell the nurse if you have chills, feel hot, or are breathing more rapidly than usual.

- Tell the nurse if you feel any pain. If you do, the nurse will give you pain medication. You'll also take antibiotics for several days to prevent infection.

Does the test have risks?

The test shouldn't be done if a person has a bleeding disorder or severe infection.

What are the normal results?

The test should show normal outlines of the kidneys. The ureters should fill uniformly and appear normal in size and course.

The normal kidney pressure is 15 centimeters of water. The normal bladder pressure ranges from 5 to 10 centimeters of water.

What do abnormal results mean?

Enlargement of the renal pelvis, calyces, or ureteropelvic junction may indicate obstruction. Subtraction of bladder pressure from kidney pressure aids diagnosis. A difference in pressure of 12 to 15 centimeters of water indicates obstruction. A difference of less than 10 centimeters of water indicates a bladder problem, such as hypertonia or neurogenic bladder.

REPRODUCTIVE SYSTEM

MAMMOGRAPHY

This commonly performed X-ray helps to detect breast cysts or cancer. Mammography can detect 90% to 95% of breast cancers. However, a biopsy of suspicious areas may be required to confirm cancer. (See *How to examine your breasts,* pages 72 and 73, and *Using light and sound to detect breast cancer,* page 74.)

If a significant breast lump is present, a mammogram may be done even during pregnancy. A lead shield placed over the mother's abdomen protects the fetus.

(Text continues on page 74.)

SELF HELP

How to examine your breasts

Women themselves discover about 90% of breast cancers by using breast self-examination techniques. It's best to examine your breasts once a month. If you haven't reached menopause, the best examination time is immediately after your menstrual period. If you're past menopause, choose any convenient, easy-to-remember day each month — the first of the month, for example. Here's how to proceed.

1 Undress to the waist, and stand or sit in front of a mirror with your arms at your sides. Observe your breasts for any change in their shape or size. Look for any puckering or dimpling of the skin.

2 Raise your arms and press your hands together behind your head. Observe your breasts as before.

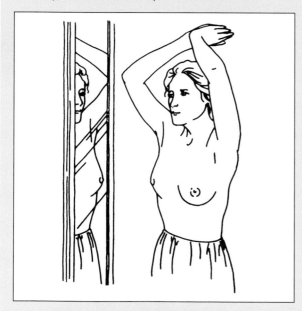

3 Press your palms firmly on your hips and observe your breasts again.

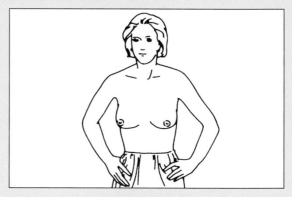

4 Now lie flat on your back. This position flattens and spreads your breasts more evenly over the chest wall. Place a small pillow under your left shoulder, and put your left hand behind your head.

5 Examine your left breast with your right hand, using a circular motion and progressing clockwise. You'll notice a ridge of firm tissue in the lower curve of your breast; this is normal. Now, repeat steps five and six on your right breast.

6 Check the area under your arm with your elbow slightly bent. If you feel a small lump that moves freely under your armpit, don't be alarmed. This area contains your lymph glands, which may become swollen when you're sick. Check the lump daily. Call the doctor if it doesn't go away in a few days or if it gets larger.

7 Gently squeeze your nipple between your thumb and forefinger, and note any discharge. Repeat this examination on your right breast, using your left hand.

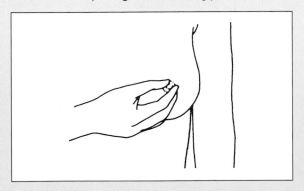

8 Finally, examine your breasts while you're in the shower or bath, lubricating your breasts with soap and water. Using the same circular, clockwise motion, gently inspect both breasts with your fingertips. After you've toweled dry, squeeze each nipple gently, and note any discharge.

9 If you feel a lump, don't panic — most lumps aren't cancerous. First, note whether you can easily lift the skin covering it and whether the lump moves when you do so.

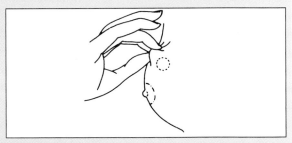

Next, notify your doctor. Be prepared to describe how the lump feels (hard or soft) and whether it moves easily under the skin.

Chances are, your doctor will want to examine the lump. Then he or she can advise you about what treatment (if any) you need.

Although self-examination is important, it's not a substitute for examination by your doctor. Be sure to see him or her annually or semiannually (if you're considered at risk).

Using light and sound to detect breast cancer

Two noninvasive tests that don't require X-rays allow safe, early detection of cancer and other breast diseases. In most cases, their diagnostic accuracy isn't as high as that of conventional mammography, but they can be repeated as often as needed without risk.

Diaphanography: The light approach

Also known as *transillumination of the breast,* diaphanography directs infrared light through the breast with a fiber-optic device, and the transmitted light is photographed with infrared film. The denser the tissue, the darker it appears on the film, which allows a trained examiner to make the following observations:

- Healthy breast tissue appears reddish yellow and translucent.
- Fluid-filled cysts and fatty tissue appear as bright spots.
- Blood vessels are dark red to black.
- Benign tumors are red.
- Malignant tumors are dark brown or black.

Diaphanography is a useful tool when used with mammography and a physical exam.

Ultrasonography: A sound technique

This test can detect breast tumors that are less than a quarter-inch in diameter. It can also help distinguish cysts from solid tumors. A transducer focuses a beam of high-frequency sound waves through the skin and into the breast. These waves then bounce back to the transducer as an echo that varies in strength with the density of the underlying tissues. A computer processes these echoes and displays a screen image of them.

Ultrasound can show all areas of a breast, including the difficult area close to the chest wall, which is hard to study with X-rays. When used with mammography, the technique increases diagnostic accuracy. When used alone, it's more accurate than mammography in examining the denser breast tissue of young women.

Why is this test done?

Mammography may be performed for the following reasons:
- To check for breast cancer
- To investigate breast masses, breast pain, or nipple discharge
- To help differentiate between benign breast disease and breast cancer.

What should you know before the test?

- You'll learn who will perform the test and where. The test takes only about 15 minutes to perform, but you may be asked to wait while the films are checked to make sure they're readable.
- Just before the test, you'll put on a hospital gown that opens in the front and be asked to remove all jewelry and clothing above the waist.

What happens during the test?

- You stand up and are asked to rest one breast on a table above an X-ray cassette.

■ The compression plate is placed on the breast, and you're asked to hold your breath. After one X-ray is taken, the machine is rotated, the breast is compressed again, and another X-ray is taken.
■ The procedure is repeated on the other breast.
■ After the X-ray films are developed, they're checked to make sure they're readable.

What are the normal results?

A mammogram should reveal normal ducts, glandular tissue, and fat architecture. No abnormal masses should be seen.

What do abnormal results mean?

Well-outlined, regular, and clear spots on a mammogram suggest benign cysts. Irregular, poorly outlined, and opaque areas suggest cancer. However, before the doctor can make a diagnosis, additional mammograms may be necessary. A biopsy may also be needed.

X-RAYS OF THE UTERUS AND FALLOPIAN TUBES

This type of X-ray is called a *hysterosalpingography*. It assists with examination of the uterus, the fallopian tubes, and the surrounding structures. In this test, X-rays are taken after the doctor injects a special dye that flows through the uterus and the fallopian tubes. The dye possesses properties that allow it to appear on X-rays.

X-rays of the uterus and fallopian tubes are generally taken as part of an infertility study. Although ultrasound tests have virtually replaced this test in detecting foreign bodies, such as a dislodged intrauterine device, they can't evaluate tubal patency, which is the main purpose of this test.

Why is this test done?

This test may be performed for the following reasons:
■ To confirm tubal abnormalities, such as adhesions and occlusion
■ To confirm uterine abnormalities, such as the presence of foreign bodies, congenital malformations, and traumatic injuries
■ To confirm the presence of fistulas or peritubal adhesions
■ To help evaluate repeated fetal loss

■ To check the outcome of surgery, especially uterine repair procedures and tubal reconstruction.

What should you know before the test?

■ You'll learn about the test, including who will perform it and where, and that it takes about 15 minutes.

■ Tell the doctor or the nurse if you have a blood clotting disorder. Also mention if you have any allergies to shellfish (such as shrimp or scallops), iodine, or the dyes used in other diagnostic tests.

■ Be prepared to feel moderate cramping from the procedure. You can receive a mild sedative.

■ You'll need to sign a form that gives your consent to perform the test. Be sure to read this form carefully and ask questions if you don't understand any portion of it.

What happens during the test?

■ You lie on the examination table with your feet in stirrups. The doctor inserts a speculum into the vagina and cleans the cervix.

■ Next, the doctor inserts a catheter into the cervix and injects dye through it. X-rays are then taken.

Normally, X-rays reveal a symmetrical uterine cavity, and the dye courses through fallopian tubes of normal caliber.

What happens after the test?

■ Tell the nurse if you feel hot or have any pain.

■ Any cramps, nausea, and dizziness should go away.

Does the test have risks?

■ This test shouldn't be performed on menstruating women or on women with undiagnosed vaginal bleeding or pelvic inflammatory disease.

■ The test can cause uterine perforation and exposure to potentially harmful radiation.

What are the normal results?

Normally, X-rays reveal a symmetrical uterine cavity. The dye courses through fallopian tubes of normal caliber, spills freely into the peritoneal cavity, and doesn't leak from the uterus.

What do abnormal results mean?

An asymmetrical uterus on the X-rays suggests intrauterine adhesions or masses, such as fibroids or foreign bodies. Impaired flow of the dye through the fallopian tubes suggests partial or complete blockage. Leakage of the dye through the uterine wall suggests fistulas. Laparoscopy (insertion of a small fiber-optic telescope) with instillation of contrast dye may help confirm findings.

SKELETAL SYSTEM

X-RAYS OF THE VERTEBRAE

The test permits examination of all or part of the spinal column. A commonly performed test, it's used to evaluate the vertebrae for deformities, fractures, dislocations, tumors, and other abnormalities. Bone X-rays determine bone density, texture, erosion, and changes in bone relationships. Joint X-rays can reveal the presence of fluid, spur formation, narrowing, and changes in the joint structure.

Why is this test done?

X-rays of the vertebrae may be performed for the following reasons:
- To detect fractures, dislocations, subluxations, and deformities
- To detect degeneration, infection, and congenital disorders
- To detect disorders of the intervertebral disks
- To determine the effects of arthritis and other conditions on the vertebrae.

What should you know before the test?

- You'll learn about the test, including who will perform the test and where and that it usually takes 15 to 30 minutes. During the test, you'll be placed in various positions for the X-ray films. Although some positions may be slightly uncomfortable, try to stay still. If you can't, the test may not be accurate.
- You won't need to fast before the test.

What happens during the test?

- Initially, you lie on your back on the table for an X-ray taken from front to back.
- You may be repositioned on your side for additional X-rays, depending on the vertebrae being tested.

What happens after the test?

You'll receive pain medications and a heating pad to relieve any discomfort.

Does the test have risks?

X-rays of the vertebrae shouldn't be performed for a woman in the first 3 months of pregnancy, unless the benefits outweigh the risks of exposing the fetus to X-rays.

What are the normal results?

Normal vertebrae show no fractures, dislocations, curvatures, or other abnormalities. Specific positions and spacing of the vertebrae vary with the person's age.

What do abnormal results mean?

The X-rays readily show vertebral displacements, fractures, dislocations, wedging, and such deformities as kyphosis, scoliosis, and lordosis. Information from the test may be used to help confirm diagnosis of a variety of disorders. These disorders include congenital abnormalities, such as torticollis (wryneck), absence of sacral or lumbar vertebrae, hemivertebrae, and Klippel-Feil syndrome; degenerative processes, such as osteoarthritis and narrowed disk spaces; benign or malignant spinal tumors; ruptured disk and cervical disk syndrome; and rheumatoid arthritis, ankylosing spondylitis, osteoporosis, and Paget's disease.

Depending on X-ray results, a definite diagnosis may require additional tests, such as a computerized axial tomography (CAT) scan.

X-RAYS OF THE JOINTS

This X-ray test, called *arthrography*, examines a joint after the injection of a special dye, air, or both to outline soft-tissue structures and the contour of the joint. The joint is put through its range of motion while a series of X-rays are taken. (See *Major movements of the knee joint*.)

This test is usually done if a person complains of lasting, unexplained joint discomfort or pain.

HOW YOUR BODY WORKS

Major movements of the knee joint

The synovial knee joint moves in three chief directions: It can extend, flex, or rotate to the side.

During extension, both the collateral ligaments and the cruciate ligaments are tensed. During flexion, the collateral ligaments are relaxed while the cruciate ligaments are tensed. During medial rotation, the collateral and cruciate ligaments are twisted.

EXTENSION

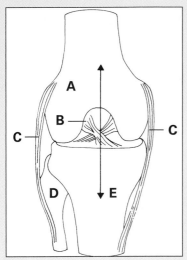

FLEXION

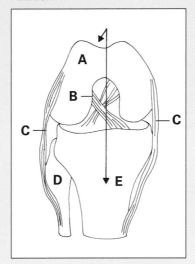

MEDIAL ROTATION

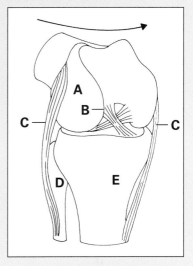

KEY
A = Femur   **B** = Cruciate ligaments   **C** = Collateral ligaments   **D** = Fibula   **E** = Tibia

Why is this test done?

X-rays of the joints may be taken for the following reasons:
- To identify acute or chronic tears or other abnormalities of the joint capsule or supporting ligaments of the knee, shoulder, ankle, hips, or wrist
- To detect internal joint derangements
- To locate synovial cysts.

What should you know before the test?

- You'll learn about the test, including who will perform it, where it will take place, and its expected duration.
- You may feel mild discomfort during injection of the local anesthetic and a brief sensation of burning and warmth and a metallic

taste in your mouth from the injection of the dye. During the test, the doctor will track the test dye as it fills the joint space and will take X-rays.

■ You'll need to remain as still as possible during the procedure, except when following instructions to change position. Your cooperation in assuming various positions is critical because X-rays must be taken quickly to ensure good quality.

■ Tell the doctor or the nurse if you have a blood clotting disorder. Also mention if you have any allergies to shellfish (such as shrimp or scallops), iodine, or the dyes used in other diagnostic tests.

■ You won't need to fast before the test.

■ You'll need to sign a form that gives your consent to perform the test. Be sure to read this form carefully and ask questions if you don't understand any portion of it.

The doctor examines a joint after the injection of a special dye, air, or both to outline soft-tissue structures and the contour of the joint.

What happens during the test?

The test may be performed on the knee or the shoulder.

Knee arthrography

■ The knee is cleaned with an antiseptic solution, and the area around the puncture site is anesthetized.

■ The doctor inserts a needle into the joint space and removes fluid, which is usually sent to a lab for testing.

■ Next, the doctor injects dye into the joint. You're asked to walk a few steps or to move your knee through a range of motions to distribute the dye in the joint space. X-rays are quickly taken with the knee held in various positions.

■ If the X-rays show no problems, the knee is bandaged. Keep the bandage in place for several days.

Shoulder arthrography

■ The skin is prepared, and a local anesthetic is injected. The doctor inserts a needle into the joint and injects dye.

■ X-rays are taken quickly to achieve maximum contrast.

What happens after the test?

■ You'll need to rest the joint for at least 12 hours.

■ You may experience some swelling or discomfort or may hear noises in the joint after the test, but these symptoms usually disappear after 1 or 2 days. Report persistent symptoms.

■ Apply ice to the joint if swelling occurs and take aspirin or Tylenol (or another brand of acetaminophen) for pain.

Does the test have risks?

■ This test shouldn't be performed on a pregnant woman.

■ It also shouldn't be performed on a person with arthritis, joint infection, or allergies to the test dye.

What are the normal results?

A normal knee arthrogram shows a characteristic wedge-shaped shadow, pointed toward the interior of the joint, that indicates a normal medial meniscus (cartilage). A normal shoulder arthrogram shows that the bicipital tendon sheath, redundant inferior joint capsule, and subscapular bursa (lubricating sac) are intact.

What do abnormal results mean?

X-rays of the joints almost always accurately detect medial meniscal tears and lacerations. They may also help identify extrameniscal lesions, such as osteochondritis dissecans, chondromalacia patellae, osteochondral fractures, cartilaginous abnormalities, synovial abnormalities, tears of the cruciate ligaments, and disruption of the joint capsule and collateral ligaments.

This test can reveal shoulder abnormalities, such as adhesive capsulitis, bicipital tenosynovitis or rupture, and rotator cuff tears, and can evaluate damage from recurrent dislocations.

LYMPH NODES

ANGIOGRAM OF THE LYMPH NODES

This test examines the lymphatic system (see *The lymphatic system: Its structure and function,* page 82). It involves a series of X-rays taken after the doctor injects a special dye into a lymphatic vessel in each foot or, less commonly, in each hand. Another name for this test is *lymphangiography.*

Dye injected into the foot lets the doctor examine the lymphatics of the leg, inguinal and iliac regions, and the retroperitoneum up to the thoracic duct. Injection into the hand allows examination of the axillary and supraclavicular nodes.

HOW YOUR BODY WORKS

The lymphatic system: Its structure and function

The lymphatic system does many important jobs:

- It transports fluids and proteins to the veins.
- It produces some of the white blood cells that fight infection and provide other immune defenses.
- It reabsorbs fats from the small intestine.

Structure of the lymphatic system
The system includes the lymphatic vessels, lymph nodes, lymphoid tissue, blood cells called lymphocytes, and reticuloendothelial cells.

Lymphatic vessels, which are like veins, eventually converge into one of two main ducts — the thoracic or right lymphatic. The thoracic duct drains the legs, the pelvis, the abdomen, and the left arm (the white area of the diagram below) as well as the left side of the head, neck, and chest. The right lymphatic duct drains the right side of the head, neck, and chest and the right arm (the shaded area of the diagram). The two ducts then empty into the veins.

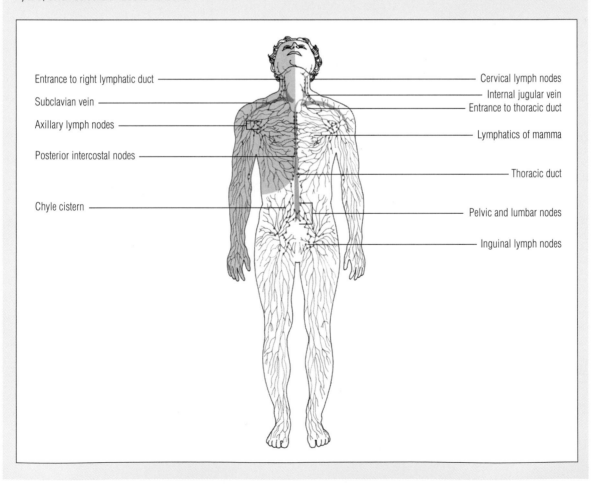

Entrance to right lymphatic duct

Subclavian vein

Axillary lymph nodes

Posterior intercostal nodes

Chyle cistern

Cervical lymph nodes

Internal jugular vein

Entrance to thoracic duct

Lymphatics of mamma

Thoracic duct

Pelvic and lumbar nodes

Inguinal lymph nodes

X-rays are taken immediately after injection to show the filling of the lymphatic system and then again 24 hours later to examine the lymph nodes. Because the dye remains in the nodes for up to 2 years, subsequent X-rays can also be taken.

Why is this test done?

An angiogram of the lymph nodes may be performed for the following reasons:

- To detect and stage lymphomas and to identify the spread of cancer to the lymph nodes
- To suggest surgical treatment or evaluate the effectiveness of chemotherapy and radiation therapy in controlling cancer
- To investigate enlarged lymph nodes that have been detected by a computerized axial tomography (CAT) scan or ultrasound.

What should you know before the test?

- You'll learn about the test, including who will perform this procedure and where and that it takes about 3 hours. Additional X-rays are also taken the following day, but these take less than 30 minutes.
- You'll learn about the blue dye that will be injected into each foot to outline the lymphatic vessels. The injection causes brief discomfort, but the dye discolors urine and stools for 48 hours and may give your skin and vision a bluish tinge for 48 hours.
- A local anesthetic will be injected before a small incision is made in each foot. The dye is then injected for the next 1½ hours using a cannula inserted into a lymphatic vessel. You must remain as still as possible during injection of the dye.
- Tell the doctor or the nurse if you have allergies to shellfish (such as shrimp or scallops), iodine, or the dyes used in other diagnostic tests.
- If this test is performed on an outpatient basis, have a friend or relative accompany you.
- Just before the test, you should urinate. You may receive a sedative and other medication.
- You'll need to sign a form that gives your consent to perform the test. Be sure to read this form carefully and ask questions if you don't understand any portion of it.

What happens during the test?

- A preliminary X-ray of the chest is taken, and the skin on each foot is cleaned with an antiseptic.

- The doctor injects a blue dye into the area between the toes, usually the first and fourth toe webs.
- The dye infiltrates the lymphatic system and, within 15 to 30 minutes, the lymphatic vessels appear as small blue lines on the upper surface of the instep of each foot.
- The doctor injects a local anesthetic into each foot and makes a small incision to expose the lymphatic vessel. Next, the doctor inserts a cannula into the vessel and slowly delivers the dye. Fluoroscopy may be used to monitor filling of the lymphatic system.
- The needles are removed, the incisions stitched, and sterile dressings applied.
- X-rays are taken of the legs, pelvis, abdomen, and chest.
- You are then taken to your room but must return 24 hours later for additional X-rays.

What happens after the test?

- You'll be checked on often. Tell the nurse if you feel short of breath, have chest pains, or feel warm.
- You'll stay in bed for 24 hours with your feet elevated to help reduce swelling. The nurse will apply ice packs to the incision sites to help reduce swelling and will give you pain medication.
- The incision site may be sore for several days after the test. The dressings usually remain in place for 2 days, making sure the wounds stay dry.
- You'll be given a follow-up X-ray, as needed.

Does the test have risks?

This test shouldn't be performed on a person with an allergy to the test dye, breathing problems, heart disease, or severe kidney or liver disease.

What are the normal results?

The lymphatic system normally fills fully and evenly with dye on the initial X-rays. On the 24-hour X-rays, the lymph nodes are fully opacified and well circumscribed.

What do abnormal results mean?

Enlarged, foamy-looking nodes indicate lymphoma, a type of cancer that originates in the lymphatic system. Other tests are needed to stage the cancer.

CAT & MRI SCANS:
Diagnosing with High-Tech Help

BRAIN & SPINE

CAT SCAN OF THE BRAIN

Doctors use a CAT scan (short for a computerized axial tomography scan) to study an area of the body, such as the brain, in much greater detail than they could by using conventional X-rays. In a CAT scan, a narrow X-ray beam is directed at the brain; at the same time, a scintillation counter, located exactly opposite the X-ray source, measures the amount of radiation that's unabsorbed as it passes through the skull and brain tissues. As the X-ray source and the scintillation counter revolve around the person's head, data from the counter is processed by a computer to create images of various sections of the brain, which are then displayed on a computer monitor.

Tumors and other brain lesions, or tissue damage, show up as areas of altered density. A CAT scan of the brain may eliminate the need for other procedures that can be painful and hazardous.

Another emerging test for obtaining detailed images of the brain is positron emission tomography. (See *Positron emission tomography: New insights into brain function.*)

Why is this test done?
A CAT scan of the brain may be performed for the following reasons:
- To check the brain's function
- To find tumors and abnormalities within the brain
- To monitor the effects of surgery, radiotherapy, or chemotherapy on brain tumors
- To detect possible blood clots after a head injury.

What should you know before the test?
- There are usually no dietary restrictions before the test. However, if a contrast dye will be used during the test, you'll be asked to fast for 4 hours before the test.
- A contrast dye — a special substance that enhances the images of the brain — may be used. You may feel flushed and warm and may experience a brief headache, a salty taste, or nausea and vomiting after this dye is injected.

Positron emission tomography: New insights into brain function

Positron emission tomography (also known by the acronym PET) is a technique for viewing the brain without surgery. Positron emission tomography produces sophisticated computer-generated images showing the details of brain function as well as brain structures.

How it works

Positron emission tomography involves the use of the radioactive forms of certain elements — oxygen, nitrogen, carbon, and fluorine — which emit tiny particles called *positrons*.

During the test, a device called a *positron emission tomography scanner* detects radiation and relays the information to a computer. The computer translates the information into an image. Positron-emitters can be used as chemical "tags" to trace the fate of various metabolites in the brain. For example, chemically tagged glucose — a form of sugar that penetrates the brain rapidly — allows the study of brain function because positron emission tomography can pinpoint glucose in the brain under various conditions.

Uses and limitations

Researchers expect this test to be useful in diagnosing many problems, such as psychiatric disorders, Parkinson's disease, MS, seizure disorders, and Alzheimer's disease.

Positron emission tomography is a costly test that has limited use, except as a research tool. However, it has already provided valuable information about the brain and may someday be widely used.

- This test involves taking a series of X-ray films of your brain. The test causes very little discomfort and lasts 15 to 30 minutes.
- A nurse or technician will explain the procedure to you.
- Your medical history will be checked for past allergic reactions to shellfish, iodine, or certain dyes.
- You may be asked to wear a hospital gown or any comfortable clothing and to remove all metal objects from the CAT scan field.
- You'll be asked to sign a consent form before the test takes place.

What happens during the test?

- You're asked to lie still on a special table; your head is held gently in place by straps and your face is left uncovered.
- The head of the table is moved into the scanner. The scanner rotates around your head, taking X-rays. It makes clacking sounds.
- If contrast dye is used, another series of scans is taken after the dye is injected and is taken up by the appropriate area of the brain.
- Information from the scans is fed into a computer and converted into images on a monitor. Photographs of selected views are taken for further study.

What happens after the test?

- If contrast dye was used, you're watched for side effects such as headache, nausea, and vomiting. You'll also be monitored for reactions such as hives, rash, or difficulty breathing. Reactions usually develop within 30 minutes.
- You may resume your usual diet.

Does the test have risks?

A pregnant woman should not undergo a CAT scan of the brain with contrast dye, especially during the first 3 months. People who are allergic to iodine or the contrast dye should also avoid the procedure.

What are the normal results?

The density of brain tissue affects its appearance on the scan. Brain tissue may appear as white, black, or shades of gray. The doctor evaluates structures according to their density, size, shape, and position.

What do abnormal results mean?

Displaced tissues or areas of altered density may indicate a tumor, blood clot, cerebral damage, infarction, swelling, or hydrocephalus.

CAT SCAN OF THE SPINE

This test provides detailed, high-resolution images of the spine. During the procedure, multiple X-ray beams are directed at the spine from different angles. X-rays pass through the body and are intercepted by radiation detectors, which produce electrical impulses that are converted by a computer into three-dimensional images. These images are displayed on a video monitor.

Why is this test done?

A CAT scan of the spine may be performed for the following reasons:
- To allow visualization of the spine
- To diagnose spinal lesions, tissue damage, and other abnormalities
- To monitor the effects of spinal surgery or therapy.

What should you know before the test?

- If contrast dye isn't ordered, you don't need to restrict food or fluids. If contrast dye is ordered, you'll be asked to fast for 4 hours before the test.
- A nurse or technician will describe the procedure, which takes 30 to 60 minutes.
- The procedure is painless, but having to remain still for a prolonged period may be slightly uncomfortable.
- If contrast dye is used, you may feel flushed and warm and may experience a brief headache, a salty taste, and nausea or vomiting after injection of the contrast dye. These reactions are normal.
- During the test, you'll be asked to wear an examining gown and to remove all metal objects and jewelry.
- Your history will be checked for past allergic reactions to iodine, shellfish, or contrast dye. If such reactions have occurred, you may receive alternative medications or the test may be performed without contrast dye.
- If you seem restless or apprehensive about the procedure, the doctor may prescribe a mild sedative.
- You'll be asked to sign a consent form before the test takes place.

You're positioned on an X-ray table inside a body scanning unit. The table slides into an opening and the scanner revolves around you, taking images at preselected intervals.

What happens during the test?

- You're positioned on an X-ray table inside a body CAT scanning unit and asked to lie very still.
- The table slides into the circular opening of the CAT scanner and the scanner revolves around you, taking images at preselected intervals.
- After the first set of scans is taken, you're removed from the scanner. Contrast dye may be administered.
- You're observed for signs and symptoms of a hypersensitivity reaction — including hives, rash, and respiratory difficulty — for 30 minutes after the contrast dye has been injected.
- After the dye is injected, you're moved back into the scanner, and another series of scans is taken. The images obtained from the scan are displayed on a video monitor during the procedure and stored on magnetic tape.

What happens after the test?

- After a scan with contrast dye, you'll be observed for side effects of the dye, such as headache, nausea, and vomiting.
- You may resume your usual diet.

Does the test have risks?

■ CAT scanning with contrast dye is not recommended for a person who is hypersensitive to iodine, shellfish, or contrast dye used in radiographic studies.

■ Some people experience strong feelings of claustrophobia or anxiety when they're inside the CAT scanner. A mild sedative may be given to help reduce the person's anxiety.

■ For people with significant back pain, painkillers are prescribed before the scan.

What are the normal results?

In the computerized axial tomography image, spinal tissue appears white, black, or gray, depending on its density.

What do abnormal results mean?

By highlighting areas of altered density and depicting structural malformations, a CAT scan can reveal different types of spinal tissue damage and abnormalities. It's particularly useful in detecting and identifying tumors. CAT scans also reveal degenerative processes and structural changes, such as spinal cord compression. Other types of disorders show as soft-tissue changes, bony overgrowth, and spurring of the vertebrae, which result in nerve root compression. Blood vessel malformations, evident after contrast dye, show as masses or clusters. Congenital spinal malformations, such as spina bifida, show as abnormally large, dark gaps between the vertebrae.

MRI SCAN OF THE BRAIN AND SPINE

MRI (which is the abbreviation for *magnetic resonance imaging*) produces computerized images of various sections of the brain and spine. These images are highly detailed. Unlike a CAT scan, which uses X-rays, an MRI scan uses magnetic fields and radio waves to produce images of the brain and spine. The magnetic fields and radio waves aren't noticed by the person undergoing the test, and no harmful effects have been reported.

The doctor uses an MRI scan to diagnose brain tumors, abscesses, swelling, bleeding, nerve damage, and other disorders that increase the fluid content of tissues. The test can also show irregularities of the spinal cord.

Why is this test done?

An MRI scan of the brain and spinal cord may be performed to diagnose brain and spinal tumors, tissue damage, or soft-tissue abnormalities.

What should you know before the test?

- This test takes up to 90 minutes to complete.
- Although MRI is painless and involves no exposure to radiation from the scanner, a radioactive contrast dye may be used. The contrast dye is injected, usually near the organ or tissue that is being observed.
- The opening for your head and body in most MRI scanners is small and deep. If you've ever experienced claustrophobia, you may need a sedative to help you relax before the test. Some of the newer MRI scanners, though, are transparent.
- During the test, you'll hear the scanner clicking, whirring, and thumping as it moves inside its housing.
- You'll be able to talk with the technician at all times during the test.
- You'll be asked to remove all metallic objects, including jewelry, hair pins, and watches. You'll also asked if you have any surgically implanted joints, pins, clips, valves, pumps, or pacemakers containing metal that could be attracted to the strong MRI magnet. If you do, you won't be able to undergo the test.
- You'll be asked to sign a consent form before the test takes place.

What happens during the test?

- You're asked to lie on a narrow bed, which then slides into the desired position inside the scanner. (See *Undergoing MRI.*)
- During the procedure you're asked to remain very still.
- The images that are generated are displayed on a monitor and recorded on film or magnetic tape for permanent storage; the radiologist may use the computer to manipulate and enhance the images.

What happens after the test?

- You may resume normal activity.
- If the test took a long time, you'll be watched for signs of light-headedness or fainting when you sit or stand up.

Undergoing MRI

The illustration below shows a person being moved into an MRI, or magnetic resonance imaging, scanner. MRI is an imaging technique based on the response of various elements to a generated magnetic field and radio signal.

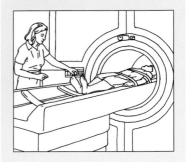

Does the test have risks?

- Because MRI works through the use of powerful magnets, it can't be performed on people with pacemakers, intracranial aneurysm clips, or other iron implants or on a person with gunshot wounds to the head.
- Because of the strong magnetic field, metallic or computer-based equipment—for example, ventilators—can't be used in the MRI area.

What are the normal results?

An MRI scan can distinctly show the brain and spine. Tissue color and shading vary, depending in part on the magnetic strength used and the amount of computer enhancement. MRI can detect nerve-related disorders, for example, MS.

What do abnormal results mean?

MRI clearly shows changes that result when water accumulates in an organ or tissue. Examples include certain brain tumors and disorders such as cerebral edema, in which fluid accumulates in the brain.

DIGESTIVE SYSTEM

CAT SCAN OF THE LIVER AND BILIARY TRACT

This test checks for problems in the biliary tract and liver. In a CAT (computerized axial tomography) scan, a series of X-rays pass through the body and show differences in tissue densities. Images of the tissues appear on a computer screen. A special dye—called a *contrast medium*—may be given intravenously or by mouth to accentuate the images.

Why is this test done?

A CAT scan of the liver and biliary tract may be performed for the following reasons:

- To detect biliary tract and liver disease
- To distinguish between two types of jaundice
- To clarify previously detected defects
- To detect suspected blood clots after abdominal injury.

What should you know before the test?

■ If you'll be receiving a contrast dye by mouth, you'll be asked to fast after midnight before the test. If a dye won't be used, fasting won't be necessary.

■ If an intravenous contrast dye is used, you may experience slight discomfort from the needle puncture and a feeling of warmth on injection. Immediately report nausea, vomiting, dizziness, headache, and itching or hives.

■ You'll be asked about any past allergies to iodine, shellfish, or the contrast dye used in other diagnostic tests.

■ The test is painless and takes approximately 90 minutes to complete.

■ A nurse or technician will explain the procedure before the test.

■ You'll be told to remain very still during the test and to hold your breath at certain intervals.

■ You'll be asked to sign a consent form before the test takes place.

What happens during the test?

■ You're positioned on an adjustable table, which is moved into a scanning chamber.

■ A series of X-ray films is taken and recorded. The information is reconstructed by a computer and appears as images on a monitor.

■ These images are studied, and selected ones are photographed.

■ The test may be repeated with contrast dye to enhance results. After the contrast dye is injected, a second series of films is taken.

What happens after the test?

■ You'll be carefully observed for allergic reactions if contrast dye was used.

■ You may resume your usual diet.

Does the test have risks?

■ A CAT scan of the biliary tract and liver is usually not recommended during pregnancy.

■ Use of an intravenous contrast dye is not recommended for people with allergies to iodine or with severe kidney or liver disease.

What are the normal results?

Normally, the liver has a uniform density that's slightly denser than the pancreas, kidneys, and spleen. Like the biliary ducts, the gallbladder is visible as a round or elliptical low-density structure. A contracted gallbladder may be impossible to visualize.

What do abnormal results mean?

Most liver defects appear as areas that are less dense than normal, and CAT scans can detect small defects. Some lesions have the same density as the liver and may be undetectable. Other defects may distort the liver or change the character of the biliary duct. Use of an intravenous contrast dye helps detect even slight biliary duct dilation.

Usually, a CAT scan can identify the cause of biliary obstructions. However, if an obstruction must be located before surgery, other tests may be performed as well.

CAT SCAN OF THE PANCREAS

During this test, a series of X-rays penetrate the upper abdomen and enable the doctor to distinguish different tissue thicknesses. Computerized images of the findings are then displayed on a monitor. A series of these cross-sectional images can provide a detailed look at the pancreas.

A CAT (computerized axial tomography) scan may be used to distinguish the pancreas and surrounding organs and vessels if enough fat is present between the structures. A type of dye, called a *contrast medium,* may be given intravenously or orally to further accentuate differences in tissue density and clarify the images.

Why is this test done?

A CAT scan of the pancreas may be performed for the following reasons:
- To detect disorders of the pancreas, such as cancer or abnormal structures called *pseudocysts*
- To detect or evaluate pancreatitis.

What should you know before the test?

- You'll be asked to fast after midnight before the test.
- A nurse or technician will explain the procedure, which is painless.
- You'll be asked to remain still during the test and to periodically hold your breath.
- You may be given an intravenous or oral contrast dye, or both, to enhance images of the pancreas. Report side effects of the dye, such as nausea, flushing, dizziness, and sweating, to the doctor or nurse.

- Your medication history will be checked for recent barium studies and for past allergic reactions to iodine, shellfish, or contrast dye used in prior tests.
- If an oral contrast dye is used, it's given before the test.

What happens during the test?

- You're positioned on an adjustable table that is placed inside a scanning booth.
- A series of X-rays is taken and recorded. The information is reconstructed as images on a monitor. These images are studied, and selected ones are photographed.
- After the first series of X-rays is completed, the images are reviewed. Then contrast dye may be administered, followed by another series of X-rays. You're observed for allergic reactions, such as itching, blood pressure changes, sweating, or dizziness.

What happens after the test?

After a CAT scan of the pancreas, you may resume your usual diet.

Does the test have risks?

A CAT scan of the pancreas should not be performed during pregnancy or, if a contrast dye is needed, on people with a history of allergic reactions to iodine or severe kidney or liver disease.

What are the normal results?

Usually, the pancreas has a uniform density, especially when an intravenous contrast dye is used. The gland normally thickens from its tail to its head and has a smooth surface.

Use of a contrast dye administered by mouth helps distinguish the stomach and duodenum and outlines the pancreas, particularly in people with little fat, such as children and thin adults.

What do abnormal results mean?

Because the tissue density of pancreatic cancer resembles normal tissue, changes in pancreatic size and shape help the doctor diagnose certain cancers and pseudocysts (abnormal or dilated cavities).

This test may also help the doctor to diagnose pancreatitis. Acute pancreatitis produces widespread enlargement of the pancreas. In chronic pancreatitis, the pancreas may appear normal, enlarged, or shrunken, depending on the severity of the disease.

Changes in pancreatic size and shape help the doctor diagnose certain types of cancer.

SKELETON

CAT SCAN OF THE SKELETON

This test takes a series of X-ray images of the bones of the skeleton. A computer constructs these images into cross-sectional views, which are displayed on a monitor. (See *Understanding your bones and joints*.)

Special techniques — such as using dyes called *contrast media* — improve the resolution and accuracy of the images. Hundreds of thousands of readings may be combined to provide three-dimensional views of the bones.

Why is this test done?

A CAT scan of the skeleton may be performed for the following reasons:
■ To allow the doctor to view the bones and joints
■ To check for bone tumors, the spread of cancer through the skeleton, and soft-tissue tumors
■ To diagnose joint abnormalities that are difficult to detect by other methods.

What should you know before the test?

■ If a contrast dye isn't ordered, you don't need to restrict food or fluids before this test. If contrast dye is ordered, you'll be asked to fast for 4 hours before the test.
■ The test takes 30 to 60 minutes and is painless.
■ A nurse or technician will explain the procedure to you. You'll be asked to lie as still as possible during the test because movement may cause distorted images.
■ If contrast dye is used, you may feel flushed and warm and may experience a brief headache, a salty taste, and nausea or vomiting after the injection. These reactions are normal.
■ You'll be given a gown to wear and asked to remove all metal objects and jewelry that may appear in the X-ray field.
■ You'll be asked to sign a consent form before the test.
■ Your medical history will be checked for past allergic reactions to iodine, shellfish, or the contrast dye in previous tests. If you've had such reactions, your doctor may prescribe medications before the test or choose not to use a contrast dye.

If contrast dye is injected, you may feel flushed and warm and may have a brief headache, a salty taste, and nausea or vomiting. These reactions are normal.

HOW YOUR BODY WORKS

Understanding your bones and joints

There are 206 bones in the normal human body. They form an underlying supporting structure called the *skeleton.* Most bones are classified by shape.

■ *Long bones* consist of a shaft and two bulbous ends. The parts of the shaft that flare to join the ends contain the bone's growth zones. Long bones are composed primarily of compact bone, which is strong and dense. Examples of long bones in the arms and legs are the humerus, radius, ulna, femur, tibia, fibula, phalanges, and metatarsals.

■ *Short bones* consist mainly of cancellous — or spongy — bone with a thin, compact bone shell, and include the tarsal and carpal bones of the feet and hands.

■ *Flat bones* have a large surface area and provide protection for soft body parts. They're made up of an inner layer of cancellous bone surrounded by compact bone. Examples are the bones of the skull over the brain area and the ribs, sternum, scapulae, ilium, and pubis, which form the torso.

■ *Irregular bones* are of various shapes and composition and include bones of the spine and certain skull bones, such as those that make up the jaw.

Joints

Joints consist of two bones joined in various ways. Like bones, joints have several forms:

■ *Fibrous joints* can move only slightly. This type of joint provides stability when a tight juncture is necessary. Examples of fibrous joints are the irregular "seams" between the bones of the skull.

■ *Cartilaginous joints* allow limited movement. Examples of cartilaginous joints are those between the vertebrae, or bones of the spine.

■ *Synovial joints* are the most common type. These joints allow angular and circular movement. To allow

freedom of movement, synovial joints have special characteristics: They're covered with a material called *cartilage* that resists pressure; where the bones meet, they glide smoothly on each other; and a fibrous capsule holds the joint together.

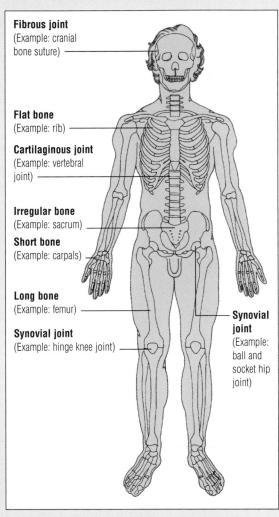

Fibrous joint
(Example: cranial bone suture)

Flat bone
(Example: rib)

Cartilaginous joint
(Example: vertebral joint)

Irregular bone
(Example: sacrum)

Short bone
(Example: carpals)

Long bone
(Example: femur)

Synovial joint
(Example: hinge knee joint)

Synovial joint
(Example: ball and socket hip joint)

■ If you're restless or apprehensive about the procedure, a mild sedative may be prescribed.

What happens during the test?

■ You're positioned on an X-ray table and asked to lie still.

■ The table slides into the circular opening of the CAT scanner. The computer-controlled scanner revolves around you, taking multiple scans.

■ After the first set of scans is taken, you're removed from the scanner and contrast dye is administered if necessary.

■ You're observed for signs and symptoms of a hypersensitivity reaction — including itching, rash, and respiratory difficulty — for 30 minutes after the contrast dye is injected.

■ After the dye is injected, you're moved back into the scanner, and another series of scans is taken. The images obtained from the scan are displayed on a video monitor during the procedure and stored on magnetic tape to create a permanent record for further study.

What happens after the test?

■ If contrast dye was used, you'll be observed for a possible delayed allergic reaction and will be given appropriate treatment if necessary.

■ You'll be encouraged to drink fluids to help eliminate the dye from your system.

■ You may resume your usual activity level and diet following the test.

Does the test have risks?

■ People who are allergic to iodine, shellfish, or contrast dye should not undergo a CAT scan with contrast enhancement.

■ Some people may experience strong feelings of claustrophobia or anxiety when inside the CAT scan machine. For such people, a mild sedative may be ordered to help reduce anxiety.

■ For a person with significant bone or joint pain, painkillers are given so the person can lie still comfortably during the scan.

What are the normal results?

The scan should reveal no problem in the bones or joints.

What do abnormal results mean?

Because it's able to display cross-sectional views of the body, CAT scanning is useful for assessing the shoulder, spine, hip, and pelvis. The scan can reveal some bone tumors and soft-tissue tumors as well as cancer that has spread from one part of the skeletal system to another. It can also reveal joint disorders that are difficult to detect by other tests.

MRI SCAN OF THE SKELETON

MRI stands for *magnetic resonance imaging.* This is a noninvasive diagnostic technique (a test in which nothing enters your body) that produces clear images of bone and soft tissue. MRI scans of the skeleton allow three-dimensional imaging of areas that can't be easily viewed with X-rays or CAT scans. It eliminates any risks associated with exposure to X-ray beams and causes no known harm to cells.

During an MRI, a powerful magnetic field is used to generate images of a person's bones on a monitor.

Why is this test done?
MRI of the skeleton may be performed for the following reasons:
- To check the bones and soft tissue
- To evaluate bone and soft-tissue tumors
- To identify changes in bone marrow composition
- To identify spinal disorders.

What should you know before the test?
- This test takes up to 90 minutes. Although MRI is painless and involves no exposure to radiation, a radioactive contrast dye may be used, depending on the type of tissue being studied.
- A nurse or technician will explain the procedure. You'll learn that the opening for your head and body in the MRI scanner is small and deep. If claustrophobia has ever been a problem for you, a sedative may help you to tolerate the scan.
- While being tested, you'll hear the scanner clicking, whirring, and thumping as it moves inside its housing. You'll be able to communicate with the technician at all times, though.
- You'll be asked to remove all metallic objects, including jewelry, hair pins, or watches before the test.

- Inform the technician if you have any surgically implanted joints, pins, clips, valves, pumps, or pacemakers containing metal. If you do, you won't be able to undergo this test.
- You'll be asked to sign a consent form before the test.

What happens during the test?

- At the scanner room door, you're checked one last time for metal objects.
- You're positioned on a narrow, padded table that moves into the scanner tunnel. Fans continuously circulate air in the tunnel, and a call bell or intercom is used to maintain verbal contact.
- You must remain still throughout the procedure.

What happens after the test?

- If the test has been prolonged, you're watched for signs of light-headedness or fainting when you stand or sit up.
- You may resume normal activity after the test.

Does the test have risks?

- MRI can't be performed on people with pacemakers, intracranial aneurysm clips, or other iron-based metal implants. Ventilators, intravenous infusion pumps, and other metallic or computer-based equipment must be kept out of the MRI area.
- If necessary, the level of oxygen in the blood, heart rhythm, and respiratory status are monitored during the test. An anesthesiologist may monitor a heavily sedated person.

What are the normal results?

Normally, MRI reveals no disorders in bones, muscles, and joints.

What do abnormal results mean?

MRI is excellent for visualizing diseases of the spinal canal and spinal cord and for identifying bone tumors. It helps delineate muscles, ligaments, and bones. The images sharply define healthy, benign, and malignant tissues.

MRI can't be performed on people with pacemakers, intracranial aneurysm clips, or other iron-based metal implants. Devices such as ventilators and intravenous infusion pumps are also kept out of the MRI area.

CHEST & HEART

CAT SCAN OF THE CHEST

This test provides cross-sectional views of the chest by passing an X-ray beam from a computerized scanner through the body at different angles. Another name for this test is *thoracic computerized axial tomography.*

CAT scanning may be done with or without an injected contrast dye. Contrast dyes are special dyes that highlight blood vessels and produce clearer images.

This test provides a three-dimensional image and is especially useful in detecting small differences in tissue density. It may provide information for diagnosing masses in the chest and Hodgkin's disease. It's also valuable for evaluating lung disorders. (See *Looking at the respiratory system,* page 102.)

Why is this test done?

A CAT scan of the chest may be performed for the following reasons:
- To provide cross-sectional views of the chest that distinguish small differences in tissue density
- To locate suspected tumors, such as those in Hodgkin's disease
- To differentiate tumors from other soft-tissue changes, such as those that indicate tuberculosis
- To distinguish tumors near the aorta from aortic aneurysms
- To detect the movement of a neck mass into the thorax
- To evaluate cancer that may move to the lungs
- To evaluate the lymph nodes in the chest area.

What should you know before the test?

- If a dye isn't used, you won't need to restrict food or fluids before the test. If the test is performed with a dye, you'll be asked to fast for 4 hours before the test.
- A nurse or technician will describe the procedure to you. The test usually takes 90 minutes and will not cause you any discomfort. Radiation exposure is minimal.
- A dye may be injected into a vein in your arm. If so, you may experience nausea, warmth, flushing of the face, or a salty taste.

HOW YOUR BODY WORKS

Looking at the respiratory system

Several organs are involved in the act of breathing — the exchange of gases between the atmosphere and the blood. These are the nose, pharynx, larynx, trachea, bronchi, and lungs. The trachea is branched, like a tree, into smaller and smaller "tubes" that carry air into the lungs. These are the primary bronchi, secondary and tertiary bronchi, bronchioles, terminal bronchioles and, finally, the alveolar sacs.

The alveolar sacs are composed of *alveoli,* which make up the main tissue of the lungs. The exchange of gases between inhaled air and the blood takes place in the alveoli. The alveoli are covered by a network of the smallest blood-carrying vessels, called *capillaries.*

In the lungs, the capillaries are further divided into *arterioles* — which carry the oxygen-rich blood away from the lungs — and *venules* — which bring oxygen-depleted blood that needs "recharging" to the lungs.

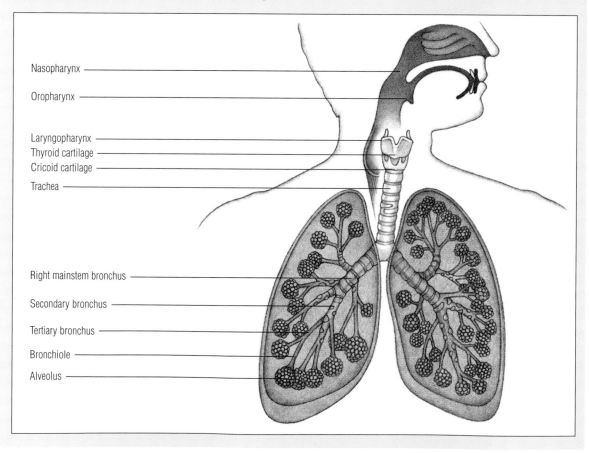

Nasopharynx

Oropharynx

Laryngopharynx
Thyroid cartilage
Cricoid cartilage
Trachea

Right mainstem bronchus

Secondary bronchus

Tertiary bronchus

Bronchiole

Alveolus

- You'll be asked to keep still during the test and to breathe normally.
- You'll be asked to remove all jewelry and metal in the X-ray field.
- You'll be asked to sign a consent form before the test takes place.
- Your history will be checked for past allergic reactions to iodine, shellfish, or contrast dyes.

What happens during the test?

- You're positioned on an X-ray table and the dye is injected. The table then moves into the center of a large ring-shaped piece of X-ray equipment. The equipment may be noisy as it scans you from different angles.
- The computer detects small differences in the densities of various tissues, water, fat, bone, and air. This information is displayed as a printout of numbers and as an image on a screen. Images may be recorded for further study.

What happens after the test?

- You'll be monitored for signs of a delayed allergic reaction to the dye, such as itching, blood pressure changes, or respiratory distress.
- You may resume your usual diet.
- You'll drink fluids to help eliminate the dye from your system.

Does the test have risks?

A CAT scan of the chest is not recommended for pregnant women or — if a dye is used — in people with a history of allergies to iodine, shellfish, or the dyes used in X-ray tests.

What are the normal results?

Black and white areas on a CAT scan of the chest help the radiologist to distinguish the density of air and bone. Shades of gray correspond to water, fat, and soft-tissue densities.

What do abnormal results mean?

A CAT scan may reveal tumors, nodules, cysts, aortic aneurysms, enlarged lymph nodes, pleural effusion, and accumulations of blood, fluid, or fat.

MRI SCAN OF THE HEART

This test helps the doctor diagnose certain heart disorders. MRI, or *magnetic resonance imaging,* uses a powerful but harmless magnetic field to "see through" bone and to show fluid-filled soft tissue in great detail, as well as produce images of organs and vessels in motion.

In this noninvasive procedure, cross-sectional images of your heart are displayed on a monitor and recorded. No X-rays are used.

Why is this test done?

An MRI scan of the heart may be performed for the following reasons:
- To check the heart's function and structure
- To identify signs of a heart attack
- To detect and evaluate cardiomyopathies (heart muscle disorders)
- To detect and evaluate diseases of the pericardium, the fluid-filled sac that surrounds the heart
- To identify masses in or around the heart
- To detect heart disease that's present at birth
- To check major blood vessels and identify vascular disorders.

What should you know before the test?

- A nurse or technician will describe this procedure to you. The test takes up to 90 minutes.
- Although MRI is painless, you may feel uncomfortable because you must remain still inside a small space throughout the test.
- If you suffer from claustrophobia, discuss this with your doctor or a nurse. You may need a sedative to tolerate the test.
- You'll be able to talk with the technician who performs the test at all times, and the procedure will be stopped if you experience problems.
- Immediately before the test, you must remove all metal objects. If you have a pacemaker or any surgically implanted joints, pins, clips, valves, or pumps containing metal that could be attracted to the strong magnetic field, you won't be able to undergo the test.
- You'll be asked to sign a consent form before the test takes place.

What happens during the test?

■ You're positioned on a narrow bed, which slides into a large cylinder that houses the MRI magnets.
■ You must remember to hold still throughout the procedure.
■ The scanner makes clicking, whirring, and thumping noises as it moves inside its housing.
■ The resulting images are displayed on a monitor and recorded on film or magnetic tape for permanent storage.
■ The technician may use the computer to manipulate and enhance the images.

What happens after the test?

If you were sedated, your status is monitored until the effects of the sedative wear off.

Does the test have risks?

■ Claustrophobic people may experience anxiety.
■ People with heart conditions are watched for signs of distress, such as chest pressure, shortness of breath, or changes in blood movement.
■ MRI can't be performed on people with pacemakers, intracranial aneurysm clips, or other iron-based metal implants.

What are the normal results?

An MRI scan should reveal a healthy heart.

What do abnormal results mean?

MRI can be used to detect and evaluate the extent of various heart diseases and defects. For example, the doctor may use information from this test in the diagnosis of cardiomyopathy, pericardial disease, and congenital heart defects. In addition, information from this test may help determine the extent of heart or blood vessel disorders.

Although MRI is painless, you may feel uncomfortable because you must remain still inside a small space throughout the test. If you suffer from claustrophobia, you may need a sedative to tolerate the test.

OTHER CAT SCANS

CAT SCAN OF STRUCTURES AROUND THE EYES

This test provides three-dimensional images of structures around the eye, especially the ocular muscles and the optic nerve. It helps the doctor identify abnormalities earlier and more accurately than other techniques, such as standard X-ray.

This test may also be called an *orbital computerized axial tomography scan.* The orbit is the bony structure that contains the eyeball.

A computer generates a series of cross-sectional images depicting the size and position of structures around the eye and their relationship to each other. In some cases, a special dye called a *contrast dye* is injected near the area that is being observed to clarify the images that are produced.

In evaluating fractures around the eye, CAT scans allow a complete three-dimensional view of the affected structures ... even the circulation of blood through abnormal tissues.

Why is this test done?

A CAT scan of the structures around the eye may be performed for the following reasons:
- To view the anatomy of the eye and its surrounding structures
- To evaluate disorders of the orbit and eye — especially expanding tissue damage and bone destruction
- To evaluate fractures of the orbit and adjoining structures
- To determine the cause of a condition called unilateral exophthalmos, which is an abnormal protrusion of the eyeball
- To help diagnose brain-related disorders that affect vision
- To evaluate conditions such as suspected circulatory disorders.

What should you know before the test?

- If contrast dye won't be used, you don't need to restrict food or fluids before this test. If the dye will be used, food and fluids are withheld for 4 hours before the test.
- A nurse or technician will describe how a series of X-ray films will be taken of your eye. During the test, a scanner rotates around your head and makes loud, clacking sounds.
- The test causes no discomfort and takes 15 to 30 minutes to perform.

■ If a dye is used, you'll be warned that you may feel flushed and warm and experience a brief headache, a salty taste, and nausea or vomiting after the dye is injected. These reactions to the contrast dye are typical.

■ You'll be asked to sign a consent form before the test takes place.

■ Your history will be checked for reactions to iodine, shellfish, or contrast dyes.

■ Before the test, you'll be asked to remove jewelry, hairpins, or other metal objects in the X-ray field to allow for precise imaging of the structures around the eye.

What happens during the test?

■ You're positioned on a special table, with your head held gently in place by straps. During the test you're asked to lie as still as possible.

■ The head of the table is moved into the scanner, which rotates around your head taking X-rays.

■ The information is stored on magnetic tapes, and the images are displayed on a screen. Photographs may be made if a permanent record is desired.

■ After this series of images is taken, a contrast dye is injected and a second series of scans is recorded.

What happens after the test?

■ If a contrast dye was used, you'll be monitored for side effects of the dye, including headache, nausea, or vomiting.

■ You may resume your usual diet.

Does the test have risks?

Use of contrast dyes is not recommended in people with known allergy to iodine, shellfish, or dyes used in other tests.

What are the normal results?

Structures around the eye are evaluated for size, shape, and position by the radiologist.

What do abnormal results mean?

A CAT scan can help the doctor identify tissue damage that obscures the normal eye structures or causes orbital enlargement, indentation of the orbital walls, or bone destruction. This test can also help determine the type of lesion, including some tumors and enlargement of the optic canal.

In evaluating fractures around the eye, CAT scans allow a complete three-dimensional view of the affected structures.

Enhancement with a contrast dye may provide information about the circulation of the blood through abnormal eye structures.

CAT SCAN OF THE KIDNEYS

In this test, a series of cross-sectional X-ray views of the kidneys are displayed on a monitor. The images of the kidneys make it possible to identify masses, such as tumors, and other lesions, or tissue damage.

An intravenous contrast medium, or dye, may be injected into your body to infiltrate the kidneys and accentuate the images that are generated. This highly accurate test is usually performed to investigate diseases found by other diagnostic procedures.

Why is this test done?

A CAT scan of the kidneys may be performed for the following reasons:
- To permit examination of the kidneys
- To detect and evaluate kidney disorders, such as tumors, obstructions, kidney stones, and fluid accumulation around the kidneys
- To guide needle placement before a biopsy
- To determine the kidney's size and location in relation to the bladder after a kidney transplant
- To locate abscesses for drainage.

What should you know before the test?

- If use of a contrast dye isn't scheduled, you won't need to restrict your diet before this test. If use of a contrast dye is scheduled, you'll be asked to fast for 4 hours before the test.
- A nurse or technician will describe the procedure to you. Expect the procedure to take about an hour, depending on the purpose of the scan.

- You may experience brief side effects from the dye, such as flushing, metallic taste, and headache, after it's injected.
- You'll be asked to sign a consent form before the test takes place.
- Your medical history will be checked for past allergic reactions to shellfish, iodine, or dyes.
- Just before the procedure, you'll be asked to put on a hospital gown and to remove any metallic objects that could interfere with the scan.
- The doctor may prescribe sedatives to reduce your anxiety about the test. They'll be given to you at the appropriate time before the test.

What happens during the test?

- You're positioned on an X-ray table and held gently in place with straps.
- The table is moved into the scanner.
- You're asked to lie still while the scanner rotates around your body.
- The scanner takes multiple images—called *tomograms*—from different angles. The equipment may make loud, clacking sounds as it rotates.
- When one series of tomograms is complete, a dye may be injected, usually through a vein. Another series of tomograms is then taken.
- After the intravenous dye is injected, you're monitored for allergic reactions, such as respiratory difficulty, hives, or rashes.
- Information from the scan is stored on a disk or on magnetic tape, fed into a computer, and converted into an image for display on a viewing screen. Photographs are taken of selected views for future reference.

What happens after the test?

- If a dye was used, you'll be monitored for signs of a possible allergic reaction.
- You may resume your usual diet.

What are the normal results?

The radiologist evaluates the position of the kidneys in relation to the surrounding structures. Normally, the density of the kidneys is slightly greater than that of the liver but less than that of bone. The size and shape of the kidneys are also determined.

The scanner takes multiple images—called tomograms—from different angles. The equipment may make loud, clacking sounds as it rotates.

What do abnormal results mean?

Kidney masses, such as tumors, appear as areas of different density than normal tissue. Such masses may alter the kidneys' shape or size.

A CAT scan may also identify other abnormalities, including obstructions, kidney stones, polycystic kidney disease, congenital anomalies, and abnormal accumulations of fluid around the kidneys. After surgical removal of a kidney, a CAT scan can detect abnormal masses, such as recurrent tumors, in a space that should be empty.

3

NUCLEAR MEDICINE SCANS:
Picturing Internal Organs

SCANNING THE THYROID

IODINE TEST OF THE THYROID GLAND

This test—which doctors call the *radioactive iodine uptake test*—is used to evaluate the thyroid gland. This important gland, located in the neck, releases two major hormones that regulate the body's metabolism. (See *Learning about the thyroid.*)

As the test begins, you receive a capsule or liquid that contains a tiny amount of radioactive iodine. After you swallow the iodine, a percentage of it accumulates in the thyroid gland, indicating the thyroid's ability to trap and retain iodine.

The test is used to accurately diagnose hyperthyroidism, a condition in which the thyroid is overactive and releases too much of its hormones. However, the test is less accurate for diagnosing hypothyroidism, a condition in which the thyroid is underactive and releases too little of its hormones.

Why is this test done?

The radioactive iodine uptake test may be performed for the following reasons:

- To check the function of the thyroid gland
- To help diagnose hyperthyroidism or hypothyroidism
- To help differentiate Graves' disease from a tumor that releases thyroid hormones.

What should you know before the test?

- You must fast after midnight on the night before the test. At the start of the test, you'll receive radioactive iodine in a capsule or liquid form. Six hours later, your thyroid will be scanned. Then, 18 hours after the first scan, your thyroid will be scanned again.
- The test is painless and exposes you to only a small, harmless amount of radiation. Its results will be available within 24 hours.
- The nurse will ask if you've ever been exposed to iodine. For instance, you may have been exposed to iodine if you had an X-ray test in which the doctor injected a special dye. Similarly, you may

HOW YOUR BODY WORKS

Learning about the thyroid

The thyroid gland is located in the neck. It has two portions called *lobes* that straddle the trachea (windpipe). The right lobe is a bit larger and higher in the neck than the left.

About 50% of normal persons have a third lobe, which has the shape of a pyramid and is called the *pyramidal lobe.*

The four small parathyroid glands, two upper and two lower, sit behind the thyroid. They're closely connected to the thyroid.

Powerful hormones released by the thyroid

The thyroid controls the body's metabolism by releasing two powerful hormones: thyroxine and triiodothyronine. Besides controlling the body's metabolism, thyroxine helps control physical and mental development, resistance to infection, and vitamin requirements. Triiodothyronine, though, is an even more potent form of thyroxine.

FRONT VIEW

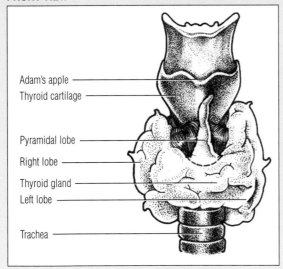

Adam's apple
Thyroid cartilage

Pyramidal lobe
Right lobe
Thyroid gland
Left lobe

Trachea

BACK VIEW

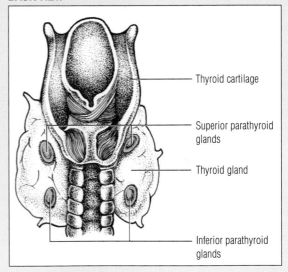

Thyroid cartilage

Superior parathyroid glands

Thyroid gland

Inferior parathyroid glands

have been exposed if you had a previous scan, used iodine preparations, or took medication for a thyroid problem.

What happens during the test?

■ After you take the dose of radioactive iodine, your thyroid gland is scanned after 6 hours and then after 24 hours.

■ During each scan, the front of your neck is placed in front of a device that detects and measures the radioactivity in your thyroid gland.

What happens after the test?

You'll be able to resume a light diet 2 hours after swallowing the iodine. When the study is complete, you'll resume a normal diet.

Does the test have risks?

The test shouldn't be performed during pregnancy and breast-feeding because the radiation could cause developmental defects in the fetus or baby.

What are the normal results?

After 6 hours, 3% to 16% of the radioactive iodine should accumulate in the thyroid. After 24 hours, the accumulation should be 8% to 29%. The rest of the iodine is excreted in the urine.

What do abnormal results mean?

Below-normal levels of iodine may indicate hypothyroidism, subacute thyroiditis, or iodine overload. Above-normal levels may indicate hyperthyroidism, early Hashimoto's thyroiditis, hypoalbuminemia, lithium ingestion, or iodine-deficient goiter.

THYROID SCAN

This test is used to examine the thyroid gland after a person ingests a small amount of a radionuclide that contains iodine or technetium. For a brief period, the radionuclide emits radiation. This radioactivity in the thyroid gland is detected by a special camera (called a *gamma camera*).

The doctor may order this scan after the discovery of a lump in the thyroid area, an enlarged thyroid gland, or an asymmetrical goiter. It's performed at the same time as the radioactive thyroid uptake test and blood tests of thyroid hormones.

Why is this test done?

The thyroid scan may be performed for the following reasons:
- To check the size, structure, and position of the thyroid gland
- To evaluate thyroid function along with other tests.

What should you know before the test?

■ You'll learn about the test, including who will perform it and where. The test itself takes about 30 minutes, but you'll need to ingest the radionuclide 20 to 30 minutes earlier (if technetium is used) or 24 hours earlier (if iodine is used). You'll need to fast after midnight on the night before the test if iodine is used, but not if technetium is used.

■ The nurse will ask about your diet and any medications that you take. Medications such as thyroid hormones and iodine preparations (Lugol's solution, some multivitamins, and cough syrups) will be discontinued 2 to 3 weeks before the test. Aspirin, blood-thinning drugs, steroids, and antihistamines will be discontinued 1 week before the test.

■ Don't use iodized salt or iodine-containing salt substitutes for 1 week before the test, and don't eat seafood during this period.

■ Just before the test, remove any jewelry, dentures, or other materials that may interfere with the scan.

What happens during the test?

■ You lie on your back with your neck extended.

■ The doctor or technician positions the gamma camera above your neck. The camera projects images of the gland on a monitor and records them on X-ray film. The doctor takes three views of the thyroid: a straight-on, frontal view and two side views.

What happens after the test?

You may resume any medications suspended for the test. And you may resume your normal diet.

Does the test have risks?

The test shouldn't be performed during pregnancy and breast-feeding because the radioactivity could cause developmental defects in the fetus or baby.

What are the normal results?

Normally, the scan shows a thyroid gland that is about 2 inches (5 centimeters) long and 1 inch (2.5 centimeters) wide. The gland should have two portions, which are called *lobes,* and should have a butterfly shape. Occasionally, a third lobe may be present; this is normal, too.

After the discovery of a lump in the thyroid area, the doctor may order a thyroid scan.

What do abnormal results mean?

The test can show areas of the thyroid that retain too much iodine. These areas are called *hot spots*. Their discovery requires follow-up testing.

The test can also show areas of the thyroid that retain little or no iodine. These areas, in contrast, are called *cold spots*. Their discovery requires an ultrasound scan to rule out cysts. In addition, a biopsy (removal and analysis of tissue) of the cold spot may be done to rule out cancer.

SCANNING THE LUNGS & HEART

BLOOD FLOW TO THE LUNGS

This test — which doctors call the *lung perfusion scan* — is used to evaluate lung perfusion, the movement of blood through the arteries that supply blood to the lungs.

The lung perfusion scan produces an image of this blood flow after the doctor injects a slightly radioactive drug into an arm vein. The drug emits tiny amounts of radiation, which is recorded by a special camera.

Why is this test done?

A lung perfusion scan may be performed for the following reasons:
- To check lung perfusion
- To detect a pulmonary embolism
- To check lung function before surgery on a person with marginal lung reserves.

What should you know before the test?

- You'll learn about the test, including who will perform it, where it will take place, and its expected duration (15 to 30 minutes). During the test, the doctor will inject a slightly radioactive drug into a vein in your arm and you'll sit in front of a camera or lie under it. Neither the camera nor the probe is radioactive.
- You won't need to fast before the test.

What happens during the test?

- The doctor injects the drug and takes a series of single stationary images with the gamma camera.
- The images, which are projected on a screen, show the distribution of radioactive particles.

What happens after the test?

If swelling occurs at the needle puncture site, warm soaks may be applied to the area.

Does the test have risks?

A lung perfusion scan shouldn't be performed in a person with allergies to the test drug.

What are the normal results?

"Hot spots" — areas with normal blood perfusion — how a high uptake of the test drug. A normal lung shows a uniform uptake pattern.

What do abnormal results mean?

"Cold spots" — areas with poor perfusion — suggest a blood clot. However, a lung ventilation scan must be done to confirm the diagnosis.

Areas of decreased blood flow without vessel blockage may indicate pneumonitis.

LUNG VENTILATION SCAN

This test is used to evaluate lung ventilation, one of the three processes that occur during breathing. (The other two processes are called *diffusion* and *perfusion.*) Ventilation refers to the movement of air from outside the body into the alveoli, the grapelike clusters in the farthest reaches of the lungs that exchange oxygen for carbon dioxide. (See *The lungs in action*, page 118.)

This scan is performed after a person inhales a mixture of air and a mildly radioactive gas that outlines areas of the lung ventilated during breathing. The scan records the distribution of the gas during three phases: the buildup of gas (wash-in phase), the time after

HOW YOUR BODY WORKS

The lungs in action

The lungs provide your body with a continuous supply of oxygen. The lungs also remove carbon dioxide from your body quickly and efficiently. This switching of the two gases takes place in grapelike clusters at the end of your breathing passages.

Alveoli do the work

These clusters, called *alveoli,* contain a network of capillaries, the body's tiniest blood vessels. The capil-laries bring blood containing carbon dioxide to the alveoli. At the same time, the breathing passages transport oxygen to the alveoli. When blood passes through the alveoli, it releases its carbon dioxide and takes on the oxygen. The now-fresh blood travels to the heart and, from there, circulates throughout the rest of body, releasing oxygen. Carbon dioxide, the other gas, passes into the breathing passages and leaves your body when you exhale.

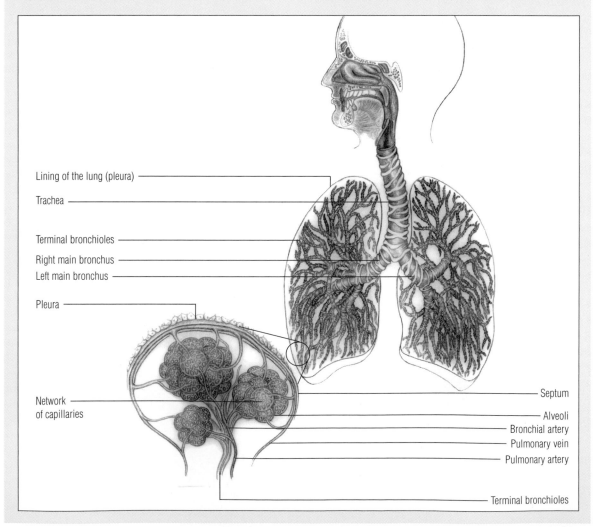

Lining of the lung (pleura)

Trachea

Terminal bronchioles

Right main bronchus

Left main bronchus

Pleura

Network of capillaries

Septum

Alveoli

Bronchial artery

Pulmonary vein

Pulmonary artery

Terminal bronchioles

rebreathing when radioactivity reaches a steady level (equilibrium phase), and after removal of the gas from the lungs (wash-out phase).

Why is this test done?

A lung ventilation scan may be performed for the following reasons:
- To help diagnose pulmonary emboli, identify areas of the lung capable of ventilation, and help evaluate breathing in a lung region
- To locate a lung region marked by poor ventilation (usually caused by smoking, chronic asthma, or emphysema)
- To distinguish between parenchymal disease, such as emphysema, sarcoidosis, lung cancer, and tuberculosis, and conditions caused by blood vessel problems such as pulmonary emboli.

During a lung ventilation scan, you must inhale a mixture of air and a mildly radioactive gas.

What should you know before the test?

- You'll learn who will perform the test, where it will take place, and that it takes 15 to 30 minutes. During the test, you'll be asked to hold your breath for a short time after inhaling a gas and to remain still while a machine scans your chest. The test uses only a small amount of radioactive gas.
- You won't need to fast before the test.
- Before the test, remove all jewelry or metal from your neck and chest.

What happens during the test?

- You inhale the air-gas mixture through a mask. As you hold your breath, the doctor checks the distribution of the gas in your lungs on a monitor.
- When you exhale, the doctor again views your lungs on the monitor.

What are the normal results?

Normal findings include an equal distribution of gas in both lungs and normal wash-in and wash-out phases.

What do abnormal results mean?

Unequal gas distribution in both lungs indicates poor ventilation or a blocked airway.

Test results may be compared to those from a lung perfusion scan. In a pulmonary embolism, perfusion is decreased but ventilation is maintained. In pneumonia or other parenchymal lung diseases, ventilation is abnormal.

TECHNETIUM SCAN OF THE HEART

Also called *hot-spot myocardial imaging* or *infarct avid imaging*, a technetium scan is used to detect a recent heart attack and determine its extent. In this test, the doctor injects a mildly radioactive element called *technetium* into a person's arm vein. The technetium accumulates in damaged heart tissue, where it shows up as "hot spots" on a scan done with a special camera.

Why is this test done?

The technetium scan may be performed for the following reasons:
- To confirm a recent heart attack in a person suffering from puzzling cardiac pain or when an electrocardiograph and blood tests don't give enough information
- To identify the size and location of a heart attack
- To determine a prognosis after a heart attack.

A technetium scan of the heart may enable the doctor to detect a recent heart attack.

What should you know before the test?

- You'll learn about the test, including who will perform the 30- to 60-minute procedure and where. Two to three hours before the test, the doctor will inject the technetium into a vein in your forearm. The injection causes only brief discomfort, and the scan itself is painless. The test involves less exposure to radiation than a chest X-ray.
- You'll need to remain quiet and motionless during the test.
- You won't need to fast before the test.
- You'll be asked to sign a form that gives your consent to do the test. Carefully read the form and ask questions if any portion of it isn't clear.

What happens during the test?

- The doctor injects the technetium into an arm vein. After 2 or 3 hours, you lie on your back on the test table and electrocardiogram electrodes are attached to your skin for continuous monitoring during the test.
- Generally, the scans are taken with you in several positions. Each scan takes 10 minutes.

What are the normal results?

A normal scan shows no technetium in the heart.

What do abnormal results mean?

The scan can reveal hot spots in a damaged heart, particularly 2 to 3 days after the start of a heart attack. However, hot spots become apparent as early as 12 hours after a heart attack. In most people who've had a heart attack, these areas disappear after 1 week. In some, they last for several months.

THALLIUM SCAN OF THE HEART

Also called *cold spot myocardial imaging,* this test helps determine if any areas of the heart aren't receiving enough blood. In the test, the doctor injects a mildly radioactive solution called *thallium* into a person's arm vein. Because thallium accumulates in healthy heart tissue but not in damaged tissue, areas of the heart with a normal blood supply and intact cells rapidly absorb it. Areas of the heart with poor blood flow and injured cells don't absorb thallium and appear as "cold spots" on a scan.

This test can be performed at rest or during exercise on a treadmill.

Persistent "cold spots" indicate a heart attack.

Why is this test done?

A thallium scan during rest may be performed for the following reasons:

- To evaluate blood flow in the heart and check for damaged areas
- To demonstrate the location and extent of a heart attack.

A thallium scan during exercise, a type of stress test, may be performed for the following reasons:

- To diagnose coronary artery disease
- To check the condition of vein grafts after bypass surgery
- To evaluate the effectiveness of drugs for chest pain
- To evaluate the effectiveness of balloon angioplasty, a procedure in which a catheter with a balloon at the tip is used to open blocked coronary arteries.

What should you know before the test?

- You'll learn about the test, including who will perform it and where it will take place. The test usually takes 45 to 90 minutes. Sometimes it's done in two stages. When that happens, additional scans are taken 3 to 6 hours after the first stage.

Treadmill stress test

The illustration below shows a stress test being performed on a treadmill. Here, the doctor is preparing to perform a special test called a *thallium scan*. The doctor injects thallium into a vein while the person continues exercising. Next the doctor will take pictures of the person's heart with a special scanner. These pictures show how well the coronary arteries supply blood to the heart during exercise.

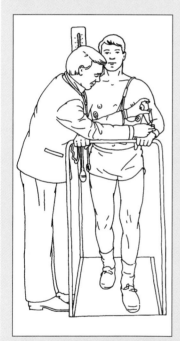

- During the test, the doctor will inject thallium into an arm vein and take scans of the heart. You may experience discomfort from the injection. During the treadmill test, you may feel some discomfort from the abrasion of your skin when electrodes are applied to your body.
- If you'll be having a treadmill test, don't drink alcohol, smoke, or take any unprescribed medications for 24 hours before the test. Don't eat or drink anything for 3 hours before the test. Before this fasting period, you should eat a light meal.
- Wear sneakers and lightweight clothing for the treadmill test. During the test, tell the doctor or nurse right away if you feel tired, are short of breath, or have chest pains.
- You'll be asked to sign a form that gives your consent to do the test. Carefully read the form and ask questions if any portion of it isn't clear.

What happens during a resting scan?

- The doctor injects thallium into a vein in your arm. After about 5 minutes, the scans are taken.
- If the doctor decides that additional scans are required, you rest and fast for several hours before they are done.

What happens during an exercise scan?

- The nurse attaches electrocardiograph electrodes to different parts of your body. These electrodes record your heart's response to different levels of exercise.
- You walk on the treadmill. (See *Treadmill stress test.*) As you reach your peak exercise level, the doctor injects thallium into a vein in your forearm. Tell the doctor or the nurse at once if you feel confused or faint, are short of breath, or have chest pains. The test is stopped for these symptoms.
- You exercise for another minute and then lie on your back under a special camera. After about 5 minutes, the scans are taken as you assume different positions on the table.
- Additional scans may be taken after you rest for 3 to 6 hours.

Does the test have risks?

- The test shouldn't be performed on a pregnant woman. It also shouldn't be done if a person has a neuromuscular impairment, an acute heart attack, an inflammation of the heart called myocarditis, narrowing of a heart valve, or a severe infection.
- The test can cause fainting, chest pain, an irregular heartbeat, and even a heart attack.

What are the normal results?

The test should show no cold spots.

What do abnormal results mean?

Persistent cold spots indicate a heart attack. Cold spots that disappear after a 3- to 6-hour rest indicate coronary artery disease, a condition that can eventually cause a heart attack.

The test can show the results of bypass surgery. For instance, if blood flow to an area of the heart improves after bypass surgery, then the new blood vessel inserted during surgery is working well.

The test can also judge how well drugs for chest pain are working and how well an alternative to bypass surgery, called angioplasty, improves blood flow in a previously blocked artery in the heart.

PERSANTINE-THALLIUM SCAN OF THE HEART

This test provides a way of examining the heart's blood vessels for people who can't tolerate exercise or a stress test. It involves the injection of two substances: the drug Persantine, then mildly radioactive thallium.

Persantine causes the body to respond as if it were actually exercising. Thallium is then used to evaluate how well the heart's blood vessels respond. Diseased vessels can't deliver thallium to the heart, and thallium lingers in diseased areas of the heart. Diseased areas appear as "cold spots" on the scan.

Why is this test done?

The Persantine-thallium scan may be performed for the following reasons:

- To identify irregular heartbeats caused by exercise or stress
- To check for damage to the heart.

What should you know before the test?

- You'll learn about the test, including who will perform it and where it will take place. The test may be done in two stages, with scans taken several hours apart.

- The nurse will tell you about the drug Persantine, which the doctor injects at the start of the test. After you get this drug, you may feel dizzy, flushed, and a little nauseated, or have a headache. These symptoms only last a brief time.
- You'll need to fast before the test. Avoid coffee and other caffeinated drinks because they may cause irregular heartbeats.
- Continue to take all your regular medications.

What happens during the test?

- At the start of the test, you lie on a table or sit. A nurse attaches electrodes to your body and performs a routine electrocardiograph, which takes 5 or 10 minutes.
- You receive Persantine and are asked to get up and walk. After Persantine takes effect, the doctor injects the thallium.
- Next, you lie on a table for about 40 minutes while the scan is performed. Then the scan is reviewed. If necessary, a second scan is performed.
- If you must return for further scanning, you should rest and not eat or drink anything in the interim.

Does the test have risks?

- The most serious risks are irregular heartbeats, chest pain, and difficulty breathing. If any of these problems occurs, the doctor will immediately treat it.
- The test can also cause nausea, headache, flushing, dizziness, and stomach pain.

What are the normal results?

The test should show no heart problems.

What do abnormal results mean?

The presence of "cold spots" usually points to coronary artery disease. However, this result could be caused by other conditions, such as sarcoidosis, myocardial fibrosis, cardiac contusion, or a spasm of one of the heart's arteries.

CARDIAC BLOOD POOL SCAN

This test is used to check the function of the ventricles, the heart's two lower chambers. (The two upper chambers are called the *atria*.) To perform this test, the doctor first gives an injection of red blood cells or a protein (albumin) that's tagged with a mildly radioactive substance called *technetium*. A scintillation camera records radioactivity as the technetium passes through the left ventricle.

Gated cardiac blood pool imaging, performed after a first-pass scan or as a separate test, has several forms. The basic principle is that multiple images are taken to show the heart in motion. This helps the doctor find problem areas in the ventricle.

Another variant of the cardiac blood pool scan, called a *MUGA scan*, may be done. (See *What is a MUGA scan?*)

Why is this test done?

A cardiac blood pool scan may be performed for the following reasons:
- To check the function of the left ventricle, the chief pumping chamber of the heart
- To detect aneurysms of the left ventricle and other motion abnormalities of the heart wall.

What should you know before the test?

- You'll learn about the test, including who will perform it, where it will take place, and its expected duration. During the test, the doctor will inject the test solution into a vein in your forearm. Then a detector positioned above your chest will record the circulation of this solution through the heart. The solution, although slightly radioactive, poses no radiation hazard and rarely produces side effects.
- You'll be directed to remain silent and motionless during the test, unless otherwise instructed.
- You'll be asked to sign a consent form. Carefully read the form and ask questions if any portion of it isn't clear.

What happens during the test?

- At the start of the test, a nurse attaches electrodes to your body so that an electrocardiogram can be performed during the test.
- You lie beneath the detector of a scintillation camera, and the doctor injects the solution.

What is a MUGA scan?

MUGA stands for a multiple-gated acquisition scan. In this test, a special camera records sequential images of the heart wall that can be studied like motion picture films. These images capture events in the heart's pumping cycle: the contraction of the heart, followed by its relaxation.

MUGA under stress

The MUGA test can be performed in two stages: at rest and after exercise. The stress MUGA test is done to detect changes in the heart's pumping performance.

Nitro MUGA

Nitro is an abbreviation for the powerful drug nitroglycerin, which is widely prescribed by doctors for chest pain. In the nitro MUGA test, a special camera records different points in the cardiac cycle after a person takes nitroglycerin. The test tells the effect nitroglycerin has on heart function.

The camera records the movement of a radioactive element called technetium *as it circulates through the heart.*

- For the next minute, the camera records the first pass of the solution through the heart so that heart valves can be located.
- Then the camera records the end of the contraction and relaxation stages of the heartbeat. In all, it records 500 to 1,000 cardiac cycles on X-ray or Polaroid film. An electrocardiograph is used to help time the taking of pictures.
- You may be asked to change your position during the test. You may also be asked to take the drug nitroglycerin or to exercise briefly.

Does the test have risks?

The test shouldn't be performed on a pregnant woman.

What are the normal results?

Normally, the left ventricle contracts symmetrically, and the technetium appears evenly distributed in the scans. Higher counts of radioactivity occur during the heart's contraction because there's more blood in the ventricle. Lower counts occur during its relaxation as the blood is ejected.

What do abnormal results mean?

The test can be used to detect coronary artery disease, which causes asymmetrical distribution of blood to the heart. The test also can detect cardiomyopathies and shunting of blood within the heart.

MISCELLANEOUS TESTS

BONE SCAN

A bone scan is used to examine the skeleton and helps doctors detect cancer and other problems long before X-ray detection is possible. In this procedure, a doctor injects a slightly radioactive solution into an arm vein. The solution accumulates in bone tissue where an abnormality is present. A special camera passes over the entire body during the test and can pinpoint these abnormal sites, which are called "hot spots."

Why is this test done?

A bone scan may be done for the following reasons:

- To detect or rule out malignant bone tumors when X-rays are normal but cancer is confirmed or suspected
- To detect difficult-to-find bone fractures
- To monitor degenerative bone disorders
- To detect bone infection
- To evaluate unexplained bone pain.

What should you know before the test?

- You'll learn about the scan, including who will perform the test and where. During the test, you may have to assume various positions on a scanner table. You must keep still for the scan.
- You'll be told that the scan, which takes about 1 hour, is painless and that the radioactive solution emits less radiation than a standard X-ray machine.
- The nurse will tell you to urinate just before the test and will give you a painkiller.
- You'll be asked to sign a form that gives your consent to do the test. Carefully read the form and ask questions if any portions of it aren't clear.

What happens during the test?

- The doctor injects the solution into a vein in your forearm. During the next 1 to 3 hours, you need to drink four to six 8-ounce glasses (about 2 liters) of water or tea.
- After this period, you lie on the scanning table. The scanner moves back and forth over your body. As it does, it detects low-level radiation emitted by the skeleton and translates this onto a film or paper chart, or both.
- The scanner takes as many views as needed to cover the specified area. You may change positions several times during the test to obtain adequate views.

What happens after the test?

You may have redness or swelling where the doctor injected the solution.

A bone scan examines the skeleton and enables the doctor to detect cancer and other problems long before they can be detected by X-rays.

Does the test have risks?

The test shouldn't be performed on a pregnant or breast-feeding woman.

What are the normal results?

The solution concentrates in bone tissue at sites of new bone formation or increased metabolism.

What do abnormal results mean?

Although a bone scan shows hot spots that identify sites of bone formation, it doesn't distinguish between normal and abnormal bone formation. But scan results can identify all types of bone cancer, infection, fracture, and other disorders if viewed in light of a person's medical and surgical history, X-rays, and other tests.

LIVER AND SPLEEN SCAN

In this test, a special camera shows images of the liver and spleen. These images show the distribution of radioactivity within the liver and spleen after a doctor injects a mildly radioactive solution of technetium into a person's arm. Roughly 80% to 90% of the solution is absorbed by the liver, 5% to 10% by the spleen, and 3% to 5% by bone marrow.

Although a person's symptoms may aid a diagnosis, results from a liver and spleen scan frequently require confirmation by an ultrasound test, a computerized axial tomography scan (commonly called a CAT scan), a gallium scan, or a biopsy (removal and analysis of tissue).

Why is this test done?

A liver and spleen scan may be performed for the following reasons:

- To screen for liver cancer and liver diseases, such as cirrhosis and hepatitis
- To detect tumors, cysts, and abscesses in the liver and spleen
- To demonstrate enlargement of the liver or spleen
- To assess the condition of the liver and spleen after abdominal injury.

What should you know before the test?

■ You'll learn about the test, including who will perform it and where it will take place. The test takes about 1 hour. You don't need to fast beforehand.

■ You'll find out that the injection isn't dangerous because the test solution contains only tiny amounts of radioactivity.

■ During the test, you must lie still and breathe quietly to ensure images of good quality; you may also be asked to briefly hold your breath. The detector head of the camera may touch your abdomen but isn't dangerous.

■ You'll be asked to sign a form that gives your consent to do the test. Carefully read the form and ask questions if any portion of it isn't clear.

Results of a liver and spleen scan frequently require confirmation by an ultrasound or other tests.

What happens during the test?

The doctor injects the technetium into a vein in your arm. After 10 to 15 minutes, your abdomen is scanned. You change positions on the table several times to get the best views of the liver and spleen.

What happens after the test?

The doctor reviews the images for clarity. If they're clear, you're allowed to leave.

Does the test have risks?

■ The test shouldn't be performed on children or on pregnant or breast-feeding women.

■ Rarely, severe reactions result from a stabilizer, such as dextran or gelatin, that's added to the technetium.

What are the normal results?

Both the liver and spleen normally appear equally bright on the image. However, distribution of the technetium is generally more uniform in the spleen than in the liver.

What do abnormal results mean?

Although the scan may fail to detect early liver disease, it shows characteristic, distinct patterns as the disease progresses. The test can also show the effects of hepatitis and cirrhosis. The spread of cancer to the liver or spleen may appear on the scan, but a biopsy must be performed to confirm the diagnosis.

The scan can identify cysts, abscesses, and tumors because they fail to absorb the technetium. Cysts appear on the scan as single or multiple defects, but an ultrasound test is required to confirm the diagnosis. Abscesses can appear in the liver or spleen, but both require a gallium scan or ultrasound test to confirm the diagnosis. Tumors require a confirming biopsy or flow studies.

The scan can demonstrate an enlarged liver or spleen, a large dependent gallbladder, and infarction of the spleen. It can evaluate liver and spleen damage after an abdominal injury.

KIDNEY SCAN

This test is used to evaluate the structure, blood flow, and function of the kidneys. It involves injection of a mildly radioactive solution into an arm vein, followed by scans of the kidneys.

Why is this test done?

A kidney scan may be performed for the following reasons:
- To detect functional and structural kidney problems (such as lesions)
- To detect renovascular hypertension and acute and chronic kidney disease, such as pyelonephritis and glomerulonephritis
- To check on the condition of a kidney transplant
- To evaluate kidney injury from trauma and blockage of the urinary tract.

What should you know before the test?

- You'll learn about the test, including who will perform it and where, and that it takes about 90 minutes. However, if certain scans are ordered, there will be a delay of 4 or more hours before the images are taken.
- You'll find out that the doctor will give you an injection that contains a tiny amount of radioactive solution. During the injection, you may feel a brief sensation of warmth and nausea.
- If you're taking any drugs for high blood pressure, the doctor may tell you to discontinue them before the test.
- You'll be asked to sign a form that gives your consent to do the test. Carefully read the form and ask questions if any portion of it isn't clear.

What happens during the test?

- You lie facedown on the examination table.
- The doctor performs a test to study blood flow through the kidneys and takes rapid-sequence photographs (one per second) for 1 minute.
- Next, the doctor does a test to measure the transit time of the radioactive solution through the kidneys.
- After the doctor injects the solution into an arm vein, images are taken for 20 minutes.
- Additional images may be obtained 4 or more hours later.

In the first stage, the doctor takes rapid-sequence photographs of blood flow through your kidneys.

What happens after the test?

After you urinate, flush the toilet immediately as a radiation precaution. You should do this every time you urinate for the next 24 hours.

What are the normal results?

The test should reveal no problems in the structure, blood flow, and function of the kidneys.

What do abnormal results mean?

The kidney scan can show poor circulation of blood through the kidneys. This circulatory problem can be caused by a kidney injury, the narrowing of the main artery in the kidneys, or a kidney infarction.

Because malignant kidney tumors usually have blood vessels within them, the test can help differentiate tumors from cysts. It can also identify the site of an obstruction in a ureter and point out congenital abnormalities, abscesses, polycystic kidney disease, acute tubular necrosis, severe infection, or rejection of a transplanted kidney.

GALLIUM SCAN OF THE BODY

This test, a total body scan, is used to check for certain tumors and inflammations that attract a mildly radioactive solution of gallium. The test is usually performed 24 to 48 hours after the doctor injects gallium into an arm vein.

Because gallium has an affinity for both benign and malignant tumors and inflammatory lesions, an exact diagnosis requires additional tests, such as ultrasound and a computerized axial tomography scan (commonly called a CAT scan).

Why is this test done?

A gallium scan may be performed for the following reasons:
- To detect cancer and its spread and inflammation when the site of the disease hasn't been clearly defined
- To evaluate malignant lymphoma and identify recurrent tumors after chemotherapy or radiation therapy
- To clarify defects in the liver when liver and spleen scanning and ultrasound tests prove inconclusive
- To evaluate lung cancer when the results of other tests conflict.

What should you know before the test?

- You'll learn about the test, including who will perform it and where, and that the scan takes 30 to 60 minutes. The scan is usually performed 24 to 48 hours after the injection of gallium.
- During the test, you may experience discomfort from the injection of gallium. However, the dosage is only slightly radioactive and isn't harmful.
- You'll receive a laxative before the test.
- You'll be asked to sign a form that gives your consent to do the test. Carefully read the form and ask questions if any portion of it isn't clear.

What happens during the test?

- The doctor injects the gallium solution into a vein in your forearm. After 24 to 48 hours, scans are taken.
- If the initial scan suggests bowel disease and additional scans are necessary, you receive a cleansing enema before continuing the test.

Does the test have risks?

A gallium scan shouldn't usually be done on children or pregnant or breast-feeding women. However, it may be performed if its potential diagnostic benefit outweighs the risks of exposure to radiation.

What are the normal results?

Gallium normally appears in the liver, spleen, bones, and large bowel.

The total body scan is usually performed 24 to 48 hours after the doctor injects gallium into an arm vein.

What do abnormal results mean?

A gallium scan may reveal inflammatory diseases. Abnormally high gallium accumulation is characteristic in inflammatory bowel diseases, such as ulcerative colitis and Crohn's disease, and in a number of cancers.

Abnormal gallium activity may be present in various sarcomas, Wilms' tumor, and neuroblastomas; cancer of the kidney, uterus, vagina, or stomach; and testicular tumors. In Hodgkin's disease and malignant lymphoma, a gallium scan may reveal abnormal activity in one or more lymph nodes.

After chemotherapy or radiation therapy, a gallium scan may be used to detect new or recurrent tumors. In a person with liver disease, the results of a gallium scan may help the doctor pinpoint the diagnosis.

In suspected lung cancer, abnormal gallium activity confirms the presence of a tumor. However, a chest X-ray should be performed to distinguish a tumor from an inflammatory lesion.

RED BLOOD CELL SURVIVAL TIME

Red blood cells, one of the main components of blood, normally die from old age. In hemolytic diseases, however, red blood cells of all ages randomly die, resulting in anemia. This test helps identify the cause of this anemia.

The test measures the lifespan of red blood cells that are removed from the body, tagged with a slightly radioactive solution of chromium, and injected back into the body. Then, over the next 3 to 4 weeks, blood samples are collected to measure the percentage of tagged cells until half of the cells disappear.

During the test period, a special camera scans the body for sites of abnormally high radioactivity, which indicates excessive red blood cell storage and destruction. Other tests may be performed with this one.

Why is this test done?

The test for red blood cell survival time may be performed for the following reasons:
- To help evaluate unexplained anemia, particularly hemolytic anemia
- To identify sites of abnormal red blood cell storage and destruction.

What should you know before the test?

■ You'll learn that the test requires regular blood samples at 3-day intervals for 3 to 4 weeks. Collecting each sample takes less than 3 minutes, and the small amount of radioactive solution used is harmless.

■ You don't need to fast before the blood tests.

■ You'll be asked to sign a form that gives your consent to do the test. Carefully read the form and ask questions if any portion of it isn't clear.

What happens during the test?

■ A blood sample is drawn from you and mixed with radioactive chromium. The mixture is injected into your arm.

■ A blood sample is drawn 30 minutes after this injection to determine blood and red blood cell volumes.

■ Additional blood samples are usually collected a day later and then at 3-day intervals for 3 to 4 weeks. (The intervals between samples may vary.) Radioactivity is calculated in each blood sample and the values are plotted to determine how long red blood cells last. Simultaneous scans are done of the chest, sacrum, liver, and spleen to detect radioactivity at sites of excessive red blood cell storage.

Does the test have risks?

This test shouldn't be done during pregnancy because it exposes a developing fetus to radiation, which may cause birth defects.

What are the normal results?

Normally, red blood cells have a half-life of 25 to 35 days.

What do abnormal results mean?

Shorter lifespans for the red blood cells indicate a blood disease. It could be leukemia, hemolytic anemia, hemoglobin C disease, spherocytosis, paroxysmal nocturnal hemoglobinuria, elliptocytosis, pernicious anemia, sickle cell anemia, or hemolytic-uremic syndrome.

HEART & BLOOD VESSELS

HEART SCAN

Called an *echocardiogram* by doctors, this test evaluates the size, shape, and motion of various structures within the heart. (See *The pump that keeps you going*.) It's a noninvasive test, which means that nothing enters your body during the procedure.

In an echocardiogram, a microphone-like transducer directs extremely high-pitched sound waves (which can't be heard by the human ear) toward the heart, which reflects these waves, producing echoes. The echoes are converted to images that are displayed on a monitor and recorded on a strip chart or videotape.

The doctor may use an echocardiogram when evaluating people with chest pain, enlarged heart silhouettes on X-rays, suspicious changes on electrocardiograms, and abnormal heart sounds.

Why is this test done?
An echocardiogram may be performed for the following reasons:
- To help the doctor diagnose and evaluate abnormalities of the heart's valves
- To measure the size of the heart's chambers
- To evaluate chambers and valves in congenital heart disorders
- To help diagnose hypertrophic and related cardiomyopathies
- To detect tumors in the atria
- To evaluate cardiac function or wall motion after a heart attack
- To detect pericardial effusion, a disorder marked by excessive fluid in the sac surrounding the heart.

What should you know before the test?
- You won't need to change your diet before the test.
- The test usually takes 15 to 30 minutes, and it's safe and painless.

HOW YOUR BODY WORKS

The pump that keeps you going

Your heart is the mechanism and the arteries, veins, and capillaries are the pathway by which blood circulates in your body. Together, they deliver oxygen and nutrients to the body's cells and remove waste.

The heart is a hollow, muscular organ located between the lungs. It's enclosed by a membranous sac called the *pericardium*, which consists of two layers, one inside the other. Pericardial fluid lubricates the layers as they glide over each other during heart movements.

The chambers

The heart pump system is made up of four chambers and an intricate set of valves:

- The atria — the two smaller upper chambers — receive blood from the systemic circulation and the pulmonary circulation.

- The two larger, thicker lower chambers — the ventricles — receive blood from the atria.

The valves

The interventricular septum divides the heart into right and left halves, and two valves separate the atria from the ventricles:

- The tricuspid valve separates the top chamber from the bottom in the right side.
- The mitral valve separates the top from bottom chambers in the left side of the heart.

The mitral valve has two movable leaflets; the tricuspid valve has three. Two crescent-shaped valves (the aortic and pulmonic) guard the entrances to the aortic and pulmonary arteries.

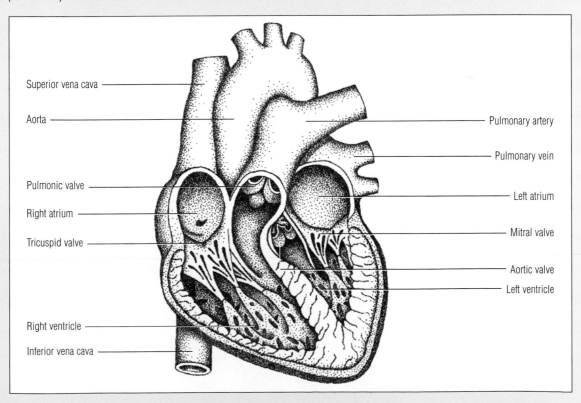

Superior vena cava
Aorta
Pulmonic valve
Right atrium
Tricuspid valve
Right ventricle
Inferior vena cava

Pulmonary artery
Pulmonary vein
Left atrium
Mitral valve
Aortic valve
Left ventricle

What happens during the test?

- The room may be darkened slightly to help the examiner see the oscilloscope screen. Other procedures, such as electrocardiography, may be performed at the same time.
- You lie on an examining table for the test.
- Conductive jelly is applied to your chest and a transducer is placed on it.
- The transducer is systematically angled to direct ultrasonic waves at specific parts of your heart.
- Significant findings are recorded on a strip chart recorder or on a videotape recorder.
- To record heart function under various conditions, you may be asked to inhale and exhale slowly or to hold your breath.
- You may be asked to inhale a gas with a slightly sweet odor (amyl nitrite) while changes in your heart function are recorded. The gas can cause dizziness, flushing, and an abnormally rapid heartbeat, but these symptoms quickly subside.

What happens after the test?

The conductive jelly is removed from your skin.

What are the normal results?

An echocardiogram can show the doctor the normal motion patterns and the structures of the four heart valves.

What do abnormal results mean?

Abnormalities in heart valves, such as mitral stenosis, readily appear on the echocardiogram. The test may also indicate that one of the heart's chambers is especially large, possibly indicating congestive heart failure. Other chamber or valve abnormalities may indicate a congenital heart disorder. The doctor can use these and other signs to choose more definitive tests.

The echocardiogram is especially sensitive in detecting pericardial effusion. Normally, the heart linings are continuous membranes, and thus produce a single or near-single echo. When fluid accumulates between these membranes, it causes an abnormal echo-free space to appear.

HEART SCAN WITH ENDOSCOPY

This test allows the doctor to see the heart's structure and function without opening the body. It combines ultrasound with endoscopy to provide a better view of your heart's structures. The medical name for this test is *transesophageal echocardiography*.

During the test, a small, microphone-like transducer is attached to the end of an endoscope and inserted into your esophagus, allowing images to be taken from the back of the heart. This causes less interference from bones and other structures near the heart and produces high-quality images of the thoracic aorta.

Heart scan with endoscopy combines two diagnostic techniques — ultrasound and endoscopy — to give the doctor a better view of your heart's structures.

Why is this test done?

The test may be performed to evaluate the following conditions:
- thoracic and aortic disorders, such as dissection and aneurysm
- conditions that affect the heart's valves, especially in the mitral valve and in people with prosthetic devices
- endocarditis
- congenital heart disease
- intracardiac clots
- cardiac tumors
- valve repairs.

What should you know before the test?

- You'll need to fast for 6 hours before the test.
- The doctor or nurse will ask if you have any conditions that might interfere with the test, such as esophageal obstruction, gastrointestinal bleeding, previous radiation therapy, severe cervical arthritis, or allergies.
- If you're having the procedure as an outpatient, arrange to have someone take you home.

What happens during the test?

- Your throat is sprayed with a topical anesthetic. You may gag when the endoscope is inserted.
- An intravenous line is inserted to sedate you before the procedure; you may feel some discomfort from the needle puncture and the pressure of the tourniquet.

- You're made as comfortable as possible during the procedure and your blood pressure and heart rate are monitored continuously.
- After the endoscope is put down your throat, ultrasound images are recorded. These images are reviewed by the doctor after the procedure.

What happens after the test?

- You'll remain in bed until the sedative wears off.
- The nurse will encourage you to cough after the procedure, either while lying on your side or sitting upright.
- You can have food or water after your gag response returns.

What are the normal results?

The test should reveal no cardiac problems.

What do abnormal results mean?

The test can reveal thoracic and aortic disorders, endocarditis, congenital heart disease, intracardiac clots, or tumors, or it can be used to evaluate valvular disease or repairs. Findings may indicate aortic dissection or an aneurysm, mitral valve disease, or congenital defects such as patent ductus arteriosus.

BLOOD VESSEL SCAN

This test — which doctors call *Doppler ultrasonography* — evaluates blood flow in your arms and legs or neck. It's a noninvasive procedure, which means nothing enters your body. It's safer, less costly, and faster than invasive tests, such as arteriography and venography. The test can accurately detect artery and vein disease that reduces blood flow by at least 50%.

In a blood vessel scan, a microphone-like transducer directs extremely high-pitch sound waves to the artery or vein being tested. The sound waves strike moving red blood cells and are reflected back to the transducer. The doctor can actually listen to the blood flow. (See *How the Doppler probe works.*)

How the Doppler probe works

If the doctor has suggested that you have this non-intrusive test, here's how it works:

- The Doppler ultrasonic probe directs high-frequency sound waves through layers of tissue.
- When these waves strike red blood cells moving through the bloodstream, their frequency changes in proportion to the rate of blood flow.
- Recording echoing waves helps the doctor detect arterial and venous obstruction but doesn't measure the quantity of blood flowing by.

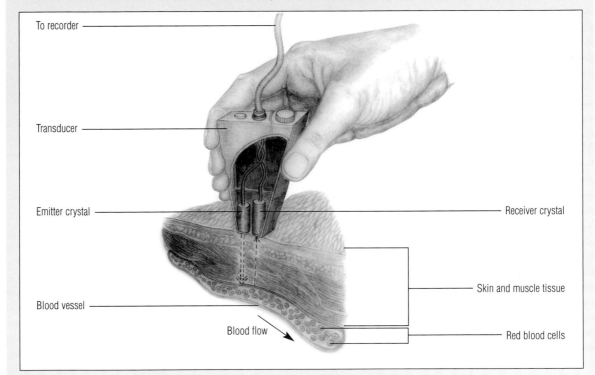

To recorder

Transducer

Emitter crystal

Receiver crystal

Skin and muscle tissue

Blood vessel

Blood flow

Red blood cells

Why is this test done?

A blood vessel scan may be performed for any of the following reasons:

- To help the doctor diagnose chronic venous insufficiency and superficial and deep vein blood clots
- To help diagnose artery disease and arterial blockage
- To monitor people who've had arterial reconstruction and bypass grafts
- To detect abnormalities of carotid artery blood flow linked to conditions such as aortic stenosis
- To evaluate possible injury to the arteries.

What should you know before the test?

The test takes about 20 minutes and doesn't involve any risk or discomfort.

What happens during the test?

- You're asked to move your arms to different positions and to perform breathing exercises as measurements are taken. A small ultrasonic probe resembling a microphone is placed at various sites along veins or arteries, and blood pressure is checked at several sites.
- You're asked to remove clothing from the area to be tested, you're draped, and you lie on an examining table or bed.

What happens after the test?

The nurse will remove all the conductive jelly left on your skin by the probe.

What are the normal results?

The examiner can hear and see that blood flow and blood pressure are within normal limits.

What do abnormal results mean?

The doctor can use the sounds of blocked arteries and veins revealed by the test to track down disease and blockages. For example, arterial narrowing or blockage reduces the blood flow velocity signal. At the lesion, the signal is high-pitched and, occasionally, turbulent. The doctor can use the test to tell how badly circulation is blocked and where.

ABDOMINAL AORTA SCAN

This test uses extremely high-pitched sound waves to examine your abdominal aorta, one of the main vessels for carrying blood away from your heart. It's safe and noninvasive, which means that nothing enters your body.

During the test, a microphone-like transducer directs the sound waves, which can't be heard by human ears, into your abdomen over a wide area from your breastbone to your navel. The echoing sound waves are displayed on a monitor to indicate internal organs, the spinal column, and the size and course of the abdominal aorta and other major vessels.

Why is this test done?

The scan may be performed for the following reasons:
- To detect and measure a suspected abdominal aortic aneurysm
- To detect and measure expansion of a known abdominal aortic aneurysm and so assess the risk of rupture.

What should you know before the test?

- You'll be asked to fast for 12 hours before the test to minimize bowel gas and movement.
- The lights in the examining room may be lowered; you'll feel only slight pressure as the transducer is moved across your abdomen. The test will take 30 to 45 minutes.
- Be assured that, if you've been diagnosed with an aneurysm, the sound waves will not cause rupture.

What happens during the test?

- You're asked to remain still during scanning and to hold your breath when requested.
- You lie on your back, and acoustic coupling gel or mineral oil is applied to your abdomen.
- After several scans of your abdomen, you may be placed on your right side and then on your left for more scans.

What happens after the test?

- The nurse will remove the acoustic coupling gel.
- You may resume your usual diet.

What are the normal results?

The examiner can see a normally sized and shaped abdominal aorta and four of its major branches.

What do abnormal results mean?

If the diameter of the abdominal aorta is too great, it suggests an aneurysm and the risk of rupture.

In a person with an abdominal aortic aneurysm, ultrasound of the abdominal aorta can help to determine the risk of rupture.

DIGESTIVE SYSTEM

GALLBLADDER AND BILE DUCT SCAN

This procedure uses extremely high-pitched sound waves to examine your gallbladder and your bile ducts. In this test, a focused beam of sound waves that can't be heard by human ears passes into the right upper quarter of your abdomen, creating echoes that vary with changes in tissue density. These echoes are converted to images on a monitor, indicating the size, shape, and position of the gallbladder and bile ducts.

Why is this test done?
A scan of the gallbladder and bile ducts may be performed for the following reasons:
- To help the doctor confirm a diagnosis of gallstones
- To diagnose acute inflammation of the gallbladder
- To distinguish between obstructive and nonobstructive jaundice.

What should you know before the test?
- You'll be asked to eat a fat-free meal in the evening and then to fast for 8 to 12 hours before the procedure. This diet change promotes accumulation of bile in your gallbladder and enhances the ultrasonic images.
- The test takes 15 to 30 minutes.
- The room may be darkened slightly to help the examiner read the screen.

What happens during the test?
- You feel only mild pressure as the transducer passes over your skin.
- You're asked to remain as still as possible during the procedure and to hold your breath at times to ensure that the gallbladder is in the same position for each scan.
- You lie on your back and the water-soluble lubricant on the face of the transducer will feel slick and cool on your skin.
- You may be asked to lie on your sides and to sit up for some of the scans.

INSIGHT INTO ILLNESS

Sites of gallstone formation

The illustration below shows potential sites of gallstone formation within the bile ducts.

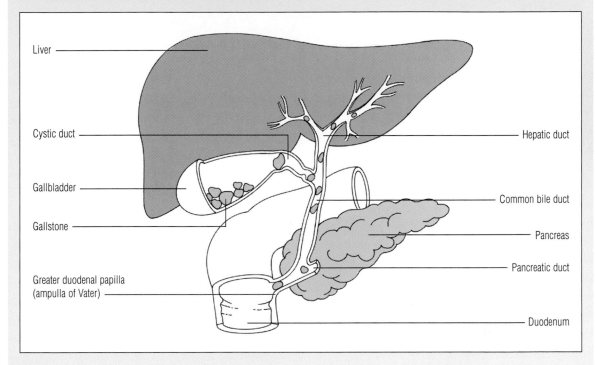

Liver

Cystic duct

Gallbladder

Gallstone

Greater duodenal papilla
(ampulla of Vater)

Hepatic duct

Common bile duct

Pancreas

Pancreatic duct

Duodenum

What happens after the test?
- The nurse will remove the lubricating jelly from your skin.
- You may resume your usual diet.

What are the normal results?
The radiologist can see that the gallbladder is of a normal shape and size, and the cystic duct and common bile ducts are properly visible.

What do abnormal results mean?
Gallstones within the gallbladder's tubes or the bile ducts typically appear as moving shadows. (See *Sites of gallstone formation.*) The doctor can also see stones in the bile ducts. The size, shape, density, and

movement of shadows in the gallbladder and ducts can lead the doctor to a long list of disorders, such as cancer, inflammation, and sludge-filled bile ducts that can lead to gallstones.

LIVER SCAN

This procedure uses extremely high-pitched sound waves, which can't be heard by human ears, to examine your liver. Images are produced on a monitor by directing these high-pitched sound waves into the right upper quarter of the abdomen. Different shades of gray show various tissue densities. Ultrasound can show the liver's internal structures and its size, shape, and position. (See *Learning about the liver.*) This test is noninvasive, which means that nothing enters your body.

Why is this test done?

A liver scan may be performed for any of the following reasons:
- To help the doctor distinguish between obstructive and non-obstructive jaundice
- To screen for liver disease
- To detect liver cancer and injury
- To determine if "cold spots" detected during liver-spleen scanning represent tumors, abscesses, or cysts.

What should you know before the test?

- You'll be asked to fast for 8 to 12 hours before the test to reduce bowel gas, which hinders the transmission of ultrasound.
- The test takes 15 to 30 minutes. It's not harmful or painful, although you may feel mild pressure as the microphone-like transducer is pressed against your skin.
- You'll be asked to remain as still as possible during the procedure and to hold your breath at times.

What happens during the test?

You lie on your back, while a water-soluble lubricant is applied to the face of the transducer and the probe is moved across your skin.

HOW YOUR BODY WORKS

Learning about the liver

The liver is your body's largest organ. It performs more than 300 functions. The liver can function even if 90% damaged. However, removal or total destruction of the liver leads to death within about 10 hours.

Locating the liver

The liver lies on your right side, just under your ribs. An adult's liver weighs about 3 pounds (1.4 kilograms) and is divided into two lobes. The right lobe has three sections and the left lobe has two. Lobules (the liver's working units) subdivide each lobe section.

You can feel the edge of your own liver, following these directions: Lie down, take a deep breath, and wrap your fingers over the lower edge of your rib cage. In a normal liver, the edge is smooth and firm.

Liver fluids: Where they go

The portal vein and the hepatic artery supply blood to the liver (about one-third of the heart's output). About 3 pints (1.4 liters) of blood flow through your liver each minute. The portal vein delivers nutrient-rich blood from the digestive tract, while the hepatic artery carries oxygen-rich blood to liver cells. The blood flows through lobular channels called *sinusoids,* which drain into the liver's central vein.

The liver also makes bile, a fluid that helps us digest fats. Bile flows through small bile ducts between liver cell plates and then drains into large bile ducts.

Liver cells: What they do

Special cells called *hepatocytes* do the liver's work. They work as the following:
- a factory — making chemical compounds, such as blood proteins, bile, and enzymes
- a warehouse — storing glycogen, iron, and vitamins
- a waste disposal plant — breaking down and excreting old red blood cells and urea and detoxifying drugs, poisons, and alcohol
- a power plant — burning carbohydrates, proteins, and fats
- a regulatory agency — maintaining blood sugar levels and regulating several hormones.

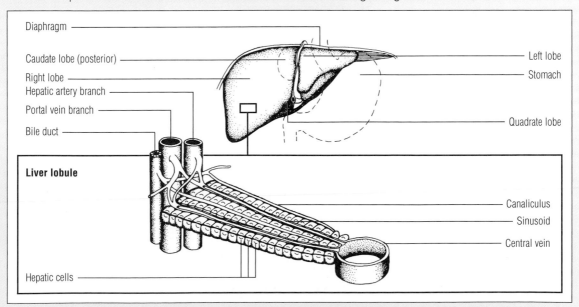

Diaphragm

Caudate lobe (posterior)

Right lobe

Hepatic artery branch

Portal vein branch

Bile duct

Left lobe

Stomach

Quadrate lobe

Liver lobule

Canaliculus

Sinusoid

Central vein

Hepatic cells

What happens after the test?

- The nurse will remove the lubricating jelly from your skin.
- You may resume your usual diet.

What are the normal results?

The liver normally appears as a homogeneous, low-level echo pattern, interrupted only by the different echo patterns of its portal and hepatic veins, the aorta, and the inferior vena cava.

What do abnormal results mean?

The doctor will look for images that indicate a long list of disorders. Dilated bile ducts point to obstructive jaundice. In cirrhosis, the scan may show variable liver size and dilated, tortuous portal branches linked to portal high hypertension. Signs of cancer in the liver vary widely — they may appear as strong or weak echoes, poorly defined or well defined. Tumors also present a varied appearance and may mimic cancers. Abscesses, cysts, and bleeding injuries all have their own characteristic look.

SPLEEN SCAN

This procedure uses extremely high-pitched sound waves to examine your spleen. A focused beam of these sound waves passes into the left upper quarter of your abdomen, creating echoes that vary with changes in tissue density. The echoes are displayed on a monitor as images that indicate the size, shape, and position of the spleen.

Why is this test done?

A spleen scan may be performed for the following reasons:

- To confirm an enlarged spleen
- To help the doctor monitor the progression of disease of the spleen and to evaluate the effectiveness of therapy
- To evaluate the spleen after abdominal injury
- To help detect cysts and an abscess of the spleen.

What should you know before the test?

■ You'll be asked to fast for 8 to 12 hours before the procedure. Fasting reduces the amount of gas in the bowel, which hinders transmission of ultrasound.
■ The procedure takes about 15 to 30 minutes.

What happens during the test?

■ You lie on an examining table with your chest uncovered.
■ The technician applies a water-soluble lubricant to the face of the microphone-like transducer and moves the ultrasound probe across your body.
■ You're asked to remain as still as possible during the procedure. You're also asked to hold your breath periodically to help the examiner get a sharp image on the screen.
■ The examining room may be darkened slightly to help the examiner see the screen.
■ Because the procedure varies depending on the size of the spleen or your physique, you may be repositioned several times. The transducer scanning angle or path is also changed.

What happens after the test?

■ A nurse or technician will remove the lubricating jelly from your skin.
■ You may resume your usual diet.

What are the normal results?

The spleen usually shows a homogeneous, low-level echo pattern, with few of its veins apparent. Its shape is usually indented by surrounding organs.

What do abnormal results mean?

The scan can show an enlarged spleen, but it usually doesn't indicate the cause. A computerized axial tomography scan (commonly called a CAT scan) can provide more specific information. The doctor may find evidence of many disorders, including an abdominal injury that's ruptured the spleen and an abscess. Used with liver-spleen scanning, ultrasound can tell cysts from solid lesions. However, ultrasound usually fails to identify tumors associated with lymphoma and chronic leukemia.

Because the procedure for ultrasound varies depending on the size of the spleen or your physique, you may be repositioned on the examining table several times.

PANCREAS SCAN

In this test, extremely high-pitched sound waves are used to examine the pancreas, the organ that secretes insulin into the bloodstream. These sound waves can't be heard by the human ear.

During the test, the doctor looks at images of the pancreas that are produced by directing the high-pitched sound waves toward the organ. When the sound waves strike the pancreas, they produce echoes, which a computer converts to visual images and displays on a monitor. The pattern varies with tissue density and indicates the size, shape, and position of the pancreas and surrounding structures. This test is noninvasive, which means that nothing enters your body.

For the ultrasound, you lie on a bed or examining table in a room that's darkened slightly to help the examiner see the screen.

Why is this test done?

A pancreas scan may be performed for any of the following reasons:
- To help the doctor detect anatomic abnormalities and diagnose pancreatitis, pseudocysts, and pancreatic cancer
- To guide the insertion of biopsy needles.

What should you know before the test?

- You'll be asked to fast for 8 to 12 hours before the procedure to reduce bowel gas.
- If you smoke, you'll be asked not to before the test.
- The test takes 30 minutes.
- The procedure isn't harmful or painful, but you may feel mild pressure from the scanner.
- You'll be asked to inhale deeply during scanning and to remain still during the procedure.

What happens during the test?

- You lie on a bed or examining table.
- The room is darkened slightly to help the examiner see the screen.
- The technician applies a water-soluble lubricant or mineral oil to your abdomen and then moves the scanner, which looks like a microphone, across your body.

What happens after the test?

- The nurse will remove the lubricating jelly from your skin.
- You may resume your usual diet.

What are the normal results?

The pancreas normally shows up as a coarse, uniform echo pattern.

What do abnormal results mean?

Changes in the size, contour, and texture of the pancreas characterize pancreatic disease. An enlarged pancreas with decreased echo strength and distinct borders suggests pancreatitis. A well-defined mass with an essentially echo-free interior indicates a pseudocyst. An ill-defined mass with scattered internal echoes or a mass in the head of the pancreas (obstructing the common bile duct) and a large gall-bladder that doesn't contract suggest pancreatic cancer. A computerized axial tomography scan (commonly called a CAT scan) and a biopsy (removal and analysis) of pancreatic tissue may be necessary to confirm a diagnosis.

MISCELLANEOUS SCANS

THYROID SCAN

This test helps the doctor define the size and shape of your thyroid gland. Ultrasonic pulses emitted from a microphone-like transducer are directed at the thyroid gland and reflected back to produce images of the organ's structure on a monitor. The test is noninvasive, which means that nothing enters your body.

After the doctor locates a lump in your neck, an ultrasound scan can help tell the difference between a cyst and a tumor. This test is also used to evaluate thyroid nodules during pregnancy because it doesn't require the use of radioactive iodine.

Why is this test done?

An ultrasound scan of the thyroid may be performed for the following reasons:

- To help the doctor evaluate thyroid structure
- To differentiate between a cyst and a tumor
- To check the size of the thyroid gland during therapy.

What should you know before the test?

■ You won't need to change your diet before the test.

■ The test takes approximately 30 minutes, it's painless and safe, and results are usually available within 24 hours.

What happens during the test?

■ You lie on the examining table with a pillow under your shoulder blades to extend your neck.

■ Your neck is coated with water-soluble gel. The technician passes the scanner across the area above your thyroid.

■ The image on the monitor is photographed for later, thorough examination by the doctor.

What happens after the test?

A nurse will remove the gel from your neck.

What are the normal results?

Normally, thyroid ultrasound shows a uniform echo pattern throughout the gland.

What do abnormal results mean?

Cysts appear as smooth-bordered, echo-free areas with enhanced sound transmission. Adenomas and cancers appear either solid and well marked or, less frequently, solid with cystic areas. Identification of a tumor is generally followed up by fine needle aspiration or surgical removal and a biopsy (removal and analysis of tissue) to determine if it's cancerous.

After the doctor locates a lump in your neck, an ultrasound scan of the thyroid can help tell the difference between a cyst and a tumor.

PELVIC SCAN

This test enables the doctor to examine the pelvic organs, such as the reproductive organs and the bladder. If you're pregnant, it helps with examination of the fetus.

In pelvic ultrasound, extremely high-pitched sound waves are reflected via a microphone-like transducer to provide images of the interior pelvic area on a monitor. This test is noninvasive, which means that nothing enters your body. Selected views may be pho-

Seeing inside the womb

Imagine seeing what you can't normally see using sounds that you can't hear. Well, that's exactly what happens when an ultrasound scan of a developing fetus is performed. When very high-pitched sound waves from a microphone-like transducer are directed at the fetus's skull, echoes return and appear as spikes on a monitor. The distance between spikes is equivalent to the distance between the top and bottom cranial walls and indicates head size. The doctor uses that measurement to determine the fetus's age.

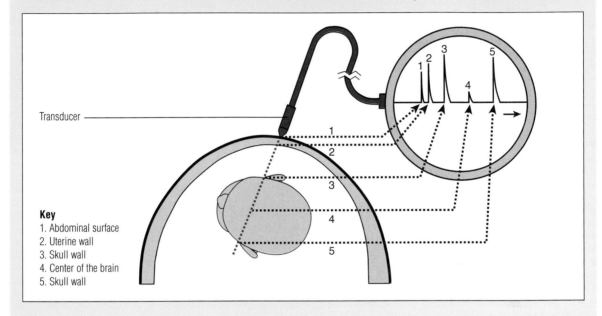

Transducer

Key
1. Abdominal surface
2. Uterine wall
3. Skull wall
4. Center of the brain
5. Skull wall

tographed for later examination by the doctor and as a permanent record of the test.

Why is this test done?

A pelvic ultrasound scan may be performed for the following reasons:
- To help the doctor evaluate symptoms that suggest pelvic disease and to confirm a tentative diagnosis
- To detect foreign bodies and distinguish between cysts and tumors
- To measure organ size
- To evaluate fetal strength, position, gestational age, and growth rate (See *Seeing inside the womb,* above, and *How a fetus grows and develops,* pages 154 and 155.)
- To detect multiple pregnancy
- To confirm fetal abnormalities and maternal abnormalities
- To guide amniocentesis by determining placental location and fetal position.

How a fetus grows and develops

The first month

At the end of 1 month, the embryo has a definite form. The head and trunk are apparent, and the tiny buds that will become the arms and legs are discernible. The heart and blood vessels have begun to work, and the umbilical cord is visible in its most primitive form.

10 TIMES ACTUAL SIZE

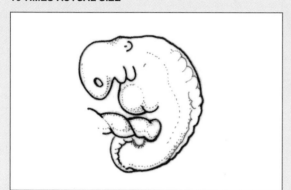

The second month

In the next month, the embryo — called a *fetus* from the seventh week on — grows to 1 inch (2.5 centimeters) in length and weighs $\frac{1}{30}$ of an ounce. The head and facial features develop as the eyes, ears, nose, lips, tongue, and tooth buds form. The arms and legs also take shape, with the fingers and toes becoming visible. Although the gender of the fetus is not yet visible, all external genitalia are present. Heart and blood vessel function is complete, and the umbilical cord has a definite form. At the end of 2 months, the fetus resembles a full-term baby except for its size.

ACTUAL SIZE

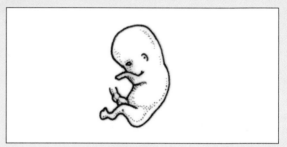

What should you know before the test?

■ Because this test requires a full bladder as a reference point to help the examiner define pelvic organs, you'll be asked to drink liquids and not to empty your bladder before the test.

■ The test can vary in length from a few minutes to several hours.

■ A water enema may be necessary to produce a better outline of the large intestine.

■ Be assured that the test will not harm a fetus.

The third month

During the third month, the fetus grows to 3 inches (7.6 centimeters) in length and weighs 1 ounce (28.4 grams). Teeth and bones begin to appear, and the kidneys start to work. Although the mother can't yet feel its activity, the fetus is moving. It opens its mouth to swallow, grasps with its tiny, but fully developed, hands, and — even though its lungs don't yet function — it prepares for breathing by inhaling and exhaling. At the end of the first trimester (3 months), its gender is apparent.

ACTUAL SIZE

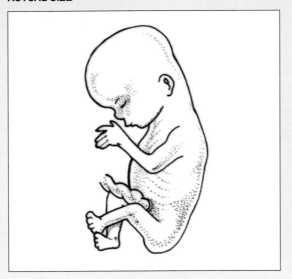

The remaining 6 months

In the remaining 6 months, fetal growth continues as internal and external structures develop at a rapid rate. In the third trimester, the fetus stores fats and minerals it will need to live outside the womb. At birth, the average full-term fetus measures 20 inches (50.8 centimeters) and weighs 7 to 7½ pounds (3.2 to 3.4 kilograms).

ONE-THIRD ACTUAL SIZE

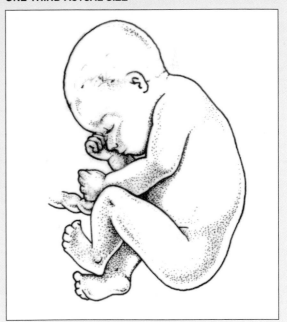

What happens during the test?

■ You lie on an examining table, and your pelvic area is coated with mineral oil or water-soluble jelly to increase sound wave conduction.

■ The technician guides the microphone-like transducer over the pelvic area. Images are observed on the oscilloscope screen.

What happens after the test?

You'll be allowed to empty your bladder immediately after the test.

Because this test requires a full bladder to help the examiner define pelvic organs, you'll drink a lot of liquids. You'll be allowed to empty your bladder immediately after the test.

What are the normal results?

The uterus is normal in size and shape. The ovaries' size, shape, and density are normal. No other masses are visible. If you're pregnant, the examiner can see that the gestational sac and fetus are of normal size in relation to gestational age.

What do abnormal results mean?

Both cystic and solid masses have homogeneous densities, but solid masses (such as fibroids) appear more dense. Inappropriate fetal size may indicate miscalculated conception or delivery date or a dead fetus. Abnormal echo patterns may indicate foreign bodies (such as an intrauterine device), multiple pregnancy, maternal abnormalities, fetal abnormalities, and fetal malpresentation (such as a breech or shoulder presentation).

KIDNEY SCAN

In this test, extremely high-pitch sound waves are transmitted from a microphone-like transducer to the kidneys and surrounding structures. The resulting echoes are converted into anatomic images and displayed on a monitor.

The doctor may use an ultrasound scan of the kidneys to detect abnormalities or to clarify those detected by other tests. Ultrasound of the ureter, bladder, and gonads also may be used to evaluate urologic disorders.

Why is this test done?

A kidney scan may be performed for any of the following reasons:
- To help the doctor determine the size, shape, and position of the kidneys, their internal structures, and surrounding tissues (See *Learning about the kidneys.*)
- To evaluate and localize urinary obstruction and abnormal fluid accumulation
- To assess and diagnose complications after kidney transplantation.

HOW YOUR BODY WORKS

Learning about the kidneys

The kidneys are reddish brown, bean-shaped organs situated in the back of the abdomen. Each kidney is about the size of a closed hand and weighs 4 to 6 ounces (113 to 170 grams). In the kidneys, the body's waste products are filtered out of the blood and excreted in the urine in combination with water.

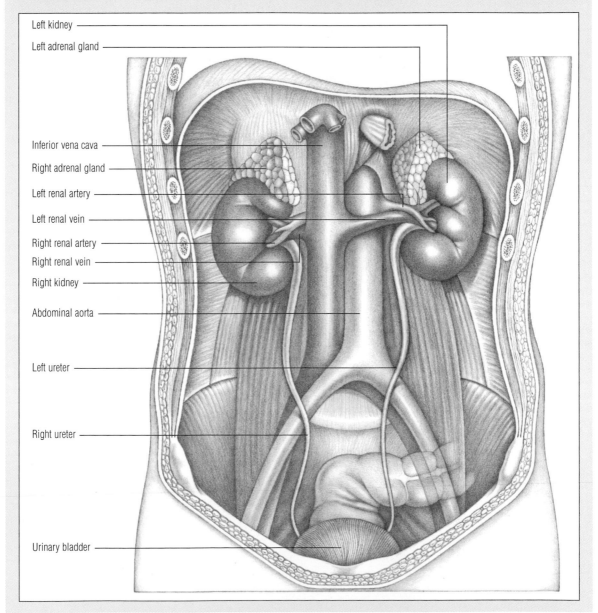

Left kidney

Left adrenal gland

Inferior vena cava

Right adrenal gland

Left renal artery

Left renal vein

Right renal artery

Right renal vein

Right kidney

Abdominal aorta

Left ureter

Right ureter

Urinary bladder

What should you know before the test?

■ You won't need to change your diet before the test.

■ The test takes about 30 minutes, and it's safe and painless.

What happens during the test?

■ You lie on the examining table and ultrasound jelly is applied to the area to be scanned.

■ You may be asked to breathe deeply to show the kidneys' movement during respiration.

What happens after the test?

The nurse will remove the ultrasound jelly from your skin.

What are the normal results?

The radiologist can see that the kidneys are of normal size and in the normal location.

What do abnormal results mean?

Cysts are usually fluid-filled, circular structures that don't reflect sound waves. Tumors produce multiple echoes and appear as irregular shapes. Abscesses found within or around the kidneys usually echo sound waves poorly. A perirenal abscess may be discovered because it displaces the kidneys.

Generally, acute kidney diseases are not detectable by ultrasound unless the kidneys are significantly scarred and decreased in size.

This test can also be used to detect inherited defects and to check the progress of a transplanted kidney.

BRAIN CIRCULATION SCAN

This scan provides information about the presence, quality, and changing nature of blood circulation to your brain by measuring the rate of blood flow through cerebral arteries. The medical name for this test is a *transcranial Doppler study*.

Narrowed blood vessels produce high blood flow rates, indicating possible narrowing or a spasm of a blood vessel. High rates may also indicate an arteriovenous malformation.

Why is this test done?

A brain circulation scan may be performed for the following reasons:
- To measure the rate of blood flow through certain vessels in the brain
- To help the doctor detect and monitor the progression of a spasm in one of the brain's blood vessels
- To determine whether a secondary route of blood flow exists before surgery for diseased vessels
- To help determine brain death.

This test provides information about the circulation in your brain. If blood is moving too quickly, it may signal narrowing or spasm of a blood vessel.

What should you know before the test?

- The test will be done while you lie on a bed or a stretcher or sit in a reclining chair. It can be performed at the bedside if you're too ill to be moved to the lab.
- The procedure usually takes less than 1 hour, depending on the number of vessels to be examined.
- You won't have to change your diet before the test.

What happens during the test?

- While you recline in a chair or on an examining table, a small amount of gel is applied to the transcranial window—an area of your head where the bone is thin enough to allow the Doppler signal to enter and be detected.
- The technician directs the signal toward the artery being studied and records the rates detected. Waveforms may be printed for later analysis.

What happens after the test?

The nurse will clean the conductive gel from your skin.

What are the normal results?

The type of waveforms and blood flow rates should indicate that vessels are functioning adequately and that spasms are absent.

What do abnormal results mean?

Although this test often is not definitive, high blood flow rates are typically abnormal and suggest that blood flow is too turbulent or the blood vessel is too narrow.

After the test and before surgery, the person may undergo an angiogram of the brain to further define cerebral blood flow patterns and to locate the exact blood vessel abnormality.

5

HEART & BRAIN MONITORING:
Checking Vital Functions

HEART MONITORING

ELECTROCARDIOGRAPHY

An electrocardiogram, commonly known as an EKG, is the most common test of the heart's condition. It's used to graphically record the electrical current generated by the beating heart. (See *The heart's electrical impulses*.) This current radiates from the heart in all directions and, on reaching the skin, is measured by electrodes. These electrodes are connected to an amplifier and strip chart recorder, which prints tracings. The doctor interprets the tracings to obtain information about the heart's functioning.

Why is this test done?
An electrocardiogram may be performed for the following reasons:
- To help identify irregular heartbeats, an enlarged or inflamed heart, heart damage, and the site and extent of a heart attack
- To check on recovery from a heart attack
- To evaluate the effectiveness of drugs for heart problems
- To check the performance of a cardiac pacemaker.

What should you know before the test?
- You'll learn about the test, including who will perform it, where it will take place, and its expected duration (5 to 10 minutes). During the test, electrodes will be attached to your arms, legs, and chest. The procedure is painless and you should relax, lie still, and breathe normally.
- Don't talk during the test because the sound of your voice may distort the electrocardiogram tracing.
- Tell the doctor or nurse if you're taking any medications.

What happens during the test?
- You lie on your back, and a nurse attaches electrodes to your chest, ankles, and wrists.
- The nurse connects leadwires after all electrodes are in place and may secure the limb electrodes with rubber straps, but won't tighten them too much.

HOW YOUR BODY WORKS

The heart's electrical impulses

Like a power plant, the heart generates and conducts its own electricity. This electricity travels through the heart to create the heartbeat.

The beat begins
The sinoatrial node, which is located in the right atrium (one of the two upper chambers of the heart), normally controls the heart rate and is called the *pacemaker.* This node has special tissue that allows it to create and send an electrical impulse through the atrium to the atrioventricular node. As an impulse passes through the atrial muscles, the atria contract.

The beat goes on
After a short delay in the atrioventricular node, the impulse travels down the bundle of His, which divides into right and left branches. Finally, the impulse reaches the Purkinje fibers, which send the impulse to the ventricles, causing them to contract.

Momentary relaxation
After contracting, the ventricles relax and begin to fill with blood, in preparation for the next impulse from the sinoatrial node.

Backup systems
The sinoatrial node fires about 60 to 100 impulses every minute. If it fails to generate the expected impulses, the atrioventricular node can take over, but at a slower rate of 40 to 60 impulses each minute. If both nodes fail, the Purkinje fibers can produce 15 to 40 impulses per minute.

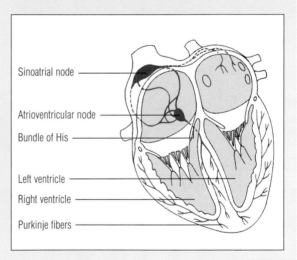

Sinoatrial node

Atrioventricular node

Bundle of His

Left ventricle

Right ventricle

Purkinje fibers

- The nurse presses the START button and the machine records and prints the electrocardiogram. (See *Performing electrocardiography,* page 164.)
- When the machine finishes, the nurse removes the electrodes.

What are the normal results?
An electrocardiogram should show no disturbances in the heart's function.

Performing electrocardiography

The photograph below shows a nurse pressing a button to start an electrocardiograph recording, a graphic recording of the electrical impulses that originate in the heart. Note the electrodes attached to the person's chest.

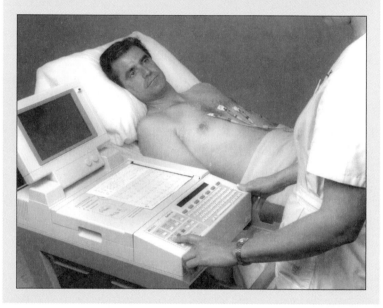

What do abnormal results mean?

An electrocardiogram may show evidence of a heart attack, enlargement of the right or left ventricle, irregular heartbeats, inflammation of the heart, and other problems. Sometimes, an electrocardiogram may only show problems during exercise or an episode of chest pain.

STRESS TEST

Referred to as an *exercise electrocardiogram* or an *exercise EKG* by doctors, this test evaluates the heart's response to physical stress. It provides important information that can't be obtained from a resting electrocardiogram.

In this test, an electrocardiogram and blood pressure readings are taken while a person walks on a treadmill or pedals a stationary bicycle. (See *Comparing two types of stress tests*, page 166.) In the multistage treadmill test, the speed and incline of the treadmill increase at predetermined intervals. In the bicycle test, the resistance in pedaling increases gradually as a person tries to maintain a specific speed.

Unless complications develop, the test goes on until a person reaches the target heart rate (set by the doctor) or feels chest pain or fatigue. A person who's had a recent heart attack or bypass surgery may walk the treadmill at a slow pace to determine his or her activity tolerance before being discharged from the hospital.

Why is this test done?
A stress test may be performed for the following reasons:
- To help diagnose the cause of chest pain
- To determine the heart's condition after surgery or a heart attack
- To check for blockages in the heart's arteries, particularly in men over age 35
- To help set limits for an exercise program
- To identify irregular heartbeats that develop during physical exercise
- To evaluate the effectiveness of drugs given for chest pain or irregular heartbeats.

What should you know before the test?
- You'll learn who will perform the test, where it will take place, and its expected duration. Electrodes will be attached to several areas on your chest and, possibly, your back. You won't feel any current from the electrodes; however, they may itch slightly.
- Expect that the test will make you tired, sweaty, and out of breath, but it poses few risks. The doctor may, in fact, stop the test if you feel tired or get chest pains.
- Don't eat, smoke, or drink alcohol or caffeinated beverages for 3 hours before the test. Continue to take any prescribed medications unless your doctor tells you otherwise.
- Wear comfortable socks and sneakers and loose, lightweight shorts or slacks. Men usually don't wear a shirt during the test, and women generally wear a bra and a lightweight short-sleeved blouse or a hospital gown with a front closure.
- Tell the doctor or nurse how you feel during the test.
- You'll be asked to sign a form that gives your permission to do the test. Read the form carefully and ask questions if any portion of it isn't clear.

Unless complications develop, the test goes on until a person reaches the target heart rate or feels chest pain or fatigue.

Comparing two types of stress tests

Treadmill test

Advantages

- Standardized and most reproducible
- Walking is familiar activity
- Constant work rate
- Attains highest maximum oxygen uptake
- Involves muscles commonly used; less chance of fatigue

Disadvantages

- Possibility of person losing balance and falling off
- Workload depends on weight; as weight increases, workload increases
- Noisy, makes communication more difficult

Bicycle test

Advantages

- Workload doesn't depend on weight
- Quieter than treadmill

Disadvantages

- Constant rate of pedaling required to maintain power
- Induces greater stress
- Attains lower maximum oxygen uptake
- Involves muscles less commonly used; greater chance of fatigue

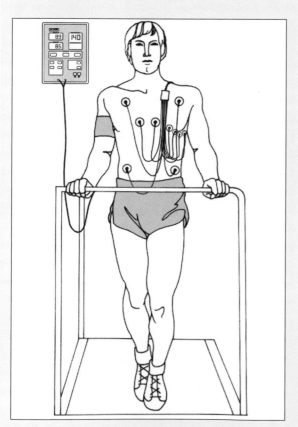

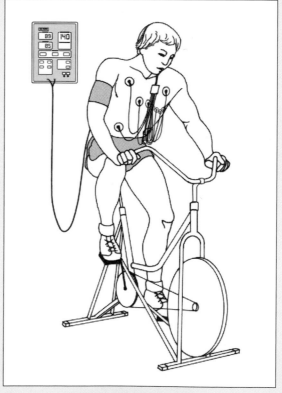

What happens during the test?

■ The electrode sites are cleaned with an alcohol swab, and excess skin oils are removed with a gauze pad or fine sandpaper.

■ Electrodes are placed on your chest. The leadwire cable is placed over your shoulder and the leadwire box is placed on your chest. The cable is secured by pinning it to your clothing or taping it to your shoulder or back. Then the leadwires are connected to the chest electrodes.

■ The monitor is started, and a tracing is obtained. The doctor checks this tracing, takes your blood pressure, and listens to your heart.

■ In a treadmill test, the treadmill is turned on to a slow speed, and you're shown how to step onto it and how to use the support railings to maintain your balance. Then the treadmill is turned off. Next, you step onto the treadmill, and it's turned on to slow speed until you get used to walking on it.

■ For a bicycle test, sit on the bicycle while the seat and handlebars are adjusted to comfortable positions. Don't grip the handlebars tightly; just use them for maintaining your balance. Pedal until you reach the desired speed, as shown on the speedometer.

■ During both tests, the doctor checks the monitor for changes in the heart's rhythm. The doctor also checks blood pressure at the end of each test level. Tell the doctor if you feel dizzy, light-headed, short of breath, or unusually tired. If your symptoms become severe, the doctor will halt the test.

■ Usually, testing stops when you reach the target heart rate. As the treadmill speed slows, you may be instructed to continue walking for several minutes to prevent nausea or dizziness. When the treadmill is turned off, you are helped to a chair, and your blood pressure and electrocardiogram are monitored for 10 to 15 minutes.

What happens after the test?

■ You may resume your usual diet.

■ If any drugs were discontinued before the test, you may resume taking them.

Does the test have risks?

■ Because a stress test places considerable demands on the heart, it's not usually performed if a person has an aneurysm, uncontrolled irregular heartbeats, an inflammation of the heart, severe anemia, uncontrolled high blood pressure, unstable angina, or congestive heart failure.

■ You may become exhausted from the test, experience chest pain or irregular heartbeats, or have significant changes in your blood pressure. The doctor will stop the test if any of these conditions develops.

What are the normal results?

In a normal exercise electrocardiogram, a person's heart rate rises in direct proportion to the workload and increased need for oxygen. Blood pressure also rises as workload increases. A normal person attains the endurance levels appropriate for his or her age.

What do abnormal results mean?

The test can detect the damage caused by a heart attack. Specific changes in electrocardiogram waveforms may indicate disease in the left coronary artery or in multiple blood vessels in the heart.

The usefulness of the test for predicting coronary artery disease varies. Much depends on the person's medical history. However, inaccurate test results are common. To detect coronary artery disease accurately, a thallium scan and stress test, exercise multiple-gated acquisition scan, or an angiogram may be necessary.

HOLTER MONITORING

This test continuously records the heart's electrical activity as a person goes about a normal routine. In effect, Holter monitoring is an around-the-clock electrocardiogram.

During the test period, which usually lasts for 24 hours but can extend up to 7 days, a person wears a small reel-to-reel or cassette tape recorder that's connected to electrodes placed on the chest. The person also keeps a diary of his or her activities and any associated symptoms. At the end of the recording period, the tape is analyzed by a computer that correlates heart abnormalities, such as irregular beats, with the activities in the diary.

Why is this test done?

Holter monitoring may be performed for the following reasons:
■ To detect irregular heartbeats missed by a stress test or resting electrocardiogram
■ To evaluate chest pain

- To check the heart's condition after a heart attack or insertion of a pacemaker
- To evaluate the effectiveness of drugs given for irregular heartbeats.

What should you know before the test?

- You'll learn that you'll wear a small tape recorder for 24 hours (or for 5 to 7 days if a self-activated monitor is being used). The nurse will show you how to position the recorder when you lie down.
- The nurse or doctor will demonstrate the proper use of specific equipment, including how to mark the tape (if applicable) at the onset of symptoms.
- If a self-activated monitor is being used, you'll be shown how to press the event button to activate the monitor if you experience any unusual sensations. Don't tamper with the monitor or disconnect the leadwires or electrodes.
- If you won't be returning to the office or hospital right after the test, the nurse or doctor will show you how to remove and store the equipment.

In effect, Holter monitoring is an around-the-clock electrocardiogram.

What happens during the test?

- The nurse or doctor cleans the electrode sites, applies the electrodes to your skin, attaches the leadwires to the electrodes, and shows you how to wear the monitor on a belt or over your shoulder.
- Continue your routine activities during the test period.
- Write in a diary your usual activities (such as walking, climbing stairs, urinating, sleeping, and sexual activity) and their time. Also write down any emotional upsets, physical symptoms (dizziness, palpitations, fatigue, chest pain, and fainting), and use of medication.
- Wear loose-fitting clothing with front-buttoning tops during the test.
- Avoid magnets, metal detectors, high-voltage areas, and electric blankets during the test.
- Check the recorder to make sure it's working properly. If the monitor light flashes, one of the electrodes may be loose and you should depress the center of each one. Notify the nurse if one comes off.

What happens after the test?

The nurse will remove all chest electrodes and clean the area.

What are the normal results?

Electrocardiogram readings are compared with the person's diary. These readings reveal changes in heart rate that normally occur during various activities. The electrocardiogram should show no significant irregular heartbeats.

What do abnormal results mean?

The test can detect many different types of irregular heartbeats. During recovery from a heart attack, this test can help determine the prognosis and the effectiveness of drug therapy.

Although Holter monitoring matches symptoms and electrocardiogram changes, it doesn't always identify the symptoms' causes. If initial monitoring proves inconclusive, the test may be repeated.

IMPEDANCE TEST OF BLOOD FLOW

This test, which doctors call *impedance phlebography* or *plethysmography*, is a painless, safe, and reliable way to measure blood flow in the leg veins. In this widely used test, electrodes are applied to the leg to record changes in electrical resistance (impedance) caused by changes in blood volume variations. These changes occur during breathing and from blocked veins.

Why is this test done?

Impedance plethysmography may be performed for the following reasons:

■ To detect blood clots in the deep veins of the leg, a condition called *deep vein thrombosis*

■ To check people who have a high risk of thrombophlebitis, a condition in which a vein is inflamed and a blood clot lodges there

■ To check for pulmonary emboli, a serious condition in which a blood clot lodges in a blood vessel in the lung. Most blood clots originate in the leg veins and travel to the lungs.

What should you know before the test?

■ You'll learn who will perform the test and where and that it takes 30 to 45 minutes. The test examines both legs and requires three to five tracings for each leg.

■ Accurate testing requires that leg muscles be relaxed and breathing be normal. If you have any pain that interferes with leg relaxation, you'll receive a mild pain reliever during the test.

- You'll be asked to put on a hospital gown.
- Just before the test, you should urinate.

What happens during the test?

- You lie on your back and raise the leg to be tested 30 degrees. Your calf should be above the level of your heart.
- Flex your knee slightly and rotate your hips by shifting weight to the same side as the leg being tested.
- Your skin will be prepped with electrode gel, and electrodes will be loosely attached to your calf. Then a pressure cuff is wrapped snugly around your thigh.
- The pressure cuff is inflated and maintained for 45 seconds or until the tracing stabilizes.
- A strip chart tracing records the increase in venous volume following cuff inflation and the decrease in venous volume 3 seconds after deflation. The test is repeated for the other leg. If necessary, 3 to 5 tracings for each leg are obtained. The tracing showing the greatest rise and fall in venous volume is reported as the test result.

What happens after the test?

A nurse will remove the gel from your skin.

What are the normal results?

A temporary blockage of a vein normally produces a sharp rise in the vein's blood volume. Release of the blockage produces a rapid flow of blood in the vein.

What do abnormal results mean?

When blood clots in a major deep vein block blood flow, the pressure in the calf veins rises, and these veins become distended. Such veins can't expand further when additional pressure is applied with an occlusive thigh cuff.

Blockage of major deep veins also decreases the rate at which blood flows from the leg. If significant blood clots are present in a major deep vein of the lower leg, both calf vein filling and outflow rate are reduced.

You lie on your back and raise the leg to be tested 30 degrees. Your calf should be above the level of your heart.

HEART CATHETERIZATION

This lengthy test checks the function of the heart and its blood vessels. In particular, it determines blood pressures and blood flow in the chambers of the heart, permits collection of blood samples, and records X-rays of the heart's ventricles or arteries. (See *The heart's blood supply*.)

To start the test, the doctor inserts a plastic catheter into a blood vessel in the arm or groin area and advances it slowly to the left or the right side of the heart. Then, the doctor injects a special dye through the catheter. The dye, which has properties that cause it to appear on X-rays, flows through a ventricle and coronary arteries, during which X-rays are taken.

The test may be done on either side of the heart. Testing the left side of the heart checks the coronary arteries, mitral and aortic valves, and left ventricle. It helps diagnose enlargement of the left ventricle, narrowing of aortic valve, insufficiency of the aortic or mitral valve, an aneurysm, and shunting (diversion) of blood from one side of the heart to the other.

Testing the right side of the heart checks the other heart valves — the tricuspid and pulmonic valves — and measures the pressure in the pulmonary artery.

Why is this test done?

Cardiac catheterization may be performed for the following reasons:
- To check for insufficiency or narrowing of the heart valves
- To identify septal defects and heart problems present at birth
- To evaluate the heart's blood supply, heart wall motion, and overall function.

What should you know before the test?

- You'll learn about the test, including who will perform it, where it will take place, and its duration (2 to 3 hours).
- You may receive a mild sedative but will remain conscious during the test. You'll be strapped to a padded table, and the table may be tilted so your heart can be examined from different angles.
- The doctors and nurses who perform the catheterization will wear gloves, masks, and gowns to protect you from infection.
- The changing X-ray plates and advancing film will make clacking noises.

HOW YOUR BODY WORKS

The heart's blood supply

Most people think of the heart as the pump that supplies the rest of the body with blood. But the heart itself has an intricate web of blood vessels to ensure that it receives its own share of blood (with accompanying oxygen and nutrients). Coronary artery disease results from conditions that slow blood flow and thus interfere with the heart's blood supply.

The illustrations show the network of vessels that supply blood to the heart.

FRONT VIEW

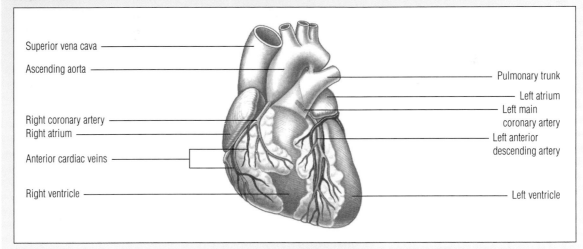

Superior vena cava

Ascending aorta

Right coronary artery

Right atrium

Anterior cardiac veins

Right ventricle

Pulmonary trunk

Left atrium

Left main coronary artery

Left anterior descending artery

Left ventricle

BACK VIEW

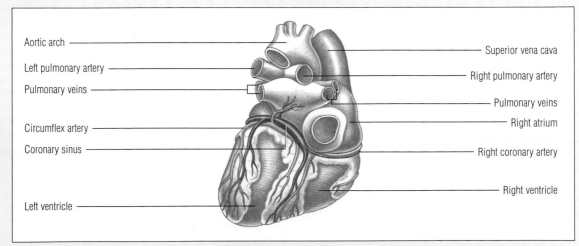

Aortic arch

Left pulmonary artery

Pulmonary veins

Circumflex artery

Coronary sinus

Left ventricle

Superior vena cava

Right pulmonary artery

Pulmonary veins

Right atrium

Right coronary artery

Right ventricle

■ For the test, you'll have an intravenous needle inserted in your arm to allow administration of medication. Electrodes for an electrocardiogram will be attached to your chest but will cause no discomfort.

■ A catheter will be inserted into an artery or vein in your arm or leg. If the skin above the vessel is hairy, it will be shaved and cleaned with an antiseptic. You'll feel a brief stinging sensation when a local anesthetic is injected to numb the incision site for catheter insertion, and you may feel pressure as the catheter moves along the blood vessel.

■ During the injection of the dye, you may feel a hot, flushing sensation or nausea that quickly passes. Follow directions to cough or breathe deeply.

■ During the test, you'll be given medication if you feel chest pain. You may also receive nitroglycerin periodically to expand the size of the heart's blood vessels.

■ Tell the doctor or nurse if you're allergic to shellfish (such as shrimp or scallops), iodine, or the dyes used in other diagnostic tests.

■ Don't eat or drink anything for at least 6 hours before the test. Continue to take any prescribed drugs unless your doctor tells you otherwise.

■ Just before the test, you should urinate and put on a hospital gown.

■ You'll be asked to sign a form that gives your permission to do the test. Read the form carefully and ask questions if any portion of it isn't clear.

What happens during the test?

■ You lie on your back on a tilt-top table and are secured by restraints. Electrocardiograph leads are applied to your skin to monitor your heart during the test and an intravenous line is inserted.

■ After injecting the local anesthetic, the doctor makes a small incision or puncture in an artery or vein. Then the doctor passes a catheter through the needle into the vessel and guides the catheter to a heart chamber or artery.

■ When the catheter is in place, the doctor injects the dye and X-rays are taken. You may be asked to cough or breathe deeply. Coughing helps counteract nausea or light-headedness caused by the dye. Deep breathing moves the diaphragm downward, making the heart easier to see.

■ During the test, you may be given nitroglycerin. After the test, the doctor removes the catheter and applies a dressing.

During the test, you may receive nitroglycerin periodically to expand the size of the heart's blood vessels.

What happens after the test?

- The nurse will check on you regularly.
- You'll rest in bed for 8 hours. If the doctor inserted the catheter into a blood vessel in the groin area, keep your leg extended for 6 to 8 hours. If the doctor inserted the catheter into a blood vessel in the arm, keep your arm extended for at least 3 hours.
- If you feel any pain, tell the nurse, who can give you medication to relieve it.
- Drink plenty of fluids high in potassium, such as orange juice.

Does the test have risks?

- A bleeding disorder, poor kidney function, or debilitation usually rules out performing the test.
- If a person has heart valve disease, antibiotics may be given before the test to guard against endocarditis.
- Complications of the test, such as a heart attack or blood clots, are rare.

Normally, the coronary arteries should have smooth and regular outlines.

What are the normal results?

Cardiac catheterization should reveal no abnormalities of heart chamber size or configuration, wall motion or thickness, direction of blood flow, or valve motion. The coronary arteries should have smooth and regular outlines.

Cardiac catheterization provides information on pressures in the heart's chambers and vessels. Higher pressures than normal are clinically significant. Lower pressures, except in shock, usually aren't significant.

The test also helps determine the ejection fraction — a comparison of the amount of blood ejected from the left ventricle during its contraction phase with the amount of blood remaining in the left ventricle at the end of its relaxation phase. A normal ejection fraction is 60% to 70%.

What do abnormal results mean?

The test can confirm coronary artery disease, poor heart function, disease of the heart valves, and septal defects.

In coronary artery disease, catheterization shows narrowing or blockages in the coronary arteries. Narrowing greater than 70% is especially significant. Narrowing of the left main coronary artery and blockage or narrowing high in the left anterior descending artery is often an indication for surgery.

Impaired wall motion can indicate coronary artery disease, aneurysm, an enlarged heart, or a heart problem present at birth. An ejection fraction under 35% generally increases the risk of complications and decreases the probability of successful surgery.

Heart valve disease is detected by a difference in pressure above and below the heart valve. The higher the difference, the greater the degree of narrowing.

Septal defects can be confirmed by measuring oxygen content in both sides of the heart. Elevated oxygen on the right side indicates a left-to-right atrial or ventricular shunt. Decreased oxygen on the left side indicates a right-to-left shunt.

HIS BUNDLE ELECTROGRAPHY

This test is used to measure the electrical impulses that produce the heartbeat and rhythm. To perform the test, the doctor inserts a small plastic catheter into a vein in the groin area and then advances the catheter into the right ventricle, one of the heart's two lower chambers.

The test measures separate conduction times as the doctor slowly withdraws the catheter from the right ventricle through the bundle of His to the sinoatrial node.

Why is this test done?
His bundle electrography may be performed for the following reasons:
- To detect irregular heartbeats
- To determine the need for a pacemaker and drug therapy and to evaluate their effects on the heart
- To find disturbances in the heart's conduction system
- To locate an abnormal site in the heart that has taken over as the heart's pacemaker
- To evaluate fainting
- To detect and locate abnormal conduction tissue in the heart.

What should you know before the test?
- You'll learn about the test, including who will perform it, where it will take place, and its duration (1 to 3 hours).

- You'll be conscious during the test. If you feel any pain, tell the doctor or nurse right away.
- Don't eat or drink anything for at least 6 hours before the test.
- Your groin area will be shaved, a catheter will be inserted into a vein, and an intravenous line may be started. You'll receive a local anesthetic but may still feel some pressure when the doctor inserts the catheter.
- Just before the test, you should urinate.
- You'll be asked to sign a form that gives your permission to do the test. Read the form carefully and ask questions if any portion of it isn't clear.

What happens during the test?

- You lie on a special X-ray table. Electrodes are applied for an electrocardiogram, which will be done during the test. The insertion site is shaved, scrubbed, and sterilized.
- The doctor injects the local anesthetic, inserts the catheter, and advances it into the right ventricle. Then the doctor slowly withdraws the catheter as recordings of conduction intervals are made. (See *A view of His bundle catheterization*, page 178.)
- After recordings and measurements are completed, the catheter is removed and a dressing is applied to the site.

What happens after the test?

- You'll rest in bed for 4 to 6 hours. A nurse will check on you regularly during this period. Tell the nurse if you feel short of breath or have chest pains.
- You may resume your usual diet.
- You'll be scheduled for a follow-up electrocardiogram to monitor your heart's functioning.

Does the test have risks?

- This test shouldn't be done if a person has a severe bleeding disorder, recent thrombophlebitis, or a pulmonary embolism.
- Possible complications of the test include irregular heartbeats, vein inflammation, blood clots in the lungs, and severe bleeding.

What are the normal results?

The test should demonstrate normal conduction intervals.

This test is used to find disturbances in the electrical system that produces your heartbeat.

A view of His bundle catheterization

In this view, the doctor has inserted an electrode catheter through the superior vena cava, right atrium, and tricuspid valve. When the doctor slowly withdraws the catheter, the tip moves downward along the ventricle wall. As it passes the bundle of His, a characteristic spike appears on the electrogram.

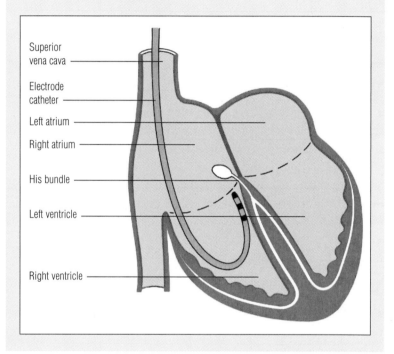

Superior
vena cava

Electrode
catheter

Left atrium

Right atrium

His bundle

Left ventricle

Right ventricle

What do abnormal results mean?

Longer-than-normal conduction intervals can be caused by acute or chronic heart disease. Shorter-than-normal intervals can be caused by atrial pacing, chronic conduction system disease, carotid sinus pressure, a recent heart attack, diseases of the atria, and use of certain drugs.

PULMONARY ARTERY CATHETERIZATION

Also known as *Swan-Ganz catheterization,* this test evaluates heart function and provides information necessary to determine therapy. It's usually performed at bedside in an intensive care unit.

During the test, the doctor slowly advances a small catheter through an arm or neck vein into the heart. Once the catheter is positioned, the doctor intermittently blocks and releases the flow of blood through the pulmonary artery. The test measures both pulmonary artery pressure and pulmonary artery wedge pressure. The catheter usually stays in place for 2 or 3 days.

Why is this test done?

Pulmonary artery catheterization may be performed for the following reasons:

- To help evaluate heart failure
- To monitor therapy for complications of a heart attack
- To check fluid status in a person with serious burns, kidney disease, or fluid accumulation in the lungs after open heart surgery
- To check the effects of drugs such as nitroglycerin.

What should you know before the test?

- You'll learn about the test, including who will perform it and where. You'll be conscious during catheterization and may feel brief local discomfort from the administration of the local anesthetic.
- The catheter insertion takes about 30 minutes but the catheter will remain in place, causing little or no discomfort, for 48 to 72 hours. You'll need to stay in bed during this period to avoid dislodging the catheter.
- While the catheter is in place, tell the doctor or nurse right away if you feel any pain.
- You'll be asked to sign a form that gives your permission to do the test. Read the form carefully and ask questions if any portion of it isn't clear.

What happens during the test?

- You lie on your back. The doctor inserts the catheter into a vein in your arm or neck.
- The doctor advances the catheter through the heart into the pulmonary artery. At each stage of the journey, the doctor checks the monitor for characteristic waveform changes.
- Next, the doctor inflates a tiny balloon at the end of the catheter and measures arterial pressures.
- When the catheter's correct position and function is established, the doctor stitches it to the skin. Ointment and an airtight dressing are applied to the insertion site. A chest X-ray is obtained.
- Pressure measurements are made at different times during the next 2 to 3 days. After they're all completed, the doctor removes the catheter.

What happens after the test?

A nurse will check on you regularly, keeping an eye on the site where the catheter was inserted for any signs of infection, such as redness, swelling, and discharge.

Does the test have risks?

- The test should be performed cautiously in a person with a heart block or an implanted pacemaker.
- The test can cause serious complications, such as a pulmonary embolism, pulmonary artery perforation, heart murmurs, blood clots, and irregular heartbeats.

Measurements of pressure in the arteries are made at different times during the next 2 to 3 days.

What are the normal results?

The test records pressures within different parts of the heart. Normal readings are:

- Right atrium pressure: 1 to 6 millimeters of mercury
- Right ventricle pressure during contraction: 20 to 30 millimeters of mercury
- Right ventricle pressure at the end of relaxation: 5 millimeters of mercury
- Pulmonary artery pressure during contraction: 20 to 30 millimeters of mercury
- Pulmonary artery pressure during relaxation: about 10 millimeters of mercury
- Mean pulmonary artery pressure: less than 20 millimeters of mercury
- Pulmonary artery wedge pressure: 6 to 12 millimeters of mercury
- Left atrial pressure: about 10 millimeters of mercury.

What do abnormal results mean?

Abnormally high pressure in the right atrium can indicate lung disease, failure of the right side of the heart, fluid overload, cardiac tamponade, tricuspid valve narrowing and insufficiency, or pulmonary high blood pressure. Abnormally high pressure in the right ventricle can be caused by pulmonary hypertension, narrowing of the pulmonic valve, right ventricular failure, severe inflammation of the heart, chronic heart failure, or ventricular septal defects.

An unusually high pulmonary artery pressure occurs in a left-to-right shunting (diversion) of blood within the heart, pulmonary high blood pressure or mitral stenosis, emphysema, a blood clot or fluid accumulation in the lungs, and left ventricular failure.

Elevated pulmonary artery wedge pressure can be caused by left ventricular failure, mitral valve narrowing and insufficiency, or cardiac tamponade.

BRAIN MONITORING

ELECTROENCEPHALOGRAPHY

Usually known by the abbreviation EEG, this test records the brain's electrical activity. It's performed by attaching electrodes to areas of the scalp. These electrodes record some of the brain's electrical activity and send this information to an electroencephalograph machine, which traces the brain waves on paper or a computer screen.

Why is this test done?

An electroencephalograph may be performed for the following reasons:
- To determine the presence and type of seizures
- To help diagnose brain abscesses and tumors
- To evaluate the brain's electrical activity in head injury, meningitis, encephalitis, mental retardation, and psychological disorders
- To confirm brain death.

An electroencephalograph can cause seizures if a person already has a seizure disorder.

What should you know before the test?

■ Don't drink caffeine-containing coffee, tea, colas, or other beverages beforehand. Otherwise, you can follow your usual diet.

■ Thoroughly wash and dry your hair to remove hair sprays, creams, or oils.

■ Tell the doctor or nurse if you take any medications—especially drugs for seizures, anxiety, insomnia, or depression. You may have to stop taking any of these medications for a day or two before the test.

■ If you're going to have a "sleep electroencephalograph," you'll need to stay awake the night before the test. Just before the test, a nurse will give you a sedative to help you sleep during the test.

■ You'll be asked to sign a form that gives your permission to do the test. Read the form carefully and ask questions if any portion of it isn't clear.

What happens during the test?

■ During the test, you relax in a reclining chair or lie on a bed, and electrodes are attached to your scalp with a special paste. The electrodes don't cause any electric shocks.

■ Before the recording procedure begins, close your eyes, relax, and remain still. Don't talk.

■ The recording may be stopped now and then to let you rest or reposition yourself.

■ After the initial recording, you may be tested under various stress-producing conditions to elicit patterns not observable while you're resting. For example, you may be asked to breathe deeply and rapidly for 3 minutes, which may elicit brain wave patterns typical of seizures or other problems. Or a bright light may be shone at you.

What happens after the test?

■ The nurse will remove the electrode paste from your hair.

■ If you received a sedative before the test, you'll feel drowsy afterward.

■ The nurse will tell you when you can take any medications that were suspended for the test.

Does the test have risks?

■ An electroencephalograph can cause seizures in a person with a seizure disorder. If a seizure occurs, the doctor will treat it right away.

What are the normal results?

An electroencephalograph records a portion of the brain's electrical activity as waves. Some of the waves are irregular, while others demonstrate frequent patterns. Among the basic waveforms are the alpha, beta, theta, and delta rhythms.

Alpha waves occur at a frequency of 8 to 12 cycles per second in a regular rhythm. They're present only when you're awake and alert but your eyes are closed. Usually, they disappear with visual activity or mental concentration.

Beta waves occur at a frequency of 13 to 30 cycles per second. They're generally associated with anxiety, depression, or the use of sedatives.

Theta waves occur at a frequency of 4 to 7 cycles per second. They're most common in children and young adults.

Delta waves occur at a frequency of 0.5 to 3.5 cycles per second. Normally, they occur only in young children and during sleep.

What do abnormal results mean?

Usually, about 100 pages of recording paper are evaluated, with particular attention paid to basic waveforms, symmetry of brain activity, brief bursts of energy, and responses to stimulation.

In seizure disorders, the electroencephalograph pattern may identify the specific type of seizure. In *absence seizures,* the electroencephalograph shows spikes and waves at a frequency of 3 cycles per second. In *generalized tonic-clonic* or *grand mal seizures*, it usually shows multiple, high-voltage, spiked waves in both hemispheres of the brain. In *complex partial seizures*, the electroencephalograph usually shows spiked waves in the affected region. And in *focal seizures*, it usually shows localized, spiked discharges.

In brain tumors or abscesses, the electroencephalograph may show slow waves (usually delta waves, but possibly beta waves). Generally, any condition that causes a diminishing level of consciousness alters the electroencephalograph pattern in proportion to the degree of consciousness lost. For example, if a person has meningitis or encephalitis, the electroencephalograph shows generalized, diffuse, and slow brain waves.

ELECTRICAL IMPULSES OF THE NERVOUS SYSTEM

A group of tests, which doctors call *evoked potential studies*, are used to measure the electrical activity of the central nervous system. They aid evaluation of visual and somatosensory pathways by measuring evoked potentials — the brain's electrical response to stimulation of the sensory organs or peripheral nerves.

The evoked potentials are recorded as electronic impulses by electrodes attached to the scalp and skin over various nerves. A computer separates these low-amplitude impulses from background brain wave activity and averages the signals from repeated stimuli. Testing may evaluate two forms of evoked potentials.

Visual evoked potentials, produced by exposing the eye to a rapidly reversing checkerboard pattern, help evaluate demyelinating diseases, injuries, and puzzling visual complaints.

Somatosensory evoked potentials, produced by electrically stimulating a peripheral sensory nerve, are used to diagnose peripheral nerve disease and locate brain and spinal cord tumors.

Why is this test done?

Evoked potential studies may be performed for the following reasons:
- To help diagnose brain and spinal cord tumors and abnormalities
- To check brain function
- To monitor comatose people and people under anesthesia
- To check on spinal cord function during spinal cord surgery
- To evaluate the brains of infants whose sensory systems can't be adequately assessed.

What should you know before the test?

- You'll learn about the test, including who will perform it, where it will take place, and that it usually lasts 45 to 60 minutes. During the test, you'll sit in a reclining chair or lay on a bed. If visual evoked potentials will be measured, electrodes will be attached to your scalp; if somatosensory evoked potentials will be measured, electrodes will be placed on your scalp, neck, lower back, wrist, knee, and ankle.
- Try to relax during the test. The electrodes won't hurt you.
- Remove all jewelry.

What happens during the test?

You lie in a reclining chair or on a bed and remain still and relax.

Visual evoked potentials

- You're placed 3 feet (1 meter) from the pattern-shift stimulator. Electrodes are attached to your scalp at different spots.
- As one eye is covered, you'll fix your gaze on a dot in the center of the screen.
- A checkerboard pattern is projected and then rapidly reversed or shifted 100 times, once or twice per second.
- A computer amplifies and averages the brain's response to each stimulus, and the results are plotted as a waveform.
- The procedure is repeated for the other eye.

Somatosensory evoked potentials

- Electrodes are attached to your skin over somatosensory pathways — typically the wrist, knee, and ankle to stimulate peripheral nerves. Other electrodes are placed on the scalp and other spots.
- Painless electrical stimulation is delivered to the peripheral nerve through the electrode. The intensity is adjusted to produce a minor muscle response such as a thumb twitch.
- Electrical stimuli are delivered 500 or more times, at a rate of 5 per second.
- A computer measures and averages the time it takes for the electrical current to reach the brain's cortex; the results, expressed in milliseconds, are recorded as waveforms.
- The test is repeated once to verify results; then the electrodes are repositioned and the entire procedure is repeated for the other side.

Painless electrical stimulation is delivered to the peripheral nerve — just enough to make a thumb twitch.

What are the normal results?

The test should reveal no abnormal waveforms.

What do abnormal results mean?

Abnormal results can occur in many conditions, such as multiple sclerosis, optic neuritis, retinopathies, amblyopia, sarcoidosis, Parkinson's disease, Huntington's disease, cervical spondylosis, brain tumors, Guillain-Barré syndrome, spinal cord injury, and others. However, the results of evoked potential studies alone can't confirm any of these diseases. Results must be interpreted in light of other tests.

Nerve conduction time: Clue to disease

Nerve conduction time is the speed at which nerves can transmit electrical messages from the body to the brain. Measuring nerve conduction time provides important information for diagnosing peripheral nerve injuries and diseases.

Performing the test

The doctor gives a person a mild electrical shock to stimulate a particular nerve. The shock is administered through the skin and underlying tissue. After each shock, a recording electrode that's placed a set distance from the site of the shock detects the response from the stimulated nerve. The lag between the shock and the response is measured. In peripheral nerve injuries and diseases, this lag time is abnormal.

NERVOUS SYSTEM MONITORING WITH ELECTROMYOGRAPHY

Electromyography, commonly abbreviated as EMG, is used to measure the electrical activity of certain skeletal muscle groups at rest and during voluntary contraction. In this test, the doctor inserts a needle electrode into a muscle and then measures the electrical discharge of the muscle, which is displayed electronically.

Why is this test done?

An electromyography may be performed for the following reasons:
- To help differentiate between primary muscle disorders, such as the muscular dystrophies, and secondary disorders
- To evaluate diseases characterized by degeneration of nerve tissue, such as amyotrophic lateral sclerosis
- To help diagnose neuromuscular disorders such as myasthenia gravis.

What should you know before the test?

- You'll learn about the test, including who will perform it, where it will take place, and its duration (1 hour). During the test, a needle will be inserted into selected muscles and you may feel some discomfort.
- Usually, you don't need to fast before the test. In some cases, cigarettes, coffee, tea, and cola may be restricted for 2 or 3 hours before the test.
- Tell the doctor or nurse if you're taking any medications.
- During the test, you may wear a hospital gown or any comfortable clothing that permits access to the muscles to be tested.
- You'll be asked to sign a form that gives your permission to do the test. Read the form carefully and ask questions if any portion of it isn't clear.

What happens during the test?

- You lie on a stretcher or bed or in a chair, depending on the muscles to be tested. Position your arm or leg so that the muscle to be tested is at rest.
- The doctor inserts the needle electrodes and places a metal plate under you. Then the muscle's electrical signal (called the *motor unit potential*) is recorded during rest and contraction.

■ Frequently, the leadwires of the recorder are attached to an audio-amplifier so that the fluctuation of voltage within the muscle can be heard.

What happens after the test?

If you feel any pain, tell the nurse, who will apply warm compresses and give you pain medication.

Does the test have risks?

This procedure shouldn't be performed on a person with a bleeding disorder.

What are the normal results?

At rest, a normal muscle exhibits little electrical activity. During voluntary contraction, however, electrical activity increases markedly.

What do abnormal results mean?

Changes in electrical activity from the norm may indicate primary muscle diseases, such as the muscular dystrophies, amyotrophic lateral sclerosis, or myasthenia gravis.

Another test, called *nerve conduction time,* may be performed to help detect peripheral nerve disorders. (See *Nerve conduction time: Clue to disease.*)

FETAL MONITORING

EXTERNAL MONITORING OF THE FETUS

This painless test checks the health of the fetus. It can be performed before or during labor. This test doesn't harm the fetus in any way and doesn't interfere with normal labor.

During the test, the doctor positions an electronic device on the mother's abdomen, over the fetus. The device records the heart rate of the fetus and, during labor, the strength and frequency of contractions.

Why is this test done?

External monitoring of the fetus may be performed for the following reasons:

- To measure the heart rate of the fetus and the frequency of contractions
- To detect distress in the fetus
- To determine the need for internal fetal monitoring.

What should you know before the test?

- If this test is being done before labor, you should eat a meal just before it. Eating increases the fetus's activity and reduces the test time.
- You'll be asked to sign a form that gives your permission to do the test. Read the form carefully and ask questions if any portion of it isn't clear.

What happens during the test?

- You lie on the examining table with your abdomen exposed.
- The doctor or nurse feels your abdomen to identify the fetal chest area and locates the most distinct heart sounds. Then an electronic device called an *ultrasound transducer* is secured over this area with an elastic band or strap. The transducer directs sound waves toward the fetus. These sound waves have a pitch so high they can't be heard by human ears. When the sound waves reach the fetus, they rebound to the transducer, which sends them to a computer for interpretation and display.

Monitoring before labor

The doctor may repeat the test weekly, if needed.

Monitoring before labor with a nonstress test

- You hold the transducer in your hand and push it each time you feel the fetus move.
- If these movements don't rouse the fetus, the nurse may shake your abdomen and repeat the test.

Monitoring before labor with a stress test

- The test can be done in two ways: by administering a drug called *oxytocin* or by nipple stimulation.
- If you receive oxytocin, the test continues until three contractions occur within 10 minutes, each lasting longer than 45 seconds.
- If nipple stimulation is used instead, you'll be asked to rub one nipple with your fingers until a contraction begins. If a second contraction doesn't occur in 2 minutes, the nurse tells you to rub the

If you're being tested before labor begins, eat a meal first. It increases the baby's activity and reduces the test time.

nipple again. If contractions don't start within 15 minutes, you rub both nipples at the same time.

Monitoring during labor
The transducer is placed over the area of greatest uterine activity during contractions (usually the fundus).

Does the test have risks?

The stress test could cause fetal distress during oxytocin administration or nipple stimulation. In such cases, the test is discontinued and the doctor is notified.

What are the normal results?

The normal heart rate for a fetus ranges from 120 to 160 beats per minute. That's roughly double the normal rate for an adult. The heart rate for a fetus may normally differ from one minute to the next by 5 to 25 beats.

The normal heart rate for a fetus ranges from 120 to 160 beats per minute. That's roughly double the normal adult rate.

What do abnormal results mean?

A heart rate of less than 120 beats per minute may indicate a heart problem, poor position of the fetus, or an inadequate supply of oxygen. A slow heart rate may also be caused by drugs taken by the mother.

A heart rate of more than 160 beats per minute may be caused by drug use by the mother or her fever, rapid heart rate, or hyperthyroidism. It can also warn of inadequate oxygen for the fetus or signal a fetal infection or irregular heartbeat.

A fluctuation of less than 5 beats per minute may be due to an irregular heartbeat, an inadequate oxygen supply, an infection, or the mother's use of drugs. Accelerations of more than 25 beats per minute may signal lack of oxygen. They may precede or follow variable decelerations and may indicate a breech position.

The nonstress test can suggest problems that may be present at birth. The stress test can also suggest these problems. If it continues to be abnormal, internal fetal monitoring or a cesarean birth may be necessary.

INTERNAL MONITORING OF THE FETUS

This test, which is performed only during labor, accurately checks on the health of the fetus. Internal monitoring can be performed only after the membranes have ruptured and the cervix has dilated 1¼ inches (3 centimeters).

To perform the test, the doctor attaches a small electrode to the fetus's scalp. The electrode allows the doctor to directly monitor the heart rate of the fetus. (See *How internal fetal monitoring works.*)

Why is this test done?

Internal monitoring of the fetus may be performed for the following reasons:

■ To check the heart rate of the fetus, especially for changes from beat to beat

■ To measure the frequency and pressure of contractions, which allows doctors to monitor the progress of labor

■ To check on the health of the fetus during labor and to determine if a cesarean section is necessary.

What should you know before the test?

■ You may be told to expect mild discomfort when the uterine catheter and scalp electrode are inserted.

■ You'll be asked to sign a form that gives your permission to do the test. Read the form carefully and ask questions if any portion of it isn't clear.

What happens during the test?

■ As you lie on the examining table, the doctor examines your vagina. Breathe through your mouth and relax your abdominal muscles.

■ After the vaginal exam, the doctor touches the scalp of the fetus, inserts a small plastic tube carrying the electrode and a wire into the cervix, and gently attaches the electrode to the fetal scalp. The doctor then removes the tube.

■ The doctor attaches the wire to a transducer, which is strapped securely to your thigh. Another cable attaches the transducer to the fetal monitor. Then monitoring begins.

■ If monitoring indicates a problem, you may receive intravenous fluids and oxygen and be turned on your side (preferably, your left). If

How internal fetal monitoring works

To perform internal fetal monitoring, the doctor attaches an electrode to the scalp of the fetus. The electrode detects each beat of the fetal heart and sends this information to an amplifier.

Subsequently, a device called a *cardiotachometer* measures the intervals between heartbeats and creates a graph of the fetal heart rate. The graph or waveform appears on a monitor.

At the same time, a catheter within the uterus measures the frequency and pressure of uterine contractions. This information also appears as a waveform on the monitor.

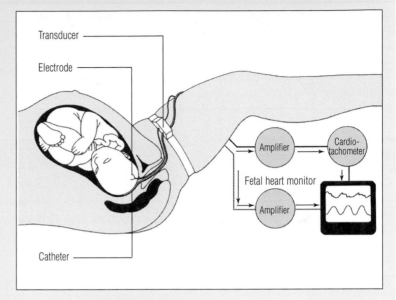

these measures return heart rate patterns to normal, labor may continue. If abnormal patterns continue, a cesarean section may be necessary.

Does the test have risks?

- Internal fetal monitoring won't be performed if the doctor is unsure about the fetus's presenting part.
- The test also won't be done if the mother has cervical or vaginal herpes lesions.
- The test carries a slight risk to the mother with a perforated uterus or an infection. It also carries a slight risk to the fetus with a scalp abscess or a blood clot.

What are the normal results?

The normal heart rate for the fetus ranges from 120 to 160 beats per minute. This rate can normally vary by 5 to 25 beats per minute.

What do abnormal results mean?

A heart rate of less than 120 beats per minute may indicate a heart problem, malpositioned fetus, or an inadequate supply of oxygen. A slow heart rate may also be caused by drugs taken by the mother, such as Inderal or narcotic pain relievers.

A heart rate of more than 160 beats per minute may be caused by drug use by the mother or her fever, rapid heart rate, or hyperthyroidism. It can also warn of inadequate oxygen for the fetus or signal a fetal infection or irregular heartbeat.

A fluctuation of less than 5 beats per minute may be caused by an irregular heartbeat, an inadequate oxygen supply, an infection, or the mother's use of drugs.

A slowing of the fetal heart rate after a contraction begins, a lag time greater than 20 seconds, and a recovery time of more than 15 seconds may be related to a uterine or placental problem, a lack of adequate oxygen for the fetus, or acidosis. Recurrent and persistently late slowing of the heart rate usually indicates serious fetal distress.

Sudden, sharp drops in heart rate, if unrelated to contractions, are commonly related to cord compression. A severe drop in heart rate indicates fetal distress.

6

ENDOSCOPY:
Peering through
the Body's Passageways

RESPIRATORY SYSTEM

EXAMINATION OF THE LARYNX

Called *direct laryngoscopy,* this test detects problems in the larynx, the upper part of the windpipe that contains the vocal cords. The larynx is sometimes referred to as the voice box.

This test lets the doctor see the larynx by the use of a fiber-optic endoscope or laryngoscope passed through the mouth and pharynx to the larynx. The doctor will use it especially for children, for people with strong gag reflexes, for people who've had no response to short-term therapy to relieve symptoms, or for people with symptoms of pharyngeal or laryngeal disease. (See *Indirect laryngoscopy: A method of viewing the larynx.*)

Why is this test done?
Laryngoscopy may be performed for the following reasons:
- To detect lesions or strictures and to remove benign tumors or foreign bodies from the larynx
- To help the doctor diagnose laryngeal cancer
- To examine the larynx when indirect laryngoscopy is inadequate.

What should you know before the test?
- You'll be told to fast for 6 to 8 hours before the test.
- The test will be performed in a dark operating room.
- You'll be given a sedative to help you relax, medication to reduce secretions and, during the procedure, a general or local anesthetic. Be assured that this procedure won't obstruct your breathing.
- The nurse will ask you to sign a consent form.
- Just before the test, you'll be asked to remove any dentures, contact lenses, and jewelry and to empty your bladder.

What happens during the test?
- You lie on your back, with your arms at your sides, and are encouraged to breathe through your nose and relax.
- You're given a general anesthetic. Alternatively, your mouth and throat may be sprayed with a local anesthetic.

Indirect laryngoscopy: A method of viewing the larynx

This procedure is usually performed in the doctor's office. It allows the doctor to see the larynx, using a warm laryngeal mirror positioned at the back of the throat, a head mirror held in front of the mouth, and a light source.

Undergoing this test
You're asked to sit erect in a chair and stick your tongue out as far as possible. The tongue is grasped with a piece of gauze and held in place with a tongue depressor. If your gag reflex is sensitive, a local anesthetic may be sprayed on the pharyngeal wall. Then, the larynx is observed at rest and when you make a noise. Polyps may also be removed during this procedure.

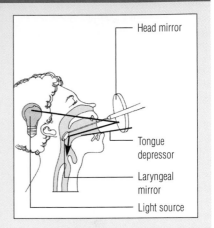

Head mirror

Tongue depressor

Laryngeal mirror

Light source

■ The laryngoscope is put through your mouth, the larynx is examined for abnormalities, and a specimen or secretions may be removed for further study. Minor surgery, such as removal of polyps or nodules, may be performed at this time.

What happens after the test?

■ The nurse may give you a soothing ice collar to minimize laryngeal swelling.

■ You'll be told to spit saliva into a basin, rather than swallow it, and to refrain from clearing your throat and coughing.

■ You'll be advised to avoid smoking until there's no evidence of complications.

■ The doctor will restrict food and fluids until your gag reflex returns (usually 2 hours). Then you may resume your usual diet, beginning with sips of water.

■ You may experience temporary loss of voice, hoarseness, or sore throat.

What are the normal results?

A normal larynx shows no evidence of inflammation, lesions, strictures, or foreign bodies.

What do abnormal results mean?

The combined results of direct laryngoscopy, a biopsy (removal and analysis of tissue), and radiography may indicate laryngeal cancer. Direct laryngoscopy may show benign lesions, strictures, or foreign bodies and, with a biopsy, may distinguish swelling of the larynx from a radiation reaction or tumor.

EXAMINATION OF THE LOWER AIRWAYS

A test called *bronchoscopy* is used to examine the lower airways. The doctor can see the larynx, windpipe, and bronchi through a flexible fiber-optic bronchoscope. A brush, biopsy forceps, or a catheter may be passed through the bronchoscope to withdraw specimens for a laboratory exam. (See *Undergoing bronchoscopy*.)

Why is this test done?

Bronchoscopy may be performed for the following reasons:

■ To let the doctor visually examine a possible tumor, obstruction, secretion, bleeding, or foreign body

■ To help the doctor diagnose lung cancer, tuberculosis, interstitial lung disease, or a fungal or parasitic lung infection

■ To remove foreign bodies, malignant or benign tumors, mucus plugs, or excessive secretions from the tracheobronchial tree.

What should you know before the test?

■ You'll be told to fast for 6 to 12 hours before the test.

■ For the test, the room will be darkened, and the procedure will take 45 to 60 minutes. Results are usually available in 1 day. A tuberculosis report may take up to 6 weeks, however.

■ Chest X-rays and blood studies will be performed before the bronchoscopy.

■ You may receive an intravenous sedative to help you relax.

■ If your test isn't being performed under general anesthesia, a local anesthetic will be sprayed into your nose and mouth to suppress the gag reflex. The spray has an unpleasant taste, and you may feel some discomfort during the procedure.

Undergoing bronchoscopy

In a bronchoscopy, the doctor inserts a flexible tube through a person's nostril into the bronchi. The bronchoscope, shown enlarged here, has four channels. Two channels (A) provide a light source. A third channel (B) allows the doctor to see. A fourth channel (C) allows the passage of medical instruments (to obtain a tissue sample for a biopsy, for instance) or medication.

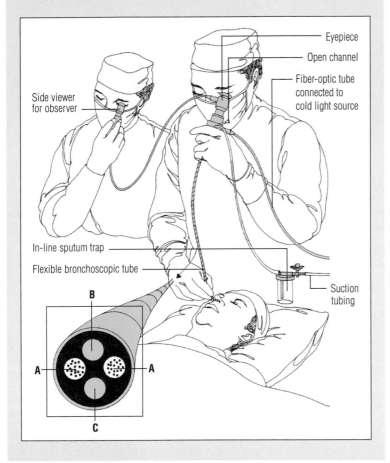

Eyepiece

Open channel

Fiber-optic tube connected to cold light source

Side viewer for observer

In-line sputum trap

Flexible bronchoscopic tube

Suction tubing

B

A   A

C

- Remember that your breathing won't be blocked during the procedure and oxygen will be administered through the bronchoscope.
- The nurse will ask you to sign a consent form and will check your history for hypersensitivity to anesthesia.
- Just before the test, you'll be asked to remove any dentures, hearing aids, or jewelry.

What happens during the test?

- You're asked to lie on an examining table or bed or to sit upright in a chair.
- The nurse urges you to remain relaxed, with your arms at your sides, and to breathe through your nose. Supplemental oxygen is available, if necessary.
- After the local anesthetic is sprayed into your throat and takes effect, a bronchoscope is introduced. The doctor inspects the anatomic structure of the windpipe and bronchi, observes the color of the mucous membrane lining, and notes masses or inflamed areas.
- The doctor may use biopsy forceps to remove a tissue specimen from a suspicious area, a bronchial brush to obtain cells from the surface of a lesion, or a suction device to remove foreign bodies or mucus plugs.

You may experience hoarseness, loss of voice, or sore throat after this test. These effects are only temporary.

What happens after the test?

- You'll rest in bed, and the nurse will instruct you to spit saliva into a basin rather than swallow it. Also, you'll have to refrain from clearing your throat and coughing, which might dislodge the clot at the biopsy site and cause hemorrhaging.
- The doctor will restrict food and fluids until your gag reflex returns (usually in 1 hour). Then you may resume your usual diet, beginning with sips of clear liquid or ice chips.
- Remember that hoarseness, loss of voice, and sore throat after this procedure are only temporary.

What are the normal results?

The windpipe normally consists of smooth muscle containing C-shaped rings of cartilage at regular intervals, and it's lined with a ciliated mucous membrane. The bronchi appear similar to the windpipe.

What do abnormal results mean?

The doctor may see abnormalities of the bronchial wall and the windpipe or find abnormal substances that require tissue and cell studies to confirm or eliminate a long list of diseases, including interstitial lung disease, bronchogenic cancer, tuberculosis, or other lung infections. Correlation of X-ray, bronchoscopic, and lab findings with the person's symptoms is essential.

EXAMINATION OF THE CHEST

Called *mediastinoscopy*, this test evaluates the lymph nodes and other structures in the chest. Using a device called an *exploring speculum* with a built-in fiber light and side slits, mediastinoscopy permits palpation and a biopsy (removal and analysis) of lymph node tissue in the chest. The doctor uses this surgical procedure when tests such as sputum cytology, lung scans, X-rays, and a bronchoscopic biopsy fail to confirm a diagnosis.

Why is this test done?

A mediastinoscopy may be performed for the following reasons:
- To help the doctor detect bronchogenic cancer, lymphoma (including Hodgkin's disease), and sarcoidosis
- To determine the stages of lung cancer.

What should you know before the test?

- You'll be told to fast after midnight before the test.
- You'll be given a general anesthetic, and the procedure will take approximately 1 hour.
- You may have temporary chest pain, tenderness at the incision site, or a sore throat (from intubation).
- A nurse will ask you to sign a consent form.
- You'll be given a sedative the night before the test and again before the procedure.

After a mediastinoscopy, you may experience chest pain, tenderness at the incision site, or a sore throat.

What happens during the test?

- After the endotracheal tube is in place, a small incision is made and the surgeon feels for the lymph nodes.
- The mediastinoscope is inserted, and tissue specimens are collected and sent to the lab for frozen section examination.
- If analysis confirms an operable, cancerous tumor, the doctor may do a thoracotomy and pneumonectomy immediately.

Does the test have risks?

Although complications are rare, the nurse will watch for signs of fever, fluid in the lungs, difficulty breathing, diminished breath sounds on the affected side, a rapid heartbeat, and high blood pressure.

What are the normal results?

Normally, lymph nodes appear as small, smooth, flat oval bodies of lymphoid tissue.

What do abnormal results mean?

Malignant lymph nodes usually indicate lung or esophageal cancer or lymphomas. The doctor uses information about the stage of lung cancer to plan therapy.

THORACOSCOPY

In this test, an endoscope is inserted directly into the chest wall to allow the doctor to examine the area around the lungs called the pleural space. It's used for both diagnostic and therapeutic purposes and can sometimes replace traditional open-chest surgery. Thoracoscopy reduces risk (by reducing the use of open-chest surgery) and postoperative pain, decreases surgical and anesthesia time, and allows faster recovery.

Thoracoscopy is used for both diagnostic and therapeutic purposes and can sometimes replace traditional open-chest surgery.

Why is this test done?

Thoracoscopy may be performed for the following reasons:
- To help the doctor diagnose pleural disease
- To obtain a biopsy specimen from the mediastinum
- To treat lung conditions, such as cysts, blebs (fluid-containing structures, similar to blisters), and fluid accumulation between the lung tissue and its lining
- To perform wedge resections.

What should you know before the test?

- The nurse will describe the procedure and remind you that, after the thoracoscopy, an open thoracotomy may be still be needed for a diagnosis or treatment and general anesthesia may be required.
- You'll be told not to eat or drink fluids for 10 to 12 hours before the procedure.
- You may be given preoperative tests (such as pulmonary function and coagulation tests, an electrocardiogram, and a chest X-ray), and you'll be asked to sign a consent form.

What happens during the test?

- After you're anesthetized, a tube is inserted, a small incision is made, and another tube with a lens is inserted.
- Two or three more small incisions are made, and more tubes are placed for the insertion of suctioning and dissection instruments.
- The camera lens and instruments are moved from site to site as needed.

What happens after the test?

- You'll be given pain relievers as needed.
- You'll have a chest tube and drainage system in place after surgery.

Does the test have risks?

- Complications, although rare, include possible hemorrhage, nerve injury, perforation of the diaphragm, air emboli, and tension pneumothorax.
- You won't be given a thoracoscopy if you have blood clotting problems or lesions near major blood vessels, if you've had previous thoracic surgery, or if you can't breathe adequately with one lung.

What are the normal results?

A normal pleural cavity contains a small amount of lubricating fluid that facilitates movement of the lung and chest wall. The layers of the lung sac are lesion-free and able to separate from each other.

What do abnormal results mean?

Lesions next to or involving the sac around the lungs or the wall between them can be seen and the doctor can take biopsies to reach a diagnosis and make decisions about treatment. After accumulated fluid is removed, sterile talc can be blown into the pleural space to promote healing and prevent future accumulations. Blebs may be removed to reduce the risk of lung collapse.

DIGESTIVE SYSTEM

EXAMINATION OF THE DIGESTIVE TRACT

This procedure's medical name is one of the longest words in the English language: *esophagogastroduodenoscopy*. In spite of its 26 letters, the word simply means a look at the lining of the upper digestive tract: the esophagus, stomach, and upper intestine. (See *The upper digestive tract.*)

During the test, the doctor can withdraw specimens for lab evaluation of abnormalities detected by X-rays. Also, it allows removal of foreign bodies by suction or forceps. The test eliminates the need for extensive exploratory surgery and can be used to detect small or surface lesions missed by X-rays.

Why is this test done?

The test may be performed for the following reasons:
- To help the doctor diagnose inflammatory disease, malignant and benign tumors, ulcers, Mallory-Weiss syndrome, and structural abnormalities (See *How a peptic ulcer forms and develops*, pages 204 and 205.)
- To evaluate the stomach and duodenum after surgery
- To obtain an emergency diagnosis of duodenal ulcer or esophageal injury such as that caused by swallowing chemicals.

What should you know before the test?

- You'll be told to fast for 6 to 12 hours before the test.
- The procedure takes about 30 minutes.
- If you require an emergency exam, your stomach contents will be withdrawn through a tube inserted through your nostril.
- A blood sample may be drawn before the procedure.
- Before the endoscope is inserted, you'll receive a sedative to help you relax, but you'll remain conscious. If the procedure is being done on an outpatient basis, you should arrange for transportation home.
- You'll be asked to sign a consent form.
- Just before the procedure, you'll be asked to remove any dentures, eyeglasses, jewelry, hairpins, combs, and constricting undergarments.

This procedure's medical name is one of the longest words in the English language: esophagogastroduodenoscopy. The exam simply looks at the lining of the upper digestive tract.

HOW YOUR BODY WORKS

The upper digestive tract

The digestive tract includes the mouth, pharynx, esophagus, stomach, small intestine (duodenum, jejunum, ileum), and large intestine (cecum, colon, rectum, anal canal). Throughout the digestive tract, peristalsis (muscle contraction) propels the food along. Sphincters close openings to prevent food from coming back up.

Saliva starts the work
Digestion begins in the mouth through chewing and the action of the enzyme amylase — secreted in saliva — which breaks down starches. Food is lubricated by the glycoprotein mucin, then swallowed as what doctors call a *bolus*. While the food is passing through the esophagus, it's also lubricated by mucous secretions. Digestion continues in the stomach through the action of glandular secretions.

The hormone gastrin, the most potent stimulus of gastric secretion, boosts the release of hydrochloric acid. In turn, the acid lowers the pH of the stomach's contents, converting secreted pepsinogen to pepsin. Pepsin begins breaking down protein into products ranging from large polypeptides to amino acids.

As the stomach churns
Through a churning motion, the stomach breaks food into tiny particles, mixes them with gastric juices, and pushes the mass toward the top of the intestine. Chyme (the liquid portion) enters the intestine in small amounts. Solid material remains in the stomach until it liquefies (usually 1 to 6 hours). Although limited amounts of water, alcohol, and certain drugs are absorbed in the stomach, chyme passes unabsorbed into the duodenum.

What happens during the test?

■ A bitter-tasting local anesthetic is sprayed into your mouth and throat to calm the gag reflex and your tongue and throat may feel swollen, making swallowing seem difficult. Let the saliva drain from the side of your mouth. A suction machine may be used to remove saliva, if necessary.

■ A mouth guard is inserted to protect your teeth and the endoscope, but it doesn't obstruct your breathing.

■ You may experience pressure in your stomach as the endoscope is moved about and a feeling of fullness when air or carbon dioxide is pumped in. The air distends and flattens your stomach wall to help the doctor see.

■ While you lie on your left side, the examiner guides the tip of the endoscope to the back of your throat and downward.

■ A camera may be attached to the endoscope to photograph areas for later study, or a measuring tube may be passed through the endoscope to determine the size of a lesion.

■ Biopsy forceps to obtain a tissue specimen for analysis or a cytology brush to obtain cells may also be passed through the scope.

INSIGHT INTO ILLNESS

How a peptic ulcer forms and develops

If you have one of the two peptic ulcer types — duodenal or gastric — this is how it forms and develops.

Duodenal ulcer

A duodenal ulcer may begin with increased stomach motility (movement), causing the stomach's contents to empty into the duodenum, the first section of intestine. The contents may move so rapidly that gastric acid hasn't yet been neutralized by the food it's digesting. Consequently, excessive acid goes to work eroding the duodenal lining. The result: inflammation and erosion. Duodenal ulcers usually affect the pylorus, the opening from the stomach.

Gastric ulcer

A gastric ulcer is probably not caused by excessive acid but by too little mucus production or a breakdown in the stomach's protective mucous membrane lining. This allows acid to permeate, inflame, and erode underlying tissues.

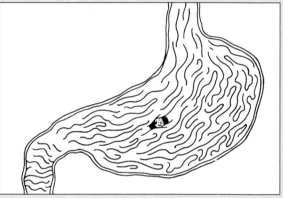

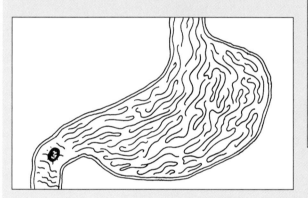

What happens after the test?

■ The doctor will withhold food and fluids until your gag reflex returns — usually in 1 hour — then you may have fluids and a light meal.

■ You may burp some of the pumped-in air and may have a sore throat for 3 or 4 days.

■ If you feel soreness at the intravenous site, the nurse will apply warm soaks.

■ If you're leaving the hospital, be sure to have transportation home. You shouldn't drive for 12 hours because you may be drowsy from sedation.

■ Immediately report persistent difficulty in swallowing, pain, fever, black stools, or bloody vomit.

How erosion works

Once tissue is inflamed, the body responds by releasing histamine. Histamine, in turn, stimulates acid secretion, which increases the capillaries' permeability to proteins such as pepsin, leading to swelling of the mucous membranes and a possible obstruction.

Unchecked, the ulcer erodes the layers of the stomach lining, damaging blood vessels in the submucous membranes and causing hemorrhage and shock. Further erosion into the muscularis and serosa causes perforation, peritonitis and, possibly, death.

Mucosa

Submucosa

Muscularis

Serosa

Does the test have risks?

■ This procedure is generally safe, but can cause perforation of the esophagus, stomach, or duodenum, especially if the person undergoing the procedure is restless or uncooperative.

■ This procedure won't be performed in people with conditions such as Zenker's diverticulum, a large aortic aneurysm, or someone with a recent ulcer perforation.

What are the normal results?

The smooth mucous membrane of the esophagus is normally yellow-pink and is marked by a fine vascular network. The healthy stomach shows an orange-red mucous membrane, and the duodenum is reddish and parts of it appear velvety.

What do abnormal results mean?

The test may reveal ulcers, benign or malignant tumors, and inflammatory disease, including esophagitis, gastritis, and duodenitis. It can discover functional and structural problems, but for some abnormalities, other tests are more accurate.

EXAMINATION OF THE LARGE INTESTINE

In this test, the doctor uses a flexible, fiber-optic endoscope to look at the lining of the large intestine. The medical name for this test is *colonoscopy*. (See *The lower digestive tract.*)

The doctor may use this procedure for people with histories of constipation or diarrhea, persistent rectal bleeding, or lower abdominal pain, or when the results of other tests are inconclusive.

Why is this test done?

A colonoscopy may be performed for the following reasons:
- To detect or evaluate inflammatory and ulcerative bowel disease
- To help the doctor diagnose colonic strictures and benign or malignant lesions
- To evaluate the colon after surgery for recurrence of polyps or malignant lesions.

What should you know before the test?

- You'll be told to take only clear liquids for 48 hours before the test.
- The test generally takes 30 to 60 minutes.
- The large intestine must be thoroughly cleaned to be clearly visible. You'll take a laxative or castor oil in the evening and an enema 3 to 4 hours before the test until the return is clear. Soapsuds enemas aren't used.
- You'll be given a sedative to help you relax about 30 minutes before the test.
- You'll be asked to sign a consent form.

HOW YOUR BODY WORKS

The lower digestive tract

Digestion and absorption occur in the lower digestive system, primarily in the small intestine, where millions of fingerlike villi increase the surface area.

Enzymes go to work

For digestion, the small intestine relies on the many enzymes produced by the pancreas or by the intestinal lining. Pancreatic enzymes empty into the intestine and begin digesting protein into amino acids, fat into fatty acids and glycerol, and starches into sugars. Intestinal enzymes convert protein to amino acids and digest complex sugars like glucose, fructose, and galactose.

Bile helps absorb vitamins

Bile also participates in digestion and absorption. After formation in the liver, bile is stored and concentrated in the gallbladder. It's released in response to a hormone secreted by the duodenum and is then emptied into the duodenum through the ampulla of Vater. Bile helps neutralize stomach acid and promotes the emulsification of fats and the absorption of the fat-soluble vitamins A, D, E, and K.

The large intestine plays its part

When food reaches the ileocecal valve and enters the large intestine (2 to 10 hours after eating), all its nutritional value has been absorbed. The first half of the large intestine absorbs water, sodium, and chloride, reducing bulk. The second half stores and further dehydrates the digestive material until defecation. The second half of the large intestine may also excrete water, potassium, and bicarbonate.

Bacteria finish the job

Bacteria in the colon putrefy undigested foods and synthesize vitamins K, B_{12}, B_2 (riboflavin), and B (thiamine). Then they produce gas, which helps propel feces toward the anus.

Intestinal gas may also be caused by swallowed air or diffusion of blood gases. Rectal distention by feces stimulates the defecation reflex, which is assisted by voluntary sphincter relaxation. Normal passage of feces through the large intestine takes 24 to 40 hours.

What happens during the test?

- You lie on your left side, with your knees flexed.
- The examiner tells you to breathe deeply and slowly through your mouth as the doctor palpates the mucous membrane of the anus and rectum and as the colonoscope is inserted.
- The colonoscope is well lubricated to ease its insertion. It initially feels cool, and you may feel an urge to defecate when it's inserted and advanced.
- Air may be pumped through the colonoscope to distend the intestinal wall and help the doctor see the lining and advance the instrument. Air normally escapes around the instrument, and you shouldn't attempt to control it.
- Suction may be used to remove blood or liquid feces that obscure the doctor's vision, but this won't cause discomfort.

INSIGHT INTO ILLNESS

Diverticula: A potentially dangerous development in the digestive tract wall

Diverticula are small pouches that form along the colon wall. They develop from a buildup of pressure that pushes the mucous layer out through a weakness in the layer of muscles around the colon.

As the illustration shows, a narrow neck connects a diverticulum to the intestinal lumen. To make things worse, fecal matter may accumulate within this pouch, cutting off its blood supply and leading to infection and inflammation.

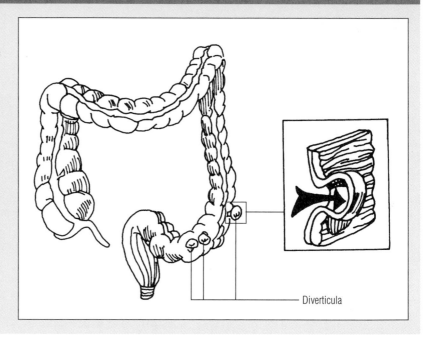

Diverticula

■ A biopsy forceps or a cytology brush may be passed through the colonoscope to obtain specimens for blood and cell exams. An electrocautery snare may be used to remove polyps.

What happens after the test?

■ If the examiner removes a tissue specimen, it will be sent immediately to the lab.
■ After you've recovered from sedation, you may resume your usual diet.
■ If a polyp has been removed, there may be some blood in your stools.

Does the test have risks?

■ Colonoscopy is usually considered a safe procedure but can cause perforation of the large intestine, excessive bleeding, and retroperitoneal emphysema.
■ The doctor won't use this procedure if you have some forms of bowel disease.

What are the normal results?

Normally, the large intestine beyond the colon appears light pink-orange and is marked by crescent-shaped folds and deep tubular pits. Blood vessels are visible beneath the intestinal mucous membrane, which glistens from mucus secretions.

What do abnormal results mean?

Visual examination of the large intestine, matched with blood and cell test results, may indicate proctitis, colitis, Crohn's disease, and malignant or benign lesions. Diverticular disease or the site of lower digestive tract bleeding can be detected through visual examination alone. (See *Diverticula: A potentially dangerous development in the digestive tract wall.*)

EXAMINATION OF THE LOWER INTESTINE

This procedure allows the doctor to look at the lining of the distal sigmoid colon, the rectum, and the anal canal. The doctor uses a proctoscope, a sigmoidoscope, and fingers to check for problems. The medical name for this test is *proctosigmoidoscopy*.

The test is usually done for people with lower abdominal pain, trouble with defecation, recent changes in bowel habits, or passage of mucus, blood, or pus.

Why is this test done?

Proctosigmoidoscopy may be performed for the following reasons:
- To help the doctor diagnose inflammatory, infectious, and ulcerative bowel disease
- To diagnose malignant and benign neoplasms
- To detect hemorrhoids, hypertrophic anal papilla, polyps, fissures, fistulas, and abscesses in the rectum and anal canal.

What should you know before the test?

■ The test requires passage of two special instruments through the anus. It takes 15 to 30 minutes.

■ You'll be told to take only clear liquids for 48 hours before the test, to avoid eating fruits and vegetables before the procedure, and to fast the morning of the procedure.

■ Laxatives or an enema may be ordered to clear the intestine to give the doctor a better view.

■ The nurse will ask you to sign a consent form and will check your history for barium tests within the past week because barium in the colon hinders accurate examination.

What happens during the test?

■ You're secured to a tilting table that rotates into horizontal and vertical positions.

■ The examiner's finger and the instrument are well lubricated to ease insertion, the instrument initially feels cool, and you may feel the urge to defecate when it's inserted and advanced.

■ The instrument stretches your intestinal wall and causes brief muscle spasms or colicky lower abdominal pain.

■ You should breathe deeply and slowly through your mouth to relax your abdominal muscles. This calms the urge to defecate and eases any discomfort.

■ Air may be pumped through the endoscope into the intestine to distend its walls. This causes air to escape around the endoscope, but you shouldn't attempt to control it.

■ A suction machine removes blood, mucus, or liquid feces that obscure the doctor's view, but it won't cause you discomfort.

■ To obtain specimens from suspicious areas of the intestinal mucous membrane, a biopsy forceps, a cytology brush, or a culture swab is passed through the sigmoidoscope.

■ Polyps may be removed for a histologic exam by insertion of an electrocautery snare through the sigmoidoscope.

■ After the sigmoidoscope is withdrawn, the proctoscope is lubricated, and you're told that it's about to be inserted. Be assured that you'll experience less discomfort during passage of the proctoscope.

■ If a biopsy (removal and analysis) of tissue from the anal canal is required, you're given a local anesthetic first.

Air may be pumped through the endoscope into the intestine to distend its walls. This causes air to escape around the endoscope, but you shouldn't attempt to control it.

What happens after the test?

- After the exam is completed, the proctoscope is withdrawn.
- If air was pumped into the intestine, you may pass gas.
- If a biopsy or polypectomy was performed, blood may appear in your stools.

Does the test have risks?

Possible complications of this procedure include rectal bleeding and, rarely, bowel perforation.

What are the normal results?

The mucous membrane of the sigmoid colon appears light pink-orange and is marked by crescent-shaped folds and deep tubular pits. The rectal mucous membrane is redder due to its rich vascular network and deepens to a purple hue. The lower two-thirds of the anus is lined with smooth gray-tan skin and joins with the hair-fringed perianal skin.

What do abnormal results mean?

The doctor can see and feel abnormalities of the anal canal and rectum, including internal and external hemorrhoids, anal fissures, anal fistulas, and abscesses. However, a biopsy, culture, and other lab tests are often necessary to detect various disorders.

REPRODUCTIVE SYSTEM

COLPOSCOPY

This test lights and magnifies the image of the vagina and cervix, letting the doctor see more than in a routine vaginal exam. The doctor uses a colposcope primarily to evaluate abnormal cells or grossly suspicious lesions and to examine the cervix and vagina after a positive (abnormal) Pap test. During the exam, a biopsy (removal and analysis of tissue) may be performed and photographs taken of suspicious lesions with the colposcope and its attachments.

Colposcopy provides more information than the doctor can obtain in a routine vaginal exam.

Why is this test done?

A colposcopy may be performed for the following reasons:
- To help the doctor confirm cervical cancer after a positive Pap test
- To evaluate vaginal or cervical lesions
- To monitor conservatively treated cervical intraepithelial neoplasia (a type of cancer)
- To monitor women whose mothers received the drug diethylstilbestrol (DES) during pregnancy.

What should you know before the test?

- You won't need to change your diet before the test.
- The test is safe and painless, and it takes 10 to 15 minutes.
- A biopsy may be performed at the time of the exam; this may cause minimal but easily controlled bleeding.

What happens during the test?

- You lie on the examining table with your feet in the stirrups and a drape over you.
- The examiner inserts the speculum and may take a specimen for a Pap test.
- The nurse may try to help you by telling you to breathe through your mouth and relax your abdominal muscles.
- After the cervix and vagina are examined, a biopsy is performed on areas that appear abnormal.

The nurse may try to help you relax by telling you to breathe through your mouth and concentrate on relaxing your abdominal muscles.

What happens after the test?

If a biopsy was done, you'll be told to abstain from intercourse and not to insert anything in your vagina (except a tampon) until healing of the biopsy site is confirmed.

Does the test have risks?

Risks include bleeding (especially during pregnancy) and infection.

What are the normal results?

Normally, cervical vessels show a network and hairpin capillary pattern. The surface contour is smooth and pink.

What do abnormal results mean?

The doctor may find abnormalities such as white areas or mosaic patterns. Other cell changes may suggest cancer or inflammatory changes (usually from infection), atrophic changes (usually from aging), and evidence of viruses.

LAPAROSCOPY

This test is used to detect abnormalities of the uterus, fallopian tubes, and ovaries. The doctor views the abdominal cavity by inserting a laparoscope (a small, fiber-optic telescope) through the abdominal wall.

This surgical technique may be used to detect abnormalities, such as cysts, adhesions, fibroids, and infection. It can also be used therapeutically to perform procedures such as the removal of adhesions, an ovarian biopsy (removal and analysis of tissue), tubal ligation, and the removal of foreign bodies.

Abdominal laparoscopy (for example, laparoscopic cholecystectomy) is used to examine and operate on abdominal organs.

Why is this test done?

Laparoscopy may be performed for the following reasons:
- To help the doctor identify the cause of pelvic pain
- To help detect endometriosis, ectopic pregnancy, or pelvic inflammatory disease
- To evaluate pelvic masses or the fallopian tubes of women who are infertile
- To determine the stage of a cancer.

What should you know before the test?

- You'll be told to fast after midnight before the test or at least 8 hours before surgery.
- The test takes only 15 to 30 minutes.
- The nurse will tell you whether you'll receive a local or general anesthetic and whether the procedure will require overnight hospitalization.
- You may experience pain at the puncture site and in the shoulder.
- You'll be asked to sign a consent form.

Laparoscopy may be performed as part of treatment during such procedures as removal of adhesions or tubal ligation.

What happens during the test?

- You're anesthetized and placed in the same position as for a Pap test—on your back with your feet in stirrups.
- The examiner puts a catheter in your bladder and then manually examines your pelvic area to detect any abnormalities that may interfere with the test.
- A tube that carries the biopsy instrument and the laparoscope is inserted into the peritoneal cavity. The examiner moves it to view the pelvis and abdomen and then may perform minor surgical procedures such as an ovarian biopsy.

What happens after the test?

- The nurse will help you walk as soon as possible after you recover from the anesthesia.
- You may resume your usual diet.
- The nurse may tell you to restrict activity for 2 to 7 days.
- Some abdominal and shoulder pain is normal and should disappear within 24 to 36 hours. You may be given a mild pain reliever.

Does the test have risks?

- Potential risks of laparoscopy include a punctured visceral organ that can bleed or spill intestinal contents into the peritoneum.
- The doctor won't use laparoscopy for people with advanced abdominal wall cancer, advanced respiratory or cardiovascular disease, intestinal obstruction, a palpable abdominal mass, a large abdominal hernia, chronic tuberculosis, or a history of peritonitis.

What are the normal results?

The uterus and fallopian tubes are normal in size and shape, free of adhesions, and motile. The ovaries are normal in size and shape; cysts and endometriosis are absent. Dye injected through the cervix flows freely.

What do abnormal results mean?

The doctor can see such abnormalities as ovarian cysts, adhesions, endometriosis, and fibroids.

SKELETAL SYSTEM

EXAMINATION OF A JOINT

This test, which is also called *arthroscopy,* is a visual exam of the interior of a joint (most often the knee) with a specially designed fiberoptic endoscope called an *arthroscope.* This endoscope is inserted through a tube that has been inserted into the joint cavity. (See *Points about joints*, page 216.)

Diagnosis by arthroscopy is highly accurate; in fact, the accuracy rate of this procedure is about 98%. During arthroscopy the doctor may also perform surgery or a biopsy (removal and analysis of tissue). Usually, a local anesthetic is used. The procedure may be performed under spinal or general anesthesia, especially if surgery is anticipated.

A camera may be attached to the arthroscope to photograph the inside of a joint for later study.

Why is this test done?
Arthroscopy may be performed for the following reasons:
- To detect and diagnose joint disorders
- To monitor disease progression
- To perform joint surgery
- To help the doctor monitor the effectiveness of therapy.

What should you know before the test?
- If surgery or other treatment is anticipated, it may be done during arthroscopy.
- You'll be told to fast after midnight before the procedure.
- If local anesthesia is to be used, you may feel brief discomfort from the injection and the pressure of the tourniquet on your leg.
- A nurse will ask you to sign a consent form.
- Just before the procedure, the nurse may shave the area of the joint and then give you a sedative to relax you for the procedure.

What happens during the test?
Although techniques vary depending on the surgeon, the following knee arthroscopy procedure is typical:
- After you lie on the operating table, an inflatable tourniquet is placed around your leg but not tightened.

Points about joints

Joints are made of two bones joined in various ways. Like bones, the joints' structures differ according to their function.

Synovial joints

Also known as *diarthroses,* these joints are the most common type. They allow angular and circular movement. To achieve freedom of movement, synovial joints have special characteristics: the bones' two contact surfaces have a smooth covering, called *articular cartilage,* that acts as a cushion. As the contact surfaces glide on each other, a fibrous capsule holds them together. The synovial membrane lines the space between the contact surfaces and secretes a clear viscous fluid called *synovial fluid,* which lubricates joint movements.

Fibrous joints

Fibrous joints, called *synarthroses,* allow only a slight range of motion and provide stability when a tight connection is necessary, as in the sutures joining the bones of your skull.

Cartilaginous joints

Cartilaginous joints, called *amphiarthroses,* allow limited movement such as between the vertebrae of your spine.

- Your leg is scrubbed according to standard surgical procedure, and a waterproof stockinette is applied.
- Your leg is elevated and wrapped from toes to lower thigh with an elastic bandage to drain as much blood from the leg as possible.
- The tourniquet is inflated and the elastic bandage removed so the local anesthetic can be given.
- If the procedure is being performed under a local anesthetic, you feel a thumping sensation when a tube containing a sharp instrument is inserted into the capsule of your knee joint. The sharp instrument is removed and the arthroscope is inserted through this tube.
- Instruments are changed, depending on the procedure.
- After a visual exam, the doctor may perform a synovial biopsy or surgery on the knee joint.

What happens after the test?

- The arthroscope is removed, the joint is irrigated by way of the tube, the tube is removed, and gentle pressure is applied to the knee to remove the normal saline solution.
- The incision site is dressed.
- You may walk as soon as you're fully awake but should avoid excessive use of the joint for a few days.
- You may resume your usual diet.

Does the test have risks?

- Complications are rare, but may include infection, swelling, synovial rupture, blood clots, numbness, and joint injury.
- The doctor won't use arthroscopy for a person with flexibility of less than 50 degrees, or for a person with local skin or wound infections.

What are the normal results?

Normally, joints are smooth and snug, cartilage appears smooth and white, and ligaments and tendons appear cablelike and silvery.

What do abnormal results mean?

An arthroscopic exam can reveal diseased tissue, ligaments, and cartilage. The doctor can see cysts and evidence of diseases such as synovitis, rheumatoid and degenerative arthritis, and foreign bodies associated with gout and other disorders.

7

BIOPSIES:
Checking for Cancer

RESPIRATORY SYSTEM

LUNG BIOPSY

This test checks the condition of the lungs after X-rays or bronchoscopy fail to identify the cause of a respiratory illness. (See *Common tissue biopsies*.)

A specimen of lung tissue is extracted by closed or open technique for a lab exam. Closed technique, performed under local anesthesia, includes both needle and transbronchial biopsies. Open technique is done under general anesthesia in the operating room.

The doctor chooses needle biopsy when the suspect lesion is readily accessible or when it originates in the lung's functional tissue, is confined to it, or is affixed to the chest wall. Needle biopsy provides a much smaller specimen than the open technique.

Transbronchial biopsy, the removal of multiple specimens through a fiber-optic bronchoscope, may be the doctor's choice for people with widespread lung disease or tumors or when the person's poor health rules out an open biopsy.

Open biopsy is used to study a well-defined lesion that may require surgery.

Why is this test done?

A lung biopsy is performed to confirm a diagnosis of widespread lung disease and lesions.

What should you know before the test?

- You'll be asked to fast after midnight before the procedure. (You may be permitted to have clear liquids the morning of the test.)
- A chest X-ray and blood studies will be done before the biopsy.
- The procedure takes 30 to 60 minutes, and test results should be available in a few days.
- The nurse will ask you to sign a consent form.
- You'll be given a mild sedative 30 minutes before the biopsy to help you relax. You'll receive a local anesthetic, but you feel a sharp, passing pain when the biopsy needle touches the lung.

Common tissue biopsies

BIOPSY TYPE AND TARGET TISSUE	EQUIPMENT

Excision
Surgical removal of an entire lesion from any tissue; may require only a local anesthetic

Scalpel

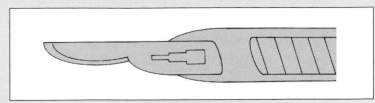

Shaving
Tissue shaved from a raised surface lesion on the skin

Scalpel

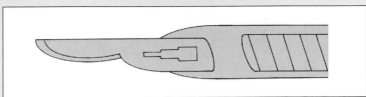

Needle
Removal of a core of tissue from bone, bone marrow, breast, lung, pleura, lymph node, liver, kidney, prostate, synovial membrane, thyroid

Cutting needle

Aspiration
Removal of a tissue sample from bone marrow or breast

Flexible or fine aspiration needle, needle guide, and aspiration syringe

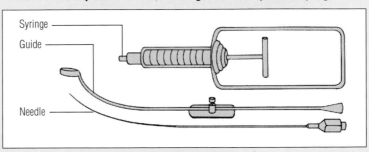

Syringe

Guide

Needle

Punch incision
Removal of a tissue specimen from core of lesion in skin or cervix

Punch

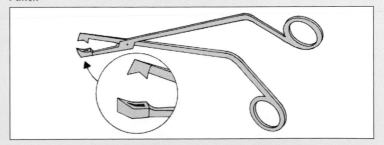

What happens during the test?

■ After the biopsy site is selected, lead markers are placed on your skin and X-rays are made to verify their correct placement.

■ You're in a sitting position, with your arms folded on a table in front of you. You're told to hold this position, to remain as still as possible, and to refrain from coughing.

■ Using a needle, the doctor anesthetizes the intercostal muscles and parietal pleura, makes a small incision with a scalpel, and introduces the biopsy needle through the incision, chest wall, and lung lining into the tumor or the pulmonary tissue.

■ When the needle is in the tumor or pulmonary tissue, the specimen is obtained and the needle is withdrawn.

■ Because coughing or movement during biopsy can cause tearing of the lung by the biopsy needle, the nurse helps to keep you calm and still.

What happens after the test?

■ A nurse will press on the biopsy site to stop the bleeding and will apply a small bandage.

■ You'll be given another X-ray immediately after the biopsy is completed.

■ You may resume your normal diet.

Does the test have risks?

You won't be given a needle biopsy if you have emphysema, blood clotting problems, or some forms of heart disease.

What are the normal results?

Normal pulmonary tissue shows uniform texture of the alveolar (air-sac) ducts, alveolar walls, bronchioles, and small vessels.

What do abnormal results mean?

Microscopic exam of a pulmonary tissue specimen can reveal abnormal cells and supplements the results of other lab tests to confirm cancer or lung disease.

PLEURAL BIOPSY

This test permits a microscopic exam of pleural tissue, the sac that covers your lungs. Tissue is removed by a needle biopsy or open biopsy.

Needle pleural biopsy is performed under local anesthesia. It usually follows thoracentesis (aspiration of pleural fluid), which is performed to determine the cause of excess fluid in the sacs that cover the lung.

Open pleural biopsy lets the doctor see the pleura and the underlying lung. It's performed in the operating room.

Why is this test done?

A pleural biopsy may be performed for the following reasons:
- To help the doctor differentiate between nonmalignant and malignant disease.
- To diagnose viral, fungal, or parasitic disease and collagen vascular disease of the pleura.

What should you know before the test?

- The needle biopsy takes 30 to 45 minutes to perform, although the needle remains in the pleura for less than 1 minute.
- Blood studies will precede the biopsy, and chest X-rays will be taken before and after the biopsy.
- The nurse will ask you to sign a consent form.
- You'll receive a local anesthetic and should feel little pain.

What happens during the test?

- You're seated on the side of the bed, with your feet resting on a stool and your arms supported by a table. You'll hold this position and remain still during the biopsy.
- The local anesthetic is administered.
- The doctor inserts a needle into the pleura, withdraws a specimen, and sends it to the lab.

What happens after the test?

The nurse will clean the skin around the biopsy site and apply an adhesive bandage.

You'll have another chest X-ray immediately after the biopsy.

You're seated on the side of the bed, with your feet resting on a stool and your arms supported by a table. You'll hold this position and remain still during the biopsy.

Does the test have risks?

You won't be given a pleural biopsy if you have a severe bleeding disorder.

What are the normal results?

The normal pleura consists primarily of cells, flattened in a uniform layer.

What do abnormal results mean?

Microscopic exam of the tissue specimen can show malignant disease, tuberculosis, or viral, fungal, parasitic, or collagen vascular disease.

DIGESTIVE SYSTEM

SMALL INTESTINE BIOPSY

The doctor performs this test to find out what may be causing poor absorption in the intestine or diarrhea. It produces larger specimens than endoscopic biopsy and allows removal of tissue from areas beyond an endoscope's reach.

In this method, several similar types of capsules are swallowed and guided to the bowel for tissue collection. A mercury-weighted bag is attached to one end of each capsule, and a thin polyethylene tube is attached to the other end. Once the bag, capsule, and tube are in place in the small bowel, suction in the tube draws the mucous membrane into the capsule and closes it, cutting off the piece of tissue within. This is an invasive procedure, but it causes little pain and complications are rare.

Why is this test done?

This biopsy is performed to help diagnose diseases of the intestine.

What should you know before the test?

- You'll be told to restrict food and fluids for at least 8 hours before the test. Aspirin and anticoagulants (blood-thinning drugs) will be withheld before the test.
- The procedure takes 45 to 60 minutes but causes little discomfort.
- The nurse will ask you to sign a consent form.
- You'll undergo a blood coagulation test before the biopsy.

What happens during the test?

- The doctor moistens the tube, capsule, and bag to ease its progress.
- The back of your throat is sprayed with a local anesthetic to decrease gagging.
- As you sit upright, the capsule is placed in your throat, and you're asked to flex your neck and swallow as the tube is advanced.
- You lie on your right side, and then the tube is advanced again. The tube's position is checked by fluoroscopy or the doctor pushes air through the tube and listens with a stethoscope for air to enter the stomach.
- Next, the tube is advanced, bit by bit, to pass the capsule through the opening between the stomach and the intestine. (The nurse may talk to you about food to stimulate your stomach and help the biopsy capsule move into your intestine.)
- When fluoroscopy confirms that the capsule has passed into your intestine, you're kept on your right side to allow the capsule to move into the second and third portions of the small bowel.
- You may hold the tube loosely to one side of your mouth if it makes you more comfortable.
- The capsule position is checked again by fluoroscopy. When the capsule is in a site the doctor has chosen, the biopsy sample can be taken.
- You lie on your back so the capsule's position can be checked again, and then the specimen is removed and sent to the lab.

While you're lying there, waiting for the test to finish, the nurse may start talking about food. The idea is to stimulate your stomach to help the biopsy capsule move into your intestine.

What happens after the test?

You can resume your normal diet.

Does the test have risks?

The biopsy won't be performed on a person who's uncooperative or who's taking aspirin or anticoagulants. It also shouldn't be performed on people with uncontrolled clotting disorders.

What are the normal results?

A normal biopsy sample consists of fingerlike villi, crypts, columnar epithelial cells, and round cells.

What do abnormal results mean?

Small intestine tissue that reveals microscopic changes in cell structure may indicate disorders called *Whipple's disease, abetalipoproteinemia, lymphoma, lymphangiectasia,* and *eosinophilic enteritis*. It may also show parasitic infections, vitamin B_{12} deficiency, and malnutrition. Such disorders require further studies.

LIVER BIOPSY

This test is used to diagnose liver disorders. Using a needle inserted through your chest, the doctor removes a core of liver tissue for microscopic analysis. This procedure is performed under local or general anesthesia. Findings may help the doctor identify liver disorders after ultrasound, a computerized axial tomography scan (commonly called a CAT scan), and other tests have failed to detect them.

Why is this test done?

This biopsy is performed to diagnose liver tissue disease, cancer, and infections.

What should you know before the test?

- You'll be told to restrict food and fluids for 4 to 8 hours before the test.
- The biopsy needle remains in the liver about 1 second, the entire procedure takes about 10 to 15 minutes, and test results are usually available in 1 day.
- The nurse will ask you to sign a consent form.
- The nurse will check your history to see if you have any hypersensitivity to the local anesthetic and to verify that you've undergone blood-clotting tests.
- You should empty your bladder just before the test.
- You may receive a local anesthetic. If so, you may experience pain similar to that of a punch in your right shoulder as the biopsy needle passes the phrenic nerve.

What happens during the test?

- You lie on your back, with your right hand under your head. Maintain this position and remain as still as possible during the procedure.
- The doctor feels around for your liver, selects the biopsy site, marks it, and injects the anesthetic.
- After the needle is inserted into your chest, the doctor asks you to take a deep breath, exhale, and hold your breath as you finish exhaling to prevent any movement of the chest wall.
- As you hold your breath, the biopsy needle is quickly inserted into the liver and withdrawn in 1 second.
- After the needle is withdrawn, you can breathe normally.

After the test, you'll be told to lie on your right side for 2 hours, with a small pillow or sandbag under your shoulder to provide extra pressure.

What happens after the test?

- You'll be told to lie on your right side for 2 hours, with a small pillow or sandbag under your shoulder to provide extra pressure. The nurse will suggest bed rest for the next 24 hours.
- If you feel pain, which may persist for several hours after the test, you may be given a pain reliever.
- You can resume your normal diet.

Does the test have risks?

You won't be given a liver biopsy if your blood doesn't clot quickly enough or if you have any of several lung, bile duct, liver, or blood diseases.

What are the normal results?

The normal liver consists of sheets of cells supported by a framework.

What do abnormal results mean?

An exam of the liver tissue may show widespread disease, such as cirrhosis or hepatitis, or infections such as tuberculosis. The test can show malignant tumors or nonmalignant lesions that require further studies.

REPRODUCTIVE SYSTEM

BREAST BIOPSY

This test permits microscopic examination of a breast tissue specimen. Once mammography, thermography, and X-rays indicate the presence of breast masses, the biopsy can confirm or rule out cancer. Tissue is removed by a needle biopsy or open biopsy.

Needle biopsy or fine needle biopsy provides a core of tissue or fluid, but is used only for fluid-filled cysts and advanced cancerous lesions. Both needle methods have limited diagnostic value because of the small and perhaps unrepresentative specimens they provide.

Open biopsy provides a complete tissue specimen, which can be sectioned to allow more accurate evaluation. All three techniques require only a local anesthetic and can often be performed without an overnight stay in the hospital. However, open biopsy may require a general anesthetic if the woman is fearful or uncooperative.

Why is this test done?

A breast biopsy is done to help the doctor differentiate between benign and malignant breast tumors.

What should you know before the test?

■ The doctor or nurse will want to discuss your medical history, including when you first noticed a lump, whether you have any pain, a change in the lump's size, or any link to your menstrual cycle. The nurse will ask about nipple discharge and nipple or skin changes, such as the characteristic "orange-peel" skin that may indicate an underlying inflammatory carcinoma. He or she will point out that breast masses don't always indicate cancer. (See *Collecting nipple discharge for lab study*.)

■ If you're going to receive a local anesthetic, you won't need to change your diet or any medications before the test.

■ If you're going to receive a general anesthetic, you'll be told to fast from midnight before the test until after the biopsy.

- The biopsy will take 15 to 30 minutes. Pretest studies, such as blood tests, urine tests, and chest X-rays, may be required.
- You'll be asked to sign a consent form.

What happens during the test?

Needle biopsy

- You're asked to undress to the waist, sit with your hands at your sides, and remain still.
- The biopsy site is cleaned, a local anesthetic is administered, and the needle is inserted into the lump.
- Fluid is withdrawn from the breast, put into a tube, and sent to the lab. (With fine-needle aspiration, a slide is made and viewed immediately under a microscope.)
- The nurse puts pressure on the biopsy site and, after bleeding stops, applies a bandage.
- Because breast fluid aspiration isn't diagnostically accurate, some doctors aspirate fluid only from cysts. If such fluid is clear yellow and the mass disappears, the aspiration procedure is both diagnostic and therapeutic. If the needle draws no fluid or if the cyst comes back two or three times, the doctor will order an open biopsy.

Open biopsy

- After you're given a general or local anesthetic, an incision is made in the breast to expose the lump.
- The examiner may then cut out a portion of tissue or remove the entire mass. If the mass is small and appears benign, it's usually removed. If it's larger or appears cancerous, a specimen is usually taken before the mass is removed.
- The specimen is sent to the lab.
- The incision is stitched, and an adhesive bandage is applied.

What happens after the test?

- If you received a local anesthetic during a needle or open biopsy, the nurse will watch your progress for a while before you can resume your normal activities.
- If you feel pain, you'll be given pain relievers.
- If you received a general anesthetic, you may remain in the hospital for at least 12 hours.

Collecting nipple discharge for lab study

Nipple discharge occurs normally during lactation. However, when this discharge occurs even though you're not breast-feeding a baby or occurs without breast masses or other signs of breast cancer, a lab study of the discharge can help find its cause. (If there were signs of breast cancer, the doctor would do a breast biopsy and other tests.)

Preparing the specimen

To prepare for taking the discharge specimen, the nurse will wash your nipple and pat it dry. Then, she will show you how to "milk" the breast to express the fluid. You'll discard the first drop and collect the next drop by moving a labeled glass slide across your nipple. (If a larger specimen is required, you'll need to collect it with a breast pump.)

What are the normal results?

Normally, breast tissue consists of cellular and noncellular connective tissue, fat lobules, and various milk ducts. It's pink, more fatty than fibrous, and shows no abnormal development of cells or tissue.

What do abnormal results mean?

Abnormal breast tissue may exhibit a wide range of malignant or benign abnormalities. Breast tumors are common in women and account for 32% of female cancers. Such tumors are rare in men (0.2% of male cancers).

If the biopsy confirms cancer, you'll need follow-up tests, including X-rays, blood studies, bone scans, and urinalysis, to determine appropriate treatment.

PROSTATE BIOPSY

This test uses a needle to withdraw a tissue specimen from the prostate. The doctor may chose to insert the needle through the perineal skin between the scrotum and the anus, through the rectum, or through the urethra. Tissue withdrawn by a needle is examined through a microscope.

Why is this test done?

A prostate biopsy may be performed for the following reasons:
- To confirm or rule out a diagnosis of prostate cancer
- To determine the cause of prostate enlargement.

What should you know before the test?

- You'll receive a local anesthetic, and the procedure takes less than 30 minutes.
- You'll be asked to sign a consent form.
- The nurse will check your history for hypersensitivity to the anesthetic or to other drugs.
- For a transrectal approach, you'll be given enemas until the return is clear. Your skin will be cleaned with an antibacterial agent to minimize the risk of infection.

- Just before the biopsy, you'll be given a sedative to make you more comfortable.
- You'll be told to remain still during the procedure and to follow instructions.

What happens during the test?
Perineal approach
- You lie on your left side with your knees to your chest or on your back with your knees up.
- You're given a local anesthetic; then a small incision is made.
- The examiner immobilizes the prostate by inserting a finger into the rectum and introduces the biopsy needle into a prostate lobe. The procedure is repeated several times for specimens, which are sent to the lab for analysis.

Transrectal approach
- This approach may be used without an anesthetic.
- You lie on the examining table on your left side.
- A biopsy needle is guided into the prostate, and you may feel pain as the needle enters and withdraws tissue.

Transurethral approach
- An endoscopic instrument is passed through the urethra, allowing the doctor a direct view of the prostate and passage of a cutting loop. The loop is rotated to obtain tissue and then withdrawn.
- After this procedure, you may remain in the hospital for 12 hours or more.

Does the test have risks?
Complications may include transient, painless passage of blood in the urine and bleeding into the prostatic urethra and bladder.

What are the normal results?
Normally, the prostate gland consists of a thin, fibrous capsule surrounding the stroma, which is made up of elastic and connective tissues and smooth-muscle fibers. The epithelial glands, found in these tissues and muscle fibers, drain into the chief excreting ducts.

What do abnormal results mean?
A microscopic exam can confirm cancer. Further tests, including bone scans, a bone marrow biopsy, and blood tests, identify the extent

of the cancer. Blood tests can tell whether the cancer is confined to the prostate. In that case, radical surgery and irradiation, although controversial, can provide a high cure rate. If discovery of cancer is delayed, treatment requires estrogen therapy, as growth of the tumor depends on secretion of testosterone.

An exam can also detect benign prostate enlargement, prostatitis, tuberculosis, lymphomas, and rectal or bladder carcinomas.

CERVICAL BIOPSY

In this test, the doctor obtains a cervical tissue specimen for microscopic study. Sharp forceps are used to remove tissue, usually several specimens from all areas with abnormal tissue or from other sites around the cervical circumference.

Doctors use this procedure for women with suspicious cervical lesions, and usually time it for one week after menstruation. Biopsy sites are selected by looking at the cervix with a colposcope — called *direct visualization,* the most accurate method — or by staining normal tissue with a dye that doesn't color abnormal tissue (called *Schiller's test*).

Why is this test done?
A cervical biopsy may be performed for the following reasons:
- To help the doctor evaluate suspicious cervical lesions
- To diagnose cervical cancer.

What should you know before the test?
- The test takes about 15 minutes, and you may experience mild discomfort during and after the biopsy.
- If you're an outpatient, you should have someone accompany you home after the biopsy.
- You'll be asked to sign a consent form.
- Just before the biopsy, you'll be asked to empty your bladder.

What happens during the test?
- You lie on an examining table with your feet in the stirrups, as you would for a Pap test.

- The nurse urges you to relax as the unlubricated speculum is inserted.

Direct visualization
- The colposcope is inserted through the speculum; the biopsy site is located and cleaned.
- The biopsy forceps are then inserted through the speculum or the colposcope, and tissue is removed from any lesion or from selected sites.

Schiller's test
- An applicator stick saturated with iodine solution is inserted through the speculum. This stains the cervix to identify lesions for biopsy.
- Samples of the unstained tissue are removed and set to the lab.

After the test, you must avoid strenuous exercise for 8 to 24 hours.

What happens after the test?
- You'll be told to avoid strenuous exercise for 8 to 24 hours after the biopsy and encouraged to rest briefly before leaving the office.
- If a tampon was inserted after the biopsy, you should leave it in place for 8 to 24 hours. Some bleeding may occur, but you should report any bleeding that is heavier than your menstrual flow. The nurse will warn you to avoid using additional tampons, which can irritate the cervix and provoke bleeding.
- You should avoid douching and intercourse for 2 weeks, or as directed by your doctor.
- A foul-smelling, gray-green vaginal discharge is normal for several days after biopsy and may persist for 3 weeks.

What are the normal results?
Normal cervical tissue is composed of several kinds of cells, loose connective tissue, and smooth-muscle fibers, with no dysplasia or abnormal cell growth.

What do abnormal results mean?
A microscopic exam of a cervical tissue specimen is used to identify abnormal cells. Results may help to differentiate between cancer that develops in the cervical tissue and cancer that originates in other body organs and spreads to the cervix.

SKELETAL SYSTEM

BONE BIOPSY

This test permits microscopic exam of a bone specimen. The doctor uses a bone biopsy for people with bone pain and tenderness. If a bone scan, a computerized axial tomography scan (commonly called a CAT scan), an X-ray, or arteriography reveals a mass or deformity, this test may be ordered.

During the test, a piece or core of bone is removed, either by a special drill needle using a local anesthetic or by surgical excision using a general anesthetic. Excision provides a larger specimen than a drill biopsy and permits immediate surgical treatment if quick analysis of the specimen reveals cancer.

Why is this test done?

A bone biopsy is performed to help the doctor distinguish between benign and malignant bone tumors.

What should you know before the test?

- For a drill biopsy, you won't need to change your diet before the test. For an open biopsy, you must fast overnight before the test.
- For a drill biopsy, you'll receive a local anesthetic but will still experience discomfort and pressure when the biopsy needle enters the bone.
- You'll be asked to sign a consent form.

What happens during the test?
Drill biopsy
- After the site is shaved and cleaned, you're given a local anesthetic.
- A special drill forces the needle into the bone and withdraws the bone sample. You're asked to hold very still during the procedure.

Open biopsy
- You're put under general anesthesia.
- An incision is made, and a piece of bone is removed and sent to the lab immediately for analysis. Further surgery can then be performed, depending on the findings.

A piece or core of bone is removed, either by a special drill needle or by surgery. Surgical excision provides a larger specimen than drill biopsy and permits immediate treatment.

What happens after the test?

Drill biopsy

The nurse will put pressure on the site with a sterile gauze pad. When the bleeding stops, the nurse will apply a topical antiseptic (povidone-iodine ointment) and an adhesive bandage or other sterile covering to close the wound and prevent infection.

Both types

- If you experience pain after the procedure, you'll be given pain killers. You'll also be monitored for signs of bone infection, such as fever, headache, pain on movement, and redness or abscess near the biopsy site.
- You may resume your normal diet.

Does the test have risks?

Possible complications include bone fracture, damage to surrounding tissue, and osteomyelitis (a bone infection).

What are the normal results?

Normal bone tissue consists of fibers of collagen and bone tissue.

What do abnormal results mean?

A bone specimen exam can reveal benign or malignant tumors. Most malignant tumors spread to bone through the blood and lymph systems from the breast, lungs, prostate, thyroid, or kidneys.

BONE MARROW ASPIRATION AND BIOPSY

This test permits microscopic examination of a bone marrow specimen. It gives the doctor reliable diagnostic information about blood disorders.

Marrow may be removed by aspiration or a needle biopsy under local anesthesia. In aspiration biopsy, a fluid specimen is removed from the bone marrow. In a needle biopsy, a core of marrow cells (not fluid) is removed. These methods are often used together to obtain the best possible marrow specimens.

Red marrow, which constitutes about 50% of an adult's marrow, actively produces red blood cells; yellow marrow contains fat cells and connective tissue and is inactive, but it can become active in response to the body's needs.

Why is this test done?

A bone marrow biopsy may be performed for the following reasons:
- To help the doctor diagnose blood diseases and anemias
- To diagnose primary and cancerous tumors
- To determine the cause of infection
- To help the doctor evaluate the stage of a disease such as Hodgkin's disease

To evaluate the effectiveness of chemotherapy and other treatments.

What should you know before the test?

- You won't need to change your diet before the test.
- The biopsy usually takes only 5 to 10 minutes. Test results are generally available in 1 day.
- More than one bone marrow specimen may be required and a blood sample will be collected before biopsy for lab testing.
- The nurse will ask you to sign a consent form.
- You'll be told which biopsy site will be used — the sternum, anterior or posterior iliac crest, vertebral spinous process, rib, or tibia.
- You'll be given a local anesthetic but will feel pressure on insertion of the biopsy needle and a brief, pulling pain on removal of the marrow.
- You'll be given a mild sedative 1 hour before the test.

What happens during the test?

- The nurse positions you and urges you to remain as still as possible.
- The nurse may talk quietly to you during the procedure, describing what's being done and answering any questions.
- After the skin over the biopsy site is prepared and the area is draped, the local anesthetic is injected.
- The doctor inserts the needle and removes a bone marrow specimen. In an aspiration biopsy, slides are prepared for immediate analysis. In a needle biopsy, a specimen is taken from the marrow cavity and sent to the lab.

To obtain the best possible marrow specimens, the doctor may use two different methods — aspiration and needle biopsy — concurrently.

What happens after the test?

■ The nurse will apply pressure to the site for 5 minutes or so.

■ If an adequate marrow specimen hasn't been obtained on the first attempt at aspiration, the needle may be repositioned within the marrow cavity or may be removed and reinserted in another site within the anesthetized area. If the second attempt fails, a needle biopsy may follow the aspiration biopsy.

Does the test have risks?

■ Bone marrow biopsy isn't used in people with severe bleeding disorders.

■ Bleeding and infection may be caused by bone marrow biopsy at any site, but the most serious complications occur at the sternum. Such complications are rare but include puncture of the heart and major vessels causing severe hemorrhage.

What are the normal results?

Yellow marrow contains fat cells and connective tissue. Red marrow contains blood-making cells, fat cells, and connective tissue. An adult has a large blood-making capacity. An infant's marrow is mainly red, reflecting a small capacity.

What do abnormal results mean?

Microscopic examination of a bone marrow specimen can be used to detect myelofibrosis, granulomas, lymphoma, or cancer. Blood analysis, including cell counts, can alert the doctor to a wide range of disorders. Some of them are iron deficiency, anemias of blood disorders, infectious mononucleosis, and several kinds of leukemia.

JOINT BIOPSY

In this test, the doctor obtains a tissue specimen from the synovial membrane that lines a joint. The doctor uses a needle to remove a tissue specimen for a microscopic exam of the thin lining of a joint capsule. In a large joint, such as the knee, preliminary arthroscopy can help the doctor select the biopsy site. Joint biopsy is performed when analysis of synovial fluid — a viscous, lubricating fluid contained within the synovial membrane — doesn't yield answers.

Why is this test done?

A joint biopsy may be performed for the following reasons:
- To diagnose gout, pseudogout, bacterial infections and lesions, and granulomatous infections
- To help the doctor diagnose lupus, rheumatoid arthritis, or Reiter's disease
- To monitor joint problems.

What should you know before the test?

- You won't need to change your diet before the test.
- You'll be given a local anesthetic to minimize discomfort, but you'll experience brief pain when the needle enters the joint.
- The procedure takes about 30 minutes, and test results are usually available in 1 or 2 days.
- You'll be asked to sign a consent form.
- The nurse will tell you which site has been chosen for the biopsy — the knee (most common), elbow, wrist, ankle, or shoulder. Usually, the most painful joint is selected.
- You'll be given a sedative to help you relax.

What happens during the test?

- The nurse puts you in position, cleans the biopsy site, and drapes the area.
- The local anesthetic is injected into the joint space; then the tube to guide the needle is forcefully thrust into the joint space.
- The biopsy needle is inserted through the tube, and a tissue segment is cut off and removed.

What happens after the test?

- A pressure bandage is applied to the incision.
- If you feel pain, you'll be given pain relievers.
- The nurse will urge you to rest the joint for 1 day before resuming normal activity.

Does the test have any risks?

Complications include infection and bleeding into the joint, but these are rare.

The nurse will tell you which site has been chosen for the biopsy — the knee, elbow, wrist, ankle, or shoulder. Usually, the most painful joint is selected.

What are the normal results?

The synovial membrane surface should be relatively smooth, except for the fingerlike villi, folds, and fat pads that project into the joint cavity. The membrane tissue produces synovial fluid and contains a capillary network, lymphatic vessels, and a few nerve fibers.

What do abnormal results mean?

A microscopic exam of synovial tissue can diagnose a long list of diseases, including gout, pseudogout, tuberculosis, sarcoidosis, amyloidosis, synovial tumors, or synovial malignancy (rare). Such an examination can also aid the diagnosis of rheumatoid arthritis.

OTHER BIOPSIES

THYROID BIOPSY

This test permits microscopic examination of a thyroid tissue specimen. The doctor uses this procedure for people with thyroid enlargement or nodules, breathing and swallowing difficulties, vocal cord paralysis, weight loss, and a sensation of fullness in the neck. It's commonly performed when noninvasive tests (tests that don't enter the body), such as thyroid ultrasound and scans, are abnormal or inconclusive.

Thyroid tissue may be obtained from your neck with a hollow needle under local anesthesia or during an open (surgical) biopsy under general anesthesia. An open biopsy provides more information than a needle biopsy. It also permits a direct exam and immediate excision of suspicious tissue.

Why is this test done?

A thyroid biopsy may be performed for the following reasons:
- To help the doctor differentiate between benign and malignant thyroid disease
- To help diagnose Hashimoto's thyroiditis, subacute granulomatous thyroiditis, hyperthyroidism, and nontoxic nodular goiter.

What should you know before the test?

- You won't need to change your diet before the test (unless you're to be given a general anesthetic).
- The test takes 15 to 30 minutes, and results should be available in 1 day.
- The nurse will ask you to sign a consent form and will check your history for hypersensitivity to anesthetics or pain relievers.
- You'll receive a local anesthetic to minimize pain during the procedure, but you may experience some pressure when the specimen is withdrawn.
- You may have a sore throat the day after the test.
- You'll be given a sedative 15 minutes before the biopsy.

What happens during the test?

- For a needle biopsy, you lie on your back, with a pillow under your shoulder blades and your head back.
- As the examiner prepares to inject the local anesthetic, you're warned not to swallow.
- The examiner withdraws a specimen with a needle and sends it to the lab.

What happens after the test?

- The nurse will apply pressure to the biopsy site to stop bleeding, and then apply a bandage.
- You'll be told to avoid straining the biopsy site by putting both hands behind your neck when you sit up.

What are the normal results?

A microscopic exam of normal tissue shows fibrous networks dividing the gland.

What do abnormal results mean?

Malignant tumors appear as well-encapsulated, solitary nodules of uniform, but abnormal, structure. The test may also show benign tumors and patterns that indicate diseases such as thyroiditis and hyperthyroidism. Because thyroid cancers are frequently small and scattered, a negative report doesn't rule out cancer.

After the test, you'll have to avoid straining the biopsy site by putting both hands behind your neck when you sit up.

LYMPH NODE BIOPSY

This test allows microscopic study of lymph node tissue. The doctor surgically removes an active lymph node or uses a needle to withdraw a nodal specimen for microscopic exam. Both techniques usually use a local anesthetic and sample the superficial nodes in the cervical, collarbone, armpit, or groin region. Surgery is preferred because it yields a larger specimen. (See *The lymphatic system*, page 240.)

Lymph nodes swell during infection, but when they're enlarged for a long time and accompanied by other symptoms, the doctor may look for diseases such as chronic lymphatic leukemia, Hodgkin's disease, infectious mononucleosis, and rheumatoid arthritis.

A complete blood count, liver function studies, liver and spleen scans, and X-rays usually precede this test.

Why is this test done?

A lymph node biopsy may be performed for the following reasons:
- To find the cause of lymph node enlargement
- To distinguish between benign and malignant lymph node tumors
- To help the doctor determine the stage of a spreading cancer.

What should you know before the test?

- If you're to have a surgical biopsy, you'll be told to eat nothing after midnight before the test and to drink only clear liquids on the morning of the test. If a general anesthetic is needed for deeper nodes, you must also restrict fluids.
- For a needle biopsy, you won't need to change your diet before the test.
- The procedure takes 15 to 30 minutes, and the analysis takes 1 day to complete.
- The nurse will ask you to sign a consent form.
- If you receive a local anesthetic, you may experience discomfort during the injection.

What happens during the test?

Excisional biopsy
- The nurse prepares the skin over the biopsy site and drapes the area.
- The doctor makes an incision, removes an entire node, and sends it to the lab.

HOW YOUR BODY WORKS

The lymphatic system

The lymphatic system is a network of capillary and venous channels. It returns excess interstitial (between-the-cells) fluids and proteins to the blood. The diagram below shows the main lymph nodes (glands) that are found throughout your body.

Cell wars

Bacteria from local tissue infection usually enter the bloodstream through the lymphatic system. When it's healthy, however, the lymphatic system provides a strong defense against bacteria and viruses. Before lymph reenters the bloodstream, afferent lymphatic vessels transport it to lymph nodes — clusters of lymphatic tissues throughout the body — where numerous lymphocytes destroy microorganisms and foreign particles.

Foreign particles that escape the lymphatic system are destroyed by white blood cells in the spleen, liver, and bone marrow.

The spleen is a germ trap

As blood circulates through the body, it flows into the spleen, where it's filtered. There, residing lymphocytes ingest abnormal or foreign cells while normal cells pass through. Bacteria that accompany digested food particles into the portal vein — which supplies the liver — are ingested by reticulum cells. Likewise, white blood cells formed in the bone marrow protect the body from invading bacteria.

Macrophages form still another defense system. These white cells in the tissues, lymph nodes, and red bone marrow migrate to inflamed areas and destroy infective particles.

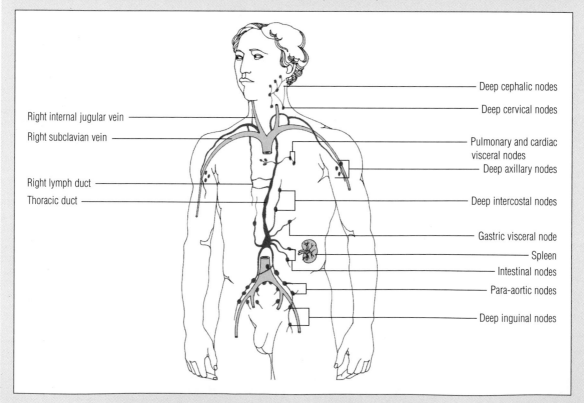

Needle biopsy
- After preparing the biopsy site and administering a local anesthetic, the doctor grasps the node between thumb and forefinger, inserts the needle directly into the node, and obtains a small core specimen.
- The needle is removed, and the specimen is sent to the lab.

What happens after the test?

- Pressure is put on the biopsy site to control bleeding, and an adhesive bandage is applied.
- You may resume your usual diet.

What are the normal results?

- The normal lymph node is encapsulated by connective tissue and is divided into smaller lobes by tissue strands.

What do abnormal results mean?

- A microscopic exam of the tissue specimen distinguishes between malignant and nonmalignant causes of lymph node enlargement. Lymphatic malignancy accounts for up to 5% of all cancers and is slightly more prevalent in males than in females.
- Hodgkin's disease, a lymphoma affecting the entire lymph system, is the leading cancer affecting adolescents and young adults.

SKIN BIOPSY

This type of biopsy provides a sample of skin for microscopic study. The doctor removes a small piece of tissue, under local anesthesia, from a lesion suspected of cancer or other problems. One of three techniques may be used: shave biopsy, punch biopsy, or excision biopsy. A shave biopsy cuts the lesion above the skin line, which allows further biopsy at the site. A punch biopsy removes an oval core from the center of a lesion. An excision biopsy removes the entire lesion. (See *How biopsies are obtained from different skin layers*, page 242.)

Lesions suspected of cancer usually have changed color, size, or appearance or fail to heal properly after injury.

How biopsies are obtained from different skin layers

Epidermal tissue specimens are generally removed by a shave biopsy. Both epidermal and dermal specimens may be obtained by a punch biopsy. Subcutaneous tissue specimens are removed by excision.

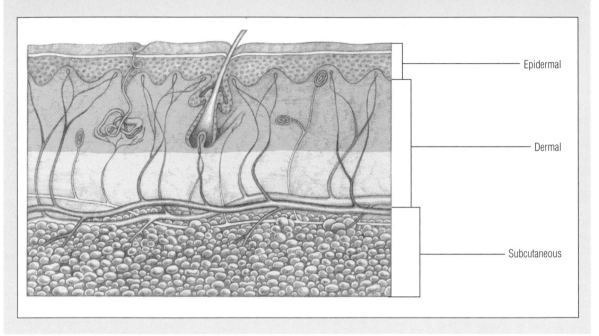

Epidermal

Dermal

Subcutaneous

Why is this test done?

A skin biopsy may be performed for the following reasons:
- To help the doctor differentiate between cancerous cells and benign growths
- To diagnose chronic bacterial or fungal skin infections.

What should you know before the test?

- You won't need to change your diet before the test.
- You'll receive a local anesthetic to minimize pain; the biopsy takes about 15 minutes, and test results are usually available in 1 day.
- The nurse will ask you to sign a consent form and will check your history for hypersensitivity to the local anesthetic.

What happens during the test?

You're given a local anesthetic.

Shave biopsy

- The protruding growth is cut off at the skin line with a scalpel and sent to the lab.
- The nurse applies pressure to the area to stop the bleeding.

Punch biopsy

The skin surrounding the lesion is pulled taut, and the doctor firmly applies the punch to the lesion and rotates it to obtain a tissue specimen. The plug is lifted with forceps or a needle and is cut off as deeply into the fat layer as possible.

Excision biopsy

The doctor uses a scalpel to totally cut out the lesion. The incision is made as wide and as deep as necessary.

What happens after the test?

- The nurse applies pressure to the site to stop the bleeding. The wound is stitched closed. If the incision is large, a skin graft may be required.
- If you have pain, the nurse will give you pain relievers.
- If you have stitches, keep the area clean and as dry as possible. Facial stitches will be removed in 3 to 5 days; trunk stitches, in 7 to 14 days.
- If you have adhesive strips, leave them in place for 14 to 21 days.

What are the normal results?

Normal skin consists of the epidermis and fibrous connective tissue (dermis).

What do abnormal results mean?

A microscopic exam of the tissue specimen may reveal a benign or malignant lesion. Malignant tumors include basal cell carcinoma, squamous cell carcinoma, and malignant melanoma. Benign growths include cysts, warts, moles, and several kinds of fibroid growths. Cultures can be used to detect chronic bacterial and fungal infections.

KIDNEY BIOPSY

In this test, doctor uses a needle to withdraw a core of kidney tissue for an exam. Also called *percutaneous renal biopsy*, this procedure may be performed during investigation of a long list of disorders. Noninvasive tests (those that don't enter the body), especially renal ultrasound and a computerized axial tomography scan (commonly called a CAT scan), have replaced a kidney biopsy in many hospitals. (See *Urinary tract brush biopsy*.)

Why is this test done?

The kidney biopsy may be performed for the following reasons:
- To help the doctor diagnose kidney disease
- To monitor progression of kidney disease and to check the effectiveness of treatment.

What should you know before the test?

- You'll be asked to fast for 8 hours before the test.
- Blood and urine specimens are collected and tested before the biopsy.
- The doctor may schedule other tests, such as intravenous pyelography, ultrasonography, or an erect film of the abdomen, to help determine the biopsy site.
- The procedure takes only 15 minutes, and the needle is in the kidney for just a few seconds.
- The nurse will ask you to sign a consent form.
You'll be given a mild sedative 30 minutes to 1 hour before the biopsy to help you relax.

What happens during the test?

- You're given a local anesthetic, but you may experience a pinching pain when the needle is inserted through your back into the kidney.
- You lie on a firm surface, with a sandbag beneath your abdomen.
- The nurse asks you to take a deep breath while your kidney is being felt by the doctor.
- The nurse asks you to hold your breath and remain immobile as the needle for the anesthetic is inserted through the back muscles and into the kidney.

The procedure takes only 15 minutes and the needle is in the kidney for just a few seconds.

Urinary tract brush biopsy

If the doctor says that X-rays show a lesion in your urinary tract, he or she may want to get a tissue specimen to analyze. The method called a *brush biopsy* is used to get the sample of cells. It's not used if you have a urinary tract infection or an obstruction at or below the biopsy site.

To prepare for the test, the nurse will check to be sure you're not sensitive to the dye that will be used in the test, or to the general, local, or spinal anesthetic that may be used. The nurse will also ask about sensitivity to any iodine-containing foods such as shellfish.

How the test is done

Just before the biopsy procedure, you'll be given a sedative and an anesthetic. You may feel some discomfort, but the procedure will be finished in 30 to 60 minutes and follows these steps:

- You lie on your back.
- Using a cystoscope, the doctor passes a guide wire up the ureter and passes a urethral catheter over the guide wire.
- A dye is sent through the catheter. The doctor uses a fluoroscope to guide the catheter to a position next to the lesion.

- The dye is washed out with normal saline solution to prevent cell distortions.
- A nylon or steel brush is passed up the catheter and the lesion is brushed. This procedure is repeated at least six times, using a new brush each time.
- As each brush is removed from the catheter, a Pap smear is made, and the brush tip is cut off and placed in formalin for 1 hour. The biopsy material is then removed from the brush tip for a lab exam.
- When the last brush is withdrawn, the catheter is irrigated with normal saline solution to remove additional cells. These cells are also sent for examination.

Because brush biopsy may cause such complications as perforation, hemorrhage, infection, or spread of the dye, the nurse will watch for any abnormal reactions and report them to the doctor.

How results are interpreted

The lab can tell the difference between malignant and benign lesions, which may appear the same on X-rays.

- After the needle is in position, you're asked to hold your breath and remain as still as possible while the needle is withdrawn.
- After a small incision is made in the anesthetized skin, you're asked to hold your breath and remain still while the doctor inserts a needle with stylet.
- You're asked to breathe deeply again, and then hold still while the tissue specimen is withdrawn.
- If an adequate tissue specimen has not been obtained, the procedure is repeated immediately.

What happens after the test?

- The nurse will apply pressure to the biopsy site for 3 to 5 minutes to stop superficial bleeding, and then will apply a bandage.

- You'll be told to lie flat on your back without moving for at least 12 hours to prevent bleeding.
- You'll be encouraged to drink fluids to minimize colic and obstruction from blood clotting.
- You may resume a normal diet.

Does the test have risks?

- You shouldn't undergo a kidney biopsy if you have severe disorders, such as kidney cancer, bleeding disorders, very high blood pressure, or only one kidney.
- Complications of the biopsy may include bleeding, a hematoma, an arteriovenous fistula, and infection.

What are the normal results?

Normally, a section of kidney tissue shows the organ's cells and healthy tissues and structure.

What do abnormal results mean?

A microscopic exam of kidney tissue can reveal cancer or other kidney disease.

VISION &
HEARING TESTS:
Evaluating Sight & Sound

EYES & VISION

EYE EXAM WITH AN OPHTHALMOSCOPE

The doctor uses a special viewing instrument called an *ophthalmoscope* to examine the back of your eye and check the optic disk, the retina and its blood vessels, and the macula. In contrast, an eye exam with a special viewing instrument called a *slit lamp* looks at the front of the eye. (See *A look at your eyes.*)

The ophthalmoscope itself is a small, hand-held instrument. It has a light source, a viewing device, a reflecting device to channel light into the person's eyes, and lenses to correct any inherent refractive error in the person's or doctor's eyes.

Why is this test done?

This eye exam may be performed to detect and evaluate problems at the back of the eye. It may also be part of a routine periodic checkup.

What should you know before the test?

- This test usually less than 5 minutes.
- You may receive eyedrops to dilate your pupils for better viewing, but you'll feel no discomfort during the test. Tell the doctor or nurse if you've ever had a bad reaction to eyedrops or if you have glaucoma.

What happens during the test?

- You sit upright in the exam chair. The doctor dims the room lights to keep reflections from interfering with the exam.
- The doctor sits or often stands about 2 feet (60 centimeters) away from you and slightly to your right. The exam usually begins with your right eye.
- Look straight ahead at some object during the full exam as the doctor checks the structures at the back of each eye.

What happens after the test?

If you received eyedrops, your near vision will be blurred for up to 2 hours. Your eyes may be sensitive to light for a while.

HOW YOUR BODY WORKS

A look at your eyes

Called by poets the "windows of the soul," the eyes can express sadness, surprise, and a range of other emotions. For doctors and scientists, the organ of vision is a delicate, complex structure that has three layers.

Outer layer

The cornea and sclera make up the outermost layer of the eye. The cornea lies at the front of the eye. A transparent structure, the cornea bends light rays that enter the eye and helps to focus the images on the retina. Adjoining the cornea is the sclera, an opaque, white, fibrous coat covering the posterior five-sixths of the eye, through which nerves and blood vessels pass to penetrate the eye's interior.

Middle layer

The middle layer, known as the *uveal tract,* consists of the iris, the ciliary body, and the choroid. The colored iris has muscle fibers that regulate the light admitted to the eye's interior through the pupil, the circular opening. Behind the iris lies a transparent lens that can change its shape to focus light rays on the retina. The ciliary body permits flexibility of the lens for clearer vision. The choroid supplies blood to the retina and conducts blood and nerve impulses to the front of the eye.

Inner layer

The third layer of the eye, the retina, consists of a complicated network of the visual cells called *rods* and *cones,* and other nerve cells lined with pigment epithelium. At the back of the retina lies the fovea. Composed entirely of cones, the fovea is the area of most acute vision.

Chambers and their fluids

The anterior, or front, chamber of the eye, which is situated behind the cornea and in front of the iris and lens, is filled with aqueous humor. This fluid nourishes the internal parts of the eye and maintains constant pressure within the eyeball.

The vitreous cavity is surrounded by the retina and the optic nerve and makes up four-fifths of the back of the eye. It's filled with vitreous humor — a clear, gelatinous substance. Vitreous humor helps maintain the transparency and shape of the eye.

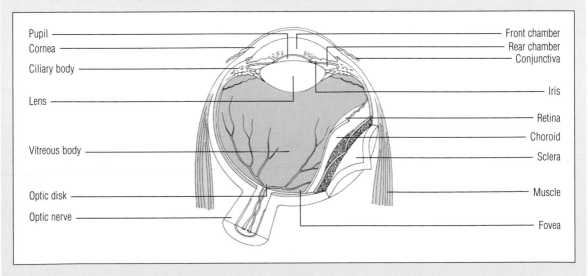

Does the test have risks?

Eyedrops shouldn't be used during the test if the person is allergic to them or has glaucoma.

What are the normal results?

The exam should show a normal optic disk, retina, macula, and other structures.

What do abnormal results mean?

The exam can identify corneal lesions, dense opacities of the aqueous or vitreous humor (such as from blood infiltration), cataracts, or a detached retina. It can also show changes characteristic of many eye diseases, such as glaucoma, optic neuritis, atrophy of the optic nerve, and inflammatory disease of the optic disk, retina, or uvea.

The exam shows the damaging effects of other diseases on the eye. High blood pressure causes spasms, hardening, and eventual blockage of the retina's blood vessels, leading to retinal swelling and hemorrhage. Diabetes may produce retinal fibroses, patches of white exudate, and tiny aneurysms (bulges) in retinal blood vessels.

EYE EXAM WITH A SLIT LAMP

Made up of a special lighting system and a binocular microscope, a slit lamp helps an eye doctor examine the front structures of the eye. Specifically, the doctor looks at the eyelids, eyelashes, conjunctiva, sclera, cornea, anterior chamber, iris, lens, and vitreous face of the eye. In contrast, an eye exam with a special viewing instrument called an *ophthalmoscope* looks at the back of the eye.

Why is this test done?

This type of eye exam may be performed to detect and evaluate problems at the front of the eye.

What should you know before the test?

- The test takes 5 to 10 minutes and requires that you remain still. The test is painless.
- Tell the doctor or nurse if you've ever had a bad reaction to eyedrops or if you have glaucoma.
- If you wear contact lenses, you'll remove them for the test (unless the test is being performed to evaluate the fit of the lens).

What happens during the test?

- You sit in the examining chair with both feet on the floor, your chin on the rest, and your forehead against the support bar. You may receive eyedrops. The doctor dims the lights in the room.
- The doctor examines the eyes starting with the lids and lashes and progressing to the vitreous face. In some cases, a special camera may be attached to the slit lamp to photograph portions of the eye.

What happens after the test?

If you received eyedrops, your near vision will be blurred for up to 2 hours. Your eyes may be sensitive to light for a while.

Does the test have risks?

Eyedrops shouldn't be used during the test if a person is allergic to them. They should also not be used in a person with glaucoma.

What are the normal results?

The exam should reveal no abnormalities in the front of the eye.

What do abnormal results mean?

The exam may detect corneal abrasions and ulcers, lens opacities, inflammation of the iris, and conjunctivitis, as well as irregularly shaped corneas. Some abnormal findings may indicate impending disorders. For example, early-stage lens opacities may signal the development of cataracts.

VISUAL ACUITY TESTS

These tests evaluate your distance and near vision. In a distance vision test, you read letters on a standardized chart, commonly called a *Snellen chart,* from a distance of 20 feet (6 meters). Charts showing the letter E in various positions and sizes are used for young children and other people who can't read. The smaller the symbol you can identify, the sharper your distance vision.

Near or reading vision may be tested as well, using a standardized card such as the Jaeger card, which has print samples in different sizes.

The Snellen test should be performed on all people with eye complaints. Near-vision testing is routine for people with eyestrain or reading difficulty and for everyone over age 40.

Why are these tests done?

Visual acuity tests may be performed for the following reasons:

- To test distance and near vision
- To check for vision problems.

What should you know before the tests?

If you wear glasses, you'll be reminded to bring them with you for the tests.

What happens during the tests?

The doctor checks distance and near vision.

Checking distance vision

- You sit 20 feet (6 meters) away from the eye chart. If you're wearing glasses, remove them so your uncorrected vision can be tested first.
- You cover one eye and are asked to read the smallest line of letters you can see on the chart. Try to read a line even if you can't see it clearly because intelligent guesses usually mean you can recognize some of the symbols' details.
- Next, cover the other eye and repeat the test.
- If you wear glasses, your corrected vision is tested using the same procedure.

Checking near vision

- Remove your glasses and cover one eye. The examiner asks you to read the Jaeger card at your customary reading distance.
- After testing one eye, the examiner tests the other. If you wear glasses, your corrected vision is also tested.

What are the normal results?

Most charts for distance vision are read at 20 feet (6 meters). If your vision is normal, you have 20/20 vision. This means that the smallest symbol you can identify at 20 feet (6 meters) is the same symbol that a person with normal vision can identify at the same distance. A person may have better-than-normal vision. For example, a person with 20/15 vision can read at 20 feet what a person with normal vision can see at 15 feet (4.5 meters).

Normal near vision is usually recorded as 14/14 because standard test charts, such as the Jaeger card, are generally held 14 inches (35 centimeters) from a person's eyes.

A normal or better-than-normal vision test doesn't necessarily indicate normal vision, however. For example, a vision problem may be present if a person consistently misses the letters on one side of all the lines. Such a finding indicates the need for further tests.

What do abnormal results mean?

If you can't read the 20/20 line on the Snellen chart, you don't have normal distance vision. (See *Sight and the aging process.*) If you can read the 20/40 line, for instance, your vision is less than normal. In this case, you would read at 20 feet what a person with normal vision would read at 40 feet (12 meters). A person who has 20/200 vision in the better corrected eye is considered legally blind.

The Jaeger card test can identify poor near vision. A result, for instance, of 14/20 means that the person can read at 14 inches what a person with normal vision can read at 20 inches (50 centimeters).

A person with less-than-normal vision needs further tests to tell if the problem results from an injury or illness or indicates the need for corrective lenses.

INSIGHT INTO ILLNESS

Sight and the aging process

The lens of the eye normally becomes less elastic as we age. This loss of elasticity hampers the ability of the lens to change its shape. As a consequence, vision often gets worse from adolescence into adulthood.

Presbyopia

A condition called *presbyopia*, or poor near vision, occurs in many middle-age people. It can be helped by wearing reading glasses.

Severe vision loss

Later in life, more serious conditions can develop. Eye tissue may become damaged and severely limit vision, especially if a person has a chronic illness, such as diabetes. Another serious condition, cataracts, often strikes elderly people. In this illness, one or both lenses become clouded and surgery may be necessary.

EARS & HEARING

BALANCE AND COORDINATION TESTS

A person who complains of dizziness or a loss of balance may undergo these screening tests. The tests evaluate balance and coordination as a person performs various movements with the eyes open and closed.

Why are these tests done?

Balance and coordination tests may be performed for the following reasons:
■ To help identify vestibular or brain disorders affecting the entire body (balance tests)
■ To help identify vestibular or brain disorders affecting the arms (coordination tests).

What should you know before the tests?

■ You'll learn about the tests, including who will perform them, where they will take place, and their duration. There's little danger of falling during the test.
■ The doctor will check your physical condition, which will influence your ability to do the tests.
■ Tell the doctor or nurse if you recently drank alcohol or took sedatives or tranquilizers.

What happens during the tests?

Testing balance
You're asked to perform as many of the following movements as possible:
■ Stand with your feet together, arms at your sides, and eyes open for 20 seconds. Try to maintain this position for another 20 seconds with your eyes closed.
■ Stand on one foot for 5 seconds, then on the other foot for 5 seconds. Next, repeat the procedure with your eyes closed.
■ Stand heel to toe for 20 seconds with your eyes opened. Then try to maintain the position with your eyes closed for another 20 seconds.
■ Walk forward and backward in a straight line, heel to toe, first with your eyes open, and then with them closed.

Testing coordination

- Sit and face the examiner, who holds out his or her index finger at your shoulder level.
- Touch the examiner's finger with your right index finger.
- Lower your arm and close your eyes. Try to touch the examiner's finger again.
- Next, repeat the entire maneuver using your left index finger.

Do the tests have risks?

When checking balance, the examiner will stand close to you to catch you if you start to fall.

What are the normal results?

A healthy person maintains balance with the eyes open and closed and can also touch the examiner's finger with the eyes open and closed.

What do abnormal results mean?

The tests can identify a vestibular lesion, which can cause swaying or falling when the person's eyes are closed. A brain lesion causes swaying or falling when eyes are open or closed.

EAR EXAM WITH AN OTOSCOPE

This test inspects the ear canal and eardrum using a hand-held instrument called an *otoscope*. (See *A look inside your ear,* page 256.) It's a basic part of any ear exam and should be performed before other ear tests. It may also be part of a routine periodic health exam. A doctor, a nurse, or an audiologist can perform this test.

Why is this test done?

An otoscopic exam may be performed for the following reasons:

- To detect foreign bodies, impacted wax, narrowing, or other problems in the ear canal
- To detect a problem in the middle ear, such as an infection or a perforated eardrum.

What should you know before the test?

This test is usually painless and takes less than 5 minutes.

HOW YOUR BODY WORKS

A look inside your ear

The ear has three parts: external, middle, and inner. Each of these parts is necessary for hearing.

External ear: Passageway for sound

The external ear consists of the auricle or pinna (the visible part) and the ear canal. These structures direct and send sound toward the eardrum. The ear canal also serves as a resonating tube, amplifying sound. The eardrum, also called the *tympanic membrane,* divides the external and middle parts of the ear.

Middle ear: The body's smallest bones within

The middle ear is a small air space that contains the body's smallest bones (ossicles): the malleus ("hammer"), the incus ("anvil"), and the stapes ("stirrups"). By their delicate vibrations, they transmit sound from the eardrum to the inner ear through a membrane called the *oval window*.

Inner ear: A sea of sound

The inner ear contains tiny organs for hearing. It also controls our sense of balance. The temporal bone surrounds and protects these interconnected, fluid-filled structures.

The organ for hearing is the cochlea. A coiled, snail-shaped tube, the cochlea contains fluid that's set in motion by the vibrations of the three tiny middle ear bones. The cochlear duct contains the organ of Corti, where sensitive hair cells convert fluid disturbances into nerve impulses. These impulses travel along the eighth cranial nerve to the brain for interpretation.

The vestibular organs, such as the semicircular canals, control balance. Changes in body position disturb the fluid in these canals and stimulate vestibular hair cells. These hair cells dispatch messages to the brain, enabling muscles to respond to position changes.

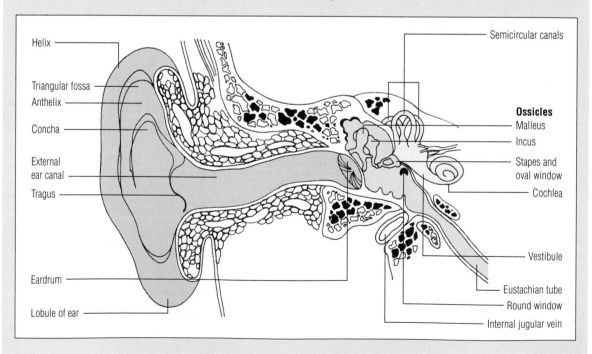

What happens during the test?

■ You sit in a chair and the examiner pulls your ear upward and backward to straighten the canal, which makes insertion of the otoscope easier.

■ The examiner looks through the otoscope's lens and check for redness, swelling, discharge, foreign bodies, or scaling in the canal.

■ Then the examiner gently advances the instrument until the eardrum is visible, checks its color and contours, and looks for any perforation. You should hold still throughout this procedure.

Does the test have risks?

■ The otoscope could irritate the ear canal, especially if it's infected.

■ The eardrum could be damaged or perforated if the otoscope is inserted too far or if the person moves abruptly during the exam.

What are the normal results?

The test should show no problems in the external and middle ear. The eardrum should look thin, translucent, shiny, and intact.

What do abnormal results mean?

Scarring, discoloration, or retraction or bulging of the eardrum indicates an infection or other problem.

HEARING TEST WITH AN AUDIOMETER

Usually performed by an audiologist, this test helps to determine the presence and degree of a hearing loss. It gives a record of the thresholds (the softest sounds) at which a person can hear a set of test tones introduced through headphones or a bone conduction (sound) vibrator.

During the test, a person will hear tones at octave frequencies between 125 and 8,000 Hertz to obtain air conduction thresholds and at frequencies between 250 and 4,000 Hertz to obtain bone conduction thresholds.

Comparison of air and bone conduction thresholds can suggest a conductive, sensorineural, or mixed hearing loss. (See *Three types of hearing loss*.) Because the test does not indicate the cause of the loss, further tests of hearing and balance as well as X-rays may be needed.

Three types of hearing loss

A hearing loss may be caused by injury or disease in any part of the ear. Doctors usually classify this loss as conductive, sensorineural, or mixed.

Conductive hearing loss

This type of hearing loss results from impaired sound transmission through the external or middle portions of the ear. These portions conduct sound vibrations to the inner ear, where the sensorineural system begins.

A conductive hearing loss may be caused by impacted wax, a perforated eardrum, a middle ear infection, or a condition called *otosclerosis*. In otosclerosis, new abnormal bone grows around the stapes, the smallest bone in the body. This new bone cements the stapes, preventing it from vibrating and sending sound to the inner ear.

Sensorineural hearing loss

A problem in the inner ear, the eighth cranial nerve, or other nerve pathways to the brain causes a sensorineural loss. The cause may be Ménière's disease, certain drugs, labyrinthitis, tumors, or MS.

Mixed hearing loss

A mixed loss is a combination problem: part conductive and part sensorineural.

Checking hearing in school children

Screening programs in nursery and elementary schools try to find children with hearing deficits. Finding such children early can avoid later problems with language development and general learning. Screening tests, performed by a nurse or audiologist and graded *pass* or *fail,* simply point out a problem and identify the need for more precise testing.

Who should be checked?

Some experts suggest yearly hearing checks for all children from preschool to grade 3. This age-group has a high rate of hearing loss.

These experts also recommend testing children with:
- speech or language problems
- learning difficulties or special needs
- classroom behavior problems, such as a lack of attention to the teacher or to classmates, unusual visual alertness, or confusion
- allergies or repeated colds or earaches
- recent placement in a new school

Why is this test done?

A hearing test with an audiometer may be performed for the following reasons:
- To determine the presence, type, and degree of hearing loss
- To check communication abilities and rehabilitation needs.

What should you know before the test?

- The test will take about 20 minutes. You and the audiologist may sit, facing each other, in a quiet room. Or, you may sit in a separate, soundproof booth.
- Just before the test, remove any jewelry or apparel that obstructs proper headphone placement.

What happens during the test?

- The audiologist checks your ear canal for impacted wax.
- Next, the audiologist presses a finger on each ear to rule out possible closure of the ear canal under pressure from the headphones. The headphones are positioned properly and the headband is tightened.
- Each ear will be checked, beginning with the ear with the better hearing (if this is known). You'll hear tones that vary in loudness and should raise your hand (or press the response button) each time you hear a tone. Respond even if the tone is very faint.

Air conduction test

- The audiologist sends a medium-pitched tone to one of your ears and reduces its loudness until you can no longer hear it. Next, the audiologist slowly increases the loudness until you can hear the tone again. Signal each time you hear the tone.
- After testing your hearing at one pitch, the audiologist changes the tone to another pitch and again varies the loudness. Altogether, the audiologist will check your hearing at seven different pitches, from very low to very high.
- After checking one ear, the audiologist repeats the test on the other ear.

Bone conduction test

- The audiologist removes the headphones and places a special vibrator on the bone behind one of your ears.
- Signal each time you hear a tone.

What happens after the test?

If test results are inconsistent, you'll need additional tests.

What are the normal results?

The normal range of hearing is 0 to 25 decibels for adults and 0 to 15 decibels for children. (See *Checking hearing in school children.*)

What do abnormal results mean?

The test indicates the degree of hearing loss. The relationship between threshold responses for air and bone conduction tones determines the type of hearing loss. In a sensorineural loss, both thresholds are depressed. In a conductive loss, air thresholds are depressed, but bone thresholds are unchanged. In a mixed hearing loss, both thresholds are abnormal, with air conduction more depressed than bone conduction.

HEARING TESTS WITH A TUNING FORK

Tuning fork tests are quick, valuable tools for detecting hearing loss and obtaining preliminary information as to its type. (See *Hearing tests: Identifying pitch and loudness.*) There are three tuning fork tests: the Weber, the Rinne, and the Schwabach.

■ The *Weber test* determines whether a person perceives the tone of the tuning fork in one ear or both.

■ The *Rinne test* compares air and bone conduction in both ears. (See *Two pathways of hearing*, page 260.)

■ The *Schwabach test* compares the person's bone conduction with that of the examiner, who is assumed to have normal hearing.

Results of these tests aren't definite. If test results indicate that the person may have a hearing problem, he or she will have to undergo another hearing test, this time with an audiometer.

Why are these tests done?

Tuning forks tests may be performed for the following reasons:

■ To check for a hearing loss

■ To help distinguish different types of hearing loss.

What should you know before the tests?

These tests are painless and take only a few minutes. Your concentration and prompt responses are essential for accurate testing.

Hearing tests: Identifying pitch and loudness

Hearing tests check a person's ability to identify sounds at different pitches and loudness levels.

Pitch

The highness or the lowness of a sound, pitch is usually called *frequency.* Measured in units known as *Hertz,* frequency is the number of times a sound vibrates in a second. Although our ears can detect frequencies of 20 to 20,000 Hertz, those between 500 and 2,000 Hertz are the most important. They're the frequencies of normal conversations in a quiet place.

Loudness

The volume of a sound — its loudness — is usually called *intensity.* It's measured in units known as *decibels.* One decibel is roughly the smallest difference in loudness that the human ear can detect. A faint whisper registers 10 to 15 decibels, whereas a normal conversation registers 50 to 60. A shout reaches 70 to 80 decibels. Louder sounds, such as a jet engine or amplified rock music, can damage hearing temporarily or even permanently.

Two pathways of hearing

Sound reaches the organ of hearing, the cochlea in the inner ear, by two routes. It can reach the cochlea by air conduction or bone conduction.

By air

In this pathway, sound travels from outside the body into the air-filled corridor called the *ear canal*. After crossing the eardrum, it passes through the air-filled spaces of the middle ear, where three tiny bones

called the *malleus* (or hammer), the *incus* (anvil), and the *stapes* (stirrups) vibrate. As they vibrate, these bones send sound to the inner ear.

By bone

In this pathway, sound travels from outside the body by conduction through surrounding bone structures and directly to the inner ear, thereby bypassing the ear canal and the middle ear.

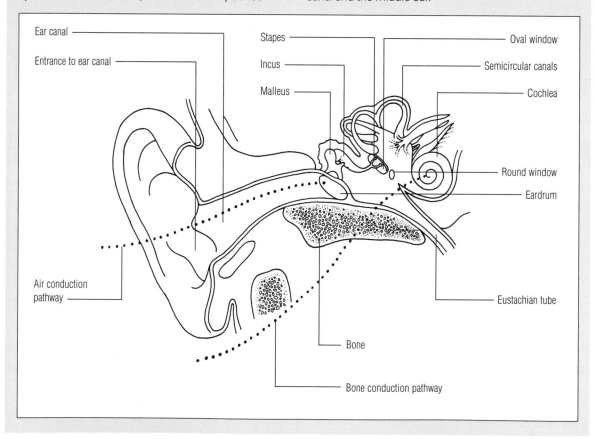

Undergoing the Weber test

This illustration shows a person undergoing the Weber tuning fork test to detect hearing loss. The base of a vibrating tuning fork is placed on the person's forehead. If the tone is louder in one ear than the other, then the person may have a conductive hearing loss in that ear.

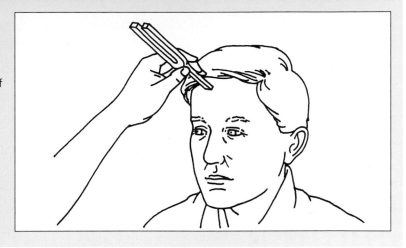

What happens during the tests?

Use hand signals to indicate whether a tone is louder in your right ear or left ear and also when you stop hearing the tone.

Weber test

■ The examiner vibrates the tuning fork and places its base on the middle of your forehead. (See *Undergoing the Weber test.*)

■ The examiner asks you if the tone is louder in your left ear or your right ear or if it's equally loud in both.

Rinne test

■ The examiner vibrates the tuning fork and places its base on a bone behind your ear.

■ Then the examiner moves the tuning fork next to your ear canal and asks which location has the louder or longer sound. After you answer, the examiner repeats the test on the other ear.

Schwabach test

■ The examiner again vibrates the tuning fork, places its base on a bone behind your ear, and asks if you hear the tone. If you do, the examiner immediately places the tuning fork behind his or her ear and listens for the tone.

■ The examiner alternates the tuning fork between the two of you until one of you stops hearing the sound.

■ The examiner repeats the test on the other ear.

What are the normal results?

A person with normal hearing will respond to the Weber test by hearing the same tone equally loud in both ears. In the Rinne test, the person will hear the air-conducted tone louder or longer than the bone-conducted tone. In the Schwabach test, the person will hear the tone for the same duration as the examiner.

What do abnormal results mean?

In the Weber test, lateralization of the tone to one ear suggests a conductive loss on that side or a sensorineural loss on the other side. If a person's hearing loss is in one ear, the Weber test may suggest the type of loss. If a person's hearing loss is in both ears, the test may help to identify the ear with the better bone conduction.

In the Rinne test, hearing the bone-conducted tone louder or longer than the air-conducted tone indicates a conductive loss. With a hearing loss in one ear, the tone may be louder when conducted by bone, but in the opposite ear. A sensorineural loss is indicated when the sound is louder by air conduction.

In the Schwabach test, hearing the tone longer than the examiner suggests a conductive loss; conversely, a shorter duration indicates a sensorineural loss.

9

SPECIAL FUNCTION TESTS:
Evaluating the Body's Responses

DIGESTION & EXCRETION

ACID PERFUSION TEST

Also called the *Bernstein test,* the acid perfusion test evaluates the competence of the lower esophageal sphincter (the valve that prevents acidic stomach juices from backing up the esophagus and irritating it). In some cases, the pyloric sphincter, which prevents backflow of bile salts, may be similarly evaluated. Esophageal irritation causes burning pains above the stomach or behind the breastbone, which radiate to the back or the arms. This test distinguishes chest pains caused by digestive tract problems from those caused by heart problems. To perform this test, the doctor delivers different liquids into the esophagus through a tube.

The acid perfusion test distinguishes chest pains caused by digestive tract problems from those caused by heart problems.

Why is this test done?

The acid perfusion test may be performed to distinguish chest pains caused by esophagitis from those caused by heart disease.

What should you know before the test?

■ This test usually lasts about 1 hour. It involves passing a tube through your nose into the esophagus, during which you may feel discomfort, a desire to cough, or a gagging sensation.
■ Follow these restrictions: no antacids for 24 hours before the test, no food for 12 hours, and no fluids or smoking for 8 hours.

What happens during the test?

■ After you're seated, the doctor inserts a thin tube through your nose into your stomach—a distance of about 12 inches (30 centimeters).
■ The doctor attaches a syringe to the tube and draws up some of the stomach contents. Next, the doctor pulls the tube back into the esophagus and delivers liquids through it. Tell the doctor if you feel any pain or a burning sensation.
■ The doctor removes the tube.

What happens after the test?

- If you feel stomach pain or burning, the nurse will give you an antacid. If you have a sore throat, the nurse will give you lozenges.
- You may resume your usual diet and any medications withheld for the test.

Does the test have risks?

- The test shouldn't be done if a person has recently had a heart attack or has a history of esophageal varices, heart failure, or other heart diseases.
- The test can cause severe coughing if the catheter enters the windpipe instead of the esophagus.
- An irregular heartbeat can develop during insertion of the catheter.

What are the normal results?

Absence of pain or burning is the normal result.

What do abnormal results mean?

Pain or burning during the test indicates esophagitis.

CYSTOMETRY

This test checks the bladder's neuromuscular function. Because cystometry results can be ambiguous, additional tests, such as cystourethrography and intravenous pyelography, may be necessary.

Why is this test done?

Cystometry may be performed for the following reasons:
- To evaluate detrusor muscle function and tone (the detrusor muscle surrounds the bladder and on contraction serves to expel urine)
- To help determine the cause of a bladder problem.

What should you know before the test?

- The test usually lasts about 40 minutes unless additional tests are ordered.
- You should urinate just before the procedure.

- You'll feel a strong urge to urinate during the test and may feel embarrassed or uncomfortable.
- You'll be asked to sign a form that gives your permission to do the test. Read the form carefully and ask questions if any portion of it isn't clear.

When the bladder reaches its full capacity, you're asked to urinate so that the full bladder pressure can be measured.

What happens during the test?

- You lie on your back on the examining table.
- The doctor inserts a thin catheter through the urethra into the bladder to measure residual urine level.
- To test the bladder's response to thermal sensation, the doctor puts a small amount of liquid into your bladder. Tell the doctor if you feel the need to urinate or if you feel nauseated, flushed, or uncomfortable.
- Next, the doctor connects the catheter to the cystometer and puts more fluid or a gas into the bladder. Let the doctor know when you *first* feel an urge to void and then when you feel you *must* urinate.
- When the bladder reaches its full capacity, you're asked to urinate so that the full bladder pressure can be measured. The bladder is then drained and, if no additional tests are required, the catheter is removed.

What happens after the test?

- Take a sitz bath or warm tub bath if you feel discomfort.
- You may have some blood in your urine. If you still have it after urinating three times, tell the doctor or nurse.

Does the test have risks?

Cystometry shouldn't be performed if a person has a urinary tract infection.

What are the normal results?

The test should show no abnormal pressures, volumes, or sensations. The bladder should be able to hold about a pint of fluid.

What do abnormal results mean?

The test can identify a condition called *neurogenic bladder,* in which a lesion in the nervous system affects urination.

ESOPHAGEAL ACIDITY TEST

This test checks the function of the lower esophageal sphincter — the circular band of muscles that tightens to prevent the backward flow of acidic digestive juices from the stomach into the esophagus. When this muscle doesn't function as it should, the esophagus becomes inflamed, causing heartburn.

The test measures the pH, or the level of acidity, within the esophagus using an electrode attached to a catheter.

Why is this test done?

The esophageal acidity test may be performed for the following reasons:
- To check the competence of the lower esophageal sphincter
- To evaluate complaints of persistent heartburn.

What should you know before the test?

- You'll learn about the test, including who will perform it, where it will take place, and its duration (about 45 minutes). During the test, a tube will be passed through your mouth into your stomach and you may experience slight discomfort, a desire to cough, or a gagging sensation.
- The doctor may tell you not to take medications, such as antacids or drugs for ulcers, for 24 hours before the test.
- You'll probably be told that you must fast and refrain from smoking after midnight before the test.

What happens during the test?

- The doctor inserts a catheter into your mouth. Swallow when it reaches the back of your throat.
- Using the catheter, the doctor positions the pH electrode at the lower esophageal sphincter. You're asked to bear down as if you're trying to have a bowel movement or to lift your legs. After you do, the doctor measures the pH in the esophagus.
- If the pH is normal, the doctor moves the catheter into your stomach and instills a solution to help fill the stomach. To test sphincter function, the doctor raises the catheter and asks you to perform the same movements again.

When the lower esophageal sphincter fails to tighten and hold back stomach acid, your esophagus becomes inflamed, causing heartburn.

What happens after the test?

- You may resume your usual diet and restart any medications that were withheld for the test.
- Tell the nurse if you have a sore throat. You can have lozenges.

Does the test have risks?

- The test can cause severe coughing if the catheter enters the windpipe instead of the esophagus.
- An irregular heartbeat can develop during the insertion of the catheter.

What are the normal results?

The pH of the esophagus normally exceeds 5.0.

What do abnormal results mean?

A severely acid pH of 1.5 to 2.0 indicates backward flow of digestive juices because the lower esophageal sphincter doesn't tighten sufficiently. Additional tests, such as a barium swallow, are necessary.

D-XYLOSE ABSORPTION TEST

This test evaluates people who have symptoms of malabsorption, such as weight loss, malnutrition, weakness, and diarrhea. The test uses a sugar called *D-xylose* that's absorbed in the small intestine, passed through the liver without being metabolized, and excreted in the urine. Because it is absorbed in the small intestine without being digested, measurement of D-xylose in the urine and blood indicates the absorptive capacity of the small intestine.

Why is this test done?

The D-xylose absorption test may be performed to help diagnose malabsorption and identify its cause.

What should you know before the test?

■ You must fast overnight before the test and will have to fast and remain in bed during the test.

■ Several blood samples will be taken during the test. You may feel some discomfort from the needle punctures and the pressure of the tourniquet.

■ Your urine will be collected for a 5- or 24-hour period.

■ Don't take any aspirin before the test.

What happens during the test?

■ During the test period, you need to stay in bed. You won't be able to eat or drink anything (other than the D-xylose).

■ The nurse inserts a needle into a vein in your arm and collects a blood sample. The nurse also collects a urine sample.

■ You receive a small amount of D-xylose dissolved in 8 ounces (240 milliliters) of water, followed by an additional 8 ounces of water.

■ The nurse collects a blood sample 2 hours later and also collects all urine during the 5 or 24 hours after D-xylose ingestion.

What happens after the test?

■ You may have an upset stomach or mild diarrhea.

■ You may resume your usual diet.

What are the normal results?

The normal results vary by a person's age:

■ Children: more than 2.0 nanomoles of D-xylose per liter of blood in 1 hour; urine, 16% to 33% of ingested D-xylose excreted in 5 hours

■ Adults under age 65: 1.7 to 2.7 nanomoles of D-xylose per liter of blood in 2 hours; urine, more than 4 grams excreted in 5 hours

■ Adults over age 65: 1.7 to 2.7 nanomoles of D-xylose per liter of blood in 2 hours; urine, more than 3.5 grams excreted in 5 hours and more than 5 grams excreted in 24 hours.

What do abnormal results mean?

Low blood and urine D-xylose levels are usually caused by malabsorption disorders, such as sprue and celiac disease. However, low levels may also be caused by enteritis, Whipple's disease, multiple jejunal diverticula, myxedema, rheumatoid arthritis, alcoholism, severe heart failure, and fluid in the abdomen.

EXTERNAL SPHINCTER ELECTROMYOGRAPHY

This test determines how well the bladder and urinary sphincter muscles work together. The urinary sphincter is a ringlike band of muscles that constricts around the urethra and helps to control urination.

External sphincter electromyography measures the electrical activity of the external urinary sphincter using skin electrodes or other devices.

The test is done primarily for people who have lost control over their urination. Often, a person who is given this test will also undergo cystometry and voiding urethrography tests.

Loss of control over urination is the primary reason for performing external sphincter electromyography.

Why is this test done?

External sphincter electromyography may be performed for the following reasons:
- To check the neuromuscular function of the external urinary sphincter
- To check the functional balance between bladder and sphincter muscle activity.

What should you know before the test?

- This test usually lasts 30 to 60 minutes.
- When a man is being tested, the nurse may shave hair from a small area behind the scrotum. When a woman is being tested, the nurse may shave a small area around the urethra.

What happens during the test?

- As you lie on the examining table, the nurse applies electrode paste and tapes the electrodes in place.
- After electrode placement, the recording starts. You're asked to alternately relax and tighten the sphincter.
- When sufficient data have been recorded, the nurse removes the electrodes gently and cleans and dries the area.

What happens after the test?

- Tell the doctor or nurse if you feel pain or observe any blood during urination.
- Take a warm bath and drink plenty of fluids.

Does the test have risks?

The test can irritate the urethra, producing painful and frequent urination and blood in the urine.

What are the normal results?

The test shows increased muscle activity when the person tightens the external urinary sphincter and decreased muscle activity when he or she relaxes it.

What do abnormal results mean?

Failure of the sphincter to relax or increased muscle activity during urination suggests a disorder, such as neurogenic bladder, spinal cord injury, multiple sclerosis, Parkinson's disease, or stress incontinence.

URINE FLOW TEST

This simple test uses a device called a *uroflowmeter* to detect and evaluate an abnormal pattern of urination. The uroflowmeter is contained in a funnel into which the person urinates. This device records flow patterns and measures the volume of urine voided per second, time of measurable urine flow, and total voiding time, including any interruptions.

Why is this test done?

The urine flow test may be performed for the following reasons:

- To evaluate bladder function
- To indicate a blockage of the bladder outlet.

What should you know before the test?

- This test usually lasts 10 to 15 minutes.
- Don't urinate for several hours before the test and drink plenty of fluids so you'll have a full bladder and a strong urge to void.
- You'll have complete privacy during the test.

What happens during the test?

- Remain still while urinating and don't strain.
- Push the flowmeter start button, count for 5 seconds, and urinate. When you're finished, count for 5 seconds and push the button again.

What are the normal results?

Normal flow rates depend on the person's age and sex and the volume of urine voided.

What do abnormal results mean?

This test can detect reduced resistance in the urethra, stress incontinence, bladder outlet obstruction, or poor tone of the detrusor muscle.

MISCELLANEOUS TESTS

COLD STIMULATION TEST FOR RAYNAUD'S SYNDROME

This test helps the doctor to detect Raynaud's syndrome, a circulatory disorder that affects the fingers and occasionally the toes (see *What Raynaud's syndrome feels like*). This test works by recording temperature changes in the fingers before and after they're put into ice water.

Why is this test done?

The cold stimulation test is performed to detect Raynaud's syndrome.

What should you know before the test?

- This test usually lasts 20 to 40 minutes. You may feel uncomfortable when your hands are briefly immersed in ice water.
- During the test, remove your watch and other jewelry from your wrists. Try to relax.

What happens during the test?

- The nurse tapes a temperature-measuring device to each of your fingers and records the temperature.
- Submerge your hands in the ice water for 20 seconds. After you remove them, the nurse records the temperature of your fingers immediately and every 5 minutes thereafter until the temperature returns to the pretest level.

Does the test have risks?

The cold stimulation test shouldn't be done if a person has gangrene or open, infected wounds on the fingers.

What are the normal results?

Normally, the temperature of the fingers returns to the pretest level within 15 minutes.

What do abnormal results mean?

If the temperature of the fingers takes longer than 20 minutes to return to the pretest level, the person may have Raynaud's syndrome.

What Raynaud's syndrome feels like

Raynaud's syndrome causes episodes during which the small arteries in the hands and sometimes the feet tighten. As a consequence, not enough blood reaches the fingers or toes, which may become pale and feel numb or tingling. Stress or exposure to cold temperatures brings on the reaction.

Who's at risk?

Raynaud's syndrome afflicts women five times more often than men. For the most part, it first strikes between the late teens and age 40.

DEXAMETHASONE SUPPRESSION TEST

In this test, the doctor measures hormone levels to screen for depression or for Cushing's syndrome, a disorder in which excessive steroid hormones appear in the blood. During the test, a person takes the drug dexamethasone, which reduces steroid hormones in healthy people. However, the drug fails to lower steroid levels in people with Cushing's syndrome or some forms of depression.

Why is this test done?

The dexamethasone suppression test may be performed for the following reasons:
- To diagnose Cushing's syndrome
- To help diagnose depression.

What should you know before the test?

- Don't eat or drink fluids for 12 hours before the test.
- Tell the doctor or nurse if you're taking any medications that may affect the test. Many drugs, including steroids, oral contraceptives, lithium, methadone, aspirin, diuretics, and morphine, can't be taken after midnight on the night before the test.
- After you receive dexamethasone, two blood samples will be taken during the test. You may feel some discomfort from the needle punctures and the pressure of the tourniquet.

What happens during the test?

- You receive a small dose of dexamethasone at 11 p.m.
- The next day, the nurse takes blood samples at 4 p.m. and 11 p.m.

A normal result doesn't rule out depression, but an abnormal result strengthens the diagnosis.

What happens after the test?

If swelling develops at the needle puncture site, warm soaks may be applied to ease discomfort.

What are the normal results?

A blood cortisol level of 138 or more nanomoles per liter indicates failure of dexamethasone suppression.

What do abnormal results mean?

A normal result doesn't rule out depression, but an abnormal result strengthens the diagnosis. An abnormal result occurs in people with Cushing's syndrome, severe stress, and depression that's likely to respond to treatment with antidepressant drugs.

PULMONARY FUNCTION TESTS

Pulmonary function tests evaluate the amount of air a person is able to breathe in and out of the lungs. A device called a *spirometer* measures the amount of air entering and leaving the lungs.

These tests are performed on people with suspected lung problems.

Why are these tests done?

Pulmonary function tests may be performed for these reasons:
- To determine the cause of shortness of breath
- To determine if a lung problem is caused by an obstructive disease (which blocks the breathing passageways) or a restrictive disease (which hinders the expansion of the lungs)
- To check the effectiveness of treatments for breathing problems
- To evaluate a person's breathing before surgery.

What should you know before the tests?

- Before the tests, you'll be shown how to use a spirometer.
- Eat only a light meal before the tests. If you're a smoker, you won't be able to smoke for 4 to 6 hours before the tests.
- The accuracy of the tests depends on your cooperation. The tests are painless and you will be allowed time to rest between each test.
- Just before the tests, you should urinate and loosen tight clothing. If you wear dentures, you can keep them in during the tests to help form a seal around the mouthpiece.
- You'll need to wear a noseclip for some of the tests.

What happens during the tests?

- To measure *tidal volume,* you breathe normally into the mouthpiece 10 times.
- To measure *expiratory reserve volume,* you breathe normally for several breaths and then exhale as completely as possible.
- To measure *vital capacity,* you inhale as deeply as possible and exhale into the mouthpiece as completely as possible, three times. The test result showing the largest volume is used.
- To measure *inspiratory capacity,* you breathe normally for several breaths and then inhale as deeply as possible.
- To measure *functional residual capacity,* you breathe normally into a spirometer that contains an inert gas (usually helium or nitrogen) in a known volume of air. After a few breaths, the concentration of inert gas in the spirometer and in the lungs reaches equilibrium. The point of equilibrium and the concentration of gas in the spirometer is recorded.
- To measure *thoracic gas volume,* you're put into an airtight box and asked to breathe through a tube. At the end of an exhalation, the tube is blocked and you're asked to pant.
- To measure *forced vital capacity* and *forced expiratory volume,* you inhale as slowly and deeply as possible and then exhale into the mouthpiece as quickly and completely as possible, three times.

To measure what doctors call vital capacity, you inhale as deeply as possible and exhale into the mouthpiece as completely as possible, three times.

■ To measure *maximal voluntary ventilation,* you breathe into the mouthpiece as quickly and deeply as possible for 15 seconds.

■ To measure *diffusing capacity for carbon monoxide,* you inhale a gas mixture and then hold your breath for 10 seconds before exhaling.

What happens after the tests?

You can resume your usual diet and daily activities.

Do the tests have risks?

Pulmonary function tests shouldn't be done if a person has chest pains (angina), has had a recent heart attack, or has a severe heart problem.

What are the normal results?

The normal results depend on a person's age, height, weight, and sex and are often expressed as a percentage. The following results are normal:

■ Tidal volume: 5 to 7 milliliters per kilogram of body weight

■ Expiratory reserve volume: 25% of vital capacity

■ Inspiratory capacity: 75% of vital capacity

■ Forced expiratory volume: 83% of vital capacity after 1 second, 94% after 2 seconds, and 97% after 3 seconds.

What do abnormal results mean?

Usually, results are considered abnormal if they're less than 80% of normal results. Abnormal results can suggest a number of obstructive lung diseases, such as emphysema and chronic bronchitis, and restrictive diseases, such as pulmonary fibrosis.

TENSILON TEST

A doctor performs this test to help determine the cause of muscle weakness. The test is named after the drug Tensilon (also known as *edrophonium),* a rapid-acting drug that improves muscle strength.

Why is this test done?

The Tensilon test may be performed for the following reasons:

■ To help diagnose myasthenia gravis, a disorder marked by faulty transmission of impulses from nerves to muscles, leading to muscular weakness

■ To tell the difference between myasthenic and cholinergic crises; a myasthenic crisis may occur in people with myasthenia gravis and is marked by difficulty in breathing; a cholinergic crisis is similar but results from drugs used to treat myasthenia gravis

■ To monitor oral cholinesterase therapy.

What should you know before the test?

■ You won't have to restrict food or fluids beforehand.

■ You'll be asked if you're taking any medications that affect muscle function, if you're receiving anticholinesterase therapy, or if you have drug hypersensitivities or respiratory disease.

■ The test usually lasts 15 to 30 minutes. During the test, a small tube will be inserted into a vein in your arm and the drug Tensilon will be given periodically. You'll be asked to make repetitive muscle movements.

■ Tensilon may produce some unpleasant effects, but someone will be with you at all times during the test and any reactions will quickly disappear.

■ To ensure accuracy, the test may be repeated several times.

What happens during the test?

■ The nurse inserts an intravenous line.

■ The doctor may initially give a small dose of Tensilon and ask you to do various exercises, such as counting to 100 until your voice diminishes or holding your arms above your shoulders until they drop. When the muscles are fatigued, the doctor injects the rest of the Tensilon.

■ After Tensilon is administered, you're asked to perform repetitive muscle movements, such as opening and closing your eyes and crossing and uncrossing your legs. The test may be repeated.

What happens after the test?

The nurse will remove the intravenous line and will check on you.

After you take Tensilon, you're asked to perform repetitive muscle movements, such as opening and closing your eyes and crossing and uncrossing your legs.

Does the test have risks?

■ Because Tensilon may cause side effects, the doctor may choose not to perform this test in people with very low blood pressure, a slow heart rate, or a blockage in the intestine or urinary tract.

■ People with respiratory ailments such as asthma should receive the drug atropine during the test to minimize the side effects of Tensilon.

What are the normal results?

People who don't have myasthenia gravis usually develop small muscle contractions in response to Tensilon.

What do abnormal results mean?

If a person has myasthenia gravis, muscle strength should improve within 30 seconds after administration of Tensilon. All people with myasthenia gravis show improved strength in this test; some, however, respond only slightly and may have to undergo a repeat test to confirm the diagnosis.

People in myasthenic crisis show brief improvement in muscle strength after Tensilon administration. Those in cholinergic crisis may experience greater weakness.

BLOOD CELL & CLOTTING TESTS:
Screening for Blood Diseases

BLOOD CELL COUNTS

RED BLOOD CELL COUNT

A red blood cell count is part of a group of tests known as the *complete blood count*. The most vital role of red blood cells is carrying oxygen from the lungs to other tissues and carrying waste gases from other tissues to the lungs for expulsion from the body. The red blood cell count is used to find out how many red blood cells are in a sample of blood. (See *Blood: Its vital functions*, page 282.)

Why is this test done?
A red blood cell count may be performed for the following reasons:
- To find out the number and sizes of red blood cells
- To evaluate the protein content and condition of red blood cells
- To support other tests for diagnosing blood problems.

What should you know before the test?
- You don't need to change your diet before the test.
- You may feel slight discomfort from the tourniquet pressure and the needle puncture.
- Drawing a blood sample takes less than 3 minutes.

What happens during the test?
- A nurse or medical technician inserts a needle into a vein, usually in your forearm. A blood sample is collected in a tube, which is then sent to a lab for testing.
- When a young child has this test, a small amount of blood is taken from the finger or earlobe.

What happens after the test?
If swelling develops at the needle puncture site, warm soaks are applied to the area to ease discomfort.

HOW YOUR BODY WORKS

Blood: Its vital functions

Blood is a fluid tissue that performs many vital functions as it circulates through the body. Most important is its ability to transport oxygen from the lungs to other body tissues and to return carbon dioxide from the tissues to the lungs to be exhaled.

Other functions performed by the blood include coagulation (clotting), which stops bleeding and helps heal injuries; regulation of body temperature; maintenance of acid-base and fluid balances in the body; movement of nutrients and hormones to body tissues; and disposal of wastes through the kidneys, lungs, and skin.

Characteristics of blood

Blood is three times thicker than water, tastes slightly salty, and is slightly alkaline, or basic, the opposite of acidic. Oxygen-rich blood flows through the body in vessels called *arteries*; oxygen-depleted blood is carried away from the organs and tissues in vessels called *veins*. Blood in the arteries is bright red; oxygen-poor blood in the veins is dark red.

Components of blood

Blood has two major components: plasma, which is the clear, straw-colored liquid portion, and the formed elements — red blood cells, white blood cells, and platelets — which help in clotting.

Red blood cells are also known as *erythrocytes* and *red corpuscles*. Red blood cells carry oxygen from the lungs to the tissues and carbon dioxide from the tissues back to the lungs to be exhaled. The white blood cells, which are also called *leukocytes,* help the body fight infection. Blood also contains several important forms of protein.

What are the normal results?

Normal red blood cell counts vary, depending on the type of sample and on the person's age and sex:

- Men: 4.2 to 5.4×10^{12} red blood cells per liter of blood
- Women: 3.6 to 5.0×10^{12} red blood cells per liter of blood
- Children: 4.6 to 4.8×10^{12} red blood cells per liter of blood
- Full-term infants: 4.4 to 5.8×10^{12} red blood cells per liter of blood at birth, decreasing to 3 to 3.8×10^{12} at age 2 months and increasing slowly thereafter.

Normal counts may be higher in people living at high altitudes.

What do abnormal results mean?

An elevated red blood cell count may indicate polycythemia. A depressed count may indicate anemia, fluid overload, or severe bleeding. Further blood tests are needed to confirm a diagnosis.

HEMATOCRIT

This test measures the percentage of red blood cells, or *hematocrit*, in a blood sample. For example, 40% hematocrit means there are 40 milliliters of red blood cells in a 100-milliliter sample.

Why is this test done?

A hematocrit test may be performed for the following reasons:
- To help diagnose blood disorders, such as polycythemia, anemia, or abnormal hydration
- To calculate the volume and concentration of blood particles.

What should you know before the test?

- You don't need to change your diet before the test.
- A small blood sample is required for this test.

What happens during the test?

- A nurse or medical technician cleans your fingertip and then punctures it with a small lancet.
- A blood sample is drawn into a small device called a *capillary tube.*
- The tube is sealed and then placed in a centrifuge to separate the red hematocrit from the clear portion of the blood.
- A small amount of blood may be taken from the finger or earlobe of a small child.

What happens after the test?

If swelling develops at the needle puncture site, warm soaks are applied to the area to ease discomfort.

What are the normal results?

Hematocrit is usually measured electronically. Normal levels vary, depending on the type of sample, the lab procedure, and the person's sex and age. (See *Hematocrit values throughout the lifespan,* page 284.)

What do abnormal results mean?

Low hematocrit suggests anemia or massive blood loss. High hematocrit indicates a problem due to blood loss or dehydration.

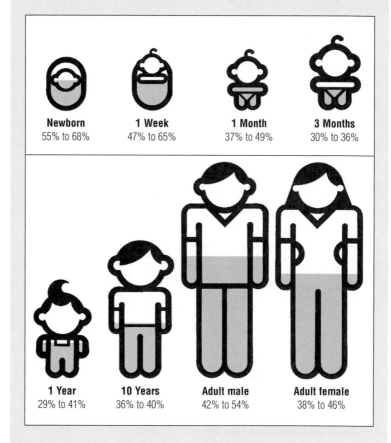

 HOW YOUR BODY WORKS

Hematocrit values throughout the lifespan

Hematocrit test results show the percentage of packed red blood cells in a whole blood sample. Values vary with a person's age. The values shown below are normal for the age-groups shown.

Newborn
55% to 68%

1 Week
47% to 65%

1 Month
37% to 49%

3 Months
30% to 36%

1 Year
29% to 41%

10 Years
36% to 40%

Adult male
42% to 54%

Adult female
38% to 46%

RED CELL INDICES

The red cell indices are calculated using the results of the red blood cell count, hematocrit, and total hemoglobin tests. These indices provide important information about the size, hemoglobin level, and hemoglobin weight of an average red cell.

Why is this test done?

Red cell indices are calculated to help diagnose anemia.

What should you know before the test?

- This test requires a blood sample, which takes less than 3 minutes to collect.
- You may feel slight discomfort from the needle puncture and tourniquet pressure.

What happens during the test?

A nurse or medical technician inserts a needle into a vein, usually in your forearm. A blood sample is collected in a tube, which is then sent to a lab for testing.

What happens after the test?

If swelling develops at the needle puncture site, warm soaks are applied to the area to ease discomfort.

What are the normal results?

The indices tested include mean corpuscular volume, mean corpuscular hemoglobin, and mean corpuscular hemoglobin concentration.

Mean corpuscular volume, the ratio of hematocrit to the red blood cell count, expresses the average size of the red blood cells and indicates whether they're microcytic (undersized), macrocytic (oversized), or normocytic (normal). Mean corpuscular hemoglobin gives the weight of hemoglobin (a type of protein) in an average red cell. Mean corpuscular hemoglobin concentration, the ratio of hemoglobin weight to hematocrit, defines the level of hemoglobin in 100 milliliters of packed red cells. It helps distinguish normochromic (normally colored) red cells from hypochromic (paler) red cells.

The range of normal red cell indices is as follows:
- Mean corpuscular volume: 84 to 99 femtoliters
- Mean corpuscular hemoglobin: 26 to 32 picograms
- Mean corpuscular hemoglobin concentration: 30% to 36%.

What do abnormal results mean?

Low mean corpuscular volume and mean corpuscular hemoglobin concentration can indicate iron deficiency anemia, pyridoxine-responsive anemia, or thalassemia. A high mean corpuscular volume suggests macrocytic anemias.

ERYTHROCYTE SEDIMENTATION RATE

This test measures the rate at which erythrocytes (red blood cells) settle in a blood sample during a specified time period. The erythrocyte sedimentation rate is a sensitive but nonspecific test that's frequently the earliest indicator of disease when other tests or physical signs are normal. The erythrocyte sedimentation rate commonly increases greatly in widespread inflammatory disorders; elevations may be prolonged in localized inflammation or cancer.

A change in the erythrocyte sedimentation rate is frequently the first indicator of disease.

Why is this test done?

The erythrocyte sedimentation rate may be measured for the following reasons:
- To evaluate the condition of red blood cells
- To monitor inflammatory or malignant disease
- To aid detection and diagnosis of such diseases as tuberculosis and connective tissue disease.

What should you know before the test?

- This test requires a blood sample, which takes less than 3 minutes to collect.
- You may feel slight discomfort from the needle puncture and tourniquet pressure.
- You don't need to change your diet before the test.

What happens during the test?

A nurse or medical technician inserts a needle into a vein, usually in your forearm. A blood sample is collected in a tube, which is then sent to a lab for testing.

What happens after the test?

If swelling develops at the needle puncture site, warm soaks are applied to the area to ease discomfort.

What are the normal results?

Normal sedimentation rates range from 0 to 20 millimeters per hour. The rates gradually increase with age.

What do abnormal results mean?

The erythrocyte sedimentation rate increases in pregnancy, anemia, acute or chronic inflammation, tuberculosis, rheumatic fever, rheumatoid arthritis, and some cancers.

Polycythemia, sickle cell anemia, hyperviscosity, and low plasma fibrinogen or globulin levels tend to slow the erythrocyte sedimentation rate.

RETICULOCYTE COUNT

Reticulocytes are immature red blood cells. They're generally larger than mature red blood cells. In this test, reticulocytes in a blood sample are counted. The number of reticulocytes is then expressed as a percentage of the total red cell count. Because only a small blood sample is used, the test result may be imprecise. Therefore, the reticulocyte count is compared with red blood cell count or hematocrit test results.

Why is this test done?

A reticulocyte count may be performed for the following reasons:
- To detect anemia or to monitor its treatment
- To distinguish between types of anemias
- To help assess blood loss or the bone marrow's response to anemia.

What should you know before the test?

- You don't need to change your diet before the test.
- This test requires a blood sample, which takes less than 3 minutes to collect.
- You may feel slight discomfort from the needle puncture and tourniquet pressure.

HOW YOUR BODY WORKS

Understanding bone marrow's role

Bone marrow is soft tissue that is found mostly in the cavities of long bones, such as the femur, or thigh bone; humerous, or upper arm bone; and sternum, or upper chest bones.

Blood from bones

Marrow produces the body's blood cells. Just before a person's birth, the marrow of all bones produces red blood cells. The amount of blood-producing marrow decreases as a person grows; by adulthood, the marrow of the sternum and ribs and of the vertebrae (backbone) and pelvis (hips) produces most red cells. Red blood cell production decreases with advancing age.

Bone marrow is either red or yellow. Red marrow, which is found mostly in the spongy tissue at the ends of bones, produces red blood cells, white blood cells, and platelets, which help the blood clot after injury. Yellow marrow, which replaces red marrow as the patient ages, is mostly inactive. It lies in the spongy tissue at the ends of a bone and in a canal that runs through the center of the bone.

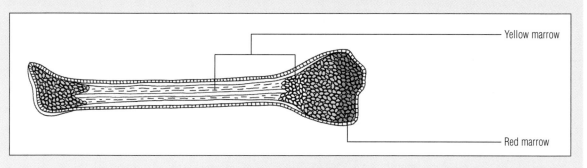

Yellow marrow

Red marrow

■ Medications that may affect test results are withheld before this test, whenever possible.

What happens during the test?

■ A nurse or medical technician inserts a needle into a vein, usually in your forearm. A blood sample is collected in a tube, which is then sent to a lab for testing.

■ A small amount of blood is taken from the finger or earlobe when an infant or child is tested.

What happens after the test?

■ If swelling develops at the needle puncture site, warm soaks are applied to the area to ease discomfort.

■ You may resume taking medications that were withheld before the test.

■ If the results of your test show an abnormal reticulocyte count, it may be repeated to detect trends or changes.

What are the normal results?

Reticulocytes compose 0.5% to 2% of the total red blood cell count. In infants the normal reticulocyte count ranges from 2% to 6% at birth, decreasing to adult levels in 1 to 2 weeks.

What do abnormal results mean?

A low reticulocyte count indicates hypoplastic or pernicious anemia.

A high reticulocyte count may occur after therapy for iron deficiency anemia or pernicious anemia. An increased reticulocyte count also may indicate hemolysis (red blood cell rupture) or a bone marrow response to anemia due to blood loss. (See *Understanding bone marrow's role.*)

TOTAL HEMOGLOBIN

Hemoglobin is a type of protein in red blood cells. Its purpose is to carry oxygen in the blood. The total hemoglobin test is used to measure the amount of hemoglobin per liter of whole blood. It's usually part of a complete blood count. Hemoglobin concentration correlates closely with the red blood cell count.

Why is this test done?

A total hemoglobin test may be performed for the following reasons:
■ To detect anemia or polycythemia or to assess your response to treatment for these disorders
■ To help the doctor calculate additional information for a complete blood count.

What should you know before the test?

■ You don't need to change your diet before the test.
■ This test requires a blood sample, which takes less than 3 minutes to collect.
■ You may feel slight discomfort from the needle puncture and tourniquet pressure.

What happens during the test?

■ A nurse or medical technician inserts a needle into a vein, usually in your forearm. A blood sample is collected in a tube, which is then sent to a lab for testing.

■ A small amount of blood is taken from the finger or earlobe when a young child is tested.

What happens after the test?

If swelling develops at the needle puncture site, warm soaks are applied to the area to ease discomfort.

What are the normal results?

Hemoglobin concentration varies, depending on the type of sample drawn (capillary blood samples for infants and venous blood samples for all others) and on the person's age and sex. (See *Hemoglobin values throughout the lifespan.*)

What do abnormal results mean?

Low hemoglobin concentration may indicate anemia, recent hemorrhage, or fluid retention. All three cause hemodilution.

Elevated hemoglobin suggests hemoconcentration from polycythemia or dehydration.

HEMOGLOBIN ELECTROPHORESIS

This test separates and measures normal and some abnormal forms of hemoglobin in the blood. In this test, a blood sample is placed on a material that allows it to separate into a series of distinctly pigmented bands. Results are compared with those of a normal sample.

Why is this test done?

This test may be performed for the following reasons:

■ To calculate the different components of hemoglobin

■ To aid the diagnosis of thalassemia.

HOW YOUR BODY WORKS

Hemoglobin values throughout the lifespan

Hemoglobin test results show the amount of hemoglobin in a person's blood. The results are expressed in grams of hemoglobin per deciliter of whole blood. Hemoglobin values vary with a person's age. For example, the normal hemoglobin range for an adult woman is 120 to 160 grams of hemoglobin for each liter of blood in her body.

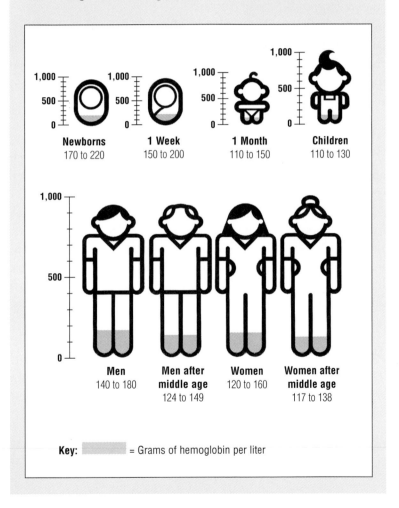

Newborns
170 to 220

1 Week
150 to 200

1 Month
110 to 150

Children
110 to 130

Men
140 to 180

Men after middle age
124 to 149

Women
120 to 160

Women after middle age
117 to 138

Key: ▭ = Grams of hemoglobin per liter

What should you know before the test?

- You don't need to change your diet before the test.
- This test requires a blood sample, which takes less than 3 minutes to collect.
- You may feel slight discomfort from the needle puncture and tourniquet pressure.
- The nurse or technician checks your history for blood transfusions within the past 4 months.

What happens during the test?

- A nurse or medical technician inserts a needle into a vein, usually in your forearm. A blood sample is collected in a tube, which is then sent to a lab for testing.
- When the test is performed on an infant or child, a small amount of blood is taken from the finger or earlobe.

What happens after the test?

If swelling develops at the needle puncture site, warm soaks are applied to the area to ease discomfort.

What are the normal results?

Various components of hemoglobin are labeled hemoglobin A, hemoglobin A_2, hemoglobin S, hemoglobin F, and so forth. In adults, hemoglobin A accounts for more than 95% of all hemoglobins; hemoglobin A_2, 2% to 3%; and hemoglobin F, less than 1%. In newborns, hemoglobin F normally accounts for half the total. Hemoglobins A and C are normally absent.

What do abnormal results mean?

This test allows identification of various types of hemoglobin. Certain types may indicate various hemolytic diseases — such as thalassemia — which are characterized by ruptured red blood cells.

INSIGHT INTO ILLNESS

Who inherits sickle cell anemia?

The most serious risk of inheriting this disorder occurs when both parents have sickle cell anemia (figure 1). Childbearing — if possible at all — is dangerous for the mother, and all offspring will have sickle cell anemia.

When one parent has sickle cell anemia and one does not (figure 2), all offspring will be carriers of sickle cell anemia. This means they carry and can pass on to their children a trait for the disorder, yet show no outward signs of the illness themselves.

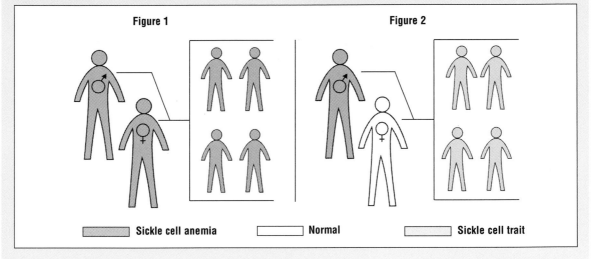

Figure 1 **Figure 2**

Sickle cell anemia Normal Sickle cell trait

SICKLE CELL TEST

Also known as the *hemoglobin S test*, this test detects *sickle cells* in the bloodstream. These are severely deformed, rigid red blood cells that may slow blood flow. Sickle cell disease almost exclusively affects people with African ancestry. The prevalence of the disease within this group is estimated at between 1 in 100 and 1 in 200. (See *Who inherits sickle cell anemia?*)

Although this test is useful as a rapid screening procedure, the results may not be accurate. The hemoglobin component test is performed to confirm the diagnosis if the presence of hemoglobin S is strongly suspected. (See *Prenatal test for sickle cell anemia,* page 294.)

INSIGHT INTO ILLNESS

Prenatal test for sickle cell anemia

When both parents of a developing fetus are suspected carriers of sickle cell trait, a reliable test is now available that can detect whether the fetus has the sickle cell trait or the disease. Many major medical centers throughout North America perform the test. Also, any doctor can request the fetal sickle cell test if both parents are suspected carriers.

An opportunity for counseling
The test requires a blood sample from both parents and an amniotic fluid sample. About 1 week is required to complete the test, which can generally be performed between the 14th and 18th weeks of pregnancy. This provides an opportunity for the parents to seek genetic counseling if the disorder is suspected.

Why is this test done?

The sickle cell test may be performed to identify sickle cell disease and sickle cell trait.

What should you know before the test?

- You don't need to restrict food or fluids before the test.
- The nurse or technician checks your history for blood transfusions within the past 3 months.
- This test requires a blood sample, which takes less than 3 minutes to collect.
- You may feel slight discomfort from the needle puncture and tourniquet pressure.

What happens during the test?

- A nurse or medical technician inserts a needle into a vein, usually in your forearm. A blood sample is collected in a tube, which is then sent to a lab for testing.
- When the test is performed on an infant or child, a small amount of blood is taken from the finger or earlobe.

What happens after the test?

If swelling develops at the needle puncture site, warm soaks are applied to the area to ease discomfort.

What are the normal results?

Results of this test are reported as positive or negative. A normal or negative result suggests the absence of hemoglobin S.

What do abnormal results mean?

A positive result may indicate the presence of sickle cells, but the hemoglobin component test is needed to further diagnose the sickling tendency. Rarely, in the absence of hemoglobin S, other abnormal hemoglobins may cause sickling.

HEINZ BODIES

Heinz bodies are particles of damaged hemoglobin that accumulate on red blood cell membranes. Although Heinz bodies are removed from red blood cells by the spleen, they can cause hemolysis (red blood cell destruction) and are a major cause of hemolytic anemias.

Why is this test done?

This test may be performed to determine the cause of anemia.

What should you know before the test?

- You don't need to change your diet before the test.
- This test requires a blood sample, which takes less than 3 minutes to collect.
- You may feel slight discomfort from the needle puncture and tourniquet pressure.
- Whenever possible, medications that may affect test results are withheld before the test.

What happens during the test?

A nurse or medical technician inserts a needle into a vein, usually in your forearm. A blood sample is collected in a tube, which is then sent to a lab for testing.

What happens after the test?

- If swelling develops at the needle puncture site, warm soaks are applied to the area to ease discomfort.
- You may resume taking medications that were withheld before the test.

What are the normal results?

A negative test result indicates an absence of Heinz bodies.

What do abnormal results mean?

A positive test result signifies the presence of Heinz bodies. This may indicate an inherited red cell enzyme deficiency, the presence of unstable hemoglobins, thalassemia, or drug-induced red cell injury. Heinz bodies may also be present after spleen surgery.

IRON AND IRON-BINDING CAPACITY

A necessary nutrient, iron is found in many foods. (See *Choosing iron-rich foods*.) After dietary iron is absorbed by the intestine, it's distributed to the liver and other areas of the body for synthesis, storage, and transport. Iron is essential to the formation and function of hemoglobin, the oxygen-transporting element of blood. This test measures the amount of iron in a blood sample.

In the bloodstream, iron is bound to a protein called *transferrin*. The second phase of this test, iron-binding capacity, measures the amount of iron that would occur in the blood if the transferrin were completely saturated with iron. (See *The iron path*, page 298.)

You need iron in your diet to be healthy. This test checks the amount of iron in a blood sample.

Why is this test done?

Iron and iron-binding capacity may be determined for the following reasons:
- To evaluate the body's capacity to store iron
- To estimate total iron storage
- To aid diagnosis of hemochromatosis
- To help distinguish iron deficiency anemia from anemia of chronic disease
- To help evaluate a person's nutrition status.

What should you know before the test?

- You don't need to change your diet before the test.
- This test requires a blood sample, which takes less than 3 minutes to collect.
- You may feel slight discomfort from the needle puncture and tourniquet pressure.
- The nurse or medical technician will check your drug history for the use of any medications that may affect test results. Usually these drugs are withheld before the test.

What happens during the test?

A nurse or medical technician inserts a needle into a vein, usually in your forearm. A blood sample is collected in a tube, which is then sent to a lab for testing.

SELF-HELP

Choosing iron-rich foods

The recommended daily iron intake is 9 to 10 mg for men of all ages. For women over 50, it is 8 mg, and for young women, 13 mg (in pregnancy, 20 mg). Consult the following list to find foods highest in iron.

Food	Quantity	Iron content (milligrams)
Oysters	3 ounces	13.2
Beef liver	3 ounces	7.5
Prune juice	½ cup	5.2
Clams	2 ounces	4.2
Walnuts	½ cup	3.75
Ground beef	3 ounces	3.0
Chickpeas	½ cup	3.0
Bran flakes	½ cup	2.8
Pork roast	3 ounces	2.7
Cashew nuts	½ cup	2.65
Shrimp	3 ounces	2.6
Raisins	½ cup	2.55
Sardines	3 ounces	2.5
Spinach	½ cup	2.4
Lima beans	½ cup	2.3
Kidney beans	½ cup	2.2
Turkey, dark meat	3 ounces	2.0
Prunes	½ cup	1.9
Roast beef	3 ounces	1.8
Green peas	½ cup	1.5
Peanuts	½ cup	1.5
Potato	1	1.1
Sweet potato	½ cup	1.0
Green beans	½ cup	1.0
Egg	1	1.0

HOW YOUR BODY WORKS

The iron path

Iron from the food you eat is absorbed and is oxidated, or gains oxygen, in the bowel. Next, it circulates to the bone marrow for hemoglobin production and to all iron-hungry body cells. In the spleen, iron is recycled back to the bone marrow or into storage. Storage areas in the liver, spleen, bone marrow, and reticuloendothelial system hold iron as ferritin until the body needs it. The body conserves iron, losing small amounts through skin, feces, urine, and menstrual blood. Normal iron metabolism is essential for red cell function.

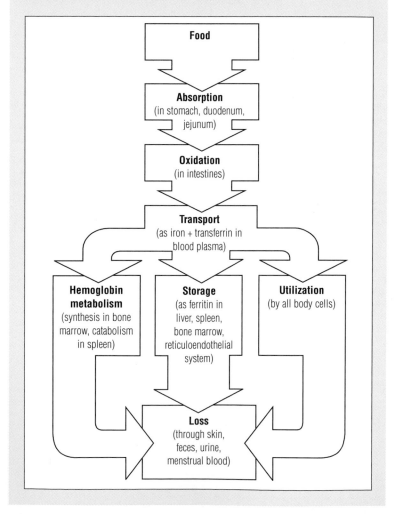

What happens after the test?

- If swelling develops at the needle puncture site, warm soaks are applied to the area to ease discomfort.
- You may resume taking medications that were withheld before the test.

What are the normal results?

Normal iron and iron-binding capacity levels are as follows:

	IRON (micromoles per liter)	IRON-BINDING CAPACITY (micromoles per liter)	PERCENT SATURATION
Men	12.5 to 26.9	53.7 to 71.6	20 to 50
Women	14.3 to 26.9	53.7 to 80.6	20 to 50

What do abnormal results mean?

In iron deficiency, iron levels decrease and iron-binding capacity increases. In people with chronic inflammations (such as rheumatoid arthritis), iron levels may be low in the presence of adequate body stores, but iron-binding capacity may be unchanged or may decrease.

Iron overload may not change iron levels until relatively late in a condition. But, in general, iron increases and iron-binding capacity remains the same.

FERRITIN

A major iron-storage protein, ferritin normally appears in small quantities in the blood. In a healthy adult, the ferritin level is directly related to the amount of available iron that's stored in the body.

Why is this test done?

Ferritin levels may be determined for the following reasons:

- To screen for iron deficiency and iron overload
- To measure iron storage

- To distinguish between iron deficiency (a condition of low iron storage) and chronic inflammation (a condition of normal storage).

What should you know before the test?

- You don't need to change your diet before this test.
- This test requires a blood sample, which takes less than 3 minutes to collect.
- You may feel slight discomfort from the needle puncture and tourniquet pressure.
- A nurse or medical technician checks your history for any transfusion within the last 4 months.

What happens during the test?

A nurse or medical technician inserts a needle into a vein, usually in your forearm. A blood sample is collected in a tube, which is then sent to a lab for testing.

What happens after the test?

If swelling develops at the needle puncture site, warm soaks are applied to the area to ease discomfort.

What are the normal results?

Normal ferritin levels vary with age and within wide ranges, as follows:
- Newborns: 25 to 200 micrograms of ferritin per liter of blood
- 1 month: 200 to 600 micrograms
- 2 to 5 months: 50 to 200 micrograms
- 6 months to 15 years: 7 to 140 micrograms
- Men: 20 to 300 micrograms
- Women: 20 to 120 micrograms.

What do abnormal results mean?

High ferritin levels may indicate acute or chronic liver disease, iron overload, leukemia, infection or inflammation, Hodgkin's disease, or chronic anemias. In these disorders, iron reserves in the bone marrow may be normal or significantly increased. Ferritin levels are characteristically normal or slightly elevated in a person with chronic kidney disease.

Low ferritin levels indicate chronic iron deficiency.

WHITE BLOOD CELL COUNT

A white blood cell count is also called a *leukocyte count*. It's part of a complete blood count. This test finds out how many white cells are in a small blood sample.

White blood cell counts may vary by as much as 2,000 on any given day, due to strenuous exercise, stress, or digestion. White blood cells help the body fight infection. The number of white blood cells may increase or decrease significantly in certain diseases, but as a diagnostic tool, the white blood cell count is useful only when a person's white cell differential and health status are considered. (See *Surround and destroy: How white blood cells fight foreign particles*, page 302.)

Why is this test done?

A white blood cell count may be performed for the following reasons:
- To detect an infection or inflammation
- To determine the need for further tests, such as the white blood cell differential or bone marrow biopsy
- To monitor a person's response to cancer therapy.

What should you know before the test?

- You should avoid strenuous exercise for 24 hours before the test. Also avoid eating a heavy meal before the test.
- This test requires a blood sample, which takes less than 3 minutes to collect.
- You may feel slight discomfort from the needle puncture and tourniquet pressure.
- If you're being treated for an infection, this test will be repeated to monitor your progress.
- Certain medications, including antibiotics, drugs for seizures, thyroid hormone antagonists, and nonsteroidal anti-inflammatory agents (such as ibuprofen) may interfere with the test results.

What happens during the test?

A nurse or medical technician inserts a needle into a vein, usually in your forearm. A blood sample is collected in a tube, which is then sent to a lab for testing.

INSIGHT INTO ILLNESS

Surround and destroy: How white blood cells fight foreign particles

In response to infection, white blood cells rush to the site of inflammation. There, phagocytosis occurs — the bacteria or other foreign particles that cause infection are engulfed and destroyed.

First, disease-fighting antibodies coat the bacteria (phase 1). Next, the white blood cell surrounds the bacteria with pseudopods, which are footlike extensions (phase 2). The foreign particles are destroyed by digestion in the white blood cell (phase 3). Finally, the white blood cell releases the digested debris (phase 4) and continues to fight infection.

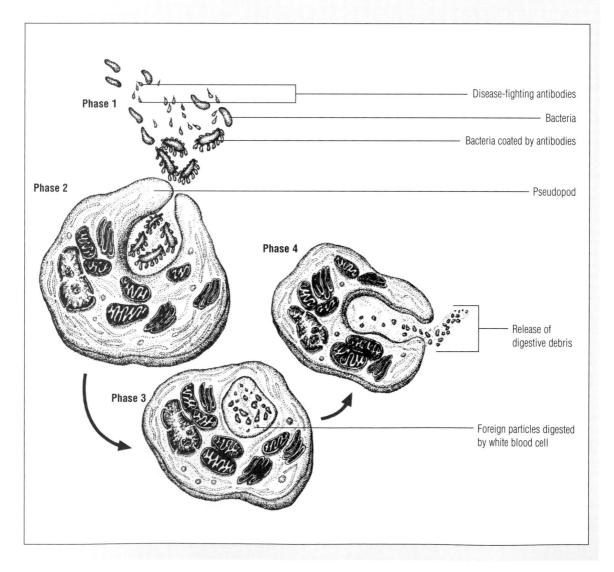

What happens after the test?

■ If swelling develops at the needle puncture site, warm soaks are applied to the area to ease discomfort.

■ You may resume activity that was restricted before the test.

■ If test results show that you have severe leukopenia, you may have little or no resistance to infection and will need protective isolation.

What are the normal results?

Normal white blood cell counts range from 4 to 10×10^9 white blood cells per liter of whole blood.

What do abnormal results mean?

An elevated white blood cell count, which doctors call *leukocytosis*, often indicates infection, such as an abscess, meningitis, appendicitis, or tonsillitis. A high count also may be caused by leukemia or by dead tissue from burns, heart attack, or gangrene.

A low white blood cell count — or leukopenia — indicates bone marrow problems. This may be caused by viral infections or from toxic reactions to poisons. Leukopenia characteristically accompanies the flu, typhoid fever, measles, infectious hepatitis, mononucleosis, and rubella.

WHITE BLOOD CELL DIFFERENTIAL

White blood cells, also called *leukocytes*, are classified into five major types: neutrophils, eosinophils, basophils, lymphocytes, and monocytes. The white blood cell differential is used to evaluate the distribution of these various leukocytes in the blood. It also tells the doctor about the structure of these cells. The information is used in evaluating the immune system.

Why is this test done?

A white blood cell differential test may be performed for the following reasons:

■ To evaluate the immune system and the body's capacity to resist and overcome infection

■ To detect and identify various types of leukemia

- To determine the stage and severity of an infection
- To detect and assess allergic reactions
- To detect parasitic infections.

What should you know before the test?

- You don't need to restrict food or fluids, but you should refrain from strenuous exercise for 24 hours before the test.
- This test requires a blood sample, which takes less than 3 minutes to collect.
- You may feel slight discomfort from the needle puncture and tourniquet pressure.
- The nurse or medical technician will check your drug history for the use of any medications that may affect test results. Usually these drugs are withheld for a period before the test.

What happens during the test?

A nurse or medical technician inserts a needle into a vein, usually in your forearm. A blood sample is collected in a tube, which is then sent to a lab for testing.

What happens after the test?

- If swelling develops at the needle puncture site, warm soaks are applied to the area to ease discomfort.
- An eosinophil count may be ordered as a follow-up test if a high or low eosinophil level is reported.

What are the normal results?

The chart below provides relative levels for the five types of white blood cells classified in the differential:

Types of cells	Adults	Boys ages 6 to 18	Girls ages 6 to 18
Neutrophils	47.6% to 76.8%	38.5% to 71.5%	41.9% to 76.5%
Lymphocytes	16.2% to 43%	19.4% to 51.4%	16.3% to 46.7%
Monocytes	0.6% to 9.6%	1.1% to 11.6%	0.9% to 9.9%
Eosinophils	0.3% to 7%	1% to 8.1%	0.8% to 8.3%
Basophils	0.3% to 2%	0.25% to 1.3%	0.3% to 1.4%

INSIGHT INTO ILLNESS

How diseases affect white blood cell count

White blood cells are classified into five major types: neutrophils, eosinophils, basophils, lymphocytes, and monocytes. Changes in the levels of these blood cell types, as revealed by lab tests, provide evidence for a wide range of diseases and other conditions.

CELL TYPE	INCREASED BY	DECREASED BY
Neutrophils 	■ Infections: osteomyelitis, otitis media, salpingitis, blood poisoning, gonorrhea, endocarditis, smallpox, chickenpox, herpes, Rocky Mountain spotted fever ■ Localized tissue death due to heart attack, burns, carcinoma ■ Metabolic disorders: diabetic acidosis, eclampsia, uremia, thyrotoxicosis ■ Stress response due to acute hemorrhage, surgery, excessive exercise, emotional distress, third trimester of pregnancy, childbirth ■ Inflammatory disease: rheumatic fever, rheumatoid arthritis, acute gout, vasculitis and myositis	■ Bone marrow depression due to radiation or cytotoxic drugs ■ Infections: typhoid, tularemia, brucellosis, hepatitis, flu, measles, German measles, mumps, infectious mononucleosis ■ Hypersplenism: liver disease and storage diseases ■ Collagen vascular disease such as lupus ■ Deficiency of folic acid or vitamin B_{12}
Eosinophils 	■ Allergic disorders: asthma, hay fever, food or drug sensitivity, serum sickness, angioneurotic edema ■ Parasitic infections: trichinosis, hookworm, roundworm, amebiasis ■ Skin diseases: eczema, pemphigus, psoriasis, dermatitis herpes ■ Cancers: chronic myelocytic leukemia, Hodgkin's disease, spread and deterioration of solid tumors ■ Miscellaneous: collagen vascular disease, adrenocortical hypofunction, ulcerative colitis, polyarteritis nodosa, postsplenectomy, pernicious anemia, scarlet fever, excessive exercise	■ Stress response due to injury, shock, burns, surgery, mental distress ■ Cushing's syndrome

(continued)

INSIGHT INTO ILLNESS

How diseases affect white blood cell count *(continued)*

CELL TYPE	INCREASED BY	DECREASED BY
Basophils 	■ Chronic myelocytic leukemia, polycythemia vera, some chronic hemolytic anemias, Hodgkin's disease, systemic mastocytosis, myxedema, ulcerative colitis, chronic hypersensitivity states, and nephrosis	■ Hyperthyroidism, ovulation, pregnancy, stress
Lymphocytes 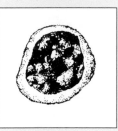	■ Infections: pertussis, brucellosis, syphilis, tuberculosis, hepatitis, infectious mononucleosis, mumps, German measles, cytomegalovirus ■ Other: thyrotoxicosis, hypoadrenalism, ulcerative colitis, immune diseases, lymphocytic leukemia	■ Severe debilitating illness, such as congestive heart failure, kidney failure, advanced tuberculosis ■ Defective lymphatic circulation, high levels of adrenal corticosteroids, immunodeficiency due to immunosuppressives
Monocytes 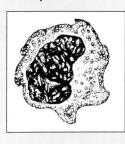	■ Infections: subacute bacterial endocarditis, tuberculosis, hepatitis, malaria, Rocky Mountain spotted fever ■ Collagen vascular disease: lupus, rheumatoid arthritis, polyarteritis nodosa ■ Carcinomas, monocytic leukemia, lymphomas	■ Immunosuppression

For an accurate diagnosis, the doctor will interpret differential test results in relation to the total white blood cell count. (See *Interpreting the white blood cell differential.*)

What do abnormal results mean?

Abnormal differential patterns provide evidence for a wide range of diseases and conditions. For example, high levels of some leukocytes are associated with various allergic diseases and reactions to parasites. (See *How diseases affect white blood cell count*, pages 305 and 306.)

BLOOD CLOTTING TESTS

BLEEDING TIME

This test measures the duration of bleeding after a small skin incision. Bleeding time depends on the elasticity of the blood vessel wall and on the number and effectiveness of platelets, which are small, disk-like structures in the blood that help blood coagulate (clot). (See *Birth of a blood clot*, page 308.)

Bleeding time may be measured by one of four methods doctors call *Duke*, *Ivy*, *template*, or *modified template*. The template methods are the most accurate because the incision size is standardized. Although this test is usually performed on a person with a personal or family history of bleeding disorders, it's also useful for screening before surgery, along with a platelet count.

Why is this test done?

Bleeding time may be determined for the following reasons:
- To measure the time required to form a clot and stop bleeding
- To assess the platelet response and constriction of blood vessels after an injury
- To detect platelet function disorders.

Interpreting the white blood cell differential

To make an accurate diagnosis, both the relative and absolute values of the differential must be considered. Considered alone, relative results may point to one disease, while masking the true disease, which would be revealed by considering the results of the white cell count.

An example

Consider a person whose white blood cell count is 6×10^9 white blood cells per liter of blood and whose differential shows 30% neutrophils and 70% lymphocytes. His relative lymphocyte count would seem to be quite high; but when this figure is multiplied by his white cell count — $6 \times 10^9 \times 70\% = 4.2 \times 10^9$ lymphocytes per liter — it is well within the normal range.

This person's neutrophil count, however, is low (30%) and when this is multiplied by the white cell count — $6 \times 10^9 \times 30\% = 1.8 \times 10^9$ neutrophils per liter — the result is a low absolute number.

This low result indicates decreased neutrophil production, which may indicate depressed bone marrow activity.

HOW YOUR BODY WORKS

Birth of a blood clot

When hemorrhage (bleeding) occurs with an injury, platelets gather at the site of injury, releasing platelet factors. These factors combine with other plasma factors to convert prothrombin to thrombin. Then thrombin converts fibrinogen to fibrin, the essential part of the clot.

BLOOD CLOT FORMATION

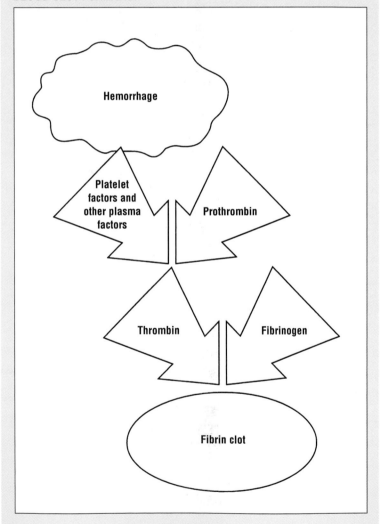

What should you know before the test?

- You don't need to change your diet before the test.
- This test requires small incisions on your forearm or earlobe. You may feel some discomfort from the incisions, the antiseptic, and the tightness of the blood pressure cuff. The test takes only 10 to 20 minutes to perform. The incisions will leave small scars that are barely visible when healed.
- The nurse or technician checks your history for recent use of drugs that prolong bleeding time. If you use such medications and are being tested to identify a suspected bleeding disorder, the test may be postponed and the drugs discontinued. If the test is part of preparation before surgery, it proceeds as scheduled.

What happens during the test?

- *Template and modified template methods*: A nurse or medical technician inflates a blood pressure cuff on your upper arm and applies a template to your forearm. For the template method, a lancet is used to make two small incisions. For the modified template method, a spring-loaded blade is used to make the incisions. The nurse gently blots drops of blood every 30 seconds until the bleeding stops in both cuts. The average bleeding time of the two cuts is calculated.
- *Ivy method:* After applying the pressure cuff, the nurse makes three small punctures, then follows a similar blotting and calculation technique.
- *Duke method:* Your shoulder is draped with a towel and a small puncture is made in your earlobe. The blotting and recording procedure is the same.

What happens after the test?

- If you have a bleeding tendency (due to hemophilia, for example), a pressure bandage is placed over the incision for 24 to 48 hours and it is checked regularly.
- If you don't have a bleeding tendency, the incision is dressed.
- You may resume taking medications that were discontinued before the test.

A test for bleeding time may be performed before surgery to ward off potential problems.

Does the test have risks?

- This test is usually not recommended for a person whose platelet count is less than 75×10^{-9} cells per liter.
- If bleeding doesn't slow down after 15 minutes, the test is discontinued.

What are the normal results?

The normal range of bleeding time is from 2 to 8 minutes in the template method; from 2 to 10 minutes in the modified template method; from 1 to 7 minutes in the Ivy method; and from 1 to 3 minutes in the Duke method.

What do abnormal results mean?

Prolonged bleeding time may indicate blood disorders, such as Hodgkin's disease, acute leukemia, disseminated intravascular coagulation, hemolytic disease of the newborn, Schönlein-Henoch purpura, severe liver disease such as cirrhosis, or severe deficiency of factors I, II, V, VII, VIII, IX, or XI.

Prolonged bleeding time in a person with a normal platelet count suggests a platelet function disorder and requires more investigation.

PLATELET COUNT

Platelets, or thrombocytes, are the smallest formed elements in blood. They promote blood clotting after an injury. A platelet count is one of the most important blood tests done.

Why is this test done?

A platelet count may be performed for the following reasons:
- To determine if blood clots normally
- To evaluate platelet production
- To assess the effects of chemotherapy or radiation therapy on platelet production
- To diagnose and monitor a severe increase or decrease in platelet count.

What should you know before the test?

- You don't need to change your diet before the test.
- This test requires a blood sample, which takes less than 3 minutes to collect.
- You may feel slight discomfort from the needle puncture and tourniquet pressure.
- The nurse or medical technician will check your drug history for the use of any medications that may affect test results. Usually these drugs are withheld for a period before the test.

What happens during the test?

The nurse or medical technician inserts a needle into a vein, usually in your forearm. A blood sample is collected in a tube, which is then sent to a lab for testing.

What happens after the test?

If swelling develops at the needle puncture site, warm soaks are applied to the area to ease discomfort.

What are the normal results?

Normal platelet counts in international units range from 130 to 370 $\times 10^9$ platelets per liter of whole blood.

What do abnormal results mean?

Thrombocytopenia (a low platelet count) can be caused by bone marrow problems, such as cancer, leukemia, or infection; folic acid or vitamin B_{12} deficiency; pooling of platelets in an enlarged spleen; increased platelet destruction due to drugs or immune disorders; or mechanical injury to platelets. A platelet count that falls below 50,000 can cause spontaneous bleeding. When it drops below 5,000, fatal central nervous system bleeding or massive gastrointestinal hemorrhage is possible.

Thrombocytosis (a high platelet count) can be caused by severe bleeding, infections, cancer, iron deficiency anemia, and recent surgery, pregnancy, or spleen removal. A high count also can be caused by inflammatory disorders.

A platelet count is one of the most important blood tests.

INSIGHT INTO ILLNESS

Fragile capillaries: A significant finding

A test result is considered *positive* when many petechiae (tiny red spots caused by bleeding under the skin) show up below the blood pressure cuff. Both the size and number of petechiae are used to determine abnormalities.

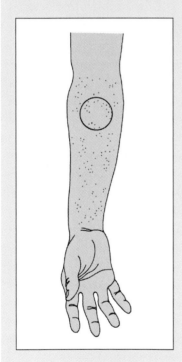

TOURNIQUET TEST

Also called the *capillary fragility test,* this test helps evaluate bleeding tendencies. It measures the ability of the capillaries, the body's smallest blood vessels, to remain intact under pressure, which is controlled by a blood pressure cuff placed around the upper arm.

Why is this test done?

The tourniquet test may be performed for the following reasons:
- To identify abnormal bleeding tendencies
- To assess the fragility of capillary walls
- To identify a low platelet count.

What should you know before the test?

- You don't need to change your diet before this test.
- The test requires use of a blood pressure cuff. You may feel slight discomfort from the pressure of the cuff on your arm.

What happens during the test?

- A nurse or medical technician checks your skin temperature and the room temperature. Normal temperatures help to ensure accurate results.
- A small space on your forearm is selected and marked. Ideally, the site is free of petechiae, which are minute, round purplish red spots caused by bleeding under the skin. If petechiae are present on the site before starting the test, they are counted and the number is recorded for future reference.
- A blood pressure cuff is fastened around your arm and inflated. This pressure is maintained for 5 minutes; then the cuff is released.
- The nurse or medical technician counts the number of petechiae that appear in the marked space.

What happens after the test?

You'll open and close your hand a few times to help blood return to your forearm.

INSIGHT INTO ILLNESS

How your doctor looks at bruises

Your doctor may use the following terms to identify what you commonly call a rash or a bruise. Types of purpuric lesions — purplish spots from blood seeping into the skin — include petechiae, ecchymoses, and hematomas.

Petechiae

These red or brown lesions are painless, round, and as tiny as pinpoints. Petechiae result from a leakage of red blood cells into skin tissue, and they usually appear and fade in groups.

Ecchymoses

These lesions are another form of blood leakage and are larger than petechiae. Ecchymoses are purple, blue, or yellow-green bruises that vary in size and shape. They can occur anywhere on the body as a result of traumatic injury. In people with bleeding disorders, ecchymoses usually appear on the arms and legs.

Hematomas

A noticeable bruise that's painful and swollen is a hematoma. Hematomas are usually the result of traumatic injury. Superficial hematomas are red, whereas deep hematomas are blue. Although their size varies widely, hematomas typically exceed 1 centimeter in diameter.

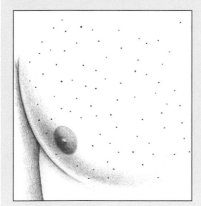 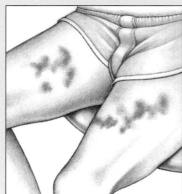 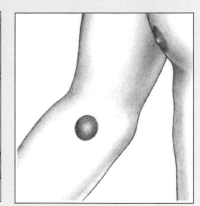

Does the test have risks?

■ This test should not be repeated on the same arm within 1 week.

■ This test is not recommended if you have disseminated intravascular coagulation or other bleeding disorders or if many petechiae are already present.

What are the normal results?

A few petechiae may normally be present before the test. Less than 10 petechiae on the forearm, 5 minutes after the test, is considered normal, or negative. More than 10 petechiae is considered a positive result.

What do abnormal results mean?

More than 10 petechiae can indicate a platelet defect or a weakness of the capillary walls, called *vascular purpura*. (See *Fragile capillaries: A significant finding,* page 312.) It may occur in a long list of bleeding disorders.

Conditions that are not related to bleeding defects, such as scarlet fever, measles, flu, chronic kidney disease, high blood pressure, and diabetes with vascular disease, may also increase capillary fragility. An abnormal number of petechiae sometimes appear before menstruation or other times in healthy people, especially women over age 40. (See *How your doctor looks at bruises,* page 313.)

PLATELET CLOTTING

Platelets are the crucial element in forming blood clots. The platelet aggregation test measures how well they are doing their job.

After injury to a blood vessel, the clot-forming elements in the blood, called *platelets*, gather at the injury site. Here the platelets clump together to form an aggregate (clot), that helps stop bleeding and promote healing. A test called the *platelet aggregation test* is used to measure how quickly the platelets in a blood sample clump together after an aggregating agent is added to the test tube.

Why is this test done?

The platelet aggregation test may be performed for the following reasons:
- To determine if blood clots properly
- To detect bleeding disorders.

What should you know before the test?

- You will be asked to fast or to maintain a nonfat diet for 8 hours before the test.

■ This test requires a blood sample, which takes less than 3 minutes to collect.

■ You may feel slight discomfort from the needle puncture and tourniquet pressure.

■ Aspirin and aspirin compounds are withheld for 14 days before the test. Azolid, Anturan, phenothiazines, antihistamines, anti-inflammatory drugs, and tricyclic antidepressants are withheld for 48 hours before the test.

■ Because many medications may alter the results of this test, you should be as drug free as possible before the test. If you've taken aspirin within the past 14 days and the test cannot be postponed, the lab is asked to verify the presence of aspirin in the sample. If test results are abnormal for this sample, you must stop taking aspirin and the test is repeated in 2 weeks. (See *Aspirin's effect on blood clotting.*)

What happens during the test?

A nurse or medical technician inserts a needle into a vein, usually in your forearm. A blood sample is collected in a tube, which is then sent to a lab for testing.

What happens after the test?

■ Pressure is applied to the needle puncture site for 5 minutes or until bleeding stops.

■ You may resume your usual diet and medications.

■ If swelling develops at the needle puncture site, warm soaks are applied to the area to ease discomfort.

What are the normal results?

Normal aggregation occurs in 3 to 5 minutes, but findings depend on temperature and vary with the lab. Aggregation curves that are obtained by using special compounds in the blood sample help to distinguish various platelet defects.

What do abnormal results mean?

Abnormal findings may indicate von Willebrand's disease, Bernard-Soulier syndrome, storage pool disease, Glanzmann's thrombasthenia, or polycythemia vera.

 HOW YOUR BODY WORKS

Aspirin's effect on blood clotting

Aspirin inhibits platelet aggregation — the ability of platelets to move together and form a mass at the site of injury. Platelet aggregation is an important stage of blood clotting. Taking aspirin may cause bleeding time to double in healthy people. In children or in people with bleeding disorders such as hemophilia, bleeding time may be even more prolonged.

Beneficial effects

On the other hand, aspirin's action on blood vessels may cause vasodilation (widening of the blood vessels). Low aspirin dosage — 80 milligrams daily or 325 milligrams every other day — may prevent thrombosis (blood clot formation) in an artery or vein that hinders the flow of blood.

ACTIVATED PARTIAL THROMBOPLASTIN TIME

The activated partial thromboplastin time test evaluates all the clotting factors of blood except platelets. This test measures the time it takes for a fibrin clot to form after special compounds called reagents are added to a blood sample. An activator, which is used to shorten clotting time, may also be added to the sample.

Why is this test done?

The activated partial thromboplastin time test may be performed for the following reasons:

- To determine if your blood clots normally
- To help check your bleeding tendencies before surgery
- To screen for clotting factor deficiencies that are present at birth
- To monitor heparin therapy.

What should you know before the test?

- You don't need to change your diet before this test.
- The test requires a blood sample, which takes less than 3 minutes to collect.
- You may feel slight discomfort from the needle puncture and tourniquet pressure.

What happens during the test?

A nurse or medical technician inserts a needle into a vein, usually in your forearm. A blood sample is collected in a tube, which is then sent to a lab for testing.

What happens after the test?

- If swelling develops at the needle puncture site, warm soaks are applied to the area to ease discomfort.
- If you're receiving heparin therapy, this test may be repeated at regular intervals to measure your response to treatment.

What are the normal results?

Normally, a fibrin clot forms 25 to 36 seconds after adding reagents to the sample. If you're on anticoagulant therapy, the doctor specifies the normal test results, adjusted for the therapy you're receiving.

What do abnormal results mean?

Prolonged activated partial thromboplastin time may indicate a deficiency of certain clotting factors or the presence of heparin, fibrin split products, fibrinolysins, or circulating anticoagulants.

PROTHROMBIN TIME

Fibrin is a type of protein that's essential to the clotting of blood. The prothrombin time test measures how long it takes for a fibrin clot to form in a specially treated blood sample.

Why is this test done?

The prothrombin time test may be performed for the following reasons:
- To see if your blood clots normally
- To provide an overall evaluation of certain clotting factors in the blood
- To monitor response to anticoagulants (drugs that are given to thin the blood).

What should you know before the test?

- You don't need to change your diet before the test.
- This test requires a blood sample, which takes less than 3 minutes to collect.
- You may feel slight discomfort from the needle puncture and tourniquet pressure.
- The nurse or medical technician checks your history for the use of medications that may affect test results.
- If this test is used to monitor the effects of blood-thinning drugs, it's performed daily when therapy begins and is repeated at longer intervals when medication levels stabilize.

If you are receiving drugs that cause your blood to become thinner, your doctor may want to measure your prothrombin time.

What happens during the test?

A nurse or medical technician inserts a needle into a vein, usually in your forearm. A blood sample is collected in a tube, which is then sent to a lab for testing.

What happens after the test?

If swelling develops at the needle puncture site, warm soaks are applied to the area to ease discomfort.

What are the normal results?

Normally, prothrombin times range from 10 to 14 seconds. The times vary, however, depending on the source of the clotting factor and the type of sensing devices that are used to measure clot formation. In a person who's receiving blood-thinning drugs, prothrombin time is usually between one and a half and two times the normal time.

What do abnormal results mean?

Prolonged prothrombin time may indicate deficiencies in several specific clotting factors. It may also be due to liver disease or therapy with blood-thinning drugs. Prolonged prothrombin time that exceeds two and a half times the control time is commonly associated with abnormal bleeding.

Prolonged prothrombin time also can be caused by a long list of drugs, thyroid hormones, vitamin A, or overuse of alcohol.

Prolonged or shortened prothrombin time can follow the use of antibiotics, barbiturates, pain relievers, or mineral oil.

CLOTTING FACTORS II, V, VII, AND X

Blood contains a number of elements, called *factors*, that help cause clotting. This test detects a deficiency of four specific factors. (See *Testing for factor XIII deficiency.*)

Why is this test done?

This test may be performed for the following reasons:

- To check blood clotting
- To identify a specific factor deficiency

INSIGHT INTO ILLNESS

Testing for factor XIII deficiency

When a person experiences poor wound healing and other symptoms of a bleeding disorder — despite normal results of coagulation screening tests — a factor XIII assay is recommended.

What is factor XIII?

Factor XIII is responsible for stabilizing the fibrin clot, the final step in the clotting process. If the clot is unstable, it breaks loose, resulting in scarring and poor wound healing. Deficiency of this factor is usually transmitted genetically but may result from liver disease or from tumors.

What happens in this test?

A plasma sample is incubated in a special solution after normal clotting takes place. The clot is observed for 24 hours. If the clot dissolves, a severe factor XIII deficiency exists.

What are the effects of factor XIII deficiency?

The effects of factor XIII deficiency include the following:

- umbilical bleeding in newborns
- recurrent bleeding under the skin, bruising or clotting in an organ or tissue, and poor wound healing
- bleeding in a joint cavity
- miscarriage (rarely)
- bleeding within the ovaries
- prolonged bleeding after injury (bleeding may begin immediately or may be delayed as long as 12 to 36 hours).

How is it treated?

Treatment with intravenous infusions of plasma or cryoprecipitate may improve the prognosis; some people even live normal lives.

- To study blood-clotting defects
- To monitor the effects of blood component therapy in a factor-deficient person.

What should you know before the test?

- You don't need to change your diet before this test.
- Oral anticoagulants are usually withheld before the test.
- This test requires a blood sample, which takes less than 3 minutes to collect.
- You may feel slight discomfort from the needle puncture and tourniquet pressure.
- If you're factor deficient and receiving blood component therapy, you may need a series of tests.

What happens during the test?

A nurse or medical technician inserts a needle into a vein, usually in your forearm. A blood sample is collected in a tube, which is then sent to a lab for testing.

What happens after the test?

- If swelling develops at the needle puncture site, warm soaks are applied to the area to ease discomfort.
- If you have a bleeding disorder, a pressure bandage may be applied to stop bleeding at the needle puncture site.

Does the test have risks?

If you have a suspected clotting problem, special care is taken to avoid excessive probing during the test, the tourniquet is removed promptly from your arm to avoid bruising, and pressure is applied to the puncture site for 5 minutes, or until the bleeding stops.

What are the normal results?

Clotting time should be between 50% and 150% of the norm.

What do abnormal results mean?

If the clotting time is prolonged, the person may be deficient in the factor being tested. Deficiency of factor II, factor VII, or factor X may indicate liver disease or vitamin K deficiency. Deficiency of factor X may also indicate scattered intravascular coagulation. Factor V deficiency suggests severe liver disease, disseminated intravascular coagulation, or fibrinogenolysis. Deficiencies of all four factors may be present at birth; absence of factor II is lethal.

CLOTTING FACTORS VIII, IX, XI, AND XII

Blood contains a number of elements, called *factors*, that help cause clotting. This test detects a deficiency of four specific factors.

Why is this test done?

This test may be performed for the following reasons:
- To check blood clotting
- To identify a specific factor deficiency
- To study blood-clotting defects
- To monitor the effects of blood component therapy in a factor-deficient person.

What should you know before the test?

- You don't need to change your diet before this test.
- The test requires a blood sample, which takes less than 3 minutes to collect.
- You may feel slight discomfort from the needle puncture and tourniquet pressure.
- Oral anticoagulants are usually withheld before the test.
- If you're factor deficient and receiving blood component therapy, a series of tests may be needed to monitor therapeutic progress.

What happens during the test?

A nurse or medical technician inserts a needle into a vein, usually in your forearm. A blood sample is collected in a tube, which is then sent to a lab for testing.

What happens after the test?

- If swelling develops at the needle puncture site, warm soaks are applied to the area to ease discomfort.
- If you have a bleeding disorder, you may need a pressure bandage to stop bleeding at the needle puncture site.
- You may resume taking any medications that were discontinued before the test.

INSIGHT INTO ILLNESS

Distinguishing between hemophilia A and hemophilia B

When blood studies confirm a hemophilia diagnosis, you're typically told you have either type A or type B hemophilia.

Hemophilia A, or classic hemophilia, occurs with deficient levels of factor VIII, and *hemophilia B*, or Christmas disease (named for a patient), results from deficient levels of factor IX.

Both types of hemophilia cause the same symptoms, but treatment differs. Knowing which type of hemophilia you have helps the doctor prescribe the most effective treatment.

Hemophilia A

If you have hemophilia A, your factor VIII assay value may be 0% to 30% of normal. Test findings reflect a prolonged activated partial thromboplastin time. However, you'll have a normal platelet count and function and normal bleeding and prothrombin times.

Hemophilia B

If you have hemophilia B, your test findings will show that your blood lacks factor IX. What's more, you'll have baseline coagulation values similar to those for hemophilia A but with normal amounts of factor VIII.

Does the test have risks?

If you're suspected of having a blood-clotting problem, excessive probing is avoided during the test, the tourniquet is removed promptly to avoid bruising, and pressure is applied to the puncture site for 5 minutes, or until the bleeding stops.

What are the normal results?

Clotting time should be between 50% and 150% of the norm.

What do abnormal results mean?

If the clotting time is prolonged, the person may be deficient in the factor being tested. Factor VIII deficiency may indicate hemophilia A, von Willebrand's disease, or factor VIII inhibitor. An acquired deficiency of factor VIII may be caused by disseminated intravascular coagulation or fibrinolysis.

Factor IX deficiency may suggest the presence of hemophilia B, liver disease, factor IX inhibitor, vitamin K deficiency, or therapy with the drug warfarin. Factor VIII and IX inhibitors occur after transfusions in people who are deficient in either factor. (See *Distinguishing between hemophilia A and hemophilia B.*)

Factor XI deficiency may appear after trauma or surgery, or briefly in newborns. Factor XII deficiency may be inherited or acquired and may also appear briefly in newborns.

THROMBIN TIME

This test is also called the *thrombin clotting time test*. In it, thrombin, an enzyme that promotes clotting, is added to a person's blood sample. Thrombin is also added to a normal, or control, sample in the lab. The clotting time for each sample is compared and recorded. This test provides a quick, but imprecise, estimate of how much fibrinogen, a clot-promoting protein, is in the blood.

Why is this test done?

The thrombin time test may be performed for the following reasons:

- To determine if your blood clots normally
- To detect fibrinogen deficiency or defect

- To help the doctor diagnose disseminated intravascular coagulation and liver disease
- To monitor the effectiveness of treatment with heparin or thrombolytic agents.

What should you know before the test?

- This test requires a blood sample, which takes less than 3 minutes to collect.
- You may feel slight discomfort from the needle puncture and tourniquet pressure.
- You don't need to change your diet before the test.
- If possible, heparin therapy is withheld before the test.

What happens during the test?

A nurse or medical technician inserts a needle into a vein, usually in your forearm. A blood sample is collected in a tube, which is then sent to a lab for testing.

What happens after the test?

If swelling develops at the needle puncture site, warm soaks are applied to the area to ease discomfort.

What are the normal results?

Normal thrombin times range from 10 to 15 seconds.

What do abnormal results mean?

A prolonged thrombin time may indicate the presence of heparin therapy, liver disease, disseminated intravascular coagulation, or hypofibrinogenemia. People with prolonged thrombin time may require measurement of fibrinogen levels. If the doctor suspects disseminated intravascular coagulation, the test for fibrin split products is also necessary.

FIBRINOGEN

Also called *factor I,* fibrinogen is a clot-promoting element in blood. Fibrinogen deficiency can produce mild to severe bleeding. This test is used to determine the amount of fibrinogen in a blood sample.

Why is this test done?

This test may be performed for the following reasons:
- To see if your blood clots normally
- To help the doctor diagnose suspected clotting or bleeding disorders caused by fibrinogen abnormalities.

Fibrinogen is an element in the blood that promotes clotting; absence of this element may cause severe bleeding.

What should you know before the test?

- You don't need to change your diet before the test.
- This test requires a blood sample, which takes less than 3 minutes to collect.
- You may feel slight discomfort from the needle puncture and tourniquet pressure.
- The nurse or medical technician will check your drug history for the use of any medications that may affect test results. Usually these drugs are withheld before the test.

What happens during the test?

A nurse or medical technician inserts a needle into a vein, usually in your forearm. A blood sample is collected in a tube, which is then sent to a lab for testing.

What happens after the test?

If swelling develops at the needle puncture site, warm soaks are applied to the area to ease discomfort.

Does the test have risks?

If you are actively bleeding, have an infection or illness, or have received a blood transfusion within 4 weeks, this test is not recommended.

What are the normal results?

Fibrinogen levels normally range from 2.0 to 3.7 grams per liter of blood.

What do abnormal results mean?

Depressed fibrinogen levels may indicate inherited blood disorders; severe liver disease; cancer of the prostate, pancreas, or lung; or bone marrow lesions. Complications or injury in childbirth may cause low fibrinogen levels.

Elevated fibrinogen levels may indicate inflammatory disorders or cancer of the stomach, breast, or kidney.

FIBRIN SPLIT PRODUCTS

After a fibrin clot forms in response to an injury, the clot is eventually broken down by plasmin, a fibrin-dissolving enzyme. The resulting fragments are known as *fibrin split products*, or *fibrinogen degradation products*. In this test, fibrin split products are detected in the diluted serum that's left in a blood sample after clotting.

Why is this test done?

A fibrin split products test may be performed for the following reasons:
- To see if your blood clots normally
- To detect fibrin split products in the circulation
- To help assess fibrin-related problems such as disseminated intravascular coagulation. (See *Causes of disseminated intravascular coagulation*, page 326.)

What should you know before the test?

- You don't need to change your diet before the test.
- This test requires a blood sample, which takes less than 3 minutes to collect.
- You may feel slight discomfort from the needle puncture and tourniquet pressure.

INSIGHT INTO ILLNESS

Causes of disseminated intravascular coagulation

Disseminated intravascular coagulation is a condition that is marked by widespread clogging of blood vessels and abnormal bleeding. Many disorders can lead to disseminated intravascular coagulation. Below are some of the most well-known causes.

Obstetric
Amniotic fluid embolism, eclampsia, retained dead fetus, retained placenta, abruptio placentae, and toxemia

Cancerous
Sarcoma, spreading carcinoma, acute leukemia, prostatic cancer, and giant hemangioma

Infectious
Acute bacteremia, septicemia, rickettsemia, and infection from viruses, fungi, or protozoa

Necrotic
Injury, destruction of brain tissue, extensive burns, heatstroke, rejection of transplant, and liver necrosis

Cardiovascular
Fat embolism, acute venous thrombosis, cardiopulmonary bypass surgery, hypovolemic shock, heart attack, and high blood pressure

Other
Snakebite, cirrhosis, transfusion of incompatible blood, purpura, and glomerulonephritis.

■ A nurse or medical technician checks your history for the use of heparin or other medications that may interfere with test results. If you're using such medications, the lab must be notified.

What happens during the test?
A nurse or medical technician inserts a needle into a vein, usually in your forearm. A blood sample is collected in a specially treated tube, which is then immediately sent to a lab for testing.

What happens after the test?
If swelling develops at the needle puncture site, warm soaks are applied to the area to ease discomfort.

What are the normal results?
Blood normally contains less than 10 micrograms of fibrin split products per milliliter. A quantitative assay shows less than 3 micrograms per milliliter of blood.

What do abnormal results mean?

Fibrin split products increase due to a long list of disorders, including alcoholic cirrhosis, disseminated intravascular coagulation and subsequent fibrinolysis, congenital heart disease, sunstroke, burns, intrauterine death, a torn placenta, pulmonary blood clot, deep-vein thrombosis, and heart attack. Fibrin split products levels usually exceed 100 micrograms per milliliter in active kidney disease or kidney transplant rejection.

PLASMINOGEN

During the healing process, an enzyme called *plasmin* dissolves clots to prevent excessive clotting and reduced blood flow. Plasmin does not circulate through the body in its active form, however, so it cannot be directly measured. This test is used to measure its circulating precursor, called *plasminogen*.

Why is this test done?

The plasminogen test may be performed for the following reasons:
- To see how well your blood clots normally
- To detect clotting disorders.

What should you know before the test?

- You don't need to change your diet before the test.
- This test requires a blood sample, which takes less than 3 minutes to collect.
- You may feel slight discomfort from the needle puncture and tourniquet pressure.
- The nurse or medical technician will check your drug history for the use of any medications that may affect test results. Usually these drugs are withheld before the test.

What happens during the test?

A nurse or medical technician inserts a needle into a vein, usually in your forearm. A blood sample is collected in a tube, which is then sent to a lab for testing.

What happens after the test?

- If swelling develops at the needle puncture site, warm soaks are applied to the area to ease discomfort.
- You may resume any medications that were withheld before the test.

What are the normal results?

Normal plasminogen levels are 10 to 20 units per milliliter of blood by immunologic methods and 80 to 120 international units per deciliter of blood by functional methods.

What do abnormal results mean?

Diminished plasminogen levels can be caused by disseminated intravascular coagulation (a condition marked by widespread clogging of blood vessels and abnormal bleeding), tumors, and some liver diseases.

11

BLOOD ELEMENT TESTS:
Surveying for Disease

BLOOD GASES & ELECTROLYTES

ARTERIAL BLOOD GAS ANALYSIS

In this test, a sample of blood is collected from an artery, which is a vessel that carries blood from the heart to other parts of the body. Arterial blood gas analysis is used to measure the partial pressures of oxygen and carbon dioxide in blood. Partial pressure is the pressure that an individual gas exerts on the walls of the arteries. Blood pH (or acidity), oxygen content, oxygen saturation, and bicarbonate content are also measured.

Why is this test done?
Arterial blood gas analysis may be performed for the following reasons:
- To evaluate how well the lungs are delivering oxygen to the blood and eliminating carbon dioxide
- To provide information about acid-base disorders
- To monitor respiratory therapy.

What should you know before the test?
- This test requires a blood sample that's collected from the radial, brachial, or femoral artery. These arteries are in the forearm, upper arm, and thigh, respectively.
- You don't need to restrict food or fluids before the test.

What happens during the test?
- Breathe normally while the test is being conducted. Your respiratory rate and rectal temperature are measured and recorded.
- A blood sample is collected from an arterial line that's already in place or by arterial puncture. You may experience a brief cramping or throbbing at the puncture site.

What happens after the test?

- After the sample is collected, pressure is applied to the puncture site for 3 to 5 minutes. Then a gauze pad is taped firmly over the area, without restricting your circulation.
- If you're receiving anticoagulants (blood-thinning drugs) or have a coagulation disorder, pressure is applied to the puncture site for longer than 5 minutes, if necessary.
- Your vital signs are monitored and you're observed for signs of circulatory impairment, such as swelling, discoloration, pain, numbness, or tingling in the bandaged arm or leg.
- You're watched for bleeding from the puncture site.

Does the test have risks?

The nurse or medical technician must wait at least 15 minutes before drawing arterial blood if you're beginning or ending oxygen therapy or if a change is being made in prescribed oxygen therapy.

What are the normal results?

Normal arterial blood gas levels fall within the following ranges:
- Partial pressure of oxygen: 75 to 100 millimeters of mercury
- Partial pressure of carbon dioxide: 35 to 45 millimeters of mercury
- pH: 7.35 to 7.42
- Oxygen content: 15% to 23%
- Oxygen saturation: 94% to 100%
- Bicarbonate: 22 to 26 milliequivalents per liter.

Blood-gas analysis shows the doctor how well your lungs deliver oxygen and eliminate carbon dioxide.

What do abnormal results mean?

Low partial pressure of oxygen, oxygen content, and oxygen saturation levels, with a high partial pressure of carbon dioxide value, may be caused by respiratory muscle weakness or paralysis, head injury, brain tumor, or drug abuse. It can also be caused by airway obstruction, possibly from mucus plugs or a tumor.

Low readings may also be caused by asthma or emphysema, by partially blocked alveoli or pulmonary capillaries, or by alveoli that are damaged or filled with fluid because of disease, hemorrhage, or near-drowning.

Low oxygen content — when respiratory functions are normal — may be caused by severe anemia, decreased blood volume, or reduced oxygen-carrying capacity.

CARBON DIOXIDE CONTENT

When the pressure of carbon dioxide in red blood cells is excessive, carbon dioxide spills out of the cells and dissolves in the plasma, which is fluid that contains blood cells. There, the carbon dioxide combines with water or dissolves to form other compounds.

This test is used to measure the concentration of all forms of carbon dioxide in blood samples. It's commonly ordered for people who have problems with respiration and is usually included in any assessment of electrolyte status. Test results are considered with pH and arterial blood gas levels.

Why is this test done?

Total carbon dioxide content may be measured for the following reasons:

- To determine the amount of carbon dioxide in the blood
- To help evaluate the acid-base balance of the blood.

What should you know before the test?

- This test requires a blood sample, which takes less than 3 minutes to collect.
- You may experience slight discomfort from the needle puncture and tourniquet pressure.
- You don't need to change your diet before the test.
- A nurse or medical technician checks your medication history for any drugs that may affect the test results, including adrenocorticotropic hormone, cortisone, thiazide diuretics, salicylates, paraldehyde, methicillin, dimercaprol, ammonium chloride, or acetazolamide. These drugs may be discontinued. Excessive ingestion of alkaline substances or licorice or accidental ingestion of ethylene glycol or methyl alcohol can also affect test results.

Eating too much licorice or accidentally drinking methyl alcohol could affect the accuracy of this test.

What happens during the test?

A nurse or medical technician inserts a needle into a vein, usually in your forearm. A blood sample is collected in a tube, which is then sent to a lab for testing.

What happens after the test?

If swelling develops at the needle puncture site, warm soaks are applied to the area to ease discomfort.

What are the normal results?

Normal total carbon dioxide levels range from 22 to 34 millimoles per liter of blood.

What do abnormal results mean?

High carbon dioxide levels may occur in acid-base disorders, primary aldosteronism, and Cushing's syndrome. Carbon dioxide levels may increase after excessive loss of acids, as in severe vomiting and continuous gastric drainage.

Decreased carbon dioxide levels are common in metabolic acidosis. Levels may also decrease in respiratory alkalosis.

CALCIUM

This test is used to measure the level of calcium in a blood sample. Calcium is an electrolyte, a substance that has an electric charge when it's dissolved in the blood.

Calcium in the blood helps regulate the body's nerve, muscle, and enzyme activity. More than 98% of the body's calcium is in the bones and teeth, however. So, when blood calcium levels fall below normal, calcium moves out of the bones and teeth and dissolves in the blood to restore the blood's calcium balance.

Because calcium is excreted daily, eating calcium-rich foods regularly is necessary to maintain a normal calcium balance. Regular sun exposure also plays a part in calcium metabolism. (See *How sunshine helps you absorb calcium*, page 336.)

Why is this test done?

Calcium levels may be measured for the following reasons:
- To determine blood calcium levels
- To help the doctor diagnose neuromuscular, skeletal, and endocrine disorders; irregular heart rhythms; blood-clotting deficiencies; and acid-base imbalance.

HOW YOUR BODY WORKS

How sunshine helps you absorb calcium

Most forms of calcium from foods are poorly absorbed from the intestinal tract because they can't be dissolved. But vitamin D — particularly vitamin D_3, which forms when you're exposed to sunshine — and parathyroid hormone play important roles in helping the intestine absorb calcium.

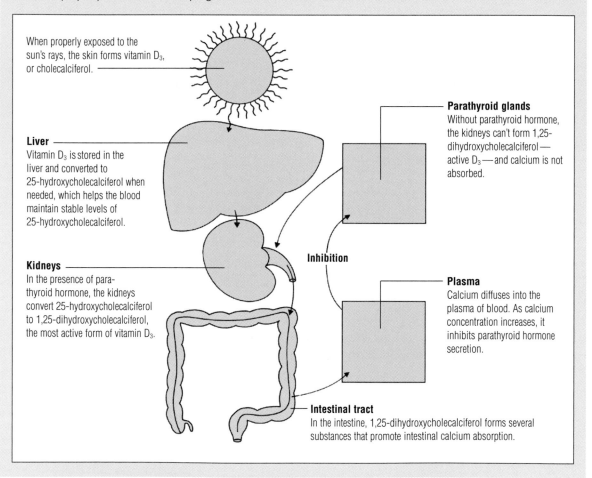

When properly exposed to the sun's rays, the skin forms vitamin D_3, or cholecalciferol.

Liver
Vitamin D_3 is stored in the liver and converted to 25-hydroxycholecalciferol when needed, which helps the blood maintain stable levels of 25-hydroxycholecalciferol.

Kidneys
In the presence of para-thyroid hormone, the kidneys convert 25-hydroxycholecalciferol to 1,25-dihydroxycholecalciferol, the most active form of vitamin D_3.

Inhibition

Parathyroid glands
Without parathyroid hormone, the kidneys can't form 1,25-dihydroxycholecalciferol — active D_3 — and calcium is not absorbed.

Plasma
Calcium diffuses into the plasma of blood. As calcium concentration increases, it inhibits parathyroid hormone secretion.

Intestinal tract
In the intestine, 1,25-dihydroxycholecalciferol forms several substances that promote intestinal calcium absorption.

What should you know before the test?

- This test requires a blood sample, which takes less than 3 minutes to collect.
- You may experience slight discomfort from the needle puncture.
- You don't need to change your diet before the test.

What happens during the test?

A nurse or medical technician inserts a needle into a vein, usually in your forearm. A blood sample is collected in a tube, which is then sent to a lab for testing.

What happens after the test?

If swelling develops at the needle puncture site, warm soaks are applied to the area to ease discomfort.

What are the normal results?

Normal calcium levels range from 2.22 to 2.52 millimoles per liter, or from 2.25 to 2.75 millimoles per liter of blood serum (the clear, fluid portion of blood). In children, calcium levels are higher than in adults. Calcium levels can be as high as 2.99 or 3 millimoles per liter during phases of rapid bone growth.

What do abnormal results mean?

Abnormally high serum calcium levels, which is called *hypercalcemia*, may occur with thyroid disorders, Paget's disease of the bone, some cancers, multiple fractures, or prolonged immobilization. High levels may also be caused by low calcium excretion, excessive calcium ingestion, or from overuse of calcium-based antacids.

Hypercalcemia can lead to deep bone pain, flank pain, and muscle weakness. Hypercalcemic crisis begins with nausea, vomiting, and dehydration, leading to stupor, coma, and cardiac arrest.

Low calcium levels, or *hypocalcemia*, may be caused by hypoparathyroidism, total parathyroid removal, or poor calcium absorption. Decreased calcium levels may also occur with Cushing's syndrome, kidney failure, acute pancreatitis, and peritonitis.

Hypocalcemia can lead to numbness and tingling or spasms of the face, arms, and legs; muscle twitching or cramping; tetany; seizures; and irregular heartbeats.

CHLORIDE

This test measures levels of chloride in blood. Chloride is an electrolyte, a substance that has an electric charge when it's dissolved in the blood. (See *Understanding body fluids.*)

Chloride helps regulate blood volume and blood pressure in the arteries. It also affects the body's acid-base balance. Chloride is absorbed through the intestines and is excreted through the kidneys.

Why is this test done?

Chloride levels may be measured for the following reasons:
- To evaluate the chloride content of blood
- To detect acidosis or alkalosis (acid-base imbalance) and electrolyte imbalances
- To help evaluate a person's fluid status.

What should you know before the test?

- This test requires a blood sample, which takes less than 3 minutes to collect.
- You may experience slight discomfort from the needle puncture and tourniquet pressure.
- You don't need to change your diet before the test.
- Your medication history is checked for the use of drugs that may affect test results. Drugs that elevate chloride levels include ammonium chloride, cholestyramine, boric acid, oxyphenbutazone, phenylbutazone, or excessive intravenous sodium chloride. Chloride levels are decreased by thiazides, furosemide, ethacrynic acid, bicarbonates, or prolonged intravenous infusion of dextrose in water.

What happens during the test?

A nurse or medical technician inserts a needle into a vein, usually in your forearm. A blood sample is collected in a tube, which is then sent to a lab for testing.

What happens after the test?

If swelling develops at the needle puncture site, warm soaks are applied to the area to ease discomfort.

HOW YOUR BODY WORKS

Understanding body fluids

Fluids, mainly water, account for 60% of an adult's total body weight. The body contains substances that conduct a weak electric current when they are dissolved in fluids. These are called *electrolytes*. Electrolytes with a positive charge are called *cations;* those carrying a negative charge are *anions*. A cation-anion balance results in electric neutrality.

Fluid compartments

Two main compartments house the body's fluids. Within its 100 trillion cells, the intracellular compartment accounts for 40% of the total body weight, which is about 25 liters (or quarts) of fluid.

In the spaces between the cells, the extracellular compartment comprises 15% of the total body weight, or approximately 15 liters of fluid. Intra-vascular fluid, or plasma in the blood, accounts for the final 5%. A change in the amount or composition of these compartments can be fatal.

Electrolytes

Electrolytes play a crucial role in the body's water distribution, osmolality (proportion of dissolved substances to liquid in a solution), acid-base balance, and neuromuscular (nerve and muscle-based) irritability.

Potassium is the principal cation (positively charged electrolyte), and phosphate is the dominant anion (negatively charged electrolyte) in the intracellular compartment. Like plasma, the interstitial fluids — which surround the cells of most tissues — contain high concentrations of sodium and chloride. Together, fluids and electrolytes nourish and maintain the body.

What are the normal results?

Normal chloride levels range from 100 to 108 millimoles per liter of blood serum (the clear, fluid portion of blood).

What do abnormal results mean?

High serum chloride levels, called *hyperchloremia*, may be caused by severe dehydration, kidney failure, head injury with hyperventilation, and primary aldosteronism. Hyperchloremia may cause stupor, rapid deep breathing, and weakness that may lead to coma. Excess chloride, which is acidic, may cause metabolic acidosis.

Low chloride levels, called *hypochloremia*, usually accompany low sodium and potassium levels. Underlying causes include prolonged vomiting, gastric suctioning, intestinal fistula, chronic kidney failure, congestive heart failure or edema with fluid retention, and Addison's disease. Hypochloremia can lead to severe muscle tension, tetany, and depressed breathing. Excessive loss of chloride may cause hypochloremic metabolic alkalosis.

MAGNESIUM

This test measures blood levels of magnesium. Magnesium is an electrolyte, a substance that has an electric charge when it's dissolved in the blood. Magnesium is vital to nerve and muscle functioning. Most is found in the bones and blood cells. A small amount occurs in the fluid around blood cells. Magnesium is absorbed through the small intestine and is excreted in urine and feces.

Why is this test done?

Magnesium levels may be measured for the following reasons:
- To determine the magnesium content in the blood
- To evaluate electrolyte status
- To check nerve and muscle functions
- To assess kidney function.

What should you know before the test?

- Don't use magnesium salts, such as milk of magnesia or Epsom salts, for at least 3 days before the test. You don't need to restrict food or fluids, however.
- This test requires a blood sample, which takes less than 3 minutes to collect.
- You may experience slight discomfort from the needle puncture and tourniquet pressure.

What happens during the test?

A nurse or medical technician inserts a needle into a vein, usually in your forearm. A blood sample is collected in a tube, which is then sent to a lab for testing.

What happens after the test?

If swelling develops at the needle puncture site, warm soaks are applied to the area to ease discomfort.

What are the normal results?

Normal magnesium levels range from 0.70 to 0.86 millimole per liter or from 0.75 to 1.25 millimoles per liter of blood serum, which is the clear, fluid portion of blood.

What do abnormal results mean?

Elevated magnesium levels, or *hypermagnesemia,* occur most commonly in kidney failure or when the kidneys excrete inadequate amounts of magnesium. Adrenal insufficiency, or Addison's disease, can also elevate serum magnesium.

Hypermagnesemia can cause lethargy; flushing; sweating; decreased blood pressure; slow, weak pulse; diminished deep-tendon reflexes; muscle weakness; and slow, shallow breathing.

Low magnesium levels, or *hypomagnesemia*, are most commonly caused by chronic alcoholism. Other causes include malabsorption syndrome, diarrhea, faulty absorption after bowel surgery, prolonged bowel or gastric aspiration, acute pancreatitis, primary aldosteronism, severe burns, excessive calcium, and some diuretic therapies.

Hypomagnesemia can lead to leg and foot cramps, hyperactive deep-tendon reflexes, irregular heartbeats, muscle weakness, seizures, twitching, tetany, and tremors.

PHOSPHATES

This test measures phosphate levels in the blood. Phosphates are electrolytes, substances that carry electric charges when they're dissolved in the blood. Phosphates affect metabolism, help maintain acid-base balance, and regulate calcium levels. Phosphates are also vital to bone formation; about 85% of the body's phosphates are in the bones.

Most phosphates are absorbed from foods, through the intestines. The kidneys excrete phosphates and regulate blood phosphate levels.

Why is this test done?

Phosphates may be tested for the following reasons:
- To determine phosphate levels in your blood
- To aid diagnosis of kidney disorders and acid-base imbalance
- To detect endocrine, skeletal, and calcium disorders.

What should you know before the test?

- This test requires a blood sample, which takes less than 3 minutes to collect.

- You may experience slight discomfort from the needle puncture and tourniquet pressure.
- You don't need to change your diet before the test.
- Your medication history is checked for drugs that alter phosphate levels, such as vitamin D, anabolic steroids, androgens, phosphate-binding antacids, acetazolamide, insulin, and epinephrine.

What happens during the test?

A nurse or medical technician inserts a needle into a vein, usually in your forearm. A blood sample is collected in a tube, which is then sent to a lab for testing.

What happens after the test?

If swelling develops at the needle puncture site, warm soaks are applied to the area to ease discomfort.

What are the normal results?

Normal phosphate levels range from 0.81 to 1.45 millimoles per liter. Children have phosphate levels as high as 2.26 millimoles per liter during periods of increased bone growth.

What do abnormal results mean?

Serum calcium and phosphate levels have an inverse relationship; if one is elevated, the other is lowered. Phosphate levels alone are of limited diagnostic use, so they are interpreted with calcium results. (See "Calcium" pages 335 to 337.)

Low phosphate levels, called *hypophosphatemia*, may be caused by malnutrition, malabsorption, hyperparathyroidism, kidney tubular acidosis, or treatment of diabetic acidosis. In children, hypophosphatemia can suppress normal growth.

High phosphate levels, or *hyperphosphatemia*, may be caused by skeletal disease, healing fractures, thyroid problems, acromegaly, diabetic acidosis, high intestinal obstruction, or kidney failure. Hyperphosphatemia is rarely a medical problem, but it can alter bone metabolism in prolonged cases.

This test measures levels of phosphates, which affect metabolism, help maintain acid-base balance, and regulate calcium levels (vital to bone formation). The kidneys excrete phosphates and regulate blood phosphate levels.

POTASSIUM

This test measures potassium levels in the blood. Potassium helps to maintain the balance among fluid solutions in cells and to regulate muscle activity, enzyme activity, and acid-base balance. Potassium also affects kidney function. It's an electrolyte, a substance that has an electric charge when it's dissolved in the blood.

The body has no efficient method to conserve potassium. The kidneys excrete nearly all that is taken in, even when the body's supply is low. Potassium deficiency can develop rapidly and is quite common. Therefore, it's essential to replenish potassium through the diet. (See *Shopping for potassium,* pages 344 and 345.)

Why is this test done?

Potassium levels may be measured for the following reasons:
- To determine the potassium content of the blood
- To evaluate excess potassium, which is called *hyperkalemia,* or potassium depletion, which is called *hypokalemia*
- To monitor kidney function, acid-base balance, and glucose metabolism
- To evaluate neuromuscular and hormone disorders
- To detect the origin of irregular heartbeats.

What should you know before the test?

- This test requires a blood sample, which takes less than 3 minutes to collect.
- You may experience slight discomfort from the needle puncture and tourniquet pressure.
- You don't need to change your diet before the test.
- Your medication history is checked for the use of drugs that may influence test results. Such medications include diuretics, penicillin G potassium, amphotericin B, methicillin, tetracycline, insulin, or glucose. When possible, these medications are discontinued for the test.

What happens during the test?

A nurse or medical technician inserts a needle into a vein, usually in your forearm. A blood sample is collected in a tube, which is then sent to a lab for testing.

SELF-HELP

Shopping for potassium

Here's a list of foods that can help you maintain your dietary intake of potassium.

FOOD	SERVING SIZE	MILLIMOLES OF POTASSIUM
Meats		
Beef	4 ounces (112 grams)	11.2
Chicken	4 ounces (112 grams)	12.0
Scallops	5 large	30.0
Veal	4 ounces (112 grams)	15.2
Vegetables		
Artichokes	1 large bud	7.7
Asparagus (frozen, cooked)	½ cup	5.5
Asparagus, raw	6 spears	7.7
Beans (dried, cooked)	½ cup	10.0
Beans, lima	½ cup	9.5
Broccoli, cooked	½ cup	7.0
Carrots, cooked	½ cup	5.7
Carrots, raw	1 large	8.8
Mushrooms, raw	4 large	10.6
Potato, baked	1 small	15.4
Spinach, fresh, cooked	½ cup	8.5
Squash, winter, baked	½ cup	12.0
Tomato, raw	1 medium	10.4
Fruits		
Apricots, dried	4 halves	5.0
Apricots, fresh	3 small	8.0
Banana	1 medium	12.8
Cantaloupe	½ small	13.0

SELF-HELP

Shopping for potassium *(continued)*

FOOD	SERVING SIZE	MILLIMOLES OF POTASSIUM
Fruits *(continued)*		
Figs, dried	7 small	17.5
Peach, fresh	1 medium	6.2
Pear, fresh	1 medium	6.2
Beverages		
Apricot nectar	1 cup (240 milliliters)	9.0
Grapefruit juice	1 cup	8.2
Orange juice	1 cup	11.4
Pineapple juice	1 cup	9.0
Prune juice	1 cup	14.4
Tomato juice	1 cup	11.6

What happens after the test?

If swelling develops at the needle puncture site, warm soaks are applied to the area to ease discomfort.

What are the normal results?

Normal potassium levels range from 3.5 to 5.0 millimoles per liter of blood serum (the clear, fluid portion of blood).

What do abnormal results mean?

Hyperkalemia occurs when excessive potassium enters the blood because of burns, crushing injuries, diabetic ketoacidosis, or heart attack. Hyperkalemia may also indicate reduced sodium excretion, possibly due to kidney failure or Addison's disease.

Hyperkalemia can lead to weakness, general discomfort, nausea, diarrhea, colicky pain, muscle irritability progressing to flaccid paralysis, oliguria, and a slow or irregular heartbeat.

Hypokalemia often is caused by aldosteronism or Cushing's syndrome, loss of body fluids, or eating too much licorice.

SELF-HELP

What you should know about sodium

North Americans consume far more sodium than their bodies need. Consider the following.

Loaded foods
- About three-fourths of the salt you consume is already in the foods you eat and drink.
- Canned, prepared, and "fast" foods are loaded with sodium; so are condiments, such as ketchup. Some foods that don't taste salty are nevertheless high in sodium, such as carbonated beverages, nondairy creamers, cookies, and cakes.
- Other high-sodium food items include baking powder, baking soda, barbecue sauce, bouillon cubes, chili sauce, cooking wine, garlic salt, softened water, and soy sauce.
- Many medicines and other nonfood items, such as alkalizers for indigestion, laxatives, aspirin, cough medicine, mouthwash, and toothpaste, contain sodium.

Reducing the load
- One teaspoon of salt contains 2 grams of sodium — which, some experts maintain, is all you need to consume on a daily basis. You can maintain this level by not salting your food.
- Even a moderate reduction in salt can lower blood pressure by 10 to 15 points.

Hypokalemia can lead to decreased reflexes; rapid, weak, irregular pulse; mental confusion; hypotension; anorexia; muscle weakness; and paresthesia. In severe cases, ventricular fibrillation, respiratory paralysis, and cardiac arrest can develop.

SODIUM

This test measures sodium levels in serum, which is the clear, fluid portion of blood. Sodium is an electrolyte, a substance that carries an electric charge when it's dissolved in the blood. It affects body water distribution, maintains pressure balance in the fluids that surround cells, and helps nerve and muscle functions. It also affects acid-base balance and influences chloride and potassium levels. Sodium is obtained largely through salt in the diet.

Why is this test done?
Sodium levels may be measured for the following reasons:
- To determine the sodium content of the blood
- To evaluate neuromuscular, kidney, and adrenal functions.

What should you know before the test?
- This test requires a blood sample, which takes less than 3 minutes to collect.
- You may experience slight discomfort from the needle puncture and tourniquet pressure.
- You don't need to change your diet before the test.
- Your medication history is checked for use of drugs that affect sodium levels. Such drugs include most diuretics, corticosteroids, lithium, chlorpropamide, vasopressin, and antihypertensives. When it's possible, medications are discontinued.

What happens during the test?
A nurse or medical technician inserts a needle into a vein, usually in your forearm. A blood sample is collected in a tube, which is then sent to a lab for testing.

What happens after the test?

If swelling develops at the needle puncture site, warm soaks are applied to ease discomfort.

What are the normal results?

Normal sodium levels are 135 to 145 millimoles per liter of blood serum, which is the clear, fluid portion of blood.

What do abnormal results mean?

Sodium imbalance can be caused by a loss or gain of sodium or from a change in the body's fluid status.

A high sodium level, which is called *hypernatremia*, may be due to eating too much salt (see *What you should know about sodium*) or drinking too little water. Other causes are water loss due to diabetes insipidus, impaired kidney function, prolonged hyperventilation, sodium retention as in aldosteronism, or severe vomiting or diarrhea.

An abnormally low sodium level, which is called *hyponatremia*, may be caused by eating too little salt or profuse sweating, gastrointestinal suctioning, diuretic therapy, diarrhea, vomiting, adrenal insufficiency, burns, or chronic poor kidney function.

ENZYMES

CREATINE KINASE

Creatine kinase is a type of protein that's known as an enzyme. This enzyme plays a role in the metabolism, or energy production, of muscle cells. Creatine kinase levels reflect normal tissue destruction. A high creatine kinase level in a blood sample indicates injury to cells, as occurs in a heart attack.

Total creatine kinase and levels of three distinct types of creatine kinase, called *isoenzymes*, are usually measured. These are CK-BB (CK$_1$), CK-MB (CK$_2$), and CK-MM (CK$_3$). The initials "M" and "B" denote muscle and brain, respectively, indicating where the isoenzymes occur. CK-BB is found mostly in brain tissue. CK-MM and CK-MB are found primarily in skeletal and heart muscles.

Isoenzyme measurements are used to determine the precise site of tissue destruction in acute heart attack. To obtain more precise information, subunits of CK-MM and CK-MB, called *isoforms*, are measured.

Why is this test done?

Creatine kinase levels may be measured for the following reasons:
- To check your heart and skeletal muscle function
- To detect and diagnose acute heart attack and recurrent heart attack
- To evaluate possible causes of chest pain
- To monitor reduced blood flow to the heart after heart surgery or other treatments that affect heart muscle
- To detect skeletal muscle disorders that do not originate in the nerves.

What should you know before the test?

- You don't need to change your diet before the test but you should avoid drinking alcoholic beverages.
- Use of aminocaproic acid or lithium may interfere with test results. When possible, these drugs are discontinued.
- If you're being evaluated for skeletal muscle disorders, avoid exercising for 24 hours before the test.
- This test requires a blood sample, which takes less than 3 minutes to collect. Multiple blood samples may be needed to detect fluctuations in creatine kinase levels.
- You may experience slight discomfort from the needle puncture and tourniquet pressure.

What happens during the test?

- A nurse or medical technician inserts a needle into a vein, usually in your forearm. A blood sample is collected in a tube, which is then sent to a lab for testing.
- The sample is collected before or within 1 hour of giving intramuscular injections because muscle injury increases the total creatine kinase level.

This enzyme tells the doctor about heart and skeletal muscle function, including the causes of chest pain.

What happens after the test?

■ If swelling develops at the needle puncture site, warm soaks are applied to the area to ease discomfort.

■ You may resume taking any medications that were withheld before the test.

What are the normal results?

Total creatine kinase levels range from 25 to 130 international units per liter for men, and from 10 to 150 international units per liter for women. Levels may be significantly higher in very muscular people. Infants up to age 1 have levels two to four times higher than adult levels, possibly reflecting birth trauma and muscle development. Normal ranges for isoenzyme levels are as follows: CK-BB, undetectable; CK-MB, undetectable to 7 international units per liter; CK-MM, 5 to 7 international units per liter (CK-MM makes up 99% of total creatine kinase normally present in blood).

What do abnormal results mean?

Detectable CK-BB isoenzyme may indicate possible brain tissue injury, widespread malignant tumors, severe shock, or kidney failure.

CK-MB isoenzyme greater than 5% of total creatine kinase indicates heart attack. In an acute heart attack or following heart surgery, CK-MB rises, peaks in 12 to 24 hours, and usually returns to normal in 24 to 48 hours. Total creatine kinase follows roughly the same pattern.

CK-MB levels may not increase in congestive heart failure or during angina pectoris not accompanied by heart tissue cell death. Serious skeletal muscle injury caused by some muscular dystrophies and other conditions may produce mild CK-MB elevation.

Increasing CK-MM levels follow skeletal muscle damage from injury, such as surgery and intramuscular injections, or from some diseases. A moderate rise in CK-MM levels develops in people with hypothyroidism. Sharp elevations occur with muscular activity caused by agitation, such as in an acute psychotic episode.

Total creatine kinase levels may be elevated in people with severe hypokalemia, carbon monoxide poisoning, malignant hyperthermia, or alcoholic cardiomyopathy. They may also be elevated following seizures and, occasionally, following lung or brain damage.

Normal levels of this type of protein may be significantly higher in very muscular people.

CREATINE KINASE COMPONENTS

Creatine kinase, an enzyme found in muscle tissue, has three components, which are called *isoenzymes*. These are CK-BB (CK_1), CK-MB (CK_2), and CK-MM (CK_3). The initials "M" and "B" denote muscle and brain, respectively, indicating where the isoenzymes occur; CK-BB is most prevalent in brain tissue; CK-MM and CK-MB are found primarily in skeletal and heart muscle.

Damage to the heart releases CK-MM, CK-MB, and another isoenzyme, called *lactate dehydrogenase*, into the blood. Subcomponents of CK-MM and CK-MB are called $CK-MM_1$, $CK-MM_2$, $CK-MB_1$, and $CK-MB_2$.

Why is this test done?

Creatine kinase isoforms may be measured for the following reasons:
- To confirm or rule out heart attack
- To evaluate skeletal muscle injury.

What should you know before the test?

- This test requires several blood samples, which are drawn at timed intervals. Each takes less than 3 minutes to collect.
- You may experience slight discomfort from the needle puncture and tourniquet pressure.
- You don't need to change your diet before the test.

What happens during the test?

- A nurse or medical technician inserts a needle into a vein, usually in your forearm. A blood sample is collected in a tube, which is then sent to a lab for testing.
- A blood sample is collected every 2 hours as needed.

What happens after the test?

If swelling develops at the needle puncture site, warm soaks are applied to the area to ease discomfort.

What are the normal results?

$CK-MB_2$ concentrations are less than 1.0. The $CK-MB_2$ to $CK-MB_1$ ratio is less than 1.5.

What do abnormal results mean?

An increase in CK-MB indicates heart attack. In more than half of the people who have a heart attack, the ratio of $CK\text{-}MB_2$ to $CK\text{-}MB_1$ is greater than 1.5 within 2 to 4 hours. By 6 hours after the heart attack, more than 90% of people have a ratio of 1.5 or greater.

LACTATE DEHYDROGENASE

Lactate dehydrogenase is a type of protein that's called an *isoenzyme*. It's involved in the body's metabolic, or energy-producing, process. When cells are damaged, levels of lactate dehydrogenase in the blood become elevated. Measuring total lactate dehydrogenase is of limited diagnostic use, however, because lactate dehydrogenase is present in almost all body tissues. Five tissue-specific forms of lactate dehydrogenase are measured in this test. These are identified by the initials "LD" and a numeral: LD_1 and LD_2 appear primarily in the heart, red blood cells, and kidneys; LD_3 is primarily in the lungs; and LD_4 and LD_5 are in the liver and the skeletal muscles.

The test helps doctors diagnose heart attack, lung damage, anemias, and liver disease.

Why is this test done?

Lactate dehydrogenase levels may be measured for the following reasons:
- To detect tissue damage
- To aid the diagnosis of heart attack, lung damage, anemias, and liver disease
- To support creatine kinase isoenzyme test results
- To monitor a person's response to some types of chemotherapy.

What should you know before the test?

- You don't need to change your diet before this test.
- A blood sample is required, which takes less than 3 minutes to collect.
- You may experience slight discomfort from the needle puncture and tourniquet pressure.
- If heart attack is suspected, the test is repeated on the next two mornings to monitor changes.

What happens during the test?

A nurse or medical technician inserts a needle into a vein, usually in your forearm. A blood sample is collected in a tube, which is then sent to a lab for testing.

What happens after the test?

If swelling develops at the needle puncture site, warm soaks are applied to the area to ease discomfort.

What are the normal results?

Total lactate dehydrogenase levels normally range from 45 to 90 international units per liter. Normal distribution is as follows:

- LD_1: 14% to 26% of total
- LD_2: 29% to 39% of total
- LD_3: 20% to 26% of total
- LD_4: 8% to 16% of total
- LD_5: 6% to 16% of total.

What do abnormal results mean?

Because many common diseases cause elevations in total lactate dehydrogenase levels, further testing is usually necessary for a diagnosis. In some disorders, total lactate dehydrogenase may be within normal limits, but abnormal proportions of each enzyme indicate specific organ tissue damage.

ASPARTATE AMINOTRANSFERASE

Aspartate aminotransferase is a type of protein called an *enzyme* that's essential to energy production in cells of the body. Aspartate aminotransferase is found in the liver, heart, skeletal muscle, kidneys, pancreas, and red blood cells. It's released into the bloodstream in proportion to the amount of cell damage due to heart or liver problems. The change in aspartate aminotransferase levels over time is a reliable monitoring mechanism.

Why is this test done?

Aspartate aminotransferase levels may be measured for the following reasons:

- To check heart and liver function
- To aid detection and differential diagnosis of acute liver disease
- To monitor a person's progress and prognosis in heart and liver diseases
- To help the doctor diagnose heart attack in correlation with creatine kinase and lactate dehydrogenase levels.

What should you know before the test?

- You don't need to change your diet before the test.
- The test usually requires three blood samples, collected on 3 consecutive days. Each sample takes less than 3 minutes to collect.
- You may experience slight discomfort from the needle puncture and tourniquet pressure.
- Drugs that may interfere with results are usually withheld before the test.

What happens during the test?

A nurse or medical technician inserts a needle into a vein, usually in your forearm. Each blood sample is collected in a tube, which is then sent to a lab for testing.

What happens after the test?

- If swelling develops at the needle puncture site, warm soaks are applied to the area to ease discomfort.
- You may resume taking medications that were withheld before the test.

What are the normal results?

Aspartate aminotransferase levels range from 8 to 20 international units per liter. Normal levels for infants are up to four times higher than those of adults.

What do abnormal results mean?

Aspartate aminotransferase levels fluctuate, reflecting the extent of cell damage. Levels are minimally elevated early in the disease process and extremely elevated during the most acute phase. Depending on when the initial sample is drawn, aspartate aminotransferase levels may increase, indicating increasing disease severity and tissue damage, or decrease, indicating disease resolution and tissue repair.

ALANINE AMINOTRANSFERASE

Alanine aminotransferase is an enzyme — or specialized protein — that's necessary for tissue energy production. Alanine aminotransferase primarily appears in the liver, with lesser amounts in the kidneys, heart, and skeletal muscle. This test is used to measure the levels of alanine aminotransferase that are released to the bloodstream after acute liver cell damage.

Why is this test done?
Alanine aminotransferase may be measured for the following reasons:
- To check liver function
- To detect and evaluate treatment of acute liver disease, especially hepatitis or cirrhosis without jaundice
- To distinguish between heart and liver tissue damage when considered with aspartate aminotransferase levels
- To assess the adverse effects that some drugs may have on the liver.

The test for this enzyme helps the doctor check for bad effects that some drugs may have on the liver.

What should you know before the test?
- This test requires a blood sample, which takes less than 3 minutes to collect.
- You may experience slight discomfort from the needle puncture and tourniquet pressure.
- You don't need to change your diet before the test.
- Drugs that may affect test results are usually withheld.

What happens during the test?
A nurse or medical technician inserts a needle into a vein, usually in your forearm. A blood sample is collected in a tube, which is then sent to a lab for testing.

What happens after the test?

■ If swelling develops at the needle puncture site, warm soaks are applied to the area to ease discomfort.

■ You may resume taking medications that were withheld before the test.

What are the normal results?

Alanine aminotransferase levels range from 8 to 20 international units per liter.

What do abnormal results mean?

Extremely high alanine aminotransferase levels—up to 50 times normal—suggest viral or severe drug-induced hepatitis or other liver disease with extensive cell damage. Moderate-to-high levels may indicate infectious mononucleosis, chronic hepatitis, intrahepatic cholestasis or cholecystitis, early or improving acute viral hepatitis or severe liver congestion due to heart failure. Slight-to-moderate elevations of alanine aminotransferase may appear in any condition that produces acute liver injury, such as active cirrhosis and drug-induced or alcoholic hepatitis. Marginal elevations occasionally occur in acute heart attack, reflecting secondary liver congestion or the release of small amounts of alanine aminotransferase from heart tissue.

ALKALINE PHOSPHATASE

Alkaline phosphatase is an enzyme, or specialized protein, that's involved in bone calcification. (See *Why enzymes cause chemical reactions,* page 356.) It also helps transport the products of metabolism and lipids, or fats, through the body.

This test is used to measure alkaline phosphatase levels in the blood. Alkaline phosphatase measurements reflect the combined activity of several alkaline phosphatase isoenzymes, or subforms, that are found in the liver, bones, kidneys, intestinal lining, and placenta. Bone and liver alkaline phosphatase are always present in the blood of adults, with liver alkaline phosphatase most prominent except during the last 3 months of pregnancy. Intestinal alkaline phosphatase can be a normal finding or it can be an abnormal finding associated with liver disease.

HOW YOUR BODY WORKS

Why enzymes cause chemical reactions

According to current theory, enzymes promote chemical reactions in the body because of their surface activity. Each reactant has its own unique three-dimensional surface, just like a puzzle piece.

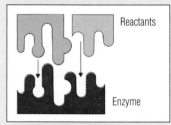

Reactants

Enzyme

An enzyme combines with reactants whose surfaces fit its own.

Reaction

To start a reaction, the reactants and an enzyme that's specific — or custom-fitted — to them combine briefly.

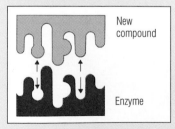

New compound

Enzyme

At the end of the reaction, the two parts separate, leaving the enzyme unchanged.

Why is this test done?

Alkaline phosphatase levels may be measured for the following reasons:
- To check your liver or bone function
- To detect and identify skeletal disease
- To detect liver lesions that cause biliary obstruction, such as tumors or abscesses
- To assess response to vitamin D in the treatment of rickets
- To supplement information from other liver function studies and gastrointestinal enzyme tests.

What should you know before the test?

- You must fast for at least 8 hours before the test because fat intake stimulates intestinal alkaline phosphatase secretion.
- This test requires a blood sample, which takes less than 3 minutes to collect.
- You may experience slight discomfort from the needle puncture and tourniquet pressure.

What happens during the test?

A nurse or medical technician inserts a needle into a vein, usually in your forearm. A blood sample is collected in a tube, which is then sent to a lab for testing.

What happens after the test?

- If swelling develops at the needle puncture site, warm soaks are applied to the area to ease discomfort.
- You may resume your regular diet.

What are the normal results?

Total alkaline phosphatase levels for men range from 90 to 239 international units per liter. For women under age 45, total alkaline phosphatase levels range from 76 to 196 international units per liter. For women over age 45, the range widens to 87 to 250 international units per liter.

What do abnormal results mean?

Although significant alkaline phosphatase elevations are possible with diseases that affect many organs, they are most likely to indicate skeletal disease or bile duct obstruction. Many acute liver diseases cause alkaline phosphatase elevations.

GAMMA GLUTAMYL TRANSFERASE

Gamma glutamyl transferase is an enzyme, or specialized protein, that's involved in the transfer of amino acids across cell membranes and possibly in other aspects of metabolism (energy production). Highest concentrations of gamma glutamyl transferase exist in the kidney tubules, but it also appears in the liver, biliary tract epithelium, pancreas, lymphocytes, brain, and testicles. This test is used to measure gamma glutamyl transferase levels in blood.

Why is this test done?

Gamma glutamyl transferase levels may be measured for the following reasons:
- To evaluate liver function
- To provide information about liver diseases, to assess liver function, and to detect alcohol ingestion
- To distinguish between skeletal disease and liver disease when alkaline phosphatase levels are elevated.

What should you know before the test?

- This test requires a blood sample, which takes less than 3 minutes to collect.
- You may experience slight discomfort from the needle puncture and tourniquet pressure.
- You don't need to change your diet before the test.

What happens during the test?

A nurse or medical technician inserts a needle into a vein, usually in your forearm. A blood sample is collected in a tube, which is then sent to a lab for testing.

What happens after the test?

If swelling develops at the needle puncture site, warm soaks are applied to the area to ease discomfort.

What are the normal results?

Usually, normal levels in women range from 5 to 24 international units per liter. In men, levels range from 8 to 37 international units per liter.

What do abnormal results mean?

Serum gamma glutamyl transferase levels are increased in any acute liver disease. Moderate increases occur in acute pancreatitis, in kidney disease, in prostatic metastases, after surgery, and sometimes with epilepsy or brain tumors. Levels also increase after alcohol ingestion. The sharpest elevations occur with obstructive jaundice and liver metastatic infiltrations. Gamma glutamyl transferase may increase 5 to 10 days after an acute heart attack.

AMYLASE

Amylase is an enzyme, or specialized protein, that's formed primarily in the pancreas and the salivary glands. It helps digest starch and glycogen in the mouth, stomach, and intestine. (See *Turning starch into sugar*.) In suspected acute pancreatic disease, measurement of amylase in the blood or the urine is the most important lab test.

Amylase helps digest starch and glycogen in the mouth, stomach, and intestine.

Why is this test done?

Amylase levels may be measured for the following reasons:
- To check pancreatic function and to diagnose acute pancreatitis
- To distinguish between acute pancreatitis and other causes of abdominal pain that require immediate surgery
- To evaluate possible pancreatic injury caused by abdominal injury or surgery.

What should you know before the test?

- This test requires a blood sample, which takes less than 3 minutes to collect.
- You may experience slight discomfort from the needle puncture and tourniquet pressure.
- You don't need to change your diet before the test, but you must abstain from alcohol.
- Drugs that may elevate amylase levels are withheld before the test.

HOW YOUR BODY WORKS

Turning starch into sugar

Starch is a polysaccharide, meaning it's composed of long chains of simple sugars. It can be digested only after it has been cooked.

Amylase takes over
Within 15 to 30 minutes after starchy foods are eaten, amylase — which is produced by the salivary glands and the pancreas — converts 70% of starch polysaccharides to disaccharides, which include simple sugars such as maltose, glucose, and oligosaccharides.

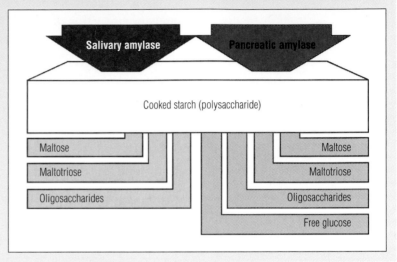

What happens during the test?

A nurse or medical technician inserts a needle into a vein, usually in your forearm. A blood sample is collected in a tube, which is then sent to a lab for testing.

What happens after the test?

- If swelling develops at the needle puncture site, warm soaks are applied to the area to ease discomfort.
- You may resume taking medications that were withheld before the test.

What are the normal results?

Serum levels range from 30 to 220 international units per liter. A general average is less than 300 international units per liter. More than 20 methods of measuring serum amylase exist, with different ranges of normal levels. Test levels cannot always be converted to a standard measurement.

What do abnormal results mean?

After the onset of acute pancreatitis, amylase levels begin to rise in 2 hours, peak at 12 to 48 hours, and return to normal in 3 to 4 days. Determination of urine levels should follow blood amylase results to rule out pancreatitis. Moderate elevations in blood amylase may accompany obstruction of the bile duct, the pancreatic duct, or at the juncture of these ducts. Other causes are pancreatic injury from perforated peptic ulcer; pancreatic cancer; and acute salivary gland disease. Impaired kidney function may increase amylase levels in blood.

Depressed levels may indicate chronic pancreatitis, pancreatic cancer, cirrhosis, hepatitis, or toxemia of pregnancy.

LIPASE

Lipase is an enzyme, or specialized protein, that's produced in the pancreas and is secreted into the duodenum, where it converts triglycerides and other fats into fatty acids and glycerol.

Destruction of pancreatic cells, which occurs in acute pancreatitis, releases large amounts of lipase into the blood. This test is used to measure blood lipase levels. It is most useful when performed with a serum or urine amylase test.

Why is this test done?

Lipase levels may be measured for the following reasons:
- To evaluate pancreas function
- To help the doctor diagnose acute pancreatitis.

What should you know before the test?

- You must fast overnight before the test.
- Cholinergics, codeine, meperidine, and morphine are usually withheld before the test.
- This test requires a blood sample, which takes less than 3 minutes to collect.
- You may experience slight discomfort from the needle puncture and tourniquet pressure.

INSIGHT INTO ILLNESS

Blocking the enzyme path

The pancreas secretes lipase, amylase, and other enzymes. These pass through the pancreatic duct into the duodenum, which is the upper portion of the intestine. In pancreatitis — inflammation of the pancreas — and obstruction of the pancreatic duct by a tumor or calculus, these enzymes can't reach their destination. Instead, they're diverted into the bloodstream.

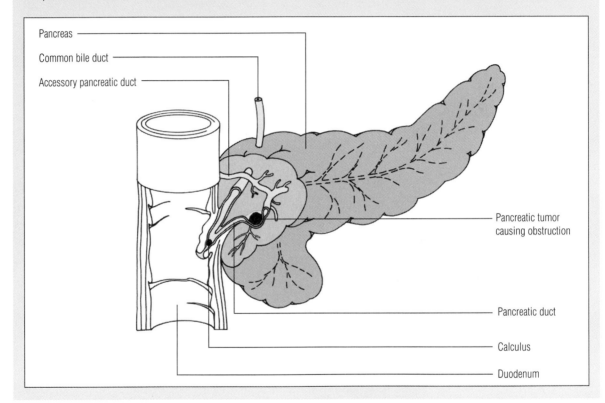

Pancreas
Common bile duct
Accessory pancreatic duct
Pancreatic tumor causing obstruction
Pancreatic duct
Calculus
Duodenum

What happens during the test?

A nurse or medical technician inserts a needle into a vein, usually in your forearm. A blood sample is collected in a tube, which is then sent to a lab for testing.

What happens after the test?

- If swelling develops at the needle puncture site, warm soaks are applied to the area to ease discomfort.
- You may resume taking medications that were withheld before the test.

What are the normal results?

Normal lipase levels are generally less than 300 international units per liter.

What do abnormal results mean?

High lipase levels suggest acute pancreatitis or pancreatic duct obstruction. (See *Blocking the enzyme path,* page 361.) After an acute attack, levels remain elevated up to 14 days. Lipase levels may also increase in other pancreatic injuries, such as perforated peptic ulcer, and with high intestinal obstruction, pancreatic cancer, or kidney disease with impaired excretion.

ACID PHOSPHATASE

Acid phosphatase is a group of enzymes, or specialized proteins, that are found primarily in the prostate gland and semen and, to a lesser extent, in the liver, spleen, red blood cells, bone marrow, and platelets. This test measures total acid phosphatase and the prostatic fraction in a blood sample.

Why is this test done?

Acid phosphatase levels may be measured for the following reasons:
- To check prostate function
- To detect prostate cancer
- To monitor response to therapy for prostate cancer (successful treatment decreases acid phosphatase levels).

What should you know before the test?

- This test requires a blood sample, which takes less than 3 minutes to collect.
- You may experience slight discomfort from the needle puncture and tourniquet pressure.
- You don't need to change your diet before this test.
- You must not use fluorides, phosphates, and clofibrate before the test.

What happens during the test?

A nurse or medical technician inserts a needle into a vein, usually in your forearm. A blood sample is collected in a tube, which is then sent to a lab for testing.

What happens after the test?

- If swelling develops at the needle puncture site, warm soaks are applied to the area to ease discomfort.
- You may resume taking medications that were withheld before the test.

What are the normal results?

Normal levels for total acid phosphatase range from approximately 0.5 to 1.9 international units per liter.

What do abnormal results mean?

High acid phosphatase levels may indicate a prostate tumor that has spread. If the tumor has spread to the bones, high acid phosphatase levels are accompanied by high alkaline phosphatase levels.

Acid phosphatase levels increase moderately in prostatic tissue damage, Paget's disease, Gaucher's disease, and occasionally in other conditions, such as multiple myeloma.

PROSTATE-SPECIFIC ANTIGEN

Antigens are any substances — such as dissolved toxins or bacteria — that evoke responses from a person's immune system. Prostate-specific antigen occurs in normal and benign prostatic tissue, as well as with prostate cancer. This test is used to measure prostate-specific antigen levels in the blood. The results are used to monitor the spread or recurrence of prostate cancer and to evaluate treatment for this disease.

Why is this test done?

Prostate-specific antigen may be measured for the following reasons:
- To monitor the course of prostate cancer
- To monitor and evaluate a person's response to treatment.

The results of this test are used to monitor the spread or recurrence of prostate cancer and to evaluate its treatment.

What should you know before the test?

- You don't need to change your diet before this test.
- The test requires a blood sample, which takes less than 3 minutes to collect. The sample is collected in the morning, if possible.
- You may experience slight discomfort from the needle puncture and tourniquet pressure.

What happens during the test?

A nurse or medical technician inserts a needle into a vein, usually in your forearm. A blood sample is collected in a tube, which is then sent to a lab for testing.

What happens after the test?

If swelling develops at the needle puncture site, warm soaks are applied to the area to ease discomfort.

What are the normal results?

Normal levels for prostate-specific antigen should not exceed 2.7 micrograms per liter of blood serum in men under age 40 or 4 micrograms per liter in men age 40 or older.

What do abnormal results mean?

About 80% of men with prostate cancer have prostate-specific antigen levels greater than 4 micrograms per liter. Prostate-specific antigen results alone do not confirm a diagnosis of prostate cancer, however; about 20% of men with benign prostatic tissue growth also have levels greater than 4 micrograms per liter. Further assessment and testing, including tissue biopsy, are needed to confirm cancer.

PLASMA RENIN ACTIVITY

Renin is an enzyme, or specialized protein, that's produced in the kidneys. Renin secretion from the kidneys is the first stage of a cycle that controls the body's sodium-potassium balance, fluid volume, and blood pressure. Renin is released into the renal veins — which are in the abdomen, near the kidneys — in response to sodium depletion and blood loss.

This test is a screening procedure for renovascular hypertension, or high blood pressure, but it doesn't confirm this diagnosis.

Why is this test done?

Plasma renin activity may be measured for the following reasons:
- To determine the cause of high blood pressure
- To screen for high blood pressure of kidney-related origin (reno-vascular hypertension)
- To help plan treatment of essential hypertension, a genetic disease that's often aggravated by excessive sodium intake
- To help identify primary aldosteronism (a disorder caused by excessive secretion of the hormone aldosterone)
- To confirm primary aldosteronism (for this, the *sodium-depleted plasma renin* test is used)
- To help identify high blood pressure linked to renovascular disease that affects one or both sides of the body (for this, *renal vein catheterization* is used).

What should you know before the test?

- A nurse or technician checks your history for the use of any substances that may affect the test results, including diuretics, antihypertensives, vasodilators, oral contraceptives, and licorice. Discontinue use of these and maintain a normal-sodium diet for 2 to 4 weeks before the test.
- For the sodium-depleted renin test, you'll receive furosemide. If you have angina or cerebrovascular insufficiency, you'll receive chlorthiazide and follow a low-salt diet for 3 days. (See *Preparing for renin testing: Pass up the salt,* page 367.)
- You'll be asked to collect your urine for 24 hours before the test.
- For several days before the test, you won't receive radiation treatments.
- The test requires a blood sample, which takes less than 3 minutes to collect. The sample is collected in the morning, if possible.
- You may experience slight discomfort from the needle puncture and tourniquet pressure.
- If a recumbent sample is ordered, you must remain in bed for at least 2 hours before the sample is obtained because posture influences renin secretion. If an upright sample is ordered, you must stand or sit upright for 2 hours before the test is performed.
- If renal vein catheterization is ordered, you'll be asked to sign an informed consent form. This procedure is done in the X-ray department. Before the test, you'll receive a local anesthetic.

Because posture influences renin secretion, one version of the test requires a blood sample after you spend 2 hours in bed.

What happens during the test?

During peripheral vein sample collection:

- A nurse or medical technician inserts a needle into a vein, usually in your forearm. A blood sample is collected in a tube, which is then sent to a lab for testing.
- The lab is notified if you're fasting and whether you're upright or supine during specimen collection.

During renal vein catheterization:

- A flexible tube, called a *catheter*, is advanced to the kidneys through the large vein in your thigh. Samples are taken from both of your renal veins and from the major vein to your heart.

What happens after the test?

After peripheral vein sample collection:

- If swelling develops at the needle puncture site, warm soaks are applied to the area to ease discomfort.
- You may resume your usual diet.
- You may resume taking medications that were discontinued before the test.

After renal vein catheterization:

- Pressure is applied to the catheterization site for 10 to 20 minutes to prevent bleeding.
- Your vital signs are monitored, and the catheterization site is checked every half hour for 2 hours, then every hour for 4 hours, to ensure that the bleeding has stopped.
- You may resume your usual diet.
- You may resume taking medications that were discontinued before the test.

Does the test have risks?

After renal vein catheterization, you're checked for blue skin coloration, loss of pulse, or skin coolness, which are signs of clot formation and clogged arteries.

What are the normal results?

Levels of plasma renin activity and of aldosterone decrease with advancing age. Results vary with the type of test.

Sodium-depleted, upright, peripheral vein: For ages 18 to 39, the range is from 0.81 to 6.67 nanograms per liter per second; the average is 3.0 nanograms per liter per second. For age 40 and over, the range

SELF-HELP

Preparing for renin testing: Pass up the salt

Before undergoing renin testing, you must severely restrict your intake of sodium for 3 days. This restriction is important to the accuracy of the test. If you are following this diet at home, observe these precautions.

- Eat only the foods included in the meal plan provided by the doctor. You may delete foods from the diet, but you may not add foods.
- Measure all portions, using standard measuring cups and spoons.
- Use 4 ounces (112 grams) *unsalted* beefsteak or ground beef for lunch and 4 ounces *unsalted* chicken for dinner. (Amount refers to weight before cooking.)
- You may eat the following *unsalted* (fresh or frozen) vegetables: asparagus, green or wax beans, cabbage, cauliflower, lettuce, and tomatoes.
- Use only the specified amount of coffee.
- If you are thirsty between meals, drink distilled water, but *no other* food or beverages.
- Prepare all foods without salt; don't use salt at the table.

Breakfast
1 egg, poached or boiled, or fried in *unsalted* fat
2 slices *unsalted* toast
1 shredded wheat biscuit or ⅔ cup *unsalted* cooked cereal
4 ounces (120 milliliters) half-and-half or milk
8 ounces (240 milliliters) coffee
1 cup orange juice
Sugar, jam or jelly, and *unsalted* butter, as desired

Lunch
4 ounces *unsalted* tomato juice
4 ounces *unsalted* beefsteak or ground beef; may be broiled, or fried in *unsalted* fat
½ cup *unsalted* potato
½ cup *unsalted* green beans or other allowed vegetable
1 serving fruit
8 ounces coffee
1 slice *unsalted* bread
Sugar, jam or jelly, and *unsalted* butter, as desired

Dinner
4 ounces *unsalted* chicken; may be baked or broiled, or fried in *unsalted* fat
½ cup *unsalted* potato
1 slice *unsalted* bread
Lettuce salad (vinegar and oil dressing)
½ cup *unsalted* green beans or other allowed vegetable
1 serving fruit
8 ounces coffee
Sugar, jam or jelly, and *unsalted* butter, as desired

is from 0.81 nanogram per liter per second; the average is 1.64 nanograms per liter per second.

Sodium-replete, upright, peripheral vein: For ages 18 to 39, the range is from 0.16 to 1.19 nanograms per liter per second; the average is 0.53 nanogram per liter per second. For age 40 and over, the range is from 0.28 to 0.83 nanogram per liter per second; the average is 0.28 nanogram per liter per second.

Renal vein catheterization: The ratio of the renin level in the renal vein to the level in the inferior vena cava is less than 1.5 to 1.0.

What do abnormal results mean?

Elevated renin levels may occasionally occur in high blood pressure of several types, cirrhosis, hypokalemia (potassium depletion), and hypovolemia (depletion of body fluid) caused by bleeding. Other causes are renin-producing kidney tumors and hypofunction of the adrenal gland (Addison's disease). High renin levels may also be found in chronic kidney failure with parenchymal disease, end-stage kidney disease, and transplant rejection.

Decreased renin levels may indicate hypervolemia due to a high-sodium diet, salt-retaining steroids, primary aldosteronism, Cushing's syndrome, licorice ingestion syndrome, or essential high blood pressure with low renin levels.

High serum and urine aldosterone levels, with low plasma renin activity, help identify primary aldosteronism. In the sodium-depleted renin test, low plasma renin confirms primary aldosteronism.

CHOLINESTERASE

The cholinesterase test measures the amounts of two similar enzymes, or specialized proteins: acetylcholinesterase and pseudocholinesterase. Acetylcholinesterase is present in nerve tissue, red cells of the spleen, and the gray matter of the brain. Pseudocholinesterase is produced primarily in the liver and appears in small amounts in the pancreas, intestine, heart, and white matter of the brain. (See *Sending an impulse from nerves to muscles.*)

When poisoning by an organophosphate (which is in nerve gases and many insecticides) is suspected, either cholinesterase may be measured. In suspected poisoning by muscle relaxant, the person lacks adequate pseudocholinesterase, which normally inactivates the muscle relaxant. In this case, measurement of pseudocholinesterase is required.

HOW YOUR BODY WORKS

Sending an impulse from nerves to muscles

Each time a nerve impulse arrives at the junction between a nerve fiber and a skeletal muscle fiber, the nerve terminals release about 300 vesicles, or bubbles, of the enzyme acetylcholine into the synaptic clefts, as seen in the diagram.

An important pause
The action of the enzyme acetylcholinesterase allows the muscle fiber to recover, or relax. Without acetylcholinesterase, muscle excitation would be continuous.

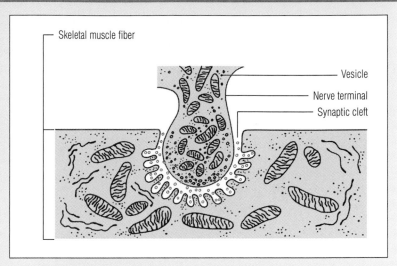

Why is this test done?

Cholinesterase levels may be measured for the following reasons:
- To check muscle function or the extent of poisoning
- To evaluate a person's potential response to cholinesterase-related substances before surgery or electroconvulsive therapy
- To determine a person's possible side effects from muscle relaxants
- To check overexposure to insecticides containing organophosphate compounds
- To check liver function and (rarely) aid diagnosis of liver disease.

What should you know before the test?

- This test requires a blood sample, which takes less than 3 minutes to collect.
- You may experience slight discomfort from the needle puncture and tourniquet pressure.
- When possible, medications that affect serum cholinesterase levels are withheld before the test.

What happens during the test?

A nurse or medical technician inserts a needle into a vein, usually in your forearm. A blood sample is collected in a tube, which is then sent to a lab for testing.

What happens after the test?

■ If swelling develops at the needle puncture site, warm soaks are applied to the area to ease discomfort.

■ You may resume taking medications that were withheld before the test.

What are the normal results?

Pseudocholinesterase levels range from 8,000 to 18,000 international units per liter of blood serum.

What do abnormal results mean?

Severely lowered pseudocholinesterase levels suggest an inherited deficiency or organophosphate insecticide poisoning. Levels near zero require emergency treatment.

Pseudocholinesterase levels are usually normal in early liver obstruction and are decreased with liver damage, such as hepatitis or cirrhosis. Levels also decline because of acute infections, chronic malnutrition, anemia, heart attack, obstructive jaundice, and cancer.

GLUCOSE-6-PHOSPHATE DEHYDROGENASE

Glucose-6-phosphate dehydrogenase is an enzyme, or specialized protein, that's found in most cells of the body. It's involved in metabolizing glucose, a form of sugar that the body uses for energy. This test can detect glucose-6-phosphate dehydrogenase deficiency, which is a hereditary condition that allows destruction of red blood cells.

About 10% of all African American men in the United States inherit mild glucose-6-phosphate dehydrogenase deficiency. Some people of Mediterranean descent inherit a severe deficiency. In some whites, fava beans may produce episodes of red blood cell destruction. Although deficiency of glucose-6-phosphate dehydrogenase provides partial immunity to one type of malaria, it causes a bad reaction to antimalarial drugs.

Why is this test done?

Glucose-6-phosphate dehydrogenase levels may be measured for the following reasons:

- To detect an inherited enzyme deficiency that affects red blood cells
- To diagnose hemolytic anemia caused by glucose-6-phosphate dehydrogenase deficiency.

What should you know before the test?

- This test requires a blood sample, which takes less than 3 minutes to collect.
- You may experience slight discomfort from the needle puncture and tourniquet pressure.
- You don't need to change your diet before the test.
- A nurse or medical technician checks your history for recent blood transfusion or ingestion of aspirin, sulfonamides, phenacetin, nitrofurantoin, vitamin K derivatives, antimalarials, or fava beans. These substances cause red blood cell destruction in people who are glucose-6-phosphate dehydrogenase–deficient.

The test may identify a specific anemia or an inherited enzyme deficiency that affects red blood cells.

What happens during the test?

A nurse or medical technician inserts a needle into a vein, usually in your forearm. A blood sample is collected in a tube, which is then sent to a lab for testing.

What happens after the test?

If swelling develops at the needle puncture site, warm soaks are applied to the area to ease discomfort.

What are the normal results?

Serum levels of glucose-6-phosphate dehydrogenase vary with the measurement method used. Results are reported as normal or abnormal.

What do abnormal results mean?

If the results of initial tests are positive, a quantitative assay for glucose-6-phosphate dehydrogenase may be performed. People with some types of genetically linked anemia exhibit symptoms only when they experience stress, illness, or exposure to drugs or agents that set off episodes of red blood cell destruction.

TAY-SACHS SCREENING

This test measures levels of hexosaminidase in blood serum or amniotic fluid. Hexosaminidase is an enzyme, or specialized protein that's found primarily in brain tissue. Deficiency of hexosaminidase A, an isoenzyme, indicates Tay-Sachs disease, a fatal disorder that affects people of Ashkenazic Jewish ancestry about 100 times more often than the general population. Both parents must carry the defective gene to transmit Tay-Sachs disease to their children.

Both parents must carry the defective gene to transmit Tay-Sachs disease to their children.

Why is this test done?
Hexosaminidase A may be measured for the following reasons:
- To identify carriers of Tay-Sachs disease
- To confirm or rule out Tay-Sachs disease in newborns
- To establish prenatal diagnosis of hexosaminidase A deficiency.

What should you know before the test?
- This test requires a blood sample, which takes less than 3 minutes to collect.
- You may experience slight discomfort from the needle puncture and tourniquet pressure.
- You don't need to change your diet before the test.
- When the test is performed prenatally, you're instructed on preparations for amniocentesis.

What happens during the test?
- A nurse or medical technician inserts a needle into a vein, usually in your forearm. A blood sample is collected in a tube, which is then sent to a lab for testing.
- When testing a newborn, blood is drawn from the baby's arm, neck, or umbilical cord. The procedure is safe and quickly performed.

What happens after the test?

- If swelling develops at the needle puncture site, warm soaks are applied to the area to ease discomfort.
- After testing a newborn, a small bandage is placed on the site of the needle puncture.
- If both you and your partner are carriers of Tay-Sachs disease, you'll be referred for genetic counseling. If either partner's blood test result is negative, the child won't get Tay-Sachs disease.

What are the normal results?

Total blood serum levels of hexosaminidase range from 5 to 12.9 international units per liter; hexosaminidase A accounts for 55% to 76% of the total.

What do abnormal results mean?

Absence of hexosaminidase A indicates Tay-Sachs disease, even though total hexosaminidase levels may be normal.

GALACTOSEMIA SCREENING

This test involves measuring levels of galactose-1-phosphate uridyl transferase. This enzyme, or specialized protein, is involved in the metabolism of lactose, a type of sugar that comes from milk. Deficiency of this enzyme may lead to galactosemia, which is a hereditary disorder. Galactosemia can impair eye, brain, and liver development, causing irreversible cataracts, mental retardation, and cirrhosis, unless it's detected and treated soon after birth.

A simple screening test for galactose-1-phosphate uridyl transferase deficiency is required in some hospitals for all newborns. Prenatal testing of amniotic fluid can also detect transferase deficiency, but this is rarely performed.

Why is this test done?

Galactose-1-phosphate uridyl transferase may be tested for the following reasons:

- To screen newborns for galactosemia
- To detect carriers of galactosemia who may transmit the disorder to their children.

What should you know before the test?

- When testing an adult, the test requires a blood sample, which takes less than 3 minutes to collect.
- You may experience slight discomfort from the needle puncture and tourniquet pressure.
- You don't need to change your diet before the test.
- Your medical history is checked for a recent exchange transfusion. If you've had a transfusion, the lab is notified or the test is postponed.

To screen for galactosemia in an infant, a small amount of umbilical cord blood or blood from a heel stick is collected.

What happens during the test?

- For a *qualitative,* or screening, test on a newborn, a small amount of umbilical cord blood or blood from a heel puncture is collected on special paper, which is then sent to a lab for testing.
- For a *quantitative* test on an adult, a nurse or medical technician inserts a needle into a vein, usually in the forearm. A blood sample is collected in a tube, which is then sent to a lab for testing.

What happens after the test?

- If swelling develops at the needle puncture site, warm soaks are applied to the area to ease discomfort.
- If test results indicate galactosemia, you're referred for nutrition counseling and provided with a galactose- and lactose-free diet for your newborn. A soybean or meat-based formula may be substituted for milk.

What are the normal results?

Normally, the qualitative test is negative. The normal range for the quantitative test is 18.5 to 28.5 international units of transferase per gram of hemoglobin.

What do abnormal results mean?

A positive qualitative test may indicate a transferase deficiency. A follow-up quantitative test is performed as soon as possible. Quantitative test results of less than 5 international units per gram of hemoglobin indicate galactosemia. Levels between 5 and 18.5 international units per gram of hemoglobin may indicate a carrier state.

ANGIOTENSIN-CONVERTING ENZYME

This test measures serum levels of angiotensin-converting enzyme, which is found in lung capillaries and, in lesser concentrations, in blood vessels and kidney tissue. Its primary function is to help regulate blood pressure in arteries. However, measurement of angiotensin-converting enzyme is of little use in diagnosing high blood pressure.

Why is this test done?

Angiotensin-converting enzyme may be measured for the following reasons:
- To diagnose sarcoidosis, Gaucher's disease, or leprosy
- To monitor a person's response to therapy for sarcoidosis.

What should you know before the test?

- You must fast for 12 hours before this test.
- The test requires a blood sample, which takes less than 3 minutes to collect.
- You may experience slight discomfort from the needle puncture and tourniquet pressure.
- Because young people have variable angiotensin-converting enzyme levels, the test may be postponed if you're under age 20.

What happens during the test?

A nurse or medical technician inserts a needle into a vein, usually in your forearm. A blood sample is collected in a tube, which is then sent to a lab for testing.

What happens after the test?

If swelling develops at the needle puncture site, warm soaks are applied to the area to ease discomfort.

What are the normal results?

Normal levels are 6.1 to 21.1 international units of angiotensin-converting enzyme per liter of blood serum.

What do abnormal results mean?

Elevated serum angiotensin-converting enzyme levels may indicate sarcoidosis, Gaucher's disease, or leprosy, but results must be correlated with the person's clinical condition. In some people, elevated angiotensin-converting enzyme levels may be caused by liver diseases, hyperthyroidism, or diabetic retinopathy.

Serum angiotensin-converting enzyme levels decline as the person responds to steroid or prednisone therapy for sarcoidosis.

FATS & LIPOPROTEINS

TRIGLYCERIDES

Triglycerides are the main storage form of fats in the body. They constitute about 95% of fatty tissue. Results of this test are used in the quantitative analysis of triglycerides in the blood. This test is not diagnostic, but it permits early detection of hyperlipemia (excessive lipids in the blood), which increases the risk of heart disease.

Why is this test done?

Triglycerides may be measured for the following reasons:
- To detect disorders of fat metabolism
- To screen for hyperlipemia
- To help identify nephrotic syndrome, which is marked by massive fluid retention and other symptoms
- To determine the risk of heart disease.

What should you know before the test?

- This test requires a blood sample, which takes less than 3 minutes to collect.
- You may experience slight discomfort from the needle puncture and tourniquet pressure.
- Abstain from food for 10 to 14 hours before the test and abstain from alcohol for 24 hours. You can have water.

■ Medications that may interfere with the accuracy of test results are withheld.

What happens during the test?

A nurse or medical technician inserts a needle into a vein, usually in your forearm. A blood sample is collected in a tube, which is then sent to a lab for testing.

What happens after the test?

■ If swelling develops at the needle puncture site, warm soaks are applied to the area to ease discomfort.
■ You may resume taking medications that were withheld before the test.
■ You may resume your regular diet.

What are the normal results?

Triglyceride levels are age- and sex-related. There's some controversy about normal ranges, although levels of 0.45 to 1.81 millimoles per liter of blood for men and 0.39 to 1.52 millimoles per liter for women are widely accepted.

What do abnormal results mean?

Increased or decreased triglyceride levels in the blood suggest an abnormality. Additional tests are required for a definitive diagnosis.

A mild-to-moderate increase in triglyceride levels indicates bile duct obstruction, diabetes, nephrotic syndrome, glandular diseases, or alcohol abuse. Markedly increased levels, without an identifiable cause, reflect hyperlipoproteinemia that's present at birth. More tests are needed to confirm this diagnosis.

Decreased serum levels are rare, mainly caused by malnutrition or a condition called *abetalipoproteinemia*.

Normal triglyceride levels are age- and sex-related, and there's some controversy about normal ranges.

CHOLESTEROL

Cholesterol is a component of cell membranes and certain structures in the blood. It's taken into the body in foods and metabolized in the liver and other body tissues. This test measures total cholesterol levels in the blood. High levels may increase a person's risk of heart disease. (See *Getting cholesterol under control.*) Further testing is needed, though, to determine the ratios of different cholesterol types, which affect the risk level.

Why is this test done?

Cholesterol may be measured for the following reasons:
- To check the body's fat metabolism
- To measure the risk of heart disease
- To aid diagnosis of nephrotic syndrome, pancreatitis, liver disease, hypothyroidism, and hyperthyroidism.

What should you know before the test?

- This test requires a blood sample, which takes less than 3 minutes to collect.
- You may experience slight discomfort from the needle puncture and tourniquet pressure.
- Don't to eat or drink for 12 hours before the test.
- Drugs that influence cholesterol levels will be withheld before the test.

What happens during the test?

A nurse or medical technician inserts a needle into a vein, usually in your forearm. A blood sample is collected in a tube, which is then sent to a lab for testing.

What happens after the test?

- If swelling develops at the needle puncture site, warm soaks are applied to the area to ease discomfort.
- You may resume taking medications that were withheld before the test.
- You may resume your usual diet.

What are the normal results?

Total cholesterol levels vary with age and sex. The normal range is 4.39 to 5.17 millimoles per liter of blood serum. Levels of 7.24 to 8.28 millimoles per liter are considered elevated.

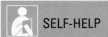 SELF-HELP

Getting cholesterol under control

Changing your diet helps reduce your cholesterol level. You'll need to reduce the amount of saturated fats you eat. This means cutting down drastically on eggs, dairy products, and fatty meats. Rely instead on poultry, fish, fruits, vegetables, and high-fiber breads. Use this list as a starting point for your new diet.

FOOD	ELIMINATE	SUBSTITUTE
Bread and cereals	Breads with whole eggs listed as a major ingredient	Oatmeal, multigrain, and bran cereals; whole-grain breads; rye bread
	Egg noodles	Pasta, rice
	Pies, cakes, doughnuts, biscuits, high-fat crackers and cookies	Angel food cake; low-fat cookies, crackers, home-baked goods
Eggs and dairy products	Whole milk, 2% milk, imitation milk	Skim milk, 1% milk, buttermilk
	Cream, half-and-half, most nondairy creamers, whipped toppings	None
	Whole milk yogurt and cottage cheese	Nonfat or low-fat yogurt, low-fat (1% or 2%) cottage cheese
	Cheese, cream cheese, sour cream, light cream cheese, light sour cream	None
	Egg yolks	Egg whites
	Ice cream	Sherbet, frozen tofu
Fats and oils	Coconut, palm, and palm kernel oils	Unsaturated vegetable oils (corn, olive, canola, safflower, sesame, soybean, and sunflower)
	Butter, lard, bacon fat	Unsaturated margarine and shortening, diet margarine
	Dressings made with egg yolks	Unsaturated or low-fat mayonnaise or salad dressings
	Chocolate	Baking cocoa
Meat, fish, and poultry	Fatty cuts of beef, lamb, or pork	Lean cuts of beef, lamb, or pork
	Organ meats, spare ribs, cold cuts, sausage, hot dogs, bacon	Poultry
	Sardines, roe	Sole, salmon, mackerel

What do abnormal results mean?

Elevated serum cholesterol, which is called *hypercholesterolemia*, may indicate risk of heart disease, as well as hepatitis, lipid disorders, bile duct blockage, nephrotic syndrome, obstructive jaundice, pancreatitis, and hypothyroidism.

Low serum cholesterol, called *hypocholesterolemia*, is commonly associated with malnutrition, liver damage, and hyperthyroidism. Abnormal cholesterol levels frequently require further testing to pinpoint the cause.

PHOSPHOLIPIDS

This test measures phospholipid levels in your blood. Phospholipids are forms of fat in the body that contain phosphorus. They're a major component of cell membranes and are involved in cell permeability and in controlling enzyme activity in the membrane. They help carry fats through the intestines and from the liver and other fat deposits to other body tissues. Phospholipids are also essential for gas exchange in the lungs.

Why is this test done?

Phospholipids may be measured for the following reasons:
- To determine how the body metabolizes fats
- To aid in the evaluation of fat metabolism
- To aid diagnosis of an underactive thyroid, diabetes, nephrotic syndrome, chronic pancreatitis, obstructive jaundice, and hypolipoproteinemia.

What should you know before the test?

- This test requires a blood sample, which takes less than 3 minutes to collect.
- You may experience slight discomfort from the needle puncture and tourniquet pressure.
- Abstain from drinking alcohol for 24 hours before the test and from food and fluids after midnight the night before the test.

What happens during the test?

A nurse or medical technician inserts a needle into a vein, usually in your forearm. A blood sample is collected in a tube, which is then sent to a lab for testing.

What happens after the test?

- If swelling develops at the needle puncture site, warm soaks are applied to the area to ease discomfort.
- You may resume your usual diet.

What are the normal results?

Normal phospholipid levels range from 5.8 to 10.3 grams per liter of blood. Although men usually have higher levels than women, levels in pregnant women exceed those of men.

What do abnormal results mean?

Elevated phospholipid levels may indicate hypothyroidism, diabetes, nephrotic syndrome, chronic pancreatitis, or obstructive jaundice.

Decreased levels may indicate primary hypolipoproteinemia.

Although men usually have higher normal phospholipid levels than women, levels in pregnant women are even higher.

LIPOPROTEIN-CHOLESTEROL FRACTIONS: HDL AND LDL

When a person's total cholesterol levels are found to be elevated, this test can isolate and measure the two primary types of cholesterol fractions in the blood. These are known as *high-density lipoproteins (HDLs)*, popularly known as "good" cholesterol, and *low-density lipoproteins (LDLs)*, or "bad" cholesterol. The relative levels of these cholesterol types have opposite effects on the incidence of heart disease. In other words, a high level of "good" high-density lipoproteins reduces the risk of heart disease. Conversely, a high level of "bad" low-density lipoproteins increases the risk of heart disease.

Why is this test done?

A lipoprotein-cholesterol test is performed to check a person's risk of heart disease.

What should you know before the test?

- This test requires a blood sample, which takes less than 3 minutes to collect.
- You may experience slight discomfort from the needle puncture and tourniquet pressure.
- Maintain your normal diet for 2 weeks before the test, but abstain from alcohol for 24 hours before the test. You may drink water, but fast and avoid exercise for 12 to 14 hours before the test.
- Medications that may influence test results are withheld before the test.

What happens during the test?

A nurse or medical technician inserts a needle into a vein, usually in your forearm. A blood sample is collected in a tube, which is then sent to a lab for testing.

What happens after the test?

- If swelling develops at the needle puncture site, warm soaks are applied to the area to ease discomfort.
- You may resume taking medications that were withheld before the test.
- You may resume your usual diet.

What are the normal results?

Normal cholesterol levels vary according to age, sex, geographic region, and ethnic group. Normal HDL levels range from 0.75 to 1.99 millimoles per liter of blood. Normal LDL levels range from 1.60 to 4.78 millimoles per liter.

What do abnormal results mean?

High LDL levels increase the risk of heart disease. Elevated HDL levels generally reflect a healthy state but can also indicate chronic hepatitis, early-stage primary biliary cirrhosis, or alcohol consumption. Rarely, a sharp increase to as high as 2.5 millimoles per liter in one type of HDL called *alpha₂-high-density lipoprotein* may indicate heart disease.

LIPOPROTEIN PHENOTYPING

Lipoproteins are the forms in which fats are transported in the blood. Lipoprotein phenotyping is used to determine levels of the four major lipoproteins: *chylomicrons, very low-density lipoproteins, low-density lipoproteins,* and *high-density lipoproteins.* Detecting altered lipoprotein patterns is the key to identifying metabolic disorders known as *hyperlipoproteinemia* or *hypolipoproteinemia.*

Why is this test done?

Lipoprotein phenotyping is performed for the following reasons:
- To evaluate how the body metabolizes fats
- To classify hyperlipoproteinemia or hypolipoproteinemia.

What should you know before the test?

- This test requires a blood sample, which takes less than 3 minutes to collect.
- You may experience slight discomfort from the needle puncture and tourniquet pressure.
- Abstain from alcohol for 24 hours before the test and fast after midnight before the test. Eat a low-fat meal the night before the test.
- A nurse or medical technician checks your drug history for the use of heparin, which may affect test results.
- You mustn't take antilipemics such as cholestyramine for about 2 weeks before the test.
- If you're hospitalized for any condition that might significantly alter lipoprotein metabolism, such as diabetes, nephrosis, or an underactive thyroid, the lab is notified.

Preparing for the test means no alcohol for 24 hours and no exercise or food for 14 hours.

What happens during the test?

A nurse or medical technician inserts a needle into a vein, usually in your forearm. A blood sample is collected in a tube, which is then sent to a lab for testing.

What happens after the test?

- If swelling develops at the needle puncture site, warm soaks are applied to the area to ease discomfort.
- You may resume taking medications that were withheld before the test.

- You may resume your regular diet.

What are the normal results?

Several types of lipoproteins normally exist in the body. The lab reports characteristic patterns among the various lipoproteins.

What do abnormal results mean?

Lipoprotein disorders are identified by characteristic patterns among a person's lipoproteins. The disorders are classified as either hyperlipoproteinemias or hypolipoproteinemias. There are six types of hyperlipoproteinemias: I, IIa, IIb, III, IV, and V. Types IIa, IIb, and IV are relatively common. All hypolipoproteinemias are rare.

PROTEINS & PIGMENTS

PROTEIN COMPONENTS

The two major proteins in blood are called *albumin* and *globulins*. This test is used to measure the levels of these proteins in blood serum, the clear fluid portion of blood. The proteins are measured and classified as five distinct fractions: albumin and alpha$_1$, alpha$_2$, beta, and gamma globulins.

Why is this test done?

Protein components are tested for the following reasons:
- To determine the protein content of blood
- To aid diagnosis of liver disease, protein deficiency, kidney disorders, and gastrointestinal and tumor-causing diseases.

What should you know before the test?

- This test requires a blood sample, which takes less than 3 minutes to collect.
- You may experience slight discomfort from the needle puncture and tourniquet pressure.
- You don't need to change your diet before the test.

INSIGHT INTO ILLNESS

How illness can affect blood protein levels

Abnormal levels of the two major proteins in the blood, albumin or the globulins, may occur in many different disorders.

Increased levels

Total proteins
- Dehydration
- Vomiting, diarrhea
- Diabetic acidosis
- Fulminating and chronic infections
- Multiple myeloma
- Monocytic leukemia
- Chronic inflammatory disease, such as rheumatoid arthritis or early-stage Laënnec's cirrhosis

Albumin
Multiple myeloma

Globulins
- Chronic syphilis
- Tuberculosis
- Subacute bacterial endocarditis
- Multiple myeloma
- Collagen diseases
- Systemic lupus erythematosus
- Rheumatoid arthritis
- Diabetes mellitus
- Hodgkin's disease

Decreased levels

Total proteins
- Malnutrition
- Gastrointestinal disease
- Blood dyscrasias
- Essential hypertension
- Hodgkin's disease
- Uncontrolled diabetes mellitus
- Malabsorption
- Hepatic dysfunction
- Toxemia of pregnancy
- Nephroses
- Surgical and traumatic shock
- Severe burns
- Hemorrhage
- Hyperthyroidism
- Benzene and carbon tetrachloride poisoning
- Congestive heart failure

Albumin
- Malnutrition
- Nephritis/nephrosis
- Diarrhea
- Plasma loss from burns
- Hepatic disease
- Hodgkin's disease
- Hypogamma-globulinemia
- Peptic ulcer
- Acute cholecystitis
- Sarcoidosis
- Collagen diseases
- Systemic lupus erythematosus
- Rheumatoid arthritis
- Essential hypertension
- Metastatic cancer
- Hyperthyroidism

Globulins
Levels vary in neoplastic and kidney diseases, liver dysfunction, and some blood disorders.

- Your medication history is checked for drugs that may influence protein levels. When possible, use of such medications is discontinued.

What happens during the test?

A nurse or medical technician inserts a needle into a vein, usually in your forearm. A blood sample is collected in a tube, which is then sent to a lab for testing.

What happens after the test?

If swelling develops at the needle puncture site, warm soaks are applied to the area to ease discomfort.

What are the normal results?

Normal total protein levels are 66 to 79 grams per liter of serum. The albumin fraction ranges from 33 to 45 grams per liter. The alpha$_1$-globulin fraction ranges from 1 to 4 grams per liter; alpha$_2$-globulin ranges from 5 to 10 grams per liter. Beta globulin ranges from 7 to 12 grams per liter; gamma globulin ranges from 5 to 16 grams per liter.

What do abnormal results mean?

For common findings, see *How illness can affect blood protein levels,* page 385.

HAPTOGLOBIN

This test measures the levels of haptoglobin, which is a type of protein that's produced in the liver. When many red blood cells are destroyed, the haptoglobin level decreases rapidly and may remain low for 5 to 7 days, until the liver produces more of it.

Why is this test done?

Haptoglobin may be measured for the following reasons:
- To determine the condition of red blood cells and the rate of their destruction
- To distinguish between types of protein in the blood

- To investigate transfusion reactions that lead to red blood cell destruction
- To establish proof of paternity.

What should you know before the test?

- This test requires a blood sample, which takes less than 3 minutes to collect.
- You may experience slight discomfort from the needle puncture and tourniquet pressure.
- You don't need to change your diet before the test.
- Your medication history is checked for drugs that may influence haptoglobin levels, including steroids and androgens.

What happens during the test?

A nurse or medical technician inserts a needle into a vein, usually in your forearm. A blood sample is collected in a tube, which is then sent to a lab for testing.

What happens after the test?

If swelling develops at the needle puncture site, warm soaks are applied to the area to ease discomfort.

What are the normal results?

Normal haptoglobin levels are 0.38 to 2.7 grams per liter of blood serum.

Haptoglobin is absent in 90% of newborns, but levels usually increase to normal by 4 months of age.

What do abnormal results mean?

Extremely low haptoglobin levels may occur in acute and chronic red blood cell destruction, severe hepatocellular disease, infectious mononucleosis, and transfusion reactions. Liver disease inhibits haptoglobin production. If your serum haptoglobin levels are very low, you must be monitored for symptoms of red blood cell destruction: chills, fever, back pain, flushing, distended neck veins, irregular heartbeat and breathing, and low blood pressure.

In about 1% of the population — including 4% of blacks — haptoglobin is permanently absent; this disorder is known as *congenital ahaptoglobinemia.*

Haptoglobin is absent in 90% of newborns, but their levels usually increase to normal by 4 months of age.

Strikingly elevated serum haptoglobin levels occur in diseases that are marked by chronic inflammatory reactions or tissue destruction, such as rheumatoid arthritis and malignant tumors.

TRANSFERRIN

Transferrin is a type of protein that's formed in the liver. It's also called *siderophilin*. Iron in the body comes from iron-rich foods or from the breakdown of red blood cells. Transferrin transports iron from the blood to the liver, spleen, and bone marrow, where it's used or stored. This test provides a quantitative analysis of transferrin levels in the blood. Results are used to evaluate iron metabolism. Iron level is usually measured at the same time.

Why is this test done?
Transferrin may be measured for the following reasons:
- To determine the cause of anemia and to evaluate iron metabolism in iron deficiency anemia
- To determine the iron-transporting capacity of the blood.

What should you know before the test?
- This test requires a blood sample, which takes less than 3 minutes to collect.
- You may experience slight discomfort from the needle puncture and tourniquet pressure.
- You don't need to change your diet before the test.
- Your medication history is checked for the use of drugs that may influence transferrin levels.

What happens during the test?
A nurse or medical technician inserts a needle into a vein, usually in your forearm. A blood sample is collected in a tube, which is then sent to a lab for testing.

What happens after the test?
If swelling develops at the needle puncture site, warm soaks are applied to the area to ease discomfort.

Iron in the body comes from iron-rich foods or from the breakdown of red blood cells.

What are the normal results?

Normal transferrin levels range from 2.2 to 4.0 grams of transferrin per liter of blood serum; 0.65 to 1.7 grams per liter are usually bound to iron.

What do abnormal results mean?

Inadequate transferrin levels may lead to impaired hemoglobin production and, possibly, anemia. Depressed serum levels may indicate inadequate production of transferrin due to liver damage or excessive protein loss from kidney disease. Decreased transferrin levels may also be caused by acute or chronic infection or cancer.

Elevated serum transferrin levels may be a sign of a severe iron deficiency.

AMINO ACID SCREENING

This test checks infants for errors of amino acid metabolism. Amino acids are the chief component of all proteins. The body contains at least 20 amino acids — 10 of these aren't formed in the body and must be acquired through the diet. Certain inborn enzyme deficiencies interfere with normal metabolism of amino acids and cause accumulation or deficiency of them. (See *Amino acids: No sooner collected than spent,* page 390.)

Why is this test done?

Amino acid screening may be performed for the following reasons:
- To determine how well an infant's body produces and uses amino acids
- To screen for inborn errors of amino acid metabolism.

What should you know before the test?

- The infant must not be given food or liquids for 4 hours before the test.
- A small amount of blood is taken from the infant's heel. Collecting the sample takes only a few minutes.

HOW YOUR BODY WORKS

Amino acids: No sooner collected than spent

Unlike carbohydrates or fats, protein is not stored by the body. Instead, the body breaks down proteins and forms an amino acid pool. From this pool, amino acids react with products of carbohydrate and fat metabolism through such processes as oxidative deamination, transamination, and ammonia transport. These reactions create new proteins as well as hormones, enzymes, or nonprotein nitrogen compounds such as creatine.

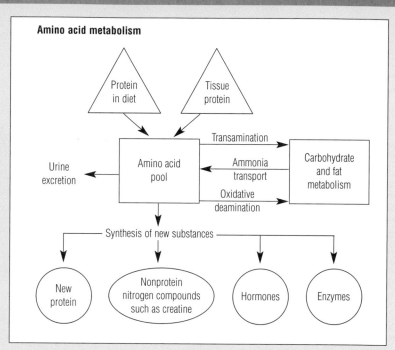

What happens during the test?

A nurse or medical technician makes a shallow skin puncture and collects a few drops of blood in a narrow tube.

What happens after the test?

- If a hematoma develops at the puncture site, warm soaks are applied to ease the infant's discomfort.
- You may resume your child's usual diet.

What are the normal results?

The test result shows a normal amino acid pattern in the blood.

What do abnormal results mean?

Excessive amino acids typically produce conditions called *overflow aminoacidurias*. Inborn abnormalities of the amino acid transport system in the kidneys produce disorders that are called *renal aminoacidurias*. Comparing blood and urine test results helps the doctor distinguish between the two types of aminoacidurias. The amino acid patterns are normal in renal aminoacidurias and abnormal in overflow aminoacidurias.

PHENYLALANINE SCREENING

This test is used to screen infants for high levels of phenylalanine in the blood. It's a routine test for newborn screening.

Phenylalanine is a naturally occurring amino acid that's essential to growth and nitrogen balance. Accumulation of phenylalanine in the blood may indicate a serious enzyme deficiency. This result may indicate a condition that's called *phenylketonuria* or *PKU*. To ensure accurate results, the test must be performed after at least 2 full days of milk or formula feeding. (See *How PKU is inherited,* page 392.)

Why is this test done?
Phenylalanine screening is performed to screen infants for possible phenylketonuria.

What should you know before the test?
This test requires a blood sample. A small amount of blood is drawn from the infant's heel.

What happens during the test?
A nurse or medical technician performs a heel puncture and collects three drops of blood on a filter paper.

What happens after the test?
If swelling develops at the puncture site, warm soaks are applied to ease the infant's discomfort.

INSIGHT INTO ILLNESS

How PKU is inherited

Phenylketonuria, also called *PKU*, is an inherited disorder that, if untreated, can cause mental retardation and other problems. In PKU, an accumulation of phenyl-alanine and other substances hinders normal nervous system development.

Hereditary risk

Being a heterozygous carrier of a trait means that, although there are no outward signs of the trait, it may be passed on to one's children. When *both* parents carry a recessive (hidden) trait for PKU, there's a 25% chance that their child will inherit both recessive genes. If so, the child will require a restricted diet to avoid retardation.

Diet therapy

Avoiding dietary phenylalanine prevents accumulation of toxic compounds and thereby prevents mental retardation. As the child matures, the body develops alternative ways to process phenylalanine.

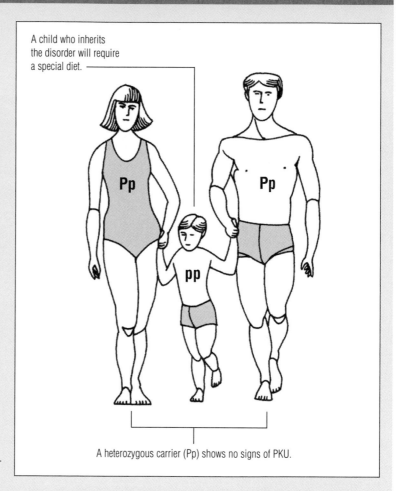

A child who inherits the disorder will require a special diet.

A heterozygous carrier (Pp) shows no signs of PKU.

What are the normal results?

A negative test indicates normal phenylalanine levels of less than 121 micromoles of phenylalanine per liter of blood. This indicates no appreciable danger of phenylketonuria.

What do abnormal results mean?

At birth, an infant with phenylketonuria usually has normal phenyl-alanine levels, but after milk or formula feeding begins, levels gradually increase. A positive test result suggests the *possibility* of phenylke-tonuria.

Diagnosis requires exact serum phenylalanine measurement and urine testing. A positive test may also be caused by liver disease, galac-tosemia, or delayed development of certain enzyme systems. Al-though this disease is a common cause of mental deficiency, early detection and continuous treatment with a low-phenylalanine diet can prevent permanent mental retardation.

AMMONIA

A form of nitrogen, ammonia helps maintain the acid-base balance in the body. This test measures levels of ammonia in the blood plasma (the clear fluid of the blood that contains suspended cells and dis-solved proteins.)

Normally, ammonia passes through the liver before it's excreted in urine. In diseases such as cirrhosis of the liver, ammonia can bypass the liver and accumulate in the blood. Plasma ammonia levels may help indicate the severity of liver damage.

Why is this test done?

Ammonia may be measured for the following reasons:
- To check liver function
- To help monitor severe liver disease and the effectiveness of ther-apy
- To recognize impending or established liver-related coma.

What should you know before the test?

- You're asked to fast overnight before the test.
- This test requires a blood sample, which takes less than 3 min-utes to collect.
- You may experience slight discomfort from the needle puncture and tourniquet pressure.
- Certain medications influence ammonia levels in the blood plas-ma and will be discontinued, if possible.

In diseases such as cirrhosis of the liver, ammonia can bypass the damaged liver and accumulate in the blood.

What happens during the test?

A nurse or medical technician inserts a needle into a vein, usually in your forearm. A blood sample is collected in a tube, which is then sent to a lab for testing.

What happens after the test?

- If swelling develops at the needle puncture site, warm soaks are applied to the area to ease discomfort.
- When plasma ammonia levels are high, you're watched for signs of liver related coma.

What are the normal results?

Normal ammonia levels are less than 28 micromoles of ammonia per liter of blood plasma.

What do abnormal results mean?

Elevated plasma ammonia levels commonly occur in severe liver disease — such as cirrhosis and acute liver necrosis — and may lead to liver-related coma. Elevated ammonia levels are also possible in Reye's syndrome, severe congestive heart failure, gastrointestinal hemorrhage, and erythroblastosis fetalis.

BLOOD UREA NITROGEN

This test measures the nitrogen found in urea, which is the chief end product of protein metabolism in the body. Urea is formed in the liver from ammonia and is excreted by the kidneys. The blood urea nitrogen level reflects protein intake and kidney function.

Why is this test done?

Blood urea nitrogen may be measured for the following reasons:
- To evaluate your kidney function and check for kidney disease
- To aid assessment of fluid use and balance in the body.

What should you know before the test?

- You don't need to restrict food or fluids before the test, but you should avoid a diet high in meat.

■ This test requires a blood sample, which takes less than 3 minutes to collect.

■ You may experience slight discomfort from the needle puncture and tourniquet pressure.

■ Your medication history is checked for use of drugs that influence blood urea nitrogen levels, and they may be discontinued.

What happens during the test?

A nurse or medical technician inserts a needle into a vein, usually in your forearm. A blood sample is collected in a tube, which is then sent to a lab for testing.

What happens after the test?

If swelling develops at the needle puncture site, warm soaks are applied to the area to ease discomfort.

What are the normal results?

Blood urea nitrogen levels normally range from 2.9 to 7.1 micromoles of nitrogen per liter of blood, with slightly higher levels in elderly people.

What do abnormal results mean?

Elevated blood urea nitrogen levels occur in kidney disease, reduced blood flow to the kidneys possibly caused by dehydration, urinary tract obstruction, and in conditions that cause protein breakdown, such as burns.

Depressed blood urea nitrogen levels occur in severe liver damage, malnutrition, and overhydration.

Depressed blood urea nitrogen levels show up in people with severe liver damage, malnutrition, and excessive liquid intake.

CREATININE

Creatinine occurs in the blood in amounts proportional to the body's muscle mass. Analysis of creatinine levels in the blood provides a more sensitive measure of kidney damage than blood urea nitrogen levels.

Why is this test done?

Creatinine levels may be measured for the following reasons:
- To check kidney function
- To screen for kidney damage.

What should you know before the test?

- This test requires a blood sample, which takes less than 3 minutes to collect.
- You may experience slight discomfort from the needle puncture and tourniquet pressure.
- You're asked to restrict food and fluids for about 8 hours before the test.
- Your history is checked for the use of drugs that may influence test results.

What happens during the test?

A nurse or medical technician inserts a needle into a vein, usually in your forearm. A blood sample is collected in a tube, which is then sent to a lab for testing.

What happens after the test?

If swelling develops at the needle puncture site, warm soaks are applied to the area to ease discomfort.

What are the normal results?

Normal creatinine concentrations in men are from 61 to 92 micromoles of creatinine per liter of blood; in women, from 46 to 69 micromoles per liter.

What do abnormal results mean?

Elevated creatinine levels generally indicate kidney disease that has seriously damaged 50% or more of the tissue. Elevated levels may also be associated with gigantism and acromegaly.

URIC ACID

Uric acid, a component of urine, normally appears in the blood-stream before being excreted. Excessive uric acid in the blood can result in gout, a form of acute arthritis. This test measures the levels of uric acid in a blood sample. Disorders of metabolism and impaired kidney excretion characteristically raise the levels of uric acid in the blood.

Why is this test done?

Uric acid levels are measured to detect gout or kidney dysfunction.

What should you know before the test?

■ This test requires a blood sample, which takes less than 3 minutes to collect.
■ You may experience slight discomfort from the needle puncture and tourniquet pressure.
■ You must fast for 8 hours before the test.
■ Your medication history is checked for use of drugs that may influence test results. They may be discontinued before the test.

Excessive uric acid in the blood is a primary sign of gout, which is a hereditary form of arthritis.

What happens during the test?

A nurse or medical technician inserts a needle into a vein, usually in your forearm. A blood sample is collected in a tube, which is then sent to a lab for testing.

What happens after the test?

If swelling develops at the needle puncture site, warm soaks are applied to the area to ease discomfort.

What are the normal results?

Uric acid concentrations in men normally range from 256 to 476 micromoles of uric acid per liter of blood; in women, from 46 to 69 micromoles per liter.

What do abnormal results mean?

Increased uric acid levels may indicate gout or impaired kidney function. Levels may also increase with congestive heart failure, glycogen storage disease, infections, hemolytic or sickle cell anemia, polycythemia, tumors, and psoriasis.

Low uric acid levels may indicate poor kidney tubular absorption, as in Fanconi's syndrome, or acute liver atrophy.

BILIRUBIN

Adults must fast at least 4 hours before the test. Fasting isn't necessary for newborns.

Bilirubin is a clear yellow or orange fluid found in bile. It's produced by the breakdown of red blood cells. This test is used to measure the levels of bilirubin in the blood. After leaving the bloodstream, bilirubin is normally excreted with bile, which aids digestion. Proper bilirubin excretion is especially important in newborns because excessive bilirubin can accumulate in the brain, causing irreparable damage.

Why is this test done?
Bilirubin may be measured for the following reasons:
- To evaluate liver function and to help diagnose obstructions in the bile system
- To evaluate the condition of red blood cells and to help diagnose anemia due to red blood cell destruction
- To aid the diagnosis of jaundice and to monitor its progress
- To determine a newborn's possible need for a transfusion or phototherapy to control excessive bilirubin.

What should you know before the test?
- This test requires a blood sample, which takes less than 3 minutes to collect.
- You (or your newborn) may experience slight discomfort from the needle puncture and tourniquet pressure.
- You don't need to restrict fluids but should fast for at least 4 hours before the test. Fasting is not necessary for newborns.
- Your medication history is checked for the use of drugs that interfere with bilirubin levels. They may be discontinued before the test.

What happens during the test?
- A nurse or medical technician inserts a needle into a vein, usually in your forearm. A blood sample is collected in a tube, which is then sent to a lab for testing.

- When a newborn is tested, a heel puncture is performed, and a small tube is filled to the designated level with blood.

What happens after the test?

If swelling develops at the needle puncture site, warm soaks are applied to the area to ease discomfort.

What are the normal results?

When measured by the *indirect serum bilirubin* method, normal adult levels are 1.1 micromoles of bilirubin per liter of blood serum or less; normal adult levels, when measured by the *direct serum bilirubin* method, are less than 8.6 micromoles of bilirubin per liter of blood serum. Total bilirubin in the newborn ranges from 17.1 to 205 micromoles per liter.

What do abnormal results mean?

Elevated indirect serum bilirubin levels often indicate liver damage and can reveal severe red blood cell destruction that causes hemolytic anemia. If cell destruction continues, both direct and indirect bilirubin results may increase. Other causes of elevated indirect levels include inborn enzyme deficiencies, such as Gilbert's disease.

Elevated direct serum bilirubin levels usually indicate bile system obstruction.

In newborns, levels of 308 micromoles of bilirubin or more per liter of blood indicate the need for blood exchange transfusion.

CARBOHYDRATES

FASTING BLOOD SUGAR

This test is also called the *fasting plasma glucose test*. Glucose is a form of sugar that's found in fruits and other foods. It's also an important component of blood and is the body's chief source of energy. This test is used to measure blood sugar levels following a 12- to 14-hour fast. Normally, increases in blood sugar levels are kept in check by the secretion of insulin. This test is commonly used to screen for diabetes, in which the absence or deficiency of insulin allows persistently high sugar levels.

Why is this test done?

The fasting blood sugar test is performed for the following reasons:
- To detect disorders of glucose metabolism
- To screen for diabetes
- To monitor drug or diet therapy in people with diabetes.

What should you know before the test?

- This test requires a blood sample, which takes less than 3 minutes to collect.
- You may experience slight discomfort from the needle puncture and tourniquet pressure.
- You must fast for 12 to 14 hours before the test.
- Before the test, you're asked to suspend the use of drugs that may affect test results. If you have diabetes, you may take your medication after the test.
- Watch for feelings of weakness, restlessness, nervousness, hunger, and sweating. Report these symptoms of hypoglycemia, or low blood sugar, immediately.

While you're fasting to prepare for the test, watch for feelings of weakness, restlessness, nervousness, hunger, and sweating.

What happens during the test?

A nurse or medical technician inserts a needle into a vein, usually in your forearm. A blood sample is collected in a tube, which is then sent to a lab for testing.

What happens after the test?

- If swelling develops at the needle puncture site, warm soaks are applied to the area to ease discomfort.
- Eat a balanced meal or a snack after the test, and resume taking medications that were withheld before the test.

What are the normal results?

Generally, normal levels, after a 12- to 14-hour fast, are 3.9 to 5.6 millimoles of true glucose for each liter of blood.

What do abnormal results mean?

Confirmation of diabetes requires fasting blood sugar levels of 7.8 millimoles per liter or more, obtained on two or more occasions.

When borderline or briefly elevated levels are reported, a 2-hour postprandial blood sugar test or the oral glucose tolerance test may be performed to confirm the diagnosis.

Increased fasting blood sugar levels can be caused by pancreatitis, recent acute illness such as heart attack, Cushing's syndrome, acromegaly, and pheochromocytoma. High blood sugar (hyperglycemia) may also stem from hyperlipoproteinemia, chronic liver disease, nephrotic syndrome, brain tumor, sepsis, or gastrectomy with dumping syndrome, and is typical in eclampsia, anoxia, and seizure disorder.

Depressed blood sugar levels can be caused by hyperinsulinism, insulinoma, von Gierke's disease, functional or reactive hypoglycemia, myxedema, adrenal insufficiency, congenital adrenal hyperplasia, hypopituitarism, malabsorption syndrome, and some liver disorders.

TWO-HOUR POSTPRANDIAL BLOOD SUGAR

This test is a valuable tool for detecting diabetes, a condition that causes persistently high blood sugar levels. It's used when someone has symptoms of diabetes, such as extreme thirst and excessive urination, or when results of the fasting plasma blood sugar test suggest diabetes.

Why is this test done?

The two-hour postprandial blood sugar test is performed for the following reasons:

- To evaluate sugar metabolism
- To aid diagnosis of diabetes
- To monitor drug or diet therapy in people with diabetes.

What should you know before the test?

- This test requires a blood sample, which takes less than 3 minutes to collect.
- You may experience slight discomfort from the needle puncture and tourniquet pressure.

How blood sugar levels vary with age

After age 50, normal blood sugar levels increase markedly and steadily, sometimes reaching 8.8 millimoles or more of glucose per liter of blood. In a younger person, a glucose concentration greater than 8.0 millimoles per liter suggests incipient diabetes and requires further evaluation.

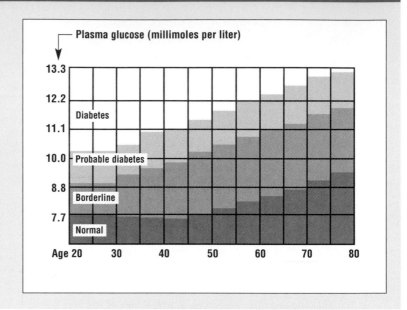

■ Eat a balanced meal or one containing 100 grams of carbohydrate before the test and then fast for 2 hours. Avoid smoking and strenuous exercise after the meal.

What happens during the test?

A nurse or medical technician inserts a needle into a vein, usually in your forearm. A blood sample is collected in a tube, which is then sent to a lab for testing.

What happens after the test?

■ If swelling develops at the needle puncture site, warm soaks are applied to the area to ease discomfort.
■ You may resume your usual diet and normal activity.

What are the normal results?

In a person who doesn't have diabetes, the postprandial blood sugar level is less than 8.0 millimoles of sugar per liter of blood; levels are slightly elevated in people who are over age 80. (See *How blood sugar levels vary with age.*)

What do abnormal results mean?

Two 2-hour postprandial blood sugar levels of 11.1 millimoles per liter or more indicate diabetes mellitus. High levels may also occur with pancreatitis, Cushing's syndrome, acromegaly, and pheochromocytoma. High levels may also be caused by hyperlipoproteinemia, chronic liver disease, nephrotic syndrome, brain tumor, sepsis, gastrectomy with dumping syndrome, eclampsia, anoxia, or seizure disorders.

Low sugar levels occur in hyperinsulinism, insulinoma, von Gierke's disease, myxedema, adrenal insufficiency, congenital adrenal hyperplasia, hypopituitarism, malabsorption syndrome, and some cases of liver insufficiency.

ORAL GLUCOSE TOLERANCE TEST

This test checks your body's ability to process glucose, a form of sugar that's your chief source of energy. During this test, sugar levels in the blood and urine are monitored for 2 hours after drinking a large dose of sugar solution. This is the most sensitive way to evaluate borderline cases of diabetes, a disorder that causes high sugar levels in the blood.

Why is this test done?

The oral glucose tolerance test is performed for the following reasons:
- To evaluate sugar metabolism
- To confirm diabetes
- To aid diagnosis of abnormally low blood sugar levels (called *hypoglycemia*) and malabsorption syndrome.

What should you know before the test?

- You're asked to eat a high-carbohydrate diet for 3 days and then to fast for 10 to 16 hours before the test. (See *Following a high-carbohydrate diet*, page 404.)
- Don't smoke, drink coffee or alcohol, or exercise strenuously for 8 hours before or during the test.
- This test requires two blood samples and usually five urine specimens. You may experience slight discomfort from the needle punctures and the pressure of the tourniquet.

SELF-HELP

Following a high carbohydrate diet

To prepare for the oral glucose tolerance test and to ensure accurate results, follow a high-carbohydrate diet like the one below for at least 3 days before the test. If you find the diet too restrictive, follow your regular diet but eat 12 extra slices of bread each day.

BREAKFAST
1 serving fruit
Eggs, as desired
5 bread exchanges*
1 cup milk
Butter or margarine
Coffee or tea, if desired

LUNCH AND DINNER
Meat, as desired
5 bread exchanges*
2 vegetables
1 serving fruit
1 cup milk
Butter or margarine
Coffee or tea, if desired

*One of the following equals one bread exchange

1 slice bread, white or whole wheat
1½-inch cube of cornbread
½ hamburger or hot dog roll
½ cup dry cereal (avoid sugar-coated
  varieties)
½ cup cooked cereal
½ cup noodles, spaghetti, or macaroni
½ cup cooked dried beans or peas
⅓ cup corn or ½ small ear of corn
1 biscuit

½ corn muffin
1 roll
5 saltine crackers
2 graham crackers
½ cup grits or rice
1 small white potato
½ cup mashed potato
¼ cup sweet potato
¼ cup baked beans
¼ cup pork and beans

■ Bring a book or other quiet diversion with you to the test because the procedure usually takes 2 hours or longer.

■ Your medication history is checked for drugs that may affect test results. Such drugs are usually withheld before the test.

■ Watch for and immediately report any feelings of weakness, restlessness, nervousness, hunger, or sweating; these may indicate hypoglycemia.

What happens during the test?

■ A nurse or medical technician first obtains a fasting blood sample. A needle is inserted into a vein, usually in your forearm. A blood sample is collected in a tube, which is then sent to a lab for testing.

- A urine specimen is collected immediately following the blood sample.
- After collecting these samples, you're given a dose of dissolved sugar to drink. The time it takes for you to finish it is recorded. You're encouraged to drink the entire solution within 5 minutes.
- A blood sample is drawn 2 hours after you drink the sugar solution.
- A urine specimen is collected at the same time.
- You may lie down if you feel faint from the needle punctures.
- You're encouraged to drink water throughout the test to promote adequate urination.

What happens after the test?

- If swelling develops at the needle puncture site, warm soaks are applied to the area to ease discomfort.
- You may resume taking medications that were withheld before the test.
- After the test, eat a balanced meal or a snack, and be alert for a hypoglycemic reaction.

Does the test have risks?

- Extended monitoring to detect hypoglycemia should not be performed on a person who is suspected of having a tumor-causing condition called *insulinoma*. Prolonged fasting may lead to fainting and coma.
- If you develop severe hypoglycemia, the test is discontinued and you'll be given orange juice with sugar added to drink. You may receive intravenous sugar to reverse the reaction.

What are the normal results?

Normal sugar levels peak at 8.9 to 10.0 millimoles of sugar per liter of blood within 30 minutes to 1 hour after consuming the oral sugar test dose. Sugar returns to fasting levels or lower within 2 to 3 hours. Urine sugar tests remain negative throughout.

What do abnormal results mean?

Depressed glucose tolerance, in which levels peak sharply before falling slowly to fasting levels, may confirm diabetes or may be caused by Cushing's disease, hemochromatosis, pheochromocytoma, or central nervous system lesions.

Bring a book or other quiet diversion with you because this test usually takes 3 hours and can last as long as 6 hours.

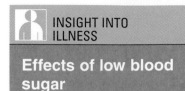

INSIGHT INTO ILLNESS

Effects of low blood sugar

Various body organs respond differently to conditions of low blood sugar. The symptoms you're most likely to notice if you have this condition are headache, sweating, and nausea.

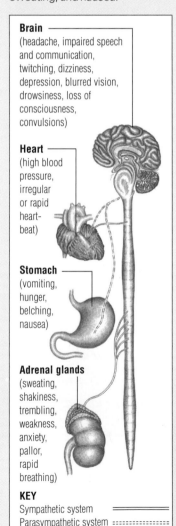

Brain
(headache, impaired speech and communication, twitching, dizziness, depression, blurred vision, drowsiness, loss of consciousness, convulsions)

Heart
(high blood pressure, irregular or rapid heartbeat)

Stomach
(vomiting, hunger, belching, nausea)

Adrenal glands
(sweating, shakiness, trembling, weakness, anxiety, pallor, rapid breathing)

KEY
Sympathetic system ══════
Parasympathetic system ┄┄┄┄┄┄

Increased glucose tolerance, in which levels may peak at less than normal, may indicate insulinoma, malabsorption syndrome, adrenocortical insufficiency (Addison's disease), or an underactive thyroid or pituitary gland.

BETA-HYDROXYBUTYRATE

This test is used to measure the levels of beta-hydroxybutyric acid in the blood. Beta-hydroxybutyrate is one of three ketone bodies that are products of fatty acid metabolism in the liver. The other two ketone bodies are acetoacetate and acetone. An accumulation of all three ketone bodies is referred to as *ketosis;* excessive formation of ketone bodies in the blood is called *ketonemia.*

Why is this test done?

Beta-hydroxybutyric acid may be measured for the following reasons:
- To evaluate ketones in your blood
- To diagnose carbohydrate deprivation, which may be caused by starvation, digestive disturbances, dietary imbalances, or frequent vomiting
- To aid diagnosis of diabetes resulting from poor carbohydrate utilization
- To aid diagnosis of glycogen storage diseases, specifically von Gierke's disease
- To monitor the effect of insulin therapy during treatment of diabetic ketoacidosis
- To monitor a person's status during emergency management of hypoglycemia, acidosis, excessive alcohol ingestion, or unexplained changes in electrolyte balance. (See *Effects of low blood sugar.*)

What should you know before the test?

- This test requires a blood sample, which takes less than 3 minutes to collect.
- You may experience slight discomfort from the needle puncture and tourniquet pressure.
- You don't need to change your diet before the test.

What happens during the test?

A nurse or medical technician inserts a needle into a vein, usually in your forearm. A blood sample is collected in a tube, which is then sent to a lab for testing.

What happens after the test?

If swelling develops at the needle puncture site, warm soaks are applied to the area to ease discomfort.

What are the normal results?

The normal value for beta-hydroxybutyrate levels is less than 38 micromoles per liter of blood serum or plasma.

What do abnormal results mean?

Elevated levels may suggest worsening of ketosis. Levels that are greater than 2 micromoles per liter require immediate treatment.

GLYCOSYLATED HEMOGLOBIN

The glycosylated hemoglobin test is also called the *total fasting hemoglobin test.* It's used for monitoring diabetes therapy.

Hemoglobin is a pigment in blood cells that assists in oxygen transport. Three minor forms of hemoglobin are measured in this test: hemoglobin A_{1a}, hemoglobin A_{1b}, and hemoglobin A_{1c}.

Measuring glycosylated hemoglobin levels gives the doctor information about the average blood sugar level during the preceding 2 to 3 months. This test requires collection of only one blood sample every 6 to 8 weeks and can therefore be used for evaluating long-term effectiveness of diabetes therapy.

Why is this test done?

The glycosylated hemoglobin test is performed to evaluate diabetes therapy.

What should you know before the test?

■ This test requires a blood sample, which takes less than 3 minutes to collect.

- You may experience slight discomfort from the needle puncture and tourniquet pressure.
- You don't need to change your diet or prescribed medication regimen before the test.

What happens during the test?

A nurse or medical technician inserts a needle into a vein, usually in your forearm. A blood sample is collected in a tube, which is then sent to a lab for testing.

What happens after the test?

- If swelling develops at the needle puncture site, warm soaks are applied to the area to ease discomfort.
- You may schedule an appointment in 6 to 8 weeks for appropriate follow-up testing.

What are the normal results?

Normal glycosylated hemoglobin levels are reported as a percentage of the total hemoglobin within a red blood cell.

What do abnormal results mean?

In diabetes, hemoglobins A_{1a} and A_{1b} constitute approximately 2.5% to 3.9% of total hemoglobin; hemoglobin A_{1c} constitutes 8% to 11.9%; and total glycosylated hemoglobin level is 10.9% to 15.5%. As effective therapy brings diabetes under control, levels approach the normal range.

With only one blood sample every 6 to 8 weeks, the test can evaluate long-term diabetes therapy.

ORAL LACTOSE TOLERANCE TEST

This test measures blood sugar levels after you drink a dose of lactose, which is a form of sugar that's found in milk. The test is used to screen for lactose intolerance. Lactose intolerance may be caused by a deficiency of the intestinal enzyme lactase, which normally splits lactose into simpler sugars. The undigested lactose remains in the intestine, which leads to symptoms such as abdominal cramps and watery diarrhea.

True congenital, or inborn, lactase deficiency is rare. Usually, lactose intolerance is acquired later in life because lactase levels generally decrease with age.

Why is this test done?

The oral lactose tolerance test is performed to determine if a person's symptoms are caused by lactose intolerance.

What should you know before the test?

- You must fast and avoid strenuous activity for 8 hours before the test.
- This test may require a stool sample.
- This test also requires the collection of four blood samples. You may feel slight discomfort from the needle punctures and the pressure of the tourniquet, but collecting each blood sample takes less than 3 minutes. The entire procedure may take as long as 2 hours.
- Your medication history is checked for drugs that may affect plasma glucose levels, and they may be discontinued.

What happens during the test?

- A nurse or medical technician first obtains a fasting blood sample. A needle is inserted into a vein, usually in your forearm. A blood sample is collected in a tube, which is then sent to a lab for testing.
- You're asked to drink the lactose solution, and the time is recorded.
- Blood samples are collected 30, 60, and 120 minutes after you drink the lactose.
- A stool sample is collected 5 hours after you drink the lactose.

What happens after the test?

- If swelling develops at the needle puncture site, warm soaks are applied to the area to ease discomfort.
- You may resume your usual diet, medications, and activities.

Does the test have risks?

You may experience symptoms of lactose intolerance, such as abdominal cramps, nausea, bloating, flatulence, and watery diarrhea. The test administrator will monitor you for these symptoms.

What are the normal results?

Normally, glucose levels in the blood increase more than 1.1 millimoles of glucose per liter over fasting levels within 15 to 60 minutes after you drink the lactose. Stool sample analysis shows normal pH of 7 to 8 and low glucose content.

What do abnormal results mean?

An increase in plasma glucose of less than 1.1 millimoles per liter indicates lactose intolerance, as does stool acidity, or pH of 5.5 or less, and high glucose content. Accompanying signs and symptoms provoked by the test also suggest but do not confirm the diagnosis, as such symptoms may appear in people with normal lactase activity after consuming the lactose. Small-bowel biopsy with lactase assay may confirm the diagnosis.

LACTIC ACID

Lactic acid, which occurs in the blood as lactate, is made primarily in muscle cells and red blood cells. It's produced during carbohydrate metabolism and is normally metabolized, or converted to energy, by the liver. Blood lactate concentration depends on the rates of production and metabolism. Levels may increase significantly during exercise.

Lactate and pyruvate, another product of carbohydrate metabolism, react together in a process that's regulated by oxygen supply. When oxygen is low, pyruvate converts to lactate. When oxygen is adequate, lactate converts to pyruvate. When the liver fails to metabolize lactose sufficiently or when excess pyruvate converts to lactate, severe elevations of lactic acid, called *lactic acidosis,* may result.

Measurement of blood lactate levels is recommended for all people with symptoms of lactic acidosis, such as rapid, deep breathing.

The test is recommended for all people with symptoms of lactic acidosis, such as rapid, deep breathing.

Why is this test done?

Lactic acid levels are measured to help determine the cause of lactic acidosis.

What should you know before the test?

▪ This test requires a blood sample, which takes less than 3 minutes to collect.

▪ You may experience slight discomfort from the needle puncture and tourniquet pressure.

▪ Fast overnight before the test, and rest for at least 1 hour before the test.

What happens during the test?

▪ A nurse or medical technician inserts a needle into a vein, usually in your forearm. A blood sample is collected in a tube, which is then sent to a lab for testing.

▪ During blood collection, don't clench your fist because this may raise blood lactate levels.

What happens after the test?

▪ If swelling develops at the needle puncture site, warm soaks are applied to the area to ease discomfort.

▪ You may resume your normal diet.

What are the normal results?

Lactate levels range from 0.93 to 1.65 millimoles of lactate per liter of blood. Pyruvate levels range from 0.08 to 0.16 millimole per liter. Normally, the lactate to pyruvate ratio is less than 10 to 1.

What do abnormal results mean?

Elevated lactate levels are usually associated with low oxygen levels in tissues and may be caused by strenuous muscle exercise, shock, hemorrhage, septicemia, heart attack, pulmonary embolism, and cardiac arrest.

Increased lactate levels may also be caused by disorders such as diabetes, leukemias and lymphomas, liver disease, or kidney failure, or from enzyme-based defects such as Von Gierke's disease.

Lactic acidosis can occur when large doses of Tylenol (or other acetaminophen-containing drugs) or alcohol are consumed.

VITAMINS

FOLIC ACID

This test is used to measure the amount of folic acid in a blood sample. It's often performed with a test for vitamin B_{12} levels. Like vitamin B_{12}, folic acid influences red blood cell production, overall body growth, and the formation of genes, which carry the genetic information in cells. Folic acid is also called *pteroylglutamic acid*, *folacin*, or *folate*.

Normally, a person's diet supplies folic acid from liver, kidney, yeast, fruits, leafy vegetables, eggs, and milk. Eating too little of these foods may cause a deficiency, especially during pregnancy. This test is called for when certain blood disorders are suspected.

Why is this test done?
Folic acid levels may be measured for the following reasons:
- To determine the folic acid level in the blood
- To help diagnose anemia from folic acid or vitamin B_{12} deficiency
- To assess folic acid stores in pregnancy.

What should you know before the test?
- You'll be instructed to fast overnight before this test.
- This test requires a blood sample, which takes less than 3 minutes to collect. You may experience slight discomfort from the needle puncture and tourniquet pressure while the sample is drawn.
- The doctor or nurse will review your medication history to see if you are taking drugs that may affect test results, such as phenytoin or pyrimethamine. When possible, such medications will be withheld. If they can't be withheld, the lab will be notified.

What happens during the test?
A nurse or medical technician inserts a needle into a vein, usually in your forearm. A blood sample is collected in a tube, which is then sent to a lab for testing.

Foods that contain folic acid include liver, kidney, yeast, fruits, leafy vegetables, eggs, and milk. Eating too little of these foods may cause a deficiency, especially during pregnancy.

What happens after the test?

- If swelling develops at the needle puncture site, warm soaks will be applied to the area to ease discomfort.
- You may resume taking medications that were discontinued before the test.

What are the normal results?

Normal levels range from 7 to 36 nanomoles of folic acid per liter of blood.

What do abnormal results mean?

Levels of folic acid in the blood below 5 nanomoles per liter may indicate blood-related abnormalities, such as anemia, decreased white blood cell count, and decreased platelet count. Low folic acid levels can also be caused by metabolism problems, inadequate dietary intake, chronic alcoholism, poor absorption, or pregnancy.

Levels greater than 5 nanomoles per liter may indicate excessive dietary intake of folic acid or folic acid supplements. Even when taken in large doses, this vitamin is nontoxic.

VITAMIN A AND CAROTENE

This test measures the amount of vitamin A—which is also called *retinol*—in the blood. Vitamin A, a fat-soluble vitamin, is derived from carotene, a substance that's found in leafy green vegetables and yellow fruits and vegetables. In a person's diet, vitamin A also is found in eggs, poultry, meat, and fish. Vitamin A is important for reproduction, bone growth, vision—especially night vision—and for forming the *epithelium,* or cells that cover and protect various organs and body parts. (See *Fat-soluble vitamins*, page 414.)

Why is this test done?

Vitamin A and carotene tests may be performed for the following reasons:

- To measure the level of vitamin A in the blood and to investigate suspected vitamin A deficiency or toxicity
- To diagnose visual disturbances, especially night blindness and a drying condition of the eyes called *xerophthalmia*

Fat-soluble vitamins

Vitamins are classified as either fat soluble or water soluble. Fat-soluble vitamins — which include vitamins A, D, E, and K — are absorbed with the fats in certain foods.

Vital but toxic too

Although these vitamins are necessary for survival, excessive or prolonged intake of most fat-soluble vitamins — especially in doses that exceed the recommended daily amounts — can have toxic effects. That's because the body stores these vitamins and does not readily excrete them.

Functions unclear

Fat-soluble vitamins have different functions that are only partially understood: Vitamin A helps to maintain night vision and cell health; vitamin D regulates the body's use of calcium and phosphorus, which are important for healthy bones; vitamin E is associated with several production processes in the body; and vitamin K is necessary for proper blood clotting.

- To diagnose some skin diseases
- To screen for poor vitamin absorption.

What should you know before the test?

- You should fast overnight before the test, but you may drink water.
- This test requires a blood sample, which takes less than 3 minutes to collect. You may experience slight discomfort from the needle puncture and tourniquet pressure while the sample is drawn.

What happens during the test?

A nurse or medical technician inserts a needle into a vein, usually in your forearm. A blood sample is collected in a tube, which is then sent to a lab for testing.

What happens after the test?

- If swelling develops at the needle puncture site, warm soaks will be applied to the area to ease discomfort.
- You may resume your usual diet.

What are the normal results?

Normal levels differ according to age and sex. For children, the range of levels is 1.05 to 2.27 nanomoles of vitamin A per liter of blood. For adults, it is 1.05 to 2.10 nanomoles per liter. Levels for men are usually 20% higher than the levels for women.

What do abnormal results mean?

Low levels of vitamin A — a condition called *hypovitaminosis A* — may indicate impaired fat absorption from various conditions such as infectious hepatitis. Low levels are also associated with a form of malnutrition known as *protein-calorie malnutrition.* Similar decreases in vitamin A levels may also be caused by chronic kidney inflammation.

High vitamin A levels — called *hypervitaminosis A* — usually indicate excessive intake of vitamin A supplements or of foods high in vitamin A. Increased levels are also associated with uncontrolled diabetes.

Low carotene levels may indicate impaired fat absorption or, rarely, insufficient carotene in the diet. Carotene levels may also be suppressed during pregnancy. Elevated carotene levels indicate excessive dietary intake of this nutrient.

VITAMIN B₂

This test is used to evaluate the amount of vitamin B₂ — or riboflavin — in the blood. Vitamin B₂ is essential for a person's growth and tissue activity. This test is more reliable than a urine vitamin B₂ test. (See *Water-soluble vitamins.*)

Why is this test done?

Vitamin B₂ testing may be performed for the following reasons:
- To evaluate vitamin B₂ levels
- To detect vitamin B₂ deficiency.

What should you know before the test?

- Maintain a normal diet before the test.
- This test requires a blood sample, which takes less than 3 minutes to collect.
- You may experience slight discomfort from the needle puncture and tourniquet pressure.

What happens during the test?

A nurse or medical technician inserts a needle into a vein, usually in your forearm. A blood sample is collected in a tube, which is then sent to a lab for testing.

What happens after the test?

- If swelling develops at the needle puncture site, warm soaks will be applied to the area to ease discomfort.
- If a deficiency is detected, you should know that good dietary sources of vitamin B₂ are milk products, liver and kidneys, fish, green leafy vegetables, and legumes.

What are the normal results?

Normal levels are 80 to 133 nanomoles of vitamin B₂ per liter of blood.

HOW YOUR BODY WORKS

Water-soluble vitamins

Vitamins are classified as either fat soluble or water soluble. Water-soluble vitamins include vitamin C and the B complex vitamins. Vitamin C is necessary for making some proteins and for maintaining healthy bone and cartilage.

B complex vitamins
- Vitamin B₁, called thiamine, prevents the disease beriberi and plays a role in energy metabolism.
- Vitamin B₂ is essential for growth and tissue function.
- Vitamin B₆, or pyridoxine, is essential to protein metabolism and contributes to cell growth and blood formation.
- Vitamin B₁₂ is essential for red blood cell production.

What do abnormal results mean?

Test results below 80 to 133 nanomoles per liter indicate vitamin B_2 deficiency. This can be caused by insufficient dietary intake of vitamin B_2, poor absorption of nutrients, or conditions that increase metabolic demands, such as stress.

VITAMIN B_{12}

This test is used to measure the amount of vitamin B_{12} in the blood. Vitamin B_{12} is also called *cyanocobalamin, antipernicious anemia factor,* or *extrinsic factor.* The test for vitamin B_{12} is often performed with a test for folic acid levels.

Vitamin B_{12} is essential to red blood cell production, nervous system health, and the formation of genes, which carry the genetic information in cells. This vitamin is found almost exclusively in animal products, such as meat, shellfish, milk, and eggs. (See *Vitamin B_{12} absorption.*)

Why is this test done?

Vitamin B_{12} testing may be performed for the following reasons:
- To determine the amount of vitamin B_{12} in the blood
- To help diagnose anemia and determine whether it's due to vitamin B_{12} or folic acid deficiency
- To help diagnose some central nervous system disorders.

What should you know before the test?

- If your folic acid level is also being measured, you'll be instructed to fast overnight before the test.
- This test requires a blood sample, which takes less than 3 minutes to collect. You may experience slight discomfort from the needle puncture and tourniquet pressure.
- Your medication history will be checked for the use of drugs — such as para-aminosalicylic acid, phenytoin, neomycin, and colchicine — that may alter test results. These drugs may be withheld before the test. If they can't be withheld, the lab will be notified.

Vitamin B$_{12}$ absorption

As vitamin B$_{12}$ is metabolized, it's absorbed at many locations in the body where it's used to produce red blood cells and support nervous system function.

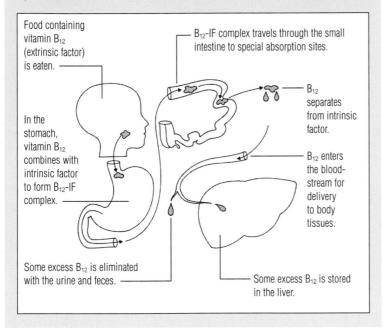

Food containing vitamin B$_{12}$ (extrinsic factor) is eaten.

B$_{12}$-IF complex travels through the small intestine to special absorption sites.

In the stomach, vitamin B$_{12}$ combines with intrinsic factor to form B$_{12}$-IF complex.

B$_{12}$ separates from intrinsic factor.

B$_{12}$ enters the bloodstream for delivery to body tissues.

Some excess B$_{12}$ is eliminated with the urine and feces.

Some excess B$_{12}$ is stored in the liver.

What happens during the test?

A nurse or medical technician inserts a needle into a vein, usually in your forearm. A blood sample is collected in a tube, which is then sent to a lab for testing.

What happens after the test?

- If swelling develops at the needle puncture site, warm soaks will be applied to the area to ease discomfort.
- You may resume your usual diet.

What are the normal results?

Normal levels range from 74 to 516 picomoles of vitamin B$_{12}$ per liter of blood.

What do abnormal results mean?

Low levels of this vitamin in the blood may indicate inadequate dietary intake, especially in strict vegetarians. Low levels are also associated with poor absorption of nutrients by the intestine, as occurs with celiac disease, poor absorption of vitamin B_{12} alone, conditions of increased metabolism such as an overactive thyroid, pregnancy, and central nervous system damage.

High levels of vitamin B_{12} may be caused by excessive dietary intake; liver disease, such as cirrhosis or acute or chronic hepatitis; and conditions known as *myeloproliferative disorders,* including some leukemias.

VITAMIN C

This test is used to measure levels of vitamin C, or ascorbic acid, in a blood sample. Vitamin C is needed to maintain healthy cartilage and bone. It also promotes iron absorption, influences folic acid metabolism, and may be necessary for withstanding the stresses of injury and infection.

This vitamin is present in generous amounts in citrus fruits, berries, tomatoes, raw cabbage, green peppers, and green leafy vegetables. Severe vitamin C deficiency, also called *scurvy,* causes fragility of tiny blood vessels, joint abnormalities, and various other symptoms.

Why is this test done?

Vitamin C testing may be performed for the following reasons:
- To detect the amount of vitamin C in the blood
- To aid diagnosis of scurvy, scurvy-like conditions, and disorders such as malnutrition and poor nutrient absorption.

What should you know before the test?

- You'll be instructed to fast overnight before the test.
- This test requires a blood sample, which takes less than 3 minutes to collect.
- You may experience slight discomfort from the needle puncture and tourniquet pressure.

Megadoses of vitamin C: Miracle cure or dangerous myth?

In the early 1970s, Nobel Laureate Linus Pauling sparked interest in vitamin C when he suggested that megadoses of this vitamin may increase a person's resistance to infections and cancer and lower blood cholesterol levels. Pauling recommended daily doses of vitamin C that are two to five times the recommended amount — 60 milligrams daily for adults — and much higher doses during times of stress or illness. He especially advocated very high doses to treat cancer and to relieve common cold symptoms.

Outcome of recent research

To date, research hasn't supported Pauling's theories. In fact, a recent study has shown that high-dose vitamin C is no more effective than a placebo, or fake pill, in the treatment of cancer. Other studies have shown that high-dose vitamin C has little or no effect on the severity of colds. But despite this, many people supplement their diets with high doses of vitamin C. And, in addition to delaying proper treatment, some of them experience severe side effects.

Dangers of vitamin C overload

The most common side effects of excessive vitamin C are diarrhea and vomiting. However, in some people, high doses of vitamin C may trigger or intensify gout and lead to the formation of kidney stones. Vitamin C also promotes iron absorption, which may lead to iron toxicity. If a person is receiving drug therapy, high doses of vitamin C may also interfere with the way medications work.

What happens during the test?

A nurse or medical technician inserts a needle into a vein, usually in your forearm. A blood sample is collected in a tube, which is then sent to a lab for testing.

What happens after the test?

- If swelling develops at the needle puncture site, warm soaks will be applied to the area to ease discomfort.
- You may resume your usual diet.

What are the normal results?

Normally, 17 micromoles of vitamin C per liter of blood is acceptable.

What do abnormal results mean?

People with levels of 11 micromoles of vitamin C per liter are considered "at risk." Levels under 11 micromoles per liter indicate vitamin C deficiency. Vitamin C levels diminish during pregnancy to a low point immediately after giving birth. Depressed levels occur with infection, fever, and anemia. Severe deficiencies result in scurvy.

High levels occur when vitamin C is consumed. Excess vitamin C is normally excreted in the urine, but excessive concentrations can cause urinary problems. (See *Megadoses of vitamin C: Miracle cure or dangerous myth?* page 419.)

VITAMIN D$_3$

Also called *cholecalciferol*, vitamin D$_3$ is important for bone growth and overall health. It's produced in the skin by the sun's ultraviolet rays. It also occurs naturally in fish liver oils, egg yolks, liver, and butter.

To become active, vitamin D is converted to a substance called *25-hydroxycholecalciferol*. This test is performed to determine the amount of 25-hydroxycholecalciferol in the blood.

Why is this test done?
Vitamin D$_3$ tests may be performed for the following reasons:
- To measure vitamin D in the body
- To evaluate skeletal diseases, such as rickets
- To help diagnose a condition called *hypercalcemia,* or excessive calcium in the blood
- To detect vitamin D toxicity
- To monitor therapy with vitamin D$_3$.

What should you know before the test?
- You don't have to restrict food or fluids before this test.
- The test requires a blood sample, which takes less than 3 minutes to collect. You may experience slight discomfort from the needle puncture and tourniquet pressure while the sample is drawn.
- The doctor or nurse will check your medication history for use of drugs that could alter test results, such as corticosteroids or anticonvulsants. If possible, these drugs are withheld. If they cannot be withheld, the lab will be notified.

Vitamin D deficiency can cause a condition known as rickets, or bone softening.

What happens during the test?
A nurse or medical technician inserts a needle into a vein, usually in your forearm. A blood sample is collected in a tube, which is then sent to a lab for testing.

What happens after the test?

■ If swelling develops at the needle puncture site, warm soaks will be applied to the area to ease discomfort.

■ You may resume taking medications that were discontinued before the test.

What are the normal results?

In summer, the range for the active form of vitamin D is from 37 to 200 nanomoles of 25-hydroxycholecalciferol per liter of blood. In winter, it's 35 to 105 nanomoles per liter.

What do abnormal results mean?

Low or undetectable levels may be caused by vitamin D deficiency, which can cause a condition known as *rickets,* or bone softening. A deficiency may be caused by a poor diet, decreased exposure to the sun, or impaired absorption of vitamin D from liver disease, pancreatitis, celiac disease, cystic fibrosis, or surgery that removes part of the stomach or small bowel.

Levels over 250 nanomoles per liter may indicate excessive self-medication or prolonged vitamin therapy. Elevated levels with excess calcium in the blood may be due to hypersensitivity to vitamin D.

TRACE ELEMENTS

MANGANESE

This test measures the amount of manganese in a blood sample. Manganese is a trace element, meaning extremely small amounts of it are present in the body. Although its function is only partially understood, manganese is known to activate several substances called *enzymes* that are essential to a person's metabolism. Dietary sources of manganese include unrefined cereals, green leafy vegetables, and nuts.

Manganese toxicity may be caused by inhaling manganese dust or fumes — a hazard in the steel and dry-cell battery industries — or from drinking contaminated water.

Why is this test done?

Manganese tests may be performed for the following reasons:
- To determine the level of manganese in the blood
- To detect manganese toxicity.

What should you know before the test?

- You don't need to restrict your diet before this test.
- The test requires a blood sample, which takes less than 3 minutes to collect. You may experience slight discomfort from the needle puncture and tourniquet pressure as the sample is drawn.
- The doctor or nurse will check your medication history for use of drugs that may influence test results, such as estrogens and glucocorticoids. When possible, such drugs will be withheld before the test. If they cannot be withheld, the lab will be notified.

What happens during the test?

A nurse or medical technician inserts a needle into a vein, usually in your forearm. A blood sample is collected in a tube, which is then sent to a lab for testing.

What happens after the test?

- If swelling develops at the needle puncture site, warm soaks will be applied to the area to ease discomfort.
- You may resume taking medications that were discontinued before the test.

What are the normal results?

Normal levels for this nutrient range from 0.04 to 1.4 micrograms of manganese per deciliter of blood.

What do abnormal results mean?

Extremely high levels indicate manganese toxicity, which requires prompt medical attention to prevent central nervous system deterioration. Low manganese levels may indicate insufficient dietary intake, although deficiency hasn't been linked to disease.

ZINC

This test measures the amount of zinc in the blood. Extremely small amounts of zinc are present in the body, but it plays a critical role in maintaining good health. Zinc deficiency — called *hypozincemia* — can seriously impair a person's metabolism, growth, and development.

Zinc occurs naturally in water and in most foods. High concentrations are found in meat, seafood, dairy products, whole grains, nuts, and legumes.

Why is this test done?

Zinc testing may be performed for the following reasons:
- To determine the concentration of zinc in the blood
- To detect zinc deficiency or toxicity.

What should you know before the test?

- You don't need to change or restrict your diet before this test.
- This test requires a blood sample, which takes less than 3 minutes to collect. You may experience slight discomfort from the needle puncture and tourniquet pressure while the sample is drawn.
- The doctor or nurse will check your drug history for use of medications — such as zinc-chelating agents and corticosteroids — that may interfere with the test results. When possible, such drugs will be withheld before the test. If they cannot be withheld, the lab will be notified.

What happens during the test?

A nurse or medical technician inserts a needle into a vein, usually in your forearm. A blood sample is collected in a tube, which is then sent to a lab for testing.

What happens after the test?

- If swelling develops at the needle puncture site, warm soaks will be applied to the area to ease discomfort.
- You may resume taking medications that were discontinued before the test.

INSIGHT INTO ILLNESS

Toxic zinc exposure: 14 high-risk jobs

Approximately 50,000 industrial workers in North America are at risk for toxic exposure to zinc oxide. Overexposure can be caused by inhaling dust or fumes in the following industries and occupations:
- Alloy manufacturing
- Brass foundry work
- Bronze foundry work
- Electric fuse manufacturing
- Gas welding
- Electroplating
- Galvanizing
- Junk metal refining
- Paint manufacturing
- Metal cutting and spraying
- Linoleum and battery manufacturing
- Rubber manufacturing
- Roof making
- Zinc manufacturing.

What are the normal results?

Normal levels range from 11 to 23 micromoles of zinc per liter of blood.

What do abnormal results mean?

Levels below 70 micrograms per deciliter indicate zinc deficiency. Low levels may be due to insufficient dietary intake, an underlying disease, or a hereditary deficiency. Markedly depressed levels are common in people with leukemia. Low zinc levels are common in persons with alcoholic cirrhosis of the liver, heart attack, ileitis, chronic kidney failure, rheumatoid arthritis, and some anemias.

Elevated and potentially toxic zinc levels may be caused by accidental ingestion or exposure while working at an industrial site. (See *Toxic zinc exposure: 14 high-risk jobs*, page 423.)

HORMONE TESTS:
Tracking the Body's Messengers

PITUITARY HORMONES

CORTICOTROPIN

This test measures the amount of corticotropin in a blood sample. Corticotropin is a hormone, a chemical that's secreted by the pituitary gland in the brain. This hormone affects the activity of another gland in the body, the adrenal gland, and causes it to secrete steroid hormones. Corticotropin also may be called *adrenocorticotropic hormone.*

This test may be ordered for people with signs of adrenal insufficiency, which means that their adrenal gland is not functioning adequately. It also may be ordered for a person with signs of Cushing's syndrome, which occurs when the adrenal gland secretes too much of its hormones. (See *Where do hormones come from?* page 428.)

Why is this test done?
Corticotropin levels may be measured for the following reasons:
- To determine if hormonal secretion is normal
- To help diagnose deficient activity by the adrenal gland
- To diagnose Cushing's syndrome.

What should you know before the test?
- A low-carbohydrate diet is generally recommended for 2 days before the test. This requirement may vary, depending on the lab. In addition, you must fast and limit your physical activity for 10 to 12 hours before the test.
- The test requires a blood sample, which takes less than 3 minutes to collect. While the sample is being drawn, you may experience slight discomfort from the needle puncture and tourniquet pressure.
- The lab needs up to 4 days to complete the analysis.
- The doctor or nurse will ask if you take any medications that may affect test results, such as corticosteroids, estrogens, amphetamines, spironolactone, calcium gluconate, or alcohol. Usually, these drugs are withheld for 48 hours or longer before the test.

HOW YOUR BODY WORKS

Where do hormones come from?

Different glands throughout the body store and secrete hormones, allowing these powerful, complex chemicals to circulate through the bloodstream. Hormones both stimulate and inhibit the activity of specific glands or organs. The glands and organs, in turn, also secrete hormones that maintain chemical balance in the body. This illustration shows the body's glands and the hormones they secrete.

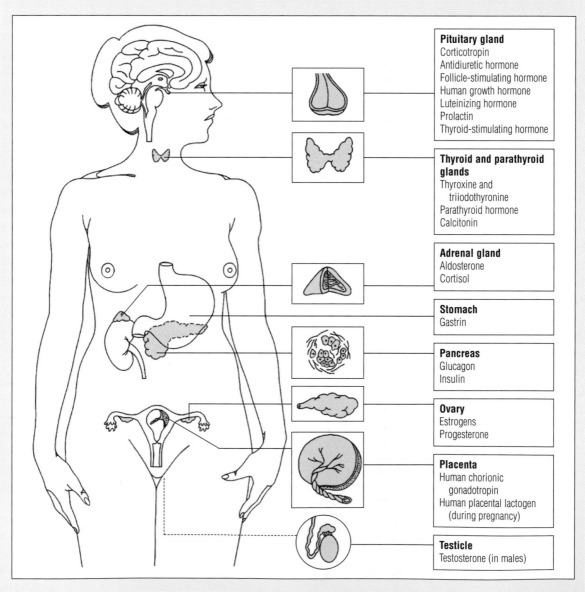

Pituitary gland
Corticotropin
Antidiuretic hormone
Follicle-stimulating hormone
Human growth hormone
Luteinizing hormone
Prolactin
Thyroid-stimulating hormone

Thyroid and parathyroid glands
Thyroxine and
    triiodothyronine
Parathyroid hormone
Calcitonin

Adrenal gland
Aldosterone
Cortisol

Stomach
Gastrin

Pancreas
Glucagon
Insulin

Ovary
Estrogens
Progesterone

Placenta
Human chorionic
    gonadotropin
Human placental lactogen
    (during pregnancy)

Testicle
Testosterone (in males)

What happens during the test?

■ If the doctor suspects you're experiencing adrenal hypofunction (inadequate adrenal gland activity), a blood sample is collected between 6 a.m. and 8 a.m.

■ If the doctor suspects you're experiencing Cushing's syndrome, a blood sample is collected between 6 p.m. and 11 p.m., which is the time of lowest hormonal secretion.

■ A nurse or medical technician inserts a needle into a vein, usually in your forearm. A blood sample is collected in a tube, which is then sent to a lab for testing.

What happens after the test?

■ If swelling develops at the needle puncture site, warm soaks are applied to the area to ease discomfort.

■ You may resume your usual diet and medications.

What are the normal results?

The Mayo Clinic in the United States sets baseline values at less than 60 picograms of corticotropin per milliliter of blood, but these values may vary, depending on the lab.

What do abnormal results mean?

The doctor interprets the test results in light of the person's signs and symptoms.

Suspected adrenal insufficiency

A higher-than-normal corticotropin level may indicate primary adrenal insufficiency, or Addison's disease. A low-normal corticotropin level suggests secondary adrenal insufficiency resulting from pituitary or hypothalamic dysfunction.

Suspected adrenal hyperfunction

An elevated corticotropin level that remains continuously high for several days suggests Cushing's disease. Moderately elevated corticotropin levels suggest pituitary-dependent adrenal hyperplasia or nonadrenal tumors such as oat cell carcinoma of the lungs.

A low-normal corticotropin level implies adrenal hyperfunction (overactivity) caused by an adrenocortical tumor or hyperplasia.

RAPID CORTICOTROPIN TEST

This is the most effective test for evaluating adrenal hypofunction, or inadequate adrenal gland activity. It may also be called the *rapid adrenocorticotropic hormone test* or the *cosyntropin test.*

In this test, baseline levels of cortisol are compared to levels of the hormone after an injection of cosyntropin, a synthetic form of corticotropin. A definitively high morning cortisol level rules out adrenal hypofunction and makes further testing unnecessary.

Why is this test done?

The rapid corticotropin test may be performed for any of the following reasons:
- To determine if your condition is due to a hormonal deficiency
- To determine if a problem with the functioning of the adrenal gland is primary hypofunction (originating from within the gland itself) or secondary hypofunction (originating from elsewhere in the body).

What should you know before the test?

- You may be required to fast for 10 to 12 hours before the test, and you must be relaxed and resting quietly for 30 minutes before the test.
- The test takes at least 1 hour to perform; three blood samples are taken and an injection is given.
- You may experience slight discomfort from the needle punctures and tourniquet pressure when the blood samples are drawn.
- You'll be instructed to refrain from taking corticotropin and all steroid medications before the test. If such drugs must be continued, the lab must be notified.

What happens during the test?

- A nurse or medical technician inserts a needle into a vein, usually in your forearm. A blood sample is collected in a tube, which is then sent to a lab for testing. This is used to determine your preinjection, or baseline, cortisol level.
- Cosyntropin is injected into a vein or muscle.

- Blood samples are collected 30 and 60 minutes after the cosyntropin injection.

What happens after the test?

- If swelling develops at the needle puncture sites, warm soaks are applied to the area to ease discomfort.
- You're observed for signs of a rare allergic reaction to cosyntropin, such as hives and itching, or an irregular heartbeat.
- You may resume your usual diet.
- Resume taking medications that were discontinued before the test.

What are the normal results?

Normally, cortisol levels rise 193 nanomoles per liter of blood or more above the baseline value, to a peak of 497 nanomoles per liter or more 60 minutes after the cosyntropin injection. Generally, a doubling of the baseline value indicates a normal response. A normal result means that the person does not have adrenal insufficiency.

What do abnormal results mean?

In people with primary adrenal hypofunction, cortisol levels remain low. However, if test results show below-normal increases in cortisol, further testing may be needed to distinguish between primary and secondary adrenal hypofunction.

GROWTH HORMONE

Human growth hormone is also called *somatotrophic hormone*. A protein secreted by the pituitary gland, it's the primary regulator of human growth. Unlike other pituitary hormones, human growth hormone has no single target gland; it affects many body tissues. Hypersecretion (overabundance) or hyposecretion (inadequacy) of this hormone may cause conditions such as dwarfism or gigantism. Altered human growth hormone levels are common in people with pituitary problems.

Human growth hormone is the primary regulator of human growth. Unlike other pituitary hormones, it has no single target gland; it affects many body tissues.

Why is this test done?

Human growth hormone levels may be measured for the following reasons:
- To help determine the cause of abnormal growth
- To distinguish dwarfism from other diagnoses; retarded growth in children also can be caused by pituitary or thyroid hypofunction
- To confirm a diagnosis of gigantism (abnormal height) or acromegaly (abnormal enlargement of the hands, feet, nose, and jaw)
- To aid diagnosis of pituitary or hypothalamic tumors
- To help evaluate human growth hormone therapy.

What should you know before the test?

- You'll be instructed to fast and to limit your physical activity for 10 to 12 hours before the test.
- This test requires a blood sample, which takes less than 3 minutes to collect. The lab requires at least 2 days for analysis. You may experience slight discomfort from the needle puncture and tourniquet pressure while the sample is being drawn.
- Another blood sample may have to be drawn the following day for comparison.
- The doctor or nurse will check your medication history for medications that affect human growth hormone levels, such as pituitary-based steroids. Usually, such medications are withheld before the test.
- You should relax and lie down for 30 minutes before the test; stress and physical activity elevate human growth hormone levels.

What happens during the test?

A nurse or medical technician inserts a needle into a vein, usually in your forearm. A blood sample is collected in a tube, which is then sent to a lab for testing.

What happens after the test?

- If swelling develops at the needle puncture site, warm soaks are applied to the area to ease discomfort.
- You may resume your usual diet.
- Resume taking medications that were discontinued before the test.

What are the normal results?

Normal human growth hormone levels for men range from undetectable to 5 micrograms of this hormone per liter of blood; for women, from undetectable to 10 micrograms per liter. Higher values in women are due to estrogen effects. Children generally have higher human growth hormone levels, ranging from undetectable to 16 micrograms per liter.

What do abnormal results mean?

Increased human growth hormone levels may indicate a pituitary or hypothalamic tumor that causes gigantism in children and acromegaly in adults and adolescents. People with diabetes sometimes have elevated human growth hormone levels without acromegaly. Growth hormone suppression testing is necessary to confirm a diagnosis.

Pituitary infarction, tumors, or cancer that has spread from another part of the body may reduce human growth hormone levels. Dwarfism may be due to low human growth hormone levels, although only 15% of all cases of growth failure are related to endocrine dysfunction. Confirmation of the diagnosis requires other lab tests.

GROWTH HORMONE SUPPRESSION TEST

This test is used to evaluate excessive amounts of human growth hormone from the pituitary gland. It may also be called the *glucose loading test.*

Normally, glucose—in the form of a sugary solution you drink during the test—should suppress the hormone's secretion. In a person with excessively high levels, failure of the glucose to suppress the secretion of growth hormone indicates a pituitary problem. This result confirms a diagnosis of acromegaly (abnormal enlargement of the hands, feet, nose, and jaw) or gigantism (abnormal height).

Why is this test done?

The growth hormone suppression test may be performed for any of the following reasons:
- To determine the cause of abnormal growth
- To assess elevated human growth hormone levels
- To confirm a diagnosis of gigantism in children and acromegaly in adults.

What should you know before the test?

- This test takes about 1 hour to complete, but the lab requires at least another 2 days to complete its analysis.
- You'll be instructed to fast and to limit your physical activity for 10 to 12 hours before the test; you may be asked to relax and lie down for 30 minutes immediately before the test.
- A nurse or technician checks your medication history. Usually, all steroids — including estrogens and progestogens — and other pituitary-based hormones are withheld before the test.
- When testing begins, you must drink a sugary solution. You may experience some nausea after drinking the solution.
- This test also requires two blood samples, each of which takes less than 3 minutes to collect. While the samples are being drawn, you may experience slight discomfort from the needle puncture and tourniquet pressure.

What happens during the test?

- A nurse or medical technician inserts a needle into a vein, usually in your forearm. A blood sample is collected in a tube, which is then sent to a lab for testing.
- You next take the sugary solution by mouth. To prevent nausea, you may drink the solution slowly.
- After about 2 hours, another blood sample is drawn and sent to the lab.

What happens after the test?

- If swelling develops at the needle puncture site, warm soaks are applied to the area to ease discomfort.
- You may resume your usual diet.
- With the doctor's permission, you may resume taking medications that were discontinued before the test.

What are the normal results?

Normally, glucose suppresses human growth hormone to levels ranging from undetectable to 3 micrograms of this hormone per liter of blood in 30 minutes to 2 hours. In children, rebound stimulation may occur after 2 to 5 hours.

What do abnormal results mean?

In a person with active acromegaly, baseline levels are elevated — 75 micrograms per liter — and aren't suppressed to less than 5 micrograms per liter during the test. Unchanged or increasing human growth hormone levels in response to glucose loading indicate excess secretion of human growth hormone and may confirm suspected acromegaly — abnormal enlargement of the hands, feet, nose, and jaw — or gigantism, which is abnormal height. This response may be verified by repeating the test after a 1-day rest.

INSULIN TOLERANCE TEST

This test measures blood levels of human growth hormone and corticotropin, another hormone, after administering insulin.

Insulin-induced hypoglycemia — or low blood sugar — stimulates secretion of human growth hormone and corticotropin. A failure of insulin to stimulate hormone secretion indicates poor functioning of the pituitary or adrenal gland and helps confirm insufficient human growth hormone or corticotropin.

Why is this test done?

The insulin tolerance test may be performed for the following reasons:

■ To evaluate hormonal secretion
■ To help the doctor diagnose human growth hormone or corticotropin deficiency
■ To identify pituitary dysfunction
■ To differentiate between primary and secondary adrenal hypofunction.

What should you know before the test?

■ You must fast and restrict physical activity for 10 to 12 hours before the test. You may be asked to relax and lie down for 90 minutes before the test.
■ The test requires intravenous administration of insulin and the collection of several blood samples.
■ You may experience slight discomfort from the needle puncture and tourniquet pressure while the blood samples are drawn.

- You may experience an increased heart rate, perspiration, hunger, and anxiety after receiving the insulin. These symptoms usually pass quickly, but if they become severe, the test will be discontinued.
- The test takes about 2 hours and results are usually available in 2 days.

What happens during the test?

- A nurse or medical technician inserts a needle into a vein, usually in your forearm. Three blood samples are collected in tubes, which are then sent to a lab for testing. These provide baseline values of glucose (sugar), human growth hormone, and corticotropin in your blood.
- Insulin is then infused into your bloodstream for 1 to 2 minutes.
- Additional blood samples are collected 15, 30, 45, 60, 90, and 120 minutes after you're given the insulin. A collection device called an *indwelling venous catheter* is used so you don't have to undergo repeated needle punctures.

What happens after the test?

- If swelling develops at the needle puncture site, warm soaks are applied to the area to ease discomfort.
- You may resume your usual diet and activities.
- Resume taking medications that were discontinued before the test.

Does the test have risks?

- This test isn't recommended for people with cardiovascular or cerebrovascular disorders, epilepsy, or low baseline cortisol levels.
- There's a risk of developing a severe hypoglycemic reaction to insulin. The nurse or technician will have a concentrated sugar solution readily available should this occur.

What are the normal results?

Normally, a person's blood sugar decreases to 50% of the fasting level 20 to 30 minutes after the insulin is given. This stimulates a 10- to 20-microgram per liter increase over baseline values in both human growth hormone and corticotropin. Peak levels occur 60 to 90 minutes after the insulin is given.

What do abnormal results mean?

Failure of the insulin to stimulate an increase in hormone levels may indicate a problem in the hypothalamus or the pituitary or adrenal gland. An increase in human growth hormone levels of less than 10 micrograms per liter may indicate a human growth hormone deficiency. However, a definitive diagnosis of deficiency requires an additional test such as the arginine test. Further testing is needed to find out where the abnormality originates.

An increase in corticotropin levels of less than 10 micrograms per liter may indicate insufficient adrenal activity. Further testing is done to confirm and supplement the diagnosis.

ARGININE TEST

Also known as the *human growth hormone stimulation test,* this test measures the level of the hormone after an injection of arginine, a substance that normally stimulates the secretion of this hormone.

The results are used to identify dysfunction of the pituitary gland in infants and children with growth retardation and to confirm human growth hormone deficiency.

Why is this test done?

The arginine test may be performed for the following reasons:
- To identify human growth hormone deficiency
- To aid the diagnosis of pituitary tumors
- To confirm human growth hormone deficiency in infants and children with low baseline levels.

What should you know before the test?

- You must fast and limit physical activity for 10 to 12 hours before the test.
- This test requires intravenous infusion of a drug and collection of several blood samples. It takes at least 2 hours to perform; results will be available in 2 days.
- You may experience slight discomfort from the needle puncture and tourniquet pressure while the blood samples are drawn.
- Before the test, the doctor or nurse will check your medication history. Usually, steroid medications, including pituitary-based hormones, are withheld before the test.

- Because human growth hormone levels might increase after exercise or excitement, you should relax and lie down for at least 90 minutes before the test.

What happens during the test?

- A nurse or medical technician inserts a needle into a vein, usually in your forearm. A blood sample is collected in a tube, which is then sent to a lab for testing.
- Arginine is provided intravenously for 30 minutes. A device called an *indwelling venous catheter* is used to avoid repeated needle punctures; this also minimizes your stress and anxiety.
- After the arginine is given, three more blood samples are collected at 30-minute intervals.

What happens after the test?

- If swelling develops at the needle puncture site, warm soaks are applied to the area to ease discomfort.
- You may resume your usual diet.
- With the doctor's permission, you may resume taking medications that were discontinued before the test.

What are the normal results?

Arginine should raise human growth hormone levels to more than 10 micrograms of hormone per liter of blood in men, 15 micrograms per liter in women, and 48 micrograms per liter in children. Such an increase may appear 30 minutes after arginine infusion is discontinued or in the samples drawn 60 and 90 minutes later.

What do abnormal results mean?

Elevated fasting levels of arginine and increases that occur during sleep help rule out human growth hormone deficiency. Failure of human growth hormone levels to increase after arginine is given indicates a low reserve of pituitary human growth hormone. In children, this deficiency causes dwarfism; in adults, it can indicate panhypopituitarism. When human growth hormone levels fail to reach 10 micrograms per liter, retesting is required at the same time of day as the original test.

FOLLICLE-STIMULATING HORMONE

A follicle is a tiny sack that surrounds each egg in a woman's ovary. Follicle-stimulating hormone is produced in the pituitary gland and stimulates the growth and maturation of the follicles. This test measures the amounts of follicle-stimulating hormone in a blood sample. The results indicate how well the gonads (sex glands) are functioning.

This test is vital to infertility studies, and it's performed more often on women than on men. Levels of follicle-stimulating hormone in the blood fluctuate widely in women. Therefore, daily testing may be necessary for 3 to 5 days, or multiple samples may be drawn on the same day.

A test for follicle-stimulating hormone is vital to infertility studies. It's performed more often on women than on men.

Why is this test done?

The follicle-stimulating hormone test may be performed for the following reasons:
- To determine if a woman's hormonal secretion is normal
- To diagnose infertility and menstrual disorders
- To diagnose precocious puberty in girls before age 9 and in boys before age 10
- To diagnose hypogonadism (inadequate sex gland activity).

What should you know before the test?

- Your don't need to fast or limit physical activity before this test.
- This test requires a blood sample, which takes less than 3 minutes to collect. While the sample is being drawn, you may experience slight discomfort from the needle puncture and tourniquet pressure.
- The doctor or nurse will check your medication history. Drugs — including those that contain estrogens or progestogens — are usually withheld for 48 hours before the test because they may interfere with test results.
- You may be asked to relax and lie down for 30 minutes before the test.

What happens during the test?

A nurse or medical technician inserts a needle into a vein, usually in your forearm. A blood sample is collected in a tube, which is then sent to a lab for testing. The lab requires at least 3 days to complete the analysis.

What happens after the test?

- If swelling develops at the needle puncture site, warm soaks are applied to the area to ease discomfort.
- You may resume your usual diet.
- With the doctor's permission, you may resume taking medications that were discontinued before the test.

What are the normal results?

Normal results vary greatly, depending on a person's age, stage of sexual development, and — for a woman — the phase of her menstrual cycle. For women who menstruate, normal results are as follows:

- Early menstrual cycle phase: 5 to 20 international units of the hormone per liter of blood
- Midcycle peak: 15 to 30
- Late cycle phase: 5 to 15.

Approximate values for adult men are 5 to 20 international units of the hormone per liter of blood; for menopausal women, 50 to 100.

What do abnormal results mean?

Low follicle-stimulating hormone levels may cause male or female infertility. Low levels may be caused by anorexia nervosa, panhypopituitarism, or hypothalamic lesions.

High follicle-stimulating hormone levels in women may indicate ovarian failure associated with Turner's syndrome or Stein-Leventhal syndrome. Elevated levels may occur with precocious puberty and in postmenopausal women. In men, abnormally high follicle-stimulating hormone levels may indicate destruction of the testes from mumps or X-ray exposure, testicular failure, seminoma, or male climacteric. Absence of the gonads at birth and early-stage acromegaly (abnormal enlargement of the hands, feet, nose, and jaw) may cause follicle-stimulating hormone levels to increase in both sexes.

LUTEINIZING HORMONE

This test measures the amount of luteinizing hormone in a blood sample. In women, luteinizing hormone is secreted during the menstrual cycle. This causes ovulation and helps the body prepare for possible conception. In men, continuous luteinizing hormone secretion stimulates the testes to release testosterone, a hormone that affects sperm production.

Why is this test done?

The luteinizing hormone test may be performed for the following reasons:

- To determine if the secretion of female hormones is normal
- To detect ovulation
- To assess male or female infertility
- To evaluate amenorrhea
- To monitor therapy designed to induce ovulation.

What should you know before the test?

- You usually don't need to fast or restrict your activities before the test.
- This test requires a blood sample, which takes less than 3 minutes to collect. While the sample is being drawn, you may experience slight discomfort from the needle puncture and tourniquet pressure.
- The doctor or nurse will check your medication history before the test. Drugs that may interfere with the test results, such as steroids — including estrogens or progesterone — are usually withheld for 48 hours before the test.

What happens during the test?

A nurse or medical technician inserts a needle into a vein, usually in your forearm. A blood sample is collected in a tube, which is then sent to a lab for testing. The lab needs at least 3 days to complete the analysis.

What happens after the test?

- If swelling develops at the needle puncture site, warm soaks are applied to the area to ease discomfort.

- With the doctor's permission, you may resume taking medications that were discontinued before the test.

What are the normal results?

Normal values may have a wide range:
- Adult men: 1 to 10 international units of luteinizing hormone per liter of blood
- Adult women: values depend on the phase of a woman's menstrual cycle: During the early phase, 1 to 20 international units per liter; during ovulation, 25 to 100; after ovulation, 0.2 to 20
- Postmenopausal women: 20 to 100
- Boys before puberty: less than 0.5
- Girls before puberty: less than 0.2.

What do abnormal results mean?

In women, absence of a midcycle peak in luteinizing hormone secretion may indicate failure to ovulate. Decreased or low-normal levels may indicate poor gonadal activity; these findings are commonly associated with faulty menstruation. High luteinizing hormone levels may indicate an inborn absence of ovaries or ovarian failure associated with Stein-Leventhal syndrome, Turner's syndrome, menopause, or early-stage acromegaly (abnormal enlargement of the hands, feet, nose, and jaw).

In men, low values may indicate gonadal dysfunction of hypothalamic or pituitary origin. High values may indicate testicular failure or damaged or absent testes.

PROLACTIN

The hormone prolactin is also known as *lactogenic hormone* or *lactogen*. It's essential for the development of the mammary glands during pregnancy and for stimulating and maintaining milk production after giving birth. Prolactin is secreted in men and nonpregnant women, but its function in them is unknown. Prolactin levels increase in response to sleep and to physical or emotional stress.

In this test, the amount of prolactin in a blood sample is measured. Prolactin levels normally increase ten- to twentyfold during preg-

HOW YOUR BODY WORKS

The secrets of milk production during pregnancy

During pregnancy, certain hormones help prepare the breasts for lactation (milk production). Estrogen causes the breasts to grow by increasing their fat content; progesterone causes fat globule growth and alveolar duct development.

After childbirth, the mother's pituitary gland secretes prolactin, a hormone that causes the release of colostrum, a liquid nutrient that precedes the flow of milk from the breasts. Usually, within 3 days, the breasts secrete large amounts of milk rather than colostrum.

The infant's sucking stimulates nerve endings at the nipple, which allows the expression of milk from the mother's breasts. Sucking also stimulates the release of another hormone, which causes milk to flow into the alveolar ducts and the lactiferous channels.

From here, the milk is available to the infant. Because the infant's sucking stimulates both milk production and milk expression, the more the infant breast-feeds, the more milk the breast produces.

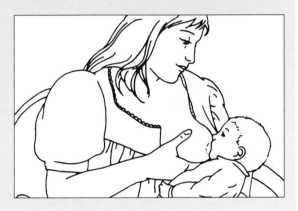

nancy. After delivery, prolactin secretion decreases to original levels in mothers who don't breast-feed; secretion increases during breast-feeding. This test is used when pituitary tumors are suspected. (See *The secrets of milk production during pregnancy*.)

Why is this test done?

Prolactin levels may be measured for the following reasons:
- To evaluate hormonal secretion
- To diagnose pituitary dysfunction
- To diagnose hypothalamic dysfunction regardless of cause
- To evaluate amenorrhea (failure to menstruate) and galactorrhea (excessive milk production).

What should you know before the test?

- You don't need to restrict food, fluids, or physical activities before this test; however, you may be asked to relax for about 30 minutes before the test.
- The doctor or nurse will check your medication history. Any drugs that may interfere with test results, such as alcohol, morphine,

Aldomet, estrogens, apomorphine, ergot alkaloids, and levodopa, will usually be withheld before the test.

■ This test requires a blood sample, which takes less than 3 minutes to collect. While the sample is being drawn, you may experience slight discomfort from the needle puncture and tourniquet pressure.

What happens during the test?

A nurse or medical technician inserts a needle into a vein, usually in your forearm. A blood sample is collected in a tube, which is then sent to a lab for testing. The lab requires at least 4 days to complete the analysis.

What happens after the test?

■ If swelling develops at the needle puncture site, warm soaks are applied to the area to ease discomfort.

■ With the doctor's permission, you may resume taking medications that were discontinued before the test.

What are the normal results?

Normal values range from undetectable to 23 micrograms of prolactin per liter of blood in non-breast-feeding women.

What do abnormal results mean?

Abnormally high prolactin levels—100 to 300 micrograms per liter—suggest Forbes-Albright syndrome. Rarely, high levels may be caused by severe endocrine disorders, such as an underactive thyroid, or some types of infertility. Additional measurements on two other occasions may be needed to diagnose slight elevations.

Decreased prolactin levels in a breast-feeding woman cause failure of milk production and may be associated with Sheehan's syndrome. Abnormally low prolactin levels have also been found occasionally with empty-sella syndrome, in which the pituitary gland is flattened and appears empty.

THYROID-STIMULATING HORMONE

Thyroid-stimulating hormone, or thyrotropin, helps increase the size, number, and activity of thyroid cells. It also stimulates the release of hormones that affect a person's metabolism and that are essential for normal growth and development.

In this test, the amount of thyroid-stimulating hormone in a blood sample is measured. The test is used to detect hypothyroidism (deficient thyroid gland activity).

Why is this test done?

Thyroid-stimulating hormone levels may be measured for the following reasons:
- To assess thyroid gland activity
- To diagnose hypothyroidism
- To help determine the cause of hypothyroidism
- To monitor drug therapy for hypothyroidism.

What should you know before the test?

- This test requires a blood sample, which takes less than 3 minutes to collect. While the sample is being drawn, you may experience slight discomfort from the needle puncture and tourniquet pressure.
- The doctor or nurse will check your drug history. Steroids, thyroid hormones, aspirin, and other drugs that may influence test results are usually discontinued before the test.
- You may be asked to relax and lie down for 30 minutes before the test.

What happens during the test?

A nurse or medical technician inserts a needle into a vein, usually in your forearm. A blood sample is collected in a tube, which is then sent to a lab for testing. The lab requires up to 2 days to complete the analysis.

What happens after the test?

- If swelling develops at the needle puncture site, warm soaks are applied to the area to ease discomfort.
- With the doctor's permission, you may resume taking medications that were discontinued before the test.

What are the normal results?

Normal results for adults and children range from undetectable to 15 milli-international units of thyroid-stimulating hormone per liter.

What do abnormal results mean?

Thyroid-stimulating hormone levels that exceed 20 milli-international units per liter of blood suggest hypothyroidism or, possibly, a goiter due to an iodine deficiency. Thyroid-stimulating hormone levels may be slightly elevated in a person with thyroid cancer whose thyroid gland functions normally.

Low or undetectable thyroid-stimulating hormone levels may be normal, but occasionally indicate hypothyroidism. Low thyroid-stimulating hormone levels also are caused by thyroiditis, and from an overactive thyroid or Graves' disease. Further testing is necessary to confirm a diagnosis.

THYROID & PARATHYROID HORMONES

THYROXINE

Thyroxine is a hormone that is secreted by the thyroid gland. Only a minute fraction of this thyroxine circulates freely in the blood. It's enough, though, to influence many functions in the body, such as metabolism, reproduction, growth, and development. (See *Step by step: The formation of thyroid hormones,* opposite, and *The thyroid gland: Creator of crucial hormones,* page 448.)

The thyroxine test is one of the most common diagnostic tools for evaluating the thyroid. It's used to measure the total circulating thyroxine level when thyroxine-binding globulin is normal.

HOW YOUR BODY WORKS

Step-by-step: The formation of thyroid hormones

You need to eat foods containing iodine to enable your thyroid gland to manufacture its important hormones. The thyroid requires approximately 1 milligram of dietary iodine every week. These diagrams show how iodine gets the job done.

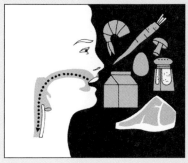

1 You ingest iodine when you eat seafoods, vegetables, eggs and dairy products, meat, and iodized salt.

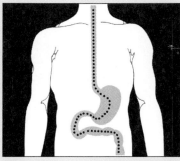

2 After digestion, the iodine contained in these foods is absorbed into the blood from the small bowel.

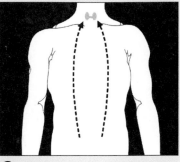

3 Iodine travels through the bloodstream and accumulates in the thyroid gland.

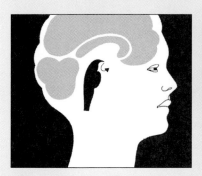

4 Meanwhile, the hypothalamus synthesizes thyrotropin-releasing hormone, which travels to the pituitary gland.

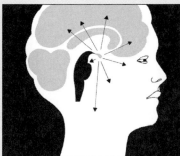

5 In the pituitary, thyrotropin-releasing hormone stimulates the production and release of thyroid-stimulating hormone.

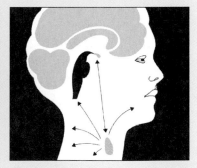

6 Thyroid-stimulating hormone then travels to the thyroid gland, where it stimulates the production of thyroxine and triiodothyronine from iodine, and triggers their release.

HOW YOUR BODY WORKS

The thyroid gland: Creator of crucial hormones

The thyroid gland straddles the upper windpipe. Its three hormones — thyroxine, triiodothyronine, and calcitonin — are synthesized in colloid follicles (see inset), where the surrounding epithelial cells prepare the hormones for release into the bloodstream.

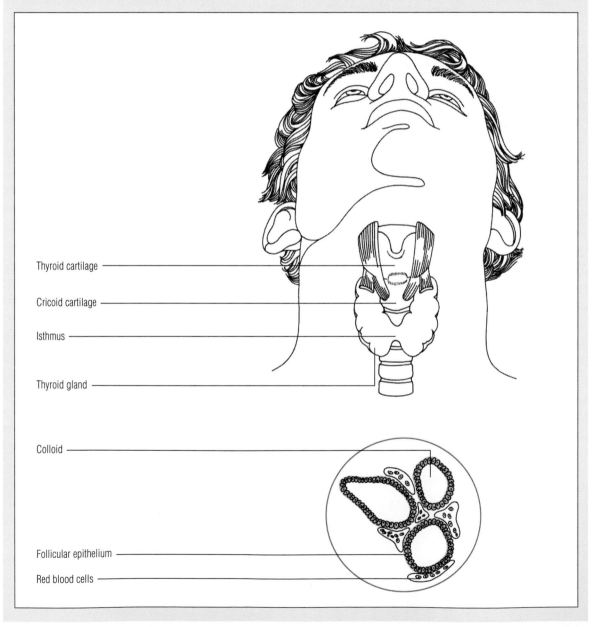

Thyroid cartilage

Cricoid cartilage

Isthmus

Thyroid gland

Colloid

Follicular epithelium

Red blood cells

Why is this test done?

Thyroxine levels may be measured for the following reasons:
- To evaluate thyroid gland activity
- To aid the diagnosis of hyperthyroidism and hypothyroidism (overactive and underactive thyroid activity)
- To monitor response to antithyroid medication in hyperthyroidism or to thyroid replacement therapy in hypothyroidism.

What should you know before the test?

- You don't need to fast or restrict your activities before this test.
- The test requires a blood sample, which takes less than 3 minutes to collect. While the sample is being drawn, you may experience slight discomfort from the needle puncture and tourniquet pressure.
- The doctor or nurse will check your medication history. Any medications that may interfere with test results will usually be withheld before the test. However, if this test is used to monitor thyroid therapy, daily thyroid supplements will be continued.

What happens during the test?

A nurse or medical technician inserts a needle into a vein, usually in your forearm. A blood sample is collected in a tube, which is then sent to a lab for testing.

What happens after the test?

- If swelling develops at the needle puncture site, warm soaks are applied to the area to ease discomfort.
- With the doctor's permission, you may resume taking medications that were discontinued before the test.

What are the normal results?

Normally, total thyroxine levels range from 64 to 174 nanomoles of hormone per liter of blood.

What do abnormal results mean?

Abnormally high levels of thyroxine indicate hyperthyroidism. Subnormal levels suggest hypothyroidism, or may be due to thyroxine suppression. In doubtful cases of hypothyroidism further hormone tests may be needed. Overt signs of hyperthyroidism likewise require further testing. Normal thyroxine levels don't necessarily indicate normal thyroid activity.

TRIIODOTHYRONINE

This test measures blood levels of triiodothyronine, a hormone secreted by the thyroid. Triiodothyronine is present in the blood in minute quantities, but it has a great impact on a person's metabolism. Results of this test are used to investigate signs of thyroid dysfunction.

Why is this test done?

Triiodothyronine levels may be measured for the following reasons:
■ To evaluate thyroid gland activity and to determine the cause of certain symptoms
■ To aid diagnosis of triiodothyronine toxicosis (poisoning)
■ To aid diagnosis of hypothyroidism and hyperthyroidism (underactive and overactive thyroid activity)
■ To monitor a person's response to thyroid replacement therapy for hypothyroidism.

What should you know before the test?

■ This test requires a blood sample, which takes less than 3 minutes to collect. While the sample is being drawn, you may experience slight discomfort from the needle puncture and tourniquet pressure.
■ The doctor or nurse will check your medication history. Any drugs that may influence thyroid activity, such as steroids, Inderal, and Questran, will usually be withheld before the test.

What happens during the test?

A nurse or medical technician inserts a needle into a vein, usually in your forearm. A blood sample is collected in a tube, which is then sent to a lab for testing.

What happens after the test?

■ If swelling develops at the needle puncture site, warm soaks are applied to the area to ease discomfort.
■ With the doctor's permission, you may resume taking medications that were discontinued before the test.

What are the normal results?

Triiodothyronine levels normally range from 1.4 to 3.5 nanomoles per liter. These values may vary with the lab performing this test.

What do abnormal results mean?

Triiodothyronine and thyroxine levels usually rise and fall in tandem, except in triiodothyronine toxicosis, when only triiodothyronine levels rise while thyroxine levels remain normal. Triiodothyronine toxicosis occurs with Graves' disease, toxic adenoma, or toxic nodular goiter.

Triiodothyronine levels normally increase during pregnancy.

Low triiodothyronine levels may appear in people with liver or kidney disease, during severe acute illness, or after injury or major surgery. Low triiodothyronine levels sometimes also occur with malnutrition.

THYROXINE-BINDING GLOBULIN

This test measures the level of thyroxine-binding globulin in a blood sample. Thyroxine-binding globulin carries thyroxine and triiodothyronine in the bloodstream. Any condition that affects thyroxine-binding globulin levels also affects the amount of thyroxine and triiodothyronine circulating in the blood. This is significant because these hormones influence many functions in the body, such as metabolism, reproduction, growth, and development.

Why is this test done?

Thyroxine-binding globulin levels may be measured for the following reasons:
- To evaluate thyroid activity
- To supplement tests for triiodothyronine or thyroxine levels
- To identify thyroxine-binding globulin abnormalities.

What should you know before the test?

- This test requires a blood sample, which takes less than 3 minutes to collect. While the sample is being drawn, you may experience slight discomfort from the needle puncture and tourniquet pressure.

■ The doctor or nurse will check your medication history. Any drugs that may interfere with the test results are withheld. These may include estrogens, anabolic steroids, Dilantin, or thyroid preparations. If these medications must be continued, the lab is notified. In some cases, the medications may be continued to determine their effect on thyroxine-binding globulin levels.

What happens during the test?

A nurse or medical technician inserts a needle into a vein, usually in your forearm. A blood sample is collected in a tube, which is then sent to a lab for testing.

What happens after the test?

■ If swelling develops at the needle puncture site, warm soaks are applied to the area to ease discomfort.
■ With the doctor's permission, you may resume taking medications that were discontinued before the test.

What are the normal results?

Any condition that affects thyroxine-binding globulin levels also affects hormones that influence many functions in the body, such as metabolism, reproduction, growth, and development.

Normal values for thyroxine-binding globulin range from 10 to 26 micrograms of thyroxine per 100 milliliters of blood. When measured by a method called *radioimmunoassay*, values for thyroxine-binding globulin range from 1.3 to 2 milligrams per deciliter.

What do abnormal results mean?

High thyroxine-binding globulin levels may indicate hypothyroidism, an inherited excess, some forms of liver disease, or a condition known as acute intermittent porphyria. Thyroxine-binding globulin levels normally increase during pregnancy and are high in newborns. Suppressed levels may indicate hyperthyroidism (an overactive thyroid) or an inborn deficiency. This can occur with nephrotic syndrome, malnutrition, acute illness, surgical stress, or active acromegaly, which is abnormal enlargement of the hands, feet, nose, and jaw.

People with thyroxine-binding globulin abnormalities require additional testing to evaluate thyroid activity more precisely.

TRIIODOTHYRONINE RESIN UPTAKE

This test measures thyroxine levels in the blood. A hormone produced in the thyroid gland, thyroxine influences many functions in the body, such as metabolism, reproduction, growth, and development. This test — which measures thyroxine indirectly — is used less frequently than more rapid tests for the major thyroid hormones.

Why is this test done?

Thyroxine levels may be measured for the following reasons:
- To evaluate thyroid activity
- To diagnose hypothyroidism and hyperthyroidism (deficient or excessive thyroid activity)
- To diagnose abnormal levels of thyroxine-binding globulin, a substance that carries thyroid hormones in the bloodstream.

What should you know before the test?

- This test requires a blood sample, which takes less than 3 minutes to collect. While the sample is being drawn, you may experience slight discomfort from the needle puncture and tourniquet pressure.
- The doctor or nurse will check your medication history, and drugs that may interfere with the test results are withheld. These may include estrogens, androgens, Dilantin, salicylates, or thyroid preparations.

What happens during the test?

A nurse or medical technician inserts a needle into a vein, usually in your forearm. A blood sample is collected in a tube, which is then sent to a lab for testing. The lab requires several days to complete the analysis.

What happens after the test?

- If swelling develops at the needle puncture site, warm soaks are applied to the area to ease discomfort.
- With the doctor's permission, you may resume taking medications that were discontinued before the test.

What are the normal results?

Normally, 25% to 35% of triiodothyronine in a blood sample is absorbed by, or binds to, the resin, a substance that's added to the test sample.

What do abnormal results mean?

A high resin uptake percentage with high thyroxine levels indicates hyperthyroidism. However, a low resin uptake percentage, together with low thyroxine levels, indicates hypothyroidism.

When thyroxine and triiodothyronine resin uptake values are discordant, it suggests that the person has a thyroxine-binding globulin abnormality.

LONG-ACTING THYROID STIMULATOR

This test determines whether a person's blood contains long-acting thyroid stimulator, an abnormal substance that mimics the action of thyroid-stimulating hormone but has more prolonged effects. Long-acting thyroid stimulator causes the thyroid gland to produce and secrete thyroid hormones in excessive amounts.

Why is this test done?

The long-acting thyroid stimulator test may be performed for the following reasons:
- To evaluate thyroid activity
- To confirm diagnosis of Graves' disease.

What should you know before the test?

- This test requires a blood sample, which takes less than 3 minutes to collect. While the sample is being drawn, you may experience slight discomfort from the needle puncture and tourniquet pressure.
- The doctor or nurse will check your medication history. Any drugs that may influence the test results are usually withheld before the test.

What happens during the test?

A nurse or medical technician inserts a needle into a vein, usually in your forearm. A blood sample is collected in a tube, which is then sent to a lab for testing.

What happens after the test?

■ If swelling develops at the needle puncture site, warm soaks are applied to the area to ease discomfort.

■ With the doctor's permission, you may resume taking medications that were discontinued before the test.

What are the normal results?

Normally, long-acting thyroid stimulator does not appear in the blood.

What do abnormal results mean?

Long-acting thyroid stimulator in a blood sample indicates Graves' disease, with or without signs of hyperthyroidism. About 80% of people with Graves' disease have detectable long-acting thyroid stimulator in their blood.

Long-acting thyroid stimulator is an abnormal substance that mimics the action of the natural hormone but has more prolonged effects.

SCREENING TEST FOR HYPOTHYROIDISM IN INFANTS

This test measures the levels of thyroxine, a thyroid hormone, in the blood of newborn infants. It's used to detect hypothyroidism (deficient thyroid activity).

Congenital hypothyroidism is characterized by low or absent levels of thyroxine at birth and affects roughly 1 in 5,000 newborns. It strikes girls three times more often than boys. If untreated, it can lead to irreversible brain damage by age 3 months. There are few signs of hypothyroidism in newborns, so most cases used to go undetected until a condition called *cretinism* became apparent or the infant died from respiratory distress.

Tests for thyroxine and thyroid-stimulating hormone are not commonly used to screen newborns, but the test is now mandatory in many provinces.

Why is this test done?

This test may be performed to screen newborns for hypothyroidism.

What should you know before the test?

- This test requires a small blood sample, which is taken from the infant's heel. It's performed before the infant is discharged from the hospital and again 4 to 6 weeks later.
- Another test is sometimes done before the infant is discharged to confirm results.

What happens during the test?

- The infant's heel is cleaned and then dried thoroughly with a gauze pad.
- A nurse or medical technician punctures the infant's heel with a small instrument called a lancet.
- Squeezing the heel gently, the nurse or technician blots a few drops of blood with a special type of paper.
- Gentle pressure is applied with a gauze pad to stop the bleeding at the puncture site.
- When the filter paper is dry, it's sent to the lab for testing.

What happens after the test?

- Heel punctures heal readily and require no special care.
- If results of the screening test indicate congenital hypothyroidism, additional testing is necessary to determine the cause of the disorder.
- If a diagnosis is confirmed, replacement therapy can restore normal thyroid gland activity. Such therapy is lifelong, and the dosage will increase until the adult requirement is reached.

What are the normal results?

Immediately after birth, thyroxine levels are considerably higher than normal adult levels. By the end of the first week, however, thyroxine levels decrease markedly:

- 1 to 5 days: 63 nanomoles or less of thyroxine per liter of blood
- 6 to 8 days: 51
- 9 to 11 days: 45
- 12 to 120 days: 39

Congenital hypothyroidism strikes girls three times more often than boys and can lead to irreversible brain damage by age 3 months.

What do abnormal results mean?

Low thyroxine levels in the newborn's blood indicate a need for additional testing to clarify a diagnosis. A complete thyroid workup — including tests for triiodothyronine, thyroxine-binding globulin, and free thyroxine levels — is necessary to confirm a diagnosis of congenital hypothyroidism before treatment begins.

CALCITONIN

This test measures levels of calcitonin, a hormone that's produced by the thyroid gland. The exact role of calcitonin in the body hasn't been fully defined. However, calcitonin affects other thyroid hormones and lowers calcium levels in the blood. This test is usually performed when a form of thyroid cancer is suspected.

Why is this test done?

Calcitonin levels may be measured for the following reasons:
- To evaluate thyroid activity
- To help diagnose thyroid cancer or tumors.

What should you know before the test?

- You'll be instructed to fast overnight before the test because food may interfere with calcitonin levels.
- This test requires a blood sample, which takes less than 3 minutes to collect. While the sample is being drawn, you may experience slight discomfort from the needle puncture and tourniquet pressure.

What happens during the test?

A nurse or medical technician inserts a needle into a vein, usually in your forearm. A blood sample is collected in a tube, which is then sent to a lab for testing. The lab requires several days to complete the analysis.

What happens after the test?

If swelling develops at the needle puncture site, warm soaks are applied to the area to ease discomfort.

Calcitonin levels in the blood are usually measured when thyroid cancer is suspected.

What are the normal results?

Normal calcitonin levels are 155 nanograms or less per liter of blood in men; in women, normal levels are 105 or less.

Normal results after calcium is provided intravenously are:
- Men: 265 nanograms per liter of blood
- Women: 120.

Normal results after a substance called *pentagastrin* is given intravenously are:
- Men: 210 nanograms per liter of blood
- Women: 105.

What do abnormal results mean?

High calcitonin levels without low calcium levels usually indicate a form of thyroid cancer. Occasionally, high calcitonin levels may be due to certain types of lung or breast cancer.

PARATHYROID HORMONE

Produced by the parathyroid glands, this hormone regulates the amount of calcium and phosphorus in the blood. The overall effect of parathyroid hormone is to raise the levels of calcium while lowering phosphorus levels.

Additional tests for measuring calcium, phosphorus, and creatinine levels along with parathyroid hormone levels are used to analyze abnormal parathyroid activity. Suppression or stimulation tests may help to confirm the findings.

Why is this test done?

Parathyroid hormone levels may be measured to evaluate parathyroid activity and disorders.

What should you know before the test?

- Because food may affect parathyroid hormone levels and interfere with the test results, you'll be instructed to fast overnight before the test.
- This test requires a blood sample, which takes less than 3 minutes to collect. While the sample is being drawn, you may experience slight discomfort from the needle puncture and tourniquet pressure.

What happens during the test?

A nurse or medical technician inserts a needle into a vein, usually in your forearm. A blood sample is collected in a tube, which is then sent to a lab for testing. The lab requires several days to complete the analysis.

What happens after the test?

- If swelling develops at the needle puncture site, warm soaks are applied to the area to ease discomfort.
- With the doctor's permission, you may resume your usual diet.

What are the normal results?

Normal parathyroid hormone levels vary, depending on the lab, and must be interpreted with calcium levels.

What do abnormal results mean?

When considered with calcium levels, abnormally high parathyroid hormone values may indicate hyperparathyroidism. Abnormally low parathyroid hormone levels may result from hypoparathyroidism and from certain malignant diseases.

ADRENAL HORMONES

ALDOSTERONE

This test measures levels of the hormone aldosterone in the blood. (See *The adrenal gland: Hormone production site*, page 460.) In the body, aldosterone helps maintain blood pressure and blood volume and regulate fluid and electrolyte balance. This test helps the doctor detect aldosteronism, a condition caused by too much aldosterone.

Why is this test done?

Aldosterone levels may be measured for the following reasons:
- To determine if a person's symptoms are due to faulty secretion of aldosterone

HOW YOUR BODY WORKS

The adrenal gland: Hormone production site

In the normal human body, two adrenal glands are found — one on top of each kidney. Each adrenal gland consists of the outer cortex, which is composed of three layers, and the medulla, or central portion. The outer layer of the cortex — the zona glomerulosa — produces the hormone aldosterone. The first inner layer — the zona fasciculata — produces the hormone cortisol. The medulla stores the catecholamines, epinephrine, and norepinephrine.

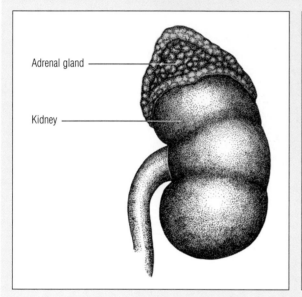

Adrenal gland

Kidney

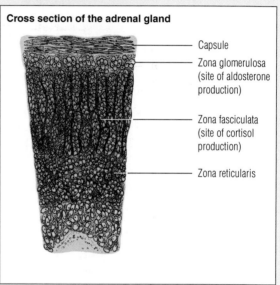

Cross section of the adrenal gland

Capsule

Zona glomerulosa (site of aldosterone production)

Zona fasciculata (site of cortisol production)

Zona reticularis

■ To help diagnose aldosteronism and determine the potential causes of this disorder.

What should you know before the test?

■ This test requires two blood samples, each of which takes less than 3 minutes to collect. While the sample is being drawn, you may experience slight discomfort from the needle puncture and tourniquet pressure.

■ You'll be instructed to maintain a low-carbohydrate, normal-salt diet for at least 2 weeks or, preferably, for 30 days before the test.

■ The doctor or nurse will check your medication history. Any drugs that alter fluid, salt, and potassium balance — especially diuretics, antihypertensives, steroids, cyclic progestational agents, and estrogens—will be withheld for at least 2 weeks or, preferably, for 30 days before the test.

- Any drugs that inhibit the secretion of the enzyme renin, such as propranolol, will usually be withheld for 1 week before the test.
- Avoid eating licorice for at least 2 weeks before the test.

What happens during the test?

- The first blood sample is collected while you're still in bed after a night's rest. A nurse or medical technician inserts a needle into a vein, usually in your forearm. A blood sample is collected in a tube, which is then sent to a lab for testing. The lab requires at least 10 days to complete the analysis.
- Another sample is collected 4 hours later, while you're standing and after you've been up and about, to evaluate the effect of a postural change.

What happens after the test?

- If swelling develops at the needle puncture site, warm soaks are applied to the area to ease discomfort.
- With the doctor's permission, you may resume taking medications that were discontinued before the test.
- You may resume your usual diet.

You'll be instructed to maintain a low-carbohydrate, normal-salt diet for at least 2 weeks or, preferably, for 30 days before the test.

What are the normal results?

Normally, aldosterone levels in a standing, nonpregnant person range from 55 to 497 picomoles of aldosterone per liter of blood. However, the range for an adult man or woman who's been standing for at least 2 hours is 111 to 860 picomoles per liter. Values for women are variable.

What do abnormal results mean?

Excessive aldosterone secretion may indicate aldosteronism resulting from certain forms of cancer, high blood pressure, congestive heart failure, cirrhosis of the liver, pregnancy, or other conditions.

Depressed serum aldosterone levels may indicate a salt-losing syndrome, toxemia of pregnancy, Addison's disease, or aldosterone deficiency.

CORTISOL

This hormone is secreted by the adrenal cortex, or outer layer of the adrenal gland. It helps the body use nutrients, mediate stress, and regulate the immune system. Cortisol secretion normally increases during the early morning hours and peaks around 8 a.m. It declines to very low levels in the evening and during the early phase of sleep. Intense heat or cold, infection, injury, exercise, obesity, and debilitating diseases influence cortisol secretion.

This test, which is used to measure cortisol levels in the blood, is usually ordered for people with signs of dysfunction of the adrenal gland. However, additional tests are generally required to confirm a diagnosis.

Cortisol is a hormone that helps the body use nutrients, mediate stress, and regulate the immune system.

Why is this test done?

Cortisol levels may be measured for the following reasons:
- To determine if a person's symptoms are due to faulty secretion of cortisol
- To help diagnose Cushing's disease or syndrome, Addison's disease, and adrenal insufficiency.

What should you know before the test?

- You'll be instructed to maintain a normal salt diet for 3 days before the test and to fast and limit physical activity for 10 to 12 hours before the test.
- You may be asked to relax and lie down for at least 30 minutes before the test.
- This test requires a blood sample, which takes less than 3 minutes to collect. While the sample is being drawn, you may experience slight discomfort from the needle puncture and tourniquet pressure.
- The doctor or nurse will check your medication history. Any medications that may interfere with plasma cortisol levels — such as estrogens, androgens, and Dilantin — will usually be withheld for 48 hours before the test.

What happens during the test?

- A nurse or medical technician inserts a needle into a vein, usually in your forearm. A blood sample is collected in a tube, which is then sent to a lab for testing. The lab requires at least 2 days to complete the analysis.

- Another blood sample may be collected later in the day.

What happens after the test?

- If swelling develops at the needle puncture site, warm soaks are applied to the area to ease discomfort.
- With the doctor's permission, you may resume eating your usual diet and taking medications that were discontinued before the test.

What are the normal results?

Normal cortisol levels in the blood range from 193 to 773 nanomoles of this hormone per liter of blood in the morning and from 55 to 497 nanomoles per liter in the afternoon. The afternoon level is usually half the morning level.

What do abnormal results mean?

High cortisol levels may indicate Cushing's disease, a rare disease of the pituitary gland, or Cushing's syndrome, which may include a cortisol excess from any cause. With Cushing's syndrome, little or no difference in values is found between morning samples and afternoon samples. Daily variations may also be absent in otherwise healthy people who are under emotional or physical stress.

Decreased cortisol levels may indicate Addison's disease. They may also be an indication of tuberculosis, fungal invasion, or hemorrhage. Low cortisol levels may also occur with impaired corticotropin secretion.

CATECHOLAMINES

This test measures catecholamines in the blood. Catecholamines are hormones, such as epinephrine, norepinephrine, and dopamine, which are secreted by the adrenal gland.

When secreted into the bloodstream, catecholamines prepare the body for the fight-or-flight reaction. They increase the heart rate, constrict blood vessels and redistribute circulating blood, activate energy reserves, and sharpen alertness. Excessive catecholamine secretion by tumors may cause high blood pressure, weight loss, sweating, headache, heart palpitations, and anxiety. (See *Fight or flight: How the body reacts to stress.*)

Catecholamine levels commonly fluctuate in response to stress, diet, smoking, kidney failure, obesity, use of certain drugs, and other conditions. If blood tests reveal high catecholamine levels, these findings must be confirmed by urine sample testing.

This test may be performed in people with high blood pressure or signs of certain adrenal tumors. It may also be performed in people with nerve-related tumors that affect endocrine activity.

Why is this test done?

Catecholamine levels may be measured for the following reasons:
- To determine if high blood pressure or other symptoms are related to improper hormonal secretion
- To rule out pheochromocytoma (a type of tumor that affects the adrenal gland) in people with high blood pressure (See *Is it high blood pressure or a rare tumor?* page 466.)
- To help identify tumors of the central nervous system, called *neuroblastomas, ganglioneuroblastomas,* and *ganglioneuromas*
- To aid diagnosis of autonomic nervous system dysfunction

What should you know before the test?

- Be sure to strictly follow the instructions you receive before this test. You'll be asked to refrain from using self-prescribed medications, especially cold or allergy remedies, for 2 weeks before the test. You'll be instructed to eliminate certain foods and beverages — such as bananas, avocados, cheese, coffee, tea, cocoa, beer, and Chianti — for 48 hours before the test and to take vitamin C, which is necessary for the formation of catecholamines.
- Don't smoke for 24 hours before the test, and fast for 10 to 12 hours.
- This test requires one or two blood samples. You may feel some discomfort from the needle punctures, but collecting the samples takes less than 20 minutes.
- The doctor or nurse will check your medication history. Any medications that affect catecholamine levels — such as amphetamines, phenothiazines, sympathomimetics, and tricyclic antidepressants — will be withheld before the test.
- Because the stress of a needle puncture may raise catecholamine levels, a device for collecting blood called an *indwelling venous catheter* may be inserted in a vein 24 hours before the test.

Catecholamine levels commonly fluctuate in response to stress, diet, smoking, kidney failure, obesity, and use of certain drugs.

HOW YOUR BODY WORKS

Fight or flight: How the body reacts to stress

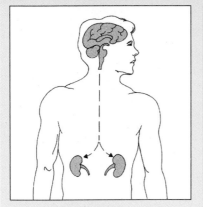

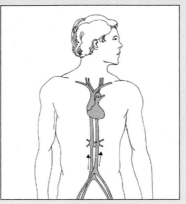

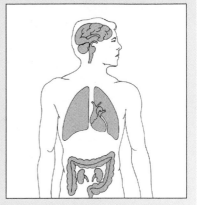

Stress — emotional or physical — causes nerve impulses to begin moving toward the adrenal glands.

Nerve impulses cause the adrenal gland to release catecholamines, primarily epinephrine and norepinephrine, into the bloodstream. This prepares the body for the fight-or-flight reaction to stress.

The fight-or-flight reaction is characterized by the following signs and symptoms:
- increased respiratory rate
- increased blood pressure, pulse rate, and cardiac output
- increased muscle strength
- increased blood supply to major organs: brain, heart
- decreased blood supply to skin, kidneys, and intestines.

- You may be asked to relax and lie down for 45 to 60 minutes before the test.
- You may be given extra blankets to keep you warm because low temperatures stimulate catecholamine secretion.

What happens during the test?

- Between 6 a.m. and 8 a.m., a nurse or medical technician collects a blood sample in a tube, which is then sent to a lab for testing. The lab requires up to 1 week to complete the analysis.
- If a second sample is required, you're asked to stand for 10 minutes before the sample is drawn.

Is it high blood pressure or a rare tumor?

The clonidine suppression test is a simple method for differentiating between essential high blood pressure and pheochromocytoma, an uncommon, but potentially fatal, tumor of the adrenal gland. Both of these conditions cause elevated catecholamine levels.

This test requires the administration of clonidine, a drug used to treat high blood pressure.

How the test is performed

To undergo this test, you're first instructed to lie on a table or bed. A blood sample is drawn to obtain your baseline (pretest) catecholamine levels. Next, you receive a dose of clonidine by mouth.

Another blood sample is collected after 3 hours to measure catecholamine levels again. Finally, the test results are compared.

What results reveal

People with pheochromocytoma show no decrease in catecholamine levels after clonidine administration. In contrast, people with high blood pressure show catecholamine levels that are reduced to normal levels.

What happens after the test?

- If swelling develops at the needle puncture site, warm soaks are applied to the area to ease discomfort.
- With the doctor's permission, you may resume eating your usual foods and taking medications that were discontinued before the test.

What are the normal results?

In one type of analysis, called *fractional analysis,* catecholamine levels (usually given in the International System of Units) range as follows:
- Reclining: epinephrine, 0 to 110 picograms of this hormone per milliliter of blood; norepinephrine, 70 to 750; dopamine, 0 to 30
- Standing: epinephrine, 0 to 140 picograms per milliliter of blood; norepinephrine, 200 to 1,700; dopamine, 0 to 30.

What do abnormal results mean?

High catecholamine levels may indicate several conditions, including pheochromocytoma, neuroblastoma, ganglioneuroblastoma, or ganglioneuroma. Elevations are possible with, but do not confirm, thyroid disorders, low blood sugar, or cardiac disease. Electroshock therapy, shock resulting from hemorrhage, endotoxins, and anaphylaxis also raise catecholamine levels.

In people with normal or low morning catecholamine levels, failure to show an increase in the sample taken after standing suggests autonomic nervous system dysfunction.

ERYTHROPOIETIN

This test measures erythropoietin, a hormone that's secreted by the kidneys and that influences red blood cell production. The test results are used to evaluate anemia (deficient red blood cell production), polycythemia (increased red blood cell production), and kidney tumors. It's also used to evaluate abuse of commercially prepared erythropoietin by athletes who believe the drug enhances performance.

Why is this test done?

Erythropoietin levels may be measured for the following reasons:
- To determine if hormonal secretion is causing changes in red blood cells
- To aid the diagnosis of anemia and polycythemia
- To aid the diagnosis of kidney tumors
- To detect abuse of erythropoietin by athletes.

What should you know before the test?

- You'll be instructed to fast for 8 to 10 hours before the test. You may also be asked to relax and lie down for 30 minutes before the test.
- This test requires a blood sample, which takes less than 3 minutes to collect. While the sample is being drawn, you may experience slight discomfort from the needle puncture and tourniquet pressure.

What happens during the test?

A nurse or medical technician inserts a needle into a vein, usually in your forearm. A blood sample is collected in a tube, which is then sent to a lab for testing. The lab requires up to 4 days to complete the analysis.

What happens after the test?

If swelling develops at the needle puncture site, warm soaks are applied to the area to ease discomfort.

What are the normal results?

The reference range is up to 24 milli-international units of erythropoietin per milliliter of blood.

What do abnormal results mean?

Low levels of erythropoietin may occur in a person with anemia whose hormone production is inadequate or absent. Congenital absence of erythropoietin can occur. Severe kidney disease may decrease the production of erythropoietin.

High levels occur in anemias as the body reestablishes its hormone balance. Inappropriate elevations may be seen in polycythemia and erythropoietin-secreting tumors.

PANCREAS & STOMACH HORMONES

INSULIN

This test measures the levels of the hormone insulin in the blood. Produced in the pancreas, insulin regulates the metabolism and transport of various nutrients in the body.

Insulin secretion reaches peak levels after meals, when metabolism and food storage are greatest. This test is usually performed with tests for glucose levels because glucose, a type of sugar, stimulates insulin secretion. (See *The pancreas: Site of insulin secretion.*)

Why is this test done?

Insulin levels may be measured for the following reasons:
- To determine if the pancreas is functioning normally
- To help diagnose hyperinsulinemia (excessive secretion of insulin by the pancreas) or hypoglycemia (low levels of sugar in the blood). These conditions may result from a tumor or abnormal growth of cells in the pancreas, severe liver disease, or a deficiency of substances that regulate sugar levels in the blood.
- To help diagnose diabetes.

What should you know before the test?

- You'll be instructed to fast for 10 to 12 hours before the test.
- You may be asked to relax and lie down for 30 minutes before the test. Agitation or stress may affect insulin levels.
- This test requires a blood sample, which takes less than 3 minutes to collect. While the sample is being drawn, you may experience slight discomfort from the needle puncture and tourniquet pressure.
- The doctor or nurse will check your medication history. Any drugs that may interfere with test results will usually be withheld before the test. Such drugs may include corticotropin, oral contraceptives, thyroid supplements, or epinephrine.
- If the results are uncertain, you may need to undergo a repeat test or a glucose tolerance test.

HOW YOUR BODY WORKS

The pancreas: Site of insulin secretion

The pancreas (shown intact, below, and magnified) is a large gland that secretes digestive enzymes and the hormones insulin and glucagon.

Parts of the pancreas

The pancreas is composed of an exocrine portion containing acinar cells that secrete digestive enzymes and an endocrine portion that secretes the hormones insulin and glucagon into the bloodstream in response to changes in blood sugar levels. The islets of Langerhans contain two main types of cells: beta cells, which produce insulin when blood sugar increases, and alpha cells, which produce glucagon when blood sugar decreases. The splenic arteries carry oxygen-rich blood to the pancreas. The mesenteric veins carry insulin and glucagon, in deoxygenated blood, away from the pancreas.

PANCREAS

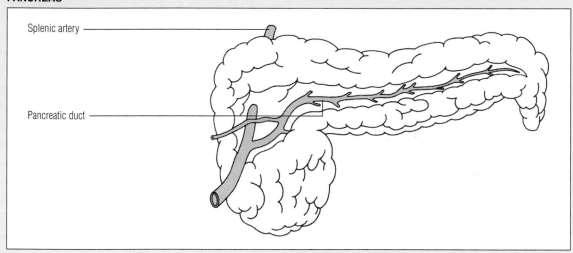

Splenic artery

Pancreatic duct

PANCREAS, MAGNIFIED AREA

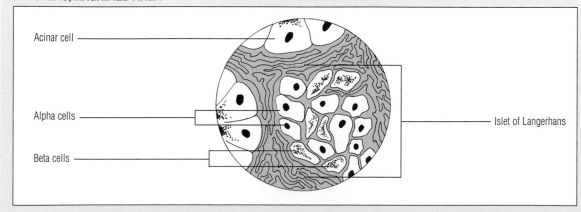

Acinar cell

Alpha cells

Beta cells

Islet of Langerhans

What happens during the test?

A nurse or medical technician inserts a needle into a vein, usually in your forearm. A blood sample is collected in a tube, which is then sent to a lab for testing.

What happens after the test?

- If swelling develops at the needle puncture site, warm soaks are applied to the area to ease discomfort.
- With the doctor's permission, you may resume eating your usual diet and taking medications that were discontinued before the test.

Does the test have risks?

In the person with a pancreatic tumor, fasting for this test may cause severe low blood sugar. Sugar should be readily available during the test to treat low blood sugar levels, if necessary.

What are the normal results?

Insulin levels normally range from 14.4 to 179 picomoles of insulin per liter of blood.

What do abnormal results mean?

Insulin levels are interpreted with sugar measurements. High insulin and low sugar levels after fasting suggests an insulinoma, a tumor of the pancreas. Prolonged fasting or further testing may be required to confirm a diagnosis. In insulin-resistant diabetes, insulin levels are high; in non-insulin-resistant diabetes, they're low.

GASTRIN

Gastrin is a hormone that's produced and stored in the stomach and, to a lesser degree, in the pancreas. It helps the body digest food by triggering the release of gastric acid. Gastrin also stimulates activity in the pancreas, intestine, and liver. Abnormal secretion of gastrin can result from tumors called *gastrinomas* and from disorders affecting the stomach, pancreas and, less commonly, the esophagus and the small intestine.

This test is used to measure gastrin levels in the blood. It's especially useful in people suspected of having gastrinomas associated with a condition called *Zollinger-Ellison syndrome*. In doubtful situations, additional testing may be needed.

Why is this test done?

Gastrin levels may be measured for the following reasons:

- To determine the cause of a person's gastrointestinal symptoms
- To confirm the diagnosis of a gastrinoma
- To help diagnose some ulcers and anemias.

What should you know before the test?

- You'll be instructed not to drink alcohol for at least 24 hours before the test and to fast for 12 hours before the test, although you may drink water.
- Because stress can increase gastrin levels, you may be asked to relax and lie down for at least 30 minutes before the test.
- This test requires a blood sample, which takes less than 3 minutes to collect. While the sample is being drawn, you may experience slight discomfort from the needle puncture and tourniquet pressure.
- The doctor or nurse will check your medication history, and drugs that may interfere with the test results — especially insulin or anticholinergics, such as atropine and Donnatal — are withheld. If these medications must be continued, the lab is notified.

Gastrin levels may be measured to determine the cause of digestive tract symptoms or to diagnose some ulcers and anemias.

What happens during the test?

A nurse or medical technician inserts a needle into a vein, usually in your forearm. A blood sample is collected in a tube, which is then sent to a lab for testing.

What happens after the test?

- If swelling develops at the needle puncture site, warm soaks are applied to the area to ease discomfort.
- With the doctor's permission, you may resume your usual diet and any medications that were discontinued before the test.

What are the normal results?

Normal gastrin levels are less than 300 nanograms of this hormone per liter of blood.

What do abnormal results mean?

Gastrin levels greater than 1,000 nanograms per liter confirm Zollinger-Ellison syndrome.

Increased levels of gastrin may occur in a few people with duodenal ulcers and in people with a condition called *achlorhydria* or with extensive stomach cancer.

SEX HORMONES

ESTROGENS

The ovaries secrete estrogens, the female sex hormones. Estrogens are responsible for the development of some female sex characteristics and for normal menstruation. In women who are in menopause, estrogen secretion drops to a constant, low level.

In this test, a blood sample is examined for levels of estradiol, estrone, and estriol, which are the principal forms of estrogen in the body.

Why is this test done?

Estrogen levels may be measured for the following reasons:
- To determine if secretion of female hormones is normal
- To determine sexual maturation and fertility
- To help diagnose sexual dysfunction, especially early or delayed puberty, menstrual disorders, or infertility
- To determine fetal well-being
- To help diagnose tumors that secrete estrogen.

What should you know before the test?

- You needn't restrict food or fluids before this test.
- This test requires a blood sample, which takes less than 3 minutes to collect. While the sample is being drawn, you may experience slight discomfort from the needle puncture and tourniquet pressure.
- The test may be repeated during the various phases of your menstrual cycle.

- The doctor or nurse will check your medication history. Steroids and other hormones — including estrogens and progestogens — will usually be withheld before the test.

What happens during the test?

A nurse or medical technician inserts a needle into a vein, usually in your forearm. A blood sample is collected in a tube, which is then sent to a lab for testing.

What happens after the test?

- If swelling develops at the needle puncture site, warm soaks are applied to the area to ease discomfort.
- With the doctor's permission, you may resume eating your usual diet and taking medications that were discontinued before the test.

Normal estrogen levels in premenopausal women vary widely. In men, the range is much narrower.

What are the normal results?

Normal estrogen levels for premenopausal women vary widely during the menstrual cycle:

- 1 to 10 days: 88 to 250 picomoles of estrogen hormones per liter of blood
- 11 to 20 days: 184 to 683
- 21 to 30 days: 268 to 547.

Estrogen levels in men range from 44 to 125 picomoles per liter of blood. In children under age 6, the normal range is 11 to 37.

What do abnormal results mean?

Low estrogen levels may indicate inadequate activity by a woman's sex organs, or ovarian failure, as in conditions called *Turner's syndrome* or *ovarian agenesis*. Low levels may also occur with menopause or with hypogonadism.

Abnormally high levels may occur with estrogen-producing tumors, in very early puberty, or in severe liver disease such as cirrhosis. High levels may also occur when a person is born with a condition that causes increased conversion of androgens (steroid hormones) to estrogen.

PROGESTERONE

Progesterone is produced by the ovaries when an egg is released, about halfway through the menstrual cycle. This hormone helps the uterine lining prepare for implantation of the egg if conception occurs. Progesterone levels continue to climb, but if pregnancy doesn't occur, they drop sharply and menstruation begins.

During pregnancy, the placenta releases about 10 times the normal monthly amount of progesterone to maintain the pregnancy. Increased secretion begins toward the end of the first trimester (3 months) and continues until delivery of the infant. Progesterone then helps the body increase stored nutrients for the developing fertilized egg.

This test, which measures progesterone levels in a blood sample, provides information for pregnancy and fertility studies. The test may be repeated several times; progesterone can also be monitored through urinalysis.

Why is this test done?

Testing for plasma progesterone may be performed for the following reasons:
- To determine if a woman's female sex hormone secretion is normal
- To help with infertility studies
- To evaluate the activity of the placenta, the tissue that surrounds the fetus during pregnancy
- To help confirm ovulation.

What should you know before the test?

- You needn't restrict food or fluids before this test.
- The test requires a blood sample, which takes less than 3 minutes to collect. While the sample is being drawn, you may experience slight discomfort from the needle puncture and tourniquet pressure.
- The doctor or nurse will check your medication history to determine if you're taking any drugs, including the hormones progesterone or estrogen, that may interfere with test results. Usually, such medications will be discontinued before the test.
- The test may be repeated at specific times during your menstrual cycle. If you're pregnant, it may be repeated with each prenatal visit.

Testing for plasma progesterone may be repeated at specific times during your menstrual cycle. If you're pregnant, it may be repeated with each prenatal visit.

What happens during the test?

A nurse or medical technician inserts a needle into a vein, usually in your forearm. A blood sample is collected in a tube, which is then sent to a lab for testing.

What happens after the test?

- If swelling develops at the needle puncture site, warm soaks are applied to the area to ease discomfort.
- With the doctor's permission, you may resume taking medications that were discontinued before the test.

What are the normal results?

During menstruation, normal results are as follows:
- Follicular phase: less than 5 nanomoles of progesterone per liter of blood
- Luteal phase: about 9.5
- Midluteal phase: 64.

   During pregnancy, normal values are as follows:
- First trimester: 48 to 159 nanomoles per liter of blood
- Second and third trimesters: 25 to 636.

What do abnormal results mean?

High progesterone levels may indicate ovulation, specific types of tumors, ovarian cysts that produce progesterone, or conditions and tumors that cause progesterone to be produced along with other steroidal hormones.

   Low progesterone levels are associated with the absence of normal menstruation due to various causes, certain complications of pregnancy, threatened miscarriage, and fetal death.

TESTOSTERONE

Testosterone is the principal androgen that promotes male characteristics. It's secreted by the testicles. (See *The testicles: Site of testosterone secretion*, page 476.)

   Testosterone induces puberty in boys and maintains male secondary sex characteristics, such as facial hair growth. Increased testosterone secretion during puberty stimulates sperm production; it also

HOW YOUR BODY WORKS

The testicles: Site of testosterone secretion

In the testicles, several hundred pyramid-shaped lobules contain one or several seminiferous tubules. Within the tissue connecting the tubules are specialized cells, which secrete the potent hormone testosterone. These cells are called *Leydig's cells.*

CROSS SECTION OF A TESTICLE

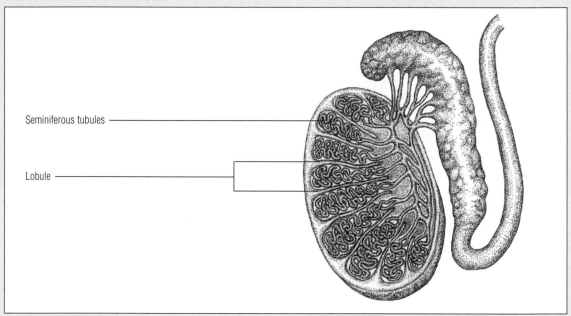

Seminiferous tubules

Lobule

MICROSCOPIC VIEW OF SEMINIFEROUS TUBULES AND LEYDIG'S CELLS

Leydig's cell

Seminiferous tubule

Leydig's cell enlarged

helps enlarge certain muscles, the genitalia, and related sex organs, such as the prostate gland.

Levels of testosterone are low before puberty; they begin to increase at the onset of puberty and continue to increase during adulthood. Production begins to taper off at about age 40, eventually dropping to about one-fifth of the peak level by age 80. In women, the adrenal glands and the ovaries secrete small amounts of testosterone.

This test is used to measure testosterone levels in the blood. When combined with other tests, it helps in the evaluation of sex gland dysfunction in men and women.

Why is this test done?

Testosterone levels may be measured for the following reasons:
- To determine if male sex hormone secretion is adequate
- To help diagnose sexual precocity in boys under age 10
- To help diagnose different forms of hypogonadism (deficient sex gland activity)
- To evaluate male infertility or other sexual dysfunction
- To evaluate abnormal hair growth and masculinization in women.

What should you know before the test?

- You needn't restrict food or fluids before this test.
- The test requires a blood sample, which takes less than 3 minutes to collect. While the sample is being drawn, you may experience slight discomfort from the needle puncture and tourniquet pressure.
- The doctor or nurse may ask you if you've received hormone therapy in the past.

What happens during the test?

A nurse or medical technician inserts a needle into a vein, usually in your forearm. A blood sample is collected in a tube, which is then sent to a lab for testing.

What happens after the test?

If swelling develops at the needle puncture site, warm soaks are applied to the area to ease discomfort.

Normal levels of testosterone in men vary widely. Levels in women are lower and their range is much narrower.

What are the normal results?

Normal levels of testosterone are as follows, although lab values vary slightly:

- Men: 10 to 42 nanomoles of testosterone per liter of blood
- Women: 1 to 3
- Prepubertal children: in boys, less than 3.5 nanomoles per liter of blood; in girls, less than 1.4.

What do abnormal results mean?

High testosterone levels in prepubertal boys may indicate true sexual precocity (early development) or false precocious puberty due to male hormone production by a testicular tumor. They can also indicate other conditions that result in precocious puberty in boys and masculinization in girls.

Increased levels can occur with a benign adrenal tumor or cancer, inadequate thyroid activity, or in the early phases of puberty. In women with ovarian tumors or other disorders, testosterone levels may increase, leading to abnormal hair growth.

Depressed testosterone levels can indicate inadequate sex gland activity, as in conditions called *Klinefelter's syndrome* or *hypogonadotropic eunuchoidism*. Low testosterone levels can also follow removal of the testes, testicular or prostate cancer, delayed male puberty, estrogen therapy, or cirrhosis.

PREGNANCY-TRIGGERED HORMONES

HUMAN CHORIONIC GONADOTROPIN

Human chorionic gonadotropin is a hormone that's produced in the placenta. If conception occurs, a test for human chorionic gonadotropin may detect this hormone in the blood 9 days after ovulation. (See *Human chorionic gonadotropin secretion: An early sign of pregnancy*.)

HOW YOUR BODY WORKS

Human chorionic gonadotropin secretion: An early sign of pregnancy

The hormone human chorionic gonadotropin is secreted if conception takes place. The fertilized egg becomes implanted in the uterine wall. There it begins to develop into the embryo and placenta. Nine days after ovulation, special cells in the tissue that will eventually form the placenta begin secreting human chorionic gonadotropin. These special cells are called *trophoblastic cells*.

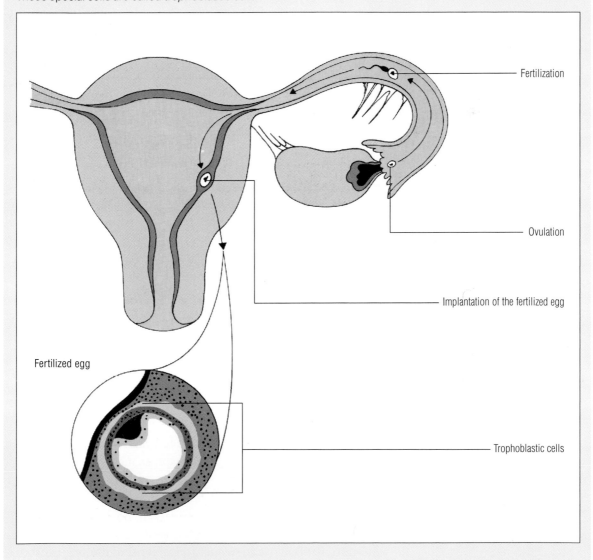

Fertilization

Ovulation

Implantation of the fertilized egg

Fertilized egg

Trophoblastic cells

Production of human chorionic gonadotropin increases steadily during the first trimester (3 months) of pregnancy, peaking around the 10th week. Levels then decrease drastically. About 2 weeks after delivery, the hormone may no longer be detectable.

This test measures the amount of human chorionic gonadotropin in a blood sample. It's more sensitive and costly than the routine pregnancy test using a urine specimen.

Why is this test done?

Human chorionic gonadotropin levels may be measured for the following reasons:
- To detect pregnancy early
- To check hormonal production in high-risk pregnancies
- To help diagnose certain tumors
- To monitor treatment for inducing ovulation and conception.

What should you know before the test?

- You needn't restrict food or fluids before this test.
- This test requires a blood sample, which takes less than 3 minutes to collect. While the sample is being drawn, you may experience slight discomfort from the needle puncture and tourniquet pressure.

What happens during the test?

A nurse or medical technician inserts a needle into a vein, usually in your forearm. A blood sample is collected in a tube, which is then sent to a lab for testing.

What happens after the test?

If swelling develops at the needle puncture site, warm soaks are applied to the area to ease discomfort.

What are the normal results?

Normal values for this hormone are less than 5 international units per liter of blood and can vary in early pregnancy.

What do abnormal results mean?

High human chorionic gonadotropin levels indicate pregnancy; significantly higher concentrations are present in a multiple pregnancy. Increased levels may also suggest several types of tumors that secrete human chorionic gonadotropin. Low levels may occur in ectopic pregnancy or pregnancy of less than 9 days.

HUMAN PLACENTAL LACTOGEN

This hormone helps prepare a pregnant woman's breasts for lactation (milk secretion) and influences fetal growth. It also indirectly provides energy for maternal metabolism and fetal nutrition. Human placental lactogen is also known as *human chorionic somatomammotropin*.

Secretion of this hormone begins about the fifth week of gestation and declines rapidly after the baby is delivered. Some experts believe this hormone may not be essential for a successful pregnancy.

This test measures human placental lactogen levels in the blood. It may be required in high-risk pregnancies or in suspected placental tissue dysfunction. Because values vary widely during the last half of pregnancy, several tests performed over several days provide the most reliable test results.

Why is this test done?

Human placental lactogen levels may be measured for the following reasons:
- To assess placental activity and fetal well-being
- To help diagnose certain tumors and to monitor treatment of tumors that secrete human placental lactogen.

What should you know before the test?

- This test requires a blood sample, which takes less than 3 minutes to collect. While the sample is being drawn, you may experience slight discomfort from the needle puncture and tourniquet pressure.
- The test may be repeated during your pregnancy.

What happens during the test?

A nurse or medical technician inserts a needle into a vein, usually in your forearm. A blood sample is collected in a tube, which is then sent to a lab for testing.

What happens after the test?

If swelling develops at the needle puncture site, warm soaks are applied to the area to ease discomfort.

What are the normal results?

For pregnant women, normal human placental lactogen levels are as listed in the chart below.

GESTATION PERIOD	HUMAN PLACENTAL LACTOGEN LEVELS
5 to 27 weeks	Less than 213 nanomoles of hormone per liter of blood
28 to 31 weeks	111 to 282
32 to 35 weeks	171 to 357
36 weeks to term	231 to 398

At term, a pregnant woman with diabetes may have levels of 400 nanomoles and higher. Normal levels for men and nonpregnant women are roughly 20 nanomoles.

What do abnormal results mean?

Human placental lactogen levels are correlated with a pregnant woman's gestational stage. For example, after 30 weeks' gestation, levels below 188 nanograms may indicate placental dysfunction. Low human placental lactogen concentrations are also characteristically associated with several pregnancy problems. Declining concentrations may help differentiate incomplete early miscarriage from a threatened miscarriage.

Low human placental lactogen concentrations don't confirm fetal distress. Conversely, concentrations over 188 nanograms after 30 weeks' gestation don't guarantee fetal well-being.

Human placental lactogen measurement over 282 nanograms after 30 weeks' gestation may suggest an unusually large placenta, commonly occurring in people with diabetes, multiple pregnancy, or a condition called *Rh isoimmunization*.

Below-normal concentrations of human placental lactogen may be associated with certain types of tumors and cancers.

IMMUNE SYSTEM TESTS:
Studying the Body's Defenses

All blood group classifications are based on the types of antigens on the surfaces of red blood cells. An antigen is a substance that triggers the body's defenses and produces an antibody to fight another substance. These antigens explain why people need their own type of blood for a transfusion.

The antigen's the thing
In 1930, a doctor identified the most important of the blood classifications — the ABO blood group system. He classified human red blood cells as A, B, AB, or O, depending on the presence or absence of antigens. He found that persons with group A blood have antigens different from people with group B blood. AB blood contains both antigens, and O has neither. Because type O has no antigens, it can be given to anyone in an emergency, with little risk of a bad reaction. The type O person is called a *universal donor*.

The universal recipient
A person with AB blood has both antigens but no anti-A or anti-B antibodies and can receive A, B, or O blood. A type AB person is called a *universal recipient*.

BLOOD COMPATIBILITY

ABO BLOOD TYPE

This test classifies blood according to either type A, type B, type AB, or type O. Different blood types are not compatible, so typing is required before a transfusion to protect the recipient from a lethal reaction.

Why is this test done?
A person's blood type is determined to check the compatibility of a donor's and a recipient's blood before transfusion. If you're scheduled for a transfusion, once your blood type is known, it can be matched with the right donor blood. (See *Why some blood types don't mix* and *Identifying compatible blood types*.)

What should you know before the test?
You won't need to change your diet before the test.

What happens during the test?
- A nurse or medical technician inserts a needle into a vein, usually in your forearm. A blood sample is collected in a tube, which is then sent to a lab for testing.
- Although you may feel a sting from the needle and pressure from the tourniquet, collecting the sample takes only a few minutes.

What happens after the test?
If swelling develops at the needle puncture site, warm soaks may be applied to ease discomfort.

Identifying compatible blood types

There are four major blood types, divided according to Rh positive and Rh negative. A transfusion is safe and effective if the donor and recipient have compatible types. The top illustration provides a guide to blood type compatibility. The bottom illustration shows the percentage distribution of blood types in Canada. The most common blood type is O Rh-positive, which is found in 39 percent of the Canadian population. The rarest is AB Rh-negative, which is found in 0.5 percent of the population.

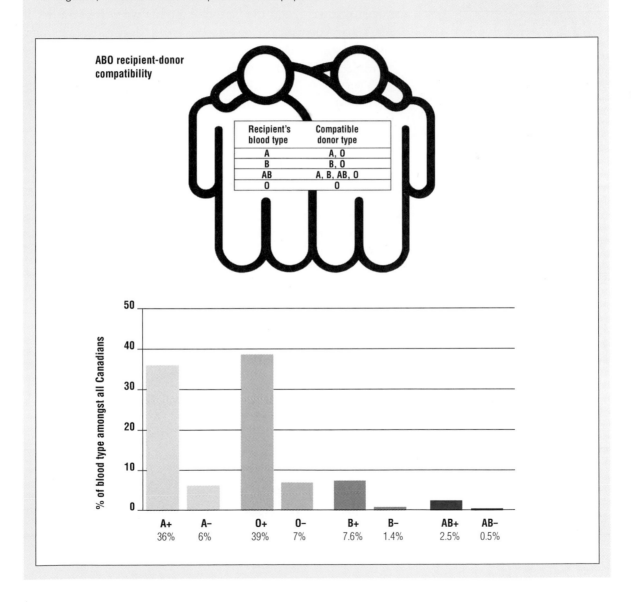

ABO recipient-donor compatibility

Recipient's blood type	Compatible donor type
A	A, O
B	B, O
AB	A, B, AB, O
O	O

% of blood type amongst all Canadians

A+	A−	O+	O−	B+	B−	AB+	AB−
36%	6%	39%	7%	7.6%	1.4%	2.5%	0.5%

Why the Rh factor matters

More than 85% of people carry the Rh antigen, called the *Rh$_o$(D) factor,* on their red blood cells. Their blood is classified Rh-positive. The remaining 15% lack this factor and their blood is typed Rh-negative.

Risk factor: Rh-negative blood
The Rh antigen is more likely to stimulate formation of antibodies to fight other blood cells than any other known antigen. Consequently, a person with Rh-positive blood does not carry any anti-Rh antibodies (because they would destroy the red blood cells). A person with Rh-negative blood, however, develops anti-Rh antibodies following exposure to Rh-positive blood (by transfusion or pregnancy). A transfusion reaction does not usually occur in such a person after the first exposure. Instead, anti-Rh antibodies develop slowly, over several weeks, causing the transfusion recipient to become sensitized to the Rh antigen. It takes a second exposure to Rh-positive blood to trigger a reaction. In infants, the reaction is called *hemolytic disease of the newborn.*

Rh TYPE: POSITIVE OR NEGATIVE

The Rh system classifies blood by the presence or absence of the Rh$_o$(D) antigen on the surface of red blood cells. In this test, a person's red blood cells are mixed with serum containing anti-Rh$_o$(D) antibodies and are observed for a reaction. If there's a reaction, the Rh$_o$(D) antigen is present, and the person's blood is typed Rh-positive. If there's no reaction, the person's blood is typed Rh-negative. (See *Why the Rh factor matters.*)

Prospective blood donors are fully tested to exclude the D^u variant of the Rh$_o$(D) antigen before being classified as Rh-negative. People who have this antigen are considered Rh-positive donors but generally can receive Rh-negative blood.

Why is this test done?
Rh typing may be performed for the following reasons:
■ To establish blood type according to the Rh system
■ To check compatibility of the donor and recipient and ensure a safe transfusion
■ To determine whether the person will require an Rh immune globulin injection to prevent complications in a future pregnancy.

What should you know before the test?
You won't need to change your diet before the test.

What happens during the test?
■ A nurse or medical technician inserts a needle into a vein, usually in your forearm. A blood sample is collected in a tube, which is then sent to a lab for testing.
■ Although you may feel a sting from the needle and pressure from the tourniquet, collecting the sample takes only a few minutes.

What happens after the test?
■ If swelling develops at the needle puncture site, warm soaks may be applied to ease discomfort.

■ If you're pregnant and your test shows that your blood is Rh-positive, you should carry a card saying that you may need to receive Rh immune globulin.

What are the normal results

Classified as Rh-positive, Rh-negative, or Rh-positive D^u, donor blood may be transfused only if compatible with the recipient's blood.

What do abnormal results mean?

If an Rh-negative woman delivers an Rh-positive baby or aborts a fetus with an unknown Rh-type, she should receive an Rh immune globulin injection within 72 hours to prevent hemolytic disease of the newborn in future births.

FETAL-MATERNAL RED BLOOD CELL TRANSFER

This test — which doctors call the *fetal-maternal erythrocyte distribution test* — measures the number of fetal red blood cells in the mother's blood. Some transfer of red blood cells from the fetus's to the mother's circulation occurs during most spontaneous or elective abortions and most normal deliveries. Usually, the amount of blood transferred is minimal and makes no difference. But transfer of significant amounts of blood from an Rh-positive fetus to an Rh-negative mother can cause the mother to develop anti-Rh-positive antibodies in her blood. During a subsequent pregnancy, the mother's antibodies are potentially fatal to an Rh-positive fetus.

Why is this test done?

The fetal-maternal red blood cell transfer test may be performed for the following reasons:
■ To detect and measure fetal-maternal blood transfer
■ To determine the amount of Rh immune globulin needed to keep the mother from developing immunization to the Rh$_o$(D) antigen
■ To determine or verify a person's blood group — an important step for a safe transfusion.

What should you know before the test?

- You won't need to change your diet before the test.
- The nurse or technician will ask whether you've recently been given dextran, intravenous contrast dye, or other drugs that may alter test results.

What happens during the test?

- A nurse or medical technician inserts a needle into a vein, usually in your forearm. A blood sample is collected in a tube, which is then sent to a lab for testing.
- Although you may feel a sting from the needle and pressure from the tourniquet, collecting the sample takes only a few minutes.

What happens after the test?

If swelling develops at the needle puncture site, warm soaks may be applied to ease discomfort.

What are the normal results?

Normally, the mother's blood contains no fetal red blood cells.

What do abnormal results mean?

If a pregnant woman has too many fetal red blood cells in her blood, she must have several doses of Rh immune globulin to keep her from developing antibodies.

Rh immune globulin should be given to an unsensitized Rh-negative mother as soon as possible (no later than 72 hours) after the birth of an Rh-positive infant or after a spontaneous or elective abortion. The Rh immune globulin prevents complications in future pregnancies. Most doctors now give Rh immune globulin as a preventive measure at 28 weeks' gestation to women who are Rh-negative but have no detectable Rh antibodies.

Who should be screened?

The following people should be screened for Rh isoimmunization or irregular antibodies: all Rh-negative mothers during their first prenatal visit and at 28 weeks' gestation and all Rh-positive mothers with histories of transfusion, a jaundiced infant, stillbirth, cesarean delivery, abortion, or miscarriage.

CROSSMATCHING

Crossmatching establishes compatibility or incompatibility of the donor's and the recipient's blood. It's the best antibody detection test available for avoiding lethal transfusion reactions. The test is available in major and minor forms.

After both the donor's and recipient's ABO blood types and Rh factor types are known, *major crossmatching* determines the compatibility of the donor's red blood cells and the recipient's serum. *Minor crossmatching* determines the compatibility of the donor's serum and the recipient's red blood cells. Because the antibody-screening test is routinely performed on all blood donors, minor crossmatching is often omitted.

Why is this test done?

Crossmatching may be performed to serve as the final check for compatibility of the donor's blood and the recipient's blood and to avoid a transfusion reaction.

What should you know before the test?

You won't need to change your diet before the test.

What happens during the test?

■ The nurse or technician asks whether you've recently been given Dextran, intravenous contrast dye, or drugs that may alter test results.
■ A nurse or medical technician inserts a needle into a vein, usually in your forearm. A blood sample is collected in a tube, which is then sent to a lab for testing.
■ Although you may feel a sting from the needle and pressure from the tourniquet, collecting the sample takes only a few minutes.

What happens after the test?

■ If swelling develops at the needle puncture site, warm soaks may be applied to ease discomfort.
■ You should carry an ABO group identification card. Such identification is helpful but doesn't replace crossmatching before a transfusion.

What are the normal results?

The absence of clumping indicates compatibility of the donor's and the recipient's blood, which means that the transfusion may proceed.

What do abnormal results mean?

A positive crossmatch (clumping) means the donor and recipient are incompatible and there is an antigen-antibody reaction. The donor's blood must be withheld and the crossmatch continued to determine the cause of the incompatibility and to identify the antibody.

DIRECT ANTIGLOBULIN TEST

The direct antiglobulin test (or direct Coombs' test) detects immunoglobulins (antibodies) on the surfaces of red blood cells. These immunoglobulins coat red blood cells when they become sensitized to an antigen, such as the Rh factor.

Why is this test done?

Direct antiglobulin testing may be performed for the following reasons:

- To diagnose a blood compatibility problem called *hemolytic disease of the newborn*
- To investigate blood transfusion reactions
- To help the doctor diagnose specific anemias that may be inherited, caused by drugs, or caused by an immune system reaction.

What should you know before the test?

You won't need to change your diet before the test.

What happens during the test?

- For a newborn, the nurse draws a sample from the umbilical cord after it's clamped and cut.
- For an adult, a nurse or medical technician inserts a needle into a vein, usually in your forearm. A blood sample is collected in a tube, which is then sent to a lab for testing.
- Although you may feel a sting from the needle and pressure from the tourniquet, collecting the sample takes only a few minutes.

What happens after the test?

■ An infant with hemolytic disease of the newborn will need more testing to monitor anemia.

■ If swelling develops at the needle puncture site, warm soaks may be applied to ease discomfort.

What are the normal results?

A negative test, in which neither antibodies nor complement (another component of the immune system) appears on the red blood cells, is normal.

What do abnormal results mean?

A positive test on a newborn's umbilical cord blood indicates that the mother's antibodies have crossed the placenta and have coated fetal red blood cells, causing hemolytic disease of the newborn. The infant may need a transfusion of compatible blood, without the antigens that have been built against the mother's antibodies, to keep from being anemic.

In an adult, a positive test result may indicate hemolytic anemia and help the doctor decide whether the anemia is caused by drugs or linked to an underlying disease, such as lymphoma. A positive test can also indicate infection. Or, a weakly positive test (showing relatively less cell agglutination) may mean the person's antibodies are reacting to transfused blood.

ANTIBODY SCREENING TEST

Also called the *indirect Coombs' test,* this test detects unexpected circulating antibodies in the person's blood. This screening test detects 95% to 99% of the circulating antibodies; another, more specific test can isolate the exact antibodies in the person's blood.

Why is this test done?

Antibody screening tests may be performed for the following reasons:

■ To detect unexpected circulating antibodies to red cell antigens in the recipient's or donor's blood before transfusion

- To determine the presence of Rh-positive antibodies in a mother's blood
- To learn whether a pregnant mother needs Rh immune globulin
- To help the doctor diagnose acquired hemolytic anemia or some other form of anemia
- To help the doctor evaluate the possibility of a transfusion reaction.

What should you know before the test?

You won't need to change your diet before the test.

What happens during the test?

- A nurse or medical technician inserts a needle into a vein, usually in your forearm. A blood sample is collected in a tube, which is then sent to a lab for testing.
- Although you may feel a sting from the needle and pressure from the tourniquet, collecting the sample takes only a few minutes.

What happens after the test?

If swelling develops at the needle puncture site, warm soaks may be applied to ease discomfort.

What are the normal results?

Normally, there's no clumping, indicating that your blood contains no circulating antibodies other than anti-A and anti-B.

What do abnormal results mean?

A positive result indicates the presence of unexpected circulating antibodies to red cell antigens. Such a reaction demonstrates donor and recipient incompatibility.

If you're pregnant and Rh-negative, a positive result may show antibodies to the Rh factor from a previous transfusion with incompatible blood or from a previous pregnancy with an Rh-positive fetus. If the positive result is strong, the fetus may develop hemolytic disease of the newborn. In that case, you'll need to have repeated tests throughout your pregnancy to evaluate your antibody levels.

WHITE CELL ANTIBODIES TEST

This test detects leukoagglutinins—antibodies that react with white blood cells—which may cause a transfusion reaction. These antibodies usually develop after a person has been exposed to foreign white cells through transfusions, pregnancies, or a graft of tissue from an unrelated donor. The doctor will use a microscope to examine the person's blood for these antibodies.

Why is this test done?

White cell antibodies tests may be performed for the following reasons:

- To detect leukoagglutinins in blood recipients who develop transfusion reactions and to distinguish this reaction from other transfusion reactions
- To detect leukoagglutinins in blood donors after transfusion of the donor's blood causes a reaction in the recipient.

What should you know before the test?

You won't need to change your diet before the test.

What happens during the test?

- A nurse or medical technician inserts a needle into a vein, usually in your forearm. A blood sample is collected in a tube, which is then sent to a lab for testing.
- Although you may feel a sting from the needle and pressure from the tourniquet, collecting the sample takes only a few minutes.

What happens after the test?

If swelling develops at the needle puncture site, warm soaks may be applied to ease discomfort.

What are the normal results?

Normally, test results are negative: The blood doesn't clump because it contains no antibodies.

What do abnormal results mean?

If the recipient has a positive white cell antibodies test, continued transfusions will require premedication with acetaminophen 1 to 2 hours before the transfusion, transfusion of specially prepared leukocyte-poor blood, or the use of leukocyte removal blood filters to prevent further reactions.

If the donor's blood shows a positive result, indicating the presence of leukoagglutinins, it means the recipient's transfusion reaction is caused by acute, noncardiogenic pulmonary edema.

IMMUNE SYSTEM COMPONENTS

T- AND B-CELL COUNTS

This test measures T cells, B cells, and so-called "null" cells to find evidence of several diseases that influence their numbers in the blood. T cells and B cells are two important types of lymphocytes — white blood cells that can recognize antigens or foreign cells through special receptors on their surfaces. Null cells alone have little diagnostic significance.

The lab marks the cell types, then counts them and compares their numbers with normal baselines.

Why is this test done?

These lymphocyte tests may be performed for the following reasons:
- To help the doctor diagnose immunodeficiency diseases
- To distinguish benign from malignant lymphocyte-producing diseases
- To monitor a person's response to therapy.

What should you know before the test?

You won't need to change your diet before the test.

What happens during the test?

■ A nurse or medical technician inserts a needle into a vein, usually in your forearm. A blood sample is collected in a tube, which is then sent to a lab for testing.

■ Although you may feel a sting from the needle and pressure from the tourniquet, collecting the sample takes only a few minutes.

What happens after the test?

If swelling develops at the needle puncture site, warm soaks may be applied to ease discomfort.

What are the normal results?

Currently, T-cell and B-cell counts are being standardized, and values may differ from one lab to another, depending on the test technique. Generally, normal results, measured as a percentage of the total lymphocyte count, are as follows:

■ T cells: 68% to 75%
■ B cells: 10% to 20%
■ Null cells: 5% to 20%.

   Normal T-cell and B-cell counts don't necessarily mean the person's immune system is strong. In autoimmune diseases, such as lupus and rheumatoid arthritis, T cells and B cells may be present in normal numbers but may not function well.

What do abnormal results mean?

An abnormal T-cell or B-cell count suggests, but doesn't confirm, specific diseases. If your cell count is abnormal, the doctor starts looking for additional signs of diseases, including:

■ an elevated B-cell count, which occurs in a form of leukemia, multiple tumors, and some kinds of anemia

■ a decreased B-cell count, found in acute lymphocytic leukemia and in certain inherited or acquired immunoglobulin deficiency diseases

■ an increased T-cell count, which occurs occasionally in infectious mononucleosis but more often in multiple tumors and acute lymphocytic leukemia

■ a decreased T-cell count, which occurs in some inherited T-cell deficiency diseases, chronic lymphocytic leukemia, and AIDS.

Natural weapons against bacteria

A group of white blood cells called *neutrophils* are the body's main bacteria fighters. They engulf and destroy bacteria and foreign particles by a process called *phagocytosis*.

In people who have recurrent bacterial infections, neutrophil function tests show whether these cells can kill offending bacteria or can move toward the infection site.

Measuring neutrophil effectiveness

The *nitroblue tetrazolium test* measures the killing ability of neutrophils. It looks for the enzymes and toxins that neutrophils make during phagocytosis.

Another test evaluates luminescence (light-emitting ability) of neutrophils, which shows how well the neutrophils are working. Finally, the neutrophils' ability to find bacteria can also be measured by placing them in separate parts of a chamber and observing their rate of migration from one area to another.

LYMPHOCYTE TRANSFORMATION TESTS

Transformation tests evaluate lymphocyte (a type of white blood cell) function, which is crucial to the immune system. These tests don't require injecting foreign cells into the skin, which eliminates the risk of immune reactions.

The lab tests match the person's white blood cells with foreign cells and evaluate what doctors call the *mitotic response,* the *antigen assay,* and the *mixed lymphocyte culture assay.* The last test is useful in matching transplant recipients and donors.

Why are these tests done?

Lymphocyte transformation tests may be performed for the following reasons:
- To assess and monitor genetic and acquired immune deficiencies
- To check compatibility of both tissue transplant recipients and donors
- To see if a person has been exposed to diseases, such as malaria, hepatitis, and mycoplasmal pneumonia.

What should you know before the tests?

You won't need to change your diet before the tests.

What happens during the tests?

- A nurse or medical technician inserts a needle into a vein, usually in your forearm. A blood sample is collected in a tube, which is then sent to a lab for testing.
- Although you may feel a sting from the needle and pressure from the tourniquet, collecting the sample takes only a few minutes.

What happens after the tests?

If swelling develops at the needle puncture site, warm soaks may be applied to ease discomfort.

What are the normal results?

Results depend on the antigens and mitogens the doctor used.

What do abnormal results mean?

In the mitogen and antigen assays, a low response or no response shows that the person has a depressed or defective immune system. An additional series of tests can monitor the effectiveness of therapy in a person with an immunodeficiency disease.

In the mixed lymphocyte culture test, if the person's white blood cells show a high reaction to a specific pathogen, it may show that he or she has been exposed to malaria, hepatitis, mycoplasmal pneumonia, periodontal disease, and certain viral infections where the person no longer has antibodies in the blood. (See *Natural weapons against bacteria.*)

IMMUNOGLOBULINS G, A, AND M

This test measures a person's disease-fighting antibodies by checking three important types of immunoglobulins. Immunoglobulins are proteins that function as specific antibodies to neutralize foreign cells. Deviations from normal immunoglobulin percentages are characteristic in many immune disorders, including cancer, liver disorders, rheumatoid arthritis, and lupus.

The test identifies immunoglobulin G, immunoglobulin A, and immunoglobulin M in a blood sample.

Why is this test done?

Immunoglobulins G, A, and M may be tested for the following reasons:

- To diagnose such conditions as multiple tumors and blood disorders
- To detect diseases, such as cirrhosis and hepatitis, that are linked to abnormally high immunoglobulin levels
- To check the effectiveness of chemotherapy or radiation therapy.

What should you know before the test?

You'll have to go without food and fluids, except for water, for 12 to 14 hours before the test.

Why your insulin may not work

An insulin antibodies test can detect insulin antibodies in the blood of people who receive insulin for treatment of diabetes mellitus. Most insulin preparations are derived from the pancreas of beef or pork and contain insulin-related peptides (impurities that are the major causes of immune reactions to the medicine). Immunoglobulin G antibodies that form in response to these peptides neutralize the insulin so that it cannot regulate sugar metabolism.

What happens during the test?

- A nurse or medical technician inserts a needle into a vein, usually in your forearm. A blood sample is collected in a tube, which is then sent to a lab for testing.
- Although you may feel a sting from the needle and pressure from the tourniquet, collecting the sample takes only a few minutes.

What happens after the test?

- If swelling develops at the needle puncture site, warm soaks may be applied to ease discomfort.
- You may resume your normal diet.

What are the normal results?

When the lab uses a method called *nephelometry,* immunoglobulin levels for adults range as follows:
- Immunoglobulin G: 7 to 18 grams per liter
- Immunoglobulin A: 0.7 to 4.4 grams per liter
- Immunoglobulin M: 0.6 to 2.9 grams per liter.

What do abnormal results mean?

In people with inherited and acquired blood diseases or tumors, the findings confirm the doctor's diagnosis. In liver and autoimmune diseases, leukemias, and lymphomas, they just support other tests, such as biopsies and white blood cell measures and physical examination. Some people can develop antibodies to their medications. (See *Why your insulin may not work.*)

   If your test results are to high or too low, the doctor will discuss the following:
- If you have abnormally low immunoglobulin levels (especially of immunoglobulin G or immunoglobulin M) you must protect yourself against bacterial infection. It helps to learn to watch for signs of infection, such as fever, chills, rash, or skin ulcers.
- If you have abnormally high immunoglobulin levels and symptoms of a blood disorder, the doctor will urge you to report bone pain and tenderness, signs of kidney failure, and frequent bone fractures.

IMMUNE COMPLEX TEST

This test checks your immune system by looking for what doctors call *immune complexes*. When immune complexes are produced faster than they can be cleared by the lymph system, the person who has been ill gets sick again. For example, a person may develop an illness after recovering from an infection or after undergoing a transfusion. In some people, the presence of immune complexes leads to drug sensitivity, rheumatoid arthritis, or lupus.

Why is this test done?

An immune complex test may be performed for the following reasons:
- To evaluate the immune system by finding circulating immune complexes in the blood
- To monitor a person's response to therapy
- To estimate the severity of disease.

What should you know before the test?

You won't need to change your diet before the test.

What happens during the test?

- A nurse or medical technician inserts a needle into a vein, usually in your forearm. A blood sample is collected in a tube, which is then sent to a lab for testing.
- Although you may feel a sting from the needle and pressure from the tourniquet, collecting the sample takes only a few minutes.

What happens after the test?

If swelling develops at the needle puncture site, warm soaks may be applied to ease discomfort.

What are the normal results?

Under normal circumstances, immune complexes are not detectable.

What do abnormal results mean?

The presence of detectable immune complexes in blood usually prompts the doctor to use other tests to diagnose a condition such as drug sensitivity, rheumatoid arthritis, or lupus.

COMPLEMENT TESTS

These tests measure a group of proteins that fight infection. *Complement* is a collective term for a system of at least 20 blood proteins that interact to destroy foreign cells and to help remove foreign materials. A complement deficiency can increase a person's susceptibility to infection and diseases.

Why are these tests done?

Complement tests may be performed for the following reasons:
- To help the doctor detect diseases that are affected by the immune system
- To check for an inherited deficiency in these proteins
- To monitor effectiveness of therapy.

What should you know before the tests?

You won't need to change your diet before the tests.

What happens during the tests?

- A nurse or medical technician inserts a needle into a vein, usually in your forearm. A blood sample is collected in a tube, which is then sent to a lab for testing.
- Although you may feel a sting from the needle and pressure from the tourniquet, collecting the sample takes only a few minutes.

What happens after the tests?

If swelling develops at the needle puncture site, warm soaks may be applied to ease discomfort.

What are the normal results?

Normal values for complement range are:
- Total complement: 3.3 to 7.3 CH_{50} units
- C1 esterase inhibitor: 0.08 to 0.23 gram per liter
- C3: 0.6 to 1.3 grams per liter
- C4: 0.1 to 0.5 gram per liter.

What do abnormal results mean?

Complement abnormalities may be genetic or acquired, but acquired abnormalities are the most common. A person with depressed total complement levels (more important than elevated levels) may have an imbalance between his production of antigen-antibody complexes and his body's ability to get rid of them. The doctor uses this information to track down the disorder in a long list of possible problems.

IMMUNE SYSTEM REACTIONS

ALLERGY TEST

This test—which doctors call the *radioallergosorbent test (RAST)*—is used to determine what causes an allergic reaction. It measures immunoglobulin E antibodies in blood and identifies specific allergens that cause rashes, asthma, hay fever, drug reactions, or other skin complaints. The radioallergosorbent test is easier to perform and more specific than skin testing; it's also less painful and less dangerous. Skin tests, however, are still the most common allergy tests.

Why is this test done?

The allergy test may be performed to identify allergens that affect the person.

What should you know before the test?

You won't need to change your diet before the test.

What happens during the test?

- A nurse or medical technician inserts a needle into a vein, usually in your forearm. A blood sample is collected in a tube, which is then sent to a lab for testing.
- Although you may feel a sting from the needle and pressure from the tourniquet, collecting the sample takes only a few minutes.

The radioallergosorbent test can tell what's causing your rashes, asthma, hay fever, drug reactions, or other skin problems. It's easier, less painful, and more reliable than the old skin tests.

What happens after the test?

If swelling develops at the needle puncture site, warm soaks may be applied to ease discomfort.

What are the normal results?

Radioallergosorbent test results are interpreted in relationship to a control or reference serum that differs among laboratories.

What do abnormal results mean?

Higher-than-normal immunoglobulin E levels in the blood suggest hypersensitivity to the specific allergen or allergens used.

WHITE BLOOD CELL ANTIGEN TEST

This test—which doctors call the *human leukocyte antigen test*—identifies a group of antigens present on the surfaces of all live cells but most easily detected on white blood cells. There are four types of human leukocyte antigens: HLA-A, HLA-B, HLA-C, and HLA-D. These antigens are essential to immunity and determine the degree of compatibility between transplant recipients and donors.

Why is this test done?

The white blood cell antigen test may be performed for the following reasons:
- To match tissue recipients and donors
- To aid genetic counseling
- To aid paternity testing.

What should you know before the test?

You won't need to change your diet before the test.

What happens during the test?

- A nurse or medical technician inserts a needle into a vein, usually in your forearm. A blood sample is collected in a tube, which is then sent to a lab for testing.
- Although you may feel a sting from the needle and pressure from the tourniquet, collecting the sample takes only a few minutes.

What happens after the test?

If swelling develops at the needle puncture site, warm soaks may be applied to ease discomfort.

What are the normal results?

In HLA-A, HLA-B, and HLA-C testing, white blood cells that react with the test antiserum break down and absorb a marker dye, which can be detected microscopically. In HLA-D testing, white blood cell incompatibility is marked by cellular and other changes.

What do abnormal results mean?

Incompatible HLA-A, HLA-B, HLA-C, or HLA-D groups may cause unsuccessful tissue transplantation. Many diseases have a strong association with certain types of human leucocyte antigens, and information from testing may help with diagnosis.

In paternity testing, if the HLA dye markers in a possible father's blood do not match the child's, it proves that he's no relation. If the man's human leukocyte antigen test shows a match with the child's, then the probability that he's the father is quite high.

This test helps predict whether an organ transplant will be successful. It's also used in paternity testing.

ANTIBODIES TO CELL NUCLEI

This test — called the *antinuclear antibodies test* — is done to evaluate the immune system. In conditions such as lupus, scleroderma, and certain infections, the body's immune system may treat portions of its own cell nuclei as if they were foreign substances and produce antinuclear antibodies against them.

Because they don't penetrate living cells, antinuclear antibodies are harmless. Sometimes, though, they form antigen-antibody complexes that cause tissue damage (as in systemic lupus erythematosus). Because several organs could be involved, the test results are used to support other evidence. Further testing is usually required for a diagnosis.

Why is this test done?

The test for antibodies to cell nuclei may be done for the following reasons:

- To screen for systemic lupus erythematosus (failure to detect antinuclear antibodies essentially rules out active systemic lupus erythematosus)
- To monitor the effectiveness of therapy for systemic lupus erythematosus.

What should you know before the test?

You won't need to change your diet before the test.

What happens during the test?

- A nurse or medical technician inserts a needle into a vein, usually in your forearm. A blood sample is collected in a tube, which is then sent to a lab for testing.
- Although you may feel a sting from the needle and pressure from the tourniquet, collecting the sample takes only a few minutes.

What happens after the test?

- If swelling develops at the needle puncture site, warm soaks may be applied to ease discomfort.
- You should keep a clean, dry bandage over the site for at least 24 hours.

What are the normal results?

Normally, the test is negative if the concentration of antinuclear antibodies is below a certain level.

What do abnormal results mean?

Low concentrations of antinuclear antibodies may point to disorders such as viral diseases, chronic liver disease, collagen vascular disease, and autoimmune diseases. The higher the concentration, the more likely it is that the person has lupus. Besides the concentration of antinuclear antibodies, patterns of antibodies that indicate other diseases can also be identified.

ANTIBODIES TO CELL MITOCHONDRIA

This test—called the *antimitochondrial antibodies test*—evaluates liver function. It's usually performed with the test for anti-smooth-muscle antibodies. Determining results requires searching for the antimitochondrial antibodies in blood samples with a microscope. These antibodies show up in several liver diseases, although their role is unknown and there's no evidence they cause liver damage. Most commonly, they're linked to cirrhosis of the liver and, sometimes, chronic active hepatitis and drug-induced jaundice. Antimitochondrial antibodies are also linked to autoimmune diseases, such as lupus, rheumatoid arthritis, pernicious anemia, and a disease of the adrenal glands called Addison's disease.

Why is this test done?

A test for antibodies to cell mitochondria may be performed for the following reasons:
- To aid diagnosis of biliary cirrhosis
- To distinguish between jaundice caused by something outside the liver and biliary cirrhosis.

What should you know before the test?

You won't need to change your diet before the test.

What happens during the test?

- A nurse or medical technician inserts a needle into a vein, usually in your forearm. A blood sample is collected in a tube, which is then sent to a lab for testing.
- Although you may feel a sting from the needle and pressure from the tourniquet, collecting the sample takes only a few minutes.

What happens after the test?

- If swelling develops at the needle puncture site, warm soaks may be applied to ease discomfort.
- Because people with liver disease may bleed excessively, the nurse will apply pressure to the venipuncture site until bleeding stops.

What are the normal results?

The blood test should show no antimitochondrial antibodies.

What do abnormal results mean?

Although antimitochondrial antibodies appear in 79% to 94% of people with primary biliary cirrhosis, this test alone doesn't confirm the diagnosis. The autoantibodies also appear in some people with chronic active hepatitis, drug-induced jaundice, and cirrhosis of unknown origins.

ANTIBODIES TO SMOOTH MUSCLE

This test — called the *anti-smooth-muscle antibodies test* — helps evaluate liver function. It measures the relative concentration of anti-smooth-muscle antibodies in blood and is usually performed with the test for antimitochondrial antibodies.

Anti-smooth-muscle antibodies appear in several liver diseases, especially chronic active hepatitis and, less often, cirrhosis of the liver. Although anti-smooth-muscle antibodies are most commonly linked to liver diseases, their role is unknown, and there's no evidence that they cause liver damage.

This test helps the doctor evaluate liver disease, especially chronic active hepatitis and cirrhosis of the liver.

Why is this test done?

A test for anti-smooth-muscle antibodies may be done to aid diagnosis of chronic active hepatitis and cirrhosis of the liver.

What should you know before the test?

You won't need to change your diet before the test.

What happens during the test?

■ A nurse or medical technician inserts a needle into a vein, usually in your forearm. A blood sample is collected in a tube, which is then sent to a lab for testing.

■ Although you may feel a sting from the needle and pressure from the tourniquet, collecting the sample takes only a few minutes.

What happens after the test?

If swelling develops at the needle puncture site, warm soaks may be applied to ease discomfort.

What are the normal results?

Normal concentration of anti-smooth-muscle antibodies in serum is less than 1 part to 20 of serum.

What do abnormal results mean?

The test for anti-smooth-muscle antibodies is not very specific. The antibodies appear in about 66% of people with chronic active hepatitis and 30% to 40% of people with cirrhosis of the liver.

Anti-smooth-muscle antibodies may also be present in people with infectious mononucleosis, acute viral hepatitis, malignant tumor of the liver, and asthma.

ANTITHYROID ANTIBODIES

The antithyroid antibodies test is done to evaluate thyroid function. In immune system disorders, such as Hashimoto's thyroiditis and Graves' disease (an overactive thyroid), the thyroid gland releases thyroglobulin into the blood. Because thyroglobulin is not normally released into circulation, antithyroglobulin antibodies are produced to attack this foreign substance. The resulting immune response may damage the thyroid gland.

Why is this test done?

A test for antithyroid antibodies may be performed to detect circulating antithyroglobulin antibodies in a person whose symptoms indicate Hashimoto's thyroiditis, Graves' disease, or other thyroid diseases.

What should you know before the test?

You won't need to change your diet before the test.

What happens during the test?

■ A nurse or medical technician inserts a needle into a vein, usually in your forearm. A blood sample is collected in a tube, which is then sent to a lab for testing.

■ Although you may feel a sting from the needle and pressure from the tourniquet, collecting the sample takes only a few minutes.

What happens after the test?

If swelling develops at the needle puncture site, warm soaks may be applied to ease discomfort.

What are the normal results?

The normal concentration of antithyroglobulin antibodies is less than 1 part per 100. Low levels of these antibodies are normal in 10% of the general population and in 20% or more of people age 70 or older.

What do abnormal results mean?

The presence of antithyroglobulin antibodies in blood can indicate autoimmune thyroid disease, Graves' disease, or myxedema (a drying and thickening of the skin). High concentrations strongly suggest Hashimoto's thyroiditis.

THYROID-STIMULATING FACTOR

This test — called the *thyroid-stimulating immunoglobulin test* by doctors — checks the function of the thyroid, a butterfly-shaped gland located in the neck. Thyroid-stimulating factor appears in the blood of most people with Graves' disease (an overactive thyroid). This disease stimulates the thyroid gland to produce and excrete excessive amounts of thyroid hormones.

Why is this test done?

The test for thyroid-stimulating factor may be done for the following reasons:

■ To help diagnose suspected thyroid disease
■ To aid diagnosis of suspected thyroid overproduction.

What should you know before the test?

You won't need to change your diet before the test.

What happens during the test?

- A nurse or medical technician inserts a needle into a vein, usually in your forearm. A blood sample is collected in a tube, which is then sent to a lab for testing.
- Although you may feel a sting from the needle and pressure from the tourniquet, collecting the sample takes only a few minutes.

What happens after the test?

If swelling develops at the needle puncture site, warm soaks may be applied to ease discomfort.

What are the normal results?

Thyroid-stimulating factor doesn't normally appear in blood. However, it may be present in 5% of people who don't have the disease.

What do abnormal results mean?

Increased thyroid-stimulating factor levels are linked to several thyroid diseases, including exophthalmos, Graves' disease, and recurrence of an underactive thyroid.

This test looks for antibodies that are attacking the thyroid gland, responding to a compound that the diseased gland would not normally release into the blood.

LUPUS TEST

A procedure called the *lupus erythematosus cell preparation* may be used to diagnose systemic lupus erythematosus, commonly known as lupus. (See *Facts about systemic lupus erythematosus*, page 512.)

Why is this test done?

The lupus test may be done for the following reasons:
- To aid diagnosis of lupus
- To monitor treatment of lupus. (About 60% of successfully treated people show no lupus erythematosus cells after 4 to 6 weeks of therapy.)

INSIGHT INTO ILLNESS

Facts about systemic lupus erythematosus

Who does it strike?

Systemic lupus erythematosus usually strikes women ages 15 to 30. It occurs in 10 times as many women as men (15 times as many women of child-bearing age) and most often in blacks.

What is it?

Lupus is a chronic inflammatory connective tissue disease of unknown cause that affects the skin, joints, and muscles. It may cause death from failure of vital organs, especially the kidneys, but it's not always fatal. Here are some of the symptoms:

- facial rash
- hair loss
- sensitivity to light
- anemia
- positive antinuclear antibody or lupus erythematosus cell test
- false-positive blood test for syphilis
- stiff joints
- mental problems or seizures.

What should you know before the test?

You won't need to change your diet before the test.

What happens during the test?

- A nurse or medical technician inserts a needle into a vein, usually in your forearm. A blood sample is collected in a tube, which is then sent to a lab for testing.
- Although you may feel a sting from the needle and pressure from the tourniquet, collecting the sample takes only a few minutes.

What happens after the test?

- If swelling develops at the needle puncture site, warm soaks may be applied to ease discomfort.
- Because many people with lupus have damaged immune systems, you must keep a clean, dry bandage over the puncture site for at least 24 hours.

What are the normal results?

Normally, no lupus erythematosus cells are present.

What do abnormal results mean?

The presence of at least two lupus erythematosus cells may indicate lupus. Such cells may also be detected in chronic active hepatitis, rheumatoid arthritis, scleroderma, and drug reactions.

CARDIOLIPIN ANTIBODIES

This test evaluates concentrations of immunoglobulin G or M antibodies in the person's blood relative to a phospholipid called *cardiolipin.* The antibodies appear in the blood of some people with lupus and others who do not have all the signs of lupus but who experience recurrent episodes of spontaneous blood clots or miscarriages.

Why is this test done?

The test for cardiolipin antibodies may be done to aid diagnosis of cardiolipin antibody syndrome in people with or without lupus who have repeated blood clots or miscarriages.

What should you know before the test?

You won't need to change your diet before the test.

What happens during the test?

- A nurse or medical technician inserts a needle into a vein, usually in your forearm. A blood sample is collected in a tube, which is then sent to a lab for testing.
- Although you may feel a sting from the needle and pressure from the tourniquet, collecting the sample takes only a few minutes.

What happens after the test?

If swelling develops at the needle puncture site, warm soaks may be applied to ease discomfort.

What are the normal results?

If serum dilution levels are low, cardiolipin antibodies aren't a problem.

What do abnormal results mean?

A high serum dilution level, along with a history of blood clots or miscarriages suggests cardiolipin antibody syndrome. The doctor may prescribe anticoagulants or platelet-inhibitor therapy to stop blood clots.

RHEUMATOID ARTHRITIS TEST

The most useful immune system test for confirming rheumatoid arthritis is called the *rheumatoid factor test*. In this disease, "renegade" immunoglobulin G antibodies, produced by lymphocytes in the synovial joints, react with other immunoglobulins to produce immune complexes, complement activation, and tissue destruction. How immunoglobulin G molecules become antigenic is still unknown, but they may be altered by aggregating with viruses or other antigens. Techniques for detecting rheumatoid factor include the sheep cell agglutination test and the latex fixation test.

This test detects immune complexes formed by "renegade" immunoglobulin G antibodies that interact with other immunoglobulins to produce complement activation and other substances. These complexes are a sign of rheumatoid arthritis.

Why is this test done?

The rheumatoid factor test may be done to help confirm a diagnosis of the disease.

What should you know before the test?

You won't need to change your diet before the test.

What happens during the test?

- A nurse or medical technician inserts a needle into a vein, usually in your forearm. A blood sample is collected in a tube, which is then sent to a lab for testing.
- Although you may feel a sting from the needle and pressure from the tourniquet, collecting the sample takes only a few minutes.

What happens after the test?

- If swelling develops at the needle puncture site, warm soaks may be applied to ease discomfort.

■ Because a person with rheumatoid arthritis may have a damaged immune system from the disease or from corticosteroid therapy, it's important to keep the puncture site covered with a clean, dry bandage for 24 hours.

What are the normal results?

The normal rheumatoid factor concentration is less than 1 part per 20 of serum.

What do abnormal results mean?

High rheumatoid factor concentrations are found in 80% of people with rheumatoid arthritis. But because people with some rheumatoid factor in their blood have other diseases and people with rheumatoid factor don't always have rheumatoid arthritis, the test isn't conclusive.

COLD ANTIBODIES TO BLOOD CELLS

Called the *cold agglutinins test* by doctors, this test detects cold agglutinins (antibodies, usually of the immunoglobulin M type) that cause red blood cells to clump at low temperatures. They may occur in small amounts in healthy people. Short-term elevations of these antibodies develop during certain infectious diseases, such as pneumonia. This test reliably detects such pneumonia within 1 to 2 weeks after infection.

Why is this test done?

A cold antibodies test may be done for the following reasons:
■ To help confirm a diagnosis of one type of pneumonia
■ To provide additional diagnostic evidence for cold agglutinin disease that is linked to many viral infections or lymph gland cancer.

What should you know before the test?

You won't need to change your diet before the test.

What happens during the test?

■ A nurse or medical technician inserts a needle into a vein, usually in your forearm. A blood sample is collected in a tube, which is then sent to a lab for testing.

■ Although you may feel a sting from the needle and pressure from the tourniquet, collecting the sample takes only a few minutes.

What happens after the test?

■ If swelling develops at the needle puncture site, warm soaks may be applied to ease discomfort.

■ If cold agglutinin disease is suspected, the nurse will urge you to keep warm. If you're exposed to low temperatures, blood-clumping may occur within hand and foot blood vessels, possibly leading to frostbite, anemia or, rarely, gangrene.

What are the normal results?

Normal concentrations are less than 1 part in 32 of serum but may be higher in elderly people.

What do abnormal results mean?

High concentrations of cold antibodies may show up independently (as with cold agglutinin disease) or with infections, lymph gland cancer, and many other diseases. Chronically high concentrations are most commonly linked to pneumonia and lymph gland cancer.

COLD SENSITIVITY ANTIBODIES

This test—which doctors call the *cryoglobulin test*—detects antibodies that may cause people to be sensitive to low temperatures. Cryoglobulins are abnormal proteins in the blood that precipitate at low temperatures and redissolve after being warmed. Their presence in the blood (called *cryoglobulinemia*) is usually, but not always, linked to immune system disease. If people with cryoglobulinemia are subjected to cold, they may experience pain and coldness of the fingers and toes (Raynaud's disease symptoms).

Why is this test done?

The cold sensitivity antibodies test may be done to detect cryoglobulinemia in people with Raynaud-like circulation symptoms.

What should you know before the test?

You'll fast for 4 to 6 hours before the test.

What happens during the test?

- A nurse or medical technician inserts a needle into a vein, usually in your forearm. A blood sample is collected in a tube, which is then sent to a lab for testing.
- Although you may feel a sting from the needle and pressure from the tourniquet, collecting the sample takes only a few minutes.

What happens after the test?

- If swelling develops at the needle puncture site, warm soaks may be applied to ease discomfort.
- You may resume your usual diet.
- If the test is positive for cryoglobulins, you should avoid cold temperatures or contact with cold objects.

People with cold-sensitive disease have to keep warm to avoid a blood-clumping reaction that can clog their blood vessels, leading to frostbite.

What are the normal results?

Normally, the blood test shows no cryoglobulins.

What do abnormal results mean?

The presence of cryoglobulins in the blood confirms cryoglobulinemia. However, this finding doesn't always mean the presence of a disease.

MYASTHENIA GRAVIS TEST

This immune system test — which doctors call the *acetylcholine receptors antibodies test* — confirms a diagnosis of myasthenia gravis. The acetylcholine receptor antibodies test is the most useful immune system test for confirming the disease, a disorder of neuromuscular transmission. In myasthenia gravis, antibodies block and destroy acetylcholine receptor sites, causing muscle weakness.

Why is this test done?

The myasthenia gravis test may be done to confirm a diagnosis of the disease and to monitor the effectiveness of therapy.

What should you know before the test?

You won't need to change your diet before the test.

What happens during the test?

- A nurse or medical technician inserts a needle into a vein, usually in your forearm. A blood sample is collected in a tube, which is then sent to a lab for testing.
- Although you may feel a sting from the needle and pressure from the tourniquet, collecting the sample takes only a few minutes.

What happens after the test?

- If swelling develops at the needle puncture site, warm soaks may be applied to ease discomfort.
- Keep a clean, dry bandage over the site for at least 24 hours.

What are the normal results?

Normal blood has no acetylcholine receptor antibodies or only a tiny concentration.

What do abnormal results mean?

Acetylcholine receptor antibodies in the blood of an adult with symptoms confirms the diagnosis of myasthenia gravis.

VIRUSES

RUBELLA TEST

This blood test diagnoses or evaluates a person's susceptibility to rubella, which is also known as *German measles*. Although rubella is generally a mild viral infection in children and young adults, it can produce severe infection in a fetus, resulting in spontaneous abortion, stillbirth, or inherited rubella syndrome. Because rubella infection normally stimulates production of immunoglobulin G and immunoglobulin M antibodies, measuring rubella antibodies can identify a current infection or an immunity resulting from past infection.

Why is this test done?

The test for rubella antibodies may be performed for the following reasons:

- To diagnose rubella, especially inherited infection in infants
- To determine susceptibility to rubella in children and in women of childbearing age.

What should you know before the test?

You won't need to change your diet before the test.

What happens during the test?

- A nurse or medical technician inserts a needle into a vein, usually in your forearm. A blood sample is collected in a tube, which is then sent to a lab for testing.
- Although you may feel a sting from the needle and pressure from the tourniquet, collecting the sample takes only a few minutes.

What happens after the test?

- If swelling develops at the needle puncture site, warm soaks may be applied to ease discomfort.
- If a current infection is suspected, a second blood sample will be needed in 2 to 3 weeks.

What are the normal results?

A high concentration of antibodies shows the person has adequate protection against rubella. The antibodies normally appear 2 to 4 days after the measles rash, peak in 2 to 3 weeks, then slowly decline but remain detectable for life.

What do abnormal results mean?

A low concentration means the person is susceptible to rubella and should be treated according to these guidelines:

- If a woman of childbearing age is found susceptible to the disease, vaccination can prevent rubella. But she must wait at least 3 months after the vaccination before becoming pregnant, or she may risk permanent damage to or death of the fetus.

If the test confirms rubella in a pregnant woman, she may need counseling to deal with permanent damage to or the loss of the fetus.

- If a pregnant woman is clinically suspected to be susceptible to rubella, she should have a follow-up rubella antibody test to detect possible subsequent infection.
- If the test confirms a current rubella infection in a pregnant woman, she may need counseling to deal with permanent damage to or the loss of her fetus.

What do the results mean in an infant?

Because maternal antibodies cross the placenta and persist in the infant's blood for up to 6 months, inherited rubella can be detected only after this period. A high concentration of antibodies in an infant age 6 months or older, who hasn't been exposed to rubella since birth, confirms a diagnosis of inherited rubella.

HEPATITIS B SCREENING TEST

This test helps identify a type of viral hepatitis by screening blood for hepatitis B surface antigen. Hepatitis B surface antigen appears in the blood of people with hepatitis B virus. It can be detected by the lab during the extended incubation period, during the first 3 weeks of acute infection, or if the person is a carrier.

Because transmission of hepatitis is one of the gravest complications linked to blood transfusion, all donors must be screened for hepatitis B before their blood is stored. This screening has helped reduce the incidence of hepatitis. However, this test doesn't screen for hepatitis A virus (infectious hepatitis).

Why is this test done?

The test for hepatitis B may be done for the following reasons:
- To screen blood donors for hepatitis B
- To screen people at high risk for contracting hepatitis B, such as hemodialysis nurses
- To help determine which type of viral hepatitis a person has.

What should you know before the test?

You won't need to change your diet before the test.

What happens during the test?

■ A nurse or medical technician inserts a needle into a vein, usually in your forearm. A blood sample is collected in a tube, which is then sent to a lab for testing.

■ Although you may feel a sting from the needle and pressure from the tourniquet, collecting the sample takes only a few minutes.

What happens after the test?

■ If swelling develops at the needle puncture site, warm soaks may be applied to ease discomfort.

■ If you're a blood donor, you'll be notified that you're positive for the antigen.

What are the normal results?

Normal blood shows no hepatitis B surface antigen.

What do abnormal results mean?

The presence of hepatitis B surface antigen in a person with hepatitis confirms hepatitis B. Hepatitis B surface antigen also may show up in about 5% of people with certain diseases other than hepatitis, such as hemophilia, Hodgkin's disease, and leukemia. Blood samples that test positive may have to be retested because inaccurate results do occur.

INFECTIOUS MONONUCLEOSIS TESTS

Called the *heterophil agglutination tests* by doctors, these tests can detect infectious mononucleosis. They're used to identify antibodies in human blood that react against foreign red blood cells. There are two types of these antibodies: Epstein-Barr virus antibodies and Forssman antibodies. Because the two types of antibodies react the same way, it takes one test to find them (the Paul-Bunnell test) and another (Davidsohn's test) to distinguish between them. (See *Spot test for mononucleosis,* page 522.)

Spot test for mononucleosis

The doctor may use one of several screening tests to diagnose mononucleosis (popularly known as *mono*). The simplest of these tests is Monospot, a rapid slide test. Monospot relies on agglutination (clumping) of horse red blood cells by mononucleosis antibodies presumed to be in the patient's serum. To confirm this reaction, serum is also mixed with a spot of guinea pig kidney cell antigen on one end of a glass slide and a spot of beef red blood cell antigen on the other end. Only the beef cell antigen is specific for mononucleosis. When horse red blood cells are added to the serum sample on each spot, clumping that occurs only on the beef cell end of the slide confirms the diagnosis.

Quick but not perfect

Monospot rivals the classic heterophil agglutination test for sensitivity. However, false-positive results may occur if the person has lymphoma, hepatitis A or B, leukemia, or pancreatic cancer.

Why are these tests done?

These tests may be performed to help distinguish infectious mononucleosis from other disorders.

What should you know before the tests?

You won't need to change your diet before the test.

What happens during the tests?

- A nurse or medical technician inserts a needle into a vein, usually in your forearm. A blood sample is collected in a tube, which is then sent to a lab for testing.
- Although you may feel a sting from the needle and pressure from the tourniquet, collecting the sample takes only a few minutes.

What happens after the tests?

- If swelling develops at the needle puncture site, warm soaks may be applied to ease discomfort.
- If the titer is positive and infectious mononucleosis is confirmed, instruct the person in the treatment plan.
- If the titer is positive but infectious mononucleosis isn't confirmed, or if the titer is negative but symptoms persist, explain that additional testing will be necessary in a few days or weeks to confirm diagnosis and plan effective treatment.

What are the normal results?

Normally, the concentration of heterophil antibodies is less than 1 part in 56, but it may be higher in elderly people.

What do abnormal results mean?

Although heterophil antibodies are present in the blood of approximately 80% of people with infectious mononucleosis 1 month after onset, a high concentration of them does not confirm this disorder. For example, a high concentration can also be caused by lupus or syphilis. A gradual increase in antibody concentration during week 3 or 4 of the illness, followed by a gradual decrease during weeks 4 to 8, proves most conclusive for infectious mononucleosis.

EPSTEIN-BARR VIRUS TEST

This test is used to diagnose infectious mononucleosis if other tests are inconclusive. Epstein-Barr virus causes infectious mononucleosis, Burkitt's lymphoma, and nose and throat cancers. This test measures Epstein-Barr virus antibodies, which combat the virus during an active infection. These antibodies can be measured precisely by a method called *indirect immunofluorescence.*

Why is this test done?

The Epstein-Barr test may be performed for the following reasons:
- To provide a laboratory diagnosis of mononucleosis missed by the Monospot test
- To determine the antibody status to Epstein-Barr virus of a person with a suppressed immune system and lymph gland involvement.

What should you know before the test?

You won't need to change your diet before the test.

What happens during the test?

- A nurse or medical technician inserts a needle into a vein, usually in your forearm. A blood sample is collected in a tube, which is then sent to a lab for testing.
- Although you may feel a sting from the needle and pressure from the tourniquet, collecting the sample takes only a few minutes.

What happens after the test?

If swelling develops at the needle puncture site, warm soaks may be applied to ease discomfort.

What are the normal results?

People who have never been infected with Epstein-Barr virus will have no detectable antibodies to the virus.

What do abnormal results mean?

Epstein-Barr virus infection can be ruled out if the person's blood has no Epstein-Barr virus antigens in the indirect immunofluorescence test. An indirect immunofluorescence test that is either immunoglobulin M-positive or Epstein-Barr nuclear antigen-negative indicates acute Epstein-Barr virus infection.

RESPIRATORY VIRUS TEST

An immune system test called the *respiratory syncytial virus test* detects a respiratory infection that's often found in children. Respiratory syncytial virus is the major viral cause of severe lower respiratory tract disease in infant, but may cause infections in people of any age. Respiratory syncytial virus infections are most common and produce the most severe disease during the first 6 months of life.

In this test, immunoglobulin G and immunoglobulin M class antibodies to the virus are measured, using a method doctors call *indirect immunofluorescence.*

Why is this test done?

The respiratory virus test may be performed to diagnose infections caused by respiratory syncytial virus.

What should you know before the test?

You or your child won't need to change your diet before the test.

What happens during the test?

- A nurse or medical technician inserts a needle into a vein, usually in your forearm. A blood sample is collected in a tube, which is then sent to a lab for testing.
- Although you may feel a sting from the needle and pressure from the tourniquet, collecting the sample takes only a few minutes.

What happens after the test?

If swelling develops at the needle puncture site, warm soaks may be applied to ease discomfort.

What are the normal results?

Blood from people who have never been infected with respiratory syncytial virus will have no detectable antibodies to the virus.

What do abnormal results mean?

The presence of immunoglobulin M or a 400% or greater increase in immunoglobulin G antibodies indicates active respiratory syncytial virus infection. In infants, blood-test diagnosis of respiratory syncytial virus infections is difficult because of the presence of the mother's immunoglobulin G antibodies. That makes the presence of immunoglobulin M antibodies more significant.

HERPES SIMPLEX VIRUS TEST

Herpes simplex virus causes various severe conditions, including genital lesions, inflammation of the eye, generalized skin lesions, and pneumonia. Severe herpes is linked to intrauterine or neonatal infections and encephalitis, especially in people with suppressed immune systems.

There are two closely related types of herpes virus. Type 1 usually causes infections above the waistline. Type 2 infections predominantly involve the external sex organs. People usually first contract this virus in early childhood as sores around the mouth or, more commonly, as a hidden infection.

Why is this test done?

This test is performed to confirm infections caused by the herpes simplex virus.

What should you know before the test?

You won't need to change your diet before the test.

What happens during the test?

■ A nurse or medical technician inserts a needle into a vein, usually in your forearm. A blood sample is collected in a tube, which is then sent to a lab for testing.

■ Although you may feel a sting from the needle and pressure from the tourniquet, collecting the sample takes only a few minutes.

What happens after the test?

If swelling develops at the needle puncture site, warm soaks may be applied to ease discomfort.

What are the normal results?

Blood from people who have never been infected with herpes simplex virus will have no detectable antibodies.

What do abnormal results mean?

The presence of antibodies suggests infection with herpes simplex. The presence of immunoglobulin M or a 400% or greater increase in immunoglobulin G antibodies indicates active herpes simplex virus infection. Reactivated infections caused by herpes simplex virus can be recognized in blood tests only by a sharp increase in immunoglobulin G antibodies.

Of the two types of herpes, Type 1 usually strikes above the waistline. Type 2 infections usually affect the genitalia.

TRANSPLANT REACTION SCREENING TEST

An immune system test called the *cytomegalovirus antibody screening test* is used to protect a person from transfusion or transplant reactions.

After an infection, cytomegalovirus remains latent in white blood cells. In a person with a damaged immune system, cytomegalovirus can come back to cause active infection. In some cases, blood or tissue from a donor with cytomegalovirus antibodies may cause active infection in recipients or in infants, especially those born prematurely.

Why is this test done?

The transplant reaction screening test may be performed for the following reasons:

- To detect previous cytomegalovirus infection in organ or blood donors and recipients
- To screen for cytomegalovirus infection in infants who require blood transfusion or tissue transplants
- To detect previous cytomegalovirus infection in people with damaged immune systems.

What should you know before the test?

You won't need to change your diet before the test.

What happens during the test?

■ A nurse or medical technician inserts a needle into a vein, usually in your forearm. A blood sample is collected in a tube, which is then sent to a lab for testing.

■ Although you may feel a sting from the needle and pressure from the tourniquet, collecting the sample takes only a few minutes.

What happens after the test?

If swelling develops at the needle puncture site, warm soaks may be applied to ease discomfort.

What are the normal results?

People who have never been infected with cytomegalovirus have no detectable antibodies to the virus.

What do abnormal results mean?

A blood sample positive for the cytomegalovirus antibody shows that the person has been infected with cytomegalovirus and that his or her blood could infect someone with a damaged immune system.

HIV INFECTION TESTS

These tests detect human immunodeficiency virus (HIV) infection. HIV is the virus that causes acquired immunodeficiency syndrome (AIDS). This virus may be transmitted when contaminated blood or blood products are exchanged from one person to another, during sexual intercourse with an infected partner, when intravenous drugs are shared, and during pregnancy or breast-feeding (passed from an infected mother to her child).

HIV is usually first identified by a test called the *enzyme-linked immunosorbent assay* (ELISA) and then confirmed by the Western blot or immunofluorescence test. Both of these tests detect antibodies to HIV, rather than the virus itself.

Why are these tests done?

The tests may be performed for the following reasons:

- To screen for HIV infection (see *How HIV destroys immunity*)
- To screen donated blood for HIV infection.

What should you know before the tests?

You won't need to fast or restrict fluids before the test to ensure reliable results. More important, the test results are confidential and will be revealed to no one without your permission.

What happens during the tests?

- A nurse or medical technician inserts a needle into a vein, usually in your forearm. A blood sample is collected in a tube, which is then sent to a lab for testing.
- Although you may feel a sting from the needle and pressure from the tourniquet, collecting the sample takes only a few minutes.

What happens after the tests?

- If swelling develops at the needle puncture site, warm soaks may be applied to ease discomfort.
- Assume that you can transmit HIV to others until conclusively proven otherwise. To prevent possible contagion, use safe-sex precautions.
- If the results are positive, get medical follow-up care, even if you have no symptoms. You should be on the lookout for early signs of AIDS, such as fever, weight loss, swollen lymph glands, rash, and persistent cough or diarrhea. Women should also report gynecologic symptoms.
- If you're found to be HIV-positive, don't share razors, toothbrushes, or utensils (which may be contaminated with blood) and clean such items with household bleach diluted 1 part to 10 in water. Practice safe sex to prevent giving HIV to another person. Don't donate blood, tissues, or an organ. Inform your doctor and dentist about your condition so that they can take the proper precautions.

What are the normal results?

The ELISA test should be negative, which means that it shows no HIV antibodies. However, this result, while certainly favorable, doesn't guarantee that a person is free from HIV infection. That's

INSIGHT INTO ILLNESS

How HIV destroys immunity

The difference between a normal and a damaged immune system is that a healthy person has the right cells to fight off infections. To understand how HIV affects immunity, consider first how a healthy immune system functions.

Normal immune function

When viruses enter the bloodstream, they're identified as foreign bodies (antigens) by cells called *macrophages*. The macrophages process the antigens and present them to T cells and B cells.

The antigen-activated T cells multiply and form several kinds of T cells. For example:

- Helper T cells stimulate B cells.
- Suppressor T cells balance them, controlling the extent of T-cell help for B cells.
- Lymphokine-producing T cells are involved in delayed hypersensitivity and other immune reactions.
- Cytotoxic, or killer, T cells directly destroy antigens.
- Memory T cells are stored to recognize and attack a reinvading antigen.

The B cells multiply, forming memory cells and plasma cells that produce antigen-specific antibodies, which then attack and kill the invading virus.

Impaired immune function

HIV selectively infects the helper T cells, impairing their ability to recognize antigens. Thus the virus is free to multiply, causing abnormal immune system function and progressive destruction.

As the person's immunity weakens, he or she becomes vulnerable to potentially fatal protozoal, viral, and fungal infections and to certain forms of cancer. Meanwhile, many more HIV particles are released and invade other T cells, further weakening the immune system.

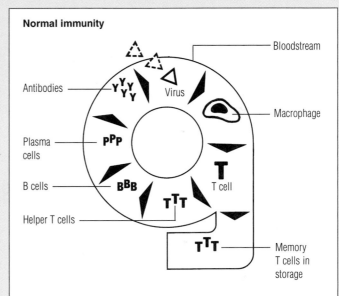

because the test doesn't identify people who've been exposed to HIV but whose bodies haven't yet created antibodies to the virus. This lag time typically varies from a few weeks to months. During this period, an HIV-infected person will test negative for HIV antibodies.

What do abnormal results mean?

A positive ELISA test indicates exposure to HIV. A positive test can't determine whether a person harbors the actively growing virus or when the person will show symptoms of AIDS. Many apparently healthy people have been exposed to HIV and have circulating antibodies. What's more, people in the later stages of AIDS may show no detectable antibodies in their blood because they can no longer mount an antibody response.

If an ELISA test is positive, the test should be repeated and then confirmed by the Western blot or an immunofluorescence test.

BACTERIA & FUNGI

STREP TEST

Called the *antistreptolysin-O test* by doctors, this test detects the immune system's response to bacteria called *streptococci* (popularly known as *strep*). It measures the relative concentrations of antibodies developed against *streptolysin O,* an antigen produced by the streptococcus bacteria.

Why is this test done?

The strep test may be performed for the following reasons:
- To confirm recent or ongoing infection with strep bacteria
- To help diagnose suspected rheumatic fever and kidney disease that may follow a strep infection
- To distinguish between rheumatic fever and rheumatoid arthritis when the person has joint pains.

What should you know before the test?

You won't need to change your diet before the test.

What happens during the test?

■ A nurse or medical technician inserts a needle into a vein, usually in your forearm. A blood sample is collected in a tube, which is then sent to a lab for testing.

■ Although you may feel a sting from the needle and pressure from the tourniquet, collecting the sample takes only a few minutes.

What happens after the test?

■ If swelling develops at the needle puncture site, warm soaks may be applied to ease discomfort.

■ The test may be repeated at regular intervals to identify active and inactive diseases by measuring changes in antibody levels.

What are the normal results?

Even healthy people have some detectable antistreptolysin-O concentration because of antibodies from previous minor strep infections.

What do abnormal results mean?

High antistreptolysin-O concentrations usually show up only after prolonged or recurrent infections. Doctors use the antibody levels from a series of tests to track down diseases. Roughly 15% to 20% of people with a disease that follows strep don't have elevated antistreptolysin-O concentrations, so this test is just one of the methods used to diagnose such diseases.

FEVER EVALUATION TESTS

Called *febrile agglutination tests* by doctors, these tests provide important diagnostic information regarding bacterial infections (such as tularemia, brucellosis, and disorders caused by salmonella) and rickettsial infections (such as Rocky Mountain spotted fever and typhus) that sometimes cause fevers of undetermined origin. In such conditions, causative organisms are difficult to isolate from blood or excretions.

These tests help pinpoint disorders that are hard to diagnose and that cause fevers of unknown origin.

Why are these tests done?

Fever evaluation tests may be performed for the following reasons:
- To support clinical findings in diagnosis of disorders caused by *Salmonella, Rickettsia, Francisella tularensis,* or *Brucella* organisms
- To identify the cause of fevers of undetermined origin.

What should you know before the tests?

You won't need to change your diet before the tests.

What happens during the tests?

- A nurse or medical technician inserts a needle into a vein, usually in your forearm. A blood sample is collected in a tube, which is then sent to a lab for testing.
- Although you may feel a sting from the needle and pressure from the tourniquet, collecting the sample takes only a few minutes.

What happens after the tests?

- If swelling develops at the needle puncture site, warm soaks may be applied to ease discomfort.
- This test requires a series of blood samples to detect a pattern of concentrations that is characteristic of the suspected disorder. Remember that a positive concentration only suggests a disorder.
- In fevers of undetermined origin and suspected infection, the hospital may have to isolate the person.

What are the normal results?

Normal antibody dilution values are as follows:
- Salmonella antibody: less than 1:80
- Brucellosis antibody: less than 1:80
- Tularemia antibody: less than 1:40
- Rickettsial antibody: less than 1:40.

What do abnormal results mean?

The doctor has to check the rise and fall of antibody dilutions to detect an active infection. If this is not possible, certain dilution levels may suggest the disorder. For all febrile agglutinins, a 400% increase in concentration is strong evidence of infection.

FUNGAL INFECTION TESTS

Blood tests (fungal serology) help the doctor diagnose specific fungal infections. Most fungi enter the body as spores inhaled into the lungs or through wounds in the skin or mucous membranes. If the body's defenses can't destroy the organisms quickly, the fungi multiply to form lesions. The person's blood and lymph vessels may then spread the fungus throughout the body. Most healthy people easily overcome a new fungal infection, but elderly people and people with deficient immune systems are more susceptible to acute or chronic infections.

Why are these tests done?

The tests may be used for the following reasons:
- To help diagnose fungal infection
- To monitor the effectiveness of therapy for fungal infection.

What should you know before the tests?

You'll restrict food and fluids for 12 to 24 hours before the test.

What happens during the tests?

- A nurse or medical technician inserts a needle into a vein, usually in your forearm. A blood sample is collected in a tube, which is then sent to a lab for testing.
- Although you may feel a sting from the needle and pressure from the tourniquet, collecting the sample takes only a few minutes.

What happens after the tests?

If swelling develops at the needle puncture site, warm soaks may be applied to ease discomfort.

What are the normal results?

Depending on the test method (complement fixation or cell agglutination procedures), a negative finding, or a normal concentration, usually indicates the absence of any fungal infection.

What do abnormal results mean?

Abnormal findings may indicate one of the following fungal infections:

- blastomycosis, a fungal condition that usually affects the lungs and produces bronchopneumonia
- coccidioidomycosis, a fungal condition that usually causes a respiratory infection but may spread throughout the body
- histoplasmosis, a fungal infection that occurs in three forms: *primary acute histoplasmosis, progressive disseminated histoplasmosis,* and *chronic pulmonary histoplasmosis,* with varying signs and symptoms
- aspergillosis, a fungal infection that occurs in four major forms: *aspergilloma* (which affects the lungs), *allergic aspergillosis* (a hypersensitive asthmatic reaction), *aspergillosis endophthalmitis* (an infection of the eye), and *disseminated aspergillosis* (an acute infection that produces blood poisoning and blood clots)
- sporotrichosis, a chronic condition that may affect the skin or lungs or may spread to the joints
- cryptococcosis, which usually starts as a lung infection without symptoms but may spread to other body regions.

CANDIDIASIS TEST

Candida albicans is a type of yeast that's commonly present in the body. It can cause an infection when the person's immune defenses have been significantly weakened.

Infection with this organism is called *candidiasis.* Candidiasis is usually limited to the skin and mucous membranes but may cause life-threatening systemic infection. Risk factors include recent antibacterial, antimetabolic, or corticosteroid therapy; immune system defects; diabetes; a debilitating disease; pregnancy; or obesity. Oral candidiasis is common and benign in children. In adults, it may be an early indication of AIDS.

When other methods fail, the doctor may use an immune system test to look for the *Candida* antibody to spot systemic candidiasis. Be aware that blood testing for these antibodies is not reliable. Medical experts continue to disagree about its usefulness.

Why is this test done?

The candidiasis test may be performed to help diagnose the infection when a culture or tissue study can't confirm it.

What should you know before the test?

You won't need to change your diet before the test.

What happens during the test?

■ A nurse or medical technician inserts a needle into a vein, usually in your forearm. A blood sample is collected in a tube, which is then sent to a lab for testing.
■ Although you may feel a sting from the needle and pressure from the tourniquet, collecting the sample takes only a few minutes.

What happens after the test?

If swelling develops at the needle puncture site, warm soaks may be applied to ease discomfort.

What are the normal results?

A normal test result is negative for the *Candida* antigen.

What do abnormal results mean?

A positive test for *Candida albicans* antigen is common in people with widespread candidiasis. However, this test yields a significant percentage of false-positive results.

When cultures and blood studies aren't definitive, doctors may look for the Candida antibody. But the test isn't considered reliable, and investigators still disagree about its usefulness.

BACTERIAL MENINGITIS TEST

Called the *bacterial meningitis antigen test,* this test can detect specific antigens of *Streptococcus pneumoniae, Neisseria meningitidis,* and *Haemophilus influenzae* type B, all of which are the major bacteria that cause meningitis. Lab technicians can use samples of blood, spinal fluid, urine, lung fluid, or joint fluid to perform the test.

Why is this test done?

The bacterial meningitis test may be performed for the following reasons:
- To identify the specific bacteria causing meningitis
- To aid diagnosis of bacterial meningitis.

What should you know before the test?

- You'll be told whether this test requires a urine specimen or a specimen of spinal fluid collected by a procedure called a *lumbar puncture.*
- If spinal fluid is to be collected, you'll be given a local anesthetic before the test, but you may feel short-term discomfort from the needle puncture.

What happens during the test?

- If a specimen of spinal fluid is required, a doctor performs the lumbar puncture procedure. This method requires insertion of a needle between the vertebrae of the lower spine. It takes about 20 minutes.
- If a urine specimen is required, you're instructed to urinate into a sterile container, which is then sent to a lab for testing.

What happens after the test?

A headache is the most common effect of lumbar puncture but your cooperation during the test minimizes the possibility of this reaction.

What are the normal results?

The test should be negative for bacterial antigens.

What do abnormal results mean?

Positive results identify the specific bacteria causing the infection: *Streptococcus pneumoniae, Neisseria meningitidis, Haemophilus influenzae* type B, or group B streptococci.

LYME DISEASE TEST

This test helps determine whether a person's symptoms are caused by Lyme disease. Lyme disease affects the skin, nervous system, heart, and joints as it goes through its various stages. It's caused by *Borrelia burgdorferi,* a bacterium commonly carried by wood ticks.

This blood test measures the antibody response to the bacteria and can identify 50% of people with early-stage Lyme disease. It can also identify all people with later complications of carditis, neuritis, and arthritis and all people who are in remission from these effects.

Why is this test done?

The test may be performed to confirm the doctor's diagnosis of Lyme disease.

What should you know before the test?

You'll have to fast for 12 hours before the blood sample is drawn, but you can drink fluids as usual.

What happens during the test?

- A nurse or medical technician inserts a needle into a vein, usually in your forearm. A blood sample is collected in a tube, which is then sent to a lab for testing.
- Although you may feel a sting from the needle and pressure from the tourniquet, collecting the sample takes only a few minutes.

What happens after the test?

If swelling develops at the needle puncture site, warm soaks may be applied to ease discomfort.

What are the normal results?

Normally, the test finds no Lyme disease antibodies. If there's a trace of antibodies, you may need repeat testing in 4 to 6 weeks.

What do abnormal results mean?

A positive test can help confirm the doctor's diagnosis, but it's not definitive. Other similar diseases and high rheumatoid factor concentrations can cause false-positive results. More than 15% of people with Lyme disease fail to develop antibodies.

This test measures the antibody response to the organism that causes Lyme disease; it can identify early stages of the disease in 50% of the cases. It's not definitive, however, because 15% of people with Lyme disease don't develop antibodies.

MISCELLANEOUS TESTS

VDRL TEST FOR SYPHILIS

The Venereal Disease Research Laboratory (VDRL) test is widely used to diagnose syphilis. Usually, a blood sample is used in the VDRL test, but this test may also be performed on a specimen of spinal fluid to test for tertiary syphilis, the stage marked by skin eruptions.

Why is this test done?

The VDRL test may be performed for the following reasons:
- To screen for syphilis
- To confirm syphilis in the presence of syphilitic lesions
- To monitor the infected person's response to treatment.

What should you know before the test?

You won't need to change your diet, but you shouldn't have any alcohol for 24 hours before the test.

What happens during the test?

- A nurse or medical technician inserts a needle into a vein, usually in your forearm. A blood sample is collected in a tube, which is then sent to a lab for testing.
- Although you may feel a sting from the needle and pressure from the tourniquet, collecting the sample takes only a few minutes.

What happens after the test?

- If swelling develops at the needle puncture site, warm soaks may be applied to ease discomfort.
- If the test is nonreactive or borderline but syphilis hasn't been ruled out, you should return for follow-up testing. Borderline test results don't necessarily mean you're free of the disease.

■ If the test is reactive, you'll need antibiotic therapy. Also, there will be mandatory inquiries from public health authorities.

■ If the test is reactive but you show no signs of syphilis, you'll need more specific tests to rule out the disease. Many uninfected people show false-positive reactions.

What are the normal results?

Normal blood shows no flocculation (thickening) when mixed with the required antigen complex and is reported as a nonreactive test.

What do abnormal results mean?

Definite flocculation is reported as a reactive test. Slight flocculation is reported as a weakly reactive test. A reactive VDRL test occurs in about 50% of people with primary syphilis and in nearly all people with secondary syphilis.

If you have syphilitic lesions, a reactive VDRL test confirms the diagnosis. If there are no lesions it means you must be repeatedly tested. However, biological false-positive reactions can be caused by conditions unrelated to syphilis; for example, infectious mononucleosis, malaria, leprosy, hepatitis, lupus, and rheumatoid arthritis.

Delayed-reaction

A nonreactive test doesn't rule out syphilis because it causes no detectable changes in the blood for 14 to 21 days after infection. However, the doctor can use a microscopic examination of matter from suspicious lesions to identify the bacteria.

A reactive VDRL test performed on spinal fluid indicates neurosyphilis, which can follow the other stages of the disease in people who don't get treatment.

FTA TEST FOR SYPHILIS

The fluorescent treponemal antibody (FTA) absorption test for syphilis is more exact than other syphilis tests. It detects antibodies to the bacteria in the blood that causes syphilis.

Why is this test done?

The FTA absorption test may be performed for the following reasons:

- To confirm primary or secondary stage syphilis
- To screen for suspected false-positive results of the VDRL test.

What should you know before the test?

You won't need to change your diet before the test.

What happens during the test?

- A nurse or medical technician inserts a needle into a vein, usually in your forearm. A blood sample is collected in a tube, which is then sent to a lab for testing.
- Although you may feel a sting from the needle and pressure from the tourniquet, collecting the sample takes only a few minutes.

What happens after the test?

- If swelling develops at the needle puncture site, warm soaks may be applied to ease discomfort.
- If the test is reactive, you'll need antibiotic treatment, and your sexual partners should also receive treatment.
- Because the disease must be reported, be prepared for inquiries from the public health authorities.
- If the test is nonreactive or findings are borderline, but syphilis has not been ruled out, you'll need to return for follow-up testing. Inconclusive results don't necessarily mean you're free of the disease.

What are the normal results?

Normally, reaction to the test is negative (no fluorescence).

What do abnormal results mean?

Antibodies in your blood—a reactive test result—do not indicate the stage or the severity of the infection. Elevated antibody levels appear in 80% to 90% of people with primary syphilis and in 100% of people with secondary syphilis. Higher antibody levels persist for several years, with or without treatment.

The absence of antibodies doesn't necessarily rule out syphilis because the infection doesn't cause detectable immunologic changes in the blood for 14 to 21 days. The doctor may find organisms earlier by examining suspicious lesions with a microscope. If you have bor-derline findings, the doctor may recommend repeated testing.

Possible sources of confusion
Although the FTA test is specific, some people with other conditions (such as lupus, genital herpes, or increased or abnormal globulins) and pregnant women may show slightly reactive levels. In addition, the test doesn't always distinguish between the organism that causes syphilis and related organisms.

CANCER SCREENING TEST

Also called the *carcinoembryonic antigen test,* this procedure detects and measures a special protein that's not normally present in adults. Carcinoembryonic antigen is secreted onto the lining of the fetus's digestive tract during the first 6 months of fetal life. Normally, this antigen is not produced after birth, but tumor growth can cause it to reappear in the blood later in life.

Because carcinoembryonic antigen levels are also raised by bile duct obstruction, alcoholic hepatitis, chronic heavy smoking, and other conditions, this test can't be used as a general indicator of can-cer, but it can help the doctor stage and monitor treatment of certain cancers.

Why is this test done?
The cancer screening test may be performed for the following rea-sons:
- To monitor the effectiveness of cancer therapy
- To assist in preoperative staging of colon and rectum cancers, check the adequacy of surgical resection, and to test for the return of the cancers.

What should you know before the test?
You won't need to change your diet before the test.

What happens during the test?

- A nurse or medical technician inserts a needle into a vein, usually in your forearm. A blood sample is collected in a tube, which is then sent to a lab for testing.
- Although you may feel a sting from the needle and pressure from the tourniquet, collecting the sample takes only a few minutes.

This test is used for preoperative staging of colon and rectum cancers. It also sheds light on lung cancers as well as some nonmalignant liver, pancreas, and bowel diseases.

What happens after the test?

If swelling develops at the needle puncture site, warm soaks may be applied to ease discomfort.

What are the normal results?

Normal blood carcinoembryonic antigen values are less than 5 nanograms per milliliter in healthy nonsmokers. However, about 5% of the population has above-normal concentrations.

What do abnormal results mean?

Persistent elevation of carcinoembryonic antigen levels suggests that the person has residual or recurrent tumor. If levels exceed normal before surgical resection, chemotherapy, or radiation therapy, their return to normal within 6 weeks suggests successful treatment.

High carcinoembryonic antigen levels show up various malignant conditions, particularly certain tumors of the gastrointestinal organs and the lungs, and in certain nonmalignant conditions, such as benign hepatic disease, hepatic cirrhosis, alcoholic pancreatitis, and inflammatory bowel disease. They also may appear in people with breast cancer or ovarian cancer.

BIRTH DEFECT AND CANCER THERAPY MONITORING

Doctors call this the *alpha-fetoprotein test*. It monitors a person's response to cancer therapy by measuring a specific blood protein. It also detects birth defects in a developing fetus, often leading to more testing, such as amniocentesis and ultrasound. Alpha-fetoprotein is produced by fetal tissue and by tumors. During fetal development, alpha-fetoprotein levels in blood and the amniotic fluid in the womb increase. Alpha-fetoprotein crosses the placenta and appears in the mother's blood.

Why is this test done?

The alpha-fetoprotein test may be performed for the following reasons:

■ To monitor the effectiveness of therapy in certain cancers, such as hepatomas and germ cell tumors, and in certain nonmalignant conditions

■ To determine the need for amniocentesis or high-resolution ultrasound in a pregnant woman.

What should you know before the test?

You won't need to change your diet before the test.

What happens during the test?

■ A nurse or medical technician inserts a needle into a vein, usually in your forearm. A blood sample is collected in a tube, which is then sent to a lab for testing.

■ Although you may feel a sting from the needle and pressure from the tourniquet, collecting the sample takes only a few minutes.

What happens after the test?

If swelling develops at the needle puncture site, warm soaks may be applied to ease discomfort.

What are the normal results?

Alpha-fetoprotein values are low to nonexistent in men and non-pregnant women.

What do abnormal results mean?

High alpha-fetoprotein in a pregnant woman's blood may suggest a neural tube defect or other spinal abnormalities in a fetus after 14 weeks' gestation. Alpha-fetoprotein levels increase sharply in approximately 90% of fetuses with no developing brain and in 50% of those with spina bifida. Definitive diagnosis requires ultrasound and amniocentesis. High alpha-fetoprotein levels may indicate that the fetus has died.

High levels in nonpregnant people may indicate a long list of digestive system cancers. Short-term, modest elevations can mean alcoholic cirrhosis and acute or chronic hepatitis.

TORCH TEST

This test helps detect exposure to pathogens involved in inherited infections in infants. TORCH is an acronym for *toxoplasmosis, rubella, cytomegalovirus, syphilis,* and *herpes simplex.* These problems are not readily apparent in newborns and may cause severe central nervous system damage. The TORCH test detects specific antibodies to these pathogens in the infant's blood.

Why is this test done?
The TORCH test may be performed to aid diagnosis of acute infections that are present in an infant at birth.

What happens during the test?
- The test requires a sample of your infant's blood.
- A nurse or a medical technician will take the sample, either with a needle or from the umbilical cord of a newborn.
- Although your infant may feel short-term discomfort, collecting the sample takes less than 3 minutes.

What are the normal results?
A normal test result is negative for TORCH agents.

What do abnormal results mean?
Depending on what antibodies are found, the doctor will use more tests to be sure of the correct diagnosis. For example, both toxoplasmosis and rubella are diagnosed by an increase in antibody concentration over time.

TUBERCULOSIS TESTS

Tuberculin skin tests help detect tuberculosis. They screen for previous infection by the tubercle bacillus. They're routinely performed in children, young adults, and other people whose X-rays suggest tuberculosis. In both the old tuberculin and purified protein derivative tests, injection of the tuberculin antigen under the skin causes a delayed hypersensitivity reaction in people with active or dormant tuberculosis. (See *Who's at risk for tuberculosis?* page 546.)

Why are these tests done?

Tuberculin skin tests may be done for the following reasons:
- To distinguish tuberculosis from other diseases, including blastomycosis, coccidioidomycosis, and histoplasmosis
- To identify persons who need to checked further for tuberculosis.

What should you know before the test?

- The tests require an injection under your skin, which may cause short-term discomfort.
- The nurse will check your history for active tuberculosis, the results of previous skin tests, or hypersensitivities. If you've had tuberculosis, the nurse won't perform the test.
- If you've had an allergic reaction to acacia, you won't be given the old tuberculin test because this product contains acacia.

What happens during the tests?

- You sit and support your extended arm on a flat surface while the nurse cleans your upper forearm with alcohol and allows the area to dry completely.
- For a Mantoux test, the needle is inserted under your skin and you feel a sting.
- For a multipuncture test, a four-pronged device punctures your skin and releases materials.

What happens after the tests?

- For either test, the nurse makes an appointment for you to return to have the skin test read — generally 48 to 72 hours later.
- A positive reaction to a skin test appears as a red, hard, raised area at the injection site. Although the area may itch, don't scratch it.

INSIGHT INTO ILLNESS

Who's at risk for tuberculosis?

Researchers may argue about the causes behind the increased incidence of tuberculosis, but they do agree that tuberculosis is on the rise. And they can identify people with the highest risk.

Generally at risk

- People disadvantaged by crowded, poorly ventilated, unsanitary living conditions (such as those in some prisons, tenement housing, or shelters for the homeless)
- Men (tuberculosis is twice as common in men than in women)
- Nonwhites (tuberculosis is four times as common in nonwhites than in whites; the typical newly diagnosed tuberculosis patient is a single, homeless, nonwhite man)
- People in close contact with a recently diagnosed tuberculosis patient
- Individuals who've previously had tuberculosis
- People with weak immune systems

Specifically at risk

- Black and Hispanic men between ages 25 and 44
- People with multiple sexual partners
- Recent immigrants from Africa, Asia, and Latin America
- People who've had a gastrectomy
- People afflicted by silicosis, diabetes, malnutrition, cancer, and diseases affecting the immune system
- Drug and alcohol abusers
- People in institutions for the chronically or mentally ill
- Nursing home residents (who are 10 times more likely to contract tuberculosis than anyone in the general populace)

- Remember that a positive reaction doesn't always indicate active tuberculosis.

Do the tests have risks?

- Tuberculin skin tests are dangerous for people with current reactions to smallpox vaccinations, any rash, skin disorder, or active tuberculosis. You should tell the doctor or nurse if you have any of those conditions.
- The nurse or technician will have epinephrine available to treat a possible acute hypersensitivity reaction.

What are the normal results?

In tuberculin skin tests, normal findings show minimal or no reactions.

What do abnormal results mean?

A positive tuberculin reaction indicates previous infection by tubercle bacilli. It doesn't distinguish between an active and dormant infection, nor does it provide a definitive diagnosis. If you have a positive reaction, a sputum smear and culture and a chest X-ray are necessary for further information.

DELAYED HYPERSENSITIVITY SKIN TESTS

These tests evaluate a person's immune system after application or injection of small doses of antigens. Skin testing is used to evaluate the immune response of people with severe recurrent infection, infection caused by unusual organisms, or suspected disorders associated with delayed hypersensitivity. Because diminished, delayed hypersensitivity may be linked to a poor chance of recovery from certain malignancies, this test may help the doctor estimate the prognosis for some cancer patients.

Why are these tests done?

Delayed hypersensitivity skin tests may be performed for the following reasons:
- To evaluate the person's immune responses
- To measure the effectiveness of immunotherapy when the person's immune response is being boosted
- To diagnose fungal diseases, bacterial diseases, and viral diseases
- To monitor the course of certain diseases.

What should you know before the tests?

You won't need to change your diet before the tests.

What happens during the tests?

- You sit and support your arm on a flat surface.
- A nurse or medical technician injects or applies the antigens.
- Although you may feel a sting from the needle, the discomfort is short-term.
- It takes about 10 minutes for each antigen to be administered.

What happens after the tests?

- Reactions should appear in 48 to 72 hours.
- Some antigens are given again after 2 weeks or, if the test is negative, a stronger dose of antigen may be given.

Do the tests have risks?

- If hypersensitivity to the antigens is suspected, they're first applied in low concentrations.
- The nurse watches for signs of a severe allergic reaction: hives, respiratory distress, and low blood pressure. If such signs develop, you're given epinephrine.

What are the normal results?

In a test called the *DNCB test,* a positive reaction (swelling, hardness, redness) appears 48 to 96 hours after the second (challenge) dose in 95% of the population. In the *recall antigen test,* a positive response (a significant reaction at the test site) appears 48 hours after injection.

What do abnormal results mean?

In the DNCB test, failure to react to the challenge dose indicates diminished, delayed hypersensitivity. In the recall antigen test several things demonstrate diminished, delayed hypersensitivity: a positive response to less than two of the six test antigens, a persistent unresponsiveness to an under-the-skin injection of higher-strength antigens, or a generalized diminished reaction.

Diminished, delayed hypersensitivity can be caused by many conditions: Hodgkin's disease; sarcoidosis; liver disease; inherited immune disease, such as DiGeorge's syndrome and Wiskott-Aldrich syndrome; uremia; acute leukemia; viral diseases, such as influenza, infectious mononucleosis, measles, mumps, and rubella; fungal diseases, such as coccidioidomycosis and cryptococcosis; bacterial diseases, such as tuberculosis; and terminal cancer. Diminished, delayed hypersensitivity can also result from immunosuppressive or steroid drugs or viral vaccination.

URINE TESTS:
Examining the Body's Excess Fluids

ANALYSIS OF URINE

ROUTINE URINALYSIS

These tests help diagnose kidney or urinary tract disease and evaluate your overall body function. (See *The kidneys and urine formation,* page 552.) The tests use several techniques, including:
- visual examination for physical characteristics (color, odor, and opacity) of urine
- refractometry to determine specific gravity and pH
- chemical tests to detect and measure protein, glucose, and ketone bodies
- microscopic inspection of sediment for blood cells, casts, and crystals.

Why is this test done?
Routine urinalysis may be performed for the following reasons:
- To screen your urine for kidney or urinary tract disease
- To help the doctor detect metabolic or systemic disease unrelated to kidney disorders.

What should you know before the test?
- You won't need to change your diet before the test.
- The nurse will ask about any current or recent medication use; many drugs may affect test results.

What happens during the test?
- You use a clean container to collect a urine specimen of at least 15 milliliters.
- Collect a specimen from your first voiding in the morning, if possible.

What are the normal results?
Harmless variations in normal values may result from diet, non-threatening conditions, specimen collection time, and other factors. The doctor looks for the following normal characteristics:
- Color: straw
- Odor: slightly aromatic

HOW YOUR BODY WORKS

The kidneys and urine formation

The kidneys, through the activity of the nephrons, continuously remove metabolic wastes, drugs, and other foreign substances. They filter excess fluids, inorganic salts, and acid and base substances from the blood for eventual excretion in the urine.

The nephron: Master filter

Each kidney has approximately 1 million nephrons. Each of these nephrons consists of an ultrafilter, called a *glomerulus,* and a tubule — a lined conduit that works to reabsorb recyclable matter and secrete foreign and waste substances.

Each tubule is made up of four sections: the proximal convoluted tubule, loop of Henle, distal convoluted tubule, and collecting tubule. As the filtrate from the glomerulus travels through the renal tubules, resorption and secretion modify it to meet the body's needs. The end result is urine.

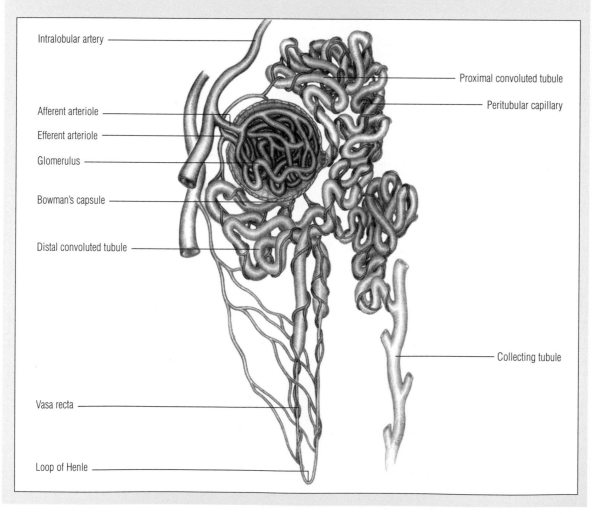

Intralobular artery

Afferent arteriole

Efferent arteriole

Glomerulus

Bowman's capsule

Distal convoluted tubule

Vasa recta

Loop of Henle

Proximal convoluted tubule

Peritubular capillary

Collecting tubule

- Appearance: clear
- Specific gravity (the ratio of the density of urine to the density of water): 1.005 to 1.035
- pH: 4.5 to 8.0
- Sugars: none
- Epithelial cells: few
- Casts: none, except occasional translucent casts
- Crystals: present
- Yeast cells: none.

What do abnormal results mean?

The following abnormal findings generally suggest diseased conditions:

- Color: Color change can result from diet, drugs, and many diseases.
- Odor: In diabetes mellitus, starvation, and dehydration, a fruity odor accompanies formation of ketone bodies. In urinary tract infections, a fetid odor commonly is associated with *Escherichia coli.* Maple syrup, urine disease, and phenylketonuria also cause distinctive odors.
- Turbidity: Turbid urine may contain red or white cells, bacteria, fat, or chyle and may reflect kidney infection.
- Specific gravity: Low specific gravity (less than 1.005) is characteristic of diabetes insipidus, nephrogenic diabetes insipidus, acute tubular necrosis, and pyelonephritis. Fixed specific gravity, in which values remain 1.010 regardless of fluid intake, occurs in chronic glomerulonephritis with severe kidney damage. High specific gravity (more than 1.035) occurs in nephrotic syndrome, dehydration, acute glomerulonephritis, congestive heart failure, liver failure, and shock.
- pH: Alkaline urine pH may result from Fanconi's syndrome, urinary tract infection, and metabolic or respiratory alkalosis. Acid urine pH is associated with kidney tuberculosis, fever, phenylketonuria, alkaptonuria, and acidosis.
- Protein: Protein in the urine suggests kidney failure or disease (including nephrosis, glomerulosclerosis, glomerulonephritis, nephrolithiasis, and polycystic kidney disease) or, possibly, multiple tumors.
- Sugars: Glycosuria usually indicates diabetes mellitus, but may be caused by a long list of diseases, including pheochromocytoma, Cushing's syndrome, impaired tubular reabsorption, advanced kidney disease, and increased intracranial pressure. Fructosuria, galac-

The color of urine can be affected by a person's diet, use of drugs, or a long list of diseases.

tosuria, and pentosuria generally suggest rare hereditary metabolic disorders (except for lactosuria during pregnancy and lactation).

■ Ketone bodies: Ketonuria occurs in diabetes mellitus or in starvation and following diarrhea or vomiting.

■ Bilirubin: Bilirubin in urine may occur in liver disease caused by obstructive jaundice, hepatotoxic drugs, or toxins or by fibrosis of the biliary canaliculi (which may occur in cirrhosis).

■ Urobilinogen: Bilirubin is changed into urobilinogen in the duodenum by intestinal bacteria. The liver reprocesses the remainder into bile. Increased urobilinogen in the urine may indicate liver damage, hemolytic disease, or severe infection. Decreased levels may occur with biliary obstruction, inflammatory disease, antimicrobial therapy, severe diarrhea, or kidney insufficiency.

■ Cells: Bloody urine indicates bleeding within the genitourinary tract, possibly caused by a long list of problems: infection, obstruction, inflammation, trauma, tumors, glomerulonephritis, kidney hypertension, lupus nephritis, kidney tuberculosis, kidney vein thrombosis, kidney stones, hydronephrosis, pyelonephritis, scurvy, malaria, parasitic infection of the bladder, subacute bacterial endocarditis, polyarteritis nodosa, and hemorrhagic disorders.

Strenuous exercise or exposure to toxic chemicals may also cause blood in the urine. An excess of white cells in urine usually implies urinary tract inflammation. White cells and white cell casts in urine suggest kidney infection. Numerous epithelial cells suggest kidney tubular degeneration.

■ Casts (plugs of gelled proteinaceous material): Casts form in the kidney's tubules and collecting ducts by agglutination of protein cells or cellular debris and are flushed loose by urine flow. Excessive numbers of casts indicate kidney disease.

■ Crystals: Some crystals normally appear in urine, but numerous calcium oxalate crystals suggest hypercalcemia. Cystine crystals (cystinuria) reflect an inborn error of metabolism.

■ Other components: Bacteria, yeast cells, and parasites in urinary sediment reflect genitourinary tract infection or contamination of external genitalia. Yeast cells, which may be mistaken for red cells, are identifiable by their oval shape, lack of color, variable size, and frequently, signs of budding. The most common parasite in sediment is *Trichomonas vaginalis,* which causes vaginitis, urethritis, and prostatovesiculitis.

KIDNEY STONE TEST

This test checks you for kidney stones. Lab analysis will reveal their composition. Kidney stones are insoluble substances most commonly formed of these mineral salts: calcium oxalate, calcium phosphate, magnesium ammonium phosphate, urate, or cystine. They may appear anywhere in the urinary tract and range in size from microscopic to several centimeters.

How kidney stones develop

You can get kidney stones from reduced urine output, increased excretion of mineral salts, holding urine, pH changes, and decreased protective substances. Stones usually form in the kidney, pass into the ureter, and are excreted in the urine. Because not all stones pass spontaneously, they may require surgical extraction. Kidney stones don't always cause symptoms, but when they do, blood in the urine is most common. If stones obstruct the ureter, they may cause severe flank pain, difficulty urinating, and urinary retention, frequency, and urgency.

The most common symptom of kidney stones is blood in the urine.

Why is this test done?

The test for kidney stones may be performed to detect and identify stones in the urine.

What should you know before the test?

- Your urine will be collected and strained.
- You don't have to restrict your diet.
- Your symptoms will go away immediately after you get rid of any stones.
- You can have medication to control pain.

What happens during the test?

- You void into the strainer.
- The strainer is carefully inspected because the stones may be tiny; they look like gravel or sand.

What are the normal results?

Normally, stones are not present in urine.

Detecting diabetes insipidus with the dehydration test

The dehydration test checks your urine to measure your kidneys' concentrating capacity after a period of dehydration and after an injection of the pituitary hormone vasopressin. Comparison of the two samples permits a reliable diagnosis of diabetes insipidus, a metabolic disorder marked by vasopressin (antidiuretic hormone) deficiency.

How the test is done
If you have this test, you'll have no fluids the evening before and the morning of the test. Your urine will be collected at hourly intervals in the morning for analysis, to see if you are dehydrated enough for the second part of the test. When you're dry enough, you'll be injected with vasopressin, and the nurse will take one more urine specimen within an hour. That specimen will be used to check for diabetes and other diseases.

What do abnormal results mean?
More than half of all kidney stones in urine are of mixed composition, containing two or more mineral salts; calcium oxalate is the most common component. When the composition of kidney stones is determined, it helps identify various metabolic disorders.

KIDNEY FUNCTION TESTS

Two tests called the *urine concentration test* and the *dilution test* help the doctor to evaluate your kidney function. The kidneys normally concentrate or dilute urine according to your fluid intake. When intake is excessive, the kidneys excrete more water in the urine. When intake is limited, they excrete less. These tests measure your kidneys' capacity to concentrate urine in response to fluid deprivation or to dilute it in response to fluid overload.

Why are these tests done?
The concentration and dilution tests may be performed to evaluate the kidneys' tubular function and detect kidney damage. (See *Detecting diabetes insipidus with the dehydration test.*)

What should you know before the tests?
- The tests require multiple urine specimens. The nurse will explain how many specimens will be collected and at what intervals.
- You should discard any urine voided during the night.
- If you're using diuretics, they should be stopped.

Concentration test
- You should have a high-protein meal and only 200 milliliters of fluid the night before the test.
- You'll limit your food and fluids for at least 14 hours before the test. (Some concentration tests require that water be withheld for 24 hours but permit relatively normal food intake.)
- Limit salt at your evening meal to prevent excessive thirst.

Dilution test
Generally, this test directly follows the concentration test and requires no additional preparation. If you're just having this test done, you'll only need to skip breakfast.

What happens during the tests?

Concentration test

You're asked to urinate into a special container at specific times: 6 a.m., 8 a.m., and 10 a.m.

Dilution test

- You should first void and discard the urine.
- You're given 1,500 milliliters of water to drink within 30 minutes.
- You're then asked to urinate into a special container. Urine specimens are collected every half hour or every hour for 4 hours thereafter.

Both tests

- You should have a balanced meal or a snack after collecting the final specimen.
- The nurse checks to make sure you void within 8 to 10 hours after the test.

What are the normal results?

In the *concentration test,* specific gravity ranges from 1.025 to 1.032, and osmolality rises above 800 nanomoles per kilogram of water in people with normal kidney function.

In the *dilution test,* specific gravity falls below 1.003 and osmolality below 100 nanomoles per kilogram for at least one specimen; 80% or more of the ingested water is eliminated in 4 hours. In elderly persons, depressed values can be associated with normal kidney function.

What do abnormal results mean?

Decreased kidney capacity to concentrate urine in response to fluid deprivation or to dilute urine in response to fluid overload may indicate tubular epithelial damage, decreased kidney blood flow, loss of functional nephrons, or pituitary or heart dysfunction.

PHOSPHATE REABSORPTION BY THE KIDNEYS

This test—which doctors call the *tubular reabsorption of phosphate test*—evaluates the parathyroid gland and measures its hormone levels. Parathyroid hormone helps maintain optimum blood levels of calcium and controls the kidneys' excretion of calcium and phosphate.

In this test, levels of phosphate and creatinine in the urine and blood are measured and these values are used to calculate the reabsorption of phosphate by tubules in the kidney.

Why is this test done?

The tubular reabsorption test may be performed for the following reasons:
- To evaluate parathyroid function
- To help the doctor diagnose primary hyperparathyroidism
- To distinguish between hypercalcemia (calcium excess) due to hyperparathyroidism and hypercalcemia due to other causes.

What should you know before the test?

- The test requires a blood sample and urine collection over a 24-hour period.
- You'll be instructed to maintain a normal phosphate diet for 3 days before the test because low phosphate intake (less than 500 milligrams per day) may elevate tubular reabsorption values and a high-phosphate diet (3,000 milligrams per day) may lower them. Common nutritional sources of phosphorus include legumes, nuts, milk, egg yolks, meat, poultry, fish, cereals, and cheese. These foods should be eaten in moderate amounts.
- You must fast after midnight the night before the test.

The doctor needs one blood sample and a container of urine collected over a 24-hour period.

What happens during the test?

- For the blood test, a nurse or medical technician inserts a needle into a vein, usually in your forearm. A blood sample is collected in a tube, which is then sent to a lab for testing.
- You're asked to urinate into a special container over a 24-hour period.
- Void and discard the urine, and then begin 24-hour collection with the next voiding.

- After you place the first specimen in the container, add the preservative given to you by the nurse or medical technician.
- Add each voiding to the container immediately. If any urine is lost, restart the test.
- Plan the start of your test so that collection ends at a time that the lab is open.
- Just before the end of the test period, make an effort to void and add that urine to the container.
- Be sure not to contaminate the specimen with toilet paper or stools.
- Occasionally, a 4-hour collection is ordered instead.

What happens after the test?

- You can eat and should drink fluids to maintain adequate urine flow after the blood test.
- If swelling develops at the needle puncture site, apply warm soaks.
- You may resume your usual diet.

What are the normal results?

Kidney tubules normally reabsorb 80% or more of phosphate.

What do abnormal results mean?

Reabsorption of less than 74% of phosphate strongly suggests primary hyperparathyroidism. Hypercalcemia is the most common manifestation of primary hyperparathyroidism. However, a person with hypercalcemia may still require additional testing to confirm primary hyperparathyroidism as the cause.

Depressed reabsorption occurs in a small number of people with kidney stones who don't have parathyroid tumor. Also, about one-fifth of people with parathyroid tumor exhibit normal reabsorption. Increased reabsorption of phosphate may be caused by uremia, kidney tubular disease, osteomalacia, sarcoidosis, and tumors.

AMYLASE

This test evaluates the function of your pancreas and salivary glands. Amylase is a starch-splitting enzyme produced primarily in the pancreas and salivary glands. It's usually secreted into the digestive tract and absorbed into the blood. Small amounts of amylase are also absorbed into the blood directly from these sources. Following glomerular filtration, amylase is excreted in the urine.

If your kidneys are working correctly, blood and urine levels of amylase usually increase together. However, within 2 or 3 days of onset of acute pancreatitis, blood amylase levels fall to normal, but elevated urine amylase persists for 7 to 10 days. One method for determining urine amylase levels is the dye-coupled starch method.

To find out how well your pancreas and salivary glands are working, doctors may examine the amount of the amylase enzyme in a urine specimen.

Why is this test done?

The amylase test may be performed for the following reasons:
- To diagnose acute pancreatitis when blood amylase levels are normal or borderline
- To help the doctor diagnose chronic pancreatitis and salivary gland disorders.

What should you know before the test?

- You won't need to change your diet before the test.
- The test requires urine collection for 2, 6, 8, or 24 hours.
- If a woman is menstruating, the test may have to be rescheduled.
- The lab requires 2 days to complete the analysis.
- If you're taking medications, some may be stopped before the test because continued use may interfere with accurate test results.

What happens during the test?

- Your urine is collected over a 2-, 6-, 8-, or 24-hour period.
- Void and discard the urine, and then begin collection with the next voiding.
- After you place the first specimen in the container, add any preservative given to you by the nurse or medical technician.
- Add each voiding to the container immediately. If any urine is lost, restart the test.
- Plan the start of your test so that collection ends at a time that the lab is open.
- Just before the end of the test period, make an effort to void and add that urine to the container.
- Be sure not to contaminate the specimen with toilet tissue or stools.

What are the normal results?

The Mayo Clinic in the United States reports urinary excretion of 10 to 80 amylase units per hour as normal.

What do abnormal results mean?

Elevated amylase levels occur in acute pancreatitis; obstruction of the pancreatic duct, intestines, or salivary duct; cancer of the head of the pancreas; mumps; acute injury of the spleen; kidney disease, with impaired absorption; perforated peptic or duodenal ulcers; and gallbladder disease. Depressed levels occur in pancreatitis, physical wasting and malnutrition, alcoholism, cancer of the liver, cirrhosis, hepatitis, and liver abscess.

ARYLSULFATASE A

This test measures an enzyme that's present throughout your body. Arylsulfatase A (ARSA) is a lysosomal enzyme found in every cell except the mature red blood cell. It's principally active in the liver, the pancreas, and the kidneys, where substances such as drugs are detoxified into sulfates. Urine ARSA levels increase in bladder cancer, colorectal cancer, and leukemia.

Why is this test done?

The arylsulfatase A test may be performed to aid diagnosis of bladder, colon, or rectal cancer; of myeloid (granulocytic) leukemia; and of an inherited lipid storage disease.

What should you know before the test?

- You won't need to change your diet before the test.
- If a woman is menstruating, her test may have to be rescheduled.
- The test requires urine collection over a 24-hour period.
- The test results are generally available in 2 or 3 days.

What happens during the test?

- You're asked to urinate into a special container over a 24-hour period.
- Void and discard the urine, and then begin 24-hour collection with the next voiding.
- After you place the first specimen in the container, add the preservative given to you by the nurse or medical technician.
- Add each voiding to the container immediately. If any urine is lost, restart the test.

- Plan the start of your test so that collection ends at a time that the lab is open.
- Just before the end of the test period, make an effort to void and add that urine to the container.
- Be sure not to contaminate the specimen with toilet paper or stools.

What are the normal results?

Normal arylsulfatase A values are as follows:
- Men: 1.4 to 19.3 international units per liter
- Women: 1.4 to 11 international units per liter
- Children: over 1 international unit per liter.

What do abnormal results mean?

Elevated ARSA levels may be caused by cancer of the bladder, the colon, or the rectum, or from myeloid leukemia.

LYSOZYME

This test evaluates your kidney function and your immune system. Lysozyme is a low-molecular-weight enzyme present in mucus, saliva, tears, skin secretions, and various internal body cells and fluids. This enzyme lyses (splits) the cell walls of some bacteria and, with other blood factors, acts to destroy them.

Lysozyme seems to be created in certain blood cells, and it first appears in blood after destruction of those cells. When blood lysozyme levels exceed three times normal, the enzyme appears in the urine. However, since kidney tissue also contains lysozyme, kidney injury alone can cause measurable excretion of this enzyme.

Why is this test done?

The lysozyme test may be performed for the following reasons:
- To aid diagnosis of acute monocytic or granulocytic leukemia and to monitor the progression of these diseases
- To evaluate kidney tubular function and to diagnose kidney damage
- To detect rejection or loss of blood supply to a transplanted kidney.

What should you know before the test?

- You won't need to change your diet before the test.
- If a woman is menstruating, she may have to reschedule the test for a later date.
- Test results should be available in 1 day.

What happens during the test?

- You're asked to urinate into a special container over a 24-hour period.
- Void and discard the urine, and then begin 24-hour collection with the next voiding.
- After you place the first specimen in the container, add the preservative given to you by the nurse or medical technician.
- Add each voiding to the container immediately. If any urine is lost, restart the test.
- Plan the start of your test so that collection ends at a time that the lab is open.
- Just before the end of the test period, make an effort to void and add that urine to the container.
- Be sure not to contaminate the specimen with toilet paper or stools.

Lysozyme is an enzyme that helps your body fight bacteria. But when it shows up in urine, that sets off alarms.

What are the normal results?

Normally, urine lysozyme values are less than 3 milligrams per liter.

What do abnormal results mean?

Elevated urine lysozyme levels may indicate impaired kidney tubular reabsorption, acute pyelonephritis, nephrotic syndrome, tuberculosis of the kidney, severe extrarenal infection, or rejection or stopped blood supply to a transplanted kidney.

Urine levels increase markedly after acute onset or relapse of monocytic or myelomonocytic leukemia and increase moderately after acute onset or relapse of granulocytic (myeloid) leukemia.

HORMONES

ALDOSTERONE

This test evaluates hormonal balance by checking the urine levels of the hormone aldosterone. Aldosterone promotes retention of sodium and excretion of potassium by the kidneys, thereby helping to regulate blood pressure and fluid and electrolyte balance. In turn, aldosterone secretion is controlled by the renin-angiotensin system. This feedback mechanism is vital to maintaining fluid and electrolyte balance.

Why is this test done?

The aldosterone test may be performed to aid diagnosis of primary and secondary aldosteronism, which may be a factor in high blood pressure.

What should you know before the test?

■ You should maintain normal levels of salt in your diet (3 grams per day) before the test and avoid high-salt foods, such as bacon, barbecue sauce, corned beef, bouillon cubes or powder, and olives.

■ Avoid strenuous physical exercise and stressful situations during the collection period.

■ If you're taking medications, some may be stopped or restricted before the test.

What happens during the test?

■ You're asked to urinate into a special container over a 24-hour period.

■ Void and discard the urine, and then begin 24-hour collection with the next voiding.

■ After you place the first specimen in the container, add the preservative given to you by the nurse or medical technician.

■ Add each voiding to the container immediately. If any urine is lost, restart the test.

■ Plan the start of your test so that collection ends at a time that the lab is open.

■ Just before the end of the test period, make an effort to void and add that urine to the container.

Aldosterone is one hormone that helps your body maintain its fluid and electrolyte balance.

- Be sure not to contaminate the specimen with toilet paper or stools.

What happens after the test?
- You can resume any medications withheld during the test.
- You can resume normal physical activity.

What are the normal results?
Normally, urine aldosterone levels range from 15.4 to 44.4 nanomoles per day.

What do abnormal results mean?
Elevated urine aldosterone levels suggest primary or secondary aldosteronism. Disorders that may cause secondary aldosteronism are severe high blood pressure, congestive heart failure, cirrhosis of the liver, nephrotic syndrome, and idiopathic cyclic edema.

Low urine aldosterone levels may be caused by Addison's disease, salt-losing syndrome, and toxemia of pregnancy.

TEST FOR CUSHING'S SYNDROME

A hormone test called the *free cortisol test* helps evaluate your adrenal gland function. It's one of the best diagnostic tools for detecting Cushing's syndrome, a disorder marked by excessive secretion of hormones by the cortex of the adrenal gland.

Why is this test done?
The test for free cortisol may be performed to aid diagnosis of Cushing's syndrome.

What should you know before the test?
You won't need to change your diet before the test, but you should avoid stressful situations and excessive physical exercise during the collection period.

What happens during the test?

- You're asked to urinate into a special container over a 24-hour period.
- Void and discard the urine, and then begin 24-hour collection with the next voiding.
- After you place the first specimen in the container, add the preservative given to you by the nurse or medical technician.
- Add each voiding to the container immediately. If any urine is lost, restart the test.
- Plan the start of your test so that collection ends at a time when the lab is open.
- Just before the end of the test period, make an effort to void and add that urine to the container.
- Be sure not to contaminate the specimen with toilet paper or stools.

What happens after the test?

You can resume your normal activities and resume taking any medications you discontinued for the test.

What are the normal results?

Normally, free cortisol values range from 66 to 298 nanomoles per day.

What do abnormal results mean?

Elevated free cortisol levels may indicate Cushing's syndrome, caused by adrenal hyperplasia, adrenal or pituitary tumor, or ectopic corticotropin production. Liver disease and obesity, which can raise plasma cortisol levels, generally don't affect urine levels of free cortisol. Low levels have little significance.

EPINEPHRINE, NOREPINEPHRINE, AND DOPAMINE

This test evaluates adrenal gland function by measuring urine levels of the major hormones epinephrine, norepinephrine, and dopamine. These hormones are known as *catecholamines*. Epinephrine is secreted by the adrenal gland; dopamine, by the central nervous system; and norepinephrine, by both.

Catecholamines help regulate metabolism and prepare the body for the fight-or-flight response to stress. Certain tumors can also secrete catecholamines.

Why is this test done?

The test for catecholamines may be performed for the following reasons:

- To aid the diagnosis of pheochromocytoma in a person with unexplained high blood pressure
- To aid the diagnosis of neuroblastoma, ganglioneuroma, and malfunction of the autonomic nervous system.

What should you know before the test?

- You won't need to change your diet before the test, but you should avoid stressful situations and excessive physical activity during the collection period.
- Either a specimen collected over 24 hours or a random specimen may be required.

What happens during the test?

- You're asked to urinate into a special container over a 24-hour period. (If a random specimen is ordered, collect it immediately after a high blood pressure episode.)
- Void and discard the urine, and then begin 24-hour collection with the next voiding.
- After you place the first specimen in the container, add the preservative given to you by the nurse or medical technician.
- Add each voiding to the container immediately. If any urine is lost, restart the test.
- Plan the start of your test so that collection ends at a time the lab is open.
- Just before the end of the test period, make an effort to void and add that urine to the container.
- Be sure not to contaminate the specimen with toilet paper or stools.

What happens after the test?

You can resume any activity or medications restricted during the test.

Catecholamines help regulate metabolism and prepare the body for the fight-or-flight response to stress.

What are the normal results?

Normally, urine catecholamine values range from undetectable to 798 nanomoles per deciliter of urine in a random specimen.

What do abnormal results mean?

In people with undiagnosed high blood pressure, elevated urine catecholamine levels following an episode of high blood pressure usually indicate a tumor. If tests indicate a tumor, the person may also be tested for multiple endocrine neoplasia.

Elevated catecholamine levels, without marked high blood pressure, may be due to brain tumors. Myasthenia gravis and progressive muscular dystrophy commonly cause urine catecholamine levels to rise above normal, but this test is rarely performed to diagnose these disorders.

ESTROGENS

The total urine estrogens test helps evaluate functioning of the ovaries or the testicles. For a pregnant woman, measuring urine estrogens helps to monitor fetal development and placental function. For a man, this test helps evaluate testicular function.

The test measures total urine levels of estradiol, estrone, and estriol — the major estrogens present in significant amounts in urine. (See *Changes in estrogen levels during the menstrual cycle.*)

Why is this test done?

The total urine estrogens test may be performed for the following reasons:
- To evaluate ovarian activity and help determine why a woman isn't menstruating and has an overproduction of estrogen
- To aid diagnosis of ovarian, adrenocortical, or testicular tumors
- To check the status of a fetus and the surrounding placenta.

What should you know before the test?

- The test requires collection of urine over a 24-hour period.
- You won't need to change your diet before the test.

HOW YOUR BODY WORKS

Changes in estrogen levels during the menstrual cycle

The quantity of total estrogens in the urine tells the doctor about the functioning of the ovaries. Estrogen excretion levels during a normal menstrual cycle show a major peak at midpoint in the cycle (ovulatory phase), and another smaller increase (luteal or premenstrual phase) just before menstruation starts.

Peaks in pregnancy

Urine estrogens rise slowly in the first trimester (3 months) of pregnancy, and then increase rapidly to reach high levels as term approaches. With menopause, the cyclical pattern fluctuates and eventually flattens out to a constant low level.

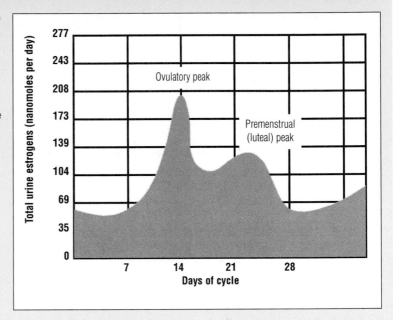

What happens during the test?

- You're asked to urinate into a special container over a 24-hour period.
- Void and discard the urine, and then begin 24-hour collection with the next voiding. After you place the first specimen in the container, add the preservative given to you by the nurse or medical technician.
- Add each voiding to the container immediately. If any urine is lost, restart the test.
- Plan the start of your test so that collection ends at a time when the lab is open.
- Just before the end of the test period, make an effort to void and add that urine to the container.
- Be sure not to contaminate the specimen with toilet paper or stools.
- If you're pregnant, the nurse will note the approximate week of development on the lab slip. If you're a nonpregnant woman, the nurse will note the stage of your menstrual cycle.

What happens after the test?

You can resume any medications withheld before the test.

What are the normal results?

In nonpregnant women, total urine estrogen levels rise and fall during the menstrual cycle, peaking shortly before midcycle, decreasing immediately following ovulation, increasing just before menstruation, and decreasing greatly as menstruation begins.

Normal values for nonpregnant women are as follows: preovulatory phase, 17 to 87 nanomoles per day; ovulatory phase, 83 to 347 nanomoles per day; shedding phase, 42 to 277 nanomoles per day. In postmenopausal women, values are less than 35 nanomoles per day. In men, values are from 14 to 87 nanomoles per day.

What do abnormal results mean?

Decreased total urine estrogen levels may reflect poor ovarian development, primary ovarian insufficiency (due to a flaw), or secondary ovarian insufficiency (due to pituitary or adrenal hypofunction or metabolic disturbances).

Elevated total estrogen levels in nonpregnant women may indicate tumors of ovarian or adrenocortical origin, adrenocortical hyperplasia, or a metabolic or liver disorder. In men, elevated total estrogen levels are associated with testicular tumors. Elevated total urine estrogen levels are normal during pregnancy.

PREGNANCY TEST

The human chorionic gonadotropin test determines whether a woman is pregnant or the status of her pregnancy. Also, the test functions as a screen for some types of cancer. Analysis of urine levels of human chorionic gonadotropin allows detection of pregnancy as early as 10 days after a missed menstrual period. Production of human chorionic gonadotropin begins after conception. During the first trimester (3 months), human chorionic gonadotropin levels increase steadily and rapidly, peaking around the tenth week of gestation and subsequently tapering off to less than 10% of peak levels.

Why is this test done?

The test for human chorionic gonadotropin may be performed for the following reasons:

- To detect and confirm pregnancy
- To aid diagnosis of a molar pregnancy or human chorionic gonadotropin-secreting tumors.

What should you know before the test?

- You won't need to change your diet before the test.
- The test uses your first urine voided in the morning or urine collection over a 24-hour period, depending on whether the doctor orders a test that is qualitative or quantitative.
- The nurse will ask about any medications that might affect human chorionic gonadotropin levels.

What happens during the test?

- For verification of pregnancy (qualitative analysis), you collect a first-voided morning specimen. If this isn't possible, collect a random specimen.
- For quantitative analysis of human chorionic gonadotropin, you're asked to urinate into a special container over a 24-hour period.
- Void and discard the urine, and then begin 24-hour collection with the next voiding.
- After you place the first specimen in the container, add the preservative given to you by the nurse or medical technician.
- Add each voiding to the container immediately. If any urine is lost, restart the test.
- Plan the start of your test so that collection ends at a time when the lab is open.
- Just before the end of the test period, make an effort to void and add that urine to the container.
- Be sure not to contaminate the specimen with toilet paper or stools.

What happens after the test?

You can resume any medications withheld during the test.

What are the normal results?

In qualitative analysis, if agglutination (a clumping of cells) fails to occur, test results are positive, indicating pregnancy. In quantitative

SELF-HELP

Over-the-counter pregnancy tests

You can get early confirmation of pregnancy through over-the-counter home pregnancy tests. These tests confirm pregnancy by detecting the presence of human chorionic gonadotropin in the urine.

Options and features

Several different kits are available. Some have a second test to use if levels of the hormone aren't immediately detectable. Each kit contains instructions for performing the test. It lists health conditions or drugs that may affect results. Remember that false-positive or false-negative results can occur. Many kits include toll-free numbers for questions about the kits or the results. Follow-up care with a doctor is recommended for all positive results.

analysis, urine human chorionic gonadotropin levels in the first trimester of a normal pregnancy may be as high as 500,000 international units per 24 hours. In the second trimester, they range from 10,000 to 25,000 international units per 24 hours, and in the third trimester, from 5,000 to 15,000 international units per 24 hours. After delivery, human chorionic gonadotropin levels decline rapidly and within a few days are undetectable.

Measurable human chorionic gonadotropin levels don't normally appear in the urine of men or nonpregnant women.

Besides lab testing, some home pregnancy test kits are also available. (See *Over-the-counter pregnancy tests,* page 571.)

What do abnormal results mean?

During pregnancy, elevated urine human chorionic gonadotropin levels may indicate multiple pregnancy or a fetus with a birth defect.

Depressed urine human chorionic gonadotropin levels may indicate threatened abortion or ectopic pregnancy.

Measurable levels of human chorionic gonadotropin in men and nonpregnant women may indicate some cancers, ovarian or testicular tumors, other tumors, or stomach, liver, pancreatic, or breast cancer.

> *To confirm that you're pregnant, collect the first urine of the morning for the test.*

PLACENTAL ESTRIOL

This test helps determine if a pregnant woman's placenta is functioning properly, which is essential to the health of the fetus. It measures urine levels of placental estriol, the predominant estrogen excreted in urine during pregnancy. A steady increase in estriol reflects a properly functioning placenta and, in most cases, a healthy, growing fetus.

Normally, estriol is secreted in much smaller amounts by the ovaries in nonpregnant women, by the testes in men, and by the adrenal cortex in both sexes.

Why is this test done?

The test for placental estriol is performed to check the status of the fetus and the placenta, especially in a high-risk pregnancy, such as one complicated by the mother's high blood pressure, diabetes, preeclampsia, toxemia, or a history of stillbirth.

What should you know before the test?

- You won't need to change your diet before the test.
- This test requires urine collection over a 24-hour period.
- The nurse will ask about any medications that might affect the test and may tell you to discontinue them.

What happens during the test?

- You're asked to urinate into a special container over a 24-hour period.
- Void and discard the urine, and then begin 24-hour collection with the next voiding.
- After you place the first specimen in the container, add the preservative given to you by the nurse or medical technician.
- Add each voiding to the container immediately. If any urine is lost, restart the test.
- Plan the start of your test so that collection ends at a time when the lab is open.
- Just before the end of the test period, make an effort to void and add that urine to the container.
- Be sure not to contaminate the specimen with toilet paper or stools.

What happens after the test?

You can resume any medications withheld during the test.

What are the normal results?

Normal values vary considerably, but a series of measurements of urine estriol levels taken during the pregnancy, when plotted on a graph, should describe a steadily rising curve. (See *Changes in estriol levels during pregnancy,* page 574.)

What do abnormal results mean?

A 40% drop from baseline values that shows up on 2 consecutive days strongly suggests the placenta isn't functioning well and the fetus will be in distress. A 20% drop over 2 weeks or failure of consecutive estriol levels to increase in a normal curve also shows a problem. These developments may require a cesarean section, depending on the mother's condition and other apparent signs of fetal distress.

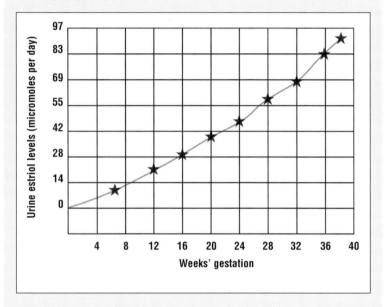

 HOW YOUR BODY WORKS

Changes in estriol levels during pregnancy

Levels of estriol in urine rise during the course of pregnancy, as shown in the graph below. Over a period of days, any significant changes in results during a series of lab tests may suggest abnormal conditions that require prompt medical care.

A check for birth defects

A chronically low urine estriol curve may be caused by fetal adrenal insufficiency, major birth defects, blood Rh-factor problems, or a placental sulfatase deficiency. Or, a high estriol level may simply indicate twins.

A high-risk pregnancy in which the mother's kidney function decreases may cause a low-normal estriol curve. Such a pregnancy may occur in a woman with high blood pressure or diabetes, for example. The pregnancy may continue, as long as no complications develop and estriol levels continue to increase.

PREGNANETRIOL

This test helps to evaluate the body's secretion of hormones. It checks urine levels of pregnanetriol, which is normally excreted in the urine in minute amounts. Elevated urine pregnanetriol levels suggest adrenogenital syndrome, a condition marked by excessive adrenal gland secretion of androgen. This condition may cause problems in the development of sexual characteristics.

Why is this test done?

The test for pregnanetriol may be performed for the following reasons:
- To aid the diagnosis of adrenogenital syndrome
- To monitor some types of hormone replacement therapy.

What should you know before the test?

You won't need to change your diet before the test.

What happens during the test?

- You're asked to urinate into a special container over a 24-hour period.
- Void and discard the urine, and then begin 24-hour collection with the next voiding.
- After you place the first specimen in the container, add the preservative given to you by the nurse or medical technician.
- Add each voiding to the container immediately. If any urine is lost, restart the test.
- Plan the start of your test so that collection ends at a time when the lab is open.
- Just before the end of the test period, make an effort to void and add that urine to the container.
- Be sure not to contaminate the specimen with toilet paper or stools.

What are the normal results?

The normal rate of pregnanetriol excretion is as follows:
- Adults: less than 10.4 micromoles per day
- Children ages 7 to 16: 0.9 to 3.3 micromoles per day
- Children younger than age 6 (including infants): up to 0.6 micromole per day.

Too much pregnanetriol at birth may cause changes in a child's physical and sexual development.

What do abnormal results mean?

Elevated urine pregnanetriol levels suggest adrenogenital syndrome, a condition marked by excessive adrenal gland secretion of androgen. Females with this condition fail to develop normal breasts or genitalia and show marked masculinization of external genitalia at birth. Males usually appear normal at birth but later develop signs of premature physical and sexual development.

VANILLYLMANDELIC ACID

This test evaluates the urine levels of vanillylmandelic acid, a metabolite that's normally most prevalent in the urine. Vanillylmandelic acid levels in the urine reflect production of major catecholamines (adrenal gland secretions) and help to detect catecholamine-secreting tumors — for example, a tumor called a *pheochromocytoma*. They also help evaluate the function of the adrenal medulla, the primary site of catecholamine production.

Why is this test done?

The test for vanillylmandelic acid may be performed for the following reasons:

- To help detect pheochromocytoma (a tumor), neuroblastoma (a malignant soft-tissue tumor that develops in infants and young children), or ganglioneuroma (a tumor of the sympathetic nervous system that develops in older children and adolescents and rarely spreads)
- To evaluate the function of the adrenal medulla.

What should you know before the test?

- You'll have to restrict foods and beverages containing phenolic acid, such as coffee, tea, bananas, citrus fruits, chocolate, and vanilla, for 3 days before the test.
- Avoid stressful situations and excessive physical activity during the urine collection period.
- The nurse will ask about medications that may affect the test.

What happens during the test?

- You're asked to urinate into a special container over a 24-hour period.
- Void and discard the urine, and then begin 24-hour collection with the next voiding.
- After you place the first specimen in the container, add the preservative given to you by the nurse or medical technician.
- Add each voiding to the container immediately. If any urine is lost, restart the test.
- Plan the start of your test so that collection ends at a time when the lab is open.
- Just before the end of the test period, make an effort to void and add that urine to the container.
- Be sure not to contaminate the specimen with toilet paper or stools.

What happens after the test?

- You can resume any medications withheld before the test.
- You may resume your normal diet and activities.

What are the normal results?

Normally, urine vanillylmandelic acid values range from 3.5 to 34.3 micromoles per day.

What do abnormal results mean?

Elevated urine vanillylmandelic acid levels may result from a catecholamine-secreting tumor. The doctor may find that more testing is necessary for a precise diagnosis.

> *Certain foods and situations affect the test results, including stressful situations and excessive physical activity.*

HOMOVANILLIC ACID

This test measures urine levels of homovanillic acid, which is a metabolite of dopamine, one of the three major catecholamines (hormones secreted by the adrenal gland). Synthesized primarily in the brain, dopamine is a precursor to epinephrine and norepinephrine, the other principal catecholamines. The liver breaks down most dopamine into homovanillic acid for eventual excretion; a minimal amount of dopamine appears in the urine.

Why is this test done?

The test for homovanillic acid may be performed for the following reasons:

- To aid the diagnosis of neuroblastoma, a malignant soft-tissue tumor that develops in infants and young children, and ganglioneuroma, a tumor of the sympathetic nervous system that develops in older children and adolescents and rarely spreads
- To rule out the diagnosis of pheochromocytoma, a tumor.

What should you know before the test?

- You won't need to change your diet before the test, but avoid stressful situations and excessive physical exercise during the collection period.
- The nurse will ask about any medications that might affect the test and then notify the doctor, who may want you to stop these medications before the test.

What happens during the test?

- You're asked to urinate into a special container over a 24-hour period.
- Void and discard the urine, and then begin 24-hour collection with the next voiding.
- After you place the first specimen in the container, add the preservative given to you by the nurse or medical technician.
- Add each voiding to the container immediately. If any urine is lost, restart the test.
- Plan the start of your test so that collection ends at a time when the lab is open.
- Just before the end of the test period, make an effort to void and add that urine to the container.
- Be sure not to contaminate the specimen with toilet paper or stools.

What happens after the test?

- You can resume taking any medications withheld before the test.
- You may resume activity restricted during the test.

What are the normal results?

Normally, the urine homovanillic acid value for adults is less than 8 milligrams per 24 hours. The range of normal urine homovanillic acid values in children varies with age.

What do abnormal results mean?

Elevated urine homovanillic acid levels suggest neuroblastoma, a malignant tumor of soft-tissues that occurs in infants and young children, or ganglioneuroma, a tumor of the sympathetic nervous system that occurs in older children and adolescents and rarely affects other body systems. Homovanillic acid levels don't usually increase in people with pheochromocytoma because this tumor secretes mainly epinephrine, which metabolizes primarily into vanillylmandelic acid. Thus, an abnormally high urine homovanillic acid level generally rules out pheochromocytoma.

HYDROXYINDOLEACETIC ACID

The analysis of urine levels of 5-hydroxyindoleacetic acid is used mainly to screen for carcinoid tumors (called *argentaffinomas*). Such tumors, found generally in the intestine or appendix, secrete an excessive amount of serotonin, which is reflected by high 5-hydroxyindoleacetic acid levels. (See *Where serotonin comes from,* page 580.)

Why is this test done?

The test for 5-hydroxyindoleacetic acid may be performed to aid diagnosis of argentaffinomas.

What should you know before the test?

- You'll be told not to eat foods containing serotonin, such as bananas, plums, pineapples, avocados, eggplants, tomatoes, or walnuts, for 4 days before the test.
- The nurse will ask about your recent use of drugs that may affect test results. The doctor may want you to discontinue their use.

What happens during the test?

- You're asked to urinate into a special container over a 24-hour period.
- Void and discard the urine, and then begin 24-hour collection with the next voiding.
- After you place the first specimen in the container, add the preservative given to you by the nurse or medical technician.
- Add each voiding to the container immediately. If any urine is lost, restart the test.

Four days before the test, you'll have to give up certain foods, including bananas, avocados, tomatoes, and walnuts.

INSIGHT INTO ILLNESS

Where serotonin comes from

The illustration below shows a microscopic view of the lining of the small intestine. Argentaffin cells in the crypts of Lieberkühn are located in the indentations between the villi in the mucous membrane of the small intestine. These cells produce serotonin. The serotonin metabolizes into 5-hydroxyindoleacetic acid. High levels of this acid in the urine can signal the presence of serotonin-secreting argentaffinomas, a type of carcinoid tumor.

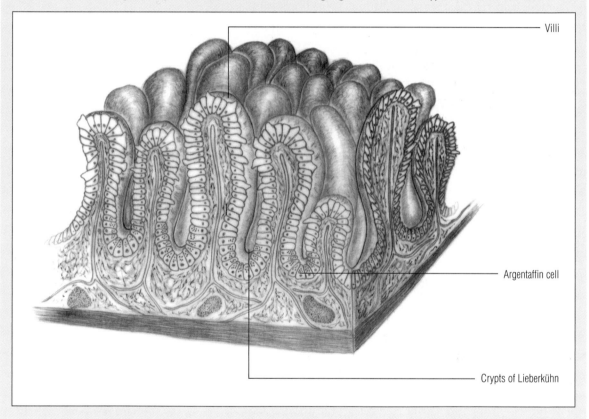

Villi

Argentaffin cell

Crypts of Lieberkühn

- Plan the start of your test so that collection ends at a time when the lab is open.
- Just before the end of the test period, make an effort to void and add that urine to the container.
- Be sure not to contaminate the specimen with toilet paper or stools.

What happens after the test?

You can resume your normal diet and any medications withheld before the test.

What are the normal results?

Normally, urine 5-hydroxyindoleacetic acid values are less than 31 micromoles per day.

What do abnormal results mean?

Marked elevation of urine 5-hydroxyindoleacetic acid levels, possibly as high as 1,046 to 3,138 micromoles per day, indicates a carcinoid tumor. However, because these tumors vary in their capacity to store and secrete serotonin, some people with carcinoid syndrome (spreading carcinoid tumors) may not show elevated levels.

Repeated testing is often necessary.

PREGNANEDIOL

When evaluating placental or ovarian function, the doctor may order a urine test that measures levels of pregnanediol, the chief metabolite of progesterone. The amount of pregnanediol in the urine provides information about production of its parent hormone, progesterone.

Progesterone is produced in nonpregnant women by the uterine lining during the latter half of each menstrual cycle, preparing the uterus for implantation of a fertilized egg. If implantation doesn't occur, progesterone secretion drops sharply. If implantation does occur, the uterine lining secretes more progesterone to further prepare the uterus for pregnancy and to begin development of the placenta. Toward the end of the first trimester (3 months), the placenta becomes the primary source of progesterone secretion, producing the progressively larger amounts needed to maintain pregnancy.

Why is this test done?

The test for pregnanediol may be performed for the following reasons:
- To evaluate placental function in pregnant women
- To evaluate ovarian function in nonpregnant women.

What should you know before the test?

- You won't need to change your diet before the test.
- If you're pregnant, this test may be repeated several times to get a sequence of measurements.
- The nurse will ask about medications that might affect the test.

What happens during the test?

- You're asked to urinate into a special container over a 24-hour period.
- Void and discard the urine, and then begin 24-hour collection with the next voiding.
- After you place the first specimen in the container, add the preservative given to you by the nurse or medical technician.
- Add each voiding to the container immediately. If any urine is lost, restart the test.
- Plan the start of your test so that collection ends at a time when the lab is open.
- Just before the end of the test period, make an effort to void and add that urine to the container.
- Be sure not to contaminate the specimen with toilet paper or stools.

What are the normal results?

In nonpregnant women, urine pregnanediol values normally range from 1.6 to 4.7 micromoles per day during the proliferative phase of the menstrual cycle. Within 24 hours after ovulation, pregnanediol levels begin to increase and continue to rise for 3 to 10 days as the uterus lining develops. During this phase, normal urine pregnanediol values range from 6.2 to 21.8 micromoles per day. In the absence of fertilization, levels drop sharply as the uterus lining degenerates and menstruation begins.

During pregnancy, urine pregnanediol levels increase markedly, peaking around the 36th week of gestation and returning to pre-pregnancy levels by between 5 and 10 days after childbirth. Normal postmenopausal values range from 0.6 to 3.1 micromoles per day. In males, urine pregnanediol levels rarely rise above 4.7 micromoles per day.

What do abnormal results mean?

During pregnancy, a decrease in urine pregnanediol levels may indicate placental insufficiency and requires immediate investigation. A

Low urine pregnanediol levels in nonpregnant women may indicate stopped ovulation, stopped menstruation, or other menstrual problems.

sharp drop in pregnanediol values may suggest fetal distress — for example, threatened abortion or fetal death. However, pregnanediol measurements are not reliable indicators of fetal viability because levels can remain normal even after fetal death, as long as the mother's circulation to the placenta remains adequate.

In nonpregnant women, abnormally low urine pregnanediol levels may occur with stopped ovulation, stopped menstruation, or other menstrual abnormalities. Elevations may indicate some types of tumors or ovarian cancer that's spreading to other parts of the body. Adrenal gland problems or bile duct obstruction may raise urine pregnanediol values in men or women. Some forms of primary liver disease produce abnormally low levels in both sexes.

PROTEINS & SUGARS

URINARY PROTEINS

This test detects proteins in your urine. Normally, the kidneys allow only proteins of low molecular weight to enter the filtrate. The kidneys' tubules then reabsorb most of these proteins. A damaged kidney allows excretion of proteins in the urine. (See *The first step in urine formation,* page 584.) A qualitative screening often precedes this test. A positive result requires quantitative analysis of a 24-hour urine specimen.

Why is this test done?
The test for proteins may be performed to aid diagnosis of illnesses marked by protein in the urine, primarily kidney disease.

What should you know before the test?
- You won't need to change your diet before the test.
- The test usually requires urine collection over a 24-hour period.
- The nurse will ask about medications that might affect the test. The doctor may want to restrict them before the test.

What happens during the test?

- You're asked to urinate into a special container over a 24-hour period.
- Void and discard the urine, and then begin 24-hour collection with the next voiding.
- After you place the first specimen in the container, add the preservative given to you by the nurse or medical technician.
- Add each voiding to the container immediately. If any urine is lost, restart the test.
- Plan the start of your test so that collection ends at a time when the lab is open.
- Just before the end of the test period, make an effort to void and add that urine to the container.
- Be sure not to contaminate the specimen with toilet paper or stools.

What happens after the test?

You can resume any medications withheld before the test.

What are the normal results?

Normal values show up to 0.15 gram of protein excreted in a day.

What do abnormal results mean?

Protein in the urine is a chief characteristic of kidney disease. When protein shows up in a single specimen, 24-hour urine collection is required to identify specific kidney problems.

What are the subtle differences?

Slight changes in the amount of protein in the urine suggest the following disorders:

- Persistent protein: kidney disease caused by increased glomerular permeability
- Minimal protein in the urine (less than 0.5 gram per 24 hours): kidney diseases in which glomerular involvement is not a major factor, such as chronic pyelonephritis
- Moderate protein (0.5 to 4 grams per 24 hours): kidney diseases, such as acute or chronic glomerulonephritis, amyloidosis, toxic nephropathies — or in diseases in which kidney failure often develops as a late complication (diabetes or heart failure, for example)
- Heavy proteinuria (more than 4 grams per 24 hours): nephrotic syndrome

■ Protein in the urine plus elevated white blood cell count: urinary tract infection

■ Protein and blood in the urine: local or diffuse urinary tract disorders. Other disorders (infections and lesions of the central nervous system, for example) can also cause detectable amounts of protein in the urine.

Some drugs damage the kidneys, causing protein in the urine. This makes the routine evaluation of urine proteins essential during these drug treatments.

Not all forms of protein in the urine have health significance; some can be caused by changes in body position. Others are linked to exercise, as well as emotional or physiologic stress, and are usually short-term.

BENCE JONES PROTEIN

This test can detect an abnormal protein in the urine. Bence Jones proteins are abnormal immunoglobulins that appear in the urine of 50% to 80% of people with multiple myeloma and in most people with a disorder called *Waldenström's macroglobulinemia.*

Screening tests, such as blood coagulation by heat and one called *Bradshaw's test,* can detect Bence Jones proteins, but urine testing is usually the doctor's choice. Both urine and blood studies are frequently used for people who may have multiple myeloma.

Why is this test done?

The Bence Jones protein test may be performed to confirm the presence of multiple myeloma in people with symptoms such as bone pain (especially in the back and thorax) and persistent anemia and fatigue.

What should you know before the test?

The test requires an early-morning urine specimen; the nurse will teach you how to collect a clean-catch specimen. (See *How to catch a midstream specimen,* page 586.)

SELF-HELP

How to catch a midstream specimen

To minimize contamination by organisms outside your urinary tract, you must get what is called a *clean-catch, midstream specimen*. To collect this specimen, follow the instructions below.

Procedure for women

- If you're menstruating, inform the doctor. He or she may want to postpone the test to avoid contamination. Or, insert a tampon to protect the specimen.
- Kneel or squat over a bedpan or straddle the toilet bowl to separate the folds of skin that cover the urinary opening.
- Separate the labia with your thumb and forefinger and clean the area around the urinary opening with three antiseptic-moistened swabs: one for each side of the opening and the third for the opening itself. Wipe with a front-to-back motion. Use another swab to dry.
- Begin voiding, and without interrupting the flow, catch about 1 ounce (30 milliliters) of urine in a sterile specimen container.

- Replace the lid of the specimen container. If you're not going to the lab immediately, refrigerate the specimen.

Procedure for men

- Be sure your bladder is full. This minimizes the risk of contamination by prostatic fluid.
- Retract your foreskin and clean the tip of your penis with an antiseptic-moistened swab, wiping in a circular motion away from the urinary opening. Use another swab to dry.
- Begin voiding into a toilet and, without interrupting the flow, catch about 1 ounce (30 milliliters) of urine in a sterile specimen container.

What happens during the test?

- You're asked to provide an early-morning urine specimen of at least 50 milliliters.
- Be careful not to contaminate the urine specimen with toilet tissue or stools.

What are the normal results?

Normal urine should contain no Bence Jones proteins.

What do abnormal results mean?

The presence of Bence Jones proteins in urine suggests multiple myeloma or Waldenström's macroglobulinemia. Very low levels, in the absence of other symptoms, may be benign.

AMINO ACID DISORDERS SCREEN

This test uses chromatography to help detect amino acid disorders. Abnormal metabolism may cause an excess of one or more amino acids to appear in blood and, as the kidneys' processing capacity is exceeded, in urine. Two types of amino acid disorders are primary (overflow) and secondary (kidney).

To screen newborns, children, and adults for inherited amino acid disorders, the doctor may use blood or urine specimens. The blood test is better for the overflow type. Urine is used to monitor certain disorders and to screen for the kidney type.

Testing for specific amino acid levels is also necessary for infants or young children with acidosis, severe vomiting and diarrhea, and abnormal urine odor. Such testing is especially important in newborns because an early diagnosis and prompt treatment of amino acid problems may prevent mental retardation.

Why is this test done?

The test for amino acids may be performed for the following reasons:
- To screen for kidney amino acid problems
- To follow up on blood-test findings when results of these tests suggest overflow amino acid problems.

What should you know before the test?

- You or your child won't need to change your diet before the test.
- The test requires a urine specimen.
- The nurse will ask about medications that might interfere with the test. (If the test is for your breast-fed infant, the nurse will ask about any drugs you're taking.)

What happens during the test?

- You're asked to urinate into a special container.
- Be sure not to contaminate the specimen with toilet paper or stools.
- If the test is for your infant, the nurse teaches you how to apply and use a pediatric urine collector.

What are the normal results?

Patterns on thin-layer chromatography are reported as normal.

What do abnormal results mean?

If thin-layer chromatography shows gross changes or abnormal patterns, blood and 24-hour urine tests are performed to identify specific amino acid abnormalities and to differentiate overflow and kidney amino acid problems.

CREATININE

This test helps evaluate your kidney function by measuring urine levels of a substance called *creatinine*. The body produces this substance in proportion to total body muscle mass. Creatinine is removed from the blood primarily by the kidneys and is excreted in the urine. Because the body doesn't recycle it, creatinine has a relatively high, constant clearance rate, making it an efficient indicator of kidney function.

Your body produces creatinine in proportion to your muscle mass and excretes it steadily in urine.

Why is this test done?

The test for creatinine is performed to help assess kidney function.

What should you know before the test?

- You won't need to restrict fluids, but you should not eat an excessive amount of meat before the test.
- You should avoid strenuous physical exercise during the collection period.
- The test usually requires urine collection over a 24-hour period.
- The nurse may ask you about medications that could interfere with the test. The doctor may restrict such drugs before the test.

What happens during the test?

- You're asked to urinate into a special container over a 24-hour period.
- Void and discard the urine, and then begin 24-hour collection with the next voiding.
- After you place the first specimen in the container, add the preservative given to you by the nurse or medical technician.
- Add each voiding to the container immediately. If any urine is lost, restart the test.

■ Plan the start of your test so that collection ends at a time when the lab is open.

■ Just before the end of the test period, make an effort to void and add that urine to the container.

■ Be sure not to contaminate the specimen with toilet paper or stools.

What happens after the test?

■ You can resume any medications withheld during the test.

■ You may resume normal diet and activity.

What are the normal results?

Normally, urine creatinine levels range from 8.8 to 16.8 millimoles per day for men and from 7 to 15 millimoles per day for women.

What do abnormal results mean?

Decreased urine creatinine levels may be caused by impaired kidney activity (associated with shock, for example) or from kidney disease due to urinary tract obstruction or other diseases. Increased levels generally have little diagnostic significance.

CREATININE CLEARANCE BY THE KIDNEYS

This test evaluates kidney function by measuring how efficiently the kidneys are clearing a substance called *creatinine* from the blood. The rate of clearance is expressed in terms of the volume of blood (in milliliters) that can be cleared of creatinine in 1 minute. Creatinine levels become abnormal when the kidneys sustain substantial damage.

Why is this test done?

The creatinine clearance test may be performed for the following reasons:

■ To check kidney function (primarily glomerular filtration)

■ To monitor progression of kidney failure.

What should you know before the test?

■ The test requires a timed urine specimen and at least one blood sample. A timed urine specimen can be taken over 2, 12, or 24 hours.

■ You won't need to change your diet before the test, but you should not eat an excessive amount of meat before the test.

■ You should avoid strenuous physical exercise during the urine collection period.

■ The nurse will ask about any medications that may interfere with the test.

What happens during the test?

■ You're asked to urinate into a special container over a prescribed period.

■ Void and discard the urine, and then begin collection with the next voiding.

■ After you place the first specimen in the container, add the preservative given to you by the nurse or medical technician.

■ Add each voiding to the container immediately. If any urine is lost, restart the test.

■ Plan the start of your test so that collection ends at a time when the lab is open.

■ Just before the end of the test period, make an effort to void and add that urine to the container.

■ Be sure not to contaminate the specimen with toilet paper or stools.

■ For the blood sample, a nurse or medical technician inserts a needle into a vein, usually in your forearm. A blood sample is collected in a tube, which is then sent to a lab for testing.

■ Although you may feel a sting from the needle and pressure from the tourniquet, collecting the sample takes only a few minutes.

What happens after the test?

■ You may resume any medications withheld before the test.

■ You may resume normal diet and activity.

■ If swelling develops at the needle puncture site, apply warm soaks.

What are the normal results?

For men, normal creatinine clearance ranges from 1.4 to 2.1 milliliters per second. For women, it ranges from 1.3 to 1.9 milliliters per second. For older people, creatinine clearance normally decreases by 0.1 milliliter per second for each decade.

What do abnormal results mean?

Low creatinine clearance may be caused by reduced kidney blood flow (associated with shock or kidney artery obstruction) or a long list of kidney disorders. It also may suggest congestive heart failure or severe dehydration.

High creatinine clearance rates generally have little diagnostic significance.

UREA CLEARANCE BY THE KIDNEYS

This test evaluates your kidney function by analyzing urine levels of urea, the main nitrogenous component in urine and the end product of protein metabolism. It's most useful for assessing overall kidney function. (See *Getting rid of urea,* page 592.)

Why is this test done?

The urea clearance test is performed to check your total kidney function.

What should you know before the test?

- The test requires two timed urine specimens and one blood sample.
- You must fast from midnight before the test and abstain from exercise before and during the test.
- The nurse will ask about any medications that might interfere with the test.

What happens during the test?

- For the blood test, a nurse or medical technician inserts a needle into a vein, usually in your forearm. A blood sample is collected in a tube, which is then sent to a lab for testing.
- Although you may feel a sting from the needle and pressure from the tourniquet, collecting the sample takes only a few minutes.
- For the urine sample, you first empty your bladder and discard the urine.
- You drink water to ensure adequate urine output.
- Collect two specimens 1 hour apart, and mark the collection time on the lab slip.

HOW YOUR BODY WORKS

Getting rid of urea

When the body has taken everything useful out of the proteins it has received, all that's left is a toxic ammonia-containing waste called *urea*, which must be disposed of quickly.

It starts with the liver...

Amino acids absorbed from proteins by the intestine pass into the liver. Since the liver stores only small amounts of these amino acids — which are later returned to the blood to make enzymes, hormones, or new protoplasm — the liver converts the leftovers into other substances, such as glucose, glycogen, or fat. Before this conversion, the amino acids lose their nitrogen-containing amino groups. The amino groups are then converted to ammonia. The ammonia then combines with carbon dioxide to form urea, which is released into the blood and flows to the kidneys.

...And ends with the kidneys

The kidneys are the last station in urea's journey outside the body. Because the ammonia contained in urea is very toxic, especially to the brain, it must be removed as quickly as it's formed. (Serious liver disease causes elevated blood ammonia levels and eventually leads to coma.)

What happens after the test?

- You can resume any medications withheld before the test.
- You may resume normal diet and activity.

What are the normal results?

Normally, the urea clearance rate ranges from 64 to 99 milliliters per minute, with maximum clearance. If the flow rate is less than 2 milliliters per minute, normal clearance is 41 to 68 milliliters per minute.

What do abnormal results mean?

Low urea clearance values may indicate decreased kidney blood flow (due to shock or kidney artery obstruction), a long list of other kidney disorders, congestive heart failure, or dehydration. High urea clearance usually is not diagnostically significant.

URIC ACID

This test measures your body's production and excretion of a waste product known as *uric acid*. The analysis of uric acid levels in urine may supplement blood uric acid testing when the doctor is working to identify disorders that alter production or excretion of uric acid (such as leukemia, gout, and kidney dysfunction).

Why is this test done?

The uric acid test may be performed for the following reasons:
- To detect enzyme deficiencies and metabolic disturbances that affect uric acid production
- To help measure the efficiency of the kidney.

What should you know before the test?

- You won't need to change your diet before the test.
- The nurse will ask about any medications you take that may interfere with the test.

What happens during the test?

- You're asked to urinate into a special container over a 24-hour period.
- Void and discard the urine, and then begin 24-hour collection with the next voiding.
- After you place the first specimen in the container, add the preservative given to you by the nurse or medical technician.
- Add each voiding to the container immediately. If any urine is lost, restart the test.
- Plan the start of your test so that collection ends at a time when the lab is open.
- Just before the end of the test period, make an effort to void and add that urine to the container.
- Be sure not to contaminate the specimen with toilet paper or stools.

What happens after the test?

You can resume any medications withheld before the test.

What are the normal results?

Normal urine uric acid values vary with diet, but generally range from 250 to 750 milligrams per 24 hours.

What do abnormal results mean?

Elevated urine uric acid levels may be caused by such problems as blood disorders, multiple tumors or, in one case of good news, early remission in pernicious anemia.

Low urine uric acid levels show up in gout (when there's normal uric acid production but inadequate excretion) and in severe kidney damage.

HEMOGLOBIN

This test checks urine for hemoglobin, the protein that gives blood its color. Its presence in urine is an abnormal finding. It indicates excessive red blood cell destruction. It may be related to some kinds of anemia, infection, strenuous exercise, or severe effects of a transfusion reaction.

When red blood cell destruction occurs within the circulation, free hemoglobin enters the plasma and binds with a material called *haptoglobin*. If hemoglobin levels exceed haptoglobin levels, the excess of unbound hemoglobin is excreted in the urine.

Why is this test done?

The test for hemoglobin may be performed to aid the diagnosis of some anemias, infection, or severe effects of transfusion reaction.

What should you know before the test?

- You won't need to change your diet before the test.
- The test requires a random urine specimen.
- Because contamination of the specimen with menstrual blood alters results, a woman who's menstruating should reschedule her test.
- You should be careful not to contaminate the specimen with toilet paper or stools.
- The nurse will ask about any medications that might affect the test.

What happens during the test?

You're asked to urinate once into a special container.

What happens after the test?

You can resume any medications withheld during the test.

What are the normal results?

Normally, hemoglobin is not present in urine.

What do abnormal results mean?

Hemoglobin in the urine may be caused by severe blood breakdown in the veins, due to a blood transfusion reaction, burns, or a crushing injury. It may be caused by acquired anemias caused by chemical or drug intoxication or malaria. Other causes include inherited anemias, such as enzyme defects and, less commonly, it may signal cystitis or ureteral stones or infection. Hemoglobin and blood in the urine also show up in kidney damage, which may be caused by acute glomerulonephritis or pyelonephritis, kidney tumor, and tuberculosis.

MYOGLOBIN

This test helps evaluate muscle injury or disease by detecting a red pigment called *myoglobin* in the urine.

Myoglobin is normally found in muscle cells. When muscle cells are extensively damaged, myoglobin gets into the blood and then quickly into the urine. The damage may be due to disease or a severe crushing injury. For example, myoglobin appears in the urine within 24 hours after a heart attack.

Why is this test done?

The test for myoglobin may be performed for the following reasons:

- To help the doctor diagnose muscle disease
- To detect extensive injury to muscle tissue
- To measure the extent of muscle damage from crushing injuries.

What should you know before the test?

- You won't need to change your diet before the test.
- The test requires a random urine specimen.
- Test results are generally available in 1 day.

What happens during the test?

You're asked to urinate once into a special container.

What are the normal results?

Normally, myoglobin does not appear in urine.

What do abnormal results mean?

Myoglobin in the urine is a sign of acute or chronic muscle disease, alcoholic muscle damage, an extensive heart attack, or simply a family trait. Myoglobin can appear after such traumas as a crushing injury, extreme hyperthermia, or severe burns. It also appears after strenuous or prolonged exercise, but disappears after rest.

PORPHYRINS

This test detects abnormal hemoglobin formation by checking the urine for substances called *porphyrins*. The test counts specific porphyrins (uroporphyrins and coproporphyrins) and their precursors (such as porphobilinogen). Porphyrins are red-orange, fluorescent compounds that are produced when the body creates heme, which is part of hemoglobin.

Porphyrins are present in all of the body's protoplasm, take part in energy storage and utilization, and are normally excreted in urine in small amounts. Elevated urine levels of porphyrins or porphyrinogens reflect impaired heme creation. That problem may be caused by inherited enzyme deficiencies (congenital porphyrias) or by disorders such as hemolytic anemias and liver disease (acquired porphyrias).

Porphyrins are present in all of the body's protoplasm, helping with energy storage and utilization.

Why is this test done?

The test for porphyrins may be performed to aid diagnosis of inherited or acquired porphyrias.

What should you know before the test?

- You won't need to change your diet before the test.
- If you're a pregnant or menstruating woman, you may want to reschedule the test to avoid making it less accurate.
- The nurse will ask about any medications that might interfere with test results. The doctor may reschedule the test or restrict drugs before the test.

What happens during the test?

- You're asked to urinate into a special container over a 24-hour period.
- Void and discard that urine, and then begin 24-hour collection with the next voiding.
- After you place the first specimen in the container, add the preservative given to you by the nurse or medical technician.
- Add each voiding to the container immediately. If any urine is lost, restart the test.
- Plan the start of your test so that collection ends at a time when the lab is open.

■ Just before the end of the test period, make an effort to void and add that urine to the container.

What happens after the test?

You may resume any medications withheld during the test.

What are the normal results?

Normal porphyrin and precursor values for urine occur in the following ranges:

■ Uroporphyrins: in women, 1.2 to 26.5 nanomoles per day; in men, undetectable to 50.5 nanomoles per day

■ Coproporphyrins: in women, 1.6 to 89 nanomoles per day; in men, undetectable to 151 nanomoles per day

■ Porphobilinogen: in both sexes, up to 6.63 micromoles per day.

What do abnormal results mean?

Increased urine levels of porphyrins and porphyrin precursors are characteristic of porphyria. Infectious hepatitis, Hodgkin's disease, central nervous system disorders, cirrhosis, and heavy metal, benzene, or carbon tetrachloride poisoning may also increase porphyrin levels.

DELTA-AMINOLEVULINIC ACID

A test called the *delta-aminolevulinic acid test* may be performed to help diagnose porphyrias, liver disease, and lead poisoning.

Why is this test done?

The test may be performed for the following reasons:

■ To screen for lead poisoning

■ To help the doctor diagnose porphyrias and certain liver disorders, such as hepatitis and liver cancer.

What should you know before the test?

■ If you or your child is having the test, you won't need to change your diet beforehand.

■ The nurse will ask about any medications that might interfere with test results. The doctor may reschedule the test or restrict drugs before the test.

What happens during the test?

■ You're asked to urinate into a special container over a 24-hour period.
■ Void once and discard the urine, and then begin 24-hour collection with the next voiding.
■ After you collect the first specimen in the container, add the preservative given to you by the nurse or medical technician.
■ Add each urine specimen to the container immediately. If any urine is lost, restart the test.
■ Plan the start of your test so that collection ends at a time when the lab is open.
■ Just before the end of the test period, make an effort to void and add that urine to the container.

What happens after the test?

The doctor will resume administration of medications withheld during the test.

What are the normal results?

Normally, urine delta-aminolevulinic acid values range from 11 to 57 micromoles per deciliter per 24 hours.

What do abnormal results mean?

Elevated urine delta-aminolevulinic acid levels may occur in lead poisoning, acute porphyria, hepatic carcinoma, or hepatitis.

Doctors can use this urine test to diagnose lead poisoning in children.

BILIRUBIN

This test helps determine the cause of jaundice. It's a screening test that detects water-soluble bilirubin in the urine. Detectable amounts of bilirubin may indicate liver disease caused by infections, bile-duct disease, or a toxic condition.

When combined with urobilinogen measurements, this test helps identify disorders that can cause jaundice. The analysis can be performed in the lab or at a person's bedside using a chemically treated strip.

Why is this test done?

The test for bilirubin may be performed to help the doctor identify the cause of jaundice.

What should you know before the test?

- You won't need to change your diet before the test.
- You'll be told that the test requires a random urine specimen.
- You'll be told that the specimen will be tested at bedside or in the lab. Bedside analysis can be performed immediately. Lab analysis is completed in 1 day.

What happens during the test?

You're asked to urinate once directly into a special container.

What are the normal results?

Normally, bilirubin is not found in urine in a routine screening test.

What do abnormal results mean?

High concentrations of direct bilirubin in urine may be evident from the specimen's appearance (dark, with a yellow foam). To diagnose jaundice, however, the doctor will correlate the bilirubin in urine with blood test results and with urine and fecal urobilinogen levels.

A nurse may quickly check out the cause of your jaundice with a bedside test, using a chemically treated strip.

UROBILINOGEN

This test helps check your liver and biliary tract function by measuring urine levels of urobilinogen. Urobilinogen is a colorless, water-soluble product that results from the reduction of bilirubin by intestinal bacteria. Absent or altered urobilinogen levels can indicate liver damage or dysfunction. Increased urine urobilinogen may indicate destruction of red blood cells. The urine sample is mixed with a chemical and the lab technician uses a microscope to watch a color reaction.

Why is this test done?

The test for urobilinogen may be performed for the following reasons:

■ To aid the diagnosis of obstructions outside the liver such as blockage of the common bile duct

■ To help diagnose liver and blood disorders.

What should you know before the test?

You won't need to change your diet except to avoid eating bananas for 48 hours before the test.

What happens during the test?

■ You're asked to urinate into a special container over a 2-hour period.

■ Void and discard the urine, and then begin 2-hour collection with the next voiding.

■ After you place the first specimen in the container, add any preservative given to you by the nurse or medical technician.

■ Add each voiding to the container immediately. If any urine is lost, restart the test.

■ Plan the start of your test so that collection ends at a time when the lab is open.

■ Just before the end of the test period, make an effort to void and add that urine to the container.

What happens after the test?

■ You may resume your normal diet.

■ You may resume any drugs withheld during the test.

What are the normal results?

Normally, urine urobilinogen values range from 0.08 to 4.2 micromoles per day in women and 0.2 to 8.5 micromoles per day in men.

What do abnormal results mean?

Absence of urine urobilinogen may be caused by complete obstructive jaundice or by broad-spectrum antibiotics, which destroy the intestinal bacterial flora. Low urine urobilinogen levels may be caused by congenital enzymatic jaundice (hyperbilirubinemia syndromes) or from treatment with drugs that acidify urine, such as ammonium chloride or ascorbic acid.

Elevated levels may indicate hemolytic jaundice, hepatitis, or cirrhosis.

COPPER REDUCTION TEST FOR SUGAR

The copper reduction test checks the urine for sugar levels, usually for the sake of diagnosing or monitoring people with diabetes.

The copper reduction test measures the concentration of substances in the urine through the reaction of these substances with a commercially prepared tablet called *Clinitest*. Clinitest reacts to glucose and to other sugars. The test is most valuable for providing diabetics with a simple, at-home method of monitoring urine glucose level. It's sometimes used as a rapid screening tool by labs.

Why is this test done?
The copper reduction test may be performed for the following reasons:
- To detect evidence of diabetes
- To monitor urine glucose levels during insulin therapy.

What should you know before the test?
- If you've been recently diagnosed as diabetic, the nurse or medical technician will teach you how to perform the Clinitest tablet test.
- The nurse will ask about any medications that might interfere with test results. The doctor may reschedule the test or restrict drugs before the test.

What happens during the test?
- First, you void, and then you drink water to ensure urine flow for the test.
- You're asked to void again after 30 to 45 minutes into a special container.
- Be sure not to contaminate the specimen with toilet tissue or stools.

The test is most valuable for helping diabetics monitor urine glucose levels at home.

The five-drop Clinitest tablet test

- Hold the medicine dropper vertically, and put five drops of urine from the specimen container into the test tube.
- Rinse the dropper with water, and add 10 drops of water to the test tube.
- Add one Clinitest tablet, and observe the color change, especially during effervescence or fizzing (the pass-through phase).
- Wait 15 seconds after effervescence subsides, and gently shake the test tube.
- If color develops at the 15-second interval, read the color against the Clinitest color chart and record the results.
- Ignore any changes that develop after 15 seconds.
- Rapid color changes (bright orange to dark brown or green-brown) in the pass-through phase in a five-drop Clinitest reaction indicate glucose in the urine of 2% or more. Record the results as over 2% without comparison to the color chart.

The two-drop Clinitest tablet test

- Hold the medicine dropper vertically, and put two drops of urine into the test tube.
- Flush urine residue from the dropper with water, and add 10 drops of water to the test tube.
- Add one Clinitest tablet, and observe the color change during the pass-through phase.
- Wait 15 seconds after effervescence stops, compare the color with the appropriate color reference chart, and record results.
- In a two-drop Clinitest reaction, rapid color changes (bright orange to dark brown or green-brown) in the pass-through phase indicate glucose in the urine of 5% or more.

What happens after the test?

- Store tablets in a well-marked, childproof bottle to prevent accidental ingestion.
- Don't use discolored tablets (dark blue). The normal color of fresh tablets is light blue, with darker blue flecks.
- During effervescence, hold the test tube near the top to avoid burning your hand; it becomes boiling hot.

Does the test have risks?

Make sure your hands are dry when handling Clinitest tablets and avoid contact with eyes, mucous membranes, gastrointestinal tract, and clothing because the sodium hydroxide and moisture produce caustic burns.

What are the normal results?

Normally, no glucose is present in urine.

What do abnormal results mean?

Glucose in the urine occurs in diabetes, adrenal and thyroid gland disorders, liver and central nervous system diseases, conditions involving low kidney function, toxic kidney tubular disease, heavy metal poisoning, pregnancy, and intravenous feeding. It also occurs with administration of large amounts of glucose and some drugs.

GLUCOSE TEST

The glucose oxidase test measures the concentration of glucose in your urine. It involves the use of commercial, plastic-coated, chemically-treated strips (Clinistix, Diastix) or Tes-Tape. The glucose oxidase test is used primarily to monitor urine glucose in people with diabetes. It's so simple and convenient that you can do it at home.

Why is this test done?

The glucose oxidase test may be performed for the following reasons:
- To detect glucose in the urine
- To monitor urine glucose levels during insulin therapy.

What should you know before the test?

- If you're newly diagnosed with diabetes, the nurse will teach you how to perform a chemical strip test.
- If you're receiving certain types of drug therapy, the nurse may recommend a Clinitest strip instead.

What happens during the test?

- First void, and then drink some water to ensure urine flow for the test.
- You urinate into a special container 30 to 45 minutes later.

The glucose oxidase test is so simple and convenient that you can do it at home.

The Clinistix test
- Dip the test area of the chemically treated strip into the specimen for 2 seconds.
- Remove excess urine by tapping the strip against a clean surface or the side of the container, and begin timing.
- Hold the strip in the air, and read the color exactly 10 seconds after taking the strip out of the urine. You read it by comparing it with the reference color blocks on the label of the container.
- Record the results.
- Ignore color changes that develop after 10 seconds.

The Diastix test
- Dip the reagent strip in the specimen for 2 seconds.
- Remove excess urine by tapping the strip against the container, and begin timing.
- Hold the strip in the air, and compare the color to the color chart exactly 30 seconds after taking the strip out of the urine.
- Record the results.
- Ignore color changes that develop after 30 seconds.

How to use Tes-Tape
- Withdraw about 1½ inches (3.8 centimeters) of the tape from the dispenser; dip 1¼ inches (3.1 centimeters) of it into the specimen for 2 seconds.
- Remove excess urine by tapping the strip against the side of the container, and begin timing.
- Hold the tape in the air, and compare the color of the darkest part of the tape to the color chart exactly 60 seconds after taking the strip out of the urine.
- If the tape indicates 0.5% or higher, wait an additional 60 seconds to make the final color comparison.
- Record the results.

What happens after the test?
- Keep the test strip container tightly closed to prevent deterioration of strips by exposure to light or moisture.
- Store it in a cool place (under 86° F [30° C]) to avoid heat degradation.
- Don't use discolored or darkened Clinistix or Diastix or dark yellow or yellow-brown Tes-Tape.

What are the normal results?

Normally, no glucose is present in urine.

What do abnormal results mean?

Glucose in the urine occurs in diabetes, adrenal and thyroid disorders, liver and central nervous system diseases, conditions involving low kidney function, toxic kidney tubular disease, heavy metal poisoning, pregnancy, and intravenous feeding. It also shows up when people are given large amounts of glucose and certain drugs.

KETONE TEST

The ketone test evaluates your fat metabolism by measuring the level of ketone bodies in your urine. Ketone bodies are the by-products of fat metabolism; they include acetoacetic acid, acetone, and beta-hydroxybutyric acid. Excessive amounts may appear in people with carbohydrate deprivation, which may occur in starvation or diabetic ketoacidosis. Commercially available tests include the Acetest tablet, Chemstrip K, Ketostix, or Keto-Diastix. Each product measures a specific ketone body. For example, Acetest measures acetone, and Ketostix measures acetoacetic acid.

Why is this test done?

The ketone test may be performed for the following reasons:
- To screen for ketones in the urine
- To identify diabetic ketoacidosis and carbohydrate deprivation
- To distinguish between a diabetic and a nondiabetic coma
- To monitor control of diabetes, ketogenic weight reduction, and treatment of diabetic ketoacidosis.

What should you know before the test?

- If you're newly diagnosed with diabetes, the nurse will tell you how to perform the test.
- The nurse will ask about any medications that might interfere with test results. The doctor may reschedule the test or restrict drugs before the test.

What happens during the test?

- First, you void, and then you drink water to ensure urine flow for the test.
- You're asked to urinate into a special container about 30 minutes later using a method to get a midstream specimen. (See *How to catch a midstream specimen,* page 586.)

How to use Acetest

- Lay the tablet on a piece of white paper, and place one drop of urine on the tablet.
- Compare the tablet color (white, lavender, or purple) with the color chart after 30 seconds.

How to use Ketostix

- Dip the chemically treated stick into the specimen and remove it immediately.
- Compare the stick color (buff or purple) with the color chart after 15 seconds.
- Record the results as negative or positive for small, moderate, or large amounts of ketones.

How to use Keto-Diastix

- Dip the chemically treated strip into the specimen, and remove it immediately.
- Tap the edge of the strip against the container or a clean, dry surface to remove excess urine.
- Hold the strip horizontally to prevent mixing the chemicals from the two areas.
- Interpret each area of the strip separately. Compare the color of the ketone section (buff or purple) with the appropriate color chart after exactly 15 seconds; compare the color of the glucose section after 30 seconds.
- Ignore color changes that occur after the specified waiting periods.
- Record the results as negative or positive for small, moderate, or large amounts of ketones.

The two-part strip is easy to use. Just hold it horizontally to prevent mixing the chemical from the two areas.

What happens after the test?

- Test the specimen within 60 minutes after it's obtained, or you must refrigerate it.
- Allow refrigerated specimens to return to room temperature before testing.
- Don't use tablets or strips that have become discolored or darkened.

What are the normal results?

Normally, no ketones are present in urine.

What do abnormal results mean?

Ketones in the urine may show up in people with uncontrolled diabetes or starvation. It also occurs as a metabolic complication of intravenous or tube feeding.

VITAMINS & MINERALS

VITAMIN B₆

The tryptophan challenge test measures your body's stores of vitamin B₆ by measuring the level of xanthurenic acid in your urine after you receive a dose of a drug called *tryptophan*. This test can detect a deficiency of vitamin B₆ long before symptoms appear. The test is especially important because, so far, there's no way to directly measure your vitamin B₆ reserve.

Vitamin B₆ deficiency can cause a form of anemia without iron deficiency, as well as central nervous system disturbances. In certain cases, vitamin B₆ deficiency may be associated with stones in the urinary tract.

Why is this test done?

The tryptophan challenge test may be performed to detect vitamin B₆ deficiency.

What happens before the test?

- You'll be given an oral dose of medication.
- The nurse will ask about any medications that might interfere with test results. The doctor may reschedule the test or restrict drugs before the test.

What happens during the test?

■ You're asked to urinate into a special container over a 24-hour period.

■ Void and discard the urine, and then begin 24-hour collection with the next voiding.

■ After you place the first specimen in the container, add the preservative given to you by the nurse or medical technician.

■ Add each voiding to the container immediately. If any urine is lost, restart the test.

■ Plan the start of your test so that collection ends at a time when the lab is open.

■ Just before the end of the test period, make an effort to void and add that urine to the container.

What are the normal results?

Normal excretion of xanthurenic acid after a tryptophan challenge dose is less than 328 micromoles per day.

What do abnormal results mean?

Urine levels of xanthurenic acid exceeding 657 micromoles per day indicate vitamin B_6 deficiency. This rare disorder may result from malnutrition, cancer, pregnancy, a family trait, or use of oral contraceptives or some drugs.

Note that if you have a vitamin B_6 deficiency, yeast, wheat, corn, liver, and kidneys are good sources of the vitamin.

VITAMIN C

This test measures levels of vitamin C (ascorbic acid) in the urine. It's particularly useful in diagnosing scurvy, an extreme deficiency of vitamin C marked by the degeneration of connective and bone-covering tissues and teeth. Although now uncommon in North America, scurvy may occur in alcoholics, people on low-fiber or low-citrus diets, and infants who've been weaned to cow's milk that doesn't contain a vitamin C supplement.

Why is this test done?

The test for vitamin C is performed to aid diagnosis of scurvy, scurvy-like conditions, and metabolic disorders such as malnutrition.

What should you know before the test?

- You won't need to change your diet before the test.
- The nurse will ask about any medications that might interfere with test results. The doctor may reschedule the test or restrict drugs before the test.

What happens during the test?

- You're asked to urinate into a special container over a 24-hour period.
- Void and discard the urine, and then begin 24-hour collection with the next voiding.
- After you place the first specimen in the container, add the preservative given to you by the nurse or medical technician.
- Add each voiding to the container immediately. If any urine is lost, restart the test.
- Plan the start of your test so that collection ends at a time when the lab is open.
- Just before the end of the test period, make an effort to void and add that urine to the container.

What are the normal results?

Normal urine vitamin C excretion is 30 milligrams per 24 hours.

What do abnormal results mean?

Low levels of vitamin C in the urine are common in people with infection, cancer, burns, or other stress-producing conditions. Decreased vitamin C levels may also indicate malnutrition, malabsorption, kidney deficiencies, or prolonged intravenous or tube feeding without vitamin C replacement. Severe vitamin C deficiency causes scurvy. (See *Scurvy: A brief history.*)

Note that if you have a vitamin C deficiency, citrus fruits, tomatoes, potatoes, cabbage, and strawberries are good dietary sources of vitamin C.

SODIUM AND CHLORIDE

This test helps determine the balance of salt and water in the body. Less significant than blood levels (and, consequently, performed less frequently), measurement of urine sodium and urine chloride con-

---

Scurvy: A brief history

Scurvy was probably the first disease to be recognized as a dietary deficiency. Although it rarely occurs now, scurvy once was common in places where fresh fruits and vegetables — major sources of vitamin C — weren't accessible in the winter.

A sailor's plague
Known as the "plague of the seas," scurvy was most prevalent in sailors because perishable foods couldn't be stored aboard ship. Famine or wartime food scarcity also caused scurvy.

When the Portuguese explorer Vasco da Gama first sailed around the Cape of Good Hope in 1497, more than half his crew died of the disease. Several centuries later, in 1747, Scottish naval surgeon James Lind found he could cure sailors of scurvy by giving them lemons and oranges.

The lime-juice cure
In an effort to duplicate Dr. Lind's success, lime juice was distributed in 1797 to the crews of British navy ships during long sea voyages, which explains the nickname "limeys," for British sailors.

centrations is used to evaluate kidney conservation of these two electrolytes and to confirm blood tests.

Why is this test done?

The tests for sodium and chloride may be given for the following reasons:

- To help evaluate fluid and electrolyte imbalance
- To monitor the effects of a low-salt diet
- To help evaluate kidney and adrenal gland disorders.

What should you know before the test?

- You won't need to change your diet before the test.
- If you're a pregnant or menstruating woman, you may want to reschedule the test to ensure more accurate results.
- The nurse will ask about any medications that might interfere with test results. The doctor may reschedule the test or restrict drugs before the test.

What happens during the test?

- You're asked to urinate into a special container over a 24-hour period.
- Void and discard the urine, and then begin 24-hour collection with the next voiding.
- After you place the first specimen in the container, add the preservative given to you by the nurse or medical technician.
- Add each voiding to the container immediately. If any urine is lost, restart the test.
- Plan the start of your test so that collection ends at a time when the lab is open.
- Just before the end of the test period, make an effort to void and add that urine to the container.
- Be sure not to contaminate the specimen with toilet paper or stools.

What are the normal results?

Normal ranges of sodium and chloride in the urine vary greatly with dietary salt intake and perspiration.

What do abnormal results mean?

Usually, levels of sodium and chloride in the urine are parallel, rising and falling together. Abnormal levels of both minerals may indicate the need for more specific testing. Elevated levels of sodium in the urine may reflect increased salt intake, adrenal failure, a diabetic condition, salt-losing tissue damage, and dehydration.

Decreased levels of sodium in the urine suggest decreased salt intake, primary aldosteronism (which causes high blood pressure), acute kidney failure, and congestive heart failure.

POTASSIUM

This test evaluates your kidney function. It measures urine levels of potassium, a major electrolyte that helps regulate acid-base balance and neuromuscular function. Potassium imbalance may cause the person to have muscle weakness, nausea, diarrhea, confusion, low blood pressure, and electrocardiogram changes. A severe imbalance may lead to cardiac arrest.

Most commonly, a blood test is performed to detect abnormally high or abnormally low potassium levels. A test of the level of potassium in the urine may be performed if doctors cannot uncover the cause of this condition through other means. If results suggest a kidney disorder, additional tests may be ordered.

Potassium imbalance may cause muscle weakness, nausea, diarrhea, confusion, low blood pressure, and electrocardiogram changes.

Why is this test done?
The test for potassium may be done to determine whether hypokalemia is caused by kidney or other disorders.

What should you know before the test?
- You won't need to change your diet before the test.
- If you're a pregnant or menstruating woman, you may want to reschedule the test to avoid making it less accurate.
- The nurse will ask about any medications that might interfere with test results. The doctor may reschedule the test or restrict drugs before the test.

What happens during the test?
- You're asked to urinate into a special container over a 24-hour period.
- Void and discard the urine, and then begin 24-hour collection with the next voiding.

- After you place the first specimen in the container, add the preservative given to you by the nurse or medical technician.
- Add each voiding to the container immediately. If any urine is lost, restart the test.
- Plan the start of your test so that collection ends at a time when the lab is open.
- Just before the end of the test period, make an effort to void and add that urine to the container.
- Refrigerate the specimen or place it on ice during the collection period.

What happens after the test?

- You may be given potassium supplements, and you may have a blood test to monitor your potassium levels.
- You may need dietary supplements and nutritional counseling.
- You may be given intravenous or oral fluids to replace lost potassium.
- You may resume drugs withheld during the test.

What are the normal results?

Normal potassium excretion is 25 to 125 millimoles per day, with an average potassium concentration of 25 to 100 millimoles per day.

What do abnormal results mean?

In a person with potassium deficiency, urine potassium concentration less than 10 millimoles per day suggests normal kidney function, indicating that potassium loss is most likely caused by a gastrointestinal disorder.

In a person with potassium deficiency lasting more than 3 days, urine potassium concentration above 10 millimoles per day indicates kidney loss of potassium. These losses may be caused by such disorders as aldosteronism or kidney problems or failure. However, disorders that don't involve the kidney, such as dehydration, starvation, Cushing's disease, or salicylate intoxication, may also elevate urine potassium levels.

CALCIUM AND PHOSPHATES

This test measures the levels of calcium and phosphates in the urine. They're essential for the formation and resorption of bone. Urine calcium and phosphate levels generally parallel levels of these minerals in the blood.

Normally absorbed in the upper intestine and excreted in feces and urine, calcium and phosphates help maintain tissue and fluid pH, electrolyte balance in cells and extracellular fluids, and permeability of cell membranes. Calcium promotes enzymatic processes, aids blood coagulation, and lowers neuromuscular irritability. Phosphates aid carbohydrate metabolism.

Why is this test done?

The test for calcium and phosphates may be performed for the following reasons:
- To evaluate calcium and phosphate metabolism and excretion
- To monitor treatment of calcium or phosphate deficiency.

What should you know before the test?

- You should be as active as possible before the test.
- The doctor may suggest you go on a diet called the *Albright-Reifenstein diet* (which contains about 130 milligrams of calcium per 24 hours) for 3 days before the test.
- If you're a pregnant or menstruating woman, you may want to reschedule the test to avoid making it less accurate.
- The nurse will ask about any medications that might interfere with test results. The doctor may reschedule the test or restrict drugs before the test.

What happens during the test?

- You're asked to urinate into a special container over a 24-hour period.
- Void and discard the urine, and then begin 24-hour collection with the next voiding.
- After you place the first specimen in the container, add the preservative given to you by the nurse or medical technician.
- Add each voiding to the container immediately. If any urine is lost, restart the test.

Before the test, you should be as active as possible, and you may be asked to follow a diet that regulates your calcium intake.

- Plan the start of your test so that collection ends at a time when the lab is open.
- Just before the end of the test period, make an effort to void and add that urine to the container.

What are the normal results?

Normal values depend on dietary intake. Men excrete less than 275 milligrams of calcium per 24 hours. Women excrete less than 250 milligrams per 24 hours. Normal excretion of phosphate in both sexes is less than 1,000 milligrams per 24 hours.

What do abnormal results mean?

A variety of disorders may affect calcium and phosphorus levels. The doctor will probably do more testing.

MAGNESIUM

The test is especially useful because magnesium deficiency is detectable in the person's urine before it shows up in the blood.

This test determines urine magnesium levels. Measurement of urine magnesium is especially useful because magnesium deficiency is detectable in the person's urine before it shows up in the blood. This test may be used to rule out magnesium deficiency as the cause of neurologic symptoms and to help evaluate glomerular function in suspected kidney disease.

Magnesium is found primarily in the bones and in intracellular fluid. An imbalance of this element in the body may cause a variety of symptoms, such as excessive perspiration, muscle weakness, visual disturbances, lethargy, confusion, hallucinations, or nausea and vomiting.

Why is this test done?

The test for magnesium may be performed for the following reasons:
- To rule out magnesium deficiency in people with symptoms of central nervous system irritation
- To detect excessive urinary excretion of magnesium
- To help evaluate glomerular function in kidney disease.

What should you know before the test?

■ You won't need to change your diet before the test.

■ If you're a pregnant or menstruating woman, you may want to reschedule the test to avoid making it less accurate.

■ The nurse will ask about any medications that might interfere with test results. The doctor may reschedule the test or restrict drugs before the test.

What happens during the test?

■ You're asked to urinate into a special container over a 24-hour period.

■ Void and discard the urine, and then begin 24-hour collection with the next voiding.

■ After you place the first specimen in the container, add the preservative given to you by the nurse or medical technician.

■ Add each voiding to the container immediately. If any urine is lost, restart the test.

■ Plan the start of your test so that collection ends at a time when the lab is open.

■ Just before the end of the test period, make an effort to void and add that urine to the container.

What are the normal results?

Normal urinary excretion of magnesium is less than 150 milligrams per 24 hours.

What do abnormal results mean?

Low urine magnesium levels may be caused by poor absorption, acute or chronic diarrhea, a diabetic condition, dehydration, pancreatitis, advanced kidney failure, and primary aldosteronism. They also may be caused by decreased dietary intake of magnesium.

Elevated urine magnesium levels may be caused by early chronic kidney disease, an adrenal gland problem, chronic alcoholism, or chronic ingestion of magnesium-containing antacids.

IRON

The hemosiderin test helps determine if the body is accumulating excessive amounts of iron. The test measures the urine level of hemosiderin—one of the two forms of storage iron deposited in body tissue.

When iron storage mechanisms fail to manage iron overload, excess iron may escape to cells unaccustomed to high iron concentrations and may produce toxic effects. Toxicity may affect the liver, the heart lining, bone marrow, pancreas, kidneys, and skin. Subsequent tissue damage is referred to as *hemochromatosis*. Hemochromatosis may occur in a rare hereditary form (primary hemochromatosis) as well as forms caused by outside influences.

> *When iron storage mechanisms fail, iron overload may produce toxic effects.*

Why is this test done?

The test for hemosiderin may be performed to aid the diagnosis of hemochromatosis.

What should you know before the test?

You'll be told that no restrictions are necessary and that the test requires a urine specimen.

What happens during the test?

You're asked to urinate once into a special container.

What are the normal results?

Normally, hemosiderin is not found in urine.

What do abnormal results mean?

The presence of hemosiderin, appearing as yellow-brown granules in urinary sediment, indicates hemochromatosis. A liver or bone marrow biopsy is necessary to confirm the condition. Hemosiderin may also suggest some forms of anemia, multiple blood transfusions, and a reaction to excessive iron injections or dietary intake of iron.

15

CULTURES:
Pinpointing
the Cause of Infection

GENERAL CULTURES

URINE CULTURE

This test detects urinary tract infections, especially bladder infections. Urine in the kidneys and bladder is normally sterile, but a urine specimen may still contain various organisms because it has passed through the nonsterile urethra and external genitalia.

Why is this test done?

The urine culture may be performed for the following reasons:
- To diagnose urinary tract infection in an adult or a child
- To check for the growth of bacteria after the doctor inserts a urinary catheter.

What should you know before the test?

- You won't need to change your diet before the test.
- The doctor or nurse will ask whether you're taking an antibiotic. He or she may discontinue the medication before the test.

What happens during the test?

- You're asked to collect a clean-voided midstream urine specimen. (If you'll be collecting a urine specimen from a baby, see *How to put a urine collector on your baby*.)
- Make sure you don't contaminate the specimen with toilet paper or feces.
- For the person with suspected tuberculosis, specimen collection may be required on three consecutive mornings.

What happens after the test?

You can resume any medications discontinued for the test.

What are the normal results?

Culture results of sterile urine are normally reported as "no growth," which usually indicates the absence of a urinary tract infection. However, a single negative culture doesn't always rule out an infection.

ADVICE FOR CAREGIVERS

How to put a urine collector on your baby

If the doctor needs samples of your baby's urine to diagnose or treat an illness, you'll be given some special equipment to collect the urine. The same plastic disposable collection bags with adhesive rings around their openings are used for boys and girls, but the methods used to attach the bags are different.

For a girl
Stretch the perineum (the skin between the anus and the labia) to smooth the skin around the vagina. Working upward from the perineum, press the bag's adhesive ring inside the labia.

For a boy
Make sure the adhesive seal attaches firmly to the skin around the scrotum and penis and doesn't pucker.

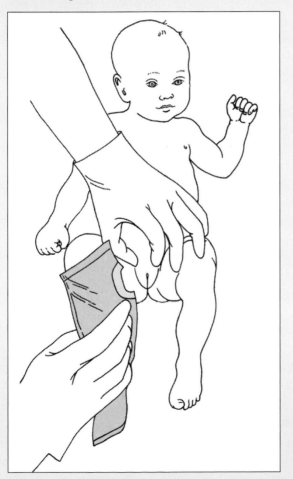

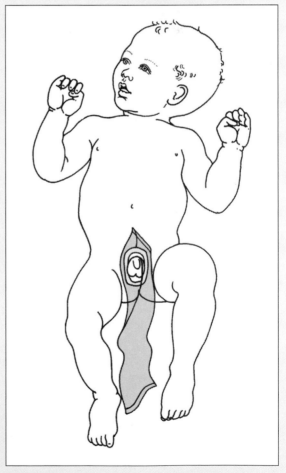

What do abnormal results mean?

Bacterial counts of 100,000 or more organisms of a single microbe species per milliliter indicate a probable urinary tract infection. Counts under 100,000 may be significant, depending on your age, sex, history, and other individual factors. A special test isolates bacteria that indicate tuberculosis of the urinary tract.

STOOL CULTURE

This test is used to determine the cause of gastrointestinal distress or to see if you're a carrier of infectious organisms. Normal bacteria in feces include several potentially harmful organisms. A bacteriologic exam is valuable for identifying organisms that cause digestive tract diseases, such as typhoid and dysentery. A sensitivity test may follow isolation of the causative organism. A stool culture may also be used to detect certain viruses, such as enterovirus, which can cause meningitis.

Why is this test done?

A stool culture may be performed for the following reasons:
- To identify harmful bacteria, especially in a debilitated person
- To help the doctor treat disease, prevent possibly life-threatening complications, and confine highly infectious diseases.

What should you know before the test?

- You won't need to change your diet before the test.
- The test may require collection of a stool specimen on 3 consecutive days.
- The nurse will ask about dietary patterns, recent antibiotic therapy that might affect the test, and recent travel that might suggest endemic infections or infestations.

What happens during the test?

You're asked to place a stool specimen directly into a special container. The specimen must represent the first, middle, and last portion of the feces passed.

What are the normal results?

Approximately 96% to 99% of normal fecal bacteria species can't survive in the open air. The remaining 1% to 4% of species include gram-negative bacilli (predominantly *Escherichia coli* and other Enterobacteriaceae), *Pseudomonas*, gram-positive cocci (mostly enterococci), and a few yeasts.

What do abnormal results mean?

The most common harmful organisms of the digestive tract are called *Shigella*, *Salmonella*, and *Campylobacter jejuni*. Isolation of these organisms in people with acute diarrhea indicates bacterial infection and may require special tests. The doctor will also look for evidence of such problems as food poisoning, staphylococcal infection, yeast infection, and aseptic meningitis.

THROAT CULTURE

A throat culture can isolate and identify harmful organisms. Culture results are considered in relation to your health status, recent antibiotic therapy, and amount of normal organisms.

Why is this test done?

A throat culture may be performed for the following reasons:

■ To isolate and identify group A beta-hemolytic streptococci, a type of microorganism; this allows for early treatment of pharyngitis and may help to prevent such complications as rheumatic heart disease or glomerulonephritis

■ To check a person who has no symptoms but who may actually have a harmful infection

■ To identify *Candida albicans* (which may cause thrush).

What should you know before the test?

■ You won't need to change your diet before the test.

■ A nurse or medical technician will use a sterile swab to collect material from your throat. You may gag during the swabbing.

■ The test takes less than 30 seconds, and test results should be available in 2 or 3 days.

The doctor may use a throat culture to check a person who has no symptoms but who may actually have a harmful infection.

- The nurse will ask about any recent antibiotic therapy and may want to know your immunization history.

What happens during the test?

- The nurse asks you to tilt your head back and close your eyes.
- With your throat well illuminated, the nurse checks for inflamed areas using a tongue depressor, and then swabs the tonsil area.

What are the normal results?

Normally, the throat contains some forms of staphylococci and *Haemophilus,* diphtheroids, pneumococci, yeasts, and enteric gram-negative bacteria.

What do abnormal results mean?

Organisms that may be harmful include the ones that can cause scarlet fever, pharyngitis, thrush, diphtheria, and whooping cough. The lab report should indicate the prevalent organisms and the quantity of pathogens cultured.

NASOPHARYNGEAL CULTURE

This test is used to isolate the cause of a nose and throat infection. It checks secretions for the presence of harmful organisms. To obtain results, a specimen is stained and then examined under a microscope. The doctor uses the information to determine the need for additional testing and to choose an effective antibiotic.

Why is this test done?

A nasopharyngeal culture may be performed for any of the following reasons:

- To identify harmful organisms causing upper respiratory tract symptoms
- To identify growth of normal nasopharyngeal organisms, which may be harmful to debilitated people or to those who have a damaged immune system

- To identify microorganisms that may cause whooping cough or meningitis (may be especially important in very young, elderly, or debilitated people and in people who don't have symptoms of illness but are nevertheless suspected of having an infection)
- Less frequently, to isolate viruses, especially to identify people who may be carrying influenza virus A or B.

What should you know before the test?

- A nurse or medical technician will collect secretions from the back of your nose and your throat using a cotton-tipped swab.
- Obtaining the specimen takes less than 15 seconds. You may feel slight discomfort and may gag.
- Initial test results are available in 48 to 72 hours. It may take longer to obtain viral test results.

What happens during the test?

- You're asked to cough before collection of the specimen. Next, you're positioned with your head tilted back.
- Using a penlight and tongue depressor, the examiner inspects your throat and the back of your nose.
- The nurse or medical technician gently passes a swab through the nostril into the nasopharynx (the upper part of the pharynx that connects with the nasal passages). Alternatively, the examiner may place a pyrex tube into your nostril and then pass the swab through this tube.

What are the normal results?

Organisms commonly found in the nasopharynx include some types of streptococci and other bacteria.

What do abnormal results mean?

Harmful organisms include some forms of streptococci, organisms that cause whooping cough and diphtheria, and excessive amounts of organisms that may cause influenza, pneumonia, or candidiasis.

A nose and throat culture may be performed to detect microorganisms that can cause whooping cough or meningitis.

SPUTUM CULTURE

This test is used to identify the organism causing a respiratory tract infection. Checking the bacteria in sputum — material raised from the lungs and bronchi — is an important aid for the doctor in the management of lung disease.

The usual method of specimen collection is to have the person cough deeply and spit out a specimen. Other methods include tracheal (windpipe) suctioning and bronchoscopy.

Why is this test done?

A sputum culture is performed to identify the cause of a lung infection. The results help the doctor diagnose bronchitis, tuberculosis, lung abscess, and pneumonia.

What should you know before the test?

Don't brush your teeth or use mouthwash before the test. (If you do, the test results will be unreliable.)

- The test requires a sputum specimen, which a nurse or medical technician will help you produce.
- If the specimen is to be collected by expectoration (spitting out), the nurse will tell you to drink fluids the night before collection to help increase sputum production.
- The nurse will teach you how to expectorate by taking three deep breaths and forcing a deep cough. It's important to remember that sputum is not the same as saliva, which is unacceptable for culturing.
- Don't brush your teeth or use mouthwash before the test. (If you do, the tests results will be unreliable.) You may rinse your mouth with water.
- If the specimen is to be collected by tracheal suctioning, you'll experience discomfort as the catheter passes into your trachea.
- If the specimen is to be collected by bronchoscopy, you'll fast for 6 hours before the procedure. You'll receive a local anesthetic just before the test to minimize discomfort during passage of the tube.
- Because the bronchoscopy requires an anesthetic, the nurse will ask you to sign a consent form.
- If the doctor suspects that you have tuberculosis, at least three morning specimens may be required.
- Test results are usually available in 48 to 72 hours. However, because cultures for tuberculosis take up to 2 months, the diagnosis of this disorder is generally based on the person's symptoms and on results of an acid-fast bacilli test, a chest X-ray, and a skin test.

What happens during the test?

■ For expectoration, the nurse asks you to cough deeply and spit into the container. If the cough doesn't produce sputum, the nurse may use chest physiotherapy or nebulization (a heated aerosol spray) to induce it.

■ For tracheal suctioning, the nurse slips a lubricated tube through your nostril and into the trachea, then suctions for up to 15 seconds. This method makes you cough.

■ For bronchoscopy, a local anesthetic is sprayed into your throat (or you gargle with a local anesthetic); then the doctor inserts the bronchoscope through your throat and into the bronchus. Secretions are collected with a bronchial brush or aspirated through the inner channel of the scope.

■ Tracheal suctioning is not used if you have abnormalities in your esophagus or if you have heart disease.

What are the normal results?

Normally, sputum is contaminated with harmless organisms, such as some types of streptococci and yeasts. These organisms are not worrisome if your overall condition is healthy.

What do abnormal results mean?

Harmful organisms most often found in sputum include the bacteria that cause pneumonia, tuberculosis, and other diseases. Isolation of the bacterium that causes tuberculosis is always a significant finding.

Diagnosis of respiratory viruses usually requires blood tests rather than a sputum culture.

BLOOD CULTURE

This test helps the doctor identify the organism causing your symptoms. A blood culture can isolate the harmful organisms that cause bacteremia (bacterial invasion of the bloodstream) and septicemia (systemic spread of such infection). The lab takes a sample of your blood, inoculates a culture medium where it can grow, and incubates it.

Why is this test done?

A blood culture may be performed for the following reasons:
- To confirm bacteremia
- To identify the causative organism in bacteremia and septicemia.

What should you know before the test?

- You won't need to change your diet before the test.
- You may be told to expect slight discomfort from the tourniquet pressure and the needle puncture.
- Drawing a blood sample takes less than 3 minutes.

What happens during the test?

A nurse or medical technician inserts a needle into a vein, usually in your forearm. A blood sample is collected in a tube, which is then sent to the lab for testing.

What happens after the test?

If swelling develops at the needle puncture site, warm soaks are applied to the area to ease discomfort.

What are the normal results?

Normally, blood cultures are sterile.

What do abnormal results mean?

Positive blood cultures do not necessarily confirm a spreading bacterial infection. Mild, short-term invasions of bacteria may occur during many infectious diseases and other disorders. Persistent, continuous, or recurrent bacteremia reliably confirms the presence of serious infection. To detect the cause, blood samples are ideally drawn on 2 consecutive days. Isolation of most organisms takes about 72 hours; however, negative cultures are held for 1 week or more before being reported negative.

WOUND CULTURE

Performed to confirm infection, a wound culture is an analysis of a specimen from a laceration or lesion. Wound cultures may be aerobic (to detect organisms that can live in the open air and usually appear in a superficial wound) or anaerobic (to detect organisms that cannot live in the presence of oxygen and that appear in postoperative wounds, ulcers, or compound fractures).

The doctor may perform this culture when a person has a fever and an inflamed, draining wound.

Why is this test done?

A wound culture may be performed to identify an infection.

What should you know before the test?

■ A drainage specimen from the wound will be withdrawn by a syringe or removed on cotton swabs.
■ Collecting the drainage specimen takes less than 3 minutes.

What happens during the test?

The nurse first cleans the area around the wound with an antiseptic solution.

Collecting an aerobic culture

The nurse will press the wound and swab as much discharge as possible or insert the swab deeply into the wound and gently rotate it.

Collecting an anaerobic culture

■ The nurse will insert the swab deeply into the wound, gently rotate it, and immediately place it in a special container.
■ Alternatively, the nurse may insert a needle into the wound, withdraw 1 to 5 milliliters of discharge into the syringe, and inject the discharge into a tube.
■ The wound is then dressed.

What are the normal results?

Normally, no harmful organisms are present in a clean wound.

The doctor may perform this culture when a person has a fever and an inflamed, draining wound.

What do abnormal results mean?

The most common aerobic organisms in a wound infection include *Staphylococcus aureus*, group A beta-hemolytic streptococci, *Proteus*, *Escherichia coli*, and other such bacteria. The most common anaerobic organisms are certain species of *Clostridium* and *Bacteroides*.

STOMACH CULTURE

Used to diagnose tuberculosis, this test requires removal of a small amount of the stomach's contents and cultivation of any microbes present. It's performed in conjunction with a chest X-ray and a skin test. This test is especially useful when a sputum specimen can't be obtained.

In an infant with an infection, gastric aspiration also provides a specimen for rapid identification of bacteria.

The microbes in your stomach can be cultured to show whether you have tuberculosis. In infants, they can reveal the cause of an infection.

Why is this test done?

A stomach culture may be performed for the following reasons:
- To help the doctor diagnose tuberculosis
- To identify the causative agent in an infant with an infection.

What should you know before the test?

- You or your infant will fast for 8 hours before the test.
- The same procedure may be performed on three consecutive mornings.
- The doctor or nurse will ask about any recent medications you've taken that could affect test results. Use of such medications may be discontinued.
- You or your infant should remain in bed each morning until the specimen is collected, to prevent premature emptying of stomach contents.
- The examiner will insert a tube through your nostril and into your stomach to withdraw the specimen. The tube may make you gag, but it will pass more easily if you relax and follow instructions about breathing and swallowing.
- Just before the procedure, the nurse will check your heart rate.
- It may take as long as 2 months to obtain test results.

What happens during the test?

As soon as you awaken in the morning, the examiner inserts the tube through your nose and collects stomach contents.

What happens after the test?

- You can resume your normal diet and any medications discontinued before the test.
- You'll be told not to blow your nose for at least 4 hours to prevent bleeding.

Does the test have risks?

You won't be given the test if you're pregnant or have a condition such as an esophageal disorder, cancer, recent severe gastric hemorrhage, aortic aneurysm, or heart failure.

What are the normal results?

Normally, the culture specimen shows no harmful organisms.

What do abnormal results mean?

Isolation and identification of the organism *Mycobacterium tuberculosis* indicates active tuberculosis. Other species of *Mycobacterium* may cause lung disease that produces the same symptoms as tuberculosis. Treatment of these diseases may be difficult and commonly requires further studies to help the doctor find an effective antibiotic.

Harmful bacteria causing an infant's infection may also be identified through culture.

INTESTINAL CULTURE

This test requires putting a tube into the duodenum (the top part of the intestine), withdrawing some contents, and cultivating the microbes found there. The culture will help the doctor identify harmful organisms that may cause intestinal diseases, such as duodenitis, cholecystitis, or cholangitis. Occasionally, a specimen may be obtained during surgery.

Why is this test done?

An intestine culture may be performed for the following reasons:
- To detect bacterial infection of the bile ducts and duodenum
- To differentiate between infection and gallstones
- To rule out bacterial infection as the cause of persistent stomach pain, nausea, vomiting, and diarrhea.

What should you know before the test?

- You'll have to restrict food and fluids for 12 hours before the test.
- A tube will be inserted through your nostril and into your stomach. Although this procedure is uncomfortable, it isn't dangerous.
- The passage of the tube may cause gagging, but following the examiner's instructions about proper positioning, breathing, swallowing, and relaxing will minimize discomfort.
- To increase your comfort level, you should empty your bladder before the procedure.

Normally, an intestine culture reveals no harmful organisms. The bacterial count is relatively low.

What happens during the test?

- After the tube is inserted, you lie on your left side with your feet elevated.
- The examiner may use a fluoroscope to confirm the correct position of the tube.
- The examiner withdraws duodenal contents.

What happens after the test?

- You'll be kept in bed until you feel stronger.
- You can resume your normal diet.

Does the test have risks?

You shouldn't undergo this test if you're pregnant, have had a heart attack or a recent severe stomach hemorrhage, or have acute pancreatitis or cholecystitis, abnormalities of the esophagus, an aortic aneurysm, or congestive heart failure.

What are the normal results?

Normally, an intestine culture contains small amounts of white blood cells and tissue cells with no harmful organisms. The bacterial count is usually relatively low: less than 100,000 per milliliter of body fluid.

What do abnormal results mean?

Generally, bacterial counts of 100,000 or more per milliliter of body fluid or the presence of harmful organisms, such as *Escherichia coli*, *Staphylococcus aureus*, and *Salmonella*, in any number indicates infection.

Numerous white blood cells, copious mucous debris, and bile-stained cells in the bile fluid suggest inflammation of the bile ducts. Other findings can suggest inflammation of the pancreas, the duodenum, or bile ducts. To make a definitive diagnosis, the doctor may require more testing.

GENITAL CULTURES

CULTURE FOR GONORRHEA

This test confirms gonorrhea, a disease that's almost always caused by sexual transmission of the organism *Neisseria gonorrhoeae*. A stained smear of genital discharge can confirm gonorrhea in 90% of men with characteristic symptoms, but a culture is often necessary, especially in women with no symptoms. Specimens may be taken from the urethra (the usual site in men), endocervix (the usual site in women), anal canal, or throat.

Why is this test done?

This culture is performed to confirm gonorrhea.

What should you know before the test?

Test results are usually available within 24 to 72 hours.

For women
You'll be told not to douche for 24 hours before the test.

For men
- You'll be told not to urinate during the hour preceding the test.
- Men sometimes experience nausea, sweating, weakness, and fainting due to stress or discomfort when the cotton swab or wire loop is introduced into the urethra.

What happens during the test?
Endocervical culture
■ You lie on the examining table with your feet in stirrups (much like when you have a Pap test). You're draped, and the examiner instructs you to take deep breaths.

■ The examiner inserts a vaginal speculum that's lubricated with warm water and wipes mucus from the cervix with cotton balls.

■ The examiner inserts a dry, sterile cotton swab into the endocervical canal to collect the specimen.

Urethral culture
■ You lie on the examining table, covered with a drape.

■ The examiner cleans around the urethral opening with a sterile gauze pad or a cotton ball, then inserts a thin swab or a wire loop into the urethra, and rotates the swab or loop from side to side.

■ In another method, the urethra may be milked, bringing urethral secretions to the opening for collection on a cotton swab.

Rectal culture
After the examiner has obtained an endocervical or urethral specimen (while you're still on the examining table), a sterile cotton swab is inserted into the anal canal to obtain another specimen.

Throat culture
■ You sit with your head tilted back.

■ The nurse checks your throat for inflamed areas using a tongue depressor, then rubs a sterile swab from side to side over the tonsil area to collect the specimen.

What happens after the test?
■ You'll be told to avoid all sexual contact until test results are available.

■ If the test confirms gonorrhea, this finding must be reported to the local health department.

■ The nurse will explain that treatment usually begins after confirmation of positive culture, except in a person who has symptoms of gonorrhea or a person who's had intercourse with someone known to have gonorrhea.

■ A repeat culture is required 1 week after completion of treatment to evaluate therapy.

If the test confirms gonorrhea, this finding must be reported to the local health department.

What are the normal results?

Normally, *Neisseria gonorrhoea* does not appear in the culture.

What do abnormal results mean?

A positive culture confirms gonorrhea.

CULTURE FOR HERPES

This test detects infection by the herpes simplex virus. About 85% of the people with this common infection don't experience noticeable symptoms at first. The rest have local lesions. After the initial infection, the person becomes a carrier who's subject to recurrent attacks. Symptoms depend on the location of the infection.

Herpes simplex type 1 is transmitted primarily by contact with oral secretions and occurs primarily in children. Herpes simplex type 2 is transmitted primarily by contact with genital secretions, mainly affects the genitalia, and usually occurs in adolescents and young adults. (See *The genital herpes cycle*, page 634.) In a person with a damaged immune system, infection with herpes simplex may lead to numerous illnesses.

Approximately 50% of the strains of herpes simplex virus can be detected within 24 hours after the lab receives the specimen. Five to 7 days are required to detect the remaining strains of herpes simplex.

About 85% of the people with this common infection don't have noticeable symptoms at first.

Why is this test done?

This culture may be performed to confirm a diagnosis of herpes simplex virus infection.

What should you know before the test?

The nurse will explain that specimens will be collected from suspected lesions.

What happens during the test?

The examiner collects a specimen for culture in a special collection device. For the throat, skin, eye, or genital area, the examiner uses a special swab.

INSIGHT INTO ILLNESS

The genital herpes cycle

After the initial genital herpes infection, a latent (inactive) period follows. During this time, the virus enters the nerves surrounding the lesions and remains there permanently.

Repeated outbreaks of herpes may develop at any time, again followed by a latent stage when healing is complete. These outbreaks may recur as often as three to eight times yearly. Although the cycle continues indefinitely, some people remain symptom-free for years.

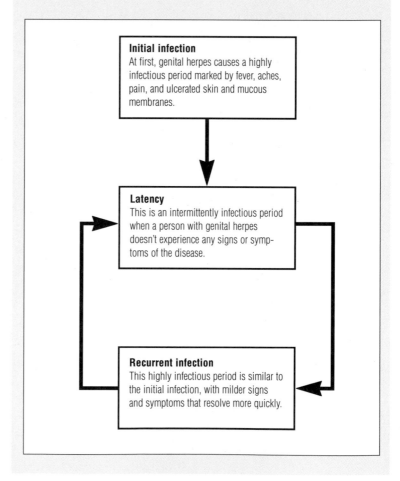

Initial infection
At first, genital herpes causes a highly infectious period marked by fever, aches, pain, and ulcerated skin and mucous membranes.

Latency
This is an intermittently infectious period when a person with genital herpes doesn't experience any signs or symptoms of the disease.

Recurrent infection
This highly infectious period is similar to the initial infection, with milder signs and symptoms that resolve more quickly.

SELF-HELP

How to prevent genital herpes from destroying your relationship

Genital herpes can cause long-term problems in a sexual relationship. Your herpes-free partner always runs the risk of acquiring the disease through sexual intercourse. You may feel like hiding your condition from your partner or hesitate to initiate a relationship.

Guidelines for decreasing the risk of transmission
Avoid having sexual intercourse from the time symptoms first occur until 10 days after the lesions heal. Although herpes can be transmitted at any time, transmission occurs less frequently during symptom-free periods.

Understand that the use of condoms doesn't guarantee protection against herpes, but it does decrease the risk.

A tough topic: Talking about herpes
If you're in a relationship, approach your partner with honesty, but avoid shocking revelations like "I have something terrible to tell you." Instead, broach the subject of herpes with discretion at a convenient time. Use neutral words and terms. For instance, think of herpes as "an infection that comes and goes" rather than "incurable."

What are the normal results?

Normally, herpes simplex virus doesn't appear in specimens from people with healthy immune systems who show no outward signs of the disease.

What do abnormal results mean?

Isolation of the virus from local lesions helps to confirm a diagnosis of herpes virus infection. If you're diagnosed with genital herpes, seek medical advice about treatment and informing sexual partners. (See *How to prevent genital herpes from destroying your relationship*.)

CULTURE FOR CHLAMYDIA

The most common sexually transmitted disease in North America is caused by a bacterium-like organism called *Chlamydia trachomatis*. This organism is identified in the lab by culturing in cells susceptible to the infection. After the culture has been incubated, the lab can detect *Chlamydia*-infected cells by looking for antibodies or by iodine staining.

Why is this test done?

This culture is performed to confirm infections caused by the organism *Chlamydia trachomatis.*

What should you know before the test?

- The nurse will describe the procedure for collecting a specimen for culture, which varies depending on the site of infection.
- If the specimen is to be collected from your genital tract, you'll be instructed not to urinate for 3 to 4 hours before the specimen is taken.

What happens during the test?

- The examiner obtains a specimen from the infected site. In adults, these sites may include the eye, urethra (not the pus-filled discharge), endocervix, or rectum.
- For a man, the examiner may obtain a urethral specimen with a cotton-tipped applicator. For a woman, the examiner may collect a specimen from the endocervix using a swab or brush.
- You're advised to avoid all sexual contact until after test results are available.

What are the normal results?

Normally, *Chlamydia trachomatis* does not appear in the culture.

What do abnormal results mean?

A positive culture confirms *Chlamydia trachomatis* infection. If you're diagnosed with chlamydia, you should seek medical advice about treatment and inform any sexual partners about your infection.

FLUID ANALYSIS:
Evaluating the Body's Other Liquids

LUNGS & DIGESTIVE TRACT

LUNG PARASITES

This test is used to check your sputum or phlegm for parasites or their eggs that might be living in your lungs. Lung parasite infestation is rare in North America, but if the doctor suspects you've been exposed, he or she will look for parasites such as hookworms. The specimen is obtained by coughing and spitting or by suctioning of the windpipe.

Why is this test done?
The sputum may be examined to identify parasites in your lungs.

What should you know before the test?
■ The test requires a sputum specimen or, if necessary, suctioning of the windpipe.
■ Early morning collection is preferred because secretions accumulate overnight.
■ You can help sputum production by drinking fluids the night before collection.

What happens during the test?
You're asked to spit by taking three deep breaths and forcing a deep cough. The sputum you produce is put into a container and sent to a lab.

If you have suctioning
■ If suctioning of your windpipe is required to provide a sample, you'll feel some short-term discomfort from the catheter.
■ The doctor or nurse passes a catheter through your nostril, without using suction. You cough when the catheter passes into your voice box.
■ The nurse applies suction for 5 or 10 seconds—no longer than 15 seconds—and then removes the catheter and sends the sample to the lab.

What are the normal results?

Normally, no parasites or eggs are found.

What do abnormal results mean?

The doctor can match the parasite to the type of lung infection you have. The parasite, in its adult state, may also cause an intestinal infection. Examples of parasites that may be found include *Entamoeba histolytica* (amebiasis), *Ascaris lumbricoides* (roundworm), *Echinococcus granulosus*, *Strongyloides stercoralis* (threadworm), *Paragonimus westermani* (lung fluke), or *Necator americanus* (hookworm).

LUNG FLUID

This test, which doctors call *pleural fluid analysis*, is used to check the space around your lungs for excess fluid. The pleura, a two-layer membrane that covers the lungs and lines the chest cavity, keeps a little lubricating fluid between its layers to minimize friction when you breathe. Increased fluid in this space may be caused by diseases such as cancer or tuberculosis or from blood or lymphatic disorders. Too much of it can cause difficult breathing. (See *The pleura: Protecting your lungs*.)

Why is this test done?

Pleural fluid analysis may be performed to find the cause and nature of excess liquid around the lungs.

What should you know before the test?

- You won't need to change your diet before the test.
- The doctor may use chest X-rays or ultrasound before the test to help locate the fluid.
- You'll be given a local anesthetic before the test; you may feel a stinging sensation when it's injected.
- You'll be asked not to cough, breathe deeply, or move during the test to minimize the risk of injury to the lung.
- The nurse may shave the area around the needle insertion site.

HOW YOUR BODY WORKS

The pleura: Protecting your lungs

If your doctor has ordered a pleural fluid analysis, understanding the function of pleura (the sacs that surround the lungs) may help you prepare for this test.

The pleural layers protect your lungs. The outer *parietal pleura* lines the inside of the chest. The inner *visceral pleura* envelops the lung itself. Between the parietal pleura and the visceral pleura, the *pleural space* contains a thin film of fluid. This lubricates the pleural surfaces and prevents friction between the layers when they expand as you inhale.

Where the breath goes

You breathe through hollow tubes in the lungs. Beginning at your mouth, the largest tube, called the *trachea (windpipe) leads to hollow tubes called bronchi*, which resemble tree branches. These gradually become smaller, until each bronchus eventually branches into *bronchioles* and finally terminates in clusters of air sacs. In these tiny air sacs, called alveoli, the exchange of oxygen and carbon dioxide takes place.

Any disorder of the pleura interferes with smooth and efficient gas exchange, thus hindering respiration.

LEFT LUNG

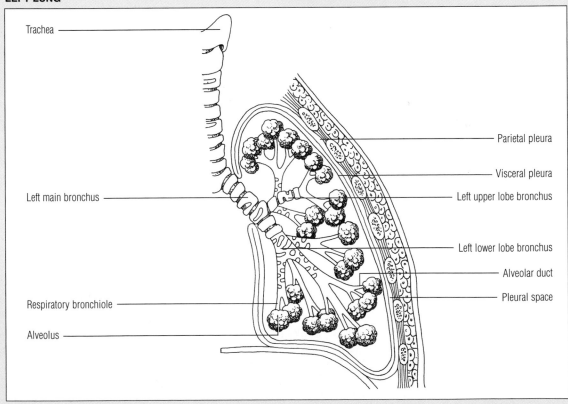

Trachea

Left main bronchus

Respiratory bronchiole

Alveolus

Parietal pleura

Visceral pleura

Left upper lobe bronchus

Left lower lobe bronchus

Alveolar duct

Pleural space

The doctor draws off lung fluid for analysis or to relieve lung compression and breathing problems.

What happens during the test?

- A nurse or medical technician asks you to sit at the edge of the bed with a chair or stool supporting your feet and your head and arms resting on a padded overbed table. If you can't sit up, you may be positioned on your side with your arm above your head.
- The nurse reminds you not to cough, breathe deeply, or move suddenly during the procedure.
- During thoracentesis (pleural fluid aspiration), the doctor punctures the chest wall with a large needle and withdraws a specimen of pleural fluid for analysis or draws off liquid through the needle to relieve lung compression and breathing problems.
- You may feel some pressure during withdrawal of the fluid.
- After the needle is removed, the nurse applies light pressure and a small adhesive bandage to the puncture site.
- You must remain on your side for at least 1 hour to seal the puncture site; notify the nurse if you have trouble breathing.

Does the test have risks?

This procedure isn't used for people who have histories of bleeding disorders.

What are the normal results?

Normally, the pleural cavity maintains negative pressure and contains less than 20 milliliters of fluid.

What do abnormal results mean?

Too much fluid is caused by the abnormal formation or reabsorption of pleural fluid. Certain characteristics classify pleural fluid as either a transudate (a low-protein fluid that's leaked from normal blood vessels) or an exudate (a protein-rich fluid that's leaked from blood vessels with increased permeability). Pleural fluid may contain blood, chyle, or pus and dead tissue.

The doctor will analyze the fluids to determine the cause, which may include high blood pressure, congestive heart failure, cirrhosis of the liver, nephritis, lymphatic drainage interference, infections, lung damage, rheumatoid arthritis, complications of pneumonia, cancer, and a variety of infections.

Cultures of pleural fluid may reveal bacteria or other pathogens.

STOMACH ACID SECRETION TEST

This procedure, which doctors call the *basal gastric secretion test*, is used to measure your stomach's secretion of acid. The test is done while you fast by withdrawing some stomach contents through a tube running from your nose to your stomach.

The doctor may perform this test if you have obscure stomach pain, loss of appetite, and weight loss. Because certain factors around you — such as the sight or odor of food — and psychological stress stimulate stomach acid secretion, accurate testing requires that you be relaxed and isolated from all sources of sensory stimulation. Although abnormal stomach acid secretion can suggest various stomach and duodenal disorders, the doctor may follow this test with the stomach acid stimulation test to obtain a complete evaluation.

Why is this test done?

The stomach acid secretion test may be performed to determine the output of stomach acid that occurs while you're fasting.

What should you know before the test?

■ You'll fast for 12 hours and restrict fluids and smoking for 8 hours before the test.
■ The procedure takes approximately 1½ hours (or 2½ hours, if followed by the stomach acid stimulation test).
■ If you're using antacids or other medications, they may be stopped for 24 hours before the test.
■ The nurse will check your pulse rate and blood pressure just before the test. Then you'll be encouraged to relax.

What happens during the test?

■ While you're seated, a nurse inserts a tube through your nose and into your stomach. You may initially feel discomfort and may cough or gag.
■ The tube is attached to a large syringe used to withdraw your stomach contents.
■ To ensure complete emptying of the stomach, you assume three positions in sequence — on your back, and then on your right and left sides — while the stomach contents are withdrawn.

■ The tube from your nose to your stomach is connected to a suction machine that applies continuous low suction. The suction can also be performed manually with a syringe.

What happens after the test?

You can resume your usual diet and any medications that were withheld before the test, unless the stomach acid stimulation test will also be performed.

What are the normal results?

Normally, basal secretion ranges from 0.2 to 3.8 milliequivalents per hour in women and 1 to 5 milliequivalents per hour in men.

What do abnormal results mean?

Abnormal results don't provide specific enough information to make a diagnosis, and the doctor will consider them with the results of the stomach acid stimulation test. A high rate of secretion may suggest an intestinal ulcer or, if it's very high, a condition called *Zollinger-Ellison syndrome*. A low amount of secretion may indicate stomach cancer or a benign stomach ulcer. Absence of secretion may indicate pernicious anemia.

The stomach acid secretion test goes hand in hand with the stomach acid stimulation test.

STOMACH ACID STIMULATION TEST

This test, which doctors call the *gastric acid stimulation test*, is used to find out if the stomach is secreting acid properly. It measures the secretion of stomach acid for 1 hour after you receive an injection of pentagastrin or a similar drug that stimulates stomach acid output. The doctor uses this test when the stomach acid secretion test suggests a problem. The stomach acid stimulation test is commonly performed immediately afterward. Although this test can detect abnormal stomach acid secretion, X-ray studies and endoscopy are necessary to determine the cause of such secretions.

Why is this test done?

The stomach acid stimulation test may be performed to help the doctor diagnose a duodenal ulcer, Zollinger-Ellison syndrome, pernicious anemia, and stomach cancer.

What should you know before the test?

- You'll be told not to eat, drink, or smoke after midnight before the test.
- If you're taking antacids or some other drugs, they may be stopped.

What happens during the test?

- The test takes 1 hour.
- The test may cause discomfort, such as abdominal pain, nausea, vomiting, flushing, transitory dizziness, faintness, and numbness of extremities. You should report symptoms immediately.
- After stomach acid secretions are collected for the stomach acid secretion test, the tube from your nose to your stomach remains in place.
- You'll receive an injection of pentagastrin. After 15 minutes, the examiner collects a specimen of stomach acid secretions from the tube every 15 minutes for 1 hour.

What happens after the test?

You may resume your usual diet and any medications withheld for the test.

What are the normal results?

Following stimulation, stomach acid secretion ranges from 11 to 21 milliequivalents per hour for women and 18 to 28 milliequivalents per hour for men.

What do abnormal results mean?

A high level of stomach acid secretion may indicate a duodenal ulcer; an extremely high level suggests Zollinger-Ellison syndrome. A low level of secretion may indicate stomach cancer; an absence of hydrochloric acid, which is normally found in secretions, may indicate pernicious anemia.

ABDOMINAL FLUID

This procedure, which doctors call *peritoneal fluid analysis*, is used to determine the cause of excess fluids in the abdomen or to detect abdominal injury. A sample of peritoneal fluid is withdrawn by a procedure called *paracentesis*. Peritoneal fluid is drawn from the peritoneum, a membrane sac that lines the abdominal and pelvic wall.

Why is this test done?

The analysis of peritoneal fluid may be performed for the following reasons:
- To determine the cause of fluid-filled sacs in the abdomen
- To detect abdominal injury.

What should you know before the test?

- You won't need to change your diet before the test.
- The test requires a peritoneal fluid sample. You'll receive a local anesthetic to make you comfortable; the procedure takes about 45 minutes.
- If you have severe pressure in your abdomen, the procedure will relieve your discomfort and allow you to breathe more easily.
- You should void any urine just before the test. This helps prevent accidental bladder injury during needle insertion.

What happens during the test?

- You sit on a bed or in a chair with your feet flat on the floor and your back well supported.
- You're draped to keep you from chilling.
- You're given a local anesthetic; you may feel a stinging sensation when it's injected.
- This procedure requires inserting a trocar (a sharp stylet inside a tube) through the abdominal wall after administration of the local anesthetic. If the fluid is being removed to provide relief, the trocar may be connected to a drainage system. However, if only a small amount of fluid is needed for a diagnosis, the test may be done with a needle.
- You may feel some pressure during withdrawal of the fluid.

This procedure is sometimes used to remove excess fluid from the abdominal cavity.

Does the test have risks?

The test must be performed very cautiously with pregnant women and people with bleeding tendencies or unstable vital signs.

What are the normal results?

Normally, the peritoneal fluid is sterile, odorless, and clear to pale yellow in color.

What do abnormal results mean?

The following are some of the abnormalities and the disorders they suggest:

- Milk-colored peritoneal fluid may be caused by fluid from a damaged thoracic duct, suggesting cancers, tuberculosis, parasitic infection, or liver cirrhosis.
- Cloudy or turbid fluid may indicate peritonitis due to primary bacterial infection, ruptured bowel (after injury), pancreatitis, strangulated intestine, or appendicitis.
- Bloody fluid may result from a benign or malignant tumor, hemorrhagic pancreatitis, or damage incurred during the test.
- Bile-stained, green fluid may indicate a ruptured gallbladder, acute pancreatitis, or perforated intestine or duodenal ulcer.

Lab tests on any red blood cells, protein, hormones, or even fungi found in the fluid will point to other possible disorders.

PARASITES IN THE DIGESTIVE TRACT

This procedure, which doctors call the *test for duodenal parasites*, is used to diagnose parasitic infection of the digestive tract by investigating duodenal contents. It's performed by passing a tube from the person's nose into the duodenum (top of the small intestine) or by using a special capsule to withdraw a specimen.

Why is this test done?

The test for duodenal parasites may be performed when the person has symptoms of parasitic infection but stool examinations are negative.

Intestinal parasites may include viruses, bacteria, fungi, single-celled amoeba, or several types of worms.

What should you know before the test?

- You'll restrict food and fluids for 12 hours before the test.
- A doctor or nurse will collect the specimen by putting a tube into your nose and stomach or by using a weighted gelatine capsule with a string attached.
- If the test is to be done with a tube through your nose, be aware that you may gag during the tube's passage. Following the examiner's instructions about positioning, breathing, and swallowing will minimize discomfort.
- You'll be told to empty your bladder just before the procedure.

What happens during the test?

Tube insertion

- After the tube is inserted, you lie on your left side, with your feet elevated, to allow your stomach's action to move the tube into the duodenum.
- Fluoroscopy may be used to confirm that the tube is in position and suction can start.

Capsule and string

- The doctor tapes the free end of the string to your cheek.
- You swallow the gelatin capsule with water.
- The string remains in place for 4 hours and then is pulled out gently and placed in a sterile container.

What happens after the test?

You can resume your normal diet.

Does the test have risks?

The test won't be given if you're a pregnant woman or have any of the following conditions: acute cholecystitis; acute pancreatitis; esophageal varices, stenosis, diverticula, or malignant cancers; recent, severe stomach hemorrhage; aortic aneurysm; or congestive heart failure.

What are the normal results?

Normally, no eggs or parasites appear.

What do abnormal results mean?

Diagnosis depends upon the type of parasite found. Finding *Giardia lamblia* indicates giardiasis, possibly causing malabsorption syndrome; *Strongyloides stercoralis* suggests strongyloidiasis; *Ancylostoma duodenale* and *Necator americanus* imply hookworm disease. Infestation of the bile ducts by liver flukes, such as *Clonorchis sinensis* and *Fasciola hepatica,* are rare in North America.

BLOOD IN FECES

This test, which doctors call the *fecal occult blood test,* is used to detect abnormal gastrointestinal bleeding. Fecal occult blood is detected by microscopic analysis or by chemical tests for hemoglobin. Normally, feces contain small amounts of blood (2 to 2.5 milliliters per day), so the test is for larger quantities. Additional tests are required to pinpoint the origin of the bleeding. (See *Common sites and causes of gastrointestinal blood loss*, page 650.)

Why is this test done?

The fecal occult blood test may be performed for the following reasons:
- To detect gastrointestinal bleeding
- To aid an early diagnosis of colorectal cancer.

What should you know before the test?

- You'll be told to maintain a high-fiber diet and to refrain from eating red meats, poultry, fish, turnips, and horseradish for 48 to 72 hours before the test as well as throughout the collection period.
- The test requires collection of three stool specimens. Occasionally, only a random specimen is collected.
- If you're taking certain medications, they may be stopped for 48 hours before and during the test.

What happens during the test?

- You collect three stool specimens or a random specimen from the toilet, using a tongue depressor or a small applicator.
- You should be careful not to contaminate the specimen with urine or toilet paper.
- A lab technician or the nurse tests the specimen.

Common sites and causes of gastrointestinal blood loss

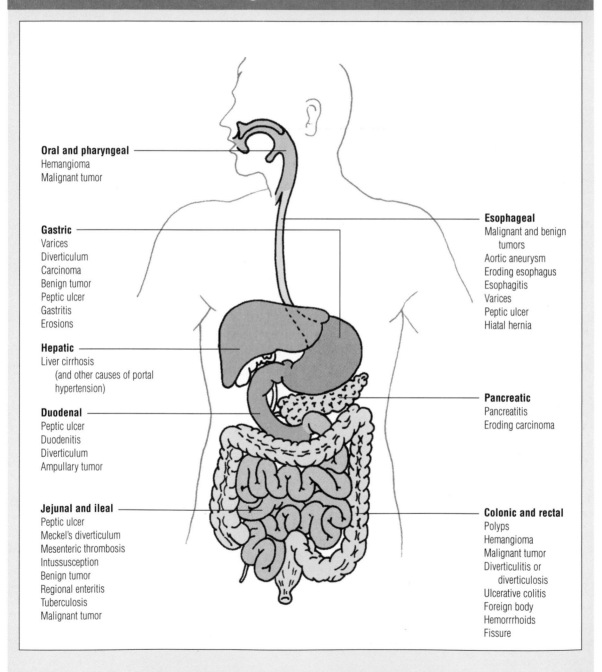

Oral and pharyngeal
Hemangioma
Malignant tumor

Gastric
Varices
Diverticulum
Carcinoma
Benign tumor
Peptic ulcer
Gastritis
Erosions

Hepatic
Liver cirrhosis
   (and other causes of portal
   hypertension)

Duodenal
Peptic ulcer
Duodenitis
Diverticulum
Ampullary tumor

Jejunal and ileal
Peptic ulcer
Meckel's diverticulum
Mesenteric thrombosis
Intussusception
Benign tumor
Regional enteritis
Tuberculosis
Malignant tumor

Esophageal
Malignant and benign
   tumors
Aortic aneurysm
Eroding esophagus
Esophagitis
Varices
Peptic ulcer
Hiatal hernia

Pancreatic
Pancreatitis
Eroding carcinoma

Colonic and rectal
Polyps
Hemangioma
Malignant tumor
Diverticulitis or
   diverticulosis
Ulcerative colitis
Foreign body
Hemorrrhoids
Fissure

What happens after the test?

After the test you can resume your usual diet and medication schedule.

What are the normal results?

Normally, less than 2.5 milliliters of blood are found.

What do abnormal results mean?

Too much blood in the feces indicates gastrointestinal bleeding, which may be caused by many disorders, such as varices, peptic ulcer, cancer, ulcerative colitis, dysentery, or hemorrhagic disease. This test is particularly important for early diagnosis of colorectal cancer. Further tests, such as barium swallow, analyses of stomach contents, and endoscopic procedures, are necessary to define the site and extent of bleeding.

FATS IN FECES

This test, which doctors call the *fecal lipids test*, is used to evaluate your digestion of fats. When bile and pancreas secretions are adequate, dietary fats are almost completely absorbed in the small intestine. When they aren't, this procedure is used to extract unabsorbed fat from the feces and weigh it to evaluate the problem.

Why is this test done?

The fecal lipids test may be performed to confirm steatorrhea (excessive fat in the feces) and to investigate signs of poor absorption in the digestive tract, such as weight loss, abdominal distention, and scaly skin.

What should you know before the test?

- You'll be told not to drink alcohol and to maintain a high-fat diet (3.5 ounces [100 grams] per day) for 3 days before the test and during the collection period.
- The test requires a 72-hour stool collection.
- If you're taking medications that could affect the test results, they may be stopped.
- The nurse will teach you how to do a timed, 72-hour stool collection.
- The lab requires 1 or 2 days to complete the analysis.

What happens during the test?

■ You collect stool specimens from the toilet over a 72-hour period, using depressors or a commercially available kit.

■ Be sure to avoid contaminating the stool specimens with toilet tissue or urine.

What happens after the test?

You may resume your usual diet and any medications withheld before the test.

What are the normal results?

Fecal fats normally comprise less than 20% of excreted solids, with excretion of less than 7 grams per 24 hours.

What do abnormal results mean?

Both digestive and absorptive disorders cause excessive fat in the feces. Digestive disorders may affect the production and release of pancreatic lipase or bile. Absorptive disorders may affect the integrity of the intestine. Investigating these disorders may lead the doctor to consider a long list of potential problems with the pancreas, liver, intestines, and lymph glands.

Symptoms that may prompt a doctor to order this test include weight loss, abdominal distention, and scaly skin.

STOOL TEST FOR INTESTINAL PARASITES

This test is used to look for intestinal parasitic infection. Examination of a stool specimen can reveal several types of intestinal parasites or their eggs. Some of these parasites are harmless. Others cause intestinal disease.

In North America, the most common parasites include the roundworms *Ascaris lumbricoides* and *Necator americanus* (hookworms); the pinworm *Enterobius follicularis;* the tapeworms *Diphyllobothrium latum, Taenia saginata*, and *T. solium* (rare); the amoeba *Entamoeba histolytica*; and the flagellate *Giardia lamblia*.

Why is this test done?

The examination of stool specimens is done to confirm or rule out intestinal parasitic infection and disease.

What should you know before the test?

■ You'll be told to avoid treatments with castor or mineral oil, bismuth, magnesium or antidiarrheal compounds, barium enemas, and antibiotics for 7 to 10 days before the test.

■ The test requires three stool specimens — one every other day or every third day. Up to six specimens may be required to confirm the presence of *Entamoeba histolytica.*

■ If you have diarrhea, the nurse will ask about your recent dietary and travel history. The nurse will also ask about other drugs that might influence the test and whether you've taken them within the past 2 weeks.

■ The nurse will teach you how to collect and store the specimens.

What happens during the test?

■ Collect the specimen from the toilet with a tongue depressor or a commercially available kit.

■ Be careful not to contaminate the specimen with toilet paper or urine. Don't collect a specimen from the toilet bowl. Any contamination can kill the parasites and invalidate the test.

■ If you're bedridden, the nurse collects the specimen in a bedpan and transfers it to a special container. (See *Checking for pinworms.*)

What are the normal results?

Normally, no parasites or eggs appear in stools.

What do abnormal results mean?

The presence of parasites confirms the suspected disorders and may lead to more tests.

Since injury to the person is difficult to detect — even when a worm's eggs or larvae appear — the number of worms usually correlates with the person's clinical symptoms. The information is used to distinguish between worm infestation and worm-caused diseases.

Parasites may be causing damage in other parts of the body. For example, the roundworm *Ascaris* may perforate the bowel wall, causing peritonitis, or may migrate to the lungs, causing pneumonia. Hookworms can cause a form of anemia due to bloodsucking and hemorrhage, especially in people with iron-deficient diets. The tapeworm *D. latum* may cause a form of anemia by removing vitamin B_{12}.

INSIGHT INTO ILLNESS

Checking for pinworms

The eggs of the pinworm seldom appear in feces because the female migrates to the person's anus and deposits her eggs there. To collect the eggs, the nurse places a piece of cellophane tape, sticky side out, on the end of a tongue depressor and presses it firmly to the anal area.

When eggs are found

The tape is transferred, sticky side down, to a slide. Since the female pinworm usually deposits her eggs at night, the best time to collect the specimen is early in the morning, before the person bathes or defecates.

INFECTIOUS DIARRHEA VIRUS

This procedure involves the examination of a stool sample for antigens to the rotavirus. This virus is the most frequent cause of infectious diarrhea in infants and young children. They're most prevalent in children ages 3 months to 2 years during the winter. Rotavirus causes diarrhea, vomiting, fever, and abdominal pain. Symptoms of infection may range from mild in adults to severe in young children, especially hospitalized infants.

Because human rotaviruses do not multiply well in lab cell cultures, a quick test with a sensitive, specific enzyme may be needed to catch them.

Why is this test done?

This stool examination is done to obtain a lab diagnosis of rotavirus gastroenteritis.

What should you know before the test?

- The test requires a stool specimen.
- If possible, collect the specimens when the disease is first suspected or during the acute stage of the infection to ensure detection of the viral antigens.

What happens during the test?

- Usually, a nurse or medical technician collects a 1-gram stool specimen in a screw-capped tube or vial. If a microbiological transport swab is used, it must be heavily stained with feces to detect the rotavirus.
- The child or adult being tested should be given extra fluids to avoid dehydration caused by vomiting and diarrhea.

What are the normal results?

Normally, there are no rotaviruses in stools.

What do abnormal results mean?

The detection of rotavirus by enzyme immunoassay indicates a current infection with the organism. The severity of disease is generally greater in young children than in adults. Rotavirus infections are easily transmitted in group settings such as nursing homes, preschools, and day-care centers. Transmission is presumed to occur from person-to-person by the fecal-oral route—making hand washing the best defense.

REPRODUCTIVE SYSTEM

CHROMOSOME ANALYSIS

Chromosome analysis is done to study the relationship between the microscopic appearance of chromosomes and an individual's phenotype—the expression of the genes in physical, biochemical, or physiologic traits.

Ideally, chromosomes are studied during the middle phase of mitosis (cell division). Cells are harvested, stained, and then examined under a microscope. These cells are then photographed to record the karyotype—the systematic arrangement of chromosomes in groupings according to size and shape.

Only rapidly dividing cells, such as bone marrow or neoplastic cells, permit direct, immediate study. In other cells, mitosis is stimulated by the addition of phytohemagglutinin. Indications for the test determine the specimen required (blood, bone marrow, amniotic fluid, skin, or placental tissue) and the specific analytic procedure.

Why is this test done?

The chromosome analysis may be performed to identify chromosomal abnormalities as the underlying cause of malformation, irregular development, or disease.

What should you know before the test?

■ The test will require a sample of your blood or a specimen of tissue, bone marrow, or amniotic fluid (to test a fetus).
■ The length of time before results will be available varies according to the specimen required. For example, test results on a blood sample

Chromosomes and sex characteristics

A mammal's eggs fertilized by sperm bearing an X chromosome become females (XX), while those fertilized by sperm bearing a Y chromosome become males (XY).

The Y chromosome causes the indifferent gonad to organize testes. The testes then secrete testosterone, causing the male body type. In the absence of the Y chromosome and testosterone secretion, ovaries form, and the embryo becomes a female.

How people with female chromosomes develop testes
Occasionally, female XX embryos develop testes and become males, or male XY embryos develop ovaries and become females. Also, either type of embryo may have a combination of testicular and ovarian tissue (true hermaphroditism). It's believed that only a small portion of the Y chromosome causes testes to form. Therefore, XX persons with testes have probably conserved this critical portion of the Y chromosome, which remains active.

Reasons for chromosome studies

Listed below are common specimens used in chromosome analysis and the reasons for their use.

Blood
- To evaluate abnormal appearance or development suggesting chromosomal irregularity
- To evaluate couples with a history of miscarriages or to identify balanced translocation carriers
- To detect chromosomal rearrangements in rare genetic diseases predisposing patient to malignant neoplasms

Blood or bone marrow
To identify Philadelphia chromosome and confirm chronic myelogenous leukemia

Skin
To evaluate abnormal appearance or development suggesting chromosomal irregularity

Amniotic fluid
To evaluate a developing fetus with possible chromosomal abnormality

Placental tissue
To evaluate products of conception after a miscarriage to determine if abnormality is fetal or placental in origin

are generally available in 72 to 96 hours. Analysis of skin biopsy specimens or amniotic fluid cells may take several weeks.

What happens during the test?

- A nurse or medical technician collects the sample, depending on the doctor's preferred method.
- If it's a blood sample, a nurse or medical technician inserts a needle into a vein, usually in your forearm. The blood sample is collected in a tube, which is then sent to a lab for testing.
- Although you may feel a sting from the needle and pressure from the tourniquet, collecting the sample takes only a few minutes.

What happens after the test?

If swelling develops at the needle puncture site, apply warm soaks.

What are the normal results?

The normal cell contains 46 chromosomes: 22 pairs of autosomes (nonsex chromosomes) and 1 pair of sex chromosomes (Y for the male-determining chromosome, X for the female-determining chromosome).

What do abnormal results mean?

Chromosome abnormalities may be in their numbers or their structures. The chromosome pairs may not have separated properly during cell division, or part of a chromosome may have broken off or traded parts to produce an unbalanced chromosome. The significance of chromosome analysis results depends on the specimen and indications for the test. (See *Chromosomes and sex characteristics*, page 655, and *Reasons for chromosome studies*.)

AMNIOCENTESIS

Amniocentesis, which doctors sometimes call *amniotic fluid analysis*, is used to detect fetal abnormalities. In this procedure, a doctor uses a needle to withdraw 10 to 20 milliliters of amniotic fluid from a pregnant woman for lab analysis.

This analysis may be used to detect certain birth defects, such as Down's syndrome or spina bifida. It can be used to find out the baby's sex and to detect diseases in the womb. It requires a level of amniotic fluid usually reached after the 16th week of pregnancy. The doctor may recommend amniocentesis if the mother is over age 35, if she's had a miscarriage, or if there's a family history of genetic, chromosomal, or neural tube defects.

Why is this test done?

Aspirating amniotic fluid may be performed for the following reasons:

- To detect fetal abnormalities, particularly chromosomal and neural tube defects
- To detect hemolytic disease of the newborn
- To diagnose metabolic disorders, amino acid disorders, and mucopolysaccharidoses
- To determine fetal age and maturity, especially lung maturity
- To assess fetal health by detecting the presence of meconium or blood or measuring amniotic levels of estriol and fetal thyroid hormone
- To identify fetal gender when one or both parents are carriers of a sex-linked disorder.

What should you know before the test?

- You won't need to change your diet before the test.
- The test requires a specimen of amniotic fluid; a nurse or doctor will perform the test.
- Normal test results can't guarantee a normal fetus because some fetal disorders are undetectable.
- You'll be asked to sign a consent form.
- You'll feel a stinging sensation when the local anesthetic is injected.
- You should empty your bladder just before the test to minimize the risk of puncturing the bladder and aspirating urine instead of amniotic fluid.

What happens during the test?

- The doctor locates a pool of amniotic fluid after finding the fetus and placental position, usually through palpation and ultrasound.
- Your skin is prepared with antiseptic and alcohol; then the anesthetic is injected.

How the doctor aspirates amniotic fluid

After the doctor knows the position of the placenta and fetus, the aspirating needle is inserted through the abdominal wall at a right angle.

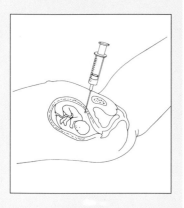

- The doctor inserts a needle with a stylet into the amniotic cavity.
- A 10-milliliter syringe is attached to the needle; then the fluid is aspirated and placed in a test tube.
- The needle is withdrawn, and an adhesive bandage is placed over the needle insertion site.

What happens after the test?

- The doctor will monitor the fetal heart rate and your vital signs.
- The doctor will tell you to report any abdominal pain or cramping, chills, fever, vaginal bleeding or leakage of vaginal fluid, or unusually high or low fetal activity immediately.

Does the test have risks?

Although side effects are rare, there's a small chance of miscarriage, injury to the fetus or placenta, bleeding, premature labor, infection, and Rh sensitization from fetal bleeding into the mother's circulation. Due to the severity of possible complications, amniocentesis isn't used as a general screening test. (See *How the doctor aspirates amniotic fluid.*)

Another method of detecting fetal chromosomal and biochemical disorders in early pregnancy is chorionic villi sampling. (See *Answers to questions about chorionic villi sampling.*)

What are the normal results?

Normal amniotic fluid is clear, but may contain white flecks of a material called *vernix caseosa* when the fetus is near term.

What do abnormal results mean?

Blood in amniotic fluid is usually the mother's and doesn't indicate an abnormality. However, it does inhibit cell growth and crowd out other constituents. The other matter that's found in the fluid includes the following, along with their indications:

- Large amounts of bilirubin, a byproduct of red blood cell breakdown, may indicate hemolytic disease of the newborn.
- Meconium, found in the fetal gastrointestinal tract, passes into the amniotic fluid when low oxygen causes fetal distress and relaxation of the anal sphincter.
- Creatinine, a product of fetal urine, increases in the amniotic fluid as the fetal kidneys mature.

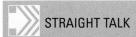

Answers to questions about chorionic villi sampling

What is chorionic villi sampling?
Chorionic villi sampling, or biopsy, is a prenatal test for quick detection of fetal disorders that's done in the first trimester (3 months) of pregnancy.

What are chorionic villi?
The chorionic villi are fingerlike projections that surround the embryonic membrane and eventually form the placenta. Cells are fetal rather than maternal, so they can be checked for fetal abnormalities.

What are the benefits of this test?
Preliminary results may be available within hours; complete results within a few days. In contrast, amniocentesis cannot be performed before the 16th week of pregnancy, and the results aren't available for at least 2 weeks. Thus, chorionic villi sampling can detect fetal abnormalities as much as 10 weeks sooner than amniocentesis.

Chorionic villi sampling can be used to detect about 200 diseases prenatally. For example, direct analysis of rapidly dividing fetal cells can detect chromosome disorders. DNA analysis can detect blood disorders and lysomal enzyme assays can screen for lysosomal storage disorders such as Tay-Sachs disease.

When should it be performed?
Samples are best obtained between the 8th and 10th weeks of pregnancy — when the fetus has grown large enough to make the procedure less difficult. After the 10th week, it may be more dangerous.

What is the downside?
The test is reliable unless the sample contains too few cells or the cells fail to grow in the culture. The mother's risks for this procedure appear to be somewhat greater than those for amniocentesis — a small chance of miscarriage, cramps, infection, and bleeding. However, recent research reports an incidence of limb malformations in newborns when chorionic villi sampling has been performed.

Unlike amniocentesis, chorionic villi sampling can't detect complications in cases of Rh sensitization, uncover neural tube defects, or determine pulmonary maturity. However, it may prove to be the best way to detect other serious fetal abnormalities early in pregnancy.

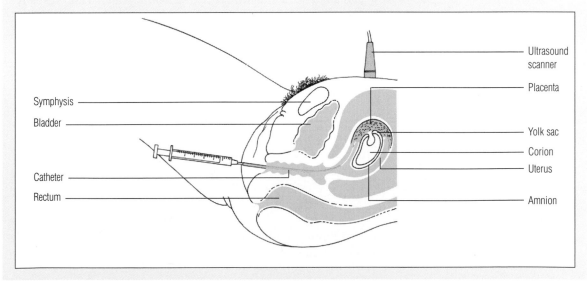

■ Alpha-fetoprotein is produced first in the yolk sac and later in the liver and gastrointestinal tract. High levels indicate neural tube defects, but the alpha-fetoprotein levels may remain normal if the defect is small and closed. Elevated alpha-fetoprotein levels may occur in multiple pregnancy and in a number of serious disorders.

■ Uric acid in the amniotic fluid increases as the fetus matures, but levels fluctuate widely and can't accurately predict maturity.

■ Estrone, estradiol, estriol, and estriol conjugates appear in amniotic fluid in varying amounts. Severe erythroblastosis fetalis decreases the estriol level.

If blood in amniotic fluid is the mother's, it doesn't usually indicate an abnormality.

■ Blood in the amniotic fluid (in about 10% of people tested) is caused by a faulty tap. If the origin is the mother's, the blood generally has no special significance. However, "portwine" fluid may be a sign of a damaged placenta, while blood of fetal origin may indicate damage to the fetal, placental, or umbilical cord vessels by the amniocentesis needle.

■ The Type II cells lining the fetal alveoli (air sacs) in the lungs produce lecithin slowly in early pregnancy and then markedly increase production around the 35th week.

■ The sphingomyelin level helps confirm fetal pulmonary maturity or suggests a risk of respiratory distress.

■ Measuring sugar levels in the fluid can aid in assessing blood sugar control in the diabetic person.

■ Insulin levels increase sharply (up to 27 times normal) in a person with poorly controlled diabetes.

■ Lab analysis can identify at least 25 different enzymes (usually in low concentrations) in amniotic fluid, but they don't explain much.

■ When the mother carries an X-linked disorder, determination of fetal sex is important. If chromosome karyotyping identifies a male fetus, there's a 50% chance he'll be affected; a female fetus won't be affected but has a 50% chance of being a carrier.

PAP TEST

The Papanicolaou (Pap) test allows for the study of cervical cells. It's a widely known test for early detection of cervical cancer. A doctor or specially trained nurse scrapes secretions from the patient's cervix and spreads them on a slide, which is sent to the lab for analysis. The test relies on the shedding of malignant cells from the cervix and shows cell maturity, metabolic activity, and structure variations.

If a Pap test is positive or suggests malignancy, a cervical biopsy (removal and analysis of tissue) can confirm the diagnosis. The test is an important aid to the detection of cancer at a stage when the disease is often without symptoms and still curable. (See *How a Pap test is done*, page 662.)

Why is this test done?

The Pap test may be done for the following reasons:

- To detect malignant cells
- To detect inflammatory tissue changes
- To assess response to chemotherapy and radiation therapy
- To detect viral, fungal and, occasionally, parasitic invasion.

What should you know before the test?

- If you're menstruating, the test will be rescheduled. The best time to have it done is midcycle.
- You'll be told not to douche or insert vaginal medications for 24 hours before the test because doing so can wash away cellular deposits and change the vaginal pH.
- The procedure takes 5 to 10 minutes or slightly longer if the vagina, pelvic cavity, and rectum are examined too.
- The nurse or doctor will ask about your most recent Pap test, your menstrual periods, what sort of birth control you might be using, and other questions that might influence interpretation of the test results.
- The test results should be available within a few days.
- You'll be asked to empty your bladder just before the test.

What happens during the test?

- You undress from the waist down and drape yourself.
- You lie on the examining table and place your heels in the stirrups. (You may be more comfortable if you keep your shoes on.) You slide your buttocks to the edge of the table.
- The examiner puts on gloves and inserts an unlubricated speculum into your vagina. To make insertion easier, the speculum may be moistened with saline solution or warm water.

How a Pap test is done

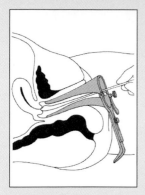

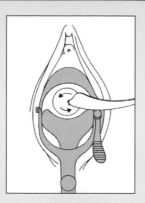

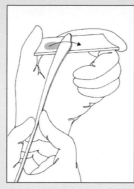

1 An unlubricated speculum is inserted into the vagina. To make insertion easier and more comfortable, the speculum is held under warm running water before insertion.

2 The cervix is exposed by opening the speculum blades. A saline-moistened Pap stick is inserted through the speculum and secretions are scraped from the cervical canal.

3 The specimen is spread on a slide.

4 Immediately, the slide is placed in a fixative solution, or sprayed with a commercial fixative.

■ After the cervix is located, the examiner collects secretions from the cervix and material from the endocervical canal with a saline-moistened cotton-tipped swab or wooden spatula.

What are the normal results?

Normally, no malignant cells or other abnormalities are present.

What do abnormal results mean?

Usually, malignant cells have relatively large nuclei and only small amounts of cytoplasm. They show abnormal nuclear chromatin patterns and marked variation in size, shape, and staining properties and may have prominent nucleoli. The results are reported in four grades of cells from normal to conclusively malignant. To confirm a suggestive or positive cytology report, the test may be repeated or followed by a biopsy.

SEMEN ANALYSIS

Semen analysis is a simple, inexpensive, and reasonably definitive test that's used in a broad range of applications. Analysis can check a man's fertility by measuring the volume of his semen, counting sperm, and examining sperm cells under a microscope. Motility and appearance are studied microscopically after staining a drop of semen.

If analysis detects an abnormality, additional tests (for example, liver, thyroid, pituitary, or adrenal function tests) may be performed. Significant abnormalities — such as greatly decreased sperm count or motility, or marked increase in abnormal forms — may require a testicular biopsy (removal and analysis of tissue).

Why is this test done?

Semen analysis may be performed for the following reasons:

- To evaluate male fertility in an infertile couple
- To prove the effectiveness of vasectomy
- To detect semen on the body or clothing of a suspected rape victim or elsewhere at the crime scene. (See *Semen identification: A tool for investigating crime*, page 664.)
- To identify blood group substances to exonerate or incriminate a criminal suspect
- To rule out paternity on grounds of complete sterility.

What happens before and during the test?

Evaluation of fertility in men

- The doctor or nurse will give you written instructions and suggest that the most useful semen specimen requires masturbation, ideally in a doctor's office or a lab.
- You'll need to follow the instructions given you about avoiding sex before the test because this may increase your sperm count. Some doctors specify a fixed number of days, usually between 2 and 5. Others advise a period of continence equal to the usual interval between episodes of sexual intercourse.
- If you prefer to collect the specimen at home, you must deliver it to the lab within 3 hours after collection. Don't expose the specimen to extreme temperatures or to direct sunlight (which can also increase its temperature). Ideally, the specimen should remain at

Semen identification: A tool for investigating crime

Sperm cells (or their fragments) can live in the vagina for more than 72 hours after sexual intercourse. This allows detection and positive identification of semen from vaginal smears or from stains on clothing, other fabrics, skin, or hair. Identification is often necessary for legal purposes, usually in connection with rape or homicide investigations. Sperm taken from the vagina of an exhumed body that has been properly embalmed and remains reasonably intact can also be identified.

Gathering the evidence
To decide which stains or fluids require further investigation, clothing or other fabrics can be scanned with ultraviolet light to detect the typical green-white fluorescence of semen. Semen and sperm can be collected by soaking samples of clothing, fabric, or hair in saline solution. Suspect deposits

of dried semen can be gently sponged from the victim's skin.

How forensic scientists identify semen
The two most common tests to identify semen are acid phosphatase concentration (the more sensitive test) and microscopic examination for the presence of sperm. Acid phosphatase appears in semen in significantly greater concentrations than in any other body fluid. In microscopic examination, sperm cells or their head fragments can be identified on stained smears prepared directly from vaginal scrapings or aspirates, or from the concentrated sediment of material rinsed from clothing or the vagina.

Semen analysis can demonstrate that the semen of a suspect in a rape or homicide investigation is different from or consistent with semen found in or on the victim's body.

body temperature until liquefaction is complete (about 20 minutes). To deliver a semen specimen to the lab during cold weather, carry the specimen in an inside pocket.

■ Alternatives to collection by masturbation include coitus interruptus or the use of a condom. For collection by coitus interruptus, you should withdraw immediately before ejaculation, and deposit the semen in a specimen container. For collection by condom, first wash the condom with soap and water, rinse it thoroughly, and allow it to dry completely. (Powders or lubricants applied to the condom may be spermicidal.) After collection, tie the condom, place it in a glass jar, and promptly deliver it to the lab.

Evaluation of fertility in women
■ Fertility may also be determined by collecting semen from the woman after intercourse. This method measures the sperm's ability to penetrate the cervical mucus and remain active.

■ For the postcoital cervical mucus test, you report for examination during the ovulatory phase of your menstrual cycle, as determined by basal temperature records, and as soon as possible after sexual intercourse (within 8 hours).

- You're put in the same position as for a Pap smear and the doctor inserts a speculum into your vagina to collect the specimen. You may feel some pressure but no pain during this procedure, which takes only a few minutes.

Semen collection from a rape victim

- You'll be asked to empty your bladder just before the test, but don't wipe the vulva afterward because this may remove semen.
- The examiner tries to obtain a semen specimen from your vagina.
- You're put into the same position as if you were having a Pap test.
- If the doctor is using vaginal lavage to rinse out a specimen, you should expect a cold sensation when the saline solution is introduced.

What are the normal results?

Normal semen volume ranges from 2 to 50 milliliters and is slightly alkaline with a pH of 5 to 10. Paradoxically, the semen volume of men in infertile couples is frequently increased. Continence for 1 week or more progressively increases semen volume (sperm counts increase with abstinence up to 10 days, sperm motility decreases, and sperm condition stays the same).

Other normal characteristics of semen are that it coagulates immediately and liquefies within 20 minutes. Normal sperm count is 20 million or more per milliliter. At least 30% of sperm cells appear normal, and at least 25% of sperm cells show motility (the ability to swim) within 2 hours of collection.

What do abnormal results mean?

Abnormal semen does *not* mean infertility. Only one viable sperm cell is needed to fertilize an egg. Although a normal sperm count is more than 20 million per milliliter, many men with sperm counts below 1 million per milliliter have fathered normal children.

Only men who can't deliver *any* viable sperm in their ejaculate during sexual intercourse are absolutely sterile. Nevertheless, subnormal sperm counts, decreased sperm motility, and abnormal morphology are usually associated with decreased fertility. Other tests may be necessary to evaluate the person's general health, metabolic status, or the function of specific endocrine glands (pituitary, thyroid, adrenal, or gonadal).

Abnormal semen does not mean infertility. Only one viable sperm cell is needed to fertilize an egg.

MISCELLANEOUS TESTS

SPINAL CORD FLUID

This test, which doctors commonly call *cerebrospinal fluid analysis,* analyzes the fluid within the spinal cord. For qualitative analysis, spinal fluid is most commonly obtained by lumbar puncture (usually taken from between the third and fourth lumbar vertebrae in the lower spine). A sample of this fluid for lab analysis is frequently obtained during other neurologic tests such as myelography.

Why is this test done?

The analysis of spinal fluid may be performed for the following reasons:
- To measure spinal fluid pressure, which helps the doctor detect obstruction of its circulation
- To aid the diagnosis of viral or bacterial meningitis, cranial hemorrhage, tumors, and brain abscesses
- To aid the diagnosis of neurosyphilis and chronic central nervous system infections.

What should you know before the test?

- You won't need to change your diet before the test.
- A doctor will perform the procedure, and it usually takes at least 15 minutes. You'll receive a local anesthetic.
- A headache is the most common side effect of a lumbar puncture, but your cooperation during the test helps minimize this effect.
- You'll be asked to sign a consent form.

What happens during the test?

- You lie on your side at the edge of the bed, with your knees drawn up to your abdomen and your chin on your chest.
- If the sitting position is preferred, you sit up and bend your chest and head toward your knees. The nurse helps you maintain this position throughout the procedure.

INSIGHT INTO ILLNESS

Spinal fluid test results

TEST	ABNORMAL RESULTS	WHAT ABNORMAL RESULTS IMPLY
Fluid pressure	Above normal	Hemorrhage, tumor, or fluid accumulation caused by injury
	Below normal	Spinal obstruction above test puncture site
Appearance (normally clear)	Cloudy	Infection or various microorganisms
	Bloody	Hemorrhage, spinal cord obstruction, or injury from the test
	Brown, orange, or yellow	Red blood cell breakdown
Protein level	Well above normal	Tumors, injury, hemorrhage, diabetes, poly-neuritis, or blood in spinal fluid
	Well below normal	Rapid spinal fluid production
Gamma globulin level	Above normal	Multiple sclerosis or similar disease, neuro-syphilis, Guillain-Barré syndrome
Glucose level	Above normal	High blood sugar
	Below normal	Low blood sugar, infection, meningitis, mumps, hemorrhage
White blood cell count	More than five white blood cells	Meningitis, acute infection, onset of chronic illness, tumor, abscess, infarction, multiple sclerosis or similar disease
Red blood cell count	Red blood cells present	Hemorrhage or injury from the test
Venereal disease research lab test or other blood tests	Positive	Neurosyphilis
Chloride level	Below normal	Tuberculosis, meningitis, or similar infection
Gram stain test	Infective organisms present	Bacterial meningitis

- After the skin is prepared for injection, the area is draped. You may experience a transient burning sensation when the local anesthetic is injected.
- When the doctor inserts the spinal needle between the vertebrae of the lower spine, you may feel some transient local pain.
- You should report any pain or sensations that differ from or continue after this expected discomfort because such sensations may indicate irritation or puncture of a nerve root, requiring repositioning of the needle.

■ You should remain still and breathe normally; movement and hyperventilation can alter pressure readings or cause injury.

What happens after the test?

■ After the specimen is collected, you'll probably be told to lie flat for 8 hours. Although you must not raise your head, you can turn from side to side.

■ You'll be encouraged to drink fluids through a flexible straw.

What are the normal results?

Normally, spinal fluid pressure is recorded and the appearance of the specimen is checked. Three tubes are collected routinely and are sent to the lab for analysis of protein, sugar, and cells as well as for serologic testing, such as the Venereal Disease Research Laboratory Test for Neurosyphilis. A separate specimen is also sent to the lab for culture and sensitivity testing. Electrolyte analysis and Gram stain may be ordered as supplementary tests. (For a summary of possible findings in spinal fluid analysis, see *Spinal fluid test results,* page 667.)

JOINT FLUID

This test, which doctors call *synovial fluid analysis,* helps determine the cause of joint inflammation and swelling and also helps relieve your pain. In synovial fluid aspiration, or arthrocentesis, a sterile needle is inserted into a joint space—most commonly the knee—to obtain a fluid specimen for analysis.

Why is this test done?

Synovial fluid analysis may be performed for the following reasons:

■ To help the doctor diagnose arthritis

■ To identify the cause and nature of joint effusion

■ To relieve the pain and distention resulting from accumulation of fluid within the joint

■ To administer a drug locally (usually a corticosteroid).

What should you know before the test?

- You'll be told to fast for 6 to 12 hours before the test if glucose testing of synovial fluid is ordered. Otherwise, you won't need to change your diet before the test.
- You'll be told that you'll receive a local anesthetic. You may still feel transient pain when the needle penetrates the joint capsule.
- You'll be asked to sign a consent form.
- The doctor or nurse may ask if you're taking any medications that might interfere with the test. When possible, administration of such medications will be discontinued before the test.

What happens during the test?

- After the local anesthetic is administered, the aspirating needle is quickly inserted through the skin, tissue under the skin, and synovial membrane into the joint space.
- As much fluid as possible is withdrawn into the syringe.
- The joint (except for the area around the puncture site) may be wrapped with an elastic bandage to compress the free fluid into this portion of the sac, ensuring collection of the most fluid.
- If a corticosteroid is being injected, a nurse applies pressure to the puncture site for about 2 minutes to prevent bleeding and then applies a sterile dressing.
- If synovial fluid glucose levels are being measured, the examiner takes a blood sample.

Most people can enjoy their usual activities immediately after this test is completed.

What happens after the test?

- You'll apply ice or cold packs to the affected joint for 24 to 36 hours after aspiration to decrease pain and swelling. Use pillows for support. If a large quantity of fluid was aspirated, you'll use an elastic bandage to stabilize the joint.
- If your condition permits, you may resume your normal diet and normal activity immediately after the procedure. However, avoid excessive use of the joint for a few days after the test, even if pain and swelling subside.

What are the normal results?

Examination of synovial fluid in the lab can take many forms. Routine examination includes gross analysis for color, clarity, quantity, viscosity, pH, and the presence of a mucin clot as well as microscopic analysis for white blood cell count and differential. Special examination includes microbiological analysis for formed elements (including crystals) and bacteria, serologic analysis, and chemical analysis for such components as glucose, protein, and enzymes.

What do abnormal results mean?

Examination of synovial fluid may reveal various joint diseases, including noninflammatory disease (traumatic arthritis and osteoarthritis), inflammatory disease (lupus, rheumatic fever, pseudogout, gout, and rheumatoid arthritis), and septic disease (tuberculous and septic arthritis).

FLUID AROUND THE HEART

This test, which doctors call *pericardial fluid analysis*, detects excessive fluid around your heart. It also helps the doctor determine the cause of excess fluid and plan appropriate therapy.

The fluid examined during the test is withdrawn from inside the pericardial sac of the heart. (See *The sac that guards your heart.*) Testing is usually performed on people with pericardial effusion (an accumulation of excess pericardial fluid), which may result from inflammation (as in pericarditis), rupture, or penetrating injury. Obtaining a specimen for analysis requires needle aspiration of pericardial fluid, a procedure called *pericardiocentesis*.

Why is this test done?

Pericardial fluid analysis may be performed to help the doctor identify the cause of pericardial effusion and to help determine appropriate therapy.

What should you know before the test?

- You won't need to change your diet before the test.
- This test takes 10 to 20 minutes.
- You'll be given a local anesthetic before the aspiration needle is inserted to relieve any discomfort.
- Although fluid aspiration isn't painful, you may experience pressure upon insertion of the needle into the pericardial sac.

HOW YOUR BODY WORKS

The sac that guards your heart

The pericardium, a fluid-filled sac, surrounds the heart wall. It consists of two layers. The *visceral pericardium* (also called the *epicardium*) serves as the pericardium's inner wall and the heart wall's outer layer. The *parietal pericardium*, a smooth, translucent membrane, serves as the pericardium's outer wall. The cavity between the parietal and visceral pericardium contains 20 to 50 milliliters of lymphlike lubricating fluid.

The important functions of the pericardium
Besides lubricating and isolating the beating heart, the pericardium also:
- holds the heart in a fixed position
- prevents the great vessels from kinking
- restrains ventricular dilation during exertion, preventing overstretching of the myocardium, a layer of the heart wall.

PERICARDIUM

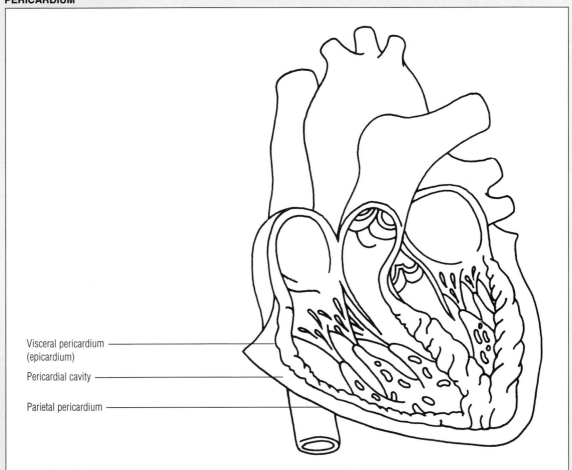

Visceral pericardium
(epicardium)

Pericardial cavity

Parietal pericardium

Once you're comfortable and well-supported, you remain still during the procedure.

- You may be asked to briefly hold your breath to aid needle insertion and placement.
- An intravenous line will be started at a slow rate in case medications need to be administered.
- Your vital signs, including pulse and blood pressure, will be monitored after the procedure.
- The doctor or nurse will ask about the use of any drugs that might interfere with obtaining accurate test results.
- You'll be asked to sign a consent form.

What happens during the test?

- You lie down with your chest elevated 60 degrees.
- Once you're comfortable and well-supported, you remain still during the procedure.
- You're given a local anesthetic.
- The doctor inserts a needle through your chest wall into the pericardial sac. Fluid is gently aspirated into the syringe.
- During needle insertion, your heart rate and rhythm are carefully monitored on an electrocardiograph.

What happens after the test?

- When the needle is withdrawn, a nurse will apply pressure to the site with sterile gauze pads for 3 to 5 minutes and then apply a bandage.
- The nurse will check blood pressure readings, pulse, respiration, and heart sounds every 15 minutes until you're stable and then every half hour for 2 hours, every hour for 4 hours, and every 4 hours thereafter. This monitoring is routine.

Does the test have risks?

Pericardiocentesis must be performed cautiously because of the risk of complications, such as myocardial or coronary artery laceration, ventricular fibrillation or vasovagal arrest, pleural infection, or accidental puncture of the lung, liver, or stomach. If possible, echocardiography may be performed before pericardiocentesis. This helps minimize the risk of complications.

What are the normal results?

Normally, 10 to 50 milliliters of sterile fluid are present in the pericardium. Pericardial fluid is clear and straw-colored, without evidence of pathogens, blood, or malignant cells.

What do abnormal results mean?

Generally, pericardial effusions are classified as transudates or exudates. Transudates are protein-poor effusions that are usually caused by mechanical problems. They may be related to the presence of a tumor. Most exudates are caused by inflammation and contain large amounts of protein. If the test reveals exudate effusions, it may signal pericarditis, cancer, heart attack, tuberculosis, rheumatoid disease, or lupus.

The doctor will also look for such problems as turbid or milky liquid caused by the accumulation of lymph or pus in the pericardial sac or from tuberculosis or rheumatoid disease.

Bloody pericardial fluid may indicate a long list of problems, from a heart attack to cancer.

SWEAT TEST

Also called *iontophoresis*, this test is a quantitative measurement of electrolyte concentrations (primarily sodium and chloride) in sweat and is usually performed using a drug that makes the person sweat. It involves putting electrodes on the body and is used almost exclusively in children to confirm cystic fibrosis.

Why is this test done?

The sweat test may be performed to confirm cystic fibrosis.

What should you know before the test?

■ A doctor or nurse will explain the test to the child (if the child is old enough to understand) and, if necessary, will clarify this explanation using clear, simple terms.

■ The child won't need to change his or her diet, medications, or activity before the test.

■ This test takes 20 to 45 minutes (depending on the equipment used).

■ The child may feel a slight tickling sensation during the procedure but won't feel any pain.

■ A child's parents are usually encouraged to assist with preparations and to stay with the child during the test. Your presence will minimize the child's anxiety.

This test may tickle a bit.

What happens during the test?

- The doctor washes the area that will undergo the sweat test with distilled water and dries it. (The right forearm is commonly used or, when the child's arm is too small to secure electrodes, the right thigh.)
- The doctor applies two electrodes to the area to be measured and secures them with straps. Lead wires to the analyzer are given a mild electric current for 15 to 20 seconds. The test continues at 15- to 20-second intervals for 5 minutes.
- You may want to distract the child with a book, a toy, or another diversion if he or she becomes nervous or frightened during the test.
- The doctor collects the sweat in a special container to send to the lab.

What happens after the test?

- The nurse will wash the area that was tested with soap and water and dry it thoroughly. If the area looks red, the nurse will reassure the child that this is normal and will disappear within a few hours.
- The child may resume his or her usual activities.

Does the test have risks?

The examiner will stop the test immediately if the child complains of a burning sensation, which usually indicates that the positive electrode is exposed or positioned improperly. The examiner then will adjust the electrode and continue the test.

What are the normal results?

Normal sodium values in sweat range from 10 to 30 milliequivalents per liter. Normal chloride values range from 10 to 35 milliequivalents per liter.

What do abnormal results mean?

Concentrations of sodium and chloride greater than 60 milliequivalents per liter, along with typical symptoms of cystic fibrosis, confirm the diagnosis.

PARASITES IN THE URINARY TRACT

This test is performed to identify the cause of infection in the urinary tract and the reproductive system. Samples of urine or vaginal, urethral, or prostatic secretions are examined under a microscope to detect infection by protozoan parasites called *Trichomonas vaginalis*. These parasites are usually transmitted sexually. This test is performed more often on women than men, since women show symptoms more often.

Why is this test done?

The test may be done to confirm trichomoniasis.

What should you know before the test?

- For a woman, the test requires a specimen of vaginal secretions or urethral discharge. You'll be asked not to douche before the test.
- For a man, the test requires a specimen of urethral or prostatic secretions.

What happens during the test?

Vaginal secretion

- You lie on your back, draped, on an exam table, as you would for a Pap test, with your feet in stirrups. (Shoes may make that more comfortable.)
- The examiner inserts an unlubricated speculum into your vagina and collects any discharge with a cotton swab, which is placed in a container and sent to the lab.

Prostatic material

The examiner massages the prostate to produce secretions. The secretions are collected with a cotton swab, which is placed in a container and sent to the lab.

Urethral discharge

The examiner collects the discharge with a cotton swab, which is placed in a container and sent to the lab.

Urine

You void once into a special container, taking care to collect the first portion of the urine stream. The container is then taken to the lab.

What are the normal results?

Trichomonads are normally absent from the urogenital tract.

What do abnormal results mean?

The presence of trichomonads in any of the samples confirms trichomoniasis. In approximately 25% of women and in most infected men, trichomonads may be present without any harmful results.

INDEX

Note: t indicates table; i indicates illustration.

Note: t indicates table; i indicates illustration.

Note: t indicates table; i indicates illustration.

Note: t indicates table; i indicates illustration.

Note: t indicates table; i indicates illustration.

Note: t indicates table; i indicates illustration.

Note: t indicates table; i indicates illustration.

Note: t indicates table; i indicates illustration.

Note: t indicates table; i indicates illustration.

Note: t indicates table; i indicates illustration.

Note: t indicates table; i indicates illustration.

Note: t indicates table; i indicates illustration.

Note: t indicates table; i indicates illustration.

Note: t indicates table; i indicates illustration.

CLASSIC BOOK OF CHILDREN'S STORIES

FIVE FAMOUS BOOKS IN ONE VOLUME

ALICE IN WONDERLAND

ROBINSON CRUSOE

THE ARABIAN NIGHTS

GULLIVER'S TRAVELS

LITTLE WOMEN

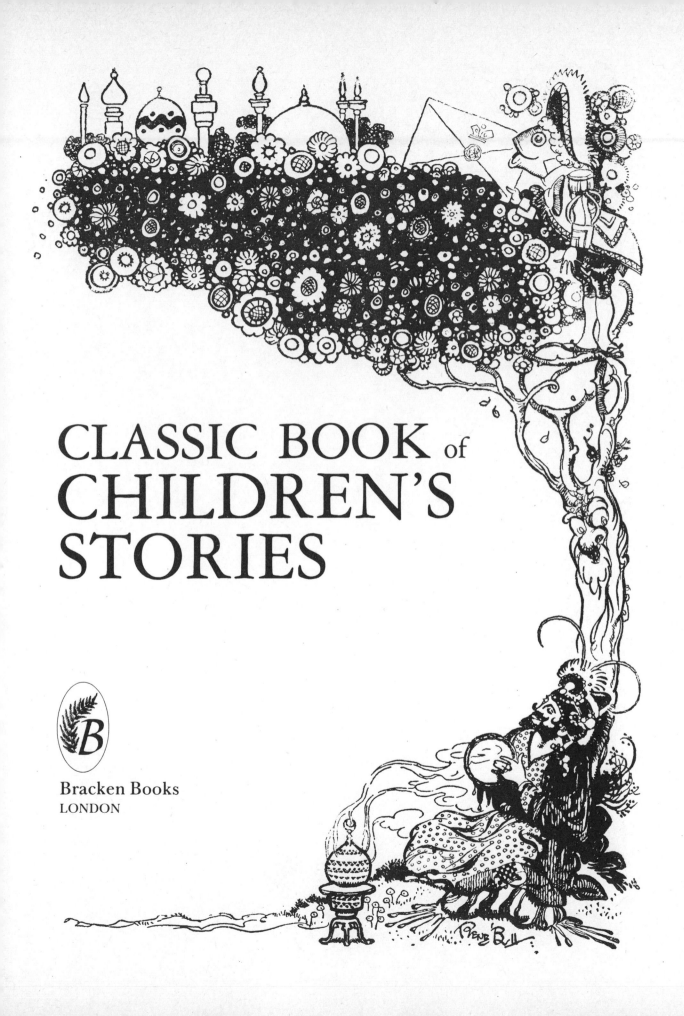

CLASSIC BOOK of CHILDREN'S STORIES

Bracken Books
LONDON

First published 1934

This edition published 1986 by Bracken Books,
a division of Bestseller Publications Limited, Brent House,
24 Friern Park, London N12 9DA, England.

Copyright © Bracken Books, 1986.
ISBN 0 946495 53 X

Printed in Hungary

CONTENTS

ILLUSTRATIONS
IN COLOUR

GULLIVER'S TRAVELS

by DEAN SWIFT

CHAPTER I

MY father had a small estate in Nottinghamshire ; I was the third of five sons. He sent me to Emanuel College in Cambridge, at fourteen years old, where I resided three years, and applied myself close to my studies ; but the charge of maintaining me, although I had a very scanty allowance, being too great for a narrow fortune, I was bound apprentice to Mr. James Bates, an eminent surgeon in London, with whom I continued four years ; and my father now and then sending me small sums of money, I laid them out in learning navigation, and other parts of the mathematics, useful to those who intend to travel, as I always believed it would be some time or other my fortune to do. When I left Mr. Bates, I went down to my father ; where, by the assistance of him and my Uncle John, and some other relations, I got forty pounds, and a promise of thirty pounds a year to maintain me at Leyden : there I studied physic two years and seven months, knowing it would be useful in long voyages.

Soon after my return from Leyden, I was recommended by my good master, Mr. Bates, to be surgeon to the *Swallow*, Captain Abraham Pannell, commander ; with whom I continued three years and a half, making a voyage or two into the Levant, and some other parts. When I came back, I resolved to settle in London, to which Mr. Bates, my master, encouraged me, and by him I was recommended to several patients.

But, my good master, Bates, dying in two years after, and I having few friends, my business began to fail ; so I determined to go again to sea. I was surgeon successively in two ships, and made several voyages for six years to the East and West Indies, by which I got some addition to my fortune.

The last of these voyages not proving very fortunate, I grew weary of the sea, and intended to stay at home with my wife and family. I removed from the Old Jewry to Fetter Lane, and from thence to Wapping, hoping to get business among the sailors ; but it would not turn to account. After three years' expectation that things would mend, I accepted an advantageous offer from Captain William Pritchard, master of the *Antelope*, who was making a voyage to the South Seas. We set sail from Bristol, 4th May, 1699, and our voyage at first was very prosperous.

In our passage to the East Indies, we were driven by a violent storm to the north-west of Van Diemen's Land. Twelve of our crew were dead by immoderate labour and ill food ; the rest were in a very weak condition. On the fifth of November, which was the beginning of summer in those parts, the weather being very hazy, the seamen spied a rock, within half a cable's length of the ship ; but the wind was so strong, that we were driven directly upon it, and immediately split.

Six of the crew, of whom I was one, having let down the boat into the sea, made a shift to get clear of the ship and the rock. We rowed about three leagues, till we were able to work no longer, being already spent with labour while we were in the ship. We therefore trusted ourselves to the mercy of the waves, and in about half an hour the boat was overset by a sudden flurry from the north. What became of my companions in the boat, as well as of those who escaped on the rock, or were left in the vessel, I cannot tell ; but conclude they were all lost.

For my own part, I swam as fortune directed me, and was pushed forward by wind and tide. I often let my legs drop, and could feel no bottom : but when I was almost gone, and able to struggle no longer, I found myself within my depth ; and by this time the storm was much abated. The declivity was so small, that I walked near a mile before I got to the shore, which I conjectured was about eight o'clock in the evening.

I then advanced forward near half a mile, but could not discover any sign of houses or inhabitants ; at least I was in so weak a condition that I did not observe them. I was extremely tired, and with that, and the heat of the weather, I found myself much inclined to sleep. I lay down on the grass, which was very short and soft, where I slept sounder than ever I remembered to have done in my life, and, as I reckoned, about nine hours ; for when I awaked it was just daylight.

I attempted to rise, but was not able to stir : for as I happened to lie on my back, I found my arms and legs were strongly fastened on each side to the ground ; and my hair, which was long and thick, tied down in the same manner. I likewise felt several slender ligatures across my body, from my arm-pits to my thighs. I could only look upwards, the sun began to grow hot, and the light offended my eyes. I heard a confused noise about me, but, in the posture I lay, could see nothing except the sky. In a little time I felt something alive moving on my left leg, which, advancing gently forward over my breast, came almost up to my chin ; when, bending my eyes downward as much as I could, I perceived it to be a human creature not six inches high, with a bow and arrow in his hands, and a quiver at his back. In the meantime, I felt at least forty more of the same kind (as I conjectured) following the first.

I was in the utmost astonishment, and roared so loud that they all ran back in a fright ; and some of them, as I was afterwards told, were hurt with the falls they got by leaping from my sides upon the ground. However, they soon returned, and one of them, who ventured so far as to get a full sight of my face, lifting up his hands and eyes by way of admiration, cried out in a shrill but distinct voice, *Hekinah degul :* the others repeated the same words several times, but I then knew not what they meant.

I lay all this while, as the reader may believe, in great uneasiness ; at length, struggling to get loose, I had the fortune to break the strings, and wrench out the pegs that fastened my left arm to the ground ; for, by lifting it up to my face, I discovered the methods they had taken to bind me, and, at the same time, with a violent pull, which gave me excessive pain, I a little

I attempted to rise, but was not able to stir

loosened the strings that tied down my hair on the left side, so that I was just able to turn my head about two inches. But the creatures ran off a second time, before I could seize them ; whereupon there was a great shout in a very shrill accent, and after it ceased, I heard one of them cry aloud, *Tolgo phonac ;* when in an instant I felt above a hundred arrows discharged on my left hand, which pricked me like so many needles ; and, besides, they shot another flight into the air, as we do bombs in Europe, whereof many, I suppose, fell on my body (though I felt them not), and some on my face, which I immediately covered with my left hand.

When this shower of arrows was over, I fell a-groaning with grief and pain, and then striving again to get loose, they discharged another volley larger than the first, and some of them attempted with spears to stick me in the sides ; but, by good luck, I had on me a buff jerkin, which they could not pierce.

I thought it the most prudent method to lie still, and my design was to continue so till night, when my left hand being already loose, I could easily free myself : and as for the inhabitants, I had reason to believe I might be a match for the greatest army they could bring against me, if they were all of the same size with him that I saw. But fortune disposed otherways of me.

When the people observed I was quiet, they discharged no more arrows : but by the noise I heard, I knew their numbers increased ; and about four yards from me, over against my right ear, I heard a knocking for above an hour, like that of people at work ; when turning my head that way, as well as the pegs and strings would permit me, I saw a stage erected, about a foot and half from the ground, capable of holding four of the inhabitants, with two or three ladders to mount it : from whence one of them, who seemed to be a person of quality, made me a long speech, whereof I understood not one syllable.

But I should have mentioned, that before the principal person began his oration, he cried out three times, *Langro dehul san* (these words and the former were afterwards repeated and explained to me). Whereupon immediately about fifty of the inhabitants came and cut the strings that fastened the left side of my head, which gave me the liberty of turning it to the right, and of observing the person and gesture of him that was to speak. He appeared to be of a middle age, and taller than any of the other three who attended him, whereof one was a page that held up his train and seemed to be somewhat longer than my middle finger ; the other two stood one on each side to support him. He acted every part of an orator, and I could observe many periods of threatening, and others of promises, pity, and kindness.

I answered in a few words, but in the most submissive manner, lifting up my left hand and both my eyes to the sun, as calling him for a witness ; and, being almost famished with hunger, having not eaten a morsel for some hours before I left the ship, I found the demands of nature so strong upon me, that I could not forbear showing my impatience (perhaps against the strict rules of decency) by putting my finger frequently to my mouth, to signify that I wanted food.

The *Hurgo* (for so they call a great lord, as I afterwards learned) understood me very well. He descended from the stage, and commanded that several ladders should be applied to my sides, on which above a hundred of the inhabitants mounted, and walked towards my mouth, laden with baskets full of meat, which had been provided and sent thither by the king's orders, upon the first intelligence he received of me. I observed there was the flesh of several animals, but could not distinguish them by the taste. There were shoulders, legs, and loins, shaped like those of mutton, and very well dressed, but smaller than the wings of a lark. I ate them by two or three at a mouthful, and took three loaves at a time, about the bigness of musket bullets. They supplied me as they could, showing a thousand marks of wonder and astonishment at my bulk and appetite.

I then made another sign that I wanted drink. They found by my eating that a small quantity would not suffice me, and being a most ingenious people, they slung up with great dexterity one of their largest hogsheads, then rolled it towards my hand, and beat out the top ; I drank it off at a draught, which I might well do, for it did not hold half a pint, and tasted like a small wine of Burgundy, but much more delicious. They brought me a second hogshead, which I drank in the same manner, and made signs for more ; but they had none to give me.

When I had performed these wonders, they shouted for joy, and danced upon my breast, repeating several times as they did at first, *Hekinah degul*. They made me a sign that I should throw down the two hogsheads, but first warning the people below to stand out of the way, crying aloud, *Borach mevolah ;* and when they saw the vessels in the air, there was a universal shout of *Hekinah degul*.

After some time, when they observed that I made no more demands for meat, there appeared before me a person of high rank from his Imperial Majesty. His Excellency, having mounted on the small of my right leg, advanced forwards up to my face, with about a dozen of his retinue. And producing his credentials under the Signet Royal, which he applied close to my eyes, spoke about ten minutes, without any signs of anger, but with a kind of determinate resolution ; often pointing forwards, which, as I afterwards found, was towards the capital city, about half a mile distant, whither, it was agreed by his Majesty in council, that I must be conveyed. I answered in few words, but to no purpose, and made a sign with my hand that was loose, putting it to the other (but over his Excellency's head, for fear of hurting him or his train) and then to my own head and body, to signify that I desired my liberty.

It appeared that he understood me well enough, for he shook his head by way of disapprobation, and held his hand in a posture, to show that I must be carried as a prisoner. However, he made other signs to let me understand that I should have meat and drink enough, and very good treatment. Whereupon I once more thought of attempting to break my bonds ; but again, when I felt the smart of their arrows upon my face and hands, which were all in blisters, and many of the darts still sticking in them ; and observing likewise that the number of my enemies increased, I gave tokens to let them know that they might do with me what they pleased. Upon this, the Hurgo and his train withdrew, with much civility and cheerful countenances.

Soon after I heard a general shout, with frequent repetitions of the words, *Peplom selan*, and I felt great numbers of people on my left side, relaxing the cords to such a degree, that I was able to turn upon my right. But before this, they had daubed my face and both my hands with a sort of ointment very pleasant to the smell, which in a few minutes removed all the smart of their arrows. These circumstances, added to the refreshment I had received by their victuals and drink, which were very nourishing, disposed me to sleep. I slept about eight hours, as I was afterwards assured ; and it was no wonder, for the physicians, by the emperor's order, had mingled a sleepy potion in the hogsheads of wine.

It seems that, upon the first moment I was discovered sleeping on the ground after my landing, the emperor had early notice of it by an express ; and determined in council that I should be tied in the manner I have related (which was done in the night while I slept) ; that plenty of meat and drink should be sent to me, and a machine prepared to carry me to the capital city.

These people are most excellent mathematicians, and arrived to a great perfection in mechanics, by the countenance and encouragement of the emperor, who is a renowned patron of learning. This prince hath several machines fixed on wheels, for the carriage of trees and other great weights. He often builds his largest men-of-war, whereof some are nine feet long, in the woods where the timber grows, and has them carried on these engines three or four hundred yards to the sea.

Five hundred carpenters and engineers were immediately set at work to prepare the greatest engine they had. It was a frame of wood raised three inches from the ground, about seven feet long, and four wide, moving upon twenty-two wheels. The shout I heard was upon the arrival of this engine, which, it seems, set out four hours after my landing. It was brought parallel to me as I lay.

But the principal difficulty was to raise and place me in this vehicle. Eighty poles, each of one foot high, were erected for this purpose, and very strong cords, of the bigness of pack-thread, were fastened by hooks to many bandages, which the workmen had girt round my neck, my hands, my body, and my legs. Nine hundred of the strongest men were employed to draw up these cords by many pulleys fastened on the poles, and thus, in less than three hours, I was raised, and slung into the engine, and there tied fast. All this I was told, for, while the whole operation was performing, I lay in a profound sleep, by the force of that soporiferous medicine infused into my liquor. Fifteen hundred of the emperor's largest horses, each about four inches and a half high, were employed to draw me towards the metropolis, which, as I said, was half a mile distant.

About four hours after we began our journey, I awaked by a very ridiculous accident ; for the carriage being stopped a while to adjust something that

The emperor ascended the turret with many principal lords

was out of order, two or three of the young natives had the curiosity to see how I looked when I was asleep; they climbed up into the engine, and advancing very softly to my face, one of them, an officer in the Guards, put the sharp end of his half-pike a good way up into my left nostril, which tickled my nose like a straw, and made me sneeze violently: whereupon they stole off unperceived, and it was three weeks before I knew the cause of my waking so suddenly.

We made a long march the remaining part of that day, and rested at night with five hundred guards on each side of me, half with torches, and half with bows and arrows, ready to shoot me if I should offer to stir. The next morning at sunrise we continued our march, and arrived within two hundred yards of the city gates about noon.

The emperor and all his court came out to meet us, but his great officers would by no means suffer his Majesty to endanger his person by mounting on my body.

At the place where the carriage stopped, there stood an ancient temple, esteemed to be the largest in the kingdom, which, having been polluted some years before by an unnatural murder, was, according to the zeal of those people, looked on as profane, and therefore had been applied to common use and all the ornaments and furniture carried away. In this edifice it was determined I should lodge.

The great gate fronting to the north was about four feet high, and almost two feet wide, through which I could easily creep. On each side of the gate was a small window, not above six inches from the ground: into that on the left side the king's smith conveyed fourscore and eleven chains, like those that hang to a lady's watch in Europe, and almost as large, which were locked to my left leg, with six-and-thirty padlocks. Over against this temple, on the other side of the great highway, at twenty feet distance, there was a turret at least five feet high. Here the emperor ascended, with many principal lords of his court, to have an opportunity of viewing me, as I was told, for I could not see them. It was reckoned, that above a hundred thousand inhabitants came out of the town upon the same errand; and, in spite of my guards, I believe there could not be fewer than ten thousand, at several times, who mounted my body by the help of ladders. But a proclamation was soon issued to forbid it, upon the pain of death.

When the workmen found it was impossible for me to break loose, they cut all the strings that bound me; whereupon I rose up with as melancholy a disposition as ever I had in my life. But the noise and astonishment of the people, at seeing me rise and walk, are not to be expressed. The chains that held my left leg were about two yards long, and gave me not only the liberty of walking backwards and forwards in a semicircle, but, being fixed within four inches of the gate, allowed me to creep in, and lie at my full length in the temple.

CHAPTER II

WHEN I found myself on my feet I looked about me, and must confess I never beheld a more entertaining prospect. The country round appeared like a continued garden, and the enclosed fields, which were generally forty feet square, resembled so many beds of flowers. These fields were intermingled with woods of half a stang, and the tallest trees, as I could judge, appeared to be seven feet high. I viewed the town on my left hand, which looked like the painted scene of a city in a theatre.

I had been for some hours extremely tired, however, so I crept into my house, and shut the door after me. But I had to come out again, and to get a little change by stepping backwards and forwards as far as my chains allowed.

I soon found that the emperor had descended from the tower, and advancing on horseback towards me, which had like to have cost him dear ; for the beast, though very well trained, yet wholly unused to such a sight, which appeared as if a mountain moved before him, reared up on his hinder feet : but that prince, who is an excellent horseman, kept his seat, till his attendants ran in and held the bridle, while his Majesty had time to dismount. When he alighted, he surveyed me round with great admiration, but kept without the length of chain. He ordered his cooks and butlers, who were already prepared, to give me victuals and drink, which they pushed forward in a sort of vehicles on wheels, till I could reach them. I took these vehicles, and soon emptied them all ; twenty of them were filled with meat, and ten with liquor. Each of the former afforded me two or three good mouthfuls, and I emptied the liquor of ten vessels, which was contained in earthen vials, into one vehicle, drinking it off at a draught, and so I did with the rest.

The empress and young princes of the blood, of both sexes, attended by many ladies, sat at some distance in their chairs ; but, upon the accident that happened to the emperor's horse, they alighted, and came near his person, which I am now going to describe. He is taller by almost the breadth of my nail than any of his court, which alone is enough to strike an awe into the beholders. His features are strong and masculine, with an Austrian lip and arched nose, his complexion olive, his countenance erect, his body and limbs well proportioned, all his motions graceful, and his deportment majestic. He was then past his prime, being twenty-eight years and three-quarters old, of which he had reigned about seven, in great felicity, and generally victorious.

For the better convenience of beholding him, I lay on my side, so that my face was parallel to his, and he stood but three yards off : however, I had him since many times in my hand, and, therefore, cannot be deceived in the description. His dress was very plain and simple, and the fashion of it, between the Asiatic and the European : but he had on his head a light helmet of gold, adorned with jewels, and a plume on the crest. He held his sword drawn in his hand, to defend himself if I should happen to break loose ; it was almost three inches long, the hilt and scabbard were gold enriched with diamonds. His voice was shrill, but very clear and articulate, and I could distinctly hear it when I stood up.

The poor man squalled terribly when I took my penknife from my pocket

The ladies and courtiers were all most magnificently clad, so that the spot they stood upon seemed to resemble a petticoat spread on the ground, embroidered with figures of gold and silver.

His Imperial Majesty spoke often to me, and I returned answers, but neither of us could understand a syllable.

There were several of his priests and lawyers present (as I conjectured by their habits) who were commanded to address themselves to me, and I spoke to them in as many languages as I had the least smattering of, which were High and Low Dutch, Latin, French, Spanish, Italian, and Lingua Franca ; but all to no purpose.

After about two hours the court retired, and I was left with a strong guard, to prevent the impertinence and probably the malice of the rabble, who were very impatient to crowd about me as near as they durst, and some of them had the impudence to shoot their arrows at me as I sat on the ground by the door of my house, whereof one very narrowly missed my left eye. But the colonel ordered six of the ringleaders to be seized, and thought no punishment so proper, as to deliver them bound into my hands, which some of the soldiers accordingly did, pushing them forwards with the butt ends of their pikes into my reach. I took them all in my right hand, put five of them into my coat pocket, and as to the sixth, I made a countenance as if I would eat him alive. The poor man squalled terribly, and the colonel and his officers were in much pain, especially when they saw me take out my penknife : but I soon put them out of fear ; for, looking mildly, and immediately cutting the string he was bound with, I set him gently on the ground, and away he ran. I treated the rest in the same manner, taking them one by one out of my pocket, and I observed both the soldiers and people were obliged at this mark of my clemency, which was represented very much to my advantage at court.

Towards night I got with some difficulty into my house, where I lay on the ground, and continued to do so about a fortnight; during which time the emperor gave orders to have a bed prepared for me. Six hundred beds of the common measure were brought in carriages, and worked up in my house. A hundred and fifty of their beds, sewn together, made up the breadth and length; and these were four double, which, however, kept me but very indifferently from the hardness of the floor, that was of smooth stone. By the same computation, they provided me with sheets, blankets, and coverlets, which were tolerable enough for one who had been so long inured to hardships.

As the news of my arrival spread through the kingdom, it brought prodigious numbers of rich, idle, and curious people to see me, so that the villages were almost emptied, and great neglect of tillage and household affairs must have ensued, if his Imperial Majesty had not provided, by several proclamations and orders of State, against this inconveniency. He directed that those who had already beheld me should return home, and not presume to come within fifty yards of my house, without licence from court; whereby the secretaries of state got considerable fees.

In the meantime, the emperor had frequent councils, to debate what course should be taken with me; and, I was afterwards assured by a particular friend, a person of great quality, who was as much in the secret as any, that the court was under many difficulties concerning me. They apprehended my breaking loose, that my diet would be very expensive, and might cause a famine. Sometime they determined to starve me, or at least to shoot me in the face and hands with poisoned arrows, which would soon despatch me.

In the midst of these consultations several officers of the army went to the door of the great council chamber, and two of them being admitted, gave an account of my behaviour to the six criminals above mentioned, which made so favourable an impression in the breast of his Majesty and the whole board in my behalf, that an imperial commission was issued out, obliging all the villages, nine hundred yards round the city, to deliver in every morning six beeves, forty sheep, and other victuals, for my sustenance; together with a proportionable quantity of bread, and wine, and other liquors; for the due payment of which his Majesty gave assignments upon his treasury. An establishment was also made of six hundred persons to be my domestics, who had board wages allowed for their maintenance and tents built for them very conveniently on each side of my door.

It was likewise ordered that three hundred tailors should make me a suit of clothes, after the fashion of the country: that six of his Majesty's greatest scholars should be employed to instruct me in their language, and, lastly, that the emperor's horses, and those of the nobility and troops of guards, should be frequently exercised in my sight, to accustom themselves to me. All these orders were duly put in execution, and, in about three weeks, I made a great progress in learning their language, during which time the emperor frequently honoured me with his visits, and was pleased to assist my masters in teaching me.

We began already to converse together in some sort ; and the first words I learned were to express my desire that he would please to give me my liberty, which I every day repeated on my knees. His answer was that this must be a work of time and that first I must swear a peace with him and his kingdom.

He desired I would not take it ill, if he gave orders to certain proper officers to search me ; for probably I might carry about me several weapons, which must needs be dangerous things if they answered the bulk of so prodigious a person. I said his Majesty should be satisfied, for I was ready to strip myself, and turn up my pockets before him. This I delivered, part in words, and part in signs. He replied, that by the laws of the kingdom I must be searched by two of his officers.

I took up the officers in my hands, put them first into my coat pockets, and then into every other pocket about me, except my two fobs, and another secret pocket which I had no mind should be searched, wherein I had some little necessaries that were of no consequence to any but myself. In one of my fobs there was a silver watch, and in the other a small quantity of gold in a purse. These gentlemen, having pen, ink, and paper, made an exact inventory of everything they saw, and, when they had done, desired I would set them down, that they might deliver it to the emperor. This inventory I afterwards translated into English, and is word for word as follows:

" *Imprimis*, In the right coat pocket of the ' Great Man-Mountain ' (for so I interpret the *Quinbus Flestrin*), after the strictest search, we found only one great piece of coarse cloth large enough to be a foot-cloth for your Majesty's chief room of state. In the left pocket we saw a huge silver chest, with a cover of the same metal, which we, the searchers, were not able to lift. We desired it should be opened, and one of us stepping into it, found himself over the knees in a sort of dust, some part whereof, flying up to our faces, set us both a-sneezing for several times together. In his right waistcoat pocket, we found a prodigious bundle of white, thin substances, folded one over another, about the bigness of three men, tied with a strong cable, and marked with black figures ; which we humbly conceive to be writings, every letter almost half as large as the palm of our hands. In the left there was a sort of engine, from the back of which were extended twenty long poles, resembling the palisadoes before your Majesty's court ; wherewith we conjecture the Man-Mountain combs his head.

" In the large pocket on the right side of his middle cover (so I translate the word *Ranfulo*, by which they meant my breeches) we saw a hollow pillar of iron, about the length of a man, fastened to a strong piece of timber, larger than the pillar ; and upon one side of the pillar were huge pieces of iron sticking out, cut into strange figures, which we know not what to make of. In the left pocket, another engine of the same kind. In the smaller pocket, on the right side, were several round flat pieces of white and red metal, of different bulk ; some of the white, which seemed to be silver, were so large and heavy, that my comrade and I could hardly lift them. In the left pocket were two black pillars, irregularly shaped ; we could not, without difficulty, reach the top of them, as we stood at the bottom of his pocket. One of them was covered, and seemed all of a piece ; but, at the upper end of the other, there appeared a white round substance, about twice the bigness of our heads. Within each of these was enclosed a prodigious plate of steel ; which, by our orders, we obliged him to show us because we apprehended they might be dangerous engines. He took them out of their cases, and told us, that in his own country his practice was to shave his beard with one of these, and to cut his meat with the other.

" Out of his right fob hung a great silver chain, with a wonderful kind of engine at the bottom. We directed him to draw out whatever was fastened to that chain ; which appeared to be a globe, half silver, and half of some transparent metal : for on the transparent side, we saw certain strange figures, circularly drawn, and thought we could touch them, till we found our fingers stopped by that lucid substance. He put his engine to our ears, which made an incessant noise, like that of a water-mill. And we conjecture, it is either some unknown animal, or the god that he worships : but we are more inclined to the latter opinion, because he assured us (if we understood him right, for he expressed himself very imperfectly) that he seldom did anything without consulting it. He called it his oracle, and said it pointed out the time for every action of his life. From the left fob he took out a net almost large enough for a fisherman, but contrived to open and shut like a purse, and served him for the same use ; we found therein several massy pieces of yellow metal, which, if they be real gold, must be of immense value.

" Having thus, in obedience to your Majesty's commands, diligently searched all his pockets, we observed a girdle about his waist, made of the hide of some prodigious animal, from which, on the left side, hung a sword of the length of five men ; and on the right, a bag or pouch, divided into two cells, each cell capable of holding three of your Majesty's subjects. In one of these cells were several globes, or balls, of a most ponderous metal, about the bigness of our heads, and required a strong hand to lift them. The other cell contained a heap of certain black grains, but of no great bulk or weight, for we could hold above fifty of them in the palms of our hands.

" This is an exact inventory of what we found about the body of the Man-Mountain, who used us with great civility, and due respect to your Majesty's commission. Signed and sealed, on the fourth day of the eighty-ninth moon of your Majesty's auspicious reign.

" CLEFRIN FRELOCK.
" MARSI FRELOCK."

When this inventory was read over to the emperor, he directed me, although in very gentle terms, to deliver up the several particulars. He first called for my scimitar which I took out, scabbard and all. In the meantime, he ordered three thousand of his choicest troops (who then attended him) to surround me at a distance, with their bows and arrows just ready to discharge : but I did not observe it, for mine eyes were wholly fixed upon his Majesty. He then desired me to draw my scimitar, which, although it had got some rust by the sea-water, was in most parts exceeding bright. I did so, and immediately all the troops gave a shout, between terror and surprise ; for the sun shone clear, and the reflection dazzled their eyes, as I waved the scimitar to and fro in my hand. His Majesty, who is a most magnanimous prince, was less daunted than I could expect ; he ordered me to return it into the scabbard, and cast it on the ground as gently as I could, about six feet from the end of my chain.

The next thing he demanded was one of the hollow iron pillars, by which he meant my pocket pistol.

I delivered up both my pistols in the same manner as I had done my scimitar, and then my pouch of powder and bullets, begging him that the former might be kept from the fire, for it would kindle with the smallest spark, and blow up his imperial palace into the air.

I likewise delivered up my watch, which the emperor was very curious to see, and commanded two of his tallest yeomen of the guards to bear it on a pole upon their shoulders, as draymen in England do a barrel of ale. He was amazed at the continual noise it made, and the motion of the minute hand, which he could easily discern (for their sight is much more acute than ours). I then gave up my silver and copper money, my purse with nine large pieces of gold, and some smaller ones; my knife and razor, my comb and silver snuff-box, my handkerchief, and journal-book.

My scimitar, pistols, and pouch were conveyed in carriages to his Majesty's stores; but the rest of my goods were returned me.

I had, as I before observed, one private pocket which escaped their search, wherein there was a pair of spectacles (which I sometimes use for the weakness of my eyes), a pocket perspective, and several other little conveniences, which I did not think myself bound in honour to discover.

CHAPTER III

MY gentleness and good behaviour had gained so far on the emperor and his court, and indeed upon the army and people in general, that I began to conceive hopes of getting my liberty in a short time. I took all possible methods to cultivate this favourable disposition. The natives came, by degrees, to be less apprehensive of any danger from me. I would sometimes lie down and let five or six of them dance on my hand; and, at last, the boys and girls would venture to come and play at hide-and-seek in my hair.

I had now made a good progress in understanding and speaking their language. The emperor had a mind, one day, to entertain me with several of the country shows, wherein they exceed all nations I have known, both for dexterity and magnificence. I was diverted with none so much as that of the rope-dancers, performed upon a slender white thread, extended about two feet, and twelve inches from the ground.

The horses of the army, and those of the royal stables, having been daily led before me, were no longer shy, but would come up to my very feet without starting. The riders would leap them over my hand as I held it on the ground, and one of the emperor's huntsmen, upon a large courser, took my foot, shoe and all: which was, indeed, a prodigious leap.

I had the good fortune to divert the emperor, one day, after a very extraordinary manner: I desired he would order several sticks of two feet high, and the thickness of an ordinary cane, to be brought me: whereupon his Majesty commanded the master of his woods to give directions accordingly, and the next morning six woodmen arrived with as many carriages drawn by eight horses to each. I took nine of these sticks, and fixing them firmly in the ground, in a quadrangular figure, two feet and a half square, I took four other sticks, and tied them parallel at each corner, about two feet from the ground; then I fastened my handkerchief to the nine sticks that stood erect, and extended it on all sides till it was as tight as the top of a drum; and the four parallel sticks, rising about five inches higher than the handkerchief, served as ledges on each side. When I had finished my work, I desired the emperor to let a troop of his best horse, twenty-four in number, come and exercise upon this plain.

His Majesty approved of the proposal, and I took them up one by one in my hands, ready mounted and armed, with the proper officers to exercise them. As soon as they got in order, they divided into two parties, performed mock skirmishes, discharged blunt arrows, drew their swords, fled and pursued, attacked and retired, and, in short, discovered the best military discipline I ever beheld. The parallel sticks secured them and their horses from falling over the stage; and the emperor was so delighted that he ordered this entertainment to be repeated several days, and once was pleased to be lifted up, and give the word of command; and, with great difficulty, persuaded even the empress herself to let me hold her in her close chair within two yards of the stage, from whence she was able to take a full view of the whole performance.

Two days afterwards, the emperor having ordered that part of his army, which quarters in and about his metropolis, to be in readiness, took a fancy of diverting himself in a very singular manner. He desired I would stand like a colossus, with my legs as far asunder as I conveniently

I stood like a colossus and the troops marched under me

could; he then commanded his general (who was an old, experienced leader, and a great patron of mine) to draw up the troops in close order, and march them under me; the foot by twenty-four in a breast, and the horse by sixteen, with drums beating, colours flying, and pikes advanced. This body consisted of three thousand foot, and a thousand horse. His Majesty gave orders, upon pain of death, that every soldier in his march should observe the strictest order.

I had sent so many memorials and petitions for my liberty, that his Majesty at length mentioned the matter first in the cabinet, and then in a full council; where it was opposed by none, except Skyresh Bolgolam, who was pleased, without any provocation, to be my mortal enemy. But it was carried against him by the whole board, and confirmed by the emperor. That minister was Galbet, or admiral of the realm, very much in his master's confidence, and a person well versed in affairs, but of a morose and sour complexion. However, he was at length persuaded to comply; but prevailed that the articles and conditions upon which I should be set free, and to which I must swear, should be drawn up by himself.

These articles were brought to me by Skyresh Bolgolam in person, attended by two under-secretaries, and several persons of distinction. After they were read, I was demanded to swear to the performance of them, first in the manner of my own country, and afterwards in the method described by their laws, which was to hold my right foot in my left hand, and to place the middle finger of my right hand on the crown of my head, and my thumb on the tip of my right ear. But, because the reader may be curious to have some idea of the style and manner of expression peculiar to that people, as well as to know the articles upon which I recovered my liberty, I have made a translation of the whole instrument, word for word, as near I as was able, which I here offer to the public.

" Golbasto Momaren Evlame Gurdilo Shefin Mully Ully Gue, most mighty Emperor of Lilliput, delight and terror of the universe, whose dominions extend five thousand *blustrugs* (about twelve miles in circumference), to the extremities of the globe; monarch of all monarchs, taller than the sons of men; whose feet press down to the centre, and whose head strikes against the sun; at whose nod the princes of the earth shake their knees; pleasant as the spring, comfortable as the summer, fruitful as autumn, dreadful as winter. His Most Sublime Majesty proposeth to the Man-Mountain, lately arrived to our celestial dominions, the following articles, which, by a solemn oath, he shall be obliged to perform :—

" 1st. The Man-Mountain shall not depart from our dominions without our licence under our great seal.

" 2nd. He shall not presume to come into our metropolis without our express order; at which time the inhabitants shall have two hours' warning to keep within their doors.

" 3rd. The said Man-Mountain shall confine his walks to our principal high roads, and not offer to walk or lie down in a meadow or field of corn.

" 4th. As he walks the said roads he shall take the utmost care not to trample upon the bodies of any of our loving subjects, their horses or carriages, nor take any of our subjects into his hands without their own consent.

" 5th. If an express requires extraordinary despatch, the Man-Mountain shall be obliged to carry in his pocket the messenger and horse a six days' journey once in every moon, and return the said messenger back (if so required) safe to our imperial presence.

" 6th. He shall be our ally against our enemies in the Island of Blefuscu, and do his utmost to destroy their fleet, which is now preparing to invade us.

" 7th. That the said Man-Mountain shall, at his times of leisure, be aiding and assisting to our workmen, in helping to raise certain great stones towards covering the wall of the principal park, and other of our royal buildings.

" 8th. That the said Man-Mountain shall, in two moons' time, deliver in an exact survey of the circumference of our dominions, by a computation of his own paces round the coast.

" Lastly. That, upon his solemn oath to observe all the above articles, the said Man-Mountain shall have a daily allowance of meat and drink sufficient for the support of 1724 of our subjects, with free access to our royal person, and other marks of our favour. Given at our palace at Belfaborac, the twelfth day of the ninety-first moon of our reign."

I swore and subscribed to these articles with great cheerfulness and content, although some of them were not so honourable as I could have wished ; which proceeded wholly from the malice of Skyresh Bolgolam, the high admiral ; whereupon my chains were immediately unlocked, and I was at full liberty. The emperor himself in person did me the honour to be by at the whole ceremony. I made my acknowledgments, by prostrating myself at his Majesty's feet, but he commanded me to rise ; and after many gracious expressions, which, to avoid the censure of vanity, I shall not repeat, he added that he hoped I should prove a useful servant, and well deserve all the favours he had already conferred upon me, or might do for the future.

CHAPTER IV

THE first request I made, after I had obtained my liberty, was that I might have licence to see Mildendo, the metropolis ; which the emperor easily granted me, but with a special charge to do no hurt either to the inhabitants or their houses. The people had notice by proclamation of my design to visit the town. The wall, which encompassed it, is two feet and a half high, and at least eleven inches broad, so that a coach and horses may be driven very safely round it ; and it is flanked with strong towers, at ten feet distance. I stepped over the great western gate, and passed very gently and sidling through the two principal streets, only in my short waistcoat, for fear of damaging the roofs and eaves of the houses with the skirts of my coat. I walked with the utmost circumspection, to avoid treading on any stragglers that might remain in the streets, although the orders were strict that all people should keep in their houses at their own peril. The garret-windows and tops of houses were so crowded with spectators that I thought, in all my travels, I had not seen a more populous place. The city is an exact square, each side of the wall being five hundred feet long.

The two great streets, which run cross, and divide it into four quarters, are five feet wide. The lanes and alleys, which I could not enter, but only viewed them as I passed, are from twelve to eighteen inches. The town is capable of holding five hundred thousand souls. The houses are from three to five storeys ; the shops and markets well provided.

The emperor's palace is in the centre of the city, where the two great streets met. It is enclosed by a wall of two feet high, and twenty feet distance from the buildings. I had his Majesty's permission to step over this wall ; and, the space being so wide between that and the palace, I could easily view it on every side. The outward court is a square of forty feet, and includes two other courts : in the inmost are the royal apartments, which I was very desirous to see, but found it extremely difficult ; for the great gates, from one square into another, were but eighteen inches high, and seven inches wide. Now, the buildings of the outer court were at least five feet high, and it was impossible for me to stride over them without infinite damage to the pile, though the walls were strongly built of hewn stone, and four inches thick. At the same time, the emperor had a great desire that I should see the magnificence of his palace ; but this I was not able to do till three days after, which I spent in cutting down with my knife some of the largest trees in the royal park, about a hundred yards distance from the city. Of these trees I made two stools, each about three feet high, and strong enough to bear my weight.

The people having received notice a second time, I went again through the city to the palace, with my two stools in my hands. When I came to the side of the outer court, I stood upon one stool, and took the other in my hand ; this I lifted over the roof, and gently set it down on the space between the first and second court, which was eight feet wide. I then stepped over the building very conveniently, from one stool to the other, and drew up the first after me with a hooked stick. By this contrivance I got into the inmost court ; and, lying down upon my side, I applied my face to the windows of the middle storeys, which were left open on purpose, and discovered the most splendid apartments that can be imagined. There I saw the empress, and the young princes, in their several lodgings, with their chief attendants about them. Her Imperial Majesty was pleased to smile very graciously upon me, and gave me her hand to kiss.

. One morning, about a fortnight after I had obtained my liberty, Reldresal, principal secretary (as they style him) of private affairs, came to my house, only attended by one servant. He ordered his coach to wait at a distance, and desired I would give him an hour's audience ; which I readily consented to, on account of his quality and personal merits, as well as the many good offices he had done me during my solicitations at court. I offered to lie down, that he might the more conveniently reach my ear ; but he chose rather to let me hold him in my hand during our conversation.

He began with compliments on my liberty ; said he might pretend to some merit in it ; but, however, added that, if it had not been for the present situation of things at court, perhaps I might not have attained it so soon.

" For," said he, " as flourishing a condition as we may appear to be in to foreigners, we labour under two mighty evils ; a violent faction at home, and the danger of an invasion by a most potent enemy from abroad. As to the first, you are to understand that, for about seventy moons past, there have been two struggling parties in this empire, under the names of Tramecksan and Slamecksan, from the high and low heels of their shoes, by which they distinguish themselves. It is alleged, indeed, that the high heels are most agreeable to our ancient constitutions ; but, however this be, his Majesty hath determined to make use of only low heels in the administration of the government, and all offices in the gift of the crown, as you cannot but observe ; and particularly, that his Majesty's imperial heels are lower at least by a *drurr* than any of his court (*drurr* is a measure about the fourteenth part of an inch).

" The animosities between these two parties run so high that they will neither eat nor drink nor talk with each other. We compute the Tramecksan, or high heels, to exceed us in number ; but the power is wholly on our side. We apprehend his Imperial Highness, the heir to the crown, to have some tendency towards the high heels ; at least, we can plainly discover that one of his heels is higher than the other, which gives him a hobble in his gait.

" Now, in the midst of these intestine disquiets, we are threatened with an invasion from the island of Blefuscu, which is the other great empire of the universe, almost as large and powerful as this of his Majesty. For, as to what we hear you affirm, that there are other kingdoms and states in the world, inhabited by human creatures as large as yourself, our philosophers are in much doubt, and would rather conjecture that you dropped from the moon, or one of the stars ; because it is certain that a hundred mortals of your bulk would, in a short time, destroy all the fruits and cattle of his Majesty's dominions. Besides, our histories of six thousand moons make no mention of any other regions than the two great empires of Lilliput and Blefuscu ; which two mighty powers have, as I was going to tell you, been engaged in a most obstinate war for six-and-thirty moons past.

" It began upon the following occasion : It is allowed on all hands that the primitive way of breaking eggs, before we eat them, was upon the larger end ; but his present Majesty's grandfather, while he was a boy, going to eat an egg, and breaking it according to the ancient practice, happened to cut one of his fingers. Whereupon the emperor, his father, published an edict, commanding all his subjects, upon great penalties, to break the smaller end of their eggs. The people so highly resented this law, that our histories tell us there have been six rebellions raised on that account, wherein one emperor lost his life and another his crown. These civil commotions were constantly fomented by the monarchs of Blefuscu ; and when they were quelled, the exiles always fled for refuge to that empire.

" It is computed that eleven thousand persons have, at several times, suffered death rather than submit to break their eggs at the smaller end. Many hundred large volumes have been published upon this controversy ; but the books of the Big-endians have been long forbidden, and the whole party rendered incapable by law of holding employments.

" During the course of these troubles the Emperors of Blefuscu did frequently expostulate by their ambassadors, accusing us of making a schism in religion, by offending against a fundamental doctrine of our great Prophet Lustrog, in the fifty-fourth chapter of the Blundecral (which is their Alcoran). This, however, is thought to be a mere strain upon the text ; for the words are these : *That all true believers break their eggs at the convenient end.* And which is the convenient end seems, in my humble opinion, to be left to every man's conscience, or, at least, in the power of the chief magistrate to determine.

" Now, the Big-endian exiles have found so much credit in the Emperor of Blefuscu's court, and so much private assistance and encouragement from their party here at home, that a bloody war hath been carried on between the two empires for six-and-twenty moons, with various success ; during which times we have lost forty capital ships, and a much greater number of smaller vessels, together with thirty thousand of our best seamen and soldiers ; and the damage received by the enemy is reckoned to be somewhat greater than ours. However, they have now equipped a numerous fleet, and are just preparing to make a descent upon us ; and his Imperial Majesty, placing great confidence in your valour and strength, hath commanded me to lay this account of his affairs before you."

I desired the secretary to present my humble duty to the emperor, and to let him know that I thought it would not become me, who was a foreigner, to interfere with parties ; but I was ready, with the hazard of my life, to defend his person and state against all invaders.

CHAPTER V

THE empire of Blefuscu is an island, situated to the north-east side of Lilliput, from whence it is parted only by a channel of eight hundred yards wide. I had not yet seen it, and upon this notice of an intended invasion, I avoided appearing on that side of the coast, for fear of being discovered by some of the enemy's ships, who had received no intelligence of me, all intercourse between the two empires having been strictly forbidden during the war, upon pain of death, and an embargo laid by our emperor upon all vessels whatsoever.

I communicated to his Majesty a project I had formed of seizing the enemy's whole fleet : which, as our scouts assured us, lay at anchor in the harbour, ready to sail with the first fair wind. I consulted the most experienced seamen upon the depth of the channel, which they had often plumbed, who told me, that in the middle, at high water, it was seventy *glumgluffs* deep, which is about six feet of European measure ; and the rest of it fifty *glumgluffs* at most. I walked towards the north-east coast, over against Blefuscu, where, lying down behind a hillock, I took out my small perspective glass, and viewed the enemy's fleet at anchor, consisting of about fifty men-of-war, and a great number of transports : I then came back to my house, and gave order (for which I had a warrant) for a great quantity of the strongest cable and bars of iron. The cable was about as thick as packthread, and the bars of the length and size of a knitting needle. I trebled the cable to make it stronger, and, for the same reason, I twisted three of the iron bars together, binding the extremities into a hook.

Having thus fixed fifty hooks to as many cables, I went back to the northeast coast, and putting off my coat, shoes, and stockings, walked into the sea, in my leathern jerkin, about half an hour before high water. I waded with what haste I could, and swam in the middle about thirty yards, till I felt ground ; I arrived at the fleet in less than half an hour. The enemy were so frightened when they saw me, that they leaped out of their ships, and swam to shore, where there could not be fewer than thirty thousand souls. I then took my tackling, and, fastening a hook to the hole at the prow of each, I tied all the cords together at the end.

While I was thus employed, the enemy discharged several thousand arrows, many of which stuck in my hands and face ; and, besides the excessive smart, gave me much disturbance at my work. My greatest apprehension was for mine eyes, which I should have infallibly lost, if I had not suddenly thought of an expedient. I kept, among other little necessaries, a pair of spectacles in a private pocket, which, as I observed before, had escaped the emperor's searchers. These I took out and fastened as strongly as I could upon my nose, and, thus armed, went on boldly with my work in spite of the enemy's arrows, many of which struck against the glasses of my spectacles, but without any other effect further than a little to discompose them.

I had now fastened all the hooks, and, taking the knot in my hand, began to pull ; but not a ship would stir, for they were all too fast held by their anchors, so that the boldest part of my enterprise remained. I therefore let go the cord, and leaving the hooks fixed to the ships, I resolutely cut with my knife the cables that fastened the anchors, receiving above two hundred shots in my face and hands ; then I took up the knotted end of the cables to which my hooks were tied, and with great ease drew fifty of the enemy's largest men-of-war after me.

The Blefuscudians, who had not the least imagination of what I intended, were at first confounded with astonishment. They had seen me cut the cables, and thought my design was only to let the ships run adrift, or fall foul on each other : but when they perceived the whole fleet moving in order, and saw me pulling at the end, they set up such a scream of grief and despair, that it is almost impossible to describe or conceive. When I had got out of danger, I stopped a while to pick out the arrows that stuck in my hands and face : and rubbed on some of the same ointment that was given me at my first arrival, as I formerly mentioned. I then took off my spectacles, and, waiting about an hour till the tide was a little fallen, I waded through the middle with my cargo, and arrived safe at the royal port of Lilliput.

The emperor and his whole court stood on the shore expecting the issue of this great adventure. They saw the ships move forward in a large half-moon, but could not discern me, who was up to my breast in water. When I advanced to the middle of the channel, they were yet in more pain, because I was under water to my neck. The emperor concluded me to be drowned, and that the enemy's fleet was approaching in a hostile manner : but he was soon eased of his fears, for the channel growing shallower every step I made, I came in a short time within hearing, and, holding up the end of the cable by which the fleet was fastened, I cried in a loud voice, " Long live the most puissant Emperor of Lilliput ! " This great prince received me at my landing with all possible encomiums, and created me a *nardac* upon the spot, which is the highest title of honour among them.

His Majesty desired I would take some other opportunity of bringing all the rest of his enemy's ships into his ports. And so unmeasurable is the ambition of princes, that he seemed to think of nothing less than reducing the whole empire of Blefuscu into a province, and governing it by a viceroy ; of destroying the Big-endian exiles, and compelling that people to break the smaller end of their eggs, by which he would remain the sole monarch of the whole world. But I endeavoured to divert him from his design, by many arguments drawn from the topics of policy, as well as justice : and I plainly protested that I would never be an instrument of bringing a free and brave people into slavery. And, when the matter was debated in council, the wisest part of the ministry were of my opinion.

This open, bold declaration of mine was so opposite to the schemes and politics of his Imperial Majesty, that he could never forgive me ; he mentioned it in a very artful manner in council, where I was told that some of the wisest appeared, at least by their silence, to be of my opinion ; but others, who were my secret enemies, could not forbear some expressions, which by a side-wind reflected on me. And from this time began an intrigue between his Majesty and a junto of ministers maliciously bent against me, which broke out in less than two months, and had like to have ended in my utter destruction.

About three weeks after this exploit, there arrived a solemn embassy from Blefuscu, with humble offers of a peace ; which was soon concluded upon conditions very advantageous to our emperor. There were six ambassadors, with a train of about five hundred persons, and their entry was very magnificent, suitable to the grandeur of their master.

When their treaty was finished, wherein I did them several good offices by the credit I now had or at least appeared to have, at court, their Excellencies, who were privately told how much I had been their friend, made me a visit in form. They began with many compliments upon my valour and generosity, invited me to that kingdom in the emperor their master's name, and desired me to show them some proofs of my prodigious strength, of which they had heard so many wonders ; wherein I readily obliged them, but shall not trouble the reader with the particulars.

When I had for some time entertained their Excellencies to their infinite satisfaction and surprise, I desired they would do me the honour to present my most humble respects to the emperor their master, the renown of whose virtues had so justly filled the whole world with admiration, and whose royal person I resolved to attend before I returned to my own country.

Accordingly, the next time I had the honour to see our emperor, I desired his general licence to wait on the Blefuscudian monarch, which he was pleased to grant me, as I could plainly perceive, in a very cold manner.

CHAPTER VI

AS the common size of the natives of Lilliput is somewhat under six inches high, so there is an exact proportion in all other animals, as well as plants and trees : for instance, the tallest horses and oxen are between four and five inches in height, the sheep an inch and half, more or less ; their geese about the bigness of a sparrow, and so the several gradations downwards, till you come to the smallest, which, to my sight, were almost invisible; but nature hath adapted the eyes of the Lilliputians to all objects proper for their view : they see with great exactness, but at no great distance. And, to show the sharpness of their sight towards objects that are near, I have been much pleased with observing a cook pulling a lark, which was not so large as a common fly, and a young girl threading an invisible needle with invisible silk. Their tallest trees are about seven feet high ; I mean some of those in the great royal park, the tops whereof I could but just reach with my fist clinched. The other vegetables are in the same proportion.

I shall say but little at present of their learning, which for many ages hath flourished in all its branches among them : but their manner of writing is very peculiar, being neither from the left to the right, like the Europeans ; nor from the right to the left, like the Arabians ; nor from up to down, like the Chinese; but aslant from one corner of the paper to the other, like ladies in England.

Their notions relating to the duties of parents and children differ extremely from ours. They will never allow that a child is under any obligation to his father or to his mother for bringing him into the world, which, considering the miseries of human life, was not a benefit in itself. Upon these, and the like reasonings, their opinion is, that parents are the last of all others to be trusted with the education of their own children ; and therefore they have in every town public nurseries, where all parents, except cottagers and labourers, are obliged to send their infants of both sexes to be reared and educated when they come to the age of twenty moons, at which time they are supposed to have some rudiments of docility. These schools are of several kinds suited to different qualities, and to both sexes. They have certain professors well skilled in preparing children for such a condition of life as befits the rank of their parents, and their own capacities as well as inclinations. I shall first say something of the male nurseries, and then of the female.

The nurseries for males of noble or eminent birth are provided with grave and learned professors, and their several deputies. The clothes and food of the children are plain and simple. They are bred up in the principles of honour, justice, courage, clemency, religion, and love of their country ; they are always employed in some business, except in the times of eating and sleeping, which are very short, and two hours for diversions, consisting of bodily exercises. They are dressed by men till four years of age, and then obliged to dress themselves, although their quality be ever so great ; and the women attendants, who are aged proportionably to ours at fifty, perform only the most menial offices. Their parents are suffered to see them only twice a year ; the visit is to last but an hour ; they are allowed to kiss the child at meeting and parting ; but a professor, who always stands by on those occasions, will not suffer them to whisper, or use any fondling expressions, or bring any presents of toys, sweetmeats, and the like.

The pension from each family for the education and entertainment of a child, upon failure of due payment, is levied by the emperor's officers.

The nurseries for children of ordinary gentlemen, merchants, traders, and handicrafts, are managed proportionably after the same manner ; only those designed for trades are put out apprentices at eleven years old, whereas those of persons of quality continue in their exercises till fifteen, which answers to twenty-one with us; but the confinement is gradually lessened for the last three years.

In the female nurseries, the young girls of quality are educated much like the males, only they are dressed by orderly servants of their own sex; but always in the presence of a professor or deputy, till they come to dress themselves, which is at five years old. And if it be found that these nurses ever presume to entertain the girls with frightful or foolish stories, or the common follies practised by chamber-maids among us, they are publicly whipped thrice about the city, imprisoned for a year, and banished for life to the most desolate part of the country.

Thus the young ladies there are as much ashamed of being cowards and fools as the men, and despise all personal ornaments beyond decency and cleanliness: neither did I perceive any difference in their education made by their difference of sex, only that the exercises of the females were not altogether so robust; and that some rules were given them relating to domestic life, and a smaller compass of learning was enjoined them; for their maxim is that, among people of quality, a wife should be always a reasonable and agreeable companion, because she cannot always be young. When the girls are twelve years old, which among them is a marriageable age, their parents or guardians take them home with great expressions of gratitude to the professors, and seldom without tears of the young lady and her companions.

In the nurseries of the females of the meaner sort, the children are instructed in all kinds of works proper for their sex and their several degrees: those intended for apprentices are dismissed at seven years old, the rest are kept to eleven.

The meaner families, who have children at these nurseries, are obliged, besides their annual pension, which is as low as possible, to return to the steward of the nursery a small monthly share of their gettings, to be a portion for the child; and therefore all parents are limited in their expenses by the law. For the Lilliputians think nothing can be more unjust than for people, in subservience to their own appetites, to bring children into the world, and leave the burthen of supporting them on the public. As to persons of quality, they give security to appropriate a certain sum for each child, suitable to their condition; and these funds are always managed with good husbandry, and the most exact justice.

The cottagers and labourers keep their children at home, their business being only to till and cultivate the earth, and therefore their education is of little consequence to the public: but the old and diseased among them are supported by hospitals; for begging is a trade unknown in this empire.

And here it may, perhaps, divert the curious reader to give some account of my domestics, and my manner of living in this country, during a residence of nine months and thirteen days. Having a head mechanically turned, and being likewise forced by necessity, I had made for myself a table and chair convenient enough, out of the largest trees in the royal park. Two hundred sempstresses were employed to make me shirts, and linen for bed and table, all of the strongest and coarsest kind they could get; which, however, they were forced to quilt together in several folds, for the thickest was some degrees finer than lawn. Their linen is usually three inches wide, and three feet make a piece. The sempstresses took my measure as I lay on the ground, one standing at my neck, and another at my knee, with a strong cord extended, that each held by the end, while the third measured the length of the cord with a rule of an inch long. Then they measured my right thumb and desired no more ; for, by a mathematical computation, that twice round the thumb is once round the wrist, and so on to the neck and waist, and by the help of my old shirt, which I displayed on the ground before them for a pattern, they fitted me exactly.

Three hundred tailors were employed in the same manner to make me clothes ; but they had another contrivance for taking my measure. I kneeled down and they raised a ladder from the ground to my neck ; upon this ladder one of them mounted, and let fall a plumb-line from my collar to the floor, which just answered the length of my coat ; but my waist and arms I measured myself. When my clothes were finished, which was done in my house (for the largest of theirs would not have been able to hold them) they looked like the patch-work made by the ladies in England, only that mine were all of a colour.

I had three hundred cooks to dress my victuals, in little convenient huts built about my house, where they and their families lived, and prepared me two dishes a-piece. I took up twenty waiters in my hand, and placed them on the table ; a hundred more attended below on the ground, some with dishes of meat, and some with barrels of wine and other liquors, slung on their shoulders, all of which the waiters above drew up as I wanted, in a very ingenious manner, by certain cords, as we draw the bucket up a well

They drew up my food by curtain cords, as we draw a bucket from a well

GULLIVER AND THE LITTLE PEOPLE.
They were amazed and terrified at my size, but I soon showed them that I was harmless.

GULLIVER AND THE EMPEROR.
The beast, unused to such a bewildering sight, reared up on his hinder feet.

in Europe. A dish of their meat was a good mouthful, and a barrel of their liquor a reasonable draught. Their mutton yields to ours, but their beef is excellent. I have had a surloin so large that I have been forced to make three bites of it ; but this is rare. My servants were astonished to see me eat it, bones and all, as in our country we do the leg of a lark. Their geese and turkeys I usually eat at a mouthful ; and I must confess they far exceed ours. Of their smaller fowl, I could take up twenty or thirty at the end of my knife.

One day his Imperial Majesty, being informed of my way of living, desired that himself and his royal consort, with the young princes of the blood of both sexes, might have the happiness (as he was pleased to call it) of dining with me. They came accordingly, and I placed them upon chairs of state upon my table, just over against me, with their guards about them. Flimnap, the lord high treasurer, attended there likewise, with his white staff ; and I observed he often looked on me with a sour countenance, which I would not seem to regard, but ate more than usual, in honour to my dear country, as well as to fill the court with admiration. I have some private reasons to believe that this visit from his Majesty gave Flimnap an opportunity of doing me ill offices to his master. That minister had always been my secret enemy, though he outwardly caressed me more than was usual to the moroseness of his nature. He represented to the emperor the low condition of his treasury ; that he was forced to take up money at great discount ; that exchequer bills would not circulate under nine per cent. below par ; that, in short, I had cost his Majesty above a million and a half of *sprugs* (their greatest gold coin, about the bigness of a spangle) ; and, upon the whole, that it would be advisable in the emperor to take the first fair occasion of dismissing me.

CHAPTER VII

BEFORE I proceed to give an account of my leaving this kingdom, it may be proper to inform the reader of a private intrigue which had been for two months forming against me.

When I was just preparing to pay my attendance on the Emperor of Blefuscu, a considerable person at court (to whom I had been very serviceable at a time when he lay under the highest displeasure of his Imperial Majesty) came to my house very privately at night in a close chair, and, without sending his name, desired admittance. The chair-men were dismissed ; I put the chair, with his lordship in it, into my coat pocket ; and, giving orders to a trusty servant to say I was indisposed and gone to sleep, I fastened the door of my house, placed the chair on the table, according to my usual custom, and sat down by it. After the common salutations were over, observing his lordship's countenance full of concern, and inquiring into the reason, he desired I would hear him with patience, in a matter that highly concerned my honour and my life. His speech was to the following effect, for I took notes of it as soon as he left me.

" You are to know," said he, " that several committees of council have been lately called in the most private manner on your account ; and it is but two days since his Majesty came to a full resolution.

" You are very sensible that Skyresh Bolgolam (galbet, or high admiral) hath been your mortal enemy almost ever since your arrival : his original reasons I know not ; but his hatred is increased since your great success against Blefuscu, by which his glory, as admiral, is much obscured. This lord, in conjunction with Flimnap the high treasurer, Limtoc the general, Lalcon the chamberlain, and Balmuff the grand justiciary, have prepared articles of impeachment against you, for treason and other capital crimes."

This preface made me so impatient, being conscious of my own merits and innocence, that I was going to interrupt ; when he entreated me to be silent, and thus proceeded :

" Out of gratitude for the favours you have done me, I procured information of the whole proceedings, and a copy of the articles, wherein I venture my head for your service.

" *Articles of Impeachment against* QUINBUS FLESTRIN (*the* MAN-MOUNTAIN).

" ARTICLE I

" That the said Quinbus Flestrin having brought the imperial fleet of Blefuscu into the royal port, and being afterwards commanded by his Imperial Majesty to seize all the other ships of the said empire of Blefuscu, and reduce that empire to a province, to be governed by a viceroy from hence, and to destroy and put to death not only all the Big-endian exiles, but likewise all the people of that empire, who would not immediately forsake the Big-endian heresy : he, the said Flestrin, like a false traitor against his most auspicious, serene, Imperial Majesty, did petition to be excused from the said service, upon pretence of unwillingness to force the consciences, or destroy the liberties and lives of innocent people.

" ARTICLE II

" That, whereas certain ambassadors arrived from the court of Blefuscu, to sue for peace in his Majesty's court : he, the said Flestrin, did, like a false traitor, aid, abet, comfort, and divert the said ambassadors, although he knew them to be servants to a prince who was lately an open enemy to his Imperial Majesty, and in open war against his said Majesty.

" ARTICLE III

" That the said Quinbus Flestrin, contrary to the duty of a faithful subject, is now preparing to make a voyage to the court and empire of Blefuscu, for which he hath received only verbal licence from his Imperial Majesty ; and under colour of the said licence doth falsely and traitorously intend to take the said voyage, and thereby to aid, comfort, and abet the Emperor of Blefuscu, so late an enemy, and in open war with his Imperial Majesty aforesaid.

" There are some other articles, but these are the most important, of which I have read you an abstract.

" In the several debates upon this impeachment, it must be confessed that his Majesty gave many marks of his great lenity, often urging the services you had done him, and endeavouring to extenuate your crimes. The treasurer and admiral insisted that you should be put to the most painful and ignominious death, by setting fire to your house at night, and the general was to attend with twenty thousand men armed with poisoned arrows, to shoot you on the face and hands. Some of your servants were to have private orders to strew a poisonous juice on your shirts and sheets, which would soon make you tear your own flesh, and die in the utmost torture. The general came into the same opinion ; so that for a long time there was a majority against you : but his Majesty resolving, if possible, to spare your life, at last brought off the chamberlain.

" Upon this incident, Reldresal, principal secretary for private affairs, who always approved himself your true friend, was commanded by the emperor to deliver his opinion, which he accordingly did : and therein justified the good thoughts you have of him. He allowed your crimes to be great, but that still there was room for mercy, the most commendable virtue in a prince, and for which his Majesty was so justly celebrated. He said the friendship between you and him was so well known to the world, that perhaps the most honourable board might think him partial ; however, in obedience to the command he had received, he would freely offer his sentiments.

" That if his Majesty, in consideration of your services, and pursuant to his own merciful disposition, would please to spare your life, and only give order to put out both your eyes, he humbly conceived that, by this expedient, justice might in some measure be satisfied, and all the world would applaud the lenity of the emperor, as well as the fair and generous proceedings of those who have the honour to be his counsellors. That the loss of your eyes would be no impediment to your bodily strength, by which you might still be useful to his Majesty. That blindness is an addition to courage, by concealing dangers from us ; that the fear you had for your eyes was the greatest difficulty in bringing over the enemy's fleet, and it would be sufficient for you to see by the eyes of the ministers, since the greatest princes do no more.

" This proposal was received with the utmost disapprobation by the whole board. Bolgolam, the admiral, could not preserve his temper ; but, rising up in fury, said he wondered how the secretary durst presume to give his opinion for preserving the life of a traitor : that the services you had performed were, by all true reasons of state, the great aggravation of your crimes ; that the same strength, which enabled you to bring over the enemy's fleet, might serve, upon the first discontent, to carry it back ; that he had good reasons to think you were a Big-endian in your heart ; and as treason begins in the heart before it appears in overt acts, so he accused you as a traitor on that account and therefore insisted you should be put to death.

" The treasurer was of the same opinion. He showed to what straits his Majesty's revenue was reduced by the charge of maintaining you, which would soon grow insupportable : that the secretary's expedient of putting out your eyes was so far from being a remedy against this evil that it would probably increase it, as it is manifest from the common practice of binding some kind of fowl, after which they fed the faster, and grew sooner fat ; that his sacred Majesty and the council, who are your judges, were in their own consciences fully convinced of your guilt, which was a sufficient argument to condemn you to death, without the formal proofs required by the strict letter of the law.

" But his Imperial Majesty, fully determined against capital punishment, was graciously pleased to say that, since the council thought the loss of your eyes too easy a censure, some other may be inflicted hereafter. And your friend, the secretary, humbly desiring to be heard again, in answer to what the treasurer had objected concerning the great charge his Majesty was at in maintaining you, said that his Excellency, who had the sole disposal of the emperor's revenue, might easily provide against that evil by gradually lessening your establishment, by which, for want of sufficient food, you would grow weak and faint, and lose your appetite, and consume in a few months ; and immediately, upon your death, five or six thousand of his Majesty's subjects might, in two or three days, cut your flesh from your bones, take it away by cart-loads, and bury it in distant parts to prevent infection, leaving the skeleton as a monument of admiration to posterity.

" Thus, by the great friendship of the secretary, the whole affair was compromised. It was strictly enjoined that the project of starving you, by degrees, should be kept a secret, but the sentence of putting out your eyes was entered on the books ; none dissenting except Bolgolam, the admiral, who, being a creature of the empress, was perpetually instigated by her Majesty to insist upon your death.

" In three days, your friend, the secretary, will be directed to come to your house, and read before you the articles of impeachment ; and then to signify the great lenity and favour of his Majesty and council, whereby you are only condemned to the loss of your eyes, which his Majesty doth not question you will gratefully and humbly submit to ; and twenty of his Majesty's surgeons will attend, in order to see the operation well performed, by discharging very sharp-pointed arrows into the balls of your eyes as you lie on the ground.

" I leave to your prudence what measures you will take ; and, to avoid suspicion, I must immediately return in as private a manner as I came."

His lordship did so, and I remained alone, under many doubts and perplexities of mind.

It was a custom introduced by this prince and his ministry (very different, as I have been assured, from the practices of former times) that after the court had decreed any cruel execution, either to gratify the monarch's resentment or the malice of a favourite, the emperor always made a speech to his whole council, expressing his great lenity and tenderness, as qualities known and confessed by all the world. This speech was immediately published through the kingdom ; nor did anything terrify the people so much as those encomiums on his Majesty's mercy ; because it was observed that the more these praises were enlarged and insisted on, the more inhuman was the punishment, and the sufferer more innocent.

Yet as to myself, I must confess, having never been designed for a courtier, either by my birth or education, I was so ill a judge of things that I could not discover the lenity and favour of this sentence, but conceived it (perhaps erroneously) rather to be rigorous than gentle. I sometimes thought of standing my trial ; for, although I could not deny the facts alleged in the several articles, yet I hoped they would admit of some extenuation. But having in my life perused many state-trials, which I ever observed to terminate as the judges thought fit to direct, I durst not rely on so dangerous a decision in so critical a juncture, and against such powerful enemies.

Once I was strongly bent upon resistance, for, while I had liberty, the whole strength of that empire could hardly subdue me, and I might easily with stones pelt the metropolis to pieces ; but I soon rejected that project with horror, by remembering the oath I had made to the emperor, the favours I received from him, and the high title of *nardac* he conferred upon me. Neither had I so soon learned the gratitude of courtiers, to persuade myself that his Majesty's present severities acquitted me of all past obligations.

At last I fixed upon a resolution, for which it is probable I may incur some censure, and not unjustly ; for I confess I owe the preserving my eyes, and consequently my liberty, to my own great rashness, and want of experience ; because, if I had then known the nature of princes and ministers, which I have since observed in many other courts, and their methods of treating criminals less obnoxious than myself, I should with great alacrity and readiness have submitted to so easy a punishment.

But hurried on by the precipitancy of youth, and having his Imperial Majesty's licence to pay my attendance upon the Emperor of Blefuscu, I took this opportunity before the three days were elapsed to send a letter to my friend the secretary, signifying my resolution of setting out that morning for Blefuscu, pursuant to the leave I had got ; and, without waiting for an answer, I went to that side of the island where our fleet lay.

I seized a large man-of-war, tied a cable to the prow, and, lifting up the anchors, I stripped myself, put my clothes (together with my coverlet, which I brought under my arm) into the vessel, and, drawing it after me, between wading and swimming, arrived at the royal port of Blefuscu, where the people had long expected me ; they lent me two guides to direct me to the capital city, which is of the same name. I held them in my hands till I came within two hundred yards of the gate, and desired them to signify my arrival to one of the secretaries, and let him know I there waited his Majesty's command. I had an answer in about an hour, that his Majesty, attended by the royal family and great officers of court, was coming out to receive me.

I advanced a hundred yards. The emperor and his train alighted from their horses, the empress and ladies from their coaches, and I did not perceive they were in any fright or concern. I lay on the ground to kiss his Majesty's and the empress's hand. I told his Majesty that I was come according to my promise, and with the licence of the emperor my master, to have the honour of seeing so mighty a monarch, and to offer him any service in my power consistent with my duty to my own prince ; not mentioning a word of my disgrace, because I had hitherto no regular information of it, and might suppose myself wholly ignorant of any such design ; neither could

I reasonably conceive that the emperor would discover the secret while I was out of his power ; wherein, however, it soon appeared I was deceived.

CHAPTER VIII

THREE days after my arrival, walking out of curiosity to the north-east coast of the island, I observed, about half a league off, in the sea, somewhat that looked like a boat overturned. I pulled off my shoes and stockings, and, wading two or three hundred yards, I found the object to approach nearer by force of the tide ; and then saw it to be a boat, which I supposed might, by some tempest, have been driven from a ship. Whereupon I returned towards the city, and desired his Imperial Majesty to lend me twenty of the tallest vessels he had left after the loss of his fleet, and three thousand seamen under the command of the vice-admiral. This fleet sailed round, while I went back the shortest way to the coast, where I first discovered the boat ; I found the tide had driven it still nearer. The seamen were all provided with cordage, which I had beforehand twisted to a sufficient strength. When the ships came up, I stripped myself, and waded till I came within a hundred yards of the boat, after which I was forced to swim till I got up to it. The seamen threw me the end of the cord, which I fastened to a hole in the fore part of the boat, and the other end to a man-of-war.

But I found all my labour to little purpose ; for, being out of my depth, I was not able to work. In this necessity, I was forced to swim behind, and push the boat forward as often as I could, with one of my hands ; and, the tide favouring me, I advanced so far, that I could just hold up my chin and feel the ground. I rested two or three minutes, and then gave the boat another shove, and so on, till the sea was no higher than my arm-pits ; and now, the most laborious part being over, I took out my other cables, which were stowed in one of the ships, and fastened them first to the boat, and then to nine of the vessels which attended me ; the wind being favourable, the seamen towed, and I shoved till we arrived within forty yards of the shore, and, waiting till the tide was out, I got dry to the boat, and by the assistance of two thousand men, with ropes and engines, I made a shift to turn it on its bottom, and found it was but little damaged.

I shall not trouble the reader with the difficulties I was under, by the help of certain paddles, which cost me ten days' making, to get my boat to the royal port of Blefuscu, where a mighty concourse of people appeared upon my arrival, full of wonder at the sight of so prodigious a vessel. I told the emperor that my good fortune had thrown this boat in my way, to carry me to some place from whence I might return into my native country, and begged his Majesty's orders for getting materials to fit it up ; together with his licence to depart ; which, after some kind expostulations, he was pleased to grant.

I did very much wonder, in all this time, not to have heard of any express relating to me from our emperor to the court of Blefuscu. But I was after-wards given privately to understand that his Imperial Majesty, never im-agining I had the least notice of his designs, believed I was only gone to

Walking by the shore I saw something half a league away, to sea

Blefuscu, in performance of my promise, according to the licence he had given me, which was well known at our court, and would return in a few days when the ceremony was ended. But he was at last in pain at my long absence ; and, after consulting with the treasurer and the rest of that cabal, a person of quality was despatched with the copy of the articles against me.

This envoy had instructions to represent to the monarch of Blefuscu the great lenity of his master, who was content to punish me no further than with the loss of my eyes ; that I had fled from justice ; and, if I did not return in two hours, I should be deprived of my title of *nardac* and declared a traitor. The envoy further added that, in order to maintain the peace and amity between both empires, his master expected that his brother of Blefuscu would give orders to have me sent back to Lilliput, bound hand and foot, to be punished as a traitor.

The emperor of Blefuscu, having taken three days to consult, returned an answer, consisting of many civilities and excuses. He said that for sending me bound, his brother knew it was impossible ; that although I had deprived him of his fleet, yet he owed great obligations to me for many good offices I had done him in making the peace : that, however, both their Majesties would soon be made easy ; for I had found a prodigious vessel on the shore, able to carry me on the sea, which he had given order to fit up with my own assistance and direction ; and he hoped, in a few weeks, both empires would be freed from so insupportable an incumbrance.

With this answer the envoy returned to Lilliput, and the monarch of Blefuscu related to me all that had passed ; offering me at the same time (but under the strictest confidence) his gracious protection, if I would continue in his service ; wherein, although I believed him sincere, yet I resolved never more to put any confidence in princes or ministers, where I could possibly avoid it ; and, therefore, with all due acknowledgments for his favourable intentions, I humbly begged to be excused. I told him, that since fortune, whether good or evil, had thrown a vessel in my way, I was resolved to venture myself in the ocean rather than be an occasion of difference between two such mighty monarchs.

Five hundred workmen were employed to make two sails to my boat, according to my directions, by quilting thirteen fold of their strongest linen together. I was at the pains of making ropes and cables, by twisting ten, twenty, or thirty of the thickest and strongest of theirs. A great stone that I happened to find, after a long search by the sea-shore, served me for an anchor. I had the tallow of three hundred cows for greasing my boat and other uses. I was at incredible pains in cutting down some of the largest timber-trees for oars and masts, wherein I was, however, much assisted by his Majesty's ship-carpenters, who helped me in smoothing them after I had done the rough work.

In about a month, when all was prepared, I sent to receive his Majesty's commands, and to take my leave. The emperor and royal family came out of the palace ; I lay down on my face to kiss his hand, which he very graciously gave me ; so did the empress, and young princes of the blood. His Majesty presented me with fifty purses of two hundred *sprugs* apiece, together with his picture at full length, which I put immediately into one of my gloves, to keep it from being hurt. The ceremonies at my departure were too many to trouble the reader with at this time.

I stored the boat with the carcasses of a hundred oxen, and three hundred sheep, with bread and drink proportionable, and as much meat ready dressed as four hundred cooks could provide. I took with me six cows and two bulls alive, with as many ewes and rams, intending to carry them into my own country and propagate the breed. And, to feed them on board, I had a good bundle of hay, and a bag of corn. I would gladly have taken a dozen of the natives, but this was a thing the emperor would by no means permit ; and, besides a diligent search into my pockets, his Majesty engaged my honour not to carry away any of his subjects, although with their own consent and desire.

Having thus prepared all things as well as I was able, I set sail on the twenty-fourth day of September, 1701, at six in the morning ; and, when I had gone about four leagues to the northward, the wind being at south-east, at six in the evening I descried a small island about half a league to the north-west. I advanced forward, and cast anchor on the lee side of the island, which seemed to be uninhabited. I then took some refreshment, and went to my rest. I slept well, and as I conjecture at least six hours, for I found the day broke in two hours after I waked. It was a clear night. I ate my breakfast before the sun was up ; and heaving anchor, the wind being favourable, I steered the same course that I had done the day before, wherein I was directed by my pocket-compass. My intention was to reach, if possible, one of those islands which I had reason to believe lay on the north-east of Van Diemen's land.

I discovered nothing all that day ; but upon the next, about three in the afternoon, when I had by my computation made twenty-four leagues from Blefuscu, I descried a sail steering to the south-east ; my course was due east. I hailed her, but could get no answer ; yet I found I gained upon her, for the wind slackened. I made all the sail I could, and in half an hour she spied me, then hung out her ancient, and discharged a gun.

It is not easy to express the joy I was in upon the unexpected hope of once more seeing my beloved country, and the dear pledges I had left in it. The ship slackened her sails, and I came up with her between five and six in the evening, September 26 ; but my heart leaped within me to see her English colours. I put my cows and sheep into my coat pockets, and got on board with all my little cargo of provisions.

The vessel was an English merchantman, returning from Japan by the North and South seas, the captain, Mr. John Biddel of Deptford, a very civil man, and an excellent sailor. We were now in the latitude of 30 degrees south ; there were about fifty men in the ship ; and here I met an old comrade of mine, one Peter Williams, who gave me a good character to the captain.

This gentleman treated me with kindness, and desired I would let him know what place I came from last, and whither I was bound ; which I did in few words, but he thought I was raving, and that the dangers I underwent had disturbed my head ; whereupon I took my black cattle and sheep out of my pocket, which, after great astonishment, clearly convinced him of my veracity. I then showed him the gold given me by the Emperor of Blefuscu, together with his Majesty's picture at full length, and some other rarities of that country. I gave him two purses of two hundred *sprugs* each, and promised, when we arrived in England, to make him a present of a cow and a sheep.

Whereupon I took my black cattle out of my pocket

We arrived in the Downs on the 13th of April, 1702. I had only one misfortune, that the rats on board carried away one of my sheep; I found her bones in a hole, picked clean from the flesh. The rest of my cattle I got safe ashore, and set them a-grazing in a bowling green at Greenwich, where the fineness of the grass made them feed very heartily, though I had always feared the contrary: neither could I possibly have preserved them in so long a voyage if the captain had not allowed me some of his best biscuit, which, rubbed to powder, and mingled with water, was their constant food. The short time I continued in England, I made a considerable profit of my showing my cattle to many persons of quality and others: and, before I began my second voyage, I sold them for six hundred pounds. Since my last return, I find the breed is considerably increased, especially the sheep, which I hope will prove much to the advantage of the woollen manufacture, by the fineness of the fleeces.

Alice in Wonderland

By LEWIS CARROLL

CHAPTER I

DOWN THE RABBIT-HOLE

ALICE was beginning to get very tired of sitting by her sister on the bank, and of having nothing to do : once or twice she had peeped into the book her sister was reading, but it had no pictures or conversations in it, " and what is the use of a book," thought Alice, " without pictures or conversations ? "

She was considering in her own mind (as well as she could, for the hot day made her feel very sleepy and stupid) whether the pleasure of making a daisy-chain would be worth the trouble of getting up and picking the daisies, when suddenly a White Rabbit with pink eyes ran close by her.

There was nothing so *very* remarkable in that ; nor did Alice think it so *very* much out of the way to hear the Rabbit say to itself, " Oh dear ! Oh dear ! I shall be too late ! " (when she thought it over afterwards, it occurred to her that she ought to have wondered at this, but at the time it all seemed quite natural) ; but when the Rabbit actually *took a watch out of its waist-coat-pocket*, and looked at it, and then hurried on, Alice started to her feet, for it flashed across her mind that she had never before seen a rabbit with either a waistcoat-pocket or a watch to take out of it, and, burning with curiosity, she ran across the field after it, and was just in time to see it pop down a large rabbit-hole under the hedge.

In another moment down went Alice after it, never once considering how in the world she was to get out again.

The rabbit-hole went straight on like a tunnel for some way, and then dipped suddenly down, so suddenly that Alice had not a moment to think about stopping herself before she found herself falling down what seemed to be a very deep well.

Either the well was very deep, or she fell very slowly, for she had plenty of time as she went down to look about her, and to wonder what was going to happen next. First, she tried to look down and make out what she was coming to, but it was too dark to see anything ; then she looked at the sides of the well, and noticed that they were filled with cupboards and book-shelves ; here and there she saw maps and pictures hung upon pegs. She took down a jar from one of the shelves as she passed ; it was labelled " ORANGE MARMALADE," but to her great disappointment it was empty : she did not like to drop the jar for fear of killing somebody under-neath, so managed to put it into one of the cupboards as she fell past it.

" Well," thought Alice to herself, " after such a fall as this, I shall think nothing of tumbling downstairs ! How brave they'll all think me at home ! Why, I wouldn't say anything about it, even if I fell off the top of the house ! " (Which was very likely true.)

Down, down, down. Would the fall *never* come to an end ? " I wonder how many miles I've fallen by this time ? " she said aloud. " I must be getting somewhere near the centre of the earth. Let me see : that would be four thousand miles down, I think "—for, you see, Alice had learned several things of this sort in her lessons in the school-room, and though this was not a *very* good opportunity for showing off her knowledge, as there was no one to listen to her, still it was good practice to say it over— " yes, that's about the right distance—but then I wonder what Latitude or Longitude I've got to ? " (Alice had not the slightest idea what Latitude was, or Longitude either, but she thought they were nice grand words to say.)

Presently she began again. " I wonder if I shall fall right *through* the earth ! How funny it'll seem to come out among the people that walk with their heads downwards ! The Antipathies, I think "—she was rather glad there *was* no one listening, this time, as it didn't sound at all the right word — " but I shall have to ask them what the name of the country is, you know. Please, Ma'am, is this New Zealand or Australia ? " (and she tried to curtsey as she spoke—fancy *curtseying* as you're falling through the air ! Do you think you could manage it ?) " And what an ignorant little girl she'll think me for asking ! No, it'll never do to ask : perhaps I shall see it written up somewhere."

Down, down, down. There was nothing else to do, so Alice soon began talking again. " Dinah'll miss me very much to-night, I should think ! " (Dinah was the cat.) " I hope they'll remember her saucer of milk at tea-time. Dinah, my dear, I wish you were down here with me ! There are no mice in the air, I'm afraid, but you might catch a bat, and that's very like a mouse, you know. But do cats eat bats, I wonder? " And here Alice began to get rather sleepy, and went on saying to herself, in a dreamy sort of way, " Do cats eat bats ? Do cats eat bats ? " and sometimes, " Do bats eat cats ? " for, you see, as she couldn't answer either question, it didn't much matter which way she put it. She felt that she was dozing off, and had just begun to dream that she was walking hand in hand with Dinah, and was saying to her very earnestly, " Now, Dinah, tell me the truth : did you ever eat a bat ? " when suddenly, thump ! thump ! down she came upon a heap of sticks and dry leaves, and the fall was over.

Alice was not a bit hurt, and she jumped up on to her feet in a moment : she looked up, but it was dark overhead ; before her another long passage, and the White Rabbit was still in sight, hurrying down it. There was not a moment to be lost : away went Alice like the wind, and was just in time to hear it say, as it turned a corner, " Oh, my ears and whiskers, how late

" Please, Ma'am, is this New Zealand or Australia?"

it's getting ! " She was close behind it when she turned the corner, but the Rabbit was no longer to be seen : she found herself in a long, low hall, which was lit up by a row of lamps hanging from the roof.

There were doors all round the hall, but they were all locked ; and when Alice had been all the way down one side and up the other, trying every door, she walked sadly down the middle, wondering how she was ever to get out again.

Suddenly she came upon a three-legged table, all made of solid glass ; there was nothing on it but a tiny golden key, and Alice's first idea was that this might belong to one of the doors of the hall ; but, alas ! either the locks were too large, or the key was too small, but at any rate it would not open any of them. However, on the second time round, she came upon a low curtain she had not noticed before, and behind it was a little door about fifteen inches high : she tried the little golden key in the lock, and to her great delight it fitted !

Alice opened the door and found that it led into a small passage, not much larger than a rat-hole : she knelt down and looked along the passage into the loveliest garden you ever saw. How she longed to get out of that dark hall, and wander about among those beds of bright flowers and those cool fountains, but she could not even get her head through the doorway ; " and even if my head would go through," thought poor Alice, " it would be of very little use without my shoulders. Oh, how I wish I could shut up like a telescope ! I think I could, if I only knew how to begin." For, you see, so many out-of-the-way things had happened lately, that Alice had begun to think that very few things indeed were really impossible.

There seemed to be no use in waiting by the little door, so she went back to the table, half hoping she might find another key on it, or at any rate a book of rules for shutting people up like telescopes : this time she found a little bottle on it (" which certainly was not here before," said Alice), and tied round the neck of the bottle was a paper label, with the words " DRINK ME " beautifully printed on it in large letters.

It was all very well to say " Drink me," but the wise little Alice was not going to do *that* in a hurry. " No, I'll look first," she said, " and see whether it's marked ' *poison* ' or not " ; for she had read several nice little stories about children who had got burnt, and eaten up by wild beasts, and other unpleasant things, all because they *would* not remember the simple rules their friends had taught them : such as, that a red-hot poker will burn you if you hold it too long ; and that, if you cut your finger *very* deeply with a knife, it usually bleeds ; and she had never forgotten that if you drink much from a bottle marked " poison," it is almost sure to disagree with you, sooner or later.

However, this bottle was *not* marked " poison," so Alice ventured to taste it, and finding it very nice (it had, in fact, a sort of mixed flavour of cherry-tart, custard, pine-apple, roast turkey, toffy, and hot buttered toast), she very soon finished it off.

    .   .   .   .

" What a curious feeling ! " said Alice. " I must be shutting up like a telescope."

And so it was indeed : she was now only ten inches high, and her face brightened up at the thought that she was now the right size for going through the little door in the garden. First, however, she waited for a few minutes to see if she was going to shrink any further : she felt a little nervous about this ; " for it might end, you know," said Alice to herself, " in my going out altogether, like a candle. I wonder what I should be like then ? " And she tried to fancy what the flame of a candle looks like after the candle is blown out, for she could not remember ever having seen such a thing.

After a while, finding that nothing more happened, she decided on going into the garden at once ; but, alas for poor Alice ! when she got to the door, she found she had forgotten the little golden key, and when she went back to the table for it, she found she could not possibly reach it : she could see it quite plainly through the glass, and she tried her best to climb up one

GULLIVER'S NEW SUIT.
Three hundred tailors were ordered to make me a new suit of clothes, one of whom had to mount a ladder to take my measurement.

GULLIVER CAPTURES THE FLEET
I drew fifty of the enemy's largest men-of-war after me with great ease.

of the legs of the table, but it was too slippery ; and when she had tired herself out with trying, the poor little thing sat down and cried.

" Come, there's no use in crying like that ! " said Alice to herself, rather sharply. " I advise you to leave off this minute ! " She generally gave herself very good advice (though she very seldom followed it), and sometimes she scolded herself so severely as to bring tears into her eyes ; and once she remembered trying to box her own ears for having cheated herself in a game of croquet she was playing against herself, for this curious child was very fond of pretending to be two people. " But it's no use now," thought poor Alice, " to pretend to be two people ! Why, there's hardly enough of me left to make *one* respectable person ! "

Soon her eye fell on a little glass box that was lying under the table : she opened it, and found in it a very small cake, on which the words " EAT ME " were beautifully marked in currants. " Well, I'll eat it," said Alice, " and if it makes me grow larger, I can reach the key ; and if it makes me smaller, I can creep under the door ; so either way I'll get into the garden, and I don't care which happens ! "

She ate a little bit, and said anxiously to herself, " Which way ? Which way ? " holding her hand on the top of her head to feel which way it was growing, and she was quite surprised to find that she remained the same size : to be sure, this is what generally happens when one eats cake, but Alice had got so much into the way of expecting nothing but out-of-the-way things to happen, that it seemed quite dull and stupid for life to go on in the common way.

So she set to work, and very soon finished off the cake.

·　·　·　·　·　·　·　·　·　·　·　·　·　·

CHAPTER II

POOL OF TEARS

" CURIOUSER and curiouser ! " cried Alice (she was so surprised, that for the moment she quite forgot how to speak good English) ; " now I'm opening out like the largest telescope that ever was ! Good-bye, feet ! " (for when she looked down at her feet, they seemed to be almost out of sight, they were getting so far off). " Oh, my poor little feet, I wonder who will put on your shoes and stockings for you now, dears ? I'm sure *I* shan't be able ! I shall be a great deal too far off to trouble myself about you : you must manage the best way you can—but I must be kind to them," thought Alice, " or perhaps they won't walk the way I want to go ! Let me see : I'll give them a new pair of boots every Christmas."

And she went on planning to herself how she would manage it. " They must go by the carrier," she thought ; " and how funny it'll seem, sending presents to one's own feet ! And how odd the directions will look !

> *Alice's Right Foot, Esq.,*
> *Hearthrug,*
> *near the Fender,*
> *(with Alice's love).*

" Oh dear, what nonsense I'm talking ! "

Just at this moment her head struck against the roof of the hall : in fact, she was now rather more than nine feet high, and she at once took up the little golden key, and hurried off to the garden door.

Poor Alice ! It was as much as she could do, lying down on one side, to look through into the garden with one eye ; but to get through was more hopeless than ever : she sat down and began to cry again.

" You ought to be ashamed of yourself," said Alice, " a great girl like

The Rabbit started violently and dropped the white kid gloves
and the fan

you " (she might well say this), " to go on crying in this way ! Stop this moment, I tell you ! " But she went on all the same, shedding gallons of tears, until there was a large pool all round her, about four inches deep and reaching half down the hall.

After a time she heard a little pattering of feet in the distance, and she hastily dried her eyes to see what was coming. It was the White Rabbit returning, splendidly dressed, with a pair of white kid gloves in one hand and a large fan in the other : he came trotting along in a great hurry, muttering to himself as he came, " Oh ! the Duchess, the Duchess ! Oh, won't she be savage if I've kept her waiting ! " Alice felt so desperate that she was ready to ask help of any one ; so, when the Rabbit came near her, she began, in a low, timid voice, " If you please, sir——" The Rabbit started violently, dropped the white kid gloves and the fan, and scurried away into the darkness as hard as he could go.

Alice took up the fan and gloves, and, as the hall was very hot, she kept fanning herself all the time she went on talking : " Dear, dear ! How queer everything is to-day ! And yesterday things went on just as usual. I wonder if I've been changed in the night ? Let me think : was I the same when I got up this morning ? I almost think I can remember feeling a little different. But if I'm not the same, the next question is, Who in the world am I ? Ah, *that's* the great puzzle ! " And she began thinking over all the children she knew that were of the same age as herself, to see if she could have been changed for any of them.

" I'm sure I'm not Ada," she said, " for her hair goes in such long ringlets, and mine doesn't go in ringlets at all ; and I'm sure I can't be Mabel, for I know all sorts of things, and she, oh ! she knows such a very little ! Besides, *she's* she, and *I'm* I, and—oh dear, how puzzling it all is ! I'll try if I know all the things I used to know. Let me see : four times five are twelve, and four times six is thirteen, and four times seven is—oh dear ! I shall never get to twenty at that rate ! However, the Multiplication Table doesn't signify : let's try Geography. London is the capital of Paris, and Paris is the capital of Rome, and Rome—no, *that's* all wrong, I'm certain ! I must have been changed for Mabel ! I'll try and say ' *How doth the little*—' " and she crossed her hands on her lap as if she were saying lessons, and began to repeat it, but her voice sounded hoarse and strange, and the words did not come the same as they used to do :—

> " *How doth the little crocodile*
> *Improve his shining tail,*
> *And pour the waters of the Nile*
> *On every golden scale !*

> " *How cheerfully he seems to grin,*
> *How neatly spread his claws,*
> *And welcomes little fishes in*
> *With gently smiling jaws !*

" I'm sure those are not the right words," said poor Alice, and her eyes filled with tears again as she went on, " I must be Mabel, after all, and I shall have to go and live in that poky little house, and have next to no toys to play with, and oh ! ever so many lessons to learn ! No, I've made up my mind about it ; if I'm Mabel, I'll stay down here ! It'll be no use their putting their heads down and saying ' Come up again, dear !' I shall only look up and say ' Who am I, then ? Tell me that first, and then, if I like being that person, I'll come up : if not, I'll stay down here till I'm somebody else '—but, oh dear ! " cried Alice, with a sudden burst of tears, " I do wish they *would* put their heads down ! I am so *very* tired of being all alone here ! "

As she said this she looked down at her hands, and was surprised to see that she had put on one of the Rabbit's little white kid gloves while she was talking. " How *can* I have done that ? " she thought. " I must be growing small again." She got up and went to the table to measure herself by it, and found that, as nearly as she could guess, she was now about two feet high, and was going on shrinking rapidly : she soon found out that the cause of this was the fan she was holding, and she dropped it hastily, just in time to save herself from shrinking away altogether.

" That *was* a narrow escape ! " said Alice, a good deal frightened at the sudden change, but very glad to find herself still in existence ; " and now for the garden ! " and she ran with all speed back to the little door : but, alas ! the little door was shut again, and the little golden key was lying on the glass table as before, " and things are worse than ever," thought the poor child, " for I never was so small as this before, never ! And I declare it's too bad, that it is ! "

As she said these words her foot slipped, and in another moment, splash ! she was up to her chin in salt water. Her first idea was that she had some-how fallen into the sea, " and in that case I can go back by railway," she said to herself. (Alice had been to the seaside once in her life, and had come to the general conclusion that wherever you go to on the English coast you find a number of bathing-machines in the sea, some children digging in the sand with wooden spades, then a row of lodging-houses, and behind them a railway station.) However, she soon made out that she was in the pool of tears which she had wept when she was nine feet high.

" I wish I hadn't cried so much ! " said Alice, as she swam about, try-ing to find her way out. " I shall be punished for it now, I suppose, by being drowned in my own tears ! That *will* be a queer thing, to be sure ! How-ever, everything is queer to-day."

Just then she heard something splashing about in the pool a little way off, and she swam nearer to make out what it was : at first she thought it must be a walrus or hippopotamus, but then she remembered how small she was now, and she soon made out that it was only a mouse that had slipped in like herself.

" Would it be of any use now," thought Alice, " to speak to this mouse? Everything is so out-of-the-way down here, that I should think very likely it can talk : at any rate there's no harm in trying." So she began : " O Mouse, do you know the way out of this pool ? I am very tired of swim-ming about here, O Mouse ! " (Alice thought this must be the right way of speaking to a mouse : she had never done such a thing before, but she remembered having seen in her brother's Latin grammar, " A mouse—of a mouse—to a mouse—a mouse—O mouse ! ") The Mouse looked at her rather inquisitively, and seemed to her to wink with one of its little eyes, but it said nothing.

" Perhaps it doesn't understand English," thought Alice ; " I dare say it's a French mouse, come over with William the Conqueror." (For, with all her knowledge of history, Alice had no very clear notion how long ago anything had happened.) So she began again : " Où est ma chatte ? " which was the first sentence in her French lesson-book. The Mouse gave a sudden leap out of the water, and seemed to quiver all over with fright. " Oh, I beg your pardon ! " cried Alice hastily, afraid that she had hurt the poor animal's feelings. " I quite forgot you didn't like cats."

" Not like cats ! " cried the Mouse, in a shrill, passionate voice. " Would *you* like cats if you were me ? "

" Well, perhaps not," said Alice, in a soothing tone : " don't be angry

about it. And yet I wish I could show you our cat Dinah : I think you'd
take a fancy to cats if you could only see her. She is such a dear quiet thing,"
Alice went on, half to herself, as she swam lazily about in the pool, " and
she sits purring so nicely by the fire, licking her paws and washing her face
—and she is such a nice soft thing to nurse—and she's such a capital one
for catching mice—oh, I beg your pardon ! " cried Alice again, for this
time the Mouse was bristling all over, and she felt certain it must be really
offended. " We won't talk about her any more if you'd rather not."

" We, indeed ! " cried the Mouse, who was trembling down to the
end of his tail, " as if I would talk on such a subject ! Our family always
hated cats : nasty, low, vulgar things ! Don't let me hear the name
again ! "

" I won't indeed ! " said Alice, in a great hurry to change the subject
of conversation. " Are you—are you fond—of—of dogs ? " The Mouse
did not answer, so Alice went on eagerly : " There is such a nice little dog
near our house I should like to show you ! A little bright-eyed terrier, you
know, with, oh, such long curly brown hair ! And it'll fetch things when
you throw them, and it'll sit up and beg for its dinner, and all sorts of things
—I can't remember half of them—and it belongs to a farmer, you know,
and he says it's so useful, it's worth a hundred pounds ! He says it kills all
the rats and—oh dear ! " cried Alice in a sorrowful tone, " I'm afraid I've
offended it again ! " For the Mouse was swimming away from her as hard
as it could go, and making quite a commotion in the pool as it went.

So she called softly after it, " Mouse, dear ! Do come back again, and
we won't talk about cats or dogs either, if you don't like them ! " When
the Mouse heard this, it turned round and swam slowly back to her: its
face was quite pale (with passion, Alice thought), and it said in a low, trembling voice, " Let us get to the shore, and then I'll tell you my history, and
you'll understand why it is I hate cats and dogs."

It was high time to go, for the pool was getting quite crowded with the
birds and animals that had fallen into it ; there was a Duck and a Dodo,
a Lory and an Eaglet, and several other curious creatures. Alice led the
way, and the whole party swam to the shore.

CHAPTER III

A CAUCUS-RACE AND A LONG TALE

THEY were indeed a queer-looking party that assembled on the
bank—the birds with draggled feathers, the animals with their fur
clinging close to them, and all dripping wet, cross, and uncomfortable.
The first question, of course, was, how to get dry again : they had a
consultation about this, and after a few minutes it seemed quite natural to
Alice to find herself talking familiarly with them, as if she had known them
all her life. Indeed, she had quite a long argument with the Lory, who at
last turned sulky, and would only say, " I am older than you, and must
know better "; and this Alice would not allow without knowing how old

it was, and, as the Lory positively refused to tell its age, there was no more to be said.

At last the Mouse, who seemed to be a person of some authority among them, called out, " Sit down, all of you, and listen to me ! *I'll* soon make you dry enough !" They all sat down at once, in a large ring, with the Mouse in the middle. Alice kept her eyes anxiously fixed on it, for she felt sure she would catch a bad cold if she did not get dry very soon.

" Ahem ! " said the Mouse with an important air. " Are you all ready ? This is the driest thing I know. Silence all round, if you please ! ' William the Conqueror, whose cause was favoured by the pope, was soon submitted to by the English, who wanted leaders, and had been of late much accustomed to usurpation and conquest. Edwin and Morcar, the earls of Mercia and Northumbria——' "

" Ugh ! " said the Lory, with a shiver.

" I beg your pardon ! " said the Mouse, frowning, but very politely, " did you speak ? "

" Not I ! " said the Lory hastily.

" I thought you did," said the Mouse. " I proceed. ' Edwin and Morcar, the earls of Mercia and Northumbria, declared for him : and even Stigand, the patriotic archbishop of Canterbury, found it advisable——' "

" Found *what* ? " said the Duck.

" Found *it*," the Mouse replied rather crossly : " of course you know what ' it ' means."

" I know what ' it ' means well enough, when *I* find a thing," said the Duck : " it's generally a frog or a worm. The question is, what did the archbishop find ? "

The Mouse did not notice this question, but hurriedly went on, " ' —found it advisable to go with Edgar Atheling to meet William and offer him the crown. William's conduct at first was moderate. But the insolence of his Normans——' How are you getting on now, my dear ? " it continued, turning to Alice as it spoke.

" As wet as ever," said Alice in a melancholy tone ; " it doesn't seem to dry me at all."

" In that case," said the Dodo solemnly, rising to its feet, " I move that the meeting adjourn, for the immediate adoption of more energetic remedies——"

" Speak English ! " said the Eaglet. " I don't know the meaning of half those long words, and what's more, I don't believe you do either ! " And the Eaglet bent down its head to hide a smile : some of the other birds tittered audibly.

" What I was going to say," said the Dodo in an offended tone, " was, that the best thing to get us dry would be a Caucus-race."

" What *is* a Caucus-race ? " said Alice ; not that she much wanted to know, but the Dodo had paused as if it thought that *somebody* ought to speak, and no one else seemed inclined to say anything.

" Why," said the Dodo, " the best way to explain it is to do it." (And, as you might like to try the thing yourself some winter day, I will tell you how the Dodo managed it.)

First it marked out a racecourse, in a sort of circle (" the exact shape doesn't matter," it said), and then all the party were placed along the course, here and there. There was no "One, two, three, and away," but they began running when they liked, and left off when they liked, so that it was not easy to know when the race was over. However, when they had been running half an hour or so, and were quite dry again, the Dodo suddenly called out, "The race is over!" and they all crowded round it, panting and asking, "But who has won?"

This question the Dodo could not answer without a great deal of thought, and it sat for a long time with one finger pressed upon its forehead (the position in which you usually see Shakespeare, in the pictures of him), while the rest waited in silence. At last the Dodo said "*Everybody* has won, and all must have prizes."

"But who is to give the prizes?" quite a chorus of voices asked.

"Why *she*, of course," said the Dodo, pointing to Alice with one finger; and the whole party at once crowded round her, calling out in a confused way, "Prizes! Prizes!"

Alice had no idea what to do, and in despair she put her hand into her pocket, and pulled out a box of comfits (luckily the salt water had not got into it), and handed them round as prizes. There was exactly one apiece all round.

"But she must have a prize herself, you know," said the Mouse.

"Of course," the Dodo replied very gravely. "What else have you got in your pocket?" he went on, turning to Alice.

"Only a thimble," said Alice sadly.

"Hand it over here," said the Dodo.

Then they all crowded round her once more, while the Dodo solemnly presented the thimble, saying, "We beg your acceptance of this elegant thimble"; and, when it had finished this short speech, they all cheered.

Alice thought the whole thing very absurd, but they all looked so grave that she did not dare to laugh; and, as she could not think of anything to say, she simply bowed, and took the thimble, looking as solemn as she could.

The next thing was to eat the comfits: this caused some noise and confusion, as the large birds complained that they could not taste theirs, and the small ones choked and had to be patted on the back. However, it was over at last, and they sat down again in a ring, and begged the Mouse to tell them something more.

"You promised to tell me your history, you know," said Alice, "and why it is you hate—C and D," she added in a whisper, half afraid that it would be offended again.

"Mine is a long and a sad tale!" said the Mouse, turning to Alice and sighing.

"It *is* a long tail, certainly," said Alice, looking down with wonder at the Mouse's tail; "but why do you call it sad?" And she kept on puzzling about it while the Mouse was speaking, so that her idea of the tale was something like this:—" Fury said to a

mouse, That he

met in the

house,

Let us

both go to

law: I will

prosecute

you. Come,

I'll take no

denial; We

must have a

trial; For

really this

morning I've

nothing

to do.'

Said the

mouse to the

cur, 'Such

a trial,

dear Sir,

With

no jury

or judge,

would be

wasting

our breath.'

'I'll be

judge, I'll

be jury,

Said

cunning

Old Fury;]

I'll try

the whole

cause,

and

condemn

you

to

death.'"

" You are not attending ! " said the Mouse to Alice severely. " What are you thinking of ? "

" I beg your pardon," said Alice very humbly : " you had got to the fifth bend, I think ? "

" I had *not* ! " cried the Mouse sharply, and very angrily.

" A knot ! " said Alice, always ready to make herself useful, and looking anxiously about her. " Oh, do let me help to undo it ! "

" I shall do nothing of the sort," said the Mouse, getting up and walking away. " You insult me by talking such nonsense ! "

" I didn't mean it ! " pleaded poor Alice. " But you are so easily offended, you know ! "

The Mouse only growled in reply.

" Please come back and finish your story ! " Alice called after it, and the others all joined in chorus, " Yes, please do ! " but the Mouse only shook its head impatiently and walked a little quicker.

" What a pity it wouldn't stay ! " sighed the Lory, as soon as it was quite out of sight ; and an old Crab took the opportunity of saying to her daughter, " Ah, my dear ! Let this be a lesson to you never to lose *your* temper ! " " Hold your tongue, Ma ! " said the young Crab, a little snappishly. " You're enough to try the patience of an oyster ! "

" I wish I had our Dinah here, I know I do ! " said Alice aloud, addressing nobody in particular. " She'd soon fetch it back ! "

" And who is Dinah, if I might venture to ask the question ? " said the Lory.

Alice replied eagerly, for she was always ready to talk about her pet : " Dinah's our cat. And she's such a capital one for catching mice, you can't think ! And oh, I wish you could see her after the birds ! Why, she'll eat a little bird as soon as look at it ! "

This speech caused a remarkable sensation among the party. Some of the birds hurried off at once : one old Magpie began wrapping itself up very carefully, remarking, " I really must be getting home ; the night-air doesn't suit my throat ! " and a Canary called out in a trembling voice to its children, " Come away, my dears ! It's high time you were all in bed ! " On various pretexts they all moved off, and Alice was soon left alone.

" I wish I hadn't mentioned Dinah ! " she said to herself in a melancholy tone. " Nobody seems to like her down here, and I'm sure she's the best cat in the world ! Oh, my dear Dinah ! I wonder if I shall ever see you any more ! " And here poor Alice began to cry again, for she felt very lonely and low-spirited. In a little while, however, she again heard a little pattering of footsteps in the distance, and she looked up eagerly, half hoping that the Mouse had changed his mind, and was coming back to finish his story.

CHAPTER IV

THE RABBIT SENDS IN A LITTLE BILL

IT was the White Rabbit, trotting slowly back again, and looking anxiously about as it went, as if it had lost something ; and she heard it muttering to itself, " The Duchess ! The Duchess ! Oh, my dear paws ! Oh, my fur and whiskers ! She'll get me executed, as sure as ferrets are ferrets ! Where *can* I have dropped them, I wonder ? " Alice guessed in a moment that it was looking for the fan and the pair of white kid gloves, and she very good-naturedly began hunting for them, but they were nowhere to be seen —everything seemed to have changed since her swim in the pool, and the great hall, with the glass table and the little door, had vanished completely.

Very soon the Rabbit noticed Alice, as she went hunting about, and called out to her in an angry tone, " Why, Mary Ann, what *are* you doing out here ? Run home this moment and fetch me a pair of gloves and a fan ! Quick now ! " And Alice was so much frightened that she ran off at once in the direction it pointed to, without trying to explain the mistake that it had made.

" He took me for his housemaid," she said to herself as she ran. " How surprised he'll be when he finds out who I am ! But I'd better take him his fan and gloves—that is, if I can find them." As she said this, she came upon a neat little house, on the door of which was a bright brass plate with the name " W. RABBIT " engraved upon it. She went in without knocking, and hurried upstairs, in great fear lest she should meet the real Mary Ann, and be turned out of the house before she had found the fan and the gloves.

" How queer it seems," Alice said to herself, " to be going messages for a rabbit ! I suppose Dinah'll be sending me on messages next ! " And

*" Why, Mary Ann, what are
you doing out here?"*

she began fancying the sort of thing that would happen : " ' Miss Alice ! Come here directly, and get ready for your walk ! ' ' Coming in a minute, nurse ! But I've got to watch this mouse-hole till Dinah comes back, and see that the mouse doesn't get out.' Only I don't think," Alice went on, " that they'd let Dinah stop in the house if it began ordering people about like that ! "

By this time she had found her way into a tidy little room with a table in the window, and on it (as she had hoped) a fan and two or three pairs of tiny white kid gloves : she took up the fan and a pair of the gloves, and was just going to leave the room, when her eye fell upon a little bottle that stood near the looking-glass. There was no label this time with the words " DRINK ME," but nevertheless she uncorked it and put it to her lips. " I know something interesting is sure to happen," she said to herself,

" whenever I eat or drink anything ; so I'll just see what this bottle does. I do hope it'll make me grow large again, for really I'm quite tired of being such a tiny little thing ! "

It did so indeed ; and much sooner than she had expected : before she had drunk half the bottle she found her head pressing against the ceiling, and had to stoop to save her neck from being broken. She hastily put down the bottle, saying to herself, " That's quite enough—I hope I shan't grow any more.—As it is, I can't get out at the door.—I do wish I hadn't drunk quite so much ! "

Alas ! it was too late to wish that ! She went on growing and growing, and very soon had to kneel down on the floor : in another minute there was not even room for this, and she tried the effect of lying down with one elbow against the door, and the other arm curled round her head. Still she went on growing, and, as a last resource, she put one arm out of the window, and one foot up the chimney, and said to herself, " Now I can do no more, whatever happens. What *will* become of me ? "

Luckily for Alice, the little magic bottle had now had its full effect, and she grew no larger : still it was very uncomfortable ; and, as there seemed to be no sort of chance of her ever getting out of the room again, no wonder she felt unhappy.

" It was much pleasanter at home," thought poor Alice, " when one wasn't always growing larger and smaller, and being ordered about by mice and rabbits. I almost wish I hadn't gone down that rabbit hole—and yet—and yet—it's rather curious, you know, this sort of life ! I do wonder what *can* have happened to me ! When I used to read fairy-tales, I fancied that kind of thing never happened, and now here I am in the middle of one ! There ought to be a book written about me, that there ought ! And when I grow up, I'll write one ; but I'm grown up now," she added in a sorrowful tone ; " at least there's no room to grow up any more *here*."

" But then," thought Alice, " shall I *never* get any older than I am now ? That'll be a comfort, one way—never to be an old woman—but then—always to have lessons to learn ! Oh, I shouldn't like *that* ! "

" Oh, you foolish Alice ! " she answered herself. " How can you learn lessons in here ? Why, there's hardly room for *you*, and no room at all for any lesson-books ! "

And so she went on, taking first one side and then the other, and making quite a conversation of it altogether ; but after a few minutes she heard a voice outside, and stopped to listen.

" Mary Ann ! Mary Ann ! " said the voice. " Fetch me my gloves this moment ! " Then came a little pattering of feet on the stairs. Alice knew it was the Rabbit coming to look for her, and she trembled till she shook the house, quite forgetting that she was now about a thousand times as large as the Rabbit, and had no reason to be afraid of it.

Presently the Rabbit came up to the door, and tried to open it ; but, as the door opened inwards, and Alice's elbow was pressed hard against it, that attempt proved a failure. Alice heard it say to itself, " Then I'll go round and get in at the window."

" *That* you won't ! " thought Alice, and, after waiting till she fancied she heard the Rabbit just under the window, she suddenly spread out her hand, and made a snatch in the air. She did not get hold of anything, but she heard a little shriek and a fall, and a crash of broken glass, from which she concluded that it was just possible it had fallen into a cucumber-frame, or something of the sort.

Next came an angry voice—the Rabbit's—" Pat ! Pat ! Where are you ? " And then a voice she had never heard before, " Sure then I'm here ! Digging for apples, yer honour ! "

" Digging for apples, indeed ! " said the Rabbit angrily. " Here ! Come and help me out of *this* ! " (Sounds of more broken glass.)

" Now tell me, Pat, what's that in the window ? "

" Sure, it's an arm, yer honour ! " (He pronounced it " arrum.")

" An arm, you goose ! Who ever saw one that size ? Why, it fills the whole window ! "

" Sure, it does, yer honour : but it's an arm for all that."

" Well, it's got no business there, at any rate : go and take it away ! "

There was a long silence after this, and Alice could only hear whispers now and then ; such as, " Sure, I don't like it, yer honour, at all, at all ! " " Do as I tell you, you coward ! " and at last she spread out her hand again, and made another snatch in the air. This time there were *two* little shrieks, and more sounds of broken glass. " What a number of cucumber-frames there must be ! " thought Alice. " I wonder what they'll do next ! As for pulling me out of the window, I only wish they *could* ! I'm sure *I* don't want to stay in here any longer ! "

She waited for some time without hearing anything more : at last came a rumbling of little cart-wheels, and the sound of a good many voices all talking together : she made out the words : " Where's the other ladder ?— Why, I hadn't to bring but one ; Bill's got the other—Bill ! Fetch it here, lad !—Here, put 'em up at this corner—No, tie 'em together first—they don't reach half high enough yet—Oh ! they'll do well enough ; don't be particular—Here, Bill ! catch hold of this rope—Will the roof bear ?—Mind that loose slate—Oh, it's coming down ! Heads below ! " (a loud crash)— " Now who did that ?—It was Bill, I fancy—Who's to go down the chimney ? —Nay, I shan't ! You do it !—*That* I won't, then !—Bill's got to go down —Here, Bill ! the master says you've got to go down the chimney ! "

" Oh ! So Bill's got to come down the chimney, has he ? " said Alice to herself. " Why, they seem to put everything upon Bill ! I wouldn't be in Bill's place for a good deal : this fireplace is narrow, to be sure ; but I *think* I can kick a little ! "

She drew her foot as far down the chimney as she could, and waited till she heard a little animal (she couldn't guess of what sort it was) scratching and scrambling about in the chimney close above her : then, saying to herself, " This is Bill," she gave one sharp kick, and waited to see what would happen next.

The first thing she heard was a general chorus of " There goes Bill ! " then the Rabbit's voice alone—" Catch him, you by the hedge ! " then silence, and then another confusion of voices—" Hold up his head—Brandy now—Don't choke him—How was it, old fellow ? What happened to you ? Tell us all about it ! "

Last came a little feeble, squeaking voice (" That's Bill," thought Alice),

" Well, I hardly know—No more, thank ye ; I'm better now—but I'm a deal too flustered to tell you—all I know is, something comes at me like a Jack-in-the-box, and up I goes like a sky-rocket ! "

" So you did, old fellow ! " said the others.

" We must burn the house down ! " said the Rabbit's voice. And Alice called out as loud as she could, " If you do, I'll set Dinah at you ! "

There was a dead silence instantly, and Alice thought to herself, " I wonder what they *will* do next ! If they had any sense, they'd take the roof off." After a minute or two, they began moving about again, and Alice heard the Rabbit say, " A barrowful will do, to begin with."

" A barrowful of *what* ? " thought Alice. But she had not long to doubt, for the next moment a shower of little pebbles came rattling in at the window, and some of them hit her in the face. " I'll put a stop to this," she said to herself, and shouted out, " You'd better not do that again ! " which produced another dead silence.

Alice noticed with some surprise that the pebbles were all turning into little cakes as they lay on the floor, and a bright idea came into her head. " If I eat one of these cakes," she thought, " it's sure to make *some* change in my size ; and, as it can't possibly make me any larger, it must make me smaller, I suppose."

So she swallowed one of the cakes, and was delighted to find that she began shrinking directly. As soon as she was small enough to get through the door, she ran out of the house, and found quite a crowd of little animals and birds waiting outside. The poor little lizard, Bill, was in the middle, being held up by two guinea-pigs, who were giving it something out of a bottle. They all made a rush at Alice the moment she appeared ; but she ran off as hard as she could, and soon found herself safe in a thick wood.

" The first thing I've got to do," said Alice to herself, as she wandered about in the wood, " is to grow to my right size again ; and the second thing is to find my way into that lovely garden. I think that will be the best plan."

It sounded an excellent plan, no doubt, and very neatly and simply arranged ; the only difficulty was, that she had not the smallest idea how to set about it ; and, while she was peering about anxiously among the trees, a little sharp bark just overhead made her look up in a great hurry.

An enormous puppy was looking down at her with large round eyes, and feebly stretching out one paw, trying to touch her. " Poor little thing ! " said Alice, in a coaxing tone, and she tried hard to whistle to it ; but she was terribly frightened all the time at the thought that it might be hungry, in which case it would be very likely to eat her up in spite of all her coaxing.

Hardly knowing what she did, she picked up a little bit of stick, and held it out to the puppy ; whereupon the puppy jumped into the air off all its feet at once, with a yelp of delight, and rushed at the stick, and made believe to worry it ; then Alice dodged behind a great thistle, to keep herself from being run over ; and the moment she appeared on the other side, the puppy made another rush at the stick, and tumbled head over heels in its hurry to get hold of it ; then Alice, thinking it was very like having a game of play with a cart-horse, and expecting every moment to be trampled under its feet, ran round the thistle again ; then the puppy began a series of short charges at the stick, running a very little way forwards each time and a long way back, and barking hoarsely all the while, till at last it sat down a good way off, panting, with its tongue hanging out of its mouth, and its great eyes half shut.

This seemed to Alice a good opportunity for making her escape ; so she set off at once, and ran till she was quite tired and out of breath, and till the puppy's bark sounded quite faint in the distance.

" And yet what a dear little puppy it was ! " said Alice, as she leant against a buttercup to rest herself, and fanned herself with one of the leaves. " I should have liked teaching it tricks very much, if—if I'd only been the right size to do it ! Oh, dear ! I'd nearly forgotten that I've got to grow up again ! Let me see—how *is* it to be managed ? I suppose I ought to eat or drink something or other ; but the great question is, what ? "

The great question certainly was, what ? Alice looked all round her at the flowers and the blades of grass, but she could not see anything that looked like the right thing to eat or drink under the circumstances. There was a large mushroom growing near her, about the same height as herself ; and, when she had looked under it, and on both sides of it, and behind it, it occurred to her that she might as well look and see what was on the top of it.

She stretched herself up on tiptoe, and peeped over the edge of the mushroom, and her eyes immediately met those of a large blue caterpillar, that was sitting on the top with its arms folded, quietly smoking a long hookah, and taking not the smallest notice of her or of anything else.

CHAPTER V

ADVICE FROM A CATERPILLAR

THE Caterpillar and Alice looked at each other for some time in silence : at last the Caterpillar took the hookah out of its mouth, and addressed her in a languid, sleepy voice.

" Who are *you* ? " said the Caterpillar.

This was not an encouraging opening for a conversation. Alice replied, rather shyly, " I—I hardly know, sir, just at present—at least I know who I *was* when I got up this morning, but I think I must have been changed several times since then."

" What do you mean by that ? " said the Caterpillar sternly. " Explain yourself ! "

" I can't explain *myself*, I'm afraid, sir," said Alice, " because I'm not myself, you see."

" I don't see," said the Caterpillar.

" I'm afraid I can't put it more clearly," Alice replied very politely, " for I can't understand it myself to begin with ; and being so many different sizes in a day is very confusing."

" It isn't," said the Caterpillar.

" Well, perhaps you haven't found it so yet," said Alice ; " but when you have to turn into a chrysalis—you will some day, you know—and then after that into a butterfly, I should think you'll feel it a little queer, won't you ? "

" Not a bit," said the Caterpillar.

" Well, perhaps your feelings may be different," said Alice ; " all I know is, it would feel very queer to *me*."

" You ! " said the Caterpillar contemptuously. " Who are *you* ? "

Which brought them back again to the beginning of the conversation.   Alice felt a little irritated at the Caterpillar's making such *very* short remarks, and she drew herself up and said, very gravely, " I think you ought to tell me who *you* are, first."

" Why ? " said the Caterpillar.

Here was another puzzling question ; and as Alice could not think of any good reason, and as the Caterpillar seemed to be in a *very* unpleasant state of mind, she turned away.

" Come   back ! "   the Caterpillar called after her. " I've something important to say ! "

This sounded promising, certainly : Alice turned and came back again.

" Keep your temper," said the Caterpillar.

" Is that all ? " said Alice, swallowing down her anger as well as she could.

" No," said the Caterpillar.

Alice thought she might

" What do you mean by that ? " said the Caterpillar sternly

as well wait, as she had nothing else to do, and perhaps after all it might tell her something worth hearing. For some minutes it puffed away without speaking, but at last it unfolded its arms, took the hookah out of its mouth again, and said, " So you think you're changed, do you ? "

" I'm afraid I am, sir," said Alice ; " I can't remember things as I used —and I don't keep the same size for ten minutes together ! "

" Can't remember *what* things ? " said the Caterpillar.

" Well, I've tried to say, ' *How doth the little busy bee*,' but it all came different ! " Alice replied, in a very melancholy voice.

" Repeat, ' *You are old, Father William,* ' " said the Caterpillar.
Alice folded her hands, and began:

> " *You are old, Father William,*" *the young man said,*
>   " *And your hair has become very white ;*
> *And yet you incessantly stand on your head—*
>   *Do you think, at your age, it is right ? "*
>
> " *In my youth,*" *Father William replied to his son,*
>   " *I feared it might injure the brain ;*
> *But, now that I'm perfectly sure I have none,*
>   *Why, I do it again and again."*
>
> " *You are old,*" *said the youth,* " *as I mentioned before,*
>   *And have grown most uncommonly fat ;*
> *Yet you turned a back-somersault in at the door—*
>   *Pray, what is the reason of that ? "*
>
> " *In my youth,*" *said the sage, as he shook his gray locks,*
>   " *I kept all my limbs very supple*
> *By the use of this ointment—one shilling the box—*
>   *Allow me to sell you a couple ? "*
>
> " *You are old,*" *said the youth,* " *and your jaws are too weak*
>   *For anything tougher than suet ;*
> *Yet you finished the goose, with the bones and the beak—*
>   *Pray, how did you manage to do it ? "*
>
> " *In my youth,*" *said his father,* " *I took to the law,*
>   *And argued each case with my wife ;*
> *And the muscular strength, which it gave to my jaw.*
>   *Has lasted the rest of my life."*
>
> " *You are old,*" *said the youth,* " *one would hardly suppose*
>   *That your eye was as steady as ever ;*
> *Yet you balanced an eel on the end of your nose—*
>   *What made you so awfully clever ? "*
>
> " *I have answered three questions, and that is enough,*"
>   *Said his father ;* " *don't give yourself airs !*
> *Do you think I can listen all day to such stuff ?*
>   *Be off, or I'll kick you downstairs ! "*

" That is not said right," said the Caterpillar.

" Not *quite* right, I'm afraid," said Alice timidly ; " some of the words have got altered."

" It is wrong from beginning to end," said the Caterpillar decidedly, and there was silence for some minutes.

" It is a very good height indeed "

The Caterpillar was the first to speak.

" What size do you want to be ? " it asked.

" Oh, I'm not particular as to size," Alice hastily replied ; " only one doesn't like changing so often, you know."

"I *don't* know," said the Caterpillar.

Alice said nothing : she had never been so much contradicted in all her life before, and she felt that she was losing her temper.

" Are you content now ? " said the Caterpillar.

" Well, I should like to be a *little* larger, sir, if you wouldn't mind," said Alice : " three inches is such a wretched height to be."

" It is a very good height indeed ! " said the Caterpillar angrily, rearing itself upright as it spoke (it was exactly three inches high).

" But I'm not used to it ! " pleaded poor Alice, in a piteous tone. And she thought to herself, " I wish the creature wouldn't be so easily offended ! "

" You'll get used to it in time," said the Caterpillar ; and it put the hookah into its mouth and began smoking again.

This time Alice waited patiently until it chose to speak again. In a minute or two the Caterpillar took the hookah out of its mouth and yawned once or twice, and shook itself. Then it got down off the mushroom, and crawled away into the grass, merely remarking as it went, " One side will make you grow taller, and the other side will make you grow shorter."

" One side of *what* ? The other side of *what* ? " thought Alice to herself.

" Of the mushroom," said the Caterpillar, just as if she had asked it aloud ; and in another moment it was out of sight.

Alice remained looking thoughtfully at the mushroom for a minute, trying to make out which were the two sides of it ; and as it was perfectly round, she found this a very difficult question. However, at last she stretched her arms round it as far as they would go, and broke off a bit of the edge with each hand.

" And now which is which ? " she said to herself, and nibbled a little of the right-hand bit to try the effect : the next moment she felt a violent blow underneath her chin ; it had struck her foot !

She was a good deal frightened by this very sudden change, but she felt that there was no time to be lost, as she was shrinking rapidly ; so she set to work at once to eat some of the other bit. Her chin was pressed so closely against her foot that there was hardly room to open her mouth ; but she did it at last, and managed to swallow a morsel of the left-hand bit.

.   .   .   .

" Come, my head's free at last ! " said Alice, in a tone of delight, which changed into alarm in another moment, when she found that her shoulders were nowhere to be found : all she could see, when she looked down, was an immense length of neck, which seemed to rise like a stalk out of a sea of green leaves that lay far below her.

" What *can* all that green stuff be ? " said Alice. " And where *have* my shoulders got to ? And oh, my poor hands, how is it I can't see you ? " She was moving them about as she spoke, but no result seemed to follow, except a little shaking among the distant green leaves.

As there seemed to be no chance of getting her hands up to her head, she tried to get her head down to them, and was delighted to find that her neck would bend about easily in any direction, like a serpent. She had just succeeded in curving it down into a graceful zigzag, and was going to dive in among the leaves, which she found to be nothing but the tops of the trees under which she had been wandering, when a sharp hiss made her draw back in a hurry ; a large pigeon had flown into her face, and was beating her violently with its wings.

" Serpent ! " screamed the Pigeon.

" I'm *not* a serpent ! " said Alice indignantly. " Leave me alone ! "

" Serpent ! I say again ! " repeated the Pigeon, but in a more subdued tone, and added with a kind of sob, " I've tried every way, and nothing seems to suit them ! "

" I haven't the least idea what you're talking about," said Alice.

" I've tried the roots of trees, and I've tried banks and I've tried hedges," the Pigeon went on, without attending to her ; " but those serpents ! There's no pleasing them ! "

Alice was more and more puzzled, but she thought there was no use in saying anything more till the Pigeon had finished.

" As if it wasn't trouble enough hatching the eggs," said the Pigeon ; " but I must be on the lookout for serpents night and day ! Why, I haven't had a wink of sleep these three weeks ! "

" I'm very sorry you've been annoyed," said Alice, who was beginning to see its meaning.

" And just as I'd taken the highest tree in the wood," continued the Pigeon, raising its voice to a shriek, " and just as I was thinking I should be free of them at last, they must needs come wriggling down from the sky ! Ugh, Serpent ! "

" But I'm *not* a serpent, I tell you ! " said Alice. " I'm a—I'm a——"

" Well ! *What* are you ? " said the Pigeon. " I can see you're trying to invent something ! "

" I—I'm a little girl," said Alice, rather doubtfully, as she remembered the number of changes she had gone through that day.

" A likely story indeed ! " said the Pigeon, in a tone of the deepest contempt. " I've seen a good many little girls in my time, but never *one* with such a neck as that ! No, no ! You're a serpent ; and there's no use denying it. I suppose you'll be telling me next that you never tasted an egg ! "

" I *have* tasted eggs, certainly," said Alice, who was a very truthful child ; " but little girls eat eggs quite as much as serpents do, you know."

" I don't believe it," said the Pigeon ; " but if they do, why, then, they're a kind of serpent, that's all I can say."

This was such a new idea to Alice, that she was quite silent for a minute or two, which gave the Pigeon the opportunity of adding, " You're looking for eggs, I know *that* well enough : and what does it matter to me whether you're a little girl or a serpent ? "

" It matters a good deal to *me*," said Alice hastily ; " but I'm not looking for eggs, as it happens ; and if I was, I shouldn't want *yours* : I don't like them raw."

" Well, be off, then ! " said the Pigeon, in a sulky tone, as it settled down again into its nest. Alice crouched down among the trees as well as she could, for her neck kept getting entangled among the branches, and every now and then she had to stop and untwist it. After a while she remembered that she still held the pieces of mushroom in her hands, and she set to work very carefully, nibbling first at one and then at the other, and growing sometimes taller and sometimes shorter, until she had succeeded in bringing herself down to her usual height.

It was so long since she had been anything near the right size, that it felt quite strange at first ; but she got used to it in a few minutes, and began talking to herself, as usual. " Come, there's half my plan done now ! How puzzling all these changes are ! I'm never sure what I'm going to be, from one minute to another ! However, I've got back to my right size : the next thing is, to get into that beautiful garden—how *is* that to be done, I wonder ? " As she said this, she came suddenly upon an open place, with a little house in it about four feet high. " Whoèver lives there," thought Alice, " it'll never do to come upon them *this* size : why, I should frighten them out of their wits ! " So she began nibbling at the right-hand bit again, and did not venture to go near the house till she had brought herself down to nine inches high.

CHAPTER VI

PIG AND PEPPER

FOR a minute or two she stood looking at the house, and wondering what to do next, when suddenly a footman in livery came running out of the wood—(she considered him to be a footman because he was in livery : otherwise, judging by his face only, she would have called him a fish)—and rapped loudly at the door with his knuckles. It was opened by another footman in livery, with a round face and large eyes like a frog ; and both footmen, Alice noticed, had powdered hair that curled all over their heads. She felt very curious to know what it was all about, and crept a little way out of the wood to listen.

The Fish-Footman began by producing from under his arm a great letter, nearly as large as himself, and this he handed over to the other, saying, in a solemn tone, " For the Duchess. An invitation from the Queen to play croquet." The Frog-Footman repeated, in the same solemn tone, only changing the order of the words a little, " From the Queen. An invitation for the Duchess to play croquet."

Then they both bowed low, and their curls got entangled together.

Alice laughed so much at this that she had to run back into the wood for fear of their hearing her ; and, when she next peeped out, the Fish-Footman was gone, and the other was sitting on the ground near the door, staring stupidly up into the sky.

Alice went timidly up to the door and knocked.

" There's no sort of use in knocking," said the Footman, " and that for two reasons. First, because I'm on the same side of the door as you are ; secondly, because they're making such a noise inside, no one could possibly hear you." And certainly there *was* a most extraordinary noise going on within—a constant howling and sneezing, and every now and then a great crash, as if a dish or kettle had been broken to pieces.

" Please, then," said Alice, " how am I to get in ? "

" There might be some sense in your knocking," the Footman went on without attending to her, " if we had the door between us. For instance, if you were *inside*, you might knock, and I could let you out, you know." He was looking up into the sky all the time he was speaking, and this Alice thought decidedly uncivil. " But perhaps he can't help it," she said to herself ; " his eyes are so *very* nearly at the top of his head. But at any rate he might answer questions. How am I to get in ? " she repeated aloud.

"I shall sit here," the Footman remarked, "till to-morrow——"

At this moment the door of the house opened, and a large plate came skimming out, straight at the Footman's head : it just grazed his nose, and broke to pieces against one of the trees behind him.

"Or next day, maybe," the Footman continued, in the same tone, exactly as if nothing had happened.

"How am I to get in ?" asked Alice again, in a louder tone.

"*Are* you to get in at all ?" said the Footman. "That's the first question, you know."

It was, no doubt ; only Alice did not like to be told so. "It's really dread-

They both bowed low

ful," she muttered to herself, "the way all the creatures argue. It's enough to drive one crazy !"

The Footman seemed to think this a good opportunity for repeating his remark, with variations. "I shall sit here," he said, "on and off, for days and days."

"But what am *I* to do ?" said Alice.

"Anything you like," said the Footman, and began whistling.

"Oh, there's no use in talking to him," said Alice desperately ; "he's perfectly idiotic !" And she opened the door and went in.

The door led right into a large kitchen, which was full of smoke from one end to the other : the Duchess was sitting on a three-legged stool in the middle, nursing a baby ; the cook was leaning over the fire, stirring a large cauldron which seemed to be full of soup.

"There's certainly too much pepper in that soup !" Alice said to herself, as well as she could for sneezing.

There was certainly too much of it in the air. Even the Duchess sneezed occasionally ; and as for the baby, it was sneezing and howling alternately without a moment's pause. The only two creatures in the kitchen that did not sneeze were the cook and a large cat which was sitting on the hearth and grinning from ear to ear.

" Please, would you tell me," said Alice, a little timidly, for she was not quite sure whether it was good manners for her to speak first, " why your cat grins like that ? "

" It's a Cheshire cat," said the Duchess, " and that's why. Pig ! "

She said the last word with such sudden violence that Alice quite jumped ; but she saw in another moment that it was addressed to the baby, and not to her, so she took courage, and went on again :

" I didn't know that Cheshire cats always grinned ; in fact, I didn't know that cats *could* grin."

" They all can," said the Duchess ; " and most of 'em do."

" I don't know of any that do," Alice said very politely, feeling quite pleased to have got into a conversation.

" You don't know much," said the Duchess ; " and that's a fact."

Alice did not at all like the tone of this remark, and thought it would be as well to introduce some other subject of conversation. While she was trying to fix on one, the cook took the cauldron of soup off the fire, and at once set to work throwing everything within her reach at the Duchess and the baby—the fire-irons came first ; then followed a shower of saucepans, plates, and dishes. The Duchess took no notice of them even when they hit her ; and the baby was howling so much already that it was quite impossible to say whether the blows hurt it or not.

" Oh, *please* mind what you're doing ! " cried Alice, jumping up and down in an agony of terror. " Oh, there goes his *precious* nose ! " as an unusually large saucepan flew close by it, and very nearly carried it off.

" If everybody minded their own business," said the Duchess, in a hoarse growl, " the world would go round a deal faster than it does."

" Which would *not* be an advantage," said Alice, who felt very glad to get an opportunity of showing off a little of her knowledge. " Just think what work it would make with the day and night ! You see, the earth takes twenty-four hours to turn round on its axis——"

" Talking of axes," said the Duchess, " chop off her head ! "

Alice glanced rather anxiously at the cook, to see if she meant to take the hint ; but the cook was busily stirring the soup, and seemed not to be listening, so she went on again : " Twenty-four hours, I *think* ; or is it twelve ? I——"

" Oh, don't bother *me*," said the Duchess ; " I never could abide figures! " And with that she began nursing her child again, singing a sort of lullaby to it as she did so, and giving it a violent shake at the end of every line :—

> " *Speak roughly to your little boy,*
> 　　*And beat him when he sneezes:*
> *He only does it to annoy,*
> 　　*Because he knows it teases.*"

(In which the cook and the baby joined):

"*Wow! wow! wow!*"

While the Duchess sang the second verse of the song, she kept tossing the baby violently up and down, and the poor little thing howled, so that Alice could hardly hear the words :

" *I speak severely to my boy,*
   I beat him when he sneezes;
For he can thoroughly enjoy
   The pepper when he pleases!"

CHORUS

"*Wow! wow! wow!*"

" Here ! you may nurse it a bit, if you like ! " said the Duchess to Alice, flinging the baby at her as she spoke. " I must go and get ready to play croquet with the Queen," and she hurried out of the room. The cook threw a frying-pan after her as she went, but it just missed her.

Alice caught the baby with some difficulty, as it was a queer-shaped little creature, and held out its arms and legs in all directions, " just like a starfish," thought Alice. The poor little thing was snorting like a steam-engine when she caught it, and kept doubling itself up and straightening itself out again, so that altogether, for the first minute or two, it was as much as she could do to hold it.

The Duchess tossed the baby up and down

As soon as she had made out the proper way of nursing it (which was to twist it up into a sort of knot, and then keep tight hold of its right ear and left foot, so as to prevent its undoing itself), she carried it out into the open air. " If I don't take this child away with me," thought Alice, " they're sure to kill it in a day or two : wouldn't it be murder to leave it behind ? " She said the last words out loud, and the little thing grunted in reply (it had left off sneezing by this time). " Don't grunt," said Alice ; " that's not at all a proper way of expressing yourself."

The baby grunted again, and Alice looked very anxiously into its face to see what was the matter with it. There could be no doubt that it had a *very* turn-up nose, much more like a snout than a real nose ; also its eyes were getting extremely small for a baby : altogether, Alice did not like the look of the thing at all. " But perhaps it was only sobbing," she thought, and looked into its eyes again, to see if there were any tears.

No, there were no tears. " If you're going to turn into a pig, my dear," said Alice seriously, " I'll have nothing more to do with you. Mind now ! " The poor little thing sobbed again (or grunted, it was impossible to say which), and they went on for some while in silence.

Alice was just beginning to think to herself, " Now what am I to do with this creature when I get it home ? " when it grunted again, so violently that she looked down into its face in some alarm. This time there could be *no* mistake about it : it was neither more nor less than a pig, and she felt that it would be quite absurd for her to carry it any farther.

So she set the little creature down, and felt quite relieved to see it trot away quietly into the wood. " If it had grown up," she said to herself, " it would have made a dreadfully ugly child ; but it makes rather a handsome pig, I think." And she began thinking over other children she knew, who might do very well as pigs, and was just saying to herself, " If one only knew the right way to change them——" when she was a little startled by seeing the Cheshire Cat sitting on a bough of a tree a few yards off.

The Cat only grinned when it saw Alice. " It looked good-natured," she thought : still it had *very* long claws and a great many teeth, so she felt that it ought to be treated with respect.

" Cheshire Puss," she began, rather timidly, as she did not at all know whether it would like the name : however, it only grinned a little wider. " Come, it's pleased so far," thought Alice, and she went on. " Would you tell me, please, which way I ought to walk from here ? "

" That depends a good deal on where you want to get to," said the Cat.

" I don't much care where——" said Alice.

" Then it doesn't matter which way you walk," said the Cat.

" So long as I get *somewhere*," Alice added, as an explanation.

" Oh, you're sure to do that," said the Cat, " if you only walk long enough."

Alice felt that this could not be denied, so she tried another question. " What sort of people live about here ? "

" In *that* direction," the Cat said, waving its right paw round, " lives a Hatter : and in *that* direction," waving the other paw, " lives a March Hare. Visit either you like : they're both mad."

" But I don't want to go among mad people," Alice remarked.

" Oh, you can't help that," said the Cat ; " we're all mad here. I'm mad. You're mad."

" How do you know I'm mad ? " said Alice.

" You must be," said the Cat, " or you wouldn't have come here."

Alice didn't think that proved it at all ; however, she went on. " And how do you know that you're mad ? "

" To begin with," said the Cat, " a dog's not mad. You grant that ? "

" I suppose so," said Alice.

" Well, then," the Cat went on, " you see, a dog growls when it's angry, and wags its tail when it's pleased. Now *I* growl when I'm pleased, and wag my tail when I'm angry. Therefore I'm mad."

" *I* call it purring, not growling," said Alice.

" Call it what you like," said the Cat. " Do you play croquet with the Queen to-day ? "

" I should like it very much," said Alice, " but I haven't been invited yet."

" You'll see me there," said the Cat, and vanished.

Alice was not much surprised at this; she was getting so well used to queer things happening. While she was still looking at the place where it had been, it suddenly appeared again.

" By the bye, what became of the baby ? " said the Cat. " I'd nearly forgotten to ask."

" It turned into a pig," Alice answered very quietly, just as if the Cat had come back in a natural way.

" I thought it would," said the Cat, and vanished again.

Alice waited a little, half expecting to see it again, but it did not appear, and after a minute or two she walked on in the direction in which the March Hare was said to live. " I've seen hatters before," she said to herself; " the March Hare will be much the most interesting, and perhaps, as this is May, it won't be raving mad—at least not so mad as it was in March." As she said this, she looked up, and there was the Cat again, sitting on a branch of a tree.

" Did you say pig, or fig ? " said the Cat.

" I said pig," replied Alice; " and I wish you wouldn't keep appearing and vanishing so suddenly : you make one quite giddy."

" All right," said the Cat; and this time it vanished quite slowly, beginning with the end of the tail, and ending with the grin, which remained some time after the rest of it had gone.

" Well ! I've often seen a cat without a grin," thought Alice; " but a grin without a cat ! It's the most curious thing I ever saw in my life ! "

She had not gone much farther before she came in sight of the house of the March Hare : she thought it must be the right house, because the chimneys were shaped like ears and the roof was thatched with fur. It was so large a house, that she did not like to go nearer till she had nibbled some more of the left-hand bit of mushroom, and raised herself to about two feet high : even then she walked up towards it rather timidly, saying to herself, " Suppose it should be raving mad after all ! I almost wish I'd gone to see the Hatter instead ! "

CHAPTER VII

A MAD TEA-PARTY

THERE was a table set out under a tree in front of the house, and the March Hare and the Hatter were having tea at it : a Dormouse was sitting between them, fast asleep, and the other two were using it as a cushion, resting their elbows on it, and talking over its head. " Very uncomfortable for the Dormouse," thought Alice ; " only, as it's asleep, I suppose it doesn't mind."

The table was a large one, but the three were all crowded together at one corner of it. " No room ! No room ! " they cried out, when they saw Alice coming. " There's *plenty* of room ! " said Alice indignantly, and she sat down in a large arm-chair at one end of the table.

" Have some wine," the March Hare said in an encouraging tone.

Alice looked all round the table, but there was nothing on it but tea. " I don't see any wine," she remarked.

" There isn't any," said the March Hare.

" Then it wasn't very civil of you to offer it," said Alice angrily.

" It wasn't very civil of you to sit down without being invited," said the March Hare.

" I didn't know it was *your* table," said Alice ; " it's laid for a great many more than three."

" Your hair wants cutting," said the Hatter. He had been looking at Alice for some time with great curiosity, and this was his first speech.

" You should learn not to make personal remarks," Alice said with some severity ; " it's very rude."

The Hatter opened his eyes very wide on hearing this ; but all he *said* was, " Why is a raven like a writing-desk ? "

" Come, we shall have some fun now ! " thought Alice. " I'm glad they've begun asking riddles. I believe I can guess that," she added aloud.

" Do you mean that you think you can find out the answer to it ? " said the March Hare.

" Exactly so," said Alice.

" Then you should say what you mean," the March Hare went on.

" I do," Alice hastily replied ; " at least—at least, I mean what I say— that's the same thing, you know."

" Not the same thing a bit ! " said the Hatter. " Why, you might just as well say that ' I see what I eat ' is the same thing as ' I eat what I see ' ! "

" You might just as well say," added the March Hare, " that ' I like what I get ' is the same thing as ' I get what I like ' ! "

" You might just as well say," added the Dormouse, who seemed to be talking in his sleep, " that ' I breathe when I sleep ' is the same thing as ' I sleep when I breathe ' ! "

" It *is* the same thing with you," said the Hatter, and here the conversation dropped, and the party sat silent for a minute, while Alice thought over all she could remember about ravens and writing-desks, which wasn't much.

The Hatter was the first to break the silence. " What day of the month is it ? " he said, turning to Alice : he had taken his watch out of his pocket, and was looking at it uneasily, shaking it every now and then, and holding it to his ear.

Alice considered a little, and said, " the fourth."

" Two days wrong ! " sighed the Hatter. " I told you butter wouldn't suit the works ! " he added, looking angrily at the March Hare.

" It was the *best* butter," the March Hare meekly replied.

" Yes, but some crumbs must have got in as well," the Hatter grumbled : " you shouldn't have put it in with the breadknife."

The March Hare took the watch and looked at it gloomily ; then he dipped it into his cup of tea, and looked at it again ; but he could think of nothing better to say than his first remark, " It was the *best* butter, you know."

Alice had been looking over his shoulder with some curiosity. " What a funny watch ! " she remarked. " It tells the day of the month, and doesn't tell what o'clock it is ! "

" Why should it ? " muttered the Hatter. " Does *your* watch tell you what year it is ? "

" Of course not," Alice replied very readily ; " but that's because it stays the same year for such a long time together."

" Which is just the case with *mine*," said the Hatter.

The March Hare dipped the watch into his cup of tea

Alice felt dreadfully puzzled. The Hatter's remark seemed to her to have no sort of meaning in it, and yet it was certainly English. " I don't quite understand you," she said, as politely as she could.

" The Dormouse is asleep again," said the Hatter, and he poured a little hot tea on to its nose.

The Dormouse shook its head impatiently, and said, without opening its eyes, " Of course, of course ; just what I was going to remark myself."

" Have you guessed the riddle yet ? " the Hatter said, turning to Alice again.

" No, I give it up," Alice replied : " what's the answer ? "

" I haven't the slightest idea," said the Hatter.

" Nor I," said the March Hare.

Alice sighed wearily. " I think you might do something better with the time," she said, " than wasting it in asking riddles that have no answers."

" If you knew Time as well as I do," said the Hatter, " you wouldn't talk about wasting *it*. It's *him*."

" I don't know what you mean," said Alice.

" Of course you don't ! " the Hatter said, tossing his head contemptuously. " I dare say you never even spoke to Time ! "

" Perhaps not," Alice cautiously replied ; " but I know I have to beat time when I learn music."

" Ah ! that accounts for it," said the Hatter. " He won't stand beating. Now, if you only kept on good terms with him, he'd do almost anything you liked with the clock. For instance, suppose it were nine o'clock in the morning, just time to begin lessons : you'd only have to whisper a hint to Time, and round goes the clock in a twinkling ! Half-past one, time for dinner ! "

(" I only wish it was," the March Hare said to itself in a whisper.)

" That would be grand, certainly," said Alice thoughtfully ; " but then—I shouldn't be hungry for it, you know."

" Not at first, perhaps," said the Hatter ; " but you could keep it to half-past one as long as you like."

" Is that the way *you* manage ? " Alice asked.

The Hatter shook his head mournfully. " Not I ! " he replied. " We quarrelled last March—just before *he* went mad, you know "—(pointing with his teaspoon at the March Hare)—" it was at the great concert given by the Queen of Hearts, and I had to sing :

> " *Twinkle, twinkle, little bat !*
> *How I wonder what you're at !*

You know the song, perhaps ? "

" I've heard something like it," said Alice.

" It goes on, you know," the Hatter continued, " in this way :

> " *Up above the world you fly,*
> *Like a tea-tray in the sky.*
> *Twinkle, twinkle*——"

Here the Dormouse shook itself, and began singing in its sleep, " *Twinkle, twinkle, twinkle, twinkle*——" and went on so long that they had to pinch it to make it stop.

" Well, I'd hardly finished the first verse," said the Hatter, " when the Queen bawled out, ' He's murdering the time ! Off with his head ! ' "

" How dreadfully savage ! " exclaimed Alice.

" And ever since that," the Hatter went on, in a mournful tone, " he won't do a thing I ask ! It's always six o'clock now."

A bright idea came into Alice's head. " Is that the reason so many tea-things are put out here ? " she asked.

"Yes, that's it," said the Hatter with a sigh: "it's always tea-time, and we've no time to wash the things between whiles."

"Then you keep moving round, I suppose?" said Alice.

"Exactly so," said the Hatter: "as the things get used up."

"But when you come to the beginning again?" Alice ventured to ask.

"Suppose we change the subject," the March Hare interrupted, yawning. "I'm getting tired of this. I vote the young lady tells us a story."

"I'm afraid I don't know one," said Alice, rather alarmed at the proposal.

"Then the Dormouse shall!" they both cried. "Wake up, Dormouse!" And they pinched it on both sides at once.

The Dormouse slowly opened his eyes. "I wasn't asleep," he said in a hoarse, feeble voice; "I heard every word you fellows were saying."

"*Once upon a time there were three sisters, and they lived at the bottom of a well*"

"Tell us a story!" said the March Hare.

"Yes, please do!" pleaded Alice.

"And be quick about it," added the Hatter, "or you'll be asleep again before it's done."

"Once upon a time there were three little sisters," the Dormouse began, in a great hurry; "and their names were Elsie, Lacie, and Tillie; and they lived at the bottom of a well——"

"What did they live on?" said Alice, who always took a great interest in questions of eating and drinking.

"They lived on treacle," said the Dormouse, after thinking a minute or two.

"They couldn't have done that, you know," Alice gently remarked; "they'd have been ill."

"So they were," said the Dormouse; "*very* ill."

Alice tried a little to fancy to herself what such an extraordinary way of living would be like, but it puzzled her too much, so she went on: "But why did they live at the bottom of a well?"

" Take some more tea," the March Hare said to Alice, very earnestly.

" I've had nothing yet," Alice replied, in an offended tone, " so I can't take more."

" You mean you can't take *less*," said the Hatter : " it's very easy to take *more* than nothing."

" Nobody asked *your* opinion," said Alice.

" Who's making personal remarks now ? " the Hatter asked triumphantly.

Alice did not quite know what to say to this ; so she helped herself to some tea and bread-and-butter, and then turned to the Dormouse, and repeated her question, " Why did they live at the bottom of a well ? "

The Dormouse again took a minute or two to think about it, and then said, " It was a treacle-well."

" There's no such thing ! " Alice was beginning very angrily, but the Hatter and the March Hare went " Sh ! sh ! " and the Dormouse sulkily remarked, " If you can't be civil, you'd better finish the story for yourself."

" No, please go on ! " Alice said very humbly, " I won't interrupt you again. I dare say there may be *one*."

" One, indeed ! " said the Dormouse indignantly, However, he consented to go on. " And so these three little sisters—they were learning to draw, you know——"

" What did they draw ? " said Alice, quite forgetting her promise.

" Treacle," said the Dormouse, without considering at all this time.

" I want a clean cup," interrupted the Hatter : " let's all move one place on."

He moved on as he spoke, and the Dormouse followed him ; the March Hare moved into the Dormouse's place, and Alice rather unwillingly took the place of the March Hare. The Hatter was the only one who got any advantage from the change ; and Alice was a good deal worse off than before, as the March Hare had just upset the milk jug into his plate.

Alice did not wish to offend the Dormouse again, so she began very cautiously : " But I don't understand. Where did they draw the treacle from ? "

" You can draw water out of a water-well," said the Hatter ; " so I should think you could draw treacle out of a treacle-well—eh, stupid ? "

" But they were *in* the well," Alice said to the Dormouse, not choosing to notice this last remark.

" Of course they were," said the Dormouse ;—" well in."

This answer so confused poor Alice, that she let the Dormouse go on for some time without interrupting it.

" They were learning to draw," the Dormouse went on, yawning and rubbing its eyes, for it was getting very sleepy ; " and they drew all manner of things—everything that begins with an M——"

" Why with an M ? " said Alice.

" Why not ? " said the March Hare.

Alice was silent.

The Dormouse had closed its eyes by this time, and was going off into a doze ; but, on being pinched by the Hatter, it woke up again with a little shriek, and went on : " That begins with an M, such as mouse-traps, and the moon, and memory, and muchness—you know you say things as ' much of a muchness '—did you ever see such a thing as a drawing of a muchness ? "

" Really, now you ask me," said Alice, very much confused, " I don't think——"

" Then you shouldn't talk," said the Hatter.

This piece of rudeness was more than Alice could bear : she got up in great disgust, and walked off ; the Dormouse fell asleep instantly, and neither of the others took the least notice of her going, though she looked back once or twice, half hoping that they would call after her : the last time she saw them, they were trying to put the Dormouse into the teapot.

" At any rate, I'll never go *there* again ! " said Alice, as she picked her way through the wood. " It's the stupidest tea-party I ever was at in all my life ! "

Just as she said this, she noticed that one of the trees had a door leading right into it. " That's very curious ! " she thought. " But everything's curious to-day. I think I may as well go in at once." And in she went.

Once more she found herself in the long hall, and close to the little glass table. " Now, I'll manage better this time," she said to herself, and began by taking the little golden key and unlocking the door that led into the garden. Then she set to work nibbling at the mushroom (she had kept a piece of it in her pocket) till she was about a foot high : then she walked down the little passage : and *then*—she found herself at last in the beautiful garden, among the bright flower-beds and the cool fountains.

CHAPTER VIII

THE QUEEN'S CROQUET GROUND

A LARGE rose-tree stood near the entrance of the garden : the roses growing on it were white, but there were three gardeners at it, busily painting them red. Alice thought this a very curious thing, and she went nearer to watch them, and just as she came up to them, she heard one of them say, " Look out now, Five ! Don't go splashing paint over me like that ! "

" I couldn't help it," said Five, in a sulky tone. " Seven jogged my elbow."

On which Seven looked up and said, " That's right, Five ! Always lay the blame on others ! "

" You'd better not talk ! " said Five. " I heard the Queen say only yesterday you deserved to be beheaded ! "

" What for ? " said the one who had spoken first.

" That's none of *your* business, Two ! " said Seven.

" Yes, it *is* his business ! " said Five. " And I'll tell him—it was for bringing the cook tulip-roots instead of onions."

Seven flung down his brush, and had just begun, " Well, of all the unjust things——" when his eye chanced to fall upon Alice, as she stood watching them, and he checked himself suddenly : the others looked round also, and all of them bowed low.

" Would you tell me, please," said Alice, a little timidly, " why you are painting those roses ? "

Five and Seven said nothing, but looked at Two. Two began, in a low voice, " Why, the fact is, you see, Miss, this here ought to have been a *red* rose-tree, and we put a white one in by mistake ; and if the Queen was to find it out, we should all have our heads cut off, you know. So you see, Miss, we're doing our best, afore she comes, to——" At this moment, Five, who had been anxiously looking across the garden, called out, " The Queen ! The Queen ! " and the three gardeners instantly threw themselves flat upon their faces. There was a sound of many footsteps, and Alice looked round, eager to see the Queen.

First came ten soldiers carrying clubs ; these were all shaped like the three gardeners, oblong and flat, with their hands and feet at the corners : next the ten courtiers ; these were ornamented all over with diamonds, and walked two and two, as the soldiers did. After these came the royal children ; there were ten of them, and the little dears came jumping merrily along hand in hand, in couples : they were all ornamented with hearts. Next came the guests, mostly Kings and Queens, and among them Alice recognised the White Rabbit : it was talking in a hurried, nervous manner, smiling at everything that was said, and went by without noticing her. Then followed the Knave of Hearts, carrying the King's crown on a crimson velvet cushion ; and, last of all this grand procession, came the KING AND QUEEN OF HEARTS.

Alice was rather doubtful whether she ought not to lie down on her face like the three gardeners, but she could not remember ever having heard of such a rule at processions ; " and besides, what would be the use of a procession," she thought, " if people had all to lie down on their faces, so that they couldn't see it ? " So she stood still where she was and waited.

When the procession came opposite to Alice, they all stopped and looked at her, and the Queen said severely, " Who is this ? " She said it to the Knave of Hearts, who only bowed and smiled in reply.

" Idiot ! " said the Queen, tossing her head impatiently ; and, turning to Alice, she went on, " What's your name, child ? "

" My name is Alice, so please your Majesty," said Alice very politely ; but she added, to herself, " Why, they're only a pack of cards, after all. I needn't be afraid of them."

" And who are *these* ? " said the Queen, pointing to the three gardeners who were lying round the rose-tree ; for, you see, as they were lying on their faces, and the pattern on their backs was the same as the rest of the pack, she could not tell whether they were gardeners, or soldiers, or courtiers, or three of her own children.

" How should I know ? " said Alice, surprised at her own courage. " It's no business of *mine*."

The Queen turned crimson with fury, and, after glaring at her for a moment like a wild beast, began screaming, " Off with her head ! Off——"

" Nonsense ! " said Alice, very loudly and decidedly, and the Queen was silent.

The King laid his hand upon her arm, and timidly said, " Consider, my dear : she is only a child ! "

The Queen turned angrily away from him, and said to the Knave, " Turn them over ! "

The Knave did so, very carefully, with one foot.

" Get up ! " said the Queen, in a shrill, loud voice, and the three gardeners instantly jumped up and began bowing to the King, the Queen, the royal children, and everybody else !

" Leave off that ! " screamed the Queen. " You make me giddy." And then, turning to the rose-tree, she went on, " What *have* you been doing here ? "

" May it please your Majesty," said Two, in a very humble tone, going down on one knee as he spoke, " we were trying——"

" *I* see ! " said the Queen, who had meanwhile been examining the roses. " Off with their heads ! " and the procession moved on, three of the soldiers remaining behind to execute the unfortunate gardeners, who ran to Alice for protection.

" You shan't be beheaded ! " said Alice, and she put them into a large flower-pot that stood near. The three soldiers wandered about for a minute or two, looking for them, and then quietly marched off after the others.

" Are their heads off ? " shouted the Queen.

" Their heads are gone, if it please your Majesty ! " the soldiers shouted in reply.

" That's right ! " shouted the Queen. " Can you play croquet ? "

The soldiers were silent, and looked at Alice, as the question was evidently meant for her.

" Yes ! " shouted Alice.

" Come on, then ! " roared the Queen, and Alice joined the procession, wondering very much what would happen next.

" It's—it's a very fine day ! " said a timid voice at her side. She was walking by the White Rabbit, who was peeping anxiously into her face.

" Very," said Alice—" where's the Duchess ? "

" Hush ! Hush ! " said the Rabbit, in a low, hurried tone. He looked anxiously over his shoulder as he spoke, and then raised himself upon tiptoe, put his mouth close to her ear, and whispered, " She's under sentence of execution."

" What for ? " said Alice.

" Did you say ' What a pity ! ' ? " the Rabbit asked.

" No, I didn't," said Alice : " I don't think it's at all a pity. I said ' What for ? ' "

" She boxed the Queen's ears——" the Rabbit began. Alice gave a little scream of laughter. " Oh, hush ! " the Rabbit whispered in a frightened tone. " The Queen will hear you ! You see she came rather late, and the Queen said——"

" Get to your places ! " shouted the Queen, in a voice of thunder, and people began running about in all directions, tumbling up against each other ; however, they got settled down in a minute or two, and the game began. Alice thought she had never seen such a curious croquet ground in her life ; it was all ridges and furrows ; the croquet balls were live hedgehogs, and the mallets live flamingoes, and the soldiers had to double themselves up and stand on their hands and feet, to make the arches.

The chief difficulty Alice found at first was in managing her flamingo : she succeeded in getting its body tucked away, comfortably enough, under her arm, with its legs hanging down, but generally, just as she had got its neck nicely straightened out, and was going to give the hedgehog a blow with its head, it *would* twist itself round and look up into her face, with such a puzzled expression that she could not help bursting out laughing : and when she had got its head down, and was going to begin again, it was very provoking to find that the hedgehog had unrolled itself, and was in the act

of crawling away : besides all this, there was generally a ridge or a furrow in the way wherever she wanted to send the hedgehog to, and, as the doubled-up soldiers were always getting up and walking off to other parts of the ground, Alice soon came to the conclusion that it was a very difficult game indeed.

The players all played at once without waiting for turns, quarrelling all the while, and fighting for the hedgehogs ; and in a very short time the Queen was in a furious passion, and went stamping about, and shouting, "Off with his head !" or " Off with her head !" about once in a minute.

Alice began to feel very uneasy : to be sure she had not as yet had any dispute with the Queen, but she knew that it might happen any minute,

Alice's chief difficulty was managing her flamingo

" and then," thought she, "what would become of me ? They're dreadfully fond of beheading people here ; the great wonder is, that there's any one left alive ! "

She was looking about for some way of escape, and wondering whether she could get away without being seen, when she noticed a curious appearance in the air : it puzzled her very much at first, but after watching it a minute or two she made it out to be a grin, and she said to herself, " It's the Cheshire Cat : now I shall have somebody to talk to."

" How are you getting on ? " said the Cat, as soon as there was mouth enough for it to speak with.

Alice waited till the eyes appeared, and then nodded. " It's no use speaking to it," she thought, " till its ears have come, or at least one of them." In another minute the whole head appeared, and then Alice put down her flamingo, and began an account of the game, feeling very glad she had some one to listen to her. The Cat seemed to think that there was enough of it now in sight, and no more of it appeared.

" I don't think they play at all fairly," Alice began, in rather a complaining tone, " and they all quarrel so dreadfully one can't hear oneself speak—and they don't seem to have any rules in particular ; at least, if there are, nobody attends to them—and you've no idea how confusing it is all the things being alive ; for instance, there's the arch I've got to go through next walking about at the other end of the ground—and I should have croqueted the Queen's hedgehog just now, only it ran away when it saw mine coming ! "

" How do you like the Queen ? " said the Cat, in a low voice.

" Not at all," said Alice ; " she's so extremely——" Just then she noticed that the Queen was close behind her listening ; so she went on, " likely to win, that it's hardly worth while finishing the game."

The Queen smiled and passed on.

" Who *are* you talking to ? " said the King, coming up to Alice, and looking at the Cat's head with great curiosity.

" It's a great friend of mine—a Cheshire Cat," said Alice. " Allow me to introduce it."

" I don't like the look of it at all," said the King ; " however, it may kiss my hand if it likes."

" I'd rather not," the Cat remarked.

" Don't be impertinent," said the King, " and don't look at me like that ! " He got behind Alice as he spoke.

" A cat may look at a king," said Alice. " I've read that in some book, but I don't remember where."

" Well, it must be removed," said the King very decidedly, and he called to the Queen, who was passing at the moment, " My dear ! I wish you would have this cat removed ! "

The Queen had only one way of settling all difficulties, great or small. " Off with his head ! " she said, without even looking round.

" I'll fetch the executioner myself," said the King eagerly, and he hurried off.

Alice thought she might as well go back and see how the game was going on, as she heard the Queen's voice in the distance, screaming with passion. She had already heard her sentence three of the players to be executed for having missed their turns, and she did not like the look of things at all, as the game was in such confusion that she never knew whether it was her turn or not. So she went off in search of her hedgehog.

The hedgehog was engaged in a fight with another hedgehog, which seemed to Alice an excellent opportunity for croqueting one of them with the other : the only difficulty was, that her flamingo was gone across to the other side of the garden, where Alice could see it trying in a helpless sort of way to fly up into a tree.

By the time she had caught the flamingo and brought it back the fight was over, and both the hedgehogs were out of sight : " But it doesn't matter much," thought Alice, " as all the arches are gone from this side of the ground." So she tucked it away under her arm, that it might not escape again, and went back to have a little more conversation with her friend.

When she got back to the Cheshire Cat, she was surprised to find quite a large crowd collected round it : there was a dispute going on between the executioner, the King, and the Queen, who were all talking at once, while all the rest were quite silent, and looked very uncomfortable.

The moment Alice appeared, she was appealed to by all three to settle the question, and they repeated their arguments to her, though, as they all spoke at once, she found it very hard to make out exactly what they said.

The executioner's argument was, that you couldn't cut off a head unless there was a body to cut it off from : that he had never had to do such a thing before, and he wasn't going to begin at *his* time of life.

The King's argument was, that anything that had a head could be beheaded, and that you weren't to talk nonsense.

The Queen's argument was, that if something wasn't done about it in less than no time, she'd have everybody executed all round. (It was this last remark that made the whole party look so grave and anxious.)

Alice could think of nothing else to say but, " It belongs to the Duchess : you'd better ask *her* about it."

" She's in prison," the Queen said to the executioner : " fetch her here." And the executioner went off like an arrow.

The Cat's head began fading away the moment he was gone, and, by the time he had come back with the Duchess, it had entirely disappeared ; so the King and the executioner ran wildly up and down looking for it, while the rest of the party went back to the game.

CHAPTER IX

THE MOCK TURTLE'S STORY

"YOU can't think how glad I am to see you again, you dear old thing ! " said the Duchess, as she tucked her arm affectionately into Alice's and they walked off together.

Alice was very glad to find her in such a pleasant temper, and thought to herself that perhaps it was only the pepper that had made her so savage when they met in the kitchen.

" When *I'm* a Duchess," she said to herself (not in a very hopeful tone though), " I won't have any pepper in my kitchen *at all*. Soup does very well without—maybe it's always pepper that makes people hot-tempered," she went on, very much pleased at having found out a new kind of rule, " and vinegar that makes them sour—and camomile that makes them bitter —and—and barley-sugar and such things that make children sweet-tempered. I only wish people knew *that* : then they wouldn't be so stingy about it, you know——"

She had quite forgotten the Duchess by this time, and was a little startled when she heard her voice close to her ear. " You're thinking about something, my dear, and that makes you forget to talk. I can't tell you just now what the moral of that is, but I shall remember it in a bit."

" Perhaps it hasn't one," Alice ventured to remark.

" Tut, tut, child ! " said the Duchess. " Everything's got a moral, if only you can find it." And she squeezed herself up closer to Alice's side as she spoke.

Alice did not much like her keeping so close to her : first, because the Duchess was *very* ugly ; and secondly, because she was exactly the right height to rest her chin on Alice's shoulder, and it was an uncomfortably sharp chin. However, she did not like to be rude, so she bore it as well as she could. " The game's going on rather better now," she said, by way of keeping up the conversation a little.

" 'Tis so," said the Duchess ; " and the moral of that is—' Oh, 'tis love, 'tis love, that makes the world go round ! ' "

" Somebody said," whispered Alice, " that it's done by everybody minding their own business ! "

" Ah, well ! It means much the same thing," said the Duchess, digging her sharp little chin into Alice's shoulder as she added, " and the moral of *that* is—' Take care of the sense, and the sounds will take care of themselves.' "

" How fond she is of finding morals in things ! " Alice thought to herself.

" I dare say you're wondering why I don't put my arm round your waist," said the Duchess, after a pause : " the reason is, that I'm doubtful about the temper of your flamingo. Shall I try the experiment ? "

" He might bite," Alice cautiously replied, not feeling at all anxious to have the experiment tried.

" Very true," said the Duchess : " flamingoes and mustard both bite. And the moral of that is—' Birds of a feather flock together.' "

" Only mustard isn't a bird," Alice remarked.

" Right, as usual," said the Duchess : " what a clear way you have of putting things ! "

" It's a mineral, I *think*," said Alice.

" Of course it is," said the Duchess, who seemed ready to agree to everything that Alice said ; " there's a large mustard-mine near here. And the moral of that is—' The more there is of mine, the less there is of yours.' "

" Oh, I know ! " exclaimed Alice, who had not attended to this last remark. " It's a vegetable. It doesn't look like one, but it is."

" I quite agree with you," said the Duchess ; " and the moral of that is—' Be what you would seem to be '—or, if you'd like it put more simply —' Never imagine yourself not to be otherwise than what it might appear to others that what you were or might have been was not otherwise than what you had been would have appeared to them to be otherwise.' "

" I think I should understand that better," Alice said very politely, " if I had it written down ; but I can't quite follow it as you say it."

" That's nothing to what I could say if I chose," the Duchess replied, in a pleased tone.

" Pray, don't trouble yourself to say it any longer than that," said Alice.

" Oh, don't talk about trouble ! " said the Duchess. " I make you a present of everything I've said as yet."

" A cheap sort of present ! " thought Alice. " I'm glad they don't give birthday presents like that ! " But she did not venture to say it out loud.

"Thinking again?" the Duchess asked, with another dig of her sharp little chin.

"I've a right to think," said Alice sharply, for she was beginning to feel a little worried.

"Just about as much right," said the Duchess, "as pigs have to fly; and the m——"

But here, to Alice's great surprise, the Duchess's voice died away, even in the middle of her favourite word "moral," and the arm that was linked into hers began to tremble. Alice looked up, and there stood the Queen in front of them, with her arms folded, frowning like a thunderstorm.

"A fine day, your Majesty!" the Duchess began, in a low, weak voice.

"Now, I give you fair warning," shouted the Queen, stamping on the ground as she spoke; "either you or your head must be off, and that in about half no time! Take your choice!"

The Duchess took her choice, and was gone in a moment.

"Let's go on with the game," the Queen said to Alice; and Alice was too much frightened to say a word, but slowly followed her back to the croquet-ground.

The other guests had taken advantage of the Queen's absence, and were resting in the shade; however, the moment they saw her, they hurried back to the game, the Queen merely remarking that a moment's delay would cost them their lives.

All the time they were playing, the Queen never left off quarrelling with the other players, and shouting,

"*As much right as pigs have to fly*"

"Off with his head!" or "Off with her head!" Those whom she sentenced were taken into custody by the soldiers, who, of course, had to leave off being arches to do this, so that by the end of half an hour or so there were no arches left, and all the players, except the King, the Queen, and Alice, were in custody and under sentence of execution.

Then the Queen left off, quite out of breath, and said to Alice, "Have you seen the Mock Turtle yet?"

"No," said Alice. "I don't even know what a Mock Turtle is."

"It's the thing Mock Turtle Soup is made from," said the Queen.

"I never saw one, or heard of one," said Alice.

"Come on, then," said the Queen, "and he shall tell you his history."

As they walked off together, Alice heard the King say, in a low voice, to the company generally, "You are all pardoned." "Come, *that's* a good thing ! " she said to herself, for she had felt quite unhappy at the number of executions the Queen had ordered.

They very soon came upon a Gryphon, lying fast asleep in the sun. (If you don't know what a Gryphon is, look at the picture.) " Up, lazy thing ! " said the Queen, " and take this young lady to see the Mock Turtle, and to hear his history. I must go back and see after some executions I have ordered," and she walked off, leaving Alice alone with the Gryphon. Alice did not quite like the look of the creature, but on the whole she thought it would be quite as safe to stay with it **as** to go after that savage Queen : so she waited.

They came upon a Gryphon lying fast asleep

The Gryphon sat up and rubbed its eyes ; then it watched the Queen till she was out of sight ; then it chuckled. " What fun ! " said the Gryphon, half to itself, half to Alice.

" What *is* the fun ? " said Alice.

" Why, *she*——" said the Gryphon. " It's all her fancy, that : they never executes nobody, you know. Come on ! "

" Everybody says ' come on ! ' here," thought Alice, as she went slowly after it : " I never was so ordered about before in all my life, never ! "

They had not gone far before they saw the Mock Turtle in the distance, sitting sad and lonely on a little ledge of rock, and, as they came nearer, Alice could hear him sighing as if his heart would break. She pitied him deeply. " What is his sorrow ? " she asked the Gryphon, and the Gryphon answered, very nearly in the same words as before, " It's all his fancy, that : he hasn't got no sorrow, you know. Come on ! "

So they went up to the Mock Turtle, who looked at them with large eyes full of tears, but said nothing.

" This here young lady," said the Gryphon, " she wants for to know your history, she do."

" I'll tell it her," said the Mock Turtle, in a deep, hollow tone : " sit down, both of you, and don't speak a word till I've finished."

So she sat down, and nobody spoke for some minutes. Alice thought to herself, " I don't see how he can *ever* finish, if he doesn't begin." But she waited patiently.

" Once," said the Mock Turtle at last, with a deep sigh, " I was a real Turtle."

These words were followed by a very long silence, broken only by an occasional exclamation of " Hjckrrh ! " from the Gryphon, and the constant heavy sobbing of the Mock Turtle. Alice was very nearly getting up and saying, " Thank you, sir, for your interesting story," but she could not help thinking there *must* be more to come, so she sat still and said nothing.

" When we were little," the Mock Turtle went on at last, more calmly, though still sobbing a little now and then, " we went to school in the sea. The master was an old Turtle—we used to call him Tortoise——"

" Why did you call him Tortoise, if he wasn't one ? " Alice asked.

" We called him Tortoise because he taught us," said the Mock Turtle angrily : " really you are very dull ! "

" You ought to be ashamed of yourself for asking such a simple question," added the Gryphon ; and then they both sat silent and looked at poor Alice, who felt ready to sink into the earth. At last the Gryphon said to the Mock Turtle, " Drive on, old fellow ! Don't be all day about it ! " and he went on in these words :

" Yes, we went to school in the sea, though you mayn't believe it——"

" I never said I didn't ! " interrupted Alice.

" You did," said the Mock Turtle.

" Hold your tongue ! " added the Gryphon, before Alice could speak again. The Mock Turtle went on :

" We had the best of educations—in fact, we went to school every day——"

" *I've* been to day-school, too," said Alice ; " you needn't be so proud as all that."

" With extras ? " asked the Mock Turtle, a little anxiously.

" Yes," said Alice, " we learned French and music."

" And washing ? " said the Mock Turtle.

" Certainly not ! " said Alice indignantly.

" Ah ! then yours wasn't a really good school," said the Mock Turtle in a tone of great relief. " Now at *ours* they had at the end of the bill, ' French, music, *and washing*—extra.' "

" You couldn't have wanted it much," said Alice ; " living at the bottom of the sea."

" I couldn't afford to learn it," said the Mock Turtle, with a sigh. " I only took the regular course."

" What was that ? " inquired Alice.

" Reeling and Writhing, of course, to begin with," the Mock Turtle replied ; " and then the different branches of Arithmetic—Ambition, Distraction, Uglification, and Derision."

" I never heard of ' Uglification,' " Alice ventured to say. " What is it ? "

The Gryphon lifted up both its paws in surprise. " Never heard of uglifying ! " it exclaimed. " You know what to beautify is, I suppose ? "

" Yes," said Alice doubtfully ; " it means—to—make—anything—prettier."

" Well, then," the Gryphon went on, " if you don't know what to uglify is, you are a simpleton."

Alice did not feel encouraged to ask any more questions about it, so she turned to the Mock Turtle and said, " What else had you to learn ? "

" Well, there was Mystery," the Mock Turtle replied, counting off the subjects on his flappers—" Mystery, ancient and modern, with Seaography ; then Drawling—the Drawling-master was an old conger-eel, that used to come once a week ; *he* taught us Drawling, Stretching, and Fainting in Coils."

" What was *that* like ? " said Alice.

" Well, I can't show it to you myself," the Mock Turtle said ; " I'm too stiff. And the Gryphon never learnt it."

" Hadn't time," said the Gryphon ; " I went to the Classical master, though. He was an old crab, *he* was."

" I never went to him," the Mock Turtle said, with a sigh ; " he taught Laughing and Grief, they used to say."

" So he did, so he did," said the Gryphon, sighing in his turn ; and both creatures hid their faces in their paws.

" And how many hours a day did you do lessons ? " said Alice, in a hurry to change the subject.

" Ten hours the first day," said the Mock Turtle ; " nine the next, and so on."

" What a curious plan ! " exclaimed Alice.

" That's the reason they're called lessons," the Gryphon remarked ; " because they lessen from day to day."

This was quite a new idea to Alice, and she thought it over a little before she made her next remark. " Then the eleventh day must have been a holiday ? "

" Of course it was," said the Mock Turtle.

" And how did you manage on the twelfth ? " Alice went on eagerly.

" That's enough about lessons," the Gryphon interrupted in a very decided tone ; " tell her something about the games now."

CHAPTER X

THE LOBSTER QUADRILLE

THE Mock Turtle sighed deeply, and drew the back of one flapper across his eyes. He looked at Alice, and tried to speak, but, for a minute or two, sobs choked his voice. " Same as if he had a bone in his throat," said the Gryphon ; and it set to work shaking him and punching him in the back. At last the Mock Turtle recovered his voice, and, with tears running down his cheeks, he went on again :

" You may not have lived much under the sea "—(" I haven't," said Alice)—" and perhaps you were never even introduced to a lobster " —(Alice began to say, " I once tasted——" but checked herself hastily, and said, " No, never ")— " so you can have no idea what a delightful thing a Lobster Quadrille is ! "

" No, indeed," said Alice. " What sort of a dance is it ? "

" Why," said the Gryphon, " you first form into a line along the seashore——"

" Two lines ! " cried the Mock Turtle. " Seals, turtles, salmon, and so on ; then, when you've cleared all the jelly-fish out of the way——"

" *That* generally takes some time," interrupted the Gryphon.

" You advance twice——"

" Each with a lobster as a partner ! " cried the Gryphon.

" Of course," the Mock Turtle said ; " advance twice, set to partners——"

" Change lobsters, and retire in same order," continued the Gryphon.

" Then, you know," the Mock Turtle went on, " you throw the——"

" The lobsters ! " shouted the Gryphon, with a bound into the air.

" As far out to sea as you can——"

The mock turtle sang, slowly and sadly

" Swim after them ! " screamed the Gryphon.

" Turn a somersault in the sea ! " cried the Mock Turtle, capering wildly about.

" Change lobsters again ! " yelled the Gryphon.

" Back to land again, and—that's all the first figure," said the Mock Turtle, suddenly dropping his voice ; and the two creatures, who had been jumping about like mad things all this time, sat down again very sadly and quietly, and looked at Alice.

" It must be a very pretty dance," said Alice timidly.

" Would you like to see a little of it ? " said the Mock Turtle.

" Very much indeed," said Alice.

" Come, let's try the first figure ! " said the Mock Turtle to the Gryphon. " We can do it without lobsters, you know. Which shall sing ? "

" Oh, *you* sing," said the Gryphon. " I've forgotten the words."

So they began solemnly dancing round and round Alice, every now and then treading on her toes when they passed too close, and waving their fore paws to mark the time, while the Mock Turtle sang this, very slowly and sadly :

" Will you walk a little faster ? " said a whiting to a snail.
" There's a porpoise close behind us, and he's treading on my tail.
See how eagerly the lobsters and the turtles all advance,
They are waiting on the shingle—will you come and join the dance ?
　Will you, won't you, will you, won't you, will you join the dance ?
　Will you, won't you, will you, won't you, won't you join the dance ?

" You can really have no notion how delightful it will be,
When they take us up and throw us, with the lobsters, out to sea ! "
But the snail replied, " Too far, too far ! " and gave a look askance—
Said he thanked the whiting kindly, but he would not join the dance.
　Would not, could not, would not, could not, would not join the dance.
　Would not, could not, would not, could not, could not join the dance.

" What matters it how far we go ? " his scaly friend replied.
" There is another shore, you know, upon the other side.
The farther off from England the nearer is to France—
Then turn not pale, beloved snail, but come and join the dance.
　Will you, won't you, will you, won't you, will you join the dance ?
　Will you, won't you, will you, won't you, won't you join the dance ? "

" Thank you, it's a very interesting dance to watch," said Alice, feeling very glad that it was over at last : " and I do so like that curious song about the whiting ! "

" Oh, as to the whiting," said the Mock Turtle, " they—you've seen them, of course ? "

" Yes," said Alice, " I've often seen them at dinn——" She checked herself hastily.

" I don't know where Dinn may be," said the Mock Turtle, " but if you've seen them so often, of course you know what they're like."

" I believe so," Alice replied thoughtfully. " They have their tails in their mouths—and they're all over crumbs."

" You're wrong about the crumbs," said the Mock Turtle ; " crumbs would all wash off in the sea. But they *have* their tails in their mouths ; and the reason is——" Here the Mock Turtle .yawned and shut his eyes. " Tell her about the reason and all that," he said to the Gryphon.

" The reason is," said the Gryphon, " that they *would* go with the lobsters to the dance. So they got thrown out to sea. So they had to fall a long way. So they got their tails fast in their mouths. So they couldn't get them out again. That's all."

" Thank you," said Alice ; " it's very interesting. I never knew so much about a whiting before."

" I can tell you more than that, if you like," said the Gryphon. " Do you know why it's called a whiting ? "

" I never thought about it," said Alice. " Why ? "

" *It does the boots and shoes,*" the Gryphon replied very solemnly.

Alice was thoroughly puzzled. " Does the boots and shoes ! " she repeated in a wondering tone.

" Why, what are *your* shoes done with ? " said the Gryphon. " I mean, what makes them so shiny ? "

Alice looked down at them, and considered a little before she gave her answer. " They're done with blacking, I believe."

" Boots and shoes under the sea," the Gryphon went on in a deep voice, " are done with whiting. Now you know."

" And what are they made of ? " Alice asked, in a tone of great curiosity.

" Soles and eels, of course," the Gryphon replied rather impatiently ; " any shrimp could have told you that."

" If I'd been the whiting," said Alice, whose thoughts were still running on the song, " I'd have said to the porpoise, ' Keep back, please : we don't want *you* with us ! ' "

" They were obliged to have him with them," the Mock Turtle said ; " no wise fish would go anywhere without a porpoise."

" Wouldn't it really ? " said Alice, in a tone of great surprise.

" Of course not," said the Mock Turtle ; " why, if a fish came to *me*, and told me he was going on a journey, I should say, ' With what porpoise ? ' "

" Don't you mean ' purpose ' ? " said Alice.

" I mean what I say," the Mock Turtle replied, in an offended tone. And the Gryphon added, " Come, let's hear some of *your* adventures."

" I could tell you my adventures—beginning from this morning," said Alice a little timidly ; " but it's no use going back to yesterday, because I was a different person then."

" Explain all that," said the Mock Turtle.

" No, no ! The adventures first," said the Gryphon, in an impatient tone ; " explanations take such a dreadful time."

So Alice began telling them her adventures from the time when she first saw the White Rabbit. She was a little nervous about it just at first, the two creatures got so close to her, one on each side, and opened their eyes and mouths so *very* wide, but she gained courage as she went on. Her listeners were perfectly quiet till she got to the part about her repeating,

" *You are old, Father William*," to the Caterpillar, and the words all coming different, and then the Mock Turtle drew a long breath, and said, " That's very curious."

" It's all about as curious as it can be," said the Gryphon.

" It all came different ! " the Mock Turtle repeated thoughtfully. " I should like to hear her try and repeat something now. Tell her to begin." He looked at the Gryphon as if he thought it had some kind of authority over Alice.

" Stand up and repeat ' *'Tis the voice of the sluggard,* ' " said the Gryphon.

" How the creatures order one about, and make one repeat lessons ! " thought Alice. " I might just as well be at school at once." However, she got up, and began to repeat it, but her head was so full of the Lobster Quadrille, that she hardly knew what she was saying, and the words came very queer indeed :

> " *'Tis the voice of the Lobster ; I heard him declare,*
> '*You have baked me too brown, I must sugar my hair.*'
> *As a duck with its eyelids, so he with his nose*
> *Trims his belt and his buttons, and turns out his toes.*
> *When the sands are all dry, he is gay as a lark,*
> *And will talk in contemptuous tones of the Shark :*
> *But, when the tide rises and sharks are around,*
> *His voice has a timid and tremulous sound.*"

" That's different from what *I* used to say when I was a child," said the Gryphon.

" Well, I never heard it before," said the Mock Turtle ; " but it sounds uncommon nonsense."

Alice said nothing ; she had sat down again with her face in her hands, wondering if anything would *ever* happen in a natural way again.

" I should like to have it explained," said the Mock Turtle.

" She can't explain it," said the Gryphon hastily. " Go on with the next verse."

" But about his toes ? " the Mock Turtle persisted. " How *could* he turn them out with his nose, you know ? "

" It's the first position in dancing," Alice said ; but she was dreadfully puzzled by the whole thing, and longed to change the subject.

" Go on with the next verse," the Gryphon repeated impatiently ; " it begins, ' *I passed by his garden.* ' "

Alice did not dare to disobey, though she felt sure it would all come wrong, and she went on in a trembling voice:—

> " *I passed by his garden, and marked, with one eye,*
> *How the Owl and the Panther were sharing a pie :*
> *The Panther took pie-crust, and gravy, and meat,*
> *While the Owl had the dish as its share of the treat.*
> *When the pie was all finished, the Owl, as a boon,*
> *Was kindly permitted to pocket the spoon :*
> *While the Panther received knife and fork with a growl,*
> *And concluded the banquet by——*"

"What *is* the use of repeating all that stuff," the Mock Turtle interrupted, "if you don't explain it as you go on ? It's by far the most confusing thing *I* ever heard ! "

"Yes, I think you'd better leave off," said the Gryphon ; and Alice was only too glad to do so.

"Shall we try another figure of the Lobster Quadrille ? " the Gryphon went on. "Or would you like the Mock Turtle to sing you a song ? "

"Oh, a song, please, if the Mock Turtle would be so kind," Alice replied, so eagerly that the Gryphon said, in a rather offended tone, "Hm ! No accounting for tastes ! Sing her ' *Turtle Soup*,' will you, old fellow ? "

The Mock Turtle sighed deeply, and began, in a voice sometimes choked with sobs, to sing this :

> " *Beautiful Soup, so rich and green,*
> *Waiting in a hot tureen !*
> *Who for such dainties would not stoop*
> *Soup of the evening, beautiful Soup !*
> *Soup of the evening, beautiful Soup !*
> *Beau—ootiful Soo—oop !*
> *Beau—ootiful Soo—oop !*
> *Soo—oop of the e—e—evening,*
> *Beautiful, beautiful Soup !*

> " *Beautiful Soup ! Who cares for fish,*
> *Game, or any other dish ?*
> *Who would not give all else for two p*
> *ennyworth only of beautiful Soup ?*
> *Pennyworth only of beautiful Soup ?*
> *Beau—ootiful Soo—oop !*
> *Beau—ootiful Soo—oop !*
> *Soo—oop of the e—e—evening,*
> *Beautiful, beauti—FUL SOUP !* "

"Chorus again ! " cried the Gryphon, and the Mock Turtle had just begun to repeat it, when a cry of " The trial's beginning ! " was heard in the distance.

"Come on ! " cried the Gryphon, and, taking Alice by the hand, it hurried off, without waiting for the end of the song.

"What trial is it ? " Alice panted, as she ran ; but the Gryphon only answered, "Come on ! " and ran the faster, while more and more faintly came, carried on the breeze that followed them, the melancholy words :

> " *Soo—oop of the e—e—evening,*
> *Beautiful, beautiful Soup !* "

CHAPTER XI

WHO STOLE THE TARTS ?

THE King and Queen of Hearts were seated on their throne when they arrived, with a great crowd assembled about them—all sorts of little birds and beasts, as well as the whole pack of cards ; the Knave was standing before them in chains, with a soldier on each side to guard him ; and near the King was the White Rabbit, with a trumpet in one hand, and a scroll of parchment in the other. In the very middle of the court was a table, with a large dish of tarts upon it: they looked so good, that it made Alice quite hungry to look at them. " I wish they'd get the trial done," she thought, " and hand round the refreshments ! " But there seemed to be no chance of this, so she began looking at everything about her, to pass away the time.

Alice had never been in a court of justice before, but she had read about them in books, and she was quite pleased to find that she knew the name of nearly everything there. " That's the judge," she said to herself, " because of his great wig."

The judge, by the way, was the King ; and as he wore his crown over the wig, he did not look at all comfortable, and it was certainly not becoming.

" And that's the jury-box," thought Alice, " and those twelve creatures " (she was obliged to say " creatures," you see, because some of them were animals, and some were birds), " I suppose they are the jurors." She said this last word two or three times over to herself, being rather proud of it : for she thought, and rightly too, that very few little girls of her age knew the meaning of it all. However, " jurymen " would have done just as well.

The twelve jurors were all writing very busily on slates. " What are they doing ? " Alice whispered to the Gryphon. " They can't have anything to put down yet, before the trial's begun."

" They're putting down their names," the Gryphon whispered in reply, " for fear they should forget them before the end of the trial."

" Stupid things ! " Alice began in a loud, indignant voice, but she stopped herself hastily, for the White Rabbit cried out, " Silence in the court ! " and the King put on his spectacles and looked anxiously round, to make out who was talking.

Alice could see, as well as if she were looking over their shoulders, that all the jurors were writing down " stupid things ! " on their slates, and she could even make out that one of them didn't know how to spell " stupid," and that he had to ask his neighbour to tell him. " A nice muddle their slates'll be in before the trial's over ! " thought Alice.

One of the jurors had a pencil that squeaked. This, of course, Alice could *not* stand, and she went round the court and got behind him, and very soon found an opportunity of taking it away. She did it so quickly that the poor little juror (it was Bill, the Lizard) could not make out at all what had become of it ; so, after hunting all about for it, he was obliged to write with one finger for the rest of the day ; and this was of very little use, as it left no mark on the slate.

" Herald, read the accusation ! " said the King.

On this the White Rabbit blew three blasts on the trumpet, and then unrolled the parchment scroll, and read as follows :

> *" The Queen of Hearts, she made some tarts,*
> *All on a summer day :*
> *The Knave of Hearts, he stole those tarts*
> *And took them quite away ! "*

" Consider your verdict," the King said to the jury.

" Not yet, not yet ! " the Rabbit hastily interrupted. " There's a great deal to come before that ! "

" Call the first witness," said the King ; and the White Rabbit blew three blasts on the trumpet, and called out, " First Witness ! "

The first witness was the Hatter. He came in with a tea-cup in one hand and a piece of bread-and-butter in the other. " I beg your pardon, your Majesty," he began, " for bringing these in : but I hadn't quite finished my tea when I was sent for."

" You ought to have finished," said the King. " When did you begin ? "

The Hatter looked at the March Hare, who had followed him into the court, arm-in-arm with the Dormouse. " Fourteenth of March, I *think* it was," he said.

" Fifteenth," said the March Hare.

" Sixteenth," added the Dormouse.

" Write that down," the King said to the jury, and the jury eagerly wrote down all three dates on their slates, and then added them up, and reduced the answer to shillings and pence.

" Take off your hat," the King said to the Hatter.

" It isn't mine," said the Hatter.

" *Stolen !* " the King exclaimed, turning to the jury, who instantly made a memorandum of the fact.

" I keep them to sell," the Hatter added, as an explanation : " I've none of my own. I'm a hatter."

Here the Queen put on her spectacles, and began staring hard at the Hatter, who turned pale and fidgeted.

" Give your evidence," said the King ; " and don't be nervous, or I'll have you executed on the spot."

This did not seem to encourage the witness at all : he kept shifting from one foot to the other, looking uneasily at the Queen, and in his con-fusion he bit a large piece out of his tea-cup instead of the bread-and-butter.

Just at this moment Alice felt a very curious sensation, which puzzled her a good deal until she made out what it was : she was beginning to grow larger again, and she thought at first she would get up and leave the court ; but on second thoughts she decided to remain where she was as long as there was room for her.

" I wish you wouldn't squeeze so," said the Dormouse, who was sitting next to her. " I can hardly breathe."

" I can't help it," said Alice very meekly : " I'm growing."

" You've no right to grow *here*," said the Dormouse.

THE MAD HATTER'S TEA-PARTY.

" You might as well say that ' I see what I eat ' is the same thing as ' I eat what I see,' " said the Hatter.

THE QUEEN OF HEARTS.
" Who is this ? " said the Queen severely, pointing at Alice.

"Don't talk nonsense," said Alice more boldly: "you know you're growing too."

"Yes, but *I* grow at a reasonable pace," said the Dormouse: "not in that ridiculous fashion." And he got up very sulkily and crossed over to the other side of the court.

All this time the Queen had never left off staring at the Hatter, and, just as the Dormouse crossed the court, she said to one of the officers of the court, "Bring me the list of the singers in the last concert!" on which the wretched Hatter trembled so, that he shook both his shoes off.

"Give your evidence," the King repeated angrily, "or I'll have you executed, whether you're nervous or not."

"I'm a poor man, your Majesty," the Hatter began in a trembling voice —"and I hadn't but just begun my tea—not above a week or so—and what with the bread-and-butter getting so thin—and the twinkling of the tea——"

"The twinkling of *what*?" said the King.

"It *began* with the tea," the Hatter replied.

"Of course twinkling begins with a T!" said the King sharply. "Do you take me for a dunce? Go on!"

"I'm a poor man," the Hatter went on, "and most things twinkled after that—only the March Hare said——"

"I didn't!" the March Hare interrupted in a great hurry.

"You did!" said the Hatter.

"I deny it!" said the March Hare.

"He denies it," said the King: "leave out that part."

"Well, at any rate, the Dormouse said——" the Hatter went on, looking anxiously round to see if he would deny it too; but the Dormouse denied nothing, being fast asleep.

"After that," continued the Hatter, "I cut some more bread-and-butter——"

"But what did the Dormouse say?" one of the jury asked.

"That I can't remember," said the Hatter.

"You *must* remember," remarked the King, "or I'll have you executed."

The miserable Hatter dropped his tea-cup and bread-and-butter, and went down on one knee. "I'm a poor man, your Majesty," he began.

"You're a *very* poor *speaker*," said the King.

Here one of the guinea-pigs cheered, and was immediately suppressed by the officers of the court. As that is rather a hard word, I will just explain to you how it was done. They had a large canvas bag, which tied up at the mouth with strings: into this they slipped the guinea-pig, head first, and then sat upon it.

"I'm glad I've seen that done," thought Alice. "I've so often read in the newspapers, at the end of trials, 'There was some attempt at applause, which was immediately suppressed by the officers of the court,' and I never understood what it meant till now."

"If that's all you know about it, you may stand down," continued the King.

"I can't go no lower," said the Hatter; "I'm on the floor as it is."

"Then you may *sit* down," the King replied.

Here the other guinea-pig cheered, and was suppressed.

"Come, that finishes the guinea-pigs!" thought Alice. "Now we shall get on better."

"I'd rather finish my tea," said the Hatter, with an anxious look at the Queen, who was reading the list of singers.

"You may go," said the King; and the Hatter hurriedly left the Court, without even waiting to put his shoes on.

"And just take his head off outside," the Queen added to one of the officers; but the Hatter was out of sight before the officer could get to the door.

"Call the next witness!" said the King.

They had a large canvas bag. Into this they supped the guinea-pig

The next witness was the Duchess's cook. She carried the pepper-box in her hand, and Alice guessed who it was, even before she got into the court, by the way the people near the door began sneezing all at once.

"Give your evidence," said the King.

"Shan't," said the cook.

The King looked anxiously at the White Rabbit, who said in a low voice, "Your Majesty must cross-examine *this* witness."

"Well, if I must, I must," the King said, with a melancholy air; and, after folding his arms and frowning at the cook till his eyes were nearly out of sight, he said in a deep voice, "What are tarts made of?"

"Pepper, mostly," said the cook.

"Treacle," said a sleepy voice behind her.

"Collar that Dormouse," the Queen shrieked out. "Behead that Dor-

mouse ! Turn that Dormouse out of court ! Suppress him ! Pinch him !
Off with his whiskers ! "

For some minutes the whole court was in confusion, getting the Dormouse turned out, and by the time they had settled down again, the cook
had disappeared.

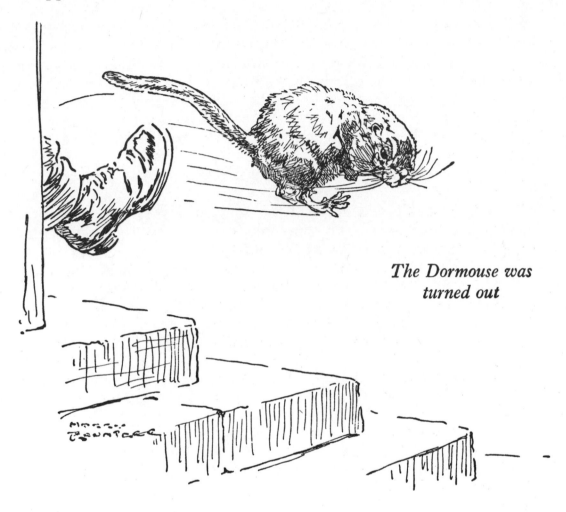

*The Dormouse was
turned out*

" Never mind ! " said the King, with an air of great relief. " Call the
next witness." And, he added in an undertone to the Queen, " Really, my
dear, *you* must cross-examine the next witness. It quite makes my forehead ache ! "

Alice watched the White Rabbit as he fumbled over the list, feeling very
curious to see what the next witness would be like, " For they haven't got
much evidence *yet*," she said to herself. Imagine her surprise, when the
White Rabbit read out, at the top of his shrill little voice, the name " Alice ! "

CHAPTER XII

ALICE'S EVIDENCE

"HERE!" cried Alice, quite forgetting in the flurry of the moment how large she had grown in the last few minutes, and she jumped up in such a hurry that she tipped over the jury-box with the edge of her skirt, upsetting all the jurymen on to the heads of the crowd below, and there they lay sprawling about, reminding her very much of a globe of goldfish she had accidentally upset the week before.

"Oh, I *beg* your pardon!" she exclaimed, in a tone of great dismay, and began picking them up again as quickly as she could, for the accident of the goldfish kept running in her head, and she had a vague sort of idea that they must be collected at once and put back into the jury-box, or they would die.

"The trial cannot proceed," said the King, in a very grave voice, "until the jurymen are back in their proper places—*all*," he repeated with great emphasis, looking hard at Alice as he said so.

Alice looked at the jury-box, and saw that, in her haste, she had put the Lizard in head downwards, and the poor little thing was waving its tail about in a melancholy way, being quite unable to move. She soon got it out again, and put it right; "Not that it signifies much," she said to herself; "I should think it would be *quite* as much use in the trial one way up as the other."

As soon as the jury had a little recovered from the shock of being upset, and their slates and pencils had been found and handed back to them, they set to work very diligently to write out a history of the accident, all except the Lizard, who seemed too much overcome to do anything but sit with its mouth open, gazing up into the roof of the court.

"What do you know about this business?" the King said to Alice.

"Nothing," said Alice.

"Nothing *whatever*?" persisted the King.

"Nothing whatever," said Alice.

"That's very important," the King said, turning to the jury. They were just beginning to write this down on their slates, when the White Rabbit interrupted: "*Un*important, your Majesty means, of course," he said in a very respectful tone, but frowning and making faces at him as he spoke.

"*Un*important, of course, I meant," the King hastily said, and went on to himself in an undertone, "important—unimportant—unimportant—important"—as if he were trying which word sounded best.

Some of the jury wrote it down "important," and some "unimportant." Alice could see this, as she was near enough to look over their slates; "But it doesn't matter a bit," she thought to herself.

At this moment the King, who had been for some time busily writing in his note-book, called out, "Silence!" and read out from his book, "Rule Forty-two. *All persons more than a mile high to leave the court.*"

Everybody looked at Alice.

" *I'm* not a mile high," said Alice.

" You are," said the King.

" Nearly two miles high," added the Queen.

" Well, I shan't go, at any rate," said Alice : " besides, that's not a regular rule ; you invented it just now."

" It's the oldest rule in the book," said the King.

" Then it ought to be Number One," said Alice.

The King turned pale, and shut his note-book hastily. " Consider your verdict," he said to the jury, in a low, trembling voice.

" There's more evidence to come yet, please your Majesty," said the White Rabbit, jumping up in a great hurry ; " this paper has just been picked up."

" What's in it ? " said the Queen.

" I haven't opened it yet," said the White Rabbit, " but it seems to be a letter, written by the prisoner to—to somebody."

" It must have been that," said the King, " unless it was written to nobody, which isn't usual, you know."

" Who is it directed to ? " said one of the jurymen.

" It isn't directed at all," said the White Rabbit ; " in fact, there's nothing written on the *outside*." He unfolded the paper as he spoke, and added, " It isn't a letter, after all : it's a set of verses."

" Are they in the prisoner's handwriting ? " asked another of the jury-men.

" No, they're not," said the White Rabbit, " and that's the queerest thing about it." (The jury all looked puzzled.)

" He must have imitated somebody else's hand," said the King. (The jury all brightened up again.)

" Please your Majesty," said the Knave, " I didn't write it, and they can't prove I did : there's no name signed at the end."

" If you didn't sign it," said the King, " that only makes the matter worse. You *must* have meant some mischief, or else you'd have signed your name like an honest man."

There was a general clapping of hands at this : it was the first really clever thing the King had said that day.

" That *proves* his guilt," said the Queen.

" It proves nothing of the sort ! " said Alice. " Why, you don't even know what they're about ! "

" Read them," said the King.

The White Rabbit put on his spectacles. " Where shall I begin, please your Majesty ? " he asked.

" Begin at the beginning," the King said gravely, " and go on till you come to the end ; then stop."

These were the verses the White Rabbit read :

> " *They told me you had been to her,*
> *And mentioned me to him :*
> *She gave me a good character,*
> *But said I could not swim.*

" *He sent them word I had not gone*
(We know it to be true):
If she should push the matter on
What would become of you?

" *I gave her one, they gave him two,*
You gave us three or more;
They all returned from him to you,
Though they were mine before.

" *If I or she should chance to be*
Involved in this affair,
He trusts to you to set them free,
Exactly as we were.

" *My notion was that you had been*
(Before she had this fit)
An obstacle that came between
Him, and ourselves, and it.

" *Don't let him know she liked them best,*
For this must ever be
A secret, kept from all the rest,
Between yourself and me."

" That's the most important piece of evidence we've heard yet," said the King, rubbing his hands ; " so now let the jury——"

" If any one of them can explain it," said Alice (she had grown so large in the last few minutes that she wasn't a bit afraid of interrupting him), " I'll give him sixpence. *I* don't believe there's an atom of meaning in it."

The jury all wrote down on the slates, " *She* doesn't believe there's an atom of meaning in it," but none of them attempted to explain the paper.

" If there's no meaning in it," said the King, " that saves a world of trouble, you know, as we needn't try to find any. And yet I don't know," he went on, spreading out the verses on his knee, and looking at them with one eye ; " I seem to see some meaning in them, after all. ' ——*said I could not swim*—' You can't swim, can you ? " he added, turning to the Knave.

The Knave shook his head sadly. " Do I look like it ? " he said. (Which he certainly did *not*, being made entirely of cardboard.)

" All right, so far," said the King, and he went on muttering over the verses to himself : " ' *We know it to be true*—' that's the jury, of course ; ' *I gave her one, they gave him two*—' why, that must be what he did with the tarts, you know——"

" But it goes on, ' *They all returned from him to you*,' " said Alice.

" Why, there they are ! " said the King triumphantly, pointing to the tarts on the table. " Nothing can be clearer than *that*. Then again—' *Before she had this fit*—' You never had fits, my dear, I think ? " he said to the Queen.

" Never ! " said the Queen furiously, throwing an inkstand at the Lizard as she spoke. (The unfortunate little Bill had left off writing on his slate with one finger, as he found it made no mark ; but he now hastily began again, using the ink, that was trickling down his face, as long as it lasted.)

" Then the words don't *fit* you," said the King, looking round the court with a smile. There was a dead silence.

" It's a pun ! " the King added, in an angry tone, and everybody laughed.

" Let the jury consider their verdict," the King said, for about the twentieth time that day.

The jury wrote down on the slates

" No, no ! " said the Queen. " Sentence first—verdict afterwards."

" Stuff and nonsense ! " said Alice loudly. " The idea of having the sentence first ! "

" Hold your tongue ! " said the Queen, turning purple.

" I won't ! " said Alice.

" Off with her head ! " the Queen shouted at the top of her voice. Nobody moved.

" Who cares for you ? " said Alice (she had grown to her full size by this time). " You're nothing but a pack of cards ! "

At this the whole pack rose up into the air, and came flying down upon her : she gave a little scream, half of fright and half of anger, and tried to beat them off, and found herself lying on the bank, with her head in the lap of her sister, who was gently brushing away some dead leaves that had fluttered down from the trees on to her face.

" Wake up, Alice dear ! " said her sister. " Why, what a long sleep you've had ! "

" Oh, I've had such a curious dream ! " said Alice, and she told her sister, as well as she could remember them, all these strange Adventures of hers that you have just been reading about ; and when she had finished, her sister kissed her, and said, " It *was* a curious dream, dear, certainly : but now run in to your tea ; it's getting late." So Alice got up and ran off, thinking while she ran, as well she might, what a wonderful dream it had been.

But her sister sat still just as she left her, leaning her head on her hand, watching the setting sun, and thinking of little Alice, and all her wonderful Adventures, till she, too, began dreaming after a fashion, and this was her dream :

First she dreamed of little Alice herself : Once again the tiny hands were clasped upon her knee, and the bright, eager eyes were looking up into hers—she could hear the very tones of her voice, and see that queer little toss of her head to keep back the wandering hair that *would* always get into her eyes—and still as she listened, or seemed to listen, the whole place around her became alive with the strange creatures of her little sister's dream.

The long grass rustled at her feet as the White Rabbit hurried by ; the frightened Mouse splashed his way through the neighbouring pool ; she could hear the rattle of the tea-cups as the March Hare and his friends shared their never-ending meal ; and the shrill voice of the Queen ordering off her unfortunate guests to execution ; once more the pig-baby was sneezing on the Duchess's knee, while plates and dishes crashed around it ; once more the shriek of the Gryphon, the squeaking of the Lizard's slate-pencil, and the choking of the suppressed guinea-pigs, filled the air, mixed up with the distant sob of the miserable Mock Turtle.

So she sat on with closed eyes, and half believed herself in Wonderland, though she knew she had but to open them again, and all would change to dull reality—the grass would be only rustling in the wind, and the pool rippling to the waving of the reeds—the rattling tea-cups would change to tinkling sheep-bells, and the Queen's shrill cries to the voice of the shepherd boy—and the sneeze of the baby, the shriek of the Gryphon, and all the other queer noises, would change (she knew) to the confused clamour of the busy farmyard—while the lowing of the cattle in the distance would take the place of the Mock Turtle's heavy sobs.

Lastly, she pictured to herself how this same little sister of hers would, in the after-time, be herself a grown woman ; and how she would keep, through all her riper years, the simple and loving heart of her childhood ; and how she would gather about her other little children, and make *their* eyes bright and eager with many a strange tale, perhaps even with the dream of Wonderland of long ago ; and how she would feel with all their simple sorrows, and find a pleasure in all their simple joys, remembering her own child-life, and the happy summer days.

THE
ARABIAN
NIGHTS

SINDBAD THE SAILOR

LONG, long ago, in the reign of the Caliph Haroun al Raschid, there dwelt in the city of Bagdad a poor man named Hindbad, who gained a living by carrying goods from place to place for other people ; in fact, he was a porter.

Though, as a rule, he did not grumble with his lot, there were times when he was not content. One of these times happened to be, when, tired out by the weight of his load, he had sat down to rest outside the house of a very rich man whose name was Sindbad.

As the soft strains of music from the house reached his ears, and the scent of rare perfumes fell upon his senses, he was struck by the difference between his lot and that of the man whose name was so like his own.

" Why should I be so poor, and he so rich ? " said Hindbad aloud ; " am I not as good a man as he ? "

Sindbad, hearing the words without seeing the speaker, sent a servant to bring Hindbad before him, and the poor man, fearing he knew not what, went into the splendid hall where Sindbad was feasting with a number of his friends.

Pointing to a seat at his right hand, Sindbad gave his guest a share of the good things on the table, and the meal being at length finished, " Tell me," said he, " why you were grumbling at your lot ? "

" Pardon me, my lord," replied Hindbad, " I was weary and sad at heart."

" Have no fear," said Sindbad kindly, " I do not blame you for your words ; but, that you may know how hard I had to work to win the riches I now enjoy, let me tell you the story of my life."

With these words he began as follows :

When I was but a young man my father died, leaving me a very large fortune, nearly the whole of which I spent in enjoying myself. At last I began to think, unless I wished to become poor, I had better try to make some more money with the little left to me, so, having bought some goods, I set sail for the Persian Gulf, hoping to sell or exchange them at a profit.

The ship called at several small islands, where we did some good trading. One day, when the vessel could not move for want of wind to fill her sails, we saw what seemed to be a little green field peeping above the water. Thinking it very strange, a party of us rowed out to it, taking some wood for a fire, and food, so that we might hold a feast.

We had all landed, and were in the middle of our meal, when we found to our horror that we were on the back of some huge sea-monster. The creature shook its great body, and lashed its tail so angrily that as many as could jumped into the boat, others into the sea, and soon all except myself were safely aboard the ship.

A fresh breeze had begun to blow, and the sails being set at once, away went the ship, leaving me still on the monster's back. Suddenly the huge creature dived under water, and I should have gone too, but that seizing a large piece of wood I kept myself afloat.

All through that day and through the night I was tossed about by the waves, but was at last thrown on to the shore of what was really an island. After a while the sun came out, warming me, and making me feel that if I wished to gain strength I must seek some food.

Dragging myself with great pain toward the middle of the island, I had the good fortune to find a few herbs. These I ate, drinking afterwards from a spring of clear, cool water.

Wishing to see on what sort of place I had been cast, I walked on until a man met me, who, hearing my strange story, took me to a cave in which were several other men. They were the servants of the ruler of the island, and had come to this part of it in order to fetch his horses back to the palace.

It was lucky for me that I met them that day ; had it not been for this I should most likely have died, as I could never have found my way to the other side of the island, where the people lived, and to which the king's servants were returning next day.

They were very kind, giving me food to eat, and taking me with them when they set out on their journey. As soon as we reached the palace they took me before the king, who also treated me with great kindness. He listened to my story, pitied my sad state, and bade me stay with him as long as I cared to do so.

Now the chief city of his kingdom, the city in which I made my home, was built on the sea-shore. Every day ships came to it from all parts of the world, and I, hoping to meet some one from my own town, spent a great deal of time watching these ships, and talking to the merchants who came and went in them.

I also grew friendly with some of the natives—Indians they were, and very wise persons ; but I never forgot to pay a daily visit to the king, with whose chief men I had many pleasant talks about the way in which their country and my own were governed.

Hearing one day of the island of Cassel, where many peculiar things were to be seen, I had a great wish to visit it, which I did, seeing many large and curious fishes on my voyage.

Shortly after my return from Cassel, the very ship in which I had set out from Bussorah, and which had sailed away leaving me struggling for life in the water, came into the harbour. Among the many bundles of goods brought from this vessel to the shore I saw those which I had bought, and on which my name was clearly written. But, on telling the captain my name, and that I wished to have my goods, he looked at me in surprise.

"How can you be Sindbad?" he asked, "when I myself saw him drowned. I fear you are not an honest man, though you look like one. I believe you are telling a lie in order to get these goods which do not belong to you."

I was at some pains to make him believe I spoke the truth, and, at last, on several of the sailors saying they were sure I was Sindbad, he let me have the goods.

Having looked through my bundle, I carried the very best of the goods to the kindly king, and asked him to take them as a gift. He seemed pleased with the gift, but not quite sure how I, a poor man cast up by the sea, had been able to get them.

I then told him of the coming of the ship, and the finding of my own bales of goods, on which he took my costly present with great pleasure, and gave me one worth far more in return. I next sold or exchanged the rest of my goods, and, having bidden his majesty good-bye, set sail for Bussorah, taking with me many articles made only on the island. These I sold for a large sum of money, for so much indeed, that I had no further need to work.

When Sindbad had finished the story of his first voyage, he ordered the band to play again, and spent the rest of the day with his guests. The poor porter, who never in all his life had been so well treated before, enjoyed himself greatly, and, when the rich man, on bidding him good-night, bade him come again the next day to hear more of his story, giving him at the same time a purse full of money, Hindbad was delighted at his good fortune.

THE SECOND VOYAGE

ALTHOUGH I had made up my mind to live quietly at home on the money gained by my first voyage, said Sindbad, when he and his poor guest were once more seated together, I soon tired of doing nothing, and having bought a large number of useful articles, once more set out to sell them to the people who lived on the various islands.

The ship carried us safely to several places where I sold my own goods and bought others ; but one day we reached what seemed to be a desert island. No living creature was to be seen, yet there were fruit-trees and flowers, and meadows, and running streams, all of which looked so tempting, that we felt obliged to land, if only to walk a little in the pleasant-looking fields.

Having no wish to wander about with the rest, I took some food and wine, found a nice, shady spot beside a stream, ate a good meal, and then fell fast asleep, wakening only when the others had returned to the vessel and sailed away without me.

I blamed myself over and over again for my folly, but, as this was not likely to help me much, I climbed a high tree in order to get a good view of the island. Far away in the distance I saw something white, and to this I went with all speed.

It was a curious thing, very large, very smooth, and rounded like a dome. While I stood wondering what it could be, all around grew dark. It was late in the day, and the sun would set in a little while, but the sky seemed to be hidden all at once by a thick cloud.

To my surprise this was not so, but the cloud was really a huge bird, bigger than I had ever dreamed a bird could be. I thought it must be the wonderful roc of which I had heard the sailors talk, and the great white dome must be its egg.

Thinking it likely the bird was coming to sit on her egg, I crept under it, and, as soon as she was settled, tied myself firmly to one of her big, strong legs.

Thus I lay until the morning, when the bird, rising high, carried me so swiftly through the air that I became dizzy, and lost my senses. On coming to myself some time later I was lying on the ground, but still tied to the leg of the huge bird.

Not wishing to go through such a terrible journey again, I made haste to get free from the bird's leg, and it was well I did so, for almost the next moment she seized a huge serpent in her bill and flew away.

I could not tell where she carried me. All around were mountains so high that they seemed to touch the sky, and so steep that no one could climb them. I was no better off here than on the island. Suddenly I forgot my trouble for a time, for, looking at the ground, I found it was covered with diamonds, big shining diamonds.

But, alas, there were other things besides, things that filled my heart with fear, and made me wish more than ever to find some way out of the lonely valley. These were serpents, larger than I had ever seen in my own land.

As the day grew brighter, however, they hid away in their homes, for fear, I supposed, of the roc, but when the night drew near they came out again in large numbers. Feeling it would be dreadful to spend the long dark night in terror lest I should be swallowed by one of the great creatures, I looked about for some place in which it might be possible to take shelter till the day dawned.

At length I found a cave, the entrance to which was so small that I could block it with a large stone. Though now feeling safer I could by no means sleep ; the hissing of the serpents outside was too fearful.

As soon as it was light I left the cave, and walked a short distance through the valley, feeling far too miserable to touch the diamonds under my feet. The food I had brought from the ship kept me from starving, but I was so weary that at last I felt obliged to lie down and sleep.

Hardly had I begun to doze, however, when I was startled by something heavy falling near me. Opening my eyes quickly I saw a large piece of raw

All round were mountains and huge, hissing serpents

meat lying at my feet. Another piece fell, and another, and several more, and as they fell heavily upon the diamonds, the lovely stones stuck firmly into the meat.

This made me think again of the sailors' stories, and I knew that the meat was being thrown into the valley by men on the mountains, in the hope that it would be fetched back by the eagles to feed their young ones, when the diamonds could be taken from their nests.

Now I thought I could see a way of escape by tying a piece of meat firmly to my back, and waiting till an eagle carried me up out of the dreadful valley. This I did, but not until I had first filled my bag with the precious stones.

I had not long to wait. One of a number of eagles picking me up bore me to his nest on the top of the mountains, where I was found by a merchant who had frightened the eagle away. At first he looked at me in surprise, and then said I had no right to steal his diamonds.

" If you will listen to me," I said gently, " you will find I am no thief, though having enough diamonds to make both myself and you rich for life. I got them from the valley, and chose the very best to be found."

The other merchants now crowded round, and all showed great surprise at my story. They wondered much at the trick I had played, but they wondered still more when I showed them the stones.

Though I begged him to take several, the merchant who had found me would take only the smallest of them, which he said was a good fortune in itself. They agreed to let me spend that night in their camp, which I did, and was then taken to the merchant's house, where I told my strange story again to his wife and children.

In the course of time I once more reached my home, and settled down to a life of ease, and made glad the hearts of my poor neighbours, by sharing my riches with them.

This being the end of Sindbad's second story, he gave Hindbad another purse of money, and asked him to return the next day.

THE THIRD VOYAGE

MY third voyage, said Sindbad the next day, was hardly begun when a very great storm arose, and the captain told us the ship was being driven towards an island, which was the home of numbers of little hairy savages not more than two feet high. He said they were very fierce, and we had better not make them angry.

As our vessel neared the land a swarm of them swam out, dragged it ashore, made us all get out, and then took the ship away with them to another island. As it was useless to stand and look after them, we walked on until we reached a beautiful palace, the courtyard of which we entered.

The yard led to a room where we saw a heap of men's bones, and a large number of spits, or long, steel skewers, on which joints of meat are roasted. As we stood looking at these things, a truly terrible ogre came into the room, making a loud noise.

In the very middle of his forehead was a huge eye, the only one he had ; his mouth was like that of a horse, and his ears flapped down on his shoulders like an elephant's. He was as tall as a high tree, and one glance at him was enough to make us all nearly die with fright.

Having taken a good look at us, the horrid ogre picked me up by my neck, and turned me round and round, but seemed to think me too thin, for, indeed, I was little more than skin and bone. Then he seized the captain, who was the fattest of us all, stuck a spit through his body, roasted, and ate him.

After this he went to sleep, and troubled us no more till the next day, when he roasted and ate another of our crew. On the third day he ate another, and we then made up our minds to kill him and try to escape. There were ten of us left, and each one taking a spit, and making its point red hot, we stuck them all together into the one eye of our terrible enemy.

Mad with pain he tried to seize us ; but we got out of the way of his fearful claw-like hands, and ran off to the shore. Here we made some rafts, but had not got afloat when two giants came in sight leading the terrible ogre who we had fondly hoped was dead.

Jumping on to the rafts we pushed off from the shore ; but the giants, wading into the water as far as they dared, threw after us some huge stones which, falling upon the rafts, sank them all but the one on which I stood with two other men. Happily we got out of their reach quickly, and, after beating about on the sea for many hours, came to another island, where we found some very good fruit.

Being now tired out we lay down to sleep, but were soon awakened by a rustling sound which, to our horror, we found was made by a huge serpent.

ALICE IN COURT.
Alice tipped over the jury-men, and they all lay sprawling on the floor.

THE END OF THE TRIAL.
The whole pack rose into the air and came flying down on top of Alice.

The horrid ogre picked me up and examined me

Before we could get away, the creature swallowed one of my comrades, and then went back to his den. The next night he came again, and caught the second of my comrades, as he was following me up a tree, where he had hoped to be quite safe.

All night I lay along one of the boughs, afraid to sleep lest the cruel monster should come back. As soon as day broke I slid down, gathered all the brushwood near, and making it into bundles placed some of them round the tree ; the others I tied to the topmost branches. When the sky began to darken in the evening, I lit them, and kept myself safe all night, for, though the serpent came, he feared to cross my circle of fire.

In the morning, feeling very miserable, I made up my mind to drown myself, but, on reaching the shore, I saw some distance off a ship passing slowly by. Unrolling my turban I waved it aloft, shouting loudly the while, until the captain sent a boat to fetch me to the ship.

Good fortune now met me once again, for this was the very captain who had sailed away without me on my second voyage. As soon as he learned who I was, he told me how glad he was to have been able to make up for that fault, by saving me now from what might have proved a worse fate.

He had taken care of my goods left on the ship, and now returned them to me with much pleasure. On reaching port I sold them at a fair price, and again returned to Bussorah with a large sum of money.

From Bussorah I went to Bagdad and bought another fine house with splendid grounds all round it. As I had done each time before, so I did now, giving a great deal of money to poor people of the city, and settling down for some time to a quiet life. But this I found very difficult to do, and at last went to sea for the fourth time, when again many wonderful things befell me.

Hindbad went home that night with a glad heart, for he was no longer poor. In his hand he held a purse of money, and it seemed as if his rich friend meant to give him the same, every day he spent with him.

THE FOURTH VOYAGE

As soon as dinner was over, Sindbad began the story of his fourth voyage. Having set all my affairs straight, he said, I travelled through a great part of Persia, buying and selling. At last, reaching the coast, I went aboard a ship, which, after calling at several places on the mainland, stood out to sea.

But soon a great storm arose ; the sails were torn in shreds, the ship was blown upon the land, and many of the passengers and sailors were drowned.

With a few of the others I clung to a plank, which was washed ashore on an island, where we found fruit and water, of which we ate and drank freely. The next morning we set out to explore the island, but before getting far were met by some black men who carried us to their homes.

They seemed very kind and gave us a tasty herb to eat.

Though feeling as hungry as my comrades, I ate none of this herb, fearing it might do me some harm. In this I was wise, for I was the only one who kept his senses. The others became dazed, and ate freely of the rice with which they were daily fed, becoming at last very fat, when the black men killed and ate them.

The horror of the whole thing, together with the very little food I ate, kept me so thin that the blacks took no notice of me, which gave me the chance of going here and there without being watched. One day, when all the people except one old man had gone out, I walked slowly till some distance away from the village, when I set off running as fast as I could, taking no heed of the old man's cries.

Resting a while now and then, I hurried on until night came. For seven days I met no one ; on the eighth I had the good fortune to come upon some white men gathering pepper, which was plentiful on the island. On hearing my story they seemed very much surprised that I had got away with my life.

They treated me with much kindness and, when their work was done, took me with them to their own island, where the king gave me some new clothes, and bade his people take great care of me. I became a great favourite with every one, and at last found a way of paying back a little of their kindness.

Seeing that all of them, even the king, rode upon the bare backs of their horses, I thought out a plan for making a saddle and bridle and stirrups. This, with the help of two workmen, I did, and gave the first set, when finished, to the king. So many costly presents were given me by those for whom I made saddles that I was soon a rich man again.

One day the king, as a token of his love, gave me a wife, thinking I should be more likely to settle down in his country, and not wish to return to my own. At first I was pleased enough to stay, but after a time I began to long for my own home in Bagdad. Therefore, keeping my eyes open, I waited for a chance to escape, which came about in a very curious manner.

My wife, who for some time had not been strong, fell sick and died, when, according to the custom of the country, I was buried with her in a deep pit on the side of a mountain near the sea.

My coffin was an open one, and when the mouth of the pit had been blocked by a huge rock, and the king with the other mourners had gone away, I rose, and by the aid of a little light that came through the corners not quite covered by the stone, looked about me.

The pit or long cave, as it really was, seemed full of dead bodies. This upset me terribly. I was afraid. At first I wished I had died in one of the storms at sea ; then I was filled with a keen desire to live. Taking some of the bread and water placed in the coffin, I groped about to find some outlet from the cave, but failed to do so.

My food was nearly all gone, when, one day, the mouth of the cave was uncovered, and I saw another burial taking place. The dead body was that of a man, and his wife being buried with him, the usual seven small loaves and a pitcher of water had been placed in her coffin. The poor woman, however, soon died, so I took the bread and water, which lasted me for several days.

Then, one morning, hearing a strange sound, I was able to follow it, until I came upon an opening in the cave, through which I crawled, and found myself on the sea-shore. The sound I had heard proved to be the heavy breathing of some creature that had come into the cave to feed upon the dead bodies.

Feeling sure now of being able to get away from my living tomb, I went back to the cave in order to get the precious stones, and jewels, and costly stuffs buried with the dead bodies, and also to bring away my bread and water. On again reaching the shore I made several neat bundles of the goods, and then settled down to wait for the passing of some ship in the hope of being picked up.

On the third day, a vessel sailed slowly out from the harbour, and I, waving the linen of my turban, shouted loudly, which at last caused the sailors to look toward me. In a few minutes a boat was lowered and three men rowed ashore to fetch me.

To account for being in so strange a place, I told them I had been ship-wrecked, but had got safely to land with a portion of my goods. The story was really a very poor one, but they seemed not to notice it, being far too busy with their own affairs.

The ship called at several ports on the islands and the mainland, where I made another large fortune by the sale of the articles brought from the cave, and at length I reached my home in safety.

As an act of thankfulness for having come safely through my troubles, I gave large sums of money to the church, to the poor, and to my own kindred, who listened in wonder to the story of my latest adventures.

Here Sindbad wished his guests good-night, bidding them all dine with him next day. He then handed to Hindbad the usual purse of one hundred sequins with which the poor man went away happy.

THE FIFTH VOYAGE

THE pleasures of my home, said Sindbad the next evening, made me forget past dangers, so, when the longing for travel came upon me, I bought many costly articles with which to carry on my trade, and sent them to the seaport town where a vessel was being built for my use.

The ship being larger than I needed for my own goods, I agreed to take several other merchants with me, and we set out in great hope of doing good business at the ports where we meant to call.

But, alas! coming one day to a desert island, where we found a young roc just ready to break from its shell, the merchants roasted and ate it, and thus brought about the deaths of every one except myself.

Just as my comrades had finished their meal, for I would by no means join in it, we saw the parent birds coming. The captain, fearing the anger of the great creatures, who looked like two large clouds floating in the sky, hurried us aboard and sailed away with all speed.

As soon as the old birds found what had been done, they swept down with a great noise, took up two huge stones, and flew after us. Stopping just above us they dropped the stones, one of which fell upon the ship, smashing it in pieces, and killing most of the sailors and merchants. Some, myself among them, sank into the water.

On coming to the surface I caught hold of a plank with one hand, and swam with the other, changing them at times, until the tide carried me to an island, the shore of which was so steep that some further toil was needed before I reached a place of safety.

In the morning, after eating of the fruits which grew in plenty, and drinking of the fresh, cool water of a brook, I wandered about, looking with pleasure at the beauty of the place.

After a time I saw a little old man making signs to me to carry him on my back over the brook. Having pity on his age, I did so, but, when I would have pulled him down on the other side, he twisted his legs so tightly round my neck, that I fell to the ground half choked.

Though he saw how faint I was he made no sign of getting off, but, opening his legs a little to let me breathe better, he dug his feet into my stomach to make me rise and carry him farther. Day after day, and night after night, he clung to me, until by good luck I got rid of him in the following way.

Coming to a spot where, a few days before, I had left the juice of some grapes in a calabash, I drank the juice, which in the meantime had become very good wine. This gave me fresh strength, and, instead of dragging myself wearily along, I danced and sang with right good-will.

The old man, seeing how light-hearted the wine had made me, signed to me to give him some. He took a deep drink, and soon became so merry that he loosed his hold on my shoulders, when I tossed him off, and killed him with a big stone, lest he should make me his victim once more.

Some sailors whom I met shortly afterwards, their ship having put into the island for water, said I was the first person they had ever known to escape from the old man of the sea, who for years had been a terror to those obliged to visit the island.

He made signs to me to carry him over the brook

One of the merchants on board, taking pity on my state, gave me a large bag, and advised me to go picking cocoa-nuts with some men whom we met in a place much visited by foreign traders. I kept close to the party, as he had bidden me, until we reached the place where the cocoa-nuts grew.

The trees were so tall that I wondered how we should get the nuts, when the men, picking up some stones, threw them at the monkeys of whom there were many on the branches. These creatures, in return, pelted us with cocoa-nuts, throwing them down so quickly that we soon filled our bags.

Day after day this was done until at length we had enough to fill the ship which waited for us in the harbour. Then, bidding the friendly merchant good-bye, I went aboard, and in due time arrived in Bagdad, none the worse for my adventures. I had done well, too, with my cocoa-nuts, having changed them for pearls and spices in the places at which we had called on the voyage.

Giving Hindbad another hundred sequins, Sindbad wished him good-night, and asked him to return next day to hear the story of his sixth voyage.

THE SIXTH VOYAGE

You will perhaps wonder why, after meeting with so many dangers, I should again venture forth, when I might have stayed quietly at home, said Sindbad, taking up his story where he had left off the day before. I wonder myself, now, yet at the time I was quite willing and eager to set out.

Travelling by way of Persia and the Indies, I at length took passage on a vessel bound on a long voyage. After being many days at sea the captain and pilot lost their way. They had no idea where we were, until the captain found his ship had got into a most dangerous current which, unless God took pity on us, would surely carry us to our death.

Almost mad with grief he left his place on deck, and went to see that his orders were carried out ; but, as the men set about changing the sails, the ropes broke, and the vessel, now quite helpless, was carried ashore and wrecked, yet not so badly but we were able to save our lives, our goods, and our provisions.

But even such comfort as was left us was taken away by the captain. " We may as well set about digging our graves," said he, " for no one ever escapes from this terrible place."

And, indeed, this seemed true, the shore being covered with wrecks, and goods of great value, and, worst of all for men in our position to see, the bones of those who had already died there, as we were only too likely to do.

The coast was very steep, and there seemed no way of climbing up, but under the hills, through a great cave, ran the very current that had brought us ashore. For some days we wandered about, heedless of the precious stones under our feet, thinking only of our sad fate. The most careful ate only a little of their share of food each day, so that some lived longer than others ; but at last I was the only one left, and, wild with grief at my folly in leaving home, I began to dig my grave, fully believing that now at least there was no more hope.

Yet it pleased God again to spare me. As I stood, lonely and miserable, looking upon the currents that had wrought our ruin, an idea came into my head. With all speed I made a raft with the pieces of timber on the shore, loaded it with the precious stones and costly stuffs lying here and there, and stepped aboard, trusting that the stream would carry me to some place where men lived, and so give me a chance of escape. If I lost my life, I should be no worse off than in staying on the coast to die.

With two small oars I guided the raft, leaving it to be carried by the current. Several days passed, and still the raft floated on in total darkness through the long tunnel. At length my food being all eaten, I sank down in a state of drowsiness, and awoke to find myself once more in the light, and surrounded by a number of black men.

Full of joy at my good fortune I rose, and gave thanks aloud to God, who had brought me to a place of safety. One of the blacks, understanding my words, stepped forward and asked how I had reached their country. They had seen my raft floating in the river, he said, and had tied it to the bank till I should awake. After eating a little food I told them of my strange adventures, the man who had first spoken to me telling the others what I said, he being the only one who understood my speech.

They looked at me in wonder, and placing me on a horse took me straight to their king. He thought my story so strange that he had it written down in letters of gold, and put away with the important papers of the kingdom. The sight of my raft and bales of goods, which the natives had taken care to bring with them, was a still further surprise. He thought my treasures very beautiful, but most of all the emeralds, of which he himself had none.

Seeing this, I begged him to accept the whole of my goods, as a token of my thankfulness to him and his people, but this he would by no means do. He said that instead of taking my riches he meant to add to them, and meanwhile, I was placed in the care of one of his chief men, who treated me with great kindness.

Though the time passed pleasantly, I could not but long to return to my home. Going therefore to pay my daily visit to the king, I told him of my wish, and begged that he would let me return to Bagdad. He agreed at once, and, giving me many valuable gifts, asked that I would carry a message of friendship to the Caliph Haroun al Raschid, together with a costly present, and a letter written upon a skin of great value. Then, sending for the captain in whose ship I was to sail, and the merchant who was to travel with me, he charged them to treat me well on the journey.

Reaching Bagdad in the course of time, I set out to fulfil my promise to the king. His gift to the Caliph was made up of four things—a beautiful cup cut out of a large ruby and filled with pearls ; the skin of a serpent supposed to keep any one who lay upon it from becoming ill ; a large quantity of wood of aloes, and of camphor ; and a beautiful slave whose clothing was rich with jewels.

The Caliph, astonished at the richness of the gift, could not keep from asking many questions about the king who had given it into my care. After telling him all he wished to know, I was free to return home, and to settle down again, this time, as I thought, for good.

The story being finished, Hindbad went away, taking with him another purse of gold ; but the next day he returned to dine with Sindbad, who, after the meal, told the story of his seventh and last voyage in these words.

THE SEVENTH VOYAGE

I was one day enjoying myself with some friends, when a slave from the palace came with a message that I should go to the Caliph at once. His Highness, having written a reply to the letter from the King of the Indies, wished me to carry it to him, together with a suitable present.

Now, though it would have given me great pleasure to serve my sovereign in any other way, I felt quite unable to face again the dangers of the sea, and, to let him know why, I told him of all the misery through which I had passed. In reply he said that though he felt very sorry for me, yet I must bear his letter and gift to the King of the Indies.

" You have but to sail to Serendib," said he, " and present my gifts to his Majesty : after that you are free to return to Bagdad."

Seeing that he would not change his mind, I at last agreed to go, and, after a fair and pleasant voyage, arrived at the king's court. The gift was a very costly one, and his Majesty showed great pleasure when it was handed to him.

After a short stay in the island I begged leave to depart, but the king gave his consent only after much pressing on my part. I went on board the vessel, taking with me a splendid gift, and hoping to have a speedy and pleasant voyage.

We had been at sea, however, only about three days, when the ship being seized by pirates, I was taken with several others and sold as a slave. The rich merchant who bought me treated me well, and, finding I was able to shoot with a bow, took me out with him to shoot elephants of which there were numbers in the forest.

Having told me to climb a tree and to wait for the animals to pass by, he gave me a supply of food, and went back to the town.

No elephants passed during the night, but in the morning I shot one out of a large herd. As soon as the others had gone, I ran quickly to my master, who, praising me highly, came back to the forest and helped to bury the huge creature. This he did in order to get the tusks, when the flesh had rotted away from them.

Every day for two whole months I shot an elephant; then one morning, as I waited in the tree for them, instead of passing by they came towards it, and looked at me steadily for a few moments. I trembled with fear, for the creatures were many in number, and seemed bent on taking my life in revenge for the death of their friends.

One great animal at last tore up the tree in which I was by the roots, lifted me from the ground where I had fallen, placed me on his back, and, closely followed by the others, carried me to a field, some distance away, which I found afterwards to be covered with the bones and teeth of dead elephants.

Having laid me on the ground they all went away, leaving me lost in wonder at their wisdom. It seemed as if they knew it was only their teeth I wanted, and they had brought me to their burying-place, so that I could get all I wished without killing any more of their number.

Here, indeed, was a great treasure, and I went quickly to tell my master of my good fortune. As I met no elephants on the way, I felt sure they had gone farther into the forest in order to leave the road open. My master, wondering why I was so long away, had meanwhile gone to the tree and found it torn from the ground, so he was overjoyed to see me, having feared the creatures had killed me in their anger.

The next day we rode to the spot on an elephant whom we loaded with as many tusks as it could carry, and on getting back home my master said that as he had become a rich man through me, I should be a slave no longer.

"The merchants of this city," he said, "have had many slaves killed by the elephants, who are indeed very cunning animals. But it has pleased God to spare your life, and to show how every one of us may become rich without the loss of any more lives. I have no doubt that when the people of this city hear about this they will all wish to help in making you a rich man, but I would rather do this by myself. I will not only set you free, I will give you enough money to live on for the rest of your life."

Having thanked the merchant for his kindness, I said, " Sir, I have no wish to take so great a gift from you. Give me leave to return to my own country a free man, and I shall be well content."

This he was quite willing to do, saying that as soon as the wind was fair, he would send me home in one of the ships that would then come to carry away the ivory.

While waiting for the ships I made several journeys to the hill with the friendly merchant, bringing home so many tusks that the storehouses were soon full of ivory. The vessels came at last, and the merchant himself, choosing the one in which I was to sail, filled it with ivory, the half of which he said was mine. Besides this splendid present he gave me a number of things found or made only in that island, and enough food to last the whole voyage : he also paid the cost of my journey.

The voyage was a good one, yet, knowing the dangers of the ocean, and how quickly storms arise, I landed at the first port we reached on the mainland, taking with me my share of the ivory which soon sold for a great deal of money.

Having bought some rare gifts for my family, I set out for Bagdad with a party of merchants. The way was long and tiring, but reaching the city at length, I went straight to the Caliph, in order to let him know that his commands had been properly carried out.

I had been so long away that he feared some danger had befallen me, so I made bold to tell him of my adventures. The story of the elephants filled him with wonder ; indeed, had he not known me to be a truthful man, he would not have believed it.

As it was he gave orders that this story, as well as all the others I had told, should be written in letters of gold, and kept in a safe place for all time.

My family, my kindred, and all my friends welcomed my return with great joy. Since that, my last voyage, I have lived a quiet life, doing much good.

" Now, friend," he added, turning to Hindbad, " I think you will agree I have earned the riches I enjoy, and the pleasures that fill my life."

" Sir," replied Hindbad, as he rose and kissed his host's hand, " I must own that your troubles have been greater than mine. You richly deserve all you have, and I hope you will from now live a happy and peaceful life."

Although he had no more stories to tell, Sindbad begged the poor porter to come to dine with him every day. " You need not do any more rough work," said he, wishing him good-night, and putting into his hand another full purse, " for Sindbad the Sailor will be your friend for the rest of your life."

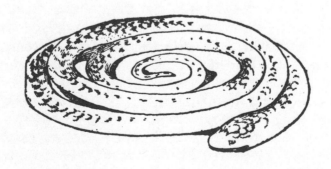

THE STORY OF ALADDIN, OR THE WONDERFUL LAMP

IN one of the large cities of China there once lived a tailor, whose name was Mustapha. Mustapha was very poor, and he found it hard to provide food for himself, his wife, and his only child, Aladdin.

Aladdin was a very naughty and lazy boy. He would never do what his parents wished him to do, but played in the streets from morning till night with boys who were as naughty as himself.

When Aladdin was old enough to learn a trade his father took him into his own shop and began to show him how he should use the needle. It was of no use. Aladdin had had his own way so long that now he could not settle down to work. His father tried him over and over again, and was at last so vexed at his son's idle habits that he became ill and soon died.

The poor widow thought that surely now her son would earn a little money. But no. Aladdin was as idle as ever. In despair, the good woman sold all the things that were in the shop, and with the money and a little she could earn by spinning cotton she got on fairly well.

One day when Aladdin was playing in the street with some more boys, a stranger saw him and stopped to look at him.

This stranger was a magician, and as he looked at Aladdin he said to himself, " This is just the kind of boy I want. He is daring and bold, and will just suit me." Going up to Aladdin, he drew him aside from his playmates.

" Is your father called Mustapha ? " the magician asked quietly. " And is he not a tailor ? "

" Yes," replied Aladdin, " but he is now dead."

Hearing this, the stranger threw his arms around the boy and kissed him, while tears seemed to flow down his cheeks.

Aladdin asked him why he wept. " Alas ! " replied the stranger, " how can I help it ? I am your uncle. Your father was my brother. I have tried to find him all over the world, and now I have come too late."

The stranger then asked Aladdin about his mother, and, putting some money into his hand, bade him go home and say he would call to see her next day.

Aladdin ran off home with glee.

" Mother," said he, " my uncle found me in the street to-day, and he bade me tell you he is coming here to-morrow."

" Your uncle found you ? " asked the good woman. " Nonsense ; you have no uncle."

" At any rate, a stranger hugged and kissed me, and gave me this gold," replied Aladdin. " He surely *must* be my uncle."

Aladdin's mother did not know what to think. She had never heard of this uncle before ; but, as Aladdin then went out, nothing more was said.

Next day the stranger again saw Aladdin playing in the street. " Here is some more money, boy," said he, kissing him again ; " take it to your mother, and tell her to buy some things for to-night's supper. I shall call on you then."

Aladdin took the money home, and, though his mother could hardly believe her senses, she spent the money in buying good food for supper. As for Aladdin, so eager was he to see his uncle once more that he went out into the street to show him the way to the house.

The stranger came. He brought some bottles of wine and some nice fruit. When these had been set on the supper table he said to the widow, " Pray, show me the place where my poor brother used to sit."

She showed him the corner of the sofa.

At once the stranger fell down before the place and began to kiss the sofa. " My poor, poor brother," said he. " How I should like to see you ! But I am too late ! Too late ! "

After a while the three sat down to supper and had a good meal. Then they talked, and the stranger said what joy it would give him to set Aladdin up in a shop, so that he might earn a good living by the sale of goods.

In the course of the next few days the stranger bought Aladdin some new clothes and took him into the rich parts of the city. Aladdin was proud to be seen in fine clothes, and thought his uncle a very kind man. " To-morrow," said the uncle to Aladdin, " I will show you some finer sights than these. Be ready for me early."

Morning came, and the two set out through the city gate. Their way led them past some large palaces with beautiful gardens round them, through which they walked. Each one was more handsome than the other, and Aladdin was full of joy on seeing them.

At last both were tired. " Let us sit down here," said the uncle to Aladdin. " I want to offer you some good advice, before I let you have the shop."

" How much farther are we going ? " asked Aladdin. " I fear I cannot walk back unless we turn soon."

" Take courage, my dear boy," said the uncle. " I wish to show you one

Aladdin took hold of the ring

garden more which is better than all the others we have seen. You are rested now. Let us go on."

Soon they came to a narrow valley where all was quiet. "This is the place I wished to reach," said the uncle. "There are wonders here which you have never yet dreamt of. I am now going to strike a light, and do you gather me some dry sticks in order to make a fire."

There were plenty of sticks near at hand, and soon Aladdin had a large heap of them. The uncle then set them on fire, and, as the blaze got big, he threw perfume into it, and spoke some strange words.

Aladdin began to feel afraid, and thought of taking to his heels. Just at that moment, however, the ground beneath them shook, and there came into sight a square stone about a foot and a half across, with a brass ring fixed right in the centre for the purpose of lifting it up.

"You have seen my power," said the uncle to Aladdin. "I want you now to do something for me."

Aladdin, though he shook with fear, said he was quite ready to do all that was wanted of him.

"Then pull that stone up by the ring," said the uncle. "It will come up easily enough if you repeat the names of your father and grandfather."

Aladdin took hold of the ring, and, strange to say, was able to lift the stone without the least effort.

"The next thing to do," went on the uncle, "is to go down that well. When you come to the bottom go through the door into a large hall; then through many halls one after the other, keeping a straight course, till you come to where you will find a lamp burning in a niche of the wall. Bring the lamp to me."

As he spoke these words he put a ring on Aladdin's finger, saying, as he did so, that it would keep him from all harm.

Then Aladdin went down the well, and found all things as the uncle had said. There were the halls, and there were gardens too, with trees in them, which bore strange-looking fruit of all colours—red, white, blue, and so on. They were, in truth, precious stones of great value.

When Aladdin came to the lamp he took it down from the wall, and, having put out the flame, carried it in his bosom. He took also some fruit from the trees, and at last came to the bottom of the well.

Up the steps he went, and saw the stranger outside waiting for him. " Give me the lamp," said the uncle; " you will be able to get out more easily."

" No, no," said Aladdin. " Help me out first, and then I will give you the lamp."

Now, I must tell you that it was the lamp the stranger wanted. He was not the real uncle of Aladdin, but had taken these means of getting it, for he alone knew where it was. He had come all the way from Africa for it, and was in a sore plight when Aladdin would not give it to him.

The stranger tried all the means he could, but Aladdin had sense enough not to part with the lamp. Seeing this, the stranger added a little more perfume to the fire, which he had all the time kept up. Then he said two magic words, and lo ! the stone which had covered up the well, and kept it from view, flew back to its place of its own accord. Then he made off as fast as he could to Africa.

Aladdin, of course, knew not what to do. He cried out many times that if his uncle would take away the stone the lamp should surely be his. But the stranger was now a long distance off, and all Aladdin's cries were in vain.

For full two days Aladdin lay helpless in the well, without either eating or drinking. On the third day, when he had quite given up all hopes of ever seeing daylight again, he joined his hands together, as he would have done had he been saying his prayers.

As he did so he chanced to rub the ring which the stranger had put on his finger.

The next instant a genie, tall and strong, stood before him. " What do you wish ? " said the genie. " I am ready to obey you as your slave, as the slave of him who has the ring on his finger, both I and the other slaves of the ring."

" Pray, then, take me out of this place," said Aladdin, hardly knowing what was going on.

In a moment Aladdin found himself on the spot where the fire had been made. He felt the fresh breeze blow upon him, and, losing no time, made the best of his way home. How he ran, to be sure !

His mother was glad to see him, and, as she set him something to eat, he told her all about the strange cave and the lamp. He also showed her the precious stones which he had culled from the trees. Then he went to bed.

Next day he rose and asked for breakfast. Alas ! there was no food in the house, for he had eaten it all the night before at supper. " If you will wait a little, my son," said his mother, " I will sell a little cotton which I have spun, and then I can buy some food."

"Nay," said Aladdin, "keep your cotton, mother, and I will sell the lamp instead."

"It will fetch a better price if I clean it," said his mother, and with that she began to rub the lamp.

Before she could turn round, a genie stood before her. "What do you wish?" roared he with a voice like thunder. "I am ready to obey you as your slave, and the slave of those who have the lamp in their hands, both I and the other slaves of the lamp."

The mother could not speak, she was so full of fear. Aladdin, however, who had seen a genie before, and had good cause to be thankful, took the lamp from his mother's hands, and said in a firm voice, "I am hungry. Bring me something to eat."

In a moment the table was spread with all sorts of good things in dishes of gold and silver.

"What is the meaning of this?" said the good woman. "Has the Sultan taken pity on us and sent them?"

It took some time for Aladdin to explain to his mother all that he knew of the ring and the lamp. Being sore afraid, she would have nothing to do with such evil spirits, as she was sure they must be. "Ah, child," said she, "put the lamp away. I would rather you threw it away or sold it, than I would run the risk of ever touching it again."

"And I," said Aladdin, "will take care what I do with the things which have been so useful to me in times of trouble."

Enough food was left from breakfast to last for two days. When this was gone Aladdin went to sell one of the silver plates. He soon found a Jew who bought it, but gave him little for it. With the money some more food was bought. This went on for some time. As often as food was wanted a plate was sold, until there was only one large dish left.

Aladdin sold this at a better price, and with the money lived for a long time. He also bought fine clothes and rings to wear. In fact, he became quite a gentleman.

It chanced, one day, that Aladdin saw the princess, the daughter of the Sultan. Now Aladdin had never seen a lady's face before, except his mother's, for in that land all ladies go about with their faces hidden under a veil. This time the princess's face was unveiled.

"How I should like to marry the princess!" said Aladdin, almost aloud. "She is so pretty."

That same night Aladdin told his mother whom he had seen, and what had passed in his mind the moment he saw her. His mother told him not to be foolish. "Who can ask such a thing of the Sultan?" said she.

"You must yourself ask," replied Aladdin in a moment.

"I?" cried his mother, with surprise. "I go to the Sultan? Not I, indeed. I will take care I do not go on any such errand."

"But indeed you must, mother; and, what is more, you shall," said Aladdin, in a pet. "You must not refuse me, or I shall die."

Thus Aladdin begged hard, but his mother would not change her mind. "Think," said she, "who you are. What have you ever done for your prince? You can ask for no favour, I am sure. And, besides, those who ask favours always give presents. Tell me, what have you to give?"

For a moment or two Aladdin could make no reply. Then he thought of the fruit which he had brought from the cave, which, he had found out, was of great value.

" The jewels, mother," said he, " will make a nice present for the Sultan."

Fetching the precious stones, he put them in rows and groups on the table. They shone so brightly that both mother and son were nearly blinded. " Here is a rich present for the Sultan," said Aladdin. " Take them to him, and I am sure you will get whatever you ask for."

" I cannot, my son," said his mother. " The Sultan will order us both to be put to death."

" Nay, do not distress yourself, dear mother," said Aladdin. " Has not the lamp been a friend to us for these years past ? and now I do not think it will desert us. At all events, try ; do, mother dear."

The good woman had now not a word to say, and in a day or two was ready to try her luck at the palace.

She took a dish with the jewels in, and folded it up in a fine linen cloth. She then took another less fine, and tied the four corners of it, that she might carry it with ease. Then she set off for the palace.

The grand vizier and all the rest of the court had gone in when she came to the gate. There was a large crowd outside, but at last the gate was opened, and she went into the divan with the others. She then placed herself right in front of the Sultan.

When the court was over the Sultan went out, and the vizier and the rest went after. The people then had to go away. For several days this sort of thing took place, and each time Aladdin was sore vexed.

One day, when the court was over and the Sultan had gone to his own room, he said to his vizier, " For some time past I have seen a woman, who has come every day I hold my court, and who carries something in her hand tied up in a linen cloth. She puts herself in front of me. Do you know what she wants ? "

The vizier did not wish the Sultan to think he had not seen her. So he said, " Oh, she seems to have come on a small errand. Some one has been selling her some bad meat."

This did not please the Sultan, for he did not think that could be the reason for a woman coming to him every day as this one had done. " The very next day the court sits," said he to the vizier, " if this woman comes, do not fail to call her, that I may hear what she has to say."

The vizier then kissed the Sultan's hand, and placed it on his head to show that he would sooner die than not do his duty.

It had now become no trouble for Aladdin's mother to go to the court, as she was quite used to it. The next time the court met there she was, right in front of the Sultan.

The vizier pointed to her, which was the order for her to go to the throne and make known her wants.

Aladdin's mother bowed and took up her place. The Sultan then spoke to her in these words : " My good woman, for a long time past I have seen you at the court, but no one has spoken to you. What is your request ? "

" I dare not tell you in the open court, in front of all these people," said the woman.

" They are a present for your highness," she said

" Then have the court cleared," said the Sultan to the vizier. " This woman shall tell us what she wants in secret."

" Now, my good woman," said the Sultan, when all had gone out, " what do you want ? "

" I am afraid even now to make it known, for you may put me to death for my pains," said Aladdin's mother.

" Whatever it may be," said the Sultan, " I pardon you from this moment ; not the least harm shall come to you from anything you may say. Be bold, and speak out."

Aladdin's mother then told the Sultan how her son had seen the princess, and wished to make her his wife. He was not in the least angry, for he had given the woman full leave to say all she wished. Before he made any reply, he pointed to her bundle and said, " What have you there, tied up so well ?"

At once the woman opened her bundle and gave the jewels to the Sultan. " They are a present for your highness," said she. " They come from my son."

The Sultan could not speak for a moment ; the jewels were so rich and rare he had never before seen any so fine. Then he looked at them one by one. " How grand ! " said he. " What say you, vizier, to such a present ? "

" They are, in truth, of great value," said the vizier.

" Ay, indeed," said the Sultan. " Must not he who sends such a present be worthy of the princess my daughter, and must I not give her to him who comes and asks for her at such a price ? "

Now, some time before this took place, the Sultan had told the vizier that he would bestow the hand of the princess on his son. The vizier was afraid, therefore, that the promise would be overlooked, and that after all his son would never be the Sultan's son-in-law, a thing upon which he had set his mind.

So the vizier stepped up to the Sultan and spoke something softly in his ear.

The Sultan started. Then, turning towards Aladdin's mother, he said to her, " Go, my good woman, return to your home, and tell your son that I cannot give my daughter to him for three months. At the end of that time do you return here."

Aladdin's mother went from the court with all speed and made quick steps for home. There she met her son, who had been awaiting her return. " What news, mother ? " asked he.

Now Aladdin saw quite clearly that his mother's visit to the Sultan had not been in vain this time : for, in the first place, she was back long before he thought she would come ; and, in the second, she looked very pleased. He thought it would give his mother joy, however, to ask her.

When she had taken off her veil, and had sat down on the sofa by his side, she said, " My son, I will tell you first that you need not give up all hope of being the Sultan's son-in-law. I gave the Sultan your present, and though he was quite taken by surprise at the request I made to him, he was not displeased. At the end of three months I am to go to the court again, when the Sultan will tell me what he has made up his mind to do."

Aladdin thought himself the most happy of men. He jumped and danced about for joy, and kissed his mother over and over again. He called her a good woman, and told her what a grand lady he would make her when he should be wedded to the princess.

The three months went by very slowly indeed. To Aladdin they seemed to be an age, but at last they were over. Aladdin did not fail to send his mother to the palace on the very next morning, to put the Sultan in mind of his promise.

She went, therefore, to the palace, as her son wished, and took up her place near the Sultan. The Sultan no sooner cast his eyes that way than he knew her face, and called to mind the strange request she had made and the exact time to which he had put it off.

The Sultan called his vizier. " I see there," said he, " that good woman who brought me the jewels three months ago. Bid her come forward, and we will hear what she has to say."

The vizier doing as he was told, called the woman, who threw herself on the ground at the foot of the throne.

After she had risen the Sultan asked what she wished. " Sire," said she, " I have come to remind you of your promise to my son. The three months have gone by. What may I tell him when I return home ? "

Now when the Sultan put the woman off for three months, he thought he should never see or hear from her again, since he knew how foolish the request was. Turning to his vizier, he asked him what he should now do.

" Sire," said the vizier, " it seems to be a very strange request, but it can be refused in an easy way without giving offence to any one. Set a very high price upon the princess your daughter, so that all his riches, however great they may be, cannot reach the value. That will be the way to put a stop to his requests."

The Sultan agreed, and in a few moments said to Aladdin's mother : " Sultans, my good woman, ought always to keep their words, and I am ready to hold to mine ; but, as I cannot give my daughter to any one unless I know him to be a rich man, tell your son I will keep my word as soon as he shall send me forty large basins of pure gold quite full of the same sort of things which you have already given to me. The basins must be brought each by a black slave, led by a white slave, young, well made, and richly dressed. These are the terms. Go, tell them to your son."

Aladdin's mother once more fell at the Sultan's feet, and then withdrew from the court. On her way home she smiled within herself at the foolish thoughts of her son. " Where, indeed," said she, " is he to find so many gold basins and such a lot of jewels to fill them ? Will he go back to the cave, the entrance to which is shut up, in order to gather them from the trees ? And where can he get all those handsome slaves whom the Sultan demands ? "

As she went into the house her mind was full of these thoughts, and, meeting her son, she said, " All hope is lost, my son ; think no more of the princess. The Sultan did, indeed, treat me with kindness, but I do not suppose for a moment that you will be able to meet his demands."

She then told him all that the vizier had said, adding, " He is even now waiting for your reply ; but, between ourselves, he may wait a long time."

" Not so long as you may think, my dear mother," said Aladdin. " I will give the Sultan a great surprise. While I am thinking what to do, do you go and get dinner and leave me to myself."

As soon as his mother had gone out to buy the dinner, Aladdin took the lamp, and, having rubbed it, the genie stood before him.

In a gentle voice—for this time Aladdin had rubbed the lamp more gently than before—the genie asked the same question : " What do you wish ? I am ready to obey you as your slave, and the slave of those who have the lamp in their hands, both I and the other slaves of the lamp."

Aladdin lost no time in telling the genie what he wanted. " The Sultan, said he, " agrees to give me the hand of the princess his daughter in marriage, but he first demands forty large basins of gold filled to the very top with that fruit of the garden from which I took the lamp that you are the slave of. He asks also that these forty basins shall be carried by as many black slaves, each led by a young and handsome white slave in rich attire. Go, get me his present as soon as you can, that I may send it to the Sultan before the court is over."

The genie said that it should be done at once.

In a very short time he came back, bringing with him the slaves and the basins full of jewels. Each basin was covered with a cloth of silver, and the slaves were richly dressed. There were so many of them that they filled the house, as well as the court in front and the garden behind.

The genie asked Aladdin if there were any further orders for him ; and on being told no, went quickly out of sight.

Aladdin's mother now coming back from the market was in the greatest surprise to see so many persons and so much riches. Having set down the food which she had brought with her, she was about to take off her veil, but Aladdin put his hand on her shoulder and stopped her.

" My dear mother," cried he, " there is no time to lose. Go with these to the court at once, and tell the Sultan they are for him."

Without waiting for her reply, Aladdin opened the door that led into the street, and told all the slaves to go out one after the other. He then put a white slave in front of each of the black ones, who carried the golden basins on their heads.

When his mother, who went with the last black slave, had gone out, he shut the door, and waited quietly in his room, thinking that now the Sultan would be sure to give him his daughter for a wife.

Every one in the street stopped to see the long line of eighty slaves. The dress of each slave was made of a rich stuff, and so covered with precious stones that those who were good judges thought each of them worth more than a kingdom.

The graceful manner of each slave caused those who saw them not to take their eyes from them, so that each person stood in the same place in the street where he was.

As the way was long it took some time to get to the palace gates, but at last they were reached.

When the first of the eighty slaves was about to pass through, the porters took him to be a king, so richly was he dressed. They were about to kiss the hem of his robe when the slave, who had had his orders from the genie, stopped them, saying, " Our master will come when the time shall be proper."

Through the gates the slaves all went one after the other, and soon found their way into the court. Their dresses were far more splendid than those of the Sultan's officers, or even the Sultan's. The slaves made two rows and stood on two sides in front of the throne.

The mother of Aladdin then threw herself at the Sultan's feet, and when she had been told to rise, said, " This, sire, is what my son sends in answer to your demands. He awaits your reply."

The Sultan hardly heard the good woman speak, for he could not take his eyes away from the slaves and the golden basins of jewels which they had brought.

At length he turned to the vizier, and, in a loud voice, so that all might hear, said, " Well, vizier, what think you of the person, whoever he may be, who has now sent me so rich and fine a present, a person whom neither of us knows or has heard of before ? Do you not think he is worthy of the princess my daughter ? "

It was the duty of the vizier to make a reply that would please the Sultan, so he answered, " Far be it from me, sire, to say nay to such a person who can send a present like this."

Then all the people in the court clapped their hands in glee, and the Sultan rose from his throne. " Go, my good woman," said he, " and tell your son that I am waiting with open arms to embrace him. The sooner he comes to claim the hand of the princess my daughter, the more pleased I shall be."

Aladdin's mother bowed and retired. The Sultan then sent everybody away but the vizier. He told the slaves to carry the golden basins and the jewels into the palace that he might show them to the Sultana and his daughter.

In the meantime, Aladdin's mother, reaching home, showed by her manner how she had got on with the Sultan. Nor did she lose a moment in telling her son what had taken place. "The Sultan awaits you," added she, "and I advise you to make yourself fit to appear before him."

Aladdin went to his own room and took down the lamp which had been so true a friend to him. No sooner had he rubbed it than the genie again showed himself ready to do his bidding.

"Genie," said Aladdin, "I want you to take me to the bath, and when I have bathed, to have a rich and handsome dress ready for me."

Aladdin had no sooner given his orders than he was lifted up and carried through the air without being seen. Then he was put into a bath of the finest marble, where he was washed and rubbed with sweet perfumes. His skin became white and fresh, and his body felt lighter and more active.

He then went to the dressing-room, where, in place of his old robe, he found one more rich and handsome than a Sultan's. By the help of the genie, who waited on him, he put on each part until he was quite dressed.

Then the genie took him home in the same way as he had carried him to the bath. "Have you any further demands?" he asked.

"Yes," said Aladdin. "Bring me a horse as soon as you can, which shall be more beautiful than any horse in the Sultan's stables, and let the saddle and bridle and the wrappings be worth more than a million pounds. Let them flash with jewels of all kinds.

"I order you also at the same time to get me twenty slaves as well and richly dressed as those who carried the basins of gold, to walk on each side and behind me, and twenty more to walk in two ranks before me. You must also get six female slaves to wait on my mother. These must be dressed more richly than the princess. I also want ten thousand pieces of gold in ten purses. These are all my commands at present. Go, and make all haste."

All in a moment the genie went and came back. He brought the horse, the slaves, ten of whom had each a purse with ten thousand pieces of gold in every one, and the six female slaves each with a fine dress for Aladdin's mother wrapped in a piece of silver cloth. These he gave to Aladdin.

Aladdin took only four of the ten purses, and gave them to his mother, as he said she might want them. He left the other six in the hands of the slaves, and told them that as they went along the streets they were to throw the coins in heaps to the people.

He then gave the six female slaves to his mother, telling her that they were for her, and that the dresses which they had in the silver cloths were for her use.

And now a start was made for the palace. Aladdin mounted his horse and began the march in the order we have told. Though he had never been on horseback in his life he rode quite well, and everybody praised the grace he showed in the saddle.

The streets were thronged with people, who shouted and cheered as the slaves threw the gold pieces among them. Aladdin was so changed in looks and dress that no one knew him, not even those with whom he had played in the streets. This all came from the power of the wonderful lamp.

At length the palace was reached. The Sultan was overjoyed to see so handsome a man as Aladdin, and so gay and rich a dress as he wore. He himself had not one so thickly covered with jewels. He came down from his throne two or three steps so as to prevent Aladdin from falling down at his feet, and holding out his hand, put Aladdin to sit between himself and the vizier.

Aladdin then rose and spoke to the Sultan in these words : " O sire, I beg you not to think me rash in asking for the hand of the princess your daughter, but I should die if I did not have her for my wife."

The Sultan was charmed with Aladdin, and made a sign. At once the air was filled with the sounds of trumpets and cymbals, and Aladdin was led by the Sultan into a saloon where a great feast was served up. The Sultan and Aladdin sat at a table together, and the vizier and the chief guards waited on them.

The Sultan talked as a friend with Aladdin, and was more and more pleased with him each moment. Then he gave orders for the marriage papers to be made ready.

Aladdin, however, did not wish the wedding to take place at once. He told the Sultan that first of all he wanted to prepare a house, good and large, fit for a princess.

" That is well," said the Sultan. " There is a large open space before my palace. Take that, and build a house upon it fit for my daughter the princess."

Then Aladdin, going home, called the genie, to whom he gave orders to build him a house on the space of ground in front of the palace. It was to be built of precious stones and to contain a room full of gold for his use.

Knowing the house would be built to his orders, Aladdin sent his mother, richly dressed and attended by her slaves, to tell the princess it was ready. She set out at once.

That same night the house was built. It rose in the air with its rooms one above another. Its walls shone and its furniture was of pure gold and pearls.

In the morning the porters opened the gates of the palace, and were not able to believe their eyes, for, till that moment, they had never seen so large and so handsome a building as that which they now saw. The Sultan saw it, and called his vizier, who put it down to magic. " We shall see," he said, " what is to come of all this finery of Aladdin's."

And now the marriage took place. There had nothing been seen like it in all the world before. There were gold and silver dishes and cups, wines of the rarest sorts, and cakes of the best.

For some time Aladdin and the princess lived in happiness. They loved each other dearly, and were a joy to the Sultan and the Sultana. Sad to say, an event took place which put an end to it all.

The magician had been away from China, but now he began to think of the lamp and what had become of it. By his magic he found out it was still Aladdin's, and that he had become a rich man and a prince. The magician once more went to the city. There he saw the fine house which Aladdin had built, and felt pretty sure that the lamp was somewhere inside. Oh, if he could only tell where !

He thought of a plan. He went to the shop of a man who made and sold lamps. " I want," said he to the man, " a dozen copper lamps. Can you make them for me ? "

" To be sure ! " replied the man. " You may have them to-morrow."

Next day the magician had the lamps sent to his inn, and he thereupon took them round the city in a basket, crying out, " Who will change old lamps for new ? "

Everybody thought the magician was mad, and laughed at him. " That man," said they, " has surely lost his senses to offer new lamps for old ones." And the children hooted after him as he went along.

By-and-by he came to the street which led to Aladdin's house and the Sultan's palace. Aladdin had gone to the hunt, but his princess sat at an open window at her spinning with her maidens. All of them heard the cry, " Who will change old lamps for new ones ? "

One of the maidens laughed at the idea of changing old lamps for new, and said that the man must be joking. Then it was agreed to try him with Aladdin's lamp. " Take it down," said the princess ; " we shall then see if he is a madman or not."

Now Aladdin had never spoken of the lamp to his wife, nor had she the least idea that it was through the lamp that so much wealth and honour had come to her husband.

The slave went down to the street with the lamp, which the magician saw and knew in a moment. " A new lamp for an old one ? " said he. " Ay, truly," said the slave ; " the princess desires it." The slave then chose out a pretty new lamp, leaving the old one with the magician, and ran off to her mistress.

No sooner did the magician get the lamp in his hands than he went back towards his inn. On the way he passed along a very quiet street, where he put down his basket of new lamps and left them. Then, instead of going to his inn, he turned through the gate of the city and got out into the country.

When night came on he drew the lamp from his bosom and rubbed it. " What do you wish ? " cried the genie, who had come in an instant. " I am ready to obey you as your slave, and the slave of those who have the lamp in their hands, both I and the other slaves of the lamp."

" I command you to take up the house, which you and the other slaves of the lamp have built, near the Sultan's palace, and carry it with me and all that is in it, dead and alive, to Africa," said the magician.

At once he and the whole palace was lifted up and carried by the genie right to the spot where the magician desired.

Next day, as soon as it was light, the Sultan cast his eyes towards the palace of Aladdin. Alas ! there was nothing left but the open space of land on which it had been built. He thought his eyes were grown dim, and that he could not see ; so he rubbed them. Still there was no Aladdin's palace. Then he called his vizier. " Look there," cried he. " The new palace is gone. It has not fallen, or the ruins would be left. Alas ! my poor daughter is gone. Where is the wretch who asked her for a wife ? I shall strike off his head."

The Sultan was told that Aladdin had been gone to the hunt these two days. " Then send thirty of my horsemen to drag him before me in chains."

The horsemen were at once sent into the forest where Aladdin had

The Sultan ordered Aladdin's head to be struck off

gone, and there they found him. "Prince Aladdin," said the chief of the horsemen, "I am sorry to have to tell you that you must come to the Sultan. I hope you will pardon me, but I must do my duty."

He then took hold of Aladdin, bound him hand and foot, and carried him to the Sultan.

The moment the Sultan saw him he ordered his head to be struck off.

"Not so fast, sire," put in the vizier. "Do you not see the people making their way into the palace? Aladdin has been kind to them, and they are now going to shield him from your wrath and save him."

The Sultan looked, and saw a huge crowd of people, with swords drawn, coming with all speed to the palace. His face showed that he was in great fear. "Put up your sword," said he to the headsman, "and you, vizier, tell the people that Aladdin is safe from harm. I pardon him."

This was done.

When all was quiet the Sultan called Aladdin to him. "What have I done, sire, to vex you?" asked Aladdin, who had not yet been told what had taken place.

"Don't talk to me," said the Sultan. "Where is my dear daughter? Where is the house you built for her on the open space in front of my palace? Where? I say. Where?"

Aladdin looked through the window of the room he was in, and lo! he too was struck dumb for a moment. "Sire," said he, "the palace is surely gone, but I have had no hand in it. Pray give me forty days in which to search for your daughter, my wife; and if I do not find her, you may kill me."

This was granted, and Aladdin left the Sultan to mourn alone. Going through the city, he asked all he met if they had seen anything done to his palace, whereupon they thought he had gone mad. Then he made up his mind to leave the city and make his search beyond it.

Towards night he found himself near a river, and the idea came to him that he would drown himself. But as he stepped down the steep bank he slipped, and in doing so rubbed the ring he was wearing on the rock.

"What do you wish?" cried the genie, who had come in an instant. "I am ready to obey you as your slave, and the slave of him who has the ring upon his finger, both I and the other slaves of the ring."

How strange that Aladdin should not have thought of the ring before! "Welcome, dear genie," cried he. "Thou hast saved my life before. Save it again by giving me back my palace and my dear wife, the princess."

"What you ask," said the genie, "is not in my power. I am only the slave of the ring; you must address yourself to the slave of the lamp."

"In that case, then," said Aladdin, "at least take me to the spot where my palace is, and place me under the window of the princess." He had barely said this before the genie, lifting him up, bore him through the air to Africa, near a large city, and in the midst of a meadow, in which the palace stood. Setting him down under one of the windows of the princess's room, he there left him.

All this was the work of an instant.

It was night, and Aladdin slept soundly beneath a tree. Next morning he was roused by the princess opening the window. He looked up and there saw her. She saw him too, and bade him come to her through a secret door.

Soon they embraced each other with tears of joy, and then Aladdin asked her what had become of the lamp. The poor princess told him all, and begged him to forgive her, which he did, saying it must be got again by some means. He felt sure that the taking away of the palace was the work of the magician.

Then Aladdin formed his plans. He went into the city and bought a drug, which he gave to the princess later in the day, asking her to put it in the magician's wine at supper that evening.

The princess hardly liked to do such a thing, even though the magician had treated her so ill; but she did it, and no sooner had he drunk his wine than he sank a helpless corpse on the floor

Aladdin lay in hiding near the palace, and at a signal went to the princess. All the slaves and servants were sent to their own rooms while Aladdin searched for the lamp. He found it in the magician's bosom, and at once rubbed it hard.

In less time than it takes to tell the story the genie came, to whom Aladdin gave orders for the palace to be carried back just as it was to China.

The Sultan, who, in the meantime, had hardly had a wink of sleep, looked once more through his window and beheld the palace in its place. Aladdin, who had risen early, thought the Sultan would lose no time in coming to see his daughter, so he went out to meet him. The Sultan came, and he and Aladdin were friends once more. Great was the joy of every one of them, and all trouble was cast aside.

Now it chanced that the magician had a brother from whom he had been parted many years. This brother found out that the magician had been put to death by poison, and that it had been done by a princess who was wedded to a rich man of low birth. He looked for this princess in all parts of the world, and at last came to the city where Aladdin lived.

In the city there also lived a holy woman whose name was Fatima. The magician's brother made his way to her, and bade her, under pain of death, to change her clothes for his. When this was done the brother, whom we will now call Fatima and speak of as a woman, went to the palace of Aladdin and began to talk with the princess.

So pleased was the princess with the holy woman that she asked her to stay with her in the palace.

That was just what Fatima wanted, so she said she would. " Rise, then," said the princess, " follow me, and we will choose your room."

Fatima did so with feeble steps, and soon the holy woman was lodged in the palace. Every day she saw the princess, and the two became fast friends.

One day, when walking through the rooms, they came to the saloon which was the best room in the palace. Fatima said she liked it very much, but there was one thing wanting—the egg of a roc hung from the centre dome.

When Aladdin came home, having been absent for some days, the princess was sad. " What is the matter, my dear ? " he asked. " Have you not all you wish for to make you happy ? "

" I thought we had the most beautiful palace in the world," said the princess, " but now I find out that there is one thing wanting to make it complete—the egg of a roc hung from the centre dome of the saloon."

" As for that," said Aladdin, " it shall be done at once." Then going to the saloon he rubbed the lamp, which he now always kept in his bosom. The genie came, and, on hearing what Aladdin wished, he gave such a wild and loud shriek that the walls of all the palace shook.

" Wretch," cried the genie, " you want me to hang my master from the dome ; but it is a good thing for you that the request is not your own. It comes from the magician's brother, who is now in this palace, dressed as a holy woman. Find him, and slay him at once."

Then Aladdin went back to the princess, and the holy woman was sent for. She came, and Aladdin asked her to cure a pain which he had in his head.

Now was the holy woman's chance to slay Aladdin and secure the lamp.

He bent his head for Fatima to place her hand upon it, when lo ! all at once Aladdin rose, seized a dagger which Fatima had already grasped from under her cloak, and thrust it into her heart.

" What have you done ? " cried the princess.

" This is not a holy woman at all," said Aladdin, " but the brother of that cruel magician who has done us both so much hurt. He has come to his fate. Now we shall indeed be happy."

These words were spoken in truth, for Aladdin and his dear princess lived for many years in each other's love ; and, when the Sultan died, Aladdin took his place and ruled his land in peace.

Ali Baba loaded his ass with some of the gold

THE STORY OF ALI BABA AND THE FORTY THIEVES

ALI BABA and Cassim were brothers who lived in a town in Persia. Cassim was rich and famous, while Ali Baba was so poor that he had to earn a living by cutting wood and selling it in the town.

One day when Ali Baba was in the forest he saw a number of horsemen coming towards him, and fearing that they might be robbers he quickly climbed a tree and hid himself.

There were forty in all, and when they came near the tree where Ali Baba was hiding they dismounted. After they had tied up their horses and fed them, they all turned and followed their captain to a rock near by. " Open Sesame," cried the leader, and a door opened in the rock. The men entered one by one, and the captain followed ; then the door closed of itself.

Ali Baba waited, and after some time he saw the robbers filing out again. When they were out of sight he went up to the rock and called out, " Open Sesame." The door flew open at the words, and Ali Baba stepping inside was surprised to find himself in a well-lighted cavern, filled with all sorts of valuable goods piled one upon another. There were bales of silk, rolls of rich carpeting, heaps of gold and silver ingots, and bags of money.

Ali Baba loaded his asses with some of the gold, and, having covered the bags with his sticks, hurried home to tell his wife of his good fortune. She was overjoyed at the sight of all the money, and wanted to count it ; but Ali Baba advised her not to take the trouble, as there was so much. " Then

I will borrow a small measure from your brother Cassim and measure it, and while I am away you can be digging a hole for it," she said.

Now, Cassim's wife, knowing how poor her sister-in-law was, felt greatly surprised that she wanted a measure. So, in order to find out what it was for, she slyly put some suet at the bottom of the measure. Ali Baba's wife going home filled it again and again with the gold, and then, being anxious to return the measure as quickly as possible, hurried off with it without noticing that a piece of gold was sticking to the bottom.

Of course Ali Baba's secret was out, and early next morning, Cassim, going to his brother, threatened to take him before the sheriff if he did not confess the whole truth about the coin. Ali Baba even had to repeat the very words to be used in order to open the door in the rock.

However, although Cassim managed to enter the cave, he was so busy picking up as much treasure as he could and thinking how wealthy he would now be that he quite forgot the magic words. He tried over and over again to remember them; but it was of no use, he only became more confused.

Now, at noon the robbers came, and when Cassim saw the door open he tried to rush out past them, but they quickly put him to death with their swords.

Next day, when Ali Baba came to the cave to look for his brother, he was horrified to find his body cut in pieces, which were hung up just inside the door. As soon as it was dark, he carried the body to his sister-in-law's house, and unloading his ass in the courtyard, told Morgiana, a very sharp and intelligent slave, what was in the bundles.

Morgiana very cleverly spread abroad the news that her master was ill, and later that he was dead. Then she led Mustapha, an old shoemaker, blindfolded to the house, and bribed him well to sew the parts of Cassim's body together. After that Cassim was buried as if he had died a natural death.

Three or four days after the funeral, Ali Baba removed to the widow's house, taking all his own goods during the day; but the money he had removed from the cave he carried at night.

Meanwhile the robbers when they went to the cave were amazed to find Cassim's body taken away. They were not only amazed, they were terrified at the thought of having been discovered and of losing their riches.

" We must find the man who knows our secret, and kill him," said the captain decidedly. " The only way in which we can discover him is by keeping a spy in the town, and, to make certain that he will do his work properly, I promise that he shall be put to death if he fails."

Without the least sign of fear, one of the robbers jumped to his feet and offered himself for the task. Every one praised him for his courage, and when he had been well disguised, he was allowed to set out.

In due course he came to the stall of Mustapha, and by means of a number of clever questions found out from the shoemaker that he had lately sewn together the pieces of a dead body.

The robber opened his eyes when he heard this, and asked to be shown the house where such a strange task had been given a shoemaker. Mustapha, on the promise of several pieces of gold, allowed himself to be blindfolded and with some difficulty managed to lead the way to Cassim's house.

In order that he should not miss the house when he returned with his companions, the robber put a white chalk mark on the door, and having thanked Mustapha, made his way back to the camp. When the captain heard of this success he decided that the robbers should enter the city and slay the man who had learned their secret.

Meanwhile, Morgiana's sharp eyes had seen the mark on her master's door ; she could not understand why it was there, but, going out, she made chalk marks exactly the same on several of the neighbours' doors.

So, when the robbers came they could not tell which was the house they were seeking. The captain was very angry, and, thinking the spy had played him a trick, exclaimed, " Let the false guide be put to death ! " on which the robber was quickly slain.

In spite of this, however, another came forward and offered to play the spy. He thought that if he marked the door with red chalk in a place not easily to be seen, all would be well. But Morgiana's quick eyes again discovered the mark, and when the robbers came they found so many doors with red marks that they were no further on than before.

The captain at once ordered the second offender to be put to death, and he himself set out to discover the house, with the help of Mustapha. When he had walked up and down in front of it long enough to fix the appearance of it firmly in his memory, he went back to the camp. " Go into all the villages about," he said, " and buy nineteen mules, with thirty-eight large leather jars, one full of oil, and the others empty."

Two days later all was ready. The mules were loaded with thirty-seven robbers in jars and one jar of oil. The captain led the way to the house. Ali Baba was sitting at the door at the time, and when the captain told him that he was on the way to the market with oil, he bade him welcome to his house. The jars were left in the garden, but the captain managed to whisper to the man in each : " When you hear me throw a few stones from my window, make haste to join me."

Fortunately, Morgiana's lamp went out for lack of oil while she was busy at her work, and there was no oil in the house. There seemed nothing for her to do but to go into the garden and take some oil out of the jars. Thus the robber's plot was found out, for instead of oil Morgiana discovered a man in the first jar she opened. " Is it time ? " he whispered. " Not yet," she replied softly.

She had to open several jars before discovering the oil, but, as soon as she got it, she ran into the house, filled a kettle with oil, boiled it, and poured enough into every jar to stifle the robber within.

Ali Baba was filled with amazement when he learned next morning that he had been entertaining the captain of the robbers. His gratitude to Morgiana knew no bounds, and he gave her her liberty with the promise of another reward later.

Meanwhile the captain, who had escaped over the wall and returned to his cave, wished to have his revenge on Ali Baba. Accordingly, he started a silk mercer's business, and was overjoyed to discover that Ali Baba's son lived opposite his shop. He gave him presents, invited him to dinner, and did everything he could think of to make friends with him.

Then Ali Baba asked his son's new friend to dine with him. This was the captain's chance. He was known at this time by the name of Cogia Houssain, and at the time appointed Ali Baba's son took him to his father's house. The faithful Morgiana was still there.

Now it happened that as Cogia Houssain said he had made a vow never to touch salt, Ali Baba gave orders to Morgiana to put no salt in the food. Of course, Morgiana could not rest till she had seen this strange visitor who did not like salt, so she helped Abdallah to carry up the dishes.

The first glance at Cogia Houssain told her that he was the captain of the robbers. " I must save my master, or this false merchant will slay him," she said to herself. Going to her room, she put on the dress of a dancer, and fastened round her waist a handsome girdle from which hung a dagger. Then, having hid her face under a mask, she said to Abdallah, " Bring your tabor, and we will amuse our master and his guest with music and dancing."

Morgiana danced gracefully round and round the room to Abdallah's music, and then suddenly seizing the dagger in her right hand, pretended to stab herself ; but as she swept past Cogia Houssain she buried it deep in his breast.

Ali Baba and his son were filled with horror ; but when Morgiana opened the pretended Cogia Houssain's cloak and showed them a dagger, and told them who he really was, Ali Baba embraced her, and gave her to his son in marriage.

In due course Ali Baba taught his son the secret of the cave, which he in turn handed down to his son, and with the riches they found they were all able to live in comfort and even splendour.

The Prince was carried high in the air

THE ENCHANTED HORSE

IN the fair land of Persia, long, long ago, the first day of each year was kept as a time of great rejoicing, when people of all countries brought before the sultan any new or wonderful things they had. On one of these feast days a poor Indian came, and he claimed to have the most wonderful horse that had ever been made by man.

"I praise my horse," said he, "not for his looks, but for what he is able to do. He will carry me to any place I wish to visit, and if your majesty chooses, I will show you his power."

"Go then," replied the sultan, "to yonder mountain and bring back to me a branch of the palm that grows at its foot."

Mounting the horse, the Indian turned a peg in the creature's neck, and the next moment was carried into the air and out of sight. In less than a quarter of an hour, he came back, bearing the palm branch in his hand.

Upon this, the sultan offered to buy the horse, but the Indian would not take money for it.

"I will take only your daughter in exchange for the horse," he said, at which the officers standing round laughed aloud; but the prince, the son of the sultan, fearing his father might make the bargain, drew near and said, "Sir, you surely will not insult the princess, my sister, by giving her in marriage to this vain fellow!"

"Son!" replied the sultan, "it may be the man will take some other reward for the animal, which is so truly wonderful, that I do not wish any other prince to become the owner of it. But, before I bargain with him, I should like to see you try the animal."

142

To this the Indian agreed, and the prince mounted ; but, before the Indian had told him what to do, he turned the peg, and was carried high into the air.

" Sir," cried the Indian, turning to the sultan in alarm, " I pray you will not blame me should any harm befall the prince, your son. I would have told him all he should know of the working of the horse had he given me the chance. Unless he finds the second peg, he cannot return to the earth again."

On hearing this, the sultan became greatly troubled, and the Indian, in order to calm him, continued, " Have no fear, your majesty. The horse will carry him safely over sea and land, and should he fail to see the second peg, he has but to wish to be in a certain place, and the horse will even carry him there."

" I hope that what you say is true," the sultan answered, " but, in case it is not, I shall keep you in prison until my son returns."

Now, the prince, on finding the horse travel on and on, rising higher and higher all the time, tried his best to stop it. At last, after some searching, he found the second peg, which he turned. No sooner had he done this than the horse began to descend, and the prince at length found himself on the roof of a great palace. It was now quite dark, for the night had come, but after a time he found a small staircase, which led him to a small room, where lay several enormous black servants fast asleep.

Passing these with great care, he entered another room, where, on a raised bed, lay a beautiful princess, and around her several women all sound asleep. Feeling that his only safety lay in begging the princess to protect him, he wakened her.

" Princess," he said when her eyes were open, " you see before you the son of the King of Persia, who finds himself in your palace, and at the mercy of your servants, unless you will have the goodness to help him."

" Prince," replied the lady, who was the daughter of the King of Bengal, " have no fear. In this country you will find nothing but welcome. As you must be in need of food and rest, I will send some of my women to see to your comfort, and in the morning I will hear your strange story."

Upon this the women led the prince to a large room filled with much beautiful furniture, and, while some got food for him, others made ready a bed, on which, as soon as he had eaten, he lay down.

In the morning the princess dressed herself with more than usual care, for she already loved the handsome prince who had come to her in so strange a manner. As soon as she was ready, " Go," said she to a servant, " to the Prince of Persia, and ask if he is ready to receive a visit from me." The prince, having heard the message, awaited her coming with great joy.

" Prince," she said, as soon as the greetings were over, " I came here because no one will come into this room. I pray you tell me to what I owe the pleasure of seeing you in my palace."

The prince told her of the coming of the poor Indian to the feast of the New Year, of his wonderful horse, and of his wish to exchange it for the hand of the Princess of Persia. He told her, too, of his own fear lest his father should consent, and also of his folly in leaving the ground without first having learned the working of the animal.

" At last," he said, " I found a second peg, and turning it, was soon brought down to the terrace on the roof of your palace. Creeping softly down the stairs and past your servants, I reached your room and wakened you. The rest of the story is known to you, and all that is now left for me to do is to thank you for your goodness, and to declare that you have already won my heart by your beauty and your kindness."

On this, the princess, blushing with pleasure, answered, " Prince, I have listened to your story with great interest, but I can hardly help shaking with fear when I think of your danger. It is well that the enchanted horse brought you to my palace. I do not, however, find myself able to believe that I have won your heart, for it is far more likely that you have given it some fair lady of Persia."

It was now time for dinner, and the princess, leading the way to a beautiful hall, sat down with the prince to a most dainty repast.

" Prince," said the princess, when dinner was over, " you may now be thinking of returning to your own country ; but you should not leave the kingdom of Bengal without first seeing the palace of the king my father."

Now, though the Prince of Persia would gladly have done this, he felt he could not visit the father of the princess in the clothing he then wore. When he told the princess this, she replied that she would supply him with all he needed, feeling sure that if her father saw the Prince of Persia, he would allow her to marry him.

The prince, however, would not agree. " If you will permit me," he said, " I will first return to Persia and let my father know of my safety ; then I will come back, not as a stranger but as a prince, and ask your hand in marriage."

Yet, as the princess seemed so little pleased to let him go, he stayed on and on until he had been two whole months in the kingdom of Bengal. Banquets and balls were given in his honour ; but at last he resolved to set out for Persia and to take the princess with him.

Placing her on the enchanted horse, therefore, he mounted behind, turned the peg, and was quickly carried to the chief city of his father's kingdom. Here he left the princess in the care of the housekeeper, at one of his father's smaller residences on the outskirts of the town, and hurried off to the sultan, who had long thought him dead.

When the sultan had heard the prince's story, he ordered that all signs of mourning in the court should be put away, and declared that he would not only consent to the marriage, but that he would himself go and meet the princess whom his son so dearly loved.

Before setting out, however, he sent for the Indian, to whom he said, " I kept you in prison in order to put you to death unless my son returned in safety. I thank God he has so returned. Go, therefore, take your horse, and never enter my kingdom again."

Now the Indian, having learned on his way from the prison about the princess whom the king's son had brought home, resolved, on leaving the palace, to carry her off. And this he did with little trouble, for the princess, thinking he had been sent to fetch her, mounted the horse with him, and was carried away over the heads of the sultan and the prince, who, though they saw her, could not help her.

The king returned in sorrow to the palace, but the prince, dressing himself as a dervish, set out to find where she had been carried, and to save her from the wicked Indian, who meant to make her his wife.

But the princess, on learning what the Indian wished, would not listen to him ; so he treated her with great violence, and one day, when he was more cruel than usual, she screamed so loudly that some horsemen passing by came to her aid.

One of these horsemen proved to be the Sultan of Cashmere, and he, hearing the princess's story, slew the Indian, and took her to his own palace, meaning to marry her for himself, for he was much struck by her wonderful beauty.

Though he had not yet asked her consent, he ordered the rejoicings to begin at once ; but the princess, having given her word to the Prince of Persia, would not marry the Sultan of Cashmere, and, in order to stop him from forcing her to do so, she pretended to go mad.

So wildly did she behave that the sultan sent for many doctors, none of whom, however, could cure her.

At last the sultan offered a reward to any doctor of any country who should restore the Princess of Bengal to health again.

Now it chanced that the Prince of Persia heard of this, and feeling sure the sick person must be his own lost princess went to Cashmere. By the sultan's leave he entered the room in which she was sitting, and singing softly to herself of the prince to whom she had given her heart.

On seeing him she took him for another doctor, for his beard had grown very long, so she flew into a great rage. But the prince, speaking so that none but she could hear, told her who he was, and that he had come to save her. On this she grew quiet, and the prince, returning to the sultan, said he thought he could cure her if he were allowed to do it in his own way. " But, sir," he said, " it would be of great help to me if I knew how the princess came to be in Cashmere, which is very far from her own country."

To this the sultan replied that she had been carried there by an Indian on an enchanted horse, which he had put in his treasury because it was such a wonderful animal.

" That horse," said the prince, " is the cause of all the trouble. The princess has been enchanted by riding on it, and I am now sure I can cure her by the aid of the animal, if your majesty will order it to be brought out into the great square before the palace."

The very next day the enchanted horse was placed in the square, and all the people and the nobles of the court stood around, to watch the new doctor cure the Princess of Bengal of her madness.

Dressed in rich garments, with jewels sparkling on her neck and wrists, the princess came from the castle, with a great many ladies, who helped her to mount the enchanted horse. In full view of the sultan and all his people she sat, while the pretended doctor walked three times round the horse, his hands crossed on his breast, and strange words coming from his lips.

Then, placing round the horse a great many vessels of fire he had ordered to be brought, he mounted behind the princess, who was quite hidden by the thick smoke, turned the peg, and, before any one knew what was happening, both of them were carried high into the air.

" Sultan of Cashmere," cried the Prince of Persia, as they passed over his head, " the next time you wish to marry a lady, you had better first ask her consent."

The enchanted horse soon carried them back to Persia, where, as soon as possible, the prince and princess were married. The Sultan of Persia was quite willing, and the King of Bengal thought his daughter greatly honoured in being chosen by so brave a man as the prince had proved himself to be.

" This is a magic carpet," the merchant told the Prince

PRINCE AHMED AND THE FAIRY PERIE BANOU

THERE was once a sultan who had three sons, Houssain, Ali, and Ahmed. He had also a niece whom he had reared among his own children. Her name was Nouronnihar, and each of the three princes, her cousins, loved her and hoped one day to marry her.

Now the sultan did not wish to favour any of his sons, though he hoped that one of them would become the husband of the princess. He said they should all three travel for a time, and the one who brought back to him the most curious and wonderful thing should marry Nouronnihar.

On a certain day, they set out dressed as merchants, each with an officer clothed as a slave, and carrying a goodly sum of money which their father had given them to pay their expenses, and to spend on buying any rare article they wished to bring home.

On the first day they travelled together till night fell, when they put up at an inn. Before setting out again, they agreed to meet at the same inn at the end of the year, so that they might return together to the palace.

Houssain, after three months of travel over desert, and mountain, and fertile country, at length reached Bisnagar, the chief town of the kingdom of that name which lies on the coast of India. Here he took a room in a khan, in the quarter of the city set apart for foreign merchants.

Every thing in Bisnagar showed that the people were very rich. The shops were filled with rare goods, and all the merchants of one trade had their shops in one street.

The buildings were so splendid, and all the goods so costly that Houssain could scarcely believe his own eyes. He walked through the city day after day in the hope of finding something, the like of which had never before been seen, and, one day, while resting in a shop, he heard a man crying a carpet for sale.

Now, as the carpet was small and the price asked very large, Houssain said to the seller, " There must be something strange about the carpet that you ask thirty purses for it ! "

" Thirty ! " said the man, " nay, I will not sell it for that now. Forty purses must be paid for this magic carpet ; why, it will carry any one who sits on it to any place where he wishes to be."

" If the carpet is what you say," said Houssain, " I will not only give you forty purses for it, but a present for yourself beside."

" Sir," cried the man, " to prove the truth of my words, I will come with you to the inner room of this shop, and sit upon the carpet with you, when, if you so desire, we shall be carried at once to the khan where you lodge."

The merchant having given them leave, Houssain and the seller spread the carpet on the floor of his back shop, when they were at once carried across the city to the khan in which the prince had taken a room.

" Surely," thought Houssain, " the princess will be mine ; no one can find a more wonderful thing than this."

He paid the forty purses asked for the carpet, and gave the seller twenty more for himself.

There were still some months to pass before the day came on which he had agreed to meet his brothers, so he resolved to remain in Bisnagar and learn all he could of the manners and customs of the country.

After seeing all the wonders of Bisnagar, Houssain decided to return to the inn. So he bade his officer sit beside him on the magic carpet, and they were at once carried there.

On the day Houssain had set out for the Indian coast, his second brother, Ali, had made his way toward Persia. On the third day he found a caravan, and went with the merchants till they reached Schiraz, which was then the capital of the kingdom.

Dressed as a jeweller, he took lodgings in a khan among other jewellers. One morning, while walking through that quarter of the city in which jewels and precious stones were sold, he chanced to hear a crier offering for sale an ivory tube about a foot long and an inch thick.

" Thirty purses for the tube ! " cried the man, and Ali, going up to a merchant who stood at his shop door, said, " Is the man mad, that he asks thirty purses for so small an article ? "

" Indeed no," replied the merchant, " he is one of our best criers. If he asks thirty purses, you may be sure the tube is worth it ; but come in and sit down a while ; he will pass the door soon, and I will ask him to show you the tube."

" This gentleman," he said to the crier some little time later, " thinks you are out of your senses to ask so much for the tube."

" You are not the only one who thinks me mad," said the crier, turning to Ali ; " but the tube is worth more than it appears to be. You see it has glass at both ends, and by looking through one of the glasses you can see anything you desire."

" Tell me through which to look," cried Ali, " and, if your words prove true, I will give you forty purses for the tube."

The crier having shown him, Ali looked through the tube and saw his father sitting on his throne, and surrounded by his council. Then, as he loved Nouronnihar best of any one in the world after his father, he wished to see her. And this he did.

She was sitting at her dressing-table, with her women all about her; and Ali thinking his present to his father would certainly be the greatest wonder, said to himself, " She will soon be my wife."

He therefore bought the tube, but spent some months in seeing the city and the places round about it before setting out for the inn. On reaching the house he was surprised to find his eldest brother had been there for three months.

" You cannot have gone far," said he to Houssain. When he learned that Houssain had spent three months in reaching the city where he had bought his present and had stayed there for four or five months after buying it, he was puzzled to know how he had got back to the inn.

" Unless you flew here, I cannot understand it," he said.

" I cannot explain," Houssain replied, " until Ahmed comes; then I will tell you."

Both the brothers were just as much puzzled about what each had bought, but, although they said nothing, each felt sure of winning the princess by the strangeness of his gift.

Now Ahmed had taken the road to Samarcande on the morning when the brothers set out on their travels, and, falling in with some travelling jewellers, he dressed himself as they did, and went with them, on reaching the city, to their inn.

The next day, in the part of the town given up to the traders, he heard a man crying an apple for sale. It was not a real apple. It had been made by a very clever doctor, who died before he could use it upon himself as the crier declared it could be used.

" This apple," said the crier, " has the power to cure all diseases; even were a man almost dead, it would bring him back to life and good health."

" If what you say is true," said Ahmed, " I will pay you forty purses for the apple."

Now it chanced that a man in the crowd had a friend who was very ill, so the crier went to the sick man's house and cured him of his sickness. Ahmed then paid him the forty purses asked for the apple, and took it away in great joy, " For," thought he, " there can be nothing more wonderful than this in all the world."

After spending a little time in seeing the beautiful parts of the kingdom of Samarcande, Ahmed joined the first caravan starting for the Indies, and in good time reached the inn where his brothers awaited him.

The greetings being over, Houssain said to his brothers, " There will be plenty of time later to speak of our travels; let us now show each other the curious things we have bought. This carpet is so wonderful that I believe you will both think it the strangest thing of which you have ever heard. It will carry whoever sits on it to any place, far or near, to which he may wish to go.

"I paid forty purses for it in Bisnagar, and when I was ready to leave the city, the carpet was the carriage which brought my servant and me here. I will allow you to see the carpet at work whenever you please."

"I must own," said Ali, when Houssain had made an end of speaking, "that the carpet is a most surprising thing ; but there are others quite as wonderful. This ivory tube will allow you to see any one you wish, simply by looking through the glass at one end of it. Take it, and judge for yourself."

Houssain, to whom Ali had offered the tube, took it, and wishing to see Nouronnihar, and to know if she were well and happy, looked through the glass, when his face became full of trouble.

The three brothers sat on the carpet and were carried home

"Alas, brothers," he cried, "the charming princess whom we all love so much is about to die. Take the glass, and you will see her in bed, with all her servants standing round and weeping." When Ali had looked at Nouronnihar, Ahmed took the glass and, having taken one glance at the dying princess, said, "It is true ; she is at death's door ; but if we can reach her quickly, we may save her life. This apple has the power to cure any disease ; the person who smells it, even though dying, will be restored to health and strength. I have seen its power, and am sure it will save Nouronnihar if we can get to her in time."

"Come, then," said Houssain, "the carpet will just hold the three of us ; but first we must direct our servants to join us at the palace."

Seating themselves on the carpet, they all wished to be carried to their cousin's room. Their arrival at the palace caused no little surprise, for they had not been expected ; but Prince Ahmed no sooner found himself in Nouronnihar's bedroom than he went to her side and put the apple to her nose.

In a few minutes she opened her eyes, sat up in bed, and, speaking as though newly wakened from a sound sleep, asked to be dressed.

Her women, however, told her how much she owed to her three cousins, and most of all to Ahmed, but for whom she would surely have died. Nouronnihar thanked them, and they, saying how glad they were to have helped her, went to the sultan, their father, to show him the wonderful things they had brought.

Now the sultan had heard that Nouronnihar, whom he loved as a daughter, had been cured by the apple, but he listened to his son's stories with great attention.

"It is true," he said, when they had finished speaking, "that Ahmed's apple cured the princess, but it was Ali's tube that told you she was ill, and Houssain's carpet that brought you here in time to save her. Thus each article is as wonderful as the other, and neither the princess nor myself can choose between them. I must find some other way of deciding whose wife she shall be.

"Fetch your bows and arrows, and meet me on the great plain beyond the city. I will give Nouronnihar to him who shoots the farthest. I thank you all for the gifts you have brought, and shall look after them with great care."

Having taken each his bow and arrow, the three princes, followed by many people, went to the plain. Houssain, being the eldest, shot first, Ali second and Ahmed last. Ahmed's arrow seemed to go farthest; but, as it could not be found, the sultan said Nouronnihar should be given to Ali, whose shot had been longer than that of Houssain, and the wedding took place a few days afterwards.

Houssain at once gave up all right to the crown, and became a dervish, and Ahmed stole away to seek the arrow he had lost. Going to the great plain, he travelled on and on till, reaching some steep rocks, he found the missing arrow.

"Surely," he said to himself, "there is something very strange in this, for no man living could shoot an arrow so far. Perhaps what I have thought my greatest sorrow may be turned into my greatest joy after all."

Seeing an opening in the rocks he passed through, when, lo! there appeared before him an iron door that had no lock. With a slight push it flew open, and Prince Ahmed, entering, found himself in the courtyard of a most beautiful palace. Just as he reached the porch, a beautiful lady, with many others quite as lovely, came toward him, saying, "Come near, Prince Ahmed, you are welcome."

Now, as Ahmed had never before seen or heard of the lady, he felt some surprise that she knew him. Having bowed low before her, he replied, "Madam, I thank you for your kind welcome; but will you do me the favour of telling me how you know me, when I have never even heard of you?"

"Prince," answered the beautiful lady, "if you will come into the hall, where we shall be more comfortable, I will tell you."

"You are surprised," she said, after they were seated on a splendid sofa, "that I know you; yet I know your brothers also, and the travels you undertook in order to win the Princess Nouronnihar. It was I who caused

A beautiful lady came forward to greet him

to be put up for sale the three articles you and they bought. It was I, also, who carried your arrow so far away, as I wished to give you greater happiness than you would have had as the husband of Nouronnihar.

" It is not strange that you know nothing of me, as I am a fairy. My name is Perie Banou, and I am the daughter of a genie. In our world it is the custom for the ladies to propose marriage, and, as I love you, and am willing to marry you, I hope you will be my husband."

Now Prince Ahmed had fallen in love with the fairy on first seeing her ; so he was quite as willing to marry her as she had hoped he would be. The wedding was a very simple one, as all weddings are in fairyland. Before the marriage feast was ready, Perie Banou took the prince through all the halls and rooms in her splendid palace ; and Prince Ahmed no longer envied his brother Ali.

He thought Perie Banou was more beautiful, more agreeable, and far more wealthy than the princess, his cousin ; so for six months he lived at her palace in great happiness. At the end of that time, however, he began to wish to see his father, and said so to his wife ; but she, fearing he might not return, begged him not to leave her.

Now Ahmed really loved his wife with all his heart, so he yielded to her wish. Often, however, as they sat talking, he spoke of his father, for whom he had great affection, and who, he feared, was sorely troubled at his long absence.

Indeed, this was so ; as the sultan grieved very much for his youngest son. On hearing he had left the palace, he had sent to all the countries near, asking that if his son had been seen anywhere, he should at once be sent back to his home.

In spite of all his care, nothing was heard of Prince Ahmed, so at last, sending for his grand vizier, he said to him, " Vizier, you know that Ahmed was my best loved son. I am so troubled about him that I shall surely die. Help me, therefore, for pity's sake, to find him."

On this, the vizier, who had a great regard for the sultan, sent for a certain witch, by whose aid, perhaps, the prince might be found.

The witch came in a little time, and, having heard what was wanted, said, " Give me until to-morrow. I may then perhaps be able to help you."

But, on the next day, all she could tell the sultan of his lost son was, that he still lived, and with this he had to be content.

At last, the fairy seeing how truly Ahmed loved her, and the wish he still had to see his father, agreed to let him go, if he would promise not to make too long a stay, nor to tell his father of his marriage.

" Beg him," she said, " to believe that you are happy ; that you could wish nothing more than you have, and tell him you came back only to set his mind at rest about you."

Mounted on a fine horse, and with twenty men, all well mounted and clothed, Prince Ahmed at length set out for his father's palace, which was not far away. As he rode slowly into the city, he was followed by crowds of people, even into the presence of his father.

The sultan met him with great joy, but could not keep from asking why he had left the court in so great a hurry.

" Sir," replied Ahmed, " it was not good that I should stay to see the happiness of my brother Ali, so I set out to find the lost arrow. And this I did. The arrow lay upon the ground at the foot of some steep rocks, on the further side of the great plain, and I thought there was meaning in the flight of the arrow that might lead to my happiness.

" So it proved to be ; for, without leaving the spot, I became very happy, and my only reason for returning is that you might cease to worry about me. I beg you to ask no questions, for I may answer none ; only give me leave to come often and see you."

The sultan would have liked to learn his son's secret, but he understood this could not be ; so he begged Ahmed to come whenever he would, saying that it would be a great joy to see him.

On the fourth day Ahmed returned to the fairy, who gave him leave to visit his father once every month. This he did, going each time in richer clothing and with more gaily dressed officers. The sultan was always full of joy at his coming, but some of the viziers, jealous of Ahmed's wealth, at length tried to set his father against him. " Some day," said they, " the people will make him their ruler in your place."

" You are mistaken," the sultan answered ; " my son loves me, and I have faith in him."

But they, far from letting the matter rest, lost no chance of making him believe that Ahmed meant to turn him off the throne. Though not letting them see how their words troubled him, he could not help thinking of them when in the quiet of his own room. At last he made up his mind to send for the witch again.

" You were right," he said to her, " in saying my son Ahmed was alive. For that I thank you. I now want you to do me another favour. I have seen him many times lately, but I cannot discover where he lives. He is here at this moment, but, as I never know when he goes away, I pray you wait in the road, watch well where he goes, and tell me."

Now the witch knew well where the prince had found his arrow, so she went there, and hid among the rocks till he came with his servants. She watched carefully; but all at once they went out of sight, and though she looked again and again about the hollow, she could find no opening of any kind.

Going back to the sultan, she told him all she had seen. "But," she added, "I will not now tell you what I think. When I am quite sure about it I will let you know, but you must ask no questions as to how I found it out."

The witch went to the sultan and told him about his son

"Do as you think fit," the sultan replied. "I will await your news. Take this diamond; it is a small payment for what you have done; when you have found the secret I will pay you much more."

Knowing that Prince Ahmed always visited his father once a month, the witch made up a cunning plan. Going to the rocks a day or two before the time of starting she waited, and, as soon as she saw him drawing near, laid her head upon the rocks as if in great pain.

"Good woman," said the prince, riding to the spot where she lay; "get up behind one of my servants; I will take you where you will be well cared for."

Upon this the witch tried to rise, and the prince, thinking she was really ill, told two of his men to set her on a horse and bring her into the fairy's palace.

"My princess," he said to his wife, who was surprised to see him return so soon, " I found this woman lying sick upon the road. I pray that she may be given the help which she needs."

The princess, telling two of her women to take the witch into a certain room and attend to her, replied, " Prince, I am glad to see you so kind-hearted, but I fear trouble will come from this. The woman is not so sick as she pretends ; but do not be uneasy, I will guard you against all the traps laid for you."

" My princess," said Ahmed, nothing moved by the fears of his wife, " I have never done wrong to any one in my life, and I do not think any one would try to wrong me."

With these words, he once more started for his father's court, where he was warmly greeted, as usual, while the sick woman was tended with great care by those into whose charge she had been given. They carried her into a grand room, and put her into a bed with the finest linen sheets and a gold coverlet.

They gave her a drink from a cup of priceless china, and when she asked to be taken to their mistress to thank her, they led her through halls filled with costly furniture to one in which Perie Banou sat upon a throne of massy gold.

" Good woman," said the fairy, on seeing her, " I am glad to have been of use to you, and to know that you are now able to continue your journey; but, before you go, you may like to see my palace—my women will show it to you."

Led by these women, who were themselves fairies, the witch passed through halls whose splendour drew from her many cries of delight, and yet this was but a small part of the fairy's wealth. At last they let her out at the iron door through which she had entered, but, though she tried her best to find it again after it had been shut, she could not do so.

However, as this was the only thing in which she had failed, she went to tell her news to the sultan.

After telling her story she added, " I fear this fairy, to whom your son is married, may lead him into wishing to rule in your stead, and this is a serious matter, which your majesty would do well to consider."

Now the sultan had been told this so often that he was beginning to believe it ; therefore, bidding the witch follow him into his council chamber, he told his favourite ministers all he had learned.

" Sir," said one of them, " I advise you to take the prince prisoner and to keep him shut up for the rest of his life."

" Sir," said the witch, thinking this would be unwise, " if you keep the prince, you must also keep his servants. This you cannot do, because they are all genies. They will fly at once to the palace of the fairy and tell her, when she will find some means to punish you.

" If you take my advice you will ask your son to bring you, by the aid of his fairy wife, so many wonderful things that he will at last grow tired and shut himself up for life in his palace. In this way you will be saved the crime of killing your own son, or even of making him a prisoner."

The sultan made up his mind to act on this advice, and the next time Ahmed came into his room, he said, " Son, though you have never told me your secret, I know of your marriage with the rich and powerful fairy. I am pleased you have done so well, and hope you will obtain for me your wife's help whenever I need it. I want you to ask her to send me a tent small enough to be carried on a man's hand, yet large enough to shelter a whole army. It is not easy to get, but I feel sure she will get it for your sake."

Now, though fairies can do many things impossible to men, Prince Ahmed felt that such a thing as his father asked could not be made even by them. Besides, he liked not to ask his wife for any favours of the kind, so he replied, " Sir, it is true I have married the fairy, though I know not how you found it out. I hope you will not insist on my asking this favour of her ; yet, if I must ask it, I will. Should I come not again, you will understand that I have failed to obtain it."

" Son," replied the sultan, " people often lose things for want of asking. You do not yet know what your wife will do to show her love for you. Ask her for the tent ; if she does not give it to you, she does not love you as she ought."

To this Ahmed made no reply. He was very vexed and left the palace two days earlier than usual. On reaching home, his face was still troubled, so that his wife, who looked always to see him return in a gay mood, asked what had happened to make him sad.

" Tell me," she said, " and whatever the cause, I will try to remove it. Perhaps the sultan, your father, is dead ; if so, I will do all I can to comfort you."

" Thanks be to God," said Ahmed, " my father is alive and well, but, in spite of all my care, he has found out about our marriage."

" I know who told him," cried the fairy. " Did I not say that sick woman would bring us trouble ? It is she who has told him. But tell me, what does your father wish ? Do not fear ; you cannot ask too much of me."

" Madam," said the prince, " though for myself I would never ask any other favour than your love, my father wishes you to send him a tent large enough to shelter his whole army, yet small enough to be carried in a man's hand."

" Prince," replied the fairy, smiling, " let so small a matter cease to trouble you ; I can easily do that, and, believe me, I shall always take pleasure in doing anything whatever, for your sake."

Then, bidding a servant bring the largest tent in the place, she laughed at the look of surprise on her husband's face when the tiny thing was brought.

" Go, set it up," she said, " that the prince may see if his father will think it large enough."

The tent proved to be even larger than his father wished, and Ahmed asked his wife's pardon for doubting her power.

" There is one thing to notice," she said in reply, " the tent becomes larger or smaller, as it is needed, without anything more being done to it."

When it was taken down and made small again, she gave it to the prince, who, the very next day, took it to his father.

The sultan's surprise was great when Ahmed placed the tent in his hands. Taking it to the great plain, he put it up, when it became large enough to cover an army twice the size of his own. However, instead of being pleased, he felt it showed that the fairy's power was great enough to do anything she wished.

Prince Ahmed threw the meat to the lions and passed in safety

He sent his best thanks by his son, and asked her to send him a little of the water of the fountain of lions, which was said to cure all disease, so that if he were taken ill he might have a remedy at hand.

Prince Ahmed was much vexed, but, on telling his wife, she agreed to send it. " For," she said, " I see he listens to the witch, and whatever she tells him to ask, I will grant. The fountain of lions is in the court of the castle, and the entrance is guarded by four lions. Do not fear ; I will give you a piece of thread, two horses—one of which you must ride while leading the other laden with the carcase of a sheep cut into four quarters—and a bottle in which to carry the water.

" You must set out early to-morrow morning, and, on passing the iron gate, throw the thread until it reaches the castle gates ; the gates will open, and you will see the lions. Throw to each a quarter of the sheep, clap spurs to your horse, and ride to the fountain. Fill the bottle, and return while the lions are still feasting."

Prince Ahmed started the next morning, and did just as his wife had told him. He was coming back again, when chancing to look behind, he saw two of the lions following him. They did not touch him, but, placing themselves one before and the other behind him, went as far as the gates of the palace, and then returned.

As soon as the sultan had the bottle, " Son," he said, " I thank you for the water, but pray tell me how you got safely away from the lions of whom I have heard."

" Sir," replied Ahmed, " all the praise is due to my wife, whose orders I have carried out."

Then the sultan, going into another room, sent for the witch, who advised him to ask Ahmed to bring him a man not more than a foot and a half high, whose beard should be thirty feet long, and who should carry on his shoulders a bar of iron weighing five hundredweight, and who should be able to speak.

" If you do this," said the sultan to his son the next day, " I will ask no further favours from you or your wife."

Ahmed went home in a rather troubled state of mind, for he thought this last favour would be too hard, even for her to grant. But the fairy set his mind at rest.

" My brother Schaibar," she said, " is just such a man. I will send for him, and you shall see I speak truly."

A golden chafing-dish with a fire in it having been placed under the porch of the palace, the fairy threw some incense upon it, when out of the thick cloud there came a man, only a foot and a half high, with a beard thirty feet long, and carrying a huge iron bar on his shoulder. He was so ugly that Prince Ahmed would have been filled with fear, but that he knew him to be his wife's brother.

" Who is that man ? " asked Schaibar, coming toward Perie Banou with a fierce scowl on his face.

On learning that Ahmed was her husband, Schaibar asked in what way he could serve him, and being told of the sultan's wish to see him, agreed to go with Ahmed to the palace.

" You wished to see me," he said to the king, " what can I do for you ? "

Instead of answering, the sultan turned his head away ; and Schaibar, being angry at such rudeness, struck him on the head and killed him, before Ahmed could do anything to stop him. Then he put to death those who had set Ahmed's father against him, even bidding the grand vizier bring out the witch, that she, too, might be punished for the evil she had done.

Schaibar next called out the people and made them swear to own Ahmed as their king, and Perie Banou as their queen. This they did very willingly, for they had always loved the young prince. When Ahmed found that neither Ali nor his wife had had anything to do with the plot against him, he gave him a large part of the kingdom, where they spent the rest of their lives. Houssain would not return, though Ahmed offered him the best of the country. All he asked of his brother was leave to live in peace on the spot he had chosen for his dwelling.

PRINCE CAMARALZAMAN AND PRINCESS BADOURA

ABOUT twenty days' sail from the coast of Persia there is an island which is called the Isle of the Children of Khaledan.

The island was ruled by King Schahzaman, who had a son named Camaralzaman. Camaralzaman was a good young prince and clever too, for he learnt without trouble all things which a prince ought to know. His father was very proud of him.

When the prince was fifteen years of age the king went to his grand vizier and said to him, " I am very proud of my son Camaralzaman, and I want to do him all the honour I can. I intend to give up my throne and let him take my place."

The vizier did not think this was a very good plan, for a king who was only fifteen years of age would not rule a kingdom so well as an older one. So he said to the king, " Let him marry first, and then we shall see what kind of a man he will make."

This idea pleased the king very much, and he sent for Camaralzaman without delay. When the prince had come to him the king said, " My son, I wish you to marry. What do you think of it ? "

Now Prince Camaralzaman had taken a dislike to ladies, and had made up his mind never to have a wife. " Sire," said he to his father, " don't you think I had better wait for a year or two before I choose a wife ? I am much too young to marry."

" Very well," said the king. " I give you time to think of it."

A full year went by, and then the king sent for Camaralzaman again.

159

" Now, my son," said the king, " you are quite old enough to have a wife. What have you to say ? "

" I have not yet thought of such a thing, indeed I haven't, father," replied Camaralzaman.

The king was sore vexed, but, not wishing to punish his son, he sent for his vizier. " What shall I do ? " he asked. " My son tells me he will not choose a wife."

The vizier said that he thought another year should be given to the prince and if at the end of that time he should still refuse, he should be made to marry.

The king agreed with his vizier that this would be a wise plan.

That year went by, but still Camaralzaman would not choose a wife. The king then asked Camaralzaman's mother to talk to him about it ; and although that lady did so, Camaralzaman was still of the same mind. " I won't marry," said he. And he meant what he said.

The king once more called his vizier. " My son still refuses to marry," said the king, " and I am going to punish him."

The vizier bowed seven times, which was a sign that he thought the prince ought to be punished. Camaralzaman was called, and the king said to him, " Camaralzaman, my son, you take no notice of my wishes. You must leave the palace, and go to live all by yourself in the tall tower. You shall have a bed, some books, and one slave to attend to you. That is all. Go."

Prince Camaralzaman was not in the least vexed at this. On the other hand, he was rather pleased to be alone. When night came he lay down on his bed quite content, and fell fast asleep. He left his lamp burning.

Now, in the tower was a well, and in the well there dwelt a fairy whose name was Maimounè. The same night that Camaralzaman lay on his bed for the first time Maimounè came up the well ready to go her nightly rounds. She saw the light burning, and went up to the couch.

" What a handsome youth," said she, " and what a pity he will not marry." Then she stooped down and kissed his cheek. After that she flew into the air, where she met a genie.

" O genie," said the fairy, " where have you come from to-night ? "

" I have come from China," said the genie, " and I have seen there a fine sight. The king is Gaiour, and he has a most lovely daughter, the most beautiful princess in the world.

" Gaiour loves the princess dearly, and has built for her seven palaces. The first is of rock crystal, the second of bronze, the third of the finest steel, the fourth of another kind of bronze, the fifth of touchstone, the sixth of silver, and the seventh of fine gold.

" There are gardens and lawns round the palaces, the whole forming a very grand place.

" The kings from all the country round want the hand of the princess in marriage, but Gaiour cannot make up his mind upon whom to bestow it, and the princess does not want to marry at all.

" Gaiour has told his daughter that she must marry some one, but she won't. I heard her say to the king, ' Speak to me no more, sire, of such a thing as marriage. If you do, I will plunge a dagger into my heart and be free.'"

" That, as you may suppose, made the king very angry, and he shut her up in a single room, and gave her only ten slaves to wait on her. Nay, more. The king thinks she is mad, and has said he will give a large reward, as well as the hand of the princess, to any one who can cure her.

" Come with me, and I will show her to you."

At this the fairy laughed. " I thought you were going to tell me something very nice," she said. " I have just seen a far more handsome prince than you have seen a lovely princess."

" That cannot be true," said the genie.

Then it was agreed that the genie should go to China and fetch the princess, who, when she was brought, should be taken to Camaralzaman's tower and laid down by his side. Very soon the genie came back with the princess.

As the two lay on the couch it was plain that they were both very beautiful. The fairy and the genie looked at them, but could not make up their minds which was the more lovely.

Just at that moment Prince Camaralzaman awoke, and seeing the princess by his side, looked into her face. " What beauty ! what charms ! Oh, my heart, my soul ! " said he. " This is without doubt the lady whom my father wishes me to marry. What a pity I did not see her sooner ! "

He was then about to kiss her on the forehead, but thinking he might wake her—a thing he did not wish to do—he took her ring from her finger and changed it for his own. Then he fell as fast asleep as he was before.

Not long afterwards the princess awoke and looked round the room. She did not know where she was. Then she reached out her hand and felt the prince.

She started with surprise, and looking at him, saw that he was the most handsome young man she had ever seen in her life. " What ! " said she to herself, " is this the person my father wishes me to marry ? I will wake him and talk to him. No, I will take his ring and wear it on my own finger."

But before she could do this she fell fast asleep again.

The genie and the fairy had watched all this without being seen by the prince or princess. When the two were once more fast asleep, the genie carried the princess home to her own room, and laid her down on her own couch.

When Prince Camaralzaman awoke next morning he looked for the princess. Lo! she was not there. He called his slave and asked him what had become of her. Of course, the slave did not know there had been a princess in the room at all, so he told him he must have had a dream. On this Prince Camaralzaman beat the slave soundly, who, as soon as he could, made his escape, and went and told the king what the prince had whipped him for.

The vizier was there, but neither he nor the king could make out what the slave was talking about. Then the king went to the tower. " What is this I hear, my son ? " asked the king.

Camaralzaman told his father about the beautiful princess, and said he would marry her at once. The king said he did not know of any princess, and thought his dear son was mad. For many days Prince Camaralzaman was sad, and no one could comfort him.

Now while all these things were taking place in the court of King Schahzaman, very much the same was happening in China. The princess, whose name was Badoura, awoke and called in a loud voice for her maidens. They rushed to her, and she asked them where the prince was.

" Prince ? " they asked. " What prince ? "

" The prince who lay on my couch last night," said Badoura. " If you do not tell me at once, I will beat you every one."

Not one of the maidens could tell the princess what she wanted to know. Then the princess took the chief maiden, who was her nurse, by the hair and gave her many slaps and blows. As soon as she could get away she ran to the queen and told her the strange story.

The queen went to see her daughter, and so did the king. They knew nothing about a prince, and both thought their dear daughter was mad. She showed them the ring which Camaralzaman had placed on her finger, and that was a strange thing to them.

For many days the princess was sad, and no one could comfort her.

The King of China could not endure to see his daughter suffer so. He gave out that if any one could cure her complaint he should wed her for his pains. This was the second time.

Many princes tried to cure her, but they could not. Indeed, so many tried one after the other that the king said he who should try and fail should have his head struck off. This kept some from trying, but in the end there were one hundred and fifty heads stuck on the walls of the city.

Still the princess was sad.

Now the nurse of the princess had a son whose name was Marzavan. He was a clever young man, and had been in many cities of the world. He came home from his travels, and heard the strange story of the princess.

Marzavan got leave to see the princess, and he told her that he hoped he would find a cure if she would wait a few days. He meant to travel till he should find some clever doctor.

Next day, losing no time, he set out. As he went from city to city he could hear nothing but the story of the Princess Badoura and the prince's ring, and the reward the man should get who should cure her of her madness.

Marzavan came at last to a city where no one talked of Badoura, but of Prince Camaralzaman and the ring of a princess. " This is strange," thought he to himself. " I must see this Camaralzaman ; perhaps he will be the very prince whom Badoura wants to marry."

Off he set once more, but the ship he was in was wrecked just as she was going into the port of the city where Prince Camaralzaman lived. Marzavan was a good swimmer, and he soon reached the shore. He found his way to the court of King Schahzaman, where he heard the full story of the prince and the ring from no less a person than the vizier himself.

" May I see the prince ? " asked Marzavan. " You may, of course," said the vizier, who led the way to Prince Camaralzaman's chamber.

The moment Marzavan saw the prince he was struck by his face. It was handsome, and just like the Princess Badoura's. He started, and Prince Camaralzaman called him to his side. Then Marzavan knew his journey would not be in vain. He felt sure he had found the proper person.

Marzavan spoke to him in a low voice and said, " Prince, the time is come when you must put an end to your sadness. The lady for whom you suffer is well known to me ; she is the Princess Badoura, daughter of the King of China, whose name is Gaiour. The princess is even now mourning for you."

Then he told the prince all about the reward King Gaiour had said he would give to the one who could cure his daughter, and added, " You, prince, are the only person who can cure her. Make haste to get well, and you shall try your luck."

Hope came at once to Prince Camaralzaman. No sooner had he heard the words of Marzavan than he seemed to get better. He rose from his couch, and let himself be dressed. In a few days he was quite well.

Then a new trouble came to him, for he felt sure his father, the king, would not be willing for him to travel so far as China. " What shall I do ? " asked he of Marzavan.

" Leave that to me," said Marzavan. " I am quite sure I can manage a small matter like that." And he did, for in a day or two he made a party for a hunt, and when the prince and he were alone he said to the prince, " Now, prince, is your chance. Let us flee."

Away they went and soon left the other huntsmen out of sight. When they came at last to the sea they took ship, and in a good many days reached the city where Princess Badoura lived.

Prince Camaralzaman changed his dress, and made out that he was a wise man from a far-off land who had come to cure the princess of her madness. He was told by the people that he had better not try, for he would be sure to lose his head like the others who had tried. But he paid no heed to their words.

Soon the vizier led Camaralzaman into the king's chamber. The king said to him, " Young man, I hardly dare think you can cure my daughter, but you may try. Take care, or your head will be struck off."

" Sire," said the prince, " the land where I come from has many wise men. I know the arts of all cures, and I am ready to restore your daughter to health and happiness. If not, I am just as ready for death."

The king then gave orders for Camaralzaman to be taken to the princess. When he got near her chamber he was so overjoyed to think he should soon see his darling again that he ran on in front of his guide.

" Where are you going, good sir ? " asked he. " You must be very ready to die to run so fast into the arms of death."

" Friend," said Camaralzaman, " I am sure to cure the princess."

Oh, how his heart beat ! He could hear the princess in her chamber moaning and he longed to be with her. But he said to his guide, " I am so sure of curing the princess that I will do it in which way you think best. I will speak to her from here, or I will go in and see her."

" I do not care in the least how you do it," said the guide. " I only know that if you do it at all you will be the wisest man in the world."

Then the prince drew from his belt some paper, on which he wrote these words : " Prince Camaralzaman to the Princess of China—Dear Princess, the heart-broken Prince Camaralzaman sends you word that he gave you his heart during your sweet sleep. He placed your ring on his finger in token of his love. He is outside your room. If you love him, come to him. If you do not, he will die."

Prince Camaralzaman gave the paper to his guide and told him to take it to the princess. The guide looked at the note in wonder, but took it in.

In a moment the note was broken open and read. Then the princess dashed past her maidens into the ante-chamber. She knew the prince at once, and fell into his embrace. Not a word was spoken, but they knew each loved the other.

The princess was a new creature. She looked happy and smiled. Her nurse was glad, and the guide ran off to tell the king what the stranger had done. "He has cured her," said he, "without even seeing her."

How glad the king was! "Whoever you may be," said he to Camaralzaman, "I will keep my promise. You may wed the princess without delay."

Then Camaralzaman told the king who he was, and that his father was the King of the Isle of the Children of Khaledan. He also told the king the story as he had heard it from his daughter, and showed him the princess's ring in proof.

That very day Prince Camaralzaman and the Princess Badoura were wed, and the whole land of China was happy, but in the night the prince dreamed that his father was sick and sad at the loss of his son. He awoke with a deep sigh, which waked the princess.

"Why weepest thou, my love?" asked she.

"Alas!" cried the prince, "I know that my father mourns my loss. We must both go to him."

The King of China gave his leave for his daughter and his son-in-law to journey to King Schahzaman, but said they must both come back in a year.

As soon as they could get ready they set out, and one evening camped near a forest. The princess was tired, and lay down to sleep. Her maidens had taken off her girdle so that she might rest at ease. There it lay near her couch.

Camaralzaman looked at it and admired the many jewels which were on it. Then he saw that a little purse was stitched to the inside, and that it had something hard in it. He opened it, and lo, there was a cornelian in it—a precious stone which the queen, the princess's mother, had given to her as a charm.

In order to look at the cornelian more closely, Prince Camaralzaman took it to the tent door, when all at once a bird darted down from the air and carried it off in his beak.

"Wretched bird!" said Camaralzaman, and started after it in the hope of getting back the stone. The bird flew a little way and then stopped. Camaralzaman was about to seize it when it flew off again. This went on for a long time, and Camaralzaman had not yet caught the bird. Night came on, and the bird perched in a high tree.

The prince dared not go back to his princess without the stone, so he laid himself down at the foot of the tree and slept.

Next day he again gave chase to the bird, and for the next ten days. On the eleventh he came to a large city, over the walls of which the bird flew and was lost to sight.

He gave chase to the bird for the next ten days

Poor Camaralzaman! what could he do? He thought of his wife, yet knew not how to get back to her. He had quite lost his way. He walked into the city and along the streets. On and on he went till he came to a garden, the gate of which was open.

The gardener was at work, and when he saw Camaralzaman he asked him to shelter in his cottage, telling him that the people of the city were very unkind to strangers.

Camaralzaman was glad to rest, and after a little time he told the gardener why he had come there. The gardener said it was a year's journey to the Isle of the Children of Khaledan, and that a ship went once a year. " If you had been here a few days sooner," said he, " you could have gone by ship. Now you must wait a twelvemonth. You may stay with me in my cottage."

Let us now turn to the Princess Badoura. For a long time she waited in her camp at the edge of the forest, but as the prince did not return she had to go on without him.

Now, in that land it was not safe for a party to be in charge of a lady, so the princess put on a suit of Prince Camaralzaman's clothes, and bade one of her maidens dress as a princess and pretend to be her.

On they went, and in six months came to the city of the Isle of Ebony. There the people thought that the princess was a prince, and led her to the king, whose name was Armanos. Princess Badoura told the king that she was Prince Camaralzaman, and that she was going to her father's court.

King Armanos was pleased to have so handsome a prince, as he thought, at his palace, and when the princess had stayed there three days he gave her in marriage to his own daughter.

What a fix Princess Badoura was in to be sure! She had said that she was Prince Camaralzaman, and if she now said she was a princess, King Armanos might put her to death. So she let herself be married to King Armanos' daughter.

When the two were in their chamber at night Princess Badoura told her wife who she was, and begged her to keep her secret. She said she would, and that she hoped the Princess Badoura might soon find her husband. Thus they lived for some time.

Prince Camaralzaman worked with the gardener in the garden. One day, when the yearly ship was about to sail for the Isle of Ebony, the gardener went to secure a passage for the prince. While he was away a strange thing took place.

Two birds came into the garden where Prince Camaralzaman was at work. They pecked at each other with all their might, till at last one of them dropped dead. The other flew away, but in a few minutes, two birds who had watched the fight from a high tree fetched him back and pecked him so much that he died on the spot where he had killed the other bird.

Prince Camaralzaman then went to this second dead bird, and what should he find in his body but the cornelian for which he had so long sought.

His joy was great, as you may suppose. He took it up and tied it to his arm so that he might never lose it again. Then he set to work with a will. While he was cutting at the root of a tree which no longer bore fruit, his axe struck something hard and made a loud noise.

Looking closely, he saw that he had opened a cave in the ground, and that in the cave were fifty large bronze jars. Each was filled with gold dust of great value.

The gardener now came back and said that Camaralzaman might sail for home in a few days, whereupon Camaralzaman told the gardener what he had found in the bird and in the cave. The gardener would not take any share in the gold dust, but said that as Camaralzaman had found it he ought to have it all.

For safety, some olives were put into the jars to cover up the gold, and into one of them Camaralzaman put the cornelian also, for safety.

Just then some sailors came to the prince and told him all was ready for the voyage, and that he must go on board that night.

It came to pass that night, however, that the gardener was taken ill and died. Prince Camaralzaman was so struck with grief at the sudden loss of his friend that he missed the ship, and it set sail without him. Another year must now pass by before he could embark.

The seamen carried away the jars of gold and the cornelian too, so that Prince Camaralzaman was in a worse plight than before.

The ship sailed to the Isle of Ebony, where the Princess Badoura saw it going into the harbour. She sent to ask whence it had come and what it had brought. She learnt that it was stored with all sorts of fine dresses and stuffs, and some jars of olives. She was also told that the merchant who owned the olives was left behind and had not sailed.

The princess bought the olives from the captain of the ship and they had them taken to the palace. When they were opened, lo! there was found in them the gold and the cornelian.

With surprise and joy she fainted away ; but the princess of the Isle of Ebony and her maidens ran to her help and soon brought her round. She took the cornelian in her hand and pressed it to her lips, kissing it all the time. Then she sent the maidens away, for she did not want them to know anything about the cornelian. They had seen her kiss it, but they did not know why she had done so.

That night she told all to the daughter of King Armanos, and, as soon as it was day, she sent for the captain of the ship and asked him about the merchant who owned the olives. From what the captain said, Princess Badoura felt sure that he was her own prince.

" Go at once," said she to the captain, " and bring him to me. He owes me some money, and if you fail to bring him you shall pay for it with your head."

The captain at once set off, and when he reached the city where Prince Camaralzaman lived he lost no time in going to the garden. He took with him some strong men, who seized the prince and dragged him by force to the ship. Not a word did they say as to why they acted so.

With a fair voyage the Isle of Ebony was reached, and no sooner did Princess Badoura know that the ship had cast anchor in the harbour than she went down to it.

Then once more she fell into the arms of her dear prince, and when her tears of joy were over she led him to the palace. It did not take long to tell the king all about their strange lives, and when he heard it he laughed with all his might.

Then, taking leave of King Armanos, the prince and princess set out for their own land. As king and queen they had a long and happy reign.

ROBINSON CRUSOE

I was born in the city of York

ROBINSON CRUSOE

CHAPTER I

I WAS born in the year 1632, in the city of York, of a good family, though not of that country, my father being a foreigner of Bremen, who settled first at Hull. He got a good estate by merchandise, and, leaving off his trade, lived afterwards at York; from whence he had married my mother, whose relations were named *Robinson*, a very good family in that country, and from whom I was called *Robinson Kreutznaer*; but, by the usual corruption of words in England, we are now called, nay, we call ourselves, and write our name, *Crusoe*; and so my companions always called me.

Being the third son of the family, and not bred to any trade, my head began to be filled very early with rambling thoughts. My father had given me a competent share of learning, as far as house-education and a country free school generally go, and designed me for the law; but I would be satisfied with nothing but going to sea; and my inclination to this led me so strongly against the will, nay, the commands of my father, and against all the entreaties and persuasions of my mother and other friends, that there seemed to be something fatal in that propension of nature, tending directly to the life of misery which was to befall me.

Being one day at Hull, whither I went casually, and without any purpose of making an elopement that time—but, I say, being there, and one of my companions being going by sea to London, in his father's ship, and prompting me to go with him, with the common allurement of a seafaring man, that it should cost me nothing for my passage, I consulted neither father nor mother any more, nor so much as sent them word of it ; but leaving them to hear of it as they might, without asking God's blessing or my father's, without any consideration of circumstances or consequences, and in an ill hour, God knows, on the 1st of September, 1651, I went on board a ship bound for London. Never any young adventurer's misfortunes, I believe, began sooner, or continued longer, than mine. The ship was no sooner got out of the Humber, than the wind began to blow, and the sea to rise in a most frightful manner ; and as I had never been at sea before, I was most inexpressibly sick in body, and terrified in mind.

The storm increased, and the sea went very high, though nothing like what I have seen many times since—no, nor what I saw a few days after : but it was enough to affect me then, who was but a young sailor, and had never known anything of the matter. I expected every wave would have swallowed us up, and that every time the ship fell down, as I thought it did in the trough or hollow of the sea, we should never rise more.

I was very grave for all that day, being also a little sea-sick still ; but towards night the weather cleared up, the wind was quite over, and a charming fine evening followed ; the sun went down perfectly clear, and rose so the next morning ; and having little or no wind, and a smooth sea, the sun shining upon it, the sight was, as I thought, the most delightful that ever I saw.

I had slept well in the night, and was now no more sea-sick, but very cheerful—looking with wonder upon the sea that was so rough and terrible the day before, and could be so calm and so pleasant in so little a time after : and now, lest my good resolutions should continue, my companion, who had indeed enticed me away, comes to me. " Well, Bob," says he, clapping me upon the shoulder, " How do you do after it ? I warrant you were frightened, weren't you, last night, when it blew but a capful of wind ? " " A capful d'ye call it ? " said I, " 'twas a terrible storm." " A storm, you fool you ! " replies he, " do you call that a storm ? why it was nothing at all ; give us but a good ship and sea-room, and we think nothing of such a squall of wind as that ; but you're but a fresh-water sailor, Bob ; come, let us make a bowl of punch, and we'll forget all that : d'ye see what charming weather 'tis now ? " To make short this sad part of my story, we went the way of all sailors ; the punch was made, and I was made half drunk with it, and in that one night's wickedness I drowned all my repentance, all my reflections upon my past conduct, all my resolutions for the future.

The sixth day of our being at sea, we came into Yarmouth Roads ; the wind having been contrary and the weather calm, we had made but little way since the storm. Here we were obliged to come to an anchor, and here we lay, the wind continuing contrary, namely, at south-west, for seven or eight days ; during which time a great many ships from Newcastle came in to the same roads, as the common harbour where the ships might wait for a wind for the river.

We had not, however, rid here so long but we should have tided it up the river, but that the wind blew too fresh ; and after we had lain four or five days, blew very hard. However, the roads being reckoned as good as a harbour, the anchorage good, and our ground-tackle very strong, our men were unconcerned, and not in the least apprehensive of danger, but spent the time in rest and mirth, after the manner of the sea ; but the eighth day, in the morning, the wind increased, and we had all hands at work to strike our top-masts, and make everything snug and close, that the ship might ride as easy as possible. By noon, the sea went very high indeed, and our ship rid forecastle in, shipped several seas, and we thought once or twice our anchor had come home ; upon which our master ordered out the sheet-anchor ; so that we rode with two anchors ahead, and the cables veered out to the better end.

By this time it blew a terrible storm indeed ; and now I began to see terror and amazement in the faces even of the seamen themselves. The master, though vigilant in the business of preserving the ship, yet, as he went in and out of the cabin by me, I could hear him, softly to himself, say several times, " Lord, be merciful to us ! we shall be all lost—we shall be all undone ! " and the like. During these first hurries, I was stupid, lying still in my cabin, which was in the steerage, and cannot describe my temper. But when the master himself came by me, and said we should all be lost, I was dreadfully frighted : I got up out of my cabin, and looked out ; but such a dismal sight I never saw : the sea went mountains high, and broke upon us every three or four minutes ; when I could look about, I could see nothing but distress round us. Two ships that rid near us, we found, had cut their masts by the board, being deep laden ; and our men cried out that a ship, which rid about a mile ahead of us, was foundered. Two more ships, being driven from their anchors, were run out of the roads to sea, at all adventures, and that with not a mast standing. The light ships fared the best, as not so much labouring in the sea ; but two or three of them drove, and came close by us, running away with only their sprit sail out before the wind.

Towards the evening, the mate and boatswain begged the master of our ship to let them cut away the foremast, which he was very unwilling to do ; but the boatswain protesting to him, that if he did not the ship would founder, he consented ; and when they had cut away the foremast, the mainmast stood so loose, and shook the ship so much, they were obliged to cut it away also, and make a clear deck.

Any one must judge what a condition I must be in at all this, who was but a young sailor, and who had been in such a fright before at but a little. But if I can express at this distance the thoughts I had about me at that time, I was in tenfold more horror of mind upon account of my former convictions, and the having returned from them to the resolutions I had wickedly taken at first, than I was at death itself ; and these, added to the terror of the storm, put me into such a condition, that I can by no words describe it. But the worst was not come yet ; the storm continued with such fury that the seamen themselves acknowledged they had never seen a worse. We had a good ship, but she was deep-laden, and wallowed in the sea, that the seamen every now and then cried out she would founder. It was my advantage, in one respect, that I did not know what they meant by founder, till I inquired. However, the storm was so violent, that I saw, what is not often seen, the master, the boatswain and some others more sensible than the rest, at their prayers, and expecting every moment when the ship would go to the bottom. In the middle of the night, and under all the rest of our distresses, one of the men that had been down on purpose to see, cried out we had sprung a leak ; another said there was four feet water in the hold. Then all hands were called to the pump. At that very word, my heart, as I thought, died within me ; and I fell backwards upon the side of my bed where I sat, into the cabin. However the men roused me, and told me that I, that was able to do nothing before, was as well able to pump as another ; at which I stirred up, and went to the pump and worked very heartily. While this was doing, the master, seeing some light colliers who, not able to ride out the storm, were obliged to slip and run away to the sea, and would come near us, ordered to fire a gun as a signal of distress. I, who knew nothing what that meant, was so surprised, that I thought the ship had broke, or some dreadful thing happened. In a word, I was so surprised that I fell down in a swoon. As this was a time when everybody had his own life to think of, nobody minded me, or what was become of me ; but another man stepped up to the pump, and thrusting me aside with his foot, let me lie, thinking I had been dead ; and it was a great while before I came to myself.

We worked on, but the water increasing in the hold, it was apparent that the ship would founder ; and though the storm began to abate a little, yet as it was not possible she could swim till we might run into a port, so the master continued firing guns for help ; and a light ship, who had rid it out just ahead of us, ventured a boat out to help us. It was with the utmost hazard the boat came near us ; but it was impossible for us to get on board, or for the boat to lie near the ship's side, till at last the men rowing very heartily, and venturing their lives to save ours, our men cast them a rope over the stern with a buoy to it, and then veered it out a great length, which they, after much labour and hazard, took hold of, and we hauled them close under our stern, and got all into their boat. It was to no purpose for them or us, after we were in the boat, to think of reaching to their own ship ; so we all agreed to let her drive, and only to pull her in towards shore as much as we could ; and our master promised them, that if the boat was staved upon shore, he would make it good to their master ; so, partly rowing, and partly driving, our boat went away to the northward, sloping towards the shore, almost as far as Winterton Ness.

We were not much more than a quarter of an hour out of our ship, but we saw her sink ; and then I understood, for the first time, what was meant by a ship foundering in the sea. I must acknowledge I had hardly eyes to look up, when the seamen told me she was sinking ; for from that moment they rather put me into the boat, than that I might be said to go in, my heart was, as it were, dead within me, partly with fright, partly with horror of mind, and the thoughts of what was yet before me.

While we were in this condition, the men yet labouring at the oar to bring the boat nearer the shore, we could see (when our boat mounting the waves, we were able to see the shore) a great many people running along the shore to assist us, when we should come near ; but we made but slow way toward the shore, nor were we able to reach the shore, till being past the lighthouse at Winterton, the shore falls off to the westward towards Cromer, and so the land broke off a little the violence of the wind. Here we got in, and though not without much difficulty, got all safe on shore, and walked afterwards on foot to Yarmouth, where, as unfortunate men, we were used with great humanity, as well by the magistrates of the town, who assigned us good quarters, as by particular merchants and owners of ships, and had money given us sufficient to carry us either to London, or back to Hull, as we thought fit.

Had I now had the sense to have gone back to Hull, and have gone home, I had been happy, and my father, an emblem of our blessed Saviour's parable, had even killed the fatted calf for me ; for, hearing the ship I went in was cast away in Yarmouth Roads, it was a great while before he had any assurance that I was not drowned.

But my ill fate pushed me on now with an obstinacy that nothing could resist ; and though I had several times loud calls from my reason and my more composed judgment to go home, yet I had no power to do it.

That evil influence which carried me first away from my father's house, that hurried me into the wild and indigested notion of raising my fortune, and that impressed those conceits so forcibly upon me, as to make me deaf to all good advice, and to the entreaties and even the command of my father —I say, the same influence, whatever it was, presented the most unfortunate of all enterprises to my view ; and I went on board a vessel bound to the coast of Africa ; or, as our sailors vulgarly call it, a voyage to Guinea.

It was my great misfortune, that in all these adventures I did not ship myself as a sailor ; whereby, though I might indeed have worked a little harder than ordinary, yet, at the same time, I had learned the duty and office of a fore-mastman, and in time might have qualified myself for a mate or lieutenant, if not for a master. But as it was always my fate to choose for the worst, so I did here ; for, having money in my pocket, and good clothes upon my back, I would always go on board in the habit of a gentleman ; and so I neither had any business in the ship, nor learned to do any.

CHAPTER II

IT was my lot, first of all, to fall into pretty good company in London, which does not always happen to such loose and unguided young fellows as I then was, the devil generally not omitting to lay some snare for them very early; but it was not so with me. I first fell acquainted with the master of a ship who had been on the coast of Guinea ; and who, having had very good success there, was resolved to go again ; and who, taking a fancy to my conversation, which was not at all disagreeable at that time, hearing me say I had a mind to see the world, told me, if I would go the voyage with him I should be at no expense—I should be his mess-mate and his companion ; and if I could carry anything with me, I should have all the advantage of it that the trade would permit ; and, perhaps, I might meet with some encouragement.

I embraced the offer; and, entering into a strict friendship with this captain, who was an honest and plain-dealing man, I went the voyage with him, and carried a small adventure with me, which, by the disinterested honesty of my friend, the captain, I increased very considerably; for I carried about forty pounds in such toys and trifles as the captain directed me to buy. This forty pounds I had mustered together by the assistance of some of my relations, whom I corresponded with, and who, I believe, got my father, or at least my mother, to contribute so much as that to my first adventure.

This was the only voyage which I may say was successful in all my adventures, and which I owe to the integrity and honesty of my friend, the captain; under whom also I got a competent knowledge of the mathematics, and the rules of navigation—learned how to keep an account of the ship's course, take an observation, and, in short, to understand some things that were needful to be understood by a sailor; for, as he took delight to instruct me, I took delight to learn; and, in a word, this voyage made me both a sailor and a merchant; for I brought home five pounds nine ounces of gold dust for my adventure, which yielded me in London, at my return, almost three hundred pounds; and this filled me with those aspiring thoughts which have since so completed my ruin.

I was now set up for a Guinea trader; and my friend, to my great misfortune, dying soon after his arrival, I resolved to go the same voyage again; and I embarked in the same vessel with one who was his mate in the former voyage, and had now got the command of the ship. This was the unhappiest voyage that ever man made; for though I did not carry quite £100 of my new gained wealth, so that I had £200 left, and which I lodged with my friend's widow, who was very just to me, yet I fell into terrible misfortunes in this voyage; and the first was this—namely, our ship, making her course towards the Canary Islands, or rather between those islands and the African shore, was surprised, in the grey of the morning, by a Moorish rover of Sallee, who gave chase to us with all the sail she could make. We crowded also as much canvas as our yards would spread, or our masts carry, to have got clear; but finding the pirate gained upon us, and would certainly come up with us in a few hours, we prepared to fight, our ship having twelve guns, and the rover eighteen. About three in the afternoon he came up with us, and bringing to, by mistake, just athwart our quarter, instead of athwart our stern, as he intended, we brought eight of our guns to bear on that side, and poured in a broadside upon him, which made him sheer off again after returning our fire, and pouring in also his small shot from near two hundred men which he had on board. However, we had not a man touched, all our men keeping close. He prepared to attack us again, and we to defend ourselves; but laying us on board the next time upon our other quarter, he entered sixty men upon our decks, who immediately fell to cutting and hacking the decks and rigging. We plied them with small shot, half-pikes, powder-chests, and such like, and cleared our deck of them twice. However, to cut short this melancholy part of our story, our ship being disabled, and three of our men killed, and eight wounded, we were obliged to yield, and were carried all prisoners into Sallee, a port belonging to the Moors.

The usage I had there was not so dreadful as at first I apprehended:

SINDBAD SEES STRANGE SIGHTS.
Many large and curious fishes were swarming in the waters.

SINDBAD ON HIS RAFT.
For several days the raft floated on in total darkness through the long tunnel.

nor was I carried up the country to the emperor's court, as the rest of our men were, but was kept by the captain of the rover, as his proper prize, and made his slave, being young and nimble, and fit for his business. At this surprising change of my circumstances, from a merchant to a miserable slave, I was perfectly overwhelmed ; and now I looked back upon my father's prophetic discourse to me, that I should be miserable, and have none to relieve me ; which I thought was now so effectually brought to pass, that I could not be worse—that now the hand of Heaven had overtaken me, and I was undone without redemption. But, alas ! this was but a taste of the misery I was to go through, as will appear in the sequel of the story.

As my new patron or master had taken me home to his house, so I was in hopes that he would take me with him when he went to sea again, believing that it would be some time or other his fate to be taken by a Spanish or Portugal man-of-war, and that then I should be set at liberty. But this hope of mine was soon taken away ; for when he went to sea, he left me on shore to look after his little garden and do the common drudgery of slaves about his house ; and when he came home again from his cruise, he ordered me to lie in the cabin to look after the ship.

Here I meditated nothing but my escape, and what method I might take to affect it ; but found no way that had the least probability in it. Nothing presented to make the supposition of it rational ; for I had nobody to communicate it to that would embark with me—no fellow-slave, no Englishman, Irishman, or Scotsman there, but myself ; so that for two years, though I often pleased myself with the imagination, yet I never had the least encouraging prospect of putting it in practice.

After about two years, an odd circumstance presented itself which put the whole thought of making some attempt for my liberty again in my head : my patron lying at home longer than usual, without fitting out his ship, which, as I heard, was for want of money, he used constantly, once or twice a week, sometimes oftener, if the weather was fair, to take the ship's pinnace, and go out into the road a-fishing ; and as he always took me and a young Moresco with him to row the boat, we made him very merry, and I proved very dexterous in catching fish ; insomuch that sometimes he would send me with a Moor, one of his kinsmen, and the youth, the Moresco, as they called him, to catch a dish of fish for him.

It happened one time that going a-fishing with him in a calm morning, a fog rose so thick, that though we were not half a league from the shore, we lost sight of it ; and rowing, we knew not whither, or which way, we laboured all day and all the next night ; and when the morning came, we found we had pulled off to sea, instead of pulling in for the shore, and that we were at least two leagues from the land : however, we got well in again, though with a great deal of labour, and some danger, for the wind began to blow pretty fresh in the morning : but, particularly, we were all very hungry.

But our patron, warned by this disaster, resolved to take more care of himself in the future ; and having lying by him the long-boat of our English ship which he had taken, he resolved he would not go a-fishing any more without a compass and some provision ; so he ordered the carpenter of his ship, who also was an English slave, to build a little state-room or cabin in the middle of the long-boat, like that of a barge, with a place to stand behind it to steer, and haul home the mainsheet; and room before for a hand or two to stand and work the sails. She sailed with what we call a shoulder-of-mutton sail; and the boom jibbed over the top of the cabin, which lay very snug and low, and had in it room for him to lie, with a slave or two, and a table to eat on, with some small lockers to put in some bottles of such liquor as he thought fit to drink, particularly his bread, rice, and coffee.

We were frequently out with this boat a-fishing; and as I was most dexterous to catch fish for him, he never went without me. It happened one day, that he had appointed to go out in this boat, either for pleasure or for fish, with two or three Moors of some distinction, and for whom he had provided extraordinary; and had therefore sent on board the boat over night a larger store of provisions than usual, and had ordered me to get ready three fusils with powder and shot, which were on board his ship; for that they designed some sport of fowling as well as fishing.

I got all things ready as he had directed and waited the next morning with the boat washed clean, her ancient and pendants out, and everything to accommodate his guests; when by-and-by my patron came on board alone, and told me his guests had put off going, upon some business that fell out, and ordered me, with the man and boy, as usual, to go out with the boat and catch them some fish, for that his friends were to sup at his house; he commanded me, too, that as soon as I had got some fish, I should bring it home to his house: all which I prepared to do.

This moment my former notions of deliverance darted into my thoughts, for now I found I was like to have a little ship at my command; and my master being gone, I prepared to furnish myself, not for fishing business, but for a voyage, though I knew not, neither did I so much as consider, whither I would steer; for anywhere to get out of that place was my way.

My first contrivance was to make a pretence to speak of this Moor, to get something for our subsistence on board; for I told him we must not presume to eat of our patron's bread. He said that was true; so he brought a large basket of rusk, or biscuit of their kind, and three jars with fresh water into the boat. I knew where my patron's case of bottles stood, which it was evident by the make were taken out of some English prize, and I conveyed them into the boat while the Moor was on shore, as if they had been there before for our master: I conveyed also a great lump of bees'-wax into the boat which weighed above half a hundredweight, with a parcel of twine or thread, a hatchet, a saw, and a hammer, all which were of great use to us afterwards, especially the wax to make candles. Another trick I tried upon him, which he innocently came into also. His name was Ishmael, whom they called Muly or Moley; so I called to him: "Moley," said I, "our patron's guns are on board the boat; can you not get a little powder and shot? It may be we may kill some alcamies (a fowl like our curlews) for ourselves, for I know he keeps the gunner's stores in the ship." "Yes," says he, "I'll bring some;" and accordingly he brought a great leather pouch which held about a pound and a half of powder or rather more, and another with shot, that had five or six pounds, with some bullets, and put all into the boat; at the same time I had found some powder of my master's in the great cabin, with which I filled one of the large bottles in the case, which was almost empty, pouring what was in it into another ; and thus furnished with everything needful, we sailed out of the port to fish. The castle, which is at the entrance of the port, knew who we were, and took no notice of us ; and we were not above a mile out of the port before we hauled in our sail, and set us down to fish. The wind blew from the north north-east, which was contrary to my desire ; for had it blown southerly, I had been sure to have made the coast of Spain, and at least reached the bay of Cadiz ; but my resolutions were, blow which way it would, I would be gone from that horrid place where I was, and leave the rest to fate.

After we had fished some time, and catched nothing—for when I had fish on my hook I would not pull them up, that he might not see them—I said to the Moor, " This will not do—our master will not be thus served —we must stand farther off." He, thinking no harm, agreed, and being in the head of the boat, set the sails ; and as I had the helm, I ran the boat out near a league farther, and then brought her to, as if I would fish ; when, giving the boy the helm, I stepped forward to where the Moor was, and making as if I stooped for something behind him, I took him by surprise with my arm under his waist, and tossed him clear overboard into the sea : he rose immediately, for he swam like a cork, and called to me, begged to be taken in, told me he would go all over the world with me. He swam so strong after the boat, that he would have reached me very quickly, there being but little wind ; upon which I stepped into the cabin, and fetching one of the fowling-pieces, I presented it at him, and told him, I had done him no hurt, and if he would be quiet I would do him none—" But," said I, " you swim well enough to reach the shore, and the sea is calm—make the best of your way to shore, and I will do you no harm ; but if you come near the boat, I'll shoot you through the head, for I am resolved to have my liberty,"—so he turned himself about, and swam for the shore, and I make no doubt but he reached it with ease, for he was an excellent swimmer.

I could have been content to have taken this Moor with me and have drowned the boy, but there was no venturing to trust him. When he was gone, I turned to the boy, whom they called Xury, and said to him : " Xury, if you will be faithful to me, I'll make you a great man ; but if you will not stroke your face to be true to me (that is, swear by Mahomet and his father's beard), I must throw you into the sea, too." The boy smiled in my face, and spoke so innocently, that I could not mistrust him ; and swore to be faithful to me, and go all over the world with me.

While I was in view of the Moor that was swimming, I stood out directly to sea with the boat, rather stretching to windward, that they might think me gone towards the Straits' mouth, as indeed any one that had been in their wits must have been supposed to do ; for who would have supposed we were sailed on to the southward, to the truly barbarian coast, where whole nations of negroes were sure to surround us with their canoes, and destroy us ; where we could never once go on shore, but we should be devoured by savage beasts, or more merciless savages of human kind ?

But as soon as it grew dusk in the evening, I changed my course, and steered directly south and by east, bending my course a little toward the east, that I might keep in with the shore ; and having a fair fresh gale of wind, and a smooth quiet sea, I made such sail, that I believe, by the next day

" I'll shoot you through the head "

at three o'clock in the afternoon, when I first made the land, I could not be less than one hundred and fifty miles south of Sallee, quite beyond the Emperor of Morocco's dominions, or, indeed, of any other king thereabouts, for we saw no people.

Yet such was the fright I had taken at the Moors, and the dreadful apprehensions I had of falling into their hands, that I would not stop, or go on shore, or come to an anchor, the wind continuing fair, till I had sailed in that manner five days ; and then the wind shifting to the southward, I concluded also that if any of our vessels were in chase of me, they also would now give over ; so I ventured to make to the coast, and come to an anchor in the mouth of a little river, I knew not what or where—neither what latitude, what country, what nation, nor what river : I neither saw, nor desired to see any people—the principal thing I wanted was fresh water. We came into this creek in the evening, resolving to swim on shore as soon as it was dark, and discover the country ; but as soon as it was quite dark, we heard such dreadful noises of the barking, roaring, and howling of wild creatures, of we knew not what kinds, that the poor boy was ready to die with fear, and begged of me not to go on shore till day. " Well, Xury," said I, " then I won't ; but it may be we may see men by day, who will be as bad to us as those lions." " Then we give them the shoot gun," says Xury, laughing, " make them run away." Such English Xury spoke by conversing among us slaves. However, I was glad to see the boy so cheerful, and I gave him a dram, out of our patron's case of bottles, to cheer him up. After all, Xury's advice was good, and I took it ; we dropped our little anchor, and lay still at night—I say still, for we slept none—for in two or three hours we saw vast great creatures (we knew not what to call them) of many sorts, come down to the seashore, and run into the water, wallowing and washing themselves for the pleasure of cooling themselves ; and they made such hideous howlings and yellings, that I never indeed heard the like.

Xury was dreadfully frighted, and indeed so was I too ; but we were both more frighted when we heard one of those mighty creatures come swimming towards our boat. We could not see him, but we might hear him by his blowing, to be a monstrous, huge, and furious beast ; Xury said it was a lion, and it might be so for aught I know. Poor Xury cried to me to weigh the anchor, and row away. " No," says I, " Xury, we can slip our cable with a buoy to it, and go to sea ; they cannot follow us far." I had no sooner said so, but I perceived the creature (whatever it was) within two oars' length, which something surprised me ; however, I immediately stepped to the cabin door, and taking up my gun, fired at him, upon which he immediately turned about, and swam to the shore again.

But it was not possible to describe the horrible noises, and hideous cries and howlings, that were raised, as well upon the edge of the shore, as higher within the country, upon the noise or report of a gun—a thing I have some reason to believe those creatures had never heard before. This convinced me that there was no going on shore for us in the night upon that coast ; and how to venture on shore in the day, was another question too ; for to have fallen into the hands of any of the savages, had been as bad as to have fallen into the paws of lions and tigers ; at least, we were equally apprehensive of the danger of it.

Be that as it would, we were obliged to go on shore somewhere or other for water, for we had not a pint left in the boat ; when or where to get it was the point. Xury said if I would let him go on shore with one of the jars, he would find if there was any water, and bring some to me. I asked him why he would go ? why I should not go, and he stay in the boat ? The boy answered with so much affection, that made me love him ever after. Says he : " If wild mans come, they eat me, you go 'way." " Well, Xury," said I, " we will both go, and if the wild mans come, we will kill them ; they shall eat neither of us." So I gave Xury a piece of rusk bread to eat, and a dram out of our patron's case of bottles, which I mentioned before ; and we hauled the boat in as near the shore as we thought was proper, and waded on shore, carrying nothing but our arms, and two jars for water.

I did not care to go out of sight of the boat, fearing the coming of canoes with savages down the river : but the boy, seeing a low place about a mile up the country, rambled to it ; and by-and-by I saw him come running towards me. I thought he was pursued by some savage, or frighted with some wild beast, and I ran forward towards him to help him ; but when I came nearer to him, I saw something hanging over his shoulders, which was a creature that he had shot, like a hare, but different in colour, and longer legs ; however, we were very glad of it, and it was very good meat ; but the great joy that poor Xury came with, was to tell me he had found good water, and seen no wild mans.

But we found afterwards that we need not take such pains for water, for a little higher up the creek where we were, we found the water fresh when the tide was out, which flows but a little way up ; so we filled our jars and feasted on the hare we had killed, and prepared to go on our way, having seen no footsteps of any human creature in that part of the country.

As I had been one voyage to the coast before, I knew very well that the islands of the Canaries, and the Cape de Verde Islands also, lay not far off from the coast. But as I had no instruments to take an observation to know what latitude we were in, and did not exactly know, or at least not remember, what latitude they were in, and knew not where to look for them, or when to stand off to sea towards them : otherwise I might now easily have found some of these islands. But my hope was, that if I stood along this coast till I came to that part where the English traded, I should find some of their vessels upon their usual design of trade, that would relieve and take us in.

By the best of my calculation, that place where I now was must be that country which, lying between the Emperor of Morocco's dominions and the negroes, lies waste and uninhabited, except by wild beasts ; the negroes having abandoned it, and gone farther south for fear of the Moors ; and the Moors not thinking it worth inhabiting, by reason of its barrenness—and, indeed, both forsaking it because of the prodigious number of tigers, lions, leopards, and other furious creatures, which harbour there ; so that the Moors use it for their hunting only, where they go like an army, two or three thousand men at a time—and, indeed, for near an hundred miles together upon this coast, we saw nothing but a waste uninhabited country by day, and heard nothing but howlings and roarings of wild beasts by night.

Once or twice in the daytime I thought I saw the Pico of Teneriffe, being the high top of the mountain Teneriffe in the Canaries, and had a great mind to venture out, in hopes of reaching thither ; but having tried twice, I was forced in again by contrary winds, the sea also going too high for my little vessel ; so I resolved to pursue my first design, and keep along the shore.

Several times I was obliged to land for fresh water, after we had left this place ; and once, in particular, being early in the morning, we came to an anchor under a little point of land which was pretty high ; and the tide beginning to flow, we lay still to go farther in. Xury, whose eyes were more about him than it seems mine were, calls softly to me, and tells me, that we had best go farther off the shore : " For," says he, " look—yonder lies a dreadful monster, on the side of that hillock, fast asleep." I looked where he pointed and saw a dreadful monster indeed, for it was a terrible great lion that lay on the side of the shore under the shade of a piece of the hill that hung, as it were, a little over him. " Xury," says I, " you shall go on shore and kill him." Xury looked frighted, and said, " Me kill ! he eat me at one mouth ! "—one mouthful he meant : however, I said no more to the boy, but bade him lie still, and I took our biggest gun, which was almost musket-bore, and loaded it with a good charge of powder, and with two slugs, and laid it down ; then I loaded another gun with two bullets ; and the third—for we had three pieces—I loaded with five smaller bullets. I took the best aim I could with the first piece to have shot him into the head, but he lay so with his leg raised a little above his nose, that the slugs hit his leg about the knee and broke the bone. He started up, growling at first, but finding his leg broke, fell down again, and then got up upon three legs, and gave the most hideous roar that ever I heard. I was a little surprised that I had not hit him on the head ; however, I took up the second piece immediately, and, though he began to move off, fired again, and shot him into the head, and had the pleasure to see him drop, and make but little noise, but lie struggling for life. Then Xury took heart, and would have me let him go on shore. " Well, go," said I ; so the boy jumped into the water, and taking a little gun in one hand, swam to shore with the other hand, and coming close to the creature, put the muzzle of the piece to his ear, and shot him into the head again, which despatched him quite.

This was game indeed to us, but this was no food ; and I was very sorry to lose three charges of powder and shot upon a creature that was good for nothing to us. However, Xury said he would have some of him ; so he comes on board, and asked me to give him the hatchet. " For what, Xury ?" said I. " Me cut off his head," said he. However, Xury could not cut off his head, but he cut off a foot, and brought it with him, and it was a monstrous great one.

I bethought myself, however, that perhaps the skin of him might, one way or other, be of some value to us ; and I resolved to take off his skin if I could. So Xury and I went to work with him ; but Xury was much the better workman at it, for I knew very ill how to do it. Indeed, it took us both up the whole day, but at last we got off the hide of him, and, spreading it on the top of our cabin, the sun effectually dried it in two days' time, and it afterwards served me to lie upon.

CHAPTER III

AFTER this stop, we made on to the southward for ten or twelve days, living very sparingly on our provisions, which began to abate very much and going no oftener into the shore than we were obliged to do for water : my design in this was, to make the River Gambia or Senegal, that is to say, anywhere about the Cape de Verde, where I was in hopes to meet with some European ship ; and if I did not, I knew not what course I had to take, but to seek for the islands, or perish there among the negroes. I knew that all the ships from Europe, which sailed either to the coast of Guinea or to Brazil, or to the East Indies, made this Cape, or those islands ; and, in a word, I put the whole of my fortune upon this single point, either that I must meet with some ship or must perish.

When I had pursued this resolution about ten days longer, as I have said, I began to see that the land was inhabited ; and in two or three places, as we sailed by, we saw people stand upon the shore to look at us : we could also perceive they were quite black, and stark naked. I was once inclined to go on shore to them ; but Xury was my better counsellor, and said to me : " No go, no go." However, I hauled in nearer the shore that I might talk to them, and I found they ran along the shore by me a good way : I observed they had no weapons in their hands except one, who had a long slender stick, which Xury said was a lance, and that they would throw them a good way with great aim ; so I kept at a distance, but talked with them by

We conversed with them by signs

signs as well as I could, and particularly made signs for something to eat ;
they beckoned to me to stop my boat, and they would fetch me some meat.
Upon this, I lowered the top of my sail, and lay by, and two of them ran up
into the country, and in less than half an hour came back, and brought with
them two pieces of dry flesh and some corn, such as is the produce of their
country ; but we neither knew what the one nor the other was ; however,
we were willing to accept it. But how to come at it was our next dispute, for
I was not for venturing on shore to them, and they were as much afraid of
us ; but they took a safe way for all, for they brought it to the shore and laid
it down, and went and stood a great way off till we fetched it on board, and
then came close to us again.

We made signs of thanks to them, for we had nothing to make them
amends ; but an opportunity offered that very instant to oblige them wonderfully ; for while we were lying by the shore, came two mighty creatures,
one pursuing the other (as we took it) with great fury from the mountains
towards the sea : whether it was the male pursuing the female, or whether
they were in sport or in rage, we could not tell, any more than we could tell
whether it was usual or strange, but I believe it was the latter ; because, in
the first place, those ravenous creatures seldom appear but in the night ;
and, in the second place, we found the people terribly frighted, especially
the women. The man that had the lance or dart did not fly from them,
but the rest did ; however, as the two creatures ran directly into the water,
they did not seem to offer to fall upon any of the negroes, but plunged themselves into the sea, and swam about as if they had come for their diversion.
At last one of them began to come nearer our boat than at first I expected ;

but I lay ready for him, for I had loaded my gun with all possible expedition, and bade Xury load both the others. As soon as he came fairly within my reach, I fired and shot him directly into the head : immediately he sank down into the water, but rose instantly and plunged up and down as if he was struggling for life, and so indeed he was ; he immediately made to the shore ; but between the wound, which was his mortal hurt, and the strangling of the water, he died just before he reached the shore.

It is impossible to express the astonishment of these poor creatures at the noise and the fire of my gun ; some of them were even ready to die for fear, and fell down as dead with the very terror. But when they saw the creature dead, and sunk in the water, and that I made signs to them to come to the shore, they took heart, and came to the shore, and began to search for the creature. I found him by his blood staining the water, and by the help of a rope, which I slung round him, and gave the negroes to haul, they dragged him on shore, and found that it was a most curious leopard, spotted, and fine to an admirable degree, and the negroes held up their hands with admiration to think what it was I had killed him with.

The other creature, frighted with the flash of fire and the noise of the gun, swam on shore, and ran up directly to the mountains from whence they came, nor could I at that distance know what it was. I found quickly the negroes were for eating the flesh of this creature, so I was willing to have them take it as a favour from me, which when I made signs to them, that they might take him, they were very thankful for. Immediately they fell to work with him, and though they had no knife, yet, with a sharpened piece of wood, they took off his skin as readily, and much more readily, than we could have done with a knife. They offered me some of the flesh, which I declined, making as if I would give it them, but made signs for the skin, which they gave me very freely, and brought me a great deal more of their provision, which, though I did not understand, yet I accepted ; then I made signs to them for some water, and held out one of my jars to them, turning it bottom upward, to show that it was empty, and that I wanted to have it filled. They called immediately to some of their friends, and there came two women, and brought a great vessel made of earth, and burned, as I suppose, in the sun ; this they set down for me, as before, and I sent Xury on shore with my jars, and filled them all three. The women were as stark naked as the men.

I was now furnished with roots and corn, such as it was, and water ; and, leaving my friendly negroes, I made forward for about eleven days more, without offering to go near the shore, till I saw the land run out a great length into the sea, at about the distance of four or five leagues before me ; and the sea being very calm, I kept a large offing to make this point ; at length, doubling the point, at about two leagues from the land, I saw plainly land on the other side to sea-ward ; then I concluded, as it was most certain, indeed, that this was the Cape de Verde, and those the islands, called from thence Cape de Verde Islands. However, they were at a great distance, and I could not tell what I had best to do ; for, if I should be taken with a fresh of wind, I might neither reach one nor the other.

In this dilemma, as I was very pensive, I stepped into the cabin and sat me down, Xury having the helm, when, on a sudden, the boy cried out :

" Master, master, a ship with a sail ! " and the foolish boy was frighted out of his wits, thinking it must needs be some of his master's ships sent to pursue us, when I knew we were gotten far enough out of their reach. I jumped out of the cabin, and immediately saw, not only the ship, but what she was, namely, that it was a Portuguese ship, and, as I thought, was bound to the coast of Guinea for negroes. But when I observed the course she steered, I was soon convinced they were bound some other way, and did not design to come any nearer to the shore ; upon which I stretched out to sea as much as I could, resolving to speak with them if possible.

With all the sail I could make, I found I should not be able to come in their way, but that they would be gone by before I could make any signal to them ; but after I had crowded to the utmost, and began to despair, they, it seems, saw me by the help of their perspective glasses, and that it was some European boat, which, as they supposed, must belong to some ship that was lost ; so they shortened sail to let me come up. I was encouraged with this ; and as I had my patron's ancient on board, I made a waft of it to them for a signal of distress, and fired a gun, both which they saw, for they told me they saw the smoke, though they did not hear the gun. Upon these signals they very kindly brought to, and lay by for me, and, in about three hours' time, I came up with them.

They asked me what I was, in Portuguese, and in Spanish, and in French ; but I understood none of them : but, at last, a Scots sailor, who was on board, called to me, and I answered him, and told him I was an Englishman —that I had made my escape out of slavery from the Moors at Sallee. They bade me come on board, and very kindly took me in, and all my goods.

It was inexpressible joy to me, as any one would believe, that I was thus delivered, as I esteemed it, from such a miserable and almost hopeless condition as I was in, and immediately offered all I had to the captain of the ship, as a return for my deliverance ; but he generously told me he would take nothing from me, but that all I had should be delivered safe to me when I came to the Brazils. " For," says he, " I have saved your life on no other terms than I would be glad to be saved myself ; and it may one time or other be my lot to be taken up in the same condition : besides," said he, " when I carry you to the Brazils, so great a way from your own country, if I should take from you what you have, you will be starved there, and then I only take away that life I have given. No, no, Seignor Inglese," says he, " Mr. Englishman, I will carry you thither in charity, and those things will help you to buy your subsistence there, and your passage home again."

As he was charitable in his proposal, so he was just in the performance to a tittle ; for he ordered the seamen, that none should offer to touch anything I had : then he took everything into his own possession, and gave me back an exact inventory of them, that I might have them ; even so much as my earthern jars.

As to my boat, it was a very good one, and that he saw, and told me he would buy it of me for the ship's use, and asked me what I would have for it ? I told him he had been so generous in everything, that I could not offer to make any price of the boat, but left it entirely to him ; upon which he told me, he would give me a note of his hand to pay me eighty pieces of eight for it at Brazil, and when it came there, if any one offered to give more, he would make it up : he offered me also sixty pieces of eight more for my boy Xury, which I was loath to take ; not that I was not willing to let the captain have him, but I was very loath to sell the poor boy's liberty, who had assisted me so faithfully in procuring my own. However, when I let him know my reason, he owned it to be just, and offered me this medium, that he would give the boy an obligation to set him free in ten years, if he turned Christian. Upon this, and Xury saying he was willing to go to him, I let the captain have him.

We had a very good voyage to the Brazils, and arrived in the Bay de Todos los Santos, or All Saints' Bay, in about twenty-two days after. And now I was once more delivered from the most miserable of all conditions of life ; and what to do next with myself I was now to consider.

The generous treatment the captain gave me, I can never enough remember. He would take nothing off me for my passage—gave me twenty ducats for the leopard's skin, and forty for the lion's skin, which I had in my boat, and caused everything I had in the ship to be punctually delivered me ; and what I was willing to sell he bought, such as the case of bottles, two of my guns, and a piece of the lump of bees'-wax, for I had made candles of the rest—in a word, I made about two hundred and twenty pieces of eight of all my cargo ; and with this stock I went on shore in the Brazils.

I had not been long here, but being recommended to the house of a good honest man like himself, who had an *ingeino*, as they call it—that is, a plantation and a sugar-house—I lived with him some time, and acquainted myself by that means with the manner of their planting and making of sugar ; and seeing how well the planters lived, and how they grew rich suddenly, I resolved, if I could get licence to settle there, I would turn planter among them ; resolving, in the meantime, to find out some way to get my money, which I had left in London, remitted to me. To this purpose, getting a kind of a letter of naturalisation, I purchased as much land that was uncured as my money would reach, and formed a plan for my plantation and settlement, and such a one as might be suitable to the stock which I proposed to myself to receive from England.

I had a neighbour, a Portuguese of Lisbon, but born of English parents, whose name was Wells, and in much such circumstances as I was. I call him neighbour, because his plantation lay next to mine, and we went on very sociably together. My stock was but low, as well as his : and we rather planted for food, than anything else, for about two years. However, we began to increase, and our land began to come into order ; so that the third year we planted some tobacco, and made each of us a large piece of ground ready for planting canes in the year to come ; but we both wanted help : and now I found more than before, I had done wrong in parting with my boy Xury.

I was, in some degree, settled in my measures for carrying on the plantation, before my kind friend, the captain of the ship that took me up at sea, went back ; for the ship remained there, in providing his loading, and preparing for his voyage, near three months ; when, telling him what little stock I had left behind me in London, he gave me this friendly and sincere advice : " Seignor Inglese," says he, for so he always called me, " if you will give me letters, and a procuration here in form to me, with orders to the person who has your money in London, to send your effects to Lisbon, to such persons as I shall direct, and in such goods as are proper for this country, I will bring you the produce of them, God willing, at my return ; but, since human affairs are all subject to changes and disasters, I would have you give orders but for one hundred pounds sterling, which, you say, is half your stock, and let the hazard be run for the first ; so that, if it comes safe, you may order the rest the same way, and if it miscarry, you may have the other half to have recourse to for your supply."

This was so wholesome advice, and looked so friendly, that I could not but be convinced it was the best course I could take ; so I accordingly prepared letters to the gentlewoman with whom I had left my money, and a procuration to the Portuguese captain, as he desired.

I wrote the English captain's widow a full account of all my adventures, my slavery, escape, and how I had met with the Portugal captain at sea, the humanity of his behaviour, and what condition I was now in, with all other necessary directions for my supply ; and when this honest captain came to Lisbon, he found means, by some of the English merchants there, to send over, not the order only, but a full account of my story, to a merchant at London, who represented it effectually to her ; whereupon, she not only delivered the money, but, out of her own pocket, sent the Portugal captain a very handsome present for his humanity and charity to me.

The merchant in London vesting this hundred pounds in English goods, such as the captain had writ for, sent them directly to him at Lisbon, and he brought them all safe to me to the Brazils ; among which, without my direction (for I was too young in my business to think of them), he had taken care to have all sorts of tools, ironwork, and utensils, necessary for my plantation, and which were of great use to me.

When this cargo arrived, I thought my fortune made, for I was surprised with joy of it ; and my good steward, the captain, had laid out the five pounds which my friend had sent him for a present for himself, to purchase, and bring me over a servant under bond for six years' service, and would not accept of any consideration, except a little tobacco, which I would have him accept, being of my own produce.

Neither was this all ; but my goods being all English manufactures, such as cloth, stuffs, baize, and things particularly valuable and desirable in the country, I found means to sell them to a very great advantage ; so that I may say I had more than four times the value of my first cargo, and was now infinitely beyond my poor neighbour, I mean in the advancement of my plantation ; for the first thing I did, I bought me a negro slave, and an European servant also—I mean another besides that which the captain brought me from Lisbon.

To come, then, by just degrees, to the particulars of this part of my story : you may suppose, that, having now lived almost four years in the Brazils, and beginning to prosper and thrive very well upon my plantation, I had not only learnt the language, but had contracted acquaintance and friendship among my fellow-planters, as well as among the merchants at St. Salvadore, which was our port ; and that in my discourse among them, I had frequently given them an account of my two voyages to the coast of Guinea, the manner of trading with the negroes there, and how easy it was to purchase upon the coast for trifles—such as beads, toys, knives, scissors, hatchets, bits of glass, and the like—not only gold dust, Guinea grains, elephants' teeth, etc., but negroes for the service of the Brazils in great numbers.

They listened always very attentively to my discourses on these heads, but especially to that part which related to buying negroes, which was a trade at that time not only not far entered into, but, as far as it was, had been carried on by the *assientos*, or permission, of the kings of Spain and Portugal, and engrossed in the public, so that few negroes were bought, and those excessively dear.

It happened, being in company with some merchants and planters of my acquaintance, and talking of those things very earnestly, three of them came to me the next morning, and told me they had been musing very much upon what I had discoursed with them of the last night, and they came to make a secret proposal to me ; and, after enjoining me secrecy, they told me that they had a mind to fit out a ship to go to Guinea ; that they had all plantations as well as I, and were straitened for nothing so much as servants ; that as it was a trade that could not be carried on, because they could not publicly sell the negroes when they came home, so they desired to make but one voyage, to bring the negroes on shore privately, and divide them among their own plantations ; and, in a word, the question was, whether I would go their supercargo in the ship, to manage the trading part upon the coast of Guinea ? and they offered me, that I should have my equal share of the negroes, without providing any part of the stock.

This was a fair proposal, it must be confessed, had it been made to any one that had not had a settlement and plantation of his own to look after, which was in a fair way of coming to be very considerable, and with a good stock upon it. But for me, that was thus entered and established, and had nothing to do but go on as I had begun for three or four years more, and to have sent for the other hundred pounds from England, and who, in that time and with that little addition, could scarce have failed of being worth three or four thousand pounds sterling, and that increasing too—for me to think of such a voyage, was the most preposterous thing that ever man in such circumstances could be guilty of.

But I, that was born to be my own destroyer, could no more resist the offer than I could restrain my first rambling designs, when my father's good counsel was lost upon me. In a word, I told them I would go with all my heart if they would undertake to look after my plantation in my absence, and would dispose of it to such as I should direct, if I miscarried. This they all engaged to do, and entered into writings, or covenants, to do so ; and I made a formal will, disposing of my plantation and effects in case of my death, making the captain of the ship that had saved my life as before, my universal heir, but obliging him to dispose of my effects as I had directed in my will, one half of the produce being to himself, and the other to be shipped to England.

In short, I took all possible caution to preserve my effects, and keep up my plantation ; had I used half as much prudence to have looked into my own interest, and have made a judgment of what I ought to have done, and not to have done, I had certainly never gone away from so prosperous an undertaking, leaving all the probable views of a thriving circumstance, and gone upon a voyage to sea, attended with all its common hazards ; to say nothing of the reasons I had to expect particular misfortunes to myself.

But I was hurried on, and obeyed blindly the dictates of my fancy, rather than my reason : and accordingly, the ship being fitted out, and the cargo furnished, and all things done as by agreement by my partners in the voyage, I went on board in an evil hour again, the 1st of September, 1659, being the same day eight years that I went from my father and mother at Hull in order to act the rebel to their authority, and the fool to my own interest.

Our ship was about one hundred and twenty tons burden, carried six guns, and fourteen men, besides the master, his boy, and myself ; we had on board no large cargo of goods, except of such toys as were fit for our trade with the negroes, such as beads, bits of glass, shells, and odd trifles, especially little looking-glasses, knives, scissors, hatchets, and the like.

The same day I went on board we set sail, standing away to the north-ward upon our own coast, with design to stretch over for the African coast, when they came about ten or twelve degrees of northern latitude, which, it seems, was the manner of their course in those days. We had very good weather, only excessively hot, all the way upon our own coast, till we came to the height of Cape St. Augustino, from whence, keeping farther off at sea, we lost sight of land, and steered as if we were bound for the isle Fernand de Noronha, holding our course north-east by north, and leaving those isles on the east. In this course we passed the Line in about twelve days' time, and were, by our last observation, in seven degrees, twenty-two minutes, northern latitude, when a violent tornado, or hurricane, took us quite out of our knowledge : it began from the south-east, came about to the north-west ; from whence it blew in such a terrible manner, that for twelve days together we could do nothing but drive, and, scudding away before it, let it carry us whither ever fate and the fury of the winds directed ; and during those twelve days, I need not say that I expected every day to be swallowed up, nor indeed, did any in the ship expect to save their lives.

In this distress, we had, besides the terror of the storm, one of our men dead of the calenture, and one man and the boy washed overboard. About the twelfth day, the weather abating a little, the master made an observation as well as he could, and found that he was in about twenty-two degrees of longitude difference west from Cape St. Augustino ; so that he found he was gotten upon the coast of Guinea, or the north part of Brazil, beyond the river Amazons, towards that of the river Oroonoque, commonly called the Great River, and began to consult with me what course he should take ; for the ship was leaky, and very much disabled, and he was going directly back to the coast of Brazil.

I was positively against that, and, looking over the charts of the sea coasts of America with him, we concluded, there was no inhabited country for us to have recourse to, till we came within the circle of the Caribbee Islands ; and therefore resolved to stand away for Barbadoes, which, by keeping off at sea, to avoid the indraft of the bay or gulf of Mexico, we might easily perform, as we hoped, in about fifteen days' sail : whereas we could

It began from the South-east

not possibly make our voyage to the coast of Africa, without some assistance, both to our ship and ourselves.

With this design we changed our course, and steered away north-west by west, in order to reach some of our English islands, where I hoped for relief : but our voyage was otherwise determined ; for, being in the latitude of twelve degrees, eighteen minutes, a second storm came upon us, which carried us away with the same impetuosity westward, and drove us so out of the very way of all human commerce, that, had all our lives been saved as to the sea, we were rather in danger of being devoured by savages than ever returning to our own country.

In this distress, the wind still blowing very hard, one of our men, early in the morning, cried out : " Land ! " and we had no sooner run out of the cabin to look out, in hopes of seeing whereabouts in the world we were, but the ship struck upon a sand, and, in a moment, her motion being so stopped, the sea broke over her in such a manner that we expected we should all have perished immediately ; and we were immediately driven into our close quarters, to shelter us from the very foam and spray of the sea.

Now, though we thought that the wind did a little abate, yet, the ship having thus struck upon the sand, and sticking too fast for us to expect her getting off, we were in a dreadful condition indeed, and had nothing to do but to think of saving our lives as well as we could. We had a boat at our stern, just before the storm ; but she was first staved by dashing against the ship's rudder, and, in the next place, she broke away, and either sunk or was driven off to sea ; so there was no hope from her. We had another boat on board, but how to get her off into the sea was a doubtful thing ;

however, there was no reason to debate, for we fancied the ship would break in pieces every minute, and some told us she was actually broken already.

In this distress, the mate of our vessel lays hold of the boat, and, with the help of the rest of the men, they got her slung over the ship's side, and getting all into her, let go, and committed ourselves, being eleven in number, to God's mercy and the wild sea; for though the storm was abated considerably, yet the sea went dreadfully high upon the shore, and might well be called *den wild zee*, as the Dutch call the sea in a storm.

And now our case was very dismal indeed; for we all saw plainly that the sea went so high that the boat could not live, and that we should be inevitably drowned. As to making sail, we had none, nor, if we had, could we have done anything with it; so we worked at the oar towards the land, though with heavy hearts, like men going to execution; for we all knew, that when the boat came nearer the shore, she would be dashed in a thousand pieces by the breach of the sea. However, we committed our souls to God in the most earnest manner; and the wind driving us towards the shore, we hastened our destruction with our own hands, pulling as well as we could towards land.

What the shore was, whether rock or sand, whether steep or shoal, we knew not; the only hope that could rationally give us the least shadow of expectation was if we might happen into some bay or gulf, or the mouth of some river, where by great chance we might have run our boat in, or got under the lee of the land, and perhaps made smooth water. But there was nothing of this appeared; but, as we made nearer and nearer the shore, the land looked more frightful than the sea.

After we had rowed, or rather driven, about a league and a half, as we reckoned it, a raging wave, mountain-like, came rolling astern of us, and plainly bade us expect a watery grave. In a word, it took us with such a fury, that it overset the boat at once; and separating us as well from the boat as from one another, gave us not time hardly to say: "O God!" for we were all swallowed up in a moment.

The wave that came upon me again buried me at once twenty or thirty feet deep in its own body; and I could feel myself carried with a mighty force and swiftness towards the shore a very great way; but I held my breath, and assisted myself to swim still forward with all my might. I was ready to burst with holding my breath, when, as I felt myself rising up, so, to my immediate relief, I found my head and hands shoot out above the surface of the water; and though it was not two seconds of time that I could keep myself so, yet it relieved me greatly, gave me breath and new courage. I was covered again with water a good while, but not so long, but I held it out; and, finding the water had spent itself and began to return, I struck forward against the return of the waves and felt ground again with my feet. I stood still a few moments to recover breath, and till the water went from me, and then took to my heels, and ran with what strength I had farther towards the shore. But neither would this deliver me from the fury of the sea, which came pouring in after me again; and twice more I was lifted up by the waves and carried forwards as before, the shore being very flat.

The last time of those two had well near been fatal to me; for the sea, having hurried me along as before, landed me, or rather dashed me, against

THE SHIPWRECK.
We lowered the boat and rowed away from the sinking ship.

CRUSOE AT HOME.
Surrounded by my household pets, I spent many happy and peaceful days.

We were all swallowed up in a moment

a piece of rock, and that with such force as it left me senseless, and indeed helpless, as to my own deliverance ; for the blow taking my side and breast, beat the breath, as it were, quite out of my body, and had it returned again immediately, I must have been strangled in the water ; but I recovered a little before the return of the waves, and, seeing I should be covered again with the water, I resolved to hold fast by a piece of the rock, and so to hold my breath, if possible, till the wave went back. Now, as the waves were not so high as at first, being near land, I held my hold till the wave abated, and then fetched another run, which brought me so near the shore, that the next wave, though it went over me, yet did not so swallow me up as to carry me away ; and the next run I took I got to the mainland, where, to my great comfort, I clambered up the cliffs of the shore, and sat me down upon the grass, free from danger, and quite out of the reach of the water.

I was now landed and safe on shore, and began to look up and thank God that my life was saved, in a case wherein there was, some minutes before, scarce any room to hope.

I walked about on the shore, lifting up my hands, and my whole being, as I may say, rapt up in the contemplation of my deliverance, making a thousand gestures and motions which I cannot describe—reflecting upon all my comrades that were drowned, and that there should not be one soul saved but myself—for, as for them, I never saw them afterwards, or any sign of them, except three of their hats, one cap, and two shoes that were not fellows.

I cast my eyes to the stranded vessel, when the breach and froth of the sea being so big, I could hardly see it, it lay so far off, and considered, Lord ! how was it possible I could get on shore ?

After I had solaced my mind with the comfortable part of my condition, I began to look round me, to see what kind of place I was in, and what was next to be done; and I soon found my comforts abate, and that, in a word, I had a dreadful deliverance : for I was wet, had no clothes to shift me, nor anything either to eat or drink to comfort me; neither did I see any prospect before me but that of perishing with hunger, or being devoured by wild beasts ; and that which was particularly afflicting to me was that I had no weapon either to hunt and kill any creature for my sustenance, or to defend myself against any other creature that might desire to kill me for theirs—in a word, I had nothing about me but a knife, a tobacco pipe, and a little tobacco in a box ; this was all my provision, and this threw me into terrible agonies of mind, that, for a while, I ran about like a madman. Night coming upon me, I began with a heavy heart to consider what would be my lot if there were any ravenous beasts in that country, seeing at night they always come abroad for their prey.

All the remedy that offered to my thoughts at that time was to get up into a thick bushy tree like a fir, but thorny, which grew near me, and where I resolved to sit all night, and consider the next day what death I should die, for as yet I saw no prospect of life. I walked about a furlong from the shore to see if I could find any fresh water to drink, which I did, to my great joy ; and having drunk and put a little tobacco in my mouth to prevent hunger, I went to the tree, and getting up into it, endeavoured to place myself so as that if I should sleep I might not fall ; and having cut me a short stick like a truncheon for my defence, I took up my lodging ; and having been excessively fatigued, I fell fast asleep, and slept as comfortably as I believe few could have done in my condition, and found myself the most refreshed with it that I think I ever was on such an occasion.

CHAPTER IV

WHEN I waked it was broad day, the weather clear, and the storm abated, so that the sea did not rage as before ; but that which surprised me most was, that the ship was lifted off in the night from the sand where she lay, by the tide, and was driven up almost as far as the rock which I first mentioned, where I had been so bruised by the dashing me against it ; this being within about a mile from the shore where I was, and the ship seeming to stand upright still, I wished myself on board, that, at least, I might save some necessary things for my use.

When I came down from my apartment in the tree, I looked about me again, and the first thing I found was the boat, which lay as the wind and the sea had tossed her up upon the land, about two miles on my right hand. I walked as far as I could upon the shore to have got to her, but found a neck, or inlet of water, between me and the boat, which was about half a mile broad : so I came back for the present, being more intent upon getting at the ship, where I hoped to find something for my present subsistence.

A little after noon, I found the sea very calm, and the tide ebbed so far out, that I could come within a quarter of a mile of the ship ; and here I found a fresh renewing of my grief : for I saw evidently, that if we had kept on board, we had been all safe,—that is to say, we had all got safe on shore, and I had not been so miserable as to be left entirely destitute of all comfort and company as I now was. This forced tears from my eyes again ; but as there was little relief in that, I resolved, if possible, to get to the ship—so I pulled off my clothes, for the weather was hot to extremity, and took the water. But when I came to the ship, my difficulty was still greater to know how to get on board ; for as she lay aground and high out of the water, there was nothing within my reach to lay hold of. I swam round her twice, and the second time I spied a small piece of a rope, which I wondered I did not see at first, hang down by the fore-chains, so low as that with great difficulty I got hold of it, and, by the help of that rope, got up into the fore-castle of the ship. Here I found that the ship was bulged, and had a great deal of water in her hold, but that she lay so on the side of a bank of hard sand, or rather earth, and her stern lay lifted up upon the bank, and her head, low almost to the water ; by this means all her quarter was free, and all that was in that part was dry ; for you may be sure my first work was to search and see what was spoiled, and what was free ; and first I found that all the ship's provisions were dry and untouched by the water ; and being very well disposed to eat, I went to the bread-room and filled my pockets with biscuit, and ate it as I went about other things, for I had no time to lose. I also found some rum in the great cabin, of which I took a large dram, and which I had indeed need enough of to spirit me for what was before me. Now I wanted nothing but a boat, to furnish myself with many things which I foresaw would be very necessary to me.

It was in vain to sit still and wish for what was not to be had ; and this extremity roused my application. We had several spare yards, and two or three large spars of wood, and a spare topmast or two in the ship ; I resolved to fall to work with these, and flung as many of them overboard as I could manage of their weight, tying every one with a rope, that they might not drive away. When this was done, I went down to the ship's side, and pulling them to me, I tied four of them fast together at both ends as well as I could, in the form of a raft, and laying two or three short pieces of plank upon them crossways, I found I could walk upon it very well, but that it was not able to bear any great weight, the pieces being too light ; so I went to work, and, with the carpenter's saw, I cut a spare topmast into three lengths, and added them to my raft, with a great deal of labour and pains ; but hope of furnishing myself with necessaries, encouraged me to go beyond what I should have been able to have done upon another occasion.

My raft was now strong enough to bear any reasonable weight ; my next care was what to load it with, and how to preserve what I laid on it from the surf of the sea ; but I was not long considering this. I first laid all the planks or boards upon it that I could get, and having considered well what I most wanted, I first got three of the seamen's chests, which I had broken open and emptied, and lowered them down upon my raft. The first of these I filled with provisions, namely, bread, rice, three Dutch cheeses, five pieces of dried goats' flesh, which we lived much upon, and a little remainder of European corn, which had been laid by for some fowls which we brought to sea with us, but the fowls were killed. There had been some barley and wheat together, but, to my great disappointment, I found afterwards that the rats had eaten or spoiled it all. As for liquors, I found several cases of bottles belonging to our skipper, in which were some cordial waters, and, in all above five or six gallons of rack : these I stowed by themselves, there being no need to put them into the chest, nor no room for them. While I was doing this, I found the tide began to flow, though very calm, and I had the mortification to see my coat, shirt, and waistcoat, which I had left on shore upon the sand, swim away ; as for my breeches, which were only linen, and open-kneed, I swam on board in them and my stockings: however, this put me upon rummaging for clothes, of which I found enough, but took no more than I wanted for present use, for I had other things which my eye was more upon : as, first, tools to work with on shore ; and it was after long searching that I found out the carpenter's chest, which was indeed a very useful prize to me, and much more valuable than a shipload of gold would have been at that time. I got it down to my raft, even whole as it was, without losing time to look into it, for I knew in general what it contained.

My next care was for some ammunition and arms. There were two very good fowling-pieces in the great cabin, and two pistols : these I secured first, with some powder-horns, and a small bag of shot, and two old rusty swords. I knew there were three barrels of powder in the ship, but knew not where our gunner had stowed them ; but with much search I found them, two of them dry and good, the third had taken water ; those two I got to my raft, with the arms. And now I thought myself pretty well freighted, and began to think how I should get to shore with them, having neither sail, oar, nor rudder, and the least capful of wind would have overset all my navigation.

I had three encouragements : 1, A smooth, calm sea ; 2, The tide rising, and setting in to the shore ; 3, What little wind there was blew me toward the land ; and thus, having found two or three broken oars belonging to the boat, and, besides the tools which were in the chest, I found two saws, an axe, and a hammer ; and with this cargo I put to sea. For a mile, or thereabouts, my raft went very well, only that I found it drive a little distant from the place where I had landed before ; by which I perceived that there was some indraft of the water, and, consequently, I hoped to find some creek or river there which I might make use of as a port to get to land with my cargo.

As I imagined, so it was ; there appeared before me a little opening of the land, and I found a strong current of the tide set into it, so I guided my raft as well as I could to keep in the middle of the stream ; but here I had like to have suffered a second shipwreck, which, if I had, I think verily would have broke my heart ; for, knowing nothing of the coast, my raft ran aground at one end of it upon a shoal, and, not being aground at the other end, it wanted but a little that all my cargo had slipped off towards that end that was afloat, and so fallen into the water. I did my utmost, by setting my back against the chests, to keep them in their places, but could not thrust off the raft with all my strength ; neither durst I stir from the posture I was in, but, holding up the chests with all my might, stood in that manner near half an hour, in which time the rising of the water brought me a little more upon a level ; and, a little after, the water still rising, my raft floated again, and I thrust her off with the oar I had into the channel ; and then, driving up higher, I at length found myself in the mouth of a little river, with land on both sides, and a strong current, or tide, running up. I looked on both sides for a proper place to get to shore ; for I was not willing to be driven too high up the river, hoping in time to see some ship at sea, and therefore resolved to place myself as near the coast as I could.

At length I spied a little cove on the right shore of the creek, to which, with great pain and difficulty, I guided my raft, and at last got so near as that, reaching ground with my oar, I could thrust her directly in ; but here I had like to have dipped all my cargo in the sea again ; for that shore lying pretty steep, that is to say, sloping, there was no place to land, but where one end of the float, if it ran on shore, would lie so high, and the other sink lower as before, that it would endanger my cargo again : all that I could do, was to wait till the tide was at the highest, keeping the raft with my oar like an anchor to hold the side of it fast to the shore, near a flat piece of ground, which I expected the water would flow over : and so it did. As soon as I found water enough—for my raft drew about a foot of water—I thrust her on upon that flat piece of ground, and there fastened, or moored her, by sticking my two broken oars into the ground—one on one side, near one end, and one on the other side, near the other end ; and thus I lay till the water ebbed away, and left my raft and all my cargo safe on shore.

My next work was to view the country, and to seek a proper place for my habitation, and where to stow my goods, to secure them from whatever might happen. Where I was, I yet knew not ; whether on the continent or on an island—whether inhabited or not inhabited—whether in danger of wild beasts or not. There was a hill, not above a mile from me, which rose up very steep and high, and which seemed to overtop some other hills which lay as in a ridge from it northward. I took out one of the fowling-pieces, and one of the pistols, and a horn of powder ; and thus armed, I travelled for discovery up to the top of that hill, where, after I had with great labour and difficulty got to the top, I saw my fate, to my great affliction, namely, that I was on an island, environed every way with the sea—no land to be seen, except some rocks which lay a great way off, and two small islands less than this, which lay about three leagues to the west.

I found also, that the island I was on was barren, and, as I saw good reason to believe, uninhabited, except by wild beasts, of which, however, I saw none ; yet I saw abundance of fowls, but knew not their kinds, neither, when I killed them, could I tell what was fit for food, and what not. At my coming back, I shot at a great bird, which I saw sitting upon a tree on the side of a great wood : I believe it was the first gun that had been fired there since the creation of the world. I had no sooner fired, but, from all parts of the wood, there arose an innumerable number of fowls of many sorts, making a confused screaming and crying, every one according to his usual note ; but not one of them of any kind that I knew. As for the creature that I killed, I took it to be a kind of hawk, its colour and beak resembling it, but had no talons or claws, more than common ; its flesh was carrion, and fit for nothing.

Contented with this discovery, I came back to my raft, and fell to work to bring my cargo on shore, which took me up the rest of that day : and what to do with myself at night I knew not, nor indeed where to rest ; for I was afraid to lie down on the ground, not knowing but some wild beast might devour me ; though, as I afterwards found, there was really no need for those fears.

However, as well as I could, I barricaded myself round with the chests and boards that I had brought on shore, and made a kind of a hut for that night's lodging. As for food, I yet saw not which way to supply myself, except that I had seen two or three creatures like hares run out of the wood where I shot the fowl.

I now began to consider that I might yet get a great many things out of the ship, which would be useful to me, and particularly some of the rigging and sails, and such other things as might come to land, and I resolved to make another voyage on board the vessel, if possible ; and as I knew that the first storm that blew must necessarily break her all in pieces, I resolved to set all other things apart, till I got everything out of the ship that I could get. Then I called a council (that is to say in my thoughts), whether I should take back the raft ; but this appeared impracticable ; so I resolved to go as before, when the tide was down, and I did so, only that I stripped before I went from my hut, having nothing on but a checked shirt and a pair of linen trousers, and a pair of pumps on my feet.

I got aboard the ship as before, and prepared a second raft ; and having had experience of the first, I neither made this so unwieldy, nor loaded it so hard, but yet I brought away several things very useful to me ; as first, in the carpenter's stores, I found two or three bags full of nails and spikes, a great screw-jack, a dozen or two of hatchets, and, above all, that most useful thing called a grindstone : all these I secured, together with several things belonging to the gunner, particularly two or three iron crows, and two barrels of musket bullets, seven muskets, and another fowling-piece, with some small quantity of powder more ; a large bag full of small shot, and a great roll of sheet lead ; but this last was so heavy I could not hoist it up to get it over the ship's side.

Besides these things, I took all the men's clothes that I could find, and a spare fore-top-sail, hammock, and some bedding ; and with this I loaded my second raft, and brought them all safe on shore, to my very great comfort.

I was under some apprehensions during my absence from the land, that at least my provisions might be devoured on shore ; but, when I came back, I found no sign of any visitor, only there sat a creature, like a wild cat, upon one of the chests, which, when I came towards it, ran away a little distance, and then stood still : she sat very composed and unconcerned, and looked full in my face, as if she had a mind to be acquainted with me. I presented my gun at her, but as she did not understand it, she was perfectly unconcerned at it, nor did she offer to stir away ; upon which I tossed her a bit of biscuit, though by the way, I was not very free of it, for my store was not great : however, I spared her a bit, I say, and she went to it, smelled of it, and ate it, and looked, as pleased, for more ; but I thanked her, and could spare no more—so she marched off.

Having got my second cargo on shore, though I was fain to open the barrels of powder, and bring them by parcels—for they were too heavy, being large casks—I went to work to make me a little tent, with the sail and some poles which I cut for that purpose ; and into this tent I brought everything that I knew would spoil either with rain or sun ; and piled all the empty chests and casks up in a circle round the tent, to fortify it from any sudden attempt, either from man or beast.

When I had done this, I blocked up the door of the tent with some boards within, and an empty chest set up on end without, and, spreading one of the beds upon the ground, laying my two pistols just at my head, and my gun at length by me, I went to bed for the first time, and slept very quietly all night, for I was very weary and heavy ; as the night before I had slept little, and had laboured very hard all day, as well to fetch all those things from the ship as to get them on shore.

I had the biggest magazine of all kinds now that ever was laid up, I believe, for one man, but I was not satisfied still : for, while the ship sat upright in that posture, I thought I ought to get everything out of her that I could : so every day, at low water, I went on board and brought away something or other, but particularly the third time I went, I brought away as much of the rigging as I could, as also all the small ropes and rope-twine I could get, with a piece of spare canvas, which was to mend the sails upon occasion, and the barrel of wet gunpowder ; in a word, I brought away all the sails first and last, only that I was fain to cut them in pieces, and bring as much at a time as I could ; for they were no more useful to be sails, but as mere canvas only.

But that which comforted me more still, was, that last of all, after I had made five or six such voyages as these, and thought I had nothing more to expect from the ship that was worth my meddling with—I say, after all this, I found a great hogshead of bread, and three large runlets of rum or spirits, and a box of sugar, and a barrel of fine flour ; this was surprising to me, because I had given over expecting any more provisions, except what was spoiled by the water. I soon emptied the hogshead of that bread, and wrapped it up, parcel by parcel, in pieces of the sails, which I cut out ; and, in a word, I got all this safe on shore also.

The next day I made another voyage ; and now, having plundered the ship of what was portable and fit to hand out, I began with the cables ; and cutting the great cable into pieces, such as I could move, I got two cables and a howser on shore, with all the iron-work I could get ; and having cut down the sprit-sail-yard, and the mizzen-yard, and everything I could, to make a large raft, I loaded it with all those heavy goods, and came away : but my good luck began now to leave me ; for this raft was so unwieldy and overladen, that, after I had entered the little cove, where I had landed the rest of my goods, not being able to guide it handily so as I did the others, it overset, and threw me and all my cargo into the water. As for myself, it was no great harm, for I was near the shore ; but as to my cargo, it was, great part of it, lost, especially the iron, which I expected would have been of great use to me ; however, when the tide was out, I got most of the pieces of cable ashore, and some of the iron, though with infinite labour ; for I was fain to dip for it into the water, a work which fatigued me very much. After this I went every day on board, and brought away what I could get.

I had been now thirteen days on shore, and had been eleven times on board the ship ; in which time I had brought away all that one pair of hands could well be supposed capable to bring, though I believe verily, had the calm held, I should have brought away the whole ship, piece by piece : but, preparing the twelfth time to go on board, I found the wind began to rise ; however, at low water, I went on board, and though I had rummaged the cabin so effectually as that nothing more could be found, yet I discovered a locker with drawers in it, in one of which I found two or three razors, and one pair of large scissors, with some ten or a dozen of good knives and forks ; in another I found about thirty-six pounds value in money, some European coin, some Brazil, some pieces of eight, some gold, some silver.

I took it away, and wrapping all this in a piece of canvas, I began to think of making another raft ; but, while I was preparing this, I found the sky overcast, and the wind began to rise, and in a quarter of an hour it blew a fresh gale from the shore. It presently occurred to me, that it was in vain to pretend to make a raft with the wind off-shore, and that it was my business to be gone before the tide of flood began, otherwise I might not be able to reach the shore at all ; accordingly, I let myself down into the water, and swam across the channel which lay between the ship and the sands, and even that with difficulty enough, partly with the weight of things I had about me, and partly the roughness of the water, for the wind rose very hastily, and, before it was quite high water, it blew a storm.

But I was gotten home to my little tent, where I lay with all my wealth about me very secure. It blew very hard all that night, and in the morning when I looked out, behold no more ship was to be seen ! I was a little surprised, but recovered myself with this satisfactory reflection, namely, that I had lost no time, nor abated no diligence, to get everything out of her that could be useful to me, and that, indeed, there was little left in her that I was able to bring away, if I had had more time.

I now gave over any more thoughts of the ship, or of anything out of her, except what might drive on shore from the wreck, as indeed divers pieces of her afterwards did ; but those things were of small use to me.

My thoughts were now wholly employed about securing myself against either savages, if any should appear, or wild beasts, if any were on the island ; and I had many thoughts of the method how to do this, and what kind of dwelling to make—whether I should make me a cave in the earth, or a tent upon the earth ; and, in short, I resolved upon both, the manner and description of which it may not be improper to give an account of.

I soon found the place I was in was not for my settlement, particularly because it was upon a low moorish ground near the sea, and I believe would not be wholesome, and more particularly because there was no fresh water near it ; so I resolved to find a more healthy and more convenient spot of ground.

I consulted several things in my situation which I found would be proper for me : First, Health and fresh water I just now mentioned ; second, Shelter from the heat of the sun ; third, Security from ravenous creatures, whether man or beast ; fourth, A view to the sea, that, if God send any ship in sight, I might not lose any advantage for my deliverance, of which I was not willing to banish all my expectation yet.

In search of a place proper for this, I found a little plain on the side of a rising hill, whose front towards this little plain was steep as a house-side, so that nothing could come down upon me from the top : on the side of this rock there was a hollow place worn a little way in, like the entrance or door of a cave, but there was not really any cave or way into the rock at all.

On the flat of the green, just below this hollow place, I resolved to pitch my tent : this plain was not above an hundred yards broad, and about twice as long, and lay like a green before my door, and at the end of it descended irregularly every way down into the low grounds by the sea-side. It was on the north-north-west side of the hill, so that I was sheltered from the heat every day, till it came to a west-and-by-south sun, or thereabouts, which in those countries is near the setting.

Before I set up my tent, I drew a half circle before the hollow place which took in about ten yards in its semi-diameter, from the rock, and twenty yards in its diameter from its beginning and ending.

In this half circle I pitched two rows of strong stakes, driving them into the ground till they stood very firm, like piles, the biggest end being out of the ground about five feet and a half, and sharpened on the top : the two rows did not stand above six inches from one another.

Then I took the pieces of cable which I had cut in the ship, and laid them in rows, one upon another, within the circle between these two rows of stakes up to the top, placing other stakes in the inside, leaning against them, about two feet and a half high, like a spur to a post ; and this fence was so strong that neither man nor beast could get into it, or over it : this cost me a great deal of time and labour, especially to cut the piles in the woods, bring them to the place, and drive them into the earth.

The entrance into this place I made to be, not by a door, but by a short ladder, to go over the top ; which ladder, when I was in, I lifted over after me : and so I was completely fenced in, and fortified, as I thought, from all the world, and consequently slept secure in the night, which otherwise I could not have done ; though, as it appeared afterwards, there was no need of all this caution from the enemies that I apprehended danger from.

Into this fence, or fortress, with infinite labour, I carried all my riches, all my provisions, ammunition, and stores, of which you have the account above ; and I made me a large tent, which, to preserve me from the rains, that in one part of the year are very violent there, I made double, namely, one smaller tent within, and one larger tent above it, and covered the uppermost with a large tarpaulin, which I had saved among the sails.

And now I lay no more, for a while, in the bed which I had brought on shore, but in a hammock, which was, indeed, a very good one, and belonged to the mate of the ship.

Into this tent I brought all my provisions, and everything that would spoil by the wet ; and having thus enclosed all my goods, I made up the entrance, which, till now, I had left open, and so passed and repassed, as I said, by a short ladder.

When I had done this, I began to work my way into the rock, and, bringing all the earth and stones that I dug down, out through my tent, I laid them up within my fence in the nature of a terrace, that so it raised the

ground within about a foot and a half ; and thus I made me a cave just
behind my tent, which served me like a cellar to my house.

It cost me much labour and many days before all these things were
brought to perfection : and, therefore, I must go back to some other things
which took up some of my thoughts. At the same time, it happened, after
I had laid my scheme for the settings of my tent, and making the cave,
that a storm of rain falling from a thick dark cloud, a sudden flash of lightning happened, and after that a great clap of thunder, as is naturally the
effect of it. I was not so much surprised with the lightning as I was with a
thought which darted into my mind, as swift as the lightning itself : Oh,
my powder ! my very heart sank within me, when I thought that, at one
blast, all my powder might be destroyed, on which, not my defence only,
but the providing me food, as I thought, entirely depended ; I was nothing
near so anxious about my own danger, though, had the powder took fire,
I had never known who had hurt me.

Such impression did this make upon me, that after the storm was over,
I laid aside all my works, my building and fortifying, and applied myself to
make bags and boxes, to separate the powder, and to keep it a little and a
little in a parcel, in hope that, whatever might come, it might not all take
fire at once, and to keep it so apart, that it should not be possible to make
one part fire another. I finished this work in about a fortnight ; and I think
my powder, which, in all, was about two hundred and forty pounds weight,
was divided in not less than a hundred parcels. As to the barrel that had
been wet, I did not apprehend any danger from that, so I placed it in my
new cave, which, in my fancy, I called my kitchen ; and the rest I hid up

It cost me much labour

and down in holes among the rocks, so that no wet might come to it, marking very carefully where I laid it.

In the interval of time, while this was doing, I went out once at least every day with my gun, as well to divert myself as to see if I could kill anything fit for food, and, as near as I could, to acquaint myself with what the island produced. The first time I went out, I presently discovered that there were goats in the island, which was a great satisfaction to me ; but then, it was attended with this misfortune to me, namely, that they were so shy, so subtle, and so swift of foot, that it was the most difficult thing in the world to come at them. But I was not discouraged at this, not doubting but I might now and then shoot one, as it soon happened ; for, after I had found their haunts a little, I laid wait in this manner for them. I observed, if they saw me in the valleys, though they were upon the rocks, they would run away as in a terrible fright ; but if they were feeding in the valleys, and I was upon the rocks, they took no notice of me ; from whence I concluded, that, by the position of their optics, their sight was so directed downwards that they did not readily see objects that were above them : so afterwards I took this method : I always climbed the rocks first, to get above them, and then had frequently a fair mark. The first shot I made among these creatures I killed a she-goat, which had a little kid by her which she gave suck to, which grieved me heartily ; but when the old one fell, the kid stood stock still by her till I came and took her up ; and not only so, but, when I carried the old one with me upon my shouders, the kid followed me quite to my enclosure ; upon which I laid down the dam, and took the kid in my arms, and carried it over my pale, in hopes to have bred it up tame ; but it would not eat, so I was forced to kill it, and eat it myself. These two supplied me with flesh a great while, for I ate sparingly, and saved my provisions (my bread especially) as much as possibly I could.

Having now fixed my habitation, I found it absolutely necessary to provide a place to make a fire on, and fuel to burn ; and what I did that for, as also how I enlarged my cave, and what conveniences I made, I shall give a full account of in its place ; but I must first give some little account of myself, and of my thoughts about living, which, it may well be supposed, were not a few.

After I had been there about ten or twelve days, it came into my thoughts that I should lose my reckoning of time for want of books, and pen and ink, and should even forget the Sabbath days from the working days ; but, to prevent this, I cut it with my knife upon a large post in capital letters, and making it into a great cross, I set it up on the shore where I first landed, namely, I came on shore here on the 30th of September, 1659. Upon the sides of this square post, I cut every day a notch with my knife, and every seventh notch was as long again as the rest, and every first day of the month as long again as that long one ; and thus I kept my calendar, or weekly, monthly, and yearly reckoning of time.

In the next place, we are to observe that, among the many things which I brought out of the ship in the several voyages, which, as above mentioned, I made to it, I got several things of less value, but not at all less useful to me, which I omitted setting down before ; as, in particular, pens, ink, and paper, several parcels in the captain's, mate's, gunner's, and carpenter's keeping, three or four compasses, some mathematical instruments, dials, perspectives, charts, and books of navigation, all which I huddled together, whether I might want them or no. Also, I found three very good Bibles, which came to me in my cargo from England, and which I had packed up among my things ; some Portuguese books also, and among them two or three Popish prayer-books, and several other books : all which I carefully secured. And I must not forget that we had in the ship a dog and two cats of whose eminent history I may have occasion to say something in its place ; for I carried both the cats with me : and as for the dog, he jumped out of the ship of himself, and swam on shore to me the day after I went on shore with my first cargo, and was a trusty servant to me many years : I wanted nothing that he could fetch me, nor any company that he could make up to me—I only wanted to have him talk to me ; but that he could not do. As I observed before, I found pen, ink, and paper, and I husbanded them to the utmost ; and I shall show, that while my ink lasted, I kept things very exact ; but after that was gone I could not, for I could not make any ink by any means that I could devise.

And this put me in mind that I wanted many things, notwithstanding all that I had amassed together ; and of these, this of ink was one, as also spade, pick-axe, and shovel, to dig or remove the earth ; needles, pins, and thread. As for linen, I soon learnt to want that without much difficulty.

This want of tools made every work I did go on heavily, and it was near a whole year before I had entirely finished my little pale, or surrounded habitation ; the piles, or stakes, which were as heavy as I could well lift, were a long time in cutting and preparing in the woods, and more by far in bringing home ; so that I spent sometimes two days in cutting and bringing home one of those posts, and a third day in driving it into the ground ; for which purpose I got a heavy piece of wood at first, but at last bethought myself of one of the iron crows, which, however, though I found it, yet it made driving those posts, or piles, very laborious and tedious work.

But what need I have been concerned at the tediousness of anything I had to do, seeing I had time enough to do it in ? Nor had I any other employment, if that had been over, at least that I could foresee, except the ranging the island to seek for food, which I did more or less every day.

I have already described my habitation, which was a tent, under the side of a rock, surrounded with a strong pale of posts and cables ; but I might now rather call it a wall, for I raised a kind of wall up againt it of turfs, about two feet thick on the outside ; and after some time—I think it was a year and a half—I raised rafters from it, leaning to the rock, and thatched or covered it with boughs of trees, and such things as I could get to keep out the rain, which I found at some times of the year very violent.

I have already observed how I brought all my goods into this pale, and into the cave which I had made behind me : but I must observe, too, that at first this was a confused heap of goods, which, as they lay in no order, so they took up all my place : I had no room to turn myself, so I set myself to enlarge my cave and works farther into the earth ; for it was a loose, sandy rock, which yielded easily to the labour I bestowed on it—and so, when I found I was pretty safe as to beasts of prey, I worked sideways to the right hand into the rock : and then, turning to the right again, worked quite out, and made me a door to come out, on the outside of my pale, or fortification.

This gave me not only egress and regress, as it were a back way to my tent and to my storehouse, but gave me room to stow my goods.

And now I began to apply myself to make such necessary things as I found I most wanted, particularly a chair and a table ; for without these I was not able to enjoy the few comforts I had in the world—I could not write, or eat, or do several things with so much pleasure without a table.

So I went to work ; and here I must needs observe, that as reason is the substance and original of the mathematics, so, by stating and squaring everything by reason, and by making the most rational judgment of things, every man may be in time master of every mechanic art. I had never handled a tool in my life, and yet in time, by labour, application, and contrivance, I found at last that I wanted nothing but I could have made it, especially if I had had tools ; however, I made abundance of things even without tools, and some with no more tools than an adze and a hatchet, which perhaps were never made that way before, and that with infinite labour—for example, if I wanted a board, I had no other way but to cut down a tree, set it on edge before me, and hew it flat on either side with my axe, till I had brought it to be as thin as a plank, and then dub it smooth with my adze. It is true, by this method I could make but one board out of a whole tree ; but this I had no remedy for but patience, any more than I had for the prodigious deal of time and labour which it took me up to make a plank or board ; but my time and labour were little worth, and so they were as well employed one way as another.

However, I made me a table and a chair, as I observed above, in the first place—and this I did out of the short pieces of boards that I brought on my raft from the ship : but, when I had wrought out some boards, as above, I made large shelves of the breadth of a foot and a half, one over another, all along one side of my cave, to lay all my tools, nails, and iron-work, and in a word, to separate everything at large in their places, that I might come easily at them. I knocked pieces into the wall of the rock to hang my guns, and all things that would hang up.

So that, had my cave been to be seen, it looked like a general magazine of all necessary things ; and I had everything so ready at my hand, that it was a great pleasure to me to see all my goods in such order, and especially to find my stock of all necessaries so great.

And now it was that I began to keep a journal of every day's employment ; for indeed at first I was in too much a hurry ; and not only hurry as to labour, but in too much discomposure of mind, and my journal would have been full of many dull things. For example, I must have said thus:— September the 30th, after I got to shore, and had escaped drowning, instead of being thankful to God for my deliverance, having first vomited with the great quantity of salt water which was gotten into my stomach, and recovering myself a little, I ran about the shore, wringing my hands, and beating my head and face, exclaiming at my misery, and crying out, I was undone, undone ! till, tired and faint, I was forced to lie down on the ground to repose, but durst not sleep for fear of being devoured.

Some days after this, and after I had been on board the ship, and got all that I could out of her, yet I could not forbear getting up to the top of a little mountain, and looking out to sea, in hopes of seeing a ship ; then fancy at a vast distance I spied a sail—please myself with the hopes of it—and then, after looking steadily till I was almost blind, lose it quite, and sit down and weep like a child, and thus increase my misery by my folly.

But having gotten over these things in some measure and having settled my household stuff and habitation, made me a table and a chair, and all as handsome about me as I could, I began to keep my journal, of which I shall here give you the copy (though in it will be told all these particulars over again), as long as it lasted ; for having no more ink, I was forced to leave it off.

CHAPTER V

THE JOURNAL

September 30, 1659.

I POOR miserable Robinson Crusoe, being shipwrecked during a dreadful storm in the offing, came on shore on this dismal, unfortunate island, which I called the Island of Despair ; all the rest of the ship's company being drowned, and myself almost dead.

All the rest of that day I spent in afflicting myself at the dismal circumstances I was brought to, namely, I had neither food, house, clothes, weapon, nor place to fly to, and in despair of any relief, saw nothing but death before me, either that I should be devoured by wild beasts, murdered by savages, or starved to death for want of food. At the approach of night I slept in a tree, for fear of wild creatures, but slept soundly, though it rained all night.

October 1.—In the morning, I saw to my great surprise, the ship had floated with the high tide, and was driven on shore again much nearer the island ; which, as it was some comfort on one hand, for seeing her sit upright, and not broken to pieces, I hoped, if the wind abated, I might get on board, and get some food and necessaries out of her for my relief ; so, on the other hand, it renewed my grief at the loss of my comrades, who, I imagined, if we had all stayed on board, might have saved the ship, or at least that they would not have been all drowned as they were ; and that had the men been saved we might perhaps have built us a boat out of the ruins of the ship, to have carried us to some other part of the world. I spent great part of this day in perplexing myself on these things ; but at length, seeing the ship almost dry, I went upon the sand as near as I could, and then swam on board. This day also it continued raining, though with no wind at all.

From the 1st of October to the 24th.—All these days entirely spent in many several voyages to get all I could out of the ship, which I brought on shore, every tide of flood, upon rafts. Much rain also in these days, though with some intervals of fair weather ; but it seems this was the rainy season.

Oct. 20.—I overset my raft, and all the goods I had upon it ; but being in shoal water, and the things being chiefly heavy, I recovered many of them when the tide was out.

Oct. 25.—It rained all night and all day, with some gusts of wind,

I began to write out a journal

during which time the ship broke in pieces, the wind blowing a little harder than before, and was no more to be seen except the wreck of her, and that only at low water. I spent this day in covering and securing the goods which I have saved, that rain might not spoil them.

Oct. 26.—I walked about the shore almost all day, to find out a place to fix my habitation, greatly concerned to secure myself from any attack in the night, either from wild beasts or men. Towards night I fixed upon a proper place under a rock, and marked out a semicircle for my encampment, which I resolved to strengthen with a work, wall, or fortification, made of double piles, lined within with cable, and without with turf.

From the 26th to the 30th I worked very hard in carrying all my goods to my new habitation, though some part of the time it rained exceedingly hard.

The 31st, in the morning, I went out into the island with my gun, to seek for some food, and discover the country; when I killed a she-goat, and her kid followed me home, which I afterwards killed also, because it would not feed.

November 1.—I set up my tent under a rock, and lay there for the first night, making it as large as I could, with stakes driven in to swing my hammock upon.

Nov. 2.—I set up all my chests and boards, and the pieces of timber, which made my rafts, and with them formed a fence round me, a little within the place I had marked out for my fortification.

Nov. 3.—I went out with my gun, and killed two fowls like ducks, which were very good food. In the afternoon, went to work to make me a table.

Nov. 4.—This morning I began to order my times of work—of going out with my gun, time of sleep, and time of diversion : namely, every morning, I walked out with my gun for two or three hours, if it did not rain, then employed myself to work till about eleven o'clock, then ate what I had to live on, and from twelve till two I lay down to sleep, the weather being excessively hot, and then in the evening to work again. The working part of this day and of the next were wholly employed in making my table, for I was yet but a very sorry workman, though time and necessity made me a complete natural mechanic soon after, as I believe it would do any one else.

Nov. 5.—This day went abroad with my gun and my dog, and killed a wild cat ; her skin pretty soft, but her flesh good for nothing ; every creature I killed I took off the skins, and preserved them. Coming back by the sea-shore, I saw many sorts of sea-fowls, which I did not understand ; but was surprised, and almost frighted, with two or three seals, which, while I was gazing at, not well knowing what they were, got into the sea, and escaped me for that time.

Nov. 6.—After my morning walk, I went to work with my table again, and finished it, though not to my liking ; nor was it long before I learned to mend it.

Nov. 7.—Now it began to be settled fair weather. The 7th, 8th, 9th, 10th, and part of the 12th (for the 11th was Sunday), I took wholly up to make me a chair, and with much ado brought it to a tolerable shape, but never to please me ; and even in the making I pulled it in pieces several times. *Note.*—I soon neglected my keeping Sundays ; for omitting my mark for them on my post, I forgot which was which.

Nov. 13.—This day it rained, which refreshed me exceedingly, and cooled the earth ; but was accompanied with terrible thunder and lightning, which frighted me dreadfully for fear of my powder. As soon as it was over, I resolved to separate my stock of powder into as many little parcels as possible, that it might not be in danger.

Nov. 14, 15, 16.—These three days I spent in making little square chests or boxes, which might hold about a pound, or two pound at most, of powder ; and so putting the powder in, I stowed it in places as secure and remote from one another as possible. On one of these three days I killed a large bird that was good to eat, but I knew not what to call it.

Nov. 17.—This day I began to dig behind my tent into the rock, to make room for my farther conveniency. *Note.*—Three things I wanted exceedingly for this work, namely, a pick-axe, a shovel, and a wheelbarrow or basket ; so I desisted from my work, and began to consider how to supply that want, and make me some tools : as for a pick-axe, I made use of the iron crows, which were proper enough, though heavy ; but the next thing was a shovel or spade ; this was so absolutely necessary, that indeed I could do nothing effectually without it, but what kind of one to make I knew not.

Nov. 18.—The next day, in searching the woods, I found a tree of that wood, or like it, which in the Brazils they call the iron tree, for its exceeding hardness : of this, with great labour, and almost spoiling my axe, I cut a piece, and brought it home too with difficulty enough, for it was exceeding heavy.

The excessive hardness of the wood, and having no other way, made me a long while upon this machine ; for I worked it effectually by little and little into the form of a shovel or spade, the handle exactly shaped like ours in England, only that the broad part having no iron shod upon it at bottom, it would not last me so long ; however, it served well enough for the uses which I had occasion to put it to ; but never was a shovel, I believe, made after that fashion, or so long a-making.

I was still deficient, for I wanted a basket or a wheelbarrow : a basket I could not make by any means, having no such things as twigs, that would bend to make wicker-ware, at least not yet found out ; and as to a wheel-barrow, I fancied I could make all but the wheel, but that I had no notion of, neither did I know how to go about it ; besides, I had no possible way to make the iron gudgeons for the spindle, or axis, of the wheel, to run in, so I gave it over ; and so, for carrying away the earth which I dug out of the cave, I made a thing like a hod, which the labourers carry mortar in when they serve the bricklayers.

This was not so difficult to me as the making the shovel ; and yet this, and the shovel, and the attempt which I made in vain to make a wheel-barrow, took me up no less than four days—I mean always excepting my morning walk with my gun, which I seldom failed ; and seldom failed also bringing home something to eat.

Nov. 23.—My other work having now stood still, because of my making these tools, when they were finished I went on, and working every day, as my strength and time allowed, I spent eighteen days entirely in widening and deepening my cave, that it might hold my goods commodiously.

Note.—During all this time I worked to make this room, or cave, spacious enough to accommodate me as a warehouse, or magazine, a kitchen, a dining-room, and a cellar : as for my lodging, I kept to the tent, except that some-times, in the wet season of the year, it rained so hard that I could not keep myself dry, which caused me afterwards to cover all my place within my pale with long poles in the form of rafters, leaning against the rock, and load them with flags and large leaves of trees like a thatch.

December 10.—I began now to think my cave, or vault, finished, when on a sudden (it seems I had made it too large) a great quantity of earth fell down from the top and one side, so much that, in short, it frighted me, and not without reason too ; for if I had been under it, I had never wanted a gravedigger. Upon this disaster I had a great deal of work to do over again ; for I had the loose earth to carry out, and, which was of more im-portance, I had the ceiling to prop up, so that I might be sure no more would come down.

Dec. 11.—This day I went to work with it accordingly, and got two shores or posts pitched upright to the top, with two pieces of boards across over each post ; this I finished the next day ; and setting more posts up with boards, in about a week more I had the roof secured ; and the posts standing in rows, served me for partitions to part off the house.

Dec. 17.—From this day to the 20th I placed shelves, and knocked up nails on the posts to hang everything up that could be hung up : and now I began to be in some order within doors.

Dec. 20.—Now I carried everything into the cave, and began to furnish my house, and set up some pieces of boards like a dresser, to order my victuals upon ; but boards began to be very scarce with me ; also, I made me another table.

Dec. 27.—Killed a young goat, and lamed another, so that I caught it, and led it home in a string ; when I had it home, I bound and splintered up its leg, which was broke. *N.B.*—I took such care of it that it lived, and the leg grew well and as strong as ever ; but by nursing it so long it grew tame, and fed upon the little green at my door, and would not go away. This was the first time that I entertained a thought of breeding up some tame creatures, that I might have food when my powder and shot are all spent.

Dec. 28, 29, 30.—Great heats, and no breeze ; so that there was no stirring abroad, except in the evening for food. This time I spent in putting all my things in order within doors.

January 1.—Very hot still : but I went abroad early and late with my gun, and lay still in the middle of the day. This evening, going farther into the valleys which lay towards the centre of the island, I found there was plenty of goats, though exceedingly shy and hard to come at ; however, I resolved to try if I could not bring my dog to hunt them down.

Jan. 2.—Accordingly, the next day I went out with my dog, and set him upon the goats ; but I was mistaken, for they all faced about upon the dog ; and he knew his danger too well, for he would not come near them.

Jan. 3.—I began my fence, or wall, which, being still jealous of my being attacked by somebody, I resolved to make very thick and strong.

N.B.—This wall being described before, I purposely omit what was said in the journal ; it is sufficient to observe, that I was no less time than from the 3rd of January to the 14th of April, working, finishing, and per-fecting this wall, though it was no more than about twenty-four yards in length, being a half circle from one place in the rock to another place about eight yards from it, the door of the cave being in the centre behind it.

All this time I worked very hard, the rains hindering me many days, nay sometimes weeks together ; but I thought I should never be perfectly secure until this wall was finished : and it is scarce credible what inexpressible labour everything was done with, especially the bringing piles out of the woods, and driving them into the ground ; for I made them much bigger than I need to have done.

When this wall was finished, and the outside double-fenced with a turf wall raised up close to it, I persuaded myself, that if any people were to come on shore there, they would not perceive anything like a habitation ; and it was very well I did so, as may be observed hereafter, upon a very remarkable occasion.

During this time I made my rounds in the woods for game every day, when the rain permitted me, and made frequent discoveries in these walks, of something or other to my advantage ; particularly, I found a kind of wild pigeons, who built, not as wood pigeons, in a tree, but rather as house pigeons, in the holes of the rocks ; and taking some young ones, I endeavoured to breed them up tame, and did so ; but when they grew older they flew away, which, perhaps, was at first for want of feeding them ; for I had nothing to give them. However, I frequently found their nests and got their young ones, which was very good meat.

And now, in the managing my household affairs, I found myself wanting in many things, which I thought at first it was impossible for me to make, as indeed, as to some of them, it was—for instance, I could never make a cask to be hooped. I had a small runlet or two, as I observed before, but I could never arrive to the capacity of making one by them, though I spent many weeks about it ; I could neither put in the heads, nor joint the staves so true to one another as to make them hold water, so I gave that also over.

In the next place, I was at great loss for candle, so that as soon as ever it was dark, which was generally by seven o'clock, I was obliged to go to bed. I remembered the lump of bees' wax with which I made candles in my African adventure, but I had none of that now. The only remedy I had was that, when I killed a goat I saved the tallow, and, with a little dish made of clay, which I baked in the sun, to which I added a wick of some oakum, I made me a lamp ; and this gave me a light, though not a clear, steady light like a candle. In the middle of all my labours, it happened that, rummaging my things, I found a little bag, which, as I hinted before, had been filled with corn for the feeding of poultry, not for this voyage, but before, as I suppose, when the ship came from Lisbon. What little remainder of corn had been in the bag was all devoured with the rats, and I saw nothing in the bag but husks and dust ; and being willing to have the bag for some other use—I think it was to put powder in, when I divided it for fear of the lightning, or some such use—I shook the husks of corn out of it, on one side of my fortification, under the rock.

It was a little before the great rains, just now mentioned, that I threw this stuff away, taking no notice of anything, and not so much as remembering that I had thrown anything there ; when about a month after, or thereabout, I saw some few stalks of something green shooting out of the ground, which I fancied might be some plant I had not seen ; but I was surprised and perfectly astonished, when, after a little longer time, I saw about ten or twelve ears come out, which were perfectly green barley, of the same kind as our European—nay, as our English barley.

I not only thought these the pure productions of Providence for my support, but, not doubting but that there was more in the place, I went all over that part of the island where I had been before, peeping in every corner, and under every rock, to see for more of it, but I could not find any. At last, it occurred to my thought, that I had shook a bag of chickens' meat out in that place, and then the wonder began to cease ; and I must confess, my religious thankfulness to God's providence began to abate too, upon discovering that all this was nothing but what was common, though I ought to have been as thankful for so strange and unforeseen a providence, as if it had been miraculous ; for it was really the work of Providence, as to me, that should order or appoint ten or twelve grains of corn to remain unspoiled, when the rats had destroyed all the rest, as if it had been dropped from heaven —as also, that I should throw it out on that particular place, where, it being in the shade of a high rock, it sprang up immediately ; whereas, if I had thrown it anywhere else at that time, it had been burnt up and destroyed.

I carefully saved the ears of corn, you may be sure, in their season, which was about the end of June, and laying up every corn, I resolved to sow them all again, hoping in time to have some quantity sufficient to supply me with bread ; but it was not till the fourth year that I could allow myself the least grain of this corn to eat, and even then but sparingly, as I shall say afterwards in its order—for I lost all that I sowed the first season, by not observing the proper time—for I sowed it just before the dry season, so that it never came up at all, at least not as it would have done—of which in its place.

Besides this barley, there were, as above, twenty or thirty stalks of rice, which I preserved with the same care, and whose use was of the same kind, or to the same purpose, namely, to make me bread, or rather food ; for I found ways to cook it up without baking, though I did that also after some time. But to return to my journal.

I worked excessively hard these three or four months to get my wall done ; and the 14th of April I closed it up, contriving to go into it, not by a door, but over the wall by a ladder, that there might be no sign in the outside of my habitation.

April 16.—I finished the ladder ; so I went up with the ladder to the top, and then pulled it up after me, and let it down in the inside. This was a complete enclosure to me ; for within I had room enough, and nothing could come at me from without, unless it could first mount my wall.

The very next day after this wall was finished, I had almost had all my labour overthrown at once, and myself killed. The case was thus : As I was busy in the inside of it, behind my tent, just in the entrance into my cave, I was terribly frighted with a most dreadful surprising thing indeed ; for on a sudden I found the earth come crumbling down from the roof of my cave, and from the edge of the hill, over my head, and two of the posts I had set up in the cave cracked in a frightful manner. I was heartily scared, but thought nothing of what was really the cause, only thinking that the top of my cave was falling in, as some of it had done before ; and for fear I should be buried in it, I ran forward to my ladder, and not thinking myself safe there neither, I got over my wall for fear of the pieces of the hill, which I expected might roll down upon me. I was no sooner stept down upon the firm ground, but I plainly saw it was a terrible earthquake, for the ground I stood on shook three times at about eight minutes' distance, with three such shocks as would have overturned the strongest building that could be supposed to have stood on the earth ; and a great piece of the top of a rock, which stood about half a mile from me, next the sea, fell down with such a terrible noise as I ever heard in all my life : I perceived also the very sea was put into violent motion by it ; and I believe the shocks were stronger under the water than on the island.

I was so amazed with the thing itself, having never felt the like, or discoursed with any one that had, that I was like one dead or stupefied ; and the motion of the earth made my stomach sick, like one that was tossed at sea ; but the noise of the falling of the rock awaked me, as it were, and, rousing me from the stupefied condition I was in, filled me with horror, and I thought of nothing then but the hill falling upon my tent and all my household goods, and burying all at once ; and thus sunk my very soul within me a second time.

After the third shock was over, and I felt no more for some time, I began to take courage ; and yet I had not heart enough to get over my wall again, for fear of being buried alive, but sat still upon the ground, greatly cast down and disconsolate, not knowing what to do. All this while I had not the least serious religious thought, nothing but the common : " Lord, have mercy upon me ! " and when it was over that went away too.

While I sat thus, I found the air overcast, and grow cloudy, as if it would rain ; soon after that, the wind rose by little and little, so that in less than half an hour it blew a most dreadful hurricane : the sea was all on a sudden covered over with foam and froth, the shore was covered with the breach of the water, the trees were torn up by the roots, and a terrible storm it was : and this held about three hours, and then began to abate, and in two hours more it was stark calm, and began to rain very hard.

All this while I sat upon the ground, very much terrified and dejected, when on a sudden it came into my thoughts, that these winds and rain being the consequence of the earthquake, the earthquake itself was spent and over and I might venture into my cave again : with this thought my spirits began to revive, and the rain also helping to persuade me, I went in and sat down in my tent ; but the rain was so violent, that my tent was ready to be beaten down with it ; and I was forced to go into my cave, though very much afraid and uneasy, for fear it should fall on my head.

This violent rain forced me to a new work, namely, to cut a hole through my new fortification, like a sink, to let water go out, which would else have drowned my cave. After I had been in my cave some time, and found still no more shocks of the earthquake follow, I began to be more composed ; and now, to support my spirits, which indeed wanted it very much, I went to my little store, and took a small cup of rum, which, however, I did then, and always, very sparingly, knowing I could have no more when that was gone.

It continued raining all that night and great part of the next day, so that I could not stir abroad ; but, my mind being more composed, I began to think of what I had best do, concluding, that if the island was subject to these earthquakes, there would be no living for me in a cave, but I must consider of building me some little hut in an open place, which I might surround with a wall as I had done here, and so make myself secure from wild beasts or men : but concluded if I stayed where I was, I should certainly, one time or other, be buried alive.

With these thoughts, I resolved to remove my tent from the place where it stood, which was just under the hanging precipice of the hill, and which, if it should be shaken again, would certainly fall upon my tent. And I spent the two next days, being the 19th and 20th of April, in contriving where and how to remove my habitation.

The fear of being swallowed up alive made me that I never slept in quiet, and yet the apprehension of lying abroad without any fence was almost equal to it ; but still, when I looked about, and saw how everything was put in order, how pleasantly concealed I was, and how safe from danger, it made me very loath to remove.

In the meantime, it occurred to me that it would require a vast deal of time for me to do this, and that I must be contented to run the venture where I was, till I had formed a camp for myself, and had secured it so as to remove to it. So, with this resolution, I composed myself for a time, and resolved that I would go to work with all speed, to build me a wall with piles and cables, etc., in a circle, as before, and set my tent up in it when it was finished ; but that I would venture to stay where I was till it was finished, and fit to remove to. This was the 21st.

April 22.—The next morning I began to consider of means to put this resolve in execution, but I was at a great loss about my tools. I had three large axes, and abundance of hatchets (for we carried the hatchets for traffic with the Indians) ; but, with much chopping, and cutting knotty hard wood, they were all full of notches and dull ; and, though I had a grindstone, I could not turn it, and grind my tools too ; this cost me as much thought as a statesman would have bestowed upon a grand point of politics, or a judge upon the life and death of a man. At length I contrived a wheel with a string, to turn it with my foot, that I might have both my hands at liberty. *Note.*— I had never seen any such thing in England, or at least not to take notice how it was done, though since I have observed it is very common there ; besides that my grindstone was very large and heavy. This machine cost me a full week's work to bring it to perfection.

CHAPTER VI

MAY 1.—In the morning, looking towards the sea-side, the tide being low, I saw something lie on the shore bigger than ordinary, and it looked like a cask. When I came to it, I found a small barrel, and two or three pieces of the ship, which were driven on shore by the hurricane ; and looking towards the wreck itself, I thought it seemed to lie higher out of the water than it used to do. I examined the barrel which was driven on shore, and soon found it was a barrel of gunpowder, but it had taken water, and the powder was caked as hard as a stone ; however, I rolled it farther on shore for the present, and went on upon the sands as near as I could to the wreck of the ship to look for more.

When I came down to the ship, I found it strangely removed : the forecastle, which lay before buried in sand, was heaved up at least six feet ; and the stern (which was broke to pieces, and parted from the rest by the force of the sea, soon after I had left rummaging her) was tossed, as it were, up, and cast on one side ; and the sand was thrown so high on that side next her stern, that whereas there was a great piece of water before, so that I could not come within a quarter of a mile of the wreck without swimming, I could now walk quite up to her when the tide was out. I was surprised with this at first, but soon concluded it must be done with the earthquake ; and, as by this violence the ship was more broken open than formerly, so many things came daily on shore, which the sea had loosened, and which the winds and waters rolled by degrees to the land.

This wholly diverted my thoughts from the design of removing my habitation ; and I busied myself mightily, that day especially, in searching whether I could make any way into the ship ; but I found nothing was to be expected of that kind, for that all the inside of the ship was choked up with sand ; however, as I had learned not to despair of anything, I resolved to pull everything to pieces that I could of the ship, concluding, that everything I could get from her would be of some use or other to me.

May 3.—I began with my saw, and cut a piece of a beam through, which I thought held some of the upper part or quarterdeck together, and when I had cut it through, I cleared away the sand as well as I could from the side which lay highest ; but the tide coming in, I was obliged to give over for that time.

May 4.—I went a-fishing, but caught not one fish that I durst eat of, till I was weary of my sport, when, just going to leave off, I caught a young dolphin. I had made me a long line of some rope yarn, but I had no hooks, yet I frequently caught fish, as much as I cared to eat ; all which I dried in the sun, and ate them dry.

May 5.—Worked on the wreck—cut another beam asunder, and brought three great fir planks off from the decks, which I tied together, and made swim on shore when the tide of flood came in.

May 6.—Worked on the wreck—got several iron bolts out of her, and other pieces of iron work ; worked very hard, and came home very much tired, and had thoughts of giving it over.

May 7.—Went to the wreck again, but with an intent not to work, but found the weight of the wreck had brought itself down, the beams being cut ; that several pieces of the ship seemed to lie loose, and the inside of the hold lay so open that I could see into it, but almost full of water and sand.

May 8.—Went to the wreck, and carried an iron crow to wrench up the deck, which lay now quite clear of the water or sand ; I wrenched open two planks, and brought them on shore also with the tide : I left the iron crow in the wreck for next day.

May 9.—Went to the wreck, and with the crow made way into the body of the wreck, and felt several casks, and loosened them with the crow, but could not break them up : I felt also the roll of English lead, and could stir it, but it was too heavy to remove.

May 10, 11, 12, 13, 14.—Went every day to the wreck, and got a great many pieces of timber, and boards, or planks, and two or three hundred-weight of iron.

May 15.—I carried two hatchets, to try if I could not cut a piece of the roll of lead, by placing the edge of one hatchet, and driving it with the other, but as it lay about a foot and a half in the water, I could not make any blow to drive the hatchet.

May 16.—It had blown hard in the night, and the wreck appeared more broken by the force of the water ; but I stayed so long in the woods to get pigeons for food, that the tide prevented me going to the wreck that day.

May 17.—I saw some pieces of the wreck blown on shore, at a great distance, near two miles off me, but resolved to see what they were, and found it was a piece of the head, but too heavy for me to bring away.

May 24.—Every day to this day I worked on the wreck, and with hard labour I loosened some things so much with the crow that the first flowing tide, several casks floated out, and two of the seamen's chests ; but the wind blowing from the shore, nothing came to land that day but pieces of timber, and a hogshead, which had some Brazil pork in it ; but the salt water and the sand had spoiled it.

I continued this work every day to the 15th of June, except the time necessary to get food, which I always appointed during this part of my

I prayed to God for the first time since the storm

employment to be when the tide was up, that I might be ready when it was ebbed out ; and by this time I had gotten timber, and plank, and iron-work enough to have built a good boat, if I had known how ; and also I got at several times, and in several pieces, near one hundredweight of the sheet lead.

June 16.—Going down to the sea-side, I found a large tortoise or turtle ; this was the first that I had seen, which it seems was only my misfortune, not any defect of the place, or scarcity ; for had I happened to be on the other side of the island, I might have had hundreds of them every day, as I found afterwards, but perhaps had paid dear for them.

June 17*th* I spent in cooking the turtle ; I found in her three score eggs ; and her flesh was to me, at that time, the most savoury and pleasant that ever I tasted in my life, having had no flesh but of goats and fowls since I landed in this horrid place.

June 18.—Rained all day, and I stayed within. I thought at this time the rain felt cold, and I was something chilly, which I knew was not usual in that latitude.

June 19.—Very ill, and shivering, as if the weather had been cold.

June 20.—No rest all night, violent pains in my head, and feverish.

June 21.—Very ill, frighted almost to death with the apprehensions of my sad condition, to be sick, and no help. Prayed to God, for the first time since the storm off Hull ; but scarce knew what I said, or why, my thoughts being all confused.

June 22.—A little better, but under dreadful apprehensions of sickness.

June 23.—Very bad again, cold and shivering, and then a violent headache.

June 24.—Much better.

June 25.—An ague—very violent ; the fit held me seven hours, cold fit and hot, with faint sweats after it.

June 26.—Better ; and, having no victuals to eat, took my gun, but found myself very weak ; however, I killed a she-goat, and with much difficulty got it home, and broiled some of it, and ate ; I would fain have stewed it, and made some broth, but had no pot.

June 27.—The ague again so violent that I lay a-bed all day, and neither ate nor drank. I was ready to perish for thirst, but so weak I had not strength to stand up, or to get myself any water to drink.

June 28.—Having been somewhat refreshed with the sleep I had had, and the fit being entirely off, I got up ; and though the fright and terror of my dream was very great, yet I considered that the fit of the ague would return again the next day, and now was my time to get something to refresh and support myself, when I should be ill : and the first thing I did, I filled a large square case-bottle with water, and set it upon my table in reach of my bed ; and to take off the chill or aguish disposition of the water, I put about a quarter of a pint of rum into it, and mixed them together ; then I got me a piece of the goat's flesh, and broiled it on the coals, but could eat very little. I walked about, but was very weak, and withal very sad and heavy-hearted, under a sense of my miserable condition, dreading the return of my distemper the next day. At night, I made my supper of three of the turtle's eggs, which I roasted in the ashes, and ate, as we call it, in the shell ; and this was the first bit of meat I had ever asked God's blessing to, even, as I could remember, in my whole life.

After I had eaten, I tried to walk, but found myself so weak that I could hardly carry the gun (for I never went out without that) ; so I went but a little way, and sat down upon the ground, looking out upon the sea, which was just before me, and very calm and smooth.

I fell asleep, and when I awaked, I found myself exceedingly refreshed, and my spirits lively and cheerful. When I got up I was stronger than I was the day before, and my stomach better, for I was hungry ; and in short, I had no fit the next day, but continued much altered for the better : this was the 29th.

The 30th was my well day, of course, and I went abroad with my gun, but did not care to travel too far : I killed a sea-fowl or two, something like a brand goose, and brought them home, but was not very forward to eat them ; so I ate some more of the turtle's eggs, which were very good. This evening I renewed the medicine, which I had supposed did me good the day before, namely, the tobacco steeped in rum ; only, I did not take so much as before, nor did I chew any of the leaf, or hold my head over the smoke ; however, I was not so well the next day, which was the 1st of July, as I hoped I should have been ; for I had a little spice of the cold fit, but it was not much.

July 2.—I renewed the medicine all the three ways, and dosed myself with it as at first, and doubled the quantity which I drank.

July 3.—I missed the fit for good and all, though I did not recover my full strength for some weeks after.

My condition began now to be, though not less miserable as to my way of living, yet much easier to my mind; and my thoughts being directed, by a constant reading the Scripture and praying to God, to things of a higher nature, I had a great deal of comfort within, which till now I knew nothing of: also, as my health and strength returned, I bestirred myself to furnish myself with everything that I wanted, and make my way of living as regular as I could.

From the 4th of July to the 14th, I was chiefly employed in walking about with my gun in my hand, a little and a little at a time, as a man that was gathering up his strength after a fit of sickness; for it is hardly to be imagined how low I was, and to what weakness I was reduced. The application which I made use of was perfectly new, and, perhaps, what had never cured an ague before; neither can I recommend it to any one to practise by this experiment; and though it did carry off the fit, yet it rather contributed to weaken me, for I had frequent convulsions in my nerves and limbs for some time.

I learnt from it also this, in particular, that being abroad in the rainy season was the most pernicious thing to my health that could be, especially in those rains which came attended with storms and hurricanes of wind; for, as the rain which came in a dry season was always most accompanied with such storms, so I found this rain was much more dangerous than the rain which fell in September and October.

I had been now in this unhappy island above ten months; all possibility of deliverance from this condition seemed to be entirely taken from me; and I firmly believed, that no human shape had ever set foot upon that place. Having now secured my habitation, as I thought, fully to my mind, I had a great desire to make a more perfect discovery of the island, and to see what other productions I might find, which yet I knew nothing of.

CHAPTER VII

IT was the 15th of July that I began to take a more particular survey of the island itself. I went up the creek first, where, as I hinted, I brought my rafts on shore. I found, after I came about two miles up, that the tide did not flow any higher, and that it was no more than a little brook of running water, very fresh and good; but this being the dry season, there was hardly any water in some parts of it, at least not enough to run into any stream, so as it could be perceived.

On the banks of this brook I found many pleasant savannas or meadows, plain, smooth, and covered with grass; and, on the rising parts of them, next to the higher grounds (where the water, as it might be supposed, never overflowed), I found a great deal of tobacco, green, and growing to a great and very strong stalk; there were divers other plants, which I had no notion of, or understanding about, and might perhaps have virtues of their own, which I could not find out.

I searched for the cassava root, which the Indians in all that climate make their bread of, but I could find none. I saw large plants of aloes, but did not then understand them; I saw several sugar-canes, but wild, and, for want of cultivation, imperfect. I contented myself with these discoveries for this time, and came back musing with myself what course I might take to know the virtue and goodness of any of the fruits or plants which I should discover, but could bring it to no conclusion ; for, in short, I had made so little observation while I was in the Brazils, that I knew little of the plants of the field : at least, very little that might serve me to any purpose now in my distress.

The next day, the 16th, I went up the same way again ; and, after going something farther than I had done the day before, I found the brook and the savannas began to cease, and the country became more woody than before. In this part I found different fruits, and particularly I found melons upon the ground in great abundance, and grapes upon the trees ; the vines had spread indeed over the trees, and the clusters of grapes were now just in their prime, very ripe and rich. This was a surprising discovery, and I was exceedingly glad of them ; but I was warned by my experience to eat sparingly of them, remembering that when I was ashore in Barbary, the eating of grapes killed several of our Englishmen who were slaves there, by throwing them into fluxes and fevers; but I found an excellent use for these grapes, and that was to cure or dry them in the sun, and keep them as dried grapes or raisins are kept, which I thought would be, as indeed they were, as wholesome and as agreeable to eat, when no grapes might be had.

I spent all that evening there, and went not back to my habitation ; which, by the way, was the first night, as I might say, I had lain from home. In the night I took my first contrivance, and got up into a tree, where I slept well, and the next morning proceeded upon my journey, travelling near four miles, as I might judge by the length of the valley, keeping still due north, with a ridge of hills on the south and north side of me.

At the end of this march I came to an opening, where the country seemed to descend to the west; and a little spring of fresh water, which issued out of the side of the hill by me, ran the other way, that is, due east ; and the country appeared so fresh, so green, so flourishing, everything being in a constant verdure, or flourish of spring, that it looked like a planted garden.

I descended a little on the side of that delicious valley, surveying it with a secret kind of pleasure (though mixed with other afflicting thoughts), to think that this was all my own, that I was king and lord of all this country indefeasibly, and had a right of possession ; and, if I could convey it, I might have it in inheritance, as completely as any lord of a manor in England. I saw here abundance of cocoa trees, orange, and lemon, and citron trees, but all wild, and few bearing any fruit ; at least, not then : however, the green limes that I gathered were not only pleasant to eat, but very wholesome ; and I mixed their juice afterwards with water, which made it very wholesome, and very cool and refreshing.

I found now I had business enough to gather and carry home ; and resolved to lay up a store, as well of grapes as limes and lemons, to furnish myself for the wet season, which I knew was approaching.

In order to do this, I gathered a great heap of grapes in one place, and a lesser heap in another place ; and a great parcel of limes and lemons in another place ; and taking a few of each with me, I travelled homeward, and resolved to come again and bring a bag or sack, or what I could make, to carry the rest home.

Accordingly, having spent three days in this journey, I came home (so I must now call my tent and my cave); but before I got thither, the grapes were spoiled; the richness of the fruit and the weight of the juice having broken them and bruised them, they were good for little or nothing: as to the limes, they were good, but I could bring but a few.

The next day, being the 19th, I went back, having made me two small bags to bring home my harvest. But I was surprised, when coming to my heap of grapes which were so rich and fine when I gathered them, I found them all spread abroad, trod to pieces, and dragged about, some here, some there, and abundance eaten and devoured. By this I concluded there were some wild creatures thereabouts, which had done this; but what they were I knew not.

However, as I found there were no laying them up on heaps, and no carrying them away in a sack, but that one way they would be destroyed, and the other way they would be crushed with their own weight, I took another course; for I gathered a large quantity of the grapes, and hung them upon the out branches of the trees, that they might cure and dry in the sun; and as for the limes and lemons, I carried as many back as I could well stand under.

When I came home from this journey, I contemplated with great pleasure on the fruitfulness of that valley, and the pleasantness of the situation, the security from storms on that side of the water and wood; and concluded, that I had pitched upon a place to fix my abode, which was by far the worst

I came all at once to an opening

part of the country. Upon the whole, I began to consider of removing my habitation, and to look out for a place, equally safe as where I now was situated, if possible, in that pleasant, fruitful part of the island.

However, I was so enamoured with this place that I spent much of my time there for the whole remaining part of the month of July; and though, upon second thoughts, I resolved, as above, not to remove, yet I built me a little kind of a bower, and surrounded it at a distance with a strong fence, being a double hedge, as high as I could reach, well staked, and filled between with brushwood; and here I lay very secure, sometimes two or three nights together, always going over it with a ladder, as before; so that I fancied now I had my country-house, and my sea-coast house, and this work took me up to the beginning of August.

I had but newly finished my fence, and began to enjoy my labour, when the rains came on, and made me stick close to my first habitation, for though I had made me a tent like the other, with a piece of sail, and spread it very well, yet I had not the shelter of a hill to keep me from storms, nor a cave behind me to retreat into when the rains were extraordinary. About the beginning of August, as I said, I had finished my bower, and begun to enjoy myself. The 3rd of August I found the grapes I had hung up were perfectly dried, and, indeed, were excellent good raisins of the sun; so I began to take them down from the trees, and it was very happy that I did so, for the rains which followed would have spoiled them, and I had lost the best part of my winter food; for I had above two hundred large bunches of them. No sooner had I taken them all down, and carried most of them home to my cave, but it began to rain; and from thence, which was the 14th of August, it rained more or less every day till the middle of October, and sometimes so violently that I could not stir out of my cave for several days.

In this season I was much surprised with the increase of my family: I had been concerned for the loss of one of my cats, who ran away from me, or, as I thought, had been dead; and I heard no more tale or tidings of her, till, to my astonishment, she came home, about the end of August, with three kittens. This was the more strange to me, because, though I had killed a wild cat, as I called it, with my gun, yet I thought it was a quite different kind from our European cats; yet the young cats were the same kind of house breed like the old ones; and both my cats being females, I thought it very strange: but from these three cats, I afterwards came to be so pestered with cats, that I was forced to kill them like vermin, or wild beasts, and to drive them from my house as much as possible.

From the 14th of August to the 26th, incessant rain, so that I could not stir, and was now very careful not to be much wet. In this confinement I began to be straitened for food; but venturing out twice, I one day killed a goat; and the last day, which was the 26th, found a very large tortoise, which was a treat to me, and my food was regulated thus: I ate a bunch of raisins for my breakfast, a piece of the goat's flesh, or of the turtle, for my dinner broiled (for, to my great misfortune, I had no vessel to boil or stew anything), and two or three of the turtle's eggs for supper.

During this confinement in my cover by the rain, I worked daily two or three hours at enlarging my cave; and, by degrees, worked it on towards one side, till I came to the outside of the hill, and made a door or way out, which came beyond my fence, or wall ; and so I came in and out this way. But I was not perfectly easy at lying so open ; for, as I had managed myself before, I was in a perfect enclosure, where as now I thought I lay exposed; and yet I could not perceive that there was any living thing to fear, the biggest creature that I had ever seen upon the island being a goat.

September the 30th.—I was now come to the unhappy anniversary of my landing—I cast up the notches on my post, and found I had been on shore three hundred and sixty-five days. I kept this day as a solemn fast, setting it apart to a religious exercise, prostrating myself to the ground with the most serious humiliation, confessing myself to God.

I had all this time observed no Sabbath day, for as at first I had no sense of religion upon my mind, I had, after some time, omitted to distinguish the weeks, by making a longer notch than ordinary for the Sabbath day, and so did not really know what any of the days were ; but now, having cast up the days as above, I found I had been there a year ; so I divided it into weeks, and set apart every seventh day for a Sabbath ; though I found, at the end of my account, I had lost a day or two of my reckoning.

A little after this my ink began to fail me, and so I contented myself to use it more sparingly, and to write down only the most remarkable events of my life, without continuing a daily memorandum of other things.

The rainy season and the dry season began now to appear regular to me, and I learned to divide them so as to provide for them accordingly. But I bought all my experience before I had it ; and this, I am going to relate, was one of the most discouraging experiments that I made at all. I have mentioned that I had saved the few ears of barley and rice which I had so surprisingly found spring up, as I thought, of themselves, and believe there were about thirty stalks of rice, and about twenty of barley ; and now I thought it a proper time to sow it after the rains, the sun being in its southern position going from me.

Accordingly, I dug up a piece of ground, as well as I could, with my wooden spade, and dividing it into two parts, I sowed my grain ; but as it was sowing, it casually occurred to my thought, that I would not sow it all at first, because I did not know when was the proper time for it ; so I sowed about two-thirds of the seeds, leaving about a handful of each.

It was a great comfort to me afterwards that I did so, for not one grain of that I sowed this time came to anything ; for the dry months following, the earth having had no rain after the seed was sown, it had no moisture to assist its growth, and never came up at all, till the wet season had come again, and then it grew as if it had been newly sown.

Finding my first seed did not grow, which I easily imagined was the drought, I sought for a moister piece of ground to make another trial in ; and I dug up a piece of ground near my new bower, and sowed the rest of my seed in February, a little before the vernal equinox ; and this, having the rainy months of March and April to water it, sprung up very pleasantly, and yielded a very good crop ; but having part of the seed left only, and not daring to sow all that I had yet, I had but a small quantity at last, my whole crop not amounting to above half a peck of each kind.

But by this experience I was made master of my business, and knew exactly when the proper season was to sow, and that I might expect two seed times and two harvests every year.

While this corn was growing, I made a little discovery which was of use to me afterwards. As soon as the rains were over, and the weather began to settle, which was about the month of November, I made a visit up the country to my bower, where, though I had not been for some months, yet I found all things just as I left them. The circle or double hedge that I had made was not only firm and entire, but the stakes which I had cut off of some trees that grew thereabouts, were all shot out, and grown with long branches as much as a willow tree usually shoots the first year after lopping its head. I could not tell what tree to call it that these stakes were cut from. I was surprised, and yet very well pleased, to see the young trees grow— and I pruned them, and led them up to grow as much alike as I could—and it is scarce credible how beautiful a figure they grew into in three years ; so that, though the hedge made a circle of about twenty-five yards in diameter, yet the trees, for such I might now call them, soon covered it ; and it was a complete shade, sufficient to lodge under all the dry season.

This made me resolve to cut some more stakes, and make me a hedge like this in a semicircle round my wall, I mean that of my first dwelling, which I did ; and placing the trees, or stakes, in a double row, at above eight yards' distance from my first fence, they grew presently, and were at first a fine cover to my habitation, and afterwards served for a defence also, as I shall observe in its order.

In the rainy season I found much employment (and very suitable also to the time), for I found great occasion of many things which I had no way to furnish myself with, but by hard labour and constant application ; parti-cularly, I tried many ways to make myself a basket ; but all the twigs I could get for the purpose proved so brittle that they would do nothing. It proved of excellent advantage to me now, that when I was a boy I used to take great delight in standing at a basket-maker's in the town where my father lived, to see them make their wicker-ware ; and being, as boys usually are, very officious to help, and a great observer of the manner how they worked those things, and sometimes lent a hand, I had by this means so full knowledge of the methods of it, that I wanted nothing but the materials ; when it came into my mind, that the twigs of that tree from whence I cut my stakes that grew, might possibly be as tough as the sallows, and willows, and osiers, in England ; and I resolved to try.

Accordingly, the next day I went to my country-house, as I called it, and, cutting some of the smaller twigs, I found them to my purpose as much as I could desire ; whereupon I came the next time prepared with a hatchet to cut down a quantity, which I soon found, for there was a great plenty of them ; these I set up to dry within my circle, or hedges, and when they were fit for use, I carried them to my cave ; and here, during the next season, I employed myself in making (as well as I could) a great many baskets both to carry earth, or to carry or lay up anything, as I had occasion ; and though I did not finish them very handsomely, yet I made them sufficiently serviceable for my purpose ; and thus afterwards I took care never to be without them ; and as my wicker-ware decayed, I made more ; especially

I made strong deep baskets to place my corn in, instead of sacks, when I should come to have any quantity of it.

Having mastered this difficulty, and employed a world of time about it, I bestirred myself to see, if possible, how to supply two wants; I had no vessels to hold anything that was liquid, except two runlets, which were almost full of rum, and some glass bottles, some of the common size, and others, which were case-bottles, square, for the holding of waters, spirits, etc. I had not so much as a pot to boil anything in, except a great kettle which I saved out of the ship, and which was too big for such cases as I desired it for, namely, to make broth, and stew a bit of meat by itself. The second thing I would fain have had was a tobacco-pipe, but it was impossible for me to make one; however, I found a contrivance for that too at last.

I employed myself in planting my second rows of stakes of piles, and in this wicker-work, all the summer, or dry season, when another business took me up more time than it could be imagined I could spare.

CHAPTER VIII

I MENTIONED before, that I had a mind to see the whole island, and that I had travelled up the brook and on to where I built my bower, and where I had an opening quite to the sea, on the other side of the island. I now resolved to travel quite across to the sea-shore on that side. So, taking my gun and hatchet, and my dog, and a larger quantity of powder and shot than usual, with two biscuit-cakes, and a great bunch of raisins in my pouch, for my store, I began my journey. When I had passed the vale where my bower stood, as above, I came within view of the sea to the west; and it being a very clear day, I fairly descried land, whether an island or continent I could not tell; but it lay very high, extending from the west to the west-south-west, at a very great distance; by my guess it could not be less than fifteen or twenty leagues off.

I could not tell what part of the world this might be, otherwise than that I knew it must be part of America; and, as I concluded by all my observations, must be near the Spanish dominions, and perhaps was all inhabited by savages, where, if I should have landed, I had been in a worse condition than I was now; and therefore I acquiesced in the dispositions of Providence, which I began now to own, and to believe ordered everything for the best— I say, I quieted my mind with this, and left afflicting myself with fruitless wishes of being there.

Besides, after some pause upon this affair, I considered, that if this land was the Spanish coast, I should certainly, one time or other, see some vessels pass or repass one way or other; but if not, then it was the savage coast between the Spanish country and Brazil, the inhabitants of which are indeed the worst of savages; for they are cannibals, or men-eaters, and fail not to murder and devour all the human bodies that fall into their hands.

With these considerations I walked very leisurely forward. I found that side of the island where I now was much pleasanter than mine—the open or savanna fields sweet, adorned with flowers and grass, and full of very fine woods. I saw abundance of parrots, and fain would I have caught one, if possible, to have kept it to be tame, and taught it to speak to me. I did, after some painstaking, catch a young parrot; for I knocked it down with a stick, and having recovered it, I brought it home, but it was some years before I could make him speak. However, at last I taught him to call me by my name very familiarly; but the accident that followed, though it be a trifle, will be very diverting in its place.

I was exceedingly diverted with this journey; I found in the low grounds, hares, as I thought them to be, and foxes, but they differed greatly from all the other kinds I had met with; nor could I satisfy myself to eat them, though I killed several; but I had no need to be venturous; for I had no want of food, and of that which was very good too; especially these three sorts; namely, goats, pigeons, and turtles, or tortoise, which added to my grapes, Leadenhall Market could not have furnished a better table than I, in proportion to the company; and though my case was deplorable enough, yet I had great cause for thankfulness, that I was not driven to any extremities for food; but rather plenty, even to dainties.

I never travelled in this journey above two miles outright in a day, or thereabouts; but I took so many turns and returns to see what discoveries I could make, that I came wearied enough to the place where I resolved to sit down for all night; and then either reposed myself in a tree, or surrounded myself with a row of stakes set upright in the ground, either from one tree to another, or so as no wild creature could come at me without waking me.

As soon as I came to the sea-shore, I was surprised to see that I had taken up my lot on the worst side of the island; for here, indeed, the shore was covered with innumerable turtles, whereas, on the other side, I had found but three in a year and a half. Here was also an infinite number of fowls of many kinds, some of which I had not seen before, and many of them very good meat; but such as I knew not the names of, except those called penguins.

I could have shot as many as I pleased, but was very sparing of my powder and shot; and therefore had more mind to kill a she-goat, if I could, which I could better feed on; and though there were many goats here, more than on the other side of the island, yet it was with much more difficulty that I could come near them—the country being flat and even, and they saw me much sooner than when I was on the hills.

I confess this side of the country was much pleasanter than mine, but yet I had not the least inclination to remove; for, as I was fixed in my habitation, it became natural to me, and I seemed, all the while I was here, to be, as it were, upon a journey and from home; however, I travelled along the shore of the sea towards the east, I suppose, about twelve miles; and then, setting up a great pole upon the shore for a mark, I concluded I would go home again; and the next journey I took should be on the other side of the island, east from my dwelling, and so round, till I came to my post again—of which in its place.

I took another way to come back than that I went, thinking I could keep all the island so much in my view, that I could not miss finding my first dwelling by viewing the country—but I found myself mistaken; for, being come about two or three miles, I found myself descended into a very large valley, but so surrounded with hills, and those hills covered with woods, that I could not see which was my way by any direction but that of the sun, nor even then, unless I knew very well the position of the sun at that time of the day.

It happened, to my further misfortune, that the weather proved hazy for three or four days, while I was in this valley ; and not being able to see the sun, I wandered about very uncomfortably, and at last was obliged to find out the sea-side, look for my post, and come back the same way I went ; and then, by easy journeys, I turned homeward, the weather being exceedingly hot, and my gun, ammunition, hatchet, and other things, very heavy.

In this journey, my dog surprised a young kid, and seized upon it ; and I running in to take hold of it, caught it, and saved it alive from the dog. I had a great mind to bring it home, if I could ; for I had often been musing whether it might not be possible to get a kid or two, and so raise a breed of tame goats, which might supply me when my powder and shot should be spent.

I made a collar for this little creature, and, with a string which I made of some rope-yarn, which I always carried about me, I led him along, though with some difficulty, till I came to my bower, and there I enclosed him, and left him, for I was very impatient to be at home, from whence I had been absent above a month.

I cannot express what a satisfaction it was to me to come into my old hutch, and lie down in my hammock-bed : this little wandering journey, without a settled place of abode, had been so unpleasant to me, that my own house, as I called it to myself, was a perfect settlement to me compared to that ; and it rendered everything about me so comfortable, that I resolved I would never go a great way from it again, while it should be my lot to stay on the island.

I reposed myself here a week, to rest and regale myself after my long journey ; during which, most of the time was taken up in the weighty affair of making a cage for my poll, who began now to be a mere domestic, and to be mighty well acquainted with me. Then I began to think of the poor kid which I had pent in within my little circle, and resolved to go and fetch it home, and give it some food ; accordingly I went, and found it where I left it ; for, indeed, it could not get out, but was almost starved for want of food. I went and cut boughs of trees, and branches of such shrubs as I could find, and threw it over, and having fed it, I tied it as I did before, to lead it away ; but it was so tame with being hungry, that I had no need to have tied it, for it followed me like a dog ; and, as I continually fed it, the creature became so loving, so gentle, and so fond, that it became from that time one of my domestics also, and would never leave me afterwards.

The rainy season of the autumnal equinox was now come, and I kept the 30th of September in the same solemn manner as before, being the anniversary of my landing on the island, having now been there two years, and no more prospect of being delivered than the first day I came there. I spent the whole day in humble and thankful acknowledgments of the many wonderful mercies which my solitary condition was attended with, and without which it might have been infinitely more miserable.

Thus, and in this disposition of mind, I began my third year ; and though I have not given the reader the trouble of so particular an account of my works this year as at first, yet in general it may be observed, that I was very seldom idle, having regularly divided my time according to the several daily employments that were before me—such as, first, my duty to God, and reading the Scriptures, which I constantly set apart some time for, thrice every day ; secondly, the going abroad with my gun for food, which generally took me up three hours every morning when it did not rain ; thirdly, the ordering, curing, preserving, and cooking what I had killed or catched for my supply—these took up great part of the day ; also it is to be considered, that in the middle of the day, when the sun was in the zenith, the violence of the heat was too great to stir out ; so that about four hours in the evening was all the time I could be supposed to work in ; with this exception, that sometimes I changed my hours of hunting and working, and went to work in the morning, and abroad with my gun in the afternoon.

To this short time allowed for labour, I desire may be added the exceeding laboriousness of my work ; the many hours which, for want of tools, want of help and want of skill, everything that I did took up out of my time—for example, I was full two-and-forty days making me a board for a long shelf, which I wanted in my cave ; whereas, two sawyers, with their tools and saw-pit, would have cut six of them out of the same tree in half a day.

My case was this : it was to be a large tree which was to be cut down, because my board was to be a broad one. The tree I was three days of cutting down, and two more cutting of the boughs, and reducing it to a log, or piece of timber. With inexpressible hacking and hewing, I reduced both the sides of it into chips, till it began to be light enough to move ; then I turned it, and made one side of it smooth and flat, as a board, from end to end ; then, turning that side downward, cut the other side till I brought the plank to be about three inches thick, and smooth on both sides.

I was now, in the months of November and December, expecting my crop of barley and rice. The ground I had manured or dug up for them was not great ; for as I observed, my seed of each was not above the quantity of half a peck, for I had lost one whole crop by sowing in the dry season ; but now my crop promised very well, when on a sudden I found I was in danger of losing it all again by enemies of several sorts, which it was scarce possible to keep from it ; at first, the goats and wild creatures which I called hares, which, tasting the sweetness of the blade, lay in it night and day, as soon as it came up, and ate it so close that it could get no time to shoot up into stalks.

This I saw no remedy for, but by making an enclosure about it with a hedge, which I did with a great deal of toil ; and the more, because it required a great deal of speed, the creatures daily spoiling my corn. However, as my arable land was but small, suited to my crop, I got it totally well fenced in about three weeks' time, and shooting some of the creatures in the daytime, I set my dog to guard it in the night, tying him up to a stake at the gate, where he would stand and bark all night long ; so in a little time the enemies forsook the place, and the corn grew very strong and well, and began to ripen apace.

But as the beasts ruined me before while my corn was in the blade, so the birds were as likely to ruin me now, when it was in the ear ; for, going along by the place to see how it throve, I saw my little crop surrounded with fowls I know not how many sorts, which stood as it were watching till I should be gone. I immediately let fly among them (for I had always my gun with me). I had no sooner shot, but there rose up a little crowd of fowls, which I had not seen at all, from among the corn itself.

This touched me sensibly ; for I foresaw that, in a few days, they would devour all my hopes ; that I should be starved, and never be able to raise a crop at all—and what to do I could not tell ; however, I resolved not to lose my corn, if possible, though I should watch it night and day. In the first place, I went among it to see what damage was already done, and found they had spoiled a good deal of it ; but that, as it was yet too green for them, the loss was not so great, but the remainder was like to be a good crop, if it could be saved.

I stayed by it to load my gun and, then coming away, I could easily see all the thieves sitting upon all the trees about me, as if they only waited till I was gone away, and the event proved it to be so ; for, as I walked off as if I was gone, I was no sooner out of their sight, but they dropped down one by one, into the corn again. I was so provoked that I could not have patience to stay till more came on, knowing that every grain they ate now was, as it might be said, a peck loaf to me in the consequence ; but, coming up to the hedge, I fired again, and killed three of them. This was what I wished for ; so I took them up, and served them as we serve notorious thieves in England, namely, hanged them in chains for a terror to others. It is impossible to imagine almost that this should have such an effect as it had ; for the fowls would not only not come at the corn, but, in short, they forsook all that part of the island, and I could never see a bird near the place as long as my scarecrows hung there.

This I was very glad of, you may be sure ; and about the latter end of December, which was our second harvest of the year, I reaped my corn.

I was sadly put to it for a scythe, or a sickle, to cut it down, and all I could do was to make one as well as I could, out of one of the broadswords, or cutlasses which I saved among the arms out of the ship. However, as my crop was but small, I had no difficulty to cut it down : in short, I reaped it my way, for I cut nothing off but the ears, and carried it away in a great basket which I had made, and so rubbed it out with my hands ; and, at the end of all my harvesting, I found that out of my half peck of seed I had near two bushels of rice, and above two bushels and a half of barley, that is to say, by my guess, for I had no measure at that time.

However, this was a great encouragement to me ; and I foresaw that in time it would please God to supply me with bread ; and yet here I was perplexed again, for I neither knew how to grind nor make meal of my corn, nor, indeed, how to clean it and part it ; nor, if made into meal how to make bread of it ; and if how to make it, yet I knew not how to bake it. These things being added to my desire of having a good quantity for store, and to secure a constant supply, I resolved not to taste any of this crop, but to preserve it all for seed against the next season, and, in the meantime, to employ all my study and hours of working to accomplish this great work of providing myself with corn and bread.

First, I had no plough to turn the earth, no spade or shovel to dig it.

Well, this I conquered by making a wooden spade, as I observed before ; but this did my work but in a wooden manner ; and though it cost me a great many days to make it, yet, for want of iron, it not only wore out the sooner, but made my work the harder, and made it be performed much worse.

However, this I bore with too, and was content to work it out with patience, and bear with the badness of the performance. When the corn was sowed, I had no harrow, but was forced to go over it myself, and drag a great heavy bough of a tree over it to scratch the earth, as it may be called, rather than rake or harrow it.

When it was growing, or grown, I have observed already how many things I wanted, to fence it, secure it, mow or reap it, cure or carry it home, thresh, part it from the chaff, and save it. Then I wanted a mill to grind it, sieves to dress it, yeast and salt to make it into bread, and an oven to bake it in ; and all these things I did without ; as shall be observed, and yet the corn was an inestimable comfort and advantage to me too. But all this, as I said, made everything laborious and tedious to me, but that there was no help for ; neither was my time so much loss to me, because, as I had divided it, a certain part of it was every day appointed to these works ; and as I resolved to use none of the corn for bread till I had a greater quantity by me, I had the next six months to apply myself wholly, by labour and invention, to furnish myself with utensils proper for the performing all the operations necessary for making the corn, when I had it fit for my use.

But first I was to prepare more land, for I had now seed enough to sow above an acre of ground. Before I did this, I had a week's work at least to make me a spade, which, when it was done, was a very sorry one indeed, and very heavy, and required double labour to work with it ; however, I went through that, and sowed my seeds in two large flat pieces of ground, as near my house as I could find them to my mind, and fenced them in with a good hedge, the stakes of which were all cut off that wood which I had set before, which I knew would grow ; so that in one year's time I knew I should have a quick or living hedge, that would want but little repair. This work was not so little as to take me up less than three months ; because great part of that time was in the wet season, when I could not go abroad.

Within doors, that is, when it rained and I could not go out, I found employment on the following occasions ; always observing, that all the while I was at work, I diverted myself with talking to my parrot, and teaching him to speak ; and I quickly learnt him to know his own name, and at last to speak it out pretty loud, POLL, which was the first word I ever heard spoken in the island by any mouth but my own. This, therefore, was not my work, but an assistant to my work ; for now, as I said, I had a great employment upon my hands, as follows : namely, I had long studied, by some means or other, to make myself some earthen vessels, which indeed I wanted sorely, but knew not where to come at them ; however, considering the heat of the climate, I did not doubt but, if I could find out any suitable clay, I might botch up some such pot as might, being dried by the sun, be hard enough and strong enough to bear handling, and to hold anything that was dry, and required to be kept so ; and as this was necessary in preparing corn, meal, etc., which was the thing I was upon, I resolved to make some as large as I could, and fit only to stand like jars to hold what should be put into them.

CHAPTER IX

IT would make the reader pity me, or rather laugh at me, to tell how many awkward ways I took to raise this paste, what odd, misshapen, ugly things I made ; how many of them fell in, and how many fell out, the clay not being stiff enough to bear its own weight ; how many cracked by the over-violent heat of the sun, being set out too hastily ; and how many fell to pieces with only removing, as well before as after they were dried : and, in a word, how, after having laboured hard to find the clay, to dig it, to temper it, to bring it home, and work it, I could not make above two large earthen ugly things—I cannot call them jars—in about two months' labour.

However, as the sun baked these two very dry and hard, I lifted them very gently up, and set them down again in two great wicker baskets, which I had made on purpose for them, that they might not break ; and, as between the pot and the basket there was a little room to spare, I stuffed it full of the rice and barley straw ; and these two pots being to stand always dry, I thought would hold my dry corn, and perhaps the meal when the corn was bruised.

Though I miscarried so much in my design for large pots, yet I made several smaller things with better success : such as little round pots, flat dishes, pitchers, and pipkins, anything my hand turned to ; and the heat of the sun baked them strangely hard.

But all this would not answer my end, which was to get an earthen pot to hold what was liquid, and bear the fire, which none of these could do. It happened after some time, making a pretty large fire for cooking my meat, when I went to put it out, after I had done with it, I found a broken piece of one of my earthenware vessels in the fire, burnt as hard as a stone, and red as a tile. I was agreeably surprised to see it, and said to myself, that certainly they might be made to burn whole, if they would burn broken.

This set me to study how to order my fire, so as to make it burn me some pots. I had no notion of a kiln such as the potters burn in, or of glazing them with lead, though I had some lead to do it with ; but I placed three large pipkins, and two or three pots, in a pile, one upon another, and placed my firewood all around it, with a great heap of embers under them. I piled the fire with fresh fuel round the outside, and upon the top, till I saw the pots in the inside red hot quite through, and observed that they did not crack at all : when I saw them clear red, I let them stand in that heat about five or six hours, till I found one of them, though it did not crack, did melt, or run ; for the sand which was mixed with the clay melted by the violence of the heat, and would have run into glass if I had gone on ; so I slacked my fire gradually, till the pots began to abate of the red colour, and watching them all night, that I might not let the fire abate too fast, in the morning I had three very good, I will not say handsome, pipkins, and two other earthen pots, as hard burnt as could be desired, and one of them perfectly glazed with the running of the sand.

After this experiment, I need not say that I wanted no sort of earthenware for my use ; but I must needs say, as to the shapes of them, they were very indifferent, as any one may suppose, when I had no way of making them but as the children make dirt pies, or as a woman would make pies that never learnt to raise paste.

No joy at a thing of so mean a nature was ever equal to mine, when I found I had made an earthen pot that would bear the fire ; and I had hardly patience to stay till they were cold, before I set one upon the fire again with some water in it, to boil me some meat, which it did admirably well ; and with a piece of kid, I made some very good broth, though I wanted oatmeal, and several other ingredients requisite to make it so good as I would have had it.

My next concern was to get me a stone mortar to stamp or beat some corn in ; for as to the mill, there was no thought of arriving to that perfection of art with one pair of hands. To supply this want, I was at a great loss ; for, of all the trades in the world, I was as perfectly unqualified for a stone-cutter as for any whatever ; neither had I any tools to go about it with. I spent many a day to find out a great stone big enough to cut hollow, and make fit for a mortar, and could find none at all, except what was in the solid rock, and which I had no way to dig, or cut out ; nor indeed were the rocks in the island of hardness sufficient, but were all of a sandy crumbling stone, which would neither bear the weight of a heavy pestle, nor would break the corn without filling it with sand ; so, after a great deal of time lost in searching for a stone, I gave it over, and resolved to look out for a great block of hard wood, which I found indeed much easier ; and, getting one as big as I had strength to stir, I rounded it, and formed it on the outside with my axe and hatchet ; and then, with the help of fire and infinite labour, made a hollow place in it, as the Indians in Brazil make their canoes. After this I made a great heavy pestle, or beater, of the wood called the iron-wood, and this I prepared and laid by against I had my next crop of corn, when I proposed to myself to grind, or rather pound, my corn, or meal, to make my bread.

My next difficulty was to make a sieve, or searce, to dress my meal, and part it from the bran and the husk, without which I did not see it possible I could have any bread. This was a most difficult thing, so much as but to think on ; for, to be sure, I had nothing like the necessary things to make it with—I mean fine thin canvas, or stuff, to searce the meal through. And here I was at a full stop for many months ; nor did I know really what to do ; linen I had none left but what was mere rags ; I had goat's hair, but neither knew I how to weave or spin it ; and had I known how, here were no tools to work it with. All the remedy that I found for this was, that at last I did remember I had among the seamen's clothes which were saved out of the ship, some neckcloths of calico, or muslin ; and with some pieces of these I made three small sieves, but proper enough for the work ; and thus I made shift for some years. How I did afterwards, I shall show in its place.

The baking part was the next thing to be considered, and how I should make bread when I came to have corn ; for, first, I had no yeast ; as to that part, there was no supplying the want, so I did not concern myself much about it. But for an oven, I was, indeed, in great pain. At length I found out an expedient for that also, which was this :—I made some earthen vessels very broad, but not deep ; that is to say, about two feet diameter, and not above nine inches deep ; these I burnt in the fire, as I had done the others, and laid them by ; and when I wanted to bake, I made a great fire upon the hearth, which I had paved with some square tiles of my own making and burning also—but I should not call them square.

When the firewood was burnt pretty much into embers, or live coals, I drew them forward upon this hearth, so as to cover it all over, and there I let them lie, till the hearth was very hot ; then, sweeping away all the embers, I set down my loaf, or loaves, and, whelming down the earthen pot upon them, drew the embers all round the outside of the port, to keep in, and add to the heat : and thus, as well as in the best oven in the world, I baked my barley-loaves, and became in a little time a good pastry-cook into the bargain ; for I made myself several cakes of the rice, and puddings : indeed, I made no pies, neither had I anything to put into them, supposing I had, except the flesh either of fowls or goats.

It need not be wondered at, if all these things took me up most part of the third year of my abode here ; for it is to be observed, that in the interval of these things I had my new harvest and husbandry to manage ; for I reaped my corn in its season, and carried it home as well as I could, and laid it up in the ear, in my large baskets, till I had time to rub it out ; for I had no floor to thrash it on, or instrument to thrash it with.

And now, indeed, my stock of corn increasing, I really wanted to build my barns bigger ; I wanted a place to lay it up in ; for the increase of the corn now yielded me so much, that I had of the barley about twenty bushels, and of the rice as much, or more ; insomuch, that I now resolved to begin to use it freely, for my bread had been quite gone a great while ; also I resolved to see what quantity would be sufficient for me a whole year, and to sow but once a year.

At length I began thinking whether it was not possible to make myself a canoe, or periagua, such as the natives of those climates make, even without tools, or, as I might say, without hands, namely, of the trunk of a great tree.

So to work I went, and felled a cedar tree. It was five feet ten inches diameter at the lower part next the stump, and four feet eleven inches diameter at the end of twenty-two feet, after which it lessened for awhile, and then parted into branches. It was not without infinite labour that I felled this tree ; I was twenty days hacking and hewing at it at the bottom ; I was fourteen more getting the branches and limbs, and the vast spreading head of it, cut off, which I hacked and hewed through with my axe and hatchet with inexpressible labour ; after this it cost me a month to shape it ; and dub it to a proportion, and to something like the bottom of a boat, that it might swim upright as it ought to do. It cost me near three months more to clear the inside, and work it out so as to make an exact boat of it : this I did indeed without fire, by mere mallet and chisel and by the dint of hard labour, till I had brought it to be a very handsome periagua, and big enough to have carried six-and-twenty men, and consequently big enough to have carried me and all my cargo.

When I had gone through this work, I was extremely delighted with it ; the boat was really much bigger than I ever saw a canoe or periagua, that was made of one tree, in my life ; many a weary stroke it had cost, you may be sure, for there remained nothing but to get it into the water ; and had I gotten it into the water I make no question but I should have begun the

I was unable to stir it

maddest voyage, and the most unlikely to be performed, that ever was undertaken.

But all my devices to get it into the water failed me, though they cost infinite labour too. I lay about one hundred yards from the water, and not more ; but the first inconvenience was, it was uphill towards the creek. Well, to take away this discouragement, I resolved to dig into the surface of the earth, and so make a declivity : this I began, and it cost me a prodigious deal of pains ; but who grudge pains that have their deliverance in view ? but when this was worked through, and this difficulty managed, it was still much at one, for I could no more stir the canoe than I could the other boat.

Then I measured the distance of ground, and resolved to cut a dock, or canal, to bring the water up to the canoe, seeing I could not bring the canoe down to the water : well, I began this work, and when I began to enter into it, and calculated how deep it was to be dug, how broad, how the stuff was to be thrown out, I found that, by the number of hands I had, being none but my own, it must have been ten or twelve years before I should have gone through with it ; for the shore lay high, so that at the upper end it must have been at least twenty feet deep ; so at length, though with great reluctance, I gave this attempt over also.

This grieved me heartily ; and now I saw, though too late, the folly of beginning a work before we count the cost, and before we judge rightly of our own strength to go through with it.

In the middle of this work I finished my fourth year in this place, and kept my anniversary with the same devotion, and with as much comfort, as ever before.

My clothes began to decay mightily : as to linen, I had none a good while, except some chequered shirts which I found in the chests of the other seamen, and which I carefully preserved, because many times I could bear no other clothes on but a shirt ; and it was a very great help to me that I had, among all the men's clothes of the ship, almost three dozen shirts. There were also several thick watch-coats of the seamen, which were left behind, but they were too hot to wear ; and though it is true that the weather was so violently hot that there was no need of clothes, yet I could not go quite naked—no, though I had been inclined to it, which I was not—nor could I abide the thoughts of it, though I was all alone.

One reason why I could not go quite naked was, I could not bear the heat of the sun so well when quite naked, as with some clothes on—nay, the very heat frequently blistered my skin ; whereas, with a shirt on, the air itself made some motion, and whistling under the shirt, was twofold cooler than without it : no more could I bring myself ever to go out in the heat of the sun without a cap or a hat ; the heat of the sun beating with such violence as it does in that place, would give me the headache presently, by darting so directly on my head, without a cap or hat on, so that I could not bear it ; whereas if I put on my hat, it would presently go away.

Upon these views I began to consider about putting the few rags I had, which I called clothes, into some order ; I had worn out all the waistcoats I had, and my business was now to try if I could not make jackets out of the great watch-coats which I had by me, and with such other materials as I had—so I set to work a-tailoring, or rather, indeed, a-botching—for I made most piteous work of it. However, I made shift to make two or three waistcoats, which I hoped would serve me a great while : as for breeches or drawers, I made but very sorry shift indeed till afterwards.

I have mentioned that I saved the skins of all the creatures that I killed —I mean four-footed ones—and I had hung them up stretched out with sticks in the sun ; by which means some of them were so dry and hard that they were fit for little ; but others, it seems, were very useful. The first thing I made of these was a great cap for my head, with the hair on the out-side to shoot off the rain : and this I performed so well, that after this I made a suit of clothes wholly of those skins—that is to say, a waistcoat and breeches open at the knees, and both loose ; for they were rather wanted to keep me cool, than to keep me warm. I must not omit to acknowledge that they were wretchedly made ; for if I was a bad carpenter, I was a worse tailor : however, they were such as I made a very good shift with ; and when I was abroad, if it happened to rain, the hair of the waistcoat and cap being outmost, I was kept very dry.

After this I spent a deal of time and pains to make me an umbrella : I was, indeed, in great want of one, and had a great mind to make one ; I had seen them made in the Brazils, where they are very useful in the great heats which are there ; and I felt the heats every jot as great here, and greater, too, being nearer the equinox ; besides, as I was obliged to be much abroad, it was a most useful thing to me, as well for the rains as the heats. I took a world of pains at it, and was a great while before I could make any-thing likely to hold ; nay, after I thought I had hit the way, I spoiled two or three before I made one to my mind ; but at last I made one that answered

I was a worse tailor

indifferently well. The main difficulty I found was to make it to let down ; I could make it to spread ; but if it did not let down too, and draw in, it would not be portable for me any way, but just over my head, which would not do. However, at last, as I said, I made one to answer : I covered it with skins, the hair upwards, so that it cast off the rain like a penthouse, and kept off the sun so effectually, that I could walk out in the hottest of the weather, with greater advantage than I could before in the coolest ; and, when I had no need of it, I could close it, and carry it under my arm.

I cannot say that, after this, for five years, any extraordinary thing happened to me ; but I lived on in the same course, in the same posture and place, just as before. The chief thing I was employed in, besides my yearly labour of planting my barley and rice, and curing my raisins, of both which I always kept up just enough to have a sufficient stock of the year's provisions beforehand—I say, besides this yearly labour, and my daily labour of going out with my gun, I had one labour to make me a canoe, which at last I finished : so that by digging a canal to it, six feet wide, and four feet deep, I brought it into the creek almost half a mile. As for the first, that was so vastly big, as I made it without considering beforehand, as I ought to do, how I should be able to launch it ; so, never being able to bring it to the water or bring the water to it, I was obliged to let it lie where it was, as a memorandum to teach me to be wiser next time. Indeed, the next time, though I could not get a tree proper for it, and was in a place where I could not get the water to it, at any less distance than, as I have said, of near a half mile ; yet, as I saw it practicable at last, I never gave it over ; and, though I was near two years about it, yet I never grudged my labour, in hopes of having a boat to go off to sea at last.

CHAPTER X

HOWEVER, though my little periagua was finished, yet the size of it was not at all answerable to the design which I had in view when I made the first—I mean of venturing over to the terra firma, where it was above forty miles broad ; accordingly, the smallness of the boat assisted to put an end to that design, and now I thought no more of it. But as I had a boat, my next design was to make a tour round the island ; for, as I had been on the other side, in one place, crossing, as I have already described it, over the land, so the discoveries I made in that journey made me very eager to see the other parts of the coast ; and now I had a boat, I thought of nothing but sailing round the island.

For this purpose, and that I might do everything with discretion and consideration, I fitted up a little mast to my boat, and made a sail to it out of some of the pieces of the ship's sails, which lay in store, and of which I had a great store by me.

Having fitted my mast and sail, and tried the boat, I found she would sail very well. Then I made little lockers and boxes at each end of my boat, to put provisions, necessaries, and ammunition, etc., into, to be kept dry, either from rain, or the spray of the sea ; and a little long hollow place I cut in the inside of the boat, where I could lay my gun, making a flap to hang down over it to keep it dry.

I fixed my umbrella also in a step at the stern, like a mast, to stand over my head, and keep the heat of the sun off me, like an awning ; and thus I every now and then took a little voyage upon the sea, but never went far out, nor far from the little creek ; but at last, being eager to view the circumference of my little kingdom, I resolved upon my tour, and accordingly I victualled my ship for the voyage.

It was the 6th of November, in the sixth year of my reign, or my captivity, which you please, that I set out on this voyage, and I found it much longer than I expected ; for though the island itself was not very large, yet when I came to the east side of it, I found a great ledge of rocks lie out about two leagues into the sea, some above water, some under it ; and beyond this a shoal of sand, lying dry half a league more : so that I was obliged to go a great way out to sea to double that point.

When I first discovered them, I was going to give over my enterprise, and come back again, not knowing how far it might oblige me to go out to sea, and, above all, doubting how I should get back again ; so I came to an anchor, for I had made me a kind of an anchor with a piece of broken grappling which I got out of the ship.

Having secured my boat, I took my gun, and went on shore, climbing up a hill, which seemed to overlook that point, where I saw the full extent of it, and resolved to venture.

In my viewing the sea from that hill where I stood, I perceived a strong, and indeed a most furious current, which ran to the east, and even came close to the point ; and I took the more notice of it, because I saw there might be some danger, that when I came into it, I might be carried out to sea by the strength of it, and not be able to make the island again. And indeed, had I not gotten first upon this hill, I believe it would have been so ; for there was the same current on the other side of the island, only that it set off at a farther distance ; and I saw there was a strong eddy under the shore—so I had nothing to do but to get out of the first current, and I should presently be in an eddy.

I lay here, however, two days ; because the wind blowing pretty fresh (at east-south-east, and that being just contrary to the said current), made a great breach of the sea upon the point ; so that it was not safe for me to keep too close to the shore for the breach, nor to go too far off because of the stream.

The third day in the morning, the wind having abated overnight, the sea was calm, and I ventured : but I am a warning-piece again to all rash and ignorant pilots ; for no sooner was I come to the point, when I was not my boat's length from the shore, but I found myself in a great depth of water and a current like the sluice of a mill. It carried my boat along with it, with such a violence that all I could do could not keep her so much as on the edge of it ; but I found it hurried me farther and farther out from the eddy, which was on the left hand. There was no wind stirring to help me, and all that I could do with my paddles signified nothing ; and now I began to give myself over for lost ; for, as the current was on both sides of the island, I knew in a few leagues' distance they must join again, and then I was irrecoverably gone—nor did I see any possibility of avoiding it ; so that I had no prospect before me but of perishing—not by the sea, for that was calm enough, but of starving for hunger. I had, indeed, found a tortoise on the shore, as big almost as I could lift, and had tossed it into the boat ; and I had a great jar of fresh water, that is to say, one of my earthen pots ; but what was all this to being driven into the vast ocean, where, to be sure, there was no shore, no mainland or island, for a thousand leagues at least ?

It is scarce possible to imagine the consternation I was in, being driven from my beloved island (for so it appeared to me now to be) into the wide ocean, almost two leagues, and in the utmost despair of ever recovering it again : however, I worked hard, till indeed my strength was almost exhausted, and kept my boat as much to the northward, that is, towards the side of the current which the eddy lay on, as possibly I could ; when about noon, as the sun passed the meridian, I thought I felt a little breeze of wind in my face, springing up from the south-south-east. I applied myself to get up my mast again, and spread my sail, standing away to the north as much as possible, to get out of the current.

Just as I had set my mast and sail, and the boat began to stretch away, I saw, even by the clearness of the water, some alteration of the current was near ; for where the current was so strong, the water was foul ; but perceiving the water clear, I found the current abate, and presently I found, to the east, at about half a mile, a breach of the sea upon some rocks : these rocks I found caused the current to part again ; and as the main stress of it ran away more southerly, leaving the rocks to the north-east, so the other returned by the repulse of the rock, and made a strong eddy, which ran back again to the north-west with a very sharp stream.

Gladly I put my boat into the stream of this eddy ; and the wind also freshening, how gladly I spread my sail to it, running cheerfully before the wind, and with a strong tide or eddy under foot.

This eddy carried me about a league on my way back again directly towards the island, but about two leagues more towards the northward than the current lay, which carried me away at first ; so that when I came near the island, I found myself open to the northern shore of it, that is to say, the other end of the island, opposite to that which I went out from.

When I had made something more than a league of way, by the help of this heavy current or eddy, I found it was spent, and served me no farther. However, I found that being between the two great currents, namely, that on the south side which had carried me away, and that on the north, which lay about two leagues on the other side—I say, between these two, in the west of the island, I found the water at least still, and running no way ; and having still a breeze of wind fair for me, I kept on steering directly for the island, though not making such fresh way as I did before.

After four o'clock in the evening, being then within about a league of the island, I found the point of the rocks which occasioned this distance stretching out, as is described before, to the southward, and, casting off the current more southwardly, had, of course, made another eddy to the north ; and this I found very strong, but not directly setting the way my course lay, which was due west, but almost full north. However, having a fresh gale, I stretched across this eddy, slanting north-west, and, in about an hour, came within about a mile of the shore, where, it being smooth water, I soon got to land.

I was now at a great loss which way to get home with my boat ; I had run so much hazard, and knew too much the cause, to think of attempting it by the way I went out ; and what might be at the other side (I mean the west side), I knew not, nor had I any mind to run any more ventures ; so I only resolved in the morning to make my way westward along the shore, and to see if there was no creek where I might lay up my frigate in safety, so as to have her again if I wanted her. In about three miles, or thereabouts, coasting the shore, I came to a very good inlet, or bay, about a mile over, which narrowed till it came to a very little rivulet, or brook, where I found a convenient harbour for my boat, and where she lay as if she had been in a little dock made on purpose for her ; here I put in, and having stowed my boat very safe, I went on shore to look about me, and see where I was.

I soon found I had but a little passed by the place where I had been before when I travelled on foot to that shore ; so, taking nothing out of my boat but my gun and my umbrella, for it was exceedingly hot, I began my march. The way was comfortable enough, after such a voyage as I had been upon, and I reached my old bower in the evening, where I found everything standing as I left it ; for I always kept it in good order, being, as I said before, my country-house.

I got over the fence, and laid me down in the shade to rest my limbs, for I was very weary, and fell asleep ; but judge if you can, you that read my story, what a surprise I must be in, when I was awaked out of my sleep by a voice calling me by my name several times, " Robin, Robin, Robin

Robinson Crusoe and his friends

Crusoe, poor Robin Crusoe! Where are you, Robin Crusoe? Where are you? Where have you been?"

I was dead asleep at first, being fatigued with rowing, or paddling, as it is called, the first part of the day, and walking the latter part, that I did not awake thoroughly, and dozing between sleeping and waking, thought I dreamed that somebody spoke to me; but as the voice continued to repeat "Robin Crusoe, Robin Crusoe!" at last I began to awake more perfectly, and was at first dreadfully frightened, and started up in the utmost consternation: but no sooner were my eyes open, but I saw my Poll sitting on the top of the hedge, and immediately knew that this was he that spoke to me; for just in such bemoaning language I had used to talk to him, and teach him; and he had learned it so perfectly, that he would sit upon my finger and lay his bill close to my face, and cry, "Poor Robin Crusoe, where are you? Where have you been? How came you here?" and such things as I taught him.

However, even though I knew it was the parrot, and that indeed it could be nobody else, it was a good while before I could compose myself. First, I was amazed how the creature got thither, and then how he should just keep about the place, and nowhere else; but as I was well satisfied it could be nobody but honest Poll, I got it over; and, holding out my hand, and calling him by his name, "Poll!" the sociable creature came to me, and sat upon my thumb, as he used to do, and continued talking to me—"Poor Robin Crusoe!" and "How did I come here?" and "Where had I been?" just as if he had been overjoyed to see me again; and so I carried him home along with me.

I dug several large pits

I had now had enough of rambling to sea for some time, and had enough to do for many days to sit still and reflect upon the danger I had been in. I would have been very glad to have had my boat again on my side of the island, but I knew not how it was practicable to get it about : as to the east side of the island, which I had gone round, I knew well enough there was no venturing that way ; my very heart would shrink, and my very blood run chill, but to think of it : and as to the other side of the island, I did not know how it might be there ; but supposing the current ran with the same force against the shore at the east, as it passed by it on the other, I might run the same risk of being driven down the stream, and carried by the island, as I had been before of being carried away from it. So with these thoughts I contented myself to be without any boat, though it had been the product of so many months' labour to make it, and of so many more to get it into the sea.

During the following year I dug large pits in which I ensnared some goats that were on the island and found them of great use to me, and very sagacious and tractable creatures, were they well used.

CHAPTER XI

I WAS somewhat impatient, as I had observed, to have the use of my boat, though loath to run any more hazard ; and therefore sometimes I sat contriving ways to get her about the island, and at other times I sat myself down contented enough without her. But I had a strange uneasiness in my mind to go down to the point of the island, where, as I have said in my last ramble, I went up the hill to see how the shore lay, and how the current set, that I might see what I had to do. This inclination increased upon me every day, and at length I resolved to travel thither by land, and following the edge of the shore, I did so ; but had any one in England been to meet such a man as I was, it must either have frightened him, or raised a great deal of laughter ; and as I frequently stood still to look at myself, I could not but smile at the notion of my travelling through Yorkshire with such an equipage, and in such a dress. Be pleased to take a sketch of my figure, as follows:—

I had a great high shapeless cap, made of goat's skin, with a flap hanging down behind, as well to keep the sun from me as to shoot the rain off from running into my neck ; nothing being so hurtful in these climates as the rain upon the flesh under the clothes.

I had a short jacket of goat's skin, the skirts coming down to about the middle of my thighs ; and a pair of open-kneed breeches of the same ; the breeches were made of the skin of an old he-goat, whose hair hung down such a length on either side, that, like pantaloons, it reached to the middle of my legs. Stockings and shoes I had none ; but I had made me a pair of something, I scarce knew what to call them, like buskins, to flap over my legs, and lace on either side like spatterdashes, but of a most barbarous shape, as indeed were all the rest of my clothes.

I had on a broad belt of goat's skin dried, which I drew together with two thongs of the same, instead of buckles ; and in a kind of a frog on either side of this, instead of a sword and dagger, hung a little saw and a hatchet —one on one side, one on the other ; I had another belt not so broad, and fastened in the same manner, which hung over my shoulder ; and at the end of it, under my left arm, hung two pouches, both made of goat's skin too, in one of which hung my powder, in the other my shot ; at my back I carried my basket, on my shoulder my gun ; and over my head a great clumsy ugly goat's skin umbrella, but which, after all, was the most necessary thing I had about me, next to my gun. As for my face, the colour of it was really not so mulatto-like as one might expect from a man not at all careful of it, and living within nine or ten degrees of the equinox. My beard I had once suffered to grow till it was about a quarter of a yard long ; but as I had both scissors and razors sufficient, I had cut it pretty short, except what grew on my upper lip, which I had trimmed into a large pair of Mahometan whiskers, such as I had seen worn by some Turks whom I saw at Sallee ; for the Moors did not wear such, though the Turks did : of these mustachios, or whiskers, I will not say they were long enough to hang my hat upon them ; but they were of length and shape monstrous enough, and such as in England would have passed for frightful.

But all this is by the bye ; for as to my figure, I had so few to observe, that it was of no manner of consequence—so I say no more to that part. In this kind of figure I went my new journey, and was out five or six days. I travelled first along the sea-shore directly to the place where I first brought my boat to an anchor, to get upon the rocks ; and, having no boat now to take care of, I went over the land a nearer way, to the same height that I was upon before ; when looking forward to the point of the rock which lay out, and which I was to double with my boat, as I said above, I was surprised to see the sea all smooth and quiet ; no rippling, no motion, no current, any more than in any other places.

I was at a strange loss to understand this, and resolved to spend some time in the observing of it, to see if nothing from the sets of the tide had occasioned it : but I was presently convinced how it was ; namely, that the tide of ebb setting from the west, and joining with the current of waters from some great river on the shore, must be the occasion of this current, and accordingly as the wind blew more forcibly from the west, or from the north, this current came near, or went farther from the shore ; for, waiting thereabouts till evening, I went up to the rock again, and then, the tide of ebb being made, I plainly saw the current again as before, only that it ran farther off, being near half a league from the shore ; whereas, in my case, it set close upon the shore, and hurried me in my canoe along with it, which at another time it would not have done.

This observation convinced me that I had nothing to do but to observe the ebbing and the flowing of the tide, and I might very easily bring my boat about the island again : but when I began to think of putting it into practice I had such a terror upon my spirits at the remembrance of the danger I had been in, that I could not think of it again with any patience ; but, on the contrary, I took up another resolution, which was more safe, though more laborious, and this was, that I would build, or rather make, me another periagua or canoe ; and so have one for one side of the island, and one for the other.

You are to understand, that now I had, as I may call it, two plantations in the island, one my little fortification, or tent, with the wall about it under the rock, with the cave behind me, which by this time I had enlarged into several apartments or caves, one within another. One of these, which was the driest and largest, and had a door out beyond my wall or fortification —that is to say, beyond where my wall joined to the rock—was all filled up with large earthen pots, of which I have given an account, and with fourteen or fifteen great baskets, which would hold five or six bushels each, where I laid up my stores of provisions, especially my corn, some in the ear, cut off short from the straws, and the other rubbed out with my hands.

As for my wall, made as before, with long stakes or piles, those piles grew all like trees, and were by this time grown so big, and spread so very much, that there was not the least appearance, to any one's view, of any habitation behind them.

Near this dwelling of mine, but a little farther within the land, and upon lower ground, lay my two pieces of corn ground, which I kept duly cultivated and sowed, and which duly yielded me their harvest in its season ; and whenever I had occasion for more corn, I had more land adjoining, as fit as that.

Besides this, I had my country seat, and I had now a tolerable plantation there also ; for first, I had my little bower, as I called it, which I kept in repair—that is to say, I kept the hedge which circled it in constantly fitted up to its usual height ; the ladder standing always in the inside ; I kept the trees, which at first were no more than stakes, but were now grown very firm and tall—I kept them always so cut that they might spread, and grow thick and wild, and make the more agreeable shade, which they did effectually to my mind. In the middle of this I had my tent always standing, being a piece of sail spread over poles set up for that purpose, and which never wanted any repair or renewing ; and under this I had made me a squab, or couch, with the skins of the creatures I had killed, and with other soft things, and a blanket laid on them, such as belonged to our sea bedding, which I had saved, and a great watch-coat to cover me ; and here, whenever I had occasion to be absent from my chief seat, I took up my country habitation.

Adjoining to this, I had my enclosures for my cattle, that is to say, my goats : and as I had taken an inconceivable deal of pains to fence and enclose this ground, I was so uneasy to see it kept entire, lest the goats should break through, that I never left off, till, with infinite labour, I had stuck the outside of the hedge so full of small stakes, and so near to one another that it was rather a pale than a hedge, and there was scarce room to put a hand through between them, which afterwards, when those stakes grew, as they all did in the next rainy season, made the enclosure strong like a wall—indeed, stronger than any wall.

This will testify for me that I was not idle, and that I spared no pains to bring to pass whatever appeared necessary for my comfortable support ; for I considered the keeping up a breed of tame creatures thus at my hand would be a living magazine of flesh, milk, butter, and cheese for me, as long as I lived in the place, if it were to be forty years ; and that keeping them in my reach depended entirely upon my perfecting my enclosures to such a degree that I might be sure of keeping them together ; which by this method, indeed, I so effectually secured, that, when these little stakes began to grow, I had planted them so very thick I was forced to pull some of them up again.

In this place also I had my grapes growing, which I principally depended on for my winter store of raisins, and which I never failed to preserve very carefully, as the best and most agreeable dainty of my whole diet ; and, indeed, they were not agreeable only, but physical, wholesome, nourishing, and refreshing to the last degree.

As this was also about half-way between my other habitation and the place where I had laid up the boat, I generally stayed and lay here on my way thither ; for I used frequently to visit my boat, and I kept all things about or belonging to her in very good order. Sometimes I went out in her to divert myself ; but no more hazardous voyages would I go, nor scarce ever above a stone's cast or two from the shore, I was so apprehensive of being hurried out of my knowledge again by the currents, or winds, or any other accident. But now I come to a new scene of my life.

It happened one day about noon, going towards my boat, I was exceedingly surprised with the print of a man's naked foot on the shore, which was very plain to be seen in the sand : I stood like one thunderstruck, or as if I had seen an apparition ; I listened, I looked round me—I could hear nothing, nor see anything : I went up to a rising ground to look farther ; I went up the shore and down the shore, but it was all one, I could see no other impression but that one ; I went to it again to see if there were any more, and to observe if it might not be my fancy ; but there was no room for that, for there was exactly the very print of a foot, toes, heel, and every part of a foot ; how it came thither I knew not, nor could in the least imagine. But after innumerable fluttering thoughts, like a man perfectly confused, and out of myself, I came home to my fortification, not feeling, as we say, the ground I went on, but terrified to the last degree, looking behind me at every two or three steps, mistaking every bush and tree, and fancying every stump at a distance to be a man ; nor is it possible to describe how many various shapes an affrighted imagination represented things to me in—how many wild ideas were formed every moment in my fancy— and what strange unaccountable whimsies came into my thoughts by the way.

When I came to my castle, for so I think I called it ever after this, I fled into it like one pursued ; whether I went over by the ladder, at first contrived, or in at the hole in the rock, which I called a door, I cannot remember ; for never frighted hare fled to cover, or fox to earth, with more terror of mind than I to this retreat.

I had no sleep that night : the farther I was from the occasion of my fright, the greater my apprehensions were ; which is something contrary to the nature of such things, and especially to the usual practice of all creatures in fear. But I was so embarrassed with my own frightful ideas of the thing, that I formed nothing but dismal imaginations to myself,

Mistaking every bush and tree

even though I was now a great way off it. Sometimes I fancied it must be the devil; and reason joined in with me upon this supposition. For how should any other thing in human shape come into the place? Where was the vessel that brought them? What marks were there of any other footsteps? And how was it possible that a man should come there? But then to think that Satan should take human shape upon him in such a place, where there could be no manner of occasion for it but to leave the print of his foot behind him, and that even for no purpose too (for he could not be sure I should see it), this was an amazement the other way: I considered that the devil might have found out abundance of other ways to have terrified me, than this of the single print of a foot; that, as I lived quite on the other side of the island, he should never have been so simple as to leave a mark in a place where it was ten thousand to one whether I should ever see it or not, and in the sand too, which the first surge of the sea upon a high wind would have defaced entirely. All this seemed inconsistent with the thing itself, and with all notions we usually entertain of the subtlety of the devil.

Abundance of such things as these assisted to argue me out of all apprehensions of its being the devil; and I presently concluded that it must be some more dangerous creature—namely, that it must be some of the savages of the mainland over against me, who had wandered out to sea in their canoes, and, either driven by the currents, or by contrary winds, had made the island, and had been on shore, but were gone away again to sea, being as loath, perhaps, to have stayed in this desolate island, as I would have been to have had them.

While these reflections were rolling upon my mind, I was very thankful in my thought, that I was so happy as not to be thereabouts, at that time, or that they did not see my boat, by which they would have concluded that some inhabitants had been in the place, and perhaps have searched farther for me. Then terrible thoughts racked my imagination, about their having found my boat, and that there were people here ; and that if so, I should certainly have them come again in greater numbers, and devour me : that if it should happen so that they should not find me, yet they would find my enclosure, destroy all my corn, carry away all my flock of tame goats, and I should perish at last for mere want.

Thus my fear banished all my religious hope ; all that former confidence in God, which was founded upon such wonderful experience as I had had of His goodness, now vanished ; as if He that had fed me by a miracle hitherto, could not preserve by His power the provision which He had made for me by His goodness. I reproached myself with my laziness, that I would not sow any more corn one year than would just serve me till the next season, as if no accident could intervene to prevent my enjoying the crop that was upon the ground. And this I thought so just a reproof, that I resolved for the future to have two or three years' corn beforehand, so that, whatever might come, I might not perish for want of bread.

It came into my thoughts one day that all this might be a mere chimera of my own, that this foot might be the print of my own foot, when I came on shore from my boat. This cheered me up a little too, and I began to persuade myself it was all a delusion—that it was nothing else but my own foot ; and why might I not come that way from my boat, as well as I was going that way to the boat. Again, I considered also, that I could by no means tell for certain where I had trod, and where I had not ; and that if at last this was only the print of my own foot, I had played the part of those fools who strive to make stories of spectres and apparitions, and then are themselves frighted at them more than anybody else.

Now I began to take courage, and to peep abroad again—for I had not stirred out of my castle for three days and nights, so that I began to starve for provision ; for I had little or nothing within doors, but some barley-cakes and water. Then I knew that my goats wanted to be milked too, which usually was my evening diversion—and the poor creatures were in great pain and inconvenience for want of it ; and, indeed, it almost spoiled some of them, and almost dried up their milk.

Heartening myself, therefore, with the belief that this was nothing but the print of one of my own feet (and so I might truly be said to start at my own shadow), I began to go abroad again, and went to my country-house to milk my flock ; but to see with what fear I went forward, how often I looked behind me, how I was ready, every now and then, to lay down my basket, and run for my life, it would have made any one have thought I was haunted with an evil conscience, or that I had been lately most terribly frighted ; and so indeed I had.

However, as I went down thus two or three days, and having seen nothing, I began to be a little bolder, and to think there was really nothing in it but my own imagination ; but I could not persuade myself fully of this, till I should go down to the shore again and see this print of a foot, and

Robinson Crusoe decked out for a hunting expedition

247

measure it by my own, and see if there was any similitude or fitness, that I might be assured it was my own foot. But when I came to the place first, it appeared evidently to me, that when I laid up my boat, I could not possibly be ashore anywhere thereabouts. Secondly, when I came to measure the mark with my own foot, I found my foot not so large by a great deal. Both these things filled my head with new imaginations, and gave me the vapours again to the highest degree ; so that I shook with cold like one in an ague, and I went home again, filled with the belief that some man or men had been on shore there ; or, in short, that the island was inhabited, and I might be surprised before I was aware ; and what course to take for my security I knew not.

Now I began sorely to repent that I had dug my cave so large as to bring a door through again, which door, as I said, came out beyond where my fortification joined to the rock. Upon maturely considering this, therefore, I resolved to draw me a second fortification in the manner of a semicircle, at a distance from my wall, just where I had planted a double row of trees about twelve years before, of which I made mention ; these trees having been planted so thick before, there wanted but a few piles to be driven between them, that they should be thicker and stronger, and my wall would soon be finished.

So that I now had a double wall, and my outer wall was thickened with pieces of timber, old cables, and everything I could think of, to make it strong : having in it seven little holes, about as big as I might put my arm out at. In the inside of this I thickened my wall to about ten feet thick, continually bringing earth out of my cave, and laying it at the foot of the wall, and walking upon it ; and through the seven holes I contrived to plant the muskets, of which I took notice that I got seven on shore out of the ship : these, I say, I planted like my cannon, and fitted them into frames that held them like a carriage, that so I could fire all the seven guns in two minutes' time. This wall I was many a weary month in finishing, and yet never thought myself safe till it was done.

When this was done, I stuck all the ground without my wall, for a great way every way, as full with stakes or sticks of the ozier-like wood, which I found so apt to grow, as they could well stand ; insomuch, that I believe I might set in near twenty thousand of them, leaving a pretty large space between them and my wall, that I might have room to see an enemy, and they might have no shelter from the young trees, if they attempted to approach my outer wall.

Thus in two years' time I had a thick grove ; and in five or six years' time I had a wood before my dwelling, grown so monstrous thick and strong, that it was, indeed, perfectly impassable ; and no man, of what kind soever, would ever imagine that there was anything beyond it, much less a habitation. As for the way I proposed myself to go in and out (for I left no avenue), it was by setting two ladders ; one to a part of the rock which was low, and then broke in, and left room to place another ladder upon that ; so when the two ladders were taken down, no man living could come down to me without mischiefing himself ; and if they had come down they were still on the outside of my outer wall.

Thus I took all the measures human prudence could suggest for my own preservation ; and it will be seen at length, that they were not altogether without just reason—though I foresaw nothing at that time more than my mere fear suggested.

While this was doing, I was not altogether careless of my other affairs, for I had a great concern upon me for my little herd of goats ; they were not only a present supply to me upon every other occasion, and to be sufficient for me without the expense of powder and shot, but also abated the fatigue of my hunting after the wild ones ; and I was loath to lose the advantage of them, and to have them all to nurse up over again.

To this purpose, after long consideration, I could think but of two ways to preserve them : one was to find another convenient place to dig a cave under ground, and to drive them into it every night ; and the other was to enclose two or three little bits of land, remote from one another, and as much concealed as I could, where I might keep about half a dozen young goats in each place, so that if any disaster happened to the flock in general, I might be able to raise them again with little trouble and time ; and this, though it would require a great deal of time and labour, I thought was the most rational design.

Accordingly, I spent some time to find out the most retired parts of the island ; and I pitched upon one which was as private, indeed, as my heart could wish, for it was a little damp piece of ground in the middle of the hollow and thick woods, where, as is observed, I almost lost myself once before, endeavouring to come back that way from the eastern part of the island. Here I found a clear piece of land, near three acres, so surrounded with woods that it was almost an enclosure by nature ; at least, it did not want near so much labour to make it so, as the other pieces of ground I had worked so hard at.

I immediately went to work with this piece of ground, and in less than a month's time I had so fenced it round that my flock, or herd, call it which you please, which were not so wild now as at first they might be supposed to be, were well enough secured in it. So, without any further delay, I removed ten she-goats and two he-goats to this piece ; and when there, I continued to perfect the fence, till I had made it as secure as the other, which, however, I did at more leisure, and it took me up the more time by a great deal.

CHAPTER XII

ALL this labour I was at the expense of, purely from my apprehensions on the account of the print of a man's foot, which I had seen ; for as yet I never saw any human creature come near the island, and I had now lived two years under these uneasinesses, which, indeed, made my life much less comfortable than it was before, as may well be imagined by any who know what it is to live in the constant snare of the fear of man.

After I had thus secured one part of my little living stock, I went about the whole island searching for another private place to make such another deposit ; when wandering more to the west point of the island than I had ever done yet, and looking out to sea, I thought I saw a boat upon the sea at a great distance. I had found a perspective glass or two in one of the seamen's chests which I saved out of our ship; but I had it not about me, and this was so remote, that I could not tell what to make of it, though I looked at it till my eyes were not able to look any longer—whether it was a boat or not, I did not know; but as I descended from the hill, I could see no more of it, so I gave it over; only I resolved to go no more without a perspective glass in my pocket.

When I was come down the hill to the shore, as I said above, being the south-west point of the island, I was perfectly confounded and amazed; nor is it possible for me to express the horror of my mind, at seeing the shore spread with skulls, hands, feet, and other bones of human bodies; and, particularly, I observed a place where there had been a fire made, and a circle dug in the earth, like a cock-pit, where I supposed the savage wretches had sat down to their inhuman feastings upon the bodies of their fellow-creatures.

I was so astonished at the sight of these things that I entertained no notions of any danger to myself from it for a long while; all my apprehensions were buried in the thoughts of such a pitch of inhuman, hellish brutality, and the horror of the degeneracy of human nature; which, though I had heard of often, yet I never had so near a view of before—in short, I turned away my face from the horrid spectacle; my stomach grew sick, and I was just at the point of fainting, when nature discharged the disorder from my stomach, and having vomited with an uncommon violence, I was a little relieved, but could not bear to stay in the place a moment; so I got me up the hill again with all the speed I could, and walked on towards my own habitation.

I was so astonished at the sight

I entertained such an abhorrence of the savage wretches that I have been speaking of, and of the wretched inhuman custom of their devouring and eating one another up, that I continued pensive and sad, and kept close within my own circle for almost two years after this.

Time, however, and the satisfaction I had that I was in no danger of being discovered by these people, began to wear off my uneasiness about them, and I began to live just in the same composed manner as before ; only with this difference, that I used more caution, and kept my eyes more about me than I did before, lest I should happen to be seen by any of them ; and particularly, I was more cautious of firing my gun, lest any of them on the island should happen to hear it ; and it was therefore a very good providence to me that I had furnished myself with a tame breed of goats, that I had no need to hunt any more about the woods, or shoot at them ; and if I did catch any more of them after this, it was by traps and snares, as I had done before—so that for two years after this, I believe I never fired my gun once off, though I never went out without it ; and, which was more, as I had saved three pistols out of the ship, I always carried them out with me, or at least two of them, sticking them in my goat-skin belt ; I likewise furbished up one of the great cutlasses that I had out of the ship, and made me a belt to put it in also : so that I was now a most formidable fellow to look at when I went abroad, if you add to the former description of myself, the particular of two pistols, and a great broadsword hanging at my side in a belt, but without a scabbard.

Things going on thus, as I have said, for some time, I seemed, excepting these cautions, to be reduced to my former calm sedate way of living.

My invention now ran quite another way ; for night and day I could think of nothing but how I might destroy some of these monsters in their cruel, bloody entertainment, and, if possible, save the victim they should bring hither to destroy. It would take up a larger volume than this whole work is intended to be, to set down all the contrivances I hatched, or rather brooded upon in my thoughts, for the destroying these creatures, or at least frightening them, so as to prevent their coming hither any more ; but all was abortive—nothing could be possible to take effect, unless I was to be there to do it myself ; and what could one man do among them, when perhaps there might be twenty or thirty of them together, with their darts, or their bows and arrows, with which they could shoot as true to a mark as I could with my gun ?

Sometimes I contrived to dig a hole under the place where they made their fire, and put in five or six pounds of gunpowder, which, when they kindled their fire, would consequently take fire, and blow up all that was near it ; but as, in the first place, I should be very loath to waste so much powder upon them, my store now being within the quantity of a barrel, so neither could I be sure of it going off at any certain time, when it might surprise them, and at best, that it would little more than just blow the fire about their ears, and fright them, but not sufficient to make them forsake the place, so I laid it aside, and then proposed that I would place myself in ambush, in some convenient place, with my three guns all double loaded, and in the middle of their bloody ceremony, let fly at them, when I should be sure to kill or wound perhaps two or three at every shot ; and then, falling in upon them with my three pistols, and my sword, I made no doubt but that, if there were twenty, I should kill them all. This fancy pleased my thoughts for some weeks, and I was so full of it that I often dreamed of it, and sometimes, that I was just going to let fly at them in my sleep.

I went so far with it in my imagination that I employed myself several days to find out proper places to put myself in ambuscade, as I said, to watch for them, and I went frequently to the place itself, which was now grown more familiar to me; and especially while my mind was thus filled with thoughts of revenge, and of a bloody putting twenty or thirty of them to the sword, as I may call it, but the horror I had at the place, and at the signals of the barbarous wretches devouring one another, abated my malice.

Well, at length I found a place in the side of the hill, where I was satisfied I might securely wait till I saw any of the boats coming, and might then, even before they would be ready to come on shore, convey myself unseen into the thickets of trees, in one of which there was a hollow large enough to conceal me entirely, and where I might sit, and observe all their bloody doings, and take my full aim at their heads, when they were so close together as that it would be next to impossible that I should miss my shot, or that I could fail wounding three or four of them at the first shot.

In this place, then, I resolved to fix my design; and, accordingly, I prepared two muskets and my ordinary fowling-piece. Two muskets I loaded with a brace of slugs each, and four or five smaller bullets, about the size of pistol bullets, and the fowling-piece I loaded with near a handful of swan-shot, of the largest size; I also loaded my pistols with about four bullets each: and in this posture, well provided with ammunition for a second and third charge, I prepared myself for my expedition.

After I had thus laid the scheme of my design, and in my imagination put in practice, I continually made my tour every morning up to the top of the hill, which was from my castle, as I called it, about three miles or more, to see if I could observe any boats upon the sea, coming near the island, or standing towards it; but I began to tire of this hard duty, after I had for two or three months constantly kept my watch, but came always back without any discovery, there having not in all that time been the least appearance, not only on or near the shore, but not on the whole ocean, so far as my eyes or glasses could reach every way.

I went and removed my boat, which I had on the other side of the island, and carried it down to the east end of the whole island, where I ran it into a little cove which I found under some high rocks, and where I knew, by reason of the currents, the savages durst not, at least would not, come with their boats, upon any account whatsoever.

With my boat I carried away everything that I had left there belonging to her, though not necessary for the bare going thither—namely, a mast and sail, which I had made for her, and a thing like an anchor, but, indeed, which could not be called either anchor or grappling—however, it was the best I could make of its kind. All these I removed, that there might not be the least shadow of any discovery, or any appearance of any boat, or of any habitation upon the island.

Besides this, I kept myself, as I said, more retired than ever, and seldom went from my cell, other than upon my constant employment—namely, to milk my she-goats, and manage my little flock in the wood, which, as it was quite on the other part of the island, was quite out of danger.

After I had been some time, I found, to my unspeakable consolation, a mere natural cave in the earth which went in a vast way, and where, I dare say, no savage, had he been at the mouth of it, would be so hardy as to venture in, nor indeed would any man else, but one who, like me, wanted nothing so much as a safe retreat.

While I was cutting down some wood here, I perceived that behind a very thick branch of low brushwood or underwood, there was a kind of hollow place ; I was curious to look into it, and getting with difficulty into the mouth of it, I found it was pretty large, that is to say, sufficient for me to stand upright in it, and perhaps another with me ; but I must confess to you I made more haste out than I did in, when, looking farther into the place which was perfectly dark, I saw two broad shining eyes of some creature, whether devil or man I knew not, which twinkled like two stars, the dim light from the cave's mouth shining directly in and making the reflection.

However, after some pause, I recovered myself, and began to call myself a thousand fools, and tell myself, that he that was afraid to see the devil was not fit to live twenty years in an island all alone, and that I durst to believe there was nothing in this cave that was more frightful than myself. Upon this, plucking up my courage, I took up a large firebrand, and in I rushed again, with the stick flaming in my hand ; I had not gone three steps in, but I was almost as much frightened as I was before, for I heard a very loud sigh, like that of a man in some pain, and it was followed by a broken noise, as if of words half expressed and then a deep sigh again. I stepped back, and was indeed struck with such a surprise that it put me into a cold sweat ; and if I had had a hat on my head, I will not answer for it that my hair might not have lifted it off. But still plucking up my spirits as well as I could, and encouraging myself a little with considering that the power and presence of God was everywhere, and was able to protect me ; upon this I stepped forward again, and by the light of the firebrand, holding it up a little over my head, I saw lying on the ground a most monstrous frightful old he-goat, just making his will, as we say, gasping for life, and dying, indeed, of mere old age.

I stirred him a little, to see if I could get him out, and he essayed to get up, but was not able to raise himself ; and I thought with myself, he might even lie there, for if he had frightened me so, he would certainly fright any of the savages if any of them should be so hardy as to come in there, while he had any life in him.

I was now recovered from my surprise, and began to look round me, when I found the cave was but very small ; that is to say, it might be about twelve feet over, but in no manner of shape, either round or square, no hands having ever been employed in making it but those of mere nature ; I observed also, that there was a place at the farther side of it that went in farther, but so low that it required me to creep upon my hands and knees to get into it, and whither it went I knew not : so, having no candle, I gave it over for some time, but resolved to come again the next day, provided with candles and a tinder-box, which I had made of the lock of one of the muskets, with some wild-fire in the pan.

Accordingly, the next day I came provided with six large candles of my own making, for I made very good candles now of goats' tallow ; and, going into this low place, I was obliged to creep upon all fours, as I have said, almost ten yards, which, by the way, I thought was a venture bold enough, considering that I knew not how far it might go, or what was beyond it. When I was got through the strait, I found the roof rose higher up, I believe near twenty feet ; but never was such a glorious sight seen in the island, I dare say, as it was, to look round the sides and roof of this vault or cave. The walls reflected an hundred thousand lights to me from my two candles ; what it was in the rock, whether diamonds or any other precious stones, or gold, which I rather supposed it to be, I knew not.

The place I was in was a most delightful cavity, or grotto, of its kind, as could be expected, though perfectly dark ; the floor was dry and level, and had a sort of small loose gravel upon it, so that there was no nauseous creature to be seen ; neither was there any damp or wet on the sides of the roof : the only difficulty in it was the entrance, which, however, as it was a place of security, and such a retreat as I wanted, I thought that was a convenience, so that I was really rejoiced at the discovery, and resolved, without any delay, to bring some of those things which I was most anxious about to this place ; particularly, I resolved to bring hither my magazine of powder, and all my spare arms, namely, two fowling-pieces (for I had three in all), and three muskets (for of them I had eight in all) ; so I kept at my castle only five which stood ready mounted, like pieces of cannon, on my outmost fence, and were ready also to take out upon any expedition.

Upon this occasion of removing my ammunition, I was obliged to open the barrel of powder which I took up out of the sea, and which had been wet, and I found that the water had penetrated about three or four inches into the powder on every side, which, caking and growing hard, had preserved the inside like a kernel in a shell, so that I had nearly sixty pounds of very good powder in the centre of the cask ; and this was an agreeable discovery to me at the time : so I carried all away thither, never keeping above two or three pounds of powder with me in my castle, for fear of a surprise of any kind ; I also carried thither all the lead I had left for bullets.

I fancied myself now like one of the ancient giants, which were said to live in caves and holes in the rocks, where none could come at them ; for I persuaded myself while I was here, if five hundred savages were to hunt me, they could never find me out ; or if they did they would not venture to attack me here.

The old goat which I found expiring died in the mouth of the cave the next day after I made this discovery ; and I found it much easier to dig a great hole there, and throw him in and cover him with earth, than to drag him out ; so I interred him there, to prevent offence to my nose.

CHAPTER XIII

IT was now the month of December, in my twenty-third year ; and this being the southern solstice—for winter I cannot call it—was the particular time of my harvest, and required my being much in the fields ; when, going out pretty early in the morning, even before it was thorough daylight, I was surprised with seeing a light of some fire upon the shore, at a distance from me of about two miles, towards the end of the island where I had observed some savages had been, as before ; but not on the other side, but, to my great affliction, it was on my side of the island.

I was, indeed, terribly surprised at the sight, and stopped short within my grove, not daring to go out, lest I might be surprised ; and yet, I had no more peace within, from the apprehensions I had, that if these savages, in rambling over the island, should find my corn standing, or cut, or any of my works and improvements, they would immediately conclude that there were people in the place, and would then never give over till they found me out. In this extremity I went back directly to my castle, pulled up the ladder after me, having made all things without look as wild and natural as I could.

Then I prepared myself within, putting myself in a posture of defence : I loaded all my cannon, as I called them—that is to say, my muskets— which were mounted upon my fortification, and all my pistols, and resolved to defend myself to the last gasp ; not forgetting seriously to recommend myself to the divine protection, and earnestly to pray to God to deliver me out of the hands of the barbarians ; and in this posture I continued about two hours, but began to be mighty impatient for intelligence abroad, for I had no spies to send out.

After sitting a while longer, and musing what I should do in this case, I was not able to bear sitting in ignorance longer ; so, setting up my ladder to the side of the hill where there was a flat place, as I observed before, and then pulling the ladder up after me, I set it up again, and mounted to the top of the hill ; and pulling out my perspective glass, which I had taken on purpose, I laid me down flat on my belly on the ground, and began to look for the place. I presently found there were no less than nine naked savages sitting round a small fire they had made ; not to warm them—for they had no need of that, the weather being extremely hot—but, as I suppose, to dress some of their barbarous diet of human flesh which they had brought with them, whether live or dead I could not know.

They had two canoes with them, which they had hauled up upon the shore ; and as it was then tide of ebb, they seemed to me to wait the return of the flood to go away again. It is not easy to imagine what confusion this sight put me into, especially seeing them come on my side the island and so near me too ; but when I observed their coming must be always with the current of the ebb, I began afterwards to be more sedate in my mind, being satisfied that I might go abroad with safety all the time of tide of flood, if they were not on shore before ; and, having made this observation, I went abroad about my harvest work with the more composure.

As I expected, so it proved ; for as soon as the tide made to the west-

I saw that they had two canoes with them

ward, I saw them all take boat, and row (or paddle, as we call it) all away :
I should have observed, that for an hour and more before they went off,
they went to dancing, and I could easily discern their postures and gestures
by my glasses : I could only perceive, by my nicest observation, that they
were stark naked, and had not the least covering upon them ; but whether
they were men or women that I could not distinguish.

As soon as I saw them shipped and gone, I took two guns upon my
shoulders, and two pistols at my girdle, and my great sword by my side,
without a scabbard ; and with all the speed I was able to make, I went away
to the hill, where I had discovered the first appearance of all. As soon as
I got thither, which was not less than two hours (for I could not go apace,
being so loaded with arms as I was), I perceived there had been three canoes
more of savages on that place ; and looking out farther, I saw they were all
at sea together, making over for the main.

This was a dreadful sight to me, especially when, going to the shore,
I could see the marks of horror which the dismal work they had been about
had left behind it, namely, the blood, the bones, and part of the flesh of
human bodies, eaten and devoured by those wretches with merriment and
sport. I was so filled with indignation at the sight, that I began now to
premeditate the destruction of the next that I saw there, let them be who or
how many soever.

I wore out a year and three months more before I ever saw any more
of the savages, and then I found them again, as I shall soon observe. It
is true, they might have been there once or twice, but either they made no
stay, or at least I did not hear them ; but in the month of May, as near as

I could calculate, and in my four-and-twentieth year. I had a very strange encounter with them, of which in its place.

On the sixteenth of May it blew a great storm of wind all day, with a great deal of lightning and thunder, and a very foul night was after it ; I know not what was the particular occasion of it ; but as I was reading in the Bible, I was surprised with the noise of a gun, as I thought, fired at sea.

I started up in the greatest haste imaginable ; and, in a trice, clapped up my ladder to the middle place of the rock, and pulled it after me, and, mounting it the second time, got to the top of the hill ; that very moment a flash of fire bade me listen for a second gun, which, accordingly, in about half a moment, I heard, and, by the sound, knew that it was from that part of the sea where I was driven out with the current in my boat.

I immediately considered that this must be some ship in distress, and that they had some comrade, or some other ship in company, and fired these guns for signals of distress, and to obtain help. I had this presence of mind that minute, as to think that though I could not help them, it might be they might help me ; so I brought together all the dry wood I could get at hand, and making a good handsome pile, I set it on fire upon the hill. The wood was dry, and blazed freely, and, though the wind blew very hard, yet it burnt fairly out, so that I was certain, if there was any such thing as a ship, they must needs see it ; and no doubt they did, for as soon as ever my fire blazed up, I heard another gun, and after that several others, all from the same quarter. I plied my fire all night long till day broke ; and when it was broad day, and the air cleared up, I saw something at a great distance at sea, full east of the island, whether a sail or a hull I could not distinguish, no, not with my glasses, the distance was so great, and the weather still something hazy also ; at least it was so out at sea.

I looked frequently at it all that day, and soon perceived that it did not move, so I presently concluded that it was a ship at anchor ; and being eager, you may be sure, to be satisfied, I took my gun in my hand, and ran towards the south-east side of the island, to the rocks, where I had been formerly carried away with the current ; and getting up there, the weather by this time being perfectly clear, I could plainly see to my great sorrow, the wreck of a ship cast away in the night upon those concealed rocks which I found when I was out in my boat ; and which rocks, as they checked the violence of the stream, and made a counter stream, or eddy, were the occasion of my recovering then from the most desperate, hopeless condition that ever I had been in all my life.

I cannot explain, by any possible energy of words, what a strange longing, or hankering of desire, I felt in my soul upon this sight—breaking out sometimes thus : " Oh ! that there had been but one or two, nay, but one soul saved out of the ship, to have escaped to me, that I might have had but one companion, one fellow-creature, to have spoken to me, and to have conversed with ! " In all the time of my solitary life I never felt so earnest, so strong a desire after the society of my fellow-creatures, or so deep a regret at the want of it.

But it was not to be ; either their fate, or mine, or both, forbade it ; for till the last year of my being on this island, I never knew whether any were saved out of that ship or no ; and had only the affliction, some days after, to see the corpse of a drowned boy come on shore, at the end of the island which was next the shipwreck : he had on no clothes but a seaman's waistcoat, a pair of open-kneed linen drawers, and a blue linen shirt ; but nothing to direct me so much as to guess what nation he was of. He had nothing in his pocket but two pieces of eight, and a tobacco pipe : the last was to me of ten times more value than the first.

It was now calm, and I had a great mind to venture out in my boat to this wreck, not doubting but I might find something on board that might be useful to me ; but that did not altogether press me so much, as the possibility that there might yet be some living creature on board, whose life I might not only save, but might, by saving that life, comfort my own to the last degree : and this thought clung so to my heart, that I could not be quiet night nor day, but I must venture out in my boat on board this wreck ; and committing the rest to God's providence, I thought the impression was so strong upon my mind that it could not be resisted, that it must come from some invisible direction, and that I should be wanting to myself if I did not go.

Under the power of this impression, I hastened back to my castle, prepared everything for my voyage, took a quantity of bread, a great pot of fresh water, a compass to steer by, a bottle of rum (for I had still a great deal of that left), a basket full of raisins ; and thus loading myself with everything necessary, I went down to my boat, got the water out of her, and got her afloat, loaded all my cargo in her, and then went home again for more : my second cargo was a great bagful of rice, the umbrella to set up over my head for shade, another large potful of fresh water, and about two dozen of my small loaves, or barley-cakes, more than before, with a bottle of goat's milk, and a cheese ; all which, with great labour and sweat, I brought to my boat ; and, praying God to direct my voyage, I put out, and rowing or paddling the canoe along the shore, I came at last to the utmost point of the island, on that side, namely, north-east. And now I was to launch out into the ocean, and either to venture or not to venture : I looked on the rapid currents which ran constantly on both sides of the island, at a distance, and which were very terrible to me, from the remembrance of the hazard I had been in before, and my heart began to fail me ; for I foresaw, that if I was driven into either of those currents, I should be carried a vast way out to sea, and perhaps out of reach or sight of the island again ; and that then, as my boat was but small, if any little gale of wind should rise, I should be inevitably lost.

These thoughts so oppressed my mind, that I began to give over my enterprise ; and having hauled my boat into a little creek on the shore, I stepped out, and sat me down upon a little spot of rising ground, very pensive and anxious, between fear and desire, about my voyage ; when, as I was musing, I could perceive that the tide was turned, and the flood came on, upon which my going was for so many hours impracticable ; upon this, it presently occurred to me, that I should go up to the highest piece of ground I could find, and observe, if I could, how the sets of the tide or currents lay, when the flood came in, that I might judge whether, if I was driven one way out, I might not expect to be driven another way home, with the same rapidness of the currents. This thought was no sooner in my

It was a dismal sight to look at

head, but I cast my eye upon a little hill which sufficiently overlooked the sea both ways, and from whence I had a clear view of the currents, or sets of the tide, and which way I was to guide myself in my return ; here I found, that as the current of the ebb set out close by the south point of the island, so the current of the flood set in close by the shore of the north side ; and that I had nothing to do but to keep to the north side of the island in my return, and I should do well enough.

Encouraged with this observation, I resolved the next morning to set out with the first of the tide ; and, reposing myself for that night in the canoe, I launched out. I made first a little out to sea full north, till I began to feel the benefit of the current, which set eastward, and which carried me at a great rate, and yet did not so hurry me as the southern side current had done before, and so as to take from me all government of the boat ; but, having a strong steerage with my paddle, I went, I say, at a great rate, directly for the wreck, and in less than two hours I came up to it.

It was a dismal sight to look at : the ship, which by its building was Spanish, stuck fast, jammed in between two rocks ; all the stern and quarter of her was beaten to pieces with the sea : and as her forecastle, which had stuck in the rocks, had run on with great violence, her mainmast and foremast were brought by the board, that is to say, broken short off ; but her boltsprit was sound, and the head and bow appeared firm. When I came close to her, a dog appeared upon her, which, seeing me coming, yelped and cried, and as soon as I called him, jumped into the sea to come to me, and I took him into the boat, but found him almost dead for hunger and thirst : I gave him a cake of my bread, and he ate it like a ravenous wolf that had been starving a fortnight in the snow ; I then gave the poor creature some fresh water, with which, if I would have let him, he would have burst himself.

After this I went on board. The first sight I met with was two men drowned in the cook-room, or forecastle of the ship, with their arms fast about one another. I concluded, as is indeed probable, that when the ship struck, it being in a storm, the sea broke so high, and so continually over her, that the men were not able to bear it, and were strangled with the constant rushing in of the water, as much as if they had been under water. Besides the dog, there was nothing left in the ship that had life, nor any goods that I could see, but what was spoiled by the water : there were some casks of liquor, whether wine or brandy I knew not, which lay lower in the hold, and which, the water being ebbed out, I could see ; but they were too big to meddle with : I saw several chests, which I believed belonged to some of the seamen, and I got two of them into the boat without examining what was in them.

Had the stern of the ship been fixed, and the fore part broken off, I am persuaded I might have made a good voyage ; for, by what I found in these two chests, I had room to suppose the ship had a great deal of wealth on board : and if I may guess by the course she steered, she must have been bound from Buenos Ayres, or the Rio de la Plata, in the south part of America, beyond the Brazils, to the Havanna, in the Gulf of Mexico, and so, perhaps, to Spain ; she had, no doubt, a great treasure in her, but of no use at that time to anybody ; and what became of the rest of her people I then knew not.

I found, besides these chests, a little cask full of liquor, of about twenty gallons, which I got into my boat with much difficulty. There were several muskets in the cabin, and a great powder-horn, with about four pounds of powder in it ; as for the muskets, I had no occasion for them, so I left them, but took the powder-horn. I took a fire-shovel and tongs, which I wanted extremely, as also two little brass kettles, a copper-pot to make chocolate, and a gridiron ; and with this cargo, and the dog, I came away, the tide beginning to make home again ; and the same evening, about an hour within night, I reached the island again, weary and fatigued to the last degree.

I reposed that night in the boat, and in the morning I resolved to harbour what I had gotten in my new cave, not to carry it home to my castle. After refreshing myself, I got all my cargo on shore ; and began to examine the particulars ; the cask of liquor I found to be a kind of rum, but not such as we had at the Brazils ; and, in a word, not at all good : but, when I came to open the chests, I found several things which I wanted ; for example, I found in one a fine case of bottles, of an extraordinary kind, and filled with cordial waters, fine, and very good ; the bottles held about three pints each, and were tipped with silver. I found two pots of very good succades or sweetmeats, so fastened also on top, that the salt water had not hurt them, and two more of the same, which the water had spoiled ; I found some very good shirts, which were very welcome to me, and about a dozen and a half of white linen handkerchiefs and coloured neckcloths ; the former were also very welcome, being exceedingly refreshing to wipe my face in a hot day. Besides this, when I came to the till in the chests, I found there three great bags of pieces of eight, which held about eleven hundred pieces in all ; and in one of them, wrapt up in a paper, six doubloons of gold, and some small bars or wedges of gold ; I suppose they might all weigh near a pound.

The other chest I found had some clothes in it, but of little value ; but, by the circumstances, it must have belonged to the gunner's mate, as there was no powder in it, but about two pounds of glazed powder in the three flasks, kept, I suppose, for charing their fowling-pieces on occasion. Upon the whole, I got very little by this voyage that was of much use to me ; for, as to the money, I had no manner of occasion for it—it was to me as the dirt under my feet ; and I would have given it all for three or four pair of English shoes and stockings, which were things I greatly wanted, but had not had on my feet now for many years : I had, indeed, got two pair of shoes now, which I took off the feet of the two drowned men whom I saw in the wreck ; and I found two pair more in one of the chests, which were very welcome to me ; but they were not like our English shoes, either for ease or service, being rather what we call pumps than shoes. I found in the seaman's chest about fifty pieces of eight in royals, but no gold : I suppose this belonged to a poorer man than the other, which seemed to belong to some officer.

Well, however, I lugged the money home to my cave, and laid it up, as I had done that before which I brought from our own ship ; but it was great pity, as I said, that the other part of the ship had not come to my share, for I am satisfied I might have loaded my canoe several times over with money, which, if I had ever escaped to England, would have lain here safe enough till I might have come again and fetched it.

Having now brought all my things on shore, and secured them, I went back to my boat, and rowed and paddled her along the shore to her old harbour, where I laid her up, and made the best of my way to my old habitation, where I found everything safe and quiet ; so I began to repose myself, live after my old fashion, and take care of my family affairs ; and for a while I lived easy enough, only that I was more vigilant than I used to be, looked out oftener, and did not go abroad so much ; and if at any time I did stir with any freedom, it was always to the east part of the island, where I was pretty well satisfied the savages never came, and where I could go without so many precautions, and such a load of arms and ammunition as I always carried with me, if I went the other way.

CHAPTER XIV

I AM now to be supposed to be retired into my castle after my late voyage to the wreck, my frigate laid up, and secured under water as usual, and my condition restored to what it was before. I had more wealth, indeed, than I had before, but was not all the richer ; for I had no more use of it than the Indians of Peru had before the Spaniards came thither.

I lived in this condition near two years more, but my unlucky head, that was always to let me know it was born to make my body miserable, was all these two years filled with projects and designs how, if it were possible, I might get away from this island; and I believe verily, if I had had the boat that I went from Sallee in, I should have ventured to sea, bound anywhere, I knew not whither.

I was surprised one morning with seeing no less than five canoes on shore, on my side the island, and the people who belonged to them all landed, and out of my sight; the number of them broke all my measures; for seeing so many, and knowing that they always come four, or six, or sometimes more, in a boat, I could not tell what to think of it, or how to take measures to attack twenty or thirty men single-handed; so, I lay still in my castle, perplexed and discomforted; however, I put myself into all the same postures for an attack that I had formerly provided, and was just ready for action if anything had presented. Having waited a good while, listening to hear if they made any noise, at length, being very impatient, I set my guns at the foot of my ladder, and clambered up to the top of the hill by my two stages, as usual, standing so, however, that my head did not appear above the hill, so that they could not perceive me by any means. Here I observed, by the help of my perspective glass, that they were no less than thirty in number; that they had a fire kindled, and they had meat dressed: how they cooked it, that I knew not, or what it was; but they were all dancing in I know not how many barbarous gestures and figures, their own way, round the fire.

When I was thus looking on them, I perceived, by my perspective, two miserable wretches dragged from the boats, where, it seems, they were laid by, and were now brought out for the slaughter: I perceived one of them immediately fall, being knocked down, I suppose, with a club or wooden sword, for that was their way; and two or three others were at work immediately, cutting him open for their cookery, while the other victim was left standing by himself, till they should be ready for him. At that very moment, this poor wretch, seeing himself a little at liberty, nature inspired him with hopes of life, and he started away from them, and ran with incredible swiftness along the sands, directly towards me—I mean towards the part of the coast where my habitation was.

I was dreadfully frightened (that I must acknowledge) when I perceived him to run my way, and especially when, as I thought, I saw him pursued by the whole body; and now I expected that part of my dream was coming to pass, and that he would certainly take shelter in my grove; but I could not depend, by any means, upon my dream for the rest of it, namely, that the other savages would not pursue him thither, and find him there. However, I kept my station, and my spirits began to recover, when I found that there were not above three men that followed him; and still more was I encouraged when I found that he outstripped them exceedingly in running, and gained ground of them—so that if he could but hold it for half an hour, I saw easily he would fairly get away from them all.

There was between them and my castle the creek, which I mentioned often at the first part of my story, when I landed my cargoes out of the ship, and this I knew he must necessarily swim over, or the poor wretch would be taken there: but when the savage escaping came thither, he made nothing of it, though the tide was then up; but plunging in, swam in about thirty strokes or thereabouts, landed, and ran on with exceeding strength and swiftness. When the three pursuers came to the creek, I found that two of them could swim, but the third could not, and that he, standing on the other side, looked at the other, but went no farther ; and soon after went softly back again, which, as it happened, was very well for him in the main.

I observed that the two who swam were yet more than twice as long swimming over the creek as the fellow was that fled from them. It came now very warmly upon my thoughts, and indeed irresistibly, that now was my time to get a servant, and perhaps a companion, or assistant, and that I was called plainly by Providence to save this poor creature's life. I immediately got down the ladders with all possible expedition, fetched my two guns, for they were both at the foot of the ladder, as I observed above ; and getting up again with the same haste to the top of the hill, I crossed towards the sea ; and having a very short cut, and all down hill, clapped myself in the way between the pursuers and the pursued, halloing aloud to him that fled, who, looking back, was at first perhaps as much frightened at me as at them ; but I beckoned with my hand to him to come back— and in the meantime I slowly advanced towards the two that followed— then rushing at once upon the foremost, I knocked him down with the stock of my piece—I was loath to fire, because I would not have the rest hear, though at that distance it would not have been easily heard—and being out of sight of the smoke, too, they would not have easily known what to make of it.

Having knocked this fellow down, the other who pursued him stopped, as if he had been frightened, and I advanced apace towards him ; but as I came nearer, I perceived presently he had a bow and arrow, and was fitting it to shoot at me ; so I was then necessitated to shoot at him first, which I did, and killed him at the first shot. The poor savage who fled, but had stopped, though he saw both his enemies fallen, and killed (as he thought), yet was so frightened with the fire and noise of my piece, that he stood stock-still, and neither came forward nor went backward, though he seemed rather inclined to fly still than to come on. I hallooed again to him, and made signs to come forward, which he easily understood, and came a little way, then stopped again, and then a little farther, and stopped again ; and I could then perceive that he stood trembling, as if he had been taken prisoner, and had just been to be killed, as his two enemies were.

I beckoned him again to come to me, and gave him all the signs of encouragement that I could think of ; and he came nearer and nearer, kneeling down every ten or twelve steps, in token of acknowledgment for saving his life. I smiled at him, and looked pleasantly, and beckoned to him to come still nearer. At length he came close to me, and then he kneeled down again, kissed the ground, and laid his head upon the ground, and, taking me by the foot, set my foot upon his head.

This, it seems, was in token of swearing to be my slave for ever. I took him up, and made much of him, and encouraged him all I could. But there was more work to do yet ; for I perceived the savage whom I knocked down was not killed, but stunned with the blow, and began to come to himself : so I pointed to him, and showed him the savage, that he was not dead ; upon this he spoke some words to me, and though I could not understand them, yet I thought they were pleasant to hear, for they were the

I killed the savage at the first shot

first sound of a man's voice that I had heard, my own excepted, for above five-and-twenty years.

But there was no time for such reflections now; the savage, who was knocked down, recovered himself so far as to sit up upon the ground; and I perceived that my savage began to be afraid; but when I saw that, I presented my other piece at the man, as if I would shoot him: upon this my savage, for so I called him now, made a motion to me to lend him my sword, which hung naked in a belt by my side—so I did: he no sooner had it, but he runs to his enemy, and at one blow cuts off his head so cleverly, no executioner in Germany could have done it sooner or better, which I thought very strange for one who, I had reason to believe, never saw a sword in his life before, except their own wooden swords: however, it seems, as I learned afterwards, they make their wooden swords so sharp, so heavy, and the wood is so hard that they will cut off heads even with them—and that at one blow too. When he had done this, he comes laughing to me in sign of triumph, and brought me the sword again, and, with abundance of gestures, which I did not understand, laid it down, with the head of the savage that he had killed, just before me.

But that which astonished him most was, to know how I had killed the other Indian so far off; so, pointing to him, he made signs to me to let him go to him; so I bade him go, as well as I could. When he came to him, he stood like one amazed, looking at him—turned him first on one side, then on the other—looked at the wound the bullet had made, which, it seems, was just in his breast, where it made a hole, and no great quantity of blood had followed; but he had bled inwardly, for he was quite dead. Then he took up his bow and arrows, and came back ; so I turned to go away, and beckoned him to follow me, making signs to him that more might come after him.

Upon this he signed to me that he should bury them with sand, that they might not be seen by the rest, if they followed ; and so I made signs again to him to do so. He fell to work, and in an instant he had scraped a hole in the sand with his hands, big enough to bury the first in, and then dragged him into it, and covered him, and did so also by the other ; I believe he had buried them both in a quarter of an hour : then calling him away, I carried him not to my castle, but quite away to my cave, on the farther part of the island ; so I did not let my dream come to pass in that part, namely, that he came into my grove for shelter.

Here I gave him bread and a bunch of raisins to eat, and a draught of water, which I found he was, indeed, in great distress for, by his running ; and, having refreshed him, I made signs for him to go lie down and sleep, pointing to a place where I had laid a great parcel of rice-straw, and a blanket upon it, which I used to sleep upon myself sometimes ; so the poor creature lay down, and went to sleep.

He was a comely, handsome fellow, perfectly well made, with straight, long limbs, not too large, tall and well shaped, and, as I reckon, about twenty-six years of age. He had a very good countenance, not a fierce and surly aspect, but seemed to have something very manly in his face, and yet he had all the sweetness and softness of an European in his countenance, too, especially when he smiled : his hair was long and black, not curled like wool ; his forehead very high and large, and a great vivacity and sparkling sharpness in his eyes. The colour of his skin was not quite black, but very tawny, and yet not of an ugly yellow nauseous tawny, as the Brazilians, and Virginians, and other natives of America are, but of a bright kind of a dun olive colour, that had in it something very agreeable, though not very easy to describe.

His face was round and plump, his nose small, not flat like the negroes, a very good mouth, thin lips, and his teeth fine, well set, and white as ivory. After he had slumbered, rather than slept, above half an hour, he waked again, and comes out of the cave to me, for I had been milking my goats, which I had in the enclosure just by : when he espied me, he came running to me, laying himself down again upon the ground, with all the possible signs of an humble, thankful disposition, making many antic gestures to show it. At last he lays his head flat upon the ground, close to my foot, and sets my other foot upon his head, as he had done before ; and, after this, he made all the signs to me of subjection, servitude, and submission imaginable, to let me know how much he would serve me as long as he lived. I understood him in many things, and let him know I was very well pleased with him. In a little time I began to speak to him, and teach him to speak to me ; and, first, I made him know his name should be Friday, which was the day I saved his life, and I called him so for the memory of the time : I likewise taught him to say Master, and then let him know that was to be my name : I likewise taught him to say Yes and No, and to know the meaning of them. I gave him some milk in an earthen pot, and let him see me drink it before him, and sop my bread in it ; and I gave him a cake of bread to do the like, which he quickly complied with, and made signs that it was very good for him.

I kept there with him all that night ; but as soon as it was day I beckoned him to come with me, and let him know I would give him some clothes, at which he seemed very glad, for he was stark naked. As we went by the place where he had buried the two men, he pointed exactly to the spot, and showed me the marks that he had made to find them again, making signs to me that we should dig them up again and eat them : at this I appeared very angry, expressed my abhorrence of it, made as if I would vomit at the thoughts of it, and beckoned with my hand to him to come away, which he did immediately, with great submission. I then led him up to the top of the hill, to see if his enemies were gone, and pulling out my glass, I looked, and saw plainly the place where they had been, but no appearance of them or of their canoes, so that it was plain that they were gone, and had left their two comrades behind them, without any search after them.

But I was not content with this discovery : but, having now more courage, and, consequently, more curiosity, I took my man Friday with me, giving him the sword in his hand, with the bow and arrows at his back, which I found he could use very dexterously, making him carry one gun for me, and I two for myself, and away we marched to the place where these creatures had been ; for I had a mind now to get some fuller intelligence of them.

When I came to the place, my very blood ran chill in my veins, and my heart sank within me, at the horror of the spectacle : indeed, it was a dreadful sight, at least it was so to me, though Friday made nothing of it ; the place was covered with human bones, the ground dyed with the blood, great pieces of flesh left here and there, half eaten, mangled, and scorched ; and, in short, all the tokens of the triumphant feast they had been making there after a victory over their enemies.

I saw three skulls, five hands, and the bones of three or four legs and feet, and abundance of other parts of the bodies ; and Friday, by his signs, made me understand that they brought over four prisoners to feast upon ; that three of them were eaten up and that he, pointing to himself, was the fourth ; that there had been a great battle between them and their next king, whose subjects, it seems, he had been one of ; and that they had taken a great number of prisoners, all which were carried to several places by those that had taken them in the fight, in order to feast upon them, as was done here by these wretches upon those they brought hither.

I caused Friday to gather all the skulls, bones, flesh, and whatever remained, and lay them together on a heap, and make a great fire upon it, and burn them all to ashes. I found Friday had still a hankering stomach after some of the flesh, and was still a cannibal in his nature ; but I discovered so much abhorrence at the very thoughts of it, and at the least appearance of it, that he durst not discover it ; for I had, by some means, let him know that I would kill him if he offered it.

When we had done this, we came back to our castle, and there I fell to work for my man Friday : and, first of all, I gave him a pair of linen drawers, which I had out of the poor gunner's chest I mentioned, and which I found in the wreck ; and which, with a little alteration, fitted him very well ; then I made him a jerkin of goat's skin, as well as my skill would allow,

Crusoe with his faithful savage, Friday

and I was now grown a tolerably good tailor ; and I gave him a cap, which I had made of a hare's skin, very convenient, and fashionable enough : and thus he was dressed, for the present, tolerably well, and mighty well was he pleased to see himself almost as well clothed as his master. It is true, he went awkwardly in these things at first ; wearing the drawers was very awkward to him, and the sleeves of the waistcoat galled his shoulders and the inside of his arms ; but a little easing them where he complained they hurt him, and using himself to them, at length he took to them very well.

The next day after I came home to my hutch with him, I began to consider where I should lodge him ; and that I might do well for him, and yet be perfectly easy myself, I made a little tent for him in the vacant place between my two fortifications, in the inside of the last, and in the outside of the first ; and as there was a door or entrance there into my cave, I made a formal framed door-case, and a door to it of boards, and set it up in the passage, a little within the entrance ; and, causing the door to open on the inside, I barred it up in the night, taking in my ladders too : so that Friday could no way come at me in the inside of my innermost wall, without making so much noise in getting over, that it must needs awaken me ; for my first wall had now a complete roof over it of long poles, covering all my tent, and leaning up to the side of the hill, which was again laid across with small sticks instead of laths, and then thatched over a great thickness with rice straw, which was strong like reeds ; and at the hole or place which was left to go in or out by the ladder, I had placed a kind of trap-door, which if it had been attempted on the outside, would not have opened at all, but would have fallen down, and made a great noise ; and as to weapons, I took them all into my side every night.

But I needed none of all this precaution ; for never man had a more faithful, loving, sincere servant than Friday was to me ; without passions, sullenness, or designs ; perfectly obliging and engaging, his very affections were tied to me like those of a child to a father ; and I dare say he would have sacrificed his life for the saving mine upon any occasion whatsoever : the many testimonies he gave me of this put it out of doubt, and soon convinced me, that I needed to use no precautions as to my safety on his account.

I was greatly delighted with my new companion, and made it my business to teach him everything that was proper to make himself useful, handy and helpful, but especially to make him speak, and understand me when I spoke : and he was the aptest scholar that ever was ; and particularly was so merry, so constantly diligent, and so pleased when he could but understand me, or make me understand him, that it was very pleasant to me to talk to him. And now my life began to be so easy, that I began to say to myself, that could I but have been safe from more savages, I cared not if I was never to remove from the place where I lived.

CHAPTER XV

AFTER I had been two or three days returned to my castle, I thought, that in order to bring Friday off from his horrid way of feeding, and from the relish of a cannibal's stomach, I ought to let him taste other flesh; so I took him out with me one morning to the woods. I went, intending to kill a kid out of my own flock, and bring it home and dress it; but as I was going, I saw a she-goat lying down in the shade, and two young kids sitting by her. I catched hold of Friday: "Hold," said I, "stand still"; and made signs to him not to stir. Immediately I presented my piece, shot, and killed one of the kids. The poor creature, who had at a distance indeed seen me kill the savage his enemy, but did not know, nor could imagine how it was done, was sensibly surprised, trembled and shook, and looked so amazed, that I thought he would have sunk down: he did not see the kid I had shot at, or perceived I had killed it, but ripped up his waistcoat to feel if he was not wounded; and, as I found presently, thought I was resolved to kill him, for he came and kneeled down to me, and embracing my knees, said a great many things I did not understand: but I could easily see that his meaning was to pray me not to kill him.

I soon found a way to convince him that I would do him no harm; and taking him up by the hand, laughed at him, and pointing to the kid which I had killed, beckoned him to run and fetch it, which he did; and while he was wondering and looking to see how the creature was killed, I loaded my gun again, and by-and-by I saw a great fowl, like a hawk, sit upon a tree within shot; so to let Friday understand a little what I would do, I called him to me again, pointing at the fowl, which was indeed a parrot, though I thought it had been a hawk—I say, pointing to the parrot, and to my gun, and to the ground under the parrot, to let him see I would make him fall, I made him understand that I would shoot and kill that bird; accordingly, I fired, and bid him look, and immediately he saw the parrot fall. He stood like one frighted again, notwithstanding all that I had said to him; and I found he was the more puzzled, because he did not see me put anything into the gun, but thought there must be some wonderful fund of death and destruction in that thing, able to kill man, beast, bird or anything, near and far off; for the astonishment this created in him was such as could not wear off for a long time; and I believe, if I would have let him, he would have worshipped me and my gun. As for the gun itself, he would not so much as touch it for several days after, but would speak to it, and talk to it, as if it had answered him, when he was by himself; which, as I afterwards learned of him, was to desire it not to kill him.

Well, after his astonishment was a little over at this, I pointed to him to run and fetch the bird I had shot, which he did, but stayed some time; for the parrot, not being quite dead, had fluttered a good way off from the place where she fell; however, he found her, took her up, and brought her to me; and as I had perceived his ignorance about the gun before, I took this advantage to charge the gun again, and not let him see me do it, that I might be ready for any other mark that might present; but nothing else offered at that time: so I brought home the kid; and the same evening I took the skin off, and cut it out as well as I could, and having a pot for that purpose, I boiled or stewed some of the flesh, and made some very good broth. After I had begun to eat some, I gave some to my man, who seemed very glad of it, and liked it very well ; but that which was strangest to him was, to see me eat salt with it. He made a sign to me that the salt was not good to eat ; and putting a little into his own mouth, he seemed to nauseate it, and would spit and sputter at it, washing his mouth with fresh water after it. On the other hand, I took some meat in my mouth without salt, and I pretended to spit and sputter for want of salt, as fast as he had done at the salt ; but it would not do, he would never care for salt with meat, or in his broth ; at least not a great while, and then but a very little.

Having thus fed him with boiled meat and broth, I was resolved to feast him the next day with roasting a piece of the kid : this I did by hanging it before the fire in a string, as I had seen many people do in England, setting two poles up, one on each side of a fire, and one cross on the top, and tying the string to the cross stick, letting the meat run continually : this Friday admired very much ; but when he came to taste the flesh, he took so many ways to tell me how well he liked it, that I could not but understand him ; and at last he told me he would never eat man's flesh any more, which I was very glad to hear.

The next day I set him to work to beating some corn out, and sifting it in the manner I used to do, as I observed before ; and he soon understood how to do it as well as I, especially after he had seen what the meaning of it was, and that it was to make bread of ; for after that I let him see me make my bread, and bake it too ; and in a little time Friday was able to do all the work for me, as well as I could do it myself.

I began now to consider, that, having two mouths to feed instead of one, I must provide more ground for my harvest, and plant a larger quantity of corn than I used to do ; so I marked out a larger piece of land, and began the fence in the same manner as before, in which Friday not only worked very willingly and very hard, but did it very cheerfully ; and I told him what it was for, that it was for corn to make more bread, because he was now with me, and that I might have enough for him and myself too : he appeared very sensible of that part, and let me know that he thought I had much more labour upon me on his account than I had for myself, and that he would work the harder for me, if I would tell him what to do.

This was the pleasantest year of all the life I led in this place. Friday began to talk pretty well, and understood the names of almost everything I had occasion to call for, and of every place I had to send him to, and talk a great deal to me ; so that, in short, I began now to have some use for my tongue again, which indeed I had very little occasion for before—that is to say, about speech. Besides the pleasure of talking to him, I had a singular satisfaction in the fellow himself : his simple unfeigned honesty appeared to me more and more every day, and I began really to love the creature ; and on his side, I believe, he loved me more than ever it was possible for him ever to love anything before.

I had a mind once to try if he had any hankering inclination to his own country again ; and having learned him English so well, that he could answer me almost any questions, I asked him whether the nation that he belonged to never conquered in battle? At which he smiled, and said, " Yes, yes, we always fight the better "—that is, he meant, always get the better in fight—and so we began the following discourse: " You always fight the better ! " said I ; " how came you to be taken prisoner, then, Friday ? "

Friday—My nation beat much for all that.

Master—How beat ? If your nation beat them, how came you to be taken ?

Friday—They more than my nation in the place where me was ; they take one, two, three, and me : my nation overbeat them in the yonder place, where me no was ; there my nation take one, two, great thousand.

Master—But why did not your side recover you from the hands of your enemies, then ?

Friday—They run, one, two, three, and me, and make go in the canoe ; my nation have no canoe that time.

Master—Well, Friday, and what does your nation do with the men they take ? Do they carry them away, and eat them as these did ?

Friday—Yes, my nation eat mans too, eat all up.

Master—Where do they carry them ?

Friday—Go to other place where they think.

Master—Do they come hither ?

Friday—Yes, yes, they come hither ; come other else place.

Master—Have you been here with them ?

Friday—Yes, I have been here [points to the north-west side of the island, which, it seems, was their side].

By this I understood that my man Friday had formerly been among the savages who used to come on shore on the farther part of the island, on the said man-eating occasions. that he was now brought for ; and some time after, when I took the courage to carry him to that side, being the same I formerly mentioned, he presently knew the place, and told me he was there once, when they ate up twenty men, two women, and one child : he could not tell twenty in English, but he numbered them by laying so many stones in a row, and pointing to me to tell them over.

I have told this passage because it introduces what follows ; that after I had had this discourse with him, I asked him how far it was from our island to the shore, and whether the canoes were not often lost—he told me there was no danger, no canoes ever lost ; but that after a little way out to sea, there was a current and a wind always one way in the morning, the other in the afternoon.

This I understood to be no more than the sets of the tide, as going out, or coming in ; but I afterwards understood it was occasioned by the great draught and reflux of the mighty river Oroonoque, in the mouth of which river, as I thought afterwards, our island lay ; and that this land which I perceived to the west and north-west, was the great island Trinidad, on the north point of the mouth of the river. I asked Friday a thousand questions about the country, the inhabitants, the sea, the coast, and what nations were near—he told me all he knew with the greatest openness imaginable. I asked him the names of the several nations of his sort of people, but could get no other name than Caribs ; from whence I easily understood that these were the Caribbees, which our maps place on that part of America which reaches from the mouth of the river Oroonoque to Guinea, and onwards to St. Martha. He told me, that up a great way beyond the moon—that was, beyond the setting of the moon, which must be west from their country—there dwelt white-bearded men, like me, and pointed to my great whiskers, which I mentioned before; and that they had killed much mans—that was his word—by which I understood he meant the Spaniards, whose cruelties in America had been spread over the whole countries, and were remembered by all the nations from father to son.

I inquired if he could tell me how I might come from this island, and get among those white men; he told me, "Yes, yes, I might go into two canoe." I could not understand what he meant by two canoe; till at last, with great difficulty, I found he meant that it must be in a large great boat as big as two canoes.

This part of Friday's discourse began to relish with me very well; and from this time I entertained some hopes, that one time or other I might find an opportunity to make my escape from this place, and that this poor savage might be a means to help me to do it.

During the long time that Friday had now been with me, and that he began to speak to me, and understand me, I was not wanting to lay a foundation of religious knowledge in his mind; particularly I asked him one time, Who made him? The poor creature did not understand me at all, but thought I had asked who was his father; but I took it by another handle, and asked him, Who made the sea, the ground he walked on, and the hills and woods? He told me it was one old Benamuckee, that lived beyond all: he could describe nothing of this great person, but that he was very old—much older, he said, than the sea or the land, than the moon or the stars. I asked him then, if this old person had made all things, why did not all things worship him? He looked very grave, and, with a perfect look of innocence, said, All things said O! to him. I asked him if the people who die in his country went away anywhere? He said, Yes, they all went to Benamuckee. Then I asked him whether those they eat up went thither too? He said Yes.

From these things I began to instruct him in the knowledge of the true God. I told him, that the great Maker of all things lived there, pointing up towards heaven; that He governs the world by the same power and providence by which He made it; that He was omnipotent, could do everything for us, give everything to us, take everything from us: and thus, by degrees, I opened his eyes. He listened with great attention, and received with pleasure the notion of Jesus Christ being sent to redeem us, and of the manner of making our prayers to God, and His being able to hear us, even in heaven: he told me one day, that if our God could hear us up beyond the sun, He must needs be a greater god than their Benamuckee, who lived but a little way off, and yet could not hear, till they went up to the great mountains, where he dwelt, to speak to him. I asked him if ever he went thither to speak to him? He said, No, they never went that were young men; none went thither but the old men, whom they called their Oowookakee; that is, as I made him explain it to me, their religious or clergy; and that they went to say O! (so he called saying prayers), and then came back, and told them what Benamuckee said.

He listened with great attention

I found it was not so easy to imprint right notions in his mind about the devil, as it was about the being of a God : nature assisted all my arguments to evidence to him even the necessity of a great First Cause, an overruling governing Power, a secret directing Providence, and of the equity and justice of paying homage to Him that made us, and the like ; but there appeared nothing of all this in the notion of an evil spirit, of his original, his being, his nature, and, above all, of his inclination to do evil, and to draw us in to do so too : and the poor creature puzzled me once in such a manner, by a question merely natural and innocent, that I scarce knew what to say to him.

I had been talking a great deal to him of the power of God, His omnipotence, His dreadful aversion to sin, His being a consuming fire to the workers of iniquity ; how, as He had made us all, He could destroy us, and all the world, in a moment : and he listened with great seriousness to me all the while. After this, I had been telling him how the devil was God's enemy in the hearts of men, and used all his malice and skill to defeat the good designs of Providence, and to ruin the kingdom of Christ in the world, and the like. " Well," says Friday, " but you say God is so strong, so great, is He not much strong, much might, as the devil ? " " Yes, yes," said I, " Friday, God is stronger than the devil ; God is above the devil ; and therefore we pray to God to tread him under our feet, and enable us to resist his temptations, and quench his fiery darts." " But," says he, again, " if God much strong, much might, as the devil, why God not kill the devil, so make him no more wicked ? "

The conversation which employed the hours between Friday and me was such as made the three years which we lived there together perfectly and completely happy, if any such thing as complete happiness can be found in a sublunary state. The savage was now a good Christian, a much better than I ; though I have reason to hope, and bless God for it, that we were equally penitent, and comforted, restored penitents.

After Friday and I became more intimately acquainted, and that he could understand almost all I said to him, and speak fluently, though in broken English, to me, I acquainted him with my own story, or at least so much of it as related to my coming into the place, how I had lived there, and how long : I let him into the mystery (for such it was to him) of gunpowder and bullets, and taught him how to shoot : I gave him a knife, which he was wonderfully delighted with ; and I made him a belt with a frog hanging to it, such as in England we wear hangers in ; and in the frog, instead of a hanger, I gave him a hatchet, which was not only as good a weapon in some cases, but much more useful upon many occasions.

I described to him the countries of Europe, and particularly England, which I came from ; how we lived, how we worshipped God, how we behaved to one another, and how we traded in ships to all the parts of the world. I gave him an account of the wreck which I had been on board of, and showed him, as near as I could, the place where she lay ; but she was all beaten in pieces long before, and quite gone. I showed him the ruins of our boat, which we lost when we escaped, and which I could not stir with my whole strength then, but was now fallen almost all to pieces. Upon seeing this boat, Friday stood musing a great while, and said nothing ; I asked him what it was he studied upon ? At last, says he, " Me see such boat like come to place at my nation."

I did not understand him a good while ; but at last, when I had examined further into it, I understood by him that a boat, such as that had been, came on shore upon the country where he lived—that is, as he explained it, was driven thither by stress of weather. I presently imagined that some European ship must have been cast away upon their coast, and the boat might get loose, and drive ashore ; but was so dull, that I never once thought of men making escape from a wreck thither, much less whence they might come—so I only inquired after a description of the boat

Friday described the boat to me well enough ; but brought me better to understand him, when he added, with some warmth, " We save the white mans from drown." Then I presently asked him if there were any white mans, as he called them, in the boat ? " Yes," he said, " the boat full of white mans." I asked him, how many ? He told upon his fingers seventeen. I asked him, what became of them ? He told me, " They live, they dwell at my nation."

This put new thoughts into my head again ; for I presently imagined that these might be the men belonging to the ship that was cast away in sight of my island, as I now called it ; and who, after the ship was struck on the rock, and they saw her inevitably lost, had saved themselves in their boat, and were landed upon that wild shore among the savages.

Upon this I inquired of him more critically, what was become of them ? He assured me they lived still there, that they had been there about four years, that the savages let them alone, and gave them victuals to live. I asked him how it came to pass they did not kill them, and eat them ? He said, " No, they make brother with them "—that is, as I understood him, a truce : and then he added, " They eat no mans but when make the war fight "—that is to say, they never eat any men but such as come to fight with them, and are taken in battle.

It was after this some considerable time, that being on the top of the hill, at the east side of the island, from whence, as I have said, I had in a clear day discovered the main or continent of America, Friday, the weather being very serene, looks very earnestly towards the mainland, and, in a kind of surprise, falls a-jumping and dancing, and calls out to me, for I was at some distance from him : I asked him what was the matter ? " Oh, joy ! " says he, " oh, glad ! there see my country, there my nation ! "

One day, walking up the same hill, but the weather being hazy at sea, so that we could not see the continent, I called to him, and said, " Friday, do not you wish yourself in your own country, your own nation ? " " Yes," he said, " I be much O glad to be at my own nation." " What would you do there ? " said I ; " would you turn wild again, eat men's flesh again, and be a savage as you were before ? " He looked full of concern, and, shaking his head, said, " No, no ! Friday tell them to live good, tell them to pray God, tell them to eat corn bread, cattle flesh, milk, no eat man again."

" Why, then," said I to him, " they will kill you ! " He looked grave at that, and then said, " No, they no kill me : they willing love learn "— he meant by this, they would be willing to learn. He added, they learned much of the bearded mans that came in the boat. Then I asked him if he would go back to them ? He smiled at that, and told me he could not swim so far. I told him I would make a canoe for him. He told me he would go if I would go with him. " I go ! " said I, " why, they will eat me if I come there ! " " No, no ! " says he, " me make them no eat you, me make they much love you "—he meant he would tell them how I had killed his enemies and saved his life, and so he would make them love me. Then he told me how kind they were to seventeen white men, or bearded men, as he called them, who came on shore in distress.

From this time, I confess, I had a mind to venture over, and see if I could possibly join with these bearded men, who, I made no doubt, were Spaniards or Portuguese ; not doubting but, if I could, we might find some method to escape from thence, being upon the continent, and a good company together, better than I could from an island forty miles off the shore, and alone without help. So, after some days, I took Friday to work again, by way of discourse, and told him I would give him a boat to go back to his own nation ; and accordingly, I carried him to my frigate, which lay on the other side of the island ; and having cleared it of water (for I always kept it sunk in the water), I brought it out, showed it him and we both went into it.

I found he was a most dexterous fellow at managing it, would make it go almost as swift and fast again as I could ; so when he was in, I said to him, " Well, now, Friday, shall we go to your nation ? " He looked very dull at my saying so, which it seems was because he thought the boat too small to go so far. I told him then I had a bigger ; so the next day I went to the place where the first boat lay which I had made, but which I could not get into the water : he said that was big enough ; but then, as I had taken no care of it, and it had lain two or three-and-twenty years there, the sun had so split and dried it, that it was in a manner rotten. Friday told me such a boat would do very well, and would carry " much enough vittle, drink, bread " —that was his way of talking.

CHAPTER XVI

UPON the whole, I was by this time so fixed upon my design of going over with him to the continent, that I told him we would go and make one as big as that, and he should go home in it. Therefore, without delay, I went to work with Friday, to find out a great tree proper to fell, and make a large periagua, or canoe, to undertake the voyage. There were trees enough in the island to have built a little fleet, not of periaguas and canoes only, but of good large vessels : but the main thing I looked at, was to get one so near the water that we might launch it when it was made, to avoid the mistake I committed at first.

At last Friday pitched upon a tree, for I found he knew much better than I what kind of wood was fittest for it ; nor can I tell to this day what wood to call the tree we cut down, except that it was very like the tree we call fustic, or between that and the Nicaragua wood, for it was much of the same colour and smell. Friday was for burning the hollow or cavity of this tree out, to make it into a boat : but I showed him how rather to cut it out with tools, which, after I showed him how to use, he did very handily ; and in about a month's hard labour we finished it, and made it very handsome, especially when, with our axes, which I showed him how to handle, we cut and hewed the outside into the true shape of a boat. After this, however, it cost us near a fortnight's time to get her along, as it were, inch by inch, upon great rollers, into the water ; but when she was in, she would have carried twenty men with great ease.

When she was in the water, and though she was so big, it amazed me to see with what dexterity, and how swift, my man Friday could manage her, turn her, and paddle her along ; so I asked him if he would, and if we might, venture over in her ? " Yes," he said, " he venture over in her very well, though great blow wind." However, I had a further design which he knew nothing of, and that was, to make a mast and sail, and to fit her with an anchor and cable. As to a mast, that was easy enough to get ; so I pitched upon a straight young cedar tree, which I found near the place, and which there was a great plenty of in the island ; and I set Friday to work to cut it down, and gave him directions how to shape and order it ; but, as to the sail, that was my particular care ; I knew I had old sails, or rather pieces of old sails, enough ; but, as I had had them now twenty-six years by me, I did not doubt but that they were all rotten. However, I found two pieces which appeared pretty good, and with these I went to work, and with a great deal of pains, and awkward tedious stitching (you may be sure) for want of needles, I at length made a three-cornered ugly thing, like what we call in England a shoulder-of-mutton sail, to go with a boom at bottom, and a little short sprit at the top, such as usually our ships' long-boats sail with.

I was near two months performing this last work, namely, rigging and fitting my mast and sails ; for I finished them very complete, making a small stay, and a sail or foresail to it, to assist if we should turn to windward ; and, which was more than all, I fixed a rudder to the stern of her, to steer with ; and though I was but a bungling shipwright, yet as I knew the usefulness, and even necessity, of such a thing, I applied myself with so much pains to do it, that at last I brought it to pass, though, considering the many dull contrivances I had for it that failed, I think it cost me almost as much labour as making the boat.

After all this was done, I had my man Friday to teach as to what belonged to the navigation of my boat ; for though he knew very well how to paddle the canoe, he knew nothing what belonged to a sail and a rudder, and was the more amazed when he saw me work the boat to and again in the sea by the rudder, and how the sail jibed and filled this way or that way, as the course we sailed changed—I say, when he saw this, he stood like one astonished and amazed : however, with a little use, I made all these things familiar to him, and he became an expert sailor, except that as to the compass I could make him understand very little of that.

I was now entered on the seven-and-twentieth year of my captivity in this place.

The rainy season was upon me, when I kept more within doors than at other times ; so I stowed our new vessel as secure as we could, bringing her up into the creek, where, as I said in the beginning, I landed my rafts from the ship ; and hauling her up to the shore, at high-water mark, I made my man Friday dig a little dock, just big enough for her to float in ; and then, when the tide was out, we made a strong dam across the end of it, to keep the water out ; and so she lay dry, as to the tide, from the sea ; and, to keep the rain off, we laid a great many boughs of trees, so thick that she was as well thatched as a house ; and thus we waited for the months of November and December, in which I designed to make my adventure.

When the settled season began to come in, as the thought of my design returned with the fair weather, I was preparing daily for the voyage ; and the first thing I did was to lay up a certain quantity of provision, being the store for the voyage, and intended, in a week or a fortnight's time, to open the dock and launch out our boat. I was busy one morning upon something of this kind, when I called to Friday, and bade him go to the sea-shore and see if he could find a turtle, or tortoise, a thing which we generally got once a week, for the sake of the eggs as well as the flesh. Friday had not been long gone when he came running back, and flew over my outward wall, or fence, like one that felt not the ground or the steps he set his feet on ; and before I had time to speak to him, he cried out to me : " Oh, master ! Oh, master ! Oh, sorrow ! Oh, bad ! " " What's the matter, Friday ? " said I. " Oh, yonder there," says he, " one, two, three canoe ! one, two, three ! " By this way of speaking, I concluded there were six ; but, on inquiry, I found there were but three. " Well, Friday," said I, " do not be frighted " ; so I heartened him up as well as I could.

However, I saw the poor fellow was most terribly scared ; for nothing ran in his head but that they were come to look for him, and would cut him in pieces and eat him. The poor fellow trembled so, that I scarce knew what to do with him. I comforted him as well as I could, and told him I was in as much danger as he, and that they would eat me as well as him. " But," said I, " Friday, we must resolve to fight them : can you fight, Friday ? " " Me shoot," says he, " but there come many great number." " No matter for that," said I again ; " our guns will fright them that we do not kill."

So I asked him, whether, if I resolved to defend him, he would defend me, and stand by me, and do just as I bade him ? He said, " Me die when you bid die, master." So I went and fetched a good dram of rum, and gave him ; for I had been so good a husband of my rum that I had a great deal left. When he had drunk it, I made him take the two fowling-pieces which we always carried, and load them with large swan-shot as big as small pistol bullets ; then I took four muskets, and loaded them with two slugs and five small bullets each ; and my two pistols I loaded with a brace of bullets each—I hung my great sword, as usual, naked by my side, and gave Friday his hatchet.

When I had thus prepared myself, I took my perspective glass, and went up to the side of the hill to see what I could discover ; and I found quickly, by my glass, that there were one-and-twenty savages, three prisoners, and three canoes ; and that their whole business seemed to be the trium-phant banquet upon these three human bodies—a barbarous feast, indeed, but nothing more than, as I had observed, was usual with them.

I observed also that they were landed, not where they had done when Friday made his escape, but nearer to my creek, where the shore was low, and where a thick wood came close almost down to the sea—this, with the abhorrence of the inhuman errand these wretches came about, so filled me with indignation, that I came down again to Friday, and told him I was resolved to go down to them and kill them all, and asked him if he would stand by me. He was now gotten over his fright, and his spirits being a little raised with the dram I had given him, he was very cheerful, and told me, as before, he would die when I bid die.

In this fit of fury, I took first and divided the arms, which I had charged, as before, between us ; I gave Friday one pistol to stick in his girdle, and three guns upon his shoulder, and I took one pistol and the other three myself ; and in this posture we marched out. I took a small bottle of rum in my pocket, and gave Friday a large bag with more powder and bullets ; and as to orders, I charged him to keep close behind me, and not to stir, shoot, or do anything till I bade him ; and, in the meantime, not to speak a word. In this posture I fetched a compass to my right hand of near a mile, as well to get over the creek as to get into the wood ; so that I might come within shot of them before I could be discovered, which I had seen by my glass it was easy to do.

I resolved I would only go place myself near them, that I might oversee their barbarous feast, and that I would act then as God should direct ; but that, unless something offered that was more a call to me than yet I knew of, I would not meddle with them.

With this resolution I entered the wood, and with all possible wariness and silence (Friday following close at my heels), I marched till I came to the skirt of the wood, on the side which was next to them—only that one corner of the wood lay between me and them—here I called softly to Friday, showing him a great tree, which was just at the corner of the wood ; I bade him go to the tree, and bring me word if he could see there plainly what they were doing ; he did so, and came immediately back to me, and told me that they might be plainly viewed there ; that they were all about the fire, eating the flesh of one of their prisoners ; and that another lay bound upon the sand, a little from them, whom he said they would kill next, and which fired the very soul within me. He told me it was not one of their nation, but one of the bearded men whom he had told me of, who came to their country in the boat. I was filled with horror at the very naming the white bearded-man, and, going to the tree, I saw plainly by my glass, a white man, who lay upon the beach of the sea, with his hands and his feet tied with flags, or things like rushes ; and that he was a European, and had clothes on.

There was another tree, and a little thicket beyond it, about fifty yards nearer to them than the place where I was, which, by going a little way about, I saw I might come at undiscovered, and that then I should be within half shot of them ; so I withheld my passion, though I was indeed enraged to the highest degree, and going back about twenty paces, I got behind some bushes, which held all the way till I came to the other tree, and then I came to a little rising ground, which gave me a full view of them at the distance of about eighty yards.

I had now not a moment to lose ; for nineteen of the dreadful wretches sat upon the ground all close huddled together, and had just sent the other two to butcher the poor Christian, and bring him, perhaps, limb by limb, to their fire ; and they were stooped down to untie the hands at his feet. I turned to Friday. " Now, Friday," said I, " do as I bid thee." Friday said he would. " Then, Friday," said I, " do exactly as you see me do ; fail in nothing." So I set down one of the muskets and the fowling-piece upon the ground and Friday did the like by his ; and with the other musket I took my aim at the savages, bidding him do the like. Then, asking him if he was ready, he said, " Yes." " Then fire at them," said I ; and the same moment I fired also.

Friday took his aim so much better than I, that on the side that he shot he killed two of them, and wounded three more ; and on my side, I killed one and wounded two. They were, you may be sure, in a dreadful consternation ; and all of them who were not hurt, jumped up upon their feet immediately, but did not know which way to run, or which way to look ; for they knew not from whence their destruction came. Friday kept his eyes close upon me, that, as I had bid him, he might observe what I did : so as soon as the first shot was made, I threw down the piece, and took up the fowling-piece, and Friday did the like ; he sees me cock and present— he did the same again. " Are you ready, Friday ? " said I. " Yes," says he. " Let fly, then," said I, " in the name of God ;" and with that I fired again among the amazed wretches, and so did Friday, and as our pieces were now loaded with what I called swan shot, or small pistol bullets, we found only two drop ; but so many were wounded, that they ran about yelling and screaming like mad creatures, all bloody, and miserably wounded most of them ; whereof three more fell quickly after, though not quite dead.

" Are you ready, Friday?" I asked

" Now, Friday," said I, laying down the discharged pieces, and taking up the musket, which was yet loaded, " follow me," said I—which he did with a deal of courage, upon which I rushed out of the wood and showed myself, and Friday close at my foot : as soon as I perceived they saw me, I shouted as loud as I could, and bade Friday do so too : and running as fast as I could, which, by the way, was not very fast, being loaded with arms as I was, I made directly towards the poor victim, who was, as I said, lying upon the beach or shore, between the place where they sat and the sea ; the two butchers who were just going to work with him, had left him at the surprise of our first fire, and fled in a terrible fright to the sea-side, and had jumped into a canoe, and three more of the rest made the same way. I turned to Friday, and bade him step forwards, and fire at them ; he under-stood me immediately, and, running about forty yards to be near them, he shot at them, and I thought he had killed them all ; for I saw them all fall on a heap into the boat—though I saw two of them get up again quickly—however, he killed two of them, and wounded the third, so that he lay down in the bottom of the boat as if he had been dead.

While my man Friday fired at them, I pulled out my knife, and cut the flags that bound the poor victim ; and loosing his hands and feet, I lifted him up, and asked him, in the Portuguese tongue, what he was ? He answered, in Latin, *Christianus ;* but was so weak and faint that he could scarce stand or speak. I took my bottle out of my pocket, and gave it him, making signs that he should drink, which he did ; and I gave him a piece of bread, which he ate : then I asked him what countryman he was ? and he said " Espagnole "; and being a little recovered, let me know, by all the signs

While Friday fired at them, I lifted him up

he could possibly make, how much he was in my debt for his deliverance. "Seignor," said I, with as much Spanish as I could make up, "we will talk afterwards, but we must fight now : if you have any strength left, take this pistol and sword, and lay about you :" he took them very thankfully, and no sooner had he arms in his hands, but, as if they had put new vigour into them, he flew upon his murderers like a fury, and had cut two of them in pieces in an instant : for the truth is, as the whole was a surprise to them, so the poor creatures were so much frightened with the noise of our pieces, that they fell down for mere amazement and fear, and had no more power to attempt their own escape, than their flesh had to resist our shot—and that was the case of those five that Friday shot in the boat ; for as three of them fell with the hurt they received, so the other two fell with the fright.

I kept my piece in my hand still, without firing, being willing to keep my charge ready, because I had given the Spaniard my pistol and sword ; so I called to Friday, and bade him run up to the tree from whence we first fired, and fetch the arms which lay there, that had been discharged, which he did with great swiftness ; and then, giving him my musket, I sat down myself to load all the rest again, and bade them come to me when they wanted. While I was loading those pieces, there happened a fierce engagement between the Spaniard and one of the savages, who made at him with one of their great wooden swords, the same weapon that was to have killed him before, if I had not prevented it : the Spaniard, who was as bold and as brave as could be imagined, though weak, had fought this Indian a good while, and had cut him two great wounds on his head ; but the savage being a stout, lusty fellow, closing in with him, had thrown him down (being faint), and was wringing my sword out his hand, when the Spaniard, though undermost, wisely quitting his sword, drew the pistol from his girdle, shot the savage through the body, and killed him upon the spot, before I, who was running to help, could come near him.

Friday being now left at his liberty, pursued the flying wretches with no weapon in his hand but his hatchet ; and with that he despatched those three, who, as I said before, were wounded at first, and fallen, and all the rest he could come up with ; and the Spaniard coming to me for a gun, I gave him one of the fowling-pieces, with which he pursued two of the savages, and wounded them both ; but, as he was not able to run, they both got from him into the wood, where Friday pursued them, and killed one of them ; but the other was too nimble for him ; and, though he was wounded, yet he plunged into the sea, and swam with all his might off to those who were left in the canoe ; which three in the canoe, with one wounded, who we knew not whether he died or no, were all that escaped our hands of one-and-twenty. The account of the rest is as follows :—

Three killed at our first shot from the tree ; two killed at the next shot ; two killed by Friday in the boat ; two killed by Friday, of those at first wounded ; one killed by Friday in the wood ; three killed by the Spaniard ; four killed, being found dropped here and there, of the wounds, or killed by Friday in his chase of them ; four escaped in the boat, whereof one was wounded, if not dead—twenty-one in all.

Those that were in the canoe worked hard to get out of gunshot ; and, though Friday made two or three shots at them, I did not find that he hit any of them. Friday would have fain had me take one of their canoes, and pursue them ; and, indeed, I was very anxious about their escape, lest, carrying the news home to their people, they should come back, perhaps, with two or three hundred of their canoes, and devour us by mere multitudes ; so I consented to pursue them by sea ; and, running to one of their canoes, I jumped in, and bade Friday follow me ; but, when I was in the canoe, I was surprised to find another poor creature lie there alive, bound hand and foot, as the Spaniard was, for the slaughter, and almost dead with fear, not knowing what the matter was ; for he had not been able to look up over the side of the boat : he was tied so hard, neck and heels, and had been tied so long, that he had really little life in him.

I immediately cut the twisted flags, or rushes, which they had bound him with, and would have helped him up ; but he could not stand or speak, but groaned most piteously, believing, it seems, still that he was only unbound in order to be killed.

When Friday came to him, I bade him speak to him, and tell him of his deliverance ; and, pulling out my bottle, made him give the poor wretch a dram, which, with the news of his being delivered, revived him, and he sat up in the boat ; but, when Friday came to hear him speak, and looked in his face, it would have moved any one to tears to have seen how Friday kissed him, embraced him, hugged him, cried, laughed, hallooed, jumped about, danced, sang, then cried again, wrung his hands, beat his own face and head, and then sang and jumped about again like a distracted creature. It was a good while before I could make him speak to me, or tell me what was the matter ; but when he came a little to himself, he told me that it was his father.

My island was now peopled, and I thought myself very rich in subjects ; and it was a merry reflection which I frequently made, how like a king I looked : first of all, the whole country was my own mere property, so that I had an undoubted right of dominion : secondly, my people were perfectly subjected ; I was absolute lord and law-giver ; they all owed their lives to me, and were ready to lay down their lives, if there had been occasion for it, for me ; it was remarkable too, I had but three subjects, and they were of three different religions. My man Friday was a Protestant, his father a Pagan and a cannibal, and the Spaniard was a Papist : however, I allowed liberty of conscience throughout my dominions ; but this by the way.

As soon as I had secured my two weak, rescued prisoners, and given them shelter, and a place to rest them upon, I began to think of making some provision for them ; and the first thing I did, I ordered Friday to take a yearling goat, betwixt a kid and a goat, out of my particular flock, to be killed : then I cut off the hind quarter, and chopping it into small pieces, I set Friday to work to boiling and stewing, and made them a very good dish, I assure you, of flesh and broth, having put some barley and rice also into the broth ; and as I cooked it without doors (for I made no fire within my inner wall), so I carried it all into the new tent ; and having set a table there for them, I sat down and ate my dinner also with them : and, as well as I could, cheered them and encouraged them, Friday being my interpreter, especially to his father, and indeed to the Spaniard too ; for the Spaniard spoke the language of the savages pretty well.

After we had dined, or rather supped, I ordered Friday to take one of the canoes, and go and fetch our muskets and other fire-arms, which, for want of time, we had left upon the place of battle ; and the next day I ordered him to go and bury the dead bodies of the savages, which lay open to the sun, and would presently be offensive ; and I also ordered him to bury the horrid remains of their barbarous feast, which I knew were pretty much, and which I could not think of doing myself ; nay, I could not bear to see them, if I went that way : all which he punctually performed, and defaced the very appearance of the savages being there ; so that when I went again, I could scarce know where it was, otherwise than by the corner of the wood pointing to the place.

I then began to enter into a little conversation with my two new subjects ; and first, I set Friday to inquire of his father what he thought of the escape of the savages in that canoe ? and whither we might expect a return of them with a power too great for us to resist ? His first opinion was, that the savages in the boat never could live out the storm which blew that night they went off, but must of necessity be drowned or driven south to those other shores, where they were as sure to be devoured as they were to be drowned if they were cast away ; but as to what they would do if they came safe on shore, he said he knew not ; but it was his opinion, that they were so dreadfully frighted with the manner of being attacked, the noise and the fire, that he believed they would tell their people they were all killed by thunder and lightning, and not by the hand of man ; and that the two which appeared (namely, Friday and I) were two heavenly spirits or furies come down to destroy them, and not men with weapons. This, he said, he knew, because he heard them all cry out so in their language to one another ; for it was impossible for them to conceive that a man should dart fire, and speak thunder, and kill at a distance, without lifting up the hand, as was done now. And this old savage was in the right ; for, as I understood since, by other hands, the savages of that part never attempted to go over to the island afterwards. They were so terrified with the accounts given by these four men (for it seems they did escape the sea), that they believed, whoever went to that enchanted island would be destroyed with fire from the gods.

This, however, I knew not, and therefore was under continual apprehensions for a good while, and kept always upon my guard ; I and all my army ; for, as there were now four of us, I would have ventured upon a hundred of them fairly in the open field at any time.

In a little time, however, no more canoes appearing, the fear of their coming wore off ; and I began to take my former thoughts of a voyage to the main into consideration, being likewise assured by Friday's father, that I might depend upon good usage from their nation on his account, if I would go.

CHAPTER XVII

BUT my thoughts were a little suspended, when I had a serious discourse with the Spaniard and understood that there were sixteen more of his countrymen and Portuguese, who, having been cast away, and made their escape to that side, lived there at peace with the savages, but were sore put to it for necessaries, and indeed for life ; I asked him all the particulars of their voyage, and found they were a Spanish ship, bound from the Rio de la Plata to the Havanna, being directed to leave their loading there, which was chiefly hides and silver, and to bring back what European goods they could meet with there ; that they had five Portuguese seamen on board, whom they took out of another wreck ; that five of their own men were drowned when first the ship was lost ; and that these escaped through infinite dangers and hazards, and arrived almost starved on the cannibal coast, where they expected to have been devoured every moment.

He told me they had some arms with them, but they were perfectly useless ; for that they had neither powder nor ball, the washing of the sea having spoiled all their powder, but a little which they used at their first landing to provide themselves some food.

I asked him what he thought would become of them there ; and if they had formed no design of making any escape ? He said they had had many consultations about it ; but that, having neither vessel nor tools to build one, nor provisions of any kind, their counsels always ended in tears and despair.

I resolved to venture to relieve them, if possible, and to send the old savage and this Spaniard over to them to treat : but when he had gotten all things in readiness to go, the Spaniard himself started an objection, which had so much prudence in it on one hand, and so much sincerity on the other hand, that I could not but be very well satisfied in it ; and, by his advice, put off the deliverance of his comrades for at least half a year. The case was this:—

He had been with us now about a month, during which time I had let him see in what manner I had provided, with the assistance of Providence, for my support; and he saw evidently what stock of corn and rice I had laid up: which, as it was more than sufficient for myself, so it was not sufficient, at least, without good husbandry, for my family, now it was increased to number four: but much less would it be sufficient if his country-men, who were, as he said, fourteen still alive, should come over; and least of all would it be sufficient to victual our vessel, if we should build one, for a voyage to any one of the Christian colonies of America. So he told me, he thought it would be more advisable to let him and the other two dig and cultivate some more land, as much as I could spare seed to sow; and that we should wait another harvest, that we might have a supply of corn for his countrymen when they should come; for want might be a temptation to them to disagree, or not to think themselves delivered, otherwise than out of one difficulty into another.

His caution was so seasonable, and his advice so good, that I could not but be very well pleased with his proposal, as well as I was satisfied with his fidelity. So we fell to digging, all four of us, as well as the wooden tools we were furnished with permitted; and, in about a month's time, by the end of which it was such time, we had gotten as much land cured and trimmed up as we sowed twenty-two bushels of barley on, and sixteen jars of rice, which was, in short, all the seed we had to spare; nor indeed did we leave ourselves barley sufficient for our own food for the six months that we had to expect our crop, that is to say, reckoning from the time we set our seed aside for sowing; for it is not to be supposed it is six months in the ground in that country.

Having now society enough, and our number being sufficient to put us out of fear of the savages, if they had come, unless their number had been very great, we went freely all over the island, wherever we found occasion; and as here we had our escape or deliverance upon our thoughts, it was impossible, at least for me, to have the means of it out of mind. To this purpose, I marked out several trees which I thought fit for our work, and I set Friday and his father to cutting them down; and then I caused the Spaniard, to whom I imparted my thoughts on that affair, to oversee and direct their work: I showed them with what indefatigable pains I had hewed a large tree into single planks, and I caused them to do the like, till they had made about a dozen large planks of good oak, near two feet broad, thirty-five feet long, and from two inches to four inches thick: what pro-digious labour it took up, any one may imagine.

At the same time, I contrived to increase my little flock of tame goats as much as I could: and to this purpose I made Friday and the Spaniard to go out one day, and myself with Friday the next day, for we took our turns; and by this means we got about twenty young kids to breed up with the rest; for whenever we shot the dam, we saved the kids, and added them to our flock: but, above all, the season for curing the grapes coming on, I caused such a prodigious quantity to be hung up in the sun, that I believe, had we been at Alicant, where the raisins of the sun are cured, we should have filled sixty or eighty barrels ; and these, with our bread, were a great part of our food, and very good living too, I assure you ; for it is an exceedingly nourishing food.

It was now harvest, and our crop in good order ; it was not the most plentiful increase I had seen in the island ; but, however, it was enough to answer our end, for from twenty-two bushels of barley, we brought in and thrashed out above two hundred and twenty bushels, and the like in proportion of the rice, which was store enough for our food to the next harvest, though all the sixteen Spaniards had been on shore with me ; or, if we had been ready for a voyage, it would very plentifully have victualled our ship, to have carried us to any part of the world, that is to say, of America. When we had thus housed and secured our magazine of corn, we fell to work to make more wicker-work, namely, great baskets, in which we kept it ; and the Spaniard was very handy and dexterous at this part, and often blamed me that I did not make some things for defence, of this kind of work ; but I saw no need of it. And now, having a full supply of food for all the guests expected, I gave the Spaniard leave to go over to the main, to see what he could do with those he left behind him there : I gave him a strict charge in writing not to bring any man with him who would not first swear, in the presence of himself and of the old savage, that he would no way injure, fight with, or attack the person he should find in the island, who was so kind to send for them, in order to their deliverance ; but that they would stand by and defend him against all such attempts ; and, wherever they went, would be entirely under, and subjected to his command ; and that this should be put in writing, and signed with their hands : how we were to have this done, when I knew they had neither pen nor ink, that, indeed, was a question which we never asked.

Under these instructions, the Spaniard and the old savage (the father of Friday) went away in one of the canoes, which they might be said to come in, or rather were brought in, when they came as prisoners to be devoured by the savages.

I gave each of them a musket with a firelock on it, and about eight charges of powder and ball, charging them to be very good husbands of both, and not to use either of them, but upon urgent occasions.

This was a cheerful work, being the first measures used by me in view of my deliverance for now twenty-seven years and some days. I gave them provisions of bread, and of dried grapes, sufficient for themselves for many days, and sufficient for their countrymen for about eight days' time ; and, wishing them a good voyage, I let them go, agreeing with them about a signal they should hang out at their return, by which I should know them again, when they came back at a distance, before they came on shore.

They went away with a fair gale on the day that the moon was at full—by my account in the month of October—but as for the exact reckoning of days, after I had once lost it, I could never recover it again ; nor had I kept the number of years so punctually as to be sure that I was right, though, as it proved when I afterwards examined my account, I found I had kept a true reckoning of years.

It was no less than eight days I waited for them, when a strange and unforeseen accident intervened, of which the like has not, perhaps, been

They went away with a fair gale

heard of in history. I was fast asleep in my hutch one morning, when my man Friday came running in to me, and called aloud, " Master, master, they are come, they are come ! "

I jumped up, and, regardless of danger, I went out as soon as I could get my clothes on, through my little grove—which, by the way, was by this time grown to be a very thick wood—I say, regardless of danger, I went without my arms, which was not my custom to do ; but I was surprised, when, turning my eyes to the sea, I presently saw a boat at about a league and a half's distance, standing in for shore, with a shoulder-of-mutton sail, as they call it, and the wind blowing pretty fair to bring them in. Also I observed presently, that they did not come from that side which the shore lay on, but from the southermost end of the island. Upon this I called Friday in, and bade him lie close, for these were not the people we looked for, and that we did not know yet whether they were friends or enemies.

In the next place, I went in to fetch my perspective glass, to see what I could make of them ; and, having taken the ladder out, I climbed up to the top of the hill, as I used to do when I was apprehensive of anything, and to take my view the plainer without being discovered.

I had scarce set my foot on the hill, when my eye plainly discovered a ship lying at an anchor, at about two leagues and a half's distance from me, south-south-east, but not above a league and a half from the shore. By my observation it appeared plainly to be an English ship, and the boat appeared to be an English long-boat.

I saw the boat draw near the shore, as if they looked for a creek to thrust in at for the convenience of landing ; however, as they did not come quite far enough, they did not see the little inlet where I formerly landed my rafts, but ran their boat on shore upon the beach, at about half a mile from me, which was very happy for me ; for otherwise they would have landed just, as I may say, at my door, and would have soon beaten me out of my castle, and, perhaps, have plundered me of all I had.

When they were on shore, I was fully satisfied they were Englishmen, at least, most of them ; one or two I thought were Dutch, but it did not prove so. There were, in all, eleven men, whereof three of them I found were unarmed and (as I thought) bound, and when the first four or five of them were jumped on shore they took those three out of the boat as prisoners. One of the three I could perceive using the most passionate gestures of entreaty, affliction, and despair, even to a kind of extravagance ; the other two, I could perceive, lifted up their hands sometimes, and appeared concerned indeed, but not to such a degree as the first.

I was perfectly confounded at the sight, and knew not what the meaning of it should be ; Friday called out to me, in English, as well as he could, " Oh, master ! you see English mans eat prisoners as well as savage mans." " Why," said I, " Friday, do you think they are going to eat them then ? " " Yes," says Friday, " they will eat them." " No, no," said I, " Friday ; I am afraid they will murder them indeed ; but you may be sure they will not eat them."

All this while I had no thought of what the matter really was, but stood trembling with the horror of the sight, expecting every moment when the three prisoners should be killed ; nay, once I saw one of the villains lift up his arm with a great cutlass (as the seamen call it) or sword, to strike one

I climbed up to the top of the hill

of the poor men ; and I expected to see him fall every moment, at which all the blood in my body seemed to run chill in my veins.

I wished heartily now for our Spaniard, and the savage that was gone with him ; or that I had any way to have come undiscovered within shot of them, that I might have rescued the three men ; for I saw no fire-arms they had among them ; but it fell out to my mind another way.

After I had observed the outrageous usage of the three men by the insolent seamen, I observed the fellows run scattering about the land, as if they wanted to see the country. I observed also, that the three other men had liberty to go where they pleased ; but they sat down all three upon the ground very pensive, and looked like men in despair.

This put me in mind of the first time when I came on shore, and began to look about me : how I gave myself over for lost, how wildly I looked round me, what dreadful apprehensions I had, and how I lodged in the tree all night for fear of being devoured by wild beasts.

As I knew nothing that night of the supply I was to receive by the providential driving of the ship nearer the land by the storms and tides, by which I have since been so long nourished and supported ; so these three poor desolate men knew nothing how certain of deliverance and supply they were, how near it was to them, and how effectually and really they were in a condition of safety, at the same time they thought themselves lost, and their case desperate.

It was just at the top of high water when these people came on shore, and while partly they stood parleying with the prisoners they brought, and partly while they rambled about to see what kind of place they were in, they had carelessly stayed till the tide was spent, and the water was ebbed considerably away, leaving their boat aground.

They had left two men in the boat, who, as I found afterwards, having drunk a little too much brandy, fell asleep ; however, one of them wakened sooner than the other, and finding the boat too fast aground for him to stir it, hallooed for the rest who were straggling about, upon which they all soon came to the boat ; but it was past all their strength to launch her, the boat being very heavy, and the shore on that side being a soft oozy sand, almost like a quicksand.

In this condition, like true seamen, who are, perhaps, the least of all mankind given to forethought, they gave it over, and away they strolled about the country again ; and I heard one of them say aloud to another (calling them off from the boat), " Why, let her alone, Jack, can't ye ? she'll float next tide." By which I was fully confirmed in the main inquiry, of what countrymen they were.

All this while I kept myself close, not once daring to stir out of my castle, any farther than to my place of observation, near the top of the hill ; and very glad I was to think how well it was fortified. I knew it was no less than ten hours before the boat could be on float again, and by that time it would be dark and I might be more at liberty to see their motions, and to hear their discourse, if they had any.

In the meantime, I fitted myself up for a battle, as before, though with more caution, knowing I had to do with another kind of enemy than I had at first ; I ordered Friday also, whom I had made an excellent marksman

I came very near them, undiscovered

with his gun, to load himself with arms—I took myself two fowling-pieces
and I gave him three muskets. My figure, indeed, was very fierce : I had
my formidable goat-skin coat on, with the great cap I mentioned, a naked
sword, two pistols in my belt, and a gun upon each shoulder.

It was my design, as I said above, not to have made any attempt till it
was dark ; but about two o'clock, being the heat of the day, I found that,
in short, they were all gone straggling into the woods, and, as I thought,
were all laid down to sleep. The three poor distressed men, too anxious for
their condition to get any sleep, were, however, set down under the shelter
of a great tree, at about a quarter of a mile from me, and, as I thought, out
of sight of any of the rest.

Upon this I resolved to discover myself to them, and learn something
of their condition. Immediately I marched in the figure above, my man
Friday at a good distance behind me, as formidable for his arms as I, but
not making quite so staring a spectre-like figure as I did.

I came as near them undiscovered as I could, and then, before any of
them saw me, I called aloud to them, in Spanish, " What are ye, gentlemen ? "

They started up at the noise, but were ten times more confounded
when they saw me, and the uncouth figure that I made—they made no
answer at all, but I thought I perceived them just going to fly from me,
when I spoke to them in English : " Gentlemen," said I, " do not be surprised at me ; perhaps you may have a friend near you, when you did not
expect it." " He must be sent directly from Heaven, then," said one of them,
very gravely, to me, pulling off his hat at the same time, " for our condition

is past the help of man." " All help is from Heaven, sir ! " said I ; " but can you put a stranger in the way how to help you, for you seem to me to be in great distress ? I saw you when you landed ; and when you seemed to make application to the brutes that came with you, I saw one of them lift up his sword to kill you."

The poor man, with tears running down his face, and trembling, looking like one astonished, returned: " Am I talking to God or man ? Is it a real man or an angel ! " " Be in no fear about that, sir," said I : " if God had sent an angel to relieve you, he would have come better clothed, and better armed after another manner than you see me in. Pray, lay aside your fears : I am a man,—an Englishman, and disposed to assist you ; you see I have one servant only—we have arms and ammunition ; tell us freely, can we serve you ? What is your case ? "

" Our case," said he, " sir, is too long to tell you while our murderers are so near ; but, in short, sir, I was commander of that ship ; my men having mutinied against me, they have been hardly prevailed on not to murder me, and at last they have set me on shore in this desolate place, with those two men with me, one my mate, the other a passenger, where we expected to perish, believing the place to be uninhabited, and know not yet what to think of it."

" Where are those brutes, your enemies ? " said I ; " do you know where they are gone ? " " There they are, sir," said he, pointing to a thicket of trees ; " my heart trembles for fear they have seen us, and heard you speak ; if they have, they will certainly murder us all."

" Have they any fire-arms ? " said I. He answered, " They had only two pieces, and one which they left in the boat." " Well, then," said I, " leave the rest to me : I see they are asleep ; it is an easy thing to kill them all, but shall we rather take them prisoners ? " He told me there were two desperate villains among them, that it was scarce safe to show any mercy to ; but if they were secured, he believed all the rest would return to their duty : I asked him which they were ? He told me he could not at that distance describe them ; but he would obey my orders in anything I would direct. " Well," said I, " let us retreat out of their view or hearing, lest they awake, and we will resolve further ; " so they willingly went back with me, till the woods covered us from them.

" Look you, sir," said I, " if I venture upon your deliverance, are you willing to make two conditions with me ? " He anticipated my proposals by telling me, that both he and the ship, if recovered, should be wholly directed and commanded by me in everything ; and if the ship was not recovered, he would live and die with me in what part of the world soever I would send him ; and the two other men said the same.

" Well," said I, " my conditions are but two : First, that while you stay on this island with me, you will not pretend to any authority here ; and if I put arms into your hands, you will upon all occasions give them up to me and do no prejudice to me or mine, upon this island, and in the meantime to be governed by orders. Second, that if the ship is, or may be recovered, you will carry me and my man to England, passage free."

He gave me all the assurance that the invention or faith of a man could devise, that he would comply with these most reasonable demands ; and besides would owe his life to me, and acknowledge it upon all occasions as long as he lived.

" Well, then," said I, " here are three muskets for you, with powder and ball ; tell me next what you think is proper to be done." He showed all the testimony of his gratitude that he was able, but offered to be wholly guided by me ; I told him I thought it was hard venturing anything, but the best method I could think of was, to fire upon them at once as they lay ; and if any were not killed at the first volley, and offered to submit, we might save them, and so put it wholly upon God's providence to direct the shot.

He said, very modestly, that he was loath to kill them if he could help it ; but that those two were incorrigible villains, and had been the authors of all the mutiny in the ship, and, if they escaped, we should be undone still ; for they would go on board, and bring the whole ship's company and destroy us all. " Well, then," said I, " necessity legitimates my advice ; for it is the only way to save our lives." However, seeing him still cautious of shedding blood, I told him they should go themselves, and manage as they found convenient.

In the middle of this discourse, we heard some of them awake, and soon after we saw two of them on their feet. I asked him if either of them were the men who he had said were the heads of the mutiny ? He said, " No." " Well, then," said I, " you may let them escape, and Providence seems to have wakened them on purpose to save themselves. Now," said I, " if the rest escape you, it is your fault."

Animated with this, he took the musket I had given him in his hand, and pistol in his belt, and his two comrades with him, with each man a piece in his hand ; the two men who were with him going first, made some noise, at which one of the seamen, who was awake, turned about, and, seeing them coming, cried out to the rest ; but it was too late then, for the moment he cried out they fired, I mean the two men, the captain wisely reserving his own piece : they had so well aimed their shot at the men they knew, that one of them was killed on the spot and the other very much wounded ; but not being dead, he started up on his feet and called eagerly for help to the other : but the captain stepping to him, told him it was too late to cry for help, he should call upon God to forgive his villainy ; and with that word knocked him down with the stock of his musket, so that he never spoke more : there were three more in the company, and one of them was also slightly wounded. By this time I was come ; and when they saw their danger, and it was in vain to resist, they begged for mercy. The captain told them he would spare their lives, if they would give him any assurance of their abhorrence of the treachery they had been guilty of, and would swear to be faithful to him in recovering the ship, and afterwards in carrying her back to Jamaica, from whence they came. They gave him all the protestations of their sincerity that could be desired, and he was willing to believe them, and spare their lives, which I was not against ; only I obliged him to keep them bound, hand and foot, while they were upon the island.

While this was doing, I sent Friday with the captain's mate to the boat with orders to secure her, and bring away the oars and sail, which they did ; and by-and-by, three straggling men, that were (happily for them) parted from the rest, came back upon hearing the guns fired ; and seeing their

Robinson Crusoe and the sailors

captain, who before was their prisoner, now their conqueror, they submitted to be bound also—and so our victory was complete.

It now remained that the captain and I should inquire into one another's circumstances. I began first, and told him my whole history, which he heard with an attention even to amazement, and particularly at the wonderful manner of my being furnished with provisions and ammunition ; and, indeed, as my whole story is a collection of wonders, it affected him deeply : but when he reflected from thence upon himself, and how I seemed to have been preserved there on purpose to save his life, the tears ran down his face, and he could not speak a word more.

After this communication was at an end, I carried him and his two men into my apartments, leading them in just where I came out, namely, at the top of the house ; where I refreshed them with such provisions as I had, and showed them all the contrivances I had made during my long, long inhabiting that place.

Then it presently occurred to me, that in a little while the ship's crew, wondering what was become of their comrades, and of the boat, would certainly come on shore in their other boat to seek for them ; and that then perhaps they might come armed, and be too strong for us : this he allowed was rational.

Upon this, I told him the first thing we had to do was to stave the boat, which lay upon the beach, so that they might not carry her off ; and taking everything out of her, leave her so far useless as not to be fit to swim ; accordingly, we went on board, took the arms which were left on board out of her, and whatever else we found there—which was a bottle of brandy and another of rum, a few biscuit cakes, a horn of powder, and a great lump of sugar in a piece of canvas—the sugar was five or six pounds ; all of which was very welcome to me, especially the brandy and sugar, of which I had had none left for many years.

When we had carried all these things on shore (the oars, mast, sail, and rudder of the boat were carried before, as above), we knocked a great hole in her bottom, that if they had come strong enough to master us, yet they could not carry off the boat. Indeed, it was not much in my thoughts, that we could be capable to recover the ship ; but my view was, that if they went away without the boat, I did not much question to make her fit again to carry us away to the Leeward Islands, and call upon our friends the Spaniards in my way, for I had them still in my thoughts.

CHAPTER XVIII

WHILE we were thus preparing our designs, and had first by main strength heaved the boat up upon the beach, so high that the tide would not float her off at high water, and had broken a hole in her bottom too big to be quickly stopped, and were sat down musing what we should do, we heard the ship fire a gun, and saw her make a waft with her ancient, as a signal for the boat to come on board ; but no boat stirred ; and they fired several times, making other signals for the boat.

At last, when all their signals and firings proved fruitless, and they found the boat did not stir, we saw them (by the help of our glasses) hoist another boat out, and row towards the shore; and we found, as they approached, that there were no less than ten men in her, and that they had fire-arms with them.

As the ship lay almost two leagues from the shore, we had a full view of them as they came, and a plain sight of the men, even of their faces; because the tide having set them a little to the east of the other boat, they rowed up under shore, to come to the same place where the other had landed, and where the boat lay.

By this means, I say, we had a full view of them, and the captain knew the persons and characters of all the men in the boat: of whom he said that there were three very honest fellows, who, he was sure, were led into this conspiracy by the rest, being overpowered and frightened; but that for the boatswain, who, it seems, was the chief officer among them, and all the rest, they were as outrageous as any of the ship's crew; and were, no doubt, made desperate in their new enterprise; and terribly apprehensive he was that they would be too powerful for us.

I smiled at him, and told him, that men in our circumstances were past the operations of fear: that seeing almost every condition that could be was better than that we were supposed to be in, we ought to expect that the consequences, whether death or life, would be sure to be a deliverance: I asked him, what he thought of the circumstances of my life, and whether a deliverance were not worth venturing for? "And where, sir," said I, "is your belief of my being preserved here on purpose to save your life, which elevated you a little while ago? For my part," said I, "there seems to be only one thing amiss in all the prospect of it." "What's that?" says he. "Why," said I, "'tis that, as you say, there are three or four honest fellows among them, which should be spared; had they been all of the wicked part of the crew, I should have thought God's providence had singled them out to deliver them into your hands: for, depend upon it, every man of them that comes ashore are our own, and shall die or live, as they behave to us."

As I spoke this with a raised voice and cheerful countenance, I found it greatly encouraged him; so we set vigorously to our business. We had, upon the first appearance of the boat's coming from the ship, considered of separating our prisoners, and had indeed secured them effectually.

Two of them, of whom the captain was less assured than ordinary, I sent with Friday, and one of the three (delivered men) to my cave, where they were remote enough, and out of danger of being heard or discovered, or of finding their way out of the woods, if they could have delivered themselves: here they left them bound, but gave them provisions, and promised them, if they continued there quietly, to give them their liberty in a day or two: but that if they attempted their escape, they should be put to death without mercy. They promised faithfully to bear their confinement with patience, and were very thankful that they had such good usage as to have provisions and a light left them; for Friday gave them candles (such as we made ourselves), for their comfort; and they did not know but that he stood sentinel over them at the entrance.

The other prisoners had better usage: two of them were kept pinioned indeed, because the captain was not free to trust them ; but the other two were taken into my service upon their captain's recommendation, and upon their solemnly engaging to live and die with us ; so, with them and the three honest men, we were seven men well armed ; and I made no doubt we should be able to deal well enough with the ten that were a-coming, considering that the captain had said there were three or four honest men amongst them also.

As soon as they got to the place where their other boat lay, they ran their boat into the beach, and came all on shore, hauling the boat up after them, which I was glad to see ; for I was afraid they would rather have left the boat at an anchor, some distance from the shore, with some hands in her to guard her ; and so we should not be able to seize the boat.

Being on shore, the first thing they did, they ran all to the other boat ; and it was easy to see they were under a great surprise to find her stripped, as above, of all that was in her, and a great hole in her bottom.

After they had mused awhile upon this, they set up two or three great shouts, hallooing with all their might to try if they could make their companions hear ; but all was to no purpose : then they came all close in a ring, and fired a volley of their small-arms, which, indeed, we heard, and the echoes made the woods ring ; but it was all one : those in the cave, we were sure, could not hear ; and those in our keeping, though they heard it well enough, yet durst give no answer to them.

They were so astonished at the surprise of this, that, as they told us afterwards, they resolved to go all on board again to their ship, and let them know there that the men were all murdered, and the long-boat staved ; accordingly, they immediately launched the boat again, and got all of them on board.

The captain was terribly amazed, and even confounded at this, believing they would go on board the ship again, and set sail, giving their comrades up for lost, and so he should still lose the ship, which he was in hopes we should have recovered ; but he was quickly as much frightened the other way.

They had not been long put off with the boat, but we perceived them all coming on shore again ; but, with this new measure in their conduct, which, it seems, they consulted together upon, namely, to leave three men in the boat, and the rest to go on shore, and go up into the country to look for their fellows.

This was a great disappointment to us ; for now we were at a loss what to do ; for our seizing those seven men on shore would be no advantage to us if we let the boat escape, because they would then row away to the ship ; and then the rest of them would be sure to weigh and set sail, and so our recovering the ship would be lost.

However, we had no remedy but to wait and see what the issue of things might present. The seven men came on shore, and the three who remained in the boat put her off to a good distance from the shore, and came to an anchor to wait for them ; so that it was impossible for us to come at them in the boat.

Those that came on shore kept close together, marching towards the top of the little hill, under which my habitation lay ; and we could see them plainly, though they could not perceive us ; we could have been very glad they would have come nearer to us, so that we might have fired at them ; or that they would have gone farther off, that we might have come abroad.

But when they were come to the brow of the hill, where they could see a great way in the valley and woods, which lay towards the north-east part, and where the island lay lowest, they shouted and hallooed till they were weary ; and not caring, it seems, to venture far from the shore, nor far from one another, they sat down together under a tree to consider of it.

The captain made a very just proposal to me upon this consultation of theirs, namely, that, perhaps, they would all fire a volley again to endeavour to make their fellows hear, and that we should all sally upon them just at the juncture when their pieces were all discharged, and they would certainly yield, and we should have them without bloodshed. I liked the proposal, provided it was done while we were near enough to come up to them before they could load their pieces again.

But this event did not happen, and we lay still a long time very irresolute what course to take ; at length I told them there would be nothing to be done, in my opinion, till night ; and then, if they did not return to the boat, perhaps we might find a way to get between them and the shore, and so might use some stratagem with them in the boat to get them on shore.

We waited a great while, though very impatient for their removing, and were very uneasy ; when, after long consultations, we saw them start all up, and march down towards the sea ; it seems they had such dreadful apprehensions upon them of the danger of the place, that they resolved to go on board the ship again, give their companions over for lost, and so go on with their intended voyage with the ship.

I ordered Friday and the captain's mate to go over the little creek westward, towards the place where the savages came on shore when Friday was rescued ; and as soon as they came to a little rising ground, at about half a mile's distance, I bade them halloo as loud as they could, and wait till they found the seamen heard them ; that as soon as ever they heard the seamen answer them, they should return it again, and then keeping out of sight take a round, always answering when the others hallooed, to draw them as far into the island, and among the woods, as possible, and then wheel about again to me, by such ways as I directed.

They were just going into the boat when Friday and the mate hallooed, and they presently heard them, and answering, ran along the shore westward, towards the voice they heard, when they were presently stopped by the creek, where, the water being up, they could not get over, and called for the boat to come up and set them over, as indeed I expected.

When they had set themselves over, I observed that the boat being gone up a good way into the creek, and, as it were, in a harbour within the land, they took one of the three men out of her to go along with them, and left only two in the boat, having fastened her to the stump of a little tree on the shore.

This was what I wished for, and immediately leaving Friday and the captain's mate to their business, I took the rest with me, and crossing the creek out of their sight, we surprised the two men before they were aware, one of them lying on the shore, and the other being in the boat ; the fellow

Friday and the mate hallooed

on shore was between sleeping and waking, and, going to start up, the captain, who was foremost, ran in upon him and knocked him down, and then called out to him in the boat to yield, or he was a dead man.

There needed very few arguments to persuade a single man to yield, when he saw five men upon him, and his comrade knocked down : besides, this was, it seems, one of the three who were not so hearty in the mutiny as the rest of the crew, and therefore was easily persuaded not only to yield, but afterwards to join very sincerely with us.

In the meantime, Friday and the captain's mate so well managed their business with the rest, that they drew them by hallooing and answering, from one hill to another, and from one wood to another, till they not only heartily tired them, but left them where they were very sure they could not reach back to the boat before it was dark ; and indeed, they were heartily tired themselves also by the time they came back to us.

We had nothing now to do but to watch for them in the dark, and to fall upon them, so as to make sure work with them.

It was several hours after Friday came back to me before they came back to their boat—and we could hear the foremost of them, long before they came quite up, calling to those behind to come along—and could also hear them answer, and complain how lame and tired they were, and not being able to come any faster, which was very welcome news to us.

At length they came up to the boat ; but it is impossible to express their confusion when they found the boat fast aground in the creek, the tide ebbed out, and their two men gone : we could hear them call to one another in a most lamentable manner, telling one another they were gotten into an enchanted island ; that either there were inhabitants in it, and they should all be murdered ; or else there were devils or spirits in it, and they should be all carried away and devoured.

They hallooed again, and called their two comrades by their names a great many times, but no answer : after some time, we could see them, by the little light there was, run about wringing their hands, like men in despair ; and that sometimes they would go and sit down in the boat to rest themselves, then come ashore, and walk about again, and so the same thing over again.

My men would fain have had me give them leave to fall upon them at once in the dark ; but I was willing to take them at some advantage, so to spare them, and kill as few of them as I could ; and especially I was unwilling to hazard the killing any of our men, knowing the other men were very well armed : I resolved to wait to see if they did not separate ; and therefore, to make sure of them, I drew my ambuscade nearer, and ordered Friday and the captain to creep upon their hands and feet as close to the ground as they could, that they might not be discovered, and get as near them as they could possibly, before they offered to fire.

They had not been long in that posture, till the boatswain, who was the principal ringleader of the mutiny, and had now shown himself the most dejected and dispirited of all the rest, came walking towards them with two more of the crew ; the captain was so eager, at having the principal rogue so much in his power, that he could hardly have patience to let him come so near as to be sure of him ; for they only heard his tongue before ; but when they came nearer, the captain and Friday, starting up on their feet, let fly at them.

The boatswain was killed upon the spot ; the next man was shot in the body, and fell just by him, though he did not die till an hour or two after ; and the third ran for it.

At the noise of the fire, I immediately advanced with my whole army, which was now eight men ; namely, myself, generalissimo ; Friday, my lieutenant-general ; the captain and his two men, and the three prisoners of war, whom we had trusted with arms.

We came upon them indeed in the dark, so that they could not see our number ; and I made the man they had left in the boat, who was now one of us, to call them by name, to try if I could bring them to a parley and so might perhaps reduce them to terms, which fell out just as we desired ; for indeed it was easy to think, as their condition then was, they would be very willing to capitulate ; so he calls out as loud as he could to one of them, " Tom Smith ! Tom Smith ! " Tom Smith answered immediately, " Who's that ? Robinson ? " For it seems he knew his voice. The other answered, " Ay, ay ; for God's sake, Tom Smith, throw down your arms, and yield, or you are all dead men this moment."

" Who must we yield to ? where are they ? " says Smith again. " Here they are," says he ; " here is our captain and fifty men with him, have been hunting you this two hours ; the boatswain is killed, Will Fry is wounded, and I am a prisoner, and if you do not yield, you are all lost."

" Will they give us quarter, then ? " says Tom Smith, " and we will yield." " I'll go and ask, if you promise to yield," says Robinson. So he asked the captain, and the captain himself then calls out, " You, Smith, you know my voice; if you lay down your arms immediately and submit, you shall have your lives, all but Will Atkins."

Upon this Will Atkins cried out, " For God's sake, captain, give me quarter ! What have I done ? They have all been as bad as I " (which, by the way, was not true either ; for it seems this Will Atkins was the first man that laid hold of the captain when they first mutinied, and used him barbarously, in tying his hands and giving him injurious language). However, the captain told him he must lay down his arms at discretion, and trust to the governor's mercy, by which he meant me ; for they all called me governor.

In a word, they all laid down their arms, and begged their lives ; and I sent the man that had parleyed with them, and two more, who bound them all ; and then my great army of fifty men, which, particularly with those three, were in all but eight, came up and seized upon them all, and upon their boat ; only that I kept myself and one more out of sight, for reasons of state.

Our next work was to repair the boat, and to think of seizing the ship ; and as for the captain, now he had leisure to parley with them, he expostulated with them upon the villainy of their practices with him, and at length, upon the further wickedness of their design ; and how certainly it must bring them to misery and distress in the end, and perhaps to the gallows.

They all appeared very penitent, begged hard for their lives ; as for that, he told them they were none of his prisoners, but the commander's of the island ; that they thought they had set him ashore in a barren uninhabited island, but it had pleased God so to direct them, that the island was inhabited, and that the governor was an Englishman ; that he might hang them all there, if he pleased ; but as he had given them all quarter, he supposed he would send them to England, to be dealt with there as justice required, except Atkins, whom he was commanded by the governor to advise to prepare for death ; for that he would be hanged in the morning.

Though this was all fiction of his own, yet it had its desired effect. Atkins fell upon his knees to beg the captain to intercede with the governor for his life ; and all the rest begged of him, for God's sake, that they might not be sent to England.

It now occurred to me, that the time of our deliverance was come, and that it would be a most easy thing to bring these fellows in to be hearty in getting possession of the ship ; so I retired in the dark from them, that they might not see what kind of a governor they had, and called the captain to me ; when I called as at a good distance, one of the men was ordered to speak again, and say to the captain, " Captain, the commander calls for you ;" and presently the captain replied, " Tell his Excellency I am just a-coming." This more perfectly amazed them ; and they all believed that the commander was just by with his fifty men.

Upon the captain's coming to me, I told him my project for seizing the ship, which he liked wonderfully well, and resolved to put it in execution the next morning.

But in order to execute it with more art, and to be secure of success, I told him we must divide the prisoners, and that he should go and take Atkins, and two more of the worst of them, and send them pinioned to the cave where the others lay ; this was committed to Friday, and the two men who came on shore with the captain.

They conveyed them to the cave, as to a prison ; and it was indeed a dismal place, especially to men in their condition.

The others I ordered to my bower, as I called it, of which I have given a full description ; and as it was fenced in, and they pinioned, the place was secure enough, considering they were upon their behaviour.

To these in the morning I sent the captain, who was to enter into a parley with them ; in a word, to try them, and tell me, whether he thought they might be trusted or no, to go on board, and surprise the ship. He talked to them of the injury done him, of the condition they were brought to ; and that though the governor had given them quarter for their lives, as to the present action, yet that if they were sent to England, they would be all hanged in chains, to be sure ; but that if they would join in such an attempt as to recover the ship, he would have the governor's engagement for their pardon.

They fell down on their knees to the captain, and promised that they would be faithful to him to the last drop, and that they should owe their lives to him, and would go with him all over the world.

" Well," says the captain, " I must go and tell the governor what you say, and see what I can do to bring him to consent to it." So he brought me an account of the temper he found them in ; and that he verily believed they would be faithful.

However, that we might be very secure, I told him he should go back again, and choose out five of them, and tell them, that they should see that they did not want men ; but he would take out those five to be his assistants, and that the governor would keep the other two, and the three that were sent prisoners to the castle (my cave), as hostages for the fidelity of those five ; and that if they proved unfaithful in the execution, the five hostages should be hanged in chains alive upon the shore.

This looked severe, and convinced them that the governor was in earnest : however, they had no way left but to accept it ; and it was now the business of the prisoners, as much as of the captain, to persuade the other five to do their duty.

Our strength was now thus ordered for the expedition :—1. The captain, his mate, and passenger. 2. Then the two prisoners of the first gang, to whom, having their characters from the captain, I had given their liberty, and trusted them with arms. 3. The other two whom I kept till now in my bower pinioned, but, upon the captain's motion, had now been released. 4. These five released at last ; so that they were twelve in all, besides five we kept prisoners in the cave for hostages.

I asked the captain if he was willing to venture with these hands on board the ship ; for, as for me and my man Friday, I did not think it was proper for us to stir, having seven men left behind ; and it was employment enough for us to keep them as under, and supply them with victuals.

As to the five in the cave, I resolved to keep them fast : but Friday went twice a-day to them, to supply them with necessaries ; and I made the other two carry provisions to a certain distance, where Friday was to take it.

When I showed myself to the two hostages, it was with the captain, who told them I was the person the governor had ordered to look after them, and that it was the governor's pleasure that they should not stir anywhere but by my direction; that if they did, they should be fetched into the castle, and be laid in irons; so that as we never suffered them to see me as governor, so I now appeared as another person, and spoke of the governor, the garrison, the castle, and the like, upon all occasions.

The captain now had no difficulty before him, but to furnish his two boats, stop the breach of one, and man them: he made his passenger captain of one, with four other men, and himself and his mate and five more went in the other; and they contrived their business very well, for they came up to the ship about midnight. As soon as they came within call of the ship, he made Robinson hail them, and tell them he had brought off the men and the boat, but that it was a long time before they had found them, and the like, holding them in a chat till they came to the ship's side; when the captain and the mate, entering first with their arms, immediately knocked down the second mate and carpenter with the butt end of their muskets. Being very faithfully seconded by their men, they secured all the rest that were upon the main and quarter decks, and began to fasten the hatches to keep those down who were below; when the other boat and their men, entering at the fore-chains, secured the forecastle of the ship, and the scuttle, which went down into the cock-room, making three men they found there prisoners.

When this was done, and all safe upon the deck, the captain ordered the mate, with three men, to break into the round-house, where the new rebel captain lay, and, having taken the alarm, was gotten up, and, with two men and a boy, had gotten fire-arms in their hands; and when the mate with a crow split open the door, the new captain and his men fired boldly among them, and wounded the mate with a musket-ball, which broke his arm, and wounded two more of the men, but killed nobody.

The mate, calling for help, rushed, however, into the round-house, wounded as he was, and with his pistol shot the new captain through the head, the bullet entering at his mouth, and came out again behind one of his ears, so that he never spoke a word; upon which the rest yielded, and the ship was taken effectually without any more lives being lost.

As soon as the ship was thus secured, the captain ordered seven guns to be fired, which was the signal agreed upon with me, to give me notice of his success; which, you may be sure, I was very glad to hear, having sat watching upon the shore for it till near two of the clock in the morning.

Having thus heard the signal plainly, I laid me down; and it having been a day of great fatigue to me, I slept very sound, till I was something surprised with the noise of a gun; and presently starting up, I heard a man call me by the name of " Governor, governor! " and presently I knew the captain's voice; when, climbing up to the top of the hill, there he stood, and pointing to the ship, he embraced me in his arms: " My dear friend and deliverer! " says he, " there's your ship, for she is all yours, and so are we, and all that belong to her." I cast my eyes to the ship, and there she rode within a little more than half a mile of the shore—for they had weighed her anchor as soon as they were masters of her—and the weather being

He shot the new captain through the head

fair, had brought her to an anchor just against the mouth of a little creek ; and the tide being up, the captain had brought the pinnace in near the place where I first landed my rafts, and so landed just at my door.

I was, at first, ready to sink down with the surprise ; for I saw my deliverance indeed visibly put into my hands, all things easy, and a large ship just ready to carry me away whither I pleased to go. At first, for some time, I was not able to answer one word ; but as he had taken me in his arms, I held fast by him, or I should have fallen to the ground.

He perceived the surprise, and immediately pulled a bottle out of his pocket, and gave me a dram of cordial, which he had brought on purpose for me ; after I drank it, I sat down upon the ground, and though it brought me to myself, yet it was a good while before I could speak a word to him.

All this while the poor man was in as great an ecstasy as I, only not under my surprise, as I was ; and he said a thousand kind tender things to me, to compose and bring me to myself ; but such was the flood of joy in my breast, that it put all my spirits into confusion—at last it broke into tears, and in a little while I recovered my speech.

Then I took my turn, and embraced him as my deliverer ; and we rejoiced together. I told him I looked upon him as a man sent from Heaven to deliver me, and that the whole transaction seemed to be a chain of wonders ; that such things as these were the testimonies we had of a secret hand of Providence governing the world, and an evidence that the eye of an infinite power could search into the remotest corner of the world, and send help to the miserable whenever He pleased.

When we had talked awhile, the captain told me, he had brought me some little refreshments, such as the ship afforded, and such as the wretches who had been so long his masters had not plundered him of. Upon this he called aloud to the boat, and bids his men bring the things ashore that were for the governor ; and indeed it was a present as if I had been one, not that I was to be carried along with them, but as if I had been to dwell upon the island still, and they were to go without me.

First, he had brought me a case of bottles full of excellent cordial waters ; six large bottles of Madeira wine, the bottles held two quarts a-piece ; two pounds of excellent good tobacco, twelve good pieces of the ship's beef, and six pieces of pork, with a bag of peas, and about a hundred weight of biscuits.

He brought me also a box of sugar, a box of flour, a bag full of lemons, and two bottles of lime juice, and abundance of other things : but besides these, and what was a thousand times more useful to me, he brought me six clean shirts, six very good neckcloths, two pair of gloves, one pair of shoes, a hat, and one pair of stockings, and a very good suit of clothes of his own, which had been worn but very little. In a word, he clothed me from head to foot.

It was a very kind and agreeable present, as any one may imagine, to one in my circumstances : but never was anything in the world of that kind so unpleasant, awkward, and uneasy, as it was to me to wear such clothes at their first putting on.

After these ceremonies passed, and after all his good things were brought into my little apartment, we began to consult what was to be done with the prisoners we had ; for it was worth considering whether we might venture to take them away with us or no, especially two of them, whom we knew to be incorrigible and refractory to the last degree ; and the captain said, he knew they were such rogues, that there was no obliging them ; and if he did carry them away it must be in irons, as malefactors, to be delivered over to justice at the first English colony he could come at ; and I found that the captain himself was very anxious about it.

Upon this, I told him, that, if he desired it, I durst undertake to bring the two men he spoke of to make it their own request that he should leave them upon the island. " I should be very glad of that," says the captain, " with all my heart."

" Well," said I, " I will send for them, and talk with them for you ; " so I caused Friday and the two hostages—for they were now discharged, their comrades having performed their promise—I say, I caused them to go to the cave, and bring up the five men, pinioned as they were, to the bower, and keep them there till I came.

After some time, I came thither dressed in my new habit, and now I was called governor again. Being all met, and the captain with me, I caused the men to be brought before me, and I told them, I had had a full account of their villainous behaviour to the captain, and how they had run away with the ship, and were preparing to commit further robberies ; but that Providence had ensnared them in their own ways, and that they were fallen into the pit which they had digged for others.

I let them know that by my direction the ship had been seized, that she lay now in the road, and they might see by-and-by, that their new captain

ROBINSON CRUSOE'S DISCOVERY.
To my utter amazement I discovered a footprint on the sand.

FRIDAY'S ESCAPE.
The savage took to his heels and ran for his life, with the natives in hot pursuit after him.

had received the reward of his villainy ; for that they might see him hanging at the yard-arm : that as to them, I wanted to know what they had to say, why I should not execute them as pirates taken in the fact, as by my commission they could not doubt I had authority to do.

One of them answered in the name of the rest, that they had nothing to say, but this, that when they were taken, the captain promised them their lives, and they humbly implored my mercy : but I told them I knew not what mercy to show them ; for, as for myself, I had resolved to quit the island with all my men, and had taken passage with the captain to go for England : and, as for the captain, he could not carry them to England, other than as prisoners in irons to be tried for mutiny, and running away with the ship, the consequence of which, they must needs know, would be the gallows ; so that I could not tell what was the best for them, unless they had a mind to take their fate in the island ; if they desired that, I did not care, as I had liberty to leave it : I had some inclination to give them their lives, if they thought they could shift on shore. They seemed very thankful for it ; said they would much rather venture to stay there, than to be carried to England to be hanged : so I left it on that issue.

However, the captain seemed to make some difficulty of it, as if he durst not leave them there : upon this, I seemed to be a little angry with the captain, and told him that they were my prisoners, not his ; and that, seeing I had offered them so much favour, I would be as good as my word ; and that if he did not think fit to consent to it, I would set them at liberty as I found them : and, if he did not like that, he might take them again if he could catch them.

Upon this, they appeared very thankful, and I accordingly set them at liberty, and bade them retire into the woods, to the place whence they came, and I would leave them some fire-arms, some ammunition, and some directions how they should live very well, if they thought fit.

Upon this, I prepared to go on board the ship, but told the captain that I would stay that night to prepare my things ; and desired him to go on board in the meantime, and keep all right in the ship, and send the boat on shore the next day for me : ordering him, in the meantime, to cause the new captain, who was killed, to be hanged at the yard-arm, that these men might see him.

When the captain was gone, I sent for the men up to me to my apartment, and entered seriously into discourse with them of their circumstances. I told them, I thought they had made a right choice : that, if the captain carried them away, they would certainly be hanged ; I showed them their captain hanging at the yard-arm of the ship, and told them they had nothing less to expect.

When they all declared their willingness to stay, I then told them I would let them into the story of my living there, and put them into the way of making it easy to them : accordingly, I gave them the whole history of the place, and of my coming to it ; showed them my fortifications, the way I made my bread, planted my corn, cured my grapes : and, in a word, all that was necessary to make them easy. I told them the story of the sixteen Spaniards that were to be expected ; for whom I left a letter, and made them promise to treat them in common with themselves.

Two came swimming to the ship's side

I left them my fire-arms, namely, five muskets, three fowling-pieces, and three swords : I had about a barrel of powder left ; for after the first year or two I used but little, and wasted none. I gave them a description of the way I managed the goats, and directions to milk and fatten them, to make both butter and cheese.

In a word, I gave them every part of my own story ; and I told them I would prevail with the captain to leave them two barrels of gunpowder more, and some garden-seed, which I told them I would have been very glad of ; also I gave them the bag of peas which the captain had brought me to eat, and bade them be sure to sow and increase them.

Having done all this, I left them the next day, and went on board the ship ; we prepared immediately to sail, but did not weigh that night. The next morning early, two of the five men came swimming to the ship's side, and, making a most lamentable complaint of the other three, begged to be taken into the ship for God's sake, for they should be murdered ; and begged the captain to take them on board, though he hanged them immediately.

Upon this the captain pretended to have no power without me ; but, after some difficulty, and after their solemn promises of amendment, they were taken on board, and were, some time after, soundly whipped and pickled : after which they proved very honest and quiet fellows.

Some time after this, I went with the boat on shore, the tide being up, with the things promised to the men, to which the captain, at my inter-cession, caused their chests and clothes to be added, which they took, and were very thankful for : I also encouraged them, by telling them, that if it lay in my way to send a vessel to take them in, I would not forget them.

When I took leave of this island, I carried on board for relics, the great goat-skin cap I had made, my umbrella, and one of my parrots : also, I forgot not to take the money I formerly mentioned, which had lain by me so long useless that it was grown rusty, or tarnished, and could hardly pass for silver, till it had been a little rubbed and handled, and also the money I found in the wreck of the Spanish ship.

And thus I left the island the 19th day of December, as I found by the ship's account, in the year 1686, after I had been upon it eight-and-twenty years, two months, and nineteen days : being delivered from the second captivity the same day of the month that I first made my escape in the barcolongo from among the Moors of Sallee.

In this vessel, after a long voyage, I arrived in England the 11th of June, in the year 1687, having been thirty and five years absent.

LITTLE WOMEN

CHAPTER I

PLAYING PILGRIMS

"CHRISTMAS won't be Christmas without any presents," grumbled Jo, lying on the rug.

" It's so dreadful to be poor ! " sighed Meg, looking down at her old dress.

" I don't think it's fair for some girls to have lots of pretty things, and other girls nothing at all," added little Amy, with an injured sniff.

" We've got father and mother, and each other anyhow," said Beth contentedly, from her corner.

The four young faces on which the firelight shone brightened at the cheerful words, but darkened again as Jo said sadly,—

" We haven't got father, and shall not have him for a long time." She didn't say " perhaps never," but each silently added it, thinking of father away where the fighting was.

Nobody spoke for a minute ; then Meg said in an altered tone,—

" You know the reason mother proposed not having any presents this Christmas was because it's going to be a hard winter for everyone ; and she thinks we ought not to spend money for pleasure when our men are suffering so in the army. We can't do much, but we can make our little sacrifices, and ought to do it gladly. But I am afraid I don't ;" and Meg shook her head, as she thought regretfully of all the pretty things she wanted.

" But I don't think the little we should spend would do any good. We've each got a dollar, and the army wouldn't be much helped by our giving that. I agree not to expect anything from mother or you, but I do want to buy *Undine and Sintram* for myself ; I've wanted it *so* long," said Jo, who was a bookworm.

" I planned to spend mine in new music," said Beth, with a little sigh, which no one heard but the hearth-brush and kettle-holder.

" I shall get a nice box of Faber's drawing pencils ; I really need them," said Amy decidedly.

" Mother didn't say anything about our money, and she won't wish us to give up everything. Let each buy what we want, and have a little fun ; I'm sure we grub hard enough to earn it," cried Jo, examining the heels of her boots in a gentlemanly manner.

" I know *I* do—teaching those dreadful children nearly all day, when I'm longing to enjoy myself at home," began Meg, in the complaining tone again.

" You don't have half such a hard time as I do," said Jo. " How would you like to be shut up for hours with a nervous, fussy old lady, who keeps you trotting, is never satisfied, and worries you till you're ready to fly out of the window or box her ears ? "

" It's naughty to fret, but I do think washing dishes and keeping things tidy is the worst work in the world. It makes me cross ; and my hands get so stiff, I can't practise good a bit." And Beth looked at her rough hands with a sigh that any one could hear that time.

" I don't believe any of you suffer as I do," cried Amy ; " for you don't have to go to school with impertinent girls, who plague you if you don't know your lessons, and laugh at your dresses, and label your father if he isn't rich, and insult you when your nose isn't nice."

" If you mean *libel*, I'd say so, and not talk about *labels*, as if pa was a pickle-bottle," advised Jo, laughing.

" I know what I mean, and you needn't be ' statirical ' about it. It's proper to use good words, and improve your *vocabilary*," returned Amy with dignity.

" Don't peck at one another, children. Don't you wish we had the money papa lost when we were little, Jo ? Dear me, how happy and good we'd be if we had no worries," said Meg, who could remember better times.

" You said the other day you thought we were a deal happier than the King children, for they were fighting and fretting all the time, in spite of their money."

" So I did, Beth. Well, I guess we are ; for though we do have to work, we make fun for ourselves, and are a pretty jolly set, as Jo would say."

" Jo does use such slang words," observed Amy, with a reproving look at the long figure stretched on the rug. Jo immediately sat up, put her hands in her apron pockets, and began to whistle.

" Don't, Jo ; it's so boyish."

" That's why I do it."

" I detest rude, unlady-like girls."

" I hate affected, niminy-piminy chits."

" Birds in their little nests agree," sang Beth, the peacemaker, with such a funny face that both sharp voices softened to a laugh, and the " pecking " ended for that time.

" Really, girls, you are both to be blamed," said Meg, beginning to lecture in her elder sisterly fashion. " You are old enough to leave off boyish tricks, and behave better, Josephine. It didn't matter so much when you were a little girl ; but now you are so tall, and turn up your hair, you should remember that you are a young lady."

" I ain't ! and if turning up my hair makes me one, I'll wear it in two tails till I'm twenty," cried Jo, pulling off her net, and shaking down a chestnut mane. " I hate to think I've got to grow up and be Miss March, and wear long gowns, and look as prim as a China-aster. It's bad enough to be a girl, anyway, when I like boy's games, and work, and manners. I can't get over my disappointment in not being a boy, and it's worse than ever now, for I'm dying to go and fight with papa, and I can only stay at home and knit like a poky old woman ; " and Jo shook the blue army-sock till the needles rattled like castanets, and her ball bounded across the room.

" Poor Jo ; it's too bad ! But it can't be helped : so you must try to be contented with making your name boyish, and playing brother to us girls," said Beth, stroking the rough head at her knee with a hand that all the dish-washing and dusting in the world could not make ungentle in its touch.

" As for you, Amy," continued Meg, " you are altogether too particular and prim. Your airs are funny now, but you'll grow up an affected little goose if you don't take care. I like your nice manners, and refined way of speaking, when you don't try to be elegant ; but your absurd words are as bad as Jo's slang."

" If Jo is a tomboy, and Amy a goose, what am I, please ? " asked Beth, ready to share the lecture.

" You're a dear, and nothing else," answered Meg warmly ; and no one contradicted her, for the " Mouse " was the pet of the family.

As young readers like to know " how people look," we will take this moment to give them a little sketch of the four sisters, who sat knitting away in the twilight, while the December snow fell quietly without, and the fire crackled cheerfully within. It was a comfortable old room, though the carpet was faded and the furniture very plain ; for a good picture or two hung on the walls, books filled the recesses, chrysanthemums and Christmas roses bloomed in the windows, and a pleasant atmosphere of home-peace pervaded it.

Margaret, the eldest of the four, was sixteen, and very pretty, being plump and fair, with large eyes, plenty of soft brown hair, a sweet mouth, and white hands, of which she was rather vain. Fifteen-year-old Jo was very tall, thin, and brown, and reminded one of a colt ; for she never seemed to know what to do with her long limbs, which were very much in her way. She had a decided mouth, a comical nose, and sharp gray eyes, which appeared to see everything, and were by turns fierce, funny or thoughtful. Her long, thick hair was her one beauty ; but it was usually bundled into a net, to be out of her way. Round shoulders had Jo, big hands and feet, a fly-away look to her clothes, and the uncomfortable appearance of a girl who was rapidly shooting up into a woman, and didn't like it. Elizabeth —or Beth, as every one called her—was a rosy, smooth-haired, bright-eyed girl of thirteen, with a shy manner, a timid voice, and a peaceful expression, which was seldom disturbed. Her father called her " Little Tranquillity," and the name suited her excellently ; for she seemed to live in a happy world of her own, only venturing out to meet the few whom she trusted and loved. Amy, though the youngest, was a most important person—in her own opinion, at least. A regular snow maiden, with blue eyes, and yellow hair curling on her shoulders ; pale and slender, and always carrying herself like a young lady mindful of her manners. What the characters of the four sisters were we will leave to be found out.

The clock struck six ; and, having swept up the hearth, Beth put a pair of slippers down to warm. Somehow the sight of the old shoes had a good effect upon the girls, for mother was coming, and every one brightened to welcome her. Meg stopped lecturing, and lit the lamp, Amy got out of the easy chair without being asked, and Jo forgot how tired she was as she sat up to hold the slippers nearer to the blaze.

" They are quite worn out ; Marmee must have a new pair."

" I thought I'd get her some with my dollar," said Beth.

" No, I shall ! " cried Amy.

" I'm the oldest," began Meg, but Jo cut in with a decided,—

" I'm the man of the family now papa is away, and *I* shall provide the slippers, for he told me to take special care of mother while he was gone."

" I'll tell you what we'll do," said Beth ; " let's each get her something for Christmas, and not get anything for ourselves."

" That's like you, dear ! What will we get ? " exclaimed Jo.

Every one thought soberly for a minute ; then Meg announced, as if the idea were suggested by the sight of her own pretty hands, " I shall give her a nice pair of gloves."

" Army shoes, best to be had," cried Jo.

" Some handkerchiefs, all hemmed," said Beth.

" I'll get a little bottle of Cologne ; she likes it, and it won't cost much, so I'll have some left to buy something for me," added Amy.

" How will we give the things ? " asked Meg.

" Put 'em on the table, and bring her in and see her open the bundles. Don't you remember how we used to do on our birthdays ? " answered Jo.

" I used to be so frightened when it was my turn to sit in the big chair with a crown on, and see you all come marching round to give the presents, with a kiss. I liked the things and the kisses, but it was dreadful to have you sit looking at me while I opened the bundles," said Beth, who was toasting her face and the bread for tea at the same time.

" Let Marmee think we are getting things for ourselves, and then surprise her. We must go shopping to-morrow afternoon, Meg ; there are lots to do about the play for Christmas night," said Jo, marching up and down with her hands behind her back, and her nose in the air.

" I don't mean to act any more after this time ; I'm getting too old for such things," observed Meg, who was as much a child as ever about " dressing-up " frolics.

" You won't stop, I know, as long as you can trail round in a white gown with your hair down and wear gold-paper jewellery. You are the best actress we've got, and there'll be an end of everything if you quit the boards," said

Jo. "We ought to rehearse to-night. Come here, Amy, and do the fainting scene, for you are as stiff as a poker in that."

"I can't help it; I never saw any one faint, and I don't choose to make myself all black and blue tumbling flat as you do. If I can go down easily, I'll drop; if I can't, I shall fall into a chair and be graceful; I don't care if Hugo comes at me with a pistol," replied Amy, who was not gifted with dramatic power, but was chosen because she was small enough to be borne out shrieking by the hero of the piece.

"Do it this way; clasp your hands so, and stagger across the room, crying frantically, 'Roderigo! save me! save me!'" and away went Jo, with a melodramatic scream which was truly thrilling.

Amy followed, but she poked her hands out stiffly before her, and jerked herself along as if she went by machinery; and her "Ow!" was more suggestive of pins being run into her than of fear and anguish. Jo gave a despairing groan and Meg laughed outright, while Beth let her bread burn as she watched the fun with interest.

"It's no use! do the best you can when the time comes, and if the audience shout, don't blame me. Come on, Meg."

Then things went smoothly, for Don Pedro edified the world in a speech of two pages without a single break; Hagar, the witch, chanted an awful incantation over her kettleful of simmering toads, with weird effect; Roderigo rent his chains asunder manfully; and Hugo died in agonies of remorse and arsenic, with a wild, "Ha! ha!"

"It's the best we've had yet," said Meg, as the dead villain sat up and rubbed his elbows.

"I don't see how you can write and act such splendid things, Jo. You're a regular Shakespeare!" exclaimed Beth, who firmly believed that her sisters were gifted with wonderful genius in all things.

"Not quite," replied Jo modestly. "I do think *The Witch's Curse: An Operatic Tragedy*, is rather a nice thing; but I'd like to try *Macbeth*, if we only had a trap-door for Banquo. I always wanted to do the killing part. 'Is that a dagger that I see before me?'" muttered Jo, rolling her eyes and clutching at the air, as she had seen a famous tragedian do.

"No, it's the toasting-fork, with ma's shoe on it instead of the bread. Beth's stage-struck!" cried Meg, and the rehearsal ended in a general burst of laughter.

"Glad to find you so merry, my girls," said a cheery voice at the door, and actors and audience turned to welcome a stout, motherly lady, with a "can-I-help-you" look about her which was truly delightful. She wasn't a particularly handsome person, but mothers are always lovely to their children, and the girls thought the gray cloak and unfashionable bonnet covered the most splendid woman in the world.

"Well, dearies, how have you go on to-day? There was so much to do, getting the boxes ready to go to-morrow, that I didn't come home to dinner. Has any one called, Beth? How is your cold, Meg? Jo, you look tired to death. Come and kiss me, baby."

As they gathered about the table, Mrs. March said, with a particularly happy face, "I've got a treat for you after supper."

A quick, bright smile went round like a streak of sunshine. Beth clapped her hands, regardless of the hot biscuit she held, and Jo tossed up her napkin, " A letter ! a letter ! Three cheers for father ! "

" Yes, a nice long letter. He is well, and thinks he shall get through the cold season better than we feared. He sends all sorts of loving wishes for Christmas, and an especial message to you girls," said Mrs. March—patting her pocket as if she had got a treasure there.

" Hurry up, and get done. Don't stop to quirk your little finger, and mince over your plate, Amy," cried Jo, choking in her tea, and dropping her bread, butter side down, on the carpet, in her haste to get at the treat.

Beth ate no more, but crept away, to sit in her shadowy corner and brood over the delight to come, till the others were ready.

" I think it was so splendid in father to go as a chaplain when he was too old to be drafted, and not strong enough for a soldier," said Meg warmly.

" Don't I wish I could go as a drummer, a *vivan*——what's its name ? or a nurse, so I could be near him and help him," exclaimed Jo, with a groan.

" It must be very disagreeable to sleep in a tent, and eat all sorts of bad-tasting things, and drink out of a tin mug," sighed Amy.

" When will he come home, Marmee ? " asked Beth, with a little quiver in her voice.

" Not for many months, dear, unless he is sick. He will stay and do his work faithfully as long as he can, and we won't ask for him back a minute sooner than he can be spared. Now come and hear the letter."

They all drew to the fire, mother in the big chair with Beth at her feet, Meg and Amy perched on either arm of the chair, and Jo leaning on the back, where no one would see any sign of emotion if the letter should happen to be touching.

Very few letters were written in those hard times that were not touching, especially those which fathers sent home. In this one little was said of the hardships endured, the dangers faced, or the homesickness conquered ; it was a cheerful, hopeful letter, full of lively descriptions of camp life, marches, and military news ; and only at the end did the writer's heart overflow with fatherly love and longing for the little girls at home.

" Give them all my dear love and a kiss. Tell them I think of them by day, pray for them by night, and find my best comfort in their affection at all times. A year seems very long to wait before I see them, but remind them that while we wait we may all work, so that these hard days need not be wasted. I know they will remember all I said to them, that they will be loving children to you, will do their duty faithfully, fight their bosom enemies bravely, and conquer themselves so beautifully, that when I come back to them I may be fonder and prouder than ever of my little women."

Everybody sniffed when they came to that part ; Jo wasn't ashamed of the great tear that dropped off the end of her nose, and Amy never minded the rumpling of her curls as she hid her face on her mother's shoulder and sobbed out, " I *am* a selfish pig ! but I'll truly try to be better, so he mayn't be disappointed in me by-and-by."

" We all will ! " cried Meg. " I think too much of my looks, and hate to work, but won't any more, if I can help it."

" I'll try and be what he loves to call me, ' a little woman,' and not be rough and wild ; but do my duty here, instead of wanting to be somewhere else," said Jo, thinking that keeping her temper at home was a much harder task than facing a rebel or two.

Beth said nothing, but wiped away her tears with the blue army-sock, and began to knit with all her might, losing no time in doing the duty that lay nearest her, while she resolved in her quiet little soul to be all that father hoped to find her when the year brought round the happy coming home.

Mrs. March broke the silence that followed Jo's words by saying in her cheery voice, " Do you remember how you used to play *Pilgrim's Progress* when you were little things ? Nothing delighted you more than to have me tie my piece-bags on your backs for burdens, give you hats and sticks, and

It was a cheerful, hopeful letter, full of lively descriptions

rolls of paper, and let you travel through the house from the cellar, which was the City of Destruction, up, up, to the house-top, where you had all the lovely things you could collect to make a Celestial City."

" What fun it was, especially going by the lions, fighting Apollyon, and passing through the Valley where the hobgoblins were," said Jo.

" I liked the place where the bundles fell off and tumbled downstairs," said Meg.

" My favourite part was when we came out on the flat roof where our flowers and arbours and pretty things were, and all stood and sang for joy up there in the sunshine," said Beth, smiling as if that pleasant moment had come back to her.

" I don't remember much about it, except that I was afraid of the cellar and the dark entry, and always liked the cake and milk we had up at the top. If I wasn't too old for such things, I'd rather like to play it over again," said Amy, who began to talk of renouncing childish things at the mature age of twelve.

"We never are too old for this, my dear, because it is a play we are playing all the time in one way or another. Our burdens are here, our road is before us, and the longing for goodness and happiness is the guide that leads us through many troubles and mistakes to the peace which is a true Celestial City. Now, my little pilgrims, suppose you begin again, not in play, but in earnest, and see how far on you can get before father comes home."

"We were in the Slough of Despond to-night, and mother came and pulled us out, as Help did in the book. We ought to have our roll of directions, like Christian. What shall we do about that?" asked Jo, delighted with the fancy which lent a little romance to the very dull task of doing her duty.

"Look under your pillows, Christmas morning, and you will find your guide-book," replied Mrs. March.

CHAPTER II

A MERRY CHRISTMAS

JO was the first to wake in the gray dawn of Christmas morning. No stockings hung at the fireplace, and for a moment she felt as much disappointed as she did long ago, when her little sock fell down because it was so full. Then she remembered her mother's promise, and slipping her hand under her pillow, drew out a little crimson-covered book. She knew it very well, for it was that beautiful old story of the best life ever lived, and Jo felt that it was a true guide-book for any pilgrim going the long journey. She woke Meg with a "Merry Christmas," and bade her see what was under her pillow. A green-covered book appeared with the same picture inside, and a few words written by their mother, which made their one present very precious in their eyes. Presently Beth and Amy woke, to rummage and find their little books also—one dove-coloured, the other blue; and all sat looking at and talking about them, while the east grew rosy with the coming day.

"Where is mother?" asked Meg, as she and Jo ran down to thank her for their gifts, half an hour later.

"Goodness only knows. Some poor creeter come a-beggin', and your ma went straight off to see what was needed. There never *was* such a woman for givin' away vittles and drink, clothes and firin'," replied Hannah, who had lived with the family since Meg was born, and was considered by them all more as a friend than a servant.

"She'll be back soon, I guess; so do your cakes, and have everything ready," said Meg, looking over the presents, which were collected in a basket and kept under the sofa, ready to be produced at the proper time. "Why, where is Amy's bottle of Cologne?" she added, as the little flask did not appear.

"She took it out a minute ago, and went off with it to put a ribbon on it, or some such notion," replied Jo, dancing about the room to take the stiffness off the new army-slippers.

" How nice my handkerchiefs look, don't they ? Hannah washed and ironed them for me, and I marked them all myself," said Beth, looking proudly at the somewhat uneven letters which had cost her such labour.

" Bless the child, she's gone and put ' Mother ' on them, instead of ' M. March ' ; how funny ! " cried Jo, taking up one.

" Isn't it right ? I thought it was better to do so, because Meg's initials are ' M. M.,' and I don't want any one to use these but Marmee," said Beth, looking troubled.

" It's all right, dear, and a very pretty idea ; quite sensible, too, for no one can ever mistake now. It will please her very much, I know," said Meg, with a frown for Jo, and a smile for Beth.

" There's mother, hide the basket, quick," cried Jo, as a door slammed, and steps sounded in the hall.

Amy came in hastily, and looked rather abashed when she saw her sisters waiting for her.

" Where have you been, and what are you hiding behind you ? " asked Meg, surprised to see, by her hood and cloak, that lazy Amy had been out so early.

" Don't laugh at me, Jo ; I didn't mean any one should know till the time came. I only meant to change the little bottle for a big one, and I gave *all* my money to get it, and I'm not going to be selfish any more."

As she spoke, Amy showed the handsome flask which replaced the cheap one ; and looked so earnest and humble in her little effort to forget herself that Meg hugged her on the spot, and Jo pronounced her " a trump," while Beth ran to the window and picked her finest rose to ornament the stately bottle.

" You see, I felt ashamed of my present after reading and talking about being good this morning, so I ran round the corner and changed it the minute I was up ; and I am *so* glad, for mine is the handsomest now."

Another bang of the street door sent the basket under the sofa, and the girls to the table, eager for breakfast.

" Merry Christmas, Marmee ! Lots of them ! Thank you for our books ; we read some, and mean to every day," they cried in chorus.

" Merry Christmas, little daughters ! I'm glad you began at once, and hope you will keep on. But I want to say one word before we sit down. Not far away from here lies a poor woman with a little new-born baby. Six children are huddled into one bed to keep from freezing, for they have no fire. There is nothing to eat over there ; and the oldest boy came to tell me they were suffering hunger and cold. My girls, will you give them your breakfast as a Christmas present ? "

They were all unusually hungry, having waited nearly an hour, and for a minute no one spoke, only a minute, for Jo exclaimed impetuously,—

" I'm so glad you came before we began ! "

" May I go and help carry the things to the poor little children ? " asked Beth eagerly.

" *I* shall take the cream and the muffins," added Amy, heroically giving up the articles she most liked.

Meg was already covering the buckwheats, and piling the bread into one big plate.

" I thought you'd do it," said Mrs. March, smiling, as if satisfied. " You shall all go and help me, and when we come back we will have bread and milk for breakfast, and make it up at dinner-time."

They were soon ready, and the procession set out. Fortunately it was early, and they went through back streets : so few people saw them, and no one laughed at the funny party.

A poor, bare, miserable room it was, with broken windows, no fire, ragged bed-clothes, a sick mother, wailing baby, and a group of pale, hungry children cuddled under one old quilt, trying to keep warm. How the big eyes stared, and the blue lips smiled, as the girls went in !

" Ach, mein Gott ! it is good angels come to us ! " cried the poor woman, crying for joy.

" Funny angels in hoods and mittens," said Jo, and set them laughing.

In a few minutes it really did seem as if kind spirits had been at work there. Hannah, who had carried wood, made a fire, and stopped up the broken panes with old hats and her own shawl. Mrs. March gave the mother tea and gruel, and comforted her with promises of help, while she dressed the little baby as tenderly as if it had been her own. The girls, meantime, spread the table, set the children round the fire, and fed them like so many hungry birds ; laughing, talking, and trying to understand the funny broken English.

" Das ist gute ! " " Der angel-kinder ! " cried the poor things, as they ate, and warmed their purple hands at the comfortable blaze. The girls had never been called angel children before, and thought it very agreeable, especially Jo, who had been considered " a Sancho " ever since she was born. That was a very happy breakfast, though they didn't get any of it ; and when they went away, leaving comfort behind, I think there were not in all the city four merrier people than the hungry little girls who gave away their breakfast and contented themselves with bread and milk on Christmas morning.

" That's loving our neighbour better than ourselves, and ·I like it," said Meg, as they set out their presents, while their mother was upstairs collecting clothes for the poor Hummels.

Not a very splendid show, but there was a great deal of love done up in the few little bundles ; and the tall vase of red roses, white chrysanthemums, and trailing vines, which stood in the middle, gave quite an elegant air to the table.

" She's coming ! Strike up, Beth ! Open the door, Amy. Three cheers for Marmee ! " cried Jo, prancing about, while Meg went to conduct mother to the seat of honour.

Beth played her gayest march, Amy threw open the door, and Meg enacted escort with great dignity. Mrs. March was both surprised and touched ; and smiled with her eyes full as she examined her presents, and read the little notes which accompanied them. The slippers went on at once, a new hand-kerchief was slipped into her pocket, well scented with Amy's Cologne, the rose was fastened in her bosom, and the nice gloves were pronounced " a perfect fit."

THE LITTLE MUSICIAN.
Beth spent many happy hours playing the piano, surrounded by her beloved family of kittens.

JO AND LAURIE.
Laurie gathered up the fallen combs and hairpins while Jo hastily tidied her hair.

Jo played male parts to her heart's content

There was a good deal of laughing, and kissing, and explaining, in the simple, loving fashion which makes these home-festivals so pleasant at the time, so sweet to remember long afterward, and then all fell to work.

The morning charities and ceremonies took so much time that the rest of the day was devoted to preparations for the evening festivities. Being still too young to go often to the theatre, and not rich enough to afford any great outlay for private performances, the girls put their wits to work, and, necessity being the mother of invention, made whatever they needed. Very clever were some of their productions : pasteboard guitars, antique lamps made of old-fashioned butter-boats, covered with silver paper, gorgeous robes of old cotton, glittering with tin spangles from a pickle factory, and armour covered with the same useful diamond-shaped bits, left in sheets when the lids of tin preserve-pots were cut out. The furniture was used to being turned topsy-turvy, and the big chamber was the scene of many innocent revels.

No gentlemen were admitted ; so Jo played male parts to her heart's content, and took immense satisfaction in a pair of russet-leather boots given her by a friend, who knew a lady who knew an actor. These boots, an old foil, and a slashed doublet once used by an artist for some picture, were Jo's chief treasures, and appeared on all occasions.

On Christmas night, a dozen girls piled on to the bed, which was the dress circle, and sat before the blue and yellow chintz curtains, in a most flattering state of expectancy. There was a good deal of rustling and whispering behind the curtain, a trifle of lamp-smoke, and an occasional giggle from Amy, who was apt to get hysterical in the excitement of the moment.

Presently a bell sounded, the curtains flew apart, and the operatic tragedy began.

"A gloomy wood," according to the one play-bill, was represented by a few shrubs in pots, a green baize on the floor, and a cave in the distance. This cave was made with a clothes-horse for a roof, bureaus for walls ; and in it was a small furnace in full blast, with a black pot on it, and an old witch bending over it. The stage was dark, and the glow of the furnace had a fine effect, especially as real steam issued from the kettle when the witch took off the cover. A moment was allowed for the first thrill to subside ; then Hugo, the villain, stalked in with a clanking sword at his side, a slouched hat, black beard, mysterious cloak, and the boots. After pacing to and fro in much agitation, he struck his forehead, and burst out in a wild strain, singing of his hatred to Roderigo, his love for Zara, and his pleasing resolution to kill the one and win the other. The gruff tones of Hugo's voice, with an occasional shout when his feelings overcame him, were very impressive, and the audience applauded the moment he paused for breath. Bowing with the air of one accustomed to public praise, he stole to the cavern, and ordered Hagar to come forth with a commanding "What ho ! minion ! 1 need thee ! "

Out came Meg, with gray horse-hair hanging about her face, a red and black robe, a staff, and cabalistic signs upon her cloak. Hugo demanded a potion to make Zara adore him and one to destroy Roderigo. Hagar, in a fine dramatic melody, promised both, and proceeded to call up the spirit who would bring the love philter :—

> " Hither, hither, from thy home,
>   Airy sprite, I bid thee come !
> Born of roses, fed on dew,
>   Charms and potions canst thou brew ?
> Bring me here, with elfin speed,
>   The fragrant philter which I need ;
> Make it sweet, and swift and strong ;
>   Spirit, answer now my song ! "

A soft strain of music sounded, and then at the back of the cave appeared a little figure in cloudy white, with glittering wings, golden hair, and a garland of roses on its head. Waving a wand, it sang :—

> " Hither I come,
>   From my airy home,
> Afar in the silver moon ;
>   Take the magic spell,
>   Oh, use it well !
> Or its power will vanish soon——"

and dropping a small gilded bottle at the witch's feet, the spirit vanished. Another chant from Hagar produced another apparition—not a lovely one, for, with a bang, an ugly black imp appeared, and having croaked a reply, tossed a dark bottle at Hugo, and disappeared with a mocking laugh. Having warbled his thanks, and put the potions in his boots, Hugo departed ; and

Hagar informed the audience that, as he had killed a few of her friends in times past, she has cursed him, and intends to thwart his plans, and be revenged on him. Then the curtain fell, and the audience reposed and ate candy while discussing the merits of the play.

A good deal of hammering went on before the curtain rose again ; but when it became evident what a masterpiece of stage carpentering had been got up, no one murmured at the delay. It was truly superb ! A tower rose to the ceiling ; half-way up appeared a window with a lamp burning at it, and behind the white curtain appeared Zara in a lovely blue and silver dress, waiting for Roderigo. He came, in gorgeous array, with plumed cap, red cloak, chestnut love-locks, a guitar, and the boots, of course. Kneeling at the foot of the tower, he sang a serenade in melting tones. Zara replied, and after a musical dialogue, consented to fly. Then came the grand effect of the play. Roderigo produced a rope-ladder with five steps to it, threw up one end, and invited Zara to descend. Timidly she crept from her lattice, put her hand on Roderigo's shoulder, and was about to leap gracefully down, when, " alas ! alas for Zara ! " she forgot her train—it caught in the window ; the tower tottered, leaned forward, fell with a crash, and buried the unhappy lovers in the ruins !

A universal shriek arose, as the russet boots waved wildly from the wreck and a golden head emerged exclaiming, " I told you so ! I told you so ! " With wonderful presence of mind Don Pedro, the cruel sire, rushed in, dragged out his daughter with a hasty aside,—

" Don't laugh ; act as if it was all right ! " and ordering Roderigo up, banished him from the kingdom with wrath and scorn. Though decidedly shaken by the fall of the tower upon him, Roderigo defied the old gentleman, and refused to stir. This dauntless example fired Zara ; she also defied her sire, and he ordered them both to the deepest dungeons of the castle. A stout little retainer came in with chains, and led them away, looking very much frightened, and evidently forgetting the speech he ought to have made.

Act Third was the castle hall ; and here Hagar appeared, having come to free the lovers and finish Hugo. She hears him coming, and hides ; sees him put the potions into two cups of wine, and bid the timid little servant " Bear them to the captives in their cells, and tell them I shall come anon." The servant takes Hugo aside to tell him something, and Hagar changes the cups for two others which are harmless. Ferdinando, the " minion," carries them away, and Hagar puts back the cup which holds the poison meant for Roderigo. Hugo, getting thirsty after a long warble, drinks it, loses his wits, and after a good deal of clutching and stamping falls flat and dies ; while Hagar informs him what she has done, in a song of exquisite power and melody.

This was a truly thrilling scene ; though some persons might have thought that the sudden tumbling down of a quantity of long hair rather marred the effect of the villain's death. He was called before the curtain, and with great propriety appeared leading Hagar, whose singing was considered more wonderful than all the rest of the performance put together.

Act Fourth displayed the despairing Roderigo on the point of stabbing himself, because he had been told that Zara has deserted him. Just as the dagger is at his heart, a lovely song is sung under his window, informing him that Zara is true, but in danger, and he can save her if he will. A key is thrown in, which unlocks the door, and in a spasm of rapture he tears off his chains, and rushes away to find and rescue his lady-love.

Act Fifth opened with a stormy scene between Zara and Don Pedro. He wishes her to go into a convent, but she won't hear of it ; and, after a touching appeal, is about to faint, when Roderigo dashes in, and demands her hand. Don Pedro refuses, because he is not rich. They shout and gesticulate tremendously, but cannot agree, and Roderigo is about to bear away the exhausted Zara, when the timid servant enters with a letter and a bag from Hagar, who has mysteriously disappeared. The letter informs the party that she bequeaths untold wealth to the young pair, and an awful doom to Don Pedro if he doesn't make them happy. The bag is opened, and several quarts of tin money shower down upon the stage, till it is quite glorified with the glitter. This entirely softens the " stern sire ; " he consents without a murmur, all join in a joyful chorus, and the curtain falls upon the lovers kneeling to receive Don Pedro's blessing, in attitudes of the most romantic grace.

Tumultuous applause followed, but received an unexpected check ; for the cot-bed on which the " dress circle " was built suddenly shut up, and extinguished the enthusiastic audience. Roderigo and Don Pedro flew to the rescue, and all were taken out unhurt, though many were speechless with laughter. The excitement had hardly subsided when Hannah appeared, with " Mrs. March's compliments, and would the ladies walk down to supper."

This was a surprise, even to the actors ; and when they saw the table they looked at one another in rapturous amazement. It was like " Marmee " to get up a little treat for them, but anything so fine as this was unheard of since the departed days of plenty. There was ice cream, actually two dishes of it—pink and white—and cake, and fruit, and distracting French bonbons, and in the middle of the table four great bouquets of hot-house flowers !

It quite took their breath away ; and they stared first at the table and then at their mother, who looked as if she enjoyed it immensely.

" Is it fairies ? " asked Amy.

" It's Santa Claus," said Beth.

" Mother did it ; " and Meg smiled her sweetest, in spite of her gray beard and white eyebrows.

" Aunt March had a good fit, and sent the supper," cried Jo, with a sudden inspiration.

" All wrong ; old Mr. Laurence sent it," replied Mrs. March.

" The Laurence boy's grandfather ! What in the world put such a thing into his head ? We don't know him," exclaimed Meg.

" Hannah told one of his servants about your breakfast party ; he is an odd old gentleman, but that pleased him. He knew my father years ago, and he sent me a polite note this afternoon, saying he hoped I would allow him to express his friendly feeling toward my children by sending them a few trifles in honour of the day. I could not refuse, and so you have a little feast at night to make up for the bread and milk breakfast."

" That boy put it into his head, I know he did ! He's a capital fellow, and I wish we could get acquainted. He looks as if he'd like to know us ;

but he's bashful, and Meg is so prim she won't let me speak to him when we pass," said Jo, as the plates went round, and the ice began to melt out of sight, with ohs ! and ahs ! of satisfaction.

" You mean the people who live in the big house next door, don't you ? " asked one of the girls. " My mother knows old Mr. Laurence, but says he's very proud, and don't like to mix with his neighbours. He keeps his grandson shut up when he isn't riding or walking with his tutor, and makes him study dreadfully hard. We invited him to our party, but he didn't come. Mother says he's very nice, though he never speaks to us girls."

" Our cat ran away once, and he brought her back, and we talked over the fence, and were getting on capitally, all about cricket and so on, when he saw Meg coming and walked off. I mean to know him some day, for he needs fun, I'm sure he does," said Jo decidedly.

" I like his manners, and he looks like a little gentleman ; so I've no objection to your knowing him if a proper opportunity comes. He brought the flowers himself, and I should have asked him in if I had been sure what was going on upstairs. He looked so wistful as he went away, hearing the frolic, and evidently having none of his own."

" It's a mercy you didn't, mother," laughed Jo, looking at her boots. " But we'll have another play some time, that he *can* see. Maybe he'll help act ; wouldn't that be jolly ! "

" I never had a bouquet before ; how pretty it is ! " and Meg examined her flowers with great interest.

" They *are* lovely, but Beth's roses are sweeter to me," said Mrs. March, sniffing at the half-dead posy in her belt.

Beth nestled up to her, and whispered softly, " I wish I could send my bunch to father. I'm afraid he isn't having such a merry Christmas as we are."

CHAPTER III

THE LAURENCE BOY

" JO! Jo ! where are you ? " cried Meg, at the foot of the garret stairs. " Here," answered a husky voice from above ; and running up, Meg found her sister eating apples and crying over the *Heir of Redclyffe*, wrapped up in a comforter on an old three-legged sofa by the window. This was Jo's favourite refuge ; and here she loved to retire with half a dozen russets and a nice book, to enjoy the quiet and the society of a pet rat who lived near by, and didn't mind her a particle. As Meg appeared, Scrabble whisked into his hole. Jo shook the tears off her cheeks, and waited to hear the news.

" Such fun ! only see ! a regular note of invitation from Mrs. Gardiner for to-morrow night ! " cried Meg, waving the precious paper, and then proceeding to read it with girlish delight.

" ' Mrs. Gardiner would be happy to see Miss March and Miss Josephine at a little dance on New Year's Eve.' Marmee is willing we should go ; now what *shall* we wear ? "

" What's the use of asking that, when you know we shall wear our poplins, because we haven't got anything else ? " answered Jo, with her mouth full.

" If I only had a silk ! " sighed Meg ; " mother says I may when I'm eighteen, perhaps ; but two years is an everlasting time to wait."

" I'm sure our pops look like silk, and they are nice enough for us. Yours is as good as new, but I forgot the burn and the tear in mine ; whatever shall I do ? The burn shows horridly, and I can't take any out."

" You must sit all you can, and keep your back out of sight ; the front is all right. I shall have a new ribbon for my hair, and Marmee will lend me

" Jo! Jo! where are you?" cried Meg, at the foot of the stairs

her little pearl pin, and my new slippers are lovely, and my gloves will do, though they aren't as nice as I'd like."

" Mine are spoilt with lemonade, and I can't get any new ones, so I shall have to go without," said Jo, who never troubled herself much about dress.

" You *must* have gloves, or I won't go," cried Meg decidedly. " Gloves are more important than anything else ; you can't dance without them, and if you don't I should be *so* mortified."

" Then I'll stay still ; I don't care much for company dancing ; it's no fun to go sailing round : I like to fly about and cut capers."

" You can't ask mother for new ones, they are so expensive, and you are so careless. She said, when you spoilt the others, that she shouldn't get you any more this winter. Can't you fix them any way ? " asked Meg anxiously.

" I can hold them crunched up in my hand, so no one will know how stained they are ; that's all I can do. No ! I'll tell you how we can manage —each wear one good one and carry a bad one ; don't you see ? "

" Your hands are bigger than mine, and you will stretch my glove dreadfully," began Meg, whose gloves were a tender point with her.

" Then I'll go without. I don't care what people say," cried Jo, taking up her book.

" You may have it, you may ! only don't stain it, and do behave nicely ; don't put your hands behind you, or stare, or say ' Christopher Columbus ! ' will you ? "

" Don't worry about me ; I'll be as prim as a dish, and not get into any scrapes, if I can help it. Now go and answer your note, and let me finish this splendid story."

So Meg went away to " accept with thanks," look over her dress, and sing blithely as she did up her one real lace frill ; while Jo finished her story, her apples, and had a game of romps with Scrabble.

On New Year's Eve the parlour was deserted, for the two younger girls played dressing-maids, and the two elder were absorbed in the all-important business of " getting ready for the party."

Simple as the toilets were, there was a great deal of running up and down, laughing and talking, and at one time a strong smell of burnt hair pervaded the house. Meg wanted a few curls about her face, and Jo undertook to pinch the papered locks with a pair of hot tongs.

" Ought they to smoke like that ? " asked Beth, from her perch on the bed.

" It's the dampness drying," replied Jo.

" What a queer smell ! it's like burnt feathers," observed Amy, smoothing her own pretty curls with a superior air.

" There, now I'll take off the papers, and you'll see a cloud of little ringlets," said Jo, putting down the tongs.

She did take off the papers, but no cloud of ringlets appeared, for the hair came with the papers, and the horrified hairdresser laid a row of little scorched bundles on the bureau before her victim.

" Oh, oh, oh ! what *have* you done ? I'm spoilt ! I can't go ! my hair, oh, my hair ! " wailed Meg, looking with despair at the uneven frizzle on her forehead.

" Just my luck ! you shouldn't have asked me to do it. I'm no end sorry, but the tongs were too hot, and so I've made a mess," groaned poor Jo, regarding the black pancakes with tears of regret.

" It isn't spoilt ; just frizzle it, and tie your ribbons so the ends come on your forehead a bit, and it will look like the last fashion. I've seen lots of girls do it so," said Amy consolingly.

" Serves me right for trying to be fine. I wish I'd let my hair alone," cried Meg petulantly.

" So do I ; it was so smooth and pretty. But it will soon grow out again," said Beth, coming to kiss and comfort the shorn sheep.

After various lesser mishaps, Meg was finished at last, and by the united exertions of the family Jo's hair was got up, and her dress on. They looked very well in their simple suits : Meg in silvery drab, with a blue velvet snood, lace frills, and the pearl pin ; Jo in maroon, with a stiff, gentlemanly linen collar, and a white chrysanthemum or two for her only ornament. Each put on one nice light glove, and carried one soiled one, and all pronounced the

effect " quite easy and nice." Meg's high-heeled slippers were dreadfully
tight, and hurt her, though she would not own it ; and Jo's nineteen hairpins
all seemed stuck straight into her head, which was not exactly comfortable ;
but, dear me, let us be elegant or die.

" Have a good time, dearies," said Mrs. March, as the sisters went daintily
down the walk. " Don't eat much supper, and come away at eleven, when
I send Hannah for you." As the gate clashed behind them, a voice cried
from a window,—

" Girls, girls ! *have* you both got nice pocket-handkerchiefs ? "

" Yes, yes, spandy nice, and Meg has Cologne on hers," cried Jo ; adding,
with a laugh, as they went on, " I do believe Marmee would ask that if we
were all running away from an earthquake."

" It is one of her aristocratic tastes, and quite proper ; for a real lady
is always known by neat boots, gloves, and handkerchief," replied Meg,
who had a good many little " aristocratic tastes " of her own.

" Now don't forget to keep the bad breadth out of sight, Jo. Is my
sash right ; and does my hair look *very* bad ? " said Meg, as she turned
from the glass in Mrs. Gardiner's dressing-room, after a prolonged gaze.

" I know I shall forget. If you see me doing anything wrong, you just
remind me by a wink, will you ? " returned Jo, giving her collar a twitch
and her head a hasty brush.

" No, winking isn't lady-like ; I'll lift my eyebrows if anything is wrong,
and nod if you are all right. Now hold your shoulders straight, and take
short steps ; and don't shake hands if you are introduced to any one, it isn't
the thing."

" How *do* you learn all the proper ways ? I never can. Isn't that music
gay ? "

Down they went, feeling a trifle timid, for they seldom went to parties,
and, informal as this little gathering was, it was an event to them. Mrs.
Gardiner, a stately old lady, greeted them kindly, and handed them over to
the eldest of her six daughters. Meg knew Sallie, and was at her ease very
soon ; but Jo, who didn't care much for girls or girlish gossip, stood about
with her back carefully against the wall, and felt as much out of place as a
colt in a flower-garden. Half a dozen jovial lads were talking about skates
in another part of the room, and she longed to go and join them ; for skating
was one of the joys of her life. She telegraphed her wishes to Meg, but the
eyebrows went up so alarmingly that she dared not stir. No one came to
talk to her, and one by one the group near her dwindled away, till she was
left alone. She could not roam about and amuse herself, for the burnt
breadth would show ; so she stared at people rather forlornly till the dancing
began. Meg was asked at once, and the tight slippers tripped about so
briskly that none would have guessed the pain their wearer suffered smilingly.
Jo saw a big red-headed youth approaching her corner, and fearing he meant
to engage her, she slipped into a curtained recess, intending to peep and
enjoy herself in peace. Unfortunately, another bashful person had chosen
the same refuge ; for, as the curtain fell behind her, she found herself face
to face with the " Laurence boy."

" Dear me, I didn't know any one was here ! " stammered Jo, preparing
to back out as speedily as she had bounced in.

" But you put it into his head, didn't you ? " said Jo

But the boy laughed, and said pleasantly, though he looked a little startled,—

" Don't mind me ; stay, if you like."

" Shan't I disturb you ? "

" Not a bit ; I only came here because I don't know many people, and felt rather strange at first, you know."

" So did I. Don't go away, please, unless you'd rather."

The boy sat down again and looked at his boots ; till Jo said, trying to be polite and easy,—

" I think I've had the pleasure of seeing you before. You live near us, don't you ? "

" Next door ; " and he looked up and laughed outright ; for Jo's prim manner was rather funny when he remembered how they had chatted about cricket when he brought the cat home.

That put Jo at her ease ; and she laughed too, as she said, in her heartiest way,—

" We did have such a good time over your nice Christmas present."

" Grandpa sent it."

" But you put it into his head, didn't you, now ? "

" How is your cat, Miss March ? " asked the boy, trying to look sober, while his black eyes shone with fun.

" Nicely, thank you, Mr. Laurence ; but I ain't Miss March, I'm only Jo," returned the young lady.

" I'm not Mr. Laurence, I'm only Laurie."

" Laurie Laurence ; what an odd name."

" My first name is Theodore, but I don't like it ; for the fellows call me Dora ; so I made them say Laurie instead."

" I hate my name too—so sentimental ! I wish every one would say Jo, instead of Josephine. How did you make the boys stop calling you Dora ? "

" I thrashed 'em."

" I can't thrash Aunt March, so I suppose I shall have to bear it ; " and Jo resigned herself with a sigh.

" Don't you like to dance, Miss Jo ? " asked Laurie, looking as if he thought the name suited her.

" I like it well enough if there is plenty of room, and every one is lively. In a place like this I'm sure to upset something, tread on people's toes, or do something dreadful ; so I keep out of mischief, and let Meg do the pretty. Don't you dance ? "

" Sometimes. You see, I've been abroad a good many years, and haven't been about enough yet to know how you do things here."

" Abroad ! " cried Jo ; " oh, tell me about it ! I love dearly to hear people describe their travels."

Laurie didn't seem to know where to begin ; but Jo's eager questions soon set him going ; and he told her how he had been at school at Vevey, where the boys never wore hats, and had a fleet of boats on the lake, and for holiday fun went walking trips about Switzerland with their teachers.

" Don't I wish I'd been there ! " cried Jo. " Did you go to Paris ? '

" We spent last winter there."

" Can you talk French ? "

" We were not allowed to speak anything else at Vevey."

" Do say some. I can read it, but can't pronounce."

" Quel nom a cette jeune demoiselle en les pantoufles jolies ? " said Laurie good-naturedly.

" How nicely you do it ! Let me see—you said, ' Who is the young lady in the pretty slippers,' didn't you ? "

" Oui, mademoiselle."

" It's my sister Margaret, and you knew it was ! Do you think she is pretty ? "

" Yes ; she makes me think of the German girls, she looks so fresh and quiet, and dances like a lady."

Jo quite glowed with pleasure at this boyish praise of her sister, and stored it up to repeat to Meg. Both peeped, and criticised, and chatted, till they felt like old acquaintances. Laurie's bashfulness soon wore off, for Jo's gentlemanly demeanour amused and set him at his ease, and Jo was her merry self again, because her dress was forgotten, and nobody lifted her eyebrows at her. She liked the " Laurence boy " better than ever, and took several good looks at him, so that she might describe him to the girls ; for they had no brothers, very few male cousins, and boys were almost unknown creatures to them.

" Curly black hair, brown skin, big black eyes, long nose, nice teeth, little hands and feet, tall as I am ; very polite for a boy, and altogether jolly. Wonder how old he is ? "

It was on the tip of Jo's tongue to ask ; but she checked herself in time, and with unusual tact tried to find out in a roundabout way.

" I suppose you are going to college soon ? I see you are pegging away at your books—no, I mean studying hard ; " and Jo blushed at the dreadful " pegging " which had escaped her.

Laurie smiled, but didn't seem shocked, and answered, with a shrug,—

" Not for two or three years yet ; I won't go before seventeen, anyway."

" Aren't you about fifteen ? " asked Jo, looking at the tall lad, whom she had imagined seventeen already.

" Sixteen, next month."

" How I wish I was going to college ; you don't look as if you liked it."

" I hate it ; nothing but grinding or sky-larking ; and I don't like the way fellows do either in this country."

" What do you like ? "

" To live in Italy, and to enjoy myself in my own way."

Jo wanted very much to ask what his own way was ; but his black brows looked rather threatening as he knit them, so she changed the subject by saying, as her foot kept time, " That's splendid polka ; why don't you go and try it ? "

" If you will come too," he answered, with a queer little French bow.

" I can't ; for I told Meg I wouldn't because——" there Jo stopped, and looked undecided whether to tell or to laugh.

" Because what ? " asked Laurie curiously.

" You won't tell ? "

" Never ! "

" Well, I have a bad trick of standing before the fire, and so I burn my frocks, and I scorched this one ; and, though it's nicely mended, it shows, and Meg told me to keep still, so no one would see it. You may laugh if you want to ; it's funny, I know."

But Laurie didn't laugh ; he only looked down a minute, and the expression of his face puzzled Jo ; when he said very gently,—

" Never mind that ; I'll tell you how we can manage ; there's a long hall out there, and we can dance grandly, and no one will see us. Please come."

Jo thanked him, and gladly went, and wishing she had two neat gloves when she saw the nice pearl-coloured ones her partner put on. The hall was empty, and they had a grand polka, for Laurie danced well, and taught her the German step, which delighted Jo, being full of swing and spring. When the music stopped they sat down on the stairs to get their breath, and Laurie was in the midst of an account of a students' festival at Heidelberg, when Meg appeared in search of her sister. She beckoned, and Jo reluctantly followed her into a side-room, where she found her on a sofa holding her foot, and looking pale.

" I've sprained my ankle. That stupid high heel turned, and gave me a horrid wrench. It aches so, I can hardly stand, and I don't know how I'm ever going to get home," she said, rocking to and fro in pain.

" I knew you'd hurt your feet with those silly things. I'm sorry ; but I don't see what you can do, except get a carriage, or stay here all night," answered Jo, softly rubbing the poor ankle as she spoke.

" I can't have a carriage without its costing ever so much ; I dare say I can't get one at all, for most people come in their own, and it's a long way to the stable, and no one to send."

" I'll go."

" No, indeed ; it's past ten, and dark as Egypt. I can't stop here, for the house is full ; Sallie has some girls staying with her. I'll rest till Hannah comes, and then do the best I can."

" I'll ask Laurie ; he will go," said Jo, looking relieved as the idea occurred to her.

" Mercy, no ! don't ask or tell any one. Get me my rubbers, and put these slippers with our things. I can't dance any more ; but as soon as supper is over, watch for Hannah, and tell me the minute she comes."

" They are going out to supper now. I'll stay with you ; I'd rather."

" No, dear ; run along, and bring me some coffee. I'm so tired, I can't stir."

So Meg reclined, with the rubbers well hidden, and Jo went blundering away to the dining-room, which she found after going into a china-closet and opening the door of a room where old Mr. Gardiner was taking a little private refreshment. Making a dive at the table, she secured the coffee, which she immediately spilt, thereby making the front of her dress as bad as the back.

" Oh, dear ! what a blunderbuss I am ! " exclaimed Jo, finishing Meg's glove by scrubbing her gown with it.

" Can I help you ? " said a friendly voice ; and there was Laurie, with a full cup in one hand and a plate of ice in the other.

" I was trying to get something for Meg, who is very tired, and some one shook me, and here I am, in a nice state," answered Jo, glancing dismally from the stained skirt to the coffee-coloured glove.

" Too bad ! I was looking for some one to give this to ; may I take it to your sister ? "

" Oh, thank you ; I'll show you where she is. I don't offer to take it myself, for I should only get into another scrape if I did."

Jo led the way, and, as if used to waiting on ladies, Laurie drew up a little table, brought a second instalment of coffee and ice for Jo, and was so obliging that even particular Meg pronounced him a " nice boy." They had a merry time over the bonbons and mottoes, and were in the midst of a quiet game of " buzz " with two or three other young people who had strayed in, when Hannah appeared. Meg forgot her foot, and rose so quickly that she was forced to catch hold of Jo, with an exclamation of pain.

" Hush ! don't say anything," she whispered ; adding aloud, " It's nothing ; I turned my foot a little—that's all," and limped upstairs to put her things on.

Hannah scolded, Meg cried, and Jo was at her wits' end, till she decided to take things into her own hands. Slipping out, she ran down, and finding a servant, asked if he could get her a carriage. It happened to be a hired waiter, who knew nothing about the neighbourhood ; and Jo was looking round for help, when Laurie, who had heard what she said, came up and offered his grandfather's carriage, which had just come for him, he said.

" It's so early—you can't mean to go yet," began Jo, looking relieved, but hesitating to accept the offer.

" I always go early—I do, truly. Please let me take you home ; it's all on my way, you know, and it rains, they say."

That settled it ; and, telling him of Meg's mishap, Jo gratefully accepted, and rushed up to bring down the rest of the party. Hannah hated rain as much as a cat does ; so she made no trouble, and they rolled away in the luxurious carriage, feeling very festive and elegant. Laurie went on the box, so Meg could keep her foot up, and the girls talked over their party in freedom.

" I had a capital time ; did you ? " asked Jo, rumpling up her hair, and making herself comfortable.

" Yes, till I hurt myself. Sallie's friend, Annie Moffat, took a fancy to me, and asked me to come and spend a week with her when Sallie does. She is going in the spring, when the Opera comes, and it will be perfectly splendid if mother only lets me go," answered Meg, cheering up at the thought.

" I saw you dancing with the red-headed man I ran away from ; was he nice ? "

" Oh, very ! his hair is auburn, not red ; and he was very polite, and I had a delicious redowa with him ! "

" He looked like a grasshopper in a fit when he did the new step. Laurie and I couldn't help laughing ; did you hear us ? "

" No ; but it was very rude. What *were* you about all that time, hidden away there ? "

Jo told her adventures, and by the time she had finished they were at home. With many thanks, they said, " Good-night," and crept in, hoping to disturb no one ; but the instant their door creaked, two little night-caps bobbed up, and two sleepy but eager voices cried out,—

" Tell about the party ! tell about the party ! "

With what Meg called " a great want of manners," Jo had saved some bonbons for the little girls, and they soon subsided, after hearing the most thrilling events of the evening.

" I declare, it really seems like being a fine young lady, to come home from my party in my carriage, and sit in my dressing-gown, with a maid to wait on me," said Meg, as Jo bound up her foot with arnica, and brushed her hair.

" I don't believe fine young ladies enjoy themselves a bit more than we do, in spite of our burnt hair, old gowns, one glove apiece, and tight slippers that sprain our ankles when we are silly enough to wear them." And I think Jo was quite right.

CHAPTER IV

BURDENS

" OH dear, how hard it does seem to take up our packs and go on," sighed Meg, the morning after the party ; for, now the holidays were over, the week of merry-making did not fit her for going on easily with the task she never liked.

" I wish it was Christmas or New Year all the time ; wouldn't it be fun ? " answered Jo, yawning dismally.

" We shouldn't enjoy ourselves half so much as we do now. But it does seem so nice to have little suppers and bouquets, and go to parties, and drive home in a carriage, and read and rest. It's like other people, you know, and I always envy girls who do such things ; I'm so fond of luxury," said Meg, trying to decide which of two shabby gowns was the least shabby.

" Well, we can't have it : so don't let's grumble, but shoulder our bundles and trudge along as cheerfully as Marmee does. I'm sure Aunt March is a regular Old Man of the Sea to me, but I suppose when I've learned to carry her without complaining, she will tumble off, or get so light that I shan't mind her."

This idea tickled Jo's fancy, and put her in good spirits ; but Meg didn't brighten, for her burden, consisting of four spoilt children, seemed heavier than ever. She hadn't heart enough even to make herself pretty, as usual, by putting on a blue neck-ribbon, and dressing her hair in the most becoming way.

" Where's the use of looking nice when no one sees me but those cross fidgets, and no one cares whether I'm pretty or not," she muttered, shutting her drawer with a jerk. " I shall have to toil and moil all my days, with only little bits of fun now and then, and get old and ugly and sour, because I'm poor and can't enjoy my life as other girls do. It's a shame ! "

So Meg went down, wearing an injured look, and wasn't at all agreeable at breakfast-time. Every one seemed rather out of sorts, and inclined to croak. Beth had a headache, and lay on the sofa trying to comfort herself with the cat and three kittens ; Amy was fretting because her lessons were not learned, and she couldn't find her rubbers ; Jo *would* whistle, and make a great racket getting ready ; Mrs. March was very busy trying to finish a letter, which must go at once ; and Hannah had the grumps, for being late didn't suit her.

" There never *was* such a cross family ! " cried Jo, losing her temper when she had upset an inkstand, broken both boot-lacings, and sat down upon her hat.

" You're the crossest person in it ! " returned Amy, washing out the sum that was all wrong with the tears that had fallen on her slate.

" Beth, if you don't keep those horrid cats down cellar I'll have them drowned," exclaimed Meg angrily, as she tried to get rid of the kitten, who had swarmed up her back, and stuck like a burr just out of reach.

Jo laughed, Meg scolded, Beth implored, and Amy wailed because she couldn't remember how much nine times twelve was.

" Girls ! girls ! do be quiet one moment. I *must* get this off by the early mail, and you drive me distracted with your worry," cried Mrs. March, crossing out the third spoiled sentence in her letter.

There was a momentary lull, broken by Hannah, who bounced in, laid two hot turnovers on the table, and bounced out again. These turnovers were an institution ; and the girls called them " muffs," for they had no others, and found the hot pies very comforting to their hands on cold mornings. Hannah never forgot to make them, no matter how busy or grumpy she might be, for the walk was long and bleak ; the poor things got no other lunch, and were seldom home before three.

" Cuddle your cats, and get over your headache, Bethy. Good-bye,

Marmee ; we are a set of rascals this morning, but we'll come home regular angels. Now, then, Meg ; " and Jo tramped away, feeling that the pilgrims were not setting out as they ought to do.

They always looked back before turning the corner, for their mother was always at the window, to nod, and smile, and wave her hand to them. Somehow, it seemed as if they couldn't have got through the day without that, for whatever their mood might be, the last glimpse of that motherly face was sure to affect them like sunshine.

" If Marmee shook her fist, instead of kissing her hand to us, it would serve us right, for more ungrateful minxes than we are were never seen," cried Jo, taking a remorseful satisfaction in the slushy road and bitter wind.

" Don't use such dreadful expressions," said Meg, from the depths of the veil in which she had shrouded herself, like a nun sick of the world.

" I like good strong words, that mean something," replied Jo, catching her hat as it took a leap off her head, preparatory to flying away altogether.

" Call yourself any names you like ; but *I* am neither a rascal nor a minx, and I don't choose to be called so."

" You're a blighted being, and decidedly cross to-day, because you can't sit in the lap of luxury all the time. Poor dear ! just wait till I make my fortune, and you shall revel in carriages, and ice-cream, and high-heeled slippers, and posies, and red-headed boys to dance with."

" How ridiculous you are, Jo ! " but Meg laughed at the nonsense, and felt better in spite of herself.

" Lucky for you I am ; for if I put on crushed airs, and tried to be dismal, as you do, we should be in a nice state. Thank goodness, I can always find something funny to keep me up. Don't croak any more, but come home jolly, there's a dear."

Jo gave her sister an encouraging pat on the shoulder as they parted for the day, each going a different way, each hugging her little warm turnover, and each trying to be cheerful in spite of wintry weather, hard work, and the unsatisfied desires of pleasure-loving youth.

When Mr. March lost his property in trying to help an unfortunate friend, the two eldest girls begged to be allowed to do something toward their own support, at least. Believing that they could not begin too early to cultivate energy, industry, and independence, their parents consented, and both fell to work with the hearty good-will which, in spite of all obstacles, is sure to succeed at last. Margaret found a place as nursery governess, and felt rich with her small salary. As she said, she *was* " fond of luxury," and her chief trouble was poverty. She found it harder to bear than the others, because she could remember a time when home was beautiful, life full of ease and pleasure, and want of any kind unknown. She tried not to be envious or discontented, but it was very natural that the young girl should long for pretty things, gay friends, accomplishments, and a happy life. At the Kings' she daily saw all she wanted, for the children's older sisters were just out, and Meg caught frequent glimpses of dainty ball-dresses and bouquets, heard lively gossip about theatres, concerts, sleighing-parties, and merry-makings of all kinds, and saw money lavished on trifles which would have been so precious to her. Poor Meg seldom complained, but a sense of injustice made her feel bitter toward every one sometimes, for she had not yet learned to know how rich she was in the blessings which alone can make life happy.

Jo happened to suit Aunt March, who was lame, and needed an active person to wait upon her. The childless old lady had offered to adopt one of the girls when the troubles came, and was much offended because her offer was declined. Other friends told the Marches that they had lost all chance of being remembered in the rich old lady's will ; but the unworldly Marches only said,—

" We can't give up our girls for a dozen fortunes. Rich or poor, we will keep together and be happy in one another."

The old lady wouldn't speak to them for a time, but happening to meet Jo at a friend's, something in her comical face and blunt manners struck the old lady's fancy, and she proposed to take her for a companion. This did not suit Jo at all ; but she accepted the place, since nothing better appeared, and, to every one's surprise, got on remarkably well with her irascible relative. There was an occasional tempest, and once Jo had marched home, declaring she couldn't bear it any longer ; but Aunt March always cleared up quickly, and sent for her back again with such urgency that she could not refuse, for in her heart she rather liked the peppery old lady.

I suspect that the real attraction was a large library of fine books, which was left to dust and spiders since Uncle March died. Jo remembered the kind old gentleman who used to let her build railroads and bridges with his big dictionaries, tell her stories about the queer pictures in his Latin books, and buy her cards of gingerbread whenever he met her in the street. The dim, dusty room, with the busts staring down from the tall bookcases, the cosy chairs, the globes, and, best of all, the wilderness of books, in which she could wander where she liked, made the library a region of bliss to her. The moment Aunt March took her nap or was busy with company, Jo hurried to this quiet place, and, curling herself up in the big chair, devoured poetry, romance, history, travels, and pictures, like a regular bookworm. But like all happiness, it did not last long ; for as sure as she had just reached the heart of the story, the sweetest verse of the song, or the most perilous adventure of her traveller, a shrill voice called " Josy-phine ! Josy-phine ! " and she had to leave her paradise to wind yarn, wash the poodle, or read Belsham's Essays by the hour together.

Jo's ambition was to do something very splendid ; what it was she had no idea, but left it for time to tell her ; and, meanwhile, found her greatest affliction in the fact that she couldn't read, run, and ride as much as she liked. A quick temper, sharp tongue, and restless spirit were always getting her into scrapes, and her life was a series of ups and downs, which were both comic and pathetic. But the training she received at Aunt March's was just what she needed ; and the thought that she was doing something to support herself made her happy, in spite of the perpetual " Josy-phine ! "

Beth was too bashful to go to school ; it had been tried, but she suffered so much that it was given up, and she did her lessons at home, with her father. Even when he went away, and her mother was called to devote her skill and energy to Soldiers' Aid Societies, Beth went faithfully on by herself, and did the best she could. She was a housewifely little creature, and helped Hannah keep home neat and comfortable for the workers, never thinking of any reward but to be loved. Long, quiet days she spent, not lonely nor idle ; for her little world was peopled with imaginary friends, and she was by nature a busy bee. There were six dolls to be taken up and dressed every morning ; for Beth was a child still, and loved her pets as well as ever ; not one whole or handsome one among them ; all were outcasts till Beth took them in ; for, when her sisters outgrew these idols, they passed to her, because Amy would have nothing old or ugly. Beth cherished them all the more tenderly for that very reason, and set up an hospital for infirm dolls. No pins ever stuck into their cotton vitals ; no harsh words or blows were ever given them ; no neglect ever saddened the heart of the most repulsive, but all were fed and clothed, nursed and caressed, with an affection which never failed. One forlorn fragment of *dollanity* had belonged to Jo ; and, having led a tempestuous life, was left a wreck in the rag-bag, from which dreary poor-house it was rescued by Beth, and taken to her refuge. Having no top to its head, she tied on a neat little cap, and, as both arms and legs were gone, she hid these deficiencies by folding it in a blanket, and devoting her best bed to this chronic invalid. If any one had known the care lavished on that dolly, I think it would have touched their hearts, even while they laughed. She brought it bits of bouquets ; she read to it, took it out to breathe the air, hidden under her coat ; she sang it lullabies, and never went to bed without kissing its dirty face, and whispering tenderly, " I hope you'll have a good night, my poor dear."

Beth had her troubles as well as the others ; and not being an angel, but a very human little girl, she often " wept a little weep," as Jo said, because she couldn't take music lessons and have a fine piano. She loved music so dearly, tried so hard to learn, and practised away so patiently at the jingling old instrument, that it did seem as if some one (not to hint Aunt March) ought to help her. Nobody did, however, and nobody saw Beth wipe the tears off the yellow keys that wouldn't keep in tune, when she was all alone. She sang like a little lark about her work, never was too tired to play for Marmee and the girls, and day after day said hopefully to herself, " I know I'll get my music sometime, if I'm good."

There are many Beths in the world, shy and quiet, sitting in corners till needed, and living for others so cheerfully that no one sees the sacrifices till the little cricket on the hearth stops chirping, and the sweet, sunshiny presence vanishes, leaving silence and shadow behind.

If anybody had asked Amy what the greatest trial of her life was, she would have answered at once, " My nose." When she was a baby, Jo had accidentally dropped her into the coal-hod, and Amy insisted that the fall had ruined her nose for ever. It was not big, nor red, like poor " Petrea's ; " it was only rather flat, and all the pinching in the world could not give it an aristocratic point. No one minded it but herself, and it was doing its best to grow, but Amy felt deeply the want of a Grecian nose, and drew whole sheets of handsome ones to console herself.

" Little Raphael," as her sisters called her, had a decided talent for drawing, and was never so happy as when copying flowers, designing fairies, or illustrating stories with queer specimens of art. Her teachers complained that, instead of doing her sums, she covered her slate with animals ; the blank pages of her atlas were used to copy maps on, and caricatures of the

" Little Raphael " had a decided talent for drawing

most ludicrous description came fluttering out of all her books at unlucky moments. She got through her lessons as well as she could, and managed to escape reprimands by being a model of deportment. She was a great favourite with her mates, being good-tempered, and possessing the happy art of pleasing without effort. Her little airs and graces were much admired, so were her accomplishments ; for, besides her drawing, she could play twelve tunes, crochet, and read French without mispronouncing more than two-thirds of the words. She had a plaintive way of saying, " When papa was rich we did so-and-so," which was very touching ; and her long words were considered " perfectly elegant " by the girls.

Amy was in a fair way to be spoilt ; for every one petted her, and her small vanities and selfishness were growing nicely. One thing, however, rather quenched her vanities : she had to wear her cousin's clothes. Now Florence's mamma hadn't a particle of taste, and Amy suffered deeply at having to wear a red instead of a blue bonnet, unbecoming gowns, and fussy aprons that did not fit. Everything was good, well made, and little worn ; but Amy's artistic eyes were much afflicted, especially this winter, when her school dress was a dull purple, with yellow dots—and no trimming.

" My only comfort," she said to Meg, with tears in her eyes, " is that mother don't take tucks in my dresses whenever I'm naughty, as Maria Parks' mother does. My dear, it's really dreadful ; for sometimes she is so bad, her frock is up to her knees, and she can't come to school. When I think of this *deggerredation*, I feel that I can bear even my flat nose and purple gown with yellow sky-rockets on it."

Meg was Amy's confidante and monitor, and, by some strange attraction of opposites, Jo was gentle Beth's. To Jo alone did the shy girl tell her thoughts ; and over her big, harum-scarum sister Beth unconsciously exercised more influence than any one in the family. The two older girls were a great deal to each other, but both took one of the younger into their keeping, and watched over them in their own way, " playing mother " they called it, and put their sisters in the places of discarded dolls, with the maternal instinct of little women.

" Has anybody got anything to tell ? It's been such a dismal day, I'm really dying for some amusement," said Meg, as they sat sewing together that evening.

" I had a queer time with aunt to-day, and, as I got the best of it, I'll tell you about it," began Jo, who dearly loved to tell stories. " I was reading that everlasting Belsham, and droning away as I always do, for aunt soon drops off, and then I take out some nice book, and read like fury, till she wakes up. I actually made myself sleepy ; and, before she began to nod, I gave such a gape that she asked me what I meant by opening my mouth wide enough to take the whole book in at once.

" ' I wish I could, and be done with it,' said I, trying not to be saucy.

" Then she gave me a long lecture on my sins, and told me to sit and think over them while she just ' lost ' herself for a moment. She never finds herself very soon ; so the minute her cap began to bob, like a top-heavy dahlia, I whipped the *Vicar of Wakefield* out of my pocket, and read away, with one eye on him, and one on aunt. I'd just got to where they all tumbled into the water, when I forgot and laughed out loud. Aunt woke up ; and, being good-natured after her nap, told me to read a bit, and show what frivolous work I preferred to the worthy and instructive Belsham. I did my very best, and she liked it, though she only said,—

" ' I don't understand what it's all about ; go back and begin it, child.'

" Back I went, and made the Primroses as interesting as ever I could. Once I was wicked enough to stop in a thrilling place, and say meekly, ' I'm afraid it tires you, ma'am ; shan't I stop now ? '

" She caught up her knitting, which had dropped out of her hands, gave me a sharp look through her specs, and said in her short way,—

" ' Finish the chapter, and don't be impertinent, miss.' "

" Did she own she liked it ? " asked Meg.

" Oh, bless you, no ! but she let old Belsham rest ; and, when I ran back after my gloves this afternoon, there she was, so hard at the *Vicar*, that she did not hear me laugh as I danced a jig in the hall, because of the good time coming. What a pleasant life she might have, if she only chose. I don't envy her much, in spite of her money, for, after all, rich people have about as many worries as poor ones, I guess," added Jo.

" That reminds me," said Meg, " that I've got something to tell. It isn't funny, like Jo's story, but I have thought about it a good deal as I came home. At the King's to-day I found everybody in a flurry, and one of the children said that her oldest brother had done something dreadful, and papa had sent him away. I heard Mrs. King crying and Mr. King talking very loud, and Grace and Ellen turned away their faces when they passed me, so I shouldn't see how red their eyes were. I didn't ask any questions, of course ; but I felt so sorry for them, and was rather glad I hadn't any wild brothers to do wicked things and disgrace the family."

"I think being disgraced in school is a great deal try*inger* than anything bad boys can do," said Amy, shaking her head, as if her experience of life had been a large one. "Susie Perkins came to school to-day with a lovely red carnelian ring; I wanted it dreadfully, and wished I was her with all my might. Well, she drew a picture of Mr. Davis, with a monstrous nose and a hump, and the words, 'Young ladies, my eye is upon you!' coming out of his mouth in a balloon thing. We were laughing over it, when all at once his eye *was* on us, and he ordered Susie to bring up her slate. She was *parry*lised with fright, but she went; and, oh, what *do* you think he did? He took her by the ear, the ear! just fancy how horrid! and led her to the recitation platform, and made her stand there half an hour, holding that slate so every one could see."

"Didn't the girls shout at the picture?" asked Jo, who relished the scrape.

"Laugh! not a one; they all sat as still as mice, and Susie cried quarts, I know she did. I didn't envy her then, for I felt that millions of carnelian rings wouldn't have made me happy after that. I never, never should have got over such an agonising mortification"; and Amy went on with her work, in the proud consciousness of virtue, and the successful utterance of two long words in a breath.

"I saw something that I liked this morning, and I meant to tell it at dinner, but I forgot," said Beth, putting Jo's topsy-turvy basket in order as she talked. "When I went to get some oysters for Hannah, Mr. Laurence was in the fish shop, but he didn't see me, for I kept behind a barrel, and he was busy with Mr. Cutter, the fishman. A poor woman came in with a pail and a mop, and asked Mr. Cutter if he would let her do some scrubbing

"Finish the chapter and don't be impertinent, miss"

for a bit of fish, because she hadn't any dinner for her children, and had been disappointed of a day's work. Mr. Cutter was in a hurry, and said, ' No,' rather crossly ; so she was going away, looking hungry and sorry, when Mr. Laurence hooked up a big fish with the crooked end of his cane, and held it out to her. She was so glad and surprised she took it right in her arms, and thanked him over and over. He told her to ' go along and cook it,' and she hurried off, so happy ! Wasn't it nice of him ? Oh, she did look so funny, hugging the big slippery fish, and hoping Mr. Laurence's bed in heaven would be ' aisy.' "

When they had laughed at Beth's story, they asked their mother for one

Mrs. March smiled, and began at once ; for she had told stories to this little audience for many years, and knew how to please them.

" Once upon a time there were four girls, who had enough to eat, and drink, and wear, a good many comforts and pleasures, kind friends and parents, who loved them dearly, and yet they were not contented." (Here the listeners stole sly looks at one another, and began to sew diligently.) " These girls were anxious to be good, and made many excellent resolutions, but somehow they did not keep them very well, and were constantly saying, ' If we only had this,' or, ' If we could only do that,' quite forgetting how much they already had, and how many pleasant things they actually could do ; so they asked an old woman what spell they could use to make them happy, and she said, ' When you feel discontented, think over your blessings, and be grateful.' " (Here Jo looked up quickly, as if about to speak, but changed her mind, seeing that the story was not done yet.)

" Being sensible girls, they decided to try her advice, and soon were surprised to see how well off they were. One discovered that money couldn't keep shame and sorrow out of rich people's houses ; another, that, though she was poor, she was a great deal happier with her youth, health, and good spirits than a certain fretful, feeble old lady, who couldn't enjoy her comforts ; a third, that, disagreeable as it was to help get dinner, it was harder still to have to go begging for it ; and the fourth, that even carnelian rings were not so valuable as good behaviour. So they agreed to stop complaining, to enjoy the blessings already possessed, and try to deserve them, lest they should be taken away entirely, instead of increased ; and I believe they were never disappointed, or sorry that they took the old woman's advice."

" Now, Marmee, that is very cunning of you to turn our own stories against us, and give us a sermon instead of a ' spin,' " cried Meg.

" I like that kind of sermon ; it's the sort father used to tell us," said Beth thoughtfully, putting the needles straight on Jo's cushion.

" I don't complain near as much as the others do, and I shall be more careful than ever now, for I've had warning from Susie's downfall," said Amy morally.

" We needed that lesson, and we won't forget it. If we do, you just say to us as Old Chloe did in *Uncle Tom*—' Tink ob yer marcies, chillen, tink ob yer marcies,' " added Jo, who could not for the life of her help getting a morsel of fun out of the little sermon, though she took it to heart as much as any of them.

CHAPTER V

BEING NEIGHBOURLY

"WHAT in the world are you going to do now, Jo?" asked Meg, one snowy afternoon, as her sister came clumping through the hall, in rubber boots, old sack and hood, with a broom in one hand and a shovel in the other.

"Going out for exercise," answered Jo, with a mischievous twinkle in her eyes.

"I should think two long walks this morning would have been enough. It's cold and dull out, and I advise you to stay, warm and dry, by the fire, as I do," said Meg, with a shiver.

"Never take advice; can't keep still all day, and not being a pussy-cat, I don't like to doze by the fire. I like adventures, and I'm going to find some."

Meg went back to toast her feet, and read *Ivanhoe*, and Jo began to dig paths with great energy. The snow was light; and with her broom she soon swept a path all round the garden, for Beth to walk in when the sun came out, and the invalid dolls needed air. Now the garden separated the Marches' house from that of Mr. Laurence; both stood in a suburb of the city, which was still country-like, with groves and lawns, large gardens and quiet streets. A low hedge parted the two estates. On one side was an old brown house, looking rather bare and shabby, robbed of the vines that in summer covered its walls, and the flowers which then surrounded it. On the other side was a stately stone mansion, plainly betokening every sort of comfort and luxury, from the big coach-house and well-kept grounds to the conservatory, and the glimpses of lovely things one caught between the rich curtains. Yet it seemed a lonely, lifeless sort of house; for no children frolicked on the lawn, no motherly face ever smiled at the windows, and few people went in and out, except the old gentleman and his grandson.

To Jo's lively fancy this fine house seemed a kind of enchanted palace, full of splendours and delights, which no one enjoyed. She had long wanted to behold these hidden glories, and to know the "Laurence boy," who looked as if he would like to be known, if he only knew how to begin. Since the party, she had been more eager than ever, and had planned many ways of making friends with him; but he had not been lately seen, and Jo began to think he had gone away, when she one day spied a brown face at an upper window, looking wistfully down into their garden, where Beth and Amy were snowballing one another.

"That boy is suffering for society and fun," she said to herself. "His grandpa don't know what's good for him, and keeps him shut up all alone. He needs a lot of jolly boys to play with, or somebody young and lively. I've a great mind to go over and tell the old gentleman so."

The idea amused Jo, who liked to do daring things, and was always scandalising Meg by her queer performances. The plan of "going over" was not forgotten; and when the snowy afternoon came, Jo resolved to try what could be done. She saw Mr. Laurence drive off, and then sallied out to dig her way down to the hedge, where she paused, and took a survey. All quiet ; curtains down at the lower windows ; servants out of sight, and nothing human visible but a curly black head leaning on a thin hand, at the upper window.

" There he is," thought Jo ; " poor boy ! all alone, and sick, this dismal day ! It's a shame ! I'll toss up a snowball, and make him look out, and then say a kind word to him."

Up went a handful of soft snow, and the head turned at once, showing a face which lost its listless look in a minute, as the big eyes brightened and the mouth began to smile. Jo nodded, and laughed, and flourished her broom as she called out,—

" How do you do ? Are you sick ? "

Laurie opened the window and croaked out as hoarsely as a raven,—

" Better, thank you. I've had a horrid cold, and been shut up a week."

" I'm sorry. What do you amuse yourself with ? "

" Nothing ; it's as dull as tombs up here."

" Don't you read ? "

" Not much ; they won't let me."

" Can't somebody read to you ? "

" Grandpa does, sometimes ; but my books don't interest him, and I hate to ask Brooke all the time."

" Have some one come and see you, then."

" There isn't any one I'd like to see. Boys make such a row, and my head is weak."

" Isn't there some nice girl who'd read and amuse you ? Girls are quiet, and like to play nurse."

" Don't know any."

" You know me," began Jo, then laughed, and stopped.

" So I do ! Will you come, please ? " cried Laurie.

" I'm not quiet and nice ; but I'll come, if mother will let me. I'll go and ask her. Shut the window like a good boy, and wait till I come."

With that Jo shouldered her broom and marched into the house, wondering what they would all say to her. Laurie was in a little flutter of excitement at the idea of having company, and flew about to get ready ; for as Mrs. March said, he was " a little gentleman," and did honour to the coming guest by brushing his curly pate, putting on a fresh collar, and trying to tidy up the room, which, in spite of half a dozen servants, was anything but neat. Presently there came a loud ring, then a decided voice, asking for " Mr. Laurie," and a surprised-looking servant came running up to announce a young lady.

" All right, show her up ; it's Miss Jo," said Laurie, going to the door of his little parlour to meet Jo, who appeared, looking rosy and kind, and quite at ease, with a covered dish in one hand and Beth's three kittens in the other.

" Here I am, bag and baggage," she said briskly. " Mother sent her love, and was glad if I could do anything for you. Meg wanted me to bring some of her blanc-mange ; she makes it very nice ; and Beth thought her cats would be comforting. I knew you'd shout at them, but I couldn't refuse, she was so anxious to do something."

It so happened that Beth's funny loan was just the thing ; for, in laughing over the kits, Laurie forgot his bashfulness, and grew sociable at once.

"That looks too pretty to eat," he said, smiling with pleasure as Jo uncovered the dish and showed the blanc-mange, surrounded by a garland of green leaves and the scarlet flowers of Amy's pet geranium.

"It isn't anything, only they all felt kindly, and wanted to show it. Tell the girl to put it away for your tea ; it's so simple, you can eat it ; and being soft, it will slip down without hurting your sore throat. What a cosy room this is !"

"It might be, if it was kept nice ; but the maids are lazy, and I don't know how to make them mind. It worries me though."

"I'll right it up in two minutes ; for it only needs to have the hearth brushed, so—and the things stood straight on the mantelpiece, so—and the books put here, and the bottles there, and your sofa turned from the light, and the pillows plumped up a bit. Now, then, you're fixed."

And so he was ; for, as she laughed and talked, Jo had whisked things into place, and given quite a different air to the room. Laurie watched her in respectful silence ; and, when she beckoned him to his sofa, he sat down with a sigh of satisfaction, saying gratefully,—

"How kind you are ! Yes, that's what it wanted. Now take the big chair, and let me do something to amuse my company."

"No ; I came to amuse you. Shall I read aloud ?" and Jo looked affectionately towards some inviting books near by.

"Thank you ; I have read all those, and, if you don't mind, I'd rather talk," answered Laurie.

"Not a bit ; I'll talk all day if you'll only set me going. Beth says I never know when to stop."

"Is Beth the rosy one, who stays at home a good deal, and sometimes goes out with a little basket ?" asked Laurie with interest.

"Yes, that's Beth ; she's my girl, and a regular good one she is too."

"The pretty one is Meg, and the curly-haired one is Amy, I believe ?"

"How did you find that out ?"

Laurie coloured up, but answered frankly, "Why, you see, I often hear you calling to one another, and when I'm alone up here, I can't help looking over at your house, you always seem to be having such good times. I beg your pardon for being so rude, but sometimes you forget to put down the curtain at the window where the flowers are ; and, when the lamps are lighted, it's like looking at a picture to see the fire, and you all round the table with your mother ; her face is right opposite, and it looks so sweet behind the flowers, I can't help watching it. I haven't got any mother, you know" ; and Laurie poked the fire to hide a little twitching of the lips that he could not control.

The solitary hungry look in his eyes went straight to Jo's warm heart. She had been so simply taught that there was no nonsense in her head, and at fifteen she was as innocent and frank as any child. Laurie was sick and lonely ; and, feeling how rich she was in home-love and happiness, she gladly tried to share it with him. Her brown face was very friendly, and her sharp voice unusually gentle, as she said,—

"We'll never draw that curtain any more, and I give you leave to look as much as you like. I just wish, though, instead of peeping, you'd come over and see us. Mother is so splendid, she'd do you heaps of good, and Beth would sing to you if *I* begged her to, and Amy would dance ; Meg and I would make you laugh over our funny stage properties, and we'd have jolly times. Wouldn't your grandpa let you ? "

" I think he would, if your mother asked him. He's very kind, though he don't look it ; and he lets me do what I like pretty much, only he's afraid I might be a bother to strangers," began Laurie, brightening more and more.

" We ain't strangers—we are neighbours ; and you needn't think you'd be a bother. We *want* to know you, and I've been trying to do it this ever so long. We haven't been here a great while, you know, but we have got acquainted with all our neighbours but you."

" You see, grandpa lives among his books, and don't mind much what happens outside. Mr. Brooke, my tutor, don't stay here, you know, and I have no one to go round with me, so I just stop at home and get on as I can."

" That's bad ; you ought to make a dive, and go visiting everywhere you are asked ; then you'll have lots of friends, and pleasant places to go to. Never mind being bashful ; it won't last long if you keep going."

Laurie turned red again, but wasn't offended at being accused of bashfulness ; for there was so much good-will in Jo, it was impossible not to take her blunt speeches as kindly as they were meant.

" Do you like your school ? " asked the boy, changing the subject, after a little pause, during which he stared at the fire, and Jo looked about her well pleased.

" Don't go to school ; I'm a business man—girl, I mean. I go to wait on my aunt, and a dear, cross old soul she is too," answered Jo.

Laurie opened his mouth to ask another question ; but remembering just in time that it wasn't manners to make too many inquiries into people's affairs, he shut it again, and looked uncomfortable. Jo liked his good breeding, and didn't mind having a laugh at Aunt March, so she gave him a lively description of the fidgety old lady, her fat poodle, the parrot that talked Spanish, and the library where she revelled. Laurie enjoyed that immensely ; and when she told about the prim old gentleman who came once to woo Aunt March, and, in the middle of a fine speech, how Poll had tweaked his wig off, to his great dismay, the boy lay back and laughed till the tears ran down his cheeks, and a maid popped her head in to see what was the matter.

" Oh ! that does me lots of good ; tell on, please," he said, taking his face out of the sofa-cushion, red and shining with merriment.

Much elated with her success, Jo did " tell on," all about their plays and plans, their hopes and fears for father, and the most interesting events of the little world in which the sisters lived. Then they got to talking about books ; and to Jo's delight she found that Laurie loved them as well as she did, and had read even more than herself.

" If you like them so much, come down and see ours. Grandpa is out, so you needn't be afraid," said Laurie, getting up.

" I'm not afraid of anything," returned Jo, with a toss of the head.

" I don't believe you are ! " exclaimed the boy, looking up at her with much admiration, though he privately thought she would have good reason to be a trifle afraid of the old gentleman, if she met him in some of his moods.

The atmosphere of the whole house being summerlike, Laurie led the way from room to room, letting Jo stop to examine whatever struck her fancy ; and so at last they came to the library, where she clapped her hands and pranced, as she always did when especially delighted. It was lined with books, and there were pictures and statues, and distracting little cabinets full of coins and curiosities, and Sleepy-Hollow chairs, and queer tables and bronzes ; and, best of all, a great, open fireplace, with quaint tiles all round it.

" What richness ! " sighed Jo, sinking into the depths of a velvet chair, and gazing about her with an air of intense satisfaction. " Theodore Laurence, you ought to be the happiest boy in the world," she added impressively.

" A fellow can't live on books," said Laurie, shaking his head, as he perched on a table opposite.

Before he could say any more a bell rang, and Jo flew up, exclaiming with alarm, " Mercy me ! it's your grandpa."

" Well, what if it is ? You are not afraid of anything, you know," returned the boy, looking wicked.

" I think I am a little afraid of him, but I don't know why I should be. Marmee said I might come, and I don't think you're any the worse for it," said Jo, composing herself, though she kept her eyes on the door.

" I'm a great deal better for it, and ever so much obliged. I'm only afraid you are very tired talking to me ; it was *so* pleasant, I couldn't bear to stop," said Laurie gratefully.

" The doctor to see you, sir " ; and the maid beckoned as she spoke.

" Would you mind if I left you for a minute ? I suppose I must see him," said Laurie.

" Don't mind me. I'm as happy as a cricket here," answered Jo.

Laurie went away, and his guest amused herself in her own way. She was standing before a fine portrait of the old gentleman when the door opened again, and, without turning, she said decidedly, " I'm sure now that I shouldn't be afraid of him, for he's got kind eyes, though his mouth is grim, and he looks as if he had a tremendous will of his own. He isn't as handsome as *my* grandfather, but I like him."

" Thank you, ma'am," said a gruff voice behind her ; and there, to her great dismay, stood old Mr. Laurence.

Poor Jo blushed till she couldn't blush any redder, and her heart began to beat uncomfortably fast as she thought of what she had said. For a minute a wild desire to run away possessed her ; but that was cowardly, and the girls would laugh at her ; so she resolved to stay, and get out of the scrape as she could. A second look showed her that the living eyes, under the bushy gray eyebrows, were kinder even than the painted ones ; and there was a sly twinkle in them, which lessened her fear a good deal. The gruff voice was gruffer than ever, as the old gentleman said abruptly, after that dreadful pause, " So you're not afraid of me, hey ? "

" Not much, sir."

" And you don't think me as handsome as your grandfather ? "

" Not quite, sir."

" And I've got a tremendous will, have I ? "

" I only said I thought so."

" But you like me, in spite of it ? "

" Yes, I do, sir."

That answer pleased the old gentleman ; he gave a short laugh, shook hands with her, and putting his finger under her chin, turned up her face, examined it gravely, and let it go, saying, with a nod, " You've got your grandfather's spirit, if you haven't his face. He *was* a fine man, my dear ; but, what is better, he was a brave and honest one, and I was proud to be his friend."

" Thank you, sir," and Jo was quite comfortable after that, for it suited her exactly.

" What have you been doing to this boy of mine, hey ? " was the next question, sharply put.

" Only trying to be neighbourly, sir " ; and Jo told how her visit came about.

" You think he needs cheering up a bit, do you ? "

" Yes, sir ; he seems a little lonely, and young folks would do him good, perhaps. We are only girls, but we should be glad to help if we could, for we don't forget the splendid Christmas present sent us," said Jo eagerly.

" Tut, tut, tut ; that was my boy's affair. How is the poor woman ? "

" Doing nicely, sir " ; and off went Jo, talking very fast, as she told about the Hummels, in whom her mother had interested richer friends than they were.

" Just her father's way of doing good. I shall come and see your mother some fine day. Tell her so. There's the tea-bell ; we have it early, on the boy's account. Come down, and go on being neighbourly."

" If you'd like to have me, sir."

" Shouldn't ask you if I didn't " ; and Mr. Laurence offered her his arm with old-fashioned courtesy.

" What *would* Meg say to this ? " thought Jo, as she was marched away, while her eyes danced with fun as she imagined herself telling the story at home.

" Hey ! why, what the dickens has come to the fellow ? " said the old gentleman, as Laurie came running downstairs, and brought up with a start of surprise at the astonishing sight of Jo arm-in-arm with the redoubtable grandfather.

" I didn't know you'd come, sir," he began, as Jo gave him a triumphant little glance.

" That's evident by the way you racket downstairs. Come to your tea, sir, and behave like a gentleman " ; and having pulled the boy's hair by way of a caress, Mr. Laurence walked on, while Laurie went through a series of comic evolutions behind their backs, which nearly produced an explosion of laughter from Jo.

The old gentleman did not say much as he drank his four cups of tea, but he watched the young people, who soon chatted away like old friends, and the change in his grandson did not escape him. There was colour, light and life in the boy's face now, vivacity in his manner, and genuine merriment in his laugh.

"She's right; the lad *is* lonely. I'll see what these little girls can do for him," thought Mr. Laurence, as he looked and listened. He liked Jo, for her odd, blunt ways suited him; and she seemed to understand the boy almost as well as if she had been one herself.

If the Laurences had been what Jo called "prim and poky," she would not have got on at all, for such people always made her shy and awkward; but finding them free and easy, she was so herself, and made a good impression. When they rose, she proposed to go, but Laurie said he had something more to show her, and took her away to the conservatory, which had been lighted for her benefit. It seemed quite fairy-like to Jo, as she went

Mr. Laurence offered her his arm with old-fashioned courtesy

up and down the walks, enjoying the blooming walls on either side—the soft light, the damp, sweet air, and the wonderful vines and trees that hung above her—while her new friend cut the finest flowers till his hands were full; then he tied them up, saying, with the happy look Jo liked to see, "Please give these to your mother, and tell her I like the medicine she sent me very much."

They found Mr. Laurence standing before the fire in the great drawing-room, but Jo's attention was entirely absorbed by a grand piano which stood open.

"Do you play?" she asked, turning to Laurie with a respectful expression.

"Sometimes," he answered modestly.

"Please do now; I want to hear it, so I can tell Beth."

"Won't you first?"

"Don't know how; too stupid to learn, but I love music dearly."

So Laurie played, and Jo listened, with her nose luxuriously buried in heliotrope and tea roses. Her respect and regard for the " Laurence boy " increased very much, for he played remarkably well, and didn't put on any airs. She wished Beth could hear him but she did not say so ; only praised him till he was quite abashed, and his grandfather came to the rescue. " That will do, that will do, young lady ; too many sugar-plums are not good for him. His music isn't bad, but I hope he will do as well in more important things. Going ? Well, I'm much obliged to you, and I hope you'll come again. My respects to your mother ; good-night, Doctor Jo."

He shook hands kindly, but looked as if something did not please him. When they got into the hall, Jo asked Laurie if she had said anything amiss ; he shook his head.

" No ; it was me : he don't like to hear me play."

" Why not ? "

" I'll tell you some day. John is going home with you, as I can't."

" No need of that ; I ain't a young lady, and it's only a step. Take care of yourself, won't you ? "

" Yes ; but you will come again, I hope ? "

" If you promise to come and see us after you are well."

" I will."

" Good-night, Laurie ! "

" Good-night, Jo ; good-night ! "

When all the afternoon's adventures had been told, the family felt inclined to go visiting in a body, for each found something very attractive in the big house on the other side of the hedge. Mrs. March wanted to talk of her father with the old man who had not forgotten him ; Meg longed to walk in the conservatory ; Beth sighed for the grand piano ; and Amy was eager to see the fine pictures and statues.

" Mother, why didn't Mr. Laurence like to have Laurie play ? " asked Jo, who was of an inquiring disposition.

" I am not quite sure, but I think it was because his son, Laurie's father, married an Italian lady, a musician, which displeased the old man, who is very proud. The lady was good and lovely and accomplished, but he did not like her, and never saw his son after he married. They both died when Laurie was a little child, and then his grandfather took him home. I fancy the boy, who was born in Italy, is not very strong, and the old man is afraid of losing him, which makes him so careful. Laurie comes naturally by his love of music, for he is like his mother, and I dare say his grandfather fears that he may want to be a musician ; at any rate, his skill reminds him of the woman he did not like, and so he ' glowered,' as Jo said."

" Dear me, how romantic ! " exclaimed Meg.

" How silly ! " said Jo ; " let him be a musician, if he wants to, and not plague his life out sending him to college, when he hates to go."

" That's why he has such handsome black eyes and pretty manners, I suppose ; Italians are always nice," said Meg, who was a little sentimental.

" What do you know about his eyes and manners ? You never spoke to him hardly," cried Jo, who was *not* sentimental.

" I saw him at the party, and what you tell shows that he knows how to behave. That was a nice little speech about the medicine mother sent him."

" He meant the blanc-mange, I suppose."

" How stupid you are, child ! he meant you, of course."

" Did he ? " and Jo opened her eyes as if it had never occurred to her before.

" I never saw such a girl ! You don't know a compliment when you get it," said Meg, with the air of a young lady who knew all about the matter.

" I think they are great nonsense, and I'll thank you not to be silly, and spoil my fun. Laurie's a nice boy, and I like him, and I won't have any sentimental stuff about compliments and such rubbish. We'll all be good to him, because he hasn't got any mother, and he *may* come over and see us, mayn't he, Marmee ? "

" Yes, Jo, your little friend is very welcome ; and I hope Meg will remember that children should be children as long as they can."

" I don't call myself a child, and I'm not in my teens yet," observed Amy. " What do you say, Beth ? "

" *I* was thinking about our *Pilgrim's Progress*," answered Beth, who had not heard a word. " How we got out of the Slough and through the Wicket Gate by resolving to be good, and up the steep hill by trying ; and that maybe the house over there, full of splendid things, is going to be our Palace Beautiful."

" We have got to get by the lions first," said Jo, as if she rather liked the prospect.

CHAPTER VI

BETH FINDS THE PALACE BEAUTIFUL

THE big house did prove a Palace Beautiful, though it took some time for all to get in, and Beth found it very hard to pass the lions. Old Mr. Laurence was the biggest one ; but, after he had called, said something funny or kind to each one of the girls, and talked over old times with their mother, nobody felt much afraid of him, except timid Beth.

What good times they had, to be sure ! Such plays and tableaux ; such sleigh-rides and skating frolics ; such pleasant evenings in the old parlour, and now and then such gay little parties at the great house. Meg could walk in the conservatory whenever she liked, and revel in bouquets ; Jo browsed over the new library voraciously, and convulsed the old gentleman with her criticisms ; Amy copied pictures and enjoyed beauty to her heart's content ; and Laurie played lord of the manor in the most delightful style.

But Beth, though yearning for the grand piano, could not pluck up courage to go to the " mansion of bliss," as Meg called it. She went once with Jo, but the old gentleman, not being aware of her infirmity, stared at her so hard from under his heavy eyebrows, and said " hey ! " so loud, that he frightened her so much her " feet chattered on the floor," she told her mother ; and she ran away, declaring she would never go there any more, not even for the dear piano. No persuasions or enticements could overcome her fear, till the fact coming to Mr. Laurence's ear in some mysterious way, he set about mending matters. During one of the brief calls he made, he artfully led the conversation to music, and talked away about great singers whom he had seen, fine organs he had heard, and told such charming anecdotes, that Beth found it impossible to stay in her distant corner, but crept nearer and nearer, as if fascinated. At the back of his chair she stopped, and stood listening with her great eyes wide open, and her cheeks red with the excitement of this unusual performance. Taking no more notice of her than if she had been a fly, Mr. Laurence talked on about Laurie's lessons and teachers; and presently, as if the idea had just occurred to him, he said to Mrs. March,—

"The boy neglects his music now, and I'm glad of it, for he was getting too fond of it. But the piano suffers for want of use; wouldn't some of your girls like to run over and practise on it now and then, just to keep it in tune, you know, ma'am?"

Beth took a step forward, and pressed her hands tightly together, to keep from clapping them, for this was an irresistible temptation; and the thought of practising on that splendid instrument quite took her breath away. Before Mrs. March could reply, Mr. Laurence went on with an odd little nod and smile,—

"They needn't see or speak to any one, but run in at any time, for I'm shut up in my study at the other end of the house. Laurie is out a great deal, and the servants are never near the drawing-room after nine o'clock." Here he rose, as if going, and Beth made up her mind to speak, for that last arrangement left nothing to be desired. "Please tell the young ladies what I say, and if they don't care to come, why, never mind." Here a little hand slipped into his, and Beth looked up at him with a face full of gratitude, as she said, in her earnest, timid way,—

"Oh, sir! they do care, very, very much!"

"Are you the musical girl?" he asked, without any startling "hey!" as he looked down at her very kindly.

"I'm Beth; I love it dearly, and I'll come if you are quite sure nobody will hear me—and be disturbed," she added, fearing to be rude, and trembling at her own boldness as she spoke.

"Not a soul, my dear. The house is empty half the day, so come and drum away as much as you like, and I shall be obliged to you."

"How kind you are, sir!"

Beth blushed like a rose under the friendly look he wore, but she was not frightened now, and gave the big hand a grateful squeeze, because she had no words to thank him for the precious gift he had given her. The old gentleman softly stroked the hair off her forehead, and, stooping down, he kissed her, saying, in a tone few people ever heard,—

"I had a little girl once with eyes like these. God bless you, my dear! Good-day, madam;" and away he went, in a great hurry.

Beth had a rapture with her mother, and then rushed up to impart the glorious news to her family of invalids, as the girls were not at home. How blithely she sang that evening, and how they all laughed at her, because she woke Amy in the night by playing the piano in her face in her sleep. Next day, having seen both the old and young gentleman out of the house, Beth, after two or three retreats, fairly got in at the side door and made her way as noiselessly as any mouse to the drawing-room, where her idol stood.

Quite by accident, of course, some pretty easy music lay on the piano; and, with trembling fingers and frequent stops to listen and look about, Beth at last touched the great instrument, and straightway forgot her fear, herself, and everything else but the unspeakable delight which the music gave her, for it was like the voice of a beloved friend.

She stayed till Hannah came to take her home to dinner; but she had no appetite, and could only sit and smile upon every one in a general state of beatitude.

After that, the little brown hood slipped through the hedge nearly every day, and the great drawing-room was haunted by a tuneful spirit that came and went unseen. She never knew that Mr. Laurence often opened his study door to hear the old-fashioned airs he liked; she never saw Laurie mount guard in the hall, to warn the servants away; she never suspected that the exercise-books and new songs which she found in the rack were put there for her special benefit; and when he talked to her about music at home, she only thought how kind he was to tell things that helped her so much. So she enjoyed herself heartily, and found, what isn't always the case, that her granted wish was all she had hoped. Perhaps it was because she was so grateful for the blessing that a greater was given her; at any rate, she deserved both.

"Mother, I'm going to work Mr. Laurence a pair of slippers. He is so kind to me, I must thank him, and I don't know any other way. Can I do it?" asked Beth, a few weeks after that eventful call of his.

"Yes, dear; it will please him very much, and be a nice way of thanking him. The girls will help you about them, and I will pay for the making-up," replied Mrs. March, who took peculiar pleasure in granting Beth's requests, because she so seldom asked anything for herself.

After many serious discussions with Meg and Jo, the pattern was chosen, the materials bought, and the slippers begun. A cluster of grave yet cheerful pansies, on a deeper purple ground, was pronounced very appropriate and pretty, and Beth worked away early and late, with occasional lifts over hard parts. She was a nimble little needle-woman, and they were finished before any one got tired of them. Then she wrote a very short, simple note, and, with Laurie's help, got them smuggled on to the study table one morning before the old gentleman was up.

When this excitement was over, Beth waited to see what would happen. All that day passed, and a part of the next, before any acknowledgment arrived, and she was beginning to fear she had offended her crotchety friend. On the afternoon of the second day she went out to do an errand, and give poor Joanna, the invalid doll, her daily exercise. As she came up the street on her return, she saw three—yes, four heads popping in and out of the parlour windows; and the moment they saw her several hands were waved, and several joyful voices screamed,—

"Here's a letter from the old gentleman; come quick and read it!"

"Oh, Beth! he's sent you——" began Amy, gesticulating with unseemly energy; but she got no farther, as they clinched her by slamming down the window.

Beth hurried in a twitter of suspense; at the door her sisters seized her and bore her to the parlour in a triumphal procession, all pointing, and all saying at once, " Look there ! look there ! " Beth did look, and turned pale with delight and surprise ; for there stood a little cabinet piano, with a letter lying on the glossy lid, directed, like a signboard, to " Miss Elizabeth March."

" For me ? " gasped Beth, holding on to Jo, and feeling as if she should tumble down, it was such an overwhelming thing altogether.

" Yes ; all for you, my precious ! Isn't it splendid of him ? Don't you think he's the dearest old man in the world ? Here's the key in the letter ; we didn't open it, but we are dying to know what he says," cried Jo, hugging her sister, and offering the note.

" You read it ; I can't, I feel so queer. Oh, it is too lovely ! " and Beth hid her face in Jo's apron, quite upset by her present.

Jo opened the paper, and began to laugh, for the first words she saw were:—

" ' MISS MARCH :

" ' *Dear Madam——* ' "

" How nice it sounds ? I wish some one would write to me so ! " said Amy, who thought the old-fashioned address very elegant.

" ' I have had many pairs of slippers in my life, but I never had any that suited me so well as yours,' " continued Jo. " ' Heart's-ease is my favourite flower, and these will always remind me of the gentle giver. I like to pay my debts, so I know you will allow " the old gentleman " to send you something which once belonged to the little granddaughter he lost. With hearty thanks and best wishes, I remain,

" ' Your grateful friend and humble servant,

" ' JAMES LAURENCE.' "

" There, Beth, that's an honour to be proud of, I'm sure ! Laurie told me how fond Mr. Laurence used to be of the child who died, and how he kept all her little things carefully. Just think ; he's given you her piano ! That comes of having big blue eyes and loving music," said Jo, trying to soothe Beth, who trembled, and looked more excited than she had ever been before.

" See the cunning brackets to hold candles, and the nice green silk, puckered up with a gold rose in the middle, and the pretty rack and stool, all complete," added Meg, opening the instrument, and displaying its beauties.

" ' Your humble servant, James Laurence ; ' only think of his writing that to you. I'll tell the girls ; they'll think it's killing," said Amy, much impressed by the note.

" Try it, honey ; let's hear the sound of the baby pianny," said Hannah, who always took a share in the family joys and sorrows.

So Beth tried it, and every one pronounced it the most remarkable piano ever heard. It had evidently been newly tuned, and put in apple-pie order ; but, perfect as it was, I think the real charm of it lay in the happiest of all happy faces which leaned over it, as Beth lovingly touched the beautiful black and white keys, and pressed the shiny pedals.

"You'll have to go and thank him," said Jo, by way of a joke; for the idea of the child's really going never entered her head.

"Yes, I mean to; I guess I'll go now, before I get frightened thinking about it;" and, to the utter amazement of the assembled family, Beth walked deliberately down the garden, through the hedge, and in at the Laurences' door.

"Well, I wish I may die if it ain't the queerest thing I ever see! The pianny has turned her head; she'd never have gone in her right mind,"

"I come to thank you, sir," began Beth

cried Hannah, staring after her, while the girls were rendered quite speechless by the miracle.

They would have been still more amazed if they had seen what Beth did afterward. If you will believe me, she went and knocked at the study door, before she gave herself time to think; and when a gruff voice called out, "Come in!" she did go in, right up to Mr. Laurence, who looked quite taken aback, and held out her hand, saying, with only a small quaver in her voice, "I come to thank you, sir, for——" but she didn't finish, for he looked so friendly that she forgot her speech; and only remembering that he had lost the little girl he loved, she put both arms round his neck and kissed him.

If the roof of the house had suddenly flown off, the old gentleman wouldn't have been more astonished; but he liked it—oh, dear, yes! he liked it amazingly; and was so touched and pleased by that confiding little kiss that all his crustiness vanished; and he just set her on his knee, and laid his wrinkled cheek against her rosy one, feeling as if he had got his own little granddaughter back again. Beth ceased to fear him from that moment, and sat there talking to him as cosily as if she had known him all her life; for love casts out fear, and gratitude can conquer pride. When she went home, he walked with her to her own gate, shook hands cordially, and touched his hat as he marched back again, looking very stately and erect, like a handsome, soldierly old gentleman, as he was.

When the girls saw that performance, Jo began to dance a jig, by way of expressing her satisfaction; Amy nearly fell out of the window in her surprise, and Meg exclaimed, with uplifted hands, "Well, I do believe the world is coming to an end!"

CHAPTER VII

JO MEETS APOLLYON

"GIRLS, where are you going?" asked Amy, coming into their room one Saturday afternoon, and finding them getting ready to go out, with an air of secrecy which excited her curiosity.

"Never mind; little girls shouldn't ask questions," returned Jo sharply.

Now if there *is* anything mortifying to our feelings when we are young it is to be told that; and to be bidden to "run away, dear," is still more trying to us. Amy bridled up at this insult, and determined to find out the secret, if she teased for an hour. Turning to Meg, who never refused her anything very long, she said coaxingly, "Do tell me! I should think you might let me go, too; for Beth is fussing over her dolls, and I haven't got anything to do, and am *so* lonely."

"I can't, dear, because you aren't invited," began Meg; but Jo broke in impatiently, "Now, Meg, be quiet, or you will spoil it all. You can't go, Amy; so don't be a baby, and whine about it."

"You are going somewhere with Laurie, I know you are; you were whispering and laughing together, on the sofa, last night, and you stopped when I came in. Aren't you going with him?"

"Yes, we are; now be still, and stop bothering." Amy held her tongue, but used her eyes, and saw Meg slip a fan into her pocket.

"I know! I know! You're going to the theatre to see the *Seven Castles*!" she cried; adding resolutely, "and I *shall* go, for mother said I might see it; and I've got my rag-money, and it was mean not to tell me in time."

"Just listen to me a minute, and be a good child," said Meg soothingly. "Mother doesn't wish you to go this week, because your eyes are not well enough yet to bear the light of this fairy piece. Next week you can go with Beth and Hannah, and have a nice time."

"I don't like that half so well as going with you and Laurie. Please let me; I've been sick with this cold so long, and shut up, I'm dying for some fun. Do, Meg! I'll be ever so good," pleaded Amy, looking as pathetic as she could.

"Suppose we take her? I don't believe mother would mind, if we bundled her up well," began Meg.

" If *she* goes, *I* shan't ; and if I don't Laurie won't like it ; and it will be very rude, after he invited only us, to go and drag in Amy. I should think she'd hate to poke herself where she isn't wanted," said Jo crossly, for she disliked the trouble of overseeing a fidgety child, when she wanted to enjoy herself.

Her tone and manner angered Amy, who began to put her boots on, saying, in her most aggravating way, " I *shall* go ; Meg says I may ; and if I pay for myself, Laurie hasn't anything to do with it."

" You can't sit with us, for our seats are reserved, and you mustn't sit alone ; so Laurie will give you his place, and that will spoil our pleasure ; or he'll get another seat for you, and that isn't proper, when you weren't asked. You shan't stir a step ; so you may just stay where you are," scolded Jo, crosser than ever, having just pricked her finger in her hurry.

Sitting on the floor, with one boot on, Amy began to cry, and Meg to reason with her, when Laurie called from below, and the two girls hurried down, leaving their sister wailing ; for now and then she forgot her grown-up ways, and acted like a spoilt child. Just as the party was setting out, Amy called over the banisters, in a threatening tone, " You'll be sorry for this, Jo March ! see if you ain't."

" Fiddlesticks ! " returned Jo, slamming the door.

They had a charming time, for *The Seven Castles of the Diamond Lake* was as brilliant and wonderful as heart could wish. But in spite of the comical, red imps, sparkling elves, and gorgeous princes and princesses, Jo's pleasure had a drop of bitterness in it ; the fairy queen's yellow curls reminded her of Amy ; and between the acts she amused herself with wondering what her sister would do to make her " sorry for it."

When they got home, they found Amy reading in the parlour. She assumed an injured air as they came in ; never lifted her eyes from her book, or asked a single question. Perhaps curiosity might have conquered resentment if Beth had not been there to inquire, and receive a glowing description of the play. On going up to put away her best hat, Jo's first look was towards the bureau ; for, in their last quarrel, Amy had soothed her feelings by turning Jo's top drawer upside down, on the floor. Everything was in its place, however, and after a hasty glance into her various closets, bags, and boxes, Jo decided that Amy had forgiven and forgotten her wrongs.

There Jo was mistaken ; for next day she made a discovery which produced a tempest. Meg, Beth, and Amy were sitting together, late in the afternoon, when Jo burst into the room, looking excited, and demanding breathlessly, " Has any one taken my story ? "

Meg and Beth said " No," at once, and looked surprised ; Amy poked the fire, and said nothing. Jo saw her colour rise, and was down upon her in a minute.

" Amy, you've got it ! "

" No, I haven't."

" You know where it is, then ! "

" No, I don't."

" That's a fib ! " cried Jo, taking her by the shoulders, and looking fierce enough to frighten a much braver child than Amy.

" It isn't. I haven't got it, don't know where it is now, and don't care."

" You know something about it, and you'd better tell at once, or I'll make you ; " and Jo gave her a slight shake.

" Scold as much as you like, you'll never get your silly old story again," cried Amy, getting excited in her turn.

" Why not ? "

" I burnt it up."

" What ! my little book I was so fond of, and worked over, and meant to finish before father got home ? Have you really burnt it ? " said Jo, turning very pale, while her eyes kindled and her hands clutched Amy nervously.

" Yes, I did ! I told you I'd make you pay for being so cross yesterday, and I have, so——"

Amy got no farther, for Jo's hot temper mastered her, and she shook Amy till her teeth chattered in her head ; crying, in a passion of grief and anger,—

" You wicked, wicked girl ! I never can write it again, and I'll never forgive you as long as I live."

Meg flew to rescue Amy, and Beth to pacify Jo, but Jo was quite beside herself ; and, with a parting box on her sister's ear, she rushed out of the room up to the old sofa in the garret, and finished her fight alone.

The storm cleared up below, for Mrs. March came home, and, having heard the story, soon brought Amy to a sense of the wrong she had done her sister. Jo's book was the pride of her heart, and was regarded by her family as a literary sprout of great promise. It was only half a dozen little fairy tales, but Jo had worked over them patiently, putting her whole heart into her work, hoping to make something good enough to print. She had just copied them with great care, and had destroyed the old manuscript, so that Amy's bonfire had consumed the loving work of several years. It seemed a small loss to others, but to Jo it was a dreadful calamity, and she felt that it never could be made up to her. Beth mourned as for a departed kitten, and Meg refused to defend her pet ; Mrs. March looked grave and grieved, and Amy felt that no one would love her till she had asked pardon for the act which she now regretted more than any of them.

When the tea-bell rang, Jo appeared, looking so grim and unapproachable that it took all Amy's courage to say meekly,—

" Please forgive me, Jo ; I'm very, very sorry."

" I never shall forgive you," was Jo's stern answer ; and, from that moment, she ignored Amy entirely.

No one spoke of the great trouble,—not even Mrs. March,—for all had learned by experience that when Jo was in that mood words were wasted.

As Jo received her good-night kiss, Mrs. March whispered gently,—

" My dear, don't let the sun go down upon your anger ; forgive each other, help each other, and begin again to-morrow."

Jo wanted to lay her head down on that motherly bosom and cry her grief and anger all away ; but tears were an unmanly weakness, and she felt so deeply injured that she really *couldn't* quite forgive yet. So she winked hard, shook her head and said, gruffly, because Amy was listening,—

" It was an abominable thing, and she don't deserve to be forgiven."

With that she marched off to bed, and there was no merry or confidential gossip that night.

Amy was much offended that her overtures of peace had been repulsed, and began to wish she had not humbled herself, to feel more injured than ever, and to plume herself on her superior virtue in a way which was particularly exasperating. Jo still looked like a thunder-cloud, and nothing went well all day. It was bitter cold in the morning ; she dropped her precious turnover in the gutter, Aunt March had an attack of fidgets, Meg was pensive, Beth *would* look grieved and wistful when she got home, and Amy kept making remarks about people who were always talking about being good, and yet wouldn't try, when other people set them a virtuous example.

" Everybody is so hateful, I'll ask Laurie to go skating. He is always kind and jolly, and will put me to rights, I know," said Jo to herself, and off she went.

Amy heard the clash of skates, and looked out with an impatient exclamation,—

" There ! she promised I should go next time, for this is the last ice we shall have. But it is no use to ask such a cross-patch to take me."

" Don't say that ; you *were* very naughty, and it *is* hard to forgive the loss of her precious little book ; but I think she might do it now, and I guess she will, if you try her at the right minute," said Meg. " Go after them ; don't say anything till Jo has got good-natured with Laurie, then take a quiet minute, and just kiss her, or do some kind thing, and I'm sure she'll be friends again, with all her heart."

" I'll try," said Amy, for the advice suited her ; and, after a flurry to get ready, she ran after the friends, who were just disappearing over the hill.

It was not far to the river, but both were ready before Amy reached them. Jo saw her coming, and turned her back ; Laurie did not see, for he was carefully skating along the shore, sounding the ice, for a warm spell had preceded the cold snap.

" I'll go on to the first bend, and see if it's all right, before we begin to race," Amy heard him say, as he shot away, looking like a young Russian in his fur-trimmed coat and cap.

Jo heard Amy panting after her run, stamping her feet, and blowing her fingers, as she tried to put her skates on ; but Jo never turned, and went slowly zigzagging down the river, taking a bitter, unhappy sort of satisfaction in her sister's troubles. She had cherished her anger till it grew strong, and took possession of her, as evil thoughts and feelings always do, unless cast out at once. As Laurie turned the bend, he shouted back,—

" Keep near the shore ; it isn't safe in the middle."

Jo heard, but Amy was just struggling to her feet, and did not catch a word. Jo glanced over her shoulder, and the little demon she was harbouring said in her ear,—

" No matter whether she heard or not ; let her take care of herself."

Laurie had vanished round the bend ; Jo was just at the turn, and Amy, far behind, striking out toward the smoother ice in the middle of the river. For a minute Jo stood still, with a strange feeling at her heart ; then she resolved to go on, but something held and turned her round, just in time to see Amy throw up her hands and go down, with the sudden crash of rotten ice, the splash of water, and a cry that made Jo's heart stand still with fear.

She tried to call Laurie, but her voice was gone ; she tried to rush forward, but her feet seemed to have no strength in them ; and, for a second, she could only stand motionless, staring, with a terror-stricken face, at the little blue hood above the black water. Something rushed swiftly by her, and Laurie's voice called out,—

" Bring a rail ; quick, quick ! "

How she did it she never knew, but the next few minutes she worked as if possessed, blindly obeying Laurie, who was quite self-possessed, and, lying flat, held Amy up by his arm and hockey, till Jo dragged a rail from the fence, and together they got the child out, more frightened than hurt.

" Now then, we must walk her home as fast as we can ; pile our things on her, while I get off these confounded skates," cried Laurie, wrapping his coat round Amy, and tugging away at the straps, which never seemed so intricate before.

Shivering, dripping, and crying, they got Amy home ; and, after an exciting time of it, she fell asleep, rolled in blankets, before a hot fire. During the bustle Jo had scarcely spoken, but flown about, looking pale and wild, with her things half off, her dress torn, and her hands cut and bruised by ice, and rails, and refractory buckles. When Amy was comfortably asleep, the house quiet, and Mrs. March sitting by the bed, she called Jo to her and began to bind up the hurt hands.

" Are you sure she is safe ? " whispered Jo, looking remorsefully at the golden head, which might have been swept away from her sight for ever, under the treacherous ice.

" Quite safe, dear ; she is not hurt, and won't even take cold, I think ; you were so sensible in covering and getting her home quickly," replied her mother cheerfully.

" Laurie did it all ; I only let her go. Mother, if she *should* die, it would be my fault ; " and Jo dropped down beside the bed, in a passion of penitent tears, telling all that had happened, bitterly condemning her hardness of heart, and sobbing out her gratitude for being spared the heavy punishment which might have come upon her.

" It's my dreadful temper ! I try to cure it ; I think I have, and then it breaks out worse than ever. Oh, mother ! what shall I do ? " cried poor Jo, in despair.

" Watch and pray, dear ; never get tired of trying, and never think it is impossible to conquer your fault," said Mrs. March, drawing the blowzy head to her shoulder, and kissing the wet cheek so tenderly, that Jo cried harder than ever.

" You don't know ; you can't guess how bad it is ! It seems as if I could do anything when I'm in a passion ; I get so savage, I could hurt any one, and enjoy it. I'm afraid I *shall* do something dreadful some day, and spoil my life, and make everybody hate me. Oh, mother ! help me, do help me ! "

" I will, my child ; I will. Don't cry so bitterly, but remember this day, and resolve, with all your soul, that you will never know another like it. Jo, dear, we all have our temptations, some far greater than yours, and it often takes us all our lives to conquer them. You think your temper is the worst in the world, but mine used to be just like it."

" Yours, mother ? Why, you are never angry ! " and, for the moment, Jo forgot remorse in surprise.

" I've been trying to cure it for forty years, and have only succeeded in controlling it. I am angry nearly every day of my life, Jo ; but I have learned not to show it ; and I still hope to learn not to feel it, though it may take me another forty years to do so."

" How did you learn to keep still ? That is what troubles me—for the sharp words fly out before I know what I'm about ; and the more I say the worse I get, till it's a pleasure to hurt people's feelings, and say dreadful things."

" Oh, mother ! do help me ! "
sobbed Jo

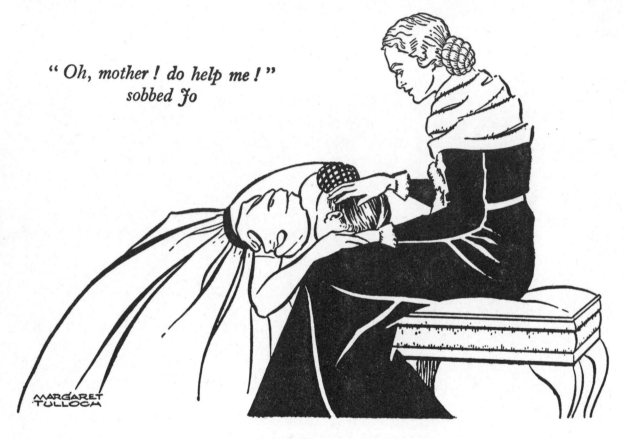

" My child, the troubles and temptations of your life are beginning, and may be many ; but you can overcome and outlive them all, if you learn to feel the strength and tenderness of your Heavenly Father as you do that of your earthly one. The more you love and trust Him, the nearer you will feel to Him, and the less you will depend on human power and wisdom. His love and care never tire or change, can never be taken from you, but may become the source of life-long peace, happiness, and strength. Believe this heartily, and go to God with all your little cares, and hopes, and sins, and sorrows, as freely and confidingly as you come to your mother."

Jo's only answer was to hold her mother close, and, in the silence which followed, the sincerest prayer she had ever prayed left her heart, without words ; for in that sad, yet happy hour, she had learned not only the bitterness of remorse and despair, but the sweetness of self-denial and self-control ; and, led by her mother's hand, she had drawn nearer to the Friend who welcomes every child with a love stronger than that of any father, tenderer than that of any mother.

Amy stirred, and sighed in her sleep ; and, as if eager to begin at once to mend her fault, Jo looked up with an expression on her face which it had never worn before.

" I let the sun go down on my anger ; I wouldn't forgive her, and to-day, if it hadn't been for Laurie, it might have been too late ! How could I have been so wicked ? " said Jo, half aloud, as she leaned over her sister, softly stroking the wet hair scattered over the pillow.

As if she heard, Amy opened her eyes, and held out her arms, with a smile that went straight to Jo's heart. Neither said a word, but they hugged one another close, in spite of the blankets, and everything was forgiven and forgotten in one hearty kiss.

CHAPTER VIII

MEG GOES TO VANITY FAIR

" I DO think it was the most fortunate thing in the world that those children should have the measles just now," said Meg, one April day, as she stood packing the " go-abroady " trunk in her room, surrounded by her sisters.

" And so nice of Annie Moffat not to forget her promise. A whole fortnight of fun will be regularly splendid," replied Jo, looking like a windmill, as she folded skirts with her long arms.

" And such lovely weather ; I'm so glad of that," added Beth, tidily sorting neck and hair ribbons in her best box, lent for the great occasion.

" I wish I was going to have a fine time, and wear all these nice things," said Amy, with her mouth full of pins, as she artistically replenished her sister's cushion.

" I wish you were all going ; but, as you can't, I shall keep my adventures to tell you when I come back. I'm sure it's the least I can do, when you have been so kind, lending me things, and helping me get ready," said Meg, glancing round the room at the very simple outfit which seemed nearly perfect in their eyes.

" What did mother give you out of the treasure-box ? " asked Amy, who had not been present at the opening of a certain cedar chest, in which Mrs. March kept a few relics of past splendour, as gifts for her girls when the proper time came.

" A pair of silk stockings, that pretty carved fan, and a lovely blue sash. I wanted the violet silk ; but there isn't time to make it over, so I must be contented with my old tarlatan."

" It will look nicely over my new muslin skirt, and the sash will set it off beautifully. I wish I hadn't smashed my coral bracelet, for you might have had it," said Jo, who loved to give and lend, but whose possessions were usually too dilapidated to be of much use.

" There is a lovely old-fashioned pearl set in the treasure-box ; but mother said real flowers were the prettiest ornament for a young girl, and Laurie promised to send me all I want," replied Meg. " Now, let me see ; there's my new gray walking-suit—just curl up the feather in my hat, Beth ;— then my poplin, for Sunday, and the small party—it looks heavy for spring, doesn't it ? the violet silk would be so nice ; oh, dear ! "

" Never mind ; you've got the tarlatan for the big party, and you always look like an angel in white," said Amy, brooding over the little store of finery in which her soul delighted.

" Annie Moffat has blue and pink bows on her night-caps ; would you put some on mine ? " she asked, as Beth brought up a pile of snowy muslins, fresh from Hannah's hands.

" No, I wouldn't ; for the smart caps won't match the plain gowns, without any trimming on them. Poor folks shouldn't rig," said Jo decidedly.

" I wonder if I shall *ever* be happy enough to have real lace on my clothes, and bows on my caps ? " said Meg impatiently.

" You said the other day that you'd be perfectly happy if you could only go to Annie Moffat's," observed Beth in her quiet way.

" So I did ! Well, I *am* happy, and I *won't* fret ; but it does seem as if the more one gets the more one wants, doesn't it ? There, now, the trays are ready, and everything in but my ball-dress, which I shall leave for mother," said Meg, cheering up, and she glanced from the half-filled trunk to the many-times pressed and mended white tarlatan, which she called her " ball-dress," with an important air.

The next day was fine, and Meg departed in style for a fortnight of novelty and pleasure. Mrs. March had consented to the visit rather reluctantly, fearing that Margaret would come back more discontented than she went. But she had begged so hard, and Sallie had promised to take good care of her, and a little pleasure seemed so delightful after a winter of hard work, that the mother yielded, and the daughter went to take her first taste of fashionable life.

The Moffats *were* very fashionable, and simple Meg was rather daunted, at first, by the splendour of the house and the elegance of its occupants. But they were kindly people, in spite of the frivolous life they led, and soon put their guest at her ease. Perhaps Meg felt, without understanding why, that they were not particularly cultivated or intelligent people, and that all their gilding could not quite conceal the ordinary material of which they were made. It certainly was agreeable to fare sumptuously, drive in a fine carriage, wear her best frock every day, and do nothing but enjoy herself. It suited her exactly ; and soon she began to imitate the manners and conversation of those about her : to put on little airs and graces, use French phrases, crimp her hair, take in her dresses, and talk about the fashions, as well as she could. The more she saw of Annie Moffat's pretty things, the more she envied her, and sighed to be rich. Home now looked bare and dismal as she thought of it, work grew harder than ever, and she felt that she was a very destitute and much-injured girl, in spite of the new gloves and silk stockings.

She had not much time for repining, however, for the three young girls were busily employed in " having a good time." They shopped, walked, rode, and called all day ; went to theatres and operas, or frolicked at home in the evening ; for Annie had many friends, and knew how to entertain them. Her older sisters were very fine young ladies, and one was engaged, which was extremely interesting and romantic, Meg thought. Mr. Moffat was a fat, jolly old gentleman, who knew her father ; and Mrs. Moffat, a fat, jolly old lady, who took as great a fancy to Meg as her daughter had done. Every one petted her ; and " Daisy," as they called her, was in a fair way to have her head turned.

When the evening for the " small party " came, she found that the poplin wouldn't do at all, for the other girls were putting on thin dresses and making themselves very fine indeed ; so out came the tarlatan, looking older, limper, and shabbier than ever, beside Sallie's crisp new one. Meg saw the girls glance at it, and then at one another, and her cheeks began to burn ; for, with all her gentleness, she was very proud. No one said a word about it, but Sallie offered to do her hair, and Annie to tie her sash, and Belle, the engaged sister, praised her white arms ; but, in their kindness, Meg saw only pity for her poverty, and her heart felt very heavy, as she stood by herself, while the others laughed and chattered, prinked, and flew about like gauzy butterflies. The hard, bitter feeling was getting pretty bad, when the maid brought in a box of flowers. Before she could speak, Annie had the cover off, and all were exclaiming at the lovely roses, heath, and ferns within.

" It's for Belle, of course ; George always sends her some, but these are altogether ravishing," cried Annie, with a great sniff.

" They are for Miss March, the man said. And here's a note," put in the maid, holding it to Meg.

" What fun ! Who are they from ? Didn't know you had a lover," cried the girls, fluttering about Meg in a high state of curiosity and surprise.

" The note is from mother, and the flowers from Laurie," said Meg simply, yet much gratified that he had not forgotten her.

" Oh, indeed ! " said Annie, with a funny look, as Meg slipped the note into her pocket, as a sort of talisman against envy, vanity, and false pride ; for the few loving words had done her good, and the flowers cheered her up by their beauty.

Feeling almost happy again, she laid by a few ferns and roses for herself, and quickly made up the rest in dainty bouquets for the breasts, hair, or skirts of her friends, offering them so prettily that Clara, the elder sister, told her she was " the sweetest little thing she ever saw ; " and they looked quite charmed with her small attention. Somehow the kind act finished her despondency ; and, when all the rest went to show themselves to Mrs. Moffat, she saw a happy, bright-eyed face in the mirror, as she laid her ferns against her rippling hair, and fastened the roses in the dress that didn't strike her as so *very* shabby now.

She enjoyed herself very much that evening, for she danced to her heart's content ; every one was very kind, and she had three compliments. Annie made her sing, and some one said she had a remarkably fine voice ; Major Lincoln asked who " the fresh little girl with the beautiful eyes was : " and Mr. Moffat insisted on dancing with her, because she " didn't dawdle, but had some spring in her," as he gracefully expressed it. So, altogether, she had a very nice time, till she overheard a bit of conversation which disturbed her extremely. She was sitting just inside the conservatory, waiting for her partner to bring her an ice, when she heard a voice ask, on the other side of the flowery wall,—

"How old is she?"

"Sixteen or seventeen, I should say," replied another voice.

"It would be a grand thing for one of those girls, wouldn't it? Sallie says they are very intimate now, and the old man quite dotes on them."

"Mrs. M. has laid her plans, I dare say, and will play her cards well, early as it is. The girl evidently doesn't think of it yet," said Mrs. Moffat.

"She told that fib about her mamma, as if she did know, and coloured

She was waiting for her partner to bring her an ice

up when the flowers came, quite prettily. Poor thing! she'd be so nice if she was only got up in style. Do you think she'd be offended if we offered to lend her a dress for Thursday?" asked another voice.

"She's proud, but I don't believe she'd mind, for that dowdy tarlatan is all she has got. She may tear it to-night, and that will be a good excuse for offering a decent one."

"We'll see; I shall ask that Laurence as a compliment to her, and we'll have fun about it afterward."

Here Meg's partner appeared, to find her looking much flushed and rather agitated. She was proud, and her pride was useful just then, for it helped her hide her mortification, anger, and disgust, at what she had just heard; for, innocent and unsuspicious as she was, she could not help understanding the gossip of her friends. She tried to forget it, but could not, and kept repeating to herself, "Mrs. M. has her plans," "that fib about her mamma," and "dowdy tarlatan," till she was ready to cry, and rush home to tell her troubles, and ask for advice. As that was impossible, she did her best to seem gay; and, being rather excited, she succeeded so well that no one dreamed what an effort she was making. She was very glad when it was all over, and she was quiet in her bed, where she could think and wonder and fume till her head ached, and her hot cheeks were cooled by a few natural tears.

Poor Meg had a restless night, and got up heavy-eyed, unhappy, half resentful towards her friends, and half ashamed of herself for not speaking out frankly, and setting everything right. Everybody dawdled that morning, and it was noon before the girls found energy enough even to take up their worsted work. Something in the manner of her friends struck Meg at once; they treated her with more respect, she thought; took quite a tender interest in what she said, and looked at her with eyes that plainly betrayed curiosity. All this surprised and flattered her, though she did not understand it till Miss Belle looked up from her writing, and said, with a sentimental air,—

"Daisy, dear, I've sent an invitation to your friend, Mr. Laurence, for Thursday. We should like to know him, and it's only a proper compliment to you."

Meg coloured, but a mischievous fancy to tease the girls made her reply demurely,—

"You are very kind, but I'm afraid he won't come."

"Why not, *chérie*?" asked Miss Belle.

"He's too old."

"My child, what do you mean? What is his age, I beg to know?" cried Miss Clara.

"Nearly seventy, I believe," answered Meg, counting stitches to hide the merriment in her eyes.

"You sly creature! Of course, we meant the young man," exclaimed Miss Belle laughing.

"There isn't any; Laurie is only a little boy;" and Meg laughed also at the queer look which the sisters exchanged, as she thus described her supposed lover.

"About your age?" Nan said.

"Nearer my sister Jo's; *I* am seventeen in August," returned Meg, tossing her head.

"It's very nice of him to send you flowers, isn't it?" said Annie, looking wise about nothing.

"Yes; he often does, to all of us; for their house is full, and we are so fond of them. My mother and old Mr. Laurence are friends, you know, so it is quite natural we children should play together;" and Meg hoped they would say no more.

"It's evident Daisy isn't out yet," said Miss Clara to Belle, with a nod.

"Quite a pastoral state of innocence all round," remarked Miss Belle, with a shrug.

"I am going out to get some little matters for my girls; can I do anything for you young ladies?" asked Mrs. Moffat, lumbering in like an elephant, in silk and lace.

"No, thank you, ma'am," replied Sallie; "I've got my new pink silk for Thursday, and don't want a thing."

" Nor I——" began Meg, but stopped, because it occurred to her that she *did* want several things, and could not have them.

" What shall you wear ? " asked Sallie.

" My old white one again, if I can mend it fit to be seen ; it got sadly torn last night," said Meg, trying to speak quite easily, but feeling very uncomfortable.

" Why don't you send home for another ? " said Sallie, who was not an observing young lady.

" I haven't got any other." It cost Meg an effort to say that, but Sallie did not see it, and exclaimed in amiable surprise,—

" Only that ? how funny——" She did not finish her speech, for Belle shook her head at her, and broke in, saying kindly,—

" Not at all ; where is the use of having a lot of dresses when she isn't out ? There's no need of sending home, Daisy, even if you had a dozen, for I've got a sweet blue silk laid away which I've outgrown, and you shall wear it to please me ; won't you, dear ? "

" You are very kind, but I don't mind my old dress, if you don't ; it does well enough for a little girl like me," said Meg.

" Now do let me please myself by dressing you up in style. I admire to do it, and you'd be a regular little beauty with a touch here and there. I shan't let any one see you till you are done, and then we'll burst upon them like Cinderella and her godmother going to the ball," said Belle, in her persuasive tone.

Meg couldn't refuse the offer so kindly made, for a desire to see if she would be " a little beauty " after touching up caused her to accept, and forget all her former uncomfortable feelings towards the Moffats.

On the Thursday evening Belle shut herself up with her maid, and, between them, they turned Meg into a fine lady. They crimpled and curled her hair, they polished her neck and arms with some fragrant powder, touched her lips with coralline salve, to make them redder, and Hortense would have added " a *soupçon* of rouge," if Meg had not rebelled. They laced her into a sky-blue dress, which was so tight she could hardly breathe, and so low in the neck that modest Meg blushed at herself in the mirror. A set of silver filigree was added, bracelets, necklace, brooch, and even ear-rings, for Hortense tied them on with a bit of pink silk which did not show. A cluster of tea rosebuds at the bosom, and a *ruche* reconciled Meg to the display of her pretty white shoulders, and a pair of high-heeled blue silk boots satisfied the last wish of her heart. A laced handkerchief, a plumy fan, and a bouquet in a silver holder finished her off, and Miss Belle surveyed her with the satisfaction of a little girl with a newly-dressed doll.

" Mademoiselle is charmante, très jolie, is she not ? " cried Hortense, clasping her hands in an affected rapture.

" Come and show yourself," said Miss Belle, leading the way to the room where the others were waiting.

As Meg went rustling after, with her long skirts trailing, her ear-rings tinkling, her curls waving, and her heart beating, she felt as if her " fun " had really begun at last, for the mirror had plainly told her that she *was* " a little beauty." Her friends repeated the pleasing phrase enthusiastically, and, for several minutes, she stood, like the jackdaw in the fable, enjoying her borrowed plumes, while the rest chattered like a party of magpies.

" While I dress, do you drill her, Nan, in the management of her skirt and those French heels, or she will trip herself up. Put your silver butterfly in the middle of that white barbe, and catch up that long curl on the left side of her head, Clara, and don't any of you disturb the charming work of my hands," said Belle, as she hurried away, looking well pleased with her success.

" I'm afraid to go down, I feel so queer and stiff, and half-dressed," said Meg to Sallie, as the bell rang, and Mrs. Moffat sent to ask the young ladies to appear at once.

" You don't look a bit like yourself, but you are very nice. I'm nowhere beside you, for Belle has heaps of taste, and you're quite French, I assure you. Let your flowers hang ; don't be so careful of them ; and be sure you don't trip," returned Sallie, trying not to care that Meg was prettier than herself.

Keeping that warning carefully in mind, Margaret got safely downstairs, and sailed into the drawing-room, where the Moffats and a few early guests were assembled. She very soon discovered that there is a charm about fine clothes which attracts a certain class of people and secures their respect. Several young ladies, who had taken no notice of her before, were very affectionate all of a sudden ; several young gentlemen, who had only stared at her at the other party, now not only stared, but asked to be introduced, and said all manner of foolish but agreeable things to her ; and several old ladies, who sat on sofas and criticised the rest of the party, inquired who she was with an air of interest. She heard Mrs. Moffat reply to one of them,—

" Daisy March—father a colonel in the army—one of our first families, but reverses of fortune, you know ; intimate friends of the Laurences ; sweet creature, I assure you ; my Ned is quite wild about her."

" Dear me ! " said the old lady, putting up her glass for another observation of Meg, who tried to look as if she had not heard and been rather shocked at Mrs. Moffat's fibs.

The " queer feeling " did not pass away, but she imagined herself acting the new part of fine lady, and so got on pretty well, though the tight dress gave her a side-ache, the train kept getting under her feet, and she was in constant fear lest her ear-rings should fly off and get lost or broken. She was flirting her fan, and laughing at the feeble jokes of a young gentleman who tried to be witty, when she suddenly stopped laughing and looked confused, for, just opposite, she saw Laurie. He was staring at her with undisguised surprise, and disapproval also, she thought ; for, though he bowed and smiled, yet something in his honest eyes made her blush, and wish she had her old dress on. To complete her confusion, she saw Belle nudge Annie, and both glance from her to Laurie, who, she was happy to see, looked unusually boyish and shy.

" Silly creatures, to put such thoughts into my head ! I won't care for it, or let it change me a bit," thought Meg, and rushed across the room to shake hands with her friend.

" I am glad you came, for I was afraid you wouldn't," she said, with her most grown-up air.

" Jo wanted me to come, and tell her how you looked, so I did," answered Laurie, without turning his eyes upon her, though he half smiled at her maternal tone.

" What shall you tell her ? " asked Meg, full of curiosity to know his opinion of her, yet feeling ill at ease with him, for the first time.

" I shall say I didn't know you, for you look so grown-up, and unlike yourself ; I'm quite afraid of you," he said, fumbling at his glove-button.

" How absurd of you ! the girls dressed me up for fun, and I rather like it. Wouldn't Jo stare if she saw me ? " said Meg, bent on making him say whether he thought her improved or not.

" Yes, I think she would," returned Laurie gravely.

" Don't you like me so ? " asked Meg.

" No, I don't," was the blunt reply.

" Why not ? " in an anxious tone.

He glanced at her frizzled head, bare shoulders, and fantastically trimmed dress with an expression that abashed her more than his answer, which had not a particle of his usual politeness about it :—

" I don't like fuss and feathers."

That was altogether too much from a lad younger than herself ; and Meg walked away, saying petulantly,—

" You are the rudest boy I ever saw."

Feeling very much ruffled, she went and stood at a quiet window, to cool her cheeks, for the tight dress gave her an uncomfortably brilliant colour. As she stood there, Major Lincoln passed by ; and, a minute after, she heard him saying to his mother,—

" They are making a fool of that little girl ; I wanted you to see her, but they have spoilt her entirely ; she's nothing but a doll to-night."

" Oh, dear ! " sighed Meg ; " I wish I'd been sensible, and worn my own things ; then I should not have disgusted other people, or felt so un-comfortable and ashamed myself."

She leaned her forehead on the cool pane, and stood half hidden by the curtains, never minding that her favourite waltz had begun, till some one touched her ; and, turning, she saw Laurie looking penitent, as he said, with his very best bow, and his hand out,—

" Please forgive my rudeness, and come and dance with me."

" I'm afraid it will be too disagreeable to you," said Meg, trying to look offended, and failing entirely.

" Not a bit of it ; I'm dying to do it. Come, I'll be good ; I don't like your gown, but I do think you are—just splendid ; " and he waved his hands, as if words failed to express his admiration.

Meg smiled, and relented, and whispered as they stood waiting to catch the time,—

" Take care my skirt doesn't trip you up ; it's the plague of my life, and I was a goose to wear it."

" Pin it round your neck, and then it will be useful," said Laurie, looking down at the little blue boots, which he evidently approved of.

Away they went, fleetly and gracefully ; for, having practised at home, they were well matched, and the blithe young couple were a pleasant sight to see, as they twirled merrily round and round, feeling more friendly than ever after their small tiff.

" Laurie, I want you to do me a favour ; will you ? " said Meg, as he stood fanning her, when her breath gave out, which it did very soon, though she would not own why.

" Won't I ! " said Laurie, with alacrity.

" Please don't tell them at home about my dress to-night. They won't understand the joke, and it will worry mother."

" Then why did you do it ? " said Laurie's eyes, so plainly that Meg hastily added,—

" I shall tell them, myself, all about it, and ' 'fess ' to mother how silly I've been. But I'd rather do it myself ; so you'll not tell, will you ? "

" I give you my word I won't ; only what shall I say when they ask me ? "

" Just say I looked nice, and was having a good time."

" I'll say the first, with all my heart ; but how about the other ? You don't look as if you were having a good time ; are you ? " and Laurie looked at her with an expression which made her answer in a whisper,—

" No, not just now. Don't think I'm horrid ; I only wanted a little fun, but this sort doesn't pay, I find, and I'm getting tired of it."

He did not speak to her again till supper-time, when he saw her drinking champagne with Ned and his friend Fisher, who were behaving " like a pair of fools," as Laurie said to himself ; for he felt a brotherly sort of right to watch over the Marches, and fight their battles whenever a defender was needed.

" Wish to-morrow was here, then," muttered Laurie, walking off, ill-pleased at the change he saw in her.

Meg danced and flirted, chattered and giggled, as the other girls did. After supper she undertook the German, and blundered through it, nearly upsetting her partner with her long skirt, and romping in a way that scandalised Laurie, who looked on and meditated a lecture. But he got no chance to deliver it, for Meg kept away from him till he came to say good-night.

" Remember ! " she said, trying to smile, for the splitting headache had already begun.

" Silence *à la mort*," replied Laurie, with a melodramatic flourish, as he went away.

This little bit of by-play excited Annie's curiosity ; but Meg was too tired for gossip, and went to bed, feeling as if she had been to a masquerade, and hadn't enjoyed herself as much as she expected. She was sick all the next day, and on Saturday went home, quite used up with her fortnight's fun, and feeling that she had sat in the lap of luxury long enough.

" It does seem pleasant to be quiet, and not have company manners on all the time. Home *is* a nice place, though it isn't splendid," said Meg, looking about her with a restful expression, as she sat with her mother and Jo on the Sunday evening.

" I'm glad to hear you say so, dear, for I was afraid home would seem dull and poor to you, after your fine quarters," replied her mother, who had given her many anxious looks that day ; for motherly eyes are quick to see any change in children's faces.

Meg had told her adventures gaily, and said over and over what a charming time she had had ; but something still seemed to weigh upon her spirits, and, when the younger girls were gone to bed, she sat thoughtfully staring at the fire, saying little, and looking worried. As the clock struck nine, and Jo proposed bed, Meg suddenly left her chair, and, taking Beth's stool, leaned her elbows on her mother's knee, saying bravely,—

" Marmee, I want to ' 'fess.' "

" I thought so. What is it, dear ? "

" Shall I go away ? " asked Jo discreetly.

" Of course not ; don't I always tell you everything ? I was ashamed to speak of it before the children, but I want you to know all the dreadful things I did at the Moffats'. "

" We are prepared," said Mrs. March, smiling, but looking a little anxious.

" I told you they rigged me up, but I didn't tell you that they powdered, and squeezed, and frizzled, and made me look like a fashion-plate. Laurie thought I wasn't proper ; I know he did, though he didn't say so ; and one man called me ' a doll.' I knew it was silly, but they flattered me, and said I was a beauty, and quantities of nonsense, so I let them make a fool of me."

" Is that all ? " asked Jo, as Mrs. March looked silently at the downcast face of her pretty daughter, and could not find it in her heart to blame her little follies.

" No ; I drank champagne, and romped, and tried to flirt, and was altogether abominable," said Meg, self-reproachfully.

" There is something more, I think ; " and Mrs. March smoothed the soft cheek, which suddenly grew rosy, as Meg answered slowly,—

" Yes ; it's very silly, but I want to tell it, because I hate to have people say and think such things about us and Laurie."

Then she told the various bits of gossip she had heard at the Moffats'; and, as she spoke, Jo saw her mother fold her lips tightly, as if ill pleased that such ideas should be put into Meg's innocent mind.

" Well, if that isn't the greatest rubbish I ever heard," cried Jo indignantly. " Why didn't you pop out and tell them so, on the spot ? "

" I couldn't, it was so embarrassing for me. I couldn't help hearing, at first, and then I was so angry and ashamed, I didn't remember that I ought to go away."

" Just wait till *I* see Annie Moffat, and I'll show you how to settle such ridiculous stuff. The idea of having ' plans,' and being kind to Laurie because he's rich, and may marry us by-and-by ! Won't he shout when I tell him what those silly things say about us poor children ! " and Jo laughed, as if, on second thoughts, the thing struck her as a good joke.

" If you tell Laurie, I'll never forgive you! She mustn't, must she, mother ? " said Meg, looking distressed.

" No ; never repeat that foolish gossip, and forget it as soon as you can," said Mrs. March gravely. " I was very unwise to let you go among people of whom I know so little ; kind, I dare say, but worldly, ill-bred, and full of these vulgar ideas about young people. I am more sorry than I can express for the mischief this visit may have done you, Meg."

" Don't be sorry ; I won't let it hurt me ; I'll forget all the bad, and remember only the good ; for I did enjoy a great deal, and thank you very much for letting me go. I'll not be sentimental or dissatisfied, mother ; I know I'm a silly little girl, and I'll stay with you till I'm fit to take care of myself. But it *is* nice to be praised and admired, and I can't help saying I like it," said Meg, looking half-ashamed of the confession.

" That is perfectly natural, and quite harmless, if the liking does not become a passion, and lead one to do foolish or unmaidenly things. Learn to know and value the praise which is worth having, and to excite the admiration of excellent people, by being modest as well as pretty, Meg."

Margaret sat thinking a moment, while Jo stood with her hands behind her, looking both interested and a little perplexed ; for it was a new thing to see Meg blushing and talking about admiration, lovers, and things of that sort, and Jo felt as if during that fortnight her sister had grown up amazingly, and was drifting away from her into a world where she could not follow.

" Mother, do you have ' plans,' as Mrs. Moffat said ? " asked Meg bashfully.

" Yes, my dear, I have a great many, all mothers do ; but mine differ somewhat from Mrs. Moffat's, I suspect. I will tell you some of them, for the time has come when a word may set this romantic little head right on a very serious subject.

" My dear girls, I *am* ambitious for you ; but not to have you make a dash in the world—marry rich men merely because they are rich, or have splendid houses, which are not homes, because love is wanting. Money is a needful and precious thing—and, when well used, a noble thing—but I never want you to think it is the first or only prize to strive for. I'd rather see you poor men's wives, if you were happy, beloved, contented, than queens on thrones, without self-respect and peace."

" Poor girls don't stand any chance, Belle says, unless they put themselves forward," sighed Meg.

" Then we'll be old maids," said Jo stoutly.

" Right, Jo ; better be happy old maids than unhappy wives, or unmaidenly girls, running about to find husbands," said Mrs. March decidedly. " Don't be troubled, Meg ; poverty seldom daunts a sincere lover. Some of the best and most honoured women I know were poor girls, but so loveworthy that they were not allowed to be old maids. Leave these things to time ; make this home happy, so that you may be fit for homes of your own, if they are offered you, and contented here if they are not. One thing remember, my girls, mother is always ready to be your confidante, father to be your friend ; and both of us trust and hope that our daughters, whether married or single, will be the pride and comfort of our lives."

" We will, Marmee, we will ! " cried both, with all their hearts, as she bade them good-night.

CHAPTER IX

EXPERIMENTS

"THE first of June ; the Kings are off to the seashore to-morrow, and I'm free ! Three months' vacation ! how I shall enjoy it ! " exclaimed Meg, coming home one warm day to find Jo laid upon the sofa in an unusual state of exhaustion, while Beth took off her dusty boots, and Amy made lemonade for the refreshment of the whole party.

" Aunt March went to-day, for which, oh be joyful ! " said Jo. " I was mortally afraid she'd ask me to go with her ; if she had, I should have felt as if I ought to do it ; but Plumfield is about as festive as a churchyard, you know, and I'd rather be excused. We had a flurry getting the old lady off, and I had a scare every time she spoke to me, for I was in such a hurry to be through that I was uncommonly helpful and sweet, and feared she'd find it impossible to part from me. I quaked till she was fairly in the carriage, and had a final fright, for, as it drove off, she popped out her head, saying, ' Josyphine, won't you——? ' I didn't hear any more, for I basely turned and fled ; I did actually run, and whisked round the corner, where I felt safe."

" Poor old Jo ! she came in looking as if bears were after her," said Beth, as she cuddled her sister's feet with a motherly air.

" Aunt March is a regular samphire, is she not ? " observed Amy, tasting ner mixture critically.

" She means *vampire*, not sea-weed ; but it don't matter ; it's too warm to be particular about one's parts of speech," murmured Jo.

" What shall you do all your vacation ? " asked Amy, changing the subject with tact.

" I shall lie a-bed late, and do nothing," replied Meg, from the depths of the rocking-chair. " I've been routed up early all winter, and had to spend my days working for other people, so now I'm going to rest and revel to my heart's content."

" Hum ! " said Jo ; " that dozy way wouldn't suit me. I've laid in a heap of books, and I'm going to improve my shining hours reading on my perch in the old apple tree, when I'm not having l——"

" Don't say ' larks ' ! " implored Amy, as a return snub for the " samphire " correction.

" I'll say ' nightingales,' then, with Laurie ; that's proper and appropriate, since he's a warbler."

" Don't let us do any lessons, Beth, for a while, but play all the time, and rest, as the girls mean to," proposed Amy.

" Well, I will, if mother don't mind. I want to learn some new songs, and my children need fixing up for the summer ; they are dreadfully out of order, and really suffering for clothes."

" May we, mother ? " asked Meg, turning to Mrs. March, who sat sewing in what they called " Marmee's corner."

" You may try your experiment for a week, and see how you like it. I

Amy put on her best frock and went off to walk

think by Saturday night you will find that all play and no work is as bad as all work and no play."

" Oh, dear, no ! it will be delicious, I'm sure," said Meg complacently.

" I now propose a toast, as my ' friend and pardner, Sairy Gamp,' says. Fun for ever and no grubbage," cried Jo, rising, glass in hand, as the lemonade went round.

They all drank it merrily, and began the experiment by lounging for the rest of the day. Next morning, Meg did not appear till ten o'clock ; her solitary breakfast did not taste good, and the room seemed lonely and untidy, for Jo had not filled the vases, Beth had not dusted, and Amy's books lay scattered about. Nothing was neat and pleasant but " Marmee's corner," which looked as usual ; and there she sat, to " rest and read," which meant yawn, and imagine what pretty summer dresses she could get with her salary. Jo spent the morning on the river with Laurie, and the afternoon reading and crying over *The Wide, Wide World* up in the apple-tree. Beth began by rummaging everything out of the big closet, where her family resided ; but getting tired before half done, she left her establishment topsy-turvy, and went to her music, rejoicing that she had no dishes to wash. Amy arranged her bower, put on her best white frock, smoothed her curls, and sat down to draw, under the honeysuckles, hoping some one would see and inquire who the young artist was. As no one appeared but an inquisitive daddy-long-legs, who examined her work with interest, she went to walk, got caught in a shower, and came home dripping.

At tea-time they compared notes, and all agreed that it had been a delightful, though unusually long day. Meg, who went shopping in the afternoon, and got a " sweet blue muslin," had discovered, after she had cut the breadths off, that it wouldn't wash, which mishap made her slightly cross. Jo had burnt the skin off her nose boating, and got a raging headache by reading too long. Beth was worried by the confusion of her closet, and the difficulty of learning three or four songs at once ; and Amy deeply regretted the damage done her frock, for Katy Brown's party was to be the next day ; and now, like Flora McFlimsy, she had " nothing to wear." But these were mere trifles, and they assured their mother that the experiment was working finely. She smiled, said nothing, and, with Hannah's help, did their neglected work, keeping home pleasant, and the domestic machinery running smoothly. It was astonishing what a peculiar and uncomfortable state of things was produced by the " resting and revelling " process. The days kept getting longer and longer ; the weather was unusually variable, and so were tempers ; an unsettled feeling possessed every one, and Satan found plenty of mischief for the idle hands to do. As the height of luxury, Meg put out some of her sewing, and then found time hang so heavily that she fell to snipping and spoiling her clothes, in her attempts to furbish them up, *à la* Moffat. Jo read till her eyes gave out, and she was sick of books ; got so fidgety that even good-natured Laurie had a quarrel with her, and so reduced in spirits that she desperately wished she had gone with Aunt March. Beth got on pretty well, for she was constantly forgetting that it was to be *all play and no work*, and fell back into her old ways, now and then ; but something in the air affected her, and, more than once, her tranquillity was much disturbed ; so much so that, on one occasion, she actually shook poor dear Joanna, and told her she was " a fright." Amy fared worst of all, for her resources were small ; and, when her sisters left her to amuse and care for herself, she soon found that accomplished and important little self a great burden. She didn't like dolls ; fairy tales were childish, and one couldn't draw all the time. Tea-parties didn't amount to much, neither did picnics, unless very well conducted. " If one could have a fine house, full of nice girls, or go travelling, the summer would be delightful ; but to stay at home with three selfish sisters and a grown-up boy was enough to try the patience of a Boaz," complained Miss Malaprop, after several days devoted to pleasure, fretting, and *ennui*.

No one would own that they were tired of the experiment ; but, by Friday night, each acknowledged to herself that they were glad the week was nearly done. Hoping to impress the lesson more deeply, Mrs. March, who had a good deal of humour, resolved to finish off the trial in an appropriate manner, so she gave Hannah a holiday, and let the girls enjoy the full effect of the play system.

When they got up on Saturday morning there was no fire in the kitchen, no breakfast in the dining-room, and no mother anywhere to be seen.

" Mercy on us ! what *has* happened ? " cried Jo, staring about her in dismay.

Meg ran upstairs, and soon came back again, looking relieved, but rather bewildered, and a little ashamed.

" Mother isn't sick, only very tired ; and she says she is going to stay quietly in her room all day, and let us do the best we can. It's a very queer thing for her to do ; she don't act a bit like herself ; but she says it *has* been a hard week for her, so we mustn't grumble, but take care of ourselves."

"That's easy enough, and I like the idea; I'm aching for something to do—that is, some new amusement, you know," added Jo quickly.

In fact, it *was* an immense relief to them all to have a little work, and they took hold with a will, but soon realised the truth of Hannah's saying, "Housekeeping ain't no joke." There was plenty of food in the larder, and, while Beth and Amy set the table, Meg and Jo got breakfast, wondering, as they did so, why servants ever talked about hard work.

"I shall take some up to mother, though she said we were not to think of her, for she'd take care of herself," said Meg, who presided, and felt quite matronly behind the teapot.

So a tray was fitted out before any one began, and taken up, with the cook's compliments. The boiled tea was very bitter, the omelette scorched, and the biscuits speckled with saleratus; but Mrs. March received her repast with thanks, and laughed heartily over it after Jo was gone.

"Poor little souls, they will have a hard time, I'm afraid; but they won't suffer, and it will do them good," she said, producing the more palatable viands with which she had provided herself, and disposing of the bad breakfast, so that their feelings might not be hurt—a motherly little deception, for which they were grateful.

Many were the complaints below, and great the chagrin of the head cook, at her failures. "Never mind, I'll get the dinner, and be servant; you be missis, keep your hands nice, see company, and give orders," said Jo, who knew still less than Meg about culinary affairs.

This obliging offer was gladly accepted, and Margaret retired to the parlour, which she hastily put in order by whisking the litter under the sofa, and shutting the blinds, to save the trouble of dusting. Jo, with perfect faith in her powers, and a friendly desire to make up the quarrel, immediately put a note in the office, inviting Laurie to dinner.

"You'd better see what you have got before you think of having company," said Meg, when informed of the hospitable but rash act.

"Oh, there's corned beef, and plenty of potatoes; and I shall get some asparagus, and a lobster, 'for a relish,' as Hannah says. We'll have lettuce, and make a salad; I don't know how, but the book tells. I'll have blanc-mange and strawberries for dessert; and coffee, too, if you want to be elegant."

"Don't try too many messes, Jo, for you can't make anything but ginger-bread and molasses candy fit to eat. I wash my hands of the dinner-party; and, since you have asked Laurie on your own responsibility, you may just take care of him."

"I don't want you to do anything but be clever to him, and help to the pudding. You'll give me your advice if I get stuck, won't you?" asked Jo, rather hurt.

"Yes; but I don't know much, except about bread, and a few trifles. You had better ask mother's leave, before you order anything," returned Meg prudently.

"Of course I shall; I ain't a fool;" and Jo went off in a huff at the doubts expressed of her powers.

"Get what you like, and don't disturb me; I'm going out to dinner, and can't worry about things at home," said Mrs. March, when Jo spoke to her. "I never enjoyed housekeeping, and I'm going to take a vacation to-day, and read, write, go visiting, and amuse myself."

The unusual spectacle of her busy mother rocking comfortably, and reading early in the morning made Jo feel as if some natural phenomenon had occurred; for an eclipse, an earthquake, or a volcanic eruption would hardly have seemed stranger.

"Everything is out of sorts, somehow," she said to herself, going downstairs. "There's Beth crying; that's a sure sign that something is wrong with this family. If Amy is bothering, I'll shake her."

Feeling very much out of sorts herself, Jo hurried into the parlour, to

" Get what you like," said Mrs. March

find Beth sobbing over Pip, the canary, who lay dead in the cage, with his little claws pathetically extended, as if imploring the food for want of which he had died.

"It's all my fault—I forgot him—there isn't a seed or drop left—oh, Pip! oh, Pip! how could I be so cruel to you!" cried Beth, taking the poor little thing in her hands, and trying to restore him.

Jo peeped into his half-open eye, felt his little heart, and finding him stiff and cold, shook her head, and offered her domino-box for a coffin.

"Put him in the oven, and maybe he will get warm, and revive," said Amy hopefully.

"He's been starved, and he shan't be baked, now he's dead. I'll make him a shroud, and he shall be buried in the grave; and I'll never have another bird, never, my Pip! for I am too bad to own one," murmured Beth, sitting on the floor with her pet folded in her hands.

"The funeral shall be this afternoon, and we will all go. Now, don't cry, Bethy; it's a pity, but nothing goes right this week, and Pip has had the worst of the experiment. Make the shroud, and lay him in my box;

and, after the dinner-party, we'll have a nice little funeral," said Jo, beginning to feel as if she had undertaken a good deal.

Leaving the others to console Beth, she departed to the kitchen, which was in a most discouraging state of confusion. Putting on a big apron, she fell to work, and got the dishes piled up ready for washing, when she discovered that the fire was out.

"Here's a sweet prospect!" muttered Jo, slamming the stove door open, and poking vigorously among the cinders.

Having re-kindled it, she thought she would go to market while the water heated. The walk revived her spirits; and, flattering herself she had made good bargains, she trudged home again, after buying a very young lobster, some very old asparagus, and two boxes of acid strawberries. By the time she had got cleared up, the dinner arrived, and the stove was red-hot. Hannah had left a pan of bread to rise, Meg had worked it up early, set it on the hearth for a second rising, and forgotten it. Meg was entertaining Sallie Gardiner, in the parlour, when the door flew open, and a floury, crocky, flushed, and dishevelled figure appeared, demanding tartly,—

"I say, isn't bread 'riz' enough when it runs over the pans?"

Sallie began to laugh; but Meg nodded, and lifted her eyebrows as high as they would go, which caused the apparition to vanish, and put the sour bread into the oven without further delay. Mrs. March went out, after peeping here and there to see how matters went, also saying a word of comfort to Beth, who sat making a winding-sheet, while the dear-departed lay in the domino-box. A strange sense of helplessness fell upon the girls as the gray bonnet vanished round the corner; and despair seized them when, a few minutes later, Miss Crocker appeared, and said she'd come to dinner. Now this lady was a thin, yellow spinster, with a sharp nose and inquisitive eyes, who saw everything, and gossiped about all she saw. They disliked her, but had been taught to be kind to her, simply because she was old and poor, and had few friends. So Meg gave her the easy chair, and tried to entertain her, while she asked questions, criticised everything, and told stories of the people whom she knew.

Language cannot describe the anxieties, experiences, and exertions which Jo underwent that morning; and the dinner she served up became a standing joke. Fearing to ask more advice, she did her best alone, and discovered that something more than energy and goodwill is necessary to make a cook. She boiled the asparagus hard for an hour, and was grieved to find the heads burnt off, and the stalks harder then ever. The bread burnt black; for the salad dressing so aggravated her that she let everything else go, till she had convinced herself that she could not make it fit to eat. The lobster was a great mystery to her, but she hammered and poked, till it was unshelled, and its meagre proportions concealed in a grove of lettuce leaves. The potatoes had to be hurried, not to keep the asparagus waiting, and were not done at last. The blanc-mange was lumpy, and the strawberries not as ripe as they looked, having been skilfully "deaconed."

"Well, they can eat beef and bread and butter, if they are hungry; only it's mortifying to have to spend your whole morning for nothing," thought Jo, so she rang the bell half an hour later than usual, and stood, hot, tired, and dispirited, surveying the feast spread for Laurie, accustomed to all sorts of elegance, and Miss Crocker, whose curious eyes would mark all failures, and whose tattling tongue would report them far and wide.

Poor Jo would gladly have gone under the table, as one thing after another was tasted and left ; while Amy giggled, Meg looked distressed, Miss Crocker pursed up her lips, and Laurie talked and laughed with all his might, to give a cheerful tone to the festive scene. Jo's one strong point was the fruit, for she had sugared it well, and had a pitcher of rich cream to eat with it. Her hot cheeks cooled a trifle, and she drew a long breath, as the pretty glass plates went round, and every one looked graciously at the little rosy islands floating in a sea of cream. Miss Crocker tasted first, made a wry face, and drank some water hastily. Jo, who had refused, thinking there might not be enough, for they dwindled sadly after the picking over, glanced at Laurie, but he was eating away manfully, though there was a slight pucker about his mouth, and he kept his eye fixed on his plate. Amy, who was fond of delicate fare, took a heaping spoonful, choked, hid her face in her napkin, and left the table precipitately.

" Oh, what is it ? " exclaimed Jo, trembling.

" Salt instead of sugar, and the cream is sour," replied Meg, with a tragic gesture.

Jo uttered a groan, and fell back in her chair, remembering that she had given a last hasty powdering to the berries out of one of the two boxes on the kitchen table, and had neglected to put the milk in the refrigerator. She turned scarlet, and was on the verge of crying, when she met Laurie's eyes, which *would* look merry, in spite of his heroic efforts ; the comical side of the affair suddenly struck her, and she laughed till the tears ran down her cheeks. So did every one else, even " Croaker," as the girls called the old lady, and the unfortunate dinner ended gaily, with bread and butter, olives and fun.

" I haven't strength of mind enough to clear up now, so we will sober ourselves with a funeral," said Jo, as they rose ; and Miss Crocker made ready to go, being eager to tell the new story at another friend's dinner table.

They did sober themselves, for Beth's sake ; Laurie dug a grave under the ferns in the grove, little Pip was laid in, with many tears, by his tender-hearted mistress, and covered with moss, while a wreath of violets and chick-weed was hung on the stone which bore his epitaph, composed by Jo, while she struggled with the dinner :—

> " Here lies Pip March,
>   Who died the 7th of June ;
> Loved and lamented sore,
>   And not forgotten soon."

At the conclusion of the ceremonies, Beth retired to her room, over-come with emotion and lobster ; but there was no place of repose, for the beds were not made, and she found her grief much assuaged by beating up pillows and putting things in order. Meg helped Jo clear away the remains of the feast, which took half the afternoon, and left them so tired that they agreed to be contented with tea and toast for supper. Laurie took Amy to drive, which was a deed of charity, for the sour cream seemed to have had a bad effect upon her temper. Mrs. March came home to find the three older girls hard at work in the middle of the afternoon ; and a glance at the closet gave her an idea of the success of one part of the experiment.

Before the housewives could rest, several people called, and there was a scramble to get ready to see them ; then tea must be got, errands done ; and one or two bits of sewing were necessary, but neglected till the last minute. As twilight fell, dewy and still, one by one they gathered in the porch, where June roses were budding beautifully, and each groaned or sighed as she sat down, as if tired or troubled.

" What a dreadful day this has been ! " began Jo, usually the first to speak.

" It has seemed shorter than usual, but *so* uncomfortable," said Meg.

" Not a bit like home," added Amy.

" It can't seem so without Marmee and little Pip," sighed Beth, glancing, with full eyes, at the empty cage above her head.

" Here's mother, dear ; and you shall have another bird to-morrow, if you want it."

As she spoke, Mrs. March came and took her place among them, looking as if her holiday had not been much pleasanter than theirs.

" Are you satisfied with your experiment, girls, or do you want another week of it ? " she asked, as Beth nestled up to her, and the rest turned towards her with brightening faces, as flowers turn toward the sun.

" I don't ! " cried Jo decidedly.

" Nor I," echoed the others.

" You think, then, that it is better to have a few duties, and live a little for others, do you ? "

" Lounging and larking don't pay," observed Jo, shaking her head. " I'm tired of it, and mean to go to work at something right off."

" Suppose you learn plain cooking ; that's a useful accomplishment, which no woman should be without," said Mrs. March, laughing audibly at the recollection of Jo's dinner-party ; for she had met Miss Crocker, and heard her account of it.

" Mother ! did you go away and let everything be, just to see how we'd get on ? " cried Meg, who had had suspicions all day.

" Yes ; I wanted you to see how the comfort of all depends on each doing her share faithfully. While Hannah and I did your work, you got on pretty well, though I don't think you were very happy or amiable ; so I thought, as a little lesson, I would show you what happens when every one thinks only of herself. Don't you feel that it is pleasanter to help one another, to have daily duties which make leisure sweet when it comes, and to bear or forbear, that home may be comfortable and lovely to us all ? "

" We do, mother, we do ! " cried the girls.

" Then let me advise you to take up your little burdens again ; for, though they seem heavy sometimes, they are good for us, and lighten as we learn to carry them. Work is wholesome, and there is plenty for every one ; it keeps us from *ennui* and mischief ; is good for health and spirits, and gives us a sense of power and independence better than money or fashion."

" We'll remember, mother ! " and they did.

CHAPTER X

CASTLES IN THE AIR

LAURIE lay luxuriously swinging to and fro in his hammock one warm September afternoon, wondering what his neighbours were about, but too lazy to go and find out. He was in one of his moods ; for the day had been unprofitable and unsatisfactory, and he was wishing he could live it over again. The hot weather made him indolent ; and he had shirked his studies, tried Mr. Brooke's patience to the utmost, displeased his grandfather by practising half the afternoon, frightened the maid-servants half out of their wits by mischievously hinting that one of his dogs was going mad, and, after high words with the stableman about some fancied neglect of his horse, he had flung himself into his hammock, to fume over the stupidity of the world in general till the peace of the lovely day quieted him in spite of himself. Staring up into the green gloom of the horse-chestnut trees above him, he dreamed dreams of all sorts, and was just imagining himself tossing on the ocean, in a voyage round the world, when the sound of voices brought him ashore in a flash. Peeping through the meshes of the hammock, he saw the Marches coming out, as if bound on some expedition.

" What in the world are those girls about now ? " thought Laurie, opening his sleepy eyes to take a good look, for there was something rather peculiar in the appearance of his neighbours. Each wore a large, flapping hat, a brown linen pouch slung over one shoulder, and carried a long staff ; Meg had a cushion, Jo a book, Beth a dipper, and Amy a portfolio. All walked quietly through the garden, out at the little back gate, and began to climb the hill that lay between the house and river.

" Well, that's cool ! " said Laurie to himself, " to have a picnic and never ask me. They can't be going in the boat, for they haven't got the key. Perhaps they forgot it ; I'll take it to them, and see what's going on."

Though possessed of half a dozen hats, it took him some time to find one ; then there was a hunt for the key, which was at last discovered in his pocket ; so that the girls were quite out of sight when he leaped the fence and ran after them. Taking the shortest way to the boat-house, he waited for them to appear ; but no one came, and he went up the hill to take an observation. A grove of pines covered one part of it, and from the heart of this green spot came a clearer sound than the soft sigh of the pines, or the drowsy chirp of the crickets.

" Here's a landscape ! " thought Laurie, peeping through the bushes, and looking wide-awake and good-natured already.

It *was* rather a pretty little picture ; for the sisters sat together in the shady nook, with sun and shadow flickering over them—the aromatic wind lifting their hair and cooling their hot cheeks—and all the little wood-people going on with their affairs as if these were no strangers, but old friends. Meg sat upon her cushion, sewing daintily with her white hands, and looking as fresh and sweet as a rose, in her pink dress, among the green. Beth was sorting the cones that lay thick under the hemlock near by, for she made pretty things of them. Amy was sketching a group of ferns, and Jo

" What in the world are those girls about now? "

was knitting as she read aloud. A shadow passed over the boy's face as he watched them, feeling that he ought to go, because uninvited ; yet lingering, because home seemed very lonely, and this quiet party in the woods most attractive to his restless spirit. He stood so still that a squirrel, busy with his harvesting, ran down a pine close beside him, saw him suddenly, and skipped back, scolding so shrilly that Beth looked, espied the wistful face behind the birches, and beckoned with a reassuring smile.

" May I come in, please ? or shall I be a bother ? " he asked, advancing slowly.

Meg lifted her eyebrows, but Jo scowled at her defiantly, and said, at once, " Of course you may. We should have asked you before, only we thought you wouldn't care for such a girl's game as this."

" I always like your games ; but if Meg don't want me, I'll go away."

" I've no objection, if you do something ; it's against the rule to be idle here," replied Meg gravely, but graciously.

" Much obliged ; I'll do anything if you'll let me stop a bit, for it's as dull as the desert of Sahara down there. Shall I sew, read, cone, draw, or do all at once ? Bring on your bears ; I'm ready ; " and Laurie sat down with a submissive expression delightful to behold.

" Finish this story while I set my heel," said Jo, handing him the book.

" Yes'm," was the meek answer, as he began, doing his best to prove his gratitude for the favour of an admission into the " Busy Bee Society."

The story was not a long one, and, when it was finished, he ventured to ask a few questions as a reward of merit.

" Please, mum, could I inquire if this highly instructive and charming institution is a new one ? "

" Would you tell him ? " asked Meg of her sisters.

" He'll laugh," said Amy warningly.

" Who cares ? " said Jo.

" I guess he'll like it," added Beth.

" Of course I shall ! I give you my word I won't laugh. Tell away, Jo, and don't be afraid."

" The idea of being afraid of you ! Well, you see, we used to play *Pilgrim's Progress*, and we have been going on with it in earnest all winter and summer."

" Yes, I know," said Laurie, nodding wisely.

" Who told you ? " demanded Jo.

" Spirits."

" No, it was me ; I wanted to amuse him one night when you were all away, and he was rather dismal. He did like it, so don't scold, Jo," said Beth meekly.

" You can't keep a secret. Never mind ; it saves trouble now."

" Go on, please," said Laurie, as Jo became absorbed in her work, looking a trifle displeased.

" Oh, didn't she tell you about this new plan of ours ? Well, we have tried not to waste our holiday, but each has had a task, and worked at it with a will. The vacation is nearly over, the stints are all done, and we are ever so glad that we didn't dawdle."

" Yes, I should think so ; " and Laurie thought regretfully of his own idle days.

" Mother likes to have us out of doors as much as possible ; so we bring our work here, and have nice times. For the fun of it we bring our things in these bags, wear the old hats, use poles to climb the hill, and play pilgrims, as we used to do years ago. We call this hill the ' Delectable Mountain,' for we can look far away and see the country where we hope to live sometime."

Jo pointed, and Laurie sat up to examine ; for through an opening in the wood one could look across the wide blue river—the meadows on the other side—far over the outskirts of the great city, to the green hills that rose to meet the sky. The sun was low, and the heavens glowed with the splendour of an autumn sunset. Gold and purple clouds lay on the hill-tops ; and rising high into the ruddy light were silvery white peaks that shone like the airy spires of some Celestial City.

" How beautiful that is ! " said Laurie softly, for he was quick to see and feel beauty of any kind.

" It's often so ; and we like to watch it, for it is never the same, but always splendid," replied Amy, wishing she could paint it.

" Jo talks about the country where we hope to live sometime ; the real country, she means, with pigs and chickens, and hay-making. It would be nice, but I wish the beautiful country up there was real, and we could ever go to it," said Beth musingly.

" There is a lovelier country even than that, where we *shall* go, by-and-by, when we are good enough," answered Meg, with her sweet voice.

" It seems so long to wait, so hard to do ; I want to fly away at once, as those swallows fly, and go in at that splendid gate."

" You'll get there, Beth, sooner or later ; no fear of that," said Jo ; " I'm the one that will have to fight and work, and climb and wait, and maybe never get in after all."

" You'll have me for company, if that's any comfort. I shall have to do a deal of travelling before I come in sight of your Celestial City. If I arrive late, you'll say a good word for me, won't you, Beth ? "

Something in the boy's face troubled his little friend ; but she said cheerfully, with her quiet eyes on the changing clouds, " If people really want to go, and really try all their lives, I think they will get in ; for I don't believe there are any locks on that door, or any guards at the gate. I always imagine it is as it is in the picture, where the shining ones stretch out their hands to welcome poor Christian as he comes up from the river."

" Wouldn't it be fun if all the castles in the air which we make could come true, and we could live in them ! " said Jo, after a little pause.

" I've made such quantities it would be hard to choose which I'd have," said Laurie, lying flat, and throwing cones at the squirrel who had betrayed him.

" You'd have to take your favourite one. What is it ? " asked Meg.

" If I tell mine, will you tell yours ? "

" Yes, if the girls will too."

" We will. Now, Laurie ! "

" After I'd seen as much of the world as I want to, I'd like to settle in Germany, and have just as much music as I choose. I'm to be a famous musician myself, and all creation is to rush to hear me ; and I'm never to be bothered about money or business, but just enjoy myself, and live for what I like. That's my favourite castle. What's yours, Meg ? "

Margaret seemed to find it a little hard to tell hers, and moved a brake before her face, as if to disperse imaginary gnats, while she said slowly, " I should like a lovely house, full of all sorts of luxurious things : nice food, pretty clothes, handsome furniture, pleasant people, and heaps of money. I am to be mistress of it, and manage it as I like, with plenty of servants, so I never need to work a bit. How I should enjoy it ! for I wouldn't be idle, but do good, and make every one love me dearly."

" Wouldn't you have a master for your castle in the air ? " asked Laurie shyly.

" I said ' pleasant people,' you know ; " and Meg carefully tied up her shoe as she spoke, so that no one saw her face.

" Why don't you say you'd have a splendid, wise, good husband, and some angelic little children ? You know your castle wouldn't be perfect without," said blunt Jo, who had no tender fancies yet, and rather scorned romance, except in books.

" You'd have nothing but horses, inkstands, and novels in yours," answered Meg petulantly.

" Wouldn't I, though ! I'd have a stable full of Arabian steeds, rooms piled with books, and I'd write out of a magic inkstand, so that my works should be as famous as Laurie's music. I want to do something splendid before I go into my castle—something heroic or wonderful—that won't be forgotten after I'm dead. I don't know what, but I'm on the watch for it, and mean to astonish you all some day. I think I shall write books, and get rich and famous ; that would suit me, so that is *my* favourite dream."

" Mine is to stay at home safe with father and mother, and help take care of the family," said Beth contentedly.

" Don't you wish for anything else ? " asked Laurie.

" Since I had my little piano I am perfectly satisfied. I only wish we may keep well, and be together ; nothing else."

" I have lots of wishes ; but the pet one is to be an artist, and go to Rome, and do fine pictures, and be the best artist in the whole world," was Amy's modest desire.

" We're an ambitious set, aren't we ? Every one of us but Beth wants to be rich and famous, and gorgeous in every respect. I do wonder if any of us will ever get our wishes," said Laurie, chewing grass, like a meditative calf.

" I've got the key to my castle in the air ; but whether I can unlock the door remains to be seen," observed Jo mysteriously.

" I've got the key to mine, but I'm not allowed to try it. Hang college ! " muttered Laurie, with an impatient sigh.

" Here's mine ! " and Amy waved her pencil.

" I haven't got any," said Meg forlornly.

" Yes, you have," said Laurie at once.

" Where ? "

" In your face."

" Nonsense ; that's of no use."

" Wait and see if it doesn't bring you something worth having," replied the boy, laughing at the thought of a charming little secret which he fancied he knew.

Meg coloured behind the brake, but asked no questions, and looked across the river with the same expectant expression which Mr. Brooke had worn when he told the story of the knight.

" If we are all alive ten years hence, let's meet, and see how many of us have got our wishes, or how much nearer we are them than now," said Jo, always ready with a plan.

" Bless me ! how old I shall be—twenty-seven ! " exclaimed Meg, who felt grown up already, having just reached seventeen.

" You and I shall be twenty-six, Teddy ; Beth twenty-four, and Amy twenty-two ; what a venerable party ! " said Jo.

" I hope I shall have done something to be proud of by that time ; but I'm such a lazy dog, I'm afraid I shall ' dawdle,' Jo."

" You need a motive, mother says ; and when you get it, she is sure you'll work splendidly."

" Is she ? By Jupiter ! I will, if I only get the chance ! " cried Laurie, sitting up with sudden energy. " I ought to be satisfied to please grandfather, and I do try, but it's working against the grain, you see, and comes hard. He wants me to be an India merchant, as he was, and I'd rather be shot ; I hate tea, and silk, and spices, and every sort of rubbish his old ships bring, and I don't care how soon they go to the bottom when I own them. Going to college ought to satisfy him, for if I give him four years, he ought to let me off from the business ; but he's set, and I've got to do just as he did, unless I break away and please myself, as my father did. If there was any one left to stay with the old gentleman, I'd do it to-morrow."

Laurie spoke excitedly, and looked ready to carry his threat into execution on the slightest provocation ; for he was growing up very fast, and, in spite of his indolent ways, had a young man's hatred of subjection—a young man's restless longing to try the world for himself.

"I advise you to sail away in one of your ships, and never come home again till you have tried your own way," said Jo, whose imagination was fired by the thought of such a daring exploit, and whose sympathy was excited by what she called " Teddy's wrongs."

"That's not right, Jo ; you mustn't talk in that way, and Laurie mustn't take your bad advice. You should do just what your grandfather wishes, my dear boy," said Meg, in her most maternal tone. " Do your best at college, and, when he sees that you try to please him, I'm sure he won't be hard or unjust to you. As you say, there is no one else to stay with and love him, and you'd never forgive yourself if you left him without his permission. Don't be dismal, or fret, but do your duty ; and you'll get your reward, as good Mr. Brooke has, by being respected and loved."

"What do you know about him ?" asked Laurie, grateful for the good advice, but objecting to the lecture, and glad to turn the conversation from himself, after his unusual outbreak.

"Only what your grandpa told mother about him ; how he took good care of his own mother till she died, and wouldn't go abroad as tutor to some nice person, because he wouldn't leave her ; and how he provides now for an old woman who nursed his mother ; and never tells any one, but is just as generous, and patient, and good as he can be."

"So he is, dear old fellow !" said Laurie heartily, as Meg paused, looking flushed and earnest with her story. " It's like grandpa to find out all about him, without letting him know, and to tell all his goodness to others, so that they might like him. Brooke couldn't understand why your mother was so kind to him, asking him over with me, and treating him in her beautiful, friendly way. He thought she was just perfect, and talked about it for days and days, and went on about you all in flaming style. If ever I do get my wish, you'll see what I'll do for Brooke."

"Begin to do something now, by not plaguing his life out," said Meg sharply.

"How do you know I do, miss ?"

"I can always tell by his face when he goes away. If you have been good, he looks satisfied, and walks briskly ; if you have plagued him, he's sober, and walks slowly, as if he wanted to go back and do his work better."

"Well, I like that ! So you keep an account of my good and bad marks in Brooke's face, do you ? I see him bow and smile as he passes your window, but I didn't know you'd got up a telegraph."

"We haven't ; don't be angry, and, oh, don't tell him I said anything ! It was only to show that I cared how you got on, and what is said here is said in confidence, you know," cried Meg, much alarmed at the thought of what might follow from her careless speech.

"*I* don't tell tales," replied Laurie, with his " high and mighty " air, as Jo called a certain expression which he occasionally wore. " Only if

C.T.B.   N

Brooke is going to be a thermometer, I must mind and have fair weather for him to report."

" Please don't be offended ; I didn't mean to preach, or tell tales, or be silly ; I only thought Jo was encouraging you in a feeling which you'd be sorry for by-and-by. You are so kind to us, we feel as if you were our brother, and just say what we think ; forgive me, I meant kindly ! " and Meg offered her hand with a gesture both affectionate and timid.

Ashamed of his momentary pique, Laurie squeezed the kind little hand, and said frankly, " I'm the one to be forgiven ; I'm cross, and have been out of sorts all day. I like to have you tell me my faults, and be sisterly ; so don't mind if I am grumpy sometimes, I thank you all the same."

Bent on showing that he was not offended, he made himself as agreeable as possible : wound cotton for Meg, recited poetry to please Jo, shook down cones for Beth, and helped Amy with her ferns—proving himself a fit person to belong to the " Busy Bee Society." In the midst of an animated discussion on the domestic habits of turtles (one of which amiable creatures having strolled up from the river), the faint sound of a bell warned them that Hannah had put the tea to " draw," and they would just have time to get home to supper.

" May I come again ? " asked Laurie.

" Yes, if you are good, and love your book, as the boys in the primer are told to do," said Meg, smiling.

" I 'll try."

" Then you may come, and I 'll teach you to knit as the Scotchmen do ; there's a demand for socks just now," added Jo, waving hers, like a big blue worsted banner, as they parted at the gate.

That night, when Beth played to Mr. Laurence in the twilight, Laurie, standing in the shadow of the curtain, listened to the little David, whose simple music always quieted his moody spirit, and watched the old man, who sat with his gray head on his hand, thinking tender thoughts of the dead child he had loved so much. Remembering the conversation of the afternoon, the boy said to himself, with the resolve to make the sacrifice cheerfully, " I 'll let my castle go, and stay with the dear old gentleman while he needs me, for I am all he has."

CHAPTER XI

SECRETS

JO was very busy up in the garret, for the October days began to grow chilly, and the afternoons were short. For two or three hours the sun lay warmly in at the high window, showing Jo seated on the old sofa writing busily, with her papers spread out upon a trunk before her, while Scrabble, the pet rat, promenaded the beams overhead, accompanied by his oldest son, a fine young fellow, who was evidently very proud of his whiskers. Quite absorbed in her work, Jo scribbled away till the last page was filled, when she signed her name with a flourish, and threw down the pen, exclaiming,—

" There, I've done my best ! If this don't suit, I shall have to wait till I can do better."

Lying back on the sofa, she read the manuscript carefully through, making dashes here and there, and putting in many exclamation points, which looked like little balloons ; then she tied it up with a smart red ribbon, and sat a minute looking at it with a sober, wistful expression, which plainly showed how earnest her work had been. Jo's desk up here was an old tin kitchen, which hung against the wall. In it she kept her papers, and a few books, safely shut away from Scrabble, who, being likewise of a literary turn, was fond of making a circulating library of such books as were left in his way, by eating the leaves. From this tin receptacle Jo produced another manuscript ; and, putting both in her pocket, crept quietly downstairs, leaving her friends to nibble her pens and taste her ink.

She put on her hat and jacket as noiselessly as possible, and, going to the back entry window, got out upon the roof of a low porch, swung herself down to the grassy bank, and took a roundabout way to the road. Once there she composed herself, hailed a passing omnibus, and rolled away to town, looking very merry and mysterious.

If any one had been watching her, he would have thought her movements decidedly peculiar ; for, on alighting, she went off at a great pace till she reached a certain number in a certain busy street. Having found the place with some difficulty, she went into the doorway, looked up the dirty stairs, and, after standing stock still a minute, suddenly dived into the street, and walked away as rapidly as she came. This manœuvre she repeated several times, to the great amusement of a black-eyed young gentleman lounging in the window of a building opposite. On returning for the third time, Jo gave herself a shake, pulled her hat over her eyes, and walked up the stairs, looking as if she was going to have all her teeth out.

There was a dentist's sign, among others, which adorned the entrance, and after staring a moment at the pair of artificial jaws which slowly opened and shut, to draw attention to a fine set of teeth, the young gentleman put on his coat, took his hat, and went down to post himself in the opposite doorway, saying, with a smile and a shiver,—

" It's like her to come alone, but if she has a bad time, she'll need some one to help her home."

In ten minutes Jo came running downstairs with a very red face, and the general appearance of a person who had just passed through a trying ordeal of some sort. When she saw the young gentleman she looked anything but pleased, and passed him with a nod ; but he followed, asking with an air of sympathy,—

" Did you have a bad time ? "

" Not very."

" You got through quick."

" Yes, thank goodness ! "

" Why did you go alone ? "

" Didn't want any one to know."

" You're the oddest fellow I ever saw. How many did you have out ? "

Jo looked at her friend as if she did not understand him ; then began to laugh, as if mightily amused at something.

" There are two which I want to have come out, but I must wait a week."

" What are you laughing at ? You are up to some mischief, Jo," said Laurie, looking mystified.

" So are you. What were you doing, sir, up in that billiard saloon ? "

" Begging your pardon, ma'am, it wasn't a billiard saloon, but a gymnasium, and I was taking a lesson in fencing."

" I am glad of that."

" Why ? "

" You can teach me ; and then, when we play *Hamlet*, you can be Laertes, and we'll make a fine thing of the fencing scene."

Laurie burst out with a hearty boy's laugh, which made several passers-by smile in spite of themselves.

" I'll teach you, whether we play *Hamlet* or not ; it's grand fun, and will straighten you up capitally. But I don't believe that was your only reason for saying, ' I'm glad,' in that decided way ; was it, now ? "

" No ; I was glad you were not in the saloon, because I hope you never go to such places. Do you ? "

" Not often."

" I wish you wouldn't."

" It's no harm, Jo. I have billiards at home, but it's no fun unless you have good players ; so, as I'm fond of it, I come sometimes and have a game with Ned Moffat or some of the other fellows."

" Oh dear, I am so sorry, for you'll get to liking it better and better, and will waste time and money, and grow like those dreadful boys. I did hope you'd stay respectable, and be a satisfaction to your friends," said Jo, shaking her head.

" Can't a fellow take a little innocent amusement now and then without losing his respectability ? " asked Laurie, looking nettled.

" That depends on how and where he takes it. I don't like Ned and his set, and wish you'd keep out of it. Mother won't let us have him at our house, though he wants to come ; and if you grow like him, she won't be willing to have us frolic together as we do now."

" Won't she ? " asked Laurie anxiously.

" No ; she can't bear fashionable young men, and she'd shut us all up in bandboxes rather than have us associate with them."

" Well, she needn't get out her bandboxes yet ; I'm not a fashionable party, and don't mean to be ; but I do like harmless larks now and then, don't you ? "

" Yes ; nobody minds them, so lark away, but don't get wild, will you ? or there will be an end of all our good times."

" I'll be a double-distilled saint."

" I can't bear saints ; just be a simple, honest, respectable boy, and we'll never desert you. I don't know what I *should* do if you acted like Mr. King's son ; he had plenty of money, but didn't know how to spend it, and got tipsy, and gambled, and ran away, and forged his father's name, I believe, and was altogether horrid."

" You think I am likely to do the same ? Much obliged."

" No, I don't—oh, *dear*, no !—but I hear people talking about money being such a temptation, and I sometimes wish you were poor ; I shouldn't worry then."

" Do you worry about me, Jo ? "

" A little, when you look moody or discontented, as you sometimes do ; for you've got such a strong will, if you once get started wrong, I'm afraid it would be hard to stop you."

Laurie walked in silence a few minutes, and Jo watched him, wishing she had held her tongue, for his eyes looked angry, though his lips still smiled as if at her warnings.

" Are you going to deliver lectures all the way home ? " he asked presently.

" Of course not ; why ? "

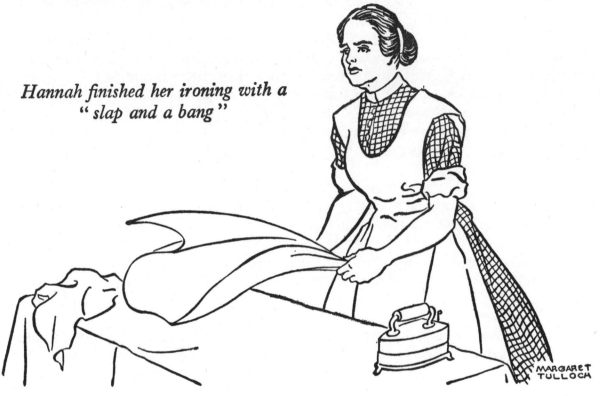

Hannah finished her ironing with a " slap and a bang "

" Because if you are, I'll take a 'bus ; if you are not, I'd like to walk with you, and tell you something very interesting."

" I won't preach any more, and I'd like to hear the news immensely."

" Very well, then ; come on. It's a secret, and if I tell you, you must tell me yours."

" I haven't got any," began Jo, but stopped suddenly, remembering that she had.

" You know you have ; you can't hide anything, so up and 'fess, or I won't tell," cried Laurie.

" Is your secret a nice one ? "

" Oh, isn't it ! all about people you know, and such fun ! You ought to hear it, and I've been aching to tell you this long time. Come, you begin."

" You'll not say anything about it at home, will you ? "

" Not a word."

" And you won't tease me in private ? "

" I never tease."

" Yes, you do ; you get everything you want out of people. I don't know how you do it, but you are a born wheedler."

" Thank you ; fire away ! "

" Well, I've left two stories with a newspaper man, and he's to give his answer next week," whispered Jo in her confidant's ear.

" Hurrah for Miss March, the celebrated American authoress ! " cried Laurie, throwing up his hat and catching it again, to the great delight of two ducks, four cats, five hens, and half a dozen Irish children ; for they were out of the city now.

" Hush ! it won't come to anything, I dare say ; but I couldn't rest till I had tried, and I said nothing about it, because I didn't want any one else to be disappointed."

" It won't fail ! Why, Jo, your stories are works of Shakespeare compared with half the rubbish that's published every day. Won't it be fun to see them in print ! And shan't we feel proud of our authoress ! "

Jo's eyes sparkled, for it's always pleasant to be believed in ; and a friend's praise is always sweeter than a dozen newspaper puffs.

" Where's *your* secret ? Play fair, Teddy, or I'll never believe you again," she said, trying to extinguish the brilliant hopes that blazed up at a word of encouragement.

" I may get into a scrape for telling ; but I didn't promise not to, so I will, for I never feel easy in my mind till I've told you any plummy bit of news I get. I know where Meg's glove is."

" Is that all ? " said Jo, looking disappointed, as Laurie nodded, and twinkled, with a face full of mysterious intelligence.

" It's quite enough for the present, as you'll agree when I tell you where it is."

" Tell, then."

Laurie bent and whispered three words in Jo's ear, which produced a comical change. She stood and stared at him for a minute, looking both surprised and displeased, then walked on, saying sharply, " How do you know ? "

" Saw it."

" Where ? "

" Pocket."

" All this time ? "

" Yes ; isn't that romantic ? "

" No ; it's horrid."

" Don't you like it ? "

" Of course I don't ; it's ridiculous ; it won't be allowed. My patience ! what would Meg say ? "

" You are not to tell any one ; mind that."

" I didn't promise."

" That was understood, and I trusted you."

" Well, I won't for the present, anyway ; but I'm disgusted, and wish you hadn't told me."

" I thought you'd be pleased."

" At the idea of anybody coming to take Meg away ? No, thank you."

" You'll feel better about it when somebody comes to take you away."

" I'd like to see any one try it," cried Jo fiercely.

" So should I ! " and Laurie chuckled at the idea.

" I don't think secrets agree with me ; I feel rumpled up in my mind since you told me that," said Jo, rather ungratefully.

" Race down this hill with me, and you'll be all right," suggested Laurie.

No one was in sight ; the smooth road sloped invitingly before her, and, finding the temptation irresistible, Jo darted away, soon leaving hat and comb behind her, and scattering hairpins as she ran. Laurie reached the goal first, and was quite satisfied with the success of his treatment ; for his Atalanta came panting up with flying hair, bright eyes, ruddy cheeks, and no signs of dissatisfaction in her face.

" I wish I was a horse ; then I could run for miles in this splendid air, and not lose my breath. It was capital ! but see what a guy it's made me. Go, pick up my things, like a cherub as you are," said Jo, dropping down under a maple-tree, which was carpeting the bank with crimson leaves.

Laurie leisurely departed to recover the lost property, and Jo bundled up her braids, hoping no one would pass by till she was tidy again. But some one did pass, and who should it be but Meg, looking particularly lady-like in her state and festival suit, for she had been making calls.

" What in the world are you doing here ? " she asked, regarding her dishevelled sister with well-bred surprise.

" Getting leaves," meekly answered Jo, sorting the rosy handful she had just swept up.

" And hairpins," added Laurie, throwing half a dozen into Jo's lap. " They grow on this road, Meg ; so do combs and brown straw hats."

" You have been running, Jo ; how could you ? When *will* you stop such romping ways ? " said Meg reprovingly, as she settled her cuffs and smoothed her hair, with which the wind had taken liberties.

" Never till I'm stiff and old, and have to use a crutch. Don't try to make me grow up before my time, Meg ; it's hard enough to have you change all of a sudden ; let me be a little girl as long as I can."

As she spoke, Jo bent over her work to hide the trembling of her lips ; for lately she had felt that Margaret was fast getting to be a woman, and Laurie's secret made her dread the separation which must surely come some time, and now seemed very near. He saw the trouble in her face, and drew Meg's attention from it by asking quickly, " Where have you been calling, all so fine ? "

" At the Gardiners' ; and Sallie has been telling me all about Belle Moffat's wedding. It was very splendid, and they have gone to spend the winter in Paris ; just think how delightful that must be ! "

" Do you envy her, Meg ? " said Laurie.

" I'm afraid I do."

" I'm glad of it ! " muttered Jo, tying on her hat with a jerk.

" Why ? " asked Meg, looking surprised.

" Because, if you care much about riches, you will never go and marry a poor man," said Jo, frowning at Laurie, who was mutely warning her to mind what she said.

" I shall never ' *go* and marry ' any one," observed Meg, walking on with great dignity, while the others followed, laughing, whispering, skipping stones, and " behaving like children," as Meg said to herself, though she might have been tempted to join them if she had not had her best dress on.

For a week or two Jo behaved so queerly that her sisters got quite bewildered. She rushed to the door when the postman rang ; was rude to Mr. Brooke whenever they met ; would sit looking at Meg, with a woebegone face, occasionally jumping up to shake, and then to kiss her, in a very mysterious manner ; Laurie and she were always making signs to one another, and talking about " Spread Eagles," till the girls declared they had both lost their wits. On the second Saturday after Jo got out of the window, Meg, as she sat sewing at her window, was scandalised by the sight of Laurie chasing Jo all over the garden, and finally capturing her in Amy's bower. What went on there Meg could not see, but shrieks of laughter were heard, followed by the murmur of voices, and a great flapping of newspapers.

" What shall we do with that girl ? She never *will* behave like a young lady," sighed Meg, as she watched the race with a disapproving face.

" I hope she won't ; she is so funny and dear as she is," said Beth, who had never betrayed that she was a little hurt at Jo's having secrets with any one but her.

" It's very trying, but we never can make her *comme la fo*," added Amy, who sat making some new frills for herself with her curls tied up in a very becoming way—two agreeable things, which made her feel unusually elegant and lady-like.

In a few minutes Jo bounced in, laid herself on the sofa, and affected to read.

" Have you anything interesting there ? " asked Meg, with condescension.

" Nothing but a story ! don't amount to much, I guess," returned Jo, carefully keeping the name of the paper out of sight.

" You'd better read it aloud ; that will amuse us, and keep you out of mischief," said Amy, in her most grown-up tone.

" What's the name ? " asked Beth, wondering why Jo kept her face behind the sheet.

" *The Rival Painters*."

" That sounds well ; read it," said Meg.

With a loud " hem ! " and a long breath, Jo began to read very fast. The girls listened with interest, for the tale was romantic, and somewhat pathetic, as most of the characters died in the end.

" I like that about the splendid picture," was Amy's approving remark, as Jo paused.

" I prefer the lovering part. Viola and Angelo are two of our favourite names ; isn't that queer ? " said Meg, wiping her eyes, for the " lovering " part was tragical.

" Who wrote it ? " asked Beth, who had caught a glimpse of Jo's face.

The reader suddenly sat up, cast away the paper, displaying a flushed countenance, and, with a funny mixture of solemnity and excitement, replied in a loud voice, " Your sister ! "

" You ? " cried Meg, dropping her work.

" It's very good," said Amy critically.

"I knew it! I knew it! Oh, my Jo, I *am* so proud!" and Beth ran to hug her sister and exult over this splendid success.

Dear me, how delighted they all were, to be sure; how Meg wouldn't believe it till she saw the words, "Miss Josephine March," actually printed in the paper; how graciously Amy criticised the artistic parts of the story, and offered hints for a sequel, which unfortunately couldn't be carried out, as the hero and heroine were dead; how Beth got excited, and skipped and sung with joy; how Hannah came in to exclaim, "Sakes alive! well, I never!" in great astonishment at "that Jo's doin's;" how proud Mrs. March was when she knew it; how Jo laughed, with tears in her eyes, as she declared she might as well be a peacock and done with it; and how the *Spread Eagle* might be said to flap his wings triumphantly over the house of March, as the paper passed from hand to hand.

"Tell us about it." "When did it come?" "How much did you get for it?" "What *will* father say?" "Won't Laurie laugh!" cried the family, all in one breath, as they clustered about Jo; for these foolish, affectionate people made a jubilee of every little household joy.

"Stop jabbering, girls, and I'll tell you everything," said Jo, wondering if Miss Burney felt any grander over her *Evelina* than she did over her *Rival Painters*. Having told how she disposed of her tales, Jo added,— "And when I went to get my answer, the man said he liked them both, but didn't pay beginners, only let them print in his paper, and noticed the stories. It was good practice, he said; and when the beginners improved any one would pay. So I let him have the two stories, and to-day this was sent to me, and Laurie caught me with it, and insisted on seeing it, so I let him; and he said it was good, and I shall write more, and he's going to get the next paid for; and, oh!—I *am* so happy, for in time I may be able to support myself and help the girls."

Jo's breath gave out here; and, wrapping her head in the paper, she bedewed her little story with a few natural tears; for to be independent, and earn the praise of those she loved, were the dearest wishes of her heart, and this seemed to be the first step toward that happy end.

CHAPTER XII

A TELEGRAM

"NOVEMBER is the most disagreeable month in the whole year," said Margaret, standing at the window one dull afternoon, looking out at the frost-bitten garden.

"That's the reason I was born in it," observed Jo pensively, quite unconscious of the blot on her nose.

"If something very pleasant should happen now, we should think it a delightful month," said Beth, who took a hopeful view of everything, even November.

"I dare say; but nothing pleasant ever *does* happen in this family," said Meg, who was out of sorts. "We go grubbing along day after day,

without a bit of change, and very little fun. We might as well be in a treadmill."

Beth, who sat at the other window, said, smiling, " Two pleasant things
are going to happen right away : Marmee is coming down the street, and
Laurie is tramping through the garden as if he had something nice to tell."

In they both came, Mrs. March with her usual question, " Any letter
from father, girls ? " and Laurie to say, in his persuasive way, " Won't some
of you come for a drive ? I've been pegging away at mathematics till my
head is in a muddle, and I'm going to freshen my wits by a brisk turn. It's
a dull day, but the air isn't bad, and I'm going to take Brooke home, so it
will be gay inside, if it isn't out. Come, Jo, you and Beth will go, won't
you ? "

" Of course we will."

" Much obliged, but I'm busy ; " and Meg whisked out her work-
basket, for she had agreed with her mother that it was best, for her at least,
not to drive often with the young gentleman.

" We three shall be ready in a minute," cried Amy, running away to
wash her hands.

" Can I do anything for you, Madam Mother ? " asked Laurie, leaning
over Mrs. March's chair, with the affectionate look and tone he always gave
her.

" No, thank you, except call at the office, if you'll be so kind, dear. It's
our day for a letter, and the penny postman hasn't been. Father is as regular
as the sun, but there's some delay on the way, perhaps."

A sharp ring interrupted her, and a minute after Hannah came in with
a letter.

" It's one of them horrid telegraph things, mum," she said, handling it
as if she were afraid it would explode, and do some damage.

At the word " telegraph," Mrs. March snatched it, read the two lines it
contained, and dropped back into her chair as white as if the little paper
had sent a bullet to her heart. Laurie dashed downstairs for water, while
Meg and Hannah supported her, and Jo read aloud in a frightened voice,—

" Mrs. March :—Your husband is very ill. Come at once.

" S. Hale,

" Blank Hospital, Washington."

How still the room was as they listened breathlessly ! how strangely
the day darkened outside ! and how suddenly the whole world seemed to
change, as the girls gathered about their mother, feeling as if all the happiness and support of their lives was about to be taken from them. Mrs.
March was herself again directly ; read the message over, and stretched
out her arms to her daughters, saying, in a tone they never forgot, " I shall
go at once, but it may be too late ; oh, children, children ; help me to bear
it ! "

For several minutes there was nothing but the sound of sobbing in the
room, mingled with broken words of comfort, tender assurances of help,
and hopeful whispers that died away in tears. Poor Hannah was the first

to recover, and with unconscious wisdom she set all the rest a good example ; for, with her, work was the panacea for most afflictions.

" The Lord keep the dear man ! I won't waste no time a cryin', but get your things ready right away, mum," she said heartily, as she wiped her face on her apron, gave her mistress a warm shake of the hand with her own hard one, and went away to work like three women in one.

" She's right ; there's no time for tears now. Be calm, girls, and let me think."

They tried to be calm, poor things, as their mother sat up, looking pale, but steady, and put away her grief to think and plan for them.

" Where's Laurie ? " she asked presently, when she had collected her thoughts, and decided on the first duties to be done.

" Here, ma'am ; oh, let me do something ! " cried the boy, hurrying from the next room, whither he had withdrawn, feeling that their first sorrow was too sacred for even his friendly eyes to see.

" Send a telegram saying I will come at once. The next train goes early in the morning ; I'll take that."

" What else ? The horses are ready ; I can go anywhere,—do anything," he said, looking ready to fly to the ends of the earth.

" Leave a note at Aunt March's. Jo, give me that pen and paper."

Tearing off the blank side of one of her newly-copied pages, Jo drew the table before her mother, well knowing that money for the long, sad journey must be borrowed, and feeling as if she could do anything to add a little to the sum for her father.

" Now go, dear ; but don't kill yourself driving at a desperate pace : there is no need for that."

Mrs. March's warning was evidently thrown away ; for five minutes later Laurie tore by the window, on his own fleet horse, riding as for life.

" Jo, run to the rooms and tell Mrs. King that I can't come. On the way get these things. I'll put them down ; they'll be needed, and I must go prepared for nursing. Hospital stores are not always good. Beth, go and ask Mr. Laurence for a couple bottles of old wine ; I'm not too proud to beg for father ; he shall have the best of everything. Amy, tell Hannah to get down the black trunk ; and, Meg, come and help me find my things, for I'm half bewildered."

Writing, thinking, and directing all at once might well bewilder the poor lady, and Meg begged her to sit quietly in her room for a little while, and let them work. Every one scattered, like leaves before a gust of wind ; and the quiet, happy household was broken up as suddenly as if the paper had been an evil spell.

Mr. Laurence came hurrying back with Beth, bringing every comfort the kind old gentleman could think of for the invalid, and friendliest promises of protection for the girls during the mother's absence, which comforted her very much. There was nothing he didn't offer, from his own dressing-gown to himself as escort. But that last was impossible. Mrs. March would not hear of the old gentleman's undertaking the long journey ; yet an expression of relief was visible when he spoke of it, for anxiety ill fits one for travelling. He saw the look, knit his eyebrows, rubbed his hands, and marched abruptly away, saying he'd be back directly. No one had time to think of him again till, as Meg ran through the entry, with a pair of rubbers in one hand and a cup of tea in the other, she came suddenly upon Mr. Brooke.

" I'm very sorry to hear of this, Miss March," he said, in the kind, quiet tone which sounded very pleasantly to her perturbed spirit. " I came to offer myself as escort to your mother. Mr. Laurence has commissions for me in Washington, and it will give me real satisfaction to be of service to her there."

Down dropped the rubbers, and the tea was very near following, as Meg put out her hand, with a face so full of gratitude, that Mr. Brooke would have felt repaid for a much greater sacrifice than the trifling one of time and comfort which he was about to make.

" How kind you all are ! Mother will accept, I'm sure ; and it will be such a relief to know that she has some one to take care of her. Thank you very, very much ! "

Meg spoke earnestly, and forgot herself entirely till something in the brown eyes looking down at her made her remember the cooling tea, and lead the way into the parlour, saying she would call her mother.

Everything was arranged by the time Laurie returned with a note from Aunt March, enclosing the desired sum, and a few lines repeating what she had often said before, that she had always told them it was absurd for March to go into the army, always predicted that no good would come of it, and she hoped they would take her advice next time. Mrs. March put the note in the fire, the money in her purse, and went on with her preparations, with her lips folded tightly in a way which Jo would have understood if she had been there.

The short afternoon wore away ; all the other errands were done, and Meg and her mother busy at some necessary needlework, while Beth and Amy got tea, and Hannah finished her ironing with what she called a " slap and a bang," but still Jo did not come. They began to get anxious ; and Laurie went off to find her, for no one ever knew what freak Jo might take into her head. He missed her, however, and she came walking in with a very queer expression of countenance, for there was a mixture of fun and fear, satisfaction and regret in it, which puzzled the family as much as did the roll of bills she laid before her mother, saying, with a little choke in her voice, " That's my contribution towards making father comfortable, and bringing him home ! "

" My dear, where did you get it ? Twenty-five dollars ! Jo, I hope you haven't done anything rash ? "

" No, it's mine honestly ; I didn't beg, borrow, or steal it. I earned it ; and I don't think you'll blame me, for I only sold what was my own."

As she spoke, Jo took off her bonnet, and a general outcry arose, for all her abundant hair was cut short.

" Your hair ! Your beautiful hair ! " " Oh, Jo, how could you ? Your one beauty." " My dear girl, there was no need of this." " She don't look like my Jo any more, but I love her dearly for it ! "

As every one exclaimed, and Beth hugged the cropped head tenderly, Jo assumed an indifferent air, which did not deceive any one a particle, and said, rumpling up the brown bush, and trying to look as if she liked it, " It doesn't affect the fate of the nation, so don't wail, Beth. It will do my brains good to have that mop taken off ; my head feels deliciously light and cool, and the barber said I could soon have a curly crop, which will be boyish, becoming, and easy to keep in order ; I'm satisfied, so please take the money, and let's have supper."

"Tell me all about it, Jo ; *I* am not quite satisfied, but I can't blame you ; for I know how willingly you sacrificed your vanity, as you call it, to your love. But, my dear, it was not necessary, and I'm afraid you will regret it one of these days," said Mrs. March.

"No, I won't ! " returned Jo stoutly, feeling much relieved that her prank was not entirely condemned.

Jo took off her bonnet and showed that her hair was cut short

"What made you do it ? " asked Amy, who would as soon have thought of cutting off her head as her pretty hair.

"Well, I was wild to do something for father," replied Jo, as they gathered about the table, for healthy young people can eat even in the midst of trouble. "I hate to borrow as much as mother does, and I knew Aunt March would croak ; she always does, if you ask for a ninepence. Meg gave all her quarterly salary towards the rent, and I only got some clothes with mine, so I felt wicked, and was bound to have some money, if I sold the nose off my face to get it."

"You needn't feel wicked, my child ; you had no winter things, and got the simplest, with your own hard earnings," said Mrs. March, with a look that warmed Jo's heart.

"I hadn't the least idea of selling my hair at first, but as I went along I kept thinking *what* I could do, and feeling as if I'd like to dive into some of the rich stores and help myself. In a barber's window I saw tails of hair with the prices marked ; and one black tail, longer, but not so thick as mine, was forty dollars. It came over me all of a sudden that I had one thing to make money out of, and, without stopping to think, I walked in, asked if they bought hair, and what they would give for mine."

" I don't see how you dared to do it," said Beth, in a tone of awe.

" Didn't you feel dreadfully when the first cut came ? " asked Meg, with a shiver.

" I took a last look at my hair while the man got his things, and that was the end of it. I never snivel over trifles like that ; I will confess, though, I felt queer when I saw the dear old hair laid out on the table, and felt only the short, rough ends on my head. It almost seemed as if I'd an arm or a leg off. The woman saw me look at it, and picked out a long lock for me to keep. I'll give it to you, Marmee, just to remember past glories by ; for a crop is so comfortable I don't think I shall ever have a mane again."

Mrs. March folded the wavy, chestnut lock, and laid it away with a short grey one in her desk. She only said, " Thank you, deary," but something in her face made the girls change the subject, and talk as cheerfully as they could about Mr. Brooke's kindness, the prospect of a fine day to-morrow, and the happy times they would have when father came home to be nursed.

No one wanted to go to bed when, at ten o'clock, Mrs. March put by the last finished job, and said, " Come, girls." Beth went to the piano and played their father's favourite hymn ; all began bravely, but broke down one by one till Beth was left alone, singing with all her heart, for to her music was always a sweet consoler.

" Go to bed, and don't talk, for we must be up early, and shall need all the sleep we can get. Good-night, my darlings," said Mrs. March, as the hymn ended, for no one cared to try another.

They kissed her quietly, and went to bed as silently as if the dear invalid lay in the next room. Beth and Amy soon fell asleep, in spite of the great trouble, but Meg lay awake, thinking the most serious thoughts she had ever known in her short life. Jo lay motionless, and her sister fancied that she was asleep, till a stifled sob made her exclaim, as she touched a wet cheek,—

" Jo, dear, what is it ? Are you crying about father ? "

" No, not now."

" What then ? "

" My—my hair," burst out poor Jo, trying vainly to smother her emotion in the pillow.

It did not sound at all comical to Meg, who kissed and caressed the afflicted heroine in the tenderest manner.

" I'm not sorry," protested Jo, with a choke. " I'd do it again to-morrow, if I could. It's only the vain, selfish part of me that goes and cries in this silly way. Don't tell any one ; it's all over now. I thought you were asleep, so I just made a little private moan for my own beauty. How came you to be awake ? "

" I can't sleep ; I'm so anxious," said Meg.

" Think about something pleasant, and you'll soon drop off."

" I tried it, but felt wider awake than ever."

" What did you think of ? "

" Handsome faces ; eyes particularly," answered Meg, smilingly, to herself in the dark.

"What colour do you like best?"

"Brown—that is, sometimes—blue are lovely."

Jo laughed, and Meg sharply ordered her not to talk, then amiably promised to make her hair curl, and fell asleep to dream of living in her castle in the air.

The clocks were striking midnight, and the rooms were very still, as a figure glided quietly from bed to bed, smoothing a coverlet here, setting a pillow there, and pausing to look long and tenderly at each unconscious face, to kiss each with lips that mutely blessed, and to pray the fervent prayers which only mothers utter. As she lifted the curtain to look out into the dreary night, the moon broke suddenly from behind the clouds, and shone upon her like a bright, benignant face, which seemed to whisper in the silence, "Be comforted, dear heart! there is light behind the clouds."

CHAPTER XIII

LETTERS

IN the cold gray dawn the sisters lit their lamp and read their chapter with an earnestness never felt before, for now the shadow of a real trouble had come, showing them how rich in sunshine their lives had been. The little books were full of help and comfort; and, as they dressed, they agreed to say good-bye cheerfully, hopefully, and send their mother on her anxious journey unsaddened by tears or complaints from them. Everything seemed very strange when they went down: so dim and still outside, so full of life and bustle within. Breakfast at that early hour seemed odd, and even Hannah's familiar face looked unnatural as she flew about her kitchen with her nightcap on. The big trunk stood ready in the hall, mother's cloak and bonnet lay on the sofa, and mother herself sat trying to eat, but looking so pale and worn with sleeplessness and anxiety that the girls found it very hard to keep their resolution. Meg's eyes kept filling in spite of herself; Jo was obliged to hide her face in the kitchen roller more than once; and the little girls' young faces wore a grave, troubled expression, as if sorrow was a new experience to them.

Nobody talked much, but, as the time drew very near, and they sat waiting for the carriage, Mrs. March said to the girls, who were all busied about her, one folding her shawl, another smoothing out the strings of her bonnet, a third putting on her over-shoes, and a fourth fastening up her travelling bag,—

"Children, I leave you to Hannah's care and Mr. Laurence's protection; Hannah is faithfulness itself, and our good neighbour will guard you as if you were his own. I have no fears for you, yet I am anxious that you should take this trouble rightly. Don't grieve and fret when I am gone, or think that you can comfort yourselves by being idle, and trying to forget. Go on with your work as usual, for work is a blessed solace. Hope, and keep busy; and, whatever happens, remember that you never can be fatherless."

"Yes, mother."

" Meg, dear, be prudent, watch over your sisters ; consult Hannah, and, in any perplexity, go to Mr. Laurence. Be patient, Jo ; don't get despondent, or do rash things ; write to me often, and be my brave girl, ready to help and cheer us all. Beth, comfort yourself with your music, and be faithful to the little home duties ; and you, Amy, help all you can, be obedient, and keep happy safe at home."

" We will, mother ! we will ! "

The rattle of an approaching carriage made them all start and listen. That was the hard minute, but the girls stood it well ; no one cried, no one ran away, or uttered a lamentation, though their hearts were very heavy as they sent loving messages to father, remembering, as they spoke, that it might be too late to deliver them. They kissed their mother quietly, clung about her tenderly, and tried to wave their hands cheerfully when she drove away.

Laurie and his grandfather came over to see her off, and Mr. Brooke looked so strong, and sensible, and kind, that the girls christened him " Mr. Greatheart," on the spot.

" Good-bye, my darlings ! God bless and keep us all," whispered Mrs. March, as she kissed one dear little face after the other, and hurried into the carriage.

As she rolled away, the sun came out, and, looking back, she saw it shining on the group at the gate, like a good omen. They saw it also, and smiled and waved their hands ; and the last thing she beheld, as she turned the corner, was the four bright faces, and behind them, like a bodyguard, old Mr. Laurence, faithful Hannah, and devoted Laurie.

" How kind every one is to us," she said, turning to find fresh proof of it in the respectful sympathy of the young man's face.

" I don't see how they can help it," returned Mr. Brooke, laughing so infectiously that Mrs. March could not help smiling ; and so the long journey began with the good omens of sunshine, smiles, and cheerful words.

" I feel as if there had been an earthquake," said Jo, as their neighbours went home to breakfast, leaving them to rest and refresh themselves.

" It seems as if half the house was gone," added Meg forlornly.

Beth opened her lips to say something, but could only point to the pile of nicely-mended hose which lay on mother's table, showing that in her last hurried moments she had thought and worked for them. It was a little thing, but it went straight to their hearts ; and, in spite of brave resolutions, they all broke down and cried bitterly.

Hannah wisely allowed them to relieve their feelings ; and, when the shower showed signs of clearing up, she came to the rescue, armed with a coffee-pot.

" Now, my dear young ladies, remember what your ma said, and don't fret ; come and have a cup of coffee all round, and then let's fall to work, and be a credit to the family."

Coffee was a treat, and Hannah showed great tact in making it that morning. No one could resist her persuasive nods, or the fragrant invitation issuing from the nose of the coffee-pot. They drew up to the table, exchanged their handkerchiefs for napkins, and, in ten minutes, were all right again.

" ' Hope and keep busy ; ' that's the motto for us, so let's see who will remember it best. I shall go to Aunt March, as usual ; oh, won't she lecture, though ! " said Jo, as she sipped with returning spirit.

"I shall go to my Kings, though I'd much rather stay at home and attend to things here," said Meg, wishing she hadn't made her eyes so red.

"No need of that ; Beth and I can keep house perfectly well," put in Amy, with an important air. "Hannah will tell us what to do ; and we'll have everything nice when you come home," added Beth, getting out her mop and dish-tub without delay.

"I think anxiety is very interesting," observed Amy, eating sugar pensively.

Beth got out her mop and dish-tub without delay

The girls couldn't help laughing, and felt better for it, though Meg shook her head at the young lady who could find consolation in a sugar-bowl.

The sight of the turnovers made Jo sober again ; and, when the two went out to their daily tasks, they looked sorrowfully back at the window where they were accustomed to see their mother's face. It was gone ; but Beth had remembered the little household ceremony, and there she was, nodding away at them like a rosy-faced mandarin.

"That's so like my Beth ! " said Jo, waving her hat, with a grateful face. "Good-bye, Meggy ; I hope the Kings won't train to-day. Don't fret about father, dear," she added, as they parted.

"And I hope Aunt March won't croak. Your hair *is* becoming, and it looks very boyish and nice," returned Meg, trying not to smile at the curly head, which looked comically small on her tall sister's shoulders.

" That's my only comfort ; " and, touching her hat, à la Laurie, away went Jo, feeling like a shorn sheep on a wintry day.

News from their father comforted the girls very much ; for, though dangerously ill, the presence of the best and tenderest of nurses had already done him good. Mr. Brooke sent a bulletin every day, and, as the head of the family, Meg insisted on reading the despatches, which grew more and more cheering as the week passed. At first, every one was eager to write, and plump envelopes were carefully poked into the letter-box, by one or other of the sisters, who felt rather important with their Washington correspondence. As one of these packets contained characteristic notes from the party, we will rob an imaginary mail, and read them :—

" MY DEAREST MOTHER,—It is impossible to tell you how happy your last letter made us, for the news was so good we couldn't help laughing and crying over it. How very kind Mr. Brooke is, and how fortunate that Mr. Laurence's business detains him near you so long, since he is so useful to you and father. The girls are all as good as gold. Jo helps me with the sewing, and insists on doing all sorts of hard jobs. I should be afraid she might overdo, if I didn't know that her ' moral fit ' wouldn't last long. Beth is as regular about her tasks as a clock, and never forgets what you told her. She grieves about father, and looks sober, except when she is at her little piano. Amy minds me nicely, and I take great care of her. She does her own hair, and I am teaching her to make button-holes, and mend her stockings. She tries very hard, and I know you will be pleased with her improvement when you come. Mr. Laurence watches over us like a motherly old hen, as Jo says ; and Laurie is very kind and neighbourly. He and Jo keep us merry, for we get pretty blue sometimes, and feel like orphans, with you so far away. Hannah is a perfect saint ; she does not scold at all, and always calls me ' Miss Margaret,' which is quite proper, you know, and treats me with respect. We are all well and busy ; but we long, day and night, to have you back. Give my dearest love to father, and believe me, ever your own

" MEG."

This note, prettily written on scented paper, was a great contrast to the next, which was scribbled on a big sheet of thin, foreign paper, ornamented with blots, and all manner of flourishes and curly-tailed letters :—

" MY PRECIOUS MARMEE,—Three cheers for dear old father ! Brooke was a trump to telegraph right off, and let us know the minute he was better. I rushed up garret when the letter came, and tried to thank God for being so good to us ; but I could only cry, and say, ' I'm glad ! I'm glad ! ' Didn't that do as well as a regular prayer ? for I felt a great many in my heart. We have such funny times ; and now I can enjoy 'em, for every one is so desperately good, it's like living in a nest of turtle-doves. You'd laugh to see Meg head the table, and try to be motherish. She gets prettier every day, and I'm in love with her sometimes. The children are regular archangels, and I—well, I'm Jo, and never shall be anything else. Oh, I must tell you that I came near having a quarrel with Laurie. I freed my mind about a silly little thing, and he was offended. I was right, but didn't speak as I ought, and he marched home, saying he wouldn't come again till I begged pardon. I declared I wouldn't, and got mad. It lasted all day; I felt bad, and wanted you very much. Laurie and I are both so proud, it's hard to beg pardon; but I thought he'd come to it, for I *was* in the right. He didn't come; and just at night I remembered what you said when Amy fell into the river. I read my little book, felt better, resolved not to let the sun set on *my* anger, and ran over to tell Laurie I was sorry. I met him at the gate, coming for the same thing. We both laughed, begged each other's pardon, and felt all good and comfortable again.

"I made a 'pome' yesterday, when I was helping Hannah wash; and, as father likes my silly little things, I put it in to amuse him. Give him the lovingest hug that ever was, and kiss yourself a dozen times for your

"Topsy-Turvy Jo."

A SONG FROM THE SUDS

"Queen of my tub, I merrily sing,
  While the white foam rises high;
And sturdily wash, and rinse, and wring,
  And fasten the clothes to dry;
Then out in the free fresh air they swing,
  Under the sunny sky.

"I wish we could wash from our hearts and souls
  The stains of the week away,
And let the water and air by their magic make
  Ourselves as pure as they;
Then on the earth there would be indeed
  A glorious washing-day!

"Along the path of a usual life
  Will heart's-ease ever bloom;
The busy mind has no time to think
  Of sorrow, or care, or gloom;
And anxious thoughts may be swept away
  As we busily wield a broom.

"I am glad a task to me is given,
  To labour at day by day;
For it brings me health, and strength, and hope,
  And I cheerfully learn to say,—
'Head you may think, Heart you may feel,
  But Hand you shall work alway!'"

"Dear Mother,—There is only room for me to send my love, and some pressed pansies from the root I have been keeping safe in the house for father to see. I read every morning, try to be good all day, and sing myself to sleep with father's tune. I can't sing ' Land of the Leal ' now ; it makes me cry. Every one is very kind, and we are as happy as we can be without you. Amy wants the rest of the page, so I must stop. I didn't forget to cover the holders, and I wind the clock and air the rooms every day.

" Kiss dear father on the cheek he calls mine. Oh, do come soon to your loving

" LITTLE BETH."

" MA CHÉRE MAMMA,—We are all well, I do my lessons always and never corroberate the girls—Meg says I mean contradick so I put in both words and you can take the properest. Meg is a great comfort to me and lets me have jelly every night at tea its so good for me Jo says because it keeps me sweet tempered. Laurie is not as respeckful as he ought to be now I am almost in my teens, he calls me Chick and hurts my feelings by talking French to me very fast when I say Merci or Bon jour as Hattie King does. The sleeves of my blue dress were all worn out and Meg put in new ones but the full front came wrong and they are more blue than the dress. I felt bad but did not fret I bear my troubles well but I do wish Hannah would put more starch in my aprons and have buck wheats every day. Can't she ? Didn't I make that interrigation point nice. Meg says my punchtuation and spelling are disgraceful and I am mortyfied but dear me I have so many things to do, I can't stop. Adieu, I send heaps of love to Papa.

" Your affectionate daughter,

" AMY CURTIS MARCH."

" DEAR MIS MARCH,—I jes drop a line to say we git on fust rate. The girls is clever and fly round right smart. Miss Meg is goin' to make a proper good housekeeper ; she hes the liking for it, and gits the hang of things surprisin' quick. Jo doos beat all for goin' ahead, but she don't stop to cal'-k'late fust, and you never know where she's like to bring up. She done out a tub of clothes on Monday but she starched em afore they was wrentched, and blued a pink calico dress till I thought I should a died a laughin. Beth is the best of little creeters, and a sight of help to me, bein so forehanded and dependable. She tries to learn everything, and really goes to market beyond her years ; likewise keep accounts, with my help, quite wonderful. We have got on very economical so fur ; I don't let the girls hev coffee only once a week, accordin to your wish, and keep em on plain wholesome vittles. Amy does well about frettin wearin her best clothes and eatin sweet stuff. Mr. Laurie is as full of didoes as usual, and turns the house upside down frequent ; but he heartens up the girls, and so I let em hev full swing. The old man sends heaps of things, and is rather wearin, but means wal, and it ain't my place to say nothin. My bread is riz, so no more at this time. I send my duty to Mr. March, and hope he's seen the last of his Pewmonia.

" Yours respectful,

" HANNAH MULLET."

" HEAD NURSE OF WARD II,—All serene on the Rappahannock, troops in fine condition, commissary department well conducted, the Home Guard under Colonel Teddy always on duty, Commander-in-chief General Laurence reviews the army daily, Quartermaster Mullet keeps order in camp, and Major Lion does picket duty at night. A salute of twenty-four guns was fired on receipt of good news from Washington, and a dress-parade took place at headquarters. Commander-in-chief sends best wishes, in which he is heartily joined by

" COLONEL TEDDY."

" DEAR MADAM,—The little girls are all well; Beth and my boy report daily; Hannah is a model servant, guards pretty Meg like a dragon. Glad the fine weather holds; pray make Brooke useful, and draw on me for funds if expenses exceed your estimate. Don't let your husband want anything. Thank God he is mending.

" Your sincere friend and servant,

" JAMES LAURENCE."

CHAPTER XIV

LITTLE FAITHFUL

FOR a week the amount of virtue in the old house would have supplied the neighbourhood. It was really amazing, for every one seemed in a heavenly frame of mind, and self-denial was all the fashion. Relieved of their first anxiety about their father, the girls insensibly relaxed their praiseworthy efforts a little, and began to fall back into the old ways. They did not forget their motto, but hoping and keeping busy seemed to grow easier; and, after such tremendous exertions, they felt that Endeavour deserved a holiday, and gave it a good many.

Jo caught a bad cold through neglecting to cover the shorn head enough, and was ordered to stay at home till she was better, for Aunt March didn't like to hear people read with colds in their heads. Jo liked this, and after an energetic rummage from garret to cellar, subsided on to the sofa to nurse her cold with arsenicum and books. Amy found that housework and art did not go well together, and returned to her mud pies. Meg went daily to her kingdom, and sewed, or thought she did, at home, but much time was spent in writing long letters to her mother, or reading the Washington despatches over and over. Beth kept on with only slight relapses into idleness or grieving. All the little duties were faithfully done each day, and many of her sisters' also, for they were forgetful, and the house seemed like a clock whose pendulum was gone a-visiting. When her heart got heavy with longings for mother, or fears for father, she went away into a certain closet, hid her face in the folds of a certain dear old gown, and made her little moan, and prayed her little prayer quietly by herself. Nobody knew what cheered her up after a sober fit, but every one felt how sweet and helpful Beth was, and fell into a way of going to her for comfort or advice in their small affairs.

All were unconscious that this experience was a test of character; and, when the first excitement was over, felt that they had done well, and deserved praise. So they did ; but their mistake was in ceasing to do well, and they learned this lesson through much anxiety and regret.

" Meg, I wish you'd go and see the Hummels ; you know mother told us not to forget them," said Beth, ten days after Mrs. March's departure.

" I'm too tired to go this afternoon," replied Meg, rocking comfortably, as she sewed.

" Can't you, Jo ? " asked Beth.

" Too stormy for me, with my cold."

" I thought it was most well."

" It's well enough for me to go out with Laurie, but not well enough to go to the Hummels," said Jo, laughing, but looking a little ashamed of her inconsistency.

" Why don't you go yourself ? " asked Meg.

" I *have* been every day, but the baby is sick, and I don't know what to do for it. Mrs. Hummel goes away to work, and Lottchen takes care of it ; but it gets sicker and sicker, and I think you or Hannah ought to go."

Beth spoke earnestly, and Meg promised she would go to-morrow.

" Ask Hannah for some nice little mess, and take it round, Beth ; the air will do you good," said Jo, adding apologetically, " I'd go, but I want to finish my story."

" My head aches, and I'm tired, so I thought maybe some of you would go," said Beth.

" Amy will be in presently, and she will run down for us," suggested Meg.

" Well, I'll rest a little, and wait for her."

So Beth lay down on the sofa, the others returned to their work, and the Hummels were forgotten. An hour passed, Amy did not come ; Meg went to her room to try on a new dress ; Jo was absorbed in her story, and Hannah was sound asleep before the kitchen fire, when Beth quietly put on her hood, filled the basket with odds and ends for the poor children, and went out into the chilly air with a heavy head, and a grieved look in her patient eyes. It was late when she came back, and no one saw her creep upstairs and shut herself in her mother's room. Half an hour after Jo went to " mother's closet " for something, and there found Beth sitting on the medicine chest, looking very grave, with red eyes, and a camphor bottle in her hand.

" Christopher Columbus ! what's the matter ? " cried Jo, as Beth put out her hand as if to warn her off, and asked quickly,—

" You've had scarlet fever, haven't you ? "

" Years ago, when Meg did. Why ? "

" Then I'll tell you—oh, Jo, the baby's dead ! "

" What baby ? "

" Mrs. Hummel's ; it died in my lap before she got home," cried Beth, with a sob.

" My poor dear, how dreadful for you ! I ought to have gone," said Jo, taking her sister in her lap as she sat down in her mother's big chair, with a remorseful face.

" It wasn't dreadful, Jo, only so sad ! I saw in a minute that it was sicker, but Lottchen said her mother had gone for a doctor, so I took baby and let Lotty rest. It seemed asleep, but all of a sudden it gave a little cry, and trembled, and then lay very still. I tried to warm its feet, and Lotty gave it some milk, but it didn't stir, and I knew it was dead."

" Don't cry, dear ! What did you do ? "

" I just sat and held it softly till Mrs. Hummel came with the doctor. He said it was dead, and looked at Heinrich and Minna, who have got sore throats. ' Scarlet fever, ma'am ; ought to have called me before,' he said crossly. Mrs. Hummel told him she was poor, and had tried to cure baby herself, but now it was too late, and she could only ask him to help the

Jo scribbled away, absorbed in her story

others, and trust to charity for his pay. He smiled then, and was kinder, but it was very sad, and I cried with them, till he turned round, all of a sudden, and told me to go home and take belladonna right away, or I'd have the fever."

" No, you won't ! " cried Jo, hugging her close, with a frightened look. " Oh, Beth, if you should be sick I never could forgive myself ! What *shall* we do ? "

" Don't be frightened, I guess I shan't have it badly ; I looked in mother's book, and saw that it begins with headache, sore throat, and queer feelings like mine, so I did take some belladonna, and I feel better," said Beth, laying her cold hands on her hot forehead, and trying to look well.

" If mother was only at home ! " exclaimed Jo, seizing the book, and feeling that Washington was an immense way off. She read a page, looked at Beth, felt her head, peeped into her throat, and then said gravely, " You've been over the baby every day for more than a week, and among the others who are going to have it, so I'm afraid you're going to have it, Beth. I'll call Hannah; she knows all about sickness."

" Don't let Amy come; she never had it, and I should hate to give it to her. Can't you and Meg have it over again ? " asked Beth anxiously.

" I guess not; don't care if I do; serve me right, selfish pig, to let you go, and stay writing rubbish myself ! " muttered Jo, as she went to consult Hannah.

The good soul was wide awake in a minute, and took the lead at once, assuring Jo that there was no need to worry; every one had scarlet fever, and if rightly treated nobody died; all of which Jo believed, and felt much relieved as they went up to call Meg.

" Now I'll tell you what we'll do," said Hannah, when she had examined and questioned Beth; " we will have Dr. Bangs, just to look at you, dear, and see that we start right; then we'll send Amy off to Aunt March's for a spell to keep her out of harm's way, and one of you girls can stay at home and amuse Beth for a day or two."

" I shall stay, of course; I'm oldest," began Meg, looking anxious and self-reproachful.

" *I* shall, because it's my fault she is sick; I told mother I'd do the errands, and I haven't," said Jo decidedly.

" Which will you have, Beth ? there ain't no need of but one," said Hannah.

" Jo, please "; and Beth leaned her head against her sister with a contented look, which effectually settled that point.

" I'll go and tell Amy," said Meg, feeling a little hurt, yet rather relieved on the whole, for she did not like nursing, and Jo did.

Amy rebelled outright, and passionately declared that she had rather have the fever than go to Aunt March. Meg reasoned, pleaded, and commanded all in vain. Amy protested that she would *not* go; and Meg left her in despair, to ask Hannah what should be done. Before she came back, Laurie walked into the parlour, to find Amy sobbing, with her head in the sofa cushions. She told her story, expecting to be consoled; but Laurie only put his hands in his pockets and walked about the room, whistling softly, as he knit his brows in deep thought. Presently he sat down beside her, and said, in his most wheedlesome tone, " Now be a sensible little woman, and do as they say. No, don't cry, but hear what a jolly plan I've got. You go to Aunt March's, and I'll come and take you out every day, driving or walking, and we'll have capital times. Won't that be better than moping here ? "

" I don't wish to be sent off, as if I was in the way," began Amy, in an injured voice.

" Bless your heart, child ! it's to keep you well. You don't want to be sick, do you ? "

" No, I'm sure I don't; but I dare say I shall be, for I've been with Beth all this time."

" That's the very reason you ought to go away at once, so that you may escape it. Change of air and care will keep you well, I dare say; or, if it don't entirely, you will have the fever more lightly. I advise you to be off as soon as you can, for scarlet fever is no joke, miss."

" But it's dull at Aunt March's, and she is so cross," said Amy, looking rather frightened.

" It won't be dull with me popping in every day to tell how Beth is, and take you out gallivanting. The old lady likes me, and I'll be as clever as possible to her, so she won't peck at us, whatever we do."

" Will you take me out in the trotting wagon with Puck ? "

" On my honour as a gentleman."

" And come every single day ? "

" See if I don't."

" And bring me back the minute Beth is well ? "

" The identical minute."

" And go to the theatre truly ? "

" A dozen theatres if we may."

" Well—I guess—I will," said Amy slowly.

" Good girl ! Sing out for Meg, and tell her you'll give in," said Laurie, with an approving pat, which annoyed Amy more than the " giving in."

Meg and Jo came running down to behold the miracle which had been wrought ; and Amy, feeling very precious and self-sacrificing, promised to go, if the doctor said Beth was going to be ill.

" How is the little dear ? " asked Laurie ; for Beth was his especial pet, and he felt more anxious about her than he liked to show.

" She is lying down on mother's bed, and feels better. The baby's death troubled her, but I dare say she has only got cold. Hannah *says* she thinks so ; but she *looks* worried, and that makes me fidgety," answered Meg.

" What a trying world it is ! " said Jo, rumpling up her hair in a fretful sort of way. " No sooner do we get out of one trouble than down comes another. There don't seem to be anything to hold on to when mother's gone ; so I'm all at sea."

" Well, don't make a porcupine of yourself ; it isn't becoming. Settle your wig, Jo, and tell me if I shall telegraph to your mother, or do anything ? " asked Laurie, who had never been reconciled to the loss of his friend's one beauty.

" That is what troubles me," said Meg. " I think we ought to tell her if Beth is really ill, but Hannah says we mustn't, for mother can't leave father, and it will only make them anxious. Beth won't be sick long, and Hannah knows just what to do, and mother said we were to mind her, so I suppose we must, but it don't seem quite right to me."

" Hum, well, I can't say ; suppose you ask grandfather, after the doctor has been ? "

" We will ; Jo, go and get Dr. Bangs at once," commanded Meg ; " we can't decide anything till he has been."

" Stay where you are, Jo ; I'm errand boy to this establishment," said Laurie, taking up his cap.

" I'm afraid you are busy," began Meg.

" No, I've done my lessons for the day."

" Do you study in vacation time ? " asked Jo.

" I follow the good example my neighbours set me," was Laurie's answer, as he swung himself out of the room.

" I have great hopes of my boy," observed Jo, watching him fly over the fence with an approving smile.

" He does very well—for a boy," was Meg's somewhat ungracious answer, for the subject did not interest her.

Dr. Bangs came, said Beth had symptoms of the fever, but thought she would have it lightly, though he looked sober over the Hummel story. Amy was ordered off at once, and provided with something to ward off danger ; she departed in great state, with Jo and Laurie as escort.

Aunt March received them with her usual hospitality.

" What do you want now ? " she asked, looking sharply over her spectacles, while the parrot sitting on the back of her chair called out,—

" Go away ; no boys allowed here."

Laurie retired to the window, and Jo told her story.

" No more than I expected, if you are allowed to go poking about among poor folks. Amy can stay and make herself useful if she isn't sick, which I've no doubt she will be,—looks like it now. Don't cry, child ; it worries me to hear people sniff."

Amy *was* on the point of crying, but Laurie slyly pulled the parrot's tail, which caused Polly to utter an astonished croak, and call out " Bless my boots ! " in such a funny way that she laughed instead.

" What do you hear from your mother ? " asked the old lady gruffly.

" Father is much better," replied Jo, trying to keep sober.

" Oh, is he ? Well, that won't last long, I fancy ; March never had any stamina," was the cheerful reply.

" Ha, ha ! never say die, take a pinch of snuff, good-bye, good-bye ! " squalled Polly, dancing on her perch and clawing at the old lady's cap, as Laurie tweaked him in the ear.

" Hold your tongue, you disrespectful old bird ! and, Jo, you'd better go at once ; it isn't proper to be gadding about so late with a rattle-pated boy like——"

" Hold your tongue, you disrespectful old bird ! " cried Polly, tumbling off the chair with a bounce and running to peck the " rattle-pated " boy, who was shaking with laughter at the last speech.

" I don't think I *can* bear it, but I'll try," thought Amy, as she was left alone with Aunt March.

" Get along, you're a fright ! " screamed Polly ; and at that rude speech Amy could not restrain a sniff.

CHAPTER XV

DARK DAYS

BETH did have the fever, and was much sicker than any one but Hannah and the doctor suspected. The girls knew nothing about illness, and Mr. Laurence was not allowed to see her, so Hannah had all her own way, and busy Dr. Bangs did his best, but left a good deal to the excellent nurse. Meg stayed at home, lest she should infect the Kings, and kept house, feeling very anxious, and a little guilty, when she wrote letters in which no mention was made of Beth's illness. She could not think it right to deceive her mother, but she had been bidden to mind Hannah, and Hannah wouldn't hear of " Mrs. March being told and worried just for sech a trifle." Jo devoted herself to Beth day and night ; not a hard task, for Beth was very patient, and bore her pain uncomplainingly as long as she could control herself. But there came a time when during the fever fits she began to talk in a hoarse, broken voice, to play on the coverlet, as if on her beloved little piano, and try to sing with a throat so swollen that there was no music left ; a time when she did not know the familiar faces round her, but addressed them by wrong names, and called imploringly for her mother. Then Jo grew frightened, Meg begged to be allowed to write the truth, and even Hannah said she " would think of it, though there was no danger *yet*." A letter from Washington added to their trouble, for Mr. March had had a relapse, and could not think of coming home for a long while.

How dark the days seemed now, how sad and lonely the house, and how heavy were the hearts of the sisters as they worked and waited, while the shadow of death hovered over the once happy home ! Then it was that Margaret, sitting alone, with tears dropping often on her work, felt how rich she had been in things more precious than any luxuries money could buy : in love, protection, peace and health, the real blessings of life. Then it was that Jo, living in the darkened room with that suffering little sister always before her eyes, and that pathetic voice sounding in her ears, learned to see the beauty and the sweetness of Beth's nature, to feel how deep and tender a place she filled in all hearts, and to acknowledge the worth of Beth's unselfish ambition : to live for others, and make home happy by the exercise of those simple virtues which all may possess, and which all should love and value more than talent, wealth or beauty. And Amy, in her exile, longed eagerly to be at home, that she might work for Beth, feeling now that no service would be hard or irksome, and remembering, with regretful grief, how many neglected tasks those willing hands had done for her. Laurie haunted the house like a restless ghost, and Mr. Laurence locked the grand piano, because he could not bear to be reminded of the young neighbour who used to make the twilight pleasant for him. Every one missed Beth. The milkman, baker, grocer, and butcher inquired how she did ; poor Mrs. Hummel came to beg pardon for her thoughtlessness, and to get a shroud for Minna ; the neighbours sent all sorts of comforts and good wishes, and even those who knew her best were surprised to find how many friends shy little Beth had made.

Meanwhile, she lay on her bed with old Joanna at her side, for even in her wanderings she did not forget her forlorn *protégée*. She longed for her cats, but would not have them brought, lest they should get sick ; and, in her quiet hours, she was full of anxiety about Jo. She sent loving messages to Amy, bade them tell her mother that she would write soon ; and often begged for pencil and paper to try to say a word, that father might not think she had neglected him. But soon even these intervals of consciousness ended, and she lay hour after hour tossing to and fro with incoherent words on her lips, or sank into a heavy sleep which brought her no refreshment.

Dr. Bangs came twice a day. Hannah sat up at night, Meg kept a telegram in her desk all ready to send off at any minute, and Jo never stirred from Beth's side.

The first of December was a wintry day indeed to them, for a bitter wind blew, snow fell fast, and the year seemed getting ready for its death. When Dr. Bangs came that morning, he looked long at Beth, held the hot hand in both his own a minute, and laid it gently down, saying in a low tone, to Hannah,—

"If Mrs. March *can* leave her husband, she'd better be sent for."

Hannah nodded without speaking, for her lips twitched nervously ; Meg dropped down into a chair as the strength seemed to go out of her limbs at the sound of those words, and Jo, after standing with a pale face for a minute, ran to the parlour, snatched up the telegram, and throwing on her things, rushed out into the storm. She was soon back, and, while noiselessly taking off her cloak, Laurie came in with a letter, saying that Mr. March was mending again. Jo read it thankfully, but the heavy weight did not seem lifted off her heart, and her face was so full of misery that Laurie asked quickly,—

"What is it ? is Beth worse ? "

"I've sent for mother," said Jo, tugging at her rubber boots with a tragical expression.

"Good for you, Jo ! Did you do it on your own responsibility ? " asked Laurie, as he seated her in the hall chair, and took off the rebellious boots, seeing how her hands shook.

"No ; the doctor told us to."

"Oh, Jo ! it's not so bad as that ? " cried Laurie, with a startled face.

"Yes, it is ; she don't know us, she don't even talk about the flocks of green doves—as she calls the vine leaves on the wall ; she don't look like my Beth, and there's nobody to help us bear it ; mother and father both gone, and God seems so far away I can't find Him."

As the tears streamed fast down poor Jo's cheeks, she stretched out her hand in a helpless sort of way, as if groping in the dark, and Laurie took it in his, whispering, as well as he could, with a lump in his throat,—

"I'm here ; hold on to me, Jo, dear ! "

She could not speak, but she did " hold on," and the warm grasp of the friendly human hand comforted her sore heart, and seemed to lead her nearer to the Divine arm which alone could uphold her in her trouble. Laurie longed to say something tender and comfortable, but no fitting words came to him, so he stood silent, gently stroking her bent head, as her mother used to do. It was the best thing he could have done ; far more soothing than the most eloquent words, for Jo felt the unspoken sympathy, and, in the silence, learned the sweet solace which affection administers to sorrow. Soon she dried the tears which had relieved her, and looked up with grateful face.

"Thank you, Teddy ; I'm better now ; I don't feel so forlorn, and will try to bear it if it comes."

"Keep hoping for the best ; that will help you lots, Jo. Soon your mother will be here, and then everything will be right."

"I'm so glad father is better ; now she won't feel so bad about leaving him. Oh, me! it does seem as if all the troubles came in a heap, and I got the heaviest part on my shoulders," sighed Jo, spreading her wet handkerchief over her knees to dry.

"Don't Meg pull fair?" asked Laurie, looking indignant.

"Oh, yes; she tries to, but she don't love Bethy as I do; and she won't miss her as I shall. Beth is my conscience, and *I can't* give her up; I can't, I can't!"

Down went Jo's face into the wet handkerchief, and she cried despairingly; for she had kept up bravely till now, and never shed a tear. Laurie drew his hand across his eyes, but could not speak till he had subdued the choky feeling in his throat, and steadied his lips. It might be unmanly, but he

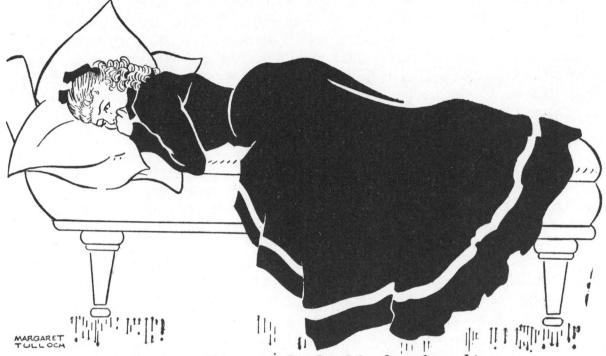

Amy was sobbing with her head in the sofa cushions

couldn't help it, and I'm glad of it. Presently, as Jo's sobs quieted, he said hopefully, "I don't think she will die; she's so good, and we all love her so much, I don't believe God will take her away yet."

"The good and dear people always do die," groaned Jo, but she stopped crying, for her friend's words cheered her up, in spite of her own doubts and fears.

"Poor girl! you're worn out. It isn't like you to be forlorn. Stop a bit; I'll hearten you up in a jiffy."

Laurie went off two stairs at a time, and Jo laid her wearied head down on Beth's little brown hood, which no one had thought of moving from the table where she left it. It must have possessed some magic, for the submissive spirit of its gentle owner seemed to enter into Jo; and, when Laurie came running down with a glass of wine, she took it with a smile, and said bravely, "I drink—health to my Beth! You are a good doctor, Teddy, and *such* a comfortable friend; how can I ever pay you?" she added, as the wine refreshed her body, as the kind words had done her troubled mind.

"I'll send in my bill, by-and-by; and to-night I'll give you something that will warm the cockles of your heart better than quarts of wine," said Laurie, beaming at her with a face of suppressed satisfaction at something.

"What is it?" cried Jo, forgetting her woes for a minute in her wonder.

"I telegraphed to your mother yesterday, and Brooke answered she'd come at once; and she'll be here to-night, and everything will be all right. Aren't you glad I did it?"

Laurie spoke very fast, and turned red and excited all in a minute, for he had kept his plot a secret, for fear of disappointing the girls or harming Beth. Jo grew quite white, flew out of her chair, and the moment he stopped speaking she electrified him by throwing her arms round his neck, and crying out, with a joyful cry, "Oh, Laurie! Oh, mother! I *am* so glad!" She did not weep again, but laughed hysterically, and trembled and clung to her friend as if she was a little bewildered by the sudden news. Laurie, though decidedly amazed, behaved with great presence of mind; he patted her back soothingly, and, finding that she was recovering, followed it up by a bashful kiss or two, which brought Jo round at once. Holding on to the banisters, she put him gently away, saying breathlessly, "Oh, don't! I didn't mean to; it was dreadful of me; but you were such a dear to go and do it, in spite of Hannah, that I couldn't help flying at you. Tell me all about it, and don't give me wine again; it makes me act so."

"I don't mind!" laughed Laurie, as he settled his tie. "Why, you see I got fidgety, and so did grandpa. We thought Hannah was overdoing the authority business, and your mother ought to know. She'd never forgive us if Beth,—well, if anything happened, you know. So I got grandpa to say it was high time we did something, and off I pelted to the office yesterday, for the doctor looked sober, and Hannah most took my head off when I proposed a telegram. I never *can* bear to be 'marmed over;' so that settled my mind, and I did it. Your mother will come, I know, and the late train is in at two a.m. I shall go for her; and you've only got to bottle up your rapture, and keep Beth quiet, till that blessed lady gets here."

"Laurie, you're an angel! How shall I ever thank you?"

"Fly at me again; I rather like it," said Laurie, looking mischievous,— a thing he had not done for a fortnight.

"No, thank you. I'll do it by proxy, when your grandpa comes. Don't tease, but go home and rest, for you'll be up half the night. Bless you, Teddy, bless you!"

Jo had backed into a corner; and, as she finished her speech, she vanished precipitately into the kitchen, and told the assembled cats that she was "happy, oh, so happy!" while Laurie departed, feeling that he made rather a neat thing of it.

"That's the interferingest chap I ever see; but I forgive him, and do hope Mrs. March is coming on right away," said Hannah, with an air of relief, when Jo told the good news.

Meg had a quiet rapture, and then brooded over the letter, while Jo set the sick-room in order, and Hannah "knocked up a couple of pies, in case of company expected." A breath of fresh air seemed to blow through the house, and something better than sunshine brightened the quiet rooms, everything appeared to feel the hopeful change ; Beth's bird began to chirp again, and a half-blown rose was discovered on Amy's bush on the window ; the fires seemed to burn with unusual cheeriness, and every time the girls met, their pale faces broke into smiles as they hugged one another, whispering encouragingly, " Mother's coming, dear ! mother's coming ! " Every one rejoiced but Beth ; she lay in that heavy stupor, alike unconscious of hope and joy, doubt and danger. It was a piteous sight,—the once rosy face so changed and vacant,—the once busy hands so weak and wasted,— the once smiling lips quite dumb,—and the once pretty, well-kept hair scattered rough and tangled on the pillow. All day she lay so, only rousing now and then to mutter, " Water ! " with lips so parched they could hardly shape the word ; all day Jo and Meg hovered over her, watching, waiting, hoping, and trusting in God and mother ; and all day the snow fell, the bitter wind raged, and the hours dragged slowly by. But night came at last ; and every time the clock struck, the sisters, still sitting on either side the bed, looked at each other with brightening eyes, for each hour brought health nearer. The doctor had been in to say that some change for the better or worse would probably take place about midnight, at which time he would return.

Hannah, quite worn out, lay down on the sofa at the bed's foot, and fell fast asleep ; Mr. Laurence marched to and fro in the parlour, feeling that he would rather face a rebel battery than Mrs. March's anxious countenance as she entered ; Laurie lay on the rug, pretending to rest, but staring into the fire with the thoughtful look which made his black eyes beautifully soft and clear.

The girls never forgot that night, for no sleep came to them as they kept their watch, with that dreadful sense of powerlessness which comes to us in hours like those.

" If God spares Beth, I never will complain again," whispered Meg earnestly.

" If God spares Beth, I'll try to love and serve Him all my life," answered Jo, with equal fervour.

" I wish I had no heart ; it aches so," sighed Meg, after a pause.

" If life is often as hard as this, I don't see how we ever shall get through it," added her sister despondently.

Here the clock struck twelve, and both forgot themselves in watching Beth, for they fancied a change passed over her wan face. The house was still as death, and nothing but the wailing of the wind broke the deep hush. Weary Hannah slept on, and no one but the sisters saw the pale shadow which seemed to fall upon the little bed. An hour went by, and nothing happened except Laurie's quiet departure for the station. Another hour— still no one came ; and anxious fears of delay in the storm, or accidents by the way, or, worst of all, a great grief at Washington, haunted the poor girls.

It was past two when Jo, who stood at the window, thinking how dreary the world looked in its winding-sheet of snow, heard a movement by the bed, and, turning quickly, saw Meg kneeling before their mother's easy chair, with her face hidden. A dreadful fear passed coldly over Jo, as she thought, " Beth is dead, and Meg is afraid to tell me."

She was back at her post in an instant, and to her excited eyes a great change seemed to have taken place. The fever-flush and the look of pain were gone, and the beloved little face looked so pale and peaceful in its utter repose that Jo felt no desire to weep or lament. Leaning low over this dearest of her sisters, she kissed the damp forehead with her heart on her lips, and softly whispered, " Good-bye, my Beth ; good-bye ! "

As if waked by the stir, Hannah started out of her sleep, hurried to the bed, looked at Beth, felt her hands, listened at her lips, and then, throwing her apron over her head, sat down to rock to and fro, exclaiming, under her breath, " The fever's turned ; she's sleepin' nat'ral ; her skin's damp ; and she breathes easy. Praise be given ! Oh, my goodness me ! "

Before the girls could believe the happy truth, the doctor came to confirm it. He was a homely man, but they thought his face quite heavenly when he smiled, and said with a fatherly look at them, " Yes, my dears, I think the little girl will pull through this time. Keep the house quiet ; let her sleep ; and when she wakes give her——"

What they were to give neither heard ; for both crept into the dark hall, and, sitting on the stairs, held each other close, rejoicing with hearts too full for words. When they went back to be kissed and cuddled by faithful Hannah, they found Beth lying as she used to do, with her cheek pillowed on her hand, the dreadful pallor gone, and breathing quietly, as if just fallen asleep.

" If mother would only come now," said Jo, as the winter night began to wane.

" See," said Meg, coming up with a white, half-opened rose, " I thought this would hardly be ready to lay in Beth's hand to-morrow if she—went away from us. But it has blossomed in the night, and now I mean to put it in my vase here, so that when the darling wakes, the first thing she sees will be the little rose and mother's face."

Never had the sun risen so beautifully, and never had the world seemed so lovely, as it did to the heavy eyes of Meg and Jo, as they looked out in the early morning, when their long, sad vigil was done.

" It looks like a fairy world," said Meg, smiling to herself, as she stood behind the curtain watching the dazzling sight.

" Hark ! " cried Jo, starting to her feet.

Yes, there was a sound of bells at the door below, a cry from Hannah, and then Laurie's voice, saying in a joyful whisper, " Girls ! she's come ! she's come ! "

CHAPTER XVI

AMY'S WILL

WHILE these things were happening at home, Amy was having hard times at Aunt March's. She felt her exile deeply, and, for the first time in her life, realised how much she was beloved and petted at home. Aunt March never petted any one ; she did not approve of it ; but she meant to be kind, for the well-behaved little girl pleased her very much, and Aunt March had a soft place in her old heart for her nephew's children, though she didn't think proper to confess it. She really did her best to make Amy happy; but, dear me, what mistakes she made! Some old people keep young at heart in spite of wrinkles and gray hairs, can sympathise with children's little cares and joys, make them feel at home, and can hide wise lessons under pleasant plays giving and receiving friendship in the sweetest way. But Aunt March had not this gift, and she worried Amy most to death with her rules and orders, her prim ways, and long, prosy talks. Finding the child more docile and amiable than her sister, the old lady felt it her duty to try and counteract, as far as possible, the bad effects of home freedom and indulgence. She took Amy in hand, and taught her as she herself had been

She lay on her bed with old Joanna at her side

taught sixty years ago; a process which carried dismay to Amy's soul, and made her feel like a fly in the web of a very strict spider.

She had to wash the cups every morning, and polish up the old-fashioned spoons, the fat silver teapot, and the glasses, till they shone. Then she must dust the room, and what a trying job that was! Not a speck escaped Aunt March's eye, and all the furniture had claw legs, and much carving, which was never dusted to suit. Then Polly must be fed, the lap-dog combed, and a dozen trips upstairs and down, to get things or deliver orders, for the old lady was very lame, and seldom left her big chair. After these tiresome labours she must do her lessons, which was a daily trial of every virtue she possessed. Then she was allowed one hour for exercise or play, and didn't she enjoy it! Laurie came, every day, and wheedled Aunt March till Amy was allowed to go out with him, when they walked and rode and had capital times. After dinner she had to read aloud, and sit still while the old lady slept, which she usually did for an hour, as she dropped off over the first page. Then patchwork or towels appeared, and Amy sewed with outward meekness and inward rebellion till dusk, when she was allowed to amuse herself as she liked till tea-time. The evenings were the worst of all, for Aunt March fell to telling long stories about her youth, which were so unutterably dull that Amy was always ready to go to bed, intending to cry over her hard fate, but usually going to sleep before she had squeezed out more than a tear or two.

If it had not been for Laurie and old Esther, the maid, she felt that she never could have got through that dreadful time. Esther was a French woman, who had lived with "Madame," as she called her mistress, for many years, and who rather tyrannised over the old lady, who could not get along without her. Her real name was Estelle ; but Aunt March ordered her to change it, and she obeyed, on condition that she was never asked to change her religion. She took a fancy to Mademoiselle, and amused her very much with odd stories of her life in France, when Amy sat with her while she got up Madame's laces. She also allowed her to roam about the great house, and examine the curious and pretty things stored away in the big wardrobes and the ancient chests ; for Aunt March hoarded like a magpie. Amy's chief delight was an Indian cabinet full of queer drawers, like pigeon-holes, and secret places in which were kept all sorts of ornaments, some precious, some merely curious, all more or less antique. To examine and arrange these things gave Amy great satisfaction, especially the jewel cases ; in which, on velvet cushions, reposed the ornaments which had adorned a belle forty years ago.

" Which would Mademoiselle choose if she had her will ? " asked Esther, who always sat near to watch over and lock up the valuables.

" I like the diamonds best, but there is no necklace among them, and I'm fond of necklaces, they are so becoming. I should choose this if I might," replied Amy, looking with great admiration at a string of gold and ebony beads, from which hung a heavy cross of the same.

" I, too, covet that, but not as a necklace ; ah, no ! to me it is a rosary, and as such I should use it like a good Catholic," said Esther, eyeing the handsome thing wistfully.

" Is it meant to use as you use the string of good-smelling wooden beads hanging over your glass ? " asked Amy.

" Truly, yes—to pray with. It would be pleasing to the saints if one used so fine a rosary as this, instead of wearing it as a vain bijou."

" You seem to take a deal of comfort in your prayers, Esther, and always come down looking quiet and satisfied. I wish I could."

" If Mademoiselle was a Catholic, she would find true comfort ; but, as that is not to be, it would be well if you went apart each day to meditate, and pray, as did the good mistress whom I served before Madame. She had a little chapel, and in it found solacement for much trouble."

" Would it be right for me to do so too ? " asked Amy, who, in her loneliness, felt the need of help of some sort, and found that she was apt to forget her little book, now that Beth was not there to remind her of it.

" It would be excellent and charming ; and I shall gladly arrange the little dressing-room for you, if you like it. Say nothing to Madame, but when she sleeps go you and sit alone a while to think good thoughts, and ask the dear God to preserve your sister."

Esther was truly pious, and quite sincere in her advice ; for she had an affectionate heart, and felt much for the sisters in their anxiety. Amy liked the idea, and gave her leave to arrange the light closet next her room, hoping it would do her good.

" I wish I knew where all these pretty things would go when Aunt March dies," she said, as she slowly replaced the shining rosary and shut the jewel cases one by one.

" To you and your sisters. I know it ; Madame confides in me ; I witnessed her will, and it is to be so," whispered Esther, smiling.

" How nice ! but I wish she'd let us have them now. Pro-cras-ti-nation is not agreeable," observed Amy, taking a last look at the diamonds.

" It is too soon yet for the young ladies to wear these things. The first one who is affianced will have the pearls—Madame has said it ; and I have a fancy that the little turquoise ring will be given to you when you go, for Madame approves your good behaviour and charming manners."

" Do you think so ? Oh, I'll be a lamb, if I can only have that lovely ring ! It's ever so much prettier than Kitty Bryant's. I do like Aunt March, after all ; " and Amy tried on the blue ring with a delighted face, and a firm resolve to earn it.

From that day she was a model of obedience, and the old lady complacently admired the success of her training. Esther fitted up the closet with a little table, placed a footstool before it, and over it a picture, taken from one of the shut-up rooms. She thought it was of no great value, but, being appropriate, she borrowed it, well knowing that Madame would never know it, nor care if she did. It was, however, a very valuable copy of one of the famous pictures of the world, and Amy's beauty-loving eyes were never tired of looking up at the sweet face of the divine mother, while tender thoughts of her own were busy at her heart. On the table she laid her little Testament and hymn-book, kept a vase always full of the best flowers Laurie brought her, and came every day to " sit alone, thinking good thoughts, and praying the dear God to preserve her sister." Esther had given her a rosary of black beads with a silver cross, but Amy hung it up, and did not use it, feeling doubtful as to its fitness for Protestant prayers.

The little girl was very sincere in all this, for, being left alone outside the safe home-nest, she felt the need of some kind hand to hold by so sorely, that she instinctively turned to the strong and tender Friend, whose fatherly love most closely surrounds His little children. She missed her mother's help to understand and rule herself ; but having been taught where to look, she did her best to find the way, and walk in it confidingly. But Amy was a young pilgrim, and just now her burden seemed very heavy. She tried to forget herself, to keep cheerful, and be satisfied with doing right, though no one saw or praised her for it. In her first effort at being very, very good, she decided to make her will, as Aunt March had done ; so that if she *did* fall ill and die, her possessions might be justly and generously divided. It cost her a pang even to think of giving up the little treasures which in her eyes were as precious as the old lady's jewels.

During one of her play hours she wrote out the important document as well as she could, with some help from Esther as to certain legal terms ; and, when the good-natured French woman had signed her name, Amy felt relieved, and laid it by to show Laurie, whom she wanted as a second witness. As it was a rainy day, she went upstairs to amuse herself in one of the large chambers, and took Polly with her for company. In this room there was a wardrobe full of old-fashioned costumes, with which Esther allowed her to play, and it was her favourite amusement to array herself in the faded brocades, and parade up and down before the long mirror, making stately curtsies, and sweeping her train about with a rustle which delighted her ears. So busy was she on this day that she did not hear Laurie's ring, nor see his face peeping in at her, as she gravely promenaded to and fro, flirting her fan and tossing her head, on which she wore a great pink turban, contrasting oddly with her blue brocade dress and yellow quilted petticoat. She was obliged to walk carefully, for she had on high-heeled shoes, and, as Laurie told Jo afterward, it was a comical sight to see her mince along in her gay suit, with Polly sidling and bridling just behind her, imitating her as well as he could, and occasionally stopping to laugh or exclaim, " Ain't we fine ? Get along, you fright ! Hold your tongue. Kiss me, dear ; ha ! ha ! "

Having with difficulty restrained an explosion of merriment, lest it should offend her majesty, Laurie tapped, and was graciously received.

" Sit down and rest while I put these things away ; then I want to consult you about a very serious matter," said Amy, when she had shown her splendour, and driven Polly into a corner. " That bird is the trial of my life," she continued, removing the pink mountain from her head, while Laurie seated himself astride of a chair. " Yesterday, when my aunt was asleep, and I was trying to be as still as a mouse, Polly began to squall and flap about in his cage ; so I went to let him out, and found a big spider there. I poked it out, and it ran under the book-case ; Polly marched straight after it, stooped down and peeped under the book-case, saying, in his funny way, with a cock of his eye, ' Come out and take a walk, my dear.' I *couldn't* help laughing, which made Poll swear, and aunt woke up and scolded us both."

" Did the spider accept the old fellow's invitation ? " asked Laurie, yawning.

" Yes ; out it came, and away ran Polly, frightened to death, and scrambled up on aunt's chair, calling out, ' Catch her ! catch her ! catch her ! ' as I chased the spider."

" That's a lie ! Oh lor ! " cried the parrot, pecking at Laurie's toes.

" I'd wring your neck if you were mine, you old torment ! " cried Laurie, shaking his fist at the bird, who put his head on one side, and gravely croaked, " Allyluyer ! bless your buttons, dear ! "

" Now I'm ready," said Amy, shutting the wardrobe, and taking a paper out of her pocket. " I want you to read that, please, and tell me if it is legal and right. I fear that I ought to do it, for life is uncertain, and I don't want any ill-feeling over my tomb."

Laurie bit his lips, and turning a little from the pensive speaker, read the following document with praiseworthy gravity, considering the spelling :—

" My last Will and Testment."

" I, Amy Curtis March, being in my sane mind, do give and bequeethe all my personal property—viz. to wit :—namely,—

" To my father, my best pictures, sketches, maps, and works of art, including frames. Also my $100, to do what he likes with.

" To my mother, all my clothes, except the blue apron with pockets—also my likeness, and my medal, with much love.

" To my dear sister Margaret, I give my turkquoise ring (if I get it), also my green box with the doves on it, also my piece of real lace for her neck, and my sketch of her as a memorial of her ' little girl.'

" To Jo I leave my breast-pin, the one mended with sealing-wax, also my bronze inkstand—she lost the cover—and my most precious plaster rabbit, because I am sorry I burnt up her story.

" To Beth (if she lives after me) I give my dolls and the little bureau, my fan, my linen collars and my new slippers if she can wear them, being thin when she gets well. And I herewith also leave her my regret that I ever made fun of old Joanna.

" To my friend and neighbour Theodore Laurence I bequeethe my paper marshay porfolio, my clay model of a horse, though he did say it hadn't any neck. Also in return for his great kindness in the hour of affliction any one of my artistic works he likes, Noter Dame is the best.

" To our venerable benefactor Mr. Laurence I leave my purple box with a looking glass in the cover which will be nice for his pens and remind him of the departed girl who thanks him for his favours to her family, specially Beth.

" I wish my favourite playmate Kitty Bryant to have the blue silk apron and my gold-bead ring with a kiss.

" To Hannah I give the band-box she wanted and all the patchwork I leave hoping she ' will remember me, when it you see.'

" And now having disposed of my most valuable property I hope all will be satisfied and not blame the dead. I forgive every one, and trust we may all meet when the trump shall sound. Amen.

" To this will and testiment I set my hand and seal on this 20th day of Nov. Anni Domino 1861.

" Amy Curtis March."

" *Witnesses :* {Estelle Valnor,
Theodore Laurence."

The last name was written in pencil, and Amy explained that he was to re-write it in ink, and seal it up for her properly.

" What put it into your head ? Did any one tell you about Beth's giving away her things ? " asked Laurie soberly, as Amy laid a bit of red tape, with sealing-wax, a taper, and a standish before him.

She explained ; and then asked anxiously, " What about Beth ? "

" I'm sorry I spoke ; but as I did I'll tell you. She felt so ill one day that she told Jo she wanted to give her piano to Meg, her bird to you, and the poor old doll to Jo, who would love it for her sake. She was sorry she had so little to give, and left locks of hair to the rest of us, and her best love to grandpa. *She* never thought of a will."

Laurie was signing and sealing as he spoke, and did not look up till a great tear dropped on the paper. Amy's face was full of trouble ; but she only said, " Don't people put sort of postscripts to their wills, sometimes ? "

" Yes ; ' codicils ' they call them."

" Put one in mine then—that I wish *all* my curls cut off, and given round to my friends. I forgot it ; but I want it done, though it will spoil my looks."

Laurie added it, smiling at Amy's last and greatest sacrifice. Then he amused her for an hour, and was much interested in all her trials. But when he came to go, Amy held him back to whisper, with trembling lips, " Is there really any danger about Beth ? "

" I'm afraid there is ; but we must hope for the best, so don't cry, dear ; " and Laurie put his arm about her with a gesture which was very comforting.

When he had gone, she went to her little chapel, and sitting in the twilight, prayed for Beth with streaming tears and an aching heart, feeling that a million turquoise rings would not console her for the loss of her gentle little sister.

CHAPTER XVII

CONFIDENTIAL

I DON'T think I have any words in which to tell the meeting of the mother and daughters ; such hours are beautiful to live, but very hard to describe, so I will leave it to the imagination of my readers, merely saying that the house was full of genuine happiness, and that Meg's tender hope was realised ; for when Beth woke from that long, healing sleep, the first objects on which her eyes fell *were* the little rose and mother's face. Too weak to wonder at anything, she only smiled, and nestled close into the loving arms about her, feeling the hungry longing was satisfied at last. Then she slept again, and the girls waited upon their mother, for she would not unclasp the thin hand which clung to hers, even in sleep. Hannah had " dished up " an astonishing breakfast for the traveller, finding it impossible to vent her excitement in any other way ; and Meg and Jo fed their mother like dutiful young storks, while they listened to her whispered account of father's state, Mr. Brooke's promise to stay and nurse him, the delays which the storm occasioned on the homeward journey, and the unspeakable comfort Laurie's hopeful face had given her when she arrived, worn out with fatigue, anxiety, and cold.

What a strange yet pleasant day that was ! so brilliant and gay without, for all the world seemed abroad to welcome the first snow ; so quiet and reposeful within, for every one slept, spent with watching, and a Sabbath stillness reigned through the house, while nodding Hannah mounted guard at the door. With a blissful sense of burdens lifted off, Meg and Jo closed their weary eyes, and lay at rest, like storm-beaten boats safe at anchor in a quiet harbour. Mrs. March would not leave Beth's side, but rested in the big chair, waking often to look at, touch, and brood over her child, like a miser over recovered treasure.

Laurie, meanwhile, posted off to comfort Amy, and told his story so well that Aunt March actually " sniffed " herself, and never once said " I told you so." Amy came out so strong on this occasion that I think the good thoughts in the little chapel really began to bear fruit. She dried her tears quickly, restrained her impatience to see her mother, and never even thought of the turquoise ring, when the old lady heartily agreed in Laurie's opinion, that she behaved " like a capital little woman." Even Polly seemed impressed, for he called her " good girl," blessed her buttons, and begged her to " come and take a walk, dear," in his most affable tone. She would very gladly have gone out to enjoy the bright wintry weather, but, discovering that Laurie was dropping with sleep, in spite of manful efforts to conceal the

MARGARET TULLOCH

Amy had to feed the parrot every day

fact, she persuaded him to rest on the sofa, while she wrote a note to her mother. She was a long time about it ; and, when she returned, he was stretched out with both arms under his head, sound asleep, while Aunt March had pulled down the curtains, and sat doing nothing in an unusual fit of benignity.

After a while, they began to think he was not going to wake till night, and I'm not sure that he would, had he not been effectually roused by Amy's cry of joy at sight of her mother. There probably were a good many happy little girls in and about the city that day, but it is my private opinion that Amy was the happiest of all, when she sat in her mother's lap and told her trials, receiving consolation and compensation in the shape of approving smiles and fond caresses. They were alone together in the chapel, to which her mother did not object when its purpose was explained to her.

" On the contrary, I like it very much, dear," she said, looking from the dusty rosary to the well-worn little book, and the lovely picture with its garland of evergreen. " It is an excellent plan to have some place where we can go to be quiet when things vex or grieve us. There are a good many hard times in this life of ours, but we can always bear them if we ask help in the right way. I think my little girl is learning this ? "

" Yes, mother ; and when I go home I mean to have a corner in the big closet to put my books, and the copy of that picture which I've tried to make. The woman's face is not good, it's too beautiful for me to draw, but the baby is done better, and I love it very much. I like to think He was a little child once, for then I don't seem so far away, and that helps me."

As Amy pointed to the smiling Christ-child on the mother's knee, Mrs. March saw something on the lifted hand that made her smile. She said nothing, but Amy understood the look, and, after a minute's pause, she added gravely,—

" I wanted to speak to you about this, but I forgot it. Aunt gave me the ring to-day ; she called me to her and kissed me, and put it on my finger, and said I was a credit to her, and she'd like to keep me always. She gave that funny guard to keep the turquoise on, as it's too big. I'd like to wear them, mother, can I ? "

" They are very pretty, but I think you're rather too young for such ornaments, Amy," said Mrs. March, looking at the plump little hand, with the band of sky blue stones on the forefinger, and the quaint guard, formed of two tiny golden hands clasped together.

" I'll try not to be vain," said Amy ; " I don't think I like it only because it's so pretty ; but I want to wear it as the girl in the story wore her bracelet : to remind me of something."

" Do you mean Aunt March ? " asked her mother, laughing.

" No, to remind me not to be selfish." Amy looked so earnest and sincere about it that her mother stopped laughing, and listened respectfully to the little plan.

" I've thought a great deal lately about ' my bundle of naughties,' and being selfish is the largest one in it ; so I'm going to try hard to cure it, if I can. Beth isn't selfish, and that's the reason every one loves her, and feels so bad at the thought of losing her. People wouldn't feel half so bad about me if I was sick, and I don't deserve to have them ; but I'd like to be loved, and missed by a great many friends, so I'm going to try to be like Beth all I can. I'm apt to forget my resolutions ; but, if I had something always about me to remind me, I guess I should do better. May I try this way ? "

" Yes ; but I have more faith in the corner of the big closet. Wear your ring, dear, and do your best ; I think you will prosper, for the sincere wish to be good is half the battle. Now I must go back to Beth. Keep up your heart, little daughter, and we will soon have you home again."

That evening, while Meg was writing to her father, to report the traveller's safe arrival, Jo slipped upstairs into Beth's room, and, finding her mother in her usual place, stood a minute twisting her fingers in her hair, with a worried gesture and an undecided look.

" What is it, deary ? " asked Mrs. March, holding out her hand with a face which invited confidence.

" I want to tell you something, mother."

" About Meg ? "

" How quick you guessed ! Yes, it's about her ; and, though it's a little thing, it fidgets me."

" Beth is asleep ; speak low, and tell me all about it. That Moffat hasn't been here, I hope ? " asked Mrs. March, rather sharply.

" No ; I should have shut the door in his face if he had," said Jo, settling herself on the floor at her mother's feet. " Last summer Meg left a pair of gloves over at the Laurences', and only one was returned. We forgot all about it till Teddy told me that Mr. Brooke had it. He kept it in his waist-coat pocket, and once it fell out, and Teddy joked him about it, and Mr. Brooke owned that he liked Meg, but didn't dare say so, she was so young and he so poor. Now, isn't it a *dread*ful state of things ? "

" Do you think Meg cares for him ? " asked Mrs. March, with an anxious look.

" Mercy me ! I don't know anything about love and such nonsense ! " cried Jo, with a funny mixture of interest and contempt. " In novels the girls show it by starting and blushing, fainting away, growing thin, and acting like fools. Now Meg don't do anything of the sort ; she eats and drinks, and sleeps, like a sensible creature ; she looks straight in my face when I talk about that man, and only blushes a little bit when Teddy jokes about lovers. I forbid him to do it, but he don't mind me as he ought."

" Then you fancy that Meg is *not* interested in John ? "

" Who ? " cried Jo, staring.

" Mr. Brooke ; I call him ' John ' now ; we fell into the way of doing so at the hospital, and he likes it."

" Oh, dear ! I know you'll take his part ; he's been good to father, and you won't send him away, but let Meg marry him, if she wants to. Mean thing ! to go petting pa and truckling to you, just to wheedle you into liking him " ; and Jo pulled her hair again with a wrathful tweak.

" My dear, don't get angry about it, and I will tell you how it happened. John went with me at Mr. Laurence's request, and was so devoted to poor father that we couldn't help getting fond of him. He was perfectly open and honourable about Meg, for he told us he loved her, but would earn a com-fortable home before he asked her to marry him. He only wanted our leave to love her and work for her, and the right to make her love him if he could. He is a truly excellent young man, and we could not refuse to listen to him ; but I will not consent to Meg's engaging herself so young."

" Of course not, it would be idiotic ! I knew there was mischief brewing ; I felt it ; and now it's worse than I imagined. I just wish I could marry Meg myself and keep her safe in the family."

This odd arrangement made Mrs. March smile, but she said gravely, " Jo, I confide in you, and don't wish you to say anything to Meg yet. When John comes back, and I see them together, I can judge better of her feelings towards him."

" She'll see his in those handsome eyes that she talks about, and then it will be all up with her. She's got such a soft heart, it will melt like butter in the sun if any one looks sentimentally at her. She read the short reports he sent more than she did your letters, and pinched me when I spoke of it, and likes brown eyes, and don't think John an ugly name, and she'll go and fall in love, and there's an end of peace, and fun, and cosy times together. I see it all ! they'll go lovering round the house, and we shall have to dodge ; Meg will be absorbed, and no good to me any more ; Brooke will scratch up a fortune somehow, carry her off, and make a hole in the family; and I shall break my heart, and everything will be abominably uncomfortable. Oh, deary me; why weren't we all boys? then there wouldn't be any bother!"

Jo leaned her chin on her knees in a disconsolate attitude, and shook her fist at the reprehensible John. Mrs. March sighed, and Jo looked up with an air of relief.

"You don't like it, mother? I'm glad of it; let's send him about his business, and not tell Meg a word of it, but all be jolly together, as we always have been."

"I did wrong to sigh, Jo. It is natural and right you should all go to homes of your own in time; but I do want to keep my girls as long as I can, and I am sorry that this happened so soon, for Meg is only seventeen, and it will be some years before John can make a home for her. Your father and I have agreed that she shall not bind herself in any way, nor be married before twenty. If she and John love one another, they can wait, and test the love by doing so. She is conscientious, and I have no fear of her treating him unkindly, my pretty, tender-hearted girl! I hope things will go happily with her."

"Hadn't you rather have her marry a rich man?" asked Jo, as her mother's voice faltered a little over the last words.

"Money is a good and useful thing, Jo, and I hope my girls will never feel the need of it too bitterly, nor be tempted by too much. I should like to know that John was firmly established in some good business, which gave him an income large enough to keep free from debt, and make Meg comfortable. I'm not ambitious for a splendid fortune, a fashionable position, or a great name for my girls. If rank and money come with love and virtue also, I should accept them gratefully, and enjoy your good fortune; but I know, by experience, how much genuine happiness can be had in a plain little house, where the daily bread is earned, and some privations give sweetness to the few pleasures. I am content to see Meg begin humbly, for, if I am not mistaken, she will be rich in the possession of a good man's heart, and that is better than a fortune."

"I understand, mother, and quite agree; but I'm disappointed about Meg, for I'd planned to have her marry Teddy by-and-by, and sit in the lap of luxury all her days. Wouldn't it be nice?" asked Jo, looking up with a brighter face.

"He is younger than she, you know," began Mrs. March, but Jo broke in,—

"Oh, that don't matter; he's old for his age, and tall; and can be quite grown-up in his manners if he likes. Then he's rich, and generous, and good, and loves us all; and I say it's a pity my plan is spoilt."

"I'm afraid Laurie is hardly grown-up enough for Meg, and altogether too much of a weathercock, just now, for any one to depend on. Don't make plans, Jo; but let time and their own hearts mate your friends. We can't meddle safely in such matters, and had better not get 'romantic rubbish,' as you call it, into our heads, lest it spoil our friendship."

"Well, I won't; but I hate to see things going all criss-cross, and getting snarled up, when a pull here, and a snip there, would straighten it out.

I wish wearing flat-irons on our heads would keep us from growing up. But buds will be roses, and kittens, cats—more's the pity ! ''

" What's that about flat-irons and cats ? '' asked Meg, as she crept into the room, with the finished letter in her hand.

" Only one of my stupid speeches. I'm going to bed ; come on, Peggy,'' said Jo, unfolding herself, like an animated puzzle.

" Quite right, and beautifully written. Please add that I send my love to John,'' said Mrs. March, as she glanced over the letter, and gave it back.

" Do you call him ' John ? '' asked Meg smiling, with her innocent eyes looking down into her mother's.

" Yes ; he has been like a son to us, and we are very fond of him,'' replied Mrs. March, returning the look with a keen one.

" I'm glad of that ; he is so lonely. Good-night, mother, dear. It is so inexpressibly comfortable to have you here,'' was Meg's quiet answer.

The kiss her mother gave her was a very tender one, and, as she went away, Mrs. March said, with a mixture of satisfaction and regret, " She does not love John yet, but will soon learn to.''

CHAPTER XVIII

LAURIE MAKES MISCHIEF, AND JO MAKES PEACE

JO'S face was a study next day, for the secret rather weighed upon her, and she found it hard not to look mysterious and important. Meg observed it, but did not trouble herself to make inquiries, for she had learned that the best way to manage Jo was by the law of contraries ; so she felt sure of being told everything if she did not ask. She was rather surprised, therefore, when the silence remained unbroken, and Jo assumed a patronising air, which decidedly aggravated Meg, who, in her turn, assumed an air of dignified reserve, and devoted herself to her mother. This left Jo to her own devices ; for Mrs. March had taken her place as nurse, and bid her rest, exercise, and amuse herself after her long confinement. Amy being gone, Laurie was her only refuge ; and, much as she enjoyed his society, she rather dreaded him just then, for he was an incorrigible tease, and she feared he would coax her secret from her.

She was quite right ; for the mischief-loving lad no sooner suspected a mystery than he settled himself to finding it out, and led Jo a trying life of it. He wheedled, bribed, ridiculed, threatened, and scolded ; affected indifference that he might surprise the truth from her ; declared he knew, then that he didn't care ; and, at last, by dint of perseverance, he satisfied himself that it concerned Meg and Mr. Brooke. Feeling indignant that he was not taken into his tutor's confidence, he set his wits to work to devise some proper retaliation for the slight.

Meg, meanwhile, had apparently forgotten the matter, and was absorbed in preparations for her father's return, but all of a sudden a change seemed to come over her, and, for a day or two, she was quite unlike herself. She started when spoken to, blushed when looked at, was very quiet, and sat over her sewing with a timid, troubled look on her face. To her mother's inquiries she answered that she was quite well, and Jo's she silenced by begging to be let alone.

"She feels it in the air—love, I mean—and she's going very fast. She's got most of the symptoms, is twittery and cross, don't eat, lies awake, and mopes in corners. I caught her singing that song about ' the silver-voiced brook,' and once she said ' John,' as you do, and then turned as red as a poppy. Whatever shall we do ? " said Jo, looking ready for any measures however violent.

"Nothing but wait. Let her alone, be kind and patient, and father's coming will settle everything," replied her mother.

"Here's a note to you, Meg, all sealed up. How odd ! Teddy never seals mine," said Jo, next day, as she distributed the contents of the little post-office.

Mrs. March and Jo were deep in their own affairs when a sound from Meg made them look up to see her staring at her note, with a frightened face.

"My child, what is it ? " cried her mother, running to her, while Jo tried to take the paper which had done the mischief.

"It's all a mistake—he didn't send it—oh, Jo, how could you do it ? " and Meg hid her face in her hands, crying as if her heart was quite broken.

"Me ! I've done nothing ! What's she talking about ? " cried Jo, bewildered.

Meg's mild eyes kindled with anger as she pulled a crumpled note from her pocket, and threw it at Jo, saying reproachfully,—

"You wrote it, and that bad boy helped you. How could you be so rude, so mean, and cruel to us both ? "

Jo hardly heard her, for she and her mother were reading the note, which was written in a peculiar hand.

"MY DEAREST MARGARET,—I can no longer restrain my passion, and must know my fate before I return. I dare not tell your parents yet, but I think they would consent if they knew that we adored one another. Mr. Laurence will help me to some good place, and then, my sweet girl, you will make me happy. I implore you to say nothing to your family yet, but to send one word of hope through Laurie to

"Your devoted,

"JOHN."

"Oh, the little villain ! that's the way he meant to pay me for keeping my word to mother. I'll give him a hearty scolding, and bring him over to beg pardon," cried Jo, burning to execute immediate justice. But her mother held her back, saying, with a look she seldom wore,—

"Stop, Jo ; you must clear yourself first. You have played so many pranks that I am afraid you have had a hand in this."

"On my word, mother, I haven't ! I never saw that note before, and don't know anything about it, as true as I live ! " said Jo, so earnestly that they believed her. "If I *had* taken a part in it, I'd have done it better than this, and have written a sensible note. I should think you'd have known

Mr. Brooke wouldn't write such stuff as that," she added, scornfully tossing down the paper.

"It's like his writing," faltered Meg, comparing it with the note in her hand.

"Oh, Meg, you didn't answer it?" cried Mrs. March quickly.

"Yes, I did!" and Meg hid her face again, overcome with shame.

"Here's a scrape! *Do* let me bring that wicked boy over to explain, and be lectured. I can't rest till I get hold of him;" and Jo made for the door again.

"Hush! let me manage this, for it is worse than I thought. Margaret, tell me the whole story," commanded Mrs. March, sitting down by Meg, yet keeping hold of Jo, lest she should fly off.

"I received the first letter from Laurie, who didn't look as if he knew anything about it," began Meg, without looking up. "I was worried at first, and meant to tell you; then I remembered how you liked Mr. Brooke, so I thought you wouldn't mind if I kept my little secret for a few days. I'm so silly that I liked to think no one knew, and, while I was deciding what to say, I felt like the girls in books, who have such things to do. Forgive me, mother; I'm paid for my silliness now. I never can look him in the face again."

"What did you say to him?" asked Mrs. March.

"I only said I was too young to do anything about it yet; that I didn't wish to have secrets from you, and he must speak to father. I was very grateful for his kindness, and would be his friend, but nothing more, for a long while."

Mrs. March smiled, as if well pleased, and Jo clapped her hands, exclaiming with a laugh,—

"You are almost equal to Caroline Percy, who was a pattern of prudence! Tell on, Meg. What did he say to that?"

"He writes in a different way entirely, telling me that he never sent any love-letter at all, and is very sorry that my roguish sister, Jo, should take liberties with our names. It's very kind and respectful, but think how dreadful for me!"

Meg leaned against her mother, looking the image of despair, and Jo tramped about the room, calling Laurie names. All of a sudden she stopped, caught up the two notes, and, after looking at them closely, said decidedly, "I don't believe Brooke ever saw either of these letters. Teddy wrote both, and keeps yours to crow over me with, because I wouldn't tell him my secret."

"Don't have any secrets, Jo; tell it to mother, and keep out of trouble, as I should have done," said Meg warningly.

"Bless you, child! mother told me."

"That will do, Jo. I'll comfort Meg while you go and get Laurie. I shall sift the matter to the bottom, and put a stop to such pranks at once."

Away ran Jo, and Mrs. March gently told Meg Mr. Brooke's real feelings. "Now, dear, what are your own? Do you love him enough to wait till he can make a home for you, or will you keep yourself quite free for the present?"

"I've been so scared and worried, I don't want to have anything to do

with lovers for a long while,—perhaps never," answered Meg petulantly.
" If John *doesn't* know anything about this nonsense, don't tell him, and
make Jo and Laurie hold their tongues. I won't be deceived and plagued
and made a fool of—it's a shame ! "

Seeing that Meg's usually gentle temper was roused, and her pride
hurt by this mischievous joke, Mrs. March soothed her by promises of
entire silence, and great discretion for the future. The instant Laurie's
step was heard in the hall, Meg fled into the study, and Mrs. March received
the culprit alone. Jo had not told him why he was wanted, fearing he wouldn't
come ; but he knew the minute he saw Mrs. March's face, and stood twirl-
ing his hat with a guilty air, which convicted him at once. Jo was dismissed,
but chose to march up and down the hall like a sentinel, having some fear
that the prisoner might bolt. The sound of voices in the parlour rose and
fell for half an hour ; but what happened during that interview the girls
never knew.

When they were called in, Laurie was standing by their mother with
such a penitent face that Jo forgave him on the spot, but did not think it
wise to betray the fact. Meg received his apology, and was much comforted
by the assurance that Brooke knew nothing of the joke.

" I'll never tell him to my dying day, wild horses shan't drag it out of
me; so you'll forgive me, Meg, and I'll do anything to show how out-and-
out sorry I am," he added, looking very much ashamed of himself.

" I'll try ; but it was a very ungentlemanly thing to do. I didn't think
you could be so sly and malicious, Laurie," replied Meg, trying to hide
her maidenly confusion under a gravely reproachful air.

" It was altogether abominable, and I don't deserve to be spoken to for
a month ; but you will, though, won't you ? " and Laurie folded his hands
together, with such an imploring gesture, and rolled up his eyes in such a
meekly repentant way as he spoke in his irresistibly persuasive tone, that it
was impossible to frown upon him, in spite of his scandalous behaviour.
Meg pardoned him, and Mrs. March's grave face relaxed, in spite of her
efforts to keep sober, when she heard him declare that he would atone for
his sins by all sorts of penances, and abase himself like a worm before the
injured damsel.

Jo stood aloof, meanwhile trying to harden her heart against him, and
succeeding only in primming up her face into an expression of entire disapprobation. Laurie looked at her once or twice, but, as she showed no
signs of relenting, he felt injured, and turned his back on her till the others
were done with him, when he made her a low bow, and walked off without
a word.

As soon as he had gone, she wished she had been more forgiving ; and,
when Meg and her mother went upstairs, she felt lonely and longed for
Teddy. After resisting for some time, she yielded to the impulse, and,
armed with a book to return, went over to the big house.

" Is Mr. Laurence in ? " asked Jo, of a housemaid, who was coming
downstairs.

" Yes, miss ; but I don't believe he's seeable just yet."

" Why not ? is he ill ? "

" La, no, miss ! but he's had a scene with Mr. Laurie, who is in one of his tantrums about something, which vexes the old gentleman, so I dursn't go nigh him."

" Where is Laurie ? "

" Shut up in his room, and he won't answer, though I've been tapping. I don't know what's to become of the dinner, for it's ready, and there's no one to eat it."

" I'll go and see what the matter is. I'm not afraid of either of them."

Up went Jo, and knocked smartly on the door of Laurie's little study.

" Stop that, or I'll open the door and make you ! " called out the young gentleman in a threatening tone.

Jo immediately pounded again ; the door flew open, and in she bounced before Laurie could recover from his surprise. Seeing that he really *was* out of temper, Jo, who knew how to manage him, assumed a contrite expression, and going artistically down upon her knees, said meekly, " Please forgive me for being so cross. I came to make it up, and can't go away till I have."

" It's all right ; get up, and don't be a goose, Jo," was the cavalier reply to her petition.

" Thank you ; I will. Could I ask what's the matter ? You don't look exactly easy in your mind."

" I've been shaken, and I won't bear it ! " growled Laurie indignantly.

" Who did it ? " demanded Jo.

" Grandfather ; if it had been any one else I'd have——" and the injured youth finished his sentence by an energetic gesture of the right arm.

" That's nothing ; I often shake you, and you don't mind," said Jo soothingly.

" Pooh ! you're a girl, and it's fun ; but I'll allow no man to shake *me*."

" I don't think any one would care to try it, if you looked as much like a thunder-cloud as you do now. Why were you treated so ? "

" Just because I wouldn't say what your mother wanted me for. I'd promised not to tell, and of course I wasn't going to break my word."

" Couldn't you satisfy your grandpa in any other way ? "

" No ; he *would* have the truth, the whole truth, and nothing but the truth. I'd have told my part of the scrape, if I could without bringing Meg in. As I couldn't, I held my tongue, and bore the scolding till the old gentleman collared me. Then I got angry, and bolted, for fear I should forget myself."

" It wasn't nice, but he's sorry, I know ; so go down and make up. I'll help you."

" Hanged if I do ! I'm not going to be lectured and pummelled by every one, just for a bit of frolic. I *was* sorry about Meg, and begged pardon like a man ; but I won't do it again, when I wasn't in the wrong."

" He didn't know that."

" He ought to trust me, and not act as if I was a baby. It's no use, Jo ; he's got to learn that I'm able to take care of myself, and don't need any one's apron-string to hold on by."

" What pepper-pots you are ! " sighed Jo. " How do you mean to settle this affair ? "

" Well, he ought to beg pardon, and believe me when I say I can't tell him what the row's about."

" Bless you ! he won't do that."

" I won't go down till he does."

" Now, Teddy, be sensible ; let it pass, and I'll explain what I can. You can't stay here, so what's the use of being melodramatic ? "

" I don't intend to stay here long, anyway. I'll slip off and take a journey somewhere, and when grandpa misses me, he'll come round fast enough."

" I dare say ; but you ought not to go and worry him."

" Don't preach. I'll go to Washington and see Brooke ; it's gay there, and I'll enjoy myself after the troubles."

" What fun you'd have ! I wish I could run off too ! " said Jo, forgetting her part of Mentor in lively visions of martial life at the capital.

" Come on, then ! Why not ? You go and surprise your father, and I'll stir up old Brooke. It would be a glorious joke ; let's do it, Jo ! We'll leave a letter saying we are all right, and trot off at once. I've got money enough ; it will do you good, and be no harm, as you go to your father."

For a moment Jo looked as if she would agree ; for, wild as the plan was, it just suited her. She was tired of care and confinement, longed for change, and thoughts of her father blended temptingly with the novel charms of camps and hospitals, liberty and fun. Her eyes kindled as they turned wistfully toward the window ; but they fell on the old house opposite, and she shook her head with sorrowful decision.

" If I was a boy, we'd run away together, and have a capital time ; but as I'm a miserable girl, I must be proper and stop at home. Don't tempt me, Teddy ; it's a crazy plan."

" That's the fun of it ! " began Laurie, who had got a wilful fit on him, and was possessed to break out of bounds in some way.

" Hold your tongue ! " cried Jo, covering her ears. " ' Prunes and prisms ' are my doom, and I may as well make up my mind to it. I came here to moralise, not to hear about things that make me skip to think of."

" I knew Meg would wet-blanket such a proposal, but I thought you had more spirit," began Laurie insinuatingly.

" Bad boy, be quiet. Sit down and think of your own sins ; don't go making me add to mine. If I get your grandpa to apologise for the shaking, will you give up running away ? " asked Jo seriously.

" Yes ; but you won't do it," answered Laurie, who wished to " make up," but felt that his outraged dignity must be appeased first.

" If I can manage the young one, I can the old one," muttered Jo, as she walked away, leaving Laurie bent over a railroad map, with his head propped up on both hands.

" Come in ! " and Mr. Laurence's gruff voice sounded gruffer than ever as Jo tapped at his door.

" It's only me, sir, come to return a book," she said blandly as she entered.

" Want any more ? " asked the old gentleman, looking grim and vexed, but trying not to show it.

" Yes, please ; I like old Sam so well I think I'll try the second volume," returned Jo, hoping to propitiate him by accepting a second dose of *Boswell's Johnson*, as he had recommended that lively work.

The shaggy eyebrows unbent a little as he rolled the steps towards the shelf where the Johnsonian literature was placed. Jo skipped up, and, sitting on the top step, affected to be searching for her book, but was really wondering how best to introduce the dangerous object of her visit. Mr. Laurence seemed to suspect that something was brewing in her mind ; for, after taking several brisk turns about the room, he faced round on her, speaking so abruptly that *Rasselas* tumbled face downward on the floor.

" What has that boy been about ? Don't try to shield him, now ! I know he has been in mischief, by the way he acted when he came home. I can't get a word from him ; and when I threatened to shake the truth out of him, he bolted upstairs and locked himself in his room."

" He did do wrong, but we forgave him, and all promised not to say a word to any one," began Jo reluctantly.

" That won't do ; he shall not shelter himself behind a promise from you soft-hearted girls. If he's done anything amiss, he shall confess, beg pardon, and be punished. Out with it, Jo ! I won't be kept in the dark."

Mr. Laurence looked so alarming, and spoke so sharply, that Jo would have gladly run away, if she could, but she was perched aloft on the steps, and he stood at the foot, a lion in the path ; so she had to stay and brave it out.

" Indeed, sir, I cannot tell ; mother forbid it. Laurie has confessed, asked pardon, and been punished quite enough. We don't keep silence to shield him, but some one else ; and it will make more trouble if you interfere. Please don't ; it was partly my fault, but it's all right now, so let's forget it, and talk about the *Rambler*, or something pleasant."

" Hang the *Rambler* ! Come down and give me your word that this harum-scarum boy of mine hasn't done anything ungrateful or impertinent. If he has, after all your kindness to him, I'll thrash him with my own hands."

The threat sounded awful, but did not alarm Jo, for she knew the irascible old man would never lift a finger against his grandson, whatever he might say to the contrary. She obediently descended, and made as light of the prank as she could without betraying Meg or forgetting the truth.

" Hum ! ha ! well, if the boy held his tongue because he'd promised, and not from obstinacy, I'll forgive him. He's a stubborn fellow, and hard to manage," said Mr. Laurence, rubbing up his hair till it looked as if he'd been out in a gale, and smoothing the frown from his brow with an air of relief.

" So am I ; but a kind word will govern me when all the king's horses and all the king's men couldn't," said Jo, trying to say a kind word for her friend, who seemed to get out of one scrape only to fall into another.

" You think I'm not kind to him, hey ? " was the sharp answer.

" Oh, dear, no, sir ; you are rather too kind sometimes, and then just a trifle hasty when he tries your patience. Don't you think you are ? "

Jo was determined to have it out now, and tried to look quite placid, though she quaked a little after her bold speech. To her great relief and surprise, the old gentleman only threw his spectacles on to the table, with a rattle, and exclaimed frankly,—

" You're right, girl, I am ! I love the boy, but he tries my patience past bearing, and I don't know how it will end, if we go on so."

" I'll tell you, he'll run away." Jo was sorry for that speech the minute it was made ; she meant to warn him that Laurie would not bear much restraint, and hoped he would be more forbearing with the lad.

Mr. Laurence's ruddy face changed suddenly, and he sat down with a troubled glance at the picture of a handsome man which hung over his table. It was Laurie's father, who *had* run away in his youth, and married against the imperious old man's will. Jo fancied he remembered and regretted the past, and she wished she had held her tongue.

" He won't do it unless he is very much worried, and only threatens it sometimes, when he gets tired of studying. I often think I should like to, especially since my hair was cut ; so, if you ever miss us, you may advertise for two boys, and look among the ships bound for India."

She laughed as she spoke, and Mr. Laurence looked relieved, evidently taking the whole as a joke.

" You hussy ! how dare you talk in that way ! where's your respect for me, and your proper bringing up ? Bless the boys and girls ! what torments they are ; yet we can't do without them," he said, pinching her cheeks good-humouredly.

" Go and bring that boy down to his dinner ; tell him it's all right, and advise him not to put on tragedy airs with his grandfather ; I won't bear it."

" He won't come, sir ; he feels badly because you didn't believe him when he said he couldn't tell. I think the shaking hurt his feelings very much."

Jo tried to look pathetic, but must have failed, for Mr. Laurence began to laugh, and she knew the day was won.

" I'm sorry for that, and ought to thank him for not shaking *me*, I suppose. What the dickens does the fellow expect ? " and the old gentleman looked a trifle ashamed of his own testiness.

" If I was you, I'd write him an apology, sir. He says he won't come down till he has one ; and talks about Washington, and goes on in an absurd way. A formal apology will make him see how foolish he is, and bring him down quite amiable. Try it ; he likes fun, and this way is better than talking. I'll carry it up and teach him his duty."

Mr. Laurence gave her a sharp look, and put on his spectacles, saying slowly, " You're a sly puss ! but I don't mind being managed by you and Beth. Here, give me a bit of paper, and let us have done with this nonsense."

The note was written in the terms which one gentleman would use to another after offering some deep insult. Jo dropped a kiss on the top of Mr. Laurence's bald head, and ran up to slip the apology under Laurie's door, advising him, through the key-hole, to be submissive, decorous, and a few other agreeable impossibilities. Finding the door locked again, she left the note to do its work, and was going quietly away, when the young gentleman slid down the banisters, and waited for her at the bottom, saying with his most virtuous expression of countenance, " What a good fellow you are, Jo ! Did you get blown up ? " he added, laughing.

" No ; he was pretty clever, on the whole."

" Ah ! I got it all round ! Even you cast me off over there, and I felt just ready to go to the deuce," he began apologetically.

" Don't talk in that way ; turn over a new leaf and begin again, Teddy, my son."

"I keep turning over new leaves, and spoiling them, as I used to spoil my copy-books; and I make so many beginnings there never will be an end," he said dolefully.

"Go and eat your dinner; you'll feel better after it. Men always croak when they are hungry"; and Jo whisked out at the front door after that.

"That's a 'label' on my 'sect,'" answered Laurie, quoting Amy, as he went to partake of humble-pie dutifully with his grandfather, who was quite saintly in temper, and overwhelmingly respectful in manner, all the rest of the day.

Every one thought the matter ended, and the little cloud blown over, but the mischief was done, for, though others forgot it, Meg remembered. She never alluded to a certain person, but she thought of him a good deal, dreamed dreams more than ever; and, once, Jo, rummaging her sister's desk for stamps, found a bit of paper scribbled over with the words, "Mrs. John Brooke;" whereat she groaned tragically, and cast it into the fire, feeling that Laurie's prank had hastened the evil day for her.

CHAPTER XIX

PLEASANT MEADOWS

LIKE sunshine after storm were the peaceful weeks which followed. The invalids improved rapidly, and Mr. March began to talk of returning early in the new year. Beth was soon able to lie on the study sofa all

"Here's another Christmas present for the March family"

day, amusing herself with the well-beloved cats, at first, and, in time, with doll's sewing, which had fallen sadly behindhand. Her once active limbs were so stiff and feeble that Jo took her a daily airing about the house in her strong arms. Meg cheerfully blackened and burnt her white hands cooking delicate messes for " the dear ; " while Amy, a loyal slave of the ring, celebrated her return by giving away as many of her treasures as she could prevail on her sisters to accept.

As Christmas approached, the usual mysteries began to haunt the house, and Jo frequently convulsed the family by proposing utterly impossible or magnificently absurd ceremonies in honour of this unusually merry Christmas. Laurie was equally impracticable, and would have had bonfires, sky-rockets, and triumphal arches, if he had had his own way. After many skirmishes and snubbings, the ambitious pair were considered effectually quenched, and went about with forlorn faces, which were rather belied by explosions of laughter when the two got together.

Several days of unusually mild weather fitly ushered in a splendid Christmas Day. Hannah " felt in her bones that it was going to be an uncommonly plummy day," and she proved herself a true prophetess, for everybody and everything seemed bound to produce a grand success. To begin with : Mr. March wrote that he would soon be with them ; then Beth felt uncommonly well that morning, and, being dressed in her mother's gift—a soft crimson merino wrapper—was borne in triumph to the window, to behold the offering of Jo and Laurie. The Unquenchables had done their best to be worthy of the name, for, like elves, they had worked by night, and conjured up a comical surprise. Out in the garden stood a stately snow-maiden, crowned with holly, bearing a basket of fruit and flowers in one hand, a great roll of new music in the other, a perfect rainbow of an Afghan round her chilly shoulders, and a Christmas carol issuing from her lips, on a pink paper streamer :—

THE JUNGFRAU TO BETH

" GOD bless you, dear Queen Bess !
    May nothing you dismay ;
But health, and peace, and happiness
    Be yours, this Christmas Day.

" Here's fruit to feed our busy bee,
    And flowers for her nose ;
Here's music for her pianee,—
    An Afghan for her toes.

" A portrait of Joanna, see,
    By Raphael No. 2,
Who laboured with great industry,
    To make it fair and true.

" Accept a ribbon red, I beg,
    For Madam Purrer's tail ;

And ice cream made by lovely Peg,—
A Mont Blanc in a pail.

" Their dearest love my makers laid
Within my breast of snow,
Accept it, and the Alpine maid,
From Laurie and from Jo."

How Beth laughed when she saw it ! How Laurie ran up and down to bring in the gifts, and what ridiculous speeches Jo made as she presented them.

" I'm so full of happiness that, if father was only here, I couldn't hold one drop more," said Beth, quite sighing with contentment as Jo carried her off to the study to rest after the excitement, and to refresh herself with some of the delicious grapes the " Jungfrau " had sent her.

" So am I," added Jo, slapping the pocket wherein reposed the long-desired *Undine and Sintram.*

" I'm sure I am," echoed Amy, poring over the engraved copy of the Madonna and Child, which her mother had given her, in a pretty frame.

" Of course I am," cried Meg, smoothing the silvery folds of her first silk dress ; for Mr. Laurence had insisted on giving it.

" How can *I* be otherwise ! " said Mrs. March gratefully, as her eyes went from her husband's letter to Beth's smiling face, and her hand caressed the brooch made of gray and golden, chestnut and dark brown hair, which the girls had just fastened on her breast.

Now and then, in this work-a-day world, things do happen in the delightful story-book fashion, and what a comfort that is ! Half an hour after every one had said they were so happy they could only hold one drop more, the drop came. Laurie opened the parlour door, and popped his head in very quietly. He might just as well have turned a somersault, and uttered an Indian war-whoop ; for his face was so full of suppressed excitement, and his voice so treacherously joyful, that every one jumped up, though he only said, in a queer breathless voice, " Here's another Christmas present for the March family."

Before the words were well out of his mouth, he was whisked away somehow, and in his place appeared a tall man, muffled up to the eyes, leaning on the arm of another tall man, who tried to say something and couldn't. Of course there was a general stampede ; and for several minutes everybody seemed to lose their wits, for the strangest things were done, and no one said a word. Mr. March became invisible in the embrace of four pairs of loving arms ; Jo disgraced herself by nearly fainting away, and had to be doctored by Laurie in the china closet ; Mr. Brooke kissed Meg entirely by mistake, as he somewhat incoherently explained ; and Amy, the dignified, tumbled over a stool, and, never stopping to get up, hugged and cried over her father's boots in the most touching manner. Mrs. March was the first to recover herself, and held up her hand with a warning, " Hush ! remember Beth ! "

But it was too late ; the study door flew open—the little red wrapper appeared on the threshold—joy put strength into the feeble limbs—and

Beth ran straight into her father's arms. Never mind just what happened after that ; for the full hearts overflowed, washing away the bitterness of the past, and leaving only the sweetness of the present.

It was not at all romantic, but a hearty laugh set everybody straight again, for Hannah was discovered behind the door, sobbing over the fat turkey, which she had forgotten to put down when she rushed up from the kitchen. As the laugh subsided, Mrs. March began to thank Mr. Brooke for his faithful care of her husband, at which Mr. Brooke suddenly remembered that Mr. March needed rest, and, seizing Laurie, he precipitately retired. Then the two invalids were ordered to repose, which they did, by both sitting in one big chair, and talking hard.

Mr. March told how he had longed to surprise them, and how, when the fine weather came, he had been allowed by his doctor to take advantage of it ; how devoted Brooke had been, and how he was altogether a most estimable and upright young man. Why Mr. March paused a minute just there, and, after a glance at Meg, who was violently poking the fire, looked at his wife with an inquiring lift of the eyebrows, I leave you to imagine ; also why Mrs. March gently nodded her head, and asked, rather abruptly, if he wouldn't have something to eat. Jo saw and understood the look ; and she stalked grimly away to get wine and beef tea, muttering to herself as she slammed the door, " I hate estimable young men with brown eyes ! "

There never *was* such a Christmas dinner as they had that day. The fat turkey was a sight to behold, when Hannah sent him up, stuffed, browned, and decorated. So was the plum-pudding, which quite melted in one's mouth ; likewise the jellies, in which Amy revelled like a fly in a honey-pot. Everything turned out well ; which was a mercy, Hannah said, " For my mind was that flustered, mum, that it's a merrycle I didn't roast the pudding, and stuff the turkey with raisins, let alone bilin' it in a cloth."

Mr. Laurence and his grandson dined with them ; also Mr. Brooke, at whom Jo glowered darkly, to Laurie's infinite amusement. Two easy chairs stood side by side at the head of the table, in which sat Beth and her father feasting, modestly, on chicken and a little fruit. They drank healths, told stories, sung songs, " reminisced," as the old folks say, and had a thoroughly good time. A sleigh-ride had been planned, but the girls would not leave their father ; so the guests departed early, and, as twilight gathered, the happy family sat together round the fire.

" Just a year ago we were groaning over the dismal Christmas we expected to have. Do you remember ? " asked Jo, breaking a short pause, which had followed a long conversation about many things.

" Rather a pleasant year on the whole ! " said Meg, smiling at the fire, and congratulating herself on having treated Mr. Brooke with dignity.

" I think it's been a pretty hard one," observed Amy, watching the light shine on her ring with thoughtful eyes.

" I'm glad it's over, because we've got you back," whispered Beth, who sat on her father's knee.

" Rather a rough road for you to travel, my little pilgrims, especially the latter part of it. But you have got on bravely ; and I think the burdens are in a fair way to tumble off very soon," said Mr. March, looking with fatherly satisfaction at the four young faces gathered round him.

" How do you know ? Did mother tell you ? " asked Jo.

" Not much ; straws show which way the wind blows ; and I've made several discoveries to-day."

" Oh, tell us what they are ! " cried Meg, who sat beside him.

" Here is one ! " and, taking up the hand which lay on the arm of his chair, he pointed to the roughened fore-finger, a burn on the back, and two or three little hard spots on the palm. " I remember a time when this hand was white and smooth, and your first care was to keep it so. It was very pretty then, but to me it is much prettier now—for in these seeming blemishes I read a little history. A burnt offering has been made of vanity ; this hardened palm has earned something better than blisters, and I'm sure the sewing done by these pricked fingers will last a long time, so much good-will went into the stitches. Meg, my dear, I value the womanly skill which keeps home happy more than white hands or fashionable accomplishments ; I'm proud to shake this good, industrious little hand, and hope I shall not soon be asked to give it away."

If Meg had wanted a reward for hours of patient labour, she received it in the hearty pressure of her father's hand, and the approving smile he gave her.

" What about Jo ? Please say something nice ; for she has tried so hard, and been so very, very good to me," said Beth, in her father's ear.

He laughed, and looked across at the tall girl who sat opposite, with an unusually mild expression on her brown face.

" In spite of the curly crop, I don't see the ' son Jo,' whom I left a year ago," said Mr. March. " I see a young lady who pins her collar straight, laces her boots neatly, and neither whistles, talks slang, nor lies on the rug, as she used to do. Her face is rather thin and pale, just now, with watching and anxiety ; but I like to look at it, for it has grown gentler, and her voice is lower ; she doesn't bounce, but moves quietly, and takes care of a certain little person in a motherly way, which delights me. I rather miss my wild girl ; but if I get a strong, helpful, tender-hearted woman in her place, I shall feel quite satisfied. I don't know whether the shearing sobered our black sheep, but I do know that in all Washington I couldn't find anything beautiful enough to be bought with the five-and-twenty dollars which my good girl sent me."

Jo's keen eyes were rather dim for a minute, and her thin face grew rosy in the firelight, as she received her father's praise feeling that she did deserve a portion of it.

" Now, Beth," said Amy, longing for her turn, ready to wait.

" There's so little of her I'm afraid to say much, for fear she will slip away altogether, though she is not so shy as she used to be," began their father cheerfully ; but, recollecting how nearly he *had* lost her, he held her close, saying tenderly, with her cheek against his own, " I've got you safe, my Beth, and I'll keep you so, please God."

After a minute's silence he looked down at Amy, who sat on the cricket at his feet, and said, with a caress of the shining hair,—

" I observed that Amy took drumsticks at dinner, ran errands for her mother all the afternoon, gave Meg her place to-night, and has waited on every one with patience and good humour. I also observe that she does not fret much, nor prink at the glass, and has not even mentioned a very pretty ring which she wears ; so I conclude that she has learned to think of other people more, and of herself less, and has decided to try to mould her character as carefully as she moulds her little clay figures. I am glad of this, for, though I should be very proud of a graceful statue made by her, I shall be infinitely prouder of a lovable daughter, with a talent for making life beautiful to herself and others."

"What are you thinking of, Beth ? " asked Jo, when Amy had thanked her father, and told about her ring.

"I read in *Pilgrim's Progress* to-day how, after many troubles, Christian and Hopeful came to a pleasant green meadow, where lilies bloomed all the year round, and there they rested happily, as we do now, before they went on to their journey's end," answered Beth ; adding, as she slipped out of her father's arms, and went slowly to the instrument, " It's singing time now, and I want to be in my old place. I'll try to sing the song of the shepherd boy which the Pilgrims heard. I made the music for father, because he likes the verses."

So, sitting at the dear little piano, Beth softly touched the keys, and, in the sweet voice they had never thought to hear again, sung, to her own accompaniment, the quaint hymn, which was a singularly fitting song for her :—

> " He that is down need fear no fall,
>   He that is low no pride ;
> He that is humble ever shall
>   Have God to be his guide.
>
> " I am content with what I have,
>   Little be it or much ;
> And, Lord ! contentment still I crave,
>   Because Thou savest such.
>
> " Fulness to them a burden is,
>   That go on Pilgrimage ;
> Here little, and hereafter bliss
>   Is best from age to age ! "

CHAPTER XX

AUNT MARCH SETTLES THE QUESTION

LIKE bees swarming after their queen, mother and daughters hovered about Mr. March the next day, neglecting everything to look at, wait upon, and listen to the new invalid, who was in a fair way to be killed by kindness. As he sat propped up in the big chair by Beth's sofa, with the other three close by, and Hannah popping in her head now and then, " to peek at the dear man," nothing seemed needed to complete their happiness. But something *was* needed, and the elder ones felt it, though none confessed the fact. Mr. and Mrs. March looked at one another with an anxious expression, as their eyes followed Meg. Jo had sudden fits of sobriety, and was seen to shake her fist at Mr. Brooke's umbrella, which had been left in the hall ; Meg was absent-minded, shy and silent, started when the bell rang, and coloured when John's name was mentioned ; Amy said, " Every one seemed waiting for something, and couldn't settle down, which was queer, since father was safe at home," and Beth innocently wondered why their neighbours didn't run over as usual.

Laurie went by in the afternoon, and, seeing Meg at the window, seemed suddenly possessed with a melodramatic fit, for he fell down upon one knee in the snow, beat his breast, tore his hair, and clasped his hands im-

He fell down upon one knee in the snow and beat his breast

ploringly, as if begging some boon ; and when Meg told him to behave himself, and go away, he wrung imaginary tears out of his handkerchief, and staggered round the corner as if in utter despair.

" What does the goose mean ? " said Meg, laughing and trying to look unconscious.

" He's showing you how your John will go on by-and-by. Touching, isn't it ? " answered Jo scornfully.

" Don't say *my John* ; it isn't proper or true ; " but Meg's voice lingered over the words as if they sounded pleasant to her. " Please don't plague me, Jo ; I've told you I don't care *much* about him, and there isn't to be anything said, but we are all to be friendly, and go on as before."

" We can't, for something *has* been said, and Laurie's mischief has spoilt you for me. I see it, and so does mother ; you are not like your own self a bit, and seem ever so far away from me. I don't mean to plague you, and will bear it like a man, but I do wish it was all settled. I hate to wait ;

so if you mean ever to do it, make haste and have it over quick," said Jo pettishly.

"*I* can't say or do anything till he speaks, and he won't because father said I was too young," began Meg, bending over her work with a queer little smile, which suggested that she did not quite agree with her father on that point.

"If he did speak you wouldn't know what to say, but would cry or blush, or let him have his own way, instead of giving a good decided No."

"I'm not so silly and weak as you think. I know just what I should say, for I've planned it all, so I needn't be taken unawares ; there's no knowing what may happen, and I wished to be prepared."

Jo couldn't help smiling at the important air which Meg had unconsciously assumed, and which was as becoming as the pretty colour varying in her cheeks.

"Would you mind telling me what you'd say ? " asked Jo, more respectfully.

"Not at all ; you are sixteen now, quite old enough to be my confidante, and my experience will be useful to you by-and-by, perhaps, in your own affairs of this sort."

"Don't mean to have any ; it's fun to watch other people philander, but I should feel like a fool doing it myself," said Jo, looking alarmed at the thought.

"I guess not, if you liked any one very much, and he liked you." Meg spoke as if to herself, and glanced out at the lane where she had often seen lovers walking together in the summer twilight.

"I thought you were going to tell your speech to that man," said Jo, rudely shortening her sister's little reverie.

"Oh, I should merely say, quite calmly and decidedly, ' Thank you, Mr. Brooke, you are very kind, but I agree with father that I am too young to enter into any engagement at present ; so please say no more, but let us be friends as we were.' "

"Hum ! that's stiff and cool enough. I don't believe you'll ever say it, and I know he won't be satisfied if you do. If he goes on like the rejected lovers in books, you'll give in, rather than hurt his feelings."

"No, I won't ! I shall tell him I've made up my mind, and shall walk out of the room with dignity."

Meg rose as she spoke, and was just going to rehearse the dignified exit, when a step in the hall made her fly into her seat, and begin to sew as if her life depended on finishing that particular seam in a given time. Jo smothered a laugh at the sudden change, and, when some one gave a modest tap, opened the door with a grim aspect, which was anything but hospitable.

"Good-afternoon, I came to get my umbrella—that is, to see how your father finds himself to-day," said Mr. Brooke, getting a trifle confused, as his eye went from one tell-tale face to the other.

"It's very well, he's in the rack, I'll get him, and tell it you are here ; " and having jumbled her father and the umbrella well together in her reply, Jo slipped out of the room to give Meg a chance to make her speech, and air her dignity. But the instant she vanished, Meg began to sidle toward the door, murmuring,—

"Mother will like to see you; pray sit down, I'll call her."

"Don't go; are you afraid of me, Margaret?" and Mr. Brooke looked so hurt that Meg thought she must have done something very rude. She blushed up to the little curls on her forehead, for he had never called her Margaret before, and she was surprised to find how natural and sweet it seemed to hear him say it. Anxious to appear friendly and at her ease, she put out her hand with a confiding gesture, and said gratefully,—

"How can I be afraid when you have been so kind to father? I only wish I could thank you for it."

"Shall I tell you how?" asked Mr. Brooke, holding the small hand fast in both his big ones, and looking down at Meg with so much love in the brown eyes that her heart began to flutter, and she both longed to run away and to stop and listen.

"Oh, no, please don't—I'd rather not," she said, trying to withdraw her hand, and looking frightened in spite of her denial.

"I won't trouble you; I only want to know if you care for me a little, Meg; I love you so much, dear," added Mr. Brooke tenderly.

This was the moment for the calm, proper speech, but Meg didn't make it, she forgot every word of it, hung her head, and answered, "I don't know," so softly that John had to stoop down to catch the foolish little reply.

He seemed to think it was worth the trouble, for he smiled to himself as if quite satisfied, pressed the plump hand gracefully, and said in his most persuasive tone, "Will you try to find out? I want to know *so* much; for I can't go to work with any heart until I learn whether I am to have my reward in the end or not."

"I'm too young," faltered Meg, wondering why she was so fluttered, yet rather enjoying it.

"I'll wait; and in the meantime you could be learning to like me. Would it be a very hard lesson, dear?"

"Not if I choose to learn it; but——"

"Please choose to learn, Meg. I love to teach, and this is easier than German," broke in John, getting possession of the other hand, so that she had no way of hiding her face, as he bent to look into it.

His tone was properly beseeching; but, stealing a shy look at him, Meg saw that his eyes were merry as well as tender, and that he wore the satisfied smile of one who had no doubt of his success. This nettled her; Annie Moffat's foolish lessons in coquetry came into her mind, and the love of power, which sleeps in the bosoms of the best of little women, woke up all of a sudden, and took possession of her. She felt excited and strange, and, not knowing what else to do, followed a capricious impulse, and, withdrawing her hands, said petulantly, "I *don't* choose; please go away; and let me be!"

Poor Mr. Brooke looked as if his lovely castle in the air was tumbling about his ears, for he had never seen Meg in such a mood before, and it rather bewildered him.

"Do you really mean that?" he asked, anxiously following her as she walked away.

"Yes, I do; I don't want to be worried about such things. Father says I needn't; it's too soon, and I'd rather not."

"Mayn't I hope you'll change your mind by-and-by? I'll wait, and say nothing till you have had more time. Don't play with me, Meg. I didn't think that of you."

"Don't think of me at all. I'd rather you wouldn't," said Meg, taking a naughty satisfaction in trying her lover's patience and her own power.

He was grave and pale now, and looked decidedly more like the novel heroes whom she admired ; but he neither slapped his forehead nor tramped about the room, as they did ; he just stood looking at her so wistfully, so tenderly, that she found her heart relenting in spite of herself. What would have happened next I cannot say, if Aunt March had not come hobbling in at this interesting minute.

The old lady couldn't resist her longing to see her nephew ; for she had met Laurie as she took her airing, and, hearing of Mr. March's arrival, drove straight out to see him. The family were all busy in the back part of the house, and she had made her way quietly in, hoping to surprise them. She did surprise two of them so much that Meg started as if she had seen a ghost, and Mr. Brooke vanished into the study.

"Bless me ! what's all this ? " cried the old lady, with a rap of her cane, as she glanced from the pale young gentleman to the scarlet young lady.

"It's father's friend. I'm *so* surprised to see you," stammered Meg, feeling that she was in for a lecture now.

"That's evident," returned Aunt March, sitting down. "But what is father's friend saying to make you look like a peony ? There's mischief going on, and I insist upon knowing what it is ! " with another rap.

"We were merely talking. Mr. Brooke came for his umbrella," began Meg, wishing that Mr. Brooke and the umbrella were safely out of the house.

"Brooke ? That boy's tutor ? Ah ! I understand now. I know all about it. Jo blundered into a wrong message in one of your pa's letters, and I made her tell me. You haven't gone and accepted him, child ? " cried Aunt March, looking scandalised.

"Hush ! he'll hear ! Shan't I call mother ? " said Meg, much troubled.

"Not yet. I've something to say to you, and I must free my mind at once. Tell me, do you mean to marry this Cook ? If you do, not one penny of my money ever goes to you. Remember that, and be a sensible girl," said the old lady impressively.

Now Aunt March possessed, in perfection, the art of rousing the spirit of opposition in the gentlest people, and enjoyed doing it. The best of us have a spice of perversity in us, especially when we are young, and in love. If Aunt March had begged Meg to accept John Brooke, she would probably have declared she couldn't think of it ; but, as she was peremptorily ordered *not* to like him, she immediately made up her mind that she would. Inclination as well as perversity made the decision easy, and, being already much excited, Meg opposed the old lady with unusual spirit.

"I shall marry whom I please, Aunt March, and you can leave your money to any one you like," she said, nodding her head with a resolute air.

"Highty tighty ! Is that the way you take my advice, miss ? You'll be sorry for it, by-and-by, when you've tried love in a cottage, and found it a failure."

" It can't be a worse one than some people find in big houses," retorted Meg.

Aunt March put on her glasses and took a look at the girl, for she did not know her in this new mood. Meg hardly knew herself, she felt so brave and independent—so glad to defend John, and assert her right to love him if she liked. Aunt March saw that she had begun wrong, and, after a little pause, made a fresh start, saying, as mildly as she could, " Now, Meg, my dear, be reasonable, and take my advice. I mean it kindly, and don't want you to spoil your whole life by making a mistake at the beginning. You ought to marry well, and help your family ; it's your duty to make a rich match, and it ought to be impressed upon you."

" Father and mother don't think so ; they like John, though he *is* poor."

" Your pa and ma, my dear, have no more wisdom than two babies."

" I'm glad of it," cried Meg stoutly.

Aunt March took no notice, but went on with her lecture. " This Rook is poor, and hasn't got any rich relations, has he ? "

" No ; but he has many warm friends."

" You can't live on friends ; try it, and see how cool they'll grow. He hasn't any business, has he ? "

" Not yet ; Mr. Laurence is going to help him."

" That won't last long. James Laurence is a crotchety old fellow, and not to be depended on. So you intend to marry a man without money, position, or business, and go on working harder than you do now, when you might be comfortable all your days by minding me, and doing better ? I thought you had more sense, Meg."

" I couldn't do better if I waited half my life ! John is good and wise ; he's got heaps of talent ; he's willing to work, and sure to get on, he's so energetic and brave. Every one likes and respects him, and I'm proud to think he cares for me, though I'm so poor and young, and silly," said Meg.

" He knows *you* have got rich relations, child ; that's the secret of his liking, I suspect."

" Aunt March, how dare you say such a thing ! John is above such meanness, and I won't listen to you a minute if you talk so," cried Meg indignantly, forgetting everything but the injustice of the old lady's suspicions. " My John wouldn't marry for money any more than I would. We are willing to work, and we mean to wait. I'm not afraid of being poor, for I've been happy so far, and I know I shall be with him, because he loves me, and I——"

Meg stopped there, remembering, all of a sudden, that she had not made up her mind ; that she had told " her John " to go away, and that he might be overhearing her inconsistent remarks.

Aunt March was very angry, for she had set her heart on having her pretty niece make a fine match, and something in the girl's happy young face made the lonely old woman feel sad and sour.

" Well, I wash my hands of the whole affair ! You are a wilful child, and you've lost more than you know by this piece of folly. No, I won't stop ; I'm disappointed in you, and haven't spirits to see your pa now. Don't expect anything from me when you are married ; your Mr. Brooke's friends must take care of you. I'm done with you for ever."

And, slamming the door in Meg's face, Aunt March drove off in high dudgeon. She seemed to take all the girl's courage with her; for, when left alone, Meg stood a moment undecided whether to laugh or cry. Before she could make up her mind, she was taken possession of by Mr. Brooke, who said, all in one breath, "I couldn't help hearing, Meg. Thank you for defending me, and Aunt March for proving that you *do* care for me."

"I didn't know how much till she abused you," began Meg.

"And I needn't go away, but may stay and be happy—may I, dear?"

Here was another fine chance to make the crushing speech and the stately exit, but Meg disgraced herself for ever in Jo's eyes by meekly whispering, "Yes, John," and hiding her face on Mr. Brooke's waistcoat.

Fifteen minutes after Aunt March's departure, Jo came softly downstairs, paused an instant at the parlour door, nodded and smiled with a satisfied expression, saying to herself, "She has sent him away as we planned, and that affair is settled. I'll go and hear the fun, and have a good laugh over it."

But poor Jo never got her laugh, for she was transfixed upon the threshold by a spectacle which held her there staring with her mouth nearly as wide open as her eyes. Going in to exult over a fallen enemy, and to praise a strong-minded sister for the banishment of an objectionable lover, it certainly *was* a shock to behold the aforesaid enemy serenely sitting on the sofa, with the strong-minded sister enthroned upon his knee, and wearing an expression of the most abject submission. Jo gave a sort of gasp, as if a cold shower-bath had suddenly fallen upon her—for such an unexpected turning of the tables actually took her breath away. At the odd sound, the lovers turned and saw her. Meg jumped up, looking both proud and shy; but "that man," as Jo called him, actually laughed, and said coolly, "Sister Jo, congratulate us."

That was adding insult to injury! and, making some wild demonstration with her hands, Jo vanished. Rushing upstairs, she startled the invalids by exclaiming, tragically, as she burst into the room, "Oh, *do* somebody go down quick! John Brooke is acting dreadfully, and Meg likes it!"

Mr. and Mrs. March left the room with speed; and casting herself upon the bed, Jo cried and scolded tempestuously as she told the awful news to Beth and Amy. The little girls, however, considered it a most agreeable and interesting event, and Jo got little comfort from them.

Nobody ever knew what went on in the parlour; but a great deal of talking was done, and quiet Mr. Brooke astonished his friends by the eloquence and spirit with which he pleaded his suit and told his plans.

The tea-bell rang before he had finished describing the paradise which he meant to earn for Meg, and he proudly took her in to supper, both looking so happy that Jo hadn't the heart to be jealous or dismal. Amy was very much impressed by John's devotion and Meg's dignity. Beth beamed at them from a distance, while Mr. and Mrs. March surveyed the young couple with such tender satisfaction that it was perfectly evident Aunt March was right in calling them as " unworldly as a pair of babies." No one ate much, but every one looked very happy.

"You can't say ' nothing pleasant ever happens now,' can you, Meg?" said Amy, trying to decide how she would group the lovers in a sketch.

"No, I'm sure I can't. How much has happened since I said that! It seems a year ago," answered Meg, who was in a blissful dream.

Meg hid her face on Mr. Brooke's waistcoat

" The joys came close upon the sorrows this time, and I rather think the changes have begun," said Mrs. March. " In most families there comes a year full of events ; this has been such an one, but it ends well, after all."

" Hope the next will end better," muttered Jo, who found it very hard to see Meg absorbed in a stranger before her face ; for Jo loved a few persons very dearly, and dreaded to have their affection lost or lessened in any way.

" I hope the third year from this *will* end better ; I mean it shall, if I live to work out my plans," said Mr. Brooke, smiling at Meg.

" Doesn't it seem very long to wait ? " asked Amy.

" I've got so much to learn before I shall be ready, it seems a short time to me," answered Meg, with a sweet gravity in her face.

" You have only to wait. *I* am to do the work," said John, beginning his labours by picking up Meg's napkin, with an expression which caused Jo to shake her head, and then say to herself, as the front door banged, " Here comes Laurie ; now we shall have a little sensible conversation."

But Jo was mistaken ; for Laurie came prancing in overflowing with spirits, bearing a great bridal-looking bouquet for " Mrs. John Brooke," and evidently labouring under the delusion that the whole affair had been brought about by his excellent management.

" I knew Brooke would have it all his own way, he always does," said Laurie, when he had presented his congratulations.

" Much obliged for that recommendation. I take it as a good omen for the future, and invite you to my wedding on the spot," answered Mr. Brooke, who felt at peace with all mankind, even his mischievous pupil.

" I'll come if I'm at the ends of the earth ; for the sight of Jo's face alone, on that occasion, would be worth a long journey. You don't look festive, ma'am ; what's the matter ? " asked Laurie, following her into a corner of the parlour, whither all had adjourned to greet Mr. Laurence.

" I don't approve of the match, but I've made up my mind to bear it, and shall not say a word against it," said Jo solemnly, with a little quiver in her voice. " You can't know how hard it is for me to give up Meg."

" You don't give her up. You only go halves," said Laurie consolingly.

" It can never be the same again. I've lost my dearest friend," sighed Jo.

" You've got me, anyhow. I'll stand by you, Jo, all the days of my life ; upon my word I will ! " and Laurie meant what he said.

" I know you will, and I'm ever so much obliged ; you are always a great comfort to me, Teddy," returned Jo, gratefully shaking hands.

" Well, now, don't be dismal, there's a good fellow. Meg is happy ; Brooke will fly round and get settled soon ; grandpa will attend to him, and it will be very jolly to see Meg in her own little house. We'll have capital times after she is gone, for I shall be through college before long, and then we'll go abroad, or some nice trip or other. Wouldn't that console you ? "

" I rather think it would ; but there's no knowing what may happen."

" That's true ! Don't you wish you could take a look forward, and see where we shall all be then ? I do," returned Laurie.

" I think not, for I might see something sad ; and every one looks so happy now, I don't believe they could be much improved ; " and Jo's eyes went slowly round the room, brightening as they looked.

Father and mother sat together, quietly re-living the first chapter of the romance which for them began some twenty years ago. Amy was drawing the lovers, who sat apart in a beautiful world of their own, the light of which touched their faces with a grace the little artist could not copy. Beth lay on her sofa talking cheerily with her old friend. Jo lounged in her favourite low seat with the grave, quiet look which best became her ; and Laurie leaned on the back of her chair, his chin on a level with her curly head.

So grouped, the curtain falls upon Meg, Jo, Beth, and Amy. Whether it ever rises again depends upon the reception given to the first act of the domestic drama called *Little Women*.